T0332464

Handbook of Research on Recent Developments in Intelligent Communication Application

Siddhartha Bhattacharyya
RCC Institute of Information Technology, India

Nibaran Das
Jadavpur University, India

Debotosh Bhattacharjee
Jadavpur University, India

Anirban Mukherjee
RCC Institute of Information Technology, India

A volume in the Advances in Wireless Technologies and Telecommunication (AWTT) Book Series

www.igi-global.com

Published in the United States of America by
IGI Global
Information Science Reference (an imprint of IGI Global)
701 E. Chocolate Avenue
Hershey PA, USA 17033
Tel: 717-533-8845
Fax: 717-533-8661
E-mail: cust@igi-global.com
Web site: http://www.igi-global.com

Library of Congress Cataloging-in-Publication Data

Names: Bhattacharyya, Siddhartha, 1975- editor. | Das, Nibaran, 1981- editor.
  | Bhattacharjee, Debotosh, 1971- editor. | Mukherjee, Anirban, editor.
Title: Handbook of research on recent developments in intelligent
  communication application / Siddhartha Bhattacharyya, Nibaran Das,
  Debotosh Bhattacharjee and Anirban Mukherjee, editors.
Description: Hershey, PA : Information Science Reference, [2017] | Includes
  bibliographical references and index.
Identifiers: LCCN 2016045758| ISBN 9781522517856 (hardcover) | ISBN
  9781522517863 (ebook)
Subjects: LCSH: Telematics--Handbooks, manuals, etc. | Data transmission
  systems--Handbooks, manuals, etc. | Wireless communication
  systems--Handbooks, manuals, etc. | Information technology--Handbooks,
  manuals, etc.
Classification: LCC TK5105.6 .H36 2017 | DDC 621.382--dc23 LC record available at https://lccn.loc.gov/2016045758

This book is published in the IGI Global book series Advances in Wireless Technologies and Telecommunication (AWTT) (ISSN: 2327-3305; eISSN: 2327-3313)

British Cataloguing in Publication Data
A Cataloguing in Publication record for this book is available from the British Library.

For electronic access to this publication, please contact: eresources@igi-global.com.

Advances in Wireless Technologies and Telecommunication (AWTT) Book Series

Xiaoge Xu

The University of Nottingham Ningbo China, China

ISSN:2327-3305
EISSN:2327-3313

MISSION

The wireless computing industry is constantly evolving, redesigning the ways in which individuals share information. Wireless technology and telecommunication remain one of the most important technologies in business organizations. The utilization of these technologies has enhanced business efficiency by enabling dynamic resources in all aspects of society.

The **Advances in Wireless Technologies and Telecommunication Book Series** aims to provide researchers and academic communities with quality research on the concepts and developments in the wireless technology fields. Developers, engineers, students, research strategists, and IT managers will find this series useful to gain insight into next generation wireless technologies and telecommunication.

COVERAGE

- Digital Communication
- Grid Communications
- Telecommunications
- Mobile Communications
- Virtual Network Operations
- Global Telecommunications
- Broadcasting
- Mobile Technology
- Network Management
- Wireless Technologies

IGI Global is currently accepting manuscripts for publication within this series. To submit a proposal for a volume in this series, please contact our Acquisition Editors at Acquisitions@igi-global.com or visit: http://www.igi-global.com/publish/.

Titles in this Series

For a list of additional titles in this series, please visit: www.igi-global.com

Handbook of Research on Advanced Trends in Microwave and Communication Engineering
Ahmed El Oualkadi (Abdelmalek Essaadi University, Morocco) and Jamal Zbitou (Hassan 1st University, Morocco)
Information Science Reference • copyright 2017 • 716pp • H/C (ISBN: 9781522507734) • US $315.00 (our price)

Handbook of Research on Wireless Sensor Network Trends, Technologies, and Applications
Narendra Kumar Kamila (C. V. Raman College of Engineering, India)
Information Science Reference • copyright 2017 • 589pp • H/C (ISBN: 9781522505013) • US $310.00 (our price)

Handbook of Research on Advanced Wireless Sensor Network Applications, Protocols, and Architectures
Niranjan K. Ray (Silicon Institute of Technology, India) and Ashok Kumar Turuk (National Institute of Technology Rourkela, India)
Information Science Reference • copyright 2017 • 502pp • H/C (ISBN: 9781522504863) • US $285.00 (our price)

Self-Organized Mobile Communication Technologies and Techniques for Network Optimization
Ali Diab (Al-Baath University, Syria)
Information Science Reference • copyright 2016 • 416pp • H/C (ISBN: 9781522502395) • US $200.00 (our price)

Advanced Methods for Complex Network Analysis
Natarajan Meghanathan (Jackson State University, USA)
Information Science Reference • copyright 2016 • 461pp • H/C (ISBN: 9781466699649) • US $215.00 (our price)

Emerging Innovations in Wireless Networks and Broadband Technologies
Naveen Chilamkurti (La Trobe University, Australia)
Information Science Reference • copyright 2016 • 292pp • H/C (ISBN: 9781466699410) • US $165.00 (our price)

Critical Socio-Technical Issues Surrounding Mobile Computing
Norshidah Mohamed (Prince Sultan University, Kingdom of Saudi Arabia and Universiti Teknologi Malaysia, Malaysia) Teddy Mantoro (USBI-Sampoerna University, Indonesia) Media Ayu (USBI-Sampoerna University, Indonesia) and Murni Mahmud (International Islamic University Malaysia, Malaysia)
Information Science Reference • copyright 2016 • 357pp • H/C (ISBN: 9781466694385) • US $210.00 (our price)

Handbook of Research on Next Generation Mobile Communication Systems
Athanasios D. Panagopoulos (National Technical University of Athens, Greece)
Information Science Reference • copyright 2016 • 604pp • H/C (ISBN: 9781466687325) • US $370.00 (our price)

www.igi-global.com

701 E. Chocolate Ave., Hershey, PA 17033
Order online at www.igi-global.com or call 717-533-8845 x100
To place a standing order for titles released in this series, contact: cust@igi-global.com
Mon-Fri 8:00 am - 5:00 pm (est) or fax 24 hours a day 717-533-8661

Prof. (Dr.) Siddhartha Bhattacharyya would like to dedicate this book to,
My parents Late Ajit Kumar Bhattacharyya and Late Hashi Bhattacharyya, my beloved wife Rashni and my maternal aunts Mrs. Biva Mukherjee, Late Ganga Bhattacharya, Mrs. Shukla Chatterjee and Mrs. Krishna Mukherjee

Dr. Nibaran Das would like to dedicate this book to,
My father Mr. Niramangal Das, my mother Mrs. Puspa Rani Das, my wife Mrs. Shyamali Das and my son Master Nandish Das

Prof. (Dr.) Debotosh Bhattacharjee would like to dedicate this book to,
Prof. (Dr.) Mita Nasipuri

Dr. Anirban Mukherjee would like to dedicate this book to,
All the students of Department of Information Technology, RCC Institute of Information Technology

Editorial Advisory Board

List of Contributors

Table of Contents

Detailed Table of Contents

    Bilal Muhammad Khan, National University of Sciences and Technology Islamabad,
        Pakistan
    Rabia Bilal, Usman Institute of Technology, Pakistan

Modulated signals used in communication systems exhibits cyclic periodicity. This is primarily due to sinusoidal product modulators, repeating preambles, coding and multiplexing in modern communication. This property of signals can be analyzed using cyclostationary analysis. SCF (Spectral correlation function) of cyclic autocorrelation (CAF) has unique features for different modulated signals and noise. Different techniques are applied to SCF for extracting features on the basis of which decision of detecting a signal or noise is made. In this chapter, study and analysis of different modulated signals used in satellite communication is presented using SCF. Also comparison of several signal detection techniques is provided on the basis of utilizing unique feature exhibit by a normalized vector calculated on SCF along frequency axis. Moreover a signal detection technique is also proposed which identifies the presence of a signal or noise in the analyzed data within the defined threshold limits.

    Srijibendu Bagchi, RCC Institute of Information Technology, India

Cognitive radio is now acknowledged as a potential solution to meet the spectrum scarcity problem in radio frequency range. To achieve this objective proper identification of vacant frequency band is necessary. In this article a detection methodology based on cepstrum estimation has been proposed that can be done through power spectral density estimation of the received signal. The detection has been studied under different channel fading conditions along with Gaussian noise. Two figures of merit are considered here; false alarm probability and detection probability. For a specific false alarm probability, the detection probabilities are calculated for different sample size and it has been established through numerical results that the proposed detector performs quite well in different channel impairments.

Chapter 3

This chapter explains the components of Radio Frequency Identification (RFID); the aspects of RFID; the barriers to RFID utilization; the privacy and security issues of RFID; the RFID applications in supply chain management; the RFID applications in the health care industry; the RFID applications in modern business; the Near Field Communication (NFC) in mobile devices; the overview of Mobile Ad-Hoc Network (MANET); the security concern of MANET; and the advanced issues of MANET in the digital age. RFID and MANET become the growing components of Information and Communication Technology (ICT) applications and can be effectively utilized in global operations. The chapter argues that RFID and MANET have the potential to increase the efficiency of operations in various industries, improve asset visibility and traceability, decrease reliance on manual processes, reduce operation costs, and provide useful data for business analytics.

Software Defined Radio (SDR) systems are the ones which can adapt to the future-proof solution and it covers both existing and emerging standards. An SDR has to possess elements of reconfigurability, intelligence and software programmable hardware. The main interest in any communication group is the sure sending of signals of info from a transmitter to a receiver. The signals are transmitted via a guide who corrupts the signal. To ensure reliable communication forward error-correcting (FEC) codes are the main part of a communication system. This chapter will discuss an SDR system built using LabVIEW for a Generic Transceiver. This chapter has covered emerging software radio standards and the technologies being used to specify and support them.

Chapter 5

Optical packet switching is connectionless networking solution through which we can get high speed data transfer and optimum bandwidth utilization using wavelength division multiplexing technique. For realizing optical packet switching the numbers of optical packet switch architectures are available in market. In this chapter the authors discuss the overall development of optical packet switching; some recently published optical packet switch architectures are discussed in the chapter and a comparison is performed between the switches through loss, cost and buffer analysis.

Having the merits of being light-weight, energy efficient, in addition to low manufacturing cost, reduced fabrication complexity, and the availability of inexpensive flexible substrates, flexible and wearable technology is being established as an appealing alternative to the conventional electronics technologies which are based on rigid substrates. Furthermore, wearable antennas have been a topic of interest for more than the past decade, and hundreds of scientific papers can be found on the subject. This large number of publications asks for some classification in order to get an overview of the trends and challenges. To this aim, an overview of antennas for wearable technologies is proposed. This chapter is organized into three major sections. In the first part, a detailed review of wearable antennas is presented. The second part of this project deals with the flexible antennas parameters and families. Materials and fabrication methods are discussed in the third part. Wearables advantages, disadvantage and challenges are summarized in the last section.

Chapter 7

The radio frequency (RF) energy harvesting is found as an attractive alternative to existing energy resources. This chapter deals with the design and performance evaluation of different rectifying antenna circuits for RF energy harvesting. The rectifying antenna i.e. rectenna consists of an antenna to grab the RF energy and rectifier to convert the RF energy to DC power. Different circularly polarized microstrip antennas e.g. shorted square ring slot antenna and crossed monopole antenna with step ground plane are studied. The antennas are combined with voltage doubler circuits with various stages and bridge rectifier. The electromagnetic simulator CST Microwave Studio is used to design and optimization of antenna structures. The rectifier circuits are designed using SPICE software. Later the prototype of the antennas and rectifiers are fabricated and tested in the laboratory environment. The detailed study on the performance of the rectenna circuits are evaluated in terms of conversion efficiency.

Robustness and reliability are two essential network parameters to be given priority in Industrial Wireless Sensor Network. But at the same time it is difficult to achieve gain in these performance metrics. Since in industries these networks are used for monitoring, control and automation processes, therefore, it also requires robust communication with minimum delay. Considering the need of high QoS in Industrial

WSN, protocols and standards were developed to fulfil the requirement of reliable data communication in harsh environment. In year 2007, HART community designed a Wireless HART standard for efficient industrial communication. This standard gain high reputation soon after its implementation and still being used as a universal solution for industries. In 2009, another standard ISA100.11a was developed, it also gives promised results but fails to eliminate WHART. Both these standards are still competing in industry and the results of these standards are more reliable in comparison to other wireless industrial protocols that exists.

Chapter 9

Modern communication infrastructures that usually keep people always on-line and inform "on-the-go" have repeatedly proved to be unreliable and unavailable during and after major disasters. In those situations the prime need is to quickly re-establish minimal communication infrastructures to start rescue operations. DTN is described by a special kind of mobile ad-hoc network where sparseness, large communication delay and lack of end to end path from source to destination exist. It is evident from this fact that data forwarding is dependent on the cooperation of multiple hops in "store-carry-forward" manner. However, nodes involved in communication may sometimes behave maliciously and may non-cooperate. So, the objective in this perspective is to develop a reliable data forwarding scheme by detecting malicious activities and encourage nodes to participate in Post Disaster Communication environment. Analysis of the proposed system, its protocols and performance studies are implemented and tested using Opportunistic Network Environment (ONE) simulator.

Chapter 10

Recently, Flying Ad-hoc Networks (FANETs), enabling ad-hoc networking between highly mobile Unmanned Aerial Vehicles (UAVs), are gaining importance in several military, commercial and civilian applications. The sensitivity of these missions requires precise and prompt data delivery. Thus, the most important communication requirements that need to be addressed while designing FANETs are of high reliability and low latency. Considering these demands, this chapter focusses on mobility models, MAC protocols and routing protocols.

Chapter 11

Security and trust are two inevitable concepts for secure Manet. There are various systems used for ensuring security and trust in case of Manet. These systems have several advantages as well as several disadvantages in terms high communication and computation overhead. In this proposed trust based system, trust of node is evaluated on the basis of ratio of signal sent and acknowledgement received. After that, priority of each node is calculated and at last Leader Election algorithm is applied to select node leader.

Bilal Muhammad Khan, National University of Sciences and Technology Islamabad, Pakistan
Rabia Bilal, Usman Institute of Technology, Pakistan

One of the critical and vital parameter of Wireless Sensor Networks (WSNs) is its lifetime. There are various methods to increase WSN lifetime, clustering technique is one of them. In clustering, selection of desired percentage of Cluster Head (CHs) is performed among the sensor nodes (SNs). Selected CHs are responsible to collect data from its member nodes, aggregates the data and finally send to the sink. In this chapter, Fuzzy-TOPSIS techniques based on multi criteria decision making to choose CH efficiently and effectively to maximize the WSN lifetime are presented. These five criteria includes; residual energy, node energy consumption rate, number of neighbor nodes, average distance between neighboring nodes and distance from sink. Threshold based intra-cluster and inter-cluster multi-hop communication mechanism is used to decrease energy consumption. Moreover impact of node density and different type mobility strategies are presented in order to investigate impact over WSN lifetime.

Sunilkumar S. Manvi, REVA University, India
Nayana Hegde, Sri Krishna Institute of Technology, India

Vehicular Cloud Communication (VCC) is the latest technology in intelligent transport system. Vehicular cloud (VC) facilitates the customers to share resources ranging from storage to computing power to renting it to other users over the Internet. Security of VANET cloud covers various aspects of security, social impact, cost effective communication. Chapter highlights a cost effective, hassle free and secure communication between the cloud and moving vehicles. Communication is established via Network as a Service (Naas). The goal of this chapter is to give a broad overview of Vehicular cloud computing, vehicular cloud applications, mobile computing, and recent literature covering security of vehicular cloud.

Arun Fera M, Thiagarajar College of Engineering, India
M. Saravanapriya, Thiagarajar College of Engineering, India
J. John Shiny, Thiagarajar College of Engineering, India

Cloud computing is one of the most vital technology which becomes part and parcel of corporate life. It is considered to be one of the most emerging technology which serves for various applications. Generally these Cloud computing systems provide a various data storage services which highly reduces the complexity of users. we mainly focus on addressing in providing confidentiality to users' data. We are proposing one mechanism for addressing this issue. Since software level security has vulnerabilities in addressing the solution to our problem we are dealing with providing hardware level of security. We are focusing on Trusted Platform Module (TPM) which is a chip in computer that is used for secure storage that is mainly used to deal with authentication problem. TPM which when used provides a trustworthy environment to the users. A detailed survey on various existing TPM related security and its implementations is carried out in our research work.

Chapter 15

Kai Li Lim, The University of Western Australia, Australia
Kah Phooi Seng, Charles Sturt University, Australia
Lee Seng Yeong, Sunway University, Malaysia
Li-Minn Ang, Charles Sturt University, Australia

This chapter presents an indoor navigation solution for visually impaired pedestrians, which employs a combination of a radio frequency identification (RFID) tag array and dead-reckoning to achieve positioning and localisation. This form of positioning aims to reduce the deployment cost and complexity of pure RFID array implementations. This is a smartphone-based navigation system that leverages the new advancements of smartphone hardware to achieve large data handling and fast pathfinding. Users interact with the system through speech recognition and synthesis. This approach allows the system to be accessible to the masses due to the ubiquity of smartphones today. Uninformed pathfinding algorithms are implemented onto this system based on our previous study on the implementation suitability of uninformed searches. Testing results showed that this navigation system is suitable for use for the visually impaired pedestrians; and the pathfinding algorithms performed consistently according to our algorithm proposals.

Chapter 16

Uday Pratap Singh, Madhav Institute of Technology and Science, India
Sanjeev Jain, Shri Mata Vaishno Devi University, India
Rajeev Kumar Singh, Madhav Institute of Technology and Science, India
Mahesh Parmar, Madhav Institute of Technology and Science, India

Two main important features of neural networks are weights and bias connection, which is still a challenging problem for researchers. In this paper we select weights and bias connection of neural network (KN) using modified differential evolution algorithm (MDEA) i.e. MDEA-NN for uncertain nonlinear systems with unknown disturbances and compare it with KN using differential evolution algorithm (DEA) i.e. DEA-KN. In this work, MDEA is based on exploitation and exploration of capability, we have implemented differential evolution algorithm and modified differential evolution algorithm, which are based on the consideration of the three main operator's mutation, crossover and selection. MDEA-KN is applied on two different uncertain nonlinear systems, and one benchmark problem known as brushless dc (BDC) motor. Proposed method is validated through statistical testing's methods which demonstrate that the difference between target and output of proposed method are acceptable.

The construction of a practical nanorobot is a definite futuristic reality. However development of a Nanorobot is associated with a multitude of challenges and limitations related mainly to its control and behavior aspects in different dynamic work environments. In this chapter a novel Nanorobot movement control algorithms in dynamic environment has being introduced. To avoid obstacles during movement trajectory, swarm intelligence based approach and for sensing, path planning, obstacle avoidance and target detection of nano-robot Quorum and RFID based approach has been utilized. Major proportion of work has been done on Microsoft Robotics Developer Studio 2008 along with two kinds of programming environment VPL and SPL. The chapter also includes a description of how nanorobotics technology has been applied in medical field. In this context, a non invasive method to treat a brain blood clot using nanorobots has being explained. Various other aspects of application of nanorobots has also been briefly mentioned.

Chapter 18

Real time analysis and interpretation of fetal heart rate (FHR) is the challenge posed to every clinician. Different algorithms had been developed, tried and subsequently incorporated into Cardiotocograph (CTG) machines for automated diagnosis. Feature extraction and accurate detection of baseline and its variability has been the focus of this chapter. Algorithms by Dawes and Redman and Ayres-de-Campos have been discussed in this chapter. The authors are pleased to propose an algorithm for extracting the variability of fetal heart. The algorithm's accuracy and degree of agreement with clinician's diagnosis had been established by various statistical methods. This algorithm has been compared with an algorithm proposed by Nidhal and the new algorithm is found to be better at detecting variability in both ante-partum and intra-partum period.

Chapter 19

Information security plays a vital role in almost every application that we handle in our day-to-day life since the communication needs to be protected in terms of the messages that we send and receive. Thus, cryptography the science of encoding the secret information provides security from being known by the unintended receivers. It ensured confidentiality, integrity, and authentication of messages. To simplify the methodology of traditional cryptography with the usage of genetic concepts lead to the field of DNA cryptography. This chapter gives an insight on various methods so far proposed related to DNA cryptography that involves the characteristics of DNA incorporating the traditional cryptographic techniques and a detailed comparison of these techniques thereby proposing the requirements for an efficient DNA-based cryptographic system. These techniques also include the area of steganography that conceals the message within a cover or a career media to eschew the attacks from the intruders.

Chapter 20

Gurkan Tuna, Trakya University, Turkey
Vehbi Cagri Gungor, Abdullah Gul University, Turkey

Underwater networking technologies have brought us unforeseen ways to explore the unexplored aquatic environment and this way provided us with a large number of different kinds of applications for environmental, scientific, commercial, and military purposes. Although precise and continuous aquatic environment monitoring capability is highly important for various underwater applications, due to the unique characteristics of underwater networks such as low communication bandwidth, high error rate, node mobility, large propagation delay, and harsh underwater environmental conditions, existing solutions cannot be applied directly to underwater networks. Therefore, new solutions considering the unique features of underwater environment are highly demanded. In this chapter, the authors mainly focus on the use of wireless micro-electromechanical systems for underwater networks and present its advantages. In addition, the authors investigate the challenges and open research issues of wireless MEMS to provide an insight into future research opportunities.

Chapter 21

Abhijit Bora, Gauhati University, India
Tulshi Bezboruah, Gauhati University, India

Quality estimation for viability of data processing and delivering through the paradigm of service oriented computing and load balancing cluster based web server for high performance of services against extensive load of consumers is an important concern in the domain of grid and distributed computing, big data analysis and internet of things. As such, this chapter proposes a quality estimation framework considering a prototype architecture for multi service multi-functional web services deploying in load balancing cluster based Apache Tomcat web server and developing a clinical database for processing disease related queries through the architecture. The high quality of service is monitored by generating extensive load of users over the system through Mercury LoadRunner load testing tool. In this chapter, the authors will discuss the methodology to study the quality of service, recorded quality metrics against different load of users and the statistical analysis along with results to establish the feasibility, applicability and adaptability of proposed quality estimation framework.

Preface

The field of communication is at the helm of affairs now-a-days. With the advancement of modern technology especially the advent of multimedia, bioinformatics and big data analytics, there has been a rapid evolution of data in these domains. Researchers have invested a lot of efforts for evolving intelligent solutions for the future in these domains. The efforts in this direction have proceeded at an explosive rate. Data processing procedures in the communication arena can greatly benefit the utilization and exploration of real data. But it is a genuine fact that most of these underlying data are unusable and imprecise in nature, thanks to the inherent uncertainty. The field of computational intelligence is blessed with several tools and techniques for handling the real life and real world uncertainties prevalent among these data sets in the communication arena. It may be noted that several classical techniques for handling this problem are reported in the literature. However, most of the classical techniques suffer from uncertainty, imprecision and vagueness. Conventional computing paradigms often fall short of offering solutions to them. Computational intelligence offers a wide range of solutions which addresses these issues to a considerable extent be it in the computational domain or in the communication networks domain. Moreover, the rapid advancement in communication sensor technologies is also a praiseworthy matter.

Computation has been one of the most astounding inventions of the present century. The communication networks are coming with flying colors. Both these fields are complementary to each other. The essence of computation lies in the dissemination of fruitful information through/via secured communication channels. Hence, the advancement of one is a boon in disguise to the advancement of another. A mammoth development has taken place in both the fields over the recent years.

As far as the field of computation is concerned, the most notable invention is the advent of intelligent machines in the form of robots which mimic human intelligence. Added to it, one can think of enormous and rapid development in data processing and mining techniques in the form of big data analytics. The advent of quantum computing has speeded up the processing capabilities of naive algorithms to a great extent. So much so forth, high performance computing (HPC) has given rise to a new era of computing paradigm where a large amount of data processing can take place effectively and efficiently. Needless to state, all these fields are motivated by the tools and technologies offered by the field of computational intelligence.

On the other hand, information networks exist to build, maintain, and develop social relationships among people, things, and places. People's behaviors are affected by information; if information contains errors or delivered information is delayed, people might not behave appropriately. Therefore, information networks are one of the most important infrastructures for our society. Information networks are built on device networks and device networks are built on energy networks. In this direction, the communication networks also have developed to a great extent. Gone are the days where it took several days to transmit information. Now, information gets transmitted at lightning speed, thanks to the advent of fiber optic communication. Mobile computing and mobile communication has also assisted mankind to communicate effectively. All these facets of communication have been mainly possible by the advancement of the underlying technology ranging from antenna design to streamlining waveform propagation characteristics. Added to these are the advancements in hardware realizations of network devices and structures.

Above all, the security of information dissemination in this information technology arena is an essential criterion. An outstanding and perpetual research initiative has always been invested in this direction resulting in robust and secure communication channels for dissemination of information.

This book is intended to encompass the recent advancements in computational intelligence as it applies to communication networks.

The proposed book would come to the benefits of several categories of students and researchers. At the students' level, this book can serve as a treatise/reference book for the special papers at the master's level aimed at inspiring possibly future researchers. Newly inducted PhD aspirants would also find the contents of this book useful as far as their compulsory course works are concerned.

At the researchers' level, those interested in interdisciplinary research would also be benefited from the book. After all, the enriched interdisciplinary contents of the book would always be a subject of interest to the faculties, existing research communities and new research aspirants from diverse disciplines of the concerned departments of premier institutes across the globe. This is expected to bring different research backgrounds (due to its cross platform characteristics) close to one another to form effective research groups all over the world. Above all, availability of the book should be ensured to as much universities and research institutes as possible through whatever graceful means it may be.

The edited volume comprises 21 well versed and self-contained chapters from diverse research domains ranging from fundamentals of communication systems to intelligent antenna design along with some reporting on recent computing paradigms.

Chapter 1 presents a cyclostationary analysis of modulated signals in modern communication systems. It elaborates the different techniques which are applied to the spectral correlation function (SCF) of signals for extracting features on the basis of which decision of detecting a signal or noise is made. The chapter also presents a comparison of several signal detection techniques on the basis of utilizing unique feature exhibit by a normalized vector calculated on SCF along frequency axis.

Cognitive radio is now acknowledged as a potential solution to meet the spectrum scarcity problem in radio frequency range. To achieve this objective proper identification of vacant frequency band is necessary. In Chapter 2, a detection methodology based on cepstrum estimation has been proposed that can be done through power spectral density estimation of the received signal. The detection has been studied under different channel fading conditions along with Gaussian noise.

RFID and MANET become the growing components of Information and Communication Technology (ICT) applications and can be effectively utilized in global operations. RFID and MANET have the potential to increase the efficiency of operations in various industries, improve asset visibility and traceability, decrease reliance on manual processes, reduce operation costs, and provide useful data for business analytics. Chapter 3 describes the various aspects and applications of Radio Frequency Identification (RFID) to the heath care industry, supply chain management and modern business.

Software Defined Radio (SDR) systems can adapt to the future-proof solution and it covers both existing and emerging standards. An SDR has to possess elements of reconfigurability, intelligence and software programmable hardware. The main interest in any communication group is the sure sending of signals of info from a transmitter to a receiver. Chapter 4 discusses an SDR system built using LabVIEW for a Generic Transceiver.

Optical packet switching is a connectionless networking solution through which we can get high speed data transfer and optimum bandwidth utilization using wavelength division multiplexing technique. A number of optical packet switch architectures are available in market for realizing optical packet switching. In Chapter 5, the authors discuss the overall development of optical packet switching. It also focuses on a comparison between the switches through loss, cost and buffer analysis.

Flexible and wearable technology, having the merits of being light-weight, energy efficient, in addition to low manufacturing cost, reduced fabrication complexity, and the availability of inexpensive flexible substrates is being established as an appealing alternative to the conventional electronics technologies which are based on rigid substrates. Furthermore, wearable antennas have been a topic of interest for more than the past decade, and hundreds of scientific papers can be found on the subject. Chapter 6 deals with an overview of antennas of wearable technologies surmising the advantages, disadvantage and challenges.

The radio frequency (RF) energy harvesting is found as an attractive alternative to existing energy resources. Chapter 7 deals with the design and performance evaluation of different rectifying antenna circuits for RF energy harvesting. This chapter throws light on the different circularly polarized microstrip antennas e.g. shorted square ring slot antenna and crossed monopole antenna with step ground plane. The chapter concludes with a detailed study on the performance of the rectenna circuits evaluated in terms of conversion efficiency.

Robustness and reliability are two essential network parameters to be given priority in Industrial Wireless Sensor Network (IWSN). But at the same time it is difficult to achieve gain in these performance metrics. Since in industries these networks are used for monitoring, control and automation processes, therefore, it also requires robust communication with minimum delay. Considering the need of high QoS in Industrial WSN, protocols and standards were developed to fulfill the requirement of reliable data communication in harsh environment. Chapter 8 discusses about a cross layer cooperative protocol for IWSN.

Chapter 9 presents a dynamic reputation based incentive scheme to encourage selfish nodes in post-disaster situation using Delay Tolerant Network (DTN). A DTN is described by a special kind of mobile ad-hoc network where sparseness, large communication delay and lack of end to end path from source to destination exist. It is evident from this fact that data forwarding is dependent on the cooperation of multiple hops in "store-carry-forward" manner. However, nodes involved in communication may sometimes behave maliciously and may non-cooperate. The primary objective of this chapter is to develop a reliable data forwarding scheme by detecting malicious activities and encourage nodes to participate in Post Disaster Communication environment.

Of late, Flying Ad-hoc Networks (FANETs), enabling ad-hoc networking between highly mobile Unmanned Aerial Vehicles (UAVs), are gaining importance in several military, commercial and civilian applications. The sensitivity of these missions requires precise and prompt data delivery. Thus, the most important communication requirements that need to be addressed while designing FANETs are of high reliability and low latency. In line with these demands, Chapter 10 focuses on the mobility models, MAC protocols and routing protocols for FANETs.

Security and trust are two inevitable concepts for secure MANET. There are various systems used for ensuring security and trust in case of MANET. These systems have several advantages as well as several disadvantages in terms of high communication and computation overhead. The goal of Chapter

11 is to implement a leader election algorithm after proper evaluation of node trust in MANET on the basis of ratio of signal sent and acknowledgement received.

One of the critical and vital parameters of Wireless Sensor Networks (WSNs) is its lifetime. There are various methods to increase WSN lifetime, clustering technique is one of them. In clustering, selection of desired percentage of Cluster Head (CHs) is performed among the sensor nodes (SNs). Selected CHs are responsible to collect data from its member nodes, aggregates the data and finally send to the sink. Chapter 12 presents Fuzzy-TOPSIS techniques based on multi criteria decision making to choose CH efficiently and effectively to maximize the WSN lifetime.

Chapter 13 highlights a cost effective, hassle free and secure communication between the cloud and moving vehicles. The goal of this chapter is to give a broad overview of Vehicular cloud computing, vehicular cloud applications, mobile computing, and recent literature covering security of vehicular cloud.

Cloud computing is one of the most vital technology which has become a part of corporate life. It is considered to be one of the most emerging technologies which serve various applications. Generally these Cloud computing systems provide various data storage services which highly reduce the complexity of users. Chapter 14 focuses on addressing the confidentiality of users' data. Since software level security has vulnerabilities in addressing this problem, the authors introduces a hardware level of security in the form of Trusted Platform Module (TPM) which is a chip in computer that is used for secure storage.

Chapter 15 presents an indoor navigation solution for visually impaired pedestrians, which employs a combination of a radio frequency identification (RFID) tag array and dead-reckoning to achieve positioning and localisation. This form of positioning aims to reduce the deployment cost and complexity of pure RFID array implementations.

The two main important features of neural networks are weights and bias connection, which is still a challenging problem for researchers. In Chapter 16, the authors select weights and bias connection of neural network (KN) using modified differential evolution algorithm (MDEA) i.e. MDEA-NN for uncertain nonlinear systems with unknown disturbances and compare it with KN using differential evolution algorithm (DEA) i.e. DEA-KN.

The construction of a practical nanorobot is a definite futuristic reality. However, the development of a Nanorobot is associated with a multitude of challenges and limitations related mainly to its control and behavioral aspects in different dynamic work environments. Chapter 17 discusses different Nanorobot movement control algorithms in dynamic environments. This chapter also includes a description of how nanorobotics technology has been applied in medical field.

Real time analysis and interpretation of fetal heart rate (FHR) is the primary challenge posed to every clinician. Different algorithms had been developed, tried and subsequently incorporated into Cardiotocograph (CTG) machines for automated diagnosis. Chapter 18 proposes an algorithm for extracting the variability of fetal heart. The algorithm's accuracy and degree of agreement with clinician's diagnosis had been established by various statistical methods.

Chapter 19 gives an insight on various methods so far proposed related to DNA cryptography that involves the characteristics of DNA incorporating the traditional cryptographic techniques and a detailed comparison of these techniques thereby proposing the requirements for an efficient DNA-based cryptographic system. These techniques also include the area of steganography that conceals the message within a cover or a career media to eschew the attacks from the intruders.

Underwater networking technologies have brought us unforeseen ways to explore the unexplored aquatic environment and this way provided us with a large number of different kinds of applications for environmental, scientific, commercial, and military purposes. Although precise and continuous aquatic environment monitoring capability is highly important for various underwater applications, due to the unique characteristics of underwater networks such as low communication bandwidth, high error rate, node mobility, large propagation delay, and harsh underwater environmental conditions, existing solutions cannot be applied directly to underwater networks. In Chapter 20, the authors mainly focus on the use of wireless micro-electromechanical systems for underwater networks and present its advantages. In addition, the authors investigate the challenges and open research issues of wireless MEMS to provide an insight into future research opportunities.

Quality estimation for viability of data processing and delivering through the paradigm of service oriented computing and load balancing cluster based web server for high performance of services against extensive load of consumers is an important concern in the domain of grid and distributed computing, big data analysis and internet of things. As such, Chapter 21 proposes a quality estimation framework considering a prototype architecture for multi service multi-functional web services deploying in load balancing cluster based Apache Tomcat web server and developing a clinical database for processing disease related queries through the architecture.

The primary objective of the book is to bring a broad spectrum of data communication applications under the purview of computational intelligence so that it is able to trigger further inspiration among various research communities to contribute in their respective fields of applications thereby orienting these application fields towards intelligence.

Once the purpose, as stated above, is achieved a larger number of research communities may be brought under one umbrella to ventilate their ideas in a more structured manner. In that case, the present endeavor may be seen as the beginning of such an effort in bringing various research applications in the complementary fields of intelligent communication close to one another.

Siddhartha Bhattacharyya
RCC Institute of Information Technology, India

Nibaran Das
Jadavpur University, India

Debotosh Bhattacharjee
Jadavpur University, India

Anirban Mukherjee
RCC Institute of Information Technology, India

Chapter 1
Blind Signal Detection Techniques for Spectrum Sensing in Satellite Communication:
Blind Signal Detection Techniques for Satellite Communication

Bilal Muhammad Khan
National University of Sciences and Technology Islamabad, Pakistan

Rabia Bilal
Usman Institute of Technology, Pakistan

ABSTRACT

Modulated signals used in communication systems exhibits cyclic periodicity. This is primarily due to sinusoidal product modulators, repeating preambles, coding and multiplexing in modern communication. This property of signals can be analyzed using cyclostationary analysis. SCF (Spectral correlation function) of cyclic autocorrelation (CAF) has unique features for different modulated signals and noise. Different techniques are applied to SCF for extracting features on the basis of which decision of detecting a signal or noise is made. In this chapter, study and analysis of different modulated signals used in satellite communication is presented using SCF. Also comparison of several signal detection techniques is provided on the basis of utilizing unique feature exhibit by a normalized vector calculated on SCF along frequency axis. Moreover a signal detection technique is also proposed which identifies the presence of a signal or noise in the analyzed data within the defined threshold limits.

DOI: 10.4018/978-1-5225-1785-6.ch001

INTRODUCTION

Motivation

Satellite cognitive radios have been proposed in recent years so that the static bandwidth of the satellite can be utilized by primary and secondary users. Cognitive radio needs spectrum sensing technique to sense the free radio channel for utilization. Cyclostationary analysis is a hot research topic in spectrum sensing because it is efficient than traditional energy detection analysis. Techniques based on this method are complex and computational hungry to be used in cognitive radios. This chapter focuses towards the modulated signals used in communication satellites since there is almost no or very little research present focusing this particular area. If computational complexity of the detection technique is minimized, the research will help in developing algorithms for spectrum sensing modules for satellite cognitive radios.

Cyclostationary and Cognitive Radios for Satellite

Cyclostationary analysis of modulated signals have been a vast topic of research for almost half a century, different aspects of this inherent property of modulated signals have been investigated in that period (Gardner, 1994). The main application of cyclostationarity of signals is in the domain of spectrum sensing as it has been a proven technique for this purpose than conventional energy detection (Yucek & Arsalan, 2009). After the advent of SDR (Software defined radio) based CR (Cognitive radios) to solve the problem of spectrum scarcity in the frequency bands (Mitola & Maguire, 1999), cyclostationary analysis have been adopted as a perfect choice for spectrum sensing (Sutton, Nolan, & Doyle, 2008; Paisana, N. Prasad, Rodrigues, & R. Prasad, 2012; Nafkha, Naoues, Cichon, & Kliks, 2014). The main focus in this context is in the terrestrial bands but their exploitation in satellite communication is still not explored (Tarchi et al., 2014). Particularly, very few initiatives at academic and industrial level have addressed the spectrum sensing aspects for CR of satellite communication (Tarchi et al., 2014). So application of cyclostationary analysis to the modulated carriers in the satellite band is an open research area. The CR for satellite needs to detect the modulated carriers while performing the spectrum sensing in order to provide opportunity spectrum holes to secondary users. There is a computational complexity associated with the cyclostationary based detection so detection technique devised for satellite CR should be low in complexity with shorter number of samples and low resolution analysis (Sutton, Nolan, & Doyle, 2008).

In satellite communication, modulated carriers are generated with modems, function generators meant for this purpose and travels at around 36000 km up to the satellite receiver. The band pipe nature of the satellite sends them back to the downlink. So this channel incorporated a lot of noisy effects in the communication signals and then intended CR should be working with these received signals having the effect of this long path channel. The importance of this scenario must be kept in mind while designing the signal detection technique for satellite CR. In this research, properties of such signals are exploited and a simpler technique incorporating all the complexity parameters discussed above is being proposed for satellite CR. The platform for the design of practical CR is of great importance. This is due to the fact that if the designed algorithm for detection is not compatible with the CR platform then the signal detection efficiency will be compromised. So USRP2 which has been a proven platform for practical SDR and CR development is used to capture the satellite signals and the lab generated satellite signals. This will enable the developed algorithm to work as a practical spectrum sensing engine for a prospective satellite CR on a real CR platform as in (Sutton, Nolan, & Doyle, 2008; Baldini, Guiliani, Capriglione, & Sithamparanathan, 2012; Aziz, & Nafkha, 2014; Nafkha, Naoues, Cichon, & Kliks, 2014).

Figure 1. GUI of GNURADIO flow graph in GRC

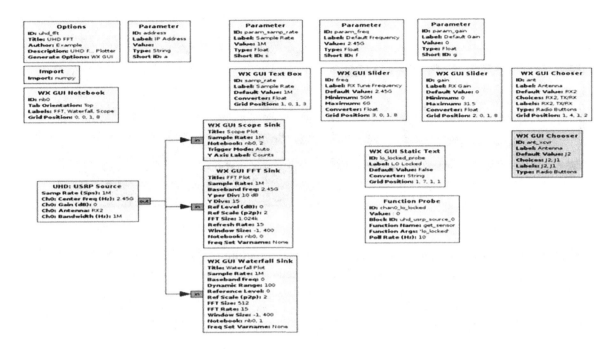

Gnu Radio

GNU Radio is an official project of GNU since 2001, it is free with open source rights software. Its development toolkit has signal processing and operation blocks using which SDR systems can be implemented. These systems can be interfaced with available low-cost RF hardware or general purpose processors (Lin, He, & He, 2009).GNU radio applications are based on python as the programming language. Main signal processing blocks in GNU radio are written in C++ programming language in processor having floating point arithmetic. In GNU radio signal processing blocks are built on C++ programming language, and they use python programming language as wrapper which connects together the signal processing block (Liangkaia, Jian, Yongtao, & Tao, 2011). In Figure 1 graphical user interface of GNU radio flow graph is shown. The application of GNU radio is known as GNU radio companion (GRC).

USRP2

The universal software radio peripheral or USRP2 is a RF hardware front end sensor and preprocessor used with GNU radio. It can convert normal computers into high bandwidth RF software radio instruments. Essentially, if a communication radio system is considered, USRP2 is the digital baseband and its daughter card is intermediate frequency (IF) equipments.in the whole system. In a standard USRP2 two parts are included:

1. A mother board with a field-programmable gate array (FPGA), with high-speed processing feature for signals;
2. At-least one or more RF daughter boards designed to cover different bands of frequencies.

Figure 2. (a) USRP2 front panel with interfaces (b) USRP2 mother board with XCVR2450 RF daughter cards

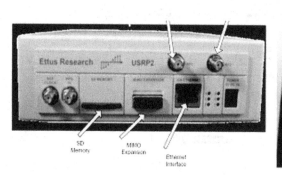

The picture of USRP2 is present in Figure 2 (a), and a picture of USRP2 mother board is present in Figure 2 (b). The elements of USRP2 include a speedy 1Gbps Ethernet port which acts as the data bridge between PC and the FPGA, there are four 14bits/sample 100 Msamples/sec high-speed analog-to-digital convertors (ADCs) and four 16 bits/sample 400Msamples/sec high-speed digital-to-analog convertors (DACs). The mother board is capable of supporting two transmit and receive daughter boards respectively. In order to change the operating frequency range we can choose different USRP2's daughter boards (Lin, He, & He, 2009). Examples are, wide-band transceiver (WBX) daughter board working at frequency range of 50-2200MHz, RFX400 daughter board working at 400-500MHz. In our experimentation, wide-band SBX transceiver with 400-4400MHz range of frequency operation is used.

LITERATURE REVIEW

In this section different approaches carried out in the literature for calculating the cyclostationary features of modulated signals are presented. The basic idea behind the approach, its significance, novelty and discrepancies are discussed. Specially, techniques using the second order statistics of the signal including the cyclic autocorrelation and the spectral correlation density for signal detection are focused.

Cyclostationary Detection

Cyclostationary for wireless signals that are present in signal processor is define by periodic variation in the statistical properties. These characteristics are time-varying with periodicity. For such wireless signals having periodicity property and modeled as cyclostationary signal, then functionality of signal processor can be enhanced by extracting cyclic features through signal detection based on features. Cyclostationary features shown by modulated carriers using signal processing of modulated sampled data is well developed in literature and has been used conventionally in wireless communication domain. The idea behind this special property of the signals is based on the fact that due to sine and cosine waves used to generate signals in a repeating manner so this introduces cyclic behavior and a part from signal's carrier frequency there exists a frequency which is a function of repetition of the parameters of such waves. This frequency is called cyclic frequency. Cyclostationary theory as first introduced by Gardner (1994) exploiting cyclo periodic features of random processes opened new threads in wide research scope. Features exhibited by the random processes and modulated signals as a function of the frequency and cyclic frequency was discovered. Detailed analysis of the cyclic periodogram was presented. The autocorrelation which is a second order statistical property for a Guassian processes having normal distribution was used by the author. Spectral analysis of autocorrelation function led to the discovery of specific peaks in the spectral density at certain location of cyclic frequency as a function of the carrier frequency. This was the first time when a proper mathematical frame work for exploring the cyclostationary behavior of the signals was proposed. The research was also used to detect cyclostationary signals leading towards development of cyclostatioanry detectors.

To implement the cyclostationary detector, cyclostationarity features of the signals are used (Lunden & Koivunen, 2007). If a signal is found in the channel, cyclic correlation values have peaks in it. If there are no peak(s), it implies that spectrum band is idle and no signal is present at the observation time. Test statistics are usually formed using the values in spectral density of correlation. For better calculations of correlation spectral peaks values large number of samples are important. A better signal detection is carried out in this way. Cyclostationary processing has added benefit of insensitivity to lower SNR and without demodulating the received signal it can detect it (Sithamparanathan & Giorgetti, 2012). As the implementation is considered, cyclostationary detector is fast Fourier transform (FFT) based and degrading SNR issues are avoidable as variance of noise is not needed in cyclic spectral analysis. This gives added advantage over the conventional energy detection method. The trade-off between good performance and high efficiency is always there for the implementation of the detection system. It is emphasized in the research literature to use longer length of observation data in order to have better signal detection estimation. Cyclostationary processing is beneficial in two important aspects. The one is its less sensitivity to low SNR (Signal to Noise ratio) and the other one is that it does not require any demodulation of the signal under consideration for extracting significant features for signal detection. Different techniques for signal detection developed in the literature have exploited the inherent properties of the parameters resulting in cyclostationary analysis. Symmetric nature and cyclic frequency location spectral peaks are two examples. These properties appear in the spectral density of the cyclostationary signal. Other techniques using complex processing for pattern matching based feature verification were also developed. The main disadvantages are high resolution analysis and complex computational requirements making them void for usage in faster spectrum sensing modules of cognitive radio designs. One such design is a satellite cognitive radio. Till date, energy based detection and processing on PSD (Power Spectral Density) of the received spectrum has been utilized for the subject of spectrum sensing for satellite cognitive radios. (Dimic, Baldini, & Kandeepan, 2014; Norris, Taylor, & Tyler, 2013).

Specific Signal Detection Techniques

Cyclostationary signals when analyzed produce features as a result. Optimum detection has been done by comparing the ideal spectral density signatures for OFDM scheme QPSK carriers with the received one in (Sutton, Nolan, & Doyle, 2008). This comparison scheme has good performance in terms of detection probability under low SNR. Also, only one FFT calculation block both for OFDM carrier generation and spectral density calculations was used reducing hardware resource utilization. But it requires high resolution complex computations in order to detect the features similar to the ideal signatures of OFDM features. Parallel implementation of cyclostationary mathematical model had been carried out in (Ge & Bostian, 2008). The method adopted was to calculate the spectral density using parallel hardware blocks instead of sequential approach. FAM (FFT Accumulation Method) is used to calculate it. A symmetry test for features in the cyclic spectrum was done to detect the signal. A very low computational time was achieved in estimating the cyclic spectrum using parallel hardware estimators. The parallelism of technique supersedes the serial implementation but the parallel threads required high resolution analysis for symmetric detection. High resolution analysis means incorporating every possible value of cyclic frequency in the analysis. Single cyclic frequency based high resolution analysis presented in (Da, Xiaoying, Hsiao-Hwa, Liang, & Miao, 2009) utilizes the maximum value of spectral density at an assumed single cycle frequency as the function of the carrier frequency with assumption of known carrier frequency and modulation type for the analyzed signal. Whole spectral density calculations were avoided and significant feature was achieved at low SNR. Detection decision is done using the threshold value achieved in case of noise and in case of signal plus noise values. The technique works with the assumption of AWGN noise. Third order cyclic cumulants for one value of cyclic frequency (the frequency of periodic repetitions) were presented in (Lin, He, & He, 2009). Covariance based matrix was calculated to detect the signal numerically by comparing with a predetermined threshold. As the order of the calculation statistics increases along with covariance matrix calculations, less efficient the technique becomes in terms of computational requirements. Circular correlation stage addition was proposed in (Lee, 2008) before the FFT stage in cyclostationary detector resulting in enhanced features achieved under lower SNR at the expense of higher computational complexity. The circular correlation stage provides a zero valued result when noise is input to the system due to random nature of the noise signal. When a true signal with cyclic periodicities inserted then it shows real values for cyclic correlation. In this way the spectral density contains features in it which were searched by the detector in terms of numerical values. Resulting enhanced features in spectral density were presented for different modulations. Timing mismatches causing feature attenuation were avoided in (Rebeiz & Cabric, 2011) by extracting feature vectors for each modulation type considered in the analysis. These feature vectors were compared separately with the calculated feature vector for the input signal for detecting the signal. The technique was proved to be robust for mitigating timing mismatches effects on the features in the spectral density. The pre-processing stage introduced to estimate the symbol rate of the incoming data had Haar wavelets. Wavelets were used to provide blindly estimated symbol rate by measuring the phase transitions from symbol changes. The frequency separation between transitions provides the estimated symbol rate Interpolated new symbol rate is used to calculate the cyclic spectrum. The proposed technique assumed a prior known carrier frequency. Wavelet based symbol rate estimation, spectral density at specific locations and comparison of feature vectors for different modulations made the technique very complex. Cyclic cumulants on BPSK modulation were applied in (Liangkaia, Jian, Yongtao, & Tao, 2011) to analyses the features of BPSK modulation using higher order statistics. In (Zhou, Li, Yang, Liu, & Wu, 2012) SDR (software defined radio) based cyclostationary analysis had been done. Coherence function was used to normalize the spectral density and carrier frequency was estimated. Spectrogram of the modulated data is used to detect the presence of the signal graphically. Carrier frequency and bit rate of the input signal was successfully estimated. The presented work enlightens only the various parameters that can be estimated using the spectral density using real time data captured from USRP. The experimentation setup of this paper provides the basic setup requirements and procedures for capturing real time data in this research. Wavelets processed spectral feature detection in the graphical plot of spectral density was carried out in (Liu et al., 2013). Reconstruction of spectral density plot was done by utilizing the smaller number of samples using non-linear or convex reconstruction algorithms. This is known as compressed sensing technique. The noise produced by the reconstruction process was removed by treating the resulting spectral density as grey image plot using Wavelets. Noise reduction and good application of Wavelets in RF domain was achieved but higher complexity with the use of two dimensional Haar wavelets was unavoidable. Practical classifier values for the cumulants were presented for BPSK, QPSK and QAM-16 modulations. The spectral density was calculated using spectral coherence function. Energy detection was used to determine the signal in the channel at the desired frequency. Then using detailed coherence function ratios for BPSK, QPSK and QAM-16 modulations were calculated. Threshold for detection was set using the mean point of the probability density function of the three modulations. The application of cumulants on the I and Q samples proved to be a good modulation classifier. Similar application of cumulants has been shown in the presented research using the resultant feature vector from the proposed technique as the input to the cumulant algorithm. Efficient spectral density algorithm on FPGA was implemented in (Badawy & Khattab, 2014) to perform the cyclostationary analysis of the signals. The detection technique under training mode saves the location of the peaks particularly produced in spectral density in look up tables with memory requirements. High complexity involves when the whole values of the analyzed data got compared with the data of the look up tables. FAM algorithm has been successfully implemented on FPGA but for the detection of signal higher memory requirement based look up tables were used. High resolution cyclostationary analysis done to make decision of a signal presence presented in (Nafkha, Naoues, Cichon, & Kliks, 2014) exploited symmetry in the correlation statistics. Spectral density estimations were carried out by using the compressed orthogonal reconstruction from samples. ANN (Artificial neural network) trained in (Ghauri, Qureshi, Shah, & Khan, 2014) were used to detect and classify modulation type of the inputted cyclostationary signals. Three layered ANN structure was used. Coherence function was first applied to get the training data for ANN. The proposed technique proved to be working well with good probability of detection and classification of the signal. Coherence function and ANN implementation makes the technique computationally demanding. A blind but complex in computation technique was presented in (Jang, 2014). It is calculating SCSD (Sum of the magnitude square of the Cyclic Spectral Density). Symmetric property of the cyclic spectral density, magnitude square, convolution between frequency shifted signal and differentiation was done to reach at the peaks and jumps in the cyclic frequency on the basis of which detection decision is done. Additional computational complexity added with two FFTs (Fast Fourier Transforms) and IFT (Inverse Fourier Transform). In (Wu, Yang, Liu, & Chakarvarthy, 2012), cyclostationary analysis for under water acoustic communication has been presented. The modulation format of BPSK and QPSK were analyzed. The detection technique works by estimating the spectral density of the input signal using dynamic multi resolution spectral correlation function. In this technique SCF is estimated with low resolution for cyclic frequency in all the regions and with high resolution at specific locations for cyclic frequency where significant features appear. Peak ratios for BPSK and QPSK are calculated by dividing the peak magnitude at cyclic frequency and frequency axes. Modulation detection was achieved in under water acoustic communication using this cyclostationary analysis detection technique. Higher detection probabilities were resulted by experimenting on real data. The technique has been found susceptible to Doppler and noise effects of underwater scenario and in practice it is more dependent on the ratio statistical values. Also large samples were used to perform the detection of modulation.

It is evident from the above discussion on different novel techniques that cylostationary analysis is computationally complex and has statistical dependence such as variance and mean due to Guassian nature of communication signal and noise. There is still room for new methods based on SCF of the modulated signals for detection. In connection to cognitive radios for satellite very less emphasis is found in the literature. So, this research fills the gap and focused on a less complex cyclo detector using low resolution and less number of samples spectrum sensing scheme. The proposed new scheme must be well performing but must use fewer resources in terms of computational operations. Also, HOS cumulants have never been tested on the features of the spectral density. The hypothesis can be formulated with the fact that if a signal sample can be used to classify modulation type applying HOS cumulants then considering the feature numerical values in form of an input vector should result in some form of static ranges or values which can help in classification of the modulation type for the detected signal.

CYCLOSTATIONARY ANALYSIS AND FAM ALGORITHM

In this section mathematical model of the cyclostationary analysis is presented. First detailed discussion on the involvement of second order statistics in determining the cyclostationary features was done. A derivation of spectral correlation density is presented. In the end, an efficient previously proposed time smoothing algorithm known as FAM (FFT Accumulation Method) with operational details is discussed.

Background

In satellite communication, modulated signals are used for different applications utilizing the band of frequencies supported by the satellite. These modulated signals are cyclostationary in nature (Gardner, 1994). Cyclostationary features are caused by the periodicity in the signal due to multiplexing, product modulation, coding and preambles induced in the generation process (Gardner, 1994). Signal's mean and autocorrelation shows periodic features. Cyclostationary based algorithms can be used to detect signals in a band exploiting cyclic correlation function and can differentiate between noise and signals (Yucek & Arsalan, 2009) CAF (Cyclic autocorrelation function) is calculated for a cyclostationary signal which is a Fourier series coefficient $R_x(\tau)$. CAF exhibits the correlation between widely separated components because of the spectral redundancy due to periodicity (Ge & Bostian, 2008). Second order statistics of the signal are calculated using the Fourier coefficients in terms of its CAF and SCF.

Cyclic Autocorrelation Function

The periodic autocorrelation function can be expressed as:

$$R_x(t,\tau) = E\left[\left(x(t)x^*(t-\tau)\right)\right] \tag{1}$$

For a cyclostationary signal $R_x(t,\tau)$ is periodic and its Fourier series decomposition yields:

$$R_x(t,\tau) = \sum_\alpha R_x^\alpha(\tau)e^{i2\pi\alpha t} \tag{2}$$

where α is the cyclic frequency. The cyclic frequency α is the occurrences of the correlation due to periodicity in time domain (Gardner, 1994). Fourier coefficient $R_x^\alpha(\tau)$ is called the CAF and can be expressed as:

$$R_x^\alpha(\tau) = \lim_{T\to\infty} \frac{1}{T} \int_{\frac{-T}{2}}^{\frac{T}{2}} R_x(t,\tau) e^{-i2\pi\alpha t} dt \tag{3}$$

where, T is the observation interval for the signal.

$R_x(t,\tau)$ can be replaced by symmetric delay conjugate product and can be expressed as:

$$R_x^\alpha(\tau) = \lim_{T\to\infty} \frac{1}{T} \int_{\frac{-T}{2}}^{\frac{T}{2}} X\left(t+\frac{\tau}{2}\right) X\left(t-\frac{\tau}{2}\right)^* e^{-i2\pi\alpha t} dt \tag{4}$$

Cyclic correlation in time domain is between two frequencies shifted x (t) values which in frequency domain are separated by α.

Let $u(t)=x(t)e^{-i\pi\alpha t}$ and $v(t)=x(t)e^{i\pi\alpha t}$ are two shifted version of $x(t)$.

$$R_x^\alpha(\tau) = \lim_{T\to\infty} \frac{1}{T} \int_{\frac{-T}{2}}^{\frac{T}{2}} u\left(t+\frac{\tau}{2}\right) v\left(t-\frac{\tau}{2}\right)^* dt \tag{5}$$

The Fourier transform of the CAF of $x(t)$ is defined as the Spectral Correlation Density (SCF). SCF is the cyclic spectrum at a given cycle frequency α. It is the density of the correlation between two spectral components separated by an amount equal to cycle frequency. SCF is also referred to as cyclic spectral density (CSD). The CSD function produces peaks when cycle frequency is exact multiple of fundamental frequency due to correlation (Yucek & Arsalan, 2009).

Spectral Correlation Function

The SCF from the CAF is given as:

$$S_x^\alpha(f) = \int_{-\infty}^{\infty} R_x^\alpha(\tau) e^{-i2\pi f\tau} d\tau \tag{6}$$

In terms of symmetric delay conjugate product between frequencies $\left(f+\frac{\alpha}{2}\right)$ and $\left(f-\frac{\alpha}{2}\right)$ for T interval, SCF in Equation 6 becomes:

$$S_x^\alpha\left(f\right) = \lim_{\Delta t \to \infty} \lim_{T \to \infty} \frac{1}{\Delta t} \frac{1}{T} \int_{-\frac{\Delta t}{2}}^{\frac{\Delta t}{2}} X_T\left(t, f + \frac{\alpha}{2}\right) X_T^*\left(t, f - \frac{\alpha}{2}\right) dt \tag{7}$$

where, $X_T\left(t, f\right)$ is the spectral component of x(t) given as:

$$X_T\left(t, f\right) = \int_{t-\frac{T}{2}}^{t+\frac{T}{2}} x\left(t\right) e^{-i2\pi f} dt \tag{8}$$

The calculated SCF is viewed on a bi-frequency plane as a function of frequency f and cyclic frequency α. A range for spectral frequency f is from $-\frac{f_s}{2}$ to $\frac{f_s}{2}$ and α is from $-f_s$ to f_s. Modulated signals have unique features pattern in their SCF that can be utilized for signal detection (Like, Chakravarthy, Ratazzi, & Wu, 2009).

FFT Accumulation Method

FAM (FFT accumulation method) is an algorithm for SCF calculation based on time smoothing method. Time smoothing method is an efficient method for SCF calculation than frequency smoothing method (Guenther, 2009; Brown & Loomis, 1993). FAM method calculates the FT (Fourier Transform) of the time smoothed correlation product of the spectral components.

Input signal $x\left(n\right)$ in Figure 3. *Time Smoothing FAM Procedure* is divided into blocks by Hamming window for reducing the spectral leakage. Complex demodulates are estimated efficiently by FFT covering all the samples in the input. Frequency shift is done to convert the signal into baseband. A step size is used instead of continuous slid through samples. Product sequences from the calculated components and complex conjugate are formed followed by a second FFT for time smoothing (Martian, Sandu, Fratu, Marghescu, & Craciunescu, 2014). The first FFT size is determined by the frequency resolution Δf and second FFT size is determined by cyclic frequency resolution $\Delta\alpha$.

$$N' = \frac{f_s}{\Delta f} \tag{9}$$

$$P = \frac{f_s}{L\Delta\alpha} \tag{10}$$

where, N' and P are the first and second FFT sizes respectively f_s is the sampling frequency.

Figure 3. Time Smoothing FAM Procedure

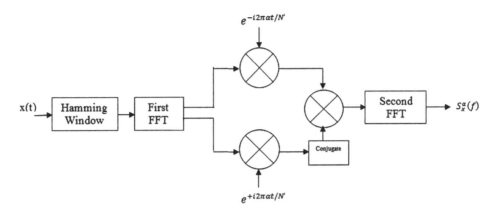

SCF OF BPSK, QPSK, AND QAM-16 MODULATIONS

Ideal features of the SCF for different modulation schemes are presented in this section. Using the cyclostationary concepts and definitions, features in the SCF of BPSK, QPSK and QAM-16 modulations can be mathematically estimated as follows.

BPSK Modulation

For BPSK modulated signal

$$y(t) = a(t)\cos\left(2\pi f_c t + \phi_0\right),$$

SCF according to (Jang, 2014; Liu, Han, Liu, & Wu, 2013) can be expressed as:

$$S_y^\alpha(f) = \begin{cases} \dfrac{1}{4}\left[S_\alpha^0\left(f - f_c\right) + S_\alpha^0\left(f + f_c\right)\right], & \alpha = 0; \\[2mm] \dfrac{1}{4}e^{j2\phi_0}S_\alpha^0\left(f\right), & \alpha = 2f_c \\[2mm] \dfrac{1}{4}e^{-j2\phi_0}S_\alpha^0\left(f\right), & \alpha = -2f_c \end{cases} \tag{11}$$

where α is the cyclic frequency, ϕ_0 is the shift in phase and S_α^0 is the Fourier transform of the autocorrelation $R_\alpha^0\left(\tau\right)$.

It is clear from the above estimate that the BPSK will show total four peaks. Two in the cyclic domain where $f = 0$ and two in the frequency domain where $\alpha = 0$ in the bi-frequency plot of SCF.

QPSK Modulation

For QPSK modulated signal

$$y(t) = \frac{1}{\sqrt{2}} \left[a(t) \cos\left(2\pi f_c t + \phi_0\right) + b(t) \cos\left(2\pi f_c t + \phi_0 + \frac{\pi}{2}\right) \right].$$

The inphase $a(t)$ and quadrature $b(t)$ can be viewed as two separate BPSKs respectively. So SCF for QPSK can be given as:

$$S_y^\alpha(f) = \left\{ \frac{1}{4} \left[S_\alpha^0\left(f - f_c\right) + S_\alpha^0\left(f + f_c\right) \right], \quad \alpha = 0; \right. \tag{12}$$

QPSK will be having two peaks in frequency domain where α =0. This is due to the cancelation of in-phase part and quadrature part in cyclic frequency domain.

QAM-16 Modulation

For QAM-16 modulated signal

$$y(t) = c(t) \cos\left(2\pi f_0 t\right) - d(t) \sin\left(2\pi f_0 t\right).$$

QAM-16 will have two peaks in the frequency domain at α = 0. Moreover, if the in-phase and quadrature part cancels out each other completely, then there will be no peaks in the cyclic frequency domain. For the case of no or little subtraction between in-phase and quadrature components, peaks may appear at locations in frequency domain.

A graphical representation of the ideal SCF of the BPSK plotted against f and α can be seen in Figure 4. The circles in blue color depicts the peaks in the SCF at specified values of cyclic frequency α, frequency resolution f and the carrier frequency f_c

BPSK modulation shows four peaks according to Equation 11. If proper values for the cyclic frequency resolution and frequency resolution are set in the analysis, ideal SCF is obtained for modulated signals present in the sampled data input to the analysis algorithm. Cyclostationary features then can be used to detect the signal from the noise.

PROPOSED DETECTION TECHNIQUE

Spectral correlation function $S_x(f, \alpha)$ is a two-dimensional function of frequency and cyclic frequency when calculated practically. It shows particular spectral peaks at certain frequency and cyclic frequency locations due to cyclostationarity. These peaks are particular features represented by SCF for particular

Figure 4. A graphical representation of Ideal BPSK SCF

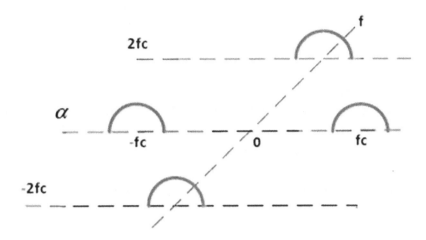

modulated signals as in our case it is BPSK, QPSK & QAM-16. The main idea behind devising a new technique is to enable a logical decision block and quantify the features shown by the SCF. For this purpose different techniques for detection have been proposed in (Sutton, Nolan, & Doyle, 2008; Ge & Bostian, 2008; Paisana, Prasad, Rodrigues, & Prasad, 2012; Xu, Chen, & Hu, 2014; Nafkha, Naoues, Cichon, & Kliks, 2014). All of these techniques in the literature use the calculated SCF further process it and reach at the detection hypothesis solution. One more method is to calculate high resolution SCF (Sutton, Nolan, & Doyle, 2008; Ge & Bostian, 2008) and use its inherent properties at particular cyclic frequency locations to detect presence of signal. In the proposed method first SCF is calculated using FAM algorithm. The frequency and cyclic frequency resolutions used are very low i.e. in order of KHz which is far greater in value from different recent and former approaches using frequency resolutions in hertz (Hz). Secondly, only 1024 maximum and 600 minimum samples have been used as input to the FAM algorithm. In simulation chapter details of the parameters of FAM algorithm has been presented. SCF containing features in its two dimensional bi-frequency plane plot for discrete input data can be expressed as cyclic periodogram (Renard, Lampe, & Horlin, 2013).

$$S_x\left(f,\alpha\right) = \frac{1}{N}\sum_{n=0}^{N-1} X_t\left(t_n, f\right) X_T^*\left(t_n, f+\alpha\right) \tag{13}$$

Let's define M as the maximum value in the calculated SCF so,

$$M = \max_{2-d\ index} S_x\left(f,\alpha\right) \tag{14}$$

Now, we define a normalized SCF as:

$$S_x\left(a,b\right) = S_x\left(f,\alpha\right) * \frac{1}{M}. \tag{15}$$

The features in the SCF can be extracted into a calculated column vector as:

$$V_i\left(K\right) = \left[Maximum\,Value\,of\,every\,column\,Index\left(1,2,3,....a\right)\right]_{\left(Row\,Wise\,shift\,\&\,compare\right)} \max_{x} S_x\left(a,b\right) \qquad (16)$$

where 'K' have values ranging from 1 to a. 'a' represents the number of rows in SCF.

The proposed detection uses only half of the values in the calculated vector to detect the presence of signal or noise in the analyzed data. This reduces the calculation complexity from 'N' vector point analysis to 'N/2' as in (Xu, Chen, & Hu, 2014).

The calculated vector $V_i\left(K\right)$ above is used by the detection block to generate the result of the hypothesis of signal and the noise in the captured spectrum band. The significant features of the SCF are presented in form of values in the index of vector V_i. This vector is a column vector. The values in the vector are in the range from $0 \underset{to}{\rightarrow} 1$. Spectral peaks in the SCF at the locations of (f=0, $\alpha = {}^{+}_{-}2f_c$), ($f = {}^{+}_{-}f_c$, α=0), (α=0), ($f = {}^{+}_{-}f_c, {}^{+}_{-}0.5f_c, \alpha = {}^{+}_{-}2f_c, {}^{+}_{-}f_c$) which are generally seen in the modulated data as in (Gardner, 1994; Rebeiz & Cabric, 2011; Ge & Bostian, 2008; Martian, Sandu, Fratu, Marghescu, & Craciunescu, 2014) are gathered in the calculated vector. Points of spectral correlation have values near to one. In case of noise, the SCF shows features only at α=0 for whole values of f (Jang, 2014). The calculated vector therefore, has more values near one. The distinction between a signal and noise thus can be made by using this response of the vector $V_i\left(K\right)$. A threshold value Υ is defined which is used to identify the number of values qualifying for distinguishing between noise and signal response. By experimentation, the values of interest in the vector are those passing $\Upsilon > 0.5$ threshold.

Let the hypothesis for detection be

$$H_0 = n\left(t\right) \qquad (17)$$

$$H_1 = y\left(t\right) + n\left(t\right) \qquad (18)$$

where n(t) is the noise and $y\left(t\right) + n\left(t\right)$ is signal with noise.

The decision is done for the two hypotheses above by calculating:

$$H_0 = No.\,of\,Values > \gamma = \frac{N}{2} \qquad (19)$$

$$H_1 = No.\,of\,Values > \gamma \neq \frac{N}{2} \qquad (20)$$

The detection procedure works as shown in Figure 5.

Figure 5. Block diagram of the detector

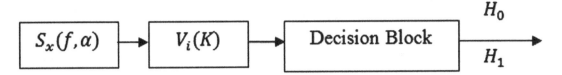

Figure 6. Block diagram of the technique

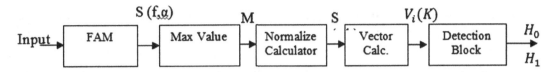

After calculating the SCF as shown in Figure 5, the vector $V_i(K)$ is extracted out containing the normalized SCF features in form of magnitudes ranging between 0 and 1. The decision block then counts the number of values in the vector above $\Upsilon > 0.5$ threshold level to decide between H_0 or H_1.

The working of the algorithm can be summarized in the following steps.

1. Estimate the SCF of the input signal using the low resolution values for frequency and cyclic frequency as parameter inputs to FAM. The resolution values are presented in Table 3.
2. Extract the maximum feature value's magnitude in the two dimensional plot of the calculated SCF using sort and compare in a nested conditional loop.
3. Normalize the whole SCF values by using this maximum value obtained in step 2.
4. Now take a one dimensional vector and extract the maximum value in magnitude from the SCF which is a matrix containing rows and columns. Sort and compare values by scanning the columns in rows.
5. Put only maximum value of the row in the vector. The vector would contain only values in the magnitude range from 0 to 1.
6. Now a search for the values passing the defined threshold is done.

Using the defined hypothesis for H_0 and H_1. If the number of peaks passing the threshold exceeds half of the number of values in the vector then detection of noise is declared else presence of the signal is declared.

Alternate to Spectral Coherence Function (SOF)

The coherence function is especially useful for cyclic frequency detection, since the coherence value is independent of the absolute power levels of the signals from the data signal $y(t)$, which simplifies choosing the threshold for detection (Martian, Sandu, Fratu, Marghescu, & Craciunescu, 2014). Additional advantage of SOF (being the normalized version of SCF) is that it helps in removing the channel effect. In literature a normalized version of the SCF is obtained for detection of signals using the Spectral Coherence Function (SOF) is given as:

$$C_y^\alpha \left(f \right) = \frac{S_y^\alpha \left(f \right)}{\sqrt{S_y^0 \left(f + \frac{\alpha}{2} \right) S_y^0 \left(f - \frac{\alpha}{2} \right)}} \qquad (21)$$

If we take a closer look at the Equation 21, it shows clearly that first SCF has to be estimated and at different cyclic frequency shifts the product value of $\alpha = 0$ SCF is used to calculate the coherence function $C_y^\alpha \left(f \right)$. Summarily, it is ratio of the whole bi-frequency SCF to the square root of the product of cyclic frequency shifted values at $\alpha = 0$. These values can also be referred to as PSD (Power Spectral Density) values (Gardner, 1994). This normalization method in comparison to the proposed technique implicates high computational complexity even if we select certain cyclic frequency locations such as $\alpha = 2f_c$ for calculating the denominator products. In the proposed technique of this research, simply maximum value of SCF in the bi-frequency plane is calculated and whole SCF of the bi-frequency plane is divided by this value using Equation 15. However, in this research the proposed method for detection has all the advantages offered by SOF with lesser amount of computational resources unlike the coherence function.

Fourth-Order Cumulants on Calculated Feature Vector for Modulation Classification

The spectrum sensing approach so far proposed has the ability to successively detect signal in the band of interest. But the type of modulation of the detected signal is unknown. One of most extensive methods used in the literature for modulation recognition is by using HOS (Higher order statistics). This is done by calculating the cyclic cumulants of 4th and above orders of the signal captured for detection purpose (Swami & Sadler, 2000; Pei-hua, Hong-xin, Xu-ying, Nan, & Yuan-yuan, 2012). The type of modulated signals in the presented work includes BPSK, QPSK and QAM-16 modulations. For BPSK only second-order statistics are enough to classify it. But for the case of QPSK and QAM-16 modulations, it lies in the higher order statistics i.e. 4th order cumulants are required to classify between these types of higher modulations.

In literature the modulation classification is done by first using the captured data (which can be complex valued or real valued data) to detect signal via energy detection method (Swami & Sadler, 2000; Narendar, Krishna, Vinod, & Madhukumar, 2012). Then cumulant values for third (Lin, He, & He, 2009) or 4th order cumulants are estimated for different modulation schemes. The Cumulant values thus estimated are used to classify the modulation types. It is evident from this approach that cumulants provides characteristic values different for different modulation types which helps in modulation recognition (Pei-hua, Hong-xin, Xu-ying, Nan, & Yuan-yuan, 2012).

For a random complex process $z\left(n \right)$, second order moments are given as:

$$C_{20} = E \left| z^2 \left(n \right) \right| \qquad (22)$$

$$C_{21} = E\left[\left|z\left(n\right)\right|^2\right] \tag{23}$$

$E[.]$ here is showing expected value of the $z\left(n\right)$ random process.

Fourth order moments and cumulants can be written in the following three ways (Swami & Sadler, 2000). 4th order cumulants can be defined as:

$$C_{40} = cum\left(z\left(n\right), z\left(n\right), z\left(n\right), z\left(n\right)\right) \tag{24}$$

$$C_{41} = cum\left(z\left(n\right), z\left(n\right), z\left(n\right), z^*\left(n\right)\right) \tag{25}$$

$$C_{42} = cum\left(z\left(n\right), z\left(n\right), z^*\left(n\right), z^*\left(n\right)\right) \tag{26}$$

For random variables a, b, c, d the fourth order cumulants can be written as:

$$cum\left(a, b, c, d\right) = E\left(abcd\right) - E\left(ab\right)E\left(cd\right) - E\left(ac\right)E\left(bd\right) - E\left(ad\right)E\left(bc\right) \tag{27}$$

Equations 24, 25, 26 can be used to express C_{40}, C_{41} *or* C_{42} using second and fourth order moments of $z\left(n\right)$ (Swami & Sadler, 2000).

The estimates of cumulants in Equation 26 using estimates of corresponding moments are given as:

$$\widehat{C_{21}} = \frac{1}{N}\sum_{N=1}^{N}\left|y\left(n\right)\right|^2 \tag{28}$$

$$\widehat{C_{20}} = \frac{1}{N}\sum_{N=1}^{N}y^2\left(n\right) \tag{29}$$

$$\widehat{C_{40}} = \frac{1}{N}\sum_{N=1}^{N}y^4\left(n\right) - 3\widehat{C_{20}^2} \tag{30}$$

$$\widehat{C_{41}} = \frac{1}{N}\sum_{N=1}^{N}y^3\left(n\right)y^*\left(n\right) - 3\widehat{C_{20}}\widehat{C_{21}} \tag{31}$$

$$\widehat{C_{42}} = \frac{1}{N}\sum_{N=1}^{N}|y\left(n\right)|^4 - \widehat{C_{20}^2} - 2\widehat{C_{21}^2} \tag{32}$$

where the subscript ^ denotes sample average.

Alternatively, in terms of moments above estimates can be written as in (Pei-hua, Hong-xin, Xu-ying, Nan, & Yuan-yuan, 2012):

$$M_{pq} = E\left[X\left(t\right)^{p-q} X^*\left(t\right)^q\right].$$ (33)

(*) means the complex conjugate. Cumulants C_{40}, C_{41}, and C_{42} then can be expressed as:

$$C_{40} = M_{40} - 3M_{20}^2$$ (34)

$$C_{41} = M_{41} - 3M_{20}M_{21}$$ (35)

$$C_{42} = M_{42} - M_{20}M_{22} - 2M_{22}$$ (36)

far detailed estimates of cumulants have been presented with special focus on fourth-order cumulants. This is because of the fact that higher order modulations of QPSK and QAM-16 shows feature values on fourth order cumulants. These feature values are used to classify these modulations after a signal is detected. One of the other main reasons for using the fourth order cumulant and not the third order cumulant is that for a random process that is symmetrically distributed, it's third order cumulants are equal to zero. Moreover, higher signal modulations have extremely small third-order cumulant value and larger fourth-order cumulant value so preference is given to fourth-order cumulant (Narendar, Krishna, Vinod, & Madhukumar, 2012). There are theoretical values for the estimated cumulants for different modulations (Swami & Sadler, 2000; Mendel, 1991) which can be used to classify the modulations. The application of cumulants after doing cyclostationary analysis re calculates the second order statistics of the signal. Particular modulation formats producing same features in the calculated moments result in the theoretical values of the cumulants. These values are approximately fixed and are used for classification of modulations after a signal has been detected by the spectrum sensing algorithm. In this research, cumulants are directly applied to the real valued vector calculated from the SCF considering it as a symmetric zero mean random variable which is having approximately a normal distribution. Its cumulant analysis being easy operator is preferred over its moments (Mendel, 1991) for characterizing the shape of the distribution (Swami & Sadler, 2000). The calculated vector serves as the random process input to the cumulants instead of the captured signal say $y\left(n\right)$. In (Wu & Iyengar, 2011) magnitudes of the FFT values obtained by calculating the second order statistics were used to calculate the second, third and fourth moments and then using these values respective cumulants can be calculated using Equation 34, 35, 36. Summarily, the idea of testing the calculated feature vector values by considering them as a random variable inputted to the cumulants will provide the required results which are present as we proceed. This application testing of cumulants on the vector has many advantages. In comparison to second and fourth order moments of a captured complex signal, the calculated vector has reduced calculation size reducing the complexity of cumulants calculation. Secondly, modulation format produces distinct features if cyclostationary analysis is done correctly. The calculated vector has these features calculated in a unique way. So it increases the probability of distinct values as output of fourth order cumulants for different modulation formats. Thirdly, a unique normalization to value equals to one approach is used in the vector so that cumulant values are least disturbed with the amplitude of the feature values and will produce the consistent values as results, normalization of cumulants has also been presented in (Swami & Sadler, 2000) for the said purpose. All these particular advantages are being utilized while calculating the fourth order cumulant values for BPSK, QPSK, QAM-16 and Noise feature vectors by the algorithm. This helps in simpler, less computational and low on resources detection and classification of modulation signals.

With such a cumulant based classifier, we can have an idea of the authenticity of the primary signal. Whether the signal present at the analyzed frequency is allowed to transmit and also we can use this identification for validation of primary user. Suppression activities of unauthorized carriers can be done by the concerned authorities such as military or the signals and frequency regulatory body.

Advantages of the Extracted Feature Vector

Some of the fringe advantages of the extracted feature vector are that the correlation spectral peaks at locations of f and α are all present in it. So when compared to noise vector, we have only certain peaky points in the vector. At low resolution, these peaky points are significant only and not there numbers of occurrences at particular locations on which many techniques are dependent as we see in the literature. There are no special pre-processing blocks, Wavelets or special high resolution analysis on particular values of cyclic frequency. There is no need for estimating the variance matrices. The said vector is not statistically bound. SCF has been estimated with low resolution FAM. Then, features are extracted from SCF in a vector with normalized values and by comparing and sorting only largest value in a row. Due to normalization, effects of noise variance are diminished as in (Renard, Lampe, & Horlin, 2013).

EXPERIMENTATION SETUP

The focus of this work is on cyclostationary analysis of signals that are used in practice by satellite uplink channels. In order to claim the use of the proposed detection technique in cognitive radios for satellite the experimentation setup should have modern SDR and CR development platforms through which signal generation and acquisition be carried out. MATLAB as being renowned simulation and analysis software platform is then used to validate the devised technique. The details of the setup and special considerations follow in the next sections.

Experimentation

The main concern of this research is to process the modulated signals used in a real satellite scenario so the experimentation involves the capture of signals from the valid sources instead of generating them in the simulation software. To gain a deeper insight into the fulfillment of requirements a flexible cognitive radio implementation platform is used (Sutton, Nolan & Doyle, 2008). The results are produced by analyzing the AWGN and multi-path fading channels both. The first approach selected for the purpose of experimentation is to generate the three modulations using the signal generator (Agilent technologies E8267D). It is a renowned fact that using signal generator at the input of the satellite RF link chain a simple modulated carrier can be uplinked on the satellite so keeping this in mind, in a setup using USRP2 N210, configured signal generator for producing BPSK, QPSK & QAM-16 modulated data is used. Spectrum analyzer (Rohde & Schwarz) is used to analyze the generated modulation's PSD and constellation. The generated modulated data is fed into the USRP2 which digitizes the captured data and decimate it. This data is provided to the computer using the gigabit interface. SBX daughter card (400-4400 MHz) is used as the RF front end for the input data to the USRP2. The sampled data is saved in a file sink for further processing it using MATLAB based detection algorithm presented above (Sutton, Nolan & Doyle, 2008; Rebeiz & Cabric, 2011; Paisana, Prasad, Rodrigues, & Prasad, 2012; Baldini, Guiliani, Capriglione, & Sithamparanathan, 2012; Aziz, & Nafkha, 2014; •). The parameters of the generated modulations are listed in the Table 1 and parameters for USRP2 data capture are presented in Table 2 respectively. GNURADIO 3.6 open source software is used to capture the data from USRP2 as it provides a GUI based flow-graph programming model. The use of USRP2 assures the fact that spectrum sensing capability of the proposed research can be utilized in a prospective design of the cognitive radio for satellites using modern flexible radio platform.

For getting the real satellite signals, an RF chain containing parabolic antenna and LNB (Low Noise Amplifier + Block down converter) is used. The frequency L band (950-1750) MHz output of the reception setup is connected with the spectrum analyzer and the USRP2 using a splitter. Real time satellite spectrum is scanned for carriers of the primary users in 1-4MHz of span. This bandwidth is well supported by the USRP2 device. A broadcasting carrier is usually using a bandwidth of 4MHz. Within this span the signal of interest is scanned and captured (Ge & Bostian, 2008). GNURADIO based flow-graph is

Table 1. Modulation parameters on signal generator

Parameter	Value
Mod Type	BPSK, QPSK, QAM-16
Symbol Rate	2Msps
Data	PN23
Frequency	2.25 GHz
Amplitude	-30dBm

Table 2. Parameters for USRP2

Parameter	Value
Sample Rate	10 MHz
Centre Frequency	2.25 GHz
Channel	0, TX/RX
Channel Gain	5dB

Table 3. FAM parameters

Parameter	Value	Unit
Fs	10	MHz
Delta α	20	KHz
Delta f	200	KHz
Np	64	Points
L	16	Points
P	32	Points
N=P*L	512	Points
FFT size	32	Points

used to capture the data using USRP2 (Rebeiz & Cabric, 2011). The saved samples in the file from the flow-graph are imported in the MATLAB for cyclostationary analysis & detection scheme simulation. A block diagram for the experimentation setup is presented below.

In Figure 7, the function generator is connected at the input of the USRP2 setup with the spectrum analyzer and the PC with GNURADIO flow graph for taking lab generated modulated data for analysis. For real time satellite signals, the function generator is disconnected and Antenna with C-band (3.4-4.2) GHz LNB with LO frequency of 5.15 GHz is connected in the input of USRP2. The Centre frequency and bandwidth for capturing the signal in the band is set by the parameters in GNURADIO flow graph.

The overall experimentation setup can be summarized in the following main steps:

1. First connect the function generator output with a splitter and configure the function generator with the modulation parameters as listed in Table 1.
2. Take the splitter's outputs and connect them to USRP2 and the spectrum analyser. Set the analyser according to the carrier frequency of function generator for taking measurement results.
3. Connect the USRP2 with the computer running GNURadio flowgraph for capturing the signals in the data file.
4. Now, generate signal from the function generator, for constellation diagrams put the spectrum analyser in the VSA (Vector Signal Analyser) mode and set the parameters for the required modulation.
5. Run the flowgraph in the computer for 5 seconds. Measure this time from the first instance of the FFT plot similarly appearing in the flowgraph as it is shown by the spectrum analyser. Replace function generator with antenna chain and repeat the steps.

Measurement Results

In Figure 8 (a), setup of configured and connected Signal generator, Spectrum Analyzer and USRP2 are shown. The generated signal from the signal generator is received on the spectrum analyzer and USRP2 both using the signal splitter. Figure 8 (b) shows running GNURADIO flow graph which is capturing the signal input to the USRP2 from signal generator. FFT plot of the real time generated BPSK modulated signal can be seen in the figure.

Configuration of the signal generator for BPSK, QPSK and QAM-16 modulations is presented in Figure 8 (c), (d) and (e) respectively. The parameters are set according to the listed parameters of Table 1.

Figure 7. Block diagram of the setup signal generator is replaced by the RF chain containing 2.4mparabolic antenna and C or Ku band LNB.

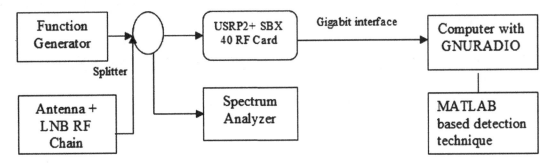

Figure 8. Experimental Setup (a), configuration (b), (c), (d), (e) and (f) and results (f), (g) and (h) of BPSK, QPSK, QAM-16 carriers

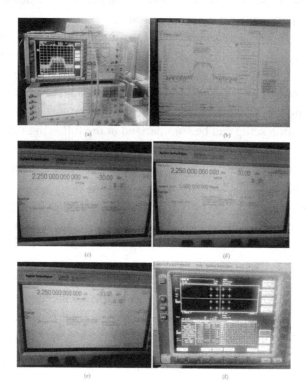

The modulated data generated is verified on the spectrum analyzer in terms of its spectrum and constellation plot. Figure 8 (f), (g) and (h) are showing the constellation plots of QAM-16, BPSK and QPSK modulated data generated by the signal generator. Same data is input to the USPR2 and collected for testing by the proposed algorithm.

After experimenting with the lab generated modulated carriers, the discussed receive only chain for capturing the satellite signals was used. The connected spectrum analyzer was used to ensure the satellite carriers having the desired modulations of BPSK, QPSK and QAM-16 along with some frequency with no transmission as can be seen in Figure 9 for noise analysis. Zoomed views of these carriers are shown in Figure 10. The marker in white color in Figure 9 is showing the noise floor. Marker labeled as *1R* in white color is showing the QPSK carrier.

The real time satellite carriers were captured by connecting the signal analyzer and USRP2 to the antenna containing the C-band LNB. Spectrum analyzer plots for BPSK, QPSK, QAM-16 and noise are shown in Figure 10 (a), (b), (c) and (d) respectively. Particular modulated carrier span is set on the spectrum analyzer to get proper view of the power spectral density on the spectrum analyzer. Noise is captured by setting the Centre frequency of USRP2 at the location in the satellite band where there is no carrier being shown on the spectrum analyzer.

Figure 9. Real-time spectrum of satellite on spectrum analyzer obtained using a receive only antenna chain

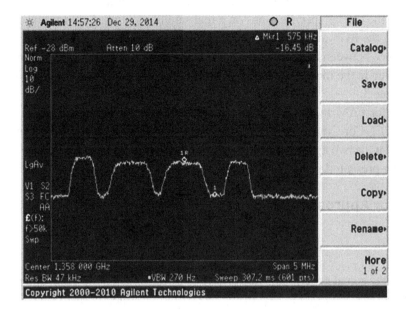

Figure 10. Spectrum of real satellite (BPSK, QPSK and QAM-16) carriers and noise

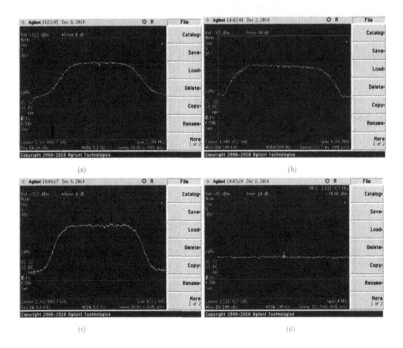

SIMULATION RESULTS

The collected samples are analyzed and plotted in MATLAB (Badawy & Khattab, 2014) using the FAM algorithm and then signal detection is done through the proposed technique. The calculated SCF with low resolution frequency and cyclic frequency is presented for BPSK, QPSK and QAM-16 modulation types. The modulation parameters using the signal generator approach as discussed in the experimentation are set according to the carrier specifications on a real satellite Uplink. SCF for noise is also presented. It can be seen from the SCF and calculated vector plots that the proposed technique can effectively identify the difference between a present signal and noise in the sampled data. The proposed technique works effectively even in the multi-path fading channel of satellite. The parameters for FAM algorithm are presented in Table 3.

The parameters for FAM in Table 3 ensure its low calculation complexity. The platform running MATLAB is an INTEL Core2duo 2.54 GHz processor with 2GB of RAM running MATLAB 7.0.8.347. The results of SCF for the two approaches along with the calculated vector (obtained using the proposed technique) are being presented in results chapter.

Signal Generator Approach

BPSK Modulation

Data obtained from the signal generator is first analyzed by the constellation plot and proper modulation is assured by getting the scatter plot in Figure 11. Input vector defined in MATLAB is used as the input data vector containing sampled data values from the GNURADIO captured file. These files were first recorded during experimentation and then were used by MATLAB to obtain the SCF features and detection results. In Figure 12, cyclic spectral density of BPSK is shown. SCF is plotted on z-axis with the

Figure 11. Constellation plot of the BPSK sampled data

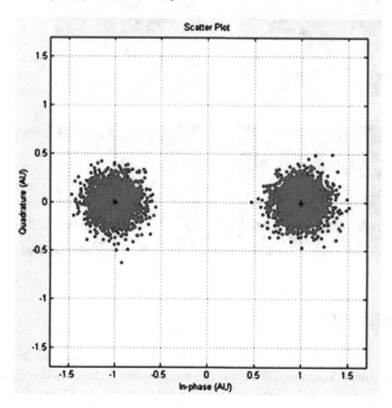

Figure 12. SCF plot of lab generated BPSK

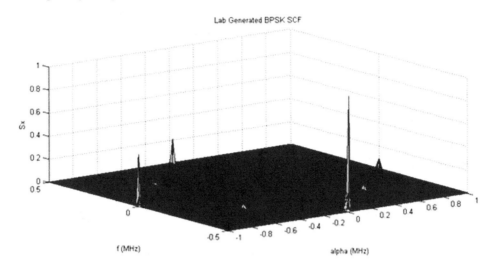

bi-plane f and α values on x and y axes respectively. Referring to the mathematical SCF of BPSK in Equation 11, the SCF plot of BPSK is having four peaks two at $\alpha = 0$ and two at $f = 0$. The frequency f and the cyclic frequency α are normalized to the value of the sampling frequency f_s. If a section through the figure is made where the cyclic frequency $\alpha = 0$, then the spectral power density of the modulated signal is obtained (Martian, Sandu, Fratu, Marghescu, & Craciunescu, 2014). It is also evident that since α and f values are normalized by f_s and peaks occurs at f_c. That means the peak locations give true f_c if we calculate it with the f_s. That is why it is blind detection no there is no need of f_c. Here f_s and f_c are sampling and carrier frequencies respectively. Determination of carrier frequency is out of scope of this thesis.

For the obtained plot of SCF in Figure 12, a graphical understanding of the features exhibit by BPSK modulated signal captured through the USRP2 can only be obtained. Now the algorithm proposed for detecting these features and based on the hypothesis for detecting signal and noise separately in the frequency band under analysis, the vector is calculated. Plot of the vector is presented in the Figure 13. The vector points or length is dependent upon the resolution of frequency set in the FAM algorithm. Making use of this lower value the proposed technique folds the SCF features and a plot is presented for understanding in Figure 13. The peaks in the plot are the spectral peaks in the SCF. This vector is fairly readable using its indexes by any computer program or hardware solving the problem of extracting SCF features which are well understandable by plotting a 3-dimensional plot.

One more advantage is that only half of the values can be utilized to detect signal or noise. If the peaks are counted from index 0 to 35, then according to Equation 20 H_1 is true resulting signal detection by the decision block.

QPSK Modulation

QPSK constellation presented in Figure 14 before applying to the algorithm ensures proper modulation data in the input vector. The SCF plot of Figure 15 has significant peaks at $\alpha = 0$. The ideal SCF should

Figure 13. Plot of lab generated BPSK feature vector

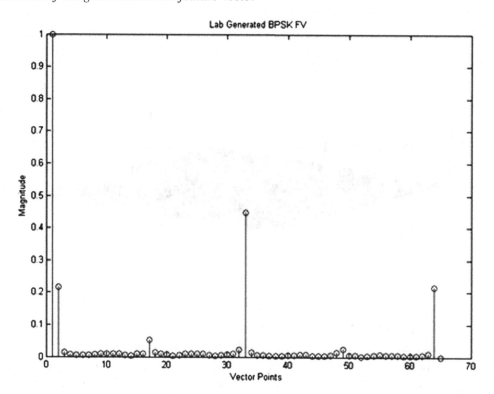

be containing only two peaks at α = 0 and no peaks in $f = 0$ axis due to the cancellation of in-phase and quadrature parts (Jang, 2014) but this is only possible when high resolution analysis is done which is computationally complex. Due to low resolution parameters used with the added advantage of less complex operation, some smaller magnitude peaks are present at the location of $f = 0$.

This phenomenon does not disturb the detection result. In Figure 16 the calculated vector shows peaks which resulted in the detection hypothesis H_1 upon the application of the devised technique. A closer look on the calculated vectors for BPSK and QPSK modulated data highlights the difference of available spectral peaks in the SCF.

QAM-16 Modulation

The captured data is first plotted and constellation for QAM-16 modulation was obtained in Figure 17. SCF is calculated using the FAM low resolution parameters. QAM-16 is a complex digital modulation. Several peaks are present in Figure 18 at α = 0, $^+_-2f_c$ and $f = 0$ axes. This is due to low resolution analysis resulting in smaller number of cancellations between in-phase and quadrature components. Figure 19 shows the plot of calculated vector containing the significant spectral peaks extracted from 3-dimensional SCF. The detection algorithm when applied resulted in hypothesis H_1. Since the number of peaks crossing the threshold value Y = 0.5 are less than $\frac{N}{2}$.

Figure 14. Constellation plot of the QPSK sampled data

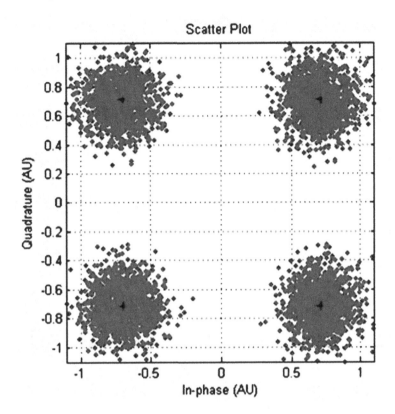

Figure 15. SCF plot of lab generated QPSK

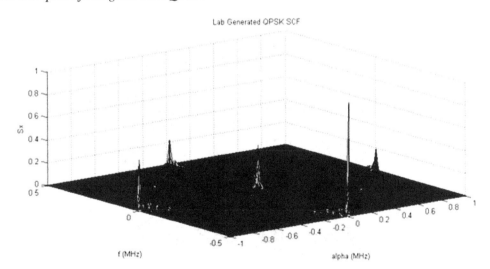

Figure 16. Plot of lab generated QPSK feature vector

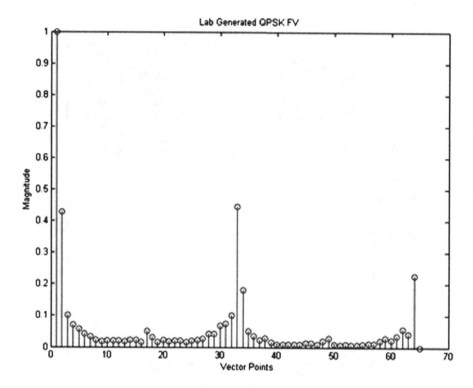

Figure 17. Constellation plot of the QAM-16 sampled data

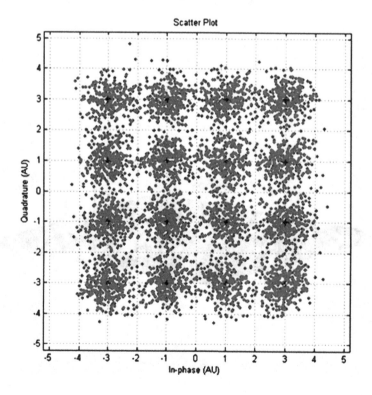

Figure 18. SCF plot of lab generated QAM-16

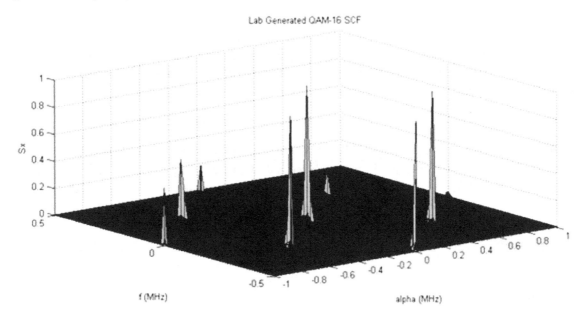

Figure 19. Plot of lab generated QAM-16 feature vector

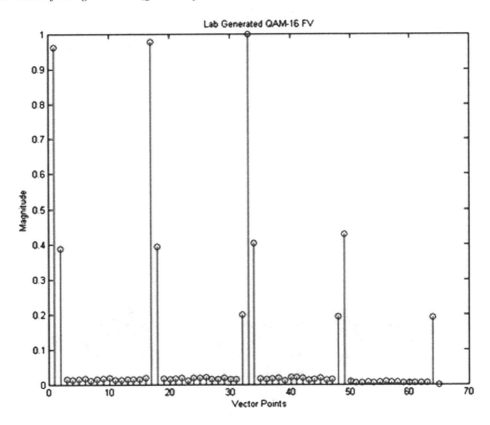

Noise

SCF plot of noise data is shown in Figure 20. There is no significant spectral peak in the whole SCF except random but symmetric peaky response at $\alpha = 0$. This is also the PSD (Power Spectral Density) of noise seen in the frequency domain spectrum. According to the basic theory in (Gardner, 1994) noise exhibits the same particular behavior as obtained in our analysis. The resultant vector from the detection algorithm is presented in Figure 21. Peaks passing the defined threshold γ are greater than $\dfrac{N}{2}$ so the detection algorithm will result in H_0. That is no signal present and only noise is detected.

Effect of varying noise variance in the analyzed data will have least effect because it is ensured through rigorous experimental testing and normalized values are present in the calculated vector and the threshold set for the worst case noise to avoid false detection.

Real Satellite Signal Approach

In this section, the analysis results for real time satellite signals are being presented. These results were obtained by applying the whole detection algorithm to the captured data from USRP2 connected with a pointed antenna with LNB operating in C-band. The antenna is pointed towards the communication satellite. Proper link was ensured between the antenna and satellite transponder using the connected spectrum analyzer. The captured signal spectrum is checked on the spectrum analyzer connected using a two port power splitter on which input signal is the LNB's output and the outputs connected with USRP2 and the spectrum analyzer. It is also worth mentioning that no sort of noise cancellation or conditioning of LNB's output had been carried out before capturing and testing the signals by the detector. The antenna and LNB used in the setup are low-cost off the shelf solution for receive only satellite link. The

Figure 20. SCF plot of lab generated noise

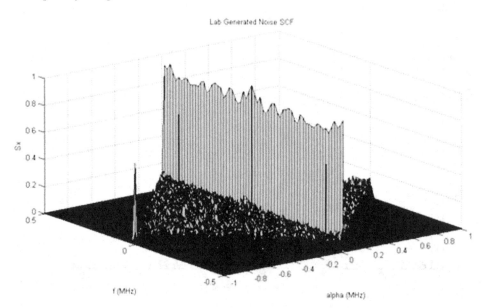

Figure 21. Plot of lab generated noise feature vector

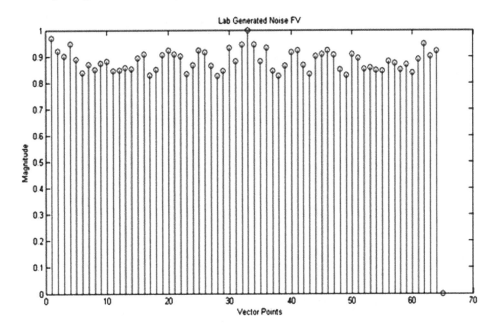

results are one of their kinds since energy detection and only PSD calculations are available so far in the literature addressing the subject of the thesis in the domain of communication satellite signals.

BPSK Modulation

Figure 22 is the plot of magnitude of the FFT in *dBm* units. It is significant to ensure that the sampled data points from USRP2 are having the same BPSK spectrum as of the measured one using the spectrum analyzer in experimentation chapter. SCF plot of Figure 23 is having the features exhibited by the BPSK carrier present in the satellite band. Since no pre-processing is done to remove the noise effects and corrections to the induced irregularities of LNB's output so SCF is different than that of the SCF of lab generated BPSK and ideal BPSK.

The normalized SCF has four bumps two at $\alpha = 0$ and two at $f = 0$ axes. These bumps are actually the peaks obtained in the lab generated BPSK SCF. The raised part in the SCF plot represents the noise floor and irregularities induced by the satellite channel and LNB's hardware. It is higher because of lower observation time & frequency resolutions (Richard, Martin, & Zhiqiang, 2011). Discussions of these effects are out of the scope here in this thesis.

Detection algorithm calculates the vector for the SCF presented in Figure 24. The raised noise floor is clearly visible since the least value in comparison to the lab generated BPSK vector has risen from nearly zero to somewhere near 0.38. The bumps in the SCF can be easily seen in the vector as features of the BPSK signal. The detection block calculates the number of peaks above the threshold of $Y = 0.5$ for $\dfrac{N}{2}$ values (where N is the total number of vector points i.e. 70) and results in H_1 hypothesis meaning detection of signal.

Figure 22. FFT plot of the BPSK satellite carrier sampled data

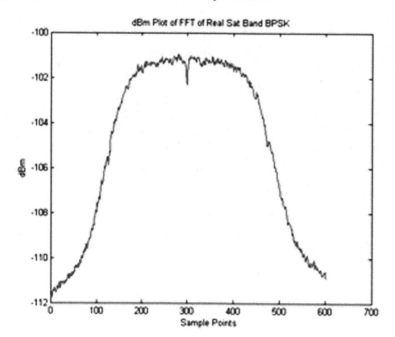

Figure 23. SCF plot of real satellite BPSK carrier

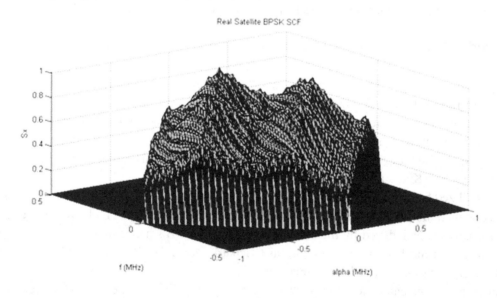

QPSK Modulation

Same procedure was repeated for QPSK data samples. First the spectrum plot is obtained from the sample data points as shown in Figure 25 with a close matching with the one measured on the spectrum analyser. The SCF plot shows particular QPSK features disturbed by the noise.

Figure 24. Plot of real satellite BPSK feature vector

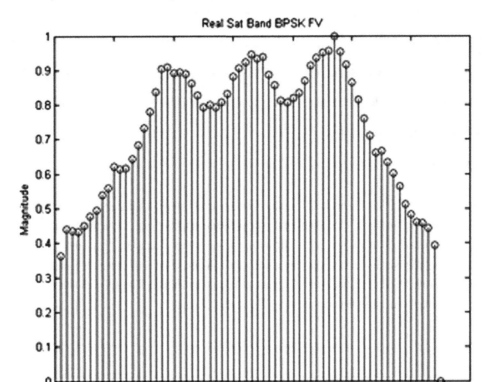

Figure 25. FFT plot of the QPSK satellite carrier sampled data

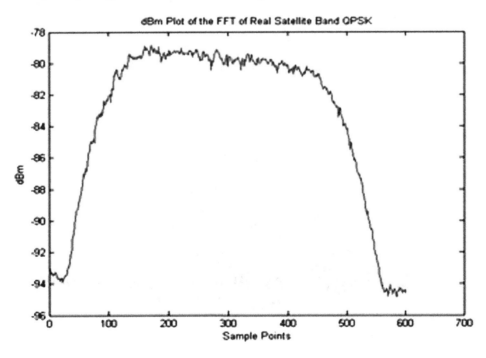

At α = 0 axis, two symmetric raised lobes are present showing the spectral features of QPSK modulation in Figure 26. The raised portion is a bit shifted too because of improper cancellation between in-phase and quadrature portions of the modulated data. But the main concentration is within the area bounded by the $\alpha = 0$ axis.

The features extracted in the calculated vector for QPSK modulation in Figure 27 are uniquely identifiable. Using the proposed detection algorithm, the values qualifying the set threshold of 0.5 are $< \dfrac{N}{2}$ so signal is detected and output is H_1.

QAM-16 Modulation

Captured data in case of QAM-16 modulation was first ensured by matching the simulated spectrum plot in Figure 28 and that obtained by spectrum analyzer presented in the experimentation measured results.

SCF of QAM-16 carrier in Figure 29 is showing raised lobes at α = 0, $^{+}_{-}2f_c$ and $f = 0$ locations. These several raised lobes are due to non cancellation of in-phase and quadrature parts of the complex modulation due to low resolution analysis. Extracted vector in Figure 30 satisfies the condition for hypothesis H_1 so detection of signal is resulted by the decision block.

Noise

The spectrum of the captured real time satellite band noise is shown in Figure 31. The noise spectrum shows rapid power level changes which is significant in processing the noise data because the shown noise spectrum is very far from the usual linear noise floor. The analysis of this type of non-linear noise floor with the proposed technique is presented for testing it under hypothesis H_0.

No particular spectral peaks are shown in the SCF of noise in the satellite frequency band. In Figure 32 the SCF for idle frequency location where there is no transmission going on is presented. In the

Figure 26. SCF plot of real satellite QPSK carrier

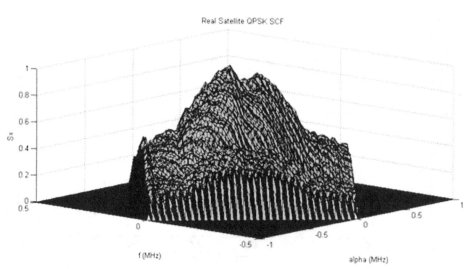

Figure 27. Plot of real satellite QPSK feature vector

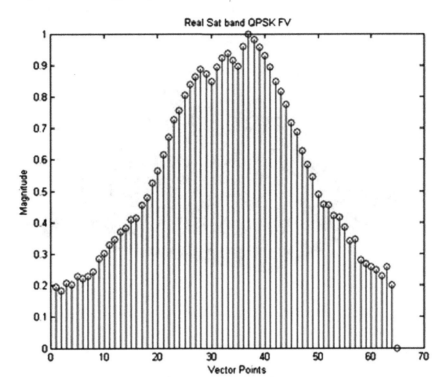

Figure 28. FFT plot of the QAM-16 satellite carrier sampled data

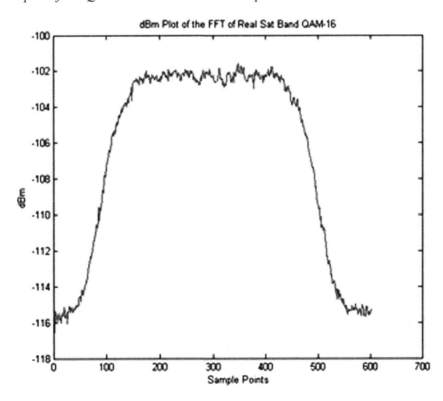

Figure 29. SCF plot of real satellite QAM-16 carrier

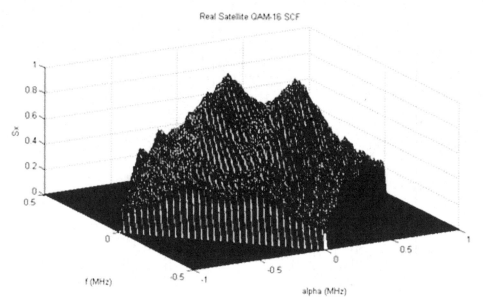

Figure 30. Plot of real satellite QAM-16 feature vector

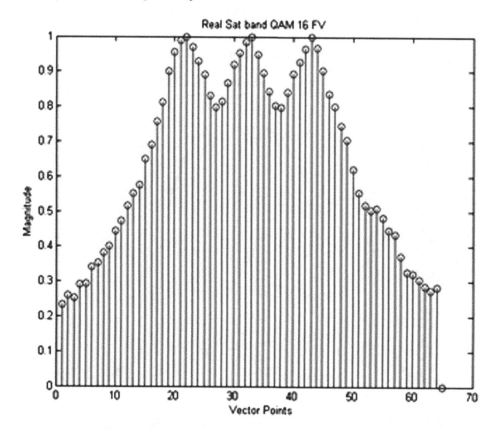

Figure 31. Plot of real satellite QAM-16 feature vector

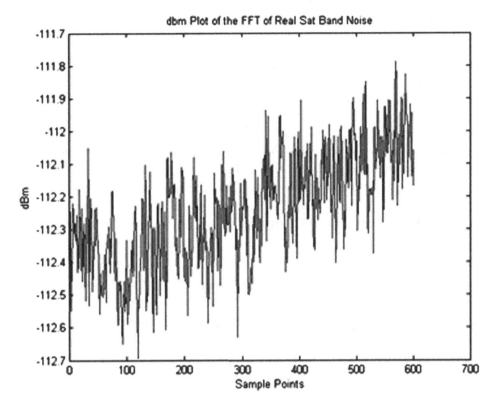

Figure 32. SCF plot of real satellite band noise

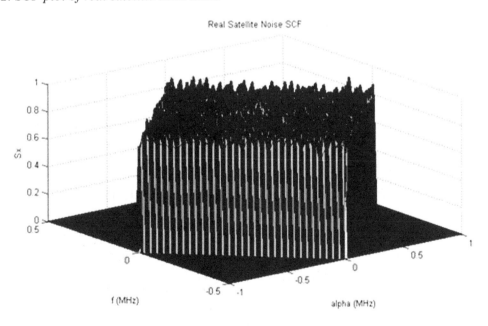

whole SCF no particular pattern is available. Since all the captured I &Q samples are same so SCF has the same spectral values in the bi-frequency plane. This is the reason for a raised noise bed in the SCF.

Figure 33 shows the calculated vector according to the proposed detection scheme from the noise SCF. All the $\frac{N}{2}$ values are passing the threshold value of 0.5 in the calculated feature vector so hypothesis H_0 is resulted by the decision block sensing an idle frequency channel equals to half the bandwidth of the sampling frequency.

So far the detection of BPSK, QPSK and QAM-16 carriers captured in the satellite band as signals in general has been presented. The algorithm then further applies fourth order cumulnats as statistical classification tool for modulation type in the detected signal. Particular values of cumulants obtained for different modulation types can assure the simple classification of the detected signal.

Modulation Classification Using Cumulants on Calculated Vector

For real constellation cumulants values follows $C_{20} = C_{21}$ and $C_{40} = C_{42}$ (Swami & Sadler, 2000). This validates the results obtained through simulations for cumulants for different modulations and noise. The classifier in the algorithm compares the incoming value with the look up table of the values in Table 4. The classification of modulation decision takes place with the result of comparison of the incoming value and the present values obtained through testing the statistics of cumulants obtained for noise and modulations. If the incoming value does not lie in the ranges presented, the classifier results in un-known modulation.

Figure 33. Plot of real satellite noise feature vector

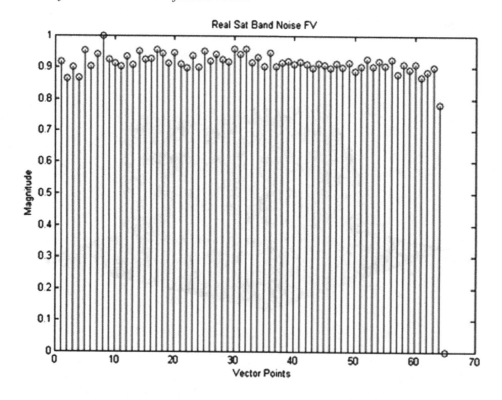

Table 4. Fourth order- cumulant values of feature vector

Cumulant	BPSK	QPSK	QAM-16	Noise
	Values for Calculated Vector (Real Satellite Signals)			
$\widehat{C40}$	-1.03995	-0.50965	-0.38224	-1.29625
$\widehat{C42}$	-1.03995	-0.50965	-0.38224	-1.29625

A plot of cumulant values for different modulations and noisy data obtained through the algorithm is shown in Figure 34. Values for modulated data from the real time satellite sampled data are present. To clarify the values of Table 4, different values obtained for BPSK, QPSK, QAM-16 and noise data by using the cumulant calculations are present in the plot of the figure. The shown values in the plot are being used by the classification block of the algorithm to differentiate between different modulations. The input data from which these values were obtained was that of the column vector Vi from Equation 16.

Trend Analysis of Cumulant Values Obtained

The values of cumulants obtained as listed in Table 4 shows the same trend as the HOS analysis on the complex valued signals. The modulation formats of BPSK, QPSK and QAM-16 have shown approximately half of the values obtained by HOS cumulants applied on the complex signal samples. The values from (Swami & Sadler, 2000) for the modulation formats are *BPSK= -2.0000, QPSK = -1.0000 and QAM-16 = -0.6047*. The trend shows that as the modulation gets more complex and dense the cu-

Figure 34. Cumulant values for BPSK, QPSK, QAM-16 and noise data

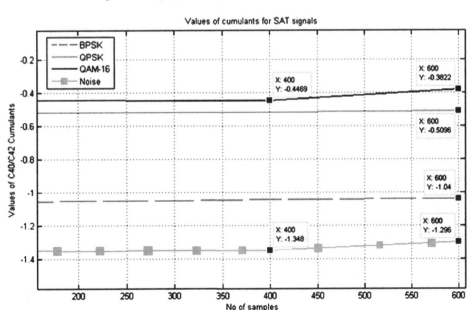

mulant values become smaller. The reason for this trend lies in the definition of cumulants. Since, the fourth order cumulants are dependent upon the second order statistics values C_{20} and C_{21} (Swami & Sadler, 2000; Mendel, 1991). For denser modulations the sum of these statistical values becomes smaller due to correlation values and cancellations of I & Q parts whether completely or partially. Figure 34 shows the trend of values obtained using cumulants for different sample sizes on the calculated feature vector obtained from the proposed technique. Remember that the feature vector contains the magnitudes FFT values of feature peaks and has only a total of 65 values which is far smaller than the sample sizes on which cumulants were calculated in (Swami & Sadler, 2000, Mendel, 1991; Wu & Iyengar, 2011). So the trend of approximately half values as compared to the theoretical values in literature is due to the lower sample size and magnitudes. Secondly, only feature values have been used in calculating cumulants. It has significantly reduced the computational complexity of the cumulant calculations and the pattern for modulations is in a great logical agreement with the theoretical pattern. The obtained values of cumulants with respect to the changing sample sizes (input to FAM from where the SCF containing the feature peaks is calculated and then feature vector is extracted) are showing lesser amount of variations. Due to normalized SCF and fixed parameters for the sample size and FAM the cumulant values obtained are consistent. The values are unique forming the same pattern as the theory suggests for the modulation formats under considerations. Noise has different and greatest value than that of the three modulations. These values are used by the classifier to decide about the type of the detected signal or noise successfully.

Comparative Analysis

In order to emphasis the valuable contributions of the discussed technique for detection of satellite signals and its classification capability, comparative analysis with other state of the art techniques built in the literature has been carried out. The cyclic spectral density resulting from cyclostationary analysis has different built-in statistical properties which are usually utilize by signal detectors specially, the symmetric property of the SCF is used. This works by checking the equality of the feature peak magnitudes at specific locations in bi-frequency SCF on cyclic frequency axis (Aziz, & Nafkha, 2014; Nafkha, Naoues, Cichon, & Kliks, 2014). For this equality decision by measuring the magnitude at symmetric SCF location, high resolution analysis is done which introduces high complexity and computational time. In the proposed research, the objective was to achieve such a detection technique which works with low resolution frequency parameters, least affected by the magnitudes of the peaks (when using low resolutions peak's magnitude attenuates), works blindly (without any prior knowledge of the signal under consideration) and should extract feature peaks form the SCF bi-frequency two variable function in a simple way. The feature vector extracted has the least possible index and values reducing post SCF calculations. Despite being less complex, the calculated SCF contains all the features exhibited by the modulations (BPSK, QPSK and QAM-16) as the theory suggests. The results from this work and other laid out techniques can be compared on the following grounds.

High Cyclic Frequency Resolution

In (Wu, Yang, Liu, & Chakarvarthy, 2012), a novel modulation detection technique has been presented for detecting acoustic signals using cyclostationary analysis. The technique works by calculating SCF at dynamic cyclic resolutions. For specific locations of cyclic frequency as a function of the carrier frequency, high resolution SCF as in Table 5 is calculated and for the rest of the bi-frequency plane low resolution calculations are done see Figure 35 (a). For signal detection decision ratio of the peaks in frequency and cyclic frequency axes is calculated. The author claims reduction in complexity by observing and analyzing short duration signals for SCF but in Figure 35 (b), the SCF misses the significant peaks at $\alpha = 2F_c$ for BPSK modulation when a little shift in F_c and a low $\Delta\alpha$ is used. This leads to false detection of modulation. The values for cyclic frequency resolutions are presented in Table 5. For the technique in (Wu, Yang, Liu, & Chakarvarthy, 2012), SCF is calculated with high and low resolutions imposing computational complexities while for the proposed technique in this research works well with low resolution cyclic frequency value.

FAM Complexity and Computational Time

For calculating the SCF, time smoothing FAM algorithm has been used in the proposed detection technique for estimating the features of the detecting signal. In Table 6, the parameters of FAM with their computing time have been listed. These parameters are mainly dependent upon the number of samples used and the resolution of frequency selected. These values have been taken from (Ge & Bostian, 2008) and since the computing time is based on the platform so same platform (Intel Core2 Duo 2.54 GHz with 2GB RAM) as mentioned in (Ge & Bostian, 2008) has been used to calculated the computing time and FAM a parameters of the proposed technique boxed in red as the last entry in the table. It can be concluded that comparatively the proposed detection technique has lesser number of samples and least computing time.

Table 5. Cyclic frequency resolutions of 5 vs. proposed technique

Δα {Dynamic SCF in Wu, Yang, Liu, & Chakarvarthy, 2012 }	Δα (Proposed Technique)
5×10^{-5} (High Resolution SCF) + 1×10^{-2} (Low Resolution SCF)	2×10^{-4} (Low Resolution SCF)

Source: Wu, Yang, Liu, & Chakarvarthy, 2012.

Figure 35. (a) SCF of BPSK, Fc=17000, Fb=4000, Fs=80000, dalpha=0.005; (b) SCF of BPSK, Fc=17020, Fb=4000, Fs=80000, dalpha=0.001

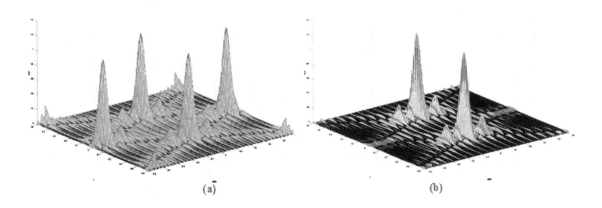

Table 6. FAM computing time and parameters in Table 1 of Ge & Bostian, 2008 vs. proposed technique

N (Samples)	N'	L	P	Resolution (Hz)	Time (s)
2^{18}	2^8	2^6	2^{12}	2^6	60.0
2^{17}	2^8	2^6	2^{11}	2^7	30.55
2^{16}	2^8	2^6	2^{10}	2^8	13.28
2^{15}	2^7	2^5	2^{10}	2^9	3.39
2^{14}	2^6	2^4	2^{10}	2^{10}	0.896
2^{13}	2^5	2^3	2^{10}	2^{11}	0.273
2^{10}	2^6	2^4	2^5	2^{11}	0.1059

Wavelet Based Technique

For wide band cyclostationary analysis, one of the techniques for detection of peaks in the calculated SCF is by using Wavelets (Liu et al., 2013). Wavelets are applied to SCF considering it as a 2-dimensional grey image. The application of wavelets significantly removes noise in the SCF introduced due to compressed sensing and helped in producing improved SCF plots. The technique comes with SCF matrix calculations using compressed sensing convex reconstruction algorithm and then it calculates the wavelet coefficients, edge magnitudes and gradients of the peaky features to remove noise and results in a de-noised SCF as shown in Figure 36 (b).

In comparison to the proposed technique of this research, the detection probability is very high in case of signal SNR = -5dB. This is because of the detection algorithm design strategy and its independence with the noise statistics due to normalized feature's magnitudes. Also, the computational complexities of wavelets are avoided in the technique.

Figure 36. (a) Before the noise reduction at SNR=-5dB, (b) after the noise reduction Figure 2 of Liu et al., 2013

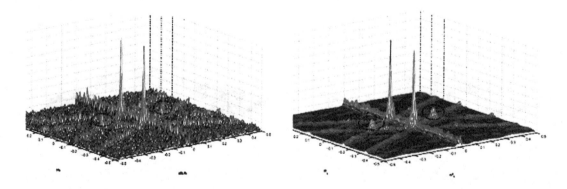

ANN Based Modulation Recognition

In (Ghauri, Qureshi, Shah, & Khan, 2014) cyclostationary analysis has been utilized to classify the modulation format of the signal. The extracted features from the signal are in terms of coherence function and cyclic domain profile as can be seen in Figure 37. The classifier used to actually perform the classification decision is an ANN (Artificial Neural Network). Classifier needs training data in large quantities as a prerequisite. Using delta rule (errors calculated and compared between desired and obtained outputs) training of ANN is carried out. The SOF (coherence function) and CDP (cyclic domain profile) requires estimation of the spectral density first. The iterative algorithm is FFBPA (Feed Forward back propagation algorithm) details of which are present in (Ghauri, Qureshi, Shah, & Khan, 2014).

Overall, in comparison to the proposed technique of cumulant based classification, the former is quite simpler and low on computation than ANN based classification. However, the classification method has a very high classification probability at SNR = 0 dB but, a large computation and signal processing is involved in calculating SCF, SOF & CDP and then ANN (FFBPA) classification.

Single Cyclic Frequency Techniques

In (Aziz, & Nafkha, 2014) a novel technique for signal detection using CAF symmetry test is presented. It is using OMP (Orthogonal Matching Point) algorithm to estimate the CAF of the signal and then check for symmetric feature of the signals at certain α. In comparison to the proposed algorithm, it is an iterative algorithm with high resolution DFT (Discrete Fourier Transform). This makes it more time consuming and complex due to iterations, number of DFT & IDFT operations. A real-time CAF symmetry check algorithm for signal detection is presented in (Nafkha, Naoues, Cichon, & Kliks, 2014). It is also using OMP algorithm and then check for the feature peak magnitude value in CAF at α & -α. The probability of detection at SNR= -15 dB is $P_d < 0.2$. which is in the proposed technique is $P_d = 0.9$. Also the FFT size of 2048 has been used in the said technique which is just 32 in our case as the first FFT size in FAM. (Jang, 2014) has an alternate to FAM technique (details are in literature review) but it has complexity of two FTs and one IFFT to reach to the detection decision when compared to the proposed technique. Also the probability of detection in lower SNR is almost the same for both the techniques.

Figure 37. Proposed algorithm for classification of PSK modulation formats
Source: Figure 8, Ghauri, Qureshi, Shah, & Khan, 2014.

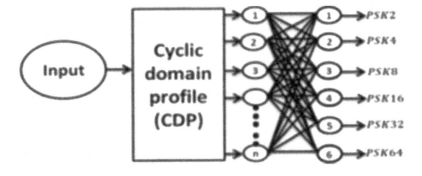

FUTURE WORK

As a future perspective, the whole algorithm can be implemented using C++ programming language and with python wrappers it can be direct implemented as a new block in GNURADIO. In this way, a real time spectrum sensing system can be demonstrated for satellite cognitive radios. The cumulant based classification provides a simpler way to identify the modulation type of the primary signal present in the channel. This classification capability enables the cognitive spectrum sensing engine to monitor the channel and validate the authenticity of the detected signal. This can be used in a manner that if the modulation type comes out to be different than known for the primary user in a specific channel, it can be reported for certain necessary actions to prevent the unauthorized use of the spectrum. Certain industry practices of suppression of such an unauthorized carrier can be carried out by the relevant satellite operator upon being reported by the secondary user utilizing the spectrum sensing engine proposed in this chapter.

CONCLUSION

In this chapter cyclostationary analysis of real time satellite signals with efficient FAM algorithm using low resolution parameters for faster execution have been presented. SCF features of real time satellite carriers are presented and a unique, less complex and simple technique for detecting signal or noise is devised. The proposed technique blindly works for BPSK, QPSK and QAM-16 modulated carriers of satellite with minimal user interaction. Also no knowledge of the interfering noise power level is required in the detection phase. This new technique works with the modern SDR based cognitive radio platform front end (USRP2) so it can be utilized in evolving satellite cognitive radio designs for the purpose of spectrum sensing. For conventional techniques, magnitude, variance and exact location of the feature peaks are very critical. This criticality has been reduced in the proposed technique by maximum value normalization as in (Renard, Lampe, & Horlin, 2013) and no dependence upon exact locations for cyclic frequency and frequency axes. Also for this technique to work only some of the feature peaks are required without any restriction of their location of occurrence. Significantly, with the processing point of view, the detector is able to work at low resolution parameters for frequency f and cyclic frequency α. Using said parameters least number of complex operations is achieved with significant features in the SCF. Only $\frac{N}{2}$ points are used to detect the presence of signal in the calculated feature vector of length N which reduces the complexity as in (Xu, Chen, & Hu, 2014). The probability of detection in lower SNR conditions is also satisfactory for the proposed technique. Further, for the classification of the modulated signals after being detected by the spectrum sensing algorithm is done using fourth order cumulants. Successive ranges for BPSK, QPSK and QAM-16 modulated carriers of satellite and lab generated signals has been achieved. With this classification capability, identification and validation of an authentic primary carrier can be done by the secondary user or any government agency. The novel application is that Cumulants were calculated on the real feature vector values extracted from the calculated SCF instead of applying them to the complex I & Q samples of the signal under analysis. It significantly reduces the calculation complexity in comparison with the conventional cumulant calculations considering the signal $y(t)$. Comparative analysis with conventional techniques revealed that this new spectrum sensing algorithm forms good connection with the background theory and shows good bond with the theoretical results.

REFERENCES

Aziz, B., & Nafkha, A. (2014). Implementation of blind cyclostationary feature detector for cognitive radios using USRP. In *Proceedings of 21st International Conference on Telecommunications (ICT)*. doi:10.1109/ICT.2014.6845077

Badawy, A., & Khattab, T. (2014). A novel peak search & save cyclostationary feature detection algorithm. In *Proceedings of Wireless Communications and Networking Conference (WCNC)*. doi:10.1109/WCNC.2014.6951976

Baldini, G., Guiliani, R., Capriglione, D., & Sithamparanathan, K. (2012). A Practical Demonstration of Spectrum Sensing for WiMAX Based on Cyclostationary Features. In *Foundation of Cognitive Radio Systems*. Available from: http://www.intechopen.com/books/foundation-of-cognitive-radio-systems/a-practical-demonstration-of-spectrum-sensing-for-wimax-based-on-cyclostationary-features

Brown, W. A., & Loomis, H. (1993). Digital Implementations of Spectral Correlation Analyzers. *IEEE Transactions on Signal Processing*, *41*(2), 703–720. doi:10.1109/78.193211

Da, S., Xiaoying, G., Hsiao-Hwa, C., Liang, Q., & Miao, X. (2009). Significant Cycle Frequency based Feature Detection for Cognitive Radio Systems. In *Proceedings of the 4th International Conference on CROWNCOM*. doi:10.1109/CROWNCOM.2009.5189106

Dimic, F., Baldini, G., & Kandeepan, S. (2014). Experimental detection of mobile satellite transmissions with cyclostationary features. *International Journal of Satellite Communications and Networking*, *33*(2), 163–183. doi:10.1002/sat.1081

Fuentes, G., Barbe, L., Moer, K. V., & Björsell, N. (2013). Discriminant Analysis for Automatic Signal Detection in Measured Power Spectra. *IEEE Transactions on Instrumentation and Measurement*, *62*(12), 3351–3360. doi:10.1109/TIM.2013.2265607

Gardner, W. A. (1994). *Cyclostationarity in Communications and Signal Processing* (W. A. Gardner, Ed.). New York: IEEE Press.

Ge, F., & Bostian, C. W. (2008). A Parallel Computing Based Spectrum Sensing Approach for Signal Detection under Conditions of Low SNR and Rayleigh Multipath Fading. In *Proceedings of 3rd IEEE Symposium on New Frontiers in Dynamic Spectrum Access Networks*. doi:10.1109/DYSPAN.2008.12

Ghauri, A., Qureshi, I., Shah, I., & Khan, N. (2014). Modulation Classification using Cyclostationary Features on Fading Channels. Research Journal of Applied Sciences. *Engineering and Technology*, *7*(24), 5331–5339.

Guenther, E. (2009). *Multi-User Signal Classification via Cyclic Spectral Analysis* (Master's Dissertation). Wright State University.

Jang, W. M. (2014). Blind Cyclostationary Spectrum Sensing in Cognitive Radios. *IEEE Communications Letters*, *18*(3), 393–396. doi:10.1109/LCOMM.2014.012714.132507

Lee, J. (2008). Blind Spectrum Sensing Techniques for Cognitive Radio System. *International Journal of Multimedia and Ubiquitous Engineering*, *3*(2), 117–128.

Liangkaia, L., Jian, C., Yongtao, L., & Tao, L. (2011). Estimation of BPSK Carrier Frequency Based on the High-Order Cyclic Cumulants. In *Proceedings of International Conference on Computer Science and Information Technology (ICCSIT 2011)*.

Like, E., Chakravarthy, V., Ratazzi, P., & Wu, Z. (2009). Signal Classification in Fading Channels Using Cyclic Spectral Analysis. *EURASIP Journal on Wireless Communications and Networking, 20*(1), 879–812.

Lin, Y., He, C., Jiang, L., & He, D. (2009). A Spectrum Sensing Method in Cognitive Radio Based on the Third Order Cyclic Cumulant. In *Proceedings of International Conference on Wireless Communications & Signal Processing (WCSP)*. doi:10.1109/WCSP.2009.5371428

Liu, X., Han, Q., Liu, Z., & Wu, Z. (2013). Novel Modulation Detection Scheme for Underwater Acoustic Communication Signal Through Short-Time Detailed Cyclostationary Features.*IEEE Wireless Communications and Networking Conference (WCNC)*.

Liu, X., Zhang, Q., Yan, X., Feng, Z., Liu, J., Zhu, Y., & Zhang, J. (2013). A Feature Detector Based on Compressed Sensing and Wavelet Transform for Wideband Cognitive Radio. In *Proceedings of 24th IEEE International Symposium on Personal, Indoor and Mobile Radio Communications: Mobile and Wireless Networks*.

Lunden, J., & Koivunen, V. (2007). Spectrum sensing in cognitive radios based on multiple cyclic frequencies. In *Proceedings of 2nd International Conference on Cognitive Radio Oriented Wireless Network Communication* (CrownCom). doi:10.1109/CROWNCOM.2007.4549769

Martian, A., Sandu, B. T., Fratu, O., Marghescu, I., & Craciunescu, R. (2014). Spectrum sensing based on spectral correlation for cognitive radio systems. In *Proceedings of 4th International conference on Wireless Communications Vehicular Technology Information Theory Aerospace & Electronics Systems (VITAE)*. doi:10.1109/VITAE.2014.6934448

Mendel, J. M. (1991). Tutorial on Higher-Order Statistics (Spectra) in Signal Processing and System Theory: Theoretical Results and Some Applications. *Proceedings of the IEEE, 79*(3), 278–305. doi:10.1109/5.75086

Mitola, J., & Maguire, G., Jr. (1999). Cognitive Radio: Making Software Radios More Personal. *IEEE Personal Communication, 6*(4), 13-18.

Nafkha, A., Naoues, M., Cichon, K., & Kliks, A. (2014). Experimental Spectrum Sensing Measurements using USRP Software Radio Platform and GNU-Radio. In *Proceedings of 9th International Conference on Cognitive Radio Oriented Wireless Networks CROWNCOM*. doi:10.4108/icst.crowncom.2014.255415

Napolitano, A. (2014). Cyclostationary Signal Processing and its Generalizations. In *Proceedings of IEEE Statistical Signal Processing Workshop*.

Narendar, M., Krishna, A., Vinod, A. P., & Madhukumar, A. S. (2012). Robust Two-Stage Spectrum Sensing and Policy Management for Cognitive Radios Using Fourth Order Cumulants. *International Journal of Information Engineering IJIE., 3*(2), 45–55.

Norris, J., Taylor, B., & Tyler, W. (2013). Methods of Detection of Bandlimited Signals on UHF MIL-SATCOM Downlinks. In *Proceedings of IEEE Military Communications Conference*. doi:10.1109/MILCOM.2013.307

Paisana, F., Prasad, N., Rodrigues, A., & Prasad, R. (2012). An alternative implementation of a cyclostationary detector. In *Proceedings of Wireless Personal Multimedia Communications*. Taipei: WPMC.

Pei-hua, L., Hong-xin, Z., Xu-ying, W., Nan, X., & Yuan-yuan, X. (2012). Modulation recognition of communication signals based on high order cumulants and support vector machine. *Journal of China Universities of Posts and Telecommunications*, *19*(1), 61–65.

Qu, Y., Li, X., Zhou, R., Chakravarthy, V., & Wu, Z. (2013). Software-Defined Radio Based Automatic Blind Hierarchical Modulation Detector via Second-Order Cyclostationary Analysis and Fourth-Order Cumulant.*IEEE Military Communications Conference*. doi:10.1109/MILCOM.2013.82

Rebeiz, E., & Cabric, D. (2011). Blind modulation classification based on spectral correlation and its robustness to timing mismatch. In *Proceedings of Military Communications Conference*. doi:10.1109/MILCOM.2011.6127676

Renard, J., Lampe, L., & Horlin, F. (2013). Nonparametric Cyclic Polyspectrum-Based Spectrum Sensing. *IEEE Wireless Communications Letters*, *2*(1), 98–101. doi:10.1109/WCL.2012.120312.120749

Richard, K., & Martin, W., & Zhiqiang, W. (2011). Using Spectral Correlation For Non-cooperative RSS-based Positioning. In *Proceedings of IEEE Statistical Signal Processing Workshop* (SSP).

Roberts, R., Brown, W., & Loomis, H. (1991). Computationally Efficient Algorithms for Cyclic Spectral Analysis. *IEEE Signal Processing Magazine*, *8*(2), 38–49. doi:10.1109/79.81008

Sithamparanathan, K., & Giorgetti, A. (2012). Cognitive Radio Techniques: Spectrum Sensing, Interference Mitigation, and Localization. Artech House. Available http://www.artechhouse.com/static/sample/Sith-203_CH03.pdf

Sutton, P. D., Nolan, K. E., & Doyle, L. E. (2008). Cyclostationary signatures in practical cognitive radio applications. *IEEE Journal on Selected Areas in Communications*, *26*(1), 13–24. doi:10.1109/JSAC.2008.080103

Swami, A., & Sadler, M. (2000). Hierarchical Digital Modulation Classification Using Cumulants. *IEEE Transactions on Communications*, *48*(3), 416–429. doi:10.1109/26.837045

Tarchi, D., Guidotti, A., Icolari, V., Varelli-Coralli, A., Sharma, S. K., Chatzinotas, S., . . . Grotz, J. (2014). Technical Challenges for Cognitive Radio Application in Satellite Communications. In *Proceedings of 9th International Conference on Cognitive Radio Oriented Wireless Networks* (CROWNCOM). doi:10.4108/icst.crowncom.2014.255727

Wu, H. C., & Iyengar, S. S. (2011). A Novel Robust Detection Algorithm for Spectrum Sensing. *IEEE Journal on Selected Areas in Communications*, *29*(2), 305–315. doi:10.1109/JSAC.2011.110204

Wu, Z., Yang, T. C., Liu, Z., & Chakarvarthy, V. (2012). Modulation Detection of Underwater Acoustic Communication Signals Through Cyclostationary Analysis. In *Proceedings of IEEE Military Communications Conference (MILCOM)*. doi:10.1109/MILCOM.2012.6415832

Xu, T., Chen, H., & Hu, H. (2014). A Low-Complexity Detection Method for Statistical Signals in OFDM Systems. *IEEE Communications Letters*, *18*(4), 632–635. doi:10.1109/LCOMM.2014.030614.140193

Yucek, T., & Arslan, H. (2009). A survey of spectrum sensing algorithms for cognitive radio applications. *IEEE Communications Surveys and Tutorials*, *11*(1), 116–130. doi:10.1109/SURV.2009.090109

Zhou, R., Li, X., Yang, T., Liu, Z., & Wu, Z. (2012). Real-time Cyclostationary Analysis for Cognitive Radio via Software Defined Radio. In *Proceedings of IEEE Globe-com*. doi:10.1109/GLOCOM.2012.6503325

KEY TERMS AND DEFINITIONS

ANN (Artificial Neural Networks): Network inspired by biological neural networks.

BPSK (Binary Phase Shift Keying): A digital modulation scheme that conveys data by changing the phase of a reference signal.

CAF (Cyclic Autocorrelation Function): A coefficient in the Fourier series expansion of the time-varying autocorrelation of a cyclostationary random process.

CR (Cognitive Radio): A form of wireless communication in which a transceiver can intelligently detect which communication channels are in use and which are not.

CSD (Cyclic Spectral Density): A method of detection and parameter estimation searching for the spectral peak.

FAM (FFT Accumulation Method): Algorithms for digital cyclic spectral analysis.

FFT (FAST Fourier Transform): Algorithm computes the discrete Fourier transform (DFT) of a sequence, or its inverse.

FPGA (Field Programmable Gate Array): An integrated circuit designed to be configured by a customer or a designer after manufacturing.

HOS (Higher Order Statistics): Functions which use the third or higher power of a sample.

LNB (Low Noise Block): The device on the front of a satellite dish that receives the very low level microwave signal from the satellite.

OFDM (Orthogonal Frequency Division Multiplexing): Scheme used as a digital multi-carrier modulation method.

PSD (Power Spectral Density): A measure of a signal's power intensity in the frequency domain.

SCF (Spectral Correlation Density): A function that describes the cross-spectral density of all pairs of frequency-shifted versions of a time-series.

SDR (Software Defined Radio): A radio communication system where components that have been typically implemented in hardware are instead implemented by means of software.

SNR (Signal to Noise Ratio): The ratio of the strength of an electrical or other signal carrying information to that of unwanted interference.

Chapter 2
Cepstrum–Based Spectrum Hole Search in Different Fading Scenario in Cognitive Radio Network

Srijibendu Bagchi
RCC Institute of Information Technology, India

ABSTRACT

Cognitive radio is now acknowledged as a potential solution to meet the spectrum scarcity problem in radio frequency range. To achieve this objective proper identification of vacant frequency band is necessary. In this article a detection methodology based on cepstrum estimation has been proposed that can be done through power spectral density estimation of the received signal. The detection has been studied under different channel fading conditions along with Gaussian noise. Two figures of merit are considered here; false alarm probability and detection probability. For a specific false alarm probability, the detection probabilities are calculated for different sample size and it has been established through numerical results that the proposed detector performs quite well in different channel impairments.

INTRODUCTION

Due to proliferation of diverse state-of-the-art wireless applications, spectrum demand is excessively high over a couple of decades. However, static spectrum allocation (SSA) policy has been revealed as a bottleneck to meet this huge requirement and consequently frequency band has become a scarce resource. Recent studies of different spectrum regulatory bodies such as FCC in USA or Ofcom in UK disclose that a significant amount of the allocated frequency band below 3 GHz is utilized intermittently thus leading to underutilization of the natural resource (FCC, 2003). Assigned spectrum utilization has been experienced to vary from 15% to 85% on temporal and geographical basis (Akyldiz et al., 2006). For example, the UHF digital TV spectrum commonly known as TV white space (TVWS) is available on a geographical basis. Medical Body Area Networks (MBAN) of 2360-2400 MHz bandwidth is also

DOI: 10.4018/978-1-5225-1785-6.ch002

obtainable in this regard (Wang et al 2011).In order to facilitate the optimum usage of available spectrum resource, dynamic spectrum access (DSA) (Shellhammer et al., 2009; Liang et al., 2011; Shin et al., 2011; Geirhofer et al., 2007) was later proposed where an unlicensed spectrum user opportunistically exploits vacant licensed frequency band (or spectrum hole) in negotiation with the licensed user or primary user (PU). In this context, the unlicensed or secondary user (SU) transmits its own data without affecting the PU transmission process. All SUs make use of cognitive radio (CR) technology to avail unutilized spectrum through DSA. A CR is proposed to be a reconfigurable device that can adjust its various parameters via intelligent sensing of its surroundings as well as maintain seamless communication. So, it may be believed that CR technology is envisioned to cater large number of unlicensed users thus facilitating proper spectrum usage. This technology really can introduce a new paradigm in the next generation wireless networks (Haykin, 2005).

Proper detection of spectrum hole (i.e. spectrum sensing) is the key necessity in this context (Tandra et al., 2009) along with other functionalities like spectrum management, spectrum sharing and spectrum mobility. On the other hand a CR is also required to be reconfigurable that necessitates:

- **Frequency Agility:** Capability of a CR device to change its operating frequency,
- **Dynamic Frequency Selection:** Dynamic detection of signals from the RF frequency band and avoiding significant co-channel interference,
- **Adaptive Modulation:** Proper modification of transmission characteristics and waveforms,
- **Transmission Power Control:** Switching capability of the device within a number of transmission power options, and
- **Dynamic Network Access:** Capability of accessing several communication networks that use different protocols.

A CR should also sustain good spectrum resource management, mobility management as well as security management. A CR device can be practically realized by software defined radio (SDR). This employs a cognitive engine for controlling different SDR based activities. The engine is responsive of hardware resources and different input parameters and it endeavors constantly to meet the radio link requirements of higher layer functionalities or user with existing resources for example spectrum and power. An SDR supports a flexible radio platform that can handle different frequency bandwidths along with various modulation techniques.

In the present article, focus is kept on the detection of vacant frequency band of a CR user. It enables a CR user to understand the existence of a licensed user in a frequency band. A CR is expected to identify vacant frequency bands correctly in spite of different channel impairments. Various techniques have been proposed so far in different literature. These techniques generally involve binary hypotheses testing where the hypotheses are framed regarding the absence or presence of PU. Here a decision is taken in favour of any one hypothesis and a CR device acts accordingly. Two types of errors may be committed in this decision making process. Firstly, a CR may falsely identify a frequency band occupied by PU when it is actually vacant. This is known as false alarm problem. In the second case, a CR may falsely identify an occupied frequency band as vacant. In this case, a CR tries to access the frequency band thus disrupting the PU transmission process. The second problem is more serious and is known as misdetection problem. A good detection technique should try to minimize both of these error probabilities but unfortunately both of them cannot be restricted simultaneously. So, one usually try to fix the false alarm probability to a certain value and minimize the misdetection probability.

The most common spectrum sensing technique is via energy detection through radiometry (Ghasemi et al., 2008; Digham et al., 2007; Cabric et al., 2006; Chen & Prasad, 2009). It is the easiest technique albeit suboptimal in nature. This technique does not require any prior knowledge of the PU signal. It compares the energy of the received signal with a threshold which is selected on the basis of false alarm probability. Naturally, if the received signal energy exceeds the threshold, the target frequency band is considered to be engaged otherwise it is treated as vacant. This technique is not very useful for weak PU signals. If the signal to noise ratio (SNR) falls below a certain value (commonly known as SNR_{wall}), the detection fails (Tandra & Sahai, 2005, 2008). Matched filter based detection is very accurate as it maximizes the SNR at the receiver (Cabric et al., 2006; Chen & Prasad, 2009). However, this technique requires prior knowledge of PU signal that may not be possible in real time scenario. Cyclostationary feature detection is more accurate as it exploits the hidden periodicities of the PU signal (Gardner, 1988; Choi et al., 2009). The natures of cyclic auto-correlation functions (and consequently spectral correlation functions) are studied in this situation. Nevertheless, this technique involves large computational complexity (Enserink & Cochran, 1994). Besides these, cooperative spectrum sensing (Chen & Prasad 2009; Ghasemi & Sousa, 2005; Mishra et al., 2006) has also become popular where a number of CR users cooperate among themselves to find vacant frequency band. This is usually effective to solve hidden terminal problems. This occurs when a CR user remains unaware regarding the interference created due to its transmission process to other spectrum users. If the interference exceeds a certain limit this may cause huge problem in the entire network. Hidden terminal problem usually occurs when a user remains in shadow region due to certain blocking. Cooperative spectrum sensing can be achieved either by centralized (Vistokoy et al., 2005) or by distributed ways (Li et al., 2009). In a centralized way, all the CR users send their sensing results or local decisions to a fusion centre and the fusion centre combines these either by soft or by hard combining. In hard combining the popular algorithms are logical AND, OR and majority rule. Also weighted cooperative spectrum sensing has been proposed in different literature. In distributed spectrum sensing a number of CR users communicate among them to take a decision of a spectrum hole. Energy efficient joint spectrum sensing by using relays is also found to be effective (Chatterjee et al., 2014). Mainly, amplify-and-forward and decode-and-forward relays are effective to handle spectrum sensing and transmission. Relays can control the interference to the licensed user. Energy efficient spectrum sensing and data transmission can also be achieved using relays. A number of literature deals with non-parametric spectrum sensing method where the noise or the signal along with noise have been considered as non-Gaussian or unknown (Bagchi, 2014; Bagchi & Rakshit, 2014). Multiband joint detection is also attractive in recent times (Quan et al., 2009). Here, spectrum sensing is performed over a wideband primary channel. Fast Fourier Transform (FFT) is performed over the received signal and then hypothesis testing is performed over each narrowband channel. However, this technique may introduce spectrum leakage due to FFT operation that may affect the detection performance (Farhang, 2008).

In this chapter, a detection methodology by cepstrum based approach has been proposed and its performance has been studied under different fading scenarios. The underlying idea behind this technique is to measure power spectral density (PSD) over the frequency band (Yao & Lee, 2007). If the PSD is higher than a threshold level, it may be inferred that the frequency band is occupied by PU. In reality, one has to estimate the PSD by finite samples of the received signal. This estimation methodology can be divided into parametric as well as non-parametric methods. The parametric or model based methods of estimation assume that the signal under study has a known mathematical form and different parameters can be estimated accordingly. This technique requires a proper selection of the nature of the spectral model. Commonly used models are autoregressive model, moving average model and autoregressive moving average model. Several algorithms have been proposed in the literature under all of these models. In the present discussion, non-parametric spectral estimation has been considered. This is useful when proper functional form of the PSD is difficult to find out. The PSD can be directly measured through periodogram estimation. It is found by averaging the square of the FFT of the finite length received signal. Otherwise, spectral estimation can be realized from the covariance sequence (Percival & Walden, 1993; Stoica & Moses, 2005). Covariance sequence decays rapidly if the lag is large. This technique ensures significant resolutions for long data lengths. However, the major problem of PSD estimation from finite samples is its high variance and does not decrease with increase in data length (Gudmundsen et al., 2008). If the bias in estimation is significant it can affect the entire detection process. Also, a problem in non-parametric method is that we should estimate the PSD theoretically with infinite values. In order to avoid it we can smooth the set of PSD values over $\left[-\pi, +\pi\right]$ by assuming it is constant over a narrower frequency band. To achieve this objective we have to eventually sacrifice the resolution that is a tradeoff is experienced between statistical variability and resolution. Thus PSD based spectral estimation may not treated as a good estimation technique when detection through parametric model is not possible. To avoid this specific problem cepstrum thresholding based smoothed non-parametric spectral estimation was later proposed. In this method, instead of direct averaging the periodogram values, the logarithm of periodogram was smoothed via thresholding of the estimated cepstrum (Childers et al., 1977; Stoica & Sandgren, 2006). One potential advantage of this technique is that the mean square error (MSE) of a non-parametric spectral estimator reduces with sample size. Here, the estimators are unbiased and consistent. If the concerned signal has moderate spectral dynamic range, the MSE of the considered estimator is much lesser than that of the periodogram at each frequency. Since, only half of the cepstral coefficients are distinct, we need not estimate the remaining coefficients. This also reduces the computational complexity. The binary hypothesis testing has been performed for the cepstral estimates to justify whether they are significant. The mean of the cepstral estimates have been taken to perform the hypothesis testing. Finally, the overall false alarm and detection probabilities can be calculated and the efficiency of the proposed technique is adjudicated by these figures of merit. It is expected to give good detection probability with increase in sample size for a fixed false alarm probability.

After transmission through wireless channel, a signal experiences fading along with noise that can degrade its quality. In this article, frequency non-selective or flat fading has been considered that may occur due to multipath effect (Simon & Alouini, 2005). Fading has been categorized by different distributions in literature. In the present article, the effectiveness of our projected technique is verified in different fading scenario by the aforesaid figures of merit. Numerical results are given in each case to validate the proposition. Overall, it is expected the novelty of cepstral estimation technique can be established through this chapter under different adverse situations.

The article is organized as follows:

- Section 2 discusses the detailed detection methodology.
- Numerical results are presented in Section 3
- Whereas concluding remarks are made in Section 4.

THE DETECTION METHODOLOGY

In this section, the significance of cepstrum has been discussed followed by the binary hypothesis testing methodology. Finally, the expressions for false alarm and detection probabilities are calculated.

Cepstrum Estimation

Let us consider a stationary, discrete time, real valued signal $\left\{y\left(t\right)\right\}_{t=0}^{N-1}$ with covariance sequence $\left\{r_k\right\}_{k=-\infty}^{\infty}$.

The PSD is defined as the DTFT of the covariance sequence.

$$\phi\left(\omega\right) = \sum_{k=-\infty}^{\infty} r_k e^{-i\omega k} \tag{1}$$

Alternatively, the PSD can also be defined as

$$\phi\left(\omega\right) = \lim_{N\to\infty} E\left\{\frac{1}{N}\left|\sum_{t=0}^{N-1} y\left(t\right)e^{-i\omega t}\right|^2\right\} \tag{2}$$

The above equations show that $\phi\left(\omega\right)$ is a periodic function where $\omega \in \left[-\pi, +\pi\right]$.

Next we can obtain the periodogram estimate from Equation 2 by neglecting the expectation and limit operation as follows

$$\hat{\phi}_p\left(\omega\right) = \frac{1}{N}\left|\sum_{t=0}^{N-1} y(t)e^{-i\omega t}\right|^2 \tag{3}$$

From equation (1), the spectral estimator can be found as given below

$$\hat{\phi}_c\left(\omega\right) = \sum_{k=-(N-1)}^{N-1} \hat{r}_k e^{-i\omega k} \tag{4}$$

where $\hat{r}_k$ is an estimate of the covariance lag r_k

In this context, the estimate of r_k denoted by $\hat{r}_k$ can be formulated as

$$\hat{r}_k = \frac{1}{N}\sum_{t=k}^{N-1} y\left(t\right)y\left(t-k\right) \tag{5}$$

where $k = 0, 1, ..., N - 1$ and $\hat{r}_{-k} = \hat{r}_k$

The integral based definition of $\hat{r}_k$ can also be obtained as

$$\hat{r}_k = \frac{1}{2\pi} \int_{-\pi}^{+\pi} \hat{\phi}(\omega) e^{i\omega k} d\omega \tag{6}$$

The Fourier grid of angular frequency axis is denoted by

$$\omega_k = \frac{2\pi}{N} k \tag{7}$$

The cepstrum of $y(t)$ can be defined as follows

$$C_k = \frac{1}{N} \sum_{p=0}^{N-1} \ln(\phi_p) e^{i\omega_k p} \tag{8}$$

where $k = 0, 1, ..., N - 1$

Otherwise the above equation can be written alternatively as

$$C_k = \frac{1}{N} \sum_{p=-\left(\frac{N}{2}-1\right)}^{\frac{N}{2}} \ln(\phi_p) e^{i\omega_k p} \tag{9}$$

In integral form, the cepstrum equation can be stated as

$$C_k = \frac{1}{2\pi} \int_{-\pi}^{+\pi} \ln(\phi(\omega)) e^{i\omega k} d\omega \tag{10}$$

Now, cepstrum estimate is obtained by replacing ϕ_p with $\hat{\phi}_p$ in equation (8)

$$\hat{C}_k = \frac{1}{N} \sum_{p=0}^{N-1} \ln(\hat{\phi}_p) e^{i\omega_k p} \tag{11}$$

where $k = 0, 1, ..., N - 1$

Next, applying inversion of equation (11) we obtain

$$\ln\left(\hat{\phi}_p\right) = \sum_{k=0}^{N-1}\hat{C}_k e^{-i\omega_p k} = \sum_{k=-\left(\frac{N}{2}-1\right)}^{\frac{N}{2}}\hat{C}_k e^{-i\omega_p k} \tag{12}$$

In order to find unbiased estimates, we can modify the cepstrum coefficients as given below:

$$\begin{cases}\overline{C}_0 = \hat{C}_0 + \gamma \\ \overline{C}_k = \hat{C}_k\end{cases} \tag{13}$$

where $k = 1,..,\dfrac{N}{2}-1$

In above equation, γ is known as Euler's constant and the value of γ is 0.577126.

Now, it can be stated that under some regularity conditions and for large sample size the estimated cepstral coefficients $\left\{\hat{C}_k\right\}_{k=0}^{\frac{N}{2}}$ can be demonstrated by independent normally distributed random variables as given by

$$\hat{C}_k \sim N\left(C_k, S_k^2\right) \tag{14}$$

where

$$S_k^2 = \begin{cases}\dfrac{\pi^2}{3N}, & if\ k = 0,\dfrac{N}{2} \\[3mm] \dfrac{\pi^2}{6N}, & if\ k = 1,..,\dfrac{N}{2}-1\end{cases} \tag{15}$$

At this stage, we assume a new estimate of C_k is $C_k^/$ and $C_k^/ = 0$ has a mean squared error (MSE) equal to C_k^2.

The estimate $\hat{C}_k$ is preferred as long as $C_k^2 \leq S_k^2$.

Next, we may assume that

$$S = \left\{k \in \left[0,\dfrac{N}{2}\right]\middle| C_k^2 \leq S_k^2\right\} \tag{16}$$

If $S^/$ be an estimate of S then by thresholding $\left\{\hat{C}_k\right\}_{k \in S^/}$, $C_k^/$ can be formulated as

$$C_k^' = \begin{cases}0, & if\ k \in S^' \\ \hat{C}_k, & else\end{cases} \quad where\ k = 0,...,\dfrac{N}{2} \tag{17}$$

Alternatively, $S^{/}$ can be re-formulated as follows

$$S' = \left\{ k \in \left[0, \frac{N}{2} \right] \mid \left| \hat{C}_k \right| \leq \gamma_{th} S_k \right\}$$
(18)

where the parameter γ_{th} is a threshold level that is to be determined from hypothesis testing problem.

Testing of Hypotheses

For the kth cepstral estimate, the binary hypotheses may be given as

H_{0k}: $C_k = 0$

H_{1k}: $C_k \neq 0$
(19)

Hence, the false alarm probability P_{fk} for the kth cepstral estimation can be calculated as follows

$$P_{fk} = \left(\left| \hat{C}_k \right| \leq \gamma_{th} S_k \mid H_{0k} \right)$$
(20)

From (20), we get

$$P_{fk} = 1 - 2Q\left(\gamma_{th} \right)$$
(21)

where

$$Q\left(x \right) = \frac{1}{\sqrt{2\pi}} \int\limits_{x}^{\infty} e^{-t^2/2} dt$$

Similarly, the detection probability for the kth cepstral estimate is given by

$$P_{dk} = \left(\left| \hat{C}_k \right| \geq \gamma_{th} S_k \mid H_{1k} \right)$$
(22)

From (22) we get

$$P_{dk} = 2Q\left(\frac{\gamma_{th} S_k - C_k}{S_k} \right)$$
(23)

In this technique, the cepstral estimates $\hat{C}_k$ for $k = 1, .., \frac{N}{2} - 1$ are considered (i.e. avoiding $\hat{C}_0$ and $\hat{C}_{\frac{N}{2}}$) as the variance is same for all these cases.

The overall detection probability has been calculated from Equation 23 by taking the average of all cepstral estimates under different channel fading conditions.

NUMERICAL RESULTS

In this section, the performance of the proposed technique has been tested under consideration of different channel fading distributions viz. Rayleigh, Rician, Log normal and Nakagami-*m* distributions. The parameter γ_{th} has been evaluated for a specific false alarm probability (0.01 and 0.05 for the current study). The parameters of the distributions have been chosen arbitrarily. The detection probability is then calculated for different sample size.

The following forms of the concerned distributions are chosen for analysis:

1. **Rayleigh:** $f(x) = \frac{x}{\sigma^2} \exp\left(-x^2 / 2\sigma^2\right)$ $x > 0$, where σ is the parameter of the distribution.

2. **Rician:** $f(x) = \frac{x}{\sigma^2} \exp\left(-(x^2 + v^2)/2\sigma^2\right) I_0\left(\frac{xv}{\sigma^2}\right)$, $x > 0$, where v and σ are the parameters of the distribution, $I_0(.)$ being the modified Bessel function of first kind with order zero.

3. **Log Normal:** $f(x) = \frac{1}{x\sigma\sqrt{2\pi}} \exp\left(-(\ln x - \mu)^2 / 2\sigma^2\right)$, $x > 0$, where μ and σ are the parameters of the distribution.

4. **Nakagami-*m*:** $f(x) = \frac{2m^m}{\Gamma(m)\omega^m} x^{2m-1} \exp\left(-\frac{m}{\omega} x^2\right)$, $x > 0$, where m and ω are known as shape and scale parameters of the distribution.

Performance Analysis for False Alarm Probability 0.01

In this sub-section, the performance of the proposed detector has been studied for false alarm probability 0.01. It is considered that for Rayleigh distribution, the parameter is 0.05 whereas for Rician distribution the two parameters (v and σ) are 0.05 and 1 respectively. For Log normal distribution μ and σ both are considered to be 0.1. Also for Nakagami-*m* distribution both the shape and scale parameters are taken as 0.1. Random samples are taken for different channel fading conditions along with Gaussian noise and also estimated cepstral coefficients are calculated based on the observed data. Finally, detection probability has been calculated for different sample sizes. As for larger sample size the estimator is unbiased and variance becomes lower, the detector usually gives better detection performance for comparatively larger sample size. The following two figures demonstrate the detection performance.

Figure 1 shows the detection probability vs. sample size plot for false alarm probability of 0.01. From the figure, we can find that the performance of the proposed detector is very consistent and improves

Figure 1. Detection probability versus. sample size plot for false alarm probability 0.01

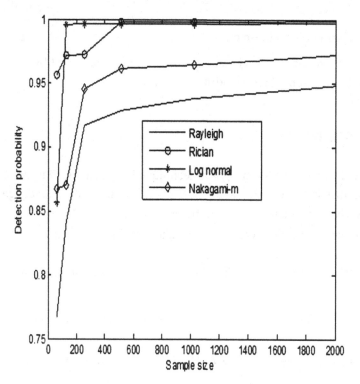

Figure 2. Detection probability versus sample size plot for false alarm probability 0.05

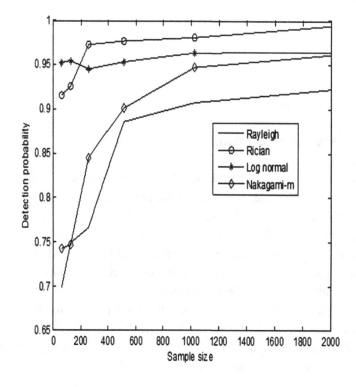

for larger sample size for different distributions of the channel fading. Since, the estimator is unbiased and consistent for large sample size, it can be naturally inferred that this technique may be treated as a potential one for larger sample size.

Performance Analysis for False Alarm Probability 0.05

Figure 2 shows the same study for false alarm probability 0.05 keeping all the distribution parameters are set as before. Here also it can be observed that the detection performance improves significantly with the sample size and the detector gives a very reliable performance for all types of channel fading. Hence, it may be concluded that for a specific false alarm probability, the proposed detector shows significant detection capability for comparatively large sample size.

FUTURE WORKS

This chapter presents a detection methodology of vacant frequency band under different fading scenarios. Four different distributions have been considered for the present study. The work may be extended for a number of other distributions. Specifically, emphasis may be given to more general distributions so that a wide class of distributions may be covered. The detection may also be performed by considering noise of non-Gaussian nature. Multi-antenna based detection methodology may also be exploited by deploying cepstral estimation technique.

CONCLUSION

In this article, different spectrum hole detection techniques have been discussed shortly and finally the detection of a primary signal through cepstrum estimation has been proposed. The details of cepstrum calculation have been discussed along with its capability of signal detection. Its performance has been studied under different channel fading conditions and it has been established that the detector is quite efficient to detect primary signal signals under different adverse situations. Numerical results have been provided to substantiate the proposition along with some future research directions. As a whole, this technique may be considered as very effective when one CR user tries to find vacant frequency band by estimating PSD of the received signal.

REFERENCES

Akyildiz, I. F., Lee, W. Y., Vuran, M. C., & Mohanty, S. (2006). NeXt generation/dynamic spectrum access/cognitive radio wireless networks: A survey. *Computer Networks, Elsevier, 50*(13), 2127–2159. doi:10.1016/j.comnet.2006.05.001

Bagchi, S. (2014). Cognitive Radio: Spectrum Sensing Under Unknown Signal and Noise Distributions. *2014 Sixth International Conference on Computational Intelligence and Communication Networks*. IEEE Computer Society. doi:10.1109/CICN.2014.101

Bagchi S & Rakshit M. (2014). Cognitive Radio: A Non-parametric Approach by Approximating Signal Plus Noise Distribution by Kaplansky Distributions in the Context of Spectrum Hole Search. *Smart Innovation, Systems and Technologies, 28*, 553-559.

Cabric, D., Tkachenko, A., & Brodersen, R. W. (2006). Spectrum Sensing Measurements of Pilot, Energy and Collaborative Detection. *IEEE Military Communications Conference (MILCOM)*. doi:10.1109/MILCOM.2006.301994

Chatterjee, S., Maity, S. P., & Acharya, T. (2014). Energy Efficient Cognitive Radio System for Joint Spectrum Sensing and Data Transmission. *IEEE J. on Emerging and Selected Topics in Circuits and Systems, 4*(3), 292–300. doi:10.1109/JETCAS.2014.2337191

Chen, K. C., & Prasad, R. (2009). *Cognitive Radio Networks*. John Wiley & Sons. Ltd. doi:10.1002/9780470742020

Childers, D. G., Skinner, D. P., & Kemerait, R. C. (1977). The cepstrum: A guide to processing. *Proceedings of the IEEE, 65*(10), 1428–1443. doi:10.1109/PROC.1977.10747

Choi, K. W., Jeon, W. S., & Jeong, D. G. (2009). Sequential Detection of Cyclostaionary Signal for Cognitive Radio Systems. *IEEE Transactions on Wireless Communications, 8*(9), 4480–4485. doi:10.1109/TWC.2009.090288

Digham, F., Alouini, M. S., & Simon, M. K. (2007). On the energy detection of unknown signals over fading channels. *IEEE Transactions on Communications, 55*(1), 21–24. doi:10.1109/TCOMM.2006.887483

Enserink, S., & Cochran, D. (1994). A Cyclostationary Feature Detector. *Signals, Systems and Computers, 1994*, 806–810.

Farhang-Boroujeny, B. (2008). Filter Bank Spectrum Sensing for Cognitive Radios. *IEEE Transactions on Signal Processing, 56*(5), 1801–1811. doi:10.1109/TSP.2007.911490

FCC. (2003). *In the Matter of Facilitating Opportunities for Flexible, Efficient and Reliable Spectrum Use Employing Cognitive Radio Technologies*. ET Docket No.03-108.

Gardner, W. A. (1988). Signal Interception: A Unifying Theoretical Framework for Feature Detection. *IEEE Transactions on Communications, 36*(8), 897–906. doi:10.1109/26.3769

Geirhofer, S., Tong, L., & Sadler, B. M. (2007). Dynamic Spectrum Access in the Time Domain: Modeling and Exploiting White Space. *IEEE Communications Magazine, 45*(5), 66–72. doi:10.1109/MCOM.2007.358851

Ghasemi, A., & Sousa, E. S. (2005). Collaborative spectrum sensing for opportunistic access in fading environment. In *Proc. IEEE DySPAN*, (pp. 131-136). doi:10.1109/DYSPAN.2005.1542627

Ghasemi, A., & Sousa, E. S. (2008). Spectrum Sensing in Cognitive Radio Networks: Requirements, Challenges and Design Trade-offs. *IEEE Communications Magazine, 46*(4), 32–39. doi:10.1109/MCOM.2008.4481338

Gudmundson, E., Sandgren, N., & Stoica, P. (2008). Automatic Smoothing of Periodogram. In *Proceedings of the 2006 IEEE International Conference on Acoustics, Speech and Signal Processing (ICASSP)*.

Haykin, S. (2005). Cognitive Radio: Brain-empowered wireless communications. *IEEE Journal on Selected Areas in Communications*, *23*(2), 201–220. doi:10.1109/JSAC.2004.839380

Li, Z., Yu, F., & Huang, M. (2009). A cooperative spectrum sensing consensus scheme in cognitive radios. *Proceedings - IEEE INFOCOM*, *2009*, 2546–2550.

Liang, Y. C., Chen, K. C., Li, G. Y., & Mahonen, P. (2011). Cognitive Radio Networking and Communications: An Overview. *IEEE Transactions on Vehicular Technology*, *60*(7), 3386–3407. doi:10.1109/TVT.2011.2158673

Mishra, S. M., Sahai, A., & Brodersen, R. W. (2006). Cooperative sensing among cognitive radios. In *Proc. IEEE Conference on Communications*.

Percival, D. B., & Walden, A. T. (1993). *Spectral Analysis for Physical applications*. Cambridge, UK: Cambridge University Press. doi:10.1017/CBO9780511622762

Quan, Z., Cui, S., Sayed, A. H., & Poor, H. V. (2009). Optimal Multiband Joint Detection for Spectrum Sensing in Cognitive Radio Networks. *IEEE Transactions on Signal Processing*, *57*(3), 1128–1140. doi:10.1109/TSP.2008.2008540

Shellhammer, S. J., Sadek, A. K., & Zhang, W. (2009). Technical Challenges for Cognitive Radio in the TV White Space Spectrum. *Information Theory and Applications Workshop*. doi:10.1109/ITA.2009.5044964

Shin, K. G., Kim, H., Min, A. W., & Kumar, A. (2010). Cognitive Radios for Dynamic Spectrum Access: From Concept to Reality. *IEEE Wireless Communications*, *17*(6), 64–74. doi:10.1109/MWC.2010.5675780

Simon, M. K., & Alouini, M. S. (2005). Digital Communications over Fading Channels. John Wiley & Sons.

Stoica, P., & Moses, R. (2005). *Spectral Analysis of Signals*. Upper Saddle River, NJ: Prentice Hall.

Stoica, P., & Sandgren, N. (2006). Cepstrum Thresholding Scheme for Nonparametric Estimation of Smooth Spectra. *IMTC 2006 - Instrumentation and Measurement Technology Conference Sorrento*, (pp. 874-878).

Stoica, P., & Sandgren, N. (2006). Smoothed nonparametric spectral estimation via cepstrum Thresholding. *IEEE Signal Processing Magazine*, 34–45. doi:10.1109/SP-M.2006.248710

Tandra, R., Mishra, M., & Sahai, A. (2009). What is a spectrum hole and what does it take to recognize one? *Proceedings of the IEEE*, *97*(5), 824–848. doi:10.1109/JPROC.2009.2015710

Tandra, R., & Sahai, A. (2005). Fundamental Limits on Detection in Low SNR Under Noise Uncertainty. *International Conference on Wireless Networks, Communication and Mobile Computing*. doi:10.1109/WIRLES.2005.1549453

Tandra, R., & Sahai, A. (2008). SNR Walls for Signal Detection. *IEEE Journal of Selected Topics in Signal Processing*, *2*(1), 4–17. doi:10.1109/JSTSP.2007.914879

Visotsky, E., Kuffner, S., & Peterson, R. (2005). On collaborative detection of TV transmissions in support of dynamic spectrum sharing. In *Proc. of IEEE DySPAN 2005*, (pp. 338–345). doi:10.1109/DYSPAN.2005.1542650

Wang, J., Ghosh, M., & Challapali, K. (2011). Emerging Cognitive Radio Applications: A Survey. *IEEE Communications Magazine, 49*(3), 74–81. doi:10.1109/MCOM.2011.5723803

Yao, F., & Lee, T. C. M. (2007). Spectral density estimation using sharpened periodograms. *IEEE Transactions on Signal Processing, 55*(9), 4711–4716. doi:10.1109/TSP.2007.896297

Chapter 3
Radio Frequency Identification and Mobile Ad–Hoc Network:
Theories and Applications

Kijpokin Kasemsap
Suan Sunandha Rajabhat University, Thailand

ABSTRACT

This chapter explains the components of Radio Frequency Identification (RFID); the aspects of RFID; the barriers to RFID utilization; the privacy and security issues of RFID; the RFID applications in supply chain management; the RFID applications in the health care industry; the RFID applications in modern business; the Near Field Communication (NFC) in mobile devices; the overview of Mobile Ad-Hoc Network (MANET); the security concern of MANET; and the advanced issues of MANET in the digital age. RFID and MANET become the growing components of Information and Communication Technology (ICT) applications and can be effectively utilized in global operations. The chapter argues that RFID and MANET have the potential to increase the efficiency of operations in various industries, improve asset visibility and traceability, decrease reliance on manual processes, reduce operation costs, and provide useful data for business analytics.

INTRODUCTION

The number of applications for radio frequency identification (RFID) systems is rapidly growing (Cui, Wang, Zhao, & Chen, 2016). Many professions, businesses, and industries have integrated the RFID technology into their procedures and it has resulted in the great advances in the accuracy of data, operational efficiencies, logistics enhancements, and other process improvements (Pang, Morgan-Morris, & Howell, 2010). RFID technology is utilized in various fields (e.g., manufacturing, retail, logistics, transportation, inventory control, health care, and business). For many companies, RFID suggests not only a new alternative to the existing tracking methods, but also a method to a wide range of previously cost-prohibitive internal control and supply chain coordination innovations (Bendoly, Citurs, & Konsynski, 2007).

DOI: 10.4018/978-1-5225-1785-6.ch003

Because of its low cost and ease of deployment, RFID technology offers the great potential for all applications that require identification (Akgün, Bayrak, & Çağlayan, 2015). As RFID can quickly identify an object without requiring physical contact, it provides efficient identification for the verification of individual objects (Chen & Wu, 2014). RFID systems rely on the significant technology of the remote and automatic identification with the small and low-cost radio frequency elements to securely complete radio frequency communications among all entities (Cheng, Liu, Chang, & Chang, 2013). RFID is a small electronic device that transmits and receives several types of data using electromagnetic radiations (Sarwar & Shah, 2015) and constitutes an important part of what has become known as the Internet of Things (IoT) that is the accessible and interconnected machine (Rekleitis, Rizomiliotis, & Gritzalis, 2014).

Mobile ad-hoc network (MANET) is recognized as one of the most important emerging wireless communication scenarios (Yang, 2010) and is a collection of communication devices or nodes that wish to communicate without any fixed infrastructure (Singh, 2016). MANET plays an important role in supporting visions toward the creation of the world of ubiquitous computing where computation is integrated into the environment, rather than having computers that are the distinct objects (Sim, Chin, & Tan, 2007). MANET is prone to confront a lot of challenges in designing a proper quality of service (QoS) model where transmission reliability has an important contribution (Das & Chaudhuri, 2017). Providing QoS assurances in MANET is difficult due to node mobility, contention for channel access, a lack of centralized coordination, and the unreliable nature of the wireless channel (Hanzo & Tafazolli, 2011).

MANET is dynamic in the sense that each node is free to join and leave the network in a non-deterministic way (Trivedi, Arora, Kapoor, & Sanyal, 2009). In MANET, the nodes need to cooperate each other to establish the multi-hop routes (Chand, 2007) for the out-of-range wireless communication (Wang, Zhang, & Naït-Abdesselam, 2015) and for maintaining the routes to other nodes in the network (Cornetta, Touhafi, Santos, & Vázquez, 2011). To minimize communication interference, the selected path may not be the shortest path or may increase the number of hops in the routing path (Zadin & Fevens, 2015). In MANET, messages hop from node to node until they reach their destination, which requires each node to be more intelligent than the conventional terminals found in other wireless networks, such as mobile networks (Fleury, Qadri, Altaf, & Ghanbari, 2011). Every node has the ability to handle the congestion in its queues during traffic overflow (Natsheh, 2009).

This chapter aims to bridge the gap in the literature on the thorough literature consolidation of RFID and MANET. The extensive literature of RFID and MANET provides a contribution to practitioners and researchers by explaining the theories and applications of RFID and MANET in order to maximize the technological impact of RFID and MANET in the digital age.

BACKGROUND

RFID is fundamentally based on the study of electromagnetic waves and radio, pioneered in the 19th century work of Faraday, Maxwell, and Marconi. The idea of using radio frequencies to reflect waves from objects dates back as far as 1886 to experiments conducted by Hertz (Wyld, 2008). RFID has been around since World War II when radio waves were used to identify the friendly aircrafts (Brown, 2011). In the 1970s, New York Port Authority introduced the RFID device used for toll collection. The development of RFID technology has been in progress for more than 50 years, and the wide variety of RFID products will become increasingly diverse with the advanced technology (Ouyang, Hou, Pang, Wang, & Xiong, 2008). Many nations have developed and implemented RFID-based automated systems in various public services (Hossain & Quaddus, 2014).

RFID systems communicate through electromagnetic waves and are categorized as radio systems. All radio systems operate in a narrow band to avoid signal interference with other radio systems (Malek & Miri, 2014). RFID technology bridges two technologies in the areas of information and communication technology (ICT), namely product code (PC) technology and wireless technology (Zayou, Besbe, & Hamam, 2014). ICT can be used in various RFID tag identification conditions, especially when the tag IDs are distributed (Jia & Feng, 2015). Barcodes identify items through the encoding of data in various sized bars using a variety of coding methodologies (Vowels, 2009). The main form of barcode-type RFID device is known as an Electronic Product Code (EPC) and the most popular standard for passive RFID tags is Class-1 Generation-2 (Picazo-Sanchez, Ortiz-Martin, Peris-Lopez, & Hernandez-Castro, 2013). In addition, EPC Global is an organization established to achieve the worldwide adoption and standardization of EPC technology (Ning, 2014).

RFID technology is an enabling technology for a wide variety of applications in next-generation network (Cho, Pack, Kwon, & Choi, 2010) and has the advantages of low entry barriers, low latency, high flexibility, and independent evolvability (Liu, Lin, Ram, & Su, 2010). RFID solutions can be utilized to reduce the operating costs through decreasing labor costs, enhancing automation, improving tracking and tracing, and preventing the loss of materials (Kasemsap, 2015a). RFID tags can incorporate additional data (e.g., details of product and manufacturer) and can transmit the measured environmental factors, such as temperature and relative humidity (Kumar, Reinitz, Simunovic, Sandeep, & Franzon, 2009). RFID allows any tagged entity to become a mobile device, thus communicating the component of the organization's overall information infrastructure (Palanisamy & Mukerji, 2013).

The growth of laptop and 802.11/Wi-Fi wireless networking have made MANET a popular research topic since the mid to late 1990s (Singh, Singh, & Mondal, 2012). MANET is the autonomous system connected by wireless communication on a peer-to-peer basis (Baqar, Aldabbas, Alwadan, Alfawair, & Janicke, 2014). As the applications of MANET increasingly grow, the size of the network greatly varies from a network of several mobile computers in a classroom to a network of hundreds of mobile units deployed in a battlefield (Dhar, 2009). Based on the physical location of the network, the velocity of the nodes can be the same or different (Mukherjee et al., 2016).

With increased mobility, route changes are more frequent compared to the Internet traffic (Khan, Kumar, Xie, & Sahoo, 2015). Every node in the network has mobility and can access the publish/subscribe service (e.g., by running a publish/subscribe middleware), while acting as the brokers for message forwarding and event matching to make the service available (Pei & Ravindran, 2010). Due to the limited transmission range of network, more than single hops is required to transfer data across the network (Patel & Prajapati, 2012).

PERSPECTIVES ON RADIO FREQUENCY IDENTIFICATION AND MOBILE AD-HOC NETWORK

This section emphasizes:

- The components of RFID;
- The aspects of RFID;
- The barriers to RFID utilization;
- The privacy and security issues of RFID;

- The RFID applications in supply chain management;
- The RFID applications in the health care industry;
- The RFID applications in modern business;
- The NFC in mobile devices;
- The overview of MANET;
- The security concern of MANET; and
- The advanced issues of MANET in the digital age.

Components of Radio Frequency Identification

RFID system consists of three major components: a reader or integrator, which sends interrogation signals to an RFID transmitter responder (transponder) or tag, which is to be identified; an RFID tag, which contains the identification code; and middleware, which maintains the interface and the software protocol to encode and decode the identification data from the reader into a mainframe or a personal computer (Karmakar, 2009). RFID systems have been developed that can calculate the location of a tag, as well as read the data it contains (Curran & Norrby, 2011). The tag receives a radio signal from the reader. The tag is activated and sends back the data to the reader. The collected information is passed on to RFID middleware for processing (Bahr & Price, 2016).

RFID system has three-layer architecture where the bottom RFID network layer manages more physical RFID networks consists of tags, readers and base stations, the top most application layer is for user applications and RFID-based services, and the integration and interfaces between these two layers are done in the RFID middleware (Kamruzzaman, Azad, Karmakar, Karmakar, & Srinivasan, 2013). Because of the incapability of the RFID system to handle vast amount of RFID tags, there are possibilities that the data cannot be efficiently processed in the RFID middleware (Lockman & Selamat, 2011).

Tags are wireless transponders that typically have no power of their own and only respond when they are in an electromagnetic field, while RFID readers are transceivers that generate such fields (Burmester & Munilla, 2013). Short-range RFID tags communicate with the RFID reader up to a few centimeters (Catarinucci, Colella, & Tarricone, 2012). Medium-range RFID tags reach almost 5 meters. Long-range RFID tags work up to almost 12 meters (Catarinucci et al., 2012). RFID tags can store a digital representation of the physical object and wirelessly transmit it to the pervasive and context-aware applications running on mobile devices (Carreton, Pinte, & Meuter, 2013). To draw full advantage from the increased functionality of the tags, it will become important to integrate these tags into the IoT, enabling the end-to-end communication over the Internet (Dominikus & Kraxberger, 2014). The IoT is an emerging paradigm, which is used to link physical objects with the Internet based on RFIF technology (Picazo-Sanchez, Ortiz-Martin, Peris-Lopez, & Bagheri, 2015). RFID reader communicates with tags at distance through wireless transmission (Yang, He, & Kun, 2013).

RFID uses radio frequency waves to transfer data between RFID reader and the item in order to identify, track, and locate that item (Andriole, 2009). RFID in the form of tags or transponders is a method of auto-identification that can be used for tracking and monitoring objects, both living and non-living (Michael & Michael, 2009). RFID facilitates the fully automated recognition of more than one transponder without direct line of sight between reader and transponders (Kaspar, 2009). RFID tags are classified into active, semi-active, and passive tags based on their on-board power supplies. Active tags have an internal battery which permits the tag to emit the stored data and to store the new data (Sinodinou, 2009). Semi-active tags contain a battery, but the battery is only used to energize the chip, and yields better longevity compared to the active tags (Karmakar, 2012). Passive tags only transmit information to the reader when they receive a radio wave signal from the reader through the antennas connected to the reader (Lim, 2013) and do not have an internal battery and cannot transmit data unless the reader activates them (Sinodinou, 2009).

In the developed RFID sensors, the complex impedance of the RFID resonant antenna is measured and correlated to the physical, chemical, or biological properties of interest (Potyrailo et al., 2009). A novel antenna structure with two crab-shaped patches and a small micro-strip dipole is proposed for ultra frequency RFID tag design, which can be directly integrated in metallic plates or other objects (Tang, Wu, Zhan, & Hu, 2014). RFID authentication is an essential part of RFID applications, which allows a reader to identify objects in an authenticated manner (Li, Mu, Susilo, Guo, & Varadharajan, 2015). The RFID authentication schemes between reader and tag based on public-key cryptography (PKC) are much better than those based on symmetric-key cryptography in terms of expanding the scale of RFID applications and the style of providing service, while the limitation of resource consumption and computation capability of RFID tags makes it difficult to apply traditional PKC to RFID authentications (Dong, Ding, & Wei, 2015).

Aspects of Radio Frequency Identification

RFID is a non-contact automatic identification technology that identifies targets to obtain relevant data using radio frequency signals without manual intervention in a variety harsh environments. Michaelides and Forster (2014) defined RFID as a type of wireless information and communication technology, which has the ability to identify, record, verify, and process data associated with various tangible items (e.g., physical location of products and the associated movement) and the supporting intangible tasks (e.g., information processing and data execution operations associated with the provision of services).

RFID has three major applications:

1. Item tracking where statically placed readers are responsible to track mobile items;
2. Item location where mobile readers are able to locate items of interest; and
3. Identification applications where RFID tags are used for identification purposes (Ahmed, 2012).

RFID technology provides much cheaper solution for object identification and tracking based on radio wave (Azad, Kamruzzaman, & Karmakar, 2012). Regarding technology acceptance model (TAM), perceived usability of RFID has a positive relationship with the levels of adoption of the technology (Ramanathan, Ramanathan, & Ko, 2015). The attitude toward using the technology arises from the perceived usefulness and the perceived ease of use (Ramanathan, Ramanathan, & Ko, 2016).

RFID technology replaces the printed barcodes and enables the electronically tagged items to be intelligently identified, tracked, and managed in real time (Kamoun & Miniaoui, 2015). RFID technology is better than barcode (Xiao et al., 2007) with respect to its tracking capabilities, multiple lending options, and more accurate operations (Abu-Shanab & Yamin, 2014). Ultra-wideband (UWB) technology is one promising wireless technique for future RFID, especially for high-throughput sensing applications (Zhang, Lu, Chen, Yan, & Zheng, 2012). A full exploitation of the RFID potential requires the study and implementation of human–computer interaction (HCI) modalities to be able to support wide usability by the target audience (Bellotti, Berta, Margarone, & de Gloria, 2008).

Critical success factors for the successful implementation of RFID systems include creating strong motivation for improvement, enhancing the desire to keep abreast of the latest technology for global competitiveness, striving for cross-organizational implementation, avoiding major process changes, starting with a small RFID project scope, facilitating vendor's investment, utilizing cost-effectiveness reusable tags, and transferring RFID knowledge from university to industry (Ngai et al., 2007). Companies with broad information technology (IT) application deployment and a critical mass of RFID implementation spending are more likely to report early returns from RFID deployments (Whitaker, Mithas, & Krishnan, 2007).

The development of RFID for wireless data transmission has presented several new opportunities for sharing, tracking, and reading digital information in various industries (Lee, 2015). RFID is used to identify objects (Wu, Sheng, Shen, & Zeadally, 2013), to organize the IoT (Miorandi, Sicari, de Pellegrini, & Chlamtac, 2012), and to provide accurate locations (Nejad, Jiang, & Kameyama, 2013). The RFID environments are characterized by a large number of items with the attached tags that move entering and leaving facilities in various locations (Vales-Alonso, Parrado-García, & Alcaraz, 2016). RFID offers the potentially flexible and low cost method of locating objects and tracking people within buildings (Parry & Symonds, 2009).

Barriers to Radio Frequency Identification Utilization

Although many companies have initiated RFID projects, they often face significant difficulties in integrating RFID systems into their existing IT landscape (Engel, Goswami, Englschalk, & Krcmar, 2015). One difficulty is the upfront estimation of the cost of the RFID integration project (Engel et al., 2015), especially the cost of RFID tags for applications involving item-level tagging (Lim, 2013). The RFID technology seems to be able to solve in the efficient way the requirements for traceability systems, however some technological problems, such as the lack of consolidated systems, and the costs are the main obstacles to the wide adoption of RFID-based traceability systems (Gandino, Sanchez, Montrucchio, & Rebaudengo, 2009). Traditionally, the traceability system is performed through the asynchronous fulfillment of checkpoints (e.g., doorways) by materials (Regattieri, Santarelli, Gamberi, & Gamberini, 2014).

The wireless channels between tags and readers are not secure in the IoT (Li, Wang, & Zheng, 2014). Before a reader processes packets from tags, the reader should detect the integrity of these packets (Li et al., 2014). To make RFID technology widely applicable, it is important to resolve the multiple tag identification problem (i.e., the problem of indicating tag collisions occurring when multiple RFID tags are simultaneously present in a reader's field) (Kim, Cho, & Kim, 2013). The RFID reader collision problem, in which an RFID reader's interrogation is interfered by other readers' transmission, is considered as an important issue to reliable operation and thus to the wide-spread deployment of RFID networks (Yoon & Vaidya, 2012). The RFID reader collision problem is caused by the interrogation zones overlap of multiple readers, and leading to the incorrect and unreliable data (Chen, Chen, & Lee, 2009).

In the active RFID systems, data collision causes serious data loss, slow identification speed, and high energy consumption (Sun, Zhang, & Mo, 2011). To enhance the quality of data, cleaning is the essential task, so that the resultant data can be applied for high-end applications (Leema & Hemalatha, 2015). As RFID-enabled technology is becoming pervasive in enterprise systems and human life, it triggers significant concerns over the malware that can infect, damage, and even destroy RFID-enabled network systems (Yan, Li, & Deng, 2013). RFID malware can spread malicious codes or data quickly to a large number of RFID systems via RFID read and write, which are the pervasive operations on RFID tags that are transported from one RFID system to another (Yan et al., 2013).

Privacy and Security Issues of Radio Frequency Identification

Since RFID utilizes the wireless medium, all the threats associated with wireless media usage exist in RFID systems (Onat & Miri, 2013). The widespread utilization of RFID technology introduces many security and privacy risks since tags contain information that can be easily obtained by anyone with a reader (Dimitriou, 2016). RFID system security issues must meet the public demand of data protection (Benssalah, Djeddou, & Drouiche, 2014) and must be addressed because security has become the bottleneck restricting the development of RFID technology (Yeh, Wang, Kuo, & Wang, 2010). Providing security and privacy services for RFID tags presents the unique set of challenges (Ma & Saxena, 2013). This is due to the constraints of RFID tags in terms of computation, memory, and power resources (Ma & Saxena, 2013).

Pervasiveness of RFID systems with inherent weaknesses has been a cause of concern about their privacy and security (Alagheband & Aref, 2013). Without adequate protection, malicious attackers can easily eavesdrop, scan, and forge the information within the tag, thus threatening the integrity of the system (Li & Liu, 2011). Therefore, a security protocol for RFID tags is needed to ensure privacy and authentication between each tag and their reader (Liu et al., 2010). Unlike barcodes, RFID tags have a longer range in which they are allowed to be scanned, subjecting them to unauthorized scanning by malicious readers and to various attacks, including cloning (Liu, Bailey, & Krishnamurthy, 2010).

Because of the increasing ubiquity of RFID devices, there is a pressing need for the development of security primitives and protocols to defeat unauthorized reading and relay attacks (Ma & Saxena, 2014). It is very challenging on designing the cryptographically strong security functions that can be incorporated into the low-cost RFID tags (Li, Deng, & Wang, 2008). To establish secure RFID network, communication between any two nodes that hold RFID tags and/or readers merged with the existing networks should be protected (Thayananthan, Alzahrani, & Qureshi, 2015). The recent shift of incorporating RFID into consumer-oriented products has raised serious concerns of customer privacy and security (Chen, 2015). These concerns are rooted in the fact that consumers are unaware that their purchases are being tracked and monitored, as well as the fear of private information being hacked or stolen through the insecure RFID systems (Chen, 2015).

Radio Frequency Identification Applications in Supply Chain Management

Supply chain networks are the integrated patterns of processes utilized within a facility and over distribution connections, adding value to customers by improving the delivery and manufacturing of products (Kasemsap, 2016a). The utilization of RFID in supply chain networks has allowed Wal-Mart to create value through greater visibility in its networks, higher product velocity, reduce human error and labor cost, and more efficient inventory management, which led to the achievement of quick response (QR) and improved customer relationship management (CRM) in the supply chain (El Khaddar, Harroud, Boulmalf, & El Koutbi, 2013). CRM is the managerial philosophy according to which the company's goal can be achieved through the identification and satisfaction of the customer's requirement (Kasemsap, 2015b). Since the introduction of RFID supplier mandates in 2003 by some of the world's leading retailers (e.g., Wal-Mart and METRO), RFID has attracted significant interest from the retail community, representing an enhancement over the existing barcode technology for managing product flows within supply chains (Tajima, 2012).

RFID technology has the potential of helping retailers provide the right product at the right place at the right time, thus maximizing sales and profits (Ajana, Harroud, Boulmalf, & Elkoutbi, 2011). Many logistics service providers have acknowledged that if they want to operate more efficiently and responsively, they must adopt technologies that help manufacturers, warehouses, and retailers effectively communicate with each other (Ramanathan, Ko, Chen, & Ramanathan, 2015). Retailers are initiating processes for collecting customer information to make their business processes more efficient. This opens up the possibility to identify a customer by attaching the RFID tag (Chowdhury & Ray, 2014). Relative advantage, competitive pressure, and value chain complexity are the significant determinants of RFID adoption in the retail industry (Bhattacharya & Wamba, 2015).

RFID technology is a promising solution for the misplaced inventory (Camdereli & Swaminathan, 2010). The decentralized supply chain benefits more from RFID technology, such that RFID adoption improves supply chain coordination (Heese, 2007). RFID provides the real-time visibility into the status of assets throughout the supply chain (Amini, Otondo, Janz, & Pitts, 2007) and has the potential to provide customers with large amounts of information at any point in the movement of products through the supply chain (Gupta, Garg, Xu, & Goh, 2009). To enlarge tracking systems to cover global supply chains, all aspects related to RFID (e.g., radio frequency, data content, transmission protocols, and message sets) need to be standardized (Permala, Rantasila, Pilli-Sihvola, & Hinkka, 2014).

RFID enables the visibility into the movement of inventories in the supply chain (Hardgrave, Aloysius, & Goyal, 2013) and allows for non-contact reading of data about products, places, times, or transactions, thus giving retailers and manufacturers alike timely and accurate data about the flow of products through their factories, warehouses, and stores (Loebecke, 2008). Misplaced inventory is the major problem in many supply chains. Suppliers who integrate the full-scale RFID systems will realize efficiencies in time, material movement, inventory planning, shipping, and warehousing both internally and externally (Singh, McCartney, Singh, & Clarke, 2008). Various modules of RFID-enabled store management system (e.g., back-store inventory, smart shelves, interactive mirrors and fitting, and self-checkout services) can be implemented for retail operations (Choi, Cheung, Yang, & Yang, 2015).

Radio Frequency Identification Applications in the Health Care Industry

Implementation of RFID technology-based health care services is on the rise (Manzoor, 2016). Health care organizations are exploiting RFID to maximize the utilization of equipment, keep tabs on medicinal drugs, boost patient flow, and increase patient safety (Watfa, Kaur, & Daruwala, 2013). RFID contributes to independent living and quality of life for many patients by reducing the need of health care providers and private nursing (D'Andrea, Ferri, & Grifoni, 2013). RFID can effectively manage health care processes, enhance quality of care, and control costs (Unnithan & Fraunholz, 2015). Certain types of mistakes may be prevented by automatically identifying the patient through RFID before surgery toward reducing medical errors (Jeong, Cheng, & Prabhu, 2011).

For medical and health care purposes, RFID systems have been mainly used for inventory control and for searching for the location of a person or material to which RFID tag is attached (Hanada, 2013). RFID technology has been proposed as the effective tracking system in health care considering that it enables automatic identification and data capture of multiple items (Noël & Connolly, 2016). The goal of most automatic identification systems is to increase efficiency and reduce errors in data capture.

RFID technology safeguards the integrity of the drug supply by automatically tracing the movement of medications from the manufacturer to the hospital patient (Littman, 2008).

RFID is an important technology of ubiquitous health care and enables a fully automated solution for information delivery, thus reducing the potential for human error (Lee & Shim, 2009). RFID can be utilized in various health care operations, ranging from care giving to telemedicine (Catarinucci, Cappelli, Colella, & Tarricone, 2008). RFID technology will help to prevent missed doses or vaccinations, prevent multiple doses being given (extra doses), and will provide a clear transfer of information from patient to health care provider to increase the vaccination rate and ensure patients have been provided with the maximum possible immunity (Hawrylak & Hart, 2014). RFID provides the ability to identify, track, and monitor patients, thus enabling better resource allocation, reduction of medical errors, and increased independence for patients (Hawrylak, Schimke, Hale, & Papa, 2012).

Radio Frequency Identification Applications in Modern Business

With the development of modern technology, the emergence of low-power miniaturized chips promotes the rapid development of RFID applications (Qian, Ngan, Liu, & Ni, 2011). RFID can be used as an advanced manufacturing technology that enables more factory automation and better performance along several dimensions (Hozak & Collier, 2008). As businesses move toward the convergence of information, RFID technology effectively provides a step closer to the reality of connecting the real world and the digital world (Soon, 2010). RFID for the supply chain has attracted global attention and many companies are using RFID in their business processes (Soon & Gutiérrez, 2011). RFID can be used to significantly improve the efficiency of business processes by providing automatic identification and data capture (Bose & Lam, 2009).

The global industry for RFID technology has been growing steadily and is expected to grow rapidly before stabilizing and settling on a steady growth path (Lee, 2013). It is important for both service and manufacturing companies to develop and implement successful strategies that integrate RFID-embedded technological initiatives and knowledge practices, technological innovations, and customer relationship building of trust if they are to survive (Smith, 2014). For example, Hong Kong International Airport has adopted the RFID technology, replacing the traditional infrared barcode system with a new 900 MHz RFID baggage handling system (Fung et al., 2007).

As RFID technology matures and organizations seek to deploy it in their business operations, a basic objective in the endeavor is that of extracting business value from the technology (Dutta, Lee, & Whang, 2007). Business units vary in their response to the RFID perspectives (Barratt & Choi, 2007). Service companies utilize RFID to reengineer service transactions and customer touchpoints (Heim, Wentworth, & Peng, 2009). The collection of real-time sales and inventory data enabled by RFID can facilitate automatic replenishment (Tajima, 2012). RFID ticketing systems constitute a particular type of pervasive information systems, thus providing the spectators of sports events with a transparent mechanism to validate the tickets (Shih, Chiu, Chang, & Yen, 2010).

Near Field Communication in Mobile Devices

Near field communication (NFC) is the radio frequency technology for the short-range communication (Karnouskos, 2007) that exchanges the data between a reader, such as a phone or sensor, and a target, such as another reader or a microchip embedded in a device (Moloney, 2014). NFC technology provides the alternative for adding a link between an object in the physical world and digital services (Isomursu & Ervasti, 2009). The integration of NFC into mobile devices has recently emerged as a disruptive innovation and a strong enabler of a wide range of new mobile applications (Kamoun, 2013), such as mobile payment (Kasemsap, 2016b).

NFC is the modern method of navigating in the indoor environments (Sakpere & Adeyeye, 2015). NFC makes it possible to utilize the basic services of the mobile phone, such as placing a call and sending a message, in a timely and effective manner (Sánchez, Nieto, Gallinas, & Vidales, 2014). The NFC controller enables the NFC communication of the mobile phone with the external NFC devices (Ahamad, Sastry, & Udgata, 2014). Hardware producers, network operators, and service providers are willing to implement the NFC technologies in order to offer the new services to their customers (Wiedmann, Reeh, & Schumacher, 2012).

NFC in mobile devices can be used to improve the attendance system, since user identification is the most important aspect that needs to be cautiously handled in various applications (Ayu, Ahmad, & Mantoro, 2016). NFC applications include using the mobile phone to emulate the physical smart cards (e.g., credit/debit cards, loyalty cards, and library cards), allowing users to exchange their contact information or electronic money with each other, and reading information from NFC tags contained in various items, such as smart posters, DVDs, and CDs (Juntunen, Tuunainen, & Luukkainen, 2012).

Overview of Mobile Ad-Hoc Network

MANET is a self-created, self-organized, and self-administering set of nodes (Gallo, Perilli, & de Bonis, 2011) connected through wireless links without the support of any fixed infrastructure (Kathirvel & Srinivasan, 2011) toward establishing an autonomous network for the specific purposes, such as emergency search and rescue (Hsin & Harn, 2013). MANET is deployed in many domestic and public applications, contributing to the new requirements concerning performance and efficiency (Kadri, Feham, & M'hamed, 2009). The mobile ad-hoc computational grid is a distributed computing infrastructure that allows mobile nodes to share the computing resources in a mobile ad-hoc environment (Shah, 2015).

The fundamental MANET is a single-hop network, in which a node can communicate with each other, such as IEEE 802.11 ad-hoc network (Wang, Li, Lin, & Shih, 2015). Since MANET is infrastructureless and multi-hop by nature, transmitting packets from any node to another node relies on services provided by the intermediate nodes (Djenouri & Badache, 2008). Internet protocol (IP) autoconfiguration of the mobile node addresses is important in the utilization of MANET (Li, Cai, & Xu, 2009). The mobile node in MANET must be assigned a free IP address before it may participate in the unicast communications (Zhou, Mutka, & Ni, 2010).

The routing protocols in MANET can be classified into two categories: table-driven protocols and on-demand protocols (Singh, Bhardwaj, & Sharma, 2015). The table-driven protocols maintain the routing table of the whole network, whereas the on-demand protocols only try to keep routes on the need-to-know bases. MANET can enhance the efficient operation by incorporating the routing functionality into mobile hosts (Cheng, 2012). Multicast in MANETs is a fundamental routing service for supporting many practical applications with one-to-many communication pattern (Qian, Tian, Chen, Huang, & Wang, 2014), such as data distribution mechanisms (Qadri & Liotta, 2011). Multicast routing provides a bandwidth-efficient method for supporting the group-oriented applications (Moamen, Hamza, & Saroit, 2014).

Security Concern of Mobile Ad-Hoc Network

Many existing works on MANET security have focused on both routing and mobility (Srinivasan & Alampalayam, 2011). Routing in MANET is multi-hop because of the limited communication range of wireless radios (Khader, 2007). The characteristics of MANET pose both challenges and opportunities in achieving security goals, such as confidentiality, authentication, integrity, availability, and access control (Wu, Wu, & Cardei, 2008). Security in the MANET is the critical job and requires the consideration of different security issues on all the layers of communication (Kumar & Dutta, 2016).

The wireless channel is accessible to both legitimate network users and malicious attackers (Singh, 2012). MANET is vulnerable to the denial of service (DoS) attacks that can adversely affect the performance of MANET (Kaur, Gaur, Suresh, & Laxmi, 2011). Byzantine attack, blackhole attack, wormhole attack, and spoofing attack are the examples of threats for MANET (Ferrag, Nafa, & Ghanemi, 2014). The security attacks aims to paralyze the member of the network (a node) or the entire network, by flooding the excessive volume of traffic to consume the key resources of the member of the network or the entire network (Sari, 2015). Flooding-based attacks impose severe effects because they are intended to consume the MANET resources, such as bandwidth, node memory, and battery power (Abdelhaq, Hassan, & Ismail, 2014).

Trust establishment is essential for any security framework of MANET (Dahshan & Irvine, 2010). In MANET, deploying a small number of mobile relays can improve the throughput, delay, and security performance (Wang & Lu, 2014). Designing the foolproof security protocol for MANET is the challenging task due to its unique characteristics, such as lack of central authority, frequent topology changes, rapid node mobility, shared radio channel, and limited availability of resources (Ali & Jawandhiya, 2012).

The intrusion detection system combined with intrusion response mechanisms is a promising approach, which mitigates the effects of security attacks (König, Hollick, Krop, & Steinmetz, 2009). The online monitoring mechanisms can collect the important MANET data that can be utilized to detect the abnormal behaviors caused by attacks (Alampalayam & Natsheh, 2008). Various types of attacks on the signaling protocol are possible, such as signaling message fabrication, interception of QoS requests, and modification of QoS parameters (Sornil, 2010).

Advanced Issues of Mobile Ad-Hoc Network in the Digital Age

Due to the new technology development, MANET becomes essential in modern operations (Harous, Aldubai, & Nasir, 2008). The transmission control protocol (TCP) is the reliable protocol of the transport layer which delivers data over the unreliable networks (Bisoy & Pattnaik, 2016). Network–wide broadcasting is broadly utilized in MANET for route discovery and for data dissemination throughout the network (Alwidian, Ababneh, & Yassein, 2013). Clustering reduces both network overhead (Majumder, De, Kar, & Singh, 2016) and the size of the routing tables in MANET (Cheng, Cao, Wang, Das, & Yang, 2009).

At the application level, user mobility prediction in combination with user's profile can provide the user with the enhanced location-based wireless services, such as route guidance, local traffic information, and online advertising (Gavalas, Konstantopoulos, Mamalis, & Pantziou, 2011). Future advances in the pervasive computing rely on the advancements in mobile communication, which includes both infrastructure-based wireless networks and non-infrastructure-based MANETs (Qadri & Fleury, 2012).

Since the topology of the network is constantly changing (Dhar, 2007), the issue of routing packets and energy conservation become the challenging tasks (Ghada, Li, & Ji, 2012). Energy consumption accounts for the energy consumed in transmitting, forwarding, and receiving the application layer data and routing-related control data (Adarbah, Ahmad, & Duffy, 2015). MANET routing protocols have two types: proactive and reactive perspectives (Meghanathan & Sugumar, 2010). The proactive routing protocols predetermine the routes for every possible source-destination pair irrespective of the requirement. The reactive routing protocols determine the route from a source to destination when required (Meghanathan & Sugumar, 2010).

Concerning the limited radio transmission range, sporadic node densities, and power limitations, MANET can become intermittently connected, and data routing process can be disrupted in the absence of an end-to-end routing path (Ma & Jamalipour, 2009). The transmission range of the nodes is limited to conserve energy and to avoid collisions that may result from the long-distance transmissions (Meghanathan, 2012). However, attenuation and interference caused by node mobility and wireless channels sharing significantly weaken the stability of communication links, especially in the ubiquitous MANET (Danyang, Lin, Xuejun, & Yubin, 2011).

FUTURE RESEARCH DIRECTIONS

The classification of the extensive literature in the domains of RFID and MANET will provide the potential opportunities for future research. RFID is a form of wireless communication that utilizes radio waves to identify and track the objects. Robots perform various operations with superior performance, ensure uniformity of production due to which rejections are minimized, and reduce losses. Cloud computing includes network access to storage, processing power, development platforms, and software (Kasemsap, 2015c). Business intelligence involves creating any type of data visualization that provides the insight into a business for the purpose of making a decision or taking an action (Kasemsap, 2016c). The use of social media has created the highly effective communication platforms where any user, virtually anywhere in the world, can freely create the content and disseminate this information in real time to a global audience (Kasemsap, 2017a). Web mining is used to create the personalized search engines which can recognize the individuals' search queries by analyzing and profiling the web user's search behavior (Kasemsap, 2017b). An examination of linkages among RFID, MANET, robots, cloud computing, business intelligence, social media, and web mining in modern operations would seem to be viable for future research efforts.

CONCLUSION

This chapter highlighted the components of RFID; the aspects of RFID; the barriers to RFID utilization; the privacy and security issues of RFID; the RFID applications in supply chain management; the RFID applications in the health care industry; the RFID applications in modern business; the NFC in mobile devices; the overview of MANET; the security concern of MANET; and the advanced issues of MANET in the digital age. RFID and MANET become the growing components of ICT applications and can be effectively in global operations. One of the major advantages of RFID is that information exchange between tags and readers is rapid, automatic and does not require direct contact or line of sight. The range and performance of an RFID system depends on a number of factors. These include operating frequency, power output of the reader, size of the tag's antenna, material composition of the item carrying the tag, and whether the tag is active or passive. RFID increases the speed and accuracy with which items can be tracked and managed, making supply chain management the most obvious application for increasing business value.

Regarding supply chain management, RFID ensures that the right products are available in the right place with no discrepancies and zero errors. RFID makes the supply chain considerably more precise and improves the efficiency and reliability of the entire chain. As real-time information is effectively made through RFID systems, administration and planning processes of supply chain can be significantly improved. RFID is being used to manage products through production, distribution, and retail. Manufacturers can especially benefit from implementing RFID applications in supply chains because they can decrease costs associated with product tracking and inventory management and increase the accuracy and timeliness of inventory data.

Concerning health care operations, RFID monitors the operating instruments and medical equipment during procedures to ensure all materials are accounted for. RFID increases accuracy, safety, and efficiency to prescription processing by utilizing barcode labels. In access control, RFID monitors the access to the restricted parts of medical office regarding privacy and security concerns. RFID accelerates the picking time and accuracy with RFID labels, which enable medical staff to locate materials and accomplish transfer operations faster. In addition, RFID wrist-banding allows for the better patient safety at the point of care toward reducing medical errors.

In business perspectives, RFID technology has the capability to both greatly enhance and protect the lives of consumers, and also revolutionize the way companies do business. As the most flexible auto-identification technology, RFID can be used to automatically track the physical world. RFID improves the shopping experience for consumers, with fewer out-of-stock items and easier returns. RFID decreases business revenue lost to theft or inaccurate accounting of products in modern business. However, privacy and security perspectives must be continuously investigated regarding RFID utilization.

MANET is the wireless communication network utilized in the commercial, military, and private sectors as the portable wireless computers. MANET allows users to access and exchange the information regardless of their geographic position or proximity to infrastructure. In contrast to the infrastructure networks, all nodes in MANET are mobile and their connections are dynamic. Unlike other mobile networks, MANET does not require a fixed infrastructure. This offers an advantageous decentralized character to the network. Decentralization makes the MANET more flexible and more robust in the digital age. RFID and MANET have the potential to increase the efficiency of operations in various industries, improve asset visibility and traceability, decrease reliance on manual processes, reduce operation costs, and provide useful data for business analytics.

REFERENCES

Abdelhaq, M., Hassan, R., & Ismail, M. (2014). Performance evaluation of mobile ad hoc networks under flooding-based attacks. *International Journal of Communication Systems*, 27(12), 4328–4345. doi:10.1002/dac.2615

Abu-Shanab, E., & Yamin, E. (2014). RFID utilization in public university libraries in Jordan. *International Journal of Digital Library Systems*, 4(2), 29–43. doi:10.4018/IJDLS.2014070103

Adarbah, H. Y., Ahmad, S., & Duffy, A. (2015). Impact of noise and interference on probabilistic broadcast schemes in mobile ad-hoc networks. *Computer Networks*, *88*, 178–186. doi:10.1016/j.comnet.2015.06.013

Ahamad, S. S., Sastry, V., & Udgata, S. K. (2014). A secure and optimized proximity mobile payment framework with formal verification. *International Journal of E-Services and Mobile Applications*, *6*(1), 66–92. doi:10.4018/ijesma.2014010104

Ahmed, N. (2012). Widespread adoption of RFID technology. In M. Khan & A. Ansari (Eds.), *Handbook of research on industrial informatics and manufacturing intelligence: Innovations and solutions* (pp. 297–314). Hershey, PA: IGI Global. doi:10.4018/978-1-4666-0294-6.ch013

Ajana, M. E., Harroud, H., Boulmalf, M., & Elkoutbi, M. (2011). FlexRFID middleware in the supply chain: Strategic values and challenges. *International Journal of Mobile Computing and Multimedia Communications*, *3*(2), 19–32. doi:10.4018/jmcmc.2011040102

Akgün, M., Bayrak, A. O., & Çağlayan, M. (2015). Attacks and improvements to chaotic map-based RFID authentication protocol. *Security and Communication Networks*, *8*(18), 4028–4040. doi:10.1002/sec.1319

Alagheband, M. R., & Aref, M. R. (2013). Unified privacy analysis of new-found RFID authentication protocols. *Security and Communication Networks*, *6*(8), 999–1009. doi:10.1002/sec.650

Alampalayam, S. K., & Natsheh, E. F. (2008). Multivariate fuzzy analysis for mobile ad hoc network threat detection. *International Journal of Business Data Communications and Networking*, *4*(3), 1–30. doi:10.4018/jbdcn.2008070101

Ali, M., & Jawandhiya, P. (2012). Security aware routing protocols for mobile ad hoc networks. In K. Lakhtaria (Ed.), *Technological advancements and applications in mobile ad-hoc networks: Research trends* (pp. 264–289). Hershey, PA: IGI Global. doi:10.4018/978-1-4666-0321-9.ch016

Alwidian, S. A., Ababneh, I. M., & Yassein, M. O. (2013). Neighborhood-based route discovery protocols for mobile ad hoc networks. *International Journal of Mobile Computing and Multimedia Communications*, *5*(3), 68–87. doi:10.4018/jmcmc.2013070105

Amini, M., Otondo, R. F., Janz, B. D., & Pitts, M. G. (2007). Simulation modeling and analysis: A collateral application and exposition of RFID technology. *Production and Operations Management*, *16*(5), 586–598. doi:10.1111/j.1937-5956.2007.tb00282.x

Andriole, S. J. (2009). Enterprise investing in radio frequency identification (RFID): The Oracle case. In S. Andriole (Ed.), *Technology due diligence: Best practices for chief information officers, venture capitalists, and technology vendors* (pp. 191–209). Hershey, PA: IGI Global. doi:10.4018/978-1-60566-018-9.ch007

Ayu, M. A., Ahmad, B. I., & Mantoro, T. (2016). Managing students' attendance using NFC-enabled mobile phones. In N. Mohamed, T. Mantoro, M. Ayu, & M. Mahmud (Eds.), *Critical socio-technical issues surrounding mobile computing* (pp. 184–203). Hershey, PA: IGI Global. doi:10.4018/978-1-4666-9438-5.ch009

Azad, A. K., Kamruzzaman, J., & Karmakar, N. C. (2012). Wireless sensor network protocols applicable to RFID system. In N. Chandra Karmakar (Ed.), *Chipless and conventional radio frequency identification: Systems for ubiquitous tagging* (pp. 251–284). Hershey, PA: IGI Global. doi:10.4018/978-1-4666-1616-5.ch013

Bahr, W., & Price, B. (2016). Radio frequency identification and its application in e-commerce. In I. Lee (Ed.), *Encyclopedia of e-commerce development, implementation, and management* (pp. 1841–1857). Hershey, PA: IGI Global. doi:10.4018/978-1-4666-9787-4.ch130

Baqar, M. A., Aldabbas, H., Alwadan, T., Alfawair, M., & Janicke, H. (2014). Review of security in VANETs and MANETs. In A. Amine, O. Mohamed, & B. Benatallah (Eds.), *Network security technologies: Design and applications* (pp. 1–27). Hershey, PA: IGI Global. doi:10.4018/978-1-4666-4789-3.ch001

Barratt, M., & Choi, T. (2007). Mandated RFID and institutional responses: Cases of decentralized business units. *Production and Operations Management*, *16*(5), 569–585. doi:10.1111/j.1937-5956.2007.tb00281.x

Bellotti, F., Berta, R., Margarone, M., & de Gloria, A. (2008). oDect: An RFID-based object detection API to support applications development on mobile devices. *Software: Practice and Experience*, *38*(12), 1241–1259. doi:10.1002/spe.864

Bendoly, E., Citurs, A., & Konsynski, B. (2007). Internal infrastructural impacts on RFID perceptions and commitment: Knowledge, operational procedures, and information-processing standards. *Decision Sciences*, *38*(3), 423–449. doi:10.1111/j.1540-5915.2007.00165.x

Benssalah, M., Djeddou, M., & Drouiche, K. (2014). Security enhancement of the authenticated RFID security mechanism based on chaotic maps. *Security and Communication Networks*, *7*(12), 2356–2372. doi:10.1002/sec.946

Bhattacharya, M., & Wamba, S. F. (2015). A conceptual framework of RFID adoption in retail using TOE framework. *International Journal of Technology Diffusion*, *6*(1), 1–32. doi:10.4018/IJTD.2015010101

Bisoy, S. K., & Pattnaik, P. K. (2016). Transmission control protocol for mobile ad hoc network. In P. Mallick (Ed.), *Research advances in the integration of big data and smart computing* (pp. 22–49). Hershey, PA: IGI Global. doi:10.4018/978-1-4666-8737-0.ch002

Bose, I., & Lam, C. W. (2009). Facing the challenges of RFID data management. In J. Symonds, J. Ayoade, & D. Parry (Eds.), *Auto-identification and ubiquitous computing applications* (pp. 230–246). Hershey, PA: IGI Global. doi:10.4018/978-1-60566-298-5.ch014

Brown, M. (2011). Ubiquitous use of RFID in the health industry. In S. Brown & M. Brown (Eds.), *Ethical issues and security monitoring trends in global healthcare: Technological advancements* (pp. 166–178). Hershey, PA: IGI Global. doi:10.4018/978-1-60960-174-4.ch012

Burmester, M., & Munilla, J. (2013). RFID grouping-proofs. In P. Lopez, J. Hernandez-Castro, & T. Li (Eds.), *Security and trends in wireless identification and sensing platform tags: Advancements in RFID* (pp. 89–119). Hershey, PA: IGI Global. doi:10.4018/978-1-4666-1990-6.ch004

Camdereli, A. Z., & Swaminathan, J. M. (2010). Misplaced inventory and radio-frequency identification (RFID) technology: Information and coordination. *Production and Operations Management, 19*(1), 1–18. doi:10.1111/j.1937-5956.2009.01057.x

Carreton, A. L., Pinte, K., & Meuter, W. D. (2013). Software abstractions for mobile RFID-enabled applications. *Software: Practice and Experience, 43*(10), 1219–1239. doi:10.1002/spe.1114

Catarinucci, L., Cappelli, M., Colella, R., & Tarricone, L. (2008). A novel low-cost multisensor-tag for RFID applications in healthcare. *Microwave and Optical Technology Letters, 50*(11), 2877–2880. doi:10.1002/mop.23837

Catarinucci, L., Colella, R., & Tarricone, L. (2012). Design, development, and performance evaluation of a compact and long-range passive UHF RFID tag. *Microwave and Optical Technology Letters, 54*(5), 1335–1339. doi:10.1002/mop.26777

Chand, N. (2007). Data caching in mobile ad-hoc networks. In D. Taniar (Ed.), *Encyclopedia of mobile computing and commerce* (pp. 172–177). Hershey, PA: IGI Global. doi:10.4018/978-1-59904-002-8.ch030

Chen, C. L., & Wu, C. Y. (2014). An RFID system yoking-proof protocol conforming to EPCglobal C1G2 standards. *Security and Communication Networks, 7*(12), 2527–2541. doi:10.1002/sec.383

Chen, E. T. (2015). RFID technology and privacy. In I. Lee (Ed.), RFID technology integration for business performance improvement (pp. 140–155). Hershey, PA: IGI Global. doi:10.4018/978-1-4666-6308-4.ch007

Chen, N. K., Chen, J. L., & Lee, C. C. (2009). Array-based reader anti-collision scheme for highly efficient RFID network applications. *Wireless Communications and Mobile Computing, 9*(7), 976–987. doi:10.1002/wcm.646

Cheng, H. (2012). Dynamic genetic algorithms with hyper-mutation schemes for dynamic shortest path routing problem in mobile ad hoc networks. *International Journal of Adaptive, Resilient and Autonomic Systems, 3*(1), 87–98. doi:10.4018/jaras.2012010105

Cheng, H., Cao, J., Wang, X., Das, S. K., & Yang, S. (2009). Stability-aware multi-metric clustering in mobile ad hoc networks with group mobility. *Wireless Communications and Mobile Computing, 9*(6), 759–771. doi:10.1002/wcm.627

Cheng, Z. Y., Liu, Y., Chang, C. C., & Chang, S. C. (2013). Authenticated RFID security mechanism based on chaotic maps. *Security and Communication Networks, 6*(2), 247–256. doi:10.1002/sec.709

Cho, K., Pack, S., Kwon, T., & Choi, Y. (2010). An extensible and ubiquitous RFID management framework over next-generation network. *International Journal of Communication Systems, 23*(9/10), 1093–1110. doi:10.1002/dac.1073

Choi, S. H., Cheung, H. H., Yang, B., & Yang, Y. X. (2015). Item-level RFID for retail Business improvement. In I. Lee (Ed.), RFID technology integration for business performance improvement (pp. 1–26). Hershey, PA: IGI Global. doi:10.4018/978-1-4666-6308-4.ch001

Chowdhury, M. U., & Ray, B. R. (2014). Security risks/vulnerability in a RFID system and possible defenses. In *Crisis management: Concepts, methodologies, tools, and applications* (pp. 1667–1681). Hershey, PA: IGI Global. doi:10.4018/978-1-4666-4707-7.ch084

Cornetta, G., Touhafi, A., Santos, D. J., & Vázquez, J. M. (2011). Power issues and energy scavenging in mobile wireless ad-hoc and sensor networks. In M. Cruz-Cunha & F. Moreira (Eds.), *Handbook of research on mobility and computing: Evolving technologies and ubiquitous impacts* (pp. 994–1020). Hershey, PA: IGI Global. doi:10.4018/978-1-60960-042-6.ch061

Cui, B., Wang, Z., Zhao, B., & Chen, X. (2016). Design and analysis of secure mechanisms based on tripartite credibility for RFID systems. *Computer Standards & Interfaces*, *44*, 110–116. doi:10.1016/j.csi.2015.06.003

Curran, K., & Norrby, S. (2011). RFID-enabled location determination within indoor environments. In K. Curran (Ed.), *Ubiquitous developments in ambient computing and intelligence: Human-centered applications* (pp. 301–324). Hershey, PA: IGI Global. doi:10.4018/978-1-60960-549-0.ch026

D'Andrea, A., Ferri, F., & Grifoni, P. (2013). RFID technologies in the health sector. In A. Moumtzoglou & A. Kastania (Eds.), *E-health technologies and improving patient safety: Exploring organizational factors* (pp. 140–147). Hershey, PA: IGI Global. doi:10.4018/978-1-4666-2657-7.ch009

Dahshan, H., & Irvine, J. (2010). A robust self-organized public key management for mobile ad hoc networks. *Security and Communication Networks*, *3*(1), 16–30. doi:10.1002/sec.131

Danyang, Q., Lin, M., Xuejun, S., & Yubin, X. (2011). Realization of route reconstructing scheme for mobile ad hoc network. In I. Khalil & E. Weippl (Eds.), *Innovations in mobile multimedia communications and applications: New technologies* (pp. 62–79). Hershey, PA: IGI Global. doi:10.4018/978-1-60960-563-6.ch005

Das, A., & Chaudhuri, A. (2017). Derivation and simulation of an efficient QoS scheme in MANET through optimised messaging based on ABCO using QualNet. In *Nature-inspired computing: Concepts, methodologies, tools, and applications* (pp. 396–425). Hershey, PA: IGI Global. doi:10.4018/978-1-5225-0788-8.ch016

Dhar, S. (2007). Applications and future trends in mobile ad hoc networks. In J. Gutierrez (Ed.), *Business data communications and networking: A research perspective* (pp. 272–300). Hershey, PA: Idea Group Publishing. doi:10.4018/978-1-59904-274-9.ch011

Dhar, S. (2009). Mobile ad hoc network. In D. Taniar (Ed.), *Mobile computing: Concepts, methodologies, tools, and applications* (pp. 952–960). Hershey, PA: IGI Global. doi:10.4018/978-1-60566-054-7.ch077

Dimitriou, T. (2016). Key evolving RFID systems: Forward/backward privacy and ownership transfer of RFID tags. *Ad Hoc Networks*, *37*, 195–208. doi:10.1016/j.adhoc.2015.08.019

Djenouri, D., & Badache, N. (2008). Struggling against selfishness and black hole attacks in MANETs. *Wireless Communications and Mobile Computing*, *8*(6), 689–704. doi:10.1002/wcm.493

Dominikus, S., & Kraxberger, S. (2014). Secure communication with RFID tags in the Internet of Things. *Security and Communication Networks*, *7*(12), 2639–2653. doi:10.1002/sec.398

Dong, Q., Ding, W., & Wei, L. (2015). Improvement and optimized implementation of cryptoGPS protocol for low-cost radio-frequency identification authentication. *Security and Communication Networks*, *8*(8), 1474–1484. doi:10.1002/sec.1096

Dutta, A., Lee, H. L., & Whang, S. (2007). RFID and operations management: Technology, value, and incentives. *Production and Operations Management*, *16*(5), 646–655. doi:10.1111/j.1937-5956.2007.tb00286.x

El Khaddar, M. A., Harroud, H., Boulmalf, M., & El Koutbi, M. (2013). FlexRFID middleware in the supply chain: Strategic values and challenges. In I. Khalil & E. Weippl (Eds.), *Contemporary challenges and solutions for mobile and multimedia technologies* (pp. 163–177). Hershey, PA: IGI Global. doi:10.4018/978-1-4666-2163-3.ch010

Engel, T., Goswami, S., Englschalk, A., & Krcmar, H. (2015). CostRFID: Design and evaluation of a cost estimation method and tool for RFID integration projects. In I. Lee (Ed.), *RFID technology integration for business performance improvement* (pp. 27–51). Hershey, PA: IGI Global. doi:10.4018/978-1-4666-6308-4.ch002

Ferrag, M. A., Nafa, M., & Ghanemi, S. (2014). Security and privacy in mobile ad hoc social networks. In D. Rawat, B. Bista, & G. Yan (Eds.), *Security, privacy, trust, and resource management in mobile and wireless communications* (pp. 222–243). Hershey, PA: IGI Global. doi:10.4018/978-1-4666-4691-9.ch010

Fleury, M., Qadri, N. N., Altaf, M., & Ghanbari, M. (2011). Robust video streaming over MANET and VANET. In C. Zhu, Y. Li, & X. Niu (Eds.), *Streaming media architectures, techniques, and applications: Recent advances* (pp. 170–200). Hershey, PA: IGI Global. doi:10.4018/978-1-61692-831-5.ch008

Fung, L. C., Chan, K. H., Lam, W. K., Leung, S. W., Wong, Y. F., Wu, P. W. K., & Tang, C. K. (2007). Electromagnetic assessment on human safety of RFID system at Hong Kong International Airport. *Microwave and Optical Technology Letters*, *49*(4), 924–928. doi:10.1002/mop.22311

Gallo, C., Perilli, M., & de Bonis, M. (2011). Mobile ad hoc networks: Protocol design and implementation. In M. Cruz-Cunha & F. Moreira (Eds.), *Handbook of research on mobility and computing: Evolving technologies and ubiquitous impacts* (pp. 31–47). Hershey, PA: IGI Global. doi:10.4018/978-1-60960-042-6.ch003

Gandino, F., Sanchez, E. R., Montrucchio, B., & Rebaudengo, M. (2009). RFID technology for agri-food tracability management. In J. Symonds, J. Ayoade, & D. Parry (Eds.), *Auto-identification and ubiquitous computing applications* (pp. 54–72). Hershey, PA: IGI Global. doi:10.4018/978-1-60566-298-5.ch004

Gavalas, D., Konstantopoulos, C., Mamalis, B., & Pantziou, G. (2011). Mobility prediction in mobile ad-hoc networks. In S. Pierre (Ed.), *Next generation mobile networks and ubiquitous computing* (pp. 226–240). Hershey, PA: IGI Global. doi:10.4018/978-1-60566-250-3.ch021

Ghada, K., Li, J., & Ji, Y. (2012). Cross-layer design for topology control and routing in MANETs. *Wireless Communications and Mobile Computing*, *12*(3), 257–267. doi:10.1002/wcm.957

Gupta, S., Garg, M., Xu, H., & Goh, M. (2009). RFID and supply chain visibility. In B. Unhelkar (Ed.), Handbook of research in mobile business, second edition: Technical, methodological and social perspectives (pp. 368–374). Hershey, PA: IGI Global. doi:10.4018/978-1-60566-156-8.ch034

Hanada, E. (2013). Effective use of RFID in medicine and general healthcare. In T. Issa, P. Isaías, & P. Kommers (Eds.), *Information systems and technology for organizations in a networked society* (pp. 335–352). Hershey, PA: IGI Global. doi:10.4018/978-1-4666-4062-7.ch018

Hanzo, L. II, & Tafazolli, R. (2011). The effects of shadow-fading on QoS-aware routing and admission control protocols designed for multi-hop MANETs. *Wireless Communications and Mobile Computing*, *11*(1), 1–22. doi:10.1002/wcm.912

Hardgrave, B. C., Aloysius, J. A., & Goyal, S. (2013). RFID-enabled visibility and retail inventory record inaccuracy: Experiments in the field. *Production and Operations Management*, *22*(4), 843–856. doi:10.1111/poms.12010

Harous, S., Aldubai, M., & Nasir, Q. (2008). An energy aware multi-path routing algorithm for mobile ad hoc networks. *International Journal of Business Data Communications and Networking*, *4*(2), 58–75. doi:10.4018/jbdcn.2008040104

Hawrylak, P. J., & Hart, C. (2014). Using radio frequency identification technology to store patients' medical information. In V. Michell, D. Rosenorn-Lanng, S. Gulliver, & W. Currie (Eds.), *Handbook of research on patient safety and quality care through health informatics* (pp. 159–178). Hershey, PA: IGI Global. doi:10.4018/978-1-4666-4546-2.ch009

Hawrylak, P. J., Schimke, N., Hale, J., & Papa, M. (2012). RFID in e-health: Technology, implementation, and security issues. In J. Rodrigues, I. de la Torre Díez, & B. Sainz de Abajo (Eds.), *Telemedicine and e-health services, policies, and applications: Advancements and developments* (pp. 347–368). Hershey, PA: IGI Global. doi:10.4018/978-1-4666-0888-7.ch013

Heese, H. S. (2007). Inventory record inaccuracy, double marginalization, and RFID adoption. *Production and Operations Management*, *16*(5), 542–553. doi:10.1111/j.1937-5956.2007.tb00279.x

Heim, G. R., Wentworth, W. R. Jr, & Peng, X. (2009). The value to the customer of RFID in service applications. *Decision Sciences*, *40*(3), 477–512. doi:10.1111/j.1540-5915.2009.00237.x

Hossain, M. A., & Quaddus, M. (2014). Mandatory and voluntary adoption of RFID. In J. Wang (Ed.), *Encyclopedia of business analytics and optimization* (pp. 1457–1475). Hershey, PA: IGI Global. doi:10.4018/978-1-4666-5202-6.ch132

Hozak, K., & Collier, D. A. (2008). RFID as an enabler of improved manufacturing performance. *Decision Sciences*, *39*(4), 859–881. doi:10.1111/j.1540-5915.2008.00214.x

Hsin, W., & Harn, L. (2013). Offline/online security in mobile ad hoc networks. In A. Elçi, J. Pieprzyk, A. Chefranov, M. Orgun, H. Wang, & R. Shankaran (Eds.), *Theory and practice of cryptography solutions for secure information systems* (pp. 199–222). Hershey, PA: IGI Global. doi:10.4018/978-1-4666-4030-6.ch009

Isomursu, M., & Ervasti, M. (2009). Touch-based access to mobile Internet: User experience findings. *International Journal of Mobile Human Computer Interaction*, *1*(4), 58–79. doi:10.4018/jmhci.2009062605

Jeong, B., Cheng, C., & Prabhu, V. (2011). Performance modeling and analysis of surgery patient identification using RFID. In J. Wang (Ed.), *Information systems and new applications in the service sector: Models and methods* (pp. 279–292). Hershey, PA: IGI Global. doi:10.4018/978-1-60960-138-6.ch016

Jia, X., & Feng, Q. Y. (2015). An improved anti-collision protocol for radio frequency identification tag. *International Journal of Communication Systems, 28*(3), 401–413. doi:10.1002/dac.2629

Juntunen, A., Tuunainen, V. K., & Luukkainen, S. (2012). Critical business model issues in deploying NFC technology for mobile services: Case mobile ticketing. *International Journal of E-Services and Mobile Applications, 4*(3), 23–41. doi:10.4018/jesma.2012070102

Kadri, B., Feham, M., & M'hamed, A. (2009). Securing reactive routing protocols in MANETs using PKI (PKI-DSR). *Security and Communication Networks, 2*(4), 341–350. doi:10.1002/sec.63

Kamoun, F. (2013). Mobile NFC services: Adoption factors and a typology of business models. In I. Lee (Ed.), *Mobile services industries, technologies, and applications in the global economy* (pp. 254–272). Hershey, PA: IGI Global. doi:10.4018/978-1-4666-1981-4.ch016

Kamoun, F., & Miniaoui, S. (2015). Towards a better understanding of organizational adoption and diffusion of RFID technology: A case study approach. *International Journal of Technology Diffusion, 6*(3), 1–20. doi:10.4018/IJTD.2015070101

Kamruzzaman, J., Azad, A. K., Karmakar, N. C., Karmakar, G., & Srinivasan, B. (2013). Security and privacy in RFID systems. In N. Karmakar (Ed.), *Advanced RFID systems, security, and applications* (pp. 16–40). Hershey, PA: IGI Global. doi:10.4018/978-1-4666-2080-3.ch002

Karmakar, N. C. (2009). Smart antennas for automatic radio frequency identification readers. In C. Sun, J. Cheng, & T. Ohira (Eds.), *Handbook on advancements in smart antenna technologies for wireless networks* (pp. 449–473). Hershey, PA: IGI Global. doi:10.4018/978-1-59904-988-5.ch021

Karmakar, N. C. (2012). Introduction to chipless and conventional radio frequency identification system. In N. Karmakar (Ed.), *Chipless and conventional radio frequency identification: Systems for ubiquitous tagging* (pp. 1–8). Hershey, PA: IGI Global. doi:10.4018/978-1-4666-1616-5.ch001

Karnouskos, S. (2007). NFC-capable mobile devices for mobile payment services. In D. Taniar (Ed.), *Encyclopedia of mobile computing and commerce* (pp. 706–710). Hershey, PA: IGI Global. doi:10.4018/978-1-59904-002-8.ch118

Kasemsap, K. (2015a). The role of radio frequency identification in modern libraries. In S. Thanuskodi (Ed.), *Handbook of research on inventive digital tools for collection management and development in modern libraries* (pp. 361–385). Hershey, PA: IGI Global. doi:10.4018/978-1-4666-8178-1.ch021

Kasemsap, K. (2015b). The role of customer relationship management in the global business environments. In T. Tsiakis (Ed.), *Trends and innovations in marketing information systems* (pp. 130–156). Hershey, PA: IGI Global. doi:10.4018/978-1-4666-8459-1.ch007

Kasemsap, K. (2015c). The role of cloud computing adoption in global business. In V. Chang, R. Walters, & G. Wills (Eds.), *Delivery and adoption of cloud computing services in contemporary organizations* (pp. 26–55). Hershey, PA: IGI Global. doi:10.4018/978-1-4666-8210-8.ch002

Kasemsap, K. (2016a). Encouraging supply chain networks and customer loyalty in global supply chain. In N. Kamath & S. Saurav (Eds.), *Handbook of research on strategic supply chain management in the retail industry* (pp. 87–112). Hershey, PA: IGI Global. doi:10.4018/978-1-4666-9894-9.ch006

Kasemsap, K. (2016b). Investigating the roles of mobile commerce and mobile payment in global business. In S. Madan & J. Arora (Eds.), *Securing transactions and payment systems for m-commerce* (pp. 1–23). Hershey, PA: IGI Global. doi:10.4018/978-1-5225-0236-4.ch001

Kasemsap, K. (2016c). The fundamentals of business intelligence. *International Journal of Organizational and Collective Intelligence*, 6(2), 12–25. doi:10.4018/IJOCI.2016040102

Kasemsap, K. (2017a). Professional and business applications of social media platforms. In V. Benson, R. Tuninga, & G. Saridakis (Eds.), *Analyzing the strategic role of social networking in firm growth and productivity* (pp. 427–450). Hershey, PA: IGI Global. doi:10.4018/978-1-5225-0559-4.ch021

Kasemsap, K. (2017b). Mastering web mining and information retrieval in the digital age. In A. Kumar (Ed.), *Web usage mining techniques and applications across industries* (pp. 1–28). Hershey, PA: IGI Global. doi:10.4018/978-1-5225-0613-3.ch001

Kaspar, C. (2009). RFID technologies and applications. In M. Pagani (Ed.), *Encyclopedia of multimedia technology and networking* (2nd ed., pp. 1232–1239). Hershey, PA: IGI Global. doi:10.4018/978-1-60566-014-1.ch167

Kathirvel, A., & Srinivasan, R. (2011). ETUS: An enhanced triple umpiring system for security and performance improvement of mobile ad hoc networks. *International Journal of Network Management*, 21(5), 341–359. doi:10.1002/nem.761

Kaur, R., Gaur, M., Suresh, L., & Laxmi, V. (2011). DoS attacks in MANETs: Detection and countermeasures. In R. Santanam, M. Sethumadhavan, & M. Virendra (Eds.), *Cyber security, cyber crime and cyber forensics: Applications and perspectives* (pp. 124–145). Hershey, PA: IGI Global. doi:10.4018/978-1-60960-123-2.ch010

Khader, O. H. (2007). FSR evaluation using the suboptimal operational values. *International Journal of Information Technology and Web Engineering*, 2(1), 47–56. doi:10.4018/jitwe.2007010104

Khan, M. S. S., Kumar, A., Xie, B., & Sahoo, P. K. (2015). Network tomography application in mobile ad-hoc network using stitching algorithm. *Journal of Network and Computer Applications*, 56, 77–87. doi:10.1016/j.jnca.2015.07.003

Kim, S. C., Cho, J. S., & Kim, S. K. (2013). Performance improvement of hybrid tag anti-collision protocol for radio frequency identification systems. *International Journal of Communication Systems*, 26(6), 705–719. doi:10.1002/dac.2389

König, A., Hollick, M., Krop, T., & Steinmetz, R. (2009). GeoSec: Quarantine zones for mobile ad hoc networks. *Security and Communication Networks*, 2(3), 271–288. doi:10.1002/sec.68

Kumar, P., Reinitz, H. W., Simunovic, J., Sandeep, K. P., & Franzon, P. D. (2009). Overview of RFID technology and its applications in the food industry. *Journal of Food Science*, 74(8), R101–R106. doi:10.1111/j.1750-3841.2009.01323.x PMID:19799677

Kumar, S., & Dutta, K. (2016). Security issues in mobile ad hoc networks: A survey. In *Mobile computing and wireless networks: Concepts, methodologies, tools, and applications* (pp. 1940–1985). Hershey, PA: IGI Global. doi:10.4018/978-1-4666-8751-6.ch086

Lee, C., & Shim, J. P. (2009). Ubiquitous healthcare: Radio frequency identification (RFID) in hospitals. In A. Lazakidou & K. Siassiakos (Eds.), *Handbook of research on distributed medical informatics and e-health* (pp. 273–281). Hershey, PA: IGI Global. doi:10.4018/978-1-60566-002-8.ch019

Lee, I. (2013). Justifying RFID investment to enable mobile service applications in manufacturing and supply chain. In I. Lee (Ed.), *Strategy, adoption, and competitive advantage of mobile services in the global economy* (pp. 325–348). Hershey, PA: IGI Global. doi:10.4018/978-1-4666-1939-5.ch018

Lee, I. (2015). *RFID technology integration for business performance improvement* (pp. 1–317). Hershey, PA: IGI Global. doi:10.4018/978-1-4666-6308-4

Leema, A. A., & Hemalatha, M. (2015). Data management issues in RFID applications. In I. Lee (Ed.), RFID technology integration for business performance improvement (pp. 179–198). Hershey, PA: IGI Global. doi:10.4018/978-1-4666-6308-4.ch009

Li, C., Wang, G., & Zheng, J. (2014). An aggregated signature-based fast RFID batch detection protocol. *Security and Communication Networks, 7*(9), 1364–1371. doi:10.1002/sec.838

Li, J. S., & Liu, K. H. (2011). A hidden mutual authentication protocol for low-cost RFID tags. *International Journal of Communication Systems, 24*(9), 1196–1211. doi:10.1002/dac.1222

Li, L., Cai, Y., & Xu, X. (2009). Domain-based autoconfiguration framework for large-scale MANETs. *Wireless Communications and Mobile Computing, 9*(7), 938–947. doi:10.1002/wcm.642

Li, N., Mu, Y., Susilo, W., Guo, F., & Varadharajan, V. (2015). Vulnerabilities of an ECC-based RFID authentication scheme. *Security and Communication Networks, 8*(17), 3262–3270. doi:10.1002/sec.1250

Li, T., Deng, R. H., & Wang, G. (2008). The security and improvement of an ultra-lightweight RFID authentication protocol. *Security and Communication Networks, 1*(2), 135–146. doi:10.1002/sec.8

Lim, M. K. (2013). Exploring value-added applications of chipless RFID systems to enhance wider adoption. In N. Karmakar (Ed.), *Advanced RFID systems, security, and applications* (pp. 221–240). Hershey, PA: IGI Global. doi:10.4018/978-1-4666-2080-3.ch010

Littman, M. K. (2008). Implementing RFID technology in hospital environments. In N. Wickramasinghe & E. Geisler (Eds.), *Encyclopedia of healthcare information systems* (pp. 705–710). Hershey, PA: IGI Global. doi:10.4018/978-1-59904-889-5.ch089

Liu, A. X., Bailey, L. A., & Krishnamurthy, A. H. (2010). RFIDGuard: A lightweight privacy and authentication protocol for passive RFID tags. *Security and Communication Networks, 3*(5), 384–393. doi:10.1002/sec.138

Liu, Y., Lin, T., Ram, S., & Su, X. (2010). A non-invasive software architecture style for RFID data provisioning. *International Journal of Applied Logistics, 1*(1), 1–15. doi:10.4018/jal.2010090201

Lockman, M. T., & Selamat, A. (2011). Multi-agent based formal verification of data in RFID middleware. In T. Matsuo & T. Fujimoto (Eds.), *E-activity and intelligent web construction: Effects of social design* (pp. 63–74). Hershey, PA: IGI Global. doi:10.4018/978-1-61520-871-5.ch006

Loebecke, C. (2008). RFID in the retail supply chain. In A. Becker (Ed.), *Electronic commerce: Concepts, methodologies, tools, and applications* (pp. 659–666). Hershey, PA: IGI Global. doi:10.4018/978-1-59904-943-4.ch054

Ma, D., & Saxena, N. (2013). Towards sensing-enabled RFID security and privacy. In P. Lopez, J. Hernandez-Castro, & T. Li (Eds.), *Security and trends in wireless identification and sensing platform tags: Advancements in RFID* (pp. 65–88). Hershey, PA: IGI Global. doi:10.4018/978-1-4666-1990-6.ch003

Ma, D., & Saxena, N. (2014). A context-aware approach to defend against unauthorized reading and relay attacks in RFID systems. *Security and Communication Networks, 7*(12), 2684–2695. doi:10.1002/sec.404

Ma, Y., & Jamalipour, A. (2009). Optimized message delivery framework using fuzzy logic for intermittently connected mobile ad hoc networks. *Wireless Communications and Mobile Computing, 9*(4), 501–512. doi:10.1002/wcm.693

Majumder, K., De, D., Kar, S., & Singh, R. (2016). Genetic-algorithm-based optimization of clustering in mobile ad hoc network. In J. Mandal, S. Mukhopadhyay, & T. Pal (Eds.), *Handbook of research on natural computing for optimization problems* (pp. 128–158). Hershey, PA: IGI Global. doi:10.4018/978-1-5225-0058-2.ch006

Malek, B., & Miri, A. (2014). Identification and authentication for RFID systems. In *Crisis management: Concepts, methodologies, tools, and applications* (pp. 1682–1704). Hershey, PA: IGI Global. doi:10.4018/978-1-4666-4707-7.ch085

Manzoor, A. (2016). RFID applications in healthcare-state-of-the-art and future trends. In T. Iyamu & A. Tatnall (Eds.), *Maximizing healthcare delivery and management through technology integration* (pp. 184–206). Hershey, PA: IGI Global. doi:10.4018/978-1-4666-9446-0.ch012

Meghanathan, N. (2012). Node stability index: A stability metric and an algorithm to determine long-living connected dominating sets for mobile ad hoc networks. *International Journal of Interdisciplinary Telecommunications and Networking, 4*(1), 31–46. doi:10.4018/jitn.2012010102

Meghanathan, N., & Sugumar, M. (2010). A beaconless minimum interference based routing protocol to minimize end-to-end delay per packet for mobile ad hoc networks. *International Journal of Interdisciplinary Telecommunications and Networking, 2*(1), 12–26. doi:10.4018/jitn.2010010102

Michael, K., & Michael, M. (2009). RFID tags and transponders: The new kid on the block. In K. Michael & M. Michael (Eds.), *Innovative automatic identification and location-based services: From bar codes to chip implants* (pp. 234–272). Hershey, PA: IGI Global. doi:10.4018/978-1-59904-795-9.ch009

Michaelides, Z., & Forster, R. (2014). The use of RFID technologies for e-enabling logistics supply chains. In *Crisis management: Concepts, methodologies, tools, and applications* (pp. 1145–1164). Hershey, PA: IGI Global. doi:10.4018/978-1-4666-4707-7.ch057

Miorandi, D., Sicari, S., de Pellegrini, F., & Chlamtac, I. (2012). Internet of Things: Vision, applications and research challenges. *Ad Hoc Networks*, *10*(7), 1497–1516. doi:10.1016/j.adhoc.2012.02.016

Moamen, A. A., Hamza, H. S., & Saroit, I. A. (2014). Secure multicast routing protocols in mobile ad-hoc networks. *International Journal of Communication Systems*, *27*(11), 2808–2831. doi:10.1002/dac.2508

Moloney, M. (2014). State of the art for near field communication: Security and privacy within the field. In D. Rawat, B. Bista, & G. Yan (Eds.), *Security, privacy, trust, and resource management in mobile and wireless communications* (pp. 408–431). Hershey, PA: IGI Global. doi:10.4018/978-1-4666-4691-9.ch017

Mukherjee, A., Dey, N., Kausar, N., Ashour, A. S., Taiar, R., & Hassanien, A. E. (2016). A disaster management specific mobility model for flying ad-hoc network. *International Journal of Rough Sets and Data Analysis*, *3*(3), 72–103. doi:10.4018/IJRSDA.2016070106

Natsheh, E. (2009). Fuzzy linguistic knowledge for active queue management in wireless ad-hoc networks. In I. Bose (Ed.), *Breakthrough perspectives in network and data communications security, design and applications* (pp. 243–257). Hershey, PA: IGI Global. doi:10.4018/978-1-60566-148-3.ch016

Nejad, K. K., Jiang, X., & Kameyama, M. (2013). RFID-based localization with non-blocking tag scanning. *Ad Hoc Networks*, *11*(8), 2264–2272. doi:10.1016/j.adhoc.2013.05.007

Ngai, E. W. T., Cheng, T. C. E., Lai, K. H., Chai, P. Y. F., Choi, Y. S., & Sin, R. K. Y. (2007). Development of an RFID-based traceability system: Experiences and lessons learned from an aircraft engineering company. *Production and Operations Management*, *16*(5), 554–568. doi:10.1111/j.1937-5956.2007.tb00280.x

Ning, Z. (2014). Computer system attacks. In *Crisis management: Concepts, methodologies, tools, and applications* (pp. 1–24). Hershey, PA: IGI Global. doi:10.4018/978-1-4666-4707-7.ch001

Noël, G. P. J. C., & Connolly, C. C. (2016). Monitoring the use of anatomical teaching material using a low-cost radio frequency identification system: A comprehensive assessment. *Anatomical Sciences Education*, *9*(2), 197–202. doi:10.1002/ase.1575 PMID:26441139

Onat, I., & Miri, A. (2013). RFID wireless link threats. In A. Miri (Ed.), *Advanced security and privacy for RFID technologies* (pp. 24–32). Hershey, PA: IGI Global. doi:10.4018/978-1-4666-3685-9.ch003

Ouyang, Y., Hou, Y., Pang, L., Wang, D., & Xiong, Z. (2008). *An intelligent RFID reader and its application in airport baggage handling system*. Paper presented at the 2008 4th IEEE International Conference on Wireless Communications, Networking and Mobile Computing (WiCOM 2008), Dalian, China. doi:10.1109/WiCom.2008.710

Palanisamy, R., & Mukerji, B. (2013). The RFID technology adoption in e-government: Issues and challenges. In V. Weerakkody (Ed.), *E-government services design, adoption, and evaluation* (pp. 93–106). Hershey, PA: IGI Global. doi:10.4018/978-1-4666-2458-0.ch006

Pang, L., Morgan-Morris, V., & Howell, A. (2010). RFID in urban planning. In C. Silva (Ed.), *Handbook of research on e-planning: ICTs for urban development and monitoring* (pp. 388–403). Hershey, PA: IGI Global. doi:10.4018/978-1-61520-929-3.ch020

Parry, D., & Symonds, J. (2009). RFID and assisted living for the elderly. In J. Symonds, J. Ayoade, & D. Parry (Eds.), *Auto-identification and ubiquitous computing applications* (pp. 119–136). Hershey, PA: IGI Global. doi:10.4018/978-1-60566-298-5.ch007

Patel, B. N., & Prajapati, S. (2012). Performance comparison of AODV and DSDV routing protocols of MANET. In K. Lakhtaria (Ed.), *Technological advancements and applications in mobile ad-hoc networks: Research trends* (pp. 144–151). Hershey, PA: IGI Global. doi:10.4018/978-1-4666-0321-9.ch008

Pei, G., & Ravindran, B. (2010). Event-based system architecture in mobile ad hoc networks (MANETs). In A. Hinze & A. Buchmann (Eds.), *Principles and applications of distributed event-based systems* (pp. 346–368). Hershey, PA: IGI Global. doi:10.4018/978-1-60566-697-6.ch015

Permala, A., Rantasila, K., Pilli-Sihvola, E., & Hinkka, V. (2014). RFID: From closed manufacturers' systems to supply chain-wide tracking. In J. Wang (Ed.), *Management science, logistics, and operations research* (pp. 53–64). Hershey, PA: IGI Global. doi:10.4018/978-1-4666-4506-6.ch004

Picazo-Sanchez, P., Ortiz-Martin, L., Peris-Lopez, P., & Bagheri, N. (2015). Weaknesses of fingerprint-based mutual authentication protocol. *Security and Communication Networks*, 8(12), 2124–2134. doi:10.1002/sec.1161

Picazo-Sanchez, P., Ortiz-Martin, L., Peris-Lopez, P., & Hernandez-Castro, J. C. (2013). Security of EPC Class-1. In P. Lopez, J. Hernandez-Castro, & T. Li (Eds.), *Security and trends in wireless identification and sensing platform tags: Advancements in RFID* (pp. 34–63). Hershey, PA: IGI Global. doi:10.4018/978-1-4666-1990-6.ch002

Potyrailo, R. A., Morris, W. G., Sivavec, T., Tomlinson, H. W., Klensmeden, S., & Lindh, K. (2009). RFID sensors based on ubiquitous passive 13.56-MHz RFID tags and complex impedance detection. *Wireless Communications and Mobile Computing*, 9(10), 1318–1330. doi:10.1002/wcm.711

Qadri, N. N., & Fleury, M. (2012). Overview of mobile ad hoc networks and their modeling. In M. Fleury & N. Qadri (Eds.), *Streaming media with peer-to-peer networks: Wireless perspectives* (pp. 96–117). Hershey, PA: IGI Global. doi:10.4018/978-1-4666-1613-4.ch006

Qadri, N. N., & Liotta, A. (2011). Peer-to-peer over mobile ad-hoc networks. In S. Pierre (Ed.), *Next generation mobile networks and ubiquitous computing* (pp. 105–121). Hershey, PA: IGI Global. doi:10.4018/978-1-60566-250-3.ch011

Qian, C., Ngan, H., Liu, Y., & Ni, L. M. (2011). Cardinality estimation for large-scale RFID systems. *IEEE Transactions on Parallel and Distributed Systems*, 22(9), 1441–1454. doi:10.1109/TPDS.2011.36

Qian, Z., Tian, X., Chen, X., Huang, W., & Wang, X. (2014). Multicast capacity in MANET with infrastructure support. *IEEE Transactions on Parallel and Distributed Systems*, 25(7), 1808–1818. doi:10.1109/TPDS.2013.79

Ramanathan, R., Ko, L. W., Chen, H., & Ramanathan, U. (2015). Green characteristics of RFID technologies: An exploration in the UK logistics sector from innovation diffusion perspective. In I. Lee (Ed.), *RFID technology integration for business performance improvement* (pp. 156–178). Hershey, PA: IGI Global. doi:10.4018/978-1-4666-6308-4.ch008

Ramanathan, R., Ramanathan, U., & Ko, L. W. (2015). An analysis of the diffusion of RFID in the UK logistics sector using a technology-acceptance perspective. In I. Lee (Ed.), *RFID technology integration for business performance improvement* (pp. 247–259). Hershey, PA: IGI Global. doi:10.4018/978-1-4666-6308-4.ch012

Ramanathan, R., Ramanathan, U., & Ko, L. W. (2016). Some lessons for promoting RFID by applying TAM theory. In I. Lee (Ed.), *Encyclopedia of e-commerce development, implementation, and management* (pp. 1900–1912). Hershey, PA: IGI Global. doi:10.4018/978-1-4666-9787-4.ch134

Regattieri, A., Santarelli, G., Gamberi, M., & Gamberini, R. (2014). The use of radio frequency identification technology in packaging systems: Experimental research on traceability. *Packaging Technology and Science, 27*(8), 591–608. doi:10.1002/pts.2052

Rekleitis, E., Rizomiliotis, P., & Gritzalis, S. (2014). How to protect security and privacy in the IoT: A policy-based RFID tag management protocol. *Security and Communication Networks, 7*(12), 2669–2683. doi:10.1002/sec.400

Sakpere, W. E., & Adeyeye, M. O. (2015). Can near field communication solve the limitations in mobile indoor navigation? In I. Lee (Ed.), *RFID technology integration for business performance improvement* (pp. 52–79). Hershey, PA: IGI Global. doi:10.4018/978-1-4666-6308-4.ch003

Sánchez, M. M., Nieto, J. A., Gallinas, R. B., & Vidales, M. Á. (2014). CommunicaME: A new proposal for facilitating communication using NFC. In M. Cruz-Cunha, F. Moreira, & J. Varajão (Eds.), *Handbook of research on enterprise 2.0: Technological, social, and organizational dimensions* (pp. 89–106). Hershey, PA: IGI Global. doi:10.4018/978-1-4666-4373-4.ch005

Sari, A. (2015). Security issues in mobile wireless ad hoc networks: A comparative survey of methods and techniques to provide security in wireless ad hoc networks. In M. Dawson & M. Omar (Eds.), *New threats and countermeasures in digital crime and cyber terrorism* (pp. 66–94). Hershey, PA: IGI Global. doi:10.4018/978-1-4666-8345-7.ch005

Sarwar, K., & Shah, M. A. (2015). Cost effective design of an RFID based healthcare service system. *International Journal of Privacy and Health Information Management, 3*(2), 51–65. doi:10.4018/IJPHIM.2015070103

Shah, S. C. (2015). Energy efficient and robust allocation of interdependent tasks on mobile ad hoc computational grid. *Concurrency and Computation, 27*(5), 1226–1254. doi:10.1002/cpe.3297

Shih, D., Chiu, Y., Chang, S., & Yen, D. C. (2010). An empirical study of factors affecting RFID's adoption in Taiwan. In J. Symonds (Ed.), *Ubiquitous and pervasive computing: Concepts, methodologies, tools, and applications* (pp. 1122–1143). Hershey, PA: IGI Global. doi:10.4018/978-1-60566-960-1.ch070

Sim, M. L., Chin, C. M., & Tan, C. M. (2007). Mobile ad-hoc networks. In D. Taniar (Ed.), *Encyclopedia of mobile computing and commerce* (pp. 424–428). Hershey, PA: IGI Global. doi:10.4018/978-1-59904-002-8.ch070

Singh, J., Bhardwaj, M., & Sharma, A. (2015). Experimental analysis of distributed routing algorithms in ad hoc mobile networks. *Procedia Computer Science, 57*, 1411–1416. doi:10.1016/j.procs.2015.07.459

Singh, R. K. (2016). Issues related to network security attacks in mobile ad hoc networks (MANET). In N. Mohamed, T. Mantoro, M. Ayu, & M. Mahmud (Eds.), *Critical socio-technical issues surrounding mobile computing* (pp. 234–256). Hershey, PA: IGI Global. doi:10.4018/978-1-4666-9438-5.ch012

Singh, S. (2012). Security threats and issues with MANET. In K. Lakhtaria (Ed.), *Technological advancements and applications in mobile ad-hoc networks: Research trends* (pp. 247–263). Hershey, PA: IGI Global. doi:10.4018/978-1-4666-0321-9.ch015

Singh, S., Singh, D. K., & Mondal, M. S. (2012). Potential area of research in MANET. In K. Lakhtaria (Ed.), *Technological advancements and applications in mobile ad-hoc networks: Research trends* (pp. 391–407). Hershey, PA: IGI Global. doi:10.4018/978-1-4666-0321-9.ch021

Singh, S. P., McCartney, M., Singh, J., & Clarke, R. (2008). RFID research and testing for packages of apparel, consumer goods and fresh produce in the retail distribution environment. *Packaging Technology and Science, 21*(2), 91–102. doi:10.1002/pts.782

Sinodinou, T. (2009). RFID technology and its impact on privacy: Is society one step before the disappearance of personal data protection? In D. Politis, P. Kozyris, & I. Iglezakis (Eds.), *Socioeconomic and legal implications of electronic intrusion* (pp. 89–107). Hershey, PA: IGI Global. doi:10.4018/978-1-60566-204-6.ch005

Smith, A. D. (2014). Case studies of RFID practices for competitive inventory management systems. In J. Wang (Ed.), *Management science, logistics, and operations research* (pp. 1–25). Hershey, PA: IGI Global. doi:10.4018/978-1-4666-4506-6.ch001

Soon, C. B. (2010). Radio frequency identification history and development. In J. Symonds (Ed.), *Ubiquitous and pervasive computing: Concepts, methodologies, tools, and applications* (pp. 65–81). Hershey, PA: IGI Global. doi:10.4018/978-1-60566-960-1.ch007

Soon, C. B., & Gutiérrez, J. A. (2011). Adoption of RFID in supply chains: A motivation and ability perspective. In J. Wang (Ed.), *Supply chain optimization, management and integration: Emerging applications* (pp. 54–63). Hershey, PA: IGI Global. doi:10.4018/978-1-60960-135-5.ch004

Sornil, O. (2010). QoS signaling security in mobile ad hoc networks. In P. Bhattarakosol (Ed.), *Intelligent quality of service technologies and network management: Models for enhancing communication* (pp. 322–332). Hershey, PA: IGI Global. doi:10.4018/978-1-61520-791-6.ch017

Srinivasan, S., & Alampalayam, S. P. (2011). Intrusion detection algorithm for MANET. *International Journal of Information Security and Privacy, 5*(3), 36–49. doi:10.4018/jisp.2011070103

Sun, Q., Zhang, H., & Mo, L. (2011). Dual-reader wireless protocols for dense active RFID identification. *International Journal of Communication Systems, 24*(11), 1431–1444. doi:10.1002/dac.1225

Tajima, M. (2012). Small manufacturers vs. large retailers on RFID adoption in the apparel supply chain. In T. Choi (Ed.), *Fashion supply chain management: Industry and business analysis* (pp. 74–99). Hershey, PA: IGI Global. doi:10.4018/978-1-60960-756-2.ch004

Tang, Z. J., Wu, X. F., Zhan, J., & Hu, S. G. (2014). Broadband UHF RFID tag antenna design matched with different RFID chips. *Microwave and Optical Technology Letters*, *56*(1), 55–57. doi:10.1002/mop.28046

Thayananthan, V., Alzahrani, A., & Qureshi, M. S. (2015). Efficient techniques of key management and quantum cryptography in RFID networks. *Security and Communication Networks*, *8*(4), 589–597. doi:10.1002/sec.1005

Trivedi, A. K., Arora, R., Kapoor, R., & Sanyal, S. (2009). Mobile ad hoc network security vulner-abilities. In M. Khosrow-Pour (Ed.), *Encyclopedia of information science and technology* (2nd ed., pp. 2557–2561). Hershey, PA: IGI Global. doi:10.4018/978-1-60566-026-4.ch407

Unnithan, C., & Fraunholz, B. (2015). Radio frequency identification technology as an analytical lens and solution in hospitals: A novel approach in BPR/BPM. In M. Tavana, A. Ghapanchi, & A. Talaei-Khoei (Eds.), *Healthcare informatics and analytics: Emerging issues and trends* (pp. 194–211). Hershey, PA: IGI Global. doi:10.4018/978-1-4666-6316-9.ch010

Vales-Alonso, J., Parrado-García, F. J., & Alcaraz, J. J. (2016). OSL: An optimization-based scheduler for RFID dense-reader environments. *Ad Hoc Networks*, *37*, 512–525. doi:10.1016/j.adhoc.2015.10.004

Vowels, S. A. (2009). Understanding RFID (radio frequency identification). In A. Cartelli & M. Palma (Eds.), *Encyclopedia of information communication technology* (pp. 782–790). Hershey, PA: IGI Global. doi:10.4018/978-1-59904-845-1.ch103

Wang, J., & Lu, K. (2014). On the mobile relay placement in hybrid MANETs with secure network coding. *Security and Communication Networks*, *7*(4), 738–749. doi:10.1002/sec.775

Wang, S., Zhang, Z., & Naït-Abdesselam, F. (2015). Towards cross-layer approaches to coping with misbehavior in mobile ad hoc networks: An anatomy of reputation systems. *Security and Communication Networks*, *8*(2), 232–244. doi:10.1002/sec.976

Wang, S. S., Li, C. C., Lin, H. W., & Shih, K. P. (2015). A passive self-configuration MAC protocol for supporting network management in IEEE 802.11-based multi-hop mobile ad hoc networks. *Journal of Network and Computer Applications*, *56*, 149–157. doi:10.1016/j.jnca.2015.05.019

Watfa, M. K., Kaur, M., & Daruwala, R. F. (2013). RFID applications in e-healthcare. In *User-driven healthcare: Concepts, methodologies, tools, and applications* (pp. 259–287). Hershey, PA: IGI Global. doi:10.4018/978-1-4666-2770-3.ch014

Whitaker, J., Mithas, S., & Krishnan, M. S. (2007). A field study of RFID deployment and return expecta-tions. *Production and Operations Management*, *16*(5), 599–612. doi:10.1111/j.1937-5956.2007.tb00283.x

Wiedmann, K., Reeh, M., & Schumacher, H. (2012). Employment and acceptance of near field commu-nication in mobile marketing. In *Wireless technologies: Concepts, methodologies, tools and applications* (pp. 1868–1890). Hershey, PA: IGI Global. doi:10.4018/978-1-61350-101-6.ch709

Wu, B., Wu, J., & Cardei, M. (2008). A survey of key management in mobile ad hoc networks. In Y. Zhang, J. Zheng, & M. Ma (Eds.), *Handbook of research on wireless security* (pp. 479–499). Hershey, PA: IGI Global. doi:10.4018/978-1-59904-899-4.ch030

Wu, Y., Sheng, Q. Z., Shen, H., & Zeadally, S. (2013). Modeling object flows from distributed and federated RFID data streams for efficient tracking and tracing. *IEEE Transactions on Parallel and Distributed Systems, 24*(10), 2036–2045. doi:10.1109/TPDS.2013.99

Wyld, D. C. (2008). Radio frequency identification (RFID) technology. In G. Garson & M. Khosrow-Pour (Eds.), *Handbook of research on public information technology* (pp. 425–440). Hershey, PA: IGI Global. doi:10.4018/978-1-59904-857-4.ch041

Xiao, Y., Yu, S., Wu, K., Ni, Q., Janecek, C., & Nordstad, J. (2007). Radio frequency identification: Technologies, applications, and research issues. *Wireless Communications and Mobile Computing, 7*(4), 457–472. doi:10.1002/wcm.365

Yan, Q., Li, Y., & Deng, R. H. (2013). Malware protection on RFID-enabled supply chain management systems in the EPCglobal Network. In A. Miri (Ed.), *Advanced security and privacy for RFID technologies* (pp. 153–175). Hershey, PA: IGI Global. doi:10.4018/978-1-4666-3685-9.ch010

Yang, C., He, J., & Kun, Y. (2013). RFID tag anti-collision protocols. In N. Karmakar (Ed.), *Advanced RFID systems, security, and applications* (pp. 133–154). Hershey, PA: IGI Global. doi:10.4018/978-1-4666-2080-3.ch007

Yang, S. J. (2010). Design issues and performance analysis for DSR routing with reclaim-based caching in MANETs. *International Journal of Network Management, 20*(1), 21–34.

Yeh, T. C., Wang, Y. J., Kuo, T. C., & Wang, S. S. (2010). Securing RFID systems conforming to EPC Class 1 Generation 2 standard. *Expert Systems with Applications, 37*(12), 7678–7683. doi:10.1016/j.eswa.2010.04.074

Yoon, W., & Vaidya, N. H. (2012). RFID reader collision problem: Performance analysis and medium access. *Wireless Communications and Mobile Computing, 12*(5), 420–430. doi:10.1002/wcm.972

Zadin, A., & Fevens, T. (2015). Minimizing communication interference for stable position-based routing in mobile ad hoc networks. *Procedia Computer Science, 52*, 460–467. doi:10.1016/j.procs.2015.05.015

Zayou, R., Besbe, M. A., & Hamam, H. (2014). Agricultural and environmental applications of RFID technology. *International Journal of Agricultural and Environmental Information Systems, 5*(2), 50–65. doi:10.4018/IJAEIS.2014040104

Zhang, Z., Lu, Z., Chen, Q., Yan, X., & Zheng, L. R. (2012). Code division multiple access/pulse position modulation ultra-wideband radio frequency identification for Internet of Things: Concept and analysis. *International Journal of Systems, 25*(9), 1103–1121. doi:10.1002/dac.2312

Zhou, H., Mutka, M. W., & Ni, L. M. (2010). Secure prophet address allocation for MANETs. *Security and Communication Networks, 3*(1), 31–43. doi:10.1002/sec.126

ADDITIONAL READING

Arce, P., & Guerri, J. C. (2015). An altruistic cross-layer recovering mechanism for ad hoc wireless networks. *Wireless Communications and Mobile Computing*, *15*(13), 1744–1758. doi:10.1002/wcm.2459

Asadpour, M., & Dashti, M. T. (2015). Scalable, privacy preserving radio-frequency identification protocol for the Internet of Things. *Concurrency and Computation*, *27*(8), 1932–1950. doi:10.1002/cpe.3165

Bashri, M. S. R., Ibrahimy, M. I., & Motakabber, S. M. A. (2014). Design of a planar wideband patch antenna for UHF RFID tag. *Microwave and Optical Technology Letters*, *56*(7), 1579–1584. doi:10.1002/mop.28389

Chen, H. D., Kuo, S. H., & Jheng, J. L. (2013). Design of compact circularly polarized radio frequency identification tag antenna for metallic object application. *Microwave and Optical Technology Letters*, *55*(7), 1481–1485. doi:10.1002/mop.27607

Choi, W., Bae, J. H., Chae, J. S., Park, C. W., & Pyo, C. (2013). Slot-array antenna for UHF RFID shelf applications. *Microwave and Optical Technology Letters*, *55*(7), 1511–1515. doi:10.1002/mop.27653

Chou, J. S. (2014). A constant-time identifying large-scale RFID tags using lines on a plane. *Transactions on Emerging Telecommunications Technologies*, *25*(11), 1083–1094. doi:10.1002/ett.2624

Deepalakshmi, P., & Radhakrishnan, S. (2014). An ant colony-based, receiver-initiated multicast mesh protocol for collaborative applications of mobile ad hoc networks. *Transactions on Emerging Telecommunications Technologies*, *25*(3), 354–369. doi:10.1002/ett.2574

Feng, G., Fan, P., & Liew, S. C. (2012). Interference minimum network topologies for ad hoc networks. *Wireless Communications and Mobile Computing*, *12*(6), 529–544. doi:10.1002/wcm.993

Fu, L., Shen, X., Zhu, L., & Wang, J. (2014). A low-cost UHF RFID tag chip with AES cryptography engine. *Security and Communication Networks*, *7*(2), 365–375. doi:10.1002/sec.723

Gerhards-Padilla, E., Aschenbruck, N., & Martini, P. (2011). TOGBAD: An approach to detect routing attacks in tactical environments. *Security and Communication Networks*, *4*(8), 793–806. doi:10.1002/sec.185

Ghosh, U., & Datta, R. (2013). IDSDDIP: A secure distributed dynamic IP configuration scheme for mobile ad hoc networks. *International Journal of Network Management*, *23*(6), 424–446. doi:10.1002/nem.1849

Gong, T., & Bhargava, B. (2013). Immunizing mobile ad hoc networks against collaborative attacks using cooperative immune model. *Security and Communication Networks*, *6*(1), 58–68. doi:10.1002/sec.530

Hu, C. C. (2012). Bandwidth-satisfied routing in multi-rate MANETs by cross-layer approach. *Wireless Communications and Mobile Computing*, *12*(2), 206–218. doi:10.1002/wcm.958

Hu, L., Yuan'an, L., Dongming, Y., Hefei, H., Sirui, D., & Mingxia, L. (2016). Study of capacity region and minimum energy of delay-tolerant unicast mobile ad hoc networks using cell-partitioned model. *Wireless Communications and Mobile Computing*, *16*(7), 825–849. doi:10.1002/wcm.2572

Husieen, N. A., Hassan, S., Ghazali, O., & Siregar, L. (2013). The robustness of RM-DSR multipath routing protocol with different network size in MANET. *International Journal of Mobile Computing and Multimedia Communications*, *5*(2), 46–57. doi:10.4018/jmcmc.2013040104

Kakuda, Y., Ohta, T., & Oda, R. (2012). A methodology for real-time self-organized autonomous clustering in mobile ad hoc networks. *Concurrency and Computation*, *24*(16), 1840–1859. doi:10.1002/cpe.1792

Kim, Y. (2013). Design of near omnidirectional UHF RFID tag with one-off seal function for liquid bottles. *Microwave and Optical Technology Letters*, *55*(2), 375–379. doi:10.1002/mop.27285

Kioumourtzis, G., Bouras, C., & Gkamas, A. (2012). Performance evaluation of ad hoc routing protocols for military communications. *International Journal of Network Management*, *22*(3), 216–234. doi:10.1002/nem.802

Kwon, O. C., Oh, H. R., Lee, Z. K., Lee, G., Park, Y., & Song, H. (2013). Entire network load-aware cooperative routing algorithm for video streaming over mobile ad hoc networks. *Wireless Communications and Mobile Computing*, *13*(12), 1135–1149. doi:10.1002/wcm.1169

Lee, W. S., & Yu, J. W. (2015). Selectable sectoral antenna array using a quadruple feeding network for item-level tagging in UHF RFID applications. *Microwave and Optical Technology Letters*, *57*(7), 1523–1526. doi:10.1002/mop.29137

Masdari, M., Jabbehdari, S., & Bagherzadeh, J. (2015). Secure publish/subscribe-based certificate status validations in mobile ad hoc networks. *Security and Communication Networks*, *8*(6), 1063–1076. doi:10.1002/sec.1062

Meghanathan, N. (2015). Correlations between centrality measures for mobile ad hoc networks. *International Journal of Wireless Networks and Broadband Technologies*, *4*(2), 15–27. doi:10.4018/IJWNBT.2015040102

Najera, P., Roman, R., & Lopez, J. (2013). User-centric secure integration of personal RFID tags and sensor networks. *Security and Communication Networks*, *6*(10), 1177–1197. doi:10.1002/sec.684

Nguyen, H., Wahman, E., Pissinou, N., Iyengar, S. S., & Makki, K. (2015). Mobile learning object authoring tool and management system for mobile ad hoc wireless networks. *International Journal of Communication Systems*, *28*(17), 2180–2196. doi:10.1002/dac.2996

Niu, J., Liu, M., Liu, Y., Shu, L., & Wu, D. (2015). A venues-aware message routing scheme for delay-tolerant networks. *Wireless Communications and Mobile Computing*, *15*(13), 1695–1710. doi:10.1002/wcm.2454

Oh, S. Y., Marfia, G., & Gerla, M. (2011). MANET QoS support without reservations. *Security and Communication Networks*, *4*(3), 316–328. doi:10.1002/sec.183

Qabajeh, L. K., Kiah, M. L. M., & Qabajeh, M. M. (2013). A more secure and scalable routing protocol for mobile ad hoc networks. *Security and Communication Networks*, *6*(3), 286–308. doi:10.1002/sec.563

Sim, C. Y. D., Chen, C. C., Cao, R., & Chen, B. S. (2015). A circular patch antenna with parasitic element for UHF RFID applications. *International Journal of RF and Microwave Computer-Aided Engineering*, *25*(8), 681–687. doi:10.1002/mmce.20905 van Assche, T., Weyn, M., & Vercauteren, C. (2014). UHF RFID feasibility research: The endless possibilities and challenges of item-level tagging in a retail store. *Microwave and Optical Technology Letters*, *56*(3), 718–727. doi:10.1002/mop.28143

Varadharajan, V., & Tupakula, U. (2015). Securing wireless mobile nodes from distributed denial-of-service attacks. *Concurrency and Computation*, *27*(15), 3794–3815. doi:10.1002/cpe.3353

Varaprasad, G. (2014). Stable routing algorithm for mobile ad hoc networks using mobile agent. *International Journal of Communication Systems*, *27*(1), 163–170. doi:10.1002/dac.2354

Wang, B., Zhuang, Y., & Li, X. (2015). Compact dual ports handheld RFID reader antenna with high isolation. *International Journal of RF and Microwave Computer-Aided Engineering*, *25*(6), 548–555. doi:10.1002/mmce.20894

Xiaonan, W., & Shan, Z. (2014). Research on mobility handover for IPv6-based MANET. *Transactions on Emerging Telecommunications Technologies*, *25*(7), 679–691. doi:10.1002/ett.2595

Xie, W., Xie, L., Zhang, C., Wang, Q., Wang, C., & Tang, C. (2014). TOA: A tag-owner-assisting RFID authentication protocol toward access control and ownership transfer. *Security and Communication Networks*, *7*(5), 934–944. doi:10.1002/sec.965

Yang, C., Huang, L., Xu, H., & Leng, B. (2016). A scale-independent way for differential estimation in dynamic radio frequency identification systems. *International Journal of Communication Systems*, *29*(4), 742–756. doi:10.1002/dac.2939

Zaid, J., Abdelghani, M. L., & Denidni, T. A. (2015). CPW-fed multiband semifractal antenna for RFID reader applications. *Microwave and Optical Technology Letters*, *57*(8), 1852–1853. doi:10.1002/mop.29198

Zhang, Y., Low, C. P., Ng, J. M., & Wang, T. (2013). Predicting group partitions in mobile ad hoc networks. *International Journal of Communication Systems*, *26*(2), 139–160. doi:10.1002/dac.1333

Zhenhua, C., Shundong, L., Qianhong, W., & Qiong, H. (2015). A distributed secret share update scheme with public verifiability for ad hoc network. *Security and Communication Networks*, *8*(8), 1485–1493. doi:10.1002/sec.1097

KEY TERMS AND DEFINITIONS

Antenna: The device used to communicate between tag and reader.

Barcode: The machine-readable printed symbol representing the textual and numerical information.

Information: The data that is accurate and organized for the specific purpose.

Mobile Ad-Hoc Network: A network that has many autonomous nodes, often composed of mobile devices or other mobile pieces, that can arrange themselves in various ways and operate without strict top-down network administration.

Near Field Communication: A short-range wireless connectivity standard that utilizes the magnetic field induction to enable communication between devices when they are touched together.

Radio Frequency Identification: An automatic identification of packages, products, and machinery through attached transponders.

Reader: A device that reads data from the tag and writes data to the tag.

Tag: A microchip with an integrated circuit packaged with an antenna used to identify the objects.

Technology: The purposeful application of information in the design, production, and utilization of products and services.

Chapter 4
Secure Baseband Techniques for Generic Transceiver Architecture for Software-Defined Radio

Nikhil Kumar Marriwala
University Institute of Engineering and Technology, India & Kurukshetra University, India

Om Prakash Sahu
NIT, India

Anil Vohra
Kurukshetra University, India

ABSTRACT

Software Defined Radio (SDR) systems are the ones which can adapt to the future-proof solution and it covers both existing and emerging standards. An SDR has to possess elements of reconfigurability, intelligence and software programmable hardware. The main interest in any communication group is the sure sending of signals of info from a transmitter to a receiver. The signals are transmitted via a guide who corrupts the signal. To ensure reliable communication forward error-correcting (FEC) codes are the main part of a communication system. This chapter will discuss an SDR system built using LabVIEW for a Generic Transceiver. This chapter has covered emerging software radio standards and the technologies being used to specify and support them.

INTRODUCTION

The term *software defined radio* has become associated with a large number of different technologies and no standard definition exists. The term is usually used to refer to a radio transceiver in which the key parameters are defined in software and in which fundamental aspects of the radio's operation can be reconfigured by the upgrading of that software.

DOI: 10.4018/978-1-5225-1785-6.ch004

A number of associated terms have also been used in the context of programmable or reconfigurable mobile systems(Paul Burns, 2002):

- **Software Defined Radio (SDR):** This is the term adopted by the SDR Forum—an international body looking at the standards aspects of software radio (Mitola, 1995).
- **Multi-Standard Terminal (MST):** This type of terminal is not necessarily a software defined radio in the context of this book, although it may be implemented in that way. It simply refers to a terminal which is capable of operation on a number of differing air interface standards (Maskell & Vinod, 2008). This type of terminal will provide either wider international roaming than would a single-standard device, or a necessary smooth upgrade path from a legacy system to a new standard, for example, the transition from Global System for Mobile communications (GSM) to wideband code-division multiple access (WCDMA) (Ramacher & Ag, 2007).
- **Reconfigurable Radio:** This term is used to encompass both software and firmware reconfiguration [e.g., through the use of programmable logic devices, such as field programmable gate array (FPGAs)]. Both forms of reconfiguration are likely to be necessary in any cost and power-efficient software radio implementation.
- **Flexible Architecture Radio (FAR):** This is a wider definition still than those above. It indicates that all aspects of the radio system are flexible, not just the baseband/digital section. A true FAR should allow parameters such as the number and type of up/downconversion stages to be altered by software as well as, for example, IF filter bandwidths and even the RF frequency band of operation. This is clearly a utopian goal for software radio (Mitola, 2001).

Further variations on the above themes are also in use; however, they all fall into one or other of the above categories.

ABOUT SOFTWARE DEFINED RADIO

Reconfigurability is a prerequisite for SDR functionality, but time and again one forgets that it can also be an enabler for low power consumption. Indeed, once flexibility is built into a transceiver, it can be used to adapt the functioning and performance of a radio to the surrounding environment. As linearity, filtering, noise, bandwidth, and so on, can be traded for power utilization in the SDR, a smart controller is able to adapt the radio at runtime to the actual performance required, and hence can reduce the average power consumption of the SDR.

The ideal SDR architecture would be an analog-to-digital converter (ADC) coupled directly to an antenna(Yuce, Tekin, & Liu, 2008). Large chunks of the RF spectrum of interest could be sampled so that digital signal processing could separate out unwanted signals, extract the signal of interest, and perform such functions as automatic gain control (AGC) and demodulation. Such an ADC would require a sampling rate, dynamic range, and signal-to-noise ratio (SNR) to cover existing and future standards with varying performance requirements. Furthermore, this topology would require tunable RF bandpass filters.

There are, however, other radio architectures that are practical today and can achieve the frequency-agile reconfigurable characteristics required for SDR transceivers. In the rest of this chapter we explore the building blocks of such transceivers and present an implementation example. There are some levels of flexibility in a radio system using SDR. It is found some differences between different levels of flexibility in a radio are as follows.

Hardware Radio (HR)

When a radio is designed for a particular use having no option to change its properties to work on other frequencies, then it is called fixed system. There is no software control over the radio. Function once set cannot be changed, e.g. FM system.

Software Controlled Radio (SCR)

Radio system has many transmitter parameters. When these parameters are controlled by software, e.g. transmitted power levels are controlled using software but the other hardware functions are fixed then it is called Software Controlled Radio.

Software Defined Radio (SDR)

It is different from SCR because here the complete system is converted to another standard by updating the software. All radio functions are modified, i.e. modulation, multiplexing, amplification, mixing, multiple access and other transmitter and receiver processes.

Ideal Software Defined Radio (ISDR)

ISDR means Ideal SDR. As the name suggest it is a theoretical concept only because in practical no system is ideal at all. Ideal SDR does not include the analog front end. Here up and down conversion is performed directly between base-band and RF frequency digitally. A number of components are excluded in ISDR. There is a number of characteristics that an SDR possesses. Recent years have shown an impressive increase in diversity of wireless services covering e.g. navigation, communication, networking and video. This evolution offers the opportunity to fundamentally improve mobility and performance by merging different services in a multi-functional reconfigurable device. A SDR transceiver, implemented as a single compact and highly configurable physical circuit, is expected to enable operation over a broad range of modes and bands while preserving low-cost, low-complexity and energy efficient implementation. The signal transmission and reception are performed by the antenna. In the receiver's first section is the Radio Frequency (RF) front end where the signal is received at a carrier frequency and down converted to an Intermediate frequency (IF) or to the baseband frequency by mixing the incoming frequency with a local oscillator frequency. The Intermediate Frequency (IF) section digitally samples the IF signal with the help of an Analog to Digital Converter (ADC). Finally, the baseband section consists of either a processor or an FPGA, which demodulates and filters the signal. The software or the code is downloaded into the processor or FPGA hardware and it produces the output in accordance with the programmed parameters (modulation type and frequency band).

In the conventional radio system, we use a large number of analog components. Since analog components are less efficient, more power consuming and more expensive. Due to advances in digital electronics, we can replace these components by the digital circuits. This is the basic idea behind the SDR. Here intermediate analog stages are replaced by digital components and an antenna is directly connected to

ADC and DAC. A fully developed SDR will have all signal elements that are programmable. The main elements of the complete SDR are:

1. **Antenna:** Which are used to transmit and receive the signal from the system.
2. **Band Pass Filters:** That are used to limit the range of frequency and also used to minimize the effect of the inter-modulation, distortions for high gain stages.
3. **LNA (Low Noise Amplifier) and Mixer:** That is used to translate the RF spectrum to a suitable frequency.
4. **Local Oscillator:** To generate the proper IF when mixed with incoming RF signal. Provide variable frequency response and easily programmable via software control.
5. **Analog to Digital Convertor:** is used to convert the intermediate frequency signal into the digital format for processing. Quite often the analog to digital convertor is the bottleneck and selection of the ADC is often a driving factor that determines the architecture of SDR, The designer is forced to select the best available ADC, realizing that under many conditions the ADC may be over-specified. Analog to digital convertor that may desirable change the sample rate, input range and potentially the active bandwidth.
6. **FPGA:** Field programmable gate array are used for programming to perform the quadrature modulation and tuning, channel filtering and data rate reduction. FPGA are also used for RF power measurement and channel linearization.

APPLICATIONS OF SDR

SDR can be used in many areas today. Some of the application areas of use of SDR are as stated:

1. **Problem-Solving:** One application is for a problem-solving program which is used to test system functionality. The application provides an interface to the low-level configuration and parameters of all components of the system. It also queries and monitors these components during operation. What makes this possible is that the mechanisms for interacting with the components are predetermined and enforced by the operating environment. Components are designed such that their operation is not disturbed by the use of their advertised monitoring interfaces.
2. **Collaboration:** In some cases, a waveform developer may desire to provide a waveform implementation or the proprietary core of a waveform. At the same time, they may wish to make their new waveform available on multiple platforms. This has been the case with iBiquity's IBOC waveform for terrestrial digital HD Radio® and Qualcomm's FLO waveform for mobile television. Since the implementation is specific to a particular processor, such as a DSP or FPGA, the integrator of the waveform must use the predetermined processor in their design. Platform-independence would make the waveform more portable, but it would not directly result in an implementation.
3. **Military:** SDR is the fundamental technology used in Joint Tactical Radio System which was initiated to develop reconfigurable radios using software that can enable seamless, real-time communication across the U.S. military.
   a. Real-time flexibility, Secure

4. **Commercial:** International connectivity.
5. **Civilian:**
   a. Portable command for crisis manage
   b. Bluetooth, WLAN, GPS, Radar, WCDMA, GPRS, GSM, DECT, AM, FM, etc.
6. **Re-Configurability:** The most obvious advantages are flexibility. They can be easily and fastly upgraded with enhanced features. They can talk and listen to multiple channels simultaneously. We can build new kinds of radios that have never existed before. Smart radios or cognitive radios are looked at the utilization of the RF spectrum in their multiband radios and configure themselves for best performance.

The ADC and DAC are connected to the antenna with only minimal analog circuitry (e.g., just the transmitting/receiving multiplexer). The idea is to shift all signal processing to the digital domain. The received signal is digitized as soon as possible, while the transmitting path has its digital-to-analog conversion as late as possible. The DSP is responsible for all signal processing, such as filtering, equalization, mixing, and (de)modulation. A first remark is that the DSP in such a system should be extremely powerful and therefore will be power hungry.

The major advantage is that this architecture offers ultimate flexibility. If another communication standard is wanted, the DSP software can be reprogrammed to perform signal processing accordingly. An SR also allows us to process all desired standards at the same time.

The downside is that the requirements for the ADC and DAC in an SR are tremendous. Due to the lack of analog mixing, the bandwidth of both the ADC and DAC is determined by the carrier frequency instead of the channel bandwidth. A single transceiver is used in an SDR. But all parts can be reconfigured by the software. By doing so, the multi-standard operation becomes possible. This reconfigurability requires new circuit design techniques. A strategy to achieve this is to make the analog front end as simple as possible, shifting the design complexity to the ADC and DAC. However, a good system-level design is required to find power-optimized solutions.

The ADC should be designed such that it can meet the specifications for the communication standard with the toughest accuracy requirement and the speed of the standard with the largest channel bandwidth. For each standard, the ADC should then be reconfigured to obtain the specifications required with minimal power consumption. For the transmitting path, a direct conversion (or homodyne) implementation might be preferable over the traditional heterodyne transmitter(Osmany, Herzel, & Scheytt, 2010).

In a direct-conversion architecture, the DAC output is directly up-converted by a single mixer stage to the carrier frequency required.

The filtering requirements of a heterodyne transmitter are very problematic for reconfigurable front ends. The often-used SAW filters are impossible to reconfigure and are hence to be avoided in SDR front ends. (Mohajer, Mohammadi, Abdipour, & Lo, n.d.)A direct-conversion architecture requires fewer filters, making it easier to implement in a reconfigurable manner. Of course, a direct-conversion transmitter also demonstrates some drawbacks [e.g., the local oscillator (LO) pulling].

SOFTWARE DEFINED RADIO ARCHITECTURES

An SDR is a transceiver in which preferably all aspects of its operation are determined by means of flexible, adaptable, general-purpose hardware whose design is under software control. Hence the term *software defined radio*, which often describes these types of systems. However, FPGAs, ASICs (containing a re-programmable element), massively parallel processor arrays, and other techniques are also available. In more common terms flexible architecture radio (FAR) and SDR are becoming gradually more adopted. This type of radio is also usually understood to be broadband (multi-band or multi-frequency in operation).

Furthermore, the many competing standards (GSM, CDMA, WCDMA, AMPS, D-AMPS, PDC) have opposed characteristics, tariffs, and so forth, and hence a multi-mode, multi-band transceiver, covering all of these systems, would certainly be a very useful device(J. Mitola, 1995).

This chapter aims to study the simplest feasible architecture for an SDR and then to demonstrate the design of a generic SDR transceiver. The concept of flexibility in a transceiver can be divided into two main areas:

1. Flexibility in the modulation format, coding, and framing.
2. Flexibility in terms of RF frequency.

The area, frequency flexibility, is indeed the most challenging of the two and is a concept which is the subject of much research(Schmidt-knorreck, Knorreck, Knopp, & Antipolis, 2012). The area of flexibility in the modulation format, coding, and framing has been addressed in the case study later in this chapter and most commercial communications receiver designs employ many of its basic principles, even if they do not aim to provide a wide choice of modulation formats.

IMPLEMENTING A DIGITAL RECEIVER

There are a number of unique aspects of a digital radio implementation which allow a wider choice of options in a receiver design. These options include the use of oversampling to achieve a lower noise floor than the chosen converter resolution would normally allow and the use of undersampling as a method of downconversion. These techniques, together with a range of new mechanisms which can add to both spurious and noise specifications, make the design of a digital receiver somewhat different to its analogue counterpart. This section will cover the major aspects of a digital receiver design, suitable for use in a software defined radio application.

Frequency Conversion Using Undersampling

Undersampling is the act of sampling a signal at a sampling rate much lower than one quarter of the Nyquist rate (i.e., much lower than half of the signal frequency). If the signal frequency is, for example, 100 MHz, then the minimum required sample frequency, the Nyquist sample rate, is 200 MHz (although practical converters would require this to be at least 250 MHz). This signal would be undersampled by employing a sample rate of >50 MHz. Undersampling is an important technique as it effectively performs a frequency mixing function on the input signal, downconverting the signal and, at the same time, performing the required (pseudo-Nyquist) sampling(Pursley & Royster, 2008). The signal is converted (aliased) down to baseband or the first Nyquist zone and sampled as if it had originally been a baseband signal. The process can be described mathematically as:

$$f_{BB} = Rem\ (f_{IF}/f_s) \tag{1}$$

where f_{IF} is the IF input frequency to the A/D converter, f_s is the sample rate and f_{BB} is the resulting baseband frequency. The 'Rem' function returns the remainder from the division of the items within the brackets, *provided that* the remainder lies in the first Nyquist zone. If the result does not lie within the first Nyquist zone, then it must be subtracted from the sample rate, f_s, to yield the correct baseband frequency.

This can be illustrated using the example above: if the 100-MHz input (IF) signal is sampled at 15 MHz, the result of the Rem function is:

100/15=6, remainder   10

$$f_{BB} = Rem\ (100/15) = 10\ MHz \tag{2}$$

Since the remainder in (*ii*) falls outside of the first Nyquist zone, which has a maximum frequency of 7.5 MHz for a 15-MHz sample rate, the result must be subtracted from f_s:

$$f_{BB} = 15 - 10 = 5\ MHz \tag{3}$$

The process of aliasing can also cause spectral reversal, and this needs to be taken into account when designing the subsequent baseband signal processing. Alternate spectral zones will be reversed and unaltered, starting with the second Nyquist zone (which will be reversed).

RADIO RECEIVER

Current radio receiver designs are, in general, narrowband and can only achieve general (or broadband) coverage by the switching or alteration of narrowband elements. Several designs, such as those used in many scanning receivers, do not try to rise above some of the fundamental receiver problems, such as blocking and image rejection, but rely on the user being able to eliminate interference by positioning of the set, or some other mechanism such as the use of a directional antenna(Selva, Reis, Lenzi, Meloni, & Barbin, 2012). Where this is not possible, the user must tolerate the problem and the restriction in frequency usage which ensues, as the price of achieving wideband coverage.

The aim of the ideas presented in this section is to propose systems and techniques for the elimination of many or all of the fundamental problems which prevent the truly universal radio receiver from becoming a reality. The ideas presented are not fully developed solutions, currently in production, but more a series of proposals as to how some of these fundamental issues might be addressed.

There are three basic problems which need to be solved:

1. The filter required in a full-duplex transceiver must be specifically and carefully designed for its intended band of operation. This filter is usually either a helical component or formed from a dielectric (such as ceramic) and hence is almost impossible to tune in any sensible fashion over a reasonable range of frequencies. A multiple-band transceiver would therefore require a number of diplexer filters and this would very quickly become prohibitive, both in terms of cost and size.

2. The front-end *preselect* filter (also known as the *band-select* or *cover* filter), utilized to reject the image signal and other particularly strong out-of-band signals, must also be either tunable or eliminated in order to allow multi-band coverage. Electronic tuning of this filter is a more realistic proposition than that of the diplexer filter mentioned earlier; however, the change in technologies (from, perhaps, lumped-element to dielectric-based) across, say, 100 MHz to 2 GHz, would make this difficult, if not impossible. The alternative to the use of such a filter would require the front-end amplifier [or low-noise amplifier (LNA)] to be able to handle the full dynamic range of signals within the broad coverage range. This may include TV transmissions of many kilowatts and microcellular transmissions of a few milliwatts, and hence a very high dynamic range amplifier is required.

3. A further consequence of eliminating the front-end filter is that the image signal is no longer suppressed and hence has the potential to interfere directly with the wanted signal in the receiver. This image signal must therefore be suppressed by some other mechanism which does not involve filtering at the input signal frequency.

Multi-Band Flexible Receiver Design

As explained earlier, that there is difficulty of producing a flexible receiver design due to the addition of wide channel bandwidths and multiple operating bands. The widening of the channel bandwidth has the following consequences:

-   The number of narrowband carriers which can enter the IF and baseband chains is increased significantly, hence increasing the potential dynamic range required in these parts of the system.
-   The sampling rate and dynamic range required of the A/D converter also increases significantly. This may well make the A/D an unrealizable part using current technology (or indeed, following medium-term advances in current technology). When we shift from a single-band to multiple bands, the receiver section faces numerous problems such as:
    -   RF pre-selection filtering becomes difficult or impossible, since the filter must now be tuned to each band of interest. Alternatively, a bank of switched filters may be employed, but this can quickly become unwieldy for a truly flexible system. This latter technique has been used in a number of military systems in the past.
    -   The channel synthesizer must tune over a far wider range than for a single-band system.
    -   The diplexer in a full-duplex transceiver must have a variable frequency of operation and a variable transmit/receive frequency split. Since the diplexer is currently realized in ceramic, SAW, or helical resonators in most portable systems, this is clearly impossible with current techniques. Again, the main obvious alternative is the use of multiple units, with switching to determine which is in use at a given point in time. As before, this can quickly become unwieldy.

It is worth examining the consequences of eliminating the inflexible components mentioned above on the overall receiver performance, since the only option is to design without these components and utilize alternative means of solving the resulting problems (if possible).

If the front-end preselect and diplexer filters are removed, then three main problems result:

Figure 1. Probable universal receiver architecture

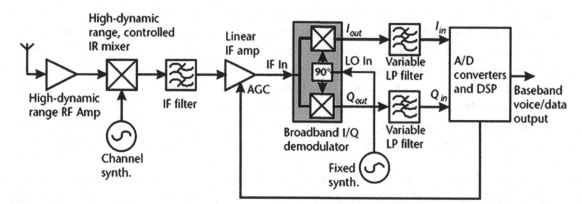

1.   All image rejection from this filter is lost, thus leaving the receiver prone to signals appearing at its image frequency.
2.   *All* radio signals within the bandwidth capability of the antenna will impinge upon the front-end low-noise amplifier in the receiver. This amplifier will therefore require a very high dynamic range to prevent overload from strong, unwanted signals (e.g., broadcast TV transmissions in a hand-portable communications receiver).
3.   Without a diplexer, the full power of the transmitter output signals may impinge upon the receiver input (depending upon what is used to replace the diplexer). The receiver must therefore be able to cope with these signals, or else utilize an alternative method of eliminating them.

One possible approach to solving these problems is shown in Figure 1.

The front-end amplifier is mandatory to have a high dynamic range and this will have implications for either its power consumption (if conventional techniques are used) or complexity (if a linearisation technique is used) or possibly both. The mixer should incorporate the image-rejection capability originally provided by the front-end filter; hence, some form of image-reject mixer will be necessary (Händel & Zetterberg, 2010).

It too will experience the full dynamic range of the input signals and hence must be able to cope with this without introducing undue levels of distortion and hence possibly blocking weak, wanted signals.

The other significant difference is the introduction of variable-bandwidth anti-alias filters prior to the A/D converters. These can then effectively perform the channel-selection filtering in the receiver and hence significantly reduce the dynamic range required of the A/D converters.

It is clear from this discussion that a number of these components have yet to be realised, although research is currently underway to solve these problems, as they are potentially key to the practical realisation of a multi-band flexible architecture radio(Rivet, Deval, Begueret, Dallet, & Belot, 2007).

Linear Transmitter

Arguably the most important element of any software defined radio system is the linear transmitter. Receiver systems have always required a high degree of linearity, as they must possess a good strong signal handling capability, in addition to good low-noise performance. In the case of transmitters, however, a high degree of linearity is a relatively recent requirement, arising predominantly from the widespread adoption of cellular networks.

Transmitters used in this type of application require a much greater degree of linearity (i.e., a much lower level of distortion) than even single-sideband (SSB) linear transmitters used in the past (e.g., for military applications). This is due to the near-far effect present in cellular systems(Paul Burns, 2002), which results in transmitter non-linearities causing significant interference to users of adjacent channels, thereby limiting system capacity. This limitation affects both uplink and downlink, depending upon which transmitter has the non-linearity problem: If it is the handset transmitter, the uplink capacity of a nearby cell will be impacted; if it is a BTS transmitter problem, the downlink capacity of a nearby cell will be impacted. Even with the high-linearity transmitters available today, many city-centre systems are currently interference limited (in terms of capacity) rather than noise limited. High linearity transmitters are therefore an enabling technology for many cellular systems, irrespective of the use (or otherwise) of a software defined radio-based architecture in their realisation.

In the case of a generic software defined radio system, a high-linearity transmitter is essential for any design that must be capable of operation on an envelope-varying modulation format. In practice, this means virtually all software defined radio systems must adopt one or other of the high-linearity amplifier or transmitter technologies. The basic architecture of a software defined radio transmitter revolves about the design of a baseband version of the desired RF spectrum, followed by a linear path translating that spectrum to a high-power RF signal. The frequency translation (upconversion) and power amplification processes, involved in creating the high power RF signal, must therefore fall into one of the following categories:

1. **Inherently Linear Processing:** The main mechanism by which this is ensured is typically by the use of back off of all stages from their 1-dB compression points. This has the obvious advantage of simplicity, in terms of design, but is typically highly inefficient (particularly in the case of the power amplifier) and costly, since it is required to significantly overrate all of the components involved.

2. **Linearisation of the RF PA:** With this option, a linearisation technique, such as those, is applied to the RF power amplifier, with inherently linear processing used for the upconversion system. This significantly reduces the size and cost of the transmitter, relative to that of option 1, but still requires the upconverter to be overrated.

3. **Linearisation of the Complete Transmitter:** Linearisation techniques exist which are capable of linearising the complete transmitter from its base-band input to its high-power RF output. This form of solution allows the upconversion processing to be more non-linear, hence requiring less backoff, and thus to be potentially cheaper.

4. **RF Synthesis Techniques:** The final option relies on the processing of constant envelope waveforms throughout the upconversion and power amplification hardware, with the desired envelope-varying RF waveform being synthesized by combining these waveforms at the output.

Comparison of Requirements

The primary constraints upon a base-station or handset linear PA or transmitter may be summarized as follows:

1. **Output Power:** The output power of a base-station PA is typically much greater than that of a handset, both in terms of overall mean power and on a power-per-carrier basis. In some micro and pico-cell applications, the power levels of the two may be similar on a power-per-carrier basis, but typically the number of carriers involved dictates that the base-station PA is of a much higher power overall.

2. **Size:** This is the most obvious difference—a handset will clearly have much less space within which the PA must be accommodated. In cellular base stations, a rack format is still common, although even here size is becoming a major issue, particularly for micro and pico BTS applications.

3. **Efficiency:** The battery life of a handset is a key selling feature (or conversely the battery size/weight for a given talk-time)—efficiency is clearly of major concern here. Efficiency is, however, of arguably similar importance in the case of the base station, due to issues of size, cooling, and running costs. An increase in base-station PA efficiency from, say, 10% to say 15%, when multiplied across a complete 3G network, can result in savings of many millions of dollars per annum in electricity costs alone. These savings will be compounded in practice by additional savings in cooling costs, and power supply costs. In addition, removing the need for air conditioning systems and the reduction and/or removal of the need for cooling fans will significantly improve BTS reliability. In a typical BTS, it is the air conditioning unit which is the single least-reliable element and failure of this subsystem frequently results in failure (due to overheating) of other subsystems (notably the RF power amplifier or transmitter).

INTRODUCTION TO LABVIEW

LabVIEW (Laboratory Virtual Instrument Engineering Workbench) is a graphically-based programming language developed by National Instruments. Its graphical nature makes it ideal for test and measurement, automation, instrument control, data acquisition, and data analysis applications. This results in significant productivity improvements over conventional programming languages. LabVIEW has a powerful built-in signal processing toolset, no coding requirements such as memory allocation or variable declarations, no compiling, highly integrated instrument control or data acquisition, and excellent display utilities for viewing these digital signals at various points in the communication system. LabVIEW Virtual Instruments (VIs) can be built and combined to produce a flexible and powerful digital communication test system. Building such a LabVIEW-based communication system will allow for new interface standards to be quickly and easily integrated (National Instruments Coorporation, n.d.). LabVIEW is a graphical programming language that uses icons instead of lines of text to create applications. In contrast to text-based programming languages, where instructions determine program execution, LabVIEW uses dataflow programming, where the flow of data determines execution. LabVIEW programs are called Virtual Instruments, or VIs, because their appearance and operation imitate physical instruments, such as oscilloscopes and multimeters. Every VI uses functions that manipulate input from the user interface or other sources and display that information or move it to other files or other computers. A Virtual Instrument (VI) is a LabVIEW programming element. A VI consists of a front panel, block diagram, and an icon that represents the program. The Front Panel is used to display controls and indicators for the user, Serves as the user interface. The Block Diagram contains the graphical source code that defines the functionality of the VI. The icon, which is a visual representation of the VI, has connectors for program inputs and outputs. It Identifies the VI so that a VI can be used in another VI. A VI within another VI is called a subVI. A subVI corresponds to a subroutine in text-based programming languages (Welch et al., 2011). Programming languages such as C and BASIC use functions and subroutines as programming elements, LabVIEW uses the VI. The Front Panel of a VI handles the function inputs and outputs, and the code diagram performs the work of the VI. Multiple VIs can be used to create large-scale applications; in fact, large scale applications may have several hundred VIs. A VI may be used as the user interface or as a subroutine in an application.

Front Panel

The Front Panel of a LabVIEW VI contains a number of entities such as knob for selecting the number of measurements per average, a control for selecting the measurement type, a digital indicator to display the output value, and a stop button. The front panel can be built with controls and indicators, which are the interactive input and output terminals of the VI, respectively. Controls are knobs, push buttons, dials, and other input devices. Indicators are graphs, LEDs, and other displays. Controls simulate instrument input devices and supply data to the block diagram of the VI(National Instruments Coorporation, n.d.). Indicators simulate instrument output devices and display data the block diagram acquires or generates. The Front Panel is the user interface of a VI. Generally the Front Panel is designed first, and then the Block Diagram is designed to perform tasks on the inputs and outputs created on the front panel. Select (Window--Show Controls Palette) is used to display the Controls palette, then select controls and indicators from the Controls palette and is then placed on the Front Panel displays. Controls simulate instrument input devices and supply data to the block diagram of the VI. Indicators simulate instrument output devices and display data the block diagram acquires or generates. Front Panel controls and indicators have optional elements that can be made visible or can be hidden. Set the visible elements for the control or indicator on the Appearance tab of the property dialog box for the front panel object. We can also set the visible elements by right-clicking an object and selecting Visible Items from the shortcut menu. LabVIEW initially configures objects in the Controls palette as controls or indicators based on their applications. For example, if a toggle switch is selected it appears on the front panel as a control because a toggle switch is usually an input device. If an LED is selected, it appears on the front panel as an indicator because an LED is usually an output device. Some palettes contain a control and an indicator for the same type or class of object. For example, the Numeric palette contains a digital control and a digital indicator. We can change a control to an indicator by right-clicking the object and selecting Change to Indicator from the shortcut menu, and can also change an indicator to a control by right-clicking the object and selecting Change to Control from the shortcut menu(National Instruments Coorporation, n.d.). We can replace a front panel object with a different control or indicator. Selecting Replace from the shortcut menu preserves as much information as possible about the original object, such as its name, description, default data, dataflow direction (control or indicator), color, size etc.

Block Diagram

After the Front Panel is built, we add code using graphical representations of functions to control the front panel objects. The Block Diagram contains this graphical source code. Front panel objects appear as terminals on the Block Diagram (BD). Objects on the block diagram include terminals, nodes, and functions. The Block Diagrams can be build by connecting the objects with wires.

Block Diagram Terminals

The Front Panel controls or indicators can be configured to appear as icon or data type terminals on the block diagram. By default, Front Panel objects appear as icon terminals. For example, a knob icon terminal represents a knob on the front panel. The DBL at the bottom of the terminal represents a data type of double-precision, floating-point numeric. A DBL terminal, represents a double-precision, floating-point numeric control or indicator. Icon terminals are used to display the types of Front Panel objects on the block diagram, in addition to the data types of the front panel objects. A terminal is any point to which we can attach a wire, other than to another wire. Terminals are entry and exit ports that exchange information between the Front Panel and Block Diagram. Data entered into the front panel controls enter the Block diagram through the control terminal. LabVIEW has control and indicator terminals, node terminals, constants, and specialized terminals on structures, such as the input and output terminals on the Formula Node.

Control and Indicator Data Types

Table 1 shows the symbols for the different types of control and indicator terminals. The color and symbol of each terminal indicate the data type of the control or indicator. Control terminals have a thicker border than indicator terminals. Also, arrows appear on front panel terminals to indicate whether the terminal is a control or an indicator. An arrow appears on the right if the terminal is a control, and an arrow appears on the left if the terminal is an indicator.

Various Key Features of LabVIEW (National Instruments Coorporation, n.d.)utilized in this implementation are as under:

- **Local Variables:** Local variables can be used to access front panel objects from more than one location in a single VI and pass data between block diagram nodes that cannot be connected with a wire. However, with a local variable we can write to it even if it is a control or read from it even if it is an indicator. In effect, with a Local Variable, we can access a Front Panel object as both an input and an output.
- **Point-by-Point Processing:** LabVIEW provides point-by-point signal generation. Point-by-point analysis functions are optimized for continuous, real-time analysis without data loss, reinitialization, or potential interruption problems. The point-by-point functions allow for the input-analysis-output process to occur continuously, in real-time.
- **Modulation-Demodulation:** The NI Modulation Toolkit can be used to implement various modulation and demodulation schemes. It extends the built-in analysis capability of LabVIEW with functions and tools for signal generation, analysis, visualization, and processing of standard and custom digital and analog modulation formats. It offers bit-error rate (BER), phase error, burst timing, and frequency deviation measurements.
- **Digital Filtering:** The filtering Coefficients used in pulse shaping and Hilbert transformation are obtained by using NI LabVIEW Digital Filter Design Toolkit. The NI LabVIEW Digital Filter Design Toolkit (DFDT) is complete filter design and analysis software that can be used to design digital filters to meet required filter specifications. With the DFDT work is done within the LabVIEW development environment to design, analyze, and implement a variety of IIR and FIR filters.

Table 1. Control and indicator data types

Control	Indicator	Data type	Color	Default Values
[SGL]	[SGL]	Single-precision floating-point numeric	Orange	0.0
[DBL]	[DBL]	Double-precision floating-point numeric	Orange	0.0
[EXT]	[EXT]	Extended-precision floating-point numeric	Orange	0.0
[CSG]	[CSG]	Complex single-precision floating-point numeric	Orange	0.0+ i0.0
[CDB]	[CDB]	Complex double-precision floating-point Numeric	Orange	0.0+ i0.0
[CXT]	[CXT]	Complex extended-precision floating-point Numeric	Orange	0.0+ i0.0
[I8]	[I8]	8-bit signed integer numeric	Blue	0
[I16]	[I16]	16-bit signed integer numeric	Blue	0
[I32]	[I32]	32-bit signed integer numeric	Blue	0
[U8]	[U8]	8-bit unsigned integer numeric	Blue	0
[U16]	[U16]	16-bit unsigned integer numeric	Blue	0
[U32]	[U32]	32-bit unsigned integer numeric	Blue	0
[ ]	[ ]	Array—Encloses the data type of its elements in square brackets and takes the color of that data type.	Varies	-----
[abc]	[abc]	String	Pink	Empty String
[TF]	[TF]	Boolean	Green	False
[cluster]	[cluster]	Cluster—Encloses several data types. Cluster data types are brown if all elements of the cluster are numeric or pink if the elements of the cluster are different types.	Pink or Brown	------
[wv]	[wv]	Waveform—Cluster of elements that carries the data, start time, and Δt of a waveform.	Brown	------

- **Other Features:** Toolkits add libraries of functions, VIs, interactive wizards, examples, utilities, and documentation to our NI LabVIEW installation, effectively reducing the time required to finish our task. Control Design tool Kit Provides a library of VIs and LabVIEW MathScript functions that are used to design, analyze, and deploy a controller for a linear time-invariant dynamic system model. This toolkit includes frequency response analysis tools such as Bode, and Nyquist, time response analysis tools such as step and impulse response analysis. Simulation Module Tool Kit Provides VIs, functions, and other tools that are used to construct and simulate all or part of a dynamic system model.

LabVIEW provides preferred interactivity and graphical-user-interface capabilities.SDR has been implemented using LabVIEW since adjustments can be made in software as needed compared to hardware-based solution. The next section covers the case study of the design of a generic transceiver for SDR implemented in LabVIEW.

LABVIEW BASED GENERIC TRANSCEIVER FOR SOFTWARE DEFINED RADIO (CASE STUDY)

In this section the building blocks of a generic transceiver for SDR Modem system built in LabVIEW are explained. The designed system consists of two parts: the Transmitter section and the Receiver section. The Transmitter section consists of four modules which are a message source module, Pulse Shaped Filter module, QAM Modulator module and Gaussian Noise module. The Receiver has been designed using an Adaptive Filter module, Hilbert Transform module, QAM Demodulator module, Sync & Tracking module. A brief description of each block follows. The Front panel of generic transceiver for SDR Modem system is shown in Figure 2.

Figure 2. Front panel for generic transceiver for SDR modem

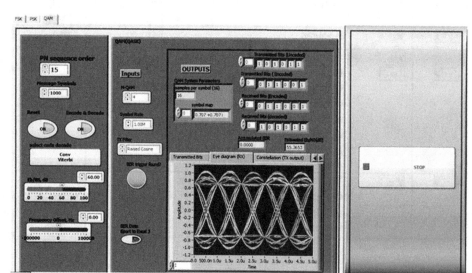

Message Source

The initial module of generic transceiver consists of a message source VI. Here Pseudo-random Noise (PN) sequences are used to spread the transmitting data in message source. PN Sequence is a definite sequence of pulses that keep on repeating itself after its period. A PN sequence is a sequence of binary numbers e.g. 0 & 1. The PN Sequence used in this design is generated by using a 5-stage Linear Feedback Shift register (LFSR) structure. In the Message source VI for achieving frame synchronization Frame Marker bits are inserted in front of PN sequences generated. The frame marker bits are a distinct pattern of bits that never occurs in the stream for message data. Thus, in this design one message sample (frame marker bit or PN sample) is generated after every four executions of this VI. Hence zero samples get generated for the remaining three executions of this message source VI. The total length of the message that is achieved is 164 for one period of frame marker bits and a PN sequence, which can be obtained by using 4 (oversampling rate) × [10(frame marker bits) + 31(period of PN sequence)]. To specify the marker bits a constant array of 10 complex numbers is used. The complex value that we get has two parts i.e. the real part and the imaginary part. The real parts of the in-phase samples is used as the frame marker bits while the imaginary part of the complex value is used as the frame marker bits of the quadrature-phase samples.

Pulse Shaped Filter

It is the process of changing the waveform of the transmitted pulse. Its purpose is to make transmitted signal more suitable to the communication channel. It is done before modulation. ISI is caused due to signal transmission at higher modulation rate from the band limited channels. By using pulse shape filtering ISI caused by channel can be controlled. The message (PN) sequences generated are sent through a raised cosine FIR filter for the creation of a band-limited baseband signal. In the VI we have used a raised cosine filter to serve as the pulse shaped filter. An FIR filter (FIR Filter Pt By Pt VI) has been used for this purpose. The Now a complex value pulse shaped message signal is constructed by combining the two outputs of the pulse shaped filter. In this VI we have obtained the filter coefficients by the filter design toolkit of LabVIEW called as the LabVIEW Digital Filter Design toolkit and stored in an array

Figure 3. Pulse Shape Filter VI

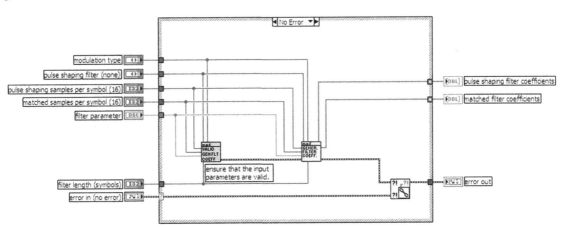

of constants toolkit. The Pulse Shape Filter VI is shown in figure 1.3. As a result, the digital sequence is smoothed or filtered to minimize any Inter-symbol interference (ISI).

Modulator

The FSK modulator accepts an M-ary value that specifies a predefined symbol map with the number of distinct symbol map values to use as symbols. The FSK instance calculates parameters for use within the modulator. The system parameters cluster from this VI wire to the corresponding parameter of the appropriate modulation VI. M-FSK specifies the M-ary number, which is the number of distinct frequency deviations to use as symbols. Bits per symbol return the number of bits represented by each symbol. This value is equal to Log_2 (M), where M is the order of the modulation. The PSK modulator converts the input bit stream into an electrical waveform suitable for transmission over the communication channel. In this design we have used the Modulator to minimize the effects of channel noise, also to match the frequency spectrum of the transmitted signal with channel characteristics QAM can be considered a logical extension of QPSK. The two independent signals are simultaneously transmitted over the same medium. The QAM modulation process involves the use of two separate product modulators that are supplied with two carriers of the same frequency, but differ in phase by -90^0. The QAM Modulator VI is shown in Figure 4.

A complex envelope is build by the output of the raised cosine filter, b $\tilde{s}(t)$ of a QAM signal given by

$$\tilde{s}(t) = \sum_{k=-\infty}^{\infty} c_k g_T\left(t - kT\right) \tag{4}$$

where c_k is the complex message made up of two real message signals a_k and $b_{k,}$ $c_{k=}$ $a_{k\,+} jb_k$

Hence the transmitted QAM signal s (t) can now be written as

$$s(t) = \Re_e\left[\tilde{s}(t)e^{jw_c t}\right] \tag{5}$$

Figure 4. Modulator VI

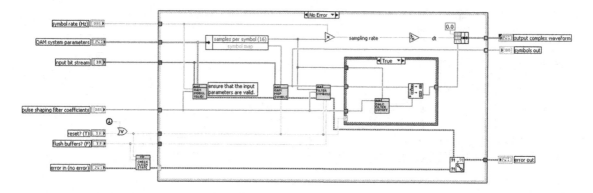

where $\Re_e$ [.] represents real part of complex value inside the square braces. The QAM modulated signal s (t) is obtained by taking the real part of the pre-envelope signal s_+ (t). The Signal is achieved by performing Multiplication between the complex carrier which consists of a cosine and a sine waveform and a complex input.

ADAPTIVE FILTER

Adaptive Filter has its usage in many applications, including the noise cancellation. The coefficients of an FIR filter are modified according to an error signal in order to adapt to a desired signal. Gaussian noise is a statistical noise which has a probability density function (PDF) of the normal Gaussian distribution. In this design we have added Gaussian noise in the SDR system. In this design we have used AWGN as a channel model in which the only impairment during wireless communication is addition of linear white noise or wideband noise with a Gaussian distribution of amplitude and a constant spectral density in watts per Hertz of bandwidth.

Demodulator

The process of recovering the original message from the modulated waveform is accomplished by the FSK demodulator. The VI used for demodulation demodulates an FSK modulated complex baseband waveform and returns the time-aligned demodulated waveform, the demodulated information bit stream, and measurement results obtained during demodulation. This VI attempts to remove the carrier and phase offset by locking to the carrier signal. Samples per symbol specify an even, positive number of samples dedicated to each symbol. Multiply this value by the symbol rate to determine the sample rate.

PSK demodulation is the process of recovering the original message from the information bearing waveform produced by the modulation is accomplished by the demodulator. Demodulates the modulated complex baseband waveform & returns the time aligned oversampled complex waveform, demodulated bit stream. This step attempts to remove carrier & phase offset by locking to the carrier signal. The demodulator used in this design performs the opposite operation of that in the modulator. The demodulator first maps the received band pass waveform into a baseband waveform, and then it recovers the sequence of symbols. Lastly the demodulator recovers the binary digits. It is possible to extract the component in phase by multiplying by a sine (or a cosine) and by a low-pass filter(Marriwala & Sahu, 2013). It involves the multiplication of complex carrier having a negative frequency with the analytic signal obtained from Hilbert Transformer block. The received QAM signal has a complex envelope which can be expressed as

$$\tilde{r}(nT) = r_+(nT)e^{-jw_c nT} = a(nT) + jb\big(nT\big) \tag{6}$$

The decoder is a Viterbi decoder which then solves for the global optimum bit sequence. The algorithm updates a path cost as it steps through each stage of the possible output sequences. At each state, it also calculates the likelihood of entering each possible new state based on the cost of the previous state. The algorithm then needs two additional zero bits after every sequence in order to force the encoder back into the zero state and to assume that the encoder ends at the all zero state(Calderbank, 1984). These two tail bits represent a fractional loss rate between the coded and that of uncoded bit sequence.

Turbo Decoding used in this system works by using a set of maximum aposteriori probability (MAP) decoders. When the data is received, it is deinterleaved back into the three streams which were sent from the transmitter:

1.   Original Data.
2.   Output from Convolutional encoder 1.
3.   Output from Convolutional Encoder 2.

The first MAP decoder takes as an input stream 1 and stream 2 and also the output from MAP decoder 2 (initialized to zeros for the first iteration). The second MAP decoder takes in an interleaved version of stream 2 (the same interleaver used to interleave the original data before it was sent to the Convolutional Encoder), stream 3, and the output from the first MAP Decoder. The two MAP Decoders then work together to converge on a solution: the most likely original bit sequence.

Sync and Tracking VI: Frame Synchronization Mode

The receiver needs to be in Synchronization with the data streams frame structure for it to make any sense of the incoming data stream. This process is referred as frame synchronization. This can be effectively accomplished with the help of some special signaling procedure taken from the transmitter. Frame synchronization is done in the system for grouping different transmitted bits into an alphabet (Marriwala, Sahu, & Vohra, 2015). For achieving the synchronization in the received and the transmitted bits, a similarity measure, is computed between the received samples and the known marker bits consisting of cross-correlation.

In the designed VI we have used a case structure to ensure that only the fourth sample is used for processing as we have seen that the demodulated signal of QAM is decimated by 4 and this structure executes only one case at a time.

Figure 5. Sync and tracking VI – frame synchronization mode

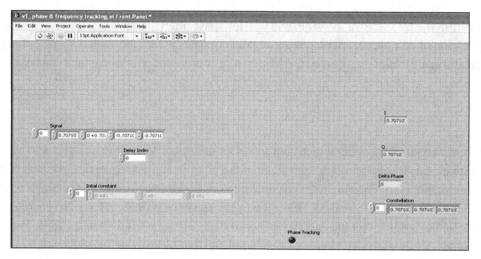

Figure 6. Phase and frequency tracking VI

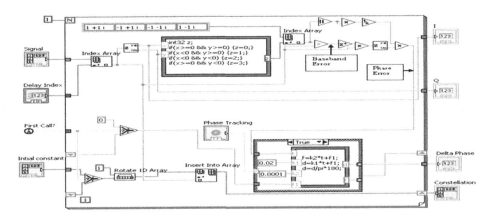

For synchronization of frame and frequency/phase tracking Sync & Tracking VI is used. Synchronization is the act of synchronizing, i.e. concurrence of events with respect to time. Figure 6 shows the block diagram for the same and also shows that the input samples are passed through Complex Queue Pt By Pt, which creates a data queue of complex numbers to obtain a beginning of a frame. A case structure is not executed until the queue is entirely filled. Extra 16 bits are added due to delays related to filtering operations in transmitter. Iinitially the value of the local variable, which is denoted by Sync, is set as true for the execution of the frame synchronization. Later, the value is changed to false so that the value is not invoked again within the case structure. The rest of the two local variables, Delay Index and Initial Const, are utilized as the two inputs in frequency and phase tracking VI module. In this design we have chosen the queue length as 51 so as to include all the marker bits in the queue. This length of the queue is calculated as under: 31[(1 period of PN sequence) + 2×10 (entire frame marker bits)].

Figure 5 depict the sync and tracking VI. In this VI complex cross-correlation is used and the VI for the same is shown in Figure 6. Through the cross-correlation VI maximum index of cross-correlation value is obtained and all data samples are taken at cross-correlation value of the queue. Accordingly, all data bits are synchronized. The cross-correlation between two complex values v and u is given by

$$R_{uv}[j] = \sum_{k=-\infty}^{\infty} \overline{u}[n]v[n+j] \tag{7}$$

Sync, Phase, and Frequency Tracking VI

Sync and Phase and Frequency Tracking module is used to adjust the LO phase needed hence the delay tracking is done at the IF frequency instead of the RF frequency. After this phase estimation is obtained by using complex data phase. Initially the phase estimation is achieved by making use of the phase of the complex data at the initial start of the frame marker bits. The constellation is achieved by real and imaginary parts of data. Local and Global variables are used both of which should contain known data values before the VI runs. The formula node used as a slicer in this design so as to find out the nearest ideal reference by using the quadrant on the I-Q plane as shown in Figure 6.

The phase error is computed from Equation 8. The phase error is multiplied by some scale factor which is small to determine the updated phase $\Delta\phi(n)$ for a second formula node corresponding to Equation 9

$$\Delta\theta(n) = \frac{\Im m\left\{\overline{\tilde{e}(nT)}\tilde{r}(nT)\right\}}{|c_n|^2} \tag{8}$$

When both frequency tracking and phase tracking are considered, the carrier phase for the receiver becomes the updated phase $\Delta\varphi(n)$ and is given by

$$\Delta\varphi(n) = k_1\Delta\theta(n) + \psi(n) \tag{9}$$

where $\psi(n)$ denotes the contribution of frequency tracking, which can be expressed as given in Equation 10

$$\psi(n) = \psi(n-1) + k_2\Delta\theta(n) \tag{10}$$

The scale factors k_1 and k_2 are assumed to be small here and usually $k_1/k_2 \geq 100$ required for phase convergence.

Notwithstanding, with a localized quantity we can correspond to it straight if it is a skillfulness or construe from it alter if it is an indicator.

CONCLUSION

This chapter covers a software-defined radio system built using LabVIEW. A software-defined radio consists of a programmable communication system where functional changes can be made by merely updating software. This chapter has covered emerging software radio standards and the technologies being used to specify and support them. We have proposed expanding the software radio definition and discussed the issues pertaining to design of a Multi-Band Flexible Receiver and a linearised transmitter using broadband quadrature techniques. We have discussed the Case Study with the design of LabVIEW Based Generic Transceiver for Software Defined Radio highlighting the multi modulation approach for the SDR. The design supports Forward Error Correction Codes (FEC) namely Convolution codes and Turbo codes for enhanced security for the data being transmitted. The proposed design is entirely reconfigurable in nature and supports multiple m-ary modulation schemes which can be changed accordingly by the user any time during the runtime. The biggest advantage of this design is that we have used phase tracking for identification of the constellation points. The analysis of the case study proves that Turbo coding gives a much improved and better minimization of the data errors than the Convolution coding.

REFERENCES

Burns. (2002). *Software Defined Radio for 3G*. Artech House.

Calderbank, P. R. (1984). *Technology as Driver of Change in Telecommunications ne Bell System – It Worked The Changing Face of Telecommunications Research*. Academic Press.

Händel, P., & Zetterberg, P. (2010). Receiver I/Q imbalance: Tone test, sensitivity analysis, and the universal software radio peripheral. *IEEE Transactions on Instrumentation and Measurement*, *59*(3), 704–714. doi:10.1109/TIM.2009.2025989

Marriwala, N., Sahu, O. P., & Vohra, A. (2013). 8-QAM Software Defined Radio Based Approach for Channel Encoding and Decoding Using Forward Error Correction. *Wireless Personal Communications*, *72*(4), 2957–2969. doi:10.1007/s11277-013-1191-z

Marriwala, N., Sahu, O. P., & Vohra, A. (2015). Novel Design of a Low Cost Flexible Transceiver Based on Multistate Digitally Modulated Signals Using Wi-Fi Protocol for Software Defined Radio. *Wireless Personal Communications*. doi:10.1007/s11277-015-3052-4

Maskell, D. L., & Vinod, A. P. (2008). *Efficient Multiplierless Channel Filters for Multi-Standard SDR*. Academic Press.

Mitola, I. J. III. (2001). Cognitive Radio for Flexible Mobile Multimedia Communications. *Mobile Networks and Applications*, *6*(5), 435–441. doi:10.1023/A:1011426600077

Mitola, J. (1995). The software radio architecture. *IEEE Communications Magazine*, *33*(5), 26–38. doi:10.1109/35.393001

Mohajer, M., Mohammadi, A., Abdipour, A., & Lo, C. Z. (n.d.). *A Software Defined Radio Direct Conversion Receiver*. Academic Press.

National Instruments Coorporation. (n.d.). *LabVIEW User Manual*. Ni.com.

Osmany, S. A., Herzel, F., & Scheytt, J. C. (2010). *Software-Defined Radio Applications*. Academic Press.

Pursley, M. B., & Royster, T. C. (2008). Low-Complexity Adaptive Transmission for Cognitive Radios in Dynamic Spectrum Access Networks. *IEEE Journal on Selected Areas in Communications*, *26*(1), 83–94. doi:10.1109/JSAC.2008.080108

Ramacher, U., & Ag, I. T. (2007). Software-Defined Radio Prospects for Multistandard Mobile Phones. *IEEE Computer Society Press Los Alamitos, CA, USA*, *40*(10), 62–69. doi:10.1109/MC.2007.362

Rivet, F., Deval, Y., Begueret, J., Dallet, D., & Belot, D. (2007). *A Universal Radio Frequency Receiver Architecture Based on Sampled Analog Signal Processing*. Academic Press.

Schmidt-knorreck, C., Knorreck, D., Knopp, R., & Antipolis, S. (2012). *IEEE 802. Receiver Design for Software Defined Radio Platforms*. doi:10.1109/DSD.2012.76

Selva, A. F. B., Reis, A. L. G., Lenzi, K. G., Meloni, L. G. P., & Barbin, S. E. (2012). *Introduction to the Software-defined Radio Approach*. Academic Press.

Yuce, M. R., Tekin, A., & Liu, W. (2008). Design and performance of a wideband sub-sampling front-end for multi-standard radios. *AEÜ. International Journal of Electronics and Communications*, *62*(1), 41–48. doi:10.1016/j.aeue.2007.02.005

Chapter 5
Design and Analysis of Optical Packet Switch Routers:
A Review

Vaibhav Shukla
Bit Mesra Ranchi, India

Aruna Jain
BIT Mesra Ranchi, India

ABSTRACT

Optical packet switching is connectionless networking solution through which we can get high speed data transfer and optimum bandwidth utilization using wavelength division multiplexing technique. For realizing optical packet switching the numbers of optical packet switch architectures are available in market. In this chapter the authors discuss the overall development of optical packet switching; some recently published optical packet switch architectures are discussed in the chapter and a comparison is performed between the switches through loss, cost and buffer analysis.

INTRODUCTION

The word telecommunication is derived from the Greek word tele + Communication which mean the communication at long distance through signals coming from a transmitter to receiver. For an effective telecommunication system an effective telecommunication medium is also required as a choice of a proper mean of transport, for this the signals has played an important role.

In past historical time, the one of the most common way of generating a signal would be with the help of light and sound. However by using these modes of communication the data transmission were insecure because, no any method of encryption of message is used.

The growth in the telecommunication sector arises in a true means when electricity came in to existence. Here the electromagnetic energy in fact provides an extremely fast data transmission. So we can say that the starting point of all present days telecommunication was the invention of electric cell by Alessandro Volta (1800).

DOI: 10.4018/978-1-5225-1785-6.ch005

After some times more advanced technologies came in to existence in to the field of telecommunication. In 1809, Thomas S. Somnering invented a telegraphic system that composed of a battery, number of wires (35 Approximate) and a group of sensors that are made by gold (Morse, 1840).

As the next advancement, step in 1843 Samuel Morre proposed a way to assign each latter and number to ternary code. This improvement makes the telegraph system more improved and accurate.

The major drawback of telegraph system is that it can be used by only trained people and it works only within a certain building or offices so it can be used by only limited peoples. So due to these drawbacks the research goes in to the other direction and the first big step in this direction was the invention of transducers that are able to transform an acoustic signal in to an electric signal and vice versa with acceptable information loss, in 1850.

After seven year G. Bell independently mange and build a prototype of early telephone machine (Bell, 1876). In telegraph and telephone systems the need of a distributed and reliable communication network soon become obvious. The routing issues in to the network was first solved by human operators and circuit communication, for this the PSTN came in to existence. But the major drawback of this system is that it did not guarantee the privacy and confidentiality of conversation.

With the last step, we have seen that the electronics is a fundamental part in the telecommunication field, at the first in the field of transmission, and soon this is used in the circuit communication also.

In the starting days of 1938 a new technology says PCM (Pulse Code Modulation) came in to existence and by using this technology the digital transmission of a voice signal by digital coding and decoding is achieved. The PCM was first used on a large scale in 1962 in United State. In the mid sixties the Paul Baron an employee of RAND Corporation gives the concept of packet switching network. According to this model the data is divided in to the small size units called the packets and each packet contains bulk of data, each packet is divided in to two parts header and payload the header contains the routing information of each packet and body contains the data that is to be transmitted.

In the starting 70's the Vincent Cerf, Bob Kahn and team developed, TCP/IP protocol suit, through which a communication of computers and heterogeneous machines through a series of physical and logical layers. The packet switching network and TCP/IP were chosen by military project ARPANET.

As the time passes the demand of higher bandwidth and fast speed network is required so in order to meet these requirements the concept of optical fiber communication came in to existence.

EVOLUTION OF OPTICAL FIBER COMMUNICATION SYSTEM

The development of fiber optic technology provided the medium through which transmission of light is possible. As the name shows, this type of communication system uses optical waves that carries signals, the bit rate distance product can be improved in optical fiber several orders of magnitude as compared to the microwave and coaxial system.

In this section the year wise growth of optical communication system is discussed. In early 1880 Alexander Graham Bell and his assistant created a photo phone which is first invention in fiber optic communication. This devise allowed transmission of sound on a beam of light. In 1880 Bell invented first wireless telephone system which is used to transmit signals between the two buildings. Due to its use of atmospheric transmission medium, the photo phone is not used practically until advancement in laser and optical fiber technology permits secure transmission of light. The photo phones are used in the military system after many years.

In 1954 Harold Hopkins and N.S. Kapany shows that light to be transmitted in to rolled fiber glass. Initially this was considered that light traverse only in the straight medium. In optical communication industry the crucial innovation are made by Van Heel, who covered a bare fiber with a transparent cladding of lower refractive index. By this the total reflection surface is protected from contamination, and crosstalk between fiber is greatly reduces.

In 1960, an attenuation of about 1dB/m occurs in glass clad fibers, which is good for medical imaging, but too high for communication.

In 1966 C.K. Kao and G Hock ham proposed an optical fiber at STC Lab, England, when they showed that the loss of 1,000dB/km in existing glass was due to the contaminants, which could potentially be removed.

In 1970 the fully developed version of optical fiber came in to existence with low attenuation which may be acceptable for communication purpose, the semiconductor lasers was developed at the same time, that were compact in size and that's why they are suitable for transmitting light through fiber optic cables for long distance communication.

After a period of time and after heavy research in 1975 the first commercial fiber optic communication came in to existence, which was operated at a wavelength of around 0.8μm and uses GaAs semiconductor lasers.

The most suitable media that are used as the carrier in there optical communication is optical fibers which were proposed in 1966 (Hecht, 1999; Agrawal, 1999; Lucky, 1999). However the common problems in these systems are extremely high loss present in this system. This problem challenged researcher and engineers to find processes through which low loss fiber could be invented. Finally in 1978 this problem was solved when optical fiber having acceptable attenuation was first invented.

The combination of advancement in semiconductor technology and low loss optical fiber made optical fiber communication system practically possible. The first system was commercially deployed in 1978 (Alexander, 1997). The whole optical fiber development is divided in to their different generations which are further discussed in to the subsections of this chapter.

OPTICAL NETWORK

The development of optical communication network took place in to different steps and they are classified in to different generations. On the basis of overall technology development the optical network is divided in to five different generations each of the generation has its own limitations which are improved in to the next generation.

First Generation Optical Network

In the first generation optical network only point to point connection between the links are possible (Agrawal, 1999). In this generation the cooper and coaxial cables are replaced by fiber cables and the switching and processing functions are performed electronically. The examples of first generation optical networks are SONET (Synchronous optical network); SDH (Synchronous digital hierarchy) and FDDI (Fiber distributed data interface).cIn general we can say that in first generation optical network the copper cables are replaced by optical fiber cables. However there are some important differences in the use of copper and fiber cables.

- Since we all know that the optical devises are much more expensive in comparison to electronic devices, so it is important to optimize the use of optical network resources.
- A number of optical signals at different carrier wavelengths may be simultaneously carried by the same fiber,
- The major difference between the optical and electronic network is that the speed at which the optical signals may be communicated is far superior in comparison to the speed at which data can be processed by electronic circuits.

Second Generation Optical Network

In second generation optical network some of the switching and routing functions are performed optically that are performed electronically in the first generation. In the second generation network the WDM (Wavelength Division Multiplexing) technology is used to divide the huge bandwidth provided by the fiber cable in the multiple wavelength channels, which can be used to support multiple transmissions simultaneously (Agrawal, 1999; Handerson, 2001). The one of the most common service in the second generation network is light path service. In the light path connection a dedicated connection is established on a wavelength between two nodes in to the network, in such a way that no electronic conversation is possible on the path between these two nodes. The some of the issues involved in second generation optical network is the development issues of OADM, wavelength convertor, routing etc.

Third Generation Optical Network

The third generation optical communication system was operated at 1.55μm and they faces loss of about 0.2 dB/km. The third generation optical network supports the connectionless optical network. In this generation any input is expected to connect to any output by just configuring the correct state of optical switches (Handerson, 2001).

Fourth Generation

In the fourth generation optical communication the use of optical amplifier came in to existence which reduces the need of repeaters and WDM technologies to increase data capacity. By overall development in this generation a bit rate of 10 Tb/S is achieved in 2001 (Feng, 2015). These two improvements caused a revolution that resulted in the doubling of system capacity every six months starting in 1992 until a bit rate of 10 Tb/s was reached by 2001. In 2006 a bit-rate of 14 Tbit/s was reached over a single 160 km line using optical amplifiers.

Fifth Generation

The focus of development for the fifth generation of fiber-optic communications is on extending the wavelength range over which a WDM system can operate. The conventional wavelength window, known as the C band, covers the wavelength range 1.53-1.57 μm, and dry fiber has a low-loss window promising an extension of that range to 1.30-1.65 μm. The concepts of optical solitions are used in the fifth generation optical communication. At the end of June 2014 Huawei shared fifth generation opti-

Figure 1. Year wise groath in optical network

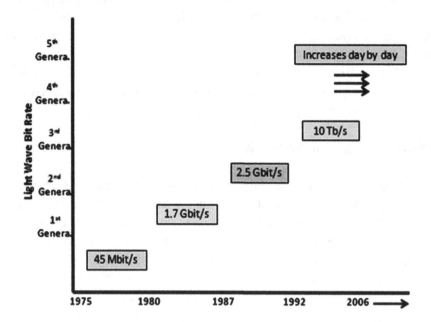

cal network concept at the next generation optical network forum in Nice, France. The fifth generation optical network architecture will direct the industry in to a bright future (Feng, 2015).

OPTICAL SWITCHING TECHNOLOGY

For the next generation optical transport technology the optical switching can be broadly divided in to the three categories optical circuit switching, optical burst switching and optical packet switching technology. The circuit and burst switching technology is used for many years in the voice and data communication. In this chapter we discuss optical packet switching technology in details.

Optical Circuit Switch Network (OCSN)

In optical circuit switching technology, before data transmission a light path is established between the source and the destination (Waheed, 2011). In OCS technology the processing of header by intermediate nodes are not required and buffering of payload is also not required in the OCS system.

Optical Burst Switch Network (OBSN)

For providing the balance between the optical packet switching and optical burst switching the optical burst switching system can be used. OBS system combines the advantages of both OCS and OPS technology. In OBS system the data is divided in to various size units, called burst which is the basic switching entity in OBS. In OBS system before transmission in the network the data is collected and form a large burst. This process removes the switching overhead of multiple packets. In OBS system since the size of burst is considered variable, so the OBS network seems to be lying between OPS and OCS network (Waheed, 2011).

Optical Packet Switch Network (OPSN)

The optical packet switching is the best available option for transferring data in optical network. OPS allow statistical sharing of wavelengths among packets that belongs to different source and destination combination. In OPS when packet arrives, the header is removed from payload and then converts the header in to electronic domain by using optical/ electrical converter and then the header is processed electronically (Ramaswami, Sivarajan, & Sasaki, 2009). Then after this the switching fabric is reconfigured, this happen on the basis of information exist in the header of packet. Since this is a time taking process so the payload at the input port is delayed. At the output port of switch the header is again converted in to optical domain with the help of electrical to optical convertor, and after this the header is assembled with payload in to a new optical packet.

There are number of problems in the deployments of optical packet switches. The packet switching requires a large buffer for storing the delayed or contended packets. Because of hardware limitations packet switching in optical domain is not yet possible. For implementing high buffering the optical RAMs are not practically available in the market. The best available option for implementing buffering in OPS system is use of fiber delay lines but the FDL stores packets for only in limited time. The length of each optical packet, in terms of the product of its transmission time and the speed of light, cannot exceed that of the available FDL in which the optical packets to be stored.

Comparison between OCSN, OBSN, and OPSN

In the further sub section of this chapter the optical packet switching technology is discussed in detailed the number optical packet switch architectures are also discussed in the chapter and an attempt has been made to perform a fair comparison between these switches.

PHOTONIC PACKET SWITCHING

As the day by day demand of internet traffic increases, the demand of high throughput, and high data transfer rate is also increases. The optical packet switching is the best available option that provides a data transfer speed up to terabit per second. Through optical packet switch network we can achieve high data transfer rate, high bandwidth utilization and high throughput hence we can say that the optical packet switching is a next generation high speed data transfer technology. The realization of optical packet switched network is possible through switches which may be optical or can be electronic in nature. By using these switches the packets are routed towards its correct destination port. The designs of optical switches are a major issue in optical network. There are number of optical packet switch architectures are available in the market. In these switches because of non feasibility of optical processor the control operations are performed through electronic controller while on the other hand the data transmission is performed in optical domain. This hybrid electronic and optical approach is referred as photonic technology. The Figure 2 shows a generic layout of photonic packet switch technology. The key function (Jajszczyk & Mouftah, 1993; Tucker & Zhong, 1999) which affects the operation and realization of switch are:

Figure 2. Generic photonic packet switches
Source: (Tucker & Zhong, 1999).

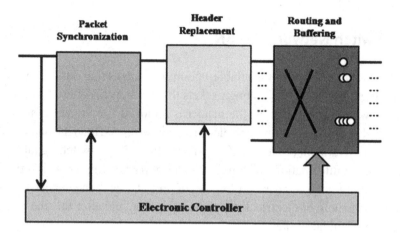

- Control,
- Packet Routing,
- Packet Synchronization, and
- Contention resolution strategies these functions are further discussed in subsections.

Control

The control unit is an important part of the switch which is used to maintain routing database. By using control unit searching in routing database is performed, decision of the outgoing port for a packet is taken and various components of the switch are configured in such a way that packet can be forwarded towards its appropriate output port in appropriate time.

Packet Routing

In each switch the distributed and centralized algorithms are used in the routing table. In the centralized control method a single processor is used to monitor the whole network. On the other hand if the network is large and can be formed by using more and more switches, then in this case the centralized controlling is not the best available option because by using this latency increases, throughput degraded and processing complexity are also increases in the switch. So for resolving these issues a distributed controlling is used in which the packet is processed independently at each node of the network. By using this type of processing the burden on the centralized processor reduces and by using this throughput of the switched network increases. There is another option, to use the hybrid technology by which we can utilize the advantages of both techniques very well.

Packet Synchronization

Whenever the optical switches are combined in to a centralized or distributed network (Franzen, Hunter, & Andonovic, 1998) the synchronization is an important parameter that must be taken into consideration.

The whole optical network is categorized in to two parts first is slotted (synchronous) and the other is unslotted (asynchronous). In the network designing phase this is difficult to decide whether all the input packets are aligned before they enter in to the switch fabric. In each case, the bit level synchronization and very fast clock recovery is required for packet header recognition and packet delineation. The packets in the slotted networks are of same size. These are combined together with header and formed a fixed time slot. The total duration of the slot is managed in such a way that it is longer than the total duration of packet. This provides a sufficient guard band between neighboring packets. In most of the cases the, optical buffering is implemented by using fiber delay lines or by using propagation delay either equal to or multiple of time slot duration. This generates a requirement that all packets received at input port of switch should have the same size and by using local clock reference they must be aligned in time slot boundary. The size of arriving packets in an unslotted network may or may not have same. In this case packets arrive and enter in to the switch without using any type of frame alignment. Hence, in this case the contention among packets occurs more frequently because the behaviors of incoming packets are more irregular. The buffering of packets in this network are more complex (Yao, Mukherjee, & Dixit, 2000).

Contention Resolution

The contention is one of the key issues in the case of optical switch network system. The situation of contention arises when two or more packets try to live the switch at the same time and for the same output port. To re-solve contention among packets, in OPS three approaches (Yao, Mukherjee, & Dixit, 2003) (alone or in combinations) seems to be viable:

1.   Use deflection routing (space dimension),
2.   Provide optical buffering by implementing the fiber delay lines (time dimension), and/or
3.   Exploit the wavelength domain and use wavelength conversion (wavelength dimension).

Wavelength Conversion

In a wavelength conversion method, if two or more than two packets, with same wavelengths arrive at the same output port then in this case the wavelength of all except one of the packet is changed in to the other wavelength and by doing this wavelength conversion process the situation of contention is re-solved. By wavelength conversion process some highly desirable properties are achieved some of them are that it does not commence the delay in the data path and in this method the sequencing of packets are not required.

Deflection Routing

The deflection routing is another method which is used to resolve the situation of contention among packets. In this method the route of all the other contending packets are deflected except one, and hence the packets are deflected towards the different output port other than the one requested, the one situation may arise that the packets may follow longer route to reach their destination so this method introduces the delays in the data path and packets may arrive out of order.

Optical Buffering

The optical buffering is one of the most effective methods for resolving the output port contention. In this method if the situation of contention arises among the packets then only one of the packets, which feel contention, is routed through the switch fabric, while all the other packets are routed towards the fiber delay lines, which are used as the optical storage for the contending packets. The optical buffering can be implemented at the input, output or shared manner within the switch.

Input Buffering

In this scheme (Figure 3), a separate buffer is used at each input port of the switch and each of the incoming packets temporarily enters in to buffer unit. In the case if buffer is vacant, output port is free and none of the packet exist in to other buffer (buffer available at other inputs) for that particular output port, then in this situation incoming packet will be forwarded towards the appropriate output and on the other hand if the buffer is not empty, then it will be placed in the buffer and will leave the buffer such that FIFO (First in First output) queue can be maintained for each output port of switch. In the input queuing process head on blocking exist and highest achievable throughput is only 0.586 (Hluchy & Karol, 1988).

Output Buffering

In output buffering process (Figure 4), a separate buffer exists at each output port of the switch and each of the arriving packets are transferred towards appropriate output port and will be processed such that FIFO can be maintained. In the output queuing method internal blocking does not occurs. Therefore, large throughput is achievable (Mishra & Jain, 2015).

Shared Buffering

To design a cost effective buffering technique a shared buffer is used in which the packets for all output ports can be stored in to the common shared buffer. In this case of shared buffering scheme the hardware complexity is low and high throughput is achievable (Arpaci & Copeland, 2009).

Figure 3. Input buffering scheme

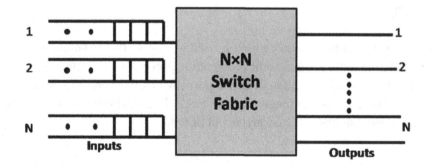

Figure 4. Output buffering scheme

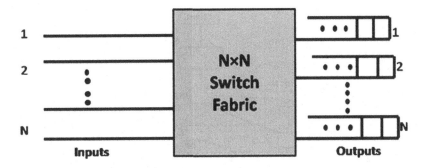

Figure 5. Shared buffering scheme

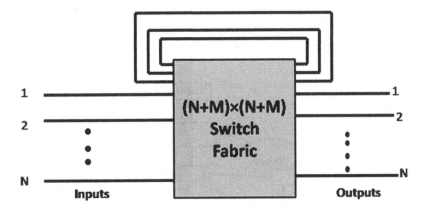

Schematic of OPS network with output buffer at each node is shown in Figure 6. Here, at each node with '*N*' input and output links a maximum of '*BN*' contending packets and for each output '*B*' packets can be stored separately(Yao, Mukherjee, & Dixit, 2000).

In Figure 7, schematic of the OPS network is presented with a shared buffer at each node. Here, at each node with 'N' input and output links we can store a maximum of 'B' contending packets in a shared manner.

It is clear from above discussion that the design of OPS node is very important; in the next section a review of OPS node switch design is presented.

DIFFERENT COMPONENTS USED IN OPTICAL SWITCHES

There are number of optical components are used in the realization of optical switches the some of the components which are frequently used in the design of switch are discussed in this section.

- **Splitter and Combiner:** The splitter and combiner are two devises which are used in opposite meaning of work. The splitter is used to divide the input signals in to equal parts and on the other hand the combiner is used to combine the n equal signals in to single one. These splitter and com-

Figure 6. Schematic of OPS network with output buffer at each node

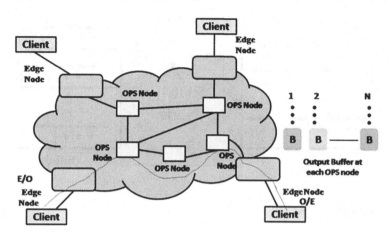

Figure 7. Schematic of OPS network with shared buffer at each node

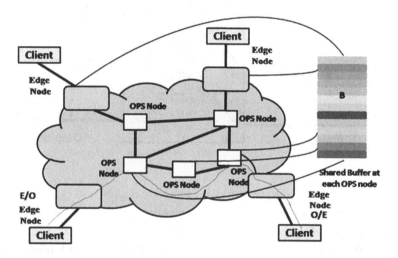

biner both are wavelength insensitive devises. The total insertion loss of splitter and combiner are large and this is approximately equal to the $10(\log_{10} N)dB$. These two devises are commonly used for broadcasting the optical signals.

- **Multiplexer and De-Multiplexer:** The multiplexer and De-multiplexer are two devises that are used to combine and separate the light signals at different wavelengths. The Demux and Mux both are wavelength sensitive devises and used in opposite nature.

- **Tunable Filters:** The tunable filters are used to select or reject the particular wavelength. The optical filters are worked on the principle of interferometer the tunable filter can be tuned to any wavelength in the allowed range of filters.

- **Tunable Wavelength Convertors:** The tunable wavelength convertor is a devise which is used to convert the one wavelength in to the other wavelength.

- **Isolator and Circulator:** An isolator is an electronic devise which is used to allow the transmission of signals only in one direction and it blocks the transmission in other direction. The two key parameters of isolators are the insertion loss of devise which is the loss in forward direction; this loss should be as small as possible.

- The circulators are special type of isolators which has more than two ports. The signal flows in one direction; in circulators.
- **Optical Amplifiers:**
  - **Semiconductor Optical Amplifier:** For amplification of optical signals the semiconductor optical amplifier is used. The size of semiconductor optical amplifier is very compact so this is one of the advantages of SOA. The SOA is very easy in use and can be easily implemented with other optical devises. The switching speed of SOA is in order of few ns. The SOA can also used as gate switch. The some of the major disadvantages of SOA are that it introduces crosstalk, it introduces the high noise figures and SOAs are polarization independent devises.
  - **Erbium Dropped Fiber Amplifier:** The invention of Erbium Dropped Fiber Amplifier (EDFA) was a great achievement in the optical communication. The EDFA amplify the signals in the optical domain so optical / electrical and electrical/ optical conversions of signals are not required. A piece of fiber is present in the EDFA, and the core of fiber piece is doped with erbium ions. In the EDFA a strong beam of laser light with proper wavelength is used as pump, is propagated in to the fiber which is used to excite the erbium ions and created population inversion. By this the amplified light is produced at the output of amplifier due to the stimulated emission. The some of the advantages of EDFA are that it produces the high gain, it introduces low noise figures, no distortion at high bit rate; on the other hand some of the disadvantages of EDFA includes dynamic controlling is required in EDFA, pump laser is necessary in EDFA and it is very difficult to integrate the EDFA with other components.

SWITCH ARCHITECTURE

The Figure 8 shows a block diagram of generic optical packet switch node architecture (Reza & Lim, 2011). The figure shows that the architecture contains set of Demux and Mux, input and output interfaces, optical buffers, wavelength converters, and a switch control unit which is used to perform the control operations of switch. In the ops node architecture first of all Demux present at each input, demultiplexed the wavelength of incoming packets in to individual wavelengths and then they are forwarded towards input interface. Each of the transmitted packet is divided in to two parts first is header which contains the addressing information and the second part is the payload which contains the actual information which is being transmitted. The input interface extracts the optical packet header and forwarded it towards the switch control unit for processing. Here in the switch control unit the header information is processed, and determine the correct output port and wavelength of packet, and gives instruction to the switch fabric to route the packet properly. In routing of packet, the switch may need to buffer it and/or convert it to a new wavelength. The switch organizer also determines a novel header for the packet, and forwards it to the output interface. When the packet arrives at the output interface, the new header is attached, and the packet is forwarded on the outgoing fiber link to the next node in its path.

A wide variety of switch architectures are available in the case of optical packet switched network system. In general we can classify the switches in to number of categories some of them are as follows:

Figure 8. Generic OPS node architecture
Source: (Reza & Lim, 2011).

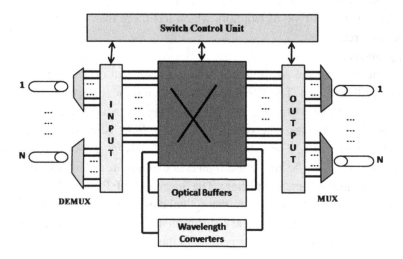

1. Space switch architecture,
2. Broadcast and select type architecture,
3. AWG based optical packet switches.

In the following subsections we discuss the switch which falls in these three categories.

Space Switch Architecture

The Figure 9 shows a schematic diagram of $N \times N$ space switch architecture (Glance, 1993). The whole switch is divided in to three unit's optical packet encoder, space switch and the optical packet buffer. The very first unit optical packet encoder works as follows, there is an optical demultiplexer which is used to divide the incoming signals in to W wavelengths. Each of these wavelengths is feed in to the TWC which converts the wavelengths in to the wavelength which are available free in to the destination optical buffer. Then with the help of space switch fabric, optical packet can be switched in to any of N output optical buffers. The splitter which is used just after TWC, then distribute same signal in to N different output fiber, one per output buffer. Each of the output fiber coming from splitter is connected with one of the fiber delay lines of destination output buffer through optical gates. The optical gates are used to forward optical packets towards the FDL this is done by keeping one optical gate open and closed rest of the gates.

Broadcast and Select Type Architecture

The Figure 10 shows broadcast and select type optical packet switch architecture. The whole switch is divided in to three blocks wavelength encoder, buffer and wavelength selector. The switch has N input and output port and D fiber delay lines are used to store the packets in such a way that each input can be delayed for an integer multiple of time slots T, up to DT (Guillemot, 1998). The first block of switch (wavelength encoder) contains N FWCs (Fixed wavelength convertors) at each input port of switch fol-

Figure 9. Spaces switch architecture (A1)

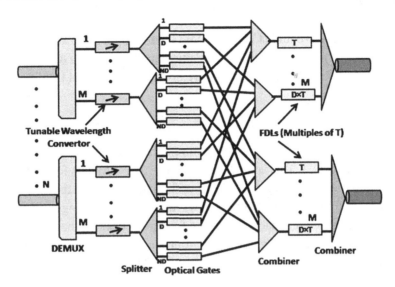

Figure 10. Broadcast and select switch architecture (A2)

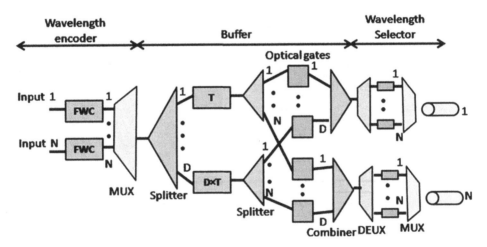

lowed by a multiplexer. The second block (buffer block) contains splitter, D fiber delay lines, optical gates and combiners. Finally the last block (wavelength selector) contains the Mux, Demux and optical gates.

In the starting time slot the wavelength of incoming packets are converted in to the fixed wavelength, through the wavelength convertor available in the wavelength encoder block. These fixed wavelengths are feed in to the multiplexer and wavelengths are converted in to the single wavelength this single wavelength is distributed in to the D fiber delay lines through a splitter. Each of the FDL has its own delay which is an integer multiple of slots. That means to say that FDL I has delay of I slots. The N optical packets are stored in to D different FDLs. In the starting of next time slot, a maximum of $D \times N$ optical packets exited from D FDLs and up to N of them are forwarded towards the destination output ports. This is achieved with the help of the combination of splitter, optical gates, demultiplexer and multiplexer. A control unit is used in to this broadcast and select switch which controls the operations of switch.

AWG Based Optical Packet Switches

There are number of Arrayed Waveguide Gratings (AWG) based optical packet switch architectures are available in the market (Li, Scott, & Deogun, 2003; Pattavina, 2005; Shukla & Srivastava, 2015). Some of the recently published AWG based architectures are discussed under this heading.

Feedback Architecture

The architecture shown in figure is feedback architecture (Chia, Hunter, Andonovic, Ball, Wright, Ferguson, Guild, & O'Mahony, 2001). This architecture uses two AWG routers for routing the packets, and shared FDL for buffering the contending packets. At each input of switch, tunable wavelength convertors are presents and these TWC are used to tune the wavelength of incoming packets as per the routing pattern of AWG router; the contending packets are then forwarded towards the recirculating buffer while the straight through packets are routed towards the appropriate output port. In the buffer another AWG is used that route the buffered packets in to appropriate direction. The problem faces by this architecture are:

1. Exit time contention may occur in this architecture.
2. Control unit complexity is high in this switch.

AWG Based Switch Architecture without Buffer

The Figure 12 shows an AWG based switch that contains a $k \times k$ AWG router for avoiding the wavelength collision at the output port of AWG the switch uses Tunable Wavelength Convertors (TWC) at the input

Figure 11. Feedback AWG and FDL based switch (A3)
Source: (Chia et al., 2001).

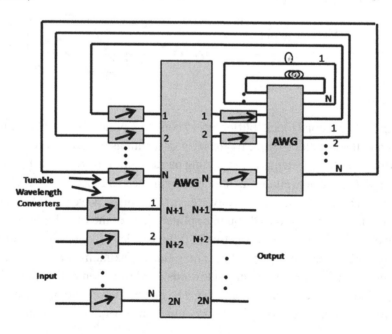

Figure 12. AWG based switch without buffer (A4)

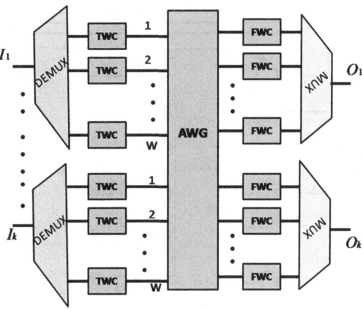

port side and FWC at the output port side (Kang, Han, Yang, So, & Kim, 2007). Whenever a burst arrives at the input whose destined output is O_i, then first check that the wavelength free at output O_i, and then if the wavelength is available free then burst is forwarded towards O_i by converting it in to available wavelength otherwise the burst is dropped.

Hybrid FDL Buffering Switch Architecture

The figure shows hybrid optical packet switch architecture (Stephen, Scott, & Deogun, 2003) which contains 2 AWG based architectures and set of TWCs as a core of switch. In this switch the wavelength routing approach is used, in which TWC and AWG works as the core part of switch. The wavelength routing switch improves there noise performance as wavelength convertor regenerates the signals. By introducing the wavelength conversion the complexity of switch is reduced in to great extent because of static configuration of AWG. At each I/O port a set of fiber delay lines are used as used in the WASPNET switch. As by using more fiber delay lines the buffering capacity of switch increases. The some of the features of switch architecture are:

1. Priority routing is used in the switch.
2. In this switch small numbers of AWGs are used so crosstalk and noise of switch reduces.
3. The system recourses and cost are reduced as the required number of wavelength is reduced.

Note that the above hybrid FDL architecture has unit length feedback FDLs, which means once a packet is sent into a fiber loop; it will come back to some input port at the next time slot. We instead use feedback FDLs with different lengths to accommodate more packets. To make the feedback FDLs more powerful, we can also give each output port a set of FDLs as the WASPNET switch did.

Figure 13. Hybrid optical packet switches (A5)

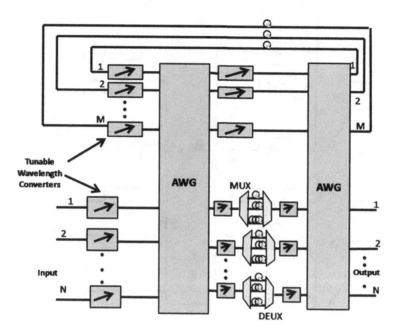

Feed Forward and Feedback AWG Based Switch

Chia et al. in 2001 proposed a feed forward and a feed backward AWG based optical switch design (Yao, Mukherjee, & Dixit, 2003). The Figure 14 shows a feed forward AWG switch architecture. In this switch design two AWG routers are used to route the incoming packets. The TWC is used at each input of switch that converts the wavelength of incoming packets and facilitates switching to correct output of first AWG router. The two AWG routers in the switch are connected with fiber delay lines through TWC and fiber delay lines lies parallel between Demux and Mux. Here the TWC present just before the second AWG router converts single wavelength at a time, hence the fiber entering in the second AWG carries no more than one wavelength channel. The controller in the switch must control the operation and does not allow multiplexer to leave more than one packet at once.

The Figure 15 shows a shared feedback delay lines based optical switch architecture (Chia et al., 2001). Here in this architecture a *2N×2N* AWG router is used for routing the packets, at input port of switch the tunable wavelength convertors are used to convert the wavelengths of incoming packets as per the routing pattern of AWG router first of all packets are converted in to appropriate wavelengths and if packet feels contention then AWG router forwarded this packet in the direction of FDL lines for buffering purpose otherwise the packet is forwarded towards its destined output port. In the loop buffer all multiplexer allows only one packet to exit at a time, no more than one packet allows to exit from the combination of FDL, Demux and Mux present in each buffer module. The advantage of this architecture is that it implements priority routing effectively.

Figure 14. A feed forward AWG based switch (A6)

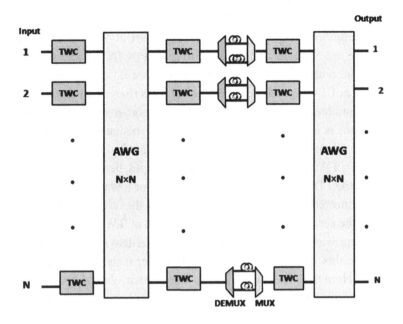

Figure 15. A feedback AWG based switch (A7)

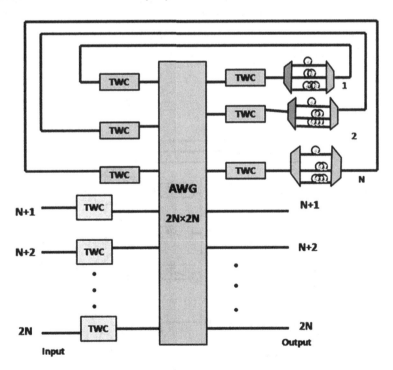

Waspnet Project: Wavelength Routed Switch

Hunter proposed a wavelength routing switch, which is the part of WASPNET project (Hunter et al., 1999). In this switch there are N inputs and output ports, total of 4N tunable wavelength converters, a 2N × 2N wavelength router and an N×N wavelength router is used as shown in the Figure 16. Hence we can say that the number of TWC and hardware requirements rises in this switch linearly with respect to N while on the other hand the hardware requirements in the other switches rises quadratically. Since each of the fiber delay lines is not associated with the output so shared buffer is used in the proposed switch, here buffering for all output packets are possible in this design. Since the wavelength of each input packet is converted by TWC as per the requirement of output, hence first wavelength router; switch the packet either towards the FDL lines for buffering purpose or towards the second router. The first N ports of first router are connected with the fiber delay lines and the other N+1 to 2N ports are connected with the input TWC and the second router through another set of TWC.

In this switch to prevent wavelength contention each packet leaving a plane must have the correct wavelength. To implement this, an additional wavelength router is used which has TWC at every input (O'Mahony, Simeonidou, Hunter, & Tzanakaki, 2001). The first wavelength router forwarded each packet towards the input of second router, which forwarded the packets in the direction of correct output port.

AWG Based Loop Buffer Switch

In this architecture the output port of the switch are directly connected with the buffer unit of switch as shown in Figure 17 (Verma, Srivastava, & Singh, 2002). In this switch a separate AWG Demux is used for separating buffer wavelengths and for combining them an AWG Mux is used. In each branch of buffer AWG two SOA gates (SOA-1 and SOA-2) are used. Here SOA-1 is used as a gate between two buffer

Figure 16. WASPNET project (A8)

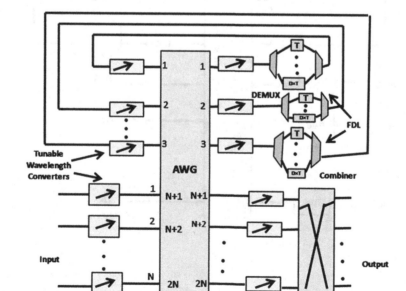

AWGs (AWG-1 and AWG-2) while on the other hand SOA-2 acts as agate switch between AWG-1 and a B×1 AWG. In the switch the TWC present at each input of switch converts the wavelength of incoming packets; by using same wavelengths the packets are circulating in to the loop buffer of switch, at the same time the SOA-1 present in the buffer is at ON state while the SOA-2 is at OFF state this happens until this is desired to read out a packet from the buffer. On the other hand if we want to remove the packets from the buffer then the SOA-1 is switched OFF and SOA-2 is switched ON and by doing this the packet is forwarded towards the output AWG. Here all the packets are appearing at the one port of AWG. The multiplexed signals are allowed to pass through the splitter and tunable filters are used to select the particular wavelength which is placed in each branch of splitter.

WDM AWG Based Optical Router

In this switch fiber loop modules are uses for storing the contending packets. The whole architecture is divided in to two sections scheduling and switching sections as shown in Figure 18, the scheduling section of switch uses a *2N×2N* AWG router. The tunable wavelength convertors are uses at each input of switch which are used to convert the wavelength of incoming packets as per the routing pattern of first AWG router, the first scheduling section AWG forwarded all the contended packets towards the fiber delay lines for buffering purpose, on the other hand straight through packets are forwarded towards the appropriate output port. In the switching section there are *N* TWCs are presents and an *N×N* AWG router route the packets towards the appropriate output port. In this switch architecture SOA (Semiconductor Optical Amplifier) can be placed in each input just after input TWC and just before the scheduling AWG router. Here, the loss of the loop as well as the loss of the directly transmitted packets can be simultaneously fully compensated by the gain of the corresponding SOA (Shukla, Jain, & Srivastava, 2014; Srivastava & Singh, 2010). Here the whole switch is controlled by an electronic controller first the controller check the header of each packet that contains the addressing information of each packet then controller decided whether to place the packet in to the buffer or forwarded straight towards the output port of the switch. On the basis of this analysis the SOA at the input tunes and compensating the loss of each packets.

Figure 17. AWG based loop buffer switch (A9)

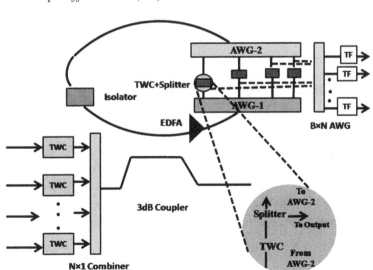

Figure 18. Design of AWG based optical switch (A10)

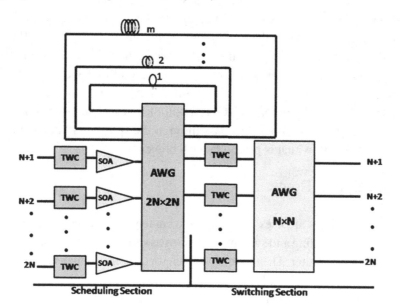

AWG Based Router

The Figure 19 shows an AWG based switched architecture proposed by H. Rastegarfar. Here a *2N×2N AWG* router is used for routing the incoming packets. The TWC present at each input of switch convert the wavelength of incoming packets as per the routing pattern of AWG. The upper N port of AWG is connected with the fiber delay lines and the other N ports are connected with the actual output port through another set of TWCs present at each output line. In the case if the situation of contention among packets arise The AWG routes these contended packets in the direction of fiber delay lines for buffering purpose. In buffer a semiconductor optical amplifier (SOA) is present at each FDL lines which are used to amplify the buffered packets. Each SOA in buffer is followed by tunable filters to limit the wideband ASE noise they generate. The TWC present in each FDL line again converted the wavelength of buffered packets as per the routing pattern of AWG. Finally a set of TF and TWC is used at each output port of switch which is used to destine the packets to corresponding output port.

LOSS ANALYSIS OF OPTICAL PACKET SWITCHES

There are some losses present in any fiber optic interconnection. The insertion loss of a connector or splice is defined as the difference in power that you see when you insert devise in to the system. For example, take a length of fiber and measure the optical power through the fiber. Note the reading (P1). Now cut the fiber in half, terminate the fibers and connect them, and measure the power again. Note the second reading (P2). The difference between the first reading (P1) and the second (P2) is the insertion loss, or the loss of optical power that occurs when you insert the connector into the line. This is measured as:

Figure 19. AWG based router (A11)

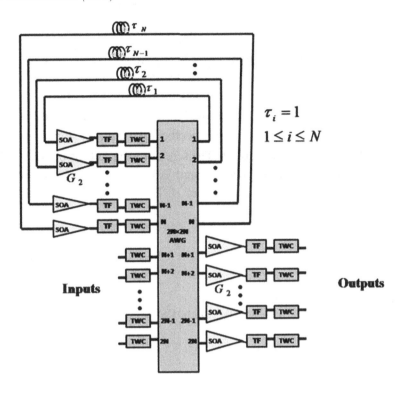

$$IL(dB) = 10 \log 10\left(\frac{P2}{P1}\right)$$

The specified insertion loss is for identical fibers.

If the core diameter (or the NA) of the side that transmits data is larger than the NA of the fiber that receives data, there is additional loss.

$$L_{dia} = 10 \log 10\left(\frac{diar}{diat}\right)^2$$

$$L_{NA} = 10 \log 10\left(\frac{NAr}{NAt}\right)^2$$

Here,

L_{dia} =Loss diameter,
L_{dir} =Loss received,
diat = diameter transmit,
LNA = Loss on optical fiber.

Additional loss can occur from Fresnel reflections. These occur when two fibers are separated so that a discontinuity exists in the refractive index. For two glass fibers separated by an air gap, Fresnel reflections are 0.32 dB.

In this section the physical layer analysis of all switches are performed and the authors of chapter calculated the total physical loss of each switch presented in this chapter. The physical loss is considered as the insertion loss of each devise used in the design of switch. The total physical loss of the switch is calculated by calculating the loss of all devises needed to realize the switch and total loss of switch is represented by L_T. The physical loss is calculated in decibel (dB) unit. The typical values of the parameters used in the calculation are shown in Table 1. The size of the packets as per the KEOPS projects as of 1.646μs as in KEOPS project, the minimum loop length is $1.646 \times 10^{-6} \times 3 \times 10^8$ i.e. 493.8 m. For a 32x32 input AWG, the maximum possible buffer modules are 16. These values are the standard loss values of different devises used in the design of switch.

Loss of switch A1:

$$L_T^{A1} = L_{Demux}L_{TWC}L_{Splitter}L_{OpticalGates}L_{Combiner}L_{Combiner} \tag{1}$$

After inserting the loss values of different devises in Equation 1 the total physical loss of switch is presented by Equation 2

$$A_T^{A} = 25.6dB \tag{2}$$

Loss of switch A2:

$$A_T^{A_2} = L_{FWC}L_{Mux}L_{Splitter}L_{Splitter}L_{OpticalGates}L_{Combiner}L_{Demux}L_{OpticalGates}L_{Mux} \tag{3}$$

Table 1. Comparison between OCSN, OBSN and OPSN

Types of WDM Network	Bandwidth Utilization	Latency	Optical Buffer	Proc/Sync Overhead	Adaptivity
OCSN	Low	High	Not Required	Low	Low
OPSN	High	Low	Required	High O/E/O is required at each node	High
OBSN	High	Low	Not Required	Low	High

Table 2. Comparison of different contention resolution techniques

Contention Resolution	Advantages	Disadvantages
Wavelength Conversion	The most efficient solution	Immature and very much expensive.
Optical Buffering	Simple in design	Increases end to end delay of packets
Deflection Routing	Extra hardware is not required in design	Packets arrive out of order.

Table 3. Value of different loss parameters

Symbol	Parameter	Value
N	Size of the switch	4
B	Size of the Buffer	4
L_{TWC}	TWC insertion loss	2.0 dB
$L_{AWG}^{2N \times 2N}$ $L_{AWG}^{N \times N}$	Loss of Scheduling and Switching AWG (32 channels)	3.0 dB
L_{FDL}	Loss of the fiber loop	0.2 dB/km
L_{3dB}	Loss of 3dB Coupler	3.0 dB
$L_{Com}^{N \times 1}$	Loss of Combiner	$10(\log_{10} N)dB$
$L_{circulator}$	Loss of circulator	1dB
L_{BPF}	Loss of Band pass Filter	1dB
$L_{3R \, Re generator}$	Loss of 3R regenerator	2dB
$L_{Splitter}^{N \times 1}$	Loss of Splitter	$10(\log_{10} N)dB$
L_{ISO}	Loss of Isolator	0.15 dB
$L_{Demux}^{N \times 1}$	Demux Loss	$1.5(\log_{2} N - 1)dB$
$L_{Mux}^{N \times 1}$	Mux Loss	$1.5(\log_{2} N - 1)dB$
L_{FBG}	Insertion loss of FBG	.15dB
L_{FF}	Fixed Filter Loss	1.0 dB
L_{F}	Loss of Fiber	.2dB
L_{SOA} L_{TF}	Loss of SOA Loss of Tunable Filter	1 dB 2 dB

Source: (Shukla, Jain, & Srivastava, 2016).

After inserting the loss of various devises in Equation 3 the total loss of the switch is given by Equation 4

$$A_T^{A_2} = 26.59dB \tag{4}$$

Loss of switch A3:

$$A_T^{A_3} = L_{TWC}L_{AWG}^{2N \times 2N}L_{TWC}L_{AWG}^{(N+m)\times(N+m)}L_{TWC}L_{AWG}^{2N \times 2N} \tag{5}$$

After inserting the loss of various devises in Equation 5 the total loss of the switch is given by Equation 6

$$A_T^{A_3} = 15dB \tag{6}$$

Loss of switch A4:

$$A_T^{A_4} = L_{Demux}L_{TWC}L_{AWG}L_{FWC}L_{Mux} \tag{7}$$

After inserting the loss of various devises in Equation 7 the total loss of the switch is calculated as in Equation 8

$$A_T^{A_4} = 10dB \tag{8}$$

Loss of switch A5:

$$A_T^{A_5} = L_{TWC}L_{AWG}L_{TWC}L_{AWG}L_{TWC}L_{AWG}L_{TWC}L_{Mux}L_{Demux}L_{TWC}L_{AWG} \tag{9}$$

After inserting the loss values of various devises in Equation 9 the total loss of the switch is given by Equation 10

$$A_T^{A_5} = 25dB \tag{10}$$

Loss of switch A6:

$$A_T^{A_6} = L_{TWC}L_{AWG}^{2N \times 2N}L_{TWC}L_{Mux}L_{Demux}L_{TWC}L_{AWG}^{2N \times 2N} \tag{11}$$

The total loss of the switch is calculated in Equation 12 by inserting various loss values in Equation 11

$$A_T^{A_6} = 15dB \tag{12}$$

Loss of switch A7:

$$A_T^{A_7} = L_{TWC} L_{AWG}^{2N \times 2N} L_{TWC} L_{Mux} L_{Demux} L_{TWC} L_{AWG}^{2N \times 2N} \tag{13}$$

After inserting the loss values of various devises in Equation 13 the total loss of switch is calculated in Equation 14

$$A_T^{A_7} = 15dB \tag{14}$$

Loss of switch A8:

$$A_T^{A_8} = L_{TWC} L_{TWC} L_{AWG}^{2N \times 2N} L_{DMUX} L_{MUX} L_{TWC} L_{TWC} L_{N \times N}^{AWG} \tag{15}$$

After inserting the loss values of different optical devises in Equation 15 the total physical loss of the switch is given as in Equation 16

$$A_T^{A_8} = 17dB \tag{16}$$

Loss of switch A9:

Here the total loss of the switch is divided in to three parts that is input loss, output loss, and loop buffer loss as represented by set of Equation shown in 17

$$A_{in}^{A_{10}} = L_{TWC} L_{Com}^{N \times 1}$$

$$A_{out}^{A_{10}} = L_{3dB} L_{Demux}^{1 \times B} L_{TWC} L_{Splitter}^{1 \times 2} L_{Demux}^{B \times N} L_{TF}$$

$$A_{loop}^{A_{10}} = L_{3dB} L_{Demux}^{1 \times B} L_{TWC} L_{Splitter}^{1 \times 2} L_{Mux}^{B \times 1} L_{ISO} L_{Fiber} \tag{17}$$

After inserting the loss values of each devise in Equation 17 the typical values of the above losses are

$$A_{in}^{A_{10}} = 8dB \quad A_{out}^{A_{10}} = 11dB$$

and

$$A_{loop}^{A_{10}} = 11.15dB \, .$$

Here, the loss of the loop is compensated by the amplifier placed in the buffer, thus $G_4 = 11.15dB$ And the packet which passes through the switch suffers a loss of

$$A_{in} + A_{out} - G_4 = 7.85dB .$$

Loss of switch A10:

$$A_T^{A_{10}} = L_{TWC} L_{SOA} L_{AWG}^{2N \times 2N} L_{TWC} L_{AWG}^{N \times N} L_{AWG}^{2N \times 2N} \tag{18}$$

By substituting the various loss parameters in the Equation 18 we can calculate the total loss of the switch A11 which is represented in Equation 19 as follows

$$A_T^{A_{10}} = 14dB \tag{19}$$

Loss of switch A11:

$$A_T^{A_{11}} = L_{TWC} L_{AWG} L_{SOA} L_{TWC} L_{TF} L_{AWG} L_{TWC} L_{TF} L_{SOA} \tag{20}$$

After inserting the loss values of different optical devises the total physical loss of the switch is

$$A_T^{A_{11}} = 18dB \tag{21}$$

In the case of analyzing the performance of switch the loss analysis is important parameters. As the loss of switch increases the more devises are required to compensate this loss, so the performance of whole switch decreases. In this section the loss of various switches are calculated, as shown in Equation 1 - 21 and Figure 20 shows a bar graph by which we can easily compare the loss values of all switches.

The Figure 20 shows the physical loss of various switches presented in this chapter from this bar graph represented in figure 20, we can say that the loss of switches A1, A2 and A5 are highest as compared to all other switches presented in this chapter, while on the other hand the loss of switches A3, A6, A7, A8, A10 and A11 are nearly same and in moderate category while the loss of switches A4 and A9 are in lowest category.

SCALABILITY ANALYSIS

Since we all know that the cost of optical components are too high (discussed in further section of chapter) and the switch having more number of components means, more loss faced by whole switch. That means, the switch having less number of components are beneficial in compare to the switch having high components count. The each switch discussed in this chapter has different components. The Table 4 shows the different components used in the switches and quantities of each component are also discussed in Table 4.

Figure 20. Bar graph of physical loss of various switches

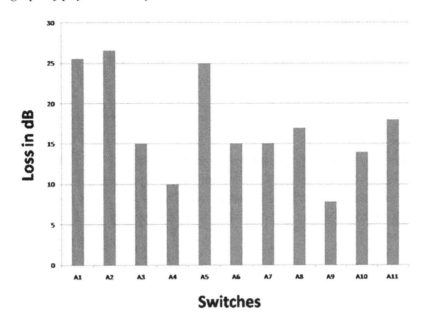

Table 4. Scalability analysis of each switch

Component Name	A1	A2	A3	A4	A5	A6	A7	A8	A9	A10	A11
TWC	NM	×	3N	N	5N	3N	3N	4N	2N	2N	3N
DEMUX	N	N	×	N	N	N	N	N	×	×	×
MUX	×	N+1	×	N	N	N	N	N	×	×	×
AWG	×	×	2	×	2	2	1	2	3	2	1
FWC	×	N	×	N	×	×	×	×	×	×	×
TF	×	×	×	×	×	×	×	×	N	×	2N
SOA	×	×	×	×	×	×	×	×	×	N	2N
Splitter	NM	M+1	×	×	×	×	×	×	N	×	×
Isolator	×	×	×	×	×	×	×	×	1	×	×
EDFA	×	×	×	×	×	×	×	×	1	×	×
3dB Coupler	×	×	×	×	×	×	×	×	1	×	×
Combiner	×	N	×	×	×	×	×	×	1	×	×

COST ANALYSIS OF SWITCHES

Since we know that the costs of optical components are too high so the cost analysis is another parameter through which the comparison is performed between different switches. In the present day's optical communication environment the components like TWC and optical regenerators are not available, so practically this is not possible to calculate the exact cost of the components. Canegem was the first scientist who represents the cost analysis and eliminated the cost of optical devises in relative units (Caenegem,

Colle, Pickavet, Demeester, Martinez, Ramos, & Marti, 2006). This cost analysis is based on the Fiber to Chip coupling (FCC) model. As in fiber to chip coupling model wavelength conversion range is not included so the cost of tunable wavelength convertor is considered to be 4. For checking the effect of wavelength conversion a more general cost effective model is proposed in Eramo and Listanti (2000), in this model the cost of TWC is represented as

$$C_{TWC} = ad^b$$

Here "a" represents as the normalization constant and the value of "b" lies between 0.5 to 5. So we can easily calculate the cost of architectures. Here in this analysis the cost of the optical fiber is neglected in each switch, and the value of N and M are considered to be 4.

Now we are going to calculate the cost of each switch, in this analysis the cost of each optical component is chosen from Table 5.

Cost of Architecture A1:

$$C_{A1} = N \left[M \left(C^{in}_{TWC} + C_{Splitter} + NDC_{Optical gates} \right) + C_{Combiner} \right] \tag{22}$$

Let suppose that the value of N=M=D and putting various cost values in Equation 22 we can calculate the total loss of switch through the Equation 23 given as below

$$C_{A1} = N^2 \left(N \right)^b + 4N^3 + 2N + 2 \tag{23}$$

Cost of Architecture A2:

$$C_{A2} = NC^{in}_{FWC} + C_{MUX} + C_{Splitter} + M \begin{bmatrix} C_{Opticalgates} + C_{Splitter} + NC_{Opticalgates} + C_{Combiner} \\ +C_{Demux} + N^2 C_{Opticalgates} + C_{Mux} \end{bmatrix} \tag{24}$$

For the sake of convenience let us consider the value of $N=M$ and after inserting various cost values in Equation 24 then the total calculated cost of A2 is given by Equation 25 as below

$$C_{A2} = N \left(N \right)^b + 4N^2 + 13N + 13 \tag{25}$$

Cost of Architecture A3:

$$C_{A3} = NC^{in}_{TWC} + C_{AWG1} + N[C^b_{TWC1} + C^b_{TWC2}] + C_{AWG2} \tag{26}$$

$$C_{A3} = 2N \left(2N \right)^b + N \left(N + M \right)^b + 2N + M$$

Table 5. Cost values of various components

Symbol	Representation	Cost
C_{TWC}	Cost of TWC	4
$C_{Combiner}^{N \times 1}$	Cost of Combiner	N+1
$C_{Splitterr}^{N \times 1}$	Cost of Splitter	N+1
C_{3db}	Cost of3dB Coupler	4
$C_{Demux}^{N \times 1}$	Cost of Demux	N+1
$C_{Mux}^{N \times 1}$	Cost of Mux	N+1
C_{EDFA}	Cost of EDFA	2
C_{ISO}	Cost of Isolator	2
C_{Regen}	Cost of Regenerator	21
C_{SOA}	Cost of SOA	2
C_{FBG}	Cost of FBG	2
C_{AWG}	Cost of AWG	2N
C_{FF}	Cost of FF	2
C_{TF}	Cost of TF	2
$C_{Circulator}$	Cost of circulator	N
C_{Fiber}	Cost of Fiber	2
C_{or}	Cost of Optical Reflector	2

Source: (Pattavina, 2005).

Now consider N=M the total cost of switch A3 is given by Equation 27 by inserting various cost values in Equation 26

$$C_{A3} = 2N(2N)^b + N(2N)^b + 2N + M$$
$$C_{A3} = 3N(2N)^b + 3N \tag{27}$$

Cost of Architecture A4:

$$C_{A4} = \left[C_{DEMUX} + NC_{TWC} + NC_{FWC} + C_{MUX} \right] + C_{AWG} \tag{28}$$

The total cost of the switch is calculated by inserting various cost values in Equation 28 so that the total cost of switch is presented by Equation 29

$$C_{A4} = 2N(N)^b + 4N + 2 \tag{29}$$

Cost of Architecture A5:

$$C_{A5} = NC_{TWC}^{in} + C_{AWG1} + MC_{TWC1}^b + MC_{TWC2}^b + NC_{TWC1}^{out}$$
$$+NC_{DEMUX} + NC_{MUX} + NC_{TWC2}^{out} + C_{AWG2} \tag{30}$$

$$C_{A5} = 2N(N)^b + (2M + N) + (N + M)^b + 6N + 2$$

In the study we consider the value of N=M so the total cost of switch is presented in Equation 31 by inserting various cost values in Equation 30

$$C_{A5} = 2N(N)^b + 3N(2N)^b + 6N + 2 \tag{31}$$

Cost of Architecture A6:

$$C_T^{A_6} = NC_{TWC} + C_{AWG}^{N \times N} + NC_{TWC} + NC_{DEMUX} + NC_{MUX} + NC_{TWC} + C_{AWG}^{N \times N} \tag{32}$$

Substituting the cost values of different components, in Equation 32 and considering a=1 we get the total cost equation of switch as shown in Equation 33

$$C_{A_6} = 3N(2N)^b + 7N + 2 \tag{33}$$

Cost of Architecture A7:

$$C_{A6} = NC_{TWC}^{in} + C_{AWG}^{2N \times 2N} + NC_{TWC1}^b + NC_{TWC2}^b + NC_{DEMUX} + NC_{MUX} \tag{34}$$

Putting the loss values of all components in Equation 34 the total cost of switch is represented in Equation 35

$$C_{A6} = N\left(2N\right)^{b} + 2N\left(N\right)^{b} + 6N + 2 \tag{35}$$

Cost of Architecture A8:

$$C_{T}^{A_8} = NC_{TWC} + NC_{TWC} + C_{AWG}^{2N \times 2N} + NC_{DMUX} + NC_{MUX} + NC_{TWC} + NC_{TWC} + C_{N \times N}^{AWG} \tag{36}$$

Substituting the cost values of different components, in Equation 36 and considering a=1 we get the total cost of switch as follows by Equation 37

$$C_{A_8} = 2N\left(2N\right)^{b} + 2N\left(N\right)^{b} + 9N + 2 \tag{37}$$

Cost of Architecture A9:

$$C_{T}^{A_9} = NC_{TWC}^{in} + C_{Com}^{N \times 1} + C_{Demux}^{B \times N} + NC_{TF} + C_{3dB} + C_{EDFA} + C_{Demux}^{1 \times B} \\ + B(C_{TWC}^{bu} + C_{Splitter}^{1 \times 2}) + C_{Mux}^{B \times 1} + C_{ISO} + C_{F} \tag{38}$$

Putting various cost values in Equation 38 and considering a=1 we get Equation 39

$$C_{T}^{A_9} = NC_{TWC}^{in} + BC_{TWC}^{bu} + 4N + 6B + 11 \\ = N\left(N\right)^{b} + B\left(N\right)^{b} + 4N + 6B + 11 \tag{39}$$

For the sake of convenience suppose the value of N=B so final cost equation is represented in (40)

$$C_{T}^{A_9} = 2N\left(N\right)^{b} + 10N + 11 \tag{40}$$

Cost of Architecture A10:

$$C_{T}^{A_2} = NC_{TWC} + NC_{SOA} + C_{AWG}^{2N \times 2N} + NC_{FDL} + C_{AWG}^{2N \times 2N} \tag{41}$$

Putting various cost values in Equation 41 and considering a=1 we get the total cost of switch by Equation 42

$$C_{A7} = N\left(2N\right)^{b} + \left(N\right)^{b} + 6N + 2 \tag{42}$$

Cost of Architecture A11:

$$C_T^{A_{11}} = NC_{TWC}^{Sc} + C_{AWG}^{2N \times 2N} + NC_{SOA}^b + NC_{TF}^b + NC_{FDL} + NC_{TWC}^b + NC_{SOA} + NC_{TF} + NC_{TWC} \quad (43)$$

Putting various cost values in Equation 43 and considering a=1 we get we get the total cost of switch by Equation 44

$$
\begin{aligned}
C_T^{A_{11}} &= Na(2N)^b + 4N + 3N + 2N + N + Na(N+1)^b + 3N + 2N + Na(N)^b \\
&= N\left[(2N)^b + (N+1)^b + (N)^b\right] + 15N
\end{aligned} \quad (44)
$$

The Figure 21 shows the cost of various switch architectures for the value of b=0.8 here for TWC the WSC model is used while for other components the FCC model is considered. As in the figure the cost of architecture A1 is highest while the cost of architectures A2, A5, A6, A8 and A11 are almost same and the cost of switches A3 and A7 and A9 are nearly same and comparable while on the other hand the cost of architecture A4 and A10 are lowest. Hence we can say that in terms of cost comparison the cost of architecture A4 and A10 are best.

Figure 22 shows the cost values of various switches for the value of b=1. In this again the cost of architecture A1 is highest; while for architecture A4 cost is second highest. The cost of the architectures A2, A5, A6, A8 and A11 are nearly same on the other hand the cost of architecture A3, A7 and A9 are same the cost of architecture A4 and A10 are lowest. Thus, by considering different values of b it is obvious that overall cost comparison remains the same and it does not change much. Thus using FCC and WSU model cost comparison of the switch architectures can be made.

Figure 21. Cost of the architectures for b=0.8

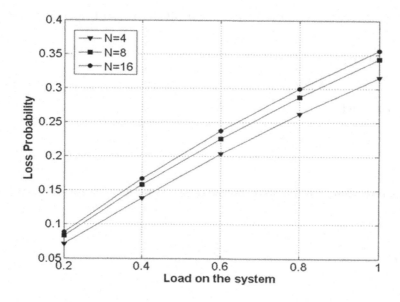

Figure 22. Cost of the architectures for b=1.0

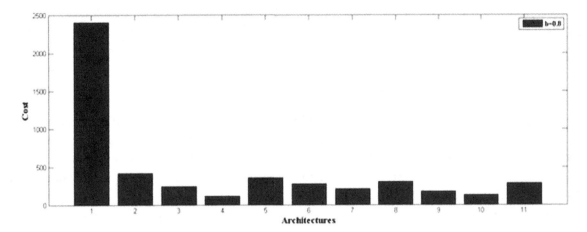

BUFFER ANALYSIS

In OPS applications, buffers are required for synchronization of incoming packets and for collision avoidance on outgoing light paths. The most practical buffer technology for OPS applications is based on fiber delay lines combined with optical switches (Ahmed, 2012; Sun, 2013; Delesques, 2013; Naiah, 2014; Ramesh & Nair, 2014; Nabih, 2014). This style of buffer has proved satisfactory in limited-scale laboratory-based demonstrations of OPS, but it is bulky and does not scale well to full size networks, especially in buffering for collision avoidance. Some solutions are also proposed where buffer-less system are proposed referred as OBS optical burst switching.

To highlight the scaling problem in large-scale OPSs, consider an OPS or router with 1000 incoming and outgoing channels, each at a data rate of 40 Gb/s. In electronic routers, the buffering capacity per port is usually equal to around 250 ms of delay per port. At the 40-Gb/s data rate, this corresponds to a buffer capacity of around 10 Gb. If single-wavelength optical fiber delay lines were used in place of electronics for this buffering, then the total length of fiber needed for buffering all ports in the router would be approximately 40 Gm, or about 150 times the distance from the earth to the moon! Even if we set aside issues of signal distortion by dispersion and the very significant problem of power consumption by the necessary inline amplifiers, these lengths of fiber are quite unrealistic just on the basis of the physical space required to house the delay lines. There have been recent suggestions that adequate network performance can be achieved with two orders of magnitude less buffering than this. In addition, wavelength-division multiplexing (WDM) of multiple stored bit streams on each delay line could reduce the total length. However, while these measures may help a little, the required buffers would still be impractically large.

In this chapter optical packet switches are broadly classified in to two categories buffered switches in which whenever the situation of contention among packets arise then the contended packets are stored in to buffer on the other hand in buffer less architectures the buffering of packets are not possible and in contention situation the packets are dropped. Table 6 describes the buffer less and buffered architectures.

Table 6. Table for analyzing bufferless and buffered switches

Category	A1	A2	A3	A4	A5	A6	A7	A8	A9	A10	A11
Buffered	×	√	√	×	√	√	√	√	√	√	√
Bufferless	√	×	×	√	×	×	×	×	×	×	×

The Table 6 shows that the architectures A1 and A4 are buffer less architectures in which no any type of buffering mechanism is used; on the other hand the switches A2, A3, A5, A6, and A7 are buffered architectures in which the effective buffering technique is used for buffering the contending packets.

For checking the effects of buffer consider a node in to the network having 4 input and output lines. Here, at the load of 0.8, 25 to 30 percent packets lost occur, depending on the size of the switch or number of input links. Since this loss is huge and we cannot neglect this so for saving these packets a deflection routing or buffering can be used. In deflection routing method no extra hardware is required while on the other hand in buffering technique an effective method is used at each node of the switch to buffer the contending packets. Hence we can say that the performance of switch which uses the effective buffering techniques is more effective then buffer less switches.

INDUSTRY APPLICATION AND FUTURE RESEARCH DIRECTIONS

Due to the fast data transfer speed and high bandwidth utilization the optical network is the first choice of present day's telecommunication industry. Over the last few years as the time passes the technology advances day by day and as the technology advancement the use of video on demand, social networking environment with the large diffusion of cell phone mobile devises and tablets have introduces the rapid growth in the internet traffic ("Broadcast Yourself", n.d.; Meeker & Wu, 2013).

Now the use of optical technology is the best available solution which is capable of providing large communication bandwidth, the optical technology is deeply employed in the present day's global communication system and easily accepts the challenge of continuous increasing data exchange. As in the

Figure 23. Four inputs and outputs node without buffer

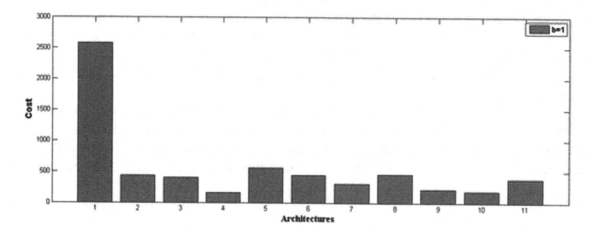

terms of network establishment the entire world is connected by optical cables across oceans and continents and the capacity of 1Tb/S is achieved. Except this the use of fiber optic communication in optical domain increases day by day, so in the modern telecommunication industry the copper cables are totally replaced by fiber cables for the deployment of optical network this extends the access data rate up to 1Gb/S, and this gives the solution of high connection demand.

On the other hand, optical technology plays a major role in the system that makes the emerging services available to the constantly growing user population: Data Centers.

For realizing the data centers the numbers of physical equipments are required, such as servers (application server, web server and data base server) switches and data storage devises, and these devises are interconnected with a complex wired network. In general we can say that the data center (DCs) stores, manages, process and exchange digital data and information.

In DCs, huge volume of packetized data is travelling to and from DCs. Cisco Global Cloud Index Study shows that more than 75% of traffic handled by DC is internal traffic.

For improving the existing data center network (in terms of speed, bandwidth, power consumption, and interconnection capabilities between DC resources) the optical packet switching captures the attention of many research groups.

The one of the major challenge in the deployment of OPS is that the transferring of packet only in the optical domain without O-E-O conversion is not possible. Electronic packet switching employs input and output buffering to perform store and forward processing needed at each switching node. This is not possible just because the unavailability of optical RAM.

Two approaches are commonly used to overcome the lack of optical RAM we can use fiber delay lines based buffers that stores packets in to optical domain. All the switches discussed in to the chapter are FDL based switches and all switch uses fiber delay lines for storing the packets when ever situation of contention among packets arises. The major drawback of using FDL lines are that, this approach significantly increases the complexity of the switch architecture and its control. The extra latency is also introduced in to the system. Moreover this method affects the signal power and by this method the packets are delayed only for fixed time, so the method does not solve the problem completely.

The second approach which is used in the OPS switches are to introduces buffering at the edges of switching network. In this method buffering can be implemented by using the electronic buffer at the edge while on the other hand switching process is in optical domain. But this method is applicable only in the systems that feature short host switch distances. In fact in the situation of contention, the packets which are to be stored at the edge of switch needs to be retransmitted. In the present days optical environment the researchers are focused in the design of hybrid buffer which contains all the quality features of electronic as well as optical buffering. Some of the switches using hybrid buffer are: Ramesh P. G. V. and Prita Nair (2014). This paper presents a scheme for hybrid burst assembly and a hybrid burst loss recovery scheme which selectively employs proactive loss recovery mechanism depending on the classification of traffic into short term and long term, respectively. Traffic prediction is made using the hidden Markov model (HMM). This dynamic hybrid approach based on HMM prediction provides overall a lower blocking probability and delay and more throughput when compared with forward segment redundancy mechanism. Ahmed Nabih et al., (2014) a hybrid optical switch (HOS) based on wavelength division multiplexing and optical code division multiplexing (WDM/OCDM) scheme is detailed. In this optical cross connect (OXC) can control and process requests for both circuit establishment and burst scheduling. The results are presented in terms of the blocking probability, probability of error, and probability of outage. Except these switches the numbers of other switches are also available that uses hybrid buffering techniques. So from this study we can say that the scope of research in the design of switch are not limited and there are number of possibilities, from this chapter we can analyze the effect of each optical component on the performance of switch which gives a brief layout of switch design.

CONCLUSION

According to the above chapter researcher wants to compare the performance of different architectures of Optical Packet Switching. In present Scenario, Telecommunication Companies are getting rise day by day and capture whole market of Communication. Time and information, which is possible through wire/wireless communication, are very important in today's environment. But wired communication bandwidth is much limited as compare to wireless communication. Therefore, to boost up the data communication rate the use of Optical packet switch in Optical Communication is probably best. In this chapter the detailed introduction of optical network is discussed. For implementation of optical network a number of optical switches are available in to the market with their pros and cons. In this chapter we have surveyed number of prominent AWG based optical packet switch architectures. A detailed analysis of each switch is presented in the paper and a comparison is performed between the switches through loss, cost, buffer and scalability analysis of switch. It is also found that the cost of TWC dominates the cost of other optical components, and its increases exponentially as the tuning range of TWC increases. So the switch having less number of TWC are more suitable. On the other hand buffer analysis presented in the chapter shows that the effective buffer technique is required in the design of switch because in the absence of buffer the packet loss increases exponentially when situation of contention arises in the switch. The study shows that this is impossible to design a switch which covers all the attributes in switch design, but this study certainly set some guidelines for the design of switch.

REFERENCES

Agrawal, G. P. (1999). *Fiber Optic Communication System* (2nd ed.). New York: John Wiley & Sons Inc.

Ahmed, I. (2012, June1). MAC-Layer Performance Enhancement Using Control Packet Buffering in Optical Burst-Switched Networks. *Journal of Lightwave Technology, 30*(11), 1578–1586. doi:10.1109/JLT.2012.2187043

Alexander. (1997). Wavelength Division. *Light Wave Magazine, 14*(7).

Arpaci, M., & Copeland, J. A. (2009). Buffer management for shared memory ATM Switches. *IEEE Communications Surveys and Tutorials, 3*(1), 2–9. doi:10.1109/COMST.2000.5340716

Bell. (1876). *Improvement in Telegraphy*. United States Patent Office, Patent no. 174,465.

Broadcast Yourself. (n.d.). Retrieved from http://www.youtube.com

Caenegem, R. V., Colle, D., Pickavet, M., Demeester, P., Martinez, J. M., Ramos, F., & Marti, J. (2006). From IP over WDM to all-optical packet switching: Economical view. *Journal of Lightwave Technology, 24*(4), 1638–1645. doi:10.1109/JLT.2006.871012

Chia, M. C., Hunter, D. K., Andonovic, I., Ball, P., Wright, I., Ferguson, S. P., & OMahony, M. J. et al. (2001). Packet loss and delay performance of feedback and feed-forward arrayed-waveguide gratings-based optical packet switches with WDM inputs-outputs. *Journal of Lightwave Technology, 19*(9), 1241–1254. doi:10.1109/50.948271

Delesques, P. (2013). Enhancement of an optical burst switch with shared electronic buffers. *Optical Network Design and Modeling, 2013*, 137–142.

Eramo, V., & Listanti, M. (2000). Packet loss in a bufferless optical WDM switch employing shared tunable wavelength converters. *Journal of Lightwave Technology, 18*(12), 1818–1833. doi:10.1109/50.908743

Feng. (2015). The fifth generation optical network flexibility, orchestration, and openness. *Industry Prospective, 2*(74), 30-32.

Franzen, A., Hunter, D. K., & Andonovic, I. (1998). Synchronization in optical packet switched network. *Proc. WAON Workshop.*

Glance. (1993). New advances on optical components needed for FDM optical networks. *The Journal of Light Wave Technology, 11*(5-6), 882-889.

Guillemot, C. G., Renaud, M., Gambini, P., Janz, C., Andonovic, I., Bauknecht, R., & Zucchelli, L. et al. (1998). Transparent optical packet switching: The European ACTS KEOPS project approach. *Journal of Lightwave Technology, 16*(12), 2117–2134. doi:10.1109/50.736580

Handerson, P. M. (2001). Introduction to optical network. *Photonics Spectra*, (September), 1–41.

Hecht, J. (1999). *City of light: the story of fiber optics* (1st ed.). New York: Oxford University Press.

Hluchy & Karol. (1988). Queuing in high performance packet switching. *IEEE J. Sel. Area Commun., 6*(9), 1587-1597.

Hunter, D. K., Nizam, M. H. M., Chia, M. C., Andonovic, I., Guild, K. M., Tzanakaki, A., & White, I. H. et al. (1999). WASPNET: A wavelength switched packet network. *IEEE Communications Magazine, 37*(3), 120–129. doi:10.1109/35.751509

Jajszczyk, A., & Mouftah, H. T. (1993). Photonic fast packet switching. *IEEE Communications Magazine, 31*(2), 58–65. doi:10.1109/35.186362

Kang, C. K., Han, K. E., Yang, W. H., So, W. h., & Kim, V. C. (2007). Analysis of AWG based elementary switches for multistage WDM optical switches. *The 9th International Conference on Advanced Communication Technology.*

Li, L., Scott, S. D., & Deogun, J. S. (2003). A novel fiber delay line buffering architecture for optical packet switching. *Proc. IEEE Globecom Conf.*

Lucky. (1999). Through a Glass Darkly- Viewing Communication in 2012 from 1961. *Proceeding of the IEEE, 87*(7), 1296-1300.

Meeker & Wu. (2013). *2013 internet trends.* Kleiner Perkins Caufield and Byere Tech. Rep.

Mishra, R. J., & Jain, A. (2015). Performance of Data Replication Algorithm in Local and Global Networks under Different Buffering Conditions. *International Journal of Intelligent Systems and Applications, 9*(9), 34–41. doi:10.5815/ijisa.2015.09.05

Morse. (1840). *Improvement in the mode of communication information by signals by the application of electromagnetism*. United States Patent Office, Patent no. 1647.

Nabih. (2014). Performance evaluation of a WDM/OCDM based hybrid optical switch utilizing efficient resource allocation. *Chinese Optics Letters, 12*(5).

Naiah, O. (2014). *The performance of OCDM/WDM with buffering based on shared fiber delay line*. IEEE ICTS.

OMahony, M. J., Simeonidou, D., Hunter, D. K., & Tzanakaki, A. (2001). The application of optical packet switching in future communication networks. *IEEE Communications Magazine, 39*(3), 128–135. doi:10.1109/35.910600

Pattavina, A. (2005). Multi- wavelength switching in IP optical nodes adopting different buffering strategies. *J. Optical Switching and Networking, 1*(1), 65–75. doi:10.1016/j.osn.2004.11.001

Ramaswami, R., Sivarajan, K., & Sasaki, G. (2009). *Optical networks: a practical perspective*. Morgan Kaufmann.

Ramesh, P. G. V., & Nair. (2014). Hybrid approach for loss recovery mechanism in OBS networks. *Chinese Optics Letters, 12*(4).

Reza, A. G., & Lim, H. (2011). Performance and Optical Cost Analysis of Shared Fiber Delay Line Based Two-Stage Optical Packet Switch. *IEEE International Conference on Advanced Information networking and Application*. doi:10.1109/AINA.2011.48

Shukla, V., Jain, A., & Srivastava, R. (2014). Physical layer analysis of arrayed waveguide based optical switch. *Int. J. Appl. Eng. Res., 9*(21), 10035–10050.

Shukla, V., Jain, A., & Srivastava, R. (2016). (in press). Design of an arrayed waveguide gratings based optical packet switch. *J. Eng. Sci. Technol., 11*(12).

Shukla, V., & Srivastava, R. (2015). WDM Fiber Delay Lines and AWG Based Optical Packet Switch Architecture. *International Journal of Recent Research Aspects*.

Srivastava, R., & Singh, Y. N. (2010). Feedback Fiber Delay Lines and AWG Based Optical Packet Switch Architecture. *Journal of Optical Switching and Networking, 7*(2), 75–84. doi:10.1016/j.osn.2010.01.002

Stephen, Scott, & Deogun. (2003). A novel fiber delay line buffering architecture for optical packet switching. In *Proceeding of IEEE 2003 GLOBECOM 2003*.

Sun. (2013). Seamlessly transformable hybrid packet and circuit switching for efficient optical networks. *Chinese Optics Letters, 11*(1).

Tucker, R. S., & Zhong, W. D. (1999). Photonic packet switching: An overview. IEICE Trans. Commun., E82 B, 254-264.

Verma, N., Srivastava, R., & Singh, Y. N. (2002). Novel design modification proposal for all optical fiber loop buffer switch. *Proc. Photonics Conf.*

Waheed. (2011). Comparing optical packet switching and optical burst switching. *Daffodil International University Journal of Science and Technology, 6*(2).

Yao, S., Mukherjee, B., & Dixit, S. (2000). *Advances in photonic packet switching: An Overview.* IEEE.

Yao, S., Mukherjee, B., & Dixit, S. (2003). A unified study of contention resolution schemes in optical packet switched networks. *Journal of Lightwave Technology, 21*(3), 672–683. doi:10.1109/JLT.2003.809573

Chapter 6
Flexible Antennas for Wearable Technologies

Amal Afyf
Mohammed V University, Morocco

Bellarbi Larbi
Mohammed V University, Morocco

Fatima Riouch
National Institute of Post and Telecommunication, Morocco

Mohamed Adel Sennouni
University Hassan the 1st, Morocco

Yaakoubi Nourdin
Maine University, France

ABSTRACT

Having the merits of being light-weight, energy efficient, in addition to low manufacturing cost, reduced fabrication complexity, and the availability of inexpensive flexible substrates, flexible and wearable technology is being established as an appealing alternative to the conventional electronics technologies which are based on rigid substrates. Furthermore, wearable antennas have been a topic of interest for more than the past decade, and hundreds of scientific papers can be found on the subject. This large number of publications asks for some classification in order to get an overview of the trends and challenges. To this aim, an overview of antennas for wearable technologies is proposed. This chapter is organized into three major sections. In the first part, a detailed review of wearable antennas is presented. The second part of this project deals with the flexible antennas parameters and families. Materials and fabrication methods are discussed in the third part. Wearables advantages, disadvantage and challenges are summarized in the last section.

INTRODUCTION

The terms "wearable technology", "wearable devices", and "wearables" all refer to electronic technologies or computers that are incorporated into items of clothing and accessories which can comfortably be worn on the body. For example, one function of an activity bracelet takes raw data from a sensor, processes it and generates a report on the number of steps taken over a given period. Sensors track motion with enough intelligence to distinguish between steps and other movements.

DOI: 10.4018/978-1-5225-1785-6.ch006

Sensors/ Antennas are an important part of wearable electronics, and continue to become smaller and more sophisticated. While there are many types of sensors that can be used, the most common is an inertial measurement unit (Accelerometer). An accelerometer can track a specific movement, its direction, and its intensity or speed. One simple example of an accelerometer is when a mobile phone or tablet (the input) is rotated and the device processes the movement and rotates the screen accordingly (the output). Other common sensors including pressure, temperature, position and humidity, support applications such as GPS. Consistently, wearable and flexible devices would often require the integration of antennas operating in specific frequency bands to provide wireless connectivity which is greatly demanded by modern information-oriented consumers. The aim of this study is to provide an overview of the current status and future perspectives in research and development of wearable technologies and sensors, to afford a comprehensive guide to various technologies and methods applied in the realization of flexible and wearable technologies along with state of the art antenna designs and implementations. Moreover, this document serves as an extensive reference in wearable topics. For these goals, it is necessary to define the field of wearable systems.

Wearable Antennas Background and Overview

History of Wearable Technologies

Wearable technology concerns any electronic products that are designed to be comfortably worn on the person as an accessory or as part of materials used in clothing. One of the major features of wearable technology is its ability to connect to the Internet, enabling data to be exchanged between a network and the device. Wearable technology is not a recent phenomenon, and dates back to head-mounted displays developed for helicopter pilots in the 1960s. Yet with recent advances in materials science that drive technology miniaturization and battery improvements, the global economy is standing on the brink of wider adoption of wearables. As computers have shrunk from room size to palm size, they have also moved from being passive accessories, such as laptops and personal digital assistants, to wearable appliances that form an integral part of our personal space. Wearable computers are always switched on and are always accessible. As computers move from desktop to coat pocket to the human body, their ability to help sort, filter and manage information will become ever more intimately connected to our daily lives. Applications of wearable technologies include wearable cameras, smart clothing, wearable apps platforms, smart glasses, health and happiness wearables, activity trackers, 3D motion sensors, and smart phone compatible watches (smart watches). In the past few years, many users often categorized these new devices as fun novelties and interesting gadgets. However, an increasing number of analysts consider wearable technologies to have more disruptive potential, to change existing industries, create new markets, and generate new jobs. As with smart phones, the possible applications of wearable technology are increasing and are closely connected to new developments in software and the emergence of the Internet of Things, the larger trend encompassing wearable technology. In Figure 1, a range of wearables' applications is illustrated.

There is a massive excitement in the industry about wearable technology. The marketing consultancy company WiFore, suggests that the "Wearable Electronics and Technology" market is estimated to exceed $14 billion in 2017, then double to reach $30 billion in 2020. Almost half of that will probably come from companies that are not players in today's consumer electronics market.

Figure 1. Wearable technologies time-line from 1975 to 2014
Wearable Technologies, Market Assessment.

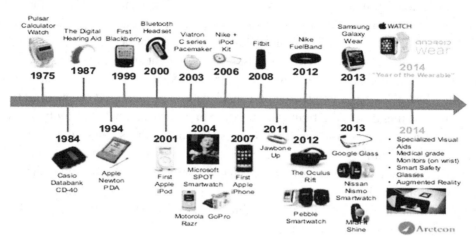

Another market research by IDTechEx analysts find that the market will be worth over $30bn in 2016, and growing in three stages: 10% annually to over $40bn in 2018, but then accelerating to 23% through to over $100bn by 2023, before slowing to 11% to reach over $150bn by 2026.

Applications of Wearables

Security (Military and Police) and Rescue Service Applications

Our main focus will be orientated towards wearable robust antennas intended to operate in various harsh environments. These antennas are mainly used for security and defense applications (Psychoudakis,

Figure 2. Global revenue from smart wearables
Source: WiFore analysis.

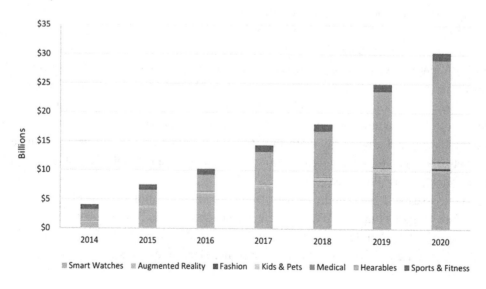

Figure 3. Global revenue from smart wearables
Source: IDTechEx analysis.

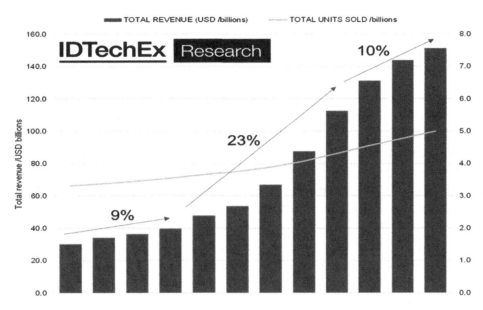

Lee, Chen, & Volakis, 2010) and within different rescue services like firefighters (Hertleer et al., 2009), mountain and water rescue workers, (Figure 4).

Frequency bands intended for security and rescue applications are regulated by special government regulatory offices. In our case, we will mainly consider the regulations and frequency allocations of the Swiss authorities (National Swiss Plan, 2014). A band of interest is the Tetrapol communication band, 380-430 MHz, widely used by different security and emergency services within the Private Mobile Radio (PMR) applications (Tetrapol, 2015). There are two common requirements for most of the wearable antennas used in security and rescue service applications: the miniaturization size and the resilience of the antenna to the environment. The wavelength of the antennas operating inside the Tetrapol band, if observed in a free space, is rather large. Antennas proposed for these applications should be small, non-protrusive, low profile and conformable so that can be easily mounted inside the uniform and placed

Figure 4. Illustrative examples of wearable antennas applications: (a) army forces; 9b) firefighters
Source: Serra, Nepa, & Manara, 2011 and Corner, 2013.

around the wearer's body. Apart from the antenna size, another important aspect is the environment and weather conditions where wearable antennas operate. As most of the wearers from the indicated groups operate outdoor, robustness against water, rain, moisture, mud, etc., is among the antenna requirements. Moreover, taking into account that the uniforms need to be washed, an integrated antenna should withstand this process. Several antenna prototypes exist in literature and on the market (Psychoudakis et al., 2010) (Hertleer et al., 2009). All the reported antennas have a size suitable for placement on the wearer. Some of the antennas are waterproof and most of them are too specific and customized and cannot be widely used for different situations. For example, the antenna presented in (Psychoudakis et al., 2010) is exclusively designed for armor vests used by the military and law enforcement agencies. It is an asymmetric dipole antenna that can be integrated only in the specified vests. Another dipole wearable antenna type is presented by the same authors in (Psychoudakis & Volakis, 2009), a conformal Asymmetric Meandered Flare (AMF) dipole antenna. The antenna's conductive surface is fabricated by using precise embroidering techniques in order to produce fully flexible antenna conformal to the wearer and his clothes, see (Figure 5). More wearable antenna prototypes operating between 0.1-1 GHz, mainly for military applications, are presented in (Matthews & Pettitt, 2009), exploiting different conductive and textile materials. A set of textile wearable antennas intended for firefighter services have been introduced by Hertler et al. A textile GPS wearable antenna and the antenna intended for voice communication between the firefighters are presented in (Vallozzi et al., 2010).

The importance of the wearable devices in the everyday operations of modern security and rescue services is reported in (Curone et al., 2007). Different parameters can be monitored with the units integrated into their garments like psychological parameters, actual position or the conditions on the field where they operate. In summary, all the concerned applications mentioned above, such as military, firefighters or rescue services require an involvement of different electronic devices and equipment in their daily activities. Depending on the type of application and activities they perform, different wearable antennas are needed. Therefore, wearable antennas play an important role in ensuring robust and reliable communication links and thus performance of these services.

Medical Applications

These applications are mainly used for health monitoring of different categories of patients and elderly people. They can monitor 24 hours a day different parameters and detect changes, for instance, blood pressure, heart rate or body temperature (Popovic, Momenroodaki, & Scheeler, 2014). With the more emphasized use of smartphones, collected data from the medical applications can be directly sent to the hospital or responsible medical doctors. Accordingly, extensive research efforts have been made to assess the accuracy of wearable sensors in classifying Activities of Daily Living (ADL). (Mathie et al., 2004) showed the feasibility of using accelerometers to identify the performance of ADL by older adults monitored in the home environment. (Sazonov et al., 2009) developed an in-shoe pressure and acceleration sensor system that was used to classify activities including sitting, standing, and walking with the ability of detecting whether subjects were simultaneously performing arm reaching movements. (Giansanti et al., 2008) developed an accelerometer-based device designed for step counting in patients with Parkinson's disease. (Aziz et al., 2007) used wearable sensors to monitor the recovery of patients after abdominal surgery. Several research projects have suggested that activity monitoring for wellness applications has great potential to increase exercise compliance in populations at risk. Long-term monitoring of physiological data can lead to improvements in the diagnosis and treatment, for instance,

Figure 5. Asymmetric Meandered Flare (AMF) wearable dipole antenna
Source: Psychoudakis & Volakis, 2009.

of cardiovascular diseases. Commercially available technology provides one with the ability to achieve long-term monitoring of heart rate, blood pressure, oxygen saturation, respiratory rate, body temperature and galvanic skin response.

Also, an area of growing interest in the field of wearable technology is the use of wearable sensors and systems to achieve early detection of changes in patient's status requiring clinical intervention. Early detection and treatment of exacerbations are important goals to prevent worsening of clinical status and the need for emergency room care or hospital admission. Remote monitoring systems can play an important role in early detection of trends in patients' health status that point towards an exacerbation event. One way to approach the problem of achieving early detection of exacerbation episodes is to detect changes in the level of activity performed by a patient (Moy, Mentzer, & Reilly 2003; Sherrill DM, Moy ML & Reilly JJ, 2005) and assume that a decrease in activity level would be indicative of the likelihood of a worsening of the clinical status of the individual undergoing monitoring. Using sophisticated machine learning algorithms, the authors were able to identify several different types of physical activities and the intensity of those activities from a single ear worn sensor. (Steele et al., 2000) and (Belza et al., 2001) measured human movement in three dimensions over 3 days and showed that the magnitude of the acceleration vector recorded in patients with chronic obstructive pulmonary disease was correlated with measures of patient's status such as the six-minute walk distance, the FEV1 (Forced Expiratory Volume in 1 sec), the severity of dyspnea, and the Physical Function domain of health-related quality of life scale. (Hecht, Ma, Porszasz, & Casaburi, 2009) presented an algorithm for a minute-by-minute analysis of patients' activity level, based on data recorded using a single unit. The system was tested in 22 patients who were monitored over a period of 14 days. The authors also implemented a simple empirically-developed algorithm to determine if the subject was wearing the device thus providing a handle on compliance. (A. Afyf et al., 2015; A. Afyf, Larbi, B., & Anouar, A. 2016) studied the possibility of implant flexible sensors into the patient bra, to detect breast cancer in early stages based on the self radiation of the body caused by heat changes.

Before showing some of the typical wearable sensors found among the medical applications, a short overview of their dedicated standards and frequency bands will be presented.

A large number of bands indicate how widely these applications are spread, emphasizing their importance. Depending on the type of devices (implanted or on the body) and the required communication. In-, On- or Off-body) different standards have been defined. The Federal Communications Commission (FCC) has established a Medical Implant Communication Service (MICS) like the band for communication with medical implants ("Federal Communications Commission (FCC)," 2014), while in Europe the same standard is regulated by the European Telecommunications Standards Institute (ETSI). In 2009, the Medical Device Radio Communications Service (Med-Radio) range, 401-406 MHz, has been created by the FCC for diagnostic and therapeutic purposes in implanted medical devices and devices worn on the body. A large number of wearable applications operate inside one of the FCC proposed Industrial Scientific Medical (ISM) bands, 902-9281MHz, 2.4-2.4835 GHz and 5.725-5.875 GHz. Some of the bands are used on a secondary basis because they are already utilized in other applications. These ISM bands are submitted to certain restrictions, like short distance operation or low emitted power, in order to allow their co-existence in the spectrum with minimal interference ("Federal Communications Commission (FCC)," 2014), ("Medical Device Radiocommunications Service (MedRadio)," 2009).

In 2002, a spectrum from 3.1-10.6 GHz has been allocated by the FCC for Ultra Wideband (UWB) applications ("Federal Communications Commission (FCC)," 2014). Many researches and different types of wearable medical applications can be found in this band, making it one of the most exploited frequency ranges for WBAN applications (Hao et al., 2012). The most recent frequency band with a potential to be used for wearable applications is the millimeter wave range between 57-64 GHz, and also known as a 60 GHz band (REED, 2007). Some research about the propagation characteristics at 60 GHz for WBAN has been done in (Alipour et al. 2010; Constantinou et al., 2012) while antenna designs are proposed in (Pellegrini et al., 2013; Wu et al., 2010) giving promising results. The large choice of frequency bands used for medical WBAN applications leads to various wearable antenna families. Several implantable and wearable antennas are presented within the following subsection. Implantable antennas are a specific group challenging to design, fabricate and package and implant. The antenna and the accompanying electronic components need to be implanted into the human or animal body, leading to a complex procedure. The antenna needs to be small, compact, built out of appropriate biocompatible materials and when implanted providing a reliable communication link towards the external units and devices (Skrivervik & Merli, 2011). An overview and analysis on the development and implantation of these antennas are presented in (Merli, 2008). Several other implantable antenna designs are shown in (Kim & Samii, 2004; Xia, Saito, Takahashi, & Ito, 2009; Kiourti et al., 2012; Curto et al., 2009). Different antenna types used for medical purposes are found in the literature, e.g. patch antenna (Chandran, Conway, & Scanlon, 2008), monopole type antenna (Ma, Edwards, & Bashir, 2008), PIFA (Lin et al., 2012), Planar Inverted Conical Antenna (PICA) (Alomainy et al., 2009), printed strip antenna (Alomainy, Hao, & Pasveer, 2007), classical dual-band patch antenna (Samii, 2007), etc.

Medical applications will remain one of the main consumers of various wearable devices. Constant progress of the wearable allows monitoring of various health activities and parameters. The fact that nowadays smartphones and other wireless devices (e.g. tablets, laptops, etc.) can act as reliable hubs and transceivers; make the wearable applications even more favorable. Wearable antennas will continue to be the crucial connection element between the on-body devices and the external units, providing reliable and on time communication.

Figure 6. Wireless body area network for ubiquitous health monitoring
Source: Ullah & Kwak, 2011.

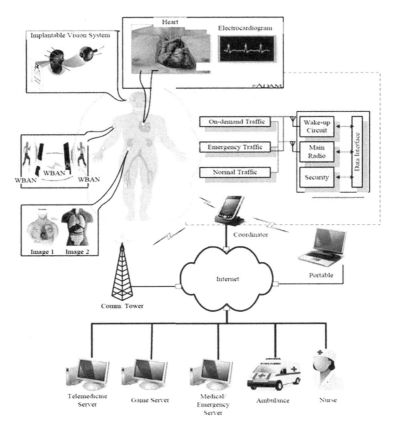

Sport, Entertainment, and Fashion Applications

Another attractive market for wearables is sport, entertainment and fashion applications (Figure 7). Nowadays consumers enjoy keeping track of performances in any kind of sports activity they do. Different wearable applications are able to track and record speed, elevation, distance and other similar parameters. Most of the tracking can be performed with the currently existing smartphones, but some separate wearable devices also exist. Several wristwatches with built-in GPS antennas, that can measure time, distance, position of the wearer or even the heart rate, can be found on the market (("Running GPS Watches," 2014; "Micoach," 2014). Wearable GPS antennas (Chen, Kuster & Chavannes, 2012; Zürcher, Staub, & Skrivervik, 2000; Skrivervik & Zürcher, 2007) play an important role in the performance of such systems. Furthermore, for the purposes of professional sportsmen, wearable devices are used in a more extensive manner. All the collected data from different wearable sensors are analyzed and used for further improvement in the sportspeople performances (Lapinski, Feldmeier, & Paradiso, 2011). Interesting examples of wearable antennas intended for integration into the shoes and thus potential use for sports applications are presented in (Gaetano et al., 2013).

Entertainment applications are also a market for the wearable technologies. They offer a lot of possibilities to this industry. Some examples of the entertainment wearable's present on the market include a bluetooth jacket ("Zegna Sport Bluetooth iJacket incorporates smart fabric," 2007), intelligent shoes

Figure 7. Illustrative examples of wearable antennas applications in sports, entertainment and fashion: (a) skiing , (b) swimming and (c) intelligent shoes
Source: *"Snow flaik tracks skiers," 2011; "Verb for shoe - very intelligent shoes," 2004.*

("Verb for shoe - very intelligent shoes," 2004) or a ski monitoring system, flaik ("Snow flaik tracks skiers," 2011). The list of wearable applications used in sports, entertainment and fashion is growing rapidly, occupying a significant part of the market (Ranck, 2012).

Other Applications

Table 1 shows an overview of the five applications for wearable technology and the products included within each of those applications.

Wearable and Flexible Antennas

Wearable sensors/ antennas are attacked to the user body forming wireless body area network (WBAN) to monitor changes in user's vital signs closely and provide real time feedback. The wearable systems typically consist of five main components:

1. **Antenna:** It is a sensing chip to sense data (such as pressure, temperature, position and humidity...) from the user's body.
2. **Microcontroller:** It is used to perform local data processing such as data compression and it also controls the functionality of other components in the sensor node.
3. **Memory:** It is used to store sensed data temporally.
4. **Radio Transceiver:** It is responsible for communication between nodes and to send/receive sensed data wirelessly.
5. **Power Supply:** The sensor nodes are powered by batteries with a lifetime of several months.

Therefore, the antenna is one of the most important elements of the optimum wearable device which should operate reliably for a long period of time without restricting the user activity and causing any behavior modification. In order to increase the battery lifetime, the energy efficiency of the device should be improved. Considering the fact that the energy consumed during radiofrequency (RF) transmission is a high percentage of the overall consumption, decreasing the number of retransmissions and improving the link budget by having higher antenna gain or pattern diversity can directly be translated into longer battery lifetime. Convenient form factor is also related to the antenna since it is one of the largest elements

Table 1. Wearable technology applications

Application	Product Categories
Healthcare and Medical	Blood Pressure Monitors/ Continous Glucose Monitoring/ Defibrillators/ Drug Delivery Products/ ECG Monitors/ Hearing Aids/ Insullin Pumps/ Smart Glasses/ Patches/ PERS/ Pulse Oximetry
Fitness and Wellness	Activity Monitors/ Emotional Measurement/ Fitness & Heart Rate Monitors/ Foot Pods & Pedometers/ Heads-up Displays/ Sleep Sensors/ Smart Glasses/ Smart Clothnig/ Smart Watches/ Audio Earbuds/ Other,
Infotainment	Bluetooth Headsets/ Head-up Displays/ Imaging Products/ Smart Glasses/ Smart Watches
Industrial	Hand-worn Terminals/ Heads-up Display/ Smart Clothing/ Smart Glasses
Military	Hand-worn Terminals/ Heads-up Display/ Smart Clothing

of the device alongside with the battery. The antennas' size plays an important role for their placement on the wearer. The gain and effective area are directly proportional to the antenna's size measured in wavelengths (Balanis, 2005). Usually, antennas that are smaller than the quarter free space wavelength are considered to be electrically small or miniature antennas (Staub et al., 1999). Before considering each of the indicated antenna family, a short overview of the miniaturization techniques will be presented.

Wearable Antenna Parameters

Conventional antenna parameters include impedance bandwidth, radiation pattern, directivity, efficiency and gain which are usually applied to fully characterize an antenna. These parameters are usually presented within the classical situation of an antenna placed in free space. However, when the antenna is in or close to a lossy medium, such as human tissue, the performance changes significantly and the parameters defining the antenna need to be revisited and redefined. In a medium with complex permittivity and non-zero conductivity, the effective permittivity $\mathscr{E}_{eff}$ and conductivity σ_{eff} are usually expressed as:

$$\varepsilon_{eff} = \varepsilon' - \frac{\sigma''}{\omega'} \tag{1}$$

$$\sigma_{eff} = \sigma' - \omega\varepsilon'' \tag{2}$$

where the permittivity and conductivity are composed of real and imaginary parts,

$$\varepsilon = \varepsilon' - j\varepsilon'' \tag{3}$$

$$\sigma = \sigma' - j\sigma'' \tag{4}$$

The permittivity of a medium is usually scaled to that of the vacuum for simplicity, $\mathscr{E}_0$ is given as $8854\times10-12$ F/m.

$$\varepsilon_r = \frac{\varepsilon_{eff}}{\varepsilon_0} \tag{5}$$

The equations above indicate the differences between free space and lossy material, hence, the imaginary part of the permittivity includes the conductivity of the material which defines the loss that is usually expressed as dissipation or loss tangent,

$$\tan \delta = \frac{\sigma_{eff}}{\omega \varepsilon_{eff}} \tag{6}$$

The biological system of the human body is an irregularly shaped dielectric medium with frequency dependent permittivity and conductivity. The distribution of the internal electromagnetic field and the scattered energy depends largely on the body's physiological parameters, geometry as well as the frequency and the polarization of the incident wave. Figure 8 shows measured permittivity and conductivity for a number of human tissues in the band 1–11 GHz. The results were obtained from a compilation study presented in (Harrison & Williams, 1965), which covers a wide range of different body tissues. Therefore, one major difference that can be identified directly when placing an antenna on a lossy medium, in this case, the human body, is the deviation in wavelength value from the free space one. The effective wavelength λ_{eff} at the specified frequency will become shorter since the wave travels more slowly in a lossy medium.

$$\lambda_{eff} = \frac{\lambda_0}{\mathrm{Re}\left[\sqrt{\varepsilon_r - j\sigma_e / \omega \varepsilon_0}\right]} \tag{7}$$

where λ_0 is the wavelength in free space. However, the effective permittivity depends on the distance between the antenna and the body and also on the location of the human electric properties which are different for various tissue types and thicknesses. The general rule of thumb is that the further the antenna is from the body the closer its performance to that in free space. This also depends on the antenna type, its structure and the matching circuit. Wire antennas operating in standalone modes and planar

Figure 8. Human tissue (a) permittivity and (b) conductivity for various organs as measured
Source: Harrison & Williams, 1965.

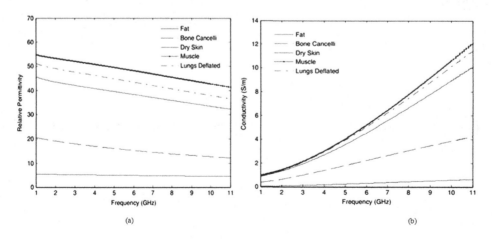

antennas directly printed on the substrate will experience changes in wavelength and hence deviation in resonance frequency, depending on the distance from the body. On the other hand, antennas with ground planes or reflectors incorporated in their design will experience less effect when placed on the body from operating frequency and impedance matching factors independent of distance from the body. An important factor in characterizing antennas is the radiation pattern and hence, gain and efficiency of the antenna. The antenna patterns and efficiency definitions are not obvious and cannot be directly derived from conventional pattern descriptors when the antenna is placed in or on a lossy medium. This is due to losses in the medium that cause waves in the far-field to attenuate more quickly and finally to zero.

Antenna efficiency is proportional to antenna gain (Hertel & Smith, 2003),

$$G(\theta,\phi) = \eta.D(\theta,\phi) \tag{8}$$

where η is the efficiency factor and D (θ,φ) is the antenna directivity which is obtained from the antenna normalized power pattern P_n that is related to the far-field amplitude F,

$$D(\theta,\phi) = \frac{P_n(\theta,\phi)}{P_n(\theta,\phi)_{average}} = \frac{\left|\vec{F}(\theta,\phi)\right|^2}{\left|\vec{F}(\theta,\phi)\right|^2_{average}} \tag{9}$$

The wearable antenna efficiency is different from that in free space, due to changes in antenna far-field patterns and also in the electric field distribution at varying distances from the body. However, the radiation efficiency of an antenna in either lossless or loss medium can be generalized as:

$$Efficiency_{radiaation} = \frac{RadiatedPower}{DeliveredPower} \tag{10}$$

An important quantity (which is in direct relation with antenna patterns and of great interest in wearable antenna designs) is the front–back ratio. This ratio defines the difference in power radiated in two opposite directions wherever the antenna is placed. The ratio varies depending on antenna location on the body and also on antenna structure.

Antenna Families

Different types of antennas are used in different situations. Wearable antennas follow similar trends and thus a wide number of various antenna types can be found in the literature. The following four antenna families are considered for the purposes of this thesis:

- Dipole antennas.
- Monopole antennas.
- Patch antennas.
- Planar Inverted-F Antennas (PIFAs).

Figure 9. Dipole antenna

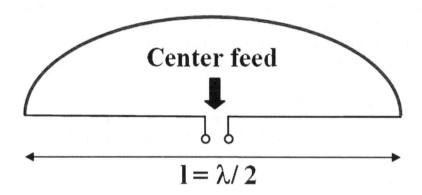

The Dipole and Related Antennas

Let us first consider the dipole as a candidate for a body-worn antenna. The dipole is the most basic design of an antenna; it is a symmetric structure, consisting of a straight thin wire conductor of a certain length and a center feeding, see for instance (Figure 9). The maximal radiation power is achieved in the plane perpendicular to the dipole. The typical radiation pattern is therefore in the shape of a torus. The dipole is a typical resonant antenna, having well-defined resonances precisely located in frequency.

Dipole antennas are widely used for wearable applications and several antenna designs are presented in the literature. In (D. Psychoudakis et al., 2010), a wearable asymmetric dipole antenna was introduced for military applications. Compared to the conventional center-fed dipole, asymmetry provides a broader frequency band and a slightly smaller size. The model is designed to be placed on the armor vest, and miniaturization techniques are applied (bending) to reduce the size. The main limitation of this antenna is that it has to be placed on flat surfaces, see (Figure 10). Similar wearable antennas, exclusively dedicated for armor vests, are presented in (Lee et al., 2011).

Volakis et al., have investigated more conventional models of dipole antennas that can be used in a larger field of applications as they are conformable. Their mounting around the wearer's body is more

Figure 10. Asymmetric wearable dipole antenna for armor vests
D. Psychoudakis et al., 2010.

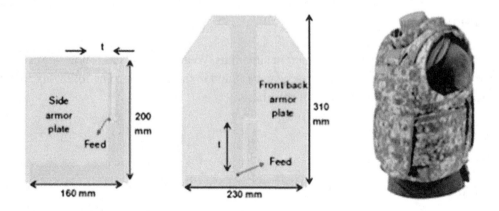

convenient compared to the previous examples. The presented antennas are based on a printed wide dipole, with slight differences between them. The first is the so-called bow-tie dipole, the second a flare dipole, while the last one is an Asymmetric Meandered Flare (AMF) and they are all shown in (Figure 11). Apart from being conformal, the dimensions of those antennas, 305 x 38 mm², allow placing several of them on the same wearer. Their overall size makes them suitable for placing at different positions of the human body like chest, back, shoulders, etc.

Table 2 gives an overview of the advantages and disadvantages of dipole antennas while placed on the wearer's body.

Figure 11. Wide printed dipole antennas for wearable applications, from left to right: Bow-Tie, Flare and Asymmetric Meandered Flare (AMF) dipole
Source: Psychoudakis & Volakis, 2009.

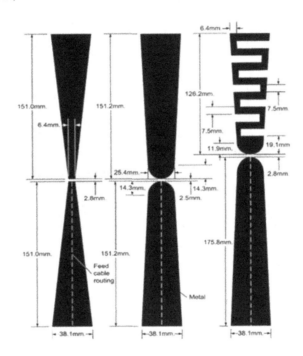

Table 2. A summary of the positive and negative aspects for dipole antennas used for wearable applications

Advantages ☺	Disadvantages ☹
Single and sharp resonant behavior, good for filtering input signal	Due to the lossy body nature the antenna requires wider operating frequency bandwidth
Radiation pattern - "Torus shape" perpendicular to the wearer's body	Radiation pattern - "Torus shape" part of the energy still penetrates into the body
Most of the models are flexible and conformal for mounting	Narrow fractional bandwidth, up to 10%
Miniaturization - bending or meandering the antenna structure	Balanced feeding, need for baluns in some cases
	The lack of the ground plane and polarization parallel to the wearer increases the penetration of the radiation inside the body

Source: Trajkovikj, Fuchs, & Skrivervik, 2011.

Monopole Antennas

The monopole antenna can be near-resonant (length is approximately a quarter-wavelength) or electrically short (length is much shorter than a quarter-wavelength). Compared to the dipole, the monopole requires a ground plane in its structure. The dimensions of the ground plane may vary from a fraction of a wavelength to many wavelengths (Weiner, 2003).

In the case of wearable applications, the presence of the ground is an advantage, since it allows some shielding of the body. The protrusion of the antenna orthogonally to the body, however, is a serious disadvantage and miniaturization is required to make the monopole low profile. Most of the monopole antennas found in the literature have planar characteristics because it is much easier to integrate planar structure into the garment or any kind of uniform (Ma et al., 2008; Lin et al., 2012).

Button Antenna as a Special Monopole Antenna Case

An especially interesting sub-group of monopole antennas is the button antenna. It is designed by loading the monopole antenna with a certain load, composed of metal in most of the cases, leading to a decrease of its height. This loading method is successfully applied to many button antennas, as it will be seen from the examples shown in this section. The existing literature gives some examples of button antennas integrated into wearable applications. For example in (Izquierdo et al., 2010), a dual-band metallic button antenna is shown for body area network applications, for covering both Off- and On-body communications. The operating frequencies of this antenna are 2.45 GHz and 5.5 GHz. For the specified frequencies the dimensions of the antenna are the following: ground plane size of 50 x 50 mm², top disc diameter 16 mm, and a total height of 8.3 mm. The 3D model of the antenna is presented in (Figure 13 a).

More complex loading shapes are also present in literature. An antenna loaded with a G-shaped metallic structure has been reported in (Salman & Talbi, 2010). This antenna operates at ISM bands and it is a dual band antenna with an overall size of 40 x 40 mm² of the ground plane and 10 mm in the height. The geometrical shape of the loading can be adapted to the desired feature of the antenna. Another monopole loaded antenna has been introduced by Koohestani et al., where a cross (Swiss flag symbol) is used as a shape for loading a vertically polarized UWB antenna (Koohestani et al., 2014), see (Figure 13 b).

Most of these antennas operate inside the ISM or UWB bands. Communication distance is aimed for a short range, from a few centimeters up to 10 meters (Alomainy et al., 2009), where the majority of

Figure 12. Monopole antenna: (a) quarter-wavelength monopole and (b) electrically short monopole

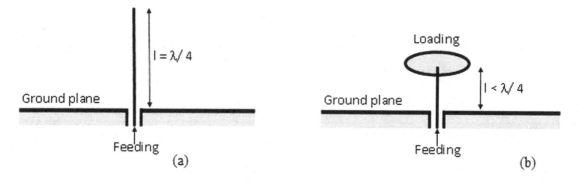

Figure 13. (a) Monopole button antenna loaded with a disc and (b) monopole antenna loaded with a cross shape structure (Swiss flag cross)
Izquierdo et al., 2010.

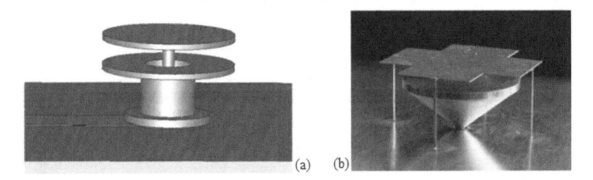

applications using button antennas are for indoor communication. Button antennas remain good candidates for applications where a compact antenna integrated into different parts of the clothes is needed for short range communication.

Patch Antennas

The microstrip patch is a planar antenna, consisting of a radiating patch on one side of a dielectric substrate, and the ground plane on the other. The radiating elements are made of conducting materials (e.g. copper, usually photo-etched). Patches can be found in any geometrical shape, but the most common have some regular shapes as square, rectangular, circular, triangular, elliptical, etc. They radiate primarily because of the fringing fields between the patch and the ground plane, see for instance (Figure 14). The radiation pattern of these antennas is perpendicular to the plane of the patch (Balanis, 2005).

Different structures can be used for feeding the patch antennas, such as microstrip line, coaxial probe, aperture coupling or proximity coupling (Balanis, 2005). The variety of the feeding techniques provides some degrees of freedom in the design phase, as well as in later stages while mounting them on the wearer's body. The microstrip patch is a candidate for any narrowband wearable application, as it has a low profile and can be made conformal for integration into the clothing. The presence of the ground plane is an additional advantage when these antennas are used in wearable applications, preventing the radiation into the wearer's body. Patch antennas are mainly used in GPS and ISM bands. Hertler et al.

Table 3. A summary of the positive and negative aspects for the monopole and button antennas when used for wearable applications

Advantages ☺	Disadvantages ☹
Presence of a ground plane	Protrusive structure
Polarization perpendicular to the wearer	
Printed monopole, planar structure	Polarization perpendicular to the wearer
Button compact antenna → easy integration	Mostly for ISM & UWB bands short distance communication

Source: Trajkovikj et al., 2011.

Figure 14. Cross section of a microstrip patch antenna

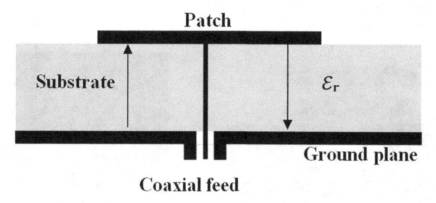

have introduced several patch based antennas operating inside the ISM and GPS bands, intended for wearable applications (Vallozzi, Van Torre, et al., 2010). All the proposed antennas are built out of specific textile materials, conductive and dielectric, and are mainly used for firefighter service applications.

An alternative shape to the conventional rectangular patch antenna can be a circular disk microstrip antenna. The main advantage of circular configuration, compared to the rectangular geometry, is that the circular disk occupies the less physical area, leading to an easier integration in arrays for instance. In (Sankaralingam & Gupta, 2009), circular disk microstrip Wireless Local Area Network (WLAN) wearable antenna is presented, operating at 2.45 GHz. Using a copper as a conducting layer, this antenna achieves a gain of 5.7 dBi, slightly lower than its rectangular counterpart which has a gain of 5.9 dBi. A complete textile patch antenna is shown in (Carter et al., 2010), where both the substrate and the patch are textile materials with good conductive and dielectric characteristics respectively. Zelt3 material is used for building the patch and the ground plane while Felt 4 is used as a substrate material. Both materials will be considered in more details in the section considering the materials. Figure 15 depicts the top view of the discussed antenna. The dimensions of this patch are 13.5 x 13.3 cm², i.e. half wavelength at 920 MHz. A summary about the suitability of patch antennas, when used in wearable applications, is shown as an overview of advantages and disadvantages (Table 4).

Planar Inverted-F Antennas (PIFAs)

A Planar Inverted-F Antenna (PIFA) is the last family of antennas enclosed in this overview which is a subject of consideration. Basically, PIFA is a kind of inverted-F antenna (IFA) with the wire radiator element replaced by a plate to expand the bandwidth. On one hand, the PIFA is derived from the monopole antenna, where by bending and shortening, its characteristic shape is achieved (Salonen et al., 1999), while on the other hand, it can also be considered as a short-circuited patch antenna (Fujimoto, 2008). The addition of the shorting strip allows a good impedance match to be achieved with a top plate, which is typically less than λ/4 long. The PIFA consists of a ground plane, a top plate element, a feed wire attached between the ground plane and the top plate, and a shorting wire or strip that is connected to the ground plane and the top plate. Figure 16 illustrates a typical PIFA configuration.

PIFA is a widely deployed antenna among many Personal Communication System (PCS) devices because of its characteristics. PIFAs have many advantages that make them very good candidates for the hand-held and mobile devices (Z. N. Chen, 2007). They are highly integrable into a casing or other

Figure 15. Patch antenna using Zelt fabric as conductor and Felt as a substrate
Source: Carter et al., 2010.

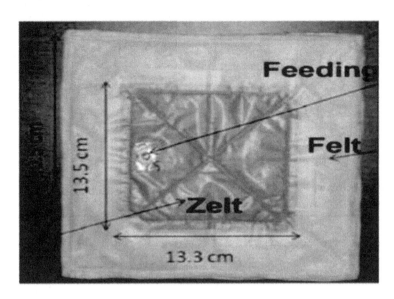

Table 4. A summary of the positive and negative aspects for patch antennas when used for wearable applications

Advantages ☺	Disadvantages ☹
Light weight and low volume	Narrow bandwidth
Conformability	Low efficiency
Low cost of fabrication	Low gain
Supports linear and circular polarization	Extraneous radiation from feeds and junctions
High level of integrability	Low power handling capacity
Mechanically robust	Surface wave excitation
Capable of multiband operations	

Source: Trajkovikj et al., 2011.

components of the environment and have a reduced backward radiation towards the users' body. In this way, the SAR is significantly reduced, which is an important aspect when it comes to the body-worn antennas (Wong, 2002). They exhibit moderate to medium gain in both vertical and horizontal states of polarization. This feature is very useful in certain situations where the antenna does not have a fixed position and different reflections are present in its environment.

For the applications where larger bandwidth is required, several different techniques can be used for its enhancement (Firoozy, 2011):

- Varying the size of the ground plane.
- Use of a thick air substrate.
- Use of parasitic resonators with resonant lengths close to main resonant frequency.

Figure 16. Configuration of PIFA

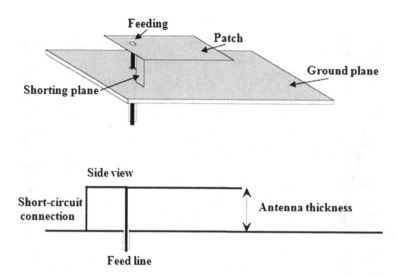

- Adjusting the location and spacing between the shorting posts.
- Use of stacked elements.
- PIFAs have two main advantages making them suitable for wearable applications:
- The presence of the ground plane in its structure which insulates the antenna from the wearer, thus reducing the coupling (favorable for off-body communications).
- Antennas low profile allows easy integration within the wearer's garments.

As an interesting candidate for UHF wearable applications, an overview of PIFAs used in WBANs is presented. A simple PIFA prototype, built out of textile materials, intended for wearable applications is presented in (Soh et al., 2010). The antenna operates at 2.45 GHz, with the overall dimensions 50 x 24 x 10 mm^3 (Figure 17). The presented antenna is characterized in free space and when placed in the vicinity of the human body.

Simulated and experimental results indicated that the textile PIFAs are able to operate with a reflection coefficient below -10 dB, and a fractional bandwidth of around 27%. On average the measured gain is 1.6 dBi while the efficiency ranges between 77- 85% (measurements obtained in free space, not on body or phantom). Two more antennas based on the PIFA concept, operating at 2.45 GHz and 5.2 GHz, are presented in the literature, the dual-band Sierpinski fractal textile PIFA and a broadband all-textile slotted PIFA (Soh et al., 2012). A modified E-shaped PIFA (Cibin et al., 2004), has been one of the pioneering antennas in the frame of this thesis project (Figure 18). It has been intended to operate inside the Tetrapol communication band, 380-400 MHz. The antenna exhibits -12 dBi gains while mounted on the body, which is better than the conventional half-wavelength dipoles. The proposed antenna has overall dimensions of 30 x 30 x 2 cm^3, which makes it suitable for mounting, but the area occupied is still fairly large. However, this antenna can be seen as a good starting example for the development of UHF wearable antennas. Table 5 summarizes the most relevant advantages and disadvantages of the PIFAs when used for wearable applications.

Figure 17. PIFA wearable antenna: (a) a 3-D model and (b) fabricated PIFAs using ShieldIt conductive textiles
Soh et al., 2010.

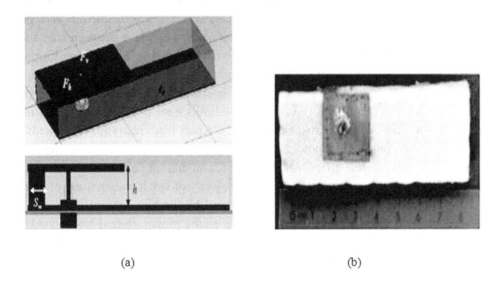

(a)   (b)

Figure 18. Modified E-PIFA structure
Cibin et al., 2004.

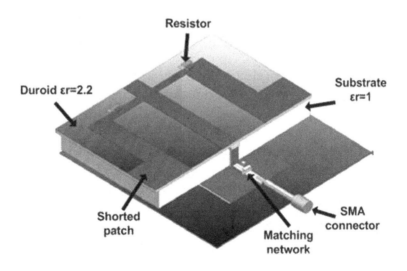

Table 5. A summary of the positive and negative aspects for the PIFAs when used for wearable applications

Advantages ☺	Disadvantages ☹
PIFA structure: good compromise fc vs. size (low profile) vs. on-body placement	PIFA structure: at UHF frequencies the size still fairly large
Moderate to medium gain	Moderate to medium efficiency
Reduced coupling to the wearer	

Source: Trajkovikj et al., 2011.

177

Miniaturization Techniques

In order to be practical, wearable antennas should often be small in size, which can be problematic for the designs especially in the UHF band. Therefore, a short overview of miniaturization techniques will be presented. Antenna miniaturization is always a matter of compromise between size and radiation characteristics (Staub et al., 1999). The fundamental physical limits on antenna EM performance related to size are well known since the early days of wireless communication (Wheeler, 1975; Chu, 1948; Harrington, 1960). The study of these limits regained a huge interest in the nineties with the boom of mobile phones (see for instance (McLean, 1996)). Lately, these limits have been refined taking into account antennas shape (Gustafsson, Sohl, & Kristensson, 2007). Apart from restrictions in bandwidth, gain, efficiency and polarization purity (Fujimoto, 2008), the process of miniaturization brings to the surface problem of feeding a small antenna efficiently. In general, antennas are either balanced or unbalanced, and their feeding should be in accordance to this. The majority of small antennas are of an unbalanced character and the reduction of their size is always followed by the reduction of their ground (often a plane). A reduced ground cannot absorb the charge flow as the proper ground would lead to spurious ground currents altering the radiation characteristics of the antenna (Staub, Zürcher, & Skrivervik, 1998).

Antennas may be small in terms of:

- **Electrical Size:** The antenna can be physically bounded by a sphere having a radius equal to $\lambda_{freespace}/2\pi$. Planar inverted-F antennas with shorting pins or/and slots are typical examples of this category.
- **Physical Size:** An antenna which is not electrically small may feature a substantial size reduction in one dimension or plane. Microstrip patch antennas with ultra low profiles belong to this category.
- **Function:** An antenna which is not electrically or physically small in size may possess additional functions without any increase in size. Dielectric resonator antennas operating in multiple modes fit this definition.

The main techniques available for antenna miniaturization are presented in (Staub et al., 1999):

- Material or lumped element loading, usually at the expense of the bandwidth of the antenna.
- Geometrical loading, by using bands and slots.
- Using grounds and short circuits.
- Using the antenna's environment to enhance the radiation.

Examples of miniaturization techniques (Staub et al., 1999) are illustrated in (Figure 19 and 20), (Bokhari et al., 1996; Zurcher, Skrivewik, & Staub, 2000), where an environment (human body) is used for the miniaturization.

Materials and Fabrication Methods

Materials play an important role in the design and fabrication of wearable antennas. The integration of the antennas into the wearers' clothes indirectly imposes the potential choice of conductive and substrate

Figure 19. Miniaturization techniques: (a) geometrical transformation steps (bending) of a monopole into Inverted-F Antenna (IFA) and (b) a capacitor–plate antenna (loaded monopole)
Staub et al., 1999.

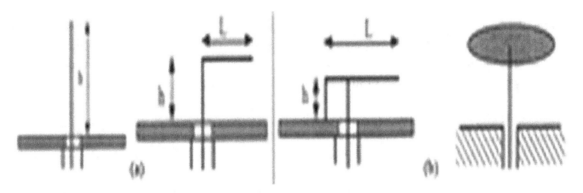

Figure 20. (a) Printed patch antenna for GPS for watch application; (b) SMILA (Smart Mono-bloc-Integrated L-Antenna)
Source: Bokhari et al., 1996; Zurcher et al., 2000.

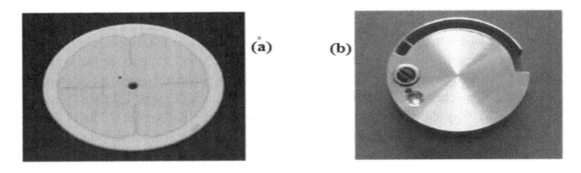

materials. A wide range of materials can be found in the literature: textiles specially treated yarns, printed conductors, polymers, etc. (Salonens et al., 2004).

Selected materials need to be combined with the set of technological and fabrication processes in order to build the final antenna structures. A set of embroidering techniques, inkjet printing, Substrate Integrated Waveguide (SIW) technology and a combination of polymers and different conductive materials are presented (Santas, Alomainy, & Hao, 2007; Rais et al., 2009).

The operating environment also influences the performance of the antenna. Apart from the body's influence on the antennas, they can be also exposed to the different harsh environment, manifested through different weather conditions like rain, humidity, snow, mud, ice, etc. This is an additional reason why a careful selection of the materials should be considered (Kaija, Lilja, & Salonen, 2010).

Material Selection

Dielectric Materials

Different types of dielectrics can be used as antenna substrates. From the EM point of view, two important characteristics matter: low permittivity and low losses improve the antenna's radiation characteristics, i.e. bandwidth and radiation efficiency (Balanis, 2005). Therefore, the efforts will be concentrated on lowering the permittivity and losses of the selected dielectric materials.

- For soft PCB processes, flexible films are the major core materials for supporting overlays, such as polyimide (PI) films ((Khaleel et al., 2012), (Virtanen et al., 2010)), polyester (commonly refers to Polyethylene TerePhthalate (PET) films (Koo et al., 2011; Casula et al., 2013), and liquid crystal polymer films (LCP) (Nikolaou et al., 2006; DeJean et al., 2005). These materials have the merits of high flexibility, low loss tangent, and availability of low thicknesses. Table 6 summarizes the advantages and disadvantages of each material (Numakura, 2007). The Kapton, as a high-performance PI film, shows good soldering tolerance for flexible antenna fabrication and withstands high temperature, which is required in thermal annealing of inkjet-printed antennas (Y. Kim, Kim, & Yoo, 2010). These soft films can hold deposited pure metal materials and conductive inks (Virtanen et al., 2010; Casula et al., 2013).
- Textile in clothing (nonconductive fabric) can be utilized as a platform for antennas, especially when combined with metal-plated textile conductors. Various types of textiles are employed, such as cotton, silk, wool, viscose, and felt (Y. Kim et al., 2010; Monti, Corchia, & Tarricone, 2013). The relative permittivity and loss tangent of such materials are highly dependent on construction (knit or woven), constituent materials, and thickness (Ouyang & Chappell, 2008). Some textiles have anisotropic qualities, such as Cordura and Ballistic fabrics (Kaivanto et al., 2011). Therefore, parameters characterization is quite essential for the selected clothing textile before the antenna design and simulation step. Nonconductive textiles can sometimes be designed with metallic pieces such as zippers and metallic buttons as the radiating parts (Mantash et al., 2011).
- Other flexible substrates are also employed for special purposes. For example, paper substrates can be utilized in screen-printing and inject printing processes based on conductive inks. The paper is widely deployed since it is a low cost, environmental friendly material and can be modified to have hydrophobic and fire retardant properties. However, it is also loss and frequency-dependent. A dispersion model is required for accurate RF simulation and analysis (Cook & Shamim, 2013).

Table 6. Properties comparison of popular film materials

Property	PI Films	LCP Films	PET Films
Thermal rating	200°C	70°C	90°C
Soldering	Applicable	Difficult	Possible
Wire bonding	Possible	No	Difficult
Moisture absorption	High	Low	Low
Dimensional stability	High	High	High
Cost	Moderate	Low	Low

Conductive Materials

Similar to conventional antennas, a typical flexible/wearable antenna consists of two parts: conductive (ground plane and radiating element) and dielectric (substrate, which acts as a platform for the radiating element).

For conductive materials, the following requirements need to be fulfilled:

- Low resistivity/ high conductivity.
- **Deformability, Flexibility:** Such as the capability for bending, crumpling and stretching.
- **Weatherproof:** Resistant to material degradation due to environmental factors such as oxidization and corrosion.
- **Tensile Strength:** The material must be able to withstand repeated pressure, deformation, etc.
- **Integration with Textiles:** The ability of the material to be sewed or embroidered.
  - Pure metallic materials are widely adopted in wearable textile-based antennas, such as silver paste (Tesla, 1892), copper gauze, and copper foils (Brown, 1984). The advantages of using such materials include high conductivity, cost effectiveness, and fabrication simplicity. It is worth noting that when the above-mentioned materials are integrated with clothing textiles, adhesive laminates or supporting foams are usually utilized instead of sewing and embroidering.
  - Metal-plated textile is another widely used conductive material in the fabrication of wearable and flexible antennas; it is often termed "electro-textile" and "E-textile". Metal-plated textiles possess the property of high ductility and can be sewed directly into clothing using textile yarns. Soft materials such as Kevlar, Nylon, and Vectran are coated with metals. The effective electrical conductivity of such textiles can reach up to 1E+6S/m; the conductive thread is the basic component of E-textiles. Different kinds/brands of E-textiles are exploited in recent published literature, such as (Jabbar, Song, & Jeong, 2010), less EMF (Rishani et al., 2012), and Zelt (Haskou et al., 2012).
  - Conductive ink, made of carbon or metal particles, is a promising material for flexible antenna design. Conductive inks have the merits of fabrication simplicity, compatibility with standard screen printing and inkjet printing process, and low cost. The effective conductivity is dependent on the material's intrinsic property, added solvent impurities, and the thermal annealing process (Declercq et al., 2010).

Material Characterization

The propagation and loss properties at the desired frequency band(s) need to be known for the candidate material prior to antenna design and fabrication. For conductive materials, conductivity and surface resistance have to be characterized, while permittivity and loss tangent have to be characterized for substrate materials. For clothing textile materials with different constructions and thicknesses, most of the parameters are unknown and need to be measured.

- Conductive materials can be characterized using waveguide cavity method and microstrip resonator method (Reina., Roa, & Prado, 2006). In waveguide cavity method, Figure 21 a, the quality factors (Q) and transmission coefficient S21 with and without the conductive textile could be measured. Then, the conductive loss is calculated, and thus, the conductivity and surface resistance of the conductive textile can be extracted. In the second method, the microstrip resonator is used instead of the waveguide cavity, as shown in Figure 21 b and the measurement steps are similar to that of the waveguide method. However, the dielectric loss of the substrate should be obtained first. Transmission line method is feasible for the same purpose (Mandal, Turicchia, & Sarpeshkar, 2010).

- For dielectric textiles, the permittivity and loss tangent properties are mainly of interest. The most popular characterization method is the resonator method. A T-resonator microstrip line method is proposed in (Wang et al., 2009) and shown in Figure 22 a. The scattering transfer cascade matrix is used to present an additional parameter S_L, as shown in Figure 22 b. The propagation factor $e\gamma$ $\binom{l\ -l}{1\ 2}$ (where l_1 and l_2 are the lengths of the two lines) is determined by the eigenvalue of scattering matrix of S_L. Effective permittivity and loss tangent can then be extracted.

Figure 21. (a) Waveguide cavity method and (b) microstrip resonator method
Source: Wu et al., 2010.

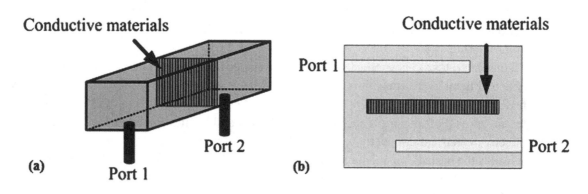

Figure 22. (a) T-resonator method and (b) matric-pencil two-line method
Source: Skrivervik & Merli, 2011; Kim & Samii, 2004.

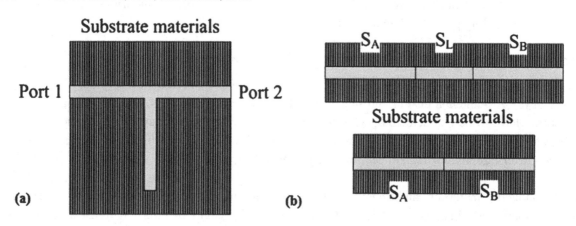

Antenna Fabrication

Based on the description of conductive and substrate materials in the previous section, there are several widely adopted fabrication processes of flexible and wearable antennas. This section reviews the commercial methods in addition to techniques used by the research and development sector. An overview of each technique, in addition to their advantages and drawbacks, is discussed:

Line Patterning

Line patterning is one of the simplest and most inexpensive solutions for fabricating RFIDs and flexible electronics (Carmo et al., 2006) .The design of a negative image of the desired pattern is first developed using a computer-aided design program, followed by depositing a conductive polymer on the substrate. The last step involves taking out the printed mask by soni-cating the substrate (by applying an ultrasonic energy) in a toluene solution for about 10 seconds. Flexible field effect transistors, filters, resistors, and RFIDs are amongst the components produced using this method.

Flexography

In flexography, a print-making process of an image is involved, which is performed by inking a protuberant surface of the printing plate matrix while the recessed (suspended) areas are left free of ink (Lilja & Salonen, 2009). Flexography gained a significant interest by RFID antenna manufacturers due to its relatively high resolution, cost-effectiveness, and roll-to-roll production capability. Furthermore, this technique requires a lower viscosity ink than the inks used in the screen-printing method, which yields dry patterned films of a thickness of < 2.5 μm. In contrast to the inks used in screen-printing, inks used in flexography must have higher conductivity to compensate for the difference in sheet resistance since the efficiency of the fabricated antennas relies directly on the electrical conductivity of the radiating element.

Screen-Printing

Screen-printing is another cost-effective technique used by flexible electronics manufacturers. This technique is characterized by its simplicity and being an additive process, which makes it environmentally friendly. A mask with the desired pattern is developed first and then applied directly on a flexible substrate/film where the conductive ink is administered and thermally treated to evaporate the excess solvent. Flexible transparent antennas and RFIDs have been successfully prototyped using this technique (Vallozzi et al., 2010). It is worth mentioning that there are some drawbacks associated with this technique, which includes the limited control over the thickness of the deposited ink, number of layers, and resolution of the deposited patterns.

Photolithography

Photolithography-based manufacturing has emerged in the 1960s targeting the PCB industry. It involves using a photoresist and chemical agents to etch away the unwanted area corrosively to produce the desired metallic patterns. This technique had gained notable popularity due to its capability of accurately producing patterns with fine details (Cibin et al., 2004). Currently, the fabrication of antennas and RF circuits based on photolithography is preferred to be conducted utilizing positive photoresists due to the fact that negative photoresists often give rise to the edge-swelling phenomenon, which compromises the consistency and resolution of the resulting pattern. When photolithography is used to produce flexible electronics, single or double-sided substrates are utilized where the desired pattern is obtained by etching regions of either or both sides. It is worth mentioning that stacking multi-flexible patterned layers are also possible using this technique. The major drawbacks of photolithography are low throughput, the involvement of hazardous chemicals, and production of by products; hence, it is not suitable for commercial production.

Thermal Evaporation

Thermal evaporation is a physical vapor deposition process, which is recognized amongst the most widely used thin-film deposition techniques. This method involves a vacuum process where a pure material coating is administered over the film surface. This process is conducted by heating a solid material inside a vacuum chamber where vapor pressure is created. Consequently, the evaporated material is deposited on the substrate. In antenna and RFID applications, the coating material is usually a pure atomic metal. It should be noted that this process is usually accompanied by a photolithographic process (Izquierdo, Huang, & Batchelor, 2006).

Sewing and Embroidering

Using sewing or embroidering machine is mainly employed in textile-based antennas, which is preferred over direct adhesion of E-textile over the fabric since no adhesive materials are introduced which may affect the electrical properties of the material (Izquierdo & Batchelor, 2008). Wrinkling and crumpling should be minimized to maintain the material qualities. For wearable antennas on clothing application, this is the most preferred fabrication process.

Inkjet Printing

Inkjet printing of antennas and RF circuits using highly conductive inks based on nanostructural materials are gaining extreme popularity nowadays. Inkjet material printers operate by releasing pico-litre sized ink droplets, which give rise to high-resolution patterns and compact designs (Izquierdo & Batchelor, 2008).

Wearable Antenna: Advantages, Disadvantages, and Challenges

Advantages

There are many advantages of using wearable sensors. Four main advantages are:

- **Medicine:** Many new technologies will help doctors monitor a patient's medical conditions through the technology without having to actually visit the doctor. Not only is this beneficial for the doctor, it will also reduce hospital costs and overall cost of healthcare
- **Every Day Use:** Many people use their cell phone or purchase a pedometer to calculate how far they have walked or ran.

- **Rescue:** Many new technologies are allowing rescue missions to be safer and more knowledgeable before entering into danger. Nowadays, we are able to map where people are in dangerous areas and establish links where help or recovery is needed.
- **Repair:** Repairing equipment would be easy with wearable technology. For instance, there is an electronic manual where pages can be flipped using the eye, which will save a lot of time.

Disadvantage

A common disadvantage with wearable antennas is radiation. A lot of research is being done regarding technology and the amount of harmful radiation generated. Radiation is electromagnetic technology that may harm human health. Fortunately, the shorter the communication distance used for a technology, the less radiation produced. Therefore, wearable technology is even less harmful than cell-phones. Also, another disadvantage for wearable technology is that many products currently still look unnatural when worn. It will be a matter of time before people start adapting and begin following the trend of wearable technology.

Challenges

There are three challenges in wearable devices that make antenna design particularly difficult:

Proximity to the Human Body

The human body is a lossy material for electromagnetic waves. This means the body converts Electric Fields into heat; put another way, the body absorbs energy from electromagnetic waves. Consequently, when an antenna is placed near the body, the result is a large reduction of the antenna efficiency of your wearable antenna. For example, if you design an antenna and measure efficiency of -3 dB (50%), when placed on the body the efficiency may easily drop to -13 dB (5%). This is a huge hit to the performance of the wireless system.

Very Limited Volumes

Wearable devices must be as small as possible. No one wants a watch with a big dipole antenna hanging out the side. Space is at an extreme premium on wearable devices, particularly for anything near the face (such as google glass). As such, industrial designers and product designers often give very little space for the antenna, which further makes the antenna design problem more difficult.

Energy Harvesting

Energy harvesting is the process of taking energy from external sources and converting these energies to electrical energy. External energy sources include kinetic (locomotion, vibration, rotation), solar cell (light), thermal, piezoelectric (using excess energy derived from motion) and even radio waves.

Pros

- Energy Harvesting helps wearable devices to become more independent from power outlets

- Solar energy works perfectly when placed on smart clothes, which can absorb and use energy straight from the sun.
- Solar energy provides energy even indoors.
- Thermoelectric harvesting energy is a solution for devices worn directly on skins (i.e. Smart Patches). The energy source is always available and provides high power.
- No wasted energy produced from your movement.

Cons

- Piezoelectric method generates comparably small amount of energy.
- Kinetic can produce energy throughout movement but is translated to low power.

CONCLUSION

This chapter provided a review of the most recent wearable and flexible antennas found in the literature. Applications such as medical, sport and Security are presented. Many antennas family included: Dipole, Monopole, Patch, and Planar Inverted-F Antennas (PIFAs) antenna, are also discussed. An overview of the electrical characterization of flexible materials used in the fabrication of wearable antennas, as well, all fabrication techniques, advantages, disadvantages and challenges were given.

It is expected that many more light-weight, high-performance wearable sensors will be available to facilitate a wide range of daily life activities. Formal and informal surveys predict an increase of interest and consequent usages of wearable devices in near future, the cost of the devices is also expected to fall resulting in of wide application in the society.

Finally, the Future of wearable technology: Smaller, Cheaper, Faster, and Personal Computing; Figure 23 illustrates some wearable products in processing.

Figure 23. Wearable sensors: future products

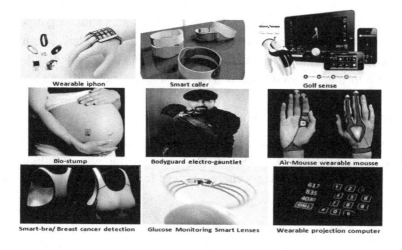

186

REFERENCES

A pervasive body sensor network for measuring postoperative recovery at home. (2007). In *Surg Innov* (pp. 83–90).

A pilot study of long-term monitoring of human movements in the home using accelerometry. (2004). *J Telemed Telecare*, 144–151.

Afyf, A., Bellarbi, L., Riouch, F., Achour, A., Errachid, A., & Sennouni, M. A. (2015). Antenna for Wireless Body Area Network (WBAN) Applications Flexible Miniaturized UWB CPW II- shaped Slot. In *IEEE Third International Workshop on RFID And Adaptive Wireless Sensor Networks* (pp. 52–56).

Afyf, A., Bellarbi, L., Riouch, F., Achour, A., Errachid, A., & Sennouni, M. A. (2015). Flexible Miniaturized UWB CPW II- shaped Slot. In *IEEE Third International Workshop on RFID And Adaptive Wireless Sensor Networks* (pp. 52–56).

Alipour, S., Parvaresh, F., Ghajari, H., & Kimball, D. F. (2010). Propagation Characteristics for a 60 GHz Wireless Body Area Network (WBAN). In *The 2010 Military Communications Conference - Unclassified Program - Waveforms and Signal Processing Track* (pp. 719–723).

Alomainy, A., Hao, Y., & Pasveer, F. (2007). Numerical and experimental evaluation of a compact sensor antenna for healthcare devices. *IEEE Transactions on Biomedical Circuits and Systems*, *1*(4), 242–249. doi:10.1109/TBCAS.2007.913127 PMID:23852005

Alomainy, A., Sani, A., Rahman, A., Santas, J. G., & Hao, Y. (2009). Transient characteristics of wearable antennas and radio propagation channels for ultrawideband body-centric wireless communications. *IEEE Transactions on Antennas and Propagation*, *57*(4), 875–884. doi:10.1109/TAP.2009.2014588

Amal, A., Larbi, B., & Anouar, A. (2016). Miniaturized Wideband Flexible CPW Antenna with Hexagonal Ring Slots for Early Breast Cancer Detection. In S. S. M. Singapore (Ed.), *Ubiquitous Networking* (pp. 211–222). Springer. doi:10.1007/978-981-287-990-5_17

An experience of health technology assessment in new models of care for subjects with Parkinson's disease by means of a new wearable device. (2008). *Telemed J E Health*, 467–472.

Automatic recognition of postures and activities in stroke patients. (2009). In IEEE Eng Med Biol Soc (pp. 2200–2203).

Balanis, C. A. (2005). *Antenna Theory Analysis and Design* (3rd ed.). John Wiley Sons, Inc.

Batchelor, J. C. (2008). A dual band belt antenna. In *International Workshop on Antenna Technology: Small Antennas and Novel Metamaterial* (pp. 374– 377).

Belza, B., Steele, B., Hunziker, J., Lakshminaryan, S., Holt, L., & Buchner, D. (2001). Correlates of physical activity in chronic obstructive pulmonary disease. In Nurs Res (pp. 195–202). doi:10.1097/00006199-200107000-00003

Bokhari, S. A., Zürcher, J. F., Mosig, J. R., & Gardiol, F. E. (1996). A small microstrip patch antenna with a convenient tuning option. *IEEE Transactions on Antennas and Propagation*, *44*(11), 1521–1528. doi:10.1109/8.542077

Brown, W. C. (1984). The history of power transmission by radio waves. *IEEE Transactions on Microwave Theory and Techniques, 32*(9), 1230–1242. doi:10.1109/TMTT.1984.1132833

Carmo, J. P., Dias, N., Mendes, P. M., Couto, C., & Correia, J. H. (2006). Low-power 2.4-GHz RF transceiver for wireless EEG module plug-and-play. In *13th IEEE International Conference on Electronics, Circuits and Systems* (pp. 1144–1147). doi:10.1109/ICECS.2006.379642

Carter, J., Saberin, J., Shah, T., Sai Ananthanarayanan, P. R., & Furse, C. (2010). Inexpensive fabric antenna for off-body wireless sensor communication. In *IEEE International Symposium on Antennas and Propagation* (pp. 9–12). http://doi.org/ doi:10.1109/APS.2010.5561753

Casula, G., Montisci, G., & Mazzarella, G. (2013). A wideband PET inkjet-printed antenna for UHF RFID. *Antennas and Wireless Propagation Letters, 12*, 1400–1403. doi:10.1109/LAWP.2013.2287307

Chandran, A. R., Conway, G. A., & Scanlon, W. G. (2008). Compact Low Profile Patch Antenna For Medical Body Area Netowrks at 868 MHz. In *IEEE Antennas and Propagation Society International Symposium* (pp. 8–11).

Chen, X. L., Kuster, N., Tan, Y. C., & Chavannes, N. (2012). Body effects on the GPS antenna of a wearable tracking device. In *6th European Conference on Antennas and Propagation, EuCAP* (pp. 3313–3316). http://doi.org/ doi:10.1109/EuCAP.2012.6205889

Chen, Z. N. (2007). *Antennas for Portable Devices* (1st ed.). Wiley-VCH. doi:10.1002/9780470319642

Chu, L. J. (1948). Small antennas. *Journal of Applied Physics, 19*(12), 1163–1175. doi:10.1063/1.1715038

Cibin, C., Leuchtmann, P., Gimersky, M., & Vahldieck, R. (2004). Modified E-Shaped Pifa Antenna for Wearable Systems. In *URSI International Symposium on Electromagnetic Theory (URSI EMTS)* (pp. 873–875).

Cibin, C., Leuchtmann, P., Gimersky, M., Vahldieck, R., & Moscibroda, S. (2004). A flexible wearable antenna. In IEEE Antennas and Propagation Society (pp. 3589–3592). doi:10.1109/APS.2004.1330122

Constantinou, C., Nechayev, Y., Wu, X., & Hall, P. (2012). Body-area Propagation at 60 GHz. In Loughborough Antennas & Propagation Conference (pp. 1–4).

Cook, B., & Shamim, A. (2013). Utilizing wideband AMC structures for high-gain inkjet-printed antennas on lossy paper substrate. *IEEE Antennas and Wireless Propagation Letters, 12*, 76–79. doi:10.1109/LAWP.2013.2240251

Corner, A. A. (2013). Body-Worn Antennas Making a Splash: Lifejacket-Integrated Antennas for Global Search and Rescue Satellite System. *IEEE Antennas and Propagation Magazine, 55*(2).

Curone, D., Dudnik, G., Loriga, G., Luprano, J., Magenes, G., Paradiso, R., … Bonfiglio, A. (2007). Smart Garments for Safety Improvement of Emergency/Disaster Operators. In *29th Annual International Conference of the IEEE Engineering in Medicine and Biology Society (EMBS)* (pp. 3962–3965). doi:10.1109/IEMBS.2007.4353201

Curto, S., McEvoy, P., Bao, X., & Ammann, M. J. (2009). Compact patch antenna for electromagnetic interaction with human tissue at 434 MHz. *IEEE Transactions on Antennas and Propagation*, *57*(9), 2564–2571. doi:10.1109/TAP.2009.2027040

Declercq, F., Couckuyt, I., Rogier, H., & Dhaene, T. (2010). Complex permittivity characterization of textile materials by means of surrogate modeling. In *IEEE Antennas and Propagation Society International Symposium* (pp. 1–4).

DeJean, G., Bairavasubramanian, R., Thompson, D., Ponchak, G. M. T., & Papapolymerou, J. (2005). Liquid crystal polymer (LCP): A new organic material for the development of multilayer dual-frequency dual-polarization flexible antenna arrays. *IEEE Antennas and Wireless Propagation Letters*, *4*(1), 22–26. doi:10.1109/LAWP.2004.841626

Federal Communications Commission (FCC). (2014). Retrieved from HTTP: //transition.fcc.gov/Bureaus/ Engineering_Technology/Orders/2002/fcc02048.pdf

Firoozy, N., & Shirazi, M. (2011). Planar Inverted-F Antenna (PIFA) Design Dissection for Cellular Communication Application. *Journal of Electromagnetic Analysis and Applications*, *03*(10), 406–411. doi:10.4236/jemaa.2011.310064

Fujimoto, K. (2008). Mobile Antenna Systems Handbook. Artech House.

Gaetano, D., McEvoy, P., Ammann, M. J., Browne, J. E., Keating, L., & Horgan, F. (2013). Footwear antennas for body area telemetry. *IEEE Transactions on Antennas and Propagation*, *61*(10), 4908–4916. doi:10.1109/TAP.2013.2272451

Gustafsson, M., Sohl, C., & Kristensson, G. (2007). Physical limitations on antennas of arbitrary shape. In Royal Society a-Mathematical Physical and Engineering Sciences (Vol. 463, pp. 2589–2607). http:// doi.org/ doi:10.1098/rspa.2007.1893

Hao, Y., Alomainy, A., Hall, P. S., Nechayev, Y. I., Parini, C. G., & Constantinou, C. C. (2012). *Antennas and Propagation for Body Centric Wireless Communications* (2nd ed.; pp. 38–41). Norwood, MA: Artech House, Inc.

Harrington, R. F. (1960). Effect of antenna size on gain, bandwidth, and efficiency. *Journal of Research of the National Bureau of Standards, Section D. Radio Propagation*, *64D*(1), 1–12. doi:10.6028/jres.064D.003

Haskou, A., Ramadan, A., Al-Husseini, M., Kasem, F., Kabalan, K. Y., & ElHajj, A. (2012). A simple estimation and verification technique for electrical characterization of textiles. In *Middle East Conference on Antennas and Propagation* (pp. 1–4). doi:10.1109/MECAP.2012.6618190

Hecht, A., Ma, S., Porszasz, J., & Casaburi, R. (2009). *Methodology for using long-term accelerometry monitoring to describe daily activity patterns in COPD*. COPD.

Hertel, T. W., & Smith, G. S. (2003). On the dispersive properties of the conical spiral antenna and its use for pulsed radiation. *IEEE Transactions on Antennas and Propagation*, *51*(7), 1426–1433. doi:10.1109/ TAP.2003.813602

Hertleer, C., Rogier, H., Member, S., Vallozzi, L., & Van Langenhove, L. (2009). A Textile Antenna for Off-Body Communication Integrated Into Protective Clothing for Firefighters. *IEEE Transactions on Antennas and Propagation, 57*(4), 919–925. doi:10.1109/TAP.2009.2014574

J., R.-T., Roa, L. M., & Prado, M. (2006). Design of antennas for a wearable sensor for homecare movement monitoring. *IEEE Engineering in Medicine and Biology Society*, (pp. 5972–5976).

Jabbar, H., Song, Y. S., & Jeong, T. T. (2010). RF energy harvesting system and circuits for charging of mobile devices. *IEEE Transactions on Consumer Electronics, 56*(1), 247–253. doi:10.1109/TCE.2010.5439152

Jr, H., & Williams, C. S. (1965). Transients in wide-angle conical antennas. *IEEE Transactions on Antennas and Propagation, 13*(2), 236–246. doi:10.1109/TAP.1965.1138399

Kaija, T., Lilja, J., & Salonen, P. (2010). Exposing textile antennas for harsh environment. In *Military Communications Conference (MILCOM)* (pp. 737–742).

Kaivanto, E., Berg, M., Salonen, E., & Maagt, P. (2011). Wearable circularly polarized antenna for personal satellite communication and navigation. *IEEE Transactions on Antennas and Propagation, 59*(12), 4490–4496. doi:10.1109/TAP.2011.2165513

Khaleel, H., Al-Rizzo, H. M., Rucker, D. G., & Mohan, S. (2012). A compact polyimide based UWB antenna for flexible electronics. *Antennas and Wireless Propagation Letters, 11*, 564–567. doi:10.1109/LAWP.2012.2199956

Kim, J., & Rahmat-Samii, Y. (2004). Implanted antennas inside a human body: Simulations, designs, and characterizations. *IEEE Transactions on Microwave Theory and Techniques, 52*(8), 1934–1943. doi:10.1109/TMTT.2004.832018

Kim, Y., Kim, H., & Yoo, H. (2010). Electrical characterization of screen-printed circuits on the fabric. *IEEE Transactions on Advanced Packaging, 33*(1), 196–205. doi:10.1109/TADVP.2009.2034536

Kiourti, A., Member, S., Costa, J. R., Member, S., Fernandes, C. A., Member, S., & Member, S. et al. (2012). Miniature Implantable Antennas for Biomedical Telemetry: From Simulation to Realization. *IEEE Transactions on Bio-Medical Engineering, 59*(11), 3140–3147. doi:10.1109/TBME.2012.2202659 PMID:22692865

Koo, T., Kim, D., Ryu, J., Seo, H., Yook, J., & Kim, J. (2011). Design of a label typed UHF RFID tag antenna for metallic objects. *Antennas and Wireless Propagation Letters, 10*, 1010–1014. doi:10.1109/LAWP.2011.2166370

Koohestani, M., Zurcher, J.-F., Moreira, A. A., & Skrivervik, A. K. (2014). A Novel, Low-Profile, Vertically-Polarized UWB Antenna for WBAN. *IEEE Transactions on Antennas and Propagation, 62*(4), 1888–1894. doi:10.1109/TAP.2014.2298886

Lapinski, M., Feldmeier, M., & Paradiso, J. A. (2011). Wearable wireless sensing for sports and ubiquitous interactivity. *IEEE Sensors, 1425–1428*. doi:10.1109/ICSENS.2011.6126902

Lee, G. Y., Psychoudakis, D., Chen, C. C., & Volakis, J. L. (2011). Omnidirectional vest-mounted body-worn antenna system for UHF operation. *IEEE Antennas and Wireless Propagation Letters, 10,* 581–583. doi:10.1109/LAWP.2011.2158381

Lilja, J., & Salonen, P. (2009). Textile material characterization for software antennas. In *IEEE Military Communications Conference* (pp. 1–7).

Lin, C. H., Li, Z., Ito, K., Takahashi, M., & Saito, K. (2012). A small tunable and wearable planar inverted-F antenna (PIFA). In *6th European Conference on Antennas and Propagation, EuCAP* (pp. 742–745). http://doi.org/ doi:10.1109/EuCAP.2012.6206554

Ma, L., Edwards, R., & Bashir, S. (2008). A wearable monopole antenna for ultra wideband with notching function. In *IET Seminar on Wideband and Ultrawideband Systems and Technologies: Evaluating current Research and Development* (pp. 1–5). doi:10.1049/ic.2008.0695

Mandal, S., Turicchia, L., & Sarpeshkar, R. (2010). A low-power, battery-free tag for body sensor networks. *IEEE Pervasive Computing / IEEE Computer Society [and] IEEE Communications Society, 9*(1), 71–77. doi:10.1109/MPRV.2010.1

Mantash, M., Tarot, A., Collardey, S., & Mahdjoubi, K. (2011). Wearable monopole zip antenna. *Electronics Letters, 47*(23), 1266–1267. doi:10.1049/el.2011.2784

Matthews, J., & Pettitt, G. (2009). Development of flexible, wearable antennas. In *3rd European Conference on Antennas and Propagation (EuCAP)* (pp. 273–277).

McLean, J. S. (1996). A re-examination of the fundamental limits on the radiation Q of\nelectrically small antennas. *IEEE Transactions on Antennas and Propagation, 44*(5), 672–676. doi:10.1109/8.496253

Medical Device Radiocommunications Service (MedRadio). (2009). Retrieved from www.fcc.gov

Merli, F. (2008). Implantable antennas for biomedical applications. In *Antennas and propagation society international Symposium* (Vol. 5110, pp. 1642–1649). http://doi.org/ doi:<ALIGNMENT.qj></ALIGNMENT>10.5075/epfl-thesis-5110

Micoach. (2014). Retrieved from http://micoach.adidas.com/

Monti, G., Corchia, L., & Tarricone, L. (2013). UHF wearable rectenna on textile materials. *IEEE Transactions on Antennas and Propagation, 61*(7), 3869–3873. doi:10.1109/TAP.2013.2254693

Moy, M., Mentzer, S., & Reilly, J. (2003). Ambulatory monitoring of cumulative freeliving activity. *IEEE Engineering in Medicine and Biology Magazine, 22*(3), 89–95. doi:10.1109/MEMB.2003.1213631 PMID:12845824

National Swiss Plan. (2014). Swiss National Frequency Allocation Plan and Specific Assignments.

Nikolaou, S., Ponchak, G., Papapolymerou, J., & Tentzeris, M. (2006). Conformal double exponentially tapered slot antenna (DETSA) on LCP for UWB applications. *IEEE Transactions on Antennas and Propagation, 54*(6), 1663–1669. doi:10.1109/TAP.2006.875915

Numakura, D. (2007). Flexible Circuit Applications and Materials. In Printed Circuit Handbook (6th ed.). McGraw-Hill.

Ouyang, Y., & Chappell, W. (2008). High-frequency properties of electro-textiles for wearable antenna applications. *IEEE Transactions on Antennas and Propagation, 56*(2), 381–389. doi:10.1109/TAP.2007.915435

Pellegrini, A., Brizzi, A., Zhang, L., Ali, K., Hao, Y., Wu, X., & Sauleau, R. et al. (2013). Antennas and propagation for body-centric wireless communications at millimeter-wave frequencies: A review. *IEEE Antennas and Propagation Magazine, 55*(4), 262–287. doi:10.1109/MAP.2013.6645205

Popovic, Z., Momenroodaki, P., & Scheeler, R. (2014). Toward wearable wireless thermometers for internal body temperature measurements. *IEEE Communications Magazine, 52*(10), 118–125. doi:10.1109/MCOM.2014.6917412

Psychoudakis, D., Lee, G., Chen, C., & Volakis, J. (2010). Military UHF body-worn antennas for armored vests. In *6th European Conference on Antennas and Propagation (EuCAP) IEEE* (pp. 1–4).

Psychoudakis, D., & Volakis, J. L. (2009). Conformal Asymmetric Meandered Flare (AMF) Antenna for Body-Worn Applications. *IEEE Antennas and Wireless Propagation Letters, 8*, 931–934. doi:10.1109/LAWP.2009.2028662

Rahmat-Samii, Y. (2007). Wearable and implantable antennas in body-centric communications. In *2nd European Conference on Antennas and Propagation (EuCAP)* (pp. 1–5).

Rais, N., Soh, P., Malek, F., Ahmad, S., Hashim, N., & Hall, P. (2009). A review of wearable antenna. In *Loughborough Antennas and Propagation Conference(LAPC)* (pp. 225–228).

Ranck, J. (n.d.). *The wearable computing market: A global analysis*. Retrieved from http://go.gigaom.com/rs/gigaom/images/ wearable-computing-the-next-big-thing-in-tech.pdf

REED., F. (2007). 60 GHz WPAN Standardization within IEEE. In *International Symposium on Signals, Systems and Electronics, (ISSSE '07)* (pp. 103–105).

Rishani, N. R., Al-Husseini, A. E.-H., & Kabalan, K. Y. (2012). Design and relative permittivity determination of an EBG-based wearable antenna. In Progress in Electromagnetics and Radio Frequency (pp. 96–99). Moscow, Russia: PIERS.

Running, G. P. S. Watches. (2014). Retrieved from http://sports.tomtom.com/en_us/

Salman, L. K. H., & Talbi, L. (2010). G-shaped wearable cuff button antenna for 2.45 GHZ ISM band applications. In *2010 14th International Symposium on Antenna Technology and Applied Electromagnetics and the American Electromagnetics Conference, ANTEM/AMEREM 2010* (pp. 14–17). http://doi.org/ doi:<ALIGNMENT.qj></ALIGNMENT>10.1109/ANTEM.2010.5552573

Salonen, P., Rahmat-Samii, Y., Hurme, H., & Kivikoski, M. (2004). Effect of conductive material on wearable antenna performance: A case study of WLAN antennas. *Antennas and Propagation Society, 1*, 455–458. doi:10.1109/APS.2004.1329672

Salonen, P., Sydanheimo, L., Keskilammi, M., & Kivikoski, M. (1999). A Small Planar Inverted-F Antenna for Wearable Applications. In *IEEE Conference Publications* (pp. 95–100). http://doi.org/doi:10.1109/ISWC.1999.806679

Sankaralingam, S., & Gupta, B. (2009). A circular disk microstrip WLAN antenna for wearable applications. In *IEEE India Council Conference* (pp. 3–6). http://doi.org/ doi:10.1109/INDCON.2009.5409355

Santas, J., Alomainy, A., & Hao, Y. (2007). Textile Antennas for On-Body Communications: Techniques and Properties. In *2nd European Conference on Antennas and Propagation (EuCAP)* (pp. 1–4.). doi:10.1049/ic.2007.1064

Sanz-Izquierdo, B., Huang, F., & Batchelor, J. C. (2006). Small size wearable button antenna. In *First European Conference on Antennas and Propagation* (pp. 1–4).

Sanz-Izquierdo, B., Miller, J. A., Batchelor, J. C., & Sobhy, M. I. (2010). Dual-Band Wearable Metallic Button Antennas and Transmission in Body Area Networks. *IET Microw. Antennas Propag.*, *4*(2), 182–190. doi:10.1049/iet-map.2009.0010

Serra, A. A., Nepa, P., & Manara, G. (2011). Cospas Sarsat rescue applications.*IEEE International Symposium on Antennas and Propagation (APSURSI)*, *3*, 1319–1322. doi:10.1109/APS.2011.5996532

Sherrill, D. M., Moy, M. L., Reilly, J. J., & Bonato, P. (2005). Using hierarchical clustering methods to classify motor activities of COPD patients from wearable sensor data. *Neuroeng Rehabil*, *2*(1), 16. doi:10.1186/1743-0003-2-16 PMID:15987518

Skrivervik, A. K., & Merli, F. (2011). Design strategies for implantable antennas. In *Loughborough Antennas and Propagation Conference* (pp. 1–5). http://doi.org/ doi:10.1109/LAPC.2011.6114011

Skrivervik, A. K., & Zürcher, J. F. (2007). Miniature antenna design at LEMA. In *19th International Conference on Applied Electromagnetics and Communications* (pp. 4–7). http://doi.org/ doi:<ALIGNMENT.qj></ALIGNMENT>10.1109/ICECOM.2007.4544410

Snow flaik tracks skiers. (2011). Retrieved from http://news.discovery.com/tech/ snow-flaik-tracks-skiers.htm

Soh, P., Boyes, S., Vandenbosch, G., Huang, Y., & Ma, Z. (2012). Dual-band Sierpinski textile PIFA efficiency measurements. In *6th European Conference on Antennas and Propagation (EuCAP)*, (pp. pp. 3322–3326).

Soh, P. J., Vandenbosch, G. A. E., Volski, V., & Nurul, H. M. R. (2010). Characterization of a Simple Broadband Textile Planar Inverted-F Antenna (PIFA) for on Body Communications. In *22nd International Conference on Applied Electromagnetics and Communications (ICECom)* (pp. 1–4).

Staub, O., Zürcher, J.-F., & Skrivervik, A. (1998). Some considerations on the correct measurement of the gain and bandwidth of electrically small antennas. *Microwave and Optical Technology Letters*, *17*(3), 156–160. doi:10.1002/(SICI)1098-2760(19980220)17:3<156::AID-MOP2>3.0.CO;2-I

Staub, O., Zurcher, J.-F., Skrivervik, A. K., & Mosig, J. R. (1999). PCS antenna design: the challenge of miniaturisation. *IEEE Antennas and Propagation Society International Symposium*, *1*. http://doi.org/ doi:10.1109/APS.1999.789198

Steele, B. L. H., Belza, B., Ferris, S., Lakshminaryan, S., & Buchner, D. (2000). *Quantitating physical activity in COPD using a triaxial accelerometer*. Chest.

Tesla, N. (1892). Experiments with alternate currents of high potential and high frequency. *Journal of the Institution of Electrical Engineers, 21*(97), 51–162. doi:10.1049/jiee-1.1892.0002

Tetrapol. (2015). *Tetrapol Factsheet Trunked radio system for emergency services.* Author.

Trajkovikj, J., Fuchs, B., & Skrivervik, A. (2011). *LEMA internal report.* LEMA.

Ullah, S., & Kwak, K. S. (2011). *Body Area Network for Ubiquitous Healthcare Applications: Theory and Implementation.* http://doi.org/<ALIGNMENT.qj></ALIGNMENT>10.1007/s10916-011-9787-x

Vallozzi, L., Van Torre, P., Hertleer, C., Rogier, H., Moeneclaey, M., & Verhaevert, J. (2010). Wireless communication for firefighters using dual-polarized textile antennas integrated in their garment. *IEEE Transactions on Antennas and Propagation, 58*(4), 1357–1368. doi:10.1109/TAP.2010.2041168

Vallozzi, L., Vandendriessche, W., Rogier, H., Hertleer, C., & Scarpello, M. L. (2010). Wearable textile GPS antenna for integration in protective garments. In *4th European Conference on Antennas and Propagation (EuCAP)* (pp. 1–4).

Vallozzi, P., Van Torre, P., Hertleer, C., Rogier, H., Moeneclaey, M., & Verhaevert, J. (2010). Wireless communication for firefighters using dual-polarized textile antennas integrated in their garment. *IEEE Transactions on Antennas and Propagation, 58*(4), 1357–1368. doi:10.1109/TAP.2010.2041168

Verb for shoe - very intelligent shoes. (2004). Retrieved from http://www.gizmag.com/go/3565/picture/7504/

Virtanen, J., Björninen, T., Ukkonen, L., & Sydänheimo, L. (2010). Passive UHF inkjet-printed narrow-line RFID tags. *Antennas and Wireless Propagation Letters, 9*, 440–443. doi:10.1109/LAWP.2010.2050050

Wang, Y., Li, L., Wang, B., & Wang, L. (2009). A body sensor network platform for in-home health monitoring application. In *4th International Conference on Ubiquitous Information Technologies Applications* (pp. 1–5). doi:10.1109/ICUT.2009.5405731

Weiner, M. M. (2003). *Monopole Antennas* (1st ed.). Taylor and Francis. doi:10.1201/9780203912676

Wheeler, H. A. (1975). Small antennas. *IEEE Transactions on Antennas and Propagation, 23*(4), 462–469. doi:10.1109/TAP.1975.1141115

Wong, K. (2002). *Compact and Broadband Microstrip Antennas* (1st ed.). Wiley-VCH. doi:10.1002/0471221112

Wu, X. Y., Akhoondzadeh-Asl, L., Wang, Z. P., & Hall, P. S. (2010). Novel Yagi-Uda antennas for on-body communication at 60GHz. In *Loughborough Antennas* (pp. 153–156). Propagation Conference. doi:10.1109/LAPC.2010.5666188

Xia, W., Saito, K., Takahashi, M., & Ito, K. (2009). Performances of an implanted cavity slot antenna embedded in the human arm. In IEEE Transactions on Antennas and Propagation (Vol. 57, pp. 894–899). http://doi.org/ doi:10.1109/TAP.2009.2014579

Zegna Sport Bluetooth iJacket incorporates smart fabric. (2007). Retrieved from http://www.gizmag.com/go/7856/

Zurcher, J.-F., Skrivewik, A. K., & Staub, O. (2000). SMILA: a miniaturized antenna for PCS applications. *IEEE Antennas and Propagation Society International Symposium, 3*, 1646–1649. http://doi.org/doi:10.1109/APS.2000.874556

Zürcher, J. F., Staub, O., & Skrivervik, A. K. (2000). SMILA: A compact and efficient antenna for mobile communications. *Microwave and Optical Technology Letters, 27*(3), 155–157. doi:10.1002/1098-2760(20001105)27:3<155::AID-MOP1>3.0.CO;2-P

Chapter 7

Performance Evaluation of Different Rectifying Antenna Systems for RF Energy Harvesting:
Rectifying Antenna Systems for RF Energy Harvesting

Saswati Ghosh
IIT Kharagpur, India

ABSTRACT

The radio frequency (RF) energy harvesting is found as an attractive alternative to existing energy resources. This chapter deals with the design and performance evaluation of different rectifying antenna circuits for RF energy harvesting. The rectifying antenna i.e. rectenna consists of an antenna to grab the RF energy and rectifier to convert the RF energy to DC power. Different circularly polarized microstrip antennas e.g. shorted square ring slot antenna and crossed monopole antenna with step ground plane are studied. The antennas are combined with voltage doubler circuits with various stages and bridge rectifier. The electromagnetic simulator CST Microwave Studio is used to design and optimization of antenna structures. The rectifier circuits are designed using SPICE software. Later the prototype of the antennas and rectifiers are fabricated and tested in the laboratory environment. The detailed study on the performance of the rectenna circuits are evaluated in terms of conversion efficiency.

INTRODUCTION

The global energy demand driven by the developed and rapidly developing countries is rising very fast (Ghosh et al., 2014). The development of a sustainable, long-term solution to meet the energy need of the world is an important area of research of the recent time. The energy harvesting techniques from surrounding energy sources e.g. heat, light, radio frequency (RF) energy are developing as environment

DOI: 10.4018/978-1-5225-1785-6.ch007

friendly energy sources (Vinoy & Prabhakar, 2014). The huge proliferation of cell tower installation in recent years and abundance of RF energy due to broadcast and cellular towers has made it an attractive means for energy harvesting. The RF energy harvesting needs a suitable module with appropriate antennas to grab the energy available in different transmission bands and a rectifying circuit for the rectification of the RF signal to DC power. Thus the device is basically a combination of antenna and rectifier and called as rectifying antenna or rectenna (Brown, 1984). The harvested DC power can be used for recharging the batteries of wireless devices like mobile phones or stored to power sensor networks. The wireless sensor networks (WSN) consists of spatially distributed sensor nodes. The WSNs play major role in the area of structural monitoring, habitat monitoring, healthcare systems etc. Energy supply has been a key limiting factor to the lifetime of WSNs as the sensors are generally powered by the onboard batteries. The batteries gradually run out of energy. The solar or other alternative energy sources are not available always (Vinoy & Prabhakar, 2014). In this situation, the energy harvesting technique using electromagnetic energy specifically in RF / microwave frequency range provides a solution to overcome these problems.

The amount of harvested power depends on the available RF power, characteristics of antenna and efficiency of the antenna and rectifier. In India, the major sources of RF radiation are the cell towers in the CDMA (Code Division Multiple Access) with frequency range 869 – 890 MHz, GSM 900 (935 – 960 MHz) and GSM 1800 (1810 – 1880 MHz) frequency bands (Arrawatia et al., 2011). However, the available RF power to the input of the RF energy harvesting system is relatively low due to the path loss and restriction on the allowable power for transmission. This requires the use of broadband, high gain antenna and efficient rectifier with impedance matched with the antenna to avoid the mismatch loss.

This chapter deals with the design and performance evaluation of different rectenna circuits for RF energy harvesting. The circularly polarized microstrip shorted square ring slot antenna and broadband crossed monopole antenna with step ground plane are used. The antennas are combined with voltage doubler circuits with various stages and bridge rectifier. The RF to DC conversion efficiency of different combinations of antenna and rectifier (rectenna) circuits are evaluated to perform a comparative study. Later the prototype of the antennas and rectifiers are fabricated and tested in the laboratory environment.

The chapter starts with a brief literature review studying and evaluating the existing rectifying antenna models for RF energy harvesting thoroughly (Section 2) leading to the main objective of the work (Section 3). The design of rectenna module with different antenna and rectifier structures are presented in Section 4. The formulation of overall efficiency of the rectenna circuits in terms of the antenna and rectifier efficiency is given in Section 5. The simulated and measured results for different antenna and rectifier circuits and discussions are presented in Section 6. This leads to the direction of future research (Section 7) and conclusion of the work (Section 8).

BACKGROUND

The rectenna i.e. rectifying antenna was invented and named by Brown (Brown, 1984). It is mainly used for receiving power where there is no physical connection. The transmission of power by radio waves was demonstrated first by Heinrich Hertz (Brown, 1984). Later Nicolas Tesla carried out the experiments on the transmission of power by radio waves (O'Neill & Genius, 1944; Cheney, 1981). The radio frequency (RF) energy harvesting had been investigated in the 1950s using the high power microwave sources. However, due to the technologies available at the time, it was then researched as a proof of the concept rather than using it as a practical energy source (Brown et al., 1965). With the advancements of low power devices in recent years, this technique has become a viable alternative to batteries in some applications – particularly, for wireless devices located in sensitive or difficult access environments. A typical rectenna consists of four main components: antenna, pre rectification filter, rectifying circuit, and DC pass filter. The first dipole rectenna was designed by Brown using aluminium rods (Brown, 1984). He also designed the thin-film printed-circuit dipole rectenna at 2.45 GHz (Brown & Triner 1982). Different types of rectenna elements were used in earlier published research works. As an important element of the rectenna, different types of antennas are used such as dipole (Degenford et al., 1964), Yagi-Uda antenna (Gutmann & Gworek, 1979), microstrip antenna (Ito et al., 1993), monopole, loop antenna, coplanar patch (Chin et al., 2005), spiral antenna (Hagerty et al., 2004), or even parabolic antenna (Fujino & Ogimura, 2004). Though the rectennas were initially designed operating over single frequency, recently works have been started on rectennas which use broadband antennas (Zhang et al., 2013; Arrawatia et al., 2016). Zhang et al. (2013) used a wideband folded dipole antenna with impedance tuning ability to avoid separate impedance matching network and thus the size of the rectenna was reduced. The broadband bent triangular omnidirectional antenna with voltage doubler circuit was designed for energy harvesting in the frequency range 0.95 – 1.85 GHz (Arrawatia et al., 2016). Since the main function of a rectifying antenna is to convert RF energy to DC power, the main design challenge lies in obtaining high conversion efficiency. This goal can be achieved using two approaches. The first approach is to receive the maximum power and deliver it to the rectifier. Another method is to suppress the harmonics generated by the rectifier that reradiate from the antenna as the power lost. The broadband antennas, large antenna arrays (Hagerty et al., 2004), and circularly polarized antennas have been used to achieve higher conversion efficiency using the first method. The broadband antenna collects relatively high RF power from different sources, and antenna array increases incident power delivered to the diode for rectification. The antenna array is an effective means of increasing the receiving power by increasing radiation gain but it also increases the size of the antenna. The circularly polarized antenna offers power reception with less polarization mismatch. The circularly polarized rectennas are preferred since the transmitting and receiving antennas do not require strict alignment in this case (Suh & Chang, 2000; Chiam et al., 2009). A truncated corner square patch microstrip antenna with gain 8.5 dBi at 5.82 GHz and microwave to DC conversion efficiency of 60% at a power density of 1.1 mWatt/cm^2 was presented in the work of Suh & Chang (2000). The paper of Chiam et al. (2009) deals with circularly polarized single element and 2×2 array to achieve gain of 3.4 dBi and 8 dBi respectively. The microstrip patch and slot antennas are mostly used for circular polarization (Nasimuddin et al., 2011; Tseng & Han, 2008). The microstrip patch showed 3-dB axial ratio bandwidth of 12 MHz and maximum gain as 4.3 dBic (Nasimuddin et al., 2011). The printed slot antenna exhibits circular polarization and impedance bandwidth of around 44% and 38% respectively (Tseng & Han, 2008). Recent works show the use of different printed and monopole antennas for dual and circular polarizations (Chen et al., 2001; Chen et al., 2012; Ghosh & Chakrabarty, 2016). The printed shorted ring slot antenna with circular polarization bandwidth of 8.1% and gain 4.0 – 5.6 dBi over the bandwidth was proposed by Chen et al., (2001). A broadband (36.5%) circular polarized antenna with comparatively low peak gain (<3 dB) was presented by Chen et al. (2012). Recently a dual band circularly polarized monopole antenna was designed for energy harvesting in the CDMA, GSM 900 and GSM 1800 bands simultaneously (Ghosh & Chakrabarty, 2016). The rectenna can also take different types of rectifying circuit such as single shunt full-wave rectifier (Alden & Ohno, 1992; Gómez et al., 2004; Fujino et al., 1996; Saka et al., 1997), full-wave bridge rectifier (Monti & Congedo, 2012), or other hybrid rectifiers (Ito et al., 1993). The circuit, especially the diode, determines the RF-DC conversion efficiency.

The schottky barrier diodes are usually used due to its shorter transit time and lower intrinsic capacitance (Monti & Congedo, 2012).

Thus it is noticed from the review of literatures, that the RF energy harvesting is found as an interesting research area due to its various applications. However, there is a need to design broadband simple and compact rectenna system with high power conversion efficiency.

MAIN FOCUS OF THE CHAPTER

This chapter aims at the design and performance evaluation of different rectenna module for ambient RF energy harvesting. The circularly polarized antenna is preferred over linearly polarized antenna due to its ability to capture radiation from all directions. Initially the microstrip shorted square ring slot antenna is studied for energy harvesting in the GSM band. Since very few literatures are found on broadband rectenna module, this chapter also presents the study of broadband crossed monopole antenna with step ground plane for energy harvesting simultaneously in the CDMA, GSM 900 and GSM 1800 bands. Different rectifier configurations e.g. bridge rectifier, voltage doubler are also tried to achieve good conversion efficiency. The prototype of the antennas and rectifiers are fabricated and tested in the laboratory environment.

The comparison of different antenna and rectifier combinations is performed in terms of conversion efficiency. This study will be helpful in the design of simple yet efficient rectenna circuit for ambient RF energy harvesting.

DESIGN OF RECTENNA MODULE

The complete RF energy scavenging module is shown in Figure 1. It consists of:

1. Antenna to receive the ambient RF energy,
2. Impedance matching network between the antenna and rectifier,
3. RF to DC converter i.e. rectifier to convert the RF energy to DC power and
4. Low power device as end user.

Figure 1. Complete RF energy scavenging rectenna module
Source: Monti & Congedo, 2012.

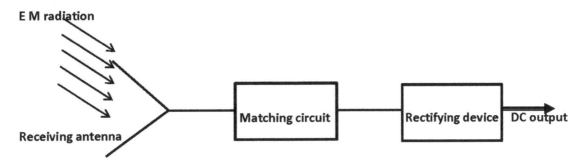

Antenna Designs

Two different circularly polarized microstrip antennas are chosen as the receiving antenna. A circularly polarized antenna simultaneously excites / receives two orthogonal electric field vectors of equal amplitude and in phase quadrature (Toh et al., 2003). The circular polarization characteristic of an antenna is determined by its axial ratio which is the ratio of orthogonal components of the E-field (Toh et al., 2003). However, it is difficult to achieve wide impedance and axial ratio bandwidth (axial ratio~3 dB) simultaneously.

Shorted Square Ring Slot Antenna

The microstrip fed printed ring slot antenna is used as receiving antenna in GSM 900 band (Chen et al., 2001). The printed square ring slot antenna is preferred because of its advantage of low profile, light weight, easy to manufacture, and wide operating bandwidth (Chang, 1996). It is noticed that by introducing a shorted section at appropriate position along the ring slot, it is possible to achieve circular polarization radiation (Morishita et al., 1991). The length of the shorted section is critical in achieving good circular polarization pattern (Morishita et al., 1991). In the present work, the antenna is designed on FR4 substrate of 1.6 mm thickness, relative permittivity ε_r of 4.4 and loss tangent 0.01. The circular polarization is achieved by introducing a section shorted with the ground plane at appropriate position along the ring slot (Figure 2). The outer and inner side of slot length is taken as L_1 and L_2 respectively. The shorted section of width g is placed perpendicular to the feed line (Chen et al., 2001). The width of the microstrip feed line (w_f) is adjusted for 50Ω impedance and attached with a quarter wave impedance transformer of width w. The impedance transformer is actually a microstrip line section of length l and width w, which is included between the outer slot boundary to 50Ω microstrip feed line for good impedance matching (Chen et al., 2001). The 50Ω microstrip line section inside the square ring slot is open circuited. The outer and inner side lengths of the printed square ring-slot antenna are taken as L_1 and L_2, respectively (Chen et al., 2001). The shorted section of width g is centered with respect to the y-axis (Figure 2). To achieve the desired circular polarization bandwidth, the mean circumference of the ring slot is taken as 1.5 times the wavelength at the center frequency of circular polarization. The dimension of the slot is calculated from the following equation:

$$f \approx \frac{1.5c}{2\left(L_1 + L_2\right) - g} \times \frac{1}{\sqrt{\varepsilon_s}} \tag{1}$$

Here f is the center circular polarization operating frequency and c is the speed of light in free space.

$$\varepsilon_s = \frac{2\varepsilon_r}{1 + \varepsilon_r} \tag{2}$$

ε_s is the effective relative permittivity considering two different media air and microwave substrate on two sides of the ring slot (Rao & Das, 1978).

Figure 2. Design of shorted square ring slot antenna; L_1 = 98; L_2 = 88; g = 50; w_f = 3.1; w = 1.9; t = 22; (All dimensions are in mm)
Source: Chen et al., 2001; Ghosh, 2015.

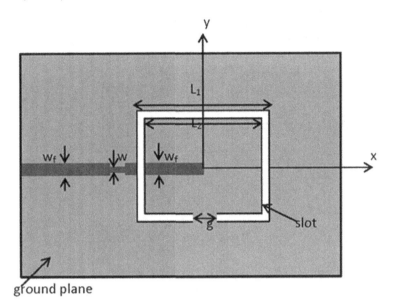

Crossed Monopole Antenna with Step Ground Plane

The crossed monopole antenna is designed to operate over the CDMA and GSM frequency bands (Figure 3). Initially a microstrip line fed patch antenna of dimension ($L_1 \times W_1$) is designed for the lower resonant frequency i.e. CDMA band using the standard formulations (Balanis, 2005; Stutzman & Thiele, 1997). The effective permittivity ε_{reff} is expressed in terms of the relative permittivity, width of patch (W) and height of the substrate (h) as follows (Balanis, 2005; Stutzman & Thiele, 1997):

For

$$W/h \rangle 1, \varepsilon_{reff} = \frac{\varepsilon_r + 1}{2} + \frac{\varepsilon_r - 1}{2}\left[1 + 12\frac{h}{W}\right]^{-\frac{1}{2}} \tag{3}$$

Generally, the length of the dipole antenna is considered as about half of wavelength. The approximate length L of the rectangular printed strip dipole is given as follows

$$L \approx \frac{\lambda}{2} = \frac{1}{2f_r\sqrt{\varepsilon_{reff}}\sqrt{\mu_0\varepsilon_0}} \tag{4}$$

The resonant frequency is considered as f_r. The dimension of the patch along its length is increased by ΔL considering the fringing effect. The length and width of the patch is determined from the equations as follows (Balanis, 2005; Stutzman & Thiele, 1997):

Figure 3. Design of the microstrip crossed monopole with step ground; Wsub=164, Lsub=186, Wg1=82, Wg2=82, Lg1=9, Lg2=45, Wf=3.1, Lf=46, W1=116, L1=140, H=38, W2=156, L2= 83 (All dimensions in mm)
Source: Ghosh & Chakrabarty, 2016.

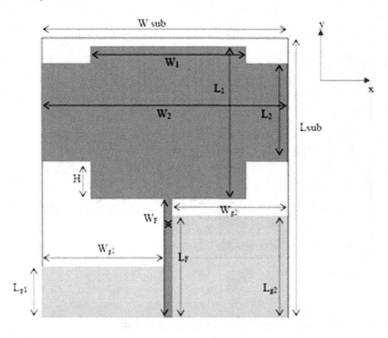

$$L = \frac{\lambda}{2} - \Delta L = \frac{1}{2f_r \sqrt{\varepsilon_{reff}} \sqrt{\mu_0 \varepsilon_0}} - 2\Delta L$$

$$W = \frac{1}{2f_r \sqrt{\mu_0 \varepsilon_0}} \sqrt{\frac{2}{\varepsilon_r + 1}} = \frac{v_0}{2f_r} \sqrt{\frac{2}{\varepsilon_r + 1}} \qquad (5)$$

$$\Delta L = 0.412 \times h \times \frac{\left(\varepsilon_{reff} + 0.3\right)\left(\dfrac{W}{h} + 0.264\right)}{\left(\varepsilon_{reff} - 0.258\right)\left(\dfrac{W}{h} + 0.8\right)}$$

To achieve the resonance at the GSM 1800 band, another patch of dimension ($L_2 \times W_2$) is attached with the original patch (Ghosh & Chakrabarty, 2016). The partial ground plane serves as the impedance matching circuit. The ground plane tunes the input impedance and the feed gap and width of the ground plane is adjusted to achieve maximum impedance bandwidth (Liang et al., 2004). However, the symmetric ground plane cannot excite circular polarization, since the horizontal current generates two components with 180o out of phase – thus produces very weak far field radiation in horizontal direction. To achieve circular polarization, an asymmetric step is introduced in the ground plane (Ghosh & Chakrabarty, 2016). The accurately chosen asymmetric ground plane produces two orthogonal electric field vectors with equal amplitude and 90o phase difference for circular polarization. The design parameters are optimized to achieve the desired axial ratio bandwidth at the same time maintaining the 10 dB return loss bandwidth (considering port impedance as 377Ω).

Rectifier Designs

The rectifier circuit is used to convert the captured RF power by the antenna to DC power. The performance of the rectenna depends on the efficiency of the rectifier chosen. Hence different types of rectifier configuration e.g. four diode bridge rectifier, voltage doubler circuits are studied.

Bridge Rectifier

The four diode bridge rectifier (Figure 4) produces twice the DC voltage compared to a center-tapped full-wave rectifier using two diodes. It provides same polarity of output for either polarity of input. The schottky diode (model no. 1N6263) from STMicroelectronics is used due to its high switching speed for the design. A capacitor is used in shunt with the load to block the RF signal with respect to the load (Monti & Congedo, 2012). The capacitor provides a low impedance path to the AC component of the output, reducing the AC voltage across, and AC current through, the resistive load. The capacitor and load resistance is chosen such that the time constant τ=RC with C and R as the capacitance and load resistance, is much longer than the time of one ripple cycle. Thus the configuration will produce a smoothed DC voltage across the load. The rectifier circuit is simulated using SPICE. The SPICE parameters of the diode are taken from available source (Kuphaldt, 2009).

Voltage Doubler Circuit

A single stage voltage doubler circuit is designed by using two diodes and two capacitors as shown in Figure 5 – 6. Its function is to rectify the full-wave peak-to-peak voltage of the incoming RF signal. A single stage voltage doubler can be used in cascade to increase the output voltage. Additional sections of diodes and capacitors are arranged in cascade to obtain the higher order voltage multiplier circuits. This

Figure 4. Circuit diagram of four diode bridge rectifier
Source: Monti & Congedo, 2012.

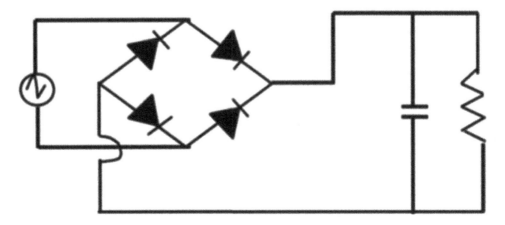

Figure 5. Single stage voltage doubler

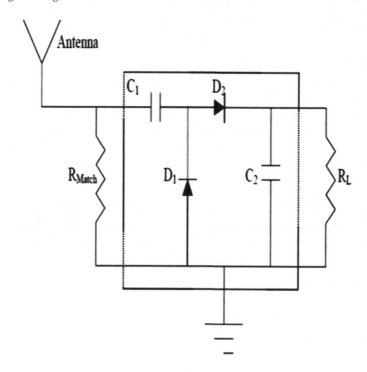

produces increased output voltage. The voltage multiplier consisting of N-stage indicates the number of stages of particular voltage multiplier. Each stage of the voltage doubler circuit is effectively considered as a single battery of internal resistance R_0 and output voltage V_0. The output voltage V_{out} is presented as follows:

$$V_{out} = \frac{V_0}{R_0 + R_L} R_L \tag{6}$$

The output voltage for n stages connected to the load R_L is expressed as follows:

$$\begin{aligned}V_{out} &= \frac{n V_0}{n R_0 + R_L} R_L \\ &= V_0 \frac{1}{\dfrac{R_0}{R_L} + \dfrac{1}{n}}\end{aligned} \tag{7}$$

The number of stages is optimized to achieve the maximum output voltage.

Figure 6. Seven stage voltage doubler

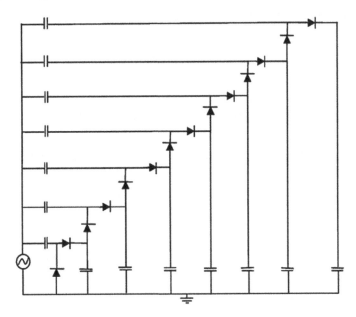

Overall Rectenna Design

The complete rectenna system generally consists of an antenna, rectifier and impedance matching network between the antenna and rectifier. In the present work, importance is given on the performance of different antenna and rectifier circuits and hence the matching network is avoided. Different combinations of antenna and rectifier are studied (Table 1).

EFFICIENCY CALCULATION

The performance of the rectenna circuit is evaluated by its efficiency. The conversion efficiency (η) of the rectifier system is generally defined by the ratio of the DC output power P_{out} at the receiver end over the AC input power P_{in} captured by the system (antenna).

$$\eta_{rectifier} = \frac{P_{out}}{P_{in}} \tag{8}$$

Table 1. Nomenclature of different rectenna modules according to the antenna and rectifier combination

Circuit	Antenna	Rectifier
Rectenna1	Shorted ring slot antenna	Bridge rectifier
Rectenna2	Shorted ring slot antenna	Seven stage voltage doubler
Rectenna3	Crossed monopole antenna with stepped ground plane	Bridge rectifier
Rectenna4	Crossed monopole antenna with stepped ground plane	Seven stage voltage doubler

The efficiency depends on the power density (P_d) distributed across the receiver aperture. The maximum incident power density can be presented as follows:

$$P_d = \frac{P_T G_T}{4\pi d^2} \tag{9}$$

Here P_T and G_T are defined as the transmitting power and gain respectively. The distance between the antennas is taken as d.

The incident power on the receiving antenna is determined by the incident power density (P_d) multiplied by the geometric area (A_G) of the antenna:

$$P_{inc} = P_d \times A_G \tag{10}$$

The effective area (A_{eff}) for the antenna is given by the following equation

$$A_{eff} = \frac{\lambda^2 G_R}{4\pi} \tag{11}$$

Here G_R is the gain of the received antenna.

Therefore, the power received by the antenna is obtained using Equations 9 and 11 as follows

$$P_{in} = P_d \times A_{eff} \tag{12}$$

Thus the power received by the antenna at various distances from the RF source is calculated using the Friis transmission equation (Paul, 2006):

$$\frac{P_R}{P_T} = G_T G_R \left[\lambda \Big/ \left(4\pi d \right) \right]^2 \tag{13}$$

In decibel, Equation 13 is written as follows:

$$10\log_{10}\left(\frac{P_R}{P_T}\right) = G_{T,dB} + G_{R,dB} - 20\log_{10} f - 20\log_{10} d + 147.56 \tag{14}$$

The efficiency of the receiving antenna is expressed as follows:

$$\eta_{antenna} = \frac{P_{in}}{P_{inc}} \tag{15}$$

Since the rectenna output is DC power, the output power (P_{out}) can be obtained from the output voltage (V_{out}) generated across the load resistance (R_L) by the following equation

$$P_{out} = \frac{V^2_{out,DC}}{R_L} \tag{16}$$

Now the overall conversion efficiency of the rectenna is obtained as follows:

$$\eta_{rectenna} = \eta_{antenna} \times \eta_{rectifier} \tag{17}$$

Using Equations 8, 10, 12, 15 and 16, the overall efficiency is achieved as follows:

$$\eta_{rectenna} = \left(\frac{V^2_{out,DC}}{R_L}\right) \frac{1}{P_d \times A_G} \tag{18}$$

RESULTS AND DISCUSSIONS

The shorted square ring slot antenna and microstrip crossed monopole with step ground are initially simulated and optimized using 3D electromagnetic simulation software Computer Simulation Technology Microwave Studio (based on FIT). The prototype antennas are also fabricated on FR4 substrate of 1.6 mm thickness, relative permittivity ε_r of 4.4 and loss tangent 0.01 for verification. The fabricated shorted square ring slot antenna is shown in Figure 7 – 8. The results for S_{11}, gain and axial ratio of antenna are shown in Figure 9 – 10. The return loss of the antenna is measured using scalar network analyzer. From the S_{11} versus frequency plot, slight shift in the resonant frequencies are noticed for the simulated and measured results (Figure 9). This occurs mainly due to the deviation in the dimension of the prototype antenna from the simulated structure. However, the 10 dB return loss bandwidth is maintained over the GSM 900 (935 – 960 MHz) band. For axial ratio measurement, the dipole antenna (Anritsu MP651A – Frequency 0.47 – 1.7 GHz) is chosen as receiving antenna and is connected with the RF analyzer. The prototype shorted square ring slot antenna is connected with the signal generator. The received power in the far field distance from the prototype antenna is measured keeping the receiving antenna in horizontal and vertical position respectively (Toh et al., 2003). The axial ratio is evaluated from the measured results of co and cross polar levels of the prototype antenna. It is noticed from the results that the axial ratio (3 dB) bandwidth is maintained over the GSM 900 (935 – 960 MHz) band (Figure 10). Also the gain over the GSM band is found to be quite high (4.2 – 4.3 dBi) (Figure 10). Next the prototype crossed monopole with step ground plane is fabricated on the FR4 substrate (Figure 11). The measured gain of the prototype antenna at the desired frequency bands are compared with the simulated results in Figure 12. It is noticed that the gain varies from 3.5 – 4.3 dBi over the desired CDMA (869 – 890 MHz) and GSM (935 – 960 MHz, 1810 – 1880 MHz) bands. Figure 13 shows that though the return loss bandwidth for both the measured and simulated data are same, the resonant frequencies differ slightly. As before, this occurs due to the fabrication errors. However, the impedance bandwidth covers the CDMA and GSM bands (Figure 13). The measured axial ratio plot shows variation from the simulated one (Figure 13). This may be due to the misalignment of the ground plane with respect to the feed line in the prototype antenna. However, the axial ratio ~3 dB is maintained over 0.8 – 1.9 GHz which also covers the impedance bandwidth.

The next step includes the design of the four diode bridge rectifier and seven stage voltage doubler circuit. The rectifier circuits are simulated using SPICE software. The schottky diode 1N6263 from ST Microelectronics is used. The load resistance is optimized to achieve the maximum output voltage. Later the bridge rectifier and seven stage voltage doubler circuit are fabricated on the FR4 substrate (Figure 14 – 15). The circuit is carefully handled while assembling the schottky diodes to avoid electrostatic discharge (ESD). The variation of output voltage for different input powers to the rectifier circuits are shown in Figure 16. It is noticed that the seven stage voltage doubler produces more output voltage for same input power as compared to the bridge rectifier as seen from the formulations (Figure 16). Thus the efficiency of the rectifier also depends on the input power and the efficiency of voltage doubler is much higher compared to the bridge rectifier (Figure 17). However, due to the limitation of the available laboratory set up, the rectifier circuits were tested upto 21 dBm input power. The highest measured efficiency is achieved as 42.25% for bridge rectifier and 90.44% for seven stage voltage doubler (Table 2). Next the efficiencies of the circularly polarized antennas are evaluated while placed at different distances from the transmitting antenna using Equations 10 – 15. It is noticed that at 950 MHz the efficiency of the shorted ring slot antenna is more compared to the crossed monopole antenna due to the smaller geometric area of the slot antenna (Table 3). Later the efficiencies of different rectenna modules

Figure 7. Front side of prototype ring slot antenna
Source: Ghosh, 2015.

Figure 8. Back side of prototype ring slot antenna
Source: Ghosh, 2015.

Figure 9. Plot of S$_{11}$ vs. frequency of the shorted square ring slot antenna
Source: Ghosh, 2015.

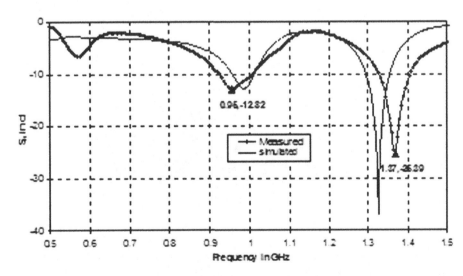

Figure 10. Gain and axial ratio vs. frequency plot of the shorted square ring slot antenna
Source: Ghosh, 2015.

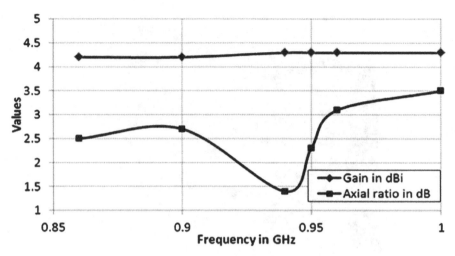

Figure 11. Prototype microstrip crossed monopole antenna with stepped ground plane
Source: Ghosh & Chakrabarty, 2016.

are compared in Table 4 at various distances from the transmitting antenna. It is noticed that Rectenna2 module shows the highest efficiency of 70.52% (output voltage=7.8V) whereas Rectenna3 module shows lowest efficiency of 25.03% (output voltage =4.6V) at a distance of 5m from the transmitting antenna.

Now, the Rectenna1 module is tested in the laboratory environment. For the measurement, a RF source transmitting in the GSM 900 band with output power of 20dBm is connected with a dipole antenna

Figure 12. Gain vs. frequency plot of the microstrip crossed monopole with step ground
Source: Ghosh & Chakrabarty, 2016.

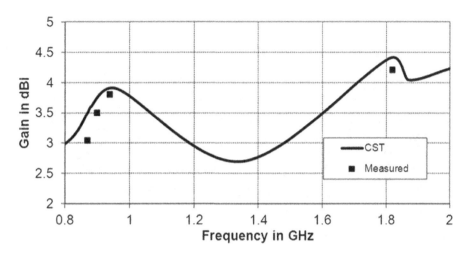

Figure 13. Plot of axial ratio and S$_{11}$ vs. frequency of the microstrip crossed monopole with step ground
Source: Ghosh & Chakrabarty, 2016.

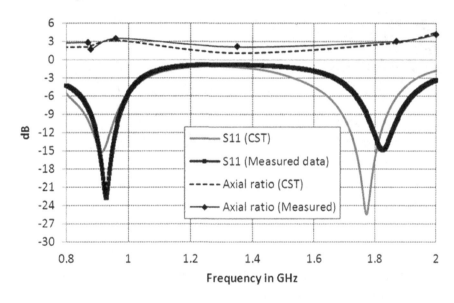

(Anritsu dipole MP651A, 470 – 1700 MHz). The dipole behaves as the RF source. The rectenna module is placed at various distances from the dipole antenna. The cable loss of 1 dB is taken into account. The power received by the circularly polarized antenna is calculated using Equation 6. The voltage developed across the load of the rectenna is measured and presented in Table 5. Also the efficiency of the overall rectenna system is computed for various distances from the transmitting antenna. It is noticed from the data presented in Table 5 that the rectenna module produces sufficient DC voltage (3.8 V) for low incident RF power density (~162μWatt/cm^2) and the overall rectenna efficiency is quite high ~ 45.47%. The gain of the cell tower antenna at 950 MHz is considered as 17 dB and input power is taken as 20

Figure 14. Prototype of four diode bridge rectifier circuit using schottky diode from STMicroelectronics 1N6263
Source: Ghosh, 2015.

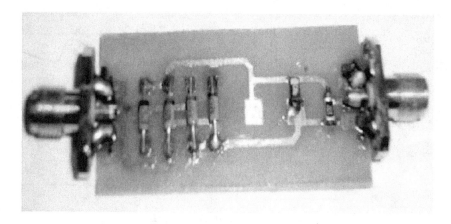

Figure 15. Prototype seven stage voltage doubler circuit using schottky diode from STMicroelectronics 1N6263

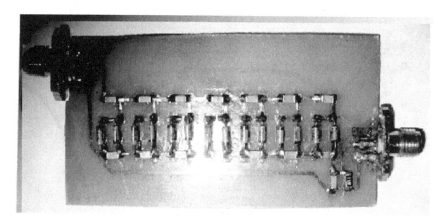

Watt. It is noticed that while used in actual site near the cell tower (at a distance of 5 m), this rectenna module produces as high as 5.2 V and can be successfully used to recharge the battery, which will be used later to power the wireless sensor networks.

FUTURE RESEARCH DIRECTIONS

This chapter presents the design and performance evaluation of different simple yet efficient rectenna modules using circularly polarized broadband / multiband antenna. However, studies need to be extended on the reduction in size of the overall rectenna. Also, for actual design, a broadband impedance matching network is required to be included between the antenna and rectifier circuit.

Figure 16. Plot of rectifier output voltage vs input power (dBm) for different rectifier configurations

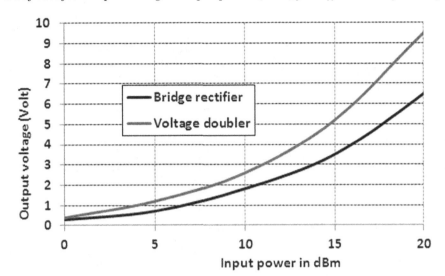

Figure 17. Plot of rectifier efficiency vs. input power (dBm) for different rectifier configurations

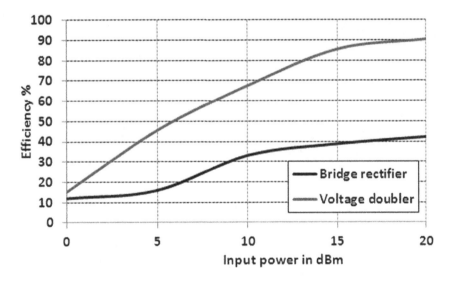

CONCLUSION

Different circularly polarized antenna along with the bridge rectifier and voltage doubler are used for the design of rectenna modules. The shorted ring slot antenna with seven stage voltage doubler is found as the most efficient rectenna module for energy harvesting in the GSM 900 band. However, the crossed monopole antenna which operates in CDMA, GSM 900 and GSM 1800 bands simultaneously is preferred due to its wide impedance and circular polarization bandwidth. Also this antenna while connected with seven stage voltage doubler shows good efficiency (54.33%) for low incident power density ($\sim$319µWatt/cm^2).

Table 2. Evaluation of rectifier efficiency for different input power

Input Power (dBm)	Input Power (mWatt)	Seven Stage Voltage Doubler			Bridge Rectifier		
		Output DC Voltage (V_{out}) in Volt	Output Power (V_{out})^2/R_L in mWatt	Rectifier Efficiency %	Output DC Voltage (V_{out}) in Volt	Output Power (V_{out})^2/R_L in mWatt	Rectifier Efficiency %
0	1	0.39	0.1521	15.21	0.34	0.12	12
5	3.16	1.2	1.44	45.57	0.71	0.50	15.95
10	10	2.6	6.76	67.6	1.82	3.31	33.12
15	31.6	5.2	27.04	85.57	3.5	12.25	38.77

Table 3. Calculation of efficiency of different antenna structures at various distances from the transmitting antenna (P_T = 20 Watt, G_T = 17 dBi, Frequency = 950 MHz)

d (m)	Power Density (Watt/m^2)	Shorted Ring Slot Antenna A_G=0.0196m^2			Crossed Monopole Antenna A_G = 0.0305 m^2		
		Received Power dBm	Received Power mwatt	Antenna Efficiency %	Received Power dBm	Received Power mwatt	Antenna Efficiency %
5	3.191	17	50.12	80.14	17.74	59.42	61.05
10	0.798	10.99	12.58	80.43	11.72	14.86	61.05
50	0.0319	-2.9	0.51	77.27	-2.07	0.62	63.9

Table 4. Comparison of efficiency of different rectenna modules at various distances from the transmitting antenna (P_T = 20 Watt, G_T = 17 dBi, Frequency = 950 MHz)

Distance (m)	Rectenna Efficiency %			
	Rectenna1	Rectenna2	Rectenna3	Rectenna4
5	32.06	70.52	25.03	54.33
10	27.34	54.69	21.36	42.12
50	7.73	10.04	7.02	8.94

Table 5. Measured results of output voltage and efficiency of Rectenna1 module in the laboratory environment

Freq in MHz	Distance in cm	Incident Power Density (Watt/m^2)	Incident Power (Watt)	P_R (dBm)	V_R (Volt)	V_R^2/R (mWatt)	Rectenna Efficiency η %
950	8	1.6203	0.0318	15.49	3.8	14.44	45.47
	20	0.259	0.0051	7.53	1.0	1	19.7
	40	0.065	0.0013	1.51	0.25	0.0625	4.9
	95	0.0115	0.00023	-6.01	0.05	0.0025	1.09

ACKNOWLEDGMENT

This work was supported by Department of Science and Technology, New Delhi, India under the SERC Women Scientist Scheme (WOS-A).

REFERENCES

Alden, A., & Ohno, T. (1992). Single foreplane high power rectenna. *Electronics Letters*, *21*(11), 1072–1073. doi:10.1049/el:19920679

Arrawatia, M., Baghini, M. S., & Kumar, G. (2011), RF energy harvesting system from cell towers in 900MHz band.*Proceedings of National Conference on Communications* (pp. 1 – 5). doi:10.1109/NCC.2011.5734733

Arrawatia, M., Baghini, M. S., & Kumar, G. (2016). Broadband bent triangular omnidirectional antenna for RF energy harvesting. *IEEE Antennas and Wireless Propagation Letters*, *15*, 36–39.

Balanis, C. A. (2005). *Antenna Theory* (3rd ed.). New York: John Wiley & Sons.

Brown, W. C. (1984). The history of power transmission by radio waves. *IEEE Transactions on Microwave Theory and Techniques*, *MTT-32*(9), 1230–1242. doi:10.1109/TMTT.1984.1132833

Brown, W. C., Mims, J. R., & Heenan, N. I. (1965), An experimental microwave-powered helicopter. *IEEE International Convention Record* (vol. 13, part 5, pp. 225 – 235).

Brown, W. C., & Triner, J. F. (1982), Experimental thin-film, etched-circuit rectenna.*IEEE MTT-S International Microwave Symposium Digest* (pp. 185–187). doi:10.1109/MWSYM.1982.1130655

Chang, K. (1996). *Microwave Circuits and Antennas*. New York: Wiley.

Chen, B., Jiao, Y.-C., Ren, F.-C., & Zhang, L. (2012). Broadband monopole antenna with wideband circular polarization. *Progress In Electromagnetics Research Letters*, *32*, 19–28. doi:10.2528/PIERL12032807

Chen, W. S., Huang, C.-C., & Wong, K.-L. (2001). Microstrip-line-fed printed shorted ring-slot antennas for circular polarization. *Microwave and Optical Technology Letters*, *31*(2), 137–140. doi:10.1002/mop.1380

Cheney, M. (1981). *Tesla, Man Out of Time*. Englewood Cliffs, NJ: Prentice-Hal.

Chiam, T. M., Ong, L. C., Karim, M. F., & Guo, Y. X. (2009), 5.8 GHz circularly polarized rectennas using schottky diode and LTC5535 rectifier for RF energy harvesting.*Proceedings of Asia-Pacific Microwave Conference* (pp. 32 – 35).

Chin, C. H. K., Xue, Q., & Chan, C. H. (2005). Design of a 5.8-GHz rectenna incorporating a new patch antenna.*IEEE Antennas and Wireless Propagation Letters*,*4*(1), 175–178. doi:10.1109/LAWP.2005.846434

Degenford, J., Sirkis, W., & Steier, W. (1964). The reflecting beam waveguide. *IEEE Transactions on Microwave Theory and Techniques*, *12*(4), 445–453. doi:10.1109/TMTT.1964.1125845

Fujino, Y., Fujita, M., Kaya, N., Kunimi, S., Ishii, M., Ogihata, N., & Ida, S. et al. (1996), A dual polarization microwave power transmission system for microwave propelled airship experiment.*Proceedings of International Symposium on Antennas and Propagation* (vol. 2, pp.393-396).

Fujino, Y., & Ogimura, K. (2004). A rectangular parabola rectenna with elliptical beam for SPS test satellite experiment. *Proc. of the Institute of Electronics, Information and Communication Engineers* (SBC-1-10, pp.S29-S20).

Ghosh, S. (2015), Design and testing of RF energy harvesting module in GSM 900 band using circularly polarized antenna.*Proceedings of IEEE International Conference on Research in Computational Intelligence and Communication Networks* (pp. 386 – 389). doi:10.1109/ICRCICN.2015.7434269

Ghosh, S., & Chakrabarty, A. (2016). Dual band circularly polarized monopole antenna design for RF energy harvesting. *Journal of the Institution of Electronics and Telecommunication Engineers*, *62*(1), 9–16.

Ghosh, S., Ghosh, S. K., & Chakrabarty, A. (2014), Design of RF energy harvesting system for wireless sensor node using circularly polarized monopole antenna. In *Proceedings of IEEE 9th International Conference on Industrial and Information Systems* (pp. 1-6).

Gómez, C., García, J. A., Mediavilla, A., & Tazón, A. (2004), A high efficiency rectenna element using E-pHEMT technology.*Proceedings of 12th GAAS Symposium* (pp.315-318).

Gutmann, R. J., & Gworek, R. B. (1979). Yagi-uda receiving elements in microwave power transmission system rectennas. *The Journal of Microwave Power*, *14*(4), 313–320. doi:10.1080/16070658.1979.11689166

Hagerty, J. A., Helmbrecht, F. B., McCalpin, W. H., Zane, R., & Popovic, Z. V. (2004). Recycling ambient microwave energy with broad-band rectenna arrays. *IEEE Transactions on Microwave Theory and Techniques*, *52*(3), 1014–1024. doi:10.1109/TMTT.2004.823585

Ito, T., Fujino, Y., & Fujita, M. (1993). Fundamental experiment of a rectenna array for microwave power receptions. *IEICE Transactions on Communications* (Vol. E *(Norwalk, Conn.)*, *76-B*(12), 1508–1513.

Kuphaldt, T. R. (2009). *Lessons in Electric Circuits*. Retrieved from www.ibiblio.org/obp/electricCircuits

Liang, J., Chiau, C. C., Chen, X., & Parini, C. G. (2004). Printed circular disc monopole antenna for ultra-wideband applications. *Electronics Letters*, *40*(20), 1246. doi:10.1049/el:20045966

Monti, G., & Congedo, F. (2012). UHF rectenna using a bowtie antenna. *Progress In Electromagnetics Research C*, *26*, 181–192. doi:10.2528/PIERC11102706

Morishita, H., Hirasawa, K., & Fujimoto, K. (1991). Analysis of a cavity backed annular slot antenna with one point shorted. *IEEE Transactions on Antennas and Propagation*, *39*(10), 1472–1478. doi:10.1109/8.97378

Nasimuddin, X., Qing, X., & Chen, Z. N. (2011). Compact asymmetric-slit microstrip antennas for circular polarization. *IEEE Transactions on Antennas and Propagation*, *59*(1), 285–288. doi:10.1109/TAP.2010.2090468

0. 'Neill. J. J. (1944). The life of Nikola Tesla. New York: Washburn.

Paul, C. R. (2006). *Introduction to Electromagnetic Compatibility* (2nd ed.). Wiley-Interscience.

Rao, J. S., & Das, B. N. (1978). Impedance characteristics of transverse slots in the ground plane of a stripline. *Proceedings of the Institution of Electrical Engineers, 125*(1), 29–32. doi:10.1049/piee.1978.0007

Saka, T., Fujino, Y., Fujita, M., & Kaya, N. (1997). An experiment of a C Band rectenna. *Proceedings of SPS* (pp.251-253).

Stutzman, W., & Thiele, G. (1997). *Antenna Theory and Design* (2nd ed.). Wiley.

Suh, Y. H., & Chang, K. (2000). A circularly polarized truncated-corner square patch microstrip rectenna for wireless power transmission. *Electronics Letters, 36*(7), 600–602. doi:10.1049/el:20000527

Toh, B. Y., Cahill, R., & Fusco, V. F. (2003). Understanding and measuring circular polarization. *IEEE Transactions on Education, 46*(3), 313–318. doi:10.1109/TE.2003.813519

Tseng, L. Y., & Han, T. Y. (2008). Microstrip-fed circular slot antenna for circular polarization. *Microwave and Optical Technology Letters, 50*(4), 1056–1058. doi:10.1002/mop.23290

Vinoy, K. J., & Prabhakar, T. V. (2014). *A universal energy harvesting scheme for operating low-power wireless sensor nodes using multiple energy resources. In Micro and Smart Devices and Systems* (pp. 453–466). Springer.

Zhang, F., Meng, F–Y., Lee, J.-C., & Wu, Q. (2013). Study of a novel compact rectenna for wireless energy harvesting. *Proceedings of IEEE International Wireless Symposium* (pp. 1 – 4). doi:10.1109/IEEE-IWS.2013.6616837

KEY TERMS AND DEFINITIONS

Asymmetric Ground Plane: Ground plane of microstrip antenna is not identical on both sides of the axis of the monopole antenna and microstrip feed line. A notch is cut in the upper left side of the ground plane to achieve the circular polarization.

Axial Ratio: The ratio between the minor and major axis of the polarization ellipse. For antenna it is defined by the ratio of orthogonal components of electric field.

Rectenna: A rectifying antenna i.e. a device used to capture and convert the electromagnetic energy to direct current (DC) electricity.

Rectenna Efficiency: It is defined by the ratio of the output DC power to the input RF power of the rectifying antenna module.

RF Energy Harvesting: The process of capturing and converting the radio frequency energy emitted from ambient or dedicated sources to usable DC voltage.

Chapter 8

Cross–Layer Cooperative Protocol for Industrial Wireless Sensor Network:
Cross–Layer Cooperative Protocol for IWSN

Bilal Muhammad Khan
National University of Sciences and Technology Islamabad, Pakistan

Rabia Bilal
Usman Institute of Technology, Pakistan

ABSTRACT

Robustness and reliability are two essential network parameters to be given priority in Industrial Wireless Sensor Network. But at the same time it is difficult to achieve gain in these performance metrics. Since in industries these networks are used for monitoring, control and automation processes, therefore, it also requires robust communication with minimum delay. Considering the need of high QoS in Industrial WSN, protocols and standards were developed to fulfil the requirement of reliable data communication in harsh environment. In year 2007, HART community designed a Wireless HART standard for efficient industrial communication. This standard gain high reputation soon after its implementation and still being used as a universal solution for industries. In 2009, another standard ISA100.11a was developed, it also gives promised results but fails to eliminate WHART. Both these standards are still competing in industry and the results of these standards are more reliable in comparison to other wireless industrial protocols that exists.

INTRODUCTION

Background

With the growing use of wireless technology for industrial communication, the need for the productive and reliable protocol also comes in demand. Wireless networks reduces the cost of network management and improves the QoS over wired network (Al-Yamin, Harb, & Abduljauwad, 2013). But still these networks

DOI: 10.4018/978-1-5225-1785-6.ch008

have some limitations which are needed to be resolved. Considering the challenges of industrial communication, protocol design with reliable and robust routing is required. Also the data communication of sensor and actuator nodes must be secure for reliable data transmission. Several methods, protocols and standards have been proposed for reliable industrial communication; however, the two standards are being used globally for wireless communication in industry. These two standards, WHART (Anna, Hekland, Petersen & Doyle, 2008) and ISA100.11a, uses proactive routing strategy and different frequency hopping techniques to maintain the network's performance. Also to overcome the issues of link breaking; graph table of mesh network are used. These standards are being used parallel to each other but none of these has eliminated the need of another in industry. Although, they have improved the performance of wireless system in industry through many factors, but they also have some drawbacks and limitations. This must be catered to further enhance the network performance. Some general solutions and protocol design are presented in this research work to eliminate the issues of communication over radio link in harsh environment. Methods proposed can be incorporated in several protocols to enhance and signify the network performance more efficiently.

Motivation and Need

Most of the industrial wireless communication are used for automation processes and controlling application. These control and monitoring mechanisms in industrial environment requires robust and secure data transmission in order to perform correct action accordingly. The delivery of false information or data may cause system to perform in an inadequate manner in such environment. Therefore, reliable and secure transmission of data is essential in industrial wireless sensor network. The atmosphere in industry causes hindrance for communication over radio link. Different industrial environments have different causes for data loss, collision and path disconnectivity. Some of these most common factors are vibration, noise, corrosion and extreme temperatures. Most of the nodes in wireless industrial network also malfunction due to corrosion and therefore does not transmit data accurately. Nodes present on field are also effected by weather changes such as rain, snow, humidity and high temperature, this increases the rate of collision and data loss in network which further degrade the network performance. Therefore the protocol design is required to maintain the network efficiency and improves network gains under challenging environment.

Problem Description

Challenges over radio link in industrial environment varies with the network topology and nodes density. Nodes in the industrial network suffered from extreme atmospheric condition and noise. Data on communication link may be lost or get erroneous in such harsh environment. In order to secure; data transmission over communication link protocol design must route the data on active and secure link. Dynamic network behavior that includes the variable data rata, node density and network traffic also deteriorate the performance of network. Communication protocol must adapt the network changes to transmit data with maximum throughput. These factors also consume more network resources; and reduces the network life time. Efficient management of power resources in therefore necessary to maximize the network life. Mobility of sensor nodes in wireless network is also a factor which degrades the network efficiency. These mobile nodes frequently break the communication link and increases the rate of packet loss. In order to improve the network performance metric in such networks; routing scheme and retransmission rate plays the key role. Updated link management with active link is therefore necessary in mobile wireless network to increase the packet delivery ratio. Since the wireless sensor network are self-healing and self-configuring networks; these abilities should be maintained by the network resources under different network scenario and network dynamics to provide optimized result and maximum gain.

AN OVERVIEW OF IWSN

Wireless Sensor Network (WSN) is a system comprises of thousands of wireless nodes spread around. These nodes use radio frequency (RF) channel to share their information and data which may be further processed to monitor or control the system. One of the emerging applications of WSN is Industrial Wireless Sensor Network (IWSN), where the wireless system is used for controlling and monitoring various industrial tasks. Wireless network shows tremendous potential and advantage over conventional wired industrial networks in terms of infrastructure (no long cable runs), cost reduction, ease of troubleshooting, ease of repair, replacement and up gradation. IWSN has the ability to operate in harsh environments and hence provide efficient performance through rapid and accurate results with enhanced reliability. Along with these gains, the challenges posed by industrial control systems are very unique. In order to operate such networks in an efficient way, wireless technology should meet the demands of industrial networks like reliability, real-time, robustness and energy efficiency. IWSN not only fulfil these demands but also provides flexibility to overall industrial network.

IWSN Structure Architecture

Wireless sensor network is an open network which provides great flexibility to the system during installation and network operation. Nodes in a wireless network are arranged in star, tree or mesh topology which is controlled by a network manager or PAN coordinator through radio communication links. Mesh topology is used to provide better reliability to the system. Deployment of mesh is very complex and costly in wired network, however, wireless network can organize it with low cost and less complexity. Figure 1 shows different network topologies for both wired and wireless network.

Unlike conventional point to point connection oriented wired network, wireless network due to their inherent connection free nature increases the flexibility of the network. This infrastructure less architecture makes the wireless network scalable, portable and reliable for both static and mobile nodes. Nodes in wireless network are self-organizing and self-healing, hence can adapt to environmental changes to perform efficiently.

IWSN provides a convenient network management, security and mesh networking in industry along with highly reliable system. Data from field devices and remote sites can communicate to SCADA(Supervisory Control And Data Acquistion) systems for process and controlling purpose. The central manager can track and monitor the devices as well as the activity over plant. Based on these observations, central manager itself can control processes or can direct commands to mobile worker on plant. This offers an efficient way of managing and controlling industrial process in real-time with reduced cost. Figure 2 shows an architecture of industrial wireless network where the central manager is monitoring and controlling several processes on plant and also at remote sites.

Figure 1. Star and Mesh topology of wired and wireless network

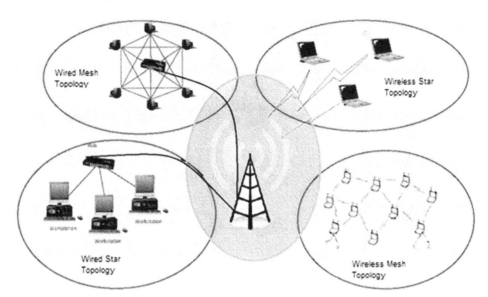

Figure 2. Industrial wireless network

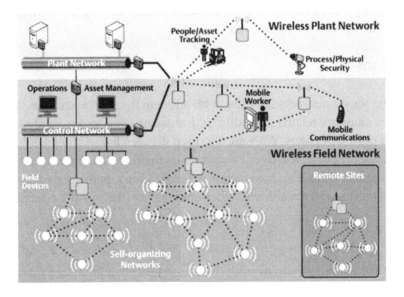

Applications of IWSN

The enhanced reliability, simple installation and convenient management of IWSN contribute to improve the productivity with high quality of services (Bal, 2014). In industry, wireless networks are used in different safety, supervisory, data acquisition and control applications ranging from alarms, monitoring, automation, logging, uploading, downloading and research purpose. Some major applications of IWSN are shown in Figure 3. Wireless sensor network can improve these processes by collecting data within

Figure 3. Applications of IWSN

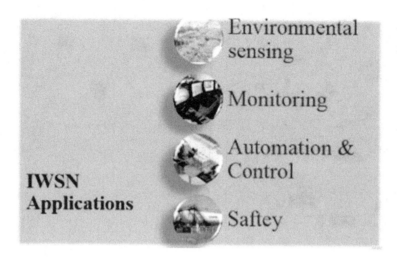

bounded time interval. It also lowers the safety risk by remotely accessing hazardous location of plant and by dealing with unplanned system failure. IWSN also offers an economical solution for difficult-to-wire areas. For moving and rotating machineries in industries, wired network requires an additional mechanical part for proper functioning. In contrast, the wireless network gives tangible cost saving by moving sensor itself along with the rotating part.

Environmental Sensing

In industries wireless sensor networks are used to monitor environmental changes at fields and plants. Agriculture industry monitors relative humidity, soil moisture, temperature and other environmental conditions for better growth of plants. WSN are also used in green house monitoring and nuclear power plant to further enhance the processes. Use of sensor nodes in oil and gas industry is to constantly monitor the resources, pumping, leakage and production at fields. These applications demand sensors at field to be energy efficient and robust towards climate conditions in order to work effectively.

Monitoring

IWSN is also being used in industry to monitor the atmospheric condition and analyze the behavior of plant and equipment which is required to enhance the yield and product quality. Data recorded through monitoring is also useful for research and development of industrial networks. Industrial equipment performance deteriorates with time which affects the optimal system performance. These equipment are needed to be monitored in order to maintain quality of service and avoid system malfunctioning. Monitoring application in IWSN demands reliable communication with accurate information from devices.

Control and Automation

Automation industry utilizes the robustness and reliability of IWSN. Mostly these networks comprise of sensor and actuator for controlling critical and non-critical processes operating in close loop. IWSN used in automation can increase the production gain by making the process fast and reliable. Such system requires a protocol which can provide better QoS in terms of robustness, reliability and real-time communication of data.

Safety

Robustness and low latency of IWSN is also required for safety critical application in industry. Wireless sensor network can be used at hazardous places to lower the injuries and equipment damage. It eliminates the need of human interaction near heavy machineries, chemicals and unsafe places.

Challenges of IWSN

In comparison with other wireless networks, IWSN requires high reliability and real-time performance, which is challenging due to its noisy surroundings. Latency, fault tolerance, synchronization, real-time constraints, network security and cross-layer design are critical issues poses by industrial applications. Figure 4 shows some challenges offered by IWSN. These challenges of IWSN can affect the network services and other performance metrics. Following are some of the factors and challenges that can degrade the network efficiency in industrial domain.

Reliability

Reliability is concerned with how much of data is received successfully at receiver end with minimum delay. In wireless sensor network, it is one of the most important factor that is considered to analyze

Figure 4. Challenges of IWSN

the network performance. Transmission of data packets in WSN generally gets affected by interference, abrupt change of channel state, weak link availability and protocol overheads. Also, highly reliable communication is required in industry to monitor and control the process with maximum accuracy; and also to lower the risk of equipment damage and injury. The industrial environment offers critical interference issues and extreme conditions such as high temperature, noise and climatic changes. Node's mobility reduces the network reliability as well by frequently breaking the communication link. Reliability of the network can be improved considering the environmental loss and other factors by using control mechanism in communication protocol. Existing data transportation schemes in IWSN should be more robust to resolve the critical issues of reliability in industries.

Latency and Real-Time Communication

Latency is defined as the time required by a data packet to reach its destination. Also to provide real-time communication data should be transmitted with minimum delay as to have live data transmission. Delay in network can introduce through number of causes including network setup time, retransmission and congestion as well as mac delays. A harsh industrial environment introduces more delays to the wireless network and makes it more challenging to provide hard real-time communication in automation industry. To improve latency in industrial environment, network traffic and interference reduction procedures should be added. Also the network setup should be robust using few control packets and less overheads. Currently industrial standards are providing soft real-time communication therefore they cannot be used for most of the time critical industrial application. More robust protocols are needed to provide hard real-time communication in industrial environments.

Climate

Climatic changes such as wind, rain, snow, humidity and temperature affect the performance of sensor nodes in large fields. Dust, dirt, high humidity level and solar radiations cause the nodes to malfunction and also reduce the signal strength. These faulty nodes then generate false data and transmit intermittently. Furthermore, rain, fog and snow have a negative impact on link connectivity and transmission range. To make the nodes robust towards climatic changes; on board self-test and error recovery should introduce.

Dynamic Network

Wireless sensor networks are based on infrastructure less architecture hence they do not follow one configured network topology. Nodes present in most of wireless networks are mobile in nature and due to their mobility the network topology changes at every instant. Also, weak communication link and noise causes the network to discover new connections among nodes and deliver data successfully. The dynamic network topology also reduces the network lifetime by increasing the routing process. Therefore, controlling the network topology is one primary task in designing a routing protocol for wireless sensor network. For various applications, standard is required which can successfully adapt and significantly enhance the performance through self-configuration and self-healing characteristics.

Power and Energy

Network life time is one critical issue in wireless networks. Due to limited resources and small size of a wireless node, the network cannot support a complex and computationally exhaustive protocol for communication. Power consumption of the network is dependent on network size, traffic load, number of retransmission, mobility and cluster size. In large network, number of transmission increases which also increases the congestion, collision, delay and packet loss. Energy consumption in industry can also decrease by incorporating clustering, reducing network traffic and by maintaining the most active link.

Security

WSN is an open system where the unauthorized user can access data easily and can provide serious security threats to industries. Most of the routing protocols are simple to keep the communication less complex but this makes the network susceptible for attackers. An intruder can pick up the data easily by designing a powerful receiver. Also, it can capture any particular node and can generate false alarm and erroneous data. Security proof protocol with strong encryption technique like AES-128 encryption can be used to secure data over communication link.

Due to the above mentioned limitations, it is challenging to establish and maintain an acceptable QoS for industrial networks. In order to overcome these challenges, several IWSN protocols and standards are produced. These protocols resolved some of the issues posed by the industrial networks; however there are still areas which need significant improvement.

IWSN Protocols

Currently two standards, Wireless HART and ISA100.11a (Low, 2013), are accepted universally for industrial wireless network. These standards are used in several industrial applications and have gained significant importance. These standards overcome the industrial challenges up to great extent; however there are some limitations which should be addressed for more efficient results.

Wireless HART

Wireless HART is the first industrial standard, released in 2007, for control and measurement which out performs all other existing industrial protocols of its time. Wireless HART commissions a self-organizing and self-healing mesh network with easy setup capability. Figure 5 shows some of the common features of HART network. HART uses IEEE 802.15.4 standard under 2.4 GHz frequency spectrum. It consumes low power for short range network to provide data rate maximum up to 250Kbps. For real-time communication HART uses synchronized time slot each of duration 10ms. Concept of super frame is also introduced to send several data frames in their respective time slots. It uses direct sequence spread spectrum (DSSS) to fragment the information and frequency hopping spread spectrum (FHSS) to select alternate channels for data transmission. To route the data packet, this protocol uses graph routing which contains redundant path for nodes. Data transmission over bad links is avoided using black listing mechanism. Security is also preserved in wireless HART through hop-by-hop data integrity using MIC with AES-128 at mac layer. The network also uses different keys for confidential data integrity such as public keys, joining keys and network keys, which enable a secure and authenticated data transmission with in a network.

Figure 5. Feature blocks of WHART

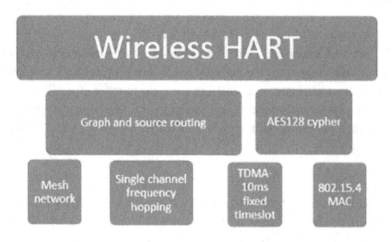

Limitations

HART uses TDMA slotting which requires all the nodes to be synchronized. Moreover, there is high possibility that nodes are not utilizing the complete time slot thus decreasing the bandwidth utilization. Black listing of channels also reduces the available channels for transmission. This can affect the bandwidth utilization and can increase interference. Graph routing, on the contrary, increases the overhead on each node; by means of demanding huge memory for redundant paths and frequent updates to maintain active route table. Wireless HART also poses the device compatibility issue and can work only with HART specific field devices.

ISA100.11a

In September 2009, the International Society of Automation proposed a comprehensive standard ISA100.11a for monitoring and control application in industries. This standard does not obsolete the need of wireless HART, but stands along with it in various industrial applications. Similar to wireless HART, it also uses 802.15.4 at physical layer but with variable TDMA slots. Some common features of ISA100.11a is presented in Figure 6. In addition to the properties of traditional 802.15.4, ISA100.11a uses time, frequency and spatial diversity. With slotted and adaptive channel hopping scheme, the communication channel switches between consecutive time slots within a super frame and among consecutive super frames (Stig & Simon, 2011). The standard uses graph and source routing, moreover it is influenced by the specification of IPV6 LoWPAN protocol to provide compatibility. Use of IPV6 provides merits of internet protocol to the wireless system. To provide better service between end-to-end users, the transport layer uses additional authentication techniques with better integrity checks and encryption. ISA100 also supports counter with cipher block chaining message authentication code along with advanced encryption standard (AES-128) to block cipher using symmetric keys. The application processes of the ISA standard are used to handle hardware, perform computation and support protocol tunneling.

Figure 6. Feature block of ISA100.11a

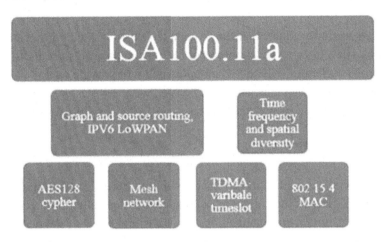

Limitations

Variable timeslot property in ISA100 is not useful for applications with constant data length because it introduces additional complexity to the network. Like wireless HART, it also offers limited number of radio channels for communication due to blacklisting. The memory exhausting graph tables for routing are sometime also unacceptable. The use of IPV6 LoWPAN in ISA100 introduces large size of header that increases complication in system design and its operation. Whereas use of compressing header techniques also provide some additional overheads. Inclusion of IP connectivity may bring security threat to these networks, since there are several mature IP hacking methods available. For real-time communication, ISA100 uses an additional contract based priority scheme which incurs complexity and overhead for its management.

Secure and reliable communication in industry is still an open issue that needs significant improvement in protocol design. Most of the existing industrial protocols uses complex routing schemes which increase the load at network manager and at each node, also results in reducing the network throughput. Since there are number of source nodes present in an industrial network, therefore, the rate of data collision in the network increases. This issues can be resolved by using different techniques of data combination or grouping the nodes based on their capability. Use of effective channel capacity can also improves the network performance in any harsh environment. Different techniques are presented in rest of this chapter to utilize the channel capacity to its maximum. Noisy surrounding in an industrial network causes data loss due to frequent path breaking. These factors includes vibration, extreme temperature, and wind. However, these can be utilized as energy harvesting resources for industrial network, which can improve the reliability of network and also its lifetime. Moreover the network dynamics is one reason that degrades the performance of any wireless network. Nodes in a network may have variable data rate and speed, which frequently changes the network topology and hence required repetitive routing. Such dynamic networks consume more network energy due to more retransmission and increased routing process. All these mentioned factors also introduces delay in a network that is not favorable for industrial communication. IWSN requires low latency for data transmission for correct action to be taken.

Methods to Enhance Network Performance

Several control mechanism are available that can be added to existing standards or can be used with some other novel approach to develop an efficient protocol for harsh industrial surroundings. Protocol design for IWSN using proposed schemes will be less complex and will provide energy efficient communication. Presented below are some techniques that can be used with any existing or new industrial protocol to enhance the reliability, robustness and energy efficiency of the wireless network.

Cognitive Radio Approach

The increased trend of wireless applications demands an opportunistic utilization of radio channels to reduce interference. In this regard the cognitive radio approach is an emerging technology which intelligently manages the spectrum for communication. The transmitter detects the occupied radio channels and then utilizes the one which is vacant. Some of the frequency channels of available network bandwidth use less often and are called as 'spectrum hole'. Using cognitive radio these 'spectrum holes' will utilize frequency spectrum efficiently.

Clustering

In dense networks, the most serious issues are packet collision and contention for accessing the medium. These issues can resolve by making clusters in which a single node among a group is selected as a cluster head. The cluster head is selected on the basis of different metrics such as its distance from gateway, node's power, number of its neighboring nodes and its location. All the nodes under specific cluster send data to their cluster head, cluster head is then responsible to forward data of whole cluster towards gateway. This would reduce the contention of channel at gateway and hence more data can be transmitted successfully. Clustering can also provide energy efficient routing by transmitting aggregated nodes information.

Aggregation

Aggregation is a technique to combine data of two or more nodes before forwarding. It can be done at physical or network layer using several coding techniques. Superposition coding, collaborative and XOR coding to name a few are available for data aggregation which can enhance the network performance by sending data in compact form. Fewer transmissions will be required to transmit all data which also improve the network latency. It further reduces the energy consumption and traffic load in a network (Arjmandi & Lahouti, 2011).

Distributed Graph Routing

Instead of using conventional graph and source routing for industrial standard, we can distribute the graph table among nodes according to their characteristic which also reduces the complexity and improves energy efficiency. Three graph tables introduced can reduce load at node and provide better communication. The 'Up-link' graph can be created which provides path from all devices to a gateway for sending node's data. 'Down-link' graph contains link of path from gateway to device in order to send individual control messages to each device. 'Broadcast' graph is used to maintain route for the transmission of common configuration and control signal from gateway to all nodes.

Cooperate Spectrum

Communication among networks, for channels within a cognitive radio network, can improve the channel capacity. Different network at the same industrial site should negotiate for frequency spectrum to avoid interference among them. Suitable protocols of spectrum sensing for the selection of next frequency channel between different networks can enhance the performance by reducing collision, data loss and interference.

Add Relaying Nodes

For reliable communication in dynamic network adding excessive relaying nodes can enhance network performance. These nodes will not be responsible for generating data or managing network instead they will only relay data among nodes. This can maintain reliability in a network even when sensor nodes reach black hole.

Cooperative Diversity

It is a technique usually used at physical layers to exploit the feature of diversity in wireless network. Methods like decode and forward (DF), amplify and forward (AF) and compress and forward (CF) are used to relay data of several nodes reliably over the network (Adam, Yanmaz, & Bettstetter, 2014). This method provides a limitation over cooperating node's data rate at physical layer, but the same procedure can be implemented at upper layers of protocol stack to achieve higher gain with larger number of nodes.

Adaptability

One way to get the optimized result in dynamic network is to introduce adaptable protocol. Control packets interval, data rate and MAC parameters can make adaptive to improve system performance. Using this scheme, the network will configure the parameters according to the surrounding atmosphere and provide high data delivery ratio with reduce packet loss.

Energy Efficiency

One technique to design an energy efficient protocol is to introduce cluster hierarchy in the network. Clustering can conserve energy by reducing network traffic and sending information towards network manager via cluster heads only. Proactive routing and routing table overheads also drain most of the node's energy. Therefore less complex routing strategy with on-demand routing should incorporate to reduce the load of routing computations. Cooperation can also improve energy efficiency by forwarding data of several nodes over single path. Energy aware routing schedule can also save network energy by transmitting data intermittently. Moreover, low power consuming components on sensor nodes can also extend the network life time (Thenral & Sikamani, 2013).

Energy Harvesting Techniques

Energy harvesting can be done at nodes by using devices which can serve as energy sources. Nodes, placed in open fields areas can make use of photovoltaic modules. These modules can utilize solar energy and can serve as unlimited energy resource for the network. Since industrial environment is surrounded by vibrations, therefore vibration harvesters can be used to transduce the vibrational energy and improve the network life. Nodes in the industrial environment can harvest energy from their surroundings in different forms, to increase the network's life time.

This chapter provides an overview of techniques and method that can be used with industrial standards to enhance their capability. Although IWSN possess several challenges, but it is preferred in industries over wired network due to its numerous advantages. It is providing efficient and affordable performance at several industrial locations where wired network lack behind. Wireless network in industrial environment requires much tougher, more reliable and robust network which can assure the maximum quality of service for end users in industries. This chapter highlights the possible solutions to the challenges offered by IWSN. By using the proposed methods, one can lead the industrial standard towards more effective and efficient performance. Out of several issues pointed out in the chapter, real-time communication and reliability are the critical issues under industrial environment and are still an open areas for research and development.

This chapter gives the detail overview of IWSN and its protocols. WSN is now essential for several industrial application which are also discussed in detail. Further the challenges offered by these networks are presented considering various aspect and factors causing them. In last protocols and standards used in this domain are discussed along with their gains and limitations. Since both industrial standards, WHART and ISA100.11a, have some limitations, therefore a new approach is needed that can overcome the challenges of these standards. Some of the techniques that can be used to increase the QoS of existing conventional IWSN protocols and standards are discussed in following chapter to optimize the results under harsh environment. Incorporating such techniques in industrial protocols will enhance the reliability and robustness of the wireless network

ADAPTABILITY AND AGGREGATION IN WSN PROTOCOL

To design a protocol providing improved network gains in harsh and dynamic environment, cooperation and adaptability at cross layer can be incorporated. These techniques are introduced in proposed Adaptive Cross Layer Protocol 'Adap-CP' in this chapter; the simulation results for the scheme are obtained and compared with conventional WSN protocol 'AODV'. Data packets of several sources are combined by piggybacking of their data; results analyzed shows that proposed scheme enhances the network gains with huge factor. Source nodes in this network were comprising their data rate due to piggy backing, however, the overall data rate and network gain has improved.

Introduction

It is challenging to provide high reliability and high quality of services to the adhoc networks with less complexity. Due to dynamic changes, interferences on radio channel and path loss increases which bounds the gains of the network. The throughput of these networks can enhance by using several cooperative and adaptive techniques at cross layer. In our scheme we are implementing the data aggregation which improves the throughput by avoiding collision and network congestion. On the other hand aggregation can increase network complexity this can be reduce by using simple aggregation technique.

Node's mobility and channel fading also degrades the network performance. To maintain and discover routes in such network is difficult and requires frequent updates. This increases the routing process over the network which in result affects the network efficiency. To reduce the overheads of route discovery several techniques have introduced in AODV routing. In proposed protocol, data aggregation can also reduce the number of route to discover for transmission and improves the latency by reducing routing delays in the network. However for high data rates congestion at MAC can increase the latency and reduces the network throughput. For various data rates MAC should be adaptable to provide high gains. This adaptability can be introduce at cross layer according to network behavior to increase the network QoS. We have made the MAC protocol adaptive so it can configure its parameter according to network requirements to produce better network services. As the number of nodes increase in the network the probability of data loss due to collision also increases. Therefore maintaining network performance for large scale is challenging.

Related Work

Adhoc network poses several challenges due to their dynamic nature. Various routing protocols are introduced to maintain link connectivity in the network. They considered throughput, end-to-end delay and packet delivery ratio as network performance metrics and conclude that reactive protocol can perform better in dynamic environment. It was found that protocols using clustering can achieve much better results.

Performance of the network also suffers with increased sources due to collision. This will introduce delay and enforces the network throughput to reduce. It makes use of node's position and customize the AODV routing by limiting RREQ to specific zone (Sungsoon, 2009). They increases the life time of the network and reduces the excessive burden on node. Using the probability of success to destination from source and choose the neighboring node with high success rate for link management was implemented.

To avoid data collision, packets of different sources can combine before transmitting towards the destination. Various data aggregation techniques are available that one can avail to improve throughput, reliability and energy consumption (Dang, Shen & Dong, 2013). A collaborative processing procedure proposed where data from several nodes is collected by a mobile agent. The introduced mobile agent works according to specific instruction of collecting data from several nodes and chose optimal shortest path for communication. Using this technique utilization of link capacity is increased with little complexity. Protocol using fusion scheme was introduced which combine two design of data aggregation together. This method make use of tree-based aggregation along with multipath aggregation and increase reliability by sending redundant data. Power saved by aggregating data is used to enhance reliability of network by increasing retransmission limit.

High data rate in network also introduce collision and contention delays at MAC. This can lower the network throughput however controlling MAC overheads and delays in an efficient manner can improve the network QoS. Cross layer protocol was design to improve performance of a network. Congestion control, path loss and delays are optimized using different schemes on three layers of protocol to make it perform efficient.

Adaptive Cross Layer Protocol (Adap-CP)

In this chapter, an efficient cross layer adaptive protocol is proposed and implemented to increase the network throughput and its efficiency. The reactive routing protocol used is AODV since it provides effective results for dynamic network with less overheads as compare to proactive routing protocol. The process introduce in the protocol to enhance network performance is data aggregation with adaptive MAC. As the routing process in the network increases with increased number of sources, it can cause more collisions and high energy consumption. This protocol reduce the need of discovering paths by aggregating data packets of several nodes. Aggregation in the network is not mandatory each time the data is generated, instead nodes aggregate their packet when needed. Hence the Adap-CP protocol works in two functioning mode:

1. Aggregated mode and
2. Non-aggregated Mode, these modes are illustrated in Figure 7.

The source generating data will search if any of its neighboring node have data to send towards similar destination. On positive response the sources goes into the aggregated mode where source forward its data to the neighboring source who piggy back its data packet and transmit towards the sink. Only two sources in same radio range are allowed to combine their data packets. A single bit header is added to inform sink that the receiving packet is aggregated data of two source, which is then decoded at receiver end. Transmission of data through single node reduces the route discovery process. Hence transmission over fewer paths reduces the routing burden over network. In other case if the source node does not find any other source in its radio range they follow the non-aggregated mode. In this mode all nodes transmit their data to the destination themselves.

Moreover aggregation also reduces the network traffic by merging the data packets. Transmitting whole data in fewer transmissions can reduce collisions and contention, and improves the throughput. It also enhance the utilization of the network bandwidth as more channels will be available for transmission. Collision at receiver end also reduces by delivering single compact data packet of several nodes instead of transmitting them from individual sources. Mechanism of protocol working modes of Adap-CP in two modes is presented in Figure 7.

Figure 7. (a) Aggregated mode, (b) non aggregated mode

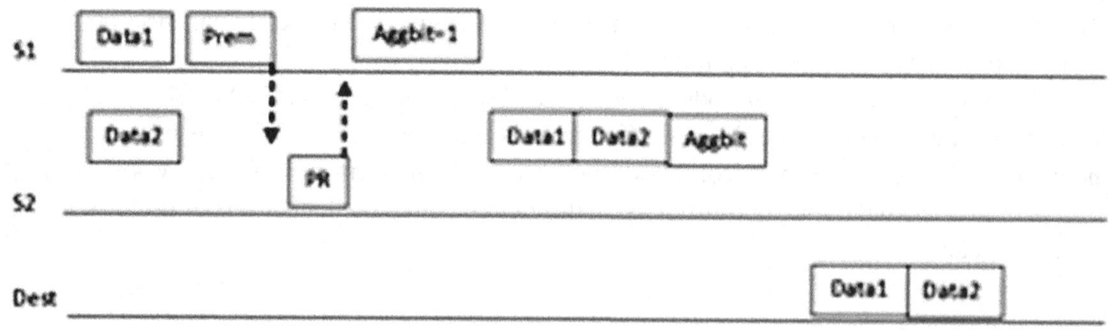

Where 'Prem' is a control bit sent to find any source node in range, 'PR' is the Positive Response by neighboring source node for data aggregation, 'NR' is negative response i.e. no source node in range and sources will send their data separately.

To further enhance the performance an adaptive MAC is introduce which is an extension to conventional 802.15.4. This MAC can provide reliability and energy efficiency along with low latency. For high data rate MAC delays are reduced with increased retransmission limit to deliver maximum packet without collision. Whereas an optimize value of MAC back off exponential and retrial limits are chosen for low data rate to improve reliability and latency. This adaptive MAC configure its parameters according to network mobility and data rate hence provides optimize results for various network states. Figure 8 shows the flow of process flow for Adap-CP.

This protocol can also resolve the problem of scalability in adhoc network and can provide better result as compare to conventional protocols. Since the network parameters in this protocol are adaptive they can configure them according to network size and data rate to maintain network performance in scalable and mobile network. The Adap-CP can produce improve results of throughput, PDR, routing computations and energy efficiency for various networks as compare to conventional adhoc protocols.

Figure 8. Adap-CP protocol flow

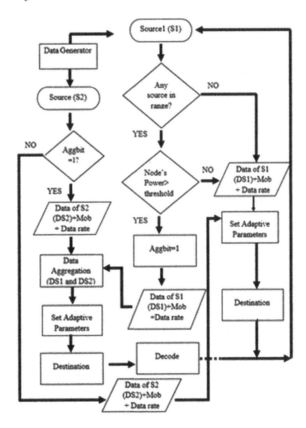

Simulation and Result Analysis

Simulation has been done using MALTAB-Simulink R2012a with true-time beta 2.0 library. The network consist of seven wireless nodes including two sources and single sink. Nodes are distributed randomly over an area of 30x30 m. Figure 9. Shows the node topology of the network. Each source generates CBR traffic with data packet of size 1Kbits. Results are obtained for both Conv-P and Adap-CP for static network with varying data rate. Mac backoff exponential and retrial limits for Conv-P are taken as 5 and 4 respectively whereas its ranging from 3-5 and 3-8 for Adap-CP. To analyze the protocol performance in worst case sources are placed in same radio range. Network performance metric such as throughput, PDR, route discovery attempts and energy has been analyzed for different network rate.

Throughput

Throughput is measured as number of successful received bits at receiver end in a second. It is initially increased by aggregating data; further efficiency is gained by using adaptive MAC parameters. Throughput of the network can express mathematically by (1)

$$Throughput = \frac{8 * No.\ of\ packets\ received}{T_{mac} + T_{rout} + T_{agg}} \tag{1}$$

$$T_{mac} = \text{No. of retrials * backoff delay} \tag{2}$$

$$T_{agg} = \left(T_{enc} + T_{dec}\right) * data\ rate \tag{3}$$

Figure 9. Network topology

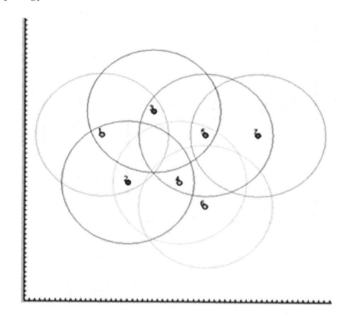

where T_{mac}, T_{rout}, T_{agg}, T_{enc}, T_{dec} are the MAC backoff delay, time required for route discovery, time required for data aggregation, time for encoding data bits, time for decoding data bits respectively.

Figure 10 , shows the throughput of Covn-P and Adap-CP with different data rates. The throughput for Conv-P is lower than Adap-CP for each data rate. This is because the contention and collision in network caused by presence of two or more source node in same radio range. Adap-CP enhance the throughput of the network by sending an aggregated data packets of such nodes. This avoids the data loss due to collision and transmit more packets by reducing routing delay. With the increase in data rate the throughput of the network increases more due to transmission of more data packets. Since probability of collision increases in Covn-P which is controlled in Adap-CP through adaptive MAC therefore high gain is observed for Adap-CP. Adap-CP provides of about 24.5% improved network throughput as compared to Conv-P.

Packet Delivery Ratio (PDR)

Packet Delivery Ratio (PDR) is used to determine efficiency of the network. It is the ratio of number of packet received with respect to the packet transmitted. PDR of the network is improved using proposed Adap-CP which gives better results maintaining high delivery ratio. It can be express using (4)

$$PDR = \frac{No.\ of\ packets\ received}{Total\ no.\ of\ packets\ transmitted} \tag{4}$$

PDR of Conv-P and Adap-CP are shown in Figure 11. PDR of Conv-P is slightly lower than Adap-CP at lower data rates. But as the data rate increases the collision of data packets and contention at MAC also increases. This increase the drops in PDR for Conv-P much more than Adap-CP which can be observe from Figure 11. For Adap-CP PDR of the network is higher for various data rate because it utilizes the channel capacity in a better way by aggregating data packets and also reduces the need of route discovery. Results shows Adap-CP provides 24% improved network PDR as compare to Conv-P.

Figure 10. Throughput of Conv-P and Adap-CP

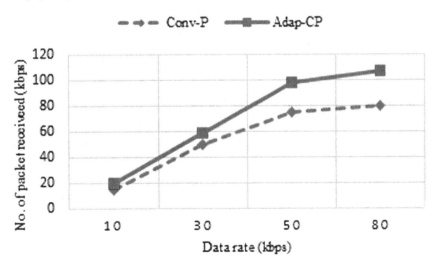

Figure 11. PDR of Conv-P and Adap-CP

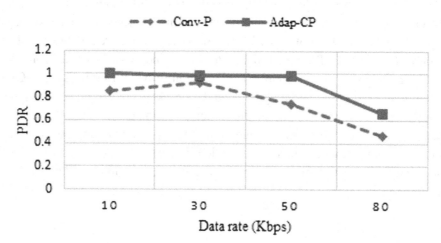

Route Discovery Attempt

Routing is essential to discover route (Agarwal, Rishiwal, & Arya, 2013) from a node to its destination. More the source nodes are available in the network the more route discovery will be required by the network. Mobility and channel fading also causes the path loss hence affect routing process. Attempt made by node for route discovery can be given by expression (5),

$$Route\ discovery\ attempt = N * mob * noise \qquad (5)$$

where N and *mob* are number of source nodes and mobility respectively.

Figure 12. shows the attempts made by each of the protocol to discover routes. Demand for route discovery is reduced significantly in Adap-CP since nodes are transmitting combine data packets. This require fewer paths to discover for packet transmission as the number of sending nodes are reduced. Whereas in Conv-P attempts for route discovery is much higher because nodes are sending their packets separately. Several nodes perform routing process to discover its path to destination. This increases the contention and delay in the network which in result affect the network latency. Around 60% of reduced demand of route discovery is achieved by Adap-CP in comparison with Conv-P.

Energy

Excess number of retransmission, route discovery process and high rate are characteristic factor for increasing energy consumption. This depletion of energy is reduced by controlling network parameters at cross layers. Equation for energy consumption in the network can be stated mathematically as (6),

$$Energy = E_{Tx} + E_{mac} + E_{agg} + E_{rout} \qquad (6)$$

Figure 12. Route discover attempt of Conv-P and Adap-CP

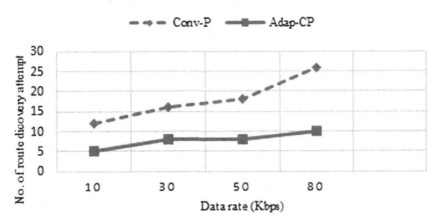

where $E_{Tx}, E_{mac,} E_{agg}, E_{rout}$ are signal transmission power, energy consumption at MAC layer, power consumption for data aggregation, energy consume during routing process respectively.

In Figure 13, power consumption for both Conv-P and Adap-CP are shown where Adap-CP has also proved to be energy efficient. The low power consumption of Adap-CP is due to adaptive MAC and reduced routing process by sending aggregated data. Most of the node's energy in Conv-P is lost in packet collision and route determining. Moreover excessive delay at high data rates also consume more energy in Conv-P which is optimize in Adap-CP. Adap-CP is designed in such a way that it gives maximum throughput with reduce power depletion. Power consumption in Adap-CP is reduced by around 35% as compare to Conv-P for network with variable data rate.

Results of Adap-CP and Conv-P shows that QoS of network can be enhanced greatly by introducing aggregation and adaptive MAC to the protocol. Adap-CP conserve power, improve latency and provides high gain. It performs efficiently with various data rate and provide improved result over several performance metrics of the network.

Figure 13. Energy consumption of Conv-P and Adap-CP

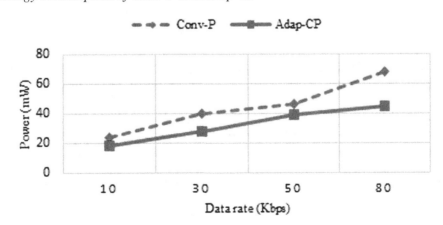

CONCLUSION

Most of the routing protocol does not work well with dynamic networks. Conventional protocols introduce high complexity and computations to maintain reliability and increase throughput of the network. This chapter proposed an enhanced cross layer adhoc protocol to improve network performance. Combination of data combination and adaptability is used at cross layer to enhance network services. The Adap-CP provides throughput gain of up to 24.5%, PDR improvement up to 24% with reducing route discovery attempts up to 60% and power reduction of about 35% in comparison with Conv-P. The enhanced performance of protocol has been analyzed for static network under differ network load capacity. This protocol can be implemented to mobile and scalable network due to its adaptive nature, it will provide better results under different network states. From result we conclude that the proposed Adap-CP can provide high network throughput for variable data rate and also improves other metrics like delay, route discovery, PDR and energy consumption. It is a comprehensive protocol that can provide multi folds network gain in several directions with less complexity and reduce computations.

REFERENCES

Adam, H., Yanmaz, E., & Bettstetter, C. (2014). Medium Access with Adaptive Relay Selection in Cooperative Wireless Networks. *IEEE Transactions o Mobile Computing, 13*(9), 2042-2057.

Agarwal, S. K., & Rishiwal, A. (2013). Fallout of different routing structures for mobility patterns in large ad-hoc network. In *Proceedings of IEEE Confluence 2013, The Next Generation Information Technology Summit,4th International Conference.*

Al-Yamin, A. M., Harb, K., & Abduljauwad, S. (2013). Industrial Wireless Sensor Networks in the perspective of Diversity and Spectral Efficiency. In *Proceeding of 11th IEEE international Conference on Communications.*

Arjmandi, H., & Lahouti, F. (2011). Resource Optimized Distributed Source Coding for Complexity Constrained Data Gathering Wireless Sensor Networks. *IEEE Sensors Journal, 11*(9), 2094–2101. doi:10.1109/JSEN.2011.2109947

Azmi, N., & Kamarudin, L. M. (2014). Interfernce issues and mitigitaion method in WSN 2.4GHz ISM band: A survey. In *Proceeding of IEEE 2nd International conference on Electronic design* (ICED).

Bal, M. (2014). Industrial Applications of collaborative Wireless Sensor Networks: A Survey. *IEEE 23rd International Symposium on Industrial Electronics*. doi:10.1109/ISIE.2014.6864830

Brown, S., & Sreenan, C. J. (2007). Study on Data Aggregation and Reliability in managing Wireless Sensor Networks. In *Proceedings of IEEE International Conference on Mobile Adhoc and Sensor Systems*. doi:10.1109/MOBHOC.2007.4428743

Christin, D., Mogre, P. S., & Hollick, M. (2010). Survey on Wireless Sensor Network Technologies for Industrial Automation the Security and Quality of Service Perspectives. *Future Internet, 2*(2), 96–125. doi:10.3390/fi2020096

Dang, K., Shen, J. Z., Dong, L. D., & Xia, Y.-X. (2013). A Graph route –Based Superframe Scheduling Scheme in WirlelessHART Mesh Networks for High Robustness. *Wireless Personal Communications*, *71*(4), 2431–2444. doi:10.1007/s11277-012-0946-2

Ding, X., Tian, Y., & Yan, Yu. (2016). A Real-Time Big Data Gathering Algorithm Based on Indoor Wireless Sensor Networks for Risk Analysis of Industrial Operations. *IEEE Transaction on Industrial Informatics*, *12*(3), 1232–1242. doi:10.1109/TII.2015.2436337

Ernst, R., & Martini, P. (2012). Adaptive HELLO for the Neighborhood Discovery Protocol. In *Proceedings of 37th Annual IEEE Conference on Local Computer Networks LCN*. doi:10.1109/LCN.2012.6423663

Ghaderi, M., Towsley, D., & Kurose, J. (2008). Reliability gain of network coding in lossy wireless networks. In *Proceedings of 28th IEEE Conference in Computer Communications*. doi:10.1109/INFO-COM.2008.284

Gupta, M. (2014). Enhanced Flooding Scheme for AODV Routing Protocol in Mobile Ad Hoc Networks. In *Proceedings of Electronic Systems Signal Processing and Computing Technologies*. ICESC. doi:10.1109/ICESC.2014.60

Hancke, G. P. (2012). Industrial Wireless Sensor Networks: A selection of challenging applications. In *Proceedings of 6th European conference on Antennas and Propagation (EUCAP)*. doi:10.1109/EuCAP.2012.6206686

Hanzo, L., & Tafazolli, R. (2006). Quality of Service Routing and Admission Control for Mobile Ad-hoc Networks with a Contention-based MAC Layer. In *Proceedings of IEEE International Conference Mobile Adhoc and Sensor Systems (MASS)*. doi:10.1109/MOBHOC.2006.278594

Hua, M., & Dong, L. (2011). A Closed-loop Adjusting strategy for wireless HART Time Synchronization. In *Proceedings of 11th International Symposium on Communication and Information Technology (ISCIT 2011)*. doi:10.1109/ISCIT.2011.6089716

Huang, J., & Liang, S. (2011). Reliability Gain of Network Coding in complicated network topology. In *Proceedings of 7th International Conference on Wireless Communication, Networking and Mobile Computing*. doi:10.1109/wicom.2011.6040178

Ismail & Ja'afar. (2007). Mobile Ad Hoc Network Overview. In *IEEE Asia Pacific Conference on Applied Electromagnetics Proceedings*.

Jamali, N. N., & El Ouadghiri, D. (2013). An enhanced on ad hoc wireless network routing based on AODV. In Proceedings of Wireless Days (WD).

Kim, Hekland, Petersen, & Doyle. (2008). When HART Goes Wireless: Understanding and Implementing the WirelessHART Standard. In *Proceedings of IEEE International Conference of Emerging Technologies and Factory Automation*.

Konstantopoulos, C., Mpitziopoulos, A., Gavalas, D., & Pantziou, G. (2010). Effecting Determination of Mobile Agent Itineraries for Data aggregation on Sensor Network. *IEEE Transactions on Knowledge and Data Engineering*, *22*(12), 1679–1693. doi:10.1109/TKDE.2009.203

Kumar, L. (2012). Scalability Performance of AODV, TORA and OLSR with Reference to Variable Network Size. *International Journal of Engineering Research and Applications, 2*(6), 82–92.

Low, A. (2013). *Evolution of Wireless Sensor Networks for Industrial Control. Technology Innovation Management Review*.

Natsheh, E., Jantan, A., Khatun, S., & Subramaniam, S. (2007). Adaptive Optimizing of Hello Messages in Wireless Ad-Hoc Networks. In: The International Arab. *Journal of Information Technology, 4*(3), 191–200.

Patel, K., Vasavada, T., & Vegas, M. (2011). Effect of Hello Message on Performance on Ad-hoc On-demand Routing Protocol. In *Proceedings of National Conference on Recent Trends in Engineering & Technology*.

Petersen & Carlsen. (2011). Wireless HART versus ISA100.11a: The Format War Hits the Factory Floor. *IEEE Industrial Electronics Magazine, 5*(4), 23-34.

Preetha, K. G., Unnikrishnan, A., & Poulose Jacob, K. (2010). A probabilistic approach to reduce the route establishment overhead in aodv algorithm for MANET. *International Journal of Distributed and Parallel Systems, 3*(2), 207–214. doi:10.5121/ijdps.2012.3218

Premalatha, J., & Balasubramanie, P. (2010). Enhancing Quality of service in MANETS by Effecting routing. In *Proceedings of International Conference on Wireless Communication and Sensor Computing*.

Priyadsrini, , & Navamani, , & Mahadevan. (2012). An Efficient Route Discovery in Manets with Improved Route Lifetime. *International Journal of Information and Electronics Engineering, 2*(4), 493–496.

Randriatsiferana, R., Lorion, R., Alicalapa, F., & Harivelo, F. (2013). Energy-efficient clustering algorithm based on energy variance for wireless sensor networks. In *IEEE International Conference on Smart Communications in network technologies* (SaCoNeT).

Razafindralambo, T., & Mitton, N. (2007). Analysis of the Impact of Hello Protocol Parameters over a Wireless Network Self Organization. In *Proceedings of the 4th ACM workshop on Performance evaluation of wireless ad hoc, sensor and ubiquitous networks*. doi:10.1145/1298197.1298206

Rohankar, R., Bhatia, R., & Shrivastava, V. (2012). Performance Analysis of Various Routing Protocols (Proactive and Reactive) for Random Mobility Models of Adhoc Networks. In *Proceedings of 1st International conference on Recent Advances in Information Technology (RAIT)*. doi:10.1109/RAIT.2012.6194441

So, J., Kim, & Gupta. (2005). Cushion: Autonomically Adaptive Data Fusion in Wireless Sensor Network. In *Proceedings of IEEE International Conference on Mobile Adhoc and Sensor Systems Conference*.

Somappa, K., Ovsthus, K., & Kristensen, L. (2014). An industrial perspective on wireless sensor networks-A survey of requirement, protocols and challenges. *IEEE Communications Surveys and Tutorials, 16*(3), 1391–1412. doi:10.1109/SURV.2014.012114.00058

Song, H., Xiuming, Z., & Mok, A. K. (2011). Reliable and Real-time communication in Industrial Messh Networks. In *Proceedings of 17th IEEE Real-Time and Embedded Technology and Applications Symposium*.

Song, J., Han, S., Mok, A. K., Chen, D., Lucas, M., Nixon, M., & Pratt, W. (2008). WirelessHART: Applying Wireless Technology in Real-Time Industrial Process Control. In *Proceedings of IEEE Real-Time and Embedded Technology and Applications Symposium*, (pp. 22-24). doi:10.1109/RTAS.2008.15

Sungsoon, C. (2009). *Adaptive Management schemes for mobile Ad-hoc Networks* (Dissertation for PHD). The University of Michigan.

Thenral, B., & Sikamani. (2013). Proficient routing method that exploits the lifetime of wireless sensor network. In *Proceedings of IEEE International Conference of Current trends in engineering and technology* (ICCTET). doi:10.1109/ICCTET.2013.6675954

Vijaya, M., & Dash, R. (2011). Influence of Routing Protocols in Performance of Wireless Mobile Adhoc Network. *Emerging Applications of Information Technology (EAIT),Second International Conference*. doi:10.1109/EAIT.2011.65

Zhai, Z., Zhang, Y., & Chen, G. (2010). A Reliable and Adaptive AODV Protocol based on Cognitive Routing for Ad Hoc Networks. In *Proceedings of 12th International Conference on Advanced Communication Technology* (ICACT).

KEY TERMS AND DEFINITIONS

AC Protocol: Adaptive Cross Layer Protocol.
ADAP-CP: ADAPtive Cross Layer Protocol.
AODV: Adhoc On-Demand Distant Vector.
Conv P: Conventional Protocol.
ISA: Industrial Standard Architecture.
IWSN: Industrial Wireless Sensor Network.
PDR: Packet Delivery Ratio.
QoS: Quality of Services.
WHART: Wireless Highway Addressable Remote Transducer.
WSN: Wireless sensor Network.
XLCI Protocol: Cross Layer Cooperative Industrial Protocol.

Chapter 9

A Dynamic Reputation-Based Incentive Scheme to Encourage Selfish Nodes in Post-Disaster Situation Using Delay-Tolerant Network

Chandrima Chakrabarti
Narula Institute of Technology, India

ABSTRACT

Modern communication infrastructures that usually keep people always on-line and inform "on-the-go" have repeatedly proved to be unreliable and unavailable during and after major disasters. In those situations the prime need is to quickly re-establish minimal communication infrastructures to start rescue operations. DTN is described by a special kind of mobile ad-hoc network where sparseness, large communication delay and lack of end to end path from source to destination exist. It is evident from this fact that data forwarding is dependent on the cooperation of multiple hops in "store-carry-forward" manner. However, nodes involved in communication may sometimes behave maliciously and may non-cooperate. So, the objective in this perspective is to develop a reliable data forwarding scheme by detecting malicious activities and encourage nodes to participate in Post Disaster Communication environment. Analysis of the proposed system, its protocols and performance studies are implemented and tested using Opportunistic Network Environment (ONE) simulator.

INTRODUCTION

Now-a-days Delay/Disruption Tolerant Network (DTN) is used in post-disaster situation to assist rescue operation. As it is a special type of wireless network with sporadic connectivity, lacks of infrastructure, very long delays due to network partitioning, are the universal aspects.

DOI: 10.4018/978-1-5225-1785-6.ch009

In DTN, messages, also called bundles, are propagated using hop by hop fashion and buffered at the next hop until the next hop appears. This propagation process is named as store-carry-forward method where the users are opportunistic in nature. As in DTN end to end communication is no longer possible, data are forwarded in hop by hop approach via intermediate nodes (Chakrabarti, & Roy, 2015; Chakrabarti *et al.*, 2014). As a result, the architecture of DTN relies on the cooperation among nodes participating in data communication (Chakrabarti, Banerjee, & Chakrabarti, 2014). However, the intermediate nodes may sometimes become selfish (Chakrabarti, & Roy, 2015; Chakrabarti *et al.* 2014; Chakrabarti, Banerjee, Chakrabarti, Chakraborty, 2014a; Banerjee *et al*, 2014; Chakrabarti, Banerjee, Chakrabarti, Chakraborty, 2014b; Banerjee, Chakrabarti, Chakraborty, Chakrabarti, 2014; Chakrabarti, 2014). Nodes may be selfish due to deficiency of its energy (battery power) or due to some malicious intention (Chakrabarti, Chakrabarti, Banejee, 2015). Therefore, how to efficiently and effectively resolve the selfishness problem has become the most challenging issue to achieve better packet delivery performance of DTNs. The most popular way is to detect and avoid those selfish nodes during data communication.

A node's selfishness may be typified as *non-cooperation* or dropping of messages (Chakrabarti *et al.*, 2014; Chakrabarti, Banerjee, Chakrabarti, Chakraborty, 2014a; Chakrabarti, Banerjee, Chakrabarti, Chakraborty, 2014b). Miao *et al.* (2012) classify selfish behavior into two categories: individual selfishness and social selfishness.

Individual selfishness is defined as the reluctance of a single node to relay others' messages, may be due to protect its limited resources or due to some malicious intention.

On the contrary, if a node belongs to a certain community, it is always willing to relay messages for the nodes within the same community/group but renounces to relay messages for the nodes outside its community/group (Wei *et al.*, 2011). This is termed as *social selfishness.*

In this paper, our objective is to assure reliable delivery of messages in DTN by avoiding the communication through selfish nodes as far as possible. We propose *a dynamic reputation based incentive scheme to detect selfish nodes and to encourage them* in a Post Disaster Communication environment. Here neighbor nodes will monitor a particular node's cooperation characteristics. Based on the cooperation characteristics of nodes in a network, Trusted Authority (TA) node publish *a universal node reputation matrix* from time to time which is consulted by each node to avoid selfish non-cooperative nodes during their data forwarding. Moreover, TA nodes will give incentives to the participated nodes, which will help them to take part in communication. We have simulated the scheme on ONE simulator and analyzed that the performance improves significantly with our proposed scheme. We also compared our performance with the "IRONMAN" scheme (Bigwood *et al.,* 2012) and with the "Pi" scheme (Lu *et al.,* 2010) using ONE simulator developed by netlab online and we got better result using our scheme with the perspective of data delivery and overhead.

The rest of the paper is organized as follows. Background describes the related research in this domain. Main focus of the chapter illustrates our reputation calculation and incentive assignment model. The simulation part depicts simulation parameters and performance of the proposed scheme. The Conclusion part concludes the paper. The last section discusses about the Future research directions.

BACKGROUND

In recent years DTN has got much attention from researchers and it has become very popular not only among the researchers but also among the common people (Chakrabarti, Chakrabarti, Chakrabarti,

2014; Chakrabarti *et al., 2014;*Banerjee, Chakraborty, Chakrabarti, 2014). A large amount of research has been done to identify the selfish nodes using reputation based strategies. Reputation implies the social tie-up pattern of a person in his associated environment. In a wireless network, when two nodes encounter each other, they can develop a perception about each other by checking their reputation values. Furthermore, recent studies on the impact of selfish behavior in DTNs show that the performance metrics (i.e., delivery ratio, delivery overhead) are severely predisposed if a major portion of the nodes is selfish (Chakrabarti *et al.,* 2014). In order to motivate a selfish node to participate in a communication, a number of incentive and reputation based schemes have been proposed. The existing incentive-based schemes can be classified into three categories (Wei *et al.,* 2011; Bigwood *et al.,* 2012; Lu *et al.,* 2010):

1. Barter based (Buttyan *et al.,* 2010; Buttyan *et al.,* 2007; Xie *et al.,* 2009),
2. Credit based (Wei *et al.,* 2011; Bigwood *et al.,* 2012; Lu *et al,* 2010; Chen *et al.,* 2010; Wei, Zhu, Cao, & Shen, 2011), and
3. Reputation based (Chakrabarti, & Roy, 2015; Zhang *et al.,* 2011; Dini *et al.,* 2010; Li *et al.,* 2010; Voss *et al.,* 2005).

In the paper inscribed by Banerjee, Chakraborty, Chakrabarti, 2014, authors performed a survey on some representative strategies in the literature belonging to each category mentioned above and finally compared the performance of these strategies for thwarting different types of selfish behavior.

Wei *et al.* 2011, proposed a user-centric reputation based incentive protocol for DTNs called Mobigame using game theory to stimulate cooperation among good nodes with selfish nodes. Here, source node is responsible for giving reward to other nodes for successful bundle forwarding by showing proper relay evidence.

Bigwood and Henderson (2012), presented an incentive mechanism to detect and punish selfish nodes and motivate unwilling nodes to participate in the network.

Dini *et al.* (2010), published the concept of carriers which are responsible for forwarding messages from one network partition to another based on probability for reaching messages towards destination where every node can compute reputation of carrier on the basis of network experience i.e. local reputation. But the drawback of this scheme is that if the message fails to reach the destination, it is not possible to identify the misbehaving carriers.

Lu *et al.* (2010), discussed that intermediate nodes can get credits from source node if the message has successfully received by the destination node. Otherwise the intermediate nodes can acquire good reputation values from the Trusted Authority for their cooperation. But the authors considered only single copy data forwarding algorithm, not multi-copy. The major drawback of this scheme is that the communication with trusted authority cannot be always guaranteed in DTN.

In the paper discussed by Zhang *et al.* (2011), authors highlighted a reputation scheme consisting of bundle forwarding, mechanism of behavior recording and computation model for stimulation of cooperation, blacklisting of node after detecting misbehavior determining degree of trust among different nodes.

Wei, Zhu, Cao, & Shen (2011), claimed that intermediate nodes are awarded good reputation only after successful message delivery. This way authors are aimed to detect selfish nodes in the network. But this scheme suffers from collusion problem and group-biasness.

Inspired by the existing research works, we aim to design a *dynamic reputation based incentive scheme to encourage selfish nodes* in DTN. In this paper, we have tried to detect the malicious activities like dropping, non forwarding, false token generation, colluding attacks and tried to avoid those nodes during data forwarding. Those nodes are stimulated eventually to improve their cooperation pattern, in turn, improves delivery ratio.

MAIN FOCUS OF THE CHAPTER

When a network starts, no reputation of a node is available to the neighbor nodes. Therefore, any node may select the forwarders nearest to it without any support from the other nodes. To guarantee reliable communication in a network like DTN, we propose to engage neighbor nodes and Trusted Authority (TA) node within a particular zone. Each TA node is assigned to screen other nodes' cooperation pattern and assign reputation based on that. Each TA node periodically prepares a node reputation matrix and broadcast it so that nodes in its environs may update their reputation table and consults this reputation table while selecting the next forwarder.

However, when a network starts, no reputation is available to the TA node for the nodes under its jurisdiction. Therefore, the nodes in any zone select the forwarders nearest to it without any support from the TA node. A node selects a forwarder:

1. Based on its own view about the cooperation characteristics (cc) table of the node.
2. Based on the neighbor nodes' view about the cooperation characteristics (cc) of the node.
3. Based on the reputation matrix published by Trusted Authority (TA) node time to time.

So, a node can select forwarder node,

Based on Its Own View About the Cooperation Characteristics (CC) Table of the Node

After a successful communication between two nodes, each node will exchange forwarder trust token (FTT) and receiver trust tokens (RTT). So, each forwarder node will get FTT and each receiver node will receive RTT from opposite side. A node issues a trust token packet to other node after encrypting it with its own private key to ensure secure communication. FTT, RTT packet may have the format shown in Tables 1 and 2.

Table 1. Sample format of FTT packet

Fttid	Forwarder Node id	Receiver Node id	No. of Exchanged Packet	Exchanged Msg id
$F1_{t1}$	N_1	N_2	1	M101

Table 2. Sample format of RTT packet

Rttid	Forwarder Node id	Receiver Node id	No. of Exchanged Packet	Exchanged Msg id
$R1_{t2}$	N_1	N_2	1	M101

According to the tables (Table 1, Table 2), two nodes N_1, N_2 are involved in exchanging message (e.g. M101), N_1 is the source, N_2 is the destination. After exchanging message, N_1 will get FTT ($F1_{t1}$) from N_2 at a particular time t1 and N2 will get RTT ($R1_{t2}$) from N1 at a particular time say, t2. Each and every intermediate node can also exchange these FTT, RTT packets. Each FTT/RTT packet has fttid / rtttid, forwarder node id, receiver node id, no. of exchanged packet and exchanged message's id. Forwarder Trust Token will be encrypted by the receiver's private key and the Receiver Trust Token will be encrypted by the forwarder's private key. Since a node cannot issue a trust token to itself as per the proposed scheme, a node cannot have a trust token encrypted by its own private key. Thus, encryption prevents a node from attempts to create false trust tokens to increase its reputation.

As a result, each node will maintain its own cooperation characteristics table.

A sample cooperation characteristics (CC) table is shown in Table 3. Here, node N_i can maintain its own cooperation value, at the same time can also maintain other node's cooperation values. CC table of N_i contain node_id, total no. of msg created at timestamp t1, total no. of msg forwarded at timestamp t2, total no. of msg received at timestamp t3, cooperation value at timestamp t4.

Here, Cooperation characteristics are measured by cooperation value. Cooperation value = total no. of messages forwarded + total no. of messages created / total no. of messages received. Suppose, node N_i created total 5 messages, forwarded 4 messages and received 10 messages. So, its cooperation value is 5+4 /10=0.9 at timestamp t4.

Cooperation characteristics (cc) are measured by the ratio of total no. of messages forwarded and created by the node with total no. of messages received by that node which are sent to that node by other nodes. The cc value is dynamically updated time to time and broadcasted in the network, so that, every node can choose forwarder node without any delay.

Based on the Neighbor Nodes' View About the Cooperation Characteristics (CC) of the Node

Each node will maintain cooperation list of other neighbor nodes by extracting values from its CC table.

So, Table 4 describes cooperation list maintained by N_i. Here, N_i maintains cooperation values of N_j with timestamp t0, N_k with timestamp t1, N_p with timestamp tp. Hence, cooperation list, maintained at each node, reflects the node's view about the cooperation characteristics of other nodes in the network.

Table 3. Sample format of cooperation characteristics table

Node_id	Total No. of msg Created	Total No. of msg Forwarded	Total No. of msg Received	Cooperation Value
N_i	5_t1	4_t2	10_t3	9 / 10 = 0.9_t4
N_j	2_t5	5_t6	11_t7	7 / 11 = 0.6_t8

Table 4. Cooperation list at Ni

	N_j	N_k	....	N_p
Ni	0.5t0	0.7t1	....	0.8t3

A node will consult this list to select a suitable cooperative forwarder. A node will show these cooperation list to only Trusted Authority (TA) nodes, when TA nodes will ask for.

Based on the Reputation Matrix Published by Trusted Authority (TA) Node Time to Time

After a few intervals, trusted Authority (TA) nodes will visit volunteer nodes to monitor the cooperation characteristics of those volunteer nodes in the network. Each node must submit all CC table, cooperation list, residual energy / resource details to Trusted Authority (TA) nodes when it is asked for. TA nodes are authorized nodes, which are employed to monitor other node's performance in a particular zone. TA node will assign reputation to the node based on:

1. CC table values,
2. Cooperation list,
3. Residual energy of a node,
4. Group biasness of that node.

From the CC table values, group biasness of a particular node can be calculated.

Group biasness of a node = No. of messages forwarded to group member nodes / Total no. of messages forwarded. So, group biasness of a node is measured as the ratio of No. of messages forwarded to group member nodes with total no. of messages forwarded. If No. of messages forwarded to group member nodes are 50% or above with respect to total no. of messages forwarded, then the node is group biased.

Each TA node periodically prepares a node reputation matrix and broadcast it so that nodes in its vicinity may update their reputation table and consults this reputation table while selecting the next forwarder.

1. If any node's cooperation values will increase and it shows no group biasness, its reputation value will also increase. TA nodes will identify this node as Good node.
2. If any node's cooperation values will remain fixed (not increased from last calculation) due to its limited resources and it shows no group biasness, its reputation value will remain fixed, not decreased. TA nodes will identify this node as Non-cooperative node.
3. If any node's cooperation values will get decrease (from last calculation) due to its limited resources and it shows no group biasness, its reputation value will remain fixed, not decreased. TA nodes will identify this node as Non-cooperative node.
4. If any node's cooperation values will increase and it shows group biasness, its reputation value will decrease. TA nodes will identify this node as Group biased node.
5. If any node's cooperation values will remain fixed or decrease (from last calculation) but it has enough resources and it shows no group biasness, its reputation value will decrease. TA nodes will identify this node as Selfish node.

After collecting reputation of all nodes, TA nodes will publish universal reputation matrix with timestamp. All nodes in the network get this information and can select forwarder node based on this universal reputation matrix.

Table 5. Reputation list at TA$_1$

	N$_j$	N$_k$	....	N$_p$
TA$_1$	Good_t0	Selfish_t1	....	Group_biased_t3

Table 5 demonstrates reputation list maintained at Trusted Authority (TA$_1$). TA$_1$ calculates reputation of N$_j$ as good at timestamp t0, reputation of N$_k$ as selfish at timestamp t1, reputation of N$_p$ as group_biased at timestamp t3.

If any node's reputation is greater than reputation threshold value, it will be declared as Good node. But, if any node's reputation is less than reputation threshold value, it will be declared as Bad node (may be non-cooperative, selfish, group biased). Bad nodes will get warning message to improve its behavior. After getting warning message twice, a particular node will be blacklisted from the network.

Proposed Scheme Based on Incentive

At the time of data exchange, nodes may follow different strategies. Suppose, node N$_i$ and N$_j$ want to exchange data, where N$_i$ is forwarder, N$_j$ is receiver. Now, using the concept of game theory (Wu *et al,* 2013) it is assumed that, both forwarder and receiver nodes have their own strategies. Strategies of forwarder node N$_i$ are as follow.

Strategies of N$_i$ - {F$^j_{t1}$, F_L$^j_{t1}$, F_G$^j_{t1}$}; where F$^j_{t1}$ denotes N$_i$ forwards packet to N$_j$ at time t1, F_L$^j_{t1}$ means N$_i$ forwards packet to N$_j$ at time t1 with energy limitation, F_G$^j_{t1}$ denotes N$_i$ forwards packet to N$_j$ at time t1 which is group biased forwarding if N$_i$ and N$_j$ belong to same group.

Similarly, receiver node N$_j$ has its own strategies as follow.

Strategies of N$_j$ - {R$^i_{t1}$, R_G$^i_{t1}$, NR$^i_{t1}$, NR_L$^i_{t1}$}; where R$^i_{t1}$ denotes N$_j$ receives packet from N$_i$ at time t1, R_G$^i_{t1}$ means N$_j$ receives packet from N$_i$ which is group biased receiving, if N$_i$ and N$_j$ belong to same group, NR$^i_{t1}$ denotes N$_j$ has not received data from N$_i$ at time t1, NR_L$^i_{t1}$ means N$_j$ has not received data from N$_i$ due to lack of energy or neighbor.

From the list of strategies, both node N$_i$ and N$_j$ can choose any of the strategies at a particular time t1 and start playing a game. Corresponding *payoff* matrix can be generated as shown in Table 6.

In the payoff matrix in Table 6, a$_{11}$, a$_{12}$, ..., a$_{34}$ are the credit points acquired by either N$_i$ or N$_j$, where a$_{21}$ > a$_{11}$ > a$_{23}$ > a$_{13}$ > a$_{24}$ > a$_{14}$ > a$_{22}$ > a$_{12}$ > a$_{33}$ > a$_{34}$ > a$_{31}$ > a$_{32}$. Credit points are exchanged based on the strategies nodes have chosen. If N$_i$ has chosen F$^j_{t1}$ strategy at t1 and N$_j$ has chosen R$^i_{t1}$ strategy at t1, then the credit point is a$_{11}$. If a$_{11}$ is positive (+ve) number then N$_i$ has got the credit point from N$_j$. So,

Table 6. Payoff matrix of the game played by N$_i$ And N$_j$

Ni	Nj			
	R$^i_{t1}$	R_G$^i_{t1}$	NR$^i_{t1}$	NR_L$^i_{t1}$
F$^j_{t1}$	a$_{11}$	a$_{12}$	a$_{13}$	a$_{14}$
F_L$^j_{t1}$	a$_{21}$	a$_{22}$	a$_{23}$	a$_{24}$
F_G$^j_{t1}$	a$_{31}$	a$_{32}$	a$_{33}$	a$_{34}$

Table 7. Credit table

Node	Credit
Ni	6
Nj	7

N_i gains a_{11} credit points from N_j. But, if a_{11} is negative (-ve) number then N_j has got credit points from N_i. So, in that case, N_i losses a_{11} credit points and N_j gains.

Here, one node must win and another must loss. The winner node will get credit point and looser node will lose credit point. The winner node will get credit point from the looser node, which is encrypted by the looser node's private key.

Table 7 depicts credit table maintained at N_i. Here, N_i has got 6 credits at timestamp t1, N_j has got 7 credits at timestamp t2.

Each node will maintain this credit point table and shows this table to the Trusted Authority (TA) node. TA node will assign that much amount of incentive based on this credit point. This kind of incentive mechanism will encourage nodes to participate in data forwarding and receiving.

SIMULATION

We have implemented our scheme using Opportunistic Network Environment (ONE) simulator developed by netlab online. The nodes are placed on default map. The details of our simulation parameters are given in Table 8.

We consider number of TA nodes are 10% of total volunteer node.

Initially, we have started the simulation with 60 neighbor nodes divided in 3 different groups, 20 in group1, 20 in group2, 10 in group3, 10% of total neighbor nodes (i.e. 5 nodes) as TA node.

Table 8. Parameters used for simulation

No. of Groups of Neighbor Nodes	3
No. of Neighbor Nodes	Varies from 60 to 200
No. of TA Node	10% of total number of volunteer nodes
Speed of Neighbor Node	0.5 m/s -1.5 m/s
Speed of TA Node	1.5 m/s – 5.5 m/s
Transmission Range	10 m
Transmission Speed	2 Mbps
Buffer Size	5 MB
Message Size	500 kB- 1MB
Movement Model	Shortest Path Map Based Movement
Routing Protocol	Spray and Wait Routing
Simulation Time	12 Hours

These results are compared with the scheme "IRONMAN" (Bigwood, & Henderson, 2011); "Pi" scheme (Lu et. al., 2010). Next, the numbers of neighbor nodes, TA nodes are gradually increased from 60 to 200 and in the same way packet delivery ratios are observed.

The performance of our proposed scheme and the "IRONMAN" scheme (Bigwood, & Henderson, 2011), "Pi" scheme (Lu *et al.*, 2010) are evaluated in terms of packet delivery probability and overhead ratio. We have used the following formulae to calculate the Delivery Probability and overhead ratio.

Delivery Probability = No. of Packets Delivered / No. of Packets Created

Overhead Ratio = (No. of packets relayed – No. of packets delivered) / No. of packets delivered

From Figure 1, it is evident that the delivery probability is better using our proposed scheme compared to the "IRONMAN" scheme (Bigwood, & Henderson, 2011), "Pi" scheme (Lu *et al.*, 2010).

We also observed the performance of our proposed scheme and the "IRONMAN" scheme (Bigwood, & Henderson, 2011), "Pi" scheme (Lu *et al.*, 2010) in terms of Overhead Ratio as represented in Figure 2 where overhead ratio decreases significantly using our proposed scheme compared to the "IRONMAN" scheme, "Pi" scheme.

FUTURE RESEARCH DIRECTIONS

This paper proposes a dynamic reputation based incentive scheme to encourage selfish nodes. This scheme is applicable in post-disaster situation. Using this scheme, selfish and non-cooperative nodes are detected. However, malicious nodes are not detected. Incentives are given to all nodes in uniform way irrespective of their cooperation pattern. But, incentives should be given to the nodes in non-uniform way. The cooperative node should get much incentives compared to the non-cooperative node. Moreover, our present scheme does not assure data integrity. In future, we focus on these issues to improve our system.

Figure 1. Simulation result of No. of neighbor node versus delivery probability using our proposed scheme and using the "IRONMAN", "Pi" schemes

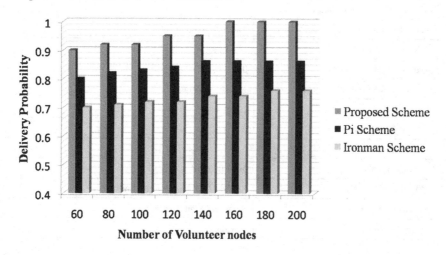

Figure 2. Simulation result of No. of neighbor node versus overhead ratio using our proposed scheme and using the "IRONMAN" scheme, "Pi" scheme

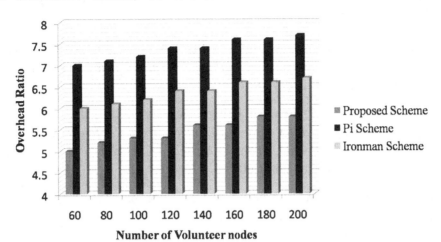

CONCLUSION

This paper presents a dynamic reputation based incentive scheme to encourage selfish nodes. This scheme is applicable in post-disaster situation.

The novelty of our reputation estimation scheme is that

1. It is distributed and dynamic in nature i.e., nodes with a bad reputation may get further opportunity to improve their reputation by participating and cooperating in future data communication.
2. It calculates reputation based on two specially encrypted tokens, FTT and RTT, issued by the forwarder and receiver nodes to each other to ensure cooperation of both parties during data communication process. Encryption prevents a node from attempts to create false trust tokens to increase its reputation.
3. Data delivery is guaranteed after awarding incentives to the nodes.

In this paper, we have tried to detect the malicious activities like dropping, non forwarding, false token generation, colluding attacks and tried to avoid those nodes during data forwarding. We have evaluated the performance in terms of delivery probability and overhead ratio. Our scheme gives better data delivery probability; overhead ratio is less compared to the "IRONMAN" scheme (Bigwood & Henderson, 2011), "Pi" scheme (Lu *et al,* 2010).

REFERENCES

Banerjee, A., Chakrabarti, C., & Chakraborty, A. (2014). A New Approach to Trace the Behaviour Pattern of Nodes in Delay Tolerant Network. In Proceedings of the ICCACCS 2014, 229-237. Kolkata, India: Springer.

Banerjee, A., Chakrabarti, C., Chakraborty, A., & Chakrabarti, S. (2014). A Comparative Survey on Detection and Prevention of Different Routing Attacks on MANET. In Proceedings of the IEMCON-2014. Kolkata, India: Elsevier Publications.

Banerjee, A., Chakraborty, A. & Chakrabarti, C. (2014). Survey on Analysis of Damage and Need Assessment in Post-Disaster Environment. *International Journal of Innovative Research in Science, Engineering and Technology, 3*(12), 18274-18279.

Bigwood, G., & Henderson, T. (2011). Ironman: Using social networks to add incentives and reputation to opportunistic networks. In *Proceedings of the IEEE International Conference on Privacy, Security, Risk, and Trust, and IEEE International Conference on Social Computing*, (pp. 65-72). Boston, MA: IEEE. doi:10.1109/PASSAT/SocialCom.2011.60

Buttyan, L., Dora, L., Felegyhazi, M., & Vajda, I. (2007). Barter-based cooperation in delay-tolerant personal wireless networks. In *Proceedings of the IEEE International Symposium on a World of Wireless, Mobile and Multimedia Networks. (WoWMoM 2007)*.Espoo, Finland: IEEE. doi:10.1109/WOWMOM.2007.4351689

Buttyan, L., Dora, L., Felegyhazi, M., & Vajda, I. (2010). Barter trade improves message delivery in opportunistic networks. *Ad Hoc Networks, 8*(1), 1–14. doi:10.1016/j.adhoc.2009.02.005

Chakrabarti, C. (2014). A Secured Message Exchange Scheme in Post–Disaster Environment Using Delay Tolerant Network. *Global Journal for Research Analysis, 3*(10), 64-66.

Chakrabarti, C., Banerjee, A., & Chakrabarti, S. (2014). A Secured Group-based Communication Scheme in Disaster Response Environment using Delay Tolerant Network. In Proceedings of the ICCACCS 2014, (pp. 217- 227). Kolkata, India: Springer.

Chakrabarti, C., Banerjee, A., Chakrabarti, S., & Chakraborty, A. (2014a). A Novel Approach for Non-Cooperative Node Detection and Avoidance using Reputation based Scheme in Mobile Ad-hoc Network. In Proceedings of the ICCACCS 2014, (pp. 279-289). Kolkata, India: Springer.

Chakrabarti, C., Banerjee, A., Chakrabarti, S., & Chakraborty, A. (2014b). A Dynamic Reputation Estimation Technique For Selfish Node Detection And Avoidance Of Non-Cooperative Nodes. In *Mobile Ad-hoc Network. Proceedings of the IEMCON-2014*. Kolkata, India: Elsevier Publications.

Chakrabarti, C., Banerjee, A., & Roy, S. (2014). An Observer based Distributed Scheme for Selfish node Detection in a Post-disaster Communication Environment using Delay Tolerant Network. In Proceedings of the Applications and Innovation in Mobile Coputing (AIMOC 2014), (pp. 151 – 156). Kolkata, India: IEEE. doi:10.1109/AIMOC.2014.6785534

Chakrabarti, C., & Chaki, R. (2011). Improved Cluster based Route Discovery Algorithm for Ad-hoc Networks. In *Proceedings of the IEEE International Conference on Communication and Industrial Application (ICCIA 2011)*, (pp. 1-4). Kolkata, India: IEEE. doi:10.1109/ICCIndA.2011.6146657

Chakrabarti, C., Chakrabarti, S., & Banerjee, A. (2015). A dynamic two hops reputation assignment scheme for selfish node detection and avoidance in delay tolerant network. In *Proceedings of the 2015 IEEE International Conference on Research in Computational Intelligence and Communication Networks (ICRCICN)*, (pp. 345-350). Kolkata, India: IEEE. doi:10.1109/ICRCICN.2015.7434262

Chakrabarti, C., Chakrabarti, S., & Chakrabarti, S. K. (2014). Towards Cluster Based Mobility Aware Secured Ad-hoc Network. In Proceedings of the IEMCON-2014, (pp. 123-128). Kolkata, India: Elsevier Publications.

Chakrabarti, C., & Roy, S. (2015). Adapting Mobility of Observers for Quick Reputation Assignment in a Sparse Post-Disaster Communication Network. In Proceedings of the Applications and Innovation in Mobile Coputing (AIMOC 2015), (pp. 29-35). Kolkata, India: IEEE. doi:10.1109/AIMOC.2015.7083826

Chen, B. B., & Chan, M. C. (2010). Mobicent: a Credit-Based Incentive System for Disruption Tolerant Network. In Proceedings of the INFOCOM, 2010, (pp. 1–9). San Diego, CA: IEEE. doi:10.1109/INFCOM.2010.5462136

Dini, G., & Duca, A. L. (2010). A reputation-based approach to tolerate misbehaving carriers in delay tolerant networks. In *Proceedings of the IEEE Symposium on Computers and Communications (ISCC 2010)*, (pp. 772–777). Riccione, Italy: IEEE. doi:10.1109/ISCC.2010.5546701

Li, N., & Das, S. K. (2010). Radon: reputation-assisted data forwarding in opportunistic networks. In *Proceedings of the Second International Workshop on Mobile Opportunistic Networking, ser. (MobiOpp '10)*, (pp. 8–14). New York: ACM. doi:10.1145/1755743.1755746

Lu, R., Lin, X., Zhu, H., Shen, X., & Preiss, B. (2010). Pi: A practical incentive protocol for delay tolerant networks. *IEEE Transactions on Wireless Communications*, 9(4), 1483–1493. doi:10.1109/TWC.2010.04.090557

Miao, J., Hasan, O., Mokhtar, S B., Brunie, L., & Yim, K. (2012). An Analysis of Strategies for Preventing Selfish Behavior in Mobile Delay Tolerant Networks. In *Proceedings of the Sixth International Conference on Innovative Mobile and Internet Services in Ubiquitous Computing (IMIS-2012)*, (pp. 208-215). Palermo, Italy: IEEE.

Netlab Online. (n.d.). *The Opportunistic Network Environment simulator (The ONE), in netlab online. Retrieved from* http://www.netlab.tkk.fi/tutkimus/dtn/theone/Ver.1.4.0

Voss, M., Heinemann, A., & Muhlhauser, M. (2005). A privacy preserving reputation system for mobile information dissemination networks. In *Proceedings of the First International Conference on Security and Privacy for Emerging Areas in Communications Networks (SecureComm 2005)*, (pp. 171– 181). Athens, Greece: IEEE. doi:10.1109/SECURECOMM.2005.7

Wei, L., Cao, Z., & Zhu, H. (2011). MobiGame: A User-Centric Reputation based Incentive Protocol for Delay/Disruption Tolerant Networks. In Proceedings of the IEEE Globecom 2011, (pp. 1-5). Houston, TX: IEEE.

Wei, L., Zhu, H., Cao, Z., & Shen, X. (2011). Mobiid: A user-centric and socialaware reputation based incentive scheme for delay/disruption tolerant networks. In Ad-hoc, Mobile, and Wireless Networks, ser. Lecture Notes in Computer Science. Springer.

Wu, F., Chen, T., Zhong, S., Qiao, C., & Chen, G. (2013). A Game-Theoretic Approach to Stimulate Cooperation for Probabilistic Routing in Opportunistic Networks. *IEEE Transactions on Wireless Communications*, 12(4), 1573–1583. doi:10.1109/TWC.2013.022113.120282

Xie, X., Chen, H., & Wu, H. (2009). Bargain-based stimulation mechanism for selfish mobile nodes in participatory sensing network. In *Proceedings of the Sixth Annual IEEE Communications Society Conference on Sensor, Mesh and Ad Hoc Communications and Networks*. Rome: IEEE. doi:10.1109/SAHCN.2009.5168911

Zhang, X., Wang, X., Liu, A., Zhang, Q., & Tang, C. (2011). Reputation-based Scheme for Delay Tolerant Networks. In *Proceedings of the IEEE International Conference on Computer Science and Network Technology*, (pp. 974-978). Harbin: IEEE.

KEY TERMS AND DEFINITIONS

Cooperation Pattern: The communication characteristics of nodes are known as cooperation pattern. In Delay Tolerant Network, due to resource limitation, all the nodes may not be cooperative. So, cooperation pattern is one of the most important parameter to judge any node's behavior.

Incentive: Incentive is a kind of stimulation given to the nodes in order to increase their cooperation in a resource-constrained environment like Delay Tolerant Network.

Intermittent Connectivity: In Delay Tolerant Network, due to nodes' movement, connectivity is not fixed always. Such inconsistent connectivity is called intermittent connectivity.

Malicious Node: The node which modifies data before, during or after transmission is known as malicious node.

Non-Cooperative Node: A node, which is unwilling to forward or receive other node's messages.

Reputation: Reputation implies the social tie-up pattern of a person in his associated environment. In a wireless network, when two nodes encounter each other, they can develop a perception about each other by checking their reputation values.

Selfish Node: A node, which drops other node's messages after receiving.

Trusted Authority: The authorized node, which is responsible to monitor other nodes' behavior or cooperation pattern, is termed as Trusted Authority node.

Chapter 10

Cross-Layer Scheme for Meeting QoS Requirements of Flying Ad-Hoc Networks:
QoS Requirements of Flying Ad-Hoc Networks

Bilal Muhammad Khan
National University of Sciences and Technology Islamabad, Pakistan

Rabia Bilal
Usman Institute of Technology, Pakistan

ABSTRACT

Recently, Flying Ad-hoc Networks (FANETs), enabling ad-hoc networking between highly mobile Unmanned Aerial Vehicles (UAVs), are gaining importance in several military, commercial and civilian applications. The sensitivity of these missions requires precise and prompt data delivery. Thus, the most important communication requirements that need to be addressed while designing FANETs are of high reliability and low latency. Considering these demands, this chapter focusses on mobility models, MAC protocols and routing protocols.

INTRODUCTION

Background

With the world turning into a global village due to technological advancements, automation in all aspects of life is gaining utmost importance. Wireless technologies have resulted in addressing the ever increasing demands of portable and flexible communication. Wireless ad-hoc networks which allow communication between devices without the need of any central infrastructure are gaining significance with monitoring and surveillance applications. A relatively new research area of ad-hoc networks is Fly-

DOI: 10.4018/978-1-5225-1785-6.ch010

ing Ad-hoc Networks (FANETs), governing the autonomous movement of Unmanned Aerial Vehicles (UAVs) (Bekmezci, Sahingoz, & Temel, 2013).

In the present day world, Unmanned Aerial Vehicles (UAVs) are considered a potential substitute of manned airplanes for several military, civilian and commercial operations. These aircrafts are used to conduct autonomous missions in remote areas in which the involvement of human personnel is considered dangerous and unsafe. Due to technological revolution in electronic and networking systems, UAVs may not only provide cost benefits but also help in efficient and adaptable mission completion for sensitive applications such as traffic monitoring, remote sensing, disaster monitoring, search operations, border surveillance and relaying networks.

The concept of single UAV systems is not new with their history associated with World Wars. Such systems comprise of an infrastructure which communicates with the UAV. This requires each UAV to be equipped with complex hardware systems to maintain its communication with the ground station, thus raising the disadvantages of high cost, reliability issues and link breakages. This led to the development of multi-UAV systems in which a network is formed between multiple UAVs which are made to communicate and collaborate so as to enhance the capability of single UAV systems. There are two distinct approaches for multi-UAV systems. The first is to form an infrastructure-based network between UAVs such that the communication between different UAVs in the network is regulated through a ground base station or satellite (Frew & Brown, 2008). This network model raises several design challenges as each UAV requires dedicated and complex hardware installment. For missions that may require higher number of UAVs, infrastructure-based multi-UAV systems are not feasible and reliable. Moreover, vigorous environmental conditions may cause link breakages between UAV and infrastructure resulting in data loss and increased delays. The second approach is to form an ad-hoc network between them. Such a network between multiple UAVs is termed as a FANET. All UAVs in the network are allowed to carry UAV to UAV communication and only a group of UAVs interact with the ground station. This eliminates the deployment of complex hardware in each UAV. Moreover, even if one of the UAVs turns down, there is no link breakage to the ground station due to ad-hoc network between UAVs.

Ad-hoc nature of FANETs allows their deployment in far-flung mission areas (Martinez-de et al., 2012). This helps in disaster management in places with impaired communication infrastructure or where prompt network establishment is required for receiving precise data from the affected region. Unlike (Mobile Ad-hoc Networks) MANETs and Vehicular Ad-hoc Networks (VANETs), FANETs have some critical requirements which need to be met. High mobility, low node density, low latency, large node distances and frequent topology change are some of the distinguishing characteristics of FANETs.

Motivation and Need

FANETs is an emerging research area and most of the research being done is in military and defense sector and hence not open source. The research has been conducted with the aim of sharing the findings with the research community so that affordable and efficient network models can be used for civilian applications to achieve desirable outcomes.

The amount of work done over the higher layers of FANETs is not enough. Moreover, a significant portion of research in FANETs focuses on the optimization and diversified use of Commercial Off-The-Shelf (COTS) equipment which adds to communication cost. Not many studies exist on Medium Access Control (MAC) and routing protocols' performance in this domain. There is a lot of room to work and make good progress in the focused arena. Hence, this work can act as a stimulator for further progress in this research domain.

FANETs are not only expected to boost performance in battlefield and military applications but they also possess a great inclination towards social applications. This research work focusses on investigating the technological aspects of FANETs that must be considered for upgrading the quality of life and environment around us.

OVERVIEW OF FANETS

FANETs is a relatively new and potential study area and holds a lot of room for further research and development. This chapter discusses the social impact of FANETs along with a detailed overview of communication requirements and challenges faced by the research community.

Social Significance of FANETs

The usage of FANETs for several military, civilian and commercial applications is expected to deliver favorable results in terms of reliable and delay bounded data delivery. Traffic monitoring, remote sensing, border surveillance, disaster management, and relaying networks are some areas where FANETs can be used to uplift the quality of life as shown in Figure 1.

FANETs as Monitoring Networks

The use of UAVs for surveillance and monitoring applications is practically being implemented since long. However, with the advent of FANETs, the concept is expected to be revolutionized in terms of reliable and delay bounded data delivery.

Figure 1. FANETs for social applications

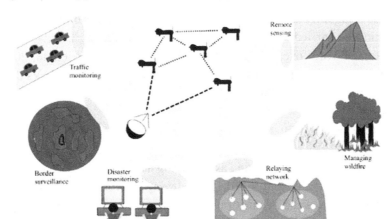

Reconnaissance Missions

In surveillance applications such as border patrol systems (Geng, Zhang, Wang, Fuh, & Teo, 2013) and urban surveillance (Semsch, Jakob, Pavlicek, Pechoucek, & Michal, 2009), UAVs are playing an important role in minimizing human intervention. Aerial reconnaissance missions range from information collection on battle fields to traffic monitoring and law enforcement activities. Monitoring tasks may include taking images of the objects and sites of interest spread over wide areas (Lim, Park, Ryoo, Choi, & Cho, 2010). For instance, in border policing swarm of UAVs can not only detect unplanned human disturbance including weapons and drugs but also illegal border crossing. The collected information can be immediately processed and transmitted to intelligence control rooms. However, the sensitivity of the data needs high accuracy for prompt action. All such surveillance missions exhibit complicated and ad-hoc nature and are intolerant to false alarms.

Traffic Monitoring

Roadway traffic monitoring is also a potential application where UAVs can replace intensive labor and complicated observing infrastructures (Coifman, McCord, Mishalani, Iswalt, & Ji, 2006). The deployment of detectors or human personnel throughout the roadway network is indeed a costly and time sensitive solution. UAVs which can monitor and report incidents or traffic management data are an economically and socially feasible option as they do not require moving on roads. Moreover, due to their high speeds, urgent event specific data can be transferred to boost up the rescue or destroy missions (George & Sousa, 2010).

Agricultural Management

Agriculture production management requires crop plant health to be monitored. Although manned aircrafts are being used in this sector but the emerging concept of small autonomous UAV swarms is believed to be more beneficial as they can perform field operations over smaller fields with more precision. This means that UAVs can focus specific sites and application of fertilizers can be performed accordingly (Huang, Thomson, Hoffmann, Lan, & Fritz, 2013).

By employing FANETs for the above discussed monitoring applications, coordination can be established amidst UAVs to achieve mission objectives cooperatively. FANETs can not only increase the coverage area but also scalability and survivability of missions (Bekmezci, Sahingoz, & Temel,2013). The type of communication carried between UAVs in such mission scenarios may include control data, video and image data and Voice over IP data (Pojda, Wolff, Sbeiti, & Wietfeld, 2011) depending on nature of the tasks assigned. Also, the scenarios and mobility patterns of the UAVs differ depending on the application and coverage requirements.

FANETs as Relaying Networks

Autonomously operated UAVs are also serving as a relaying network for MANETs and Wireless Sensor Networks (WSN) (Heimfarth & De Araujo, 2014). A relaying network is used to maintain communication links between remote source and destination which cannot communicate directly due to obstacles. To efficiently and securely transmit information collected by ground sensors to distant control centers and to increase communication range of ground relaying nodes, UAVs have been used as airborne communication relays (Jawhar, Mohamed, Al-Jaroodi, & Sheng Zhang, 2013; Cetin & Zagli, 2011). Areas such as forests and marshlands, which are inaccessible for ground vehicles due to their remote placements, can be prevented from disasters by WSN and UAV networks. Also, lifetime of the remote sensor networks can be increased by using UAVs as mobile relays since maintenance of such networks is a daunting task. Wildfire is a concerning problem all over the world. UAVs cannot only help in preventing such incidents by transmitting the sensed information related to location of the fire-prone areas but in post-fire tasks as well (Barrado *et al.*, 2010). Such event driven applications require that the information should be available to fire managers urgently so such applications tend to meet certain delay bounds.

FANETs are expected to enhance the performance of UAV relaying networks as the use of multiple UAVs can further increase the communication range. Moreover, in comparison to ground relaying networks swarms of UAVs can relay data with minimal latencies due to high mobility and robust connectivity. They move high up in the sky and are not met with terrain constraints. Also, there is clear Line of Sight (LoS) between ground nodes and UAVs which further ensures reliable delivery. The energy of sensor nodes in distant areas can be preserved by dedicating a group of nodes to directly communicate with the UAV network. This in turn minimizes the number of hops required to relay the information which in the absence of FANETs require multiple hops and ground relaying nodes. In this manner scientists can conduct quality research in dangerous remote spots, which are considered unsafe for technology personnel such as volcano-prone areas, without visiting them.

Distinguishing Features of FANETs

FANETs belong to the family of MANETs and VANETs. Figure 2 depicts block diagram of a FANET node. However, technical requirements of FANETs differ from the latter two with respect to node speed, mobility pattern, node density and energy consumption. The dissimilarities are discussed below:

- In FANETs, nodes are highly mobile with a typical UAV speed of 30-460 km/hr (Bekmezci, Sahingoz, & Temel, 2013; Huba & Shenoy,2012). Such high mobility factor accounts for challenging communication design.
- UAVs in a FANET are deployed on critical missions. A predetermined path is set to accomplish such operations. Since they fly in formations, special mobility models and path planning strategies are required for FANETs rather than commonly used Random Way Point (RWP) models in MANETs (Bouachir, Abrassart, Garcia & Larrieu, 2014).
- The UAVs comprising a FANET are scattered in the sky and they are much fewer in number forming a UAV swarm unlike large number of mobile devices or vehicles which form ad-hoc networks on ground (Bekmezci, Sahingoz & Temel, 2013).
- FANETs do not suffer from energy consumption problems because the power resource of the UAVs fulfills the energy requirement of FANET communication hardware and the constraints of battery powered devices are not met.

Figure 2. A block diagram of FANET node

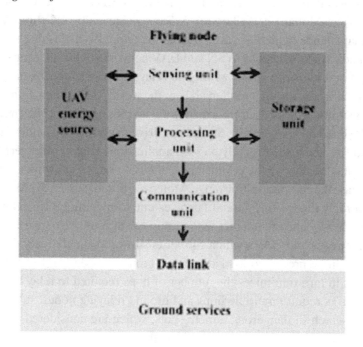

Communication Challenges

FANETs suffer challenges such as high mobility, frequent topology change, minimal delay and high reliability requirement. In order to carry efficient and vigorous communication between UAVs these challenges have to be encountered.

High Mobility

UAVs in FANETs demonstrate much rapid motion than MANETs and cannot be catered by conventional methods like mobile IP (Bekmezci, Sahingoz & Temel, 2013). Moreover, the quality of wireless links fluctuates due to high speed of UAVs which is addressed by MAC layer. Link stability and transmission range gets varied due to signal strength uncertainties. To study how link fluctuations caused by high mobility may be detrimental in FANET applications, consider a routing protocol which keeps a check on its neighbors by sending topology control messages before genuine data transmission. If the link quality goes down after the transmission of control packets, the link becomes void. Hence, the routing decisions will not be precise leading to performance degradation. MAC layer addresses this issue by maintaining Quality of Service (QoS) for one hop transmission (Cai, Yu, Li, Zhou, & Lamont, 2012) whereas routing layer ensures reliable end-to-end delivery (Pojda, Wolff, Sbeiti, & Wietfeld, 2011). One potential solution to encounter high mobility of UAVs has been addressed by predicting the location and movement of UAVs through heuristic techniques (Newaz, Pratama, & Chong, 2013). On the favorable side, when FANETs are used as relaying networks, the high mobility factor gives desired outcomes in establishment of delay tolerant links between geographically distant infrastructures.

Rapid Topology Change

Frequent topology changes result from high mobility which has to be considered in FANET design. Other factors which cause redefinition of routes include environmental obstacles such as mountains, failure of existing UAVs in the network, injection of new UAVs, possible mission updates or operational requirements. Due to weather conditions and geographical uncertainties, applications such as remote sensing become victim of bad links between UAVs (Bekmezci, Sahingoz, & Temel,2013). All such factors responsible for topological changes cause increased routing overhead, delays and low successful packet delivery rates. The topology change rate can be neglected by enlarging the transmission range of the UAVs i.e. employing a MAC layer protocol which supports large transmission range. The trade-off for adopting this solution will be complexity and energy consumption but UAVs have enough hardware support to cater such issues.

Low Latency Requirement

Search and destroy operations and disaster monitoring require minimal latency as the information needs to be transmitted at a very high rate. However, latency requirement of a FANET is application dependent. A crude way for acquiring minimal latency is that hop counts are decreased by long transmission ranges resulting in improved latency results. Moreover, the concept of priority schemes can also be used in FANETs (Shetty, Sudit, & Nagi, 2008). Priority based routing protocols can be used to attain different QoS for various message types. Congestion control protocols are vital for performing efficient collision control and coordination among UAVs (Bodanese, de Araujo, Steup, Raffo, & Becker, 2014). An appropriate choice of protocol suite can address the demand of delay bounds.

High Reliability

Affordability and accessibility of UAVs are determined by their reliability factor. FANETs are used in sensitive military and monitoring applications which require guaranteed data delivery (Coifman, McCord, Mishalani, Iswalt, & Ji, 2006; Barrado *et al.*, 2010). In FANETs, reliability is achieved by forming an ad-hoc network between UAVs so that if a UAV experiences a failed link it can still communicate to the infrastructure via other UAVs. In the absence of an ad-hoc set-up amid UAVs, each UAV needs to be connected to the infrastructure. Under such scenario if a UAV fails, important information related to the mission could be lost. Routing protocols based on data aggregation can serve the demand of highly accurate data (Huba & Shenoy, 2012). In such protocols data loss due to link failures is addressed by allowing the intended destination to request certain data from other UAVs in the network, thus ensuring the receipt of fully reliable information considering military and monitoring centric applications.

Communication Types in FANETS

UAV communication deals with exchange of data between UAVs and between UAVs and infrastructure i.e. ground station or satellite. Based on the intended destination, UAV communication in FANETs is classified into two main types as shown in Figure 3.

Figure 3. UAV-to-UAV and UAV-to-infrastructure communication scenario

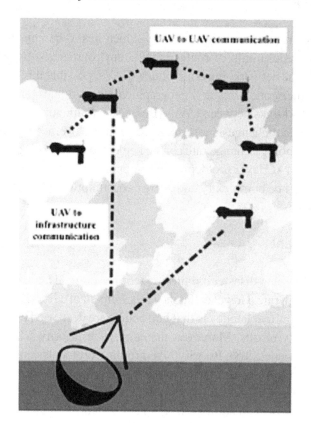

UAV to UAV

Inter-UAV communication carried in an ad-hoc manner gives rise to FANETs. Information is exchanged between UAVs without a central controller using different routing algorithms. These UAVs are in vicinity of each other and allow multi-hop communication of command and control data between them e.g. about target object in search and destroy operation. Since the FANET topology changes due to removal or addition of new UAVs, maintaining efficient UAV to UAV communication leads to several research directions. Robust routing protocols that can guarantee packets' delivery from source UAV to destination UAV are being explored (Alshabtat & Dong, 2011; Lin, Sung, Li, & Yang, 2012). Moreover, reducing packet latency between UAVs, due to rapid scenario change, is also an important research area. Although the same task could be performed using infrastructure based multi UAV systems but UAV to UAV data links in FANETs can reliably convey the information even if a UAV cannot form communication link with the infrastructure (Bekmezci, Sahingoz, & Temel, 2013).

UAV to Infrastructure

In FANETs, only a subgroup of UAVs communicates with the infrastructure. This type of communication conveys information about intended tasks over a wider scale and requires exchange of heavier data payloads. Few UAVs amongst the group send updates to the infrastructure e.g. on-site images in traffic monitoring. Extended communication range is required for the exchange of messages between UAV and satellite or ground station.

FANET Design Considerations

FANETs are characterized by rapid changes and activities during network operation. The design should be highly scalable with adaptive path planning and robust communication protocols. A brief insight of these technical requirements is summarized below:

Topologies

In order to maintain coordination and collaboration, peer-to-peer connections are formed between UAVs in a FANET scenario. The tasks can be completed using single cluster or multicluster formations. Single cluster networks can best serve to accomplish homogenous and small scale missions. However, the need for multicluster networks arises when certain UAVs have to perform multiple missions covering wide terrains. In such case, UAVs group together into small clusters with ad-hoc network within each cluster. The cluster head of each cluster is not only designated to carry downlink communication but to also communicate with cluster heads of other clusters. The clusters may be in same or different mission areas and serve to enhance the scalability of the network as shown in Figure 4. Such models are used in scenarios which involve large mission areas as search tasks can be performed more efficiently and collaboratively. For multicluster scenario, selection of cluster head is a serious design issue when one of the cluster heads goes down. Hence, FANETs should be designed for highly dynamic scenarios.

Figure 4. Clustered FANET scenario

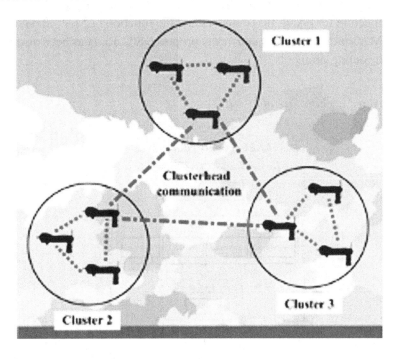

Mobility Models

Efficient communication in FANETs is also dependent on mobility models that capture trails and speed deviations of the UAVs. The selection of mobility model is application dependent. Some tasks require UAVs to move in a planned way on a predetermined path and do not exhibit random movement. Hence, random mobility models cannot be used to simulate FANETs in such scenarios. Reference Point Group Mobility Model (RPGM) can best represent motion of UAVs in performing autonomous military operations without centralized control. This model has a logical center node which governs the movement of the other nodes in its group and monitors their speed, location and direction. Many other models such as Manhattan Grid Mobility (MGM) model which can be used to emulate map based approach in which the movement of UAVs takes into account geographic restrictions (Geng, Zhang, Wang, Fuh, & Teo, 2013; Semsch, Jakob, Pavlicek, Pechoucek, & Michal, 2009) and Random Way Point (RWP) model can be used for patrolling applications where UAVs are allowed to adopt flexible trajectories. Gauss Markov mobility model can serve to model FANETs as relaying networks since the movement of UAVs is dependent on previous speed and directions (Jawhar, Mohamed, Al-Jaroodi, & Sheng Zhang, 2013; Cetin & Zagli, 2011).

Communication Protocols

Due to its unique characteristics, FANETs face communication design challenges. Being a subset of MANETs and VANETs and relatively a new research domain, existing MANET and VANET communication protocols are being tested for FANET scenarios. However, the characteristics and requirements of FANETs strongly differ from those of MANETs and FANETs. Hence, designing of dedicated communication protocols for MAC, network and transport layers still remains an open area of research in FANETs as insignificant amount of work has been done over the higher layers. Figure 5 describes the existing layered architecture for FANETs. To understand the function of MAC and network layer in this regard, widely used MAC protocol 802.11 and newly proposed 802.15.4 has been discussed below along with the essentials of routing protocols.

Figure 5. Existing layered architecture of FANETs

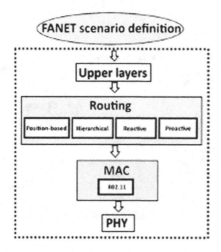

MAC Layer

MAC layer handles coordinated and scheduled transmission between several contending nodes. The important issues that FANET MAC layer should address are of variable link quality, packet delays and optimal channel utilization during real-time network operation. High bit error rates in FANETs make wireless communication links unreliable.

IEEE 802.11

For the MAC layer protocol, IEEE 802.11 has been used along with the optimization of commercial off the shelf hardware components such as directional and omnidirectional antennas. Due to its extensive availability and support for infrastructure-based as well as infrastructure-less modes, 802.11 is being used in on-going FANET research studies. Full duplex radio circuits and multipacket reception techniques have been used to obtain improved Chanel State Information (CSI) for the UAVs. Due to the availability of up-to-date information about channel state, these schemes have exhibited improved results for latency and throughput even if the channel state information is not absolutely accurate.

For bandwidth hungry applications such as hunt and destroy operations and border patrolling, IEEE 802.11 can offer maximum advantages because it supports bandwidth up to 11Mbps and a typical range of 150m which can effectively facilitate multimedia images and videos.

IEEE 802.15.4

IEEE 802.15.4 could be another potential candidate for MAC layer protocol. It provides low power consumption, cost and complexity. This protocol was basically designed for devices with low energy requirement to be used in Wireless Personal Area Networks (WPANs). It can operate at a raw data rate of 250 kbps using 2.4 GHz ISM frequency band. Less bandwidth hungry applications such as monitoring and control, wildfire management, remote sensing and relaying networks require control information to be exchanged within the network. Such applications do not necessarily require a high data rate protocol such as 802.11. UAV to UAV communication can be realized efficiently by deploying a low data rate protocol such as IEEE 802.15.4. IEEE 802.15.4 has not been exploited so far for FANETs. For both single cluster and multi-cluster scenarios 802.15.4 can be used within the cluster so as to achieve better results in terms of reduced complexity and bandwidth minimization.

In comparison to 802.11, two important modes supported by 802.15.4 are beacon enabled or synchronous mode and non-beacon enabled or asynchronous mode. In beacon enabled mode, beacons are generated by a dedicated device known as the Personal Area Network (PAN) coordinator to the nodes who wish to transmit the data. The nodes then transmit their data to the coordinator using slotted Carrier Sense Multiple Access/Collision Avoidance (CSMA/CA) scheme. The slotted CSMA/CA uses superframe structure to split the time between beacons into 16 slots. These slots are divided into Contention Access Period (CAP) and Contention Free Period (CFP). CAP provides contention based medium access whereas CFP have Guaranteed Time Slots (GTS) for data transmission. Superframe order is related to the superframe duration i.e. the active period of the node during CAP and beacon order is used to define beacon interval i.e. the time between two beacons. For multicluster and hierarchical FANETs, synchronous mode can provide the desired benefits as it offers dedicated cyclic slots for heavy traffic.

In non-beacon enabled mode, the node transmits its data to the coordinator using unslotted CSMA/CA. For single cluster or small FANETs, asynchronous mode can be used as it offers low control overhead.

IEEE 802.15.4 can be expected to provide a winning situation for in-network communication between UAVs by modifying MAC layer and determining optimal values of backoff exponential, beacon order (BO), superframe order (SO) and CAP. By minimizing the backoff exponential value, backoff delay of the nodes can be shortened and increasing contention free period length in the superframe structure of 802.15.4 may take advantage in transmitting data leading to improved throughput performance. 100% duty cycle can be achieved by adjusting SO and BO values as energy resource constrain does not occur in FANETs due to dedicated UAV hardware.

To meet certain reliability bounds in FANET applications, controlled access MAC layer protocols can prove to be very promising. TDMA scheme allows nodes to transmit in dedicated time slots. In disaster management scenarios where QoS criteria need to be met, collision free transmissions can be done exploiting TDMA. In multicluster scenario, UAVs may communicate their bandwidth requirements to the cluster head which in turn assign timeslots accordingly.

Network Layer

Dynamic nature of FANETs causes sudden changes in the network topology and thus makes routing among UAVs a daunting task. Considering UAV to UAV communication, routing protocol plays an important role in reliable end-to-end data delivery and makes routing an engaging research prospect in FANET domain. Various reactive, proactive, position-based and hierarchical routing protocols have been implemented to meet the challenges of FANETs. The routing algorithm should be such that if a link cannot be established with one of the UAVs in a FANET, the network can still route messages through other UAVs. Various types of routing strategies that can be exploited in FANETs are mentioned below:

Proactive Routing

Such routing class of protocols tends to save the entire network topology in form of routing tables which are updated on periodic or event driven basis. In FANET studies, proactive protocols have resulted in minimized routing overheads but have also raised concerns as stale routing table cannot account for high mobility (Alshabtat & Dong, 2011).

Reactive Routing

If there is no prior maintenance of routes within the network and a route discovery process is initiated only when requested, the routing protocol used falls in the category of reactive routing. Reactive protocols have proved to address the demand of frequent and unstable topological changes that may occur due to weather conditions, structural obstacles or non-functioning UAVs. However, repetitive path finding results in exhaustive search (Pojda, Wolff, Sbeiti, & Wietfeld, 2011).

Geographic Routing

Geographic routing protocols route information based on the position information of the UAVs (Lin, Sung, Li & Yang, 2012). Benefits in terms of reduced routing overhead, computation time and energy resource are obtained. Since there is clear LoS between transmitter and receiver FANET nodes, hence geographic routing protocols can make use of exact information obtained by Global Positioning System (GPS). However, due to unique challenges of FANETs, such as exceptionally high mobility, determination of accurate positioning systems still remains an open area of research.

Hierarchical Routing

Hierarchical routing protocols run in multicluster scenarios by forming UAVs into groups. By performing efficient routing between cluster heads, hierarchical routing can increase robustness of FANETs along with improved results for large geographic area. Here the issue lies with cluster formation for which FANET dedicated algorithms have been proposed.

Some of the conventional protocols from the above categories like Directional Optimized Link State Routing Protocol (DOLSR) have met the requirements of latency by the use of directional antennas to reduce the number of multipoint relay nodes (Alshabtat & Dong,2011) . A dedicated geographic routing solution named Geographic Position Mobility Oriented Routing (GPMOR) has been proposed that not only determines location but also predicts movement of the UAVs in a FANET (Lin, Sung, Li & Yang

,2012). This approach proved to be beneficial for improved packet delivery ratio results. Dynamic Source Routing (DSR) and time slotted variant of Ad-hoc On-demand Distance Vector (AODV) have also been tested for FANETs (Forsmann, Hiromoto, & Svoboda,2007).

PERFORMANCE ANALYSIS OF MOBILITY MODELS FOR FANETS

Introduction

Efficient routing in FANETs is also dependent on mobility models that capture trails and speed deviations of the UAVs. Since the destination, speed and direction of nodes is not solely random, hence mobility model of MANETs such as Random Way Point (RWP) cannot be wholly used for predicting the behavior of routing protocols in a FANET scenario. However, semi random movement may arise as a result of environment changes leading to redefining path plans. Temporal-based models which generate correlated movement of nodes can be used for critical flight missions where the movement of UAVs should be systematic. Mobility models with spatial dependency can be used to generate group movements as of swarm of UAVs which move in collaboration with each other for dedicated missions. Another class of mobility models is geographic restriction based mobility models in which movement of nodes is subjected to the environment. This type of mobility pattern can be used to generate predefined pathways for UAVs.

In this chapter four available mobility models have been evaluated which include Reference Point Group Mobility Model (RPGM), Gauss Markov (GM) mobility model, Random Way Point (RWP) mobility model and Manhattan Grid Mobility (MGM) model selected from families of spatial dependent, temporal dependent, random based and geographic restriction based mobility models, respectively. The unique presentation of this chapter involves categorization of suitable mobility models for different applications in UAV domain. The effect of dynamic FANET environment, characterized by high mobility and generated by these models, is evaluated for different routing protocols: DSR, AODV and OLSR.

Related Work

Some studies have used existing MANET mobility models while others have proposed specific models for UAV ad-hoc networks. In (Wan, Namuduri, Zhou, & Fu, 2013), smooth turn mobility model has been proposed for Airborne Networks (AN). The model accounts for spatial and temporal dependency of airborne vehicles in highly random AN networks. The trajectory of vehicles is predicted by using the correlated information of speed and acceleration which is straight and smooth at turns.

In (Kuiper & Nadjm-Tehrani, 2006) two mobility models for group surveying scenario of UAVs have been proposed. The first model is based on memoryless movement of UAVs whereas the second model uses the idea of pheromones to provide dependent and coordinated movement among UAVs. The random model provides left, right and straight movements according to fixed probabilities. The study reveals that the models provide a trade-off between maximum coverage and maximum connectivity.

In (Bouachir, Abrassart, Garcia, & Larrieu, 2014), authors propose Paparazzi Mobility Model (PPRZM) based on Paparazzi system for the UAVs. The model supports five movements: Stay-At, Way-Point, Eight, Oval and Scan. Results show that PPRZM gives more realistic results in terms of End-to-End delay as compared to Random Way Point (RWP) Mobility model. Semi-Random Circular Movement (SRCM) mobility model has been proposed for UAV MANETs in (W. Wang, Guan, B. Wang & Y Wang, 2010). The UAV movement is around a fixed point with a random radius.

Gauss Markov mobility model has been used in (Lin, Sung, Li & Yang, 2012) along with the proposed Geographic Position Mobility Oriented Routing (GPMOR). The authors have utilized the best next hop discovery property of Gauss Markov Mobility model to make their routing protocol more robust towards route failures. Similarly, an optimized 3-D version of Gauss Markov mobility model has been used in (Broyles, Jabbar, & Sterbenz, 2010) for highly dynamic AN. In (Kuiper, 2008), the authors have tested their proposed protocol location aware routing for delay-tolerant networks (LAROD) using Random Way Point mobility for reconnaissance tasks.

Mobility Models

A brief discussion on the mobility models and the movement traces used in this study are given below.

Reference Point Group Mobility (RPGM) Model

Group mobility models can be used to simulate group of UAVs in performing autonomous military operations without centralized control. RPGM model falls in the category of mobility models exhibiting spatial dependency. Nodes are divided into groups and the movement of nodes within one group is dependent on each other. Every group has a group center that moves on a predefined path and defines the movement trend of the entire group. The direction and speed of every node in the group depends on its own reference point and a random deviating vector from group center (Camp, Boleng, & Davies, 2002). Figure 6 shows movement trace of RPGM.

Gauss Markov (GM) Mobility Model

In Gauss Markov mobility model, at the start a specific speed and direction is defined for each node (Camp, Boleng & Davies, 2002). This is a memory based model with speed and direction of a node at

Figure 6. Movement trace of two nodes under RPGM mobility model in 130 x 130 m area

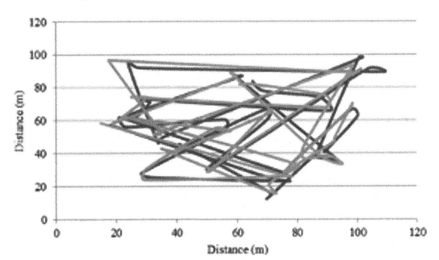

Figure 7. Movement trace of single node under GM mobility model in 130 x 130 m area

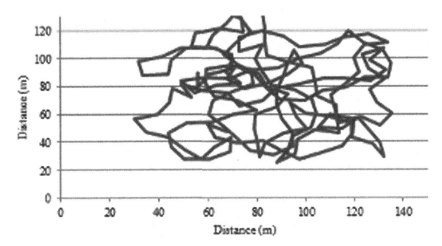

time instant T depending on speed and direction at time instant T-1. The values are updated after constant time intervals. Hence, Gauss Markov mobility model exhibits temporal dependency. The degree of randomness in the movement can be obtained through a parameter alpha (0<alpha<1). For a memoryless Gauss Markov mobility model alpha=0 and for full memory based model alpha=1.

Random Way Point (RWP) Mobility Model

Random Way Point is a commonly used model of MANETs. Initially, there is random deployment of nodes in the simulation area. The nodes remain stationary for a certain time termed as pause time and then start moving towards randomly chosen destinations. The chosen speed is uniformly distributed between [Vmin, Vmax] (Camp, Boleng, & Davies, 2002). In some applications like patrolling UAVs may be allowed to adopt flexible trajectories. Such scenarios can be modeled using Random Way Point

Figure 8. Movement trace of single node under RWP mobility model in 130 x 130 m area

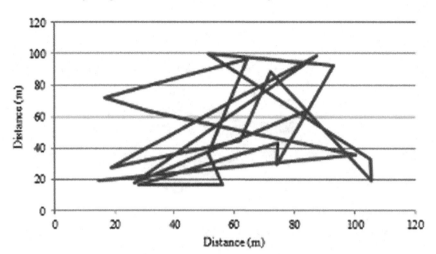

Figure 9. Movement trace of single node under MGM mobility model in 130 x 130 m area

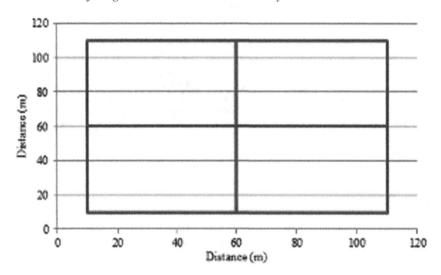

mobility model. Unlike MANETs, UAVs cannot make sharp turns that occur in RWP. So, this random based model cannot provide realistic results for FANETs.

Manhattan Grid Mobility (MGM) Model

Manhattan Grid mobility model can be used to emulate map based approach in which the movement of UAVs takes into account geographic restrictions. The nodes move on pre-defined horizontal and vertical grids. The nodes are allowed to move in north, south, east or west direction. Straight movement of nodes on the defined grids occurs with probability 0.5 and the nodes take turns on corners with probability 0.25. The speed of a node in a lane at a certain time interval is dependent not only on the previous time interval but also on the nodes moving in the same lane.

Table 1. Mobility models feasibility for FANET application scenarios

Mobility Model	Proposed Application Scenario
Manhattan Grid Mobility (MGM) model	Complex Urban Environments (Kothari, Postlethwaite & Gu, 2013)
Random Way Point (RWP) mobility model	Patrol systems (Girard, Howell & Hedrick, 2014)
Reference Point Group Mobility (RPGM) model	Disaster management, Search and destroy operations (Quaritsch et al.,2010; George & Sousa, 2010)
Gauss Markov	Multi-tier Airborne MANETs (Broyles, Jabbar, & Sterbenz, 2010)

Based on comprehensive study of FANET applications, mobility models have been categorized for various scenarios in Table 1.

Simulation Methodology

The simulations were performed on ns2 which is a discrete network simulator. To generate movement of nodes for different mobility models, BonnMotion utility was used which creates, analyzes and exports mobility scenarios to different network simulators (Aschenbruck, Ernst, Gerhards-Padilla & Schwamborn, 2010). Figure 10 shows the network topology used in for simulations. The network topology consists of 5 nodes where center node acts as a sink and a relaying node and it assigns timeslots such that two nodes contend for the medium in that duration and transmit their data to node 0 while the remaining two are in sleep mode. The effect of collision has been introduced for acquiring more comprehensive results. The nodes move with average speeds ranging from 10m/s to 100m/s (Bekmezci, Sahingoz, & Temel, 2013). The pause time was set to 5s to generate highly dynamic scenario with frequent topology changes. Constant Bit Rate (CBR) traffic model was used with packet size of 100 bytes transmitted at a constant rate of 50kbps. In FANETs a line of sight is maintained between UAVs (Bekmezci, Sahingoz, & Temel, 2013). Hence, the radio propagation model used is free space model as it works on the assumption of a

Figure 10. Network topology

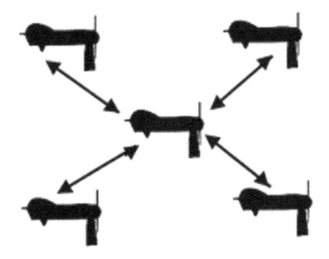

Table 2. Simulation parameters

Parameter	Value
Simulation tool	ns-2.35
Simulation time	200
MAC Protocol	802.11
Simulation Area	200 x 200
Routing Protocol	AODV, DSR, OLSR
Traffic	CBR
Number of nodes	5
Transmission Range	75m
CBR data rate	50 kbps
Speed	10,50,100,200,300,400,500 (m/s)
Channel capacity	11 Mbps
Mobility models	Reference Point Group Mobility Model (RPGM) Gauss Markov mobility model (GM) Random Way Point mobility model (RWP) Manhattan Grid Mobility model (MGM)

single clear line of sight between transmitter and receiver. The simulation parameters given in table 2 have been selected in reference to (Alshabtat & Dong, 2011; Lin, Sung, Li, & Yang, 2012).

BonnMotion generates node movement patterns according to the mobility models specified by taking certain parameters as input such as maximum minimum speed, number of nodes, speed standard deviations, group change probabilities, pause time and simulation area and duration. The traces of node movements generated for different mobility models have been presented in the previous section.

Performance Metrics

The performance evaluation parameters used for FANET topology are described below:

Packet Delivery Ratio (PDR): It gives the ratio of data packets received at the destination successfully to the data packets generated by the source. This parameter is used to determine network reliability.

$$PDR = \frac{\sum_1^N D_{packets}}{\sum_1^N S_{packets}}$$

(1)

where:

$D_{packets}$ = Data packets received at the destination UAV
$S_{packets}$ = Data packets generated by the source UAV
N = Total number of packets

- **Average End to End (E2E) Delay:** This metric tells about the average time it takes for data packets to reach the destinations successfully.

$$Average\ End-to-End\ Delay = \sum_{1}^{N}\left(T_t + T_{rt} + T_b + T_p\right) \tag{2}$$

where:

T_t = Transmission time
T_{rt} = Retransmission time
T_b = Buffering time
T_p = Processing time
N = Total number of packets

- **Routing Overhead:** Routing overhead determines the total number of routing packets that took part in the transmission.

$$Routing\ overhead = \sum_{1}^{N} R_{packets} \tag{3}$$

where:

$R_{packets}$ = Routing packets
N = Total number of packets

Results and Analysis

Packet Delivery Ratio

Figures 11-14 depict the performance of different mobility models in terms of PDR for AODV, DSR and DSDV. It can be observed that for all scenarios, DSR maintains high PDR. The use of data link acknowledgements makes DSR robust to link failures. Moreover, since routing information is overheard by intermediate nodes, they learn multiple routes to a certain destination and include them in their caches. In case one link does not work from the cache, the alternate route can be used. AODV and OLSR show a decreasing trend in delivery ratio with the increase in speed. Since OLSR is table driven protocol, the routes in the table become outdated very quickly and the rediscovery of the broken link takes time. AODV due to its on-demand nature reacts more rapidly towards route failures.

It can be observed from Figure 11 that RPGM provides higher PDR for all routing protocols. This is because the movement of all nodes in RPGM is governed by defining a maximum distance from group center. Thus, the network is in a fully connected state most of the time. Also, as the speed increases, PDR does not drop below 90% because when UAVs are moving as a swarm and are in the radio range of each other, the effect of high mobility nullifies whereas in other mobility models the increase in node

Figure 11. PDR vs. speed for RPGM

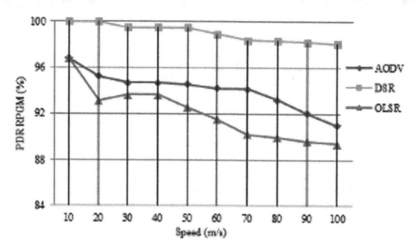

Figure 12. PDR vs. speed for RWP

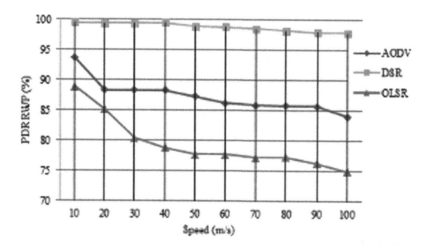

Figure 13. PDR vs. speed for GM

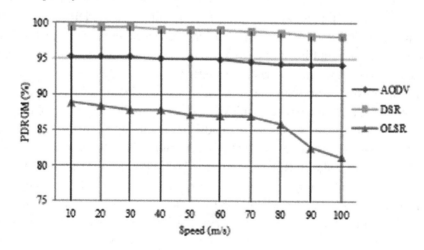

Figure 14. PDR vs. speed for MGM

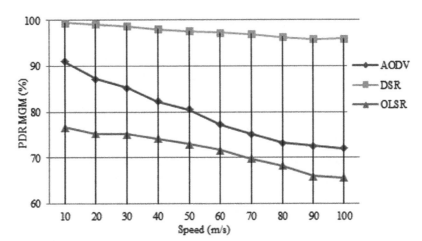

mobility causes decrease in PDR because of the uncoordinated node movements. Routing protocols play an important role by finding alternate valid routes. Thus, suitable mobility models along with appropriate routing protocol can address the issue of link breakages due to high mobility and can help in maintaining an acceptable PDR depending on the application for which FANET nodes are deployed.

Average End-to-End Delay

Figures 15-18 show average end to end delay of AODV, DSR and OLSR for mobility models. It must be noted that the delays are effective delays of data packets that successfully arrive at the destination. As shown DSR exhibits higher delays followed by AODV and OLSR. The route caching mechanism of DSR increases the end to end delay of the network. Due to high mobility the cache contains more percentage of stale routes. If the mobile source node fails to find route to the destination it starts discovery for new route. The entire process increases the packet reception time. AODV on the other hand omits route cache discovery process and shows less average delay. OLSR has routes available all the time and can provide them when required. Due to low PDR of OLSR, fewer data packets are able to reach intended destinations within the simulation time and give low average end-to-end delay of data packets.

Routing Overhead

Figures 19-22 show control or routing overhead for AODV, DSR and OLSR. DSR demonstrates lowest routing overhead than AODV and OLSR. Since DSR also takes advantage of source route caches hence the number of route request packets generated is less than that of AODV. However, with the increase in speed, routing overhead of DSR also increases because frequent link failures make route cache mechanism less effective. OLSR depicts extremely large routing overhead due to the transmission of periodic HELLO and Topology Control (TC) messages. Unlike the used topology, dense and large networks can make the most of OLSR due to multi point relay selection mechanism which guarantees improved scalability in the sharing of topology information.

Figure 15. Average E2E delay vs. speed for RPGM

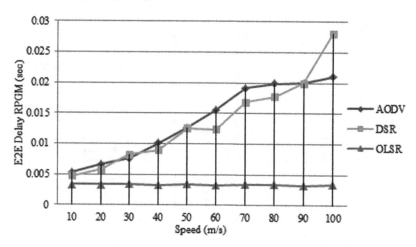

Figure 16. Average E2E delay vs. speed for RWP

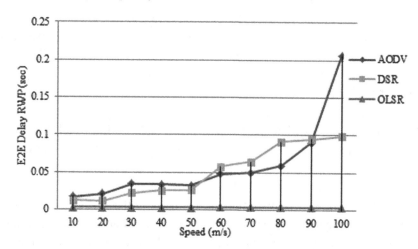

Figure 17. Average E2E delay vs. speed for GM

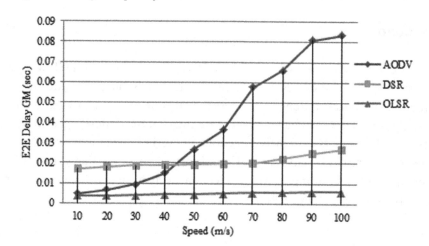

Figure 18. Average E2E delay vs. speed for MGM

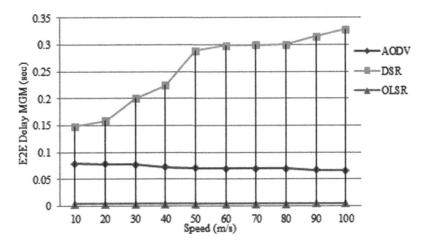

Figure 19. Routing overhead vs. speed for RPGM

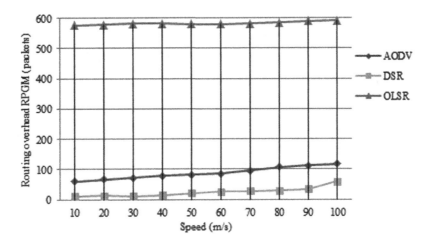

Figure 20. Routing overhead vs. speed for RWP

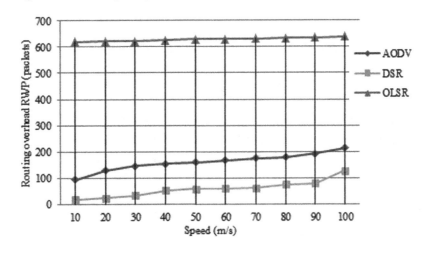

Figure 21. Routing overhead vs. speed for GM

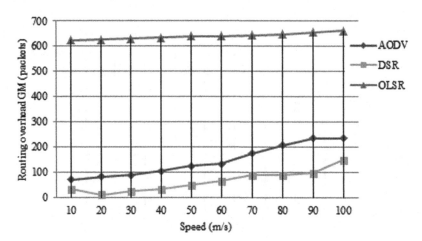

Figure 22. Routing overhead vs. speed for MGM

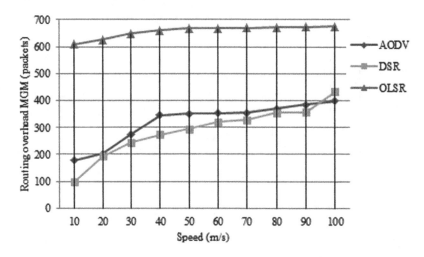

CONCLUSION

FANETs are used for critical and sensitive applications such as reconnaissance and patrolling and hence simulation analysis needs to be performed under realistic environments. Accurate mobility models are essential to foretell communication problems during protocols evaluation that may arise in real-world scenarios.

There is not a standard method to validate or select a mobility model for FANETs because different applications may require different movement patterns. Therefore, a detailed performance evaluation of mobility models has been done for the first time and different mobility models for various applications have been suggested. DSR, AODV and OLSR routing protocols have been evaluated using these models. DSR gave better results for highly dynamic environments generated by Reference Point Group Mobility, Gauss Markov, Random Way Point and Manhattan Grid mobility models.

REFERENCES

Alshabtat, A., & Dong, L. (2011). Low Latency Routing Algorithm for Unmanned Aerial Vehicles Ad-Hoc Networks. *Iranian Journal of Electrical and Computer Engineering*, 6(1), 48–54.

Aschenbruck, N., Ernst, R., Gerhards-Padilla, E., & Schwamborn, M. (2010). BonnMotion - a Mobility Scenario Generation and Analysis Tool. In *3rd International ICST Conference on Simulation Tools and Techniques (SIMUTools)*, Brussels, Belgium. doi:10.4108/ICST.SIMUTOOLS2010.8684

Barrado, C., Messeguer, R., Lopez, J., Pastor, E., Santamaria, E., & Royo, P. (2010). Wildfire monitoring using a mixed air-ground mobile network. *IEEE Pervasive Computing / IEEE Computer Society [and] IEEE Communications Society*, 9(4), 24–32. doi:10.1109/MPRV.2010.54

Bekmezci, İ., Sahingoz, O., & Temel, Ş. (2013). Flying Ad-Hoc Networks (FANETs): A survey. *Ad Hoc Networks*, 11(3), 1254–1270. doi:10.1016/j.adhoc.2012.12.004

Bodanese, J., de Araujo, G., Steup, C., Raffo, G., & Becker, L. (2014). Wireless Communication Infrastructure for a Short-Range Unmanned Aerial. In *28th International Conference on Advanced Information Networking and Applications Workshops (WAINA)*, Victoria, BC. doi:10.1109/WAINA.2014.154

Bouachir, O., Abrassart, A., Garcia, F., & Larrieu, N. (2014). A Mobility Model for UAV Ad-hoc Network. In *International Conference on Unmanned Aircraft Systems*, Orlando, FL. doi:10.1109/ICUAS.2014.6842277

Broyles, D., Jabbar, A., & Sterbenz, J. (2010). *Design and analysis of a 3-D Gauss-Markov mobility model for highly-dynamic airborne networks*. In International Telemetering Conference (ITC), San Diego, CA.

Cai, Y., Yu, F., Li, J., Zhou, Y., & Lamont, L. (2012). MAC performance improvement in UAV ad-hoc networks with full-duplex radios and multi-packet reception capability. In *IEEE International Conference on Communications (ICC)*, Ottawa, Canada. doi:10.1109/ICC.2012.6364116

Camp, T., Boleng, J., & Davies, V. (2002). A survey of mobility models for ad hoc network research. *Wireless Communication and Mobile Computing*, 2(5), 483–502. doi:10.1002/wcm.72

Cetin, O., & Zagli, I. (2011). Continuous Airborne Communication Relay Approach Using Unmanned Aerial Vehicles. *Journal of Intelligent & Robotic Systems*, 65(1-4), 549–562. doi:10.1007/s10846-011-9556-6

Coifman, B., McCord, M., Mishalani, R., Iswalt, M., & Ji, Y. (2006). Roadway traffic monitoring from an unmanned aerial vehicle. *IEEE Proceedings on Intelligent Transport Systems*.

Forsmann, J., Hiromoto, R., & Svoboda, J. (2007). A time-slotted on-demand routing protocol for mobile ad hoc unmanned vehicle systems. In *SPIE Defense and Security Symposium, Unmanned Systems Technology*, Orlando, FL. doi:10.1117/12.719355

Frew, E., & Brown, T. (2008). Networking Issues for Small Unmanned Aircraft Systems. *Journal of Intelligent & Robotic Systems*, 54(1-3), 21–37. doi:10.1007/s10846-008-9253-2

Geng, L., Zhang, Y., Wang, J., Fuh, J., & Teo, S. (2013). Mission planning of autonomous UAVs for urban surveillance with evolutionary algorithms. In *10th IEEE International Conference on Control and Automation (ICCA)*, Hangzhou, China. doi:10.1109/ICCA.2013.6564992

George, J., & Sousa, J. (2010). Search Strategies for Multiple UAV Search and Destroy Missions. *Journal of Intelligent & Robotic Systems, 61*(1-4), 355–367. doi:10.1007/s10846-010-9486-8

Girard, A., Howell, A., & Hedrick, J. (2014). Border patrol and surveillance missions using multiple unmanned air vehicles. In *43rd IEEE Conference on Decision and Control* (CDC), Nassau.

Heimfarth, T., & De Araujo, J. (2014). *Using Unmanned Aerial Vehicle to Connect Disjoint Segments of Wireless Sensor Network*. In IEEE 28th International Conference on Advanced Information Networking and Applications (AINA), Victoria, BC.

Huang, Y., Thomson, S., Hoffmann, W., Lan, Y., & Fritz, B. (2013). Development and prospect of unmanned aerial vehicle technologies for agricultural production management. *International Journal of Agricultural and Biological Engineering, 6*(3), 1–10.

Huba, W., & Shenoy, N. (2012). Airborne surveillance networks with directional antennas. In *8th International Conference on Networking and Services (ICNS)*.

Jawhar, I., Mohamed, N., Al-Jaroodi, J., & Sheng Zhang, J. (2013). Data communication in linear wireless sensor networks using unmanned aerial vehicles. In *International Conference on Unmanned Aircraft Systems (ICUAS)*, Atlanta, GA. doi:10.1109/ICUAS.2013.6564725

Kothari, M., Postlethwaite, I., & Gu, D. (2013). UAV Path Following in Windy Urban Environments. *Journal of Intelligent & Robotic Systems, 74*(3-4), 1013–1028. doi:10.1007/s10846-013-9873-z

Kuiper, E. (2008). *Mobility and Routing in a Delay-tolerant Network of Unmanned Aerial Vehicles* (PhD Dissertation). Linköping University.

Kuiper, E., & Nadjm-Tehrani, S. (2006). Mobility Models for UAV Group Reconnaissance Applications. In *International Conference on Wireless and Mobile Communications (ICWMC)*, Bucharest, Romania. doi:10.1109/ICWMC.2006.63

Lim, C., Park, S., Ryoo, C., Choi, K., & Cho, J. (2010). *A path planning algorithm for Surveillance UAVs with timing mission constrains*. In International Conference on Control Automation and Systems (ICCAS), Gyeonggi.

Lin, L., Sung, Q., Li, J., & Yang, F. (2012). A novel geographic position mobility oriented routing strategy for UAVs. *Journal of Computer Information Systems, 8*(2), 709–716.

Martinez-de Dios, J., Lferd, K., de San Bernabé, A., Núñez, G., Torres-González, A., & Ollero, A. (2012). Cooperation Between UAS and Wireless Sensor Networks for Efficient Data Collection in Large Environments. *Journal of Intelligent & Robotic Systems*. doi:10.1007/s10846-012-9733-2

Newaz, A., Pratama, F., & Chong, N. (2013). Exploration Priority Based Heuristic Approach to UAV path planning. In RO-MAN IEEE, Gyeongju.

Pojda, J., Wolff, A., Sbeiti, M., & Wietfeld, C. (2011). Performance analysis of mesh routing protocols for UAV swarming applications. In *8th International Symposium on Wireless Communication Systems (ISWCS)*, Aachen. doi:10.1109/ISWCS.2011.6125375

Quaritsch, M., Kruggl, K., Wischounig-Strucl, D., Bhattacharya, S., Shah, M., & Rinner, B. (2010). Networked UAVs as aerial sensor network for disaster management applications. *Elektrotechnik und Informationstechnik, 127*(3), 56-63.

Semsch, E., Jakob, M., & Pavlicek, D. (2009). *Autonomous UAV Surveillance in Complex Urban Environments*. In IEEE/WIC/ACM International Joint Conferences on Web Intelligence and Intelligent Agent Technologies (WI-IAT), Milan, Italy.

Shetty, V., Sudit, M., & Nagi, R. (2008). Priority-based assignment and routing of a fleet of unmanned combat aerial vehicles. *Computers & Operations Research, 35*(6), 1813–1828. doi:10.1016/j.cor.2006.09.013

Temel, S., & Bekmezci, I. (2013). *On the performance of Flying Ad-hoc Networks (FANETs) utilizing near space high altitude platforms* (HAPs). In *6th International Conference on Recent Advances in Space Technologies (RAST)*, Istanbul, Turkey. doi:10.1109/RAST.2013.6581252

Wan, Y., Namuduri, K., Zhou, Y., & Fu, S. (2013). A Smooth-Turn Mobility Model for Airborne Networks. *IEEE Transactions on Vehicular Technology, 62*(7), 3359–3370. doi:10.1109/TVT.2013.2251686

Wang, W., Guan, X., Wang, B., & Wang, Y. (2010). A novel mobility model based on semi-random circular movement in mobile ad hoc networks. *Information Sciences, 180*(3), 399–413. doi:10.1016/j.ins.2009.10.001

Chapter 11
Implementing Leader Election Algorithm after Evaluation of Node Trust in MANETs

Jayanta Das
SSVASM, India

Abhijit Das
RCCIIT, India

ABSTRACT

Security and trust are two inevitable concepts for secure Manet. There are various systems used for ensuring security and trust in case of Manet. These systems have several advantages as well as several disadvantages in terms high communication and computation overhead. In this proposed trust based system, trust of node is evaluated on the basis of ratio of signal sent and acknowledgement received. After that, priority of each node is calculated and at last Leader Election algorithm is applied to select node leader.

INTRODUCTION

Wireless sensor network (WSN) is consisting with spatially dispersed and dedicated sensors for monitoring and recording the physical conditions of the universe and organizing the collected data at a central or main location. WSN is basically a system that incorporates a gateway that provides wireless connectivity back to the wired environment and distributed sensor nodes. WSN allows us to observe the event previously which is unobserved at an excellent resolution over large spatiotemporal scales.

Wireless communication (Shantanu, 2011) is not mealy a buzz word, rather, it is an innovative paradigm that is successfully providing services to human being from wireless LANs (McGuffin, 1995) to mobile telephone communication, wireless PANs (Fegan, 2007), and sensor networks. Especially, last decade has witnessed tremendous growth in wireless communication that has helped to trigger and fueled the area of distributed computing. Now days, due to active research, the horizon of distributed computing has been further pushed to the field of Mobile Computing (Goodchild, 2003) with an objec-

DOI: 10.4018/978-1-5225-1785-6.ch011

tive to implement efficient solutions in wireless domain with minimal cost and reduced or less power consumption by handheld devices.

"Wireless networking (Amit Shrivastava, Overview of Routing Protocols in MANET's and Enhancements in Reactive Protocols) is a technology that enables two or more computers to communicate using standard network protocols, but without network cabling" (Gawali, 2012). And now there exist network protocols that are developed just for the implementation of Wireless networks. We can classify wireless network in primarily following two categories:

1. Network with existing infrastructure: is a network where exists a wireless access point or earlier wireless hardware support for every node to connect to networks. Here nodes do not require to participate in any kind of transit services. They communicate to access points to send & receive packets from other nodes. In this kind of network different access point can be able to follow different wireless protocol like 802.11 b or 802.11g and still can communicate with each other. There exist several wireless products based on this kind of technology.
2. Ad hoc network is a network where there is no existence of wireless infrastructure for networking, instead each node communicates with each other using their sole transmitter-receiver only. In this kind of network each and every node does participate voluntarily in transit packet that flow to and from different nodes. Each node does follow same routing algorithm to route different packets. Thus, this kind of network have limited homogenous feature. There are not many wireless products that follow this proposed technology.

Manet is defined as self-configuring network of mobile host which is connected by wireless network. Its specialty is to provide peer-to-peer communication without accessing any point or any wired network. The movement of mobile nodes is random and during this movement no predetermined topology is formed by mobile stations. That is why, there is no assurance to form long term guaranteed path from any node to another node. So, it is applied in that type of applications where emergency service is needed like military battlefield. Now the question is arisen that why we choose MANET for communication purpose. There are several reasons behind that. There is no requirement to install specific infrastructure and as well as low set up time and cost in case of MANET. Another thing is that Trust of node to provide appropriate security in the network. In this matter, we should discuss about Trust.

Trust is one of the prime factor for decision-making processes of any network for which absolutely plays very crucial role. If it is possible to predict regarding any faulty behavior in advance for any network, any network becomes flawless.

Some of the main features of MANET are listed below:

1. MANET can be formed or constructed without any preexisting infrastructure.
2. It follows dynamic topology where nodes may join and leave the network at any time and the multi-hop routing may keep changing as nodes join and depart from the network.
3. It does have very limited physical security, and thus increasing security is an important concern.
4. Every node in the MANET can be helpful to assist in routing of packets in the network.
5. Limited Bandwidth & Limited Power.

Security in MANET

There is very limited physical security in MANET. The type of attacks can be classified in Active attacks or Passive attacks (Loutfi, 2003). The common known security issues are Passive attacks which include eavesdropping and information disclosure. Inclusion of active attacks is Denial of service, Data modification by viruses, Trojans and worms.

There are other more specific problems with mobile ad hoc network such as vulnerability of channels and nodes, Byzantine black hole and Byzantine wormhole attack (Awerbuch, 2000). The security issue also includes attacks that may inject erroneous routing information and diverting network traffic thus making routing inefficient.

There are many methods to reduce the impact of these attacks, which include a secure routing using public and private keys to get a certification authority and use of digital signatures and priori trust relationships. The drawbacks of such a system is that the priori trust needs to be in place before the network is set up this may not always be possible in a case of disaster affected areas (Marti, 2000).

Characteristics of MANET

- **Autonomous and Infrastructure-Less:** Each node under MANET is assigned as an independent router and that router generates independent data. That is why, there is not possible to establish any predetermined communication infrastructure.
- **Multi-Hop Routing:** Acting as individual router, each node can be able to forward packet to each other which is helpful to exchange information smoothly between each node i.e. each mobile host.
- **Dynamically Changing Network Topology:** In MANET, nodes are able to move without any pre-determined manner that leads changing the network topology as well as routes between the nodes abruptly. As a result of this, a number of packets cannot be arrived at proper destination.
- **Node Heterogeneity:** The radio interface/interfaces included in each node have various transmission/receiving capabilities which lead the creation of asymmetric links. Again different software/ hardware configuration of each node is able to create various processing capabilities. To cope up the above problems, we should design complicated and robust network protocol as well as algorithm.
- **Energy Constrained Operation:** Each node has low battery power. So power-aware algorithms must be designed to provide some extra energy to each node for forwarding packets.
- **Network Scalability:** Many MANET is designed with the help of adding with tens of thousands of nodes to cope up the problem regarding large network.

Issues in MANET

There are number of issues in MANETs and can be classified as:

1. Medium access related (*e.g.*, distributed operations, hidden terminal problem, access delay, through-put, real time traffic support and resource reservation),
2. Routing algorithm related (*e.g.*, mobility, bandwidth, error prone, shared medium and resource constraint),

3. Multicasting related (*e.g.*, robustness, efficiency, scalability, security and efficient group management),
4. QoS related (*e.g.*, reliability, delay, jitter, bandwidth and QoS aware routing),
5. Security related (*e.g.*, shared medium, lack of central authority, low power at nodes, insecure operational environment and physical vulnerability),
6. Energy management related (*e.g.*, transmission power management, battery power management, process power management and device power management), and
7. Development related (*e.g.*, low cost, choice of protocol, area coverage and reconfiguration).

The above mentioned issues affect the performance of MANET. However, the performance and efficiency of distributed services running on MANET must be unaffected by these factors as far as possible. Hence, the distributed protocols, which handle various computing challenges, *e.g.*, mutual exclusion, leader election, termination detection, etc., should be introduced or developed keeping these issues aside, though these issues do affect them (Shantanu, 2011).

Applications of MANET

- A Bluetooth unit, equipped with a microchip, useful to provide wireless ad hoc communications, of voice and data between portable and/or fixed electronic devices like computers, cellular phones, printers and digital cameras.
- The IEEE 802.11 standard is able to specify two operational modes for Wireless LANs: infrastructure-based and ad hoc. In the ad hoc mode, any station that is within the transmission range of any other, after a synchronization phase, can start communicating.
- MANET is employed in military operations, communication and also at automated battlefields.
- In MANET, smart nodes can be equipped with electronic devices so that end user can control these devices at local location and as well as remote location.
- In MANET, emergency search and rescue operations can be performed successfully in case of disaster like earthquake, thunderstorms, tsunami, fire etc.
- In MANET, tracking data with respect of animal movement, weather forecasting, and patient diagnosis can be performed.
- In MANET, setting up virtual classrooms and setting ad hoc communication network during class lectures, important business meeting can be performed.

Challenges in MANET

MANET inherits all the challenges of wireless domain with enhanced complications; thus, coordinator election in ad hoc environment is more sinister than in its infrastructure counterpart. The following factors add to difficulties in developing a leader election protocol in such environment (Shrivastava et al.; Chen, 2011):

- **Dynamic System:** Election protocols are developed for conventional distributed system, usually, depends upon the network topology; while in MANET, nodes are highly mobile, hence, the topology is able to change at a very fast rate. Intuitively, node mobility is able to enforce network reconfiguration frequently which makes the network more susceptible to attacks.

- **Variation in Node Capabilities:** Every node has different battery power, computational power and memory stacks. Moreover, they may have differentiating software configuration, traffic load distribution, congestion control mechanism, transmission/receiving capabilities and bandwidths. The heterogeneity in node radio capabilities can issue result in possibly asymmetric links. Thus, designing network protocols for such heterogeneous network can be complex, requiring dynamic adaptation to the changing conditions.
- **Failure of Mobile Nodes:** Mobile nodes are generally high error prostrate unlike static wired network nodes due to limited resources at nodes.
- **No Secure Medium:** The wireless network is more immune by a wide range of passive and active attacks. Also, the security mechanisms, like secret keys, trusted authorities, are difficult to implement. Thus, the working of MANETs is often obstructed by the attacks, like man-in-middle, denial-of services, which may lead to elect a false coordinator.
- **Limited Network Scalability:** At present, most of the static environment protocols can have significant network scalability due to relatively small wireless components. However, MANET applications involve large wireless components with thousands of nodes. Hence, scalability is crucial to the successful deployment of these networks.

Although, these challenges do exist in cellular mobile systems, the coordinator election in MANET is difficult due to absence of some static node like base station (BS) and mobile switching center (MSC) in cellular systems (Shantanu, 2011).

Routing Procedure

Routing is the procedure of forwarding packet towards its destination using most efficient path. Efficiency of the path is measured in various metrics like, Number of hops, traffic, security, etc. In Ad-hoc network each host node acts as specialized router itself.

Different Routing Strategies

Routing protocol for ad-hoc network can be classified in three strategies.

1. Flat vs. Hierarchical architecture.
2. Pro- active vs. Re- active routing protocol.
3. Hybrid protocols.

Flat vs. Hierarchical Architecture

Hierarchical network architecture topology is consisting of multiple layers where top layers are more seen as master of their lower layer nodes. There are cluster of nodes and one gateway node among all clusters has a responsibility to communicate with the gateway node in other cluster. In this schema there is a clear distribution of task. Burden of storage of network topology is totally dependent on gateway nodes, where as communicating different control message is dependent on cluster nodes.

But this architecture breaks down when single node failure (Gateway node) is happened. Gateway nodes become very crucial for successful operation of network. Examples include Zone-based Hierarchical Link State (ZHLS) routing protocol (Joa-Ng, 1999). Where in flat architecture no layering of responsibility does not exist. Each and every node does follow the same routing algorithm as any other node in the network.

PROACTIVE VS. REACTIVE ROUTING PROTOCOL IN MANET

Proactive Routing Protocol

In proactive routing scheme every node continuously is able to maintain complete routing information of the network. This is completely achieved by flooding network periodically with network status information to find out any possible change in network topology.

Current routing protocol like Link State Routing (LSR) protocol (open shortest path first) and the Distance Vector Routing Protocol (Bellman-Ford algorithm) are not suitable to be implemented in mobile environment.

Destination Sequenced Distance Vector Routing protocol (DSDV) and Wireless routing protocols were helpful to propose to eliminate counting to infinity and looping problems of the distributed Bellman-Ford Algorithm.

Examples of Proactive Routing Protocols are (Misra, 1999):

1. Global State Routing (GSR).
2. Hierarchical State Routing (HSR).
3. Destination Sequenced Distance Vector Routing (DSDV).

Reactive Routing Protocol

Every node in this routing protocol is able to maintain information of only active paths to the destination nodes. A route search is required for every new destination therefore the communication overhead is lessened at the expense of delay to search the route. Rapidly changing wireless network topology may be able to break active route and cause subsequent route search (Joa-Ng, 1999).

Examples of reactive protocols are:

1. Ad hoc On-demand Distance Vector Routing (AODV).
2. Dynamic Source Routing (DSR).
3. Location Aided Routing (LAR).
4. Temporally Ordered Routing Algorithm (TORA).

Hybrid Routing Protocols in MANET

There exist a vast number of routing protocols of globally reactive and locally proactive states. Hybrid routing algorithm is ideally suited for Zone Based Routing Protocol (ZRP) (Joa-Ng, 1999).

COST BENEFITS TRADE-OFF BETWEEN PROACTIVE AND REACTIVE PROTOCOLS

Advantage: Proactive vs. Reactive

- **Proactive Protocols:** Routes are readily available when there is any requirement to be able to send packet to any other mobile node in the network. Quick response is provided to application program.
- **Reactive Protocols:** These are bandwidth efficient protocols. Routes are discovered on the basis of demand. Less Network communication overhead is needed in this protocol.

Disadvantage: Proactive vs. Reactive

- **Proactive Protocols:** These maintain the complete network graph in current state, where it is not needed to send packets to all those nodes. Consumes lots of network resources to maintain up-to-date status of network graph. "A frequent system-wide broadcast limits the size of ad-hoc network that can effectively use DSDV because the control message overhead is grown as $O (n^2)$."
- **Reactive Protocols:** These have very high response time as route is required to be discovered on demand, when there is some packet to be able to send to new destination which does not lie on active path.

Reactive Routing Protocols

Reactive routing protocols are more popular set of routing algorithms which are helpful for mobile computation because of their excellent low bandwidth consumption.

AODV

AODV is termed as Ad-hoc On Demand Distance Vector. AODV is distance vector type routing where it does not involve those nodes to maintain routes to destination that are not on active path. As long as end points are valid AODV does not have role of its part. Different route messages like Route Request, Route Replies and Route Errors are used to discover and maintain links. UDP/IP is used to be able to receive and get messages. AODV implements a destination sequence number for each route created by destination node for any request to the nodes. A route with maximum sequence number is chosen for selection. To find a new route the source node sends Route Request message to the network until and unless destination is reached or a node with fresh route is found. Then Route Reply is able to send back to the source node. The nodes on active route communicate with each other by passing hello messages periodically to its immediate or nearest neighbor. If a node does not receive a reply, then it has no option but to delete the node from its list and sends Route Error to all the members in the active members in the route. AODV does not allow link which is unidirectional (Altman & Jimenez, 2002).

DSR

This is an On-demand source routing protocol. In DSR or Demand Source Routing, the route paths are discovered after source is able to send a packet to a destination node in the ad-hoc network. The source node primarily does not have a path to the destination when the first packet is sent. The DSR has two functions first is discovery of route and the second is maintenance of route (Marti, 2000).

Location Aided Routing (LAR) (Silberschatz, 2009)

LAR or Location Aided Routing uses the basic flooding algorithm that is defined in DSR with the exception that it uses location information of a particular node which is helpful to limit the flooding in the network. The location information can be collected using the Global Positioning System (GPS). Sometimes the GPS might only be able to give the approximate location of a node. Even then the LAR protocol can be implemented. Using the location information, LAR is able to calculate the expected zone of a particular node.

Components of Wireless Environment

According to (Gopal, 2012), the wireless network is equipped with mainly three components. They are Client, router and gateways. The detailed information of these components are given below-

Clients are the end-user devices like laptop, personal digital assistant, and smart phone by which network can be accessed through different applications like e-mail, game, detection of location etc. Basically all the previously mentioned applications are mobile; mostly they have excellent routing capability in spite of having limited power. It cannot be assured that all of them are connected to the network. Instead of this it can be concluded that some of them are not connected to the network and rest of them are connected to the network.

Routers are the specific devices which are implemented for routing the network traffic. They have no power for terminating as well as originating the traffic. The routers have limited power in case of mobility but they have certain reliable characteristics. In case of specific router such as mesh router, the consumption of transmission power is low for multi-hop communication strategy. Additionally, multiple channels and multiple interfaces for enabling scalability in a multi-hop mesh environment are supported by the Medium Access Control (MAC) protocol in a mesh router.

Gateways are the specific type of routers which are enjoying direct access to the wired network. Because Gateways are equipped with multiple interfaces to connect to both wired and wireless networks, obviously the gateways are quite costly.

TRUST IN MANET AND ITS RELATED WORK

Trust

In MANET trust can be defined as a level of belief according to the behavior of nodes (or entities, agents etc.) (Dalal, 2012; Capra., 2004). The probability value of trust ranging from 0 to1, where 0 represent DISTRUST and 1 represents TRUST (Dalal, 2012; LoPresti, 2004). The different existing trust based schemes in Ad-hoc network were discussed in this paper. Jiang and Baras (Dalal, 2012) (Theodorakopoulos & Baras, 2006) proposed Ant Based Evidence Distribution Scheme. Swarm Intelligence Paradigm concept is used by this scheme. According to this scheme, MANET mobile nodes communicate with other nodes through "agents". These "agents" are called as "ants" under Ant Based Evidence Distribution Scheme. Agents are able to find the optimal path for evaluating trust with the help of the specific information. This specific information is called as "Pheromones" and is collected by ants. The features of this scheme are easily adaptive to mobility and working in effective manner under structure less network. Buckerche & Ren (Dalal, 2012) (Y.Ren, 2008) proposed Generalization Reputation Evidence protocol based scheme. The main feature of this scheme is that to provide security to MANET trusted community from malicious nodes. There is a certain reason behind this feature. The reason is that this scheme will not allow entering any node which is under suspicion into any secured or trusted network. The advantage of this scheme is that not any attack is addressed under Generalization Reputation Evidence model. Individual trust model and punishment or reward system is combined to form a new trust model. This model is known as System Level Trust Model. According to this model, punishment will be given by the system to those nodes which are suspicious or malicious and reward will be given by the system to those nodes which behave as trustworthy at most of the time. "Trust Evidence Dissemination Mechanism" (Dalal, 2012; Yu, 2010) is included under System Level Trust Model. Watchdog trust Model is one of the specific System Level Trust Model. In 2000, this model was discovered by (Marti, 2000) and discussed by (Dalal, 2012). Watchdog mechanism is able to find out suspicious or malicious nodes by applying procedure such as listening transmission of the next node, exploiting abnormal mode of operation etc. Mainly the two cases are responsible to take decision that whether the node is malicious or not. Case 1 is if node does not forward the packet within the specific period of time and case 2 is that each node is responsible to maintain buffer for storing packet. But it has been notified that if overheard packet is not same as the packet which is already stored into the packet, it has been concluded that the node is malicious. Another mechanism Pathrater is behaved like watchdog mechanism (Dalal, 2012; Marti, 2000). One special feature is additionally included in Pathrater mechanism. This feature is to calculate best route link. This link is only implemented by reliable data. The procedure to find out best route link is to calculate path metric by thorough observation of rating for each and every neighboring node in MANET. Obviously the rating should be known. This mechanism performs excellent work by calculating shortest path when reliable information is not availed. This mechanism provides a unique idea to detect the malicious node in the network. If the calculated path metric is negative, then it is concluded that at least one malicious node is existing in the network. (Dalal, 2012) discussed and (Buchegger, 2002) proposed another excellent system level based trust model in the year of 2002. This model is known as CONFIDENT. The full form of CONFIDENT is Cooperation of Nodes Fairness in Dynamic Network. According to this mechanism, abnormal behaved nodes in the network are extracted. Actually four components are required for applying this mechanism.

1. The first component is Monitor. With help of this component, next node transmission or behavior of route protocol is thoroughly monitored. In this way, this component is able to track those types of nodes which behave abnormally.
2. The second component is known as Reputation System. With the help of this component, an ALARM message is conveyed to the Trust Manager component, if any node is tracked under suspicious mode in MANET.

3. The third component is known as Trust Manager. With the help of this component, the trust is evaluated for any node under MANET.
4. The fourth or last component is known as Path Manager. With the help of this component, a list is maintained by each node in MANET.

This list consists of a list of malicious nodes. This list is swapped by a list of trustworthy nodes. The time period of this swapping operation should be random. Collaborative Reputation (Core) trust scheme is discussed in (Dalal, 2012). This scheme was invented in 2002 by Michirardi. This scheme is successfully able to draw difference between the selfish node and malicious node. Some nodes are not cooperative with other nodes in MANET because these non cooperative are saving battery life for its own communication. They do not bother for other nodes. But these nodes do not harm other nodes. These nodes are termed as "selfish" nodes. But the behavior of malicious nodes is abnormal. They act suspiciously and surely can harm other nodes. Three different types of reputation were proposed by CORE scheme. The first reputation is Subjective Reputation. According to this reputation, priority should be given to mobile node's past observation instead of current observation in case of evaluating reputation value. If malicious node is tracked, then node's subjective reputation value should be replaced by implementing watchdog mechanism. The second reputation is Indirect Reputation. According to this reputation, there is provision of giving reputation by one node to other node and in this way, the reputation value is calculated. There is also provision of updating of reputation value with the help of reply message. This reply message consists of a list of nodes with normal behavior in every function context. If any node is tracked with negative reputation value, then all requests made by this node for performing any operation are totally rejected. So it may be assumed that this node is treated as service provider, not as the requester. For a long period of time, if it has been noticed that this node will be able to provide correct services to all other nodes in MANET, this node can regain its reputation value. Regaining reputation value is achieved when current reputation value exceeds threshold reputation value. At this time, it may be concluded that this node will be able to declare itself as service provider and also as service requester. The third reputation is functional reputation. According to this reputation, the two previous reputations, subjective reputation and indirect reputation, are combined. Functional reputation value is calculated by the weight combine formula. In Dalal (2012), another trust scheme is discussed. This trust scheme was invented in 2003 by Bansal (2003). It is known as Observation Based Cooperation Enforcement in Ad-hoc network or OCEAN. There are five components available in OCEAN. The first component is Neighbor Watch which will watch the behavior of neighboring node. The second component is Route Ranker which maintains the route rank list for each neighboring node. The third component is Rank based Routing. This component extracts those types' routes in excellent manner which consists of malicious nodes. The fourth component is Malicious Traffic Rejection. This component successfully removes the suspicious traffics. These suspicious traffics are considered as misleading by this component. The fifth or last component is Second-chance Mechanism. According to this mechanism, malicious nodes are removed from faulty lists if it has been found that these malicious nodes are totally inactive for a long duration. Instead of this, constant value is assigned to the node. In 2004, one important trust scheme, secure and Objective Reputation-based Incentive or SORI scheme was discussed in 2012 in Dalal . This scheme was invented by in the year of 2004 in He (2004). SORI scheme accepts concept of reputation rating. This reputation rating is totally based on packet forwarding ratio of a node. There are three components exist in this scheme.

1. The first component is Neighbors Monitoring. This component is applied to collect information of neighboring node. This information is based about the behavior of packet forwarding.
2. The second component is Reputation Propagation. This component is responsible to provide information about sharing of other node with its neighbor.
3. The third or last component is Punishment. This component includes the process which is about removing the packet from the network. But this component has one disadvantage. It is unable to differentiate between selfish node and malicious node.

Another trust scheme was discussed in Dalal (2012). This scheme is known as Locally Aware Reputation System or LARS level trust model was proposed by Liu (2004) in 2006. This trust model is responsible to provide reputation value to its entire one hop neighboring mode. The change of reputation value is possible with the help of direct observation of neighboring node. The evaluator node or EN to its neighboring node is responsible to generate the Warning message, if evaluator node notices that the reputation value of any node is less than the threshold trustworthy value.

Characteristics of Trust

The essential features of Trust in MANET is given below (Liu, 2004):

1. For verifying trust towards an entity, a decision technique has to be fully spread because there is no supposition of being a trusted third party.
2. Confirmation of trust is customized in excellent manner without too much communication load and computation.
3. It is not possible for a decision support system in MANET to believe that node(s) are cooperative. In selfishness and resource-restricted environments, the node(s) is likely to be widespread rather than collaboration (Chen, (2011, Oct) A Survey on Trust Management for Mobile Ad-Hoc Networks, 2011, Oct).
4. There is no concept of static trust. Trust should be dynamic.
5. There is existence of subjective trust.
6. It is not possible for trust to be transitive. For example, A trusts B as well as B trusts C, that does not imply C trusts A.
7. It is possible to consider that trust is asymmetric but there is no concept of reciprocal trust.
8. It is fact that trust is context-dependent. For example, A trusts B in one aspect, but that does mean A trusts B in other aspect.

In MANETs, high computational power is required for the node(s) participating in routing. In this way it can be concluded that a node equipped with high battery power is considered as trusted, but a node equipped with low battery power is considered as distrusted. But a distrusted node cannot be treated as malicious because though it is distrusted, it cannot harm other nodes. So this node can be treated as honest node.

More Related Work for Trust Evaluation

In Jacquet (2014), nodes are created and deployed in the wireless sensor network. These nodes are termed as CH or Cluster Head, CM or Cluster Mode and BS or Base Station. Each CH is equipped with several CMs. A lightweight trust scheme is calculated between CMs or between CHs. Within each cluster, CH calculates indirect trust for its CM. So, CM does not need to maintain feedback from other CMs which reduces the communication overhead. According to dependability-enhanced trust evaluating approach, CHs accept the responsibility of large amount of data forwarding and communication tasks which lessen network consumption by preventing improper (malicious, selfish and faulty) CHs. In Das (2011), the routing services are severely affected by wormhole attack and weakened by the Byzantine attack. To overcome these attacks, the proposed trust based approach calculates the Observed Trust Value or OTV and Advertised Trust Value or ATV. The Observed Trust Value identifies to the root trust calculated by node itself on the basis of ROUTE_ACKNOWLEDGEMENT or R_ACK information. A node just below of current node advertises the Advertised Trust Value. Route Selection Value or RSV is evaluated with the Observed Trust Value and the Advertised Trust Value. Route Selection Value is treated as a parameter in choosing one of the multiple paths leading towards destination. Whatever the path chosen by Route Selection Value is the trusted and shortest path. In Kaur (2013) (Mittal, 2013), according to Seniority Based or SB trust model, trust management and maintenance are distributed among both space(k) and time(T) domains. Thus Seniority Based model describes a seniors-securing scheme to node authentication in Manet. In other words, the time varying feature of a trust relationship, while k indicates the number of senior nodes required to work as 'Certificate Authority' or CA. In the network, there are so many groups. Again each group includes several nodes. The leader of the group treats as a 'Certificate Authority' or CA, which issues group membership certificates. CAs certifies that the public key in the certificate is provided to a group member. An entity is trusted if any k trusted available senior entities claim so within a certain time period say, T. Once a node is trusted by its groups, it is universally accepted as a trusted node by the group members. Otherwise, if the seniors distrust a node, this node is treated as untrustworthy in the whole network. In Velloso (2010), a human based trust model is proposed into which a trust relationship is built. This relationship relates two nodes in an ad hoc network. The trust is evaluated absolutely on the basis of previously individual experiences and on the recommendation of others. That is why, a specific protocol known as Recommendation Exchange protocol (REP) is presented which allows nodes to swap recommendations about their neighbors. This method does not require to transmit the information about nodes over the entire network. Instead of this, the information about the current nodes and their neighbors are transmitted as well as swapped through that network which is within the radio range.

ELECTION ALGORITHM IN GENERAL

Election algorithms (Silberschatz, 2009) assume that a specific priority number is associated with each active process in the system. For ease of notation, the priority number of process p_x is x. The coordinator is always the process with the highest priority number. Hence, at the time of failure of a coordinator, the algorithm must elect that active process with highest priority number. This highest priority number must be sent to each active process in the system. Besides this, the algorithm must provide a technique for a recovered process to identify current coordinator.

The Bully Algorithm

Suppose (Bhoir, 2013) that process p_x sends a request that is not answered by the coordinator within a time interval t. In this case, the failure of coordinator is assumed and p_x tries to elect itself as the new coordinator. This operation is completed through the following algorithm.

Process p_x sends a election message to every process equipped with a higher priority number. Process p_x then waits for a time interval t for an answer from any one of the processes.

If no response is received within time t, p_x assumes that all processes with numbers higher than x have failed and elect itself as new coordinator. Process p_x restarts a new copy of the coordinator and sends a message to inform all active processes with priority number less than x that p_x is the new coordinator.

However, if an answer is received, p_x begins a time interval t′, waiting to receive a message informing it that a process with a larger priority number has been elected. (That means, some process, other than p_x, is electing itself coordinator and should report the results within time interval t′) If no message is received within time interval t′, then the process within larger number is assumed to be failed and process p_x should restart the algorithm.

If p_x is not the coordinator, then at any time during execution, p_x may receive one of the following two messages from process p_y:

- P_y is the new coordinator (y>x). Process p_x, in turn, records the information.
- P_y has started election (y<x). Process p_x sends a response to p_y and starts it own election algorithm, provided that p_x has not initiated such an election.

The process that completes its algorithm has the largest number and is elected as coordinator. It has sent its number to all active processes with less numbers. After recovering a failed process, it immediately starts the same algorithm. If there are no active processes with larger numbers, the recovered process forces all processes with less numbers to let it become the coordinator process, even if there is a currently active coordinator with a less number. For this reason, the algorithm is treated as bully algorithm.

The bully algorithm can be described in another elaborated way (Figures 1-5).

It can be assumed that all processes are very much aware about each other. It should also be very much aware that all process numbers should be unique and they have no information about each other's state.

Suppose process A notices no coordinator. At that time election message should be sent by this process to all higher numbered processes. At this time, two alternative results are expected. If there are no responses from other higher numbered processes, process A announces itself as coordinator. But if there is any response, process A retreats back and agrees that process as coordinator from which response is coming.

Suppose process B receives election message. At that time, an OK message is sent by process B to the sender by announcing that it will be ready to take over as a coordinator and at the same time process B sends a new election message to all higher numbered processes.

The above incident is continued until and unless one process is left standing by announcing that this process is actual winner for taking charge as coordinator.

Suppose process C comes back on line by sending a new election message to all higher numbered processes. Again this incident is continued until and unless a single process left standing by announcing itself as winner and it will be ready to take the charge as coordinator. As a result of this, the existing coordinator is surrendered.

Figure 1. Sending election message by source 'c'   *Figure 2. Previous coordinator has crashed*

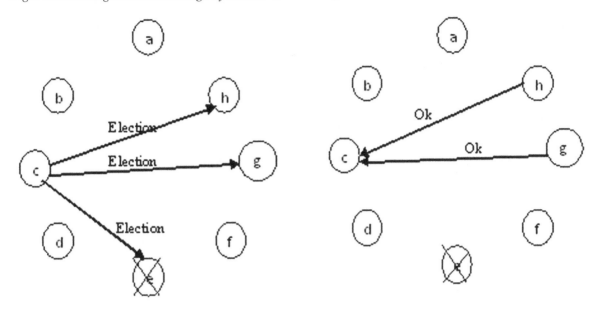

Figure 3. New election message is started   *Figure 4. Continuation of process in Figure 1c*

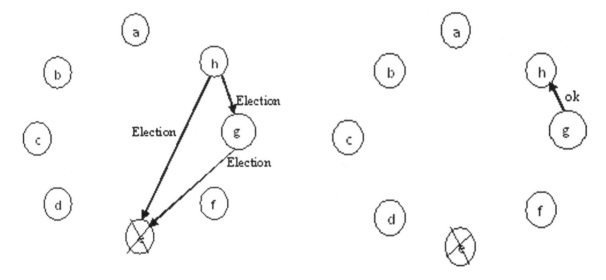

Hence this algorithm is termed as "bully".

The Ring Algorithm

According to this algorithm (showing in Figure 6), all processes are arranged as ring. Suppose process D notices no coordinator. At that time, an election message is sent by process D to its successor. The message body should contain the process number of process D. If successor is down for any reason, election message is just transferred to next successor. Suppose process E receives an election message,

Figure 5. Node 'g' as coordinator

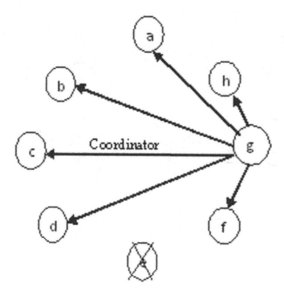

it just adds its own process number into the message body. Suppose process D receives an election message with its own process number into the message body. At that time, it changes this election message to the coordinator message by preserving body of the message. If multiple messages are circulated in this way, they will contain same list of processes. If process comes back on line, a new election message should be called.

Wireless Environment

In this environment (showing in Figures 7-12), network is unreliable and there is frequent movement of processes. Network topology is constantly changing. According to this algorithm, an election message is sent by any starting node to its neighbors. When this election message is received by any node for the

Figure 6. Ring algorithm

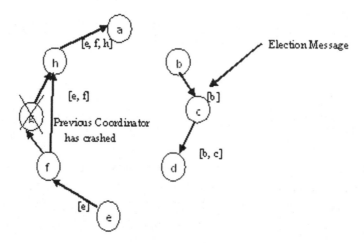

first time, it forwards this message to its neighbors and designates the sender as its parent. It waits for the responses which carry several resource information from its neighbors. When the election message is received by any node for the second time, it just OKs the message.

Kordafshari Protocol

Modified Bully protocol (Kordafshari, 2005) is able to eliminate or drop-off the message complexity of Bully protocol to O(n). When a node N_i detects that the coordinator has been crashed, it is able to initiate an election algorithm by sending election message to all higher ID nodes. Each node, that receives election messages, sends OK message with its valid ID to node N_i. If no node sends OK message to

Figure 7. Election network in wireless environment with node 5 as source

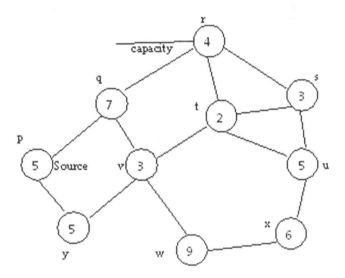

Figure 8. The build tree phase

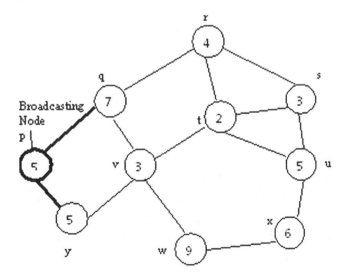

Figure 9. The build tree phase

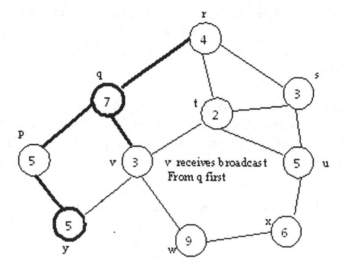

Figure 10. The build tree phase

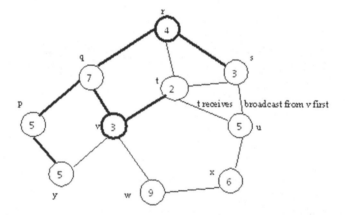

responses to node *N*i, it will be able to broadcast coordinator message to all nodes, declaring itself as a coordinator. On the other hand, if some node *N*j sends OK message to node *N*i, then node *N*i will select the node with the highest ID *N*k as coordinator and then sends to it the GRANT message. Reception of GRANT message at highest ID node *N*k, is able to initiate broadcast of coordinator message to all other nodes and informs itself as a coordinator.

Dehghan Protocol

In the protocol (Parvar, 2007), when node *N*i detects crash of leader, it is able to send an election message to all the nodes with higher ID. Each node sends its ID, in response of election message, to node *N*i. If no node is available to send its ID to node *N*i, it will broadcast coordinator message to all the nodes with piggybacking with its ID. If some node response to node *N*i, it will select the node with the highest ID as coordinator and be able to broadcast the coordinator message to all the nodes. In this manner, all nodes

Figure 11. The build tree phase

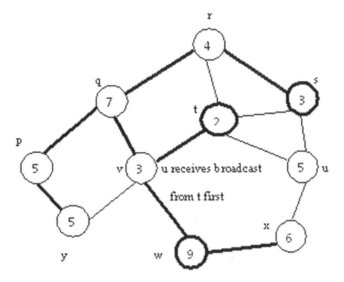

Figure 12. Reporting of best node to source

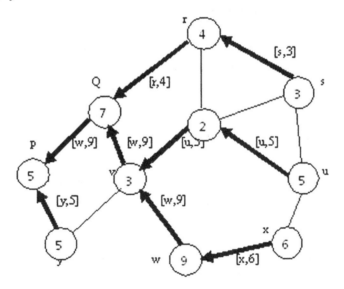

know the new leader. Now, the response message by ID with highest number may be lost destined to node N_i. In such scenario, node N_i select the second highest ID node N_j as leader number and be able to broadcast the coordinator message to all the nodes, now the new leader sends election message to nodes with greater ID to sure that there is no node with greater ID. If a message is received from nodes with greater ID, it causes the greatest one as leader. Otherwise, it remains the leader again.

Singh Protocol

Singh protocol (Kurose, 1994) is totally different from all other protocol. In the protocol, leader is elected on the basis of different criteria that mean some preference, not on the basis of node's ID. Authors suggested the need of this extrema finding approach as:

1. When a leader is elected on the basis of an ID number, it is chosen without considering regard to the preferences of the individual nodes or equivalency and performance level;
2. All existing algorithms entirely dependent on the robustness and reliability of node.

Distributed Council Election Protocol

The article, in Raz (2004) is able to focus on electing a small number of representatives (council) out of a (possible large) group of anonymous or unknown candidates. The protocol elects a group of any size in a range which is predefined. In addition, tradeoff between expected number of rounds for election and the expected number of unicast messages needed is shown. However, paper is based towards random protocols.

Election in Quasi-Static Mesh Networks

In article Abrougui (2007), leader election algorithm for wireless quasi-static mesh network is served, where some nodes' designation is as mesh routers are static and other nodes designated as mesh clients are mobile. It is relied on the construction of a spanning tree that includes all the static wireless mesh routers. Furthermore, impressive message complexity analysis and time complexity is also given.

Raychoudhury Protocol

The protocol, in Raychoudhury (2008), invents the coordinator out of the top K special nodes called 'valued' nodes. This protocol is able to execute in three phases *election*, *diffusion computation* and *coordinator*. Initially, all nodes are *WHITE*. In election phase, every node selects most valued node as *RED* among its one hop neighbors. After that, RED nodes initiate diffusion computation and also include WHITE nodes in the tree. After termination of this phase, all RED nodes are merged and eventually the highest valued RED node will be able to get the complete weight information about the network and it is able to send coordinator message to top K RED valued node, which again propagate to all WHITE nodes.

More Related Work for Leader Election Algorithm

According to Bhoir (2013) and Sinha (2014), this paper presents a comparative analysis of various leader election algorithms and a new leader election algorithm in analytical way which considers parameters such as node position, time complexity, message complexity, battery life and security. According to Gawali (2012), this paper provides the information about the various leader election technique which select the leader to solve different problems and as well as the survey information about modified election algorithm. Designating a single node as an organizer in distributed systems is a very big challenging issue that calls for effective election algorithm (Parvar, 2010). In distributed systems, nodes are communicated with each other using shared memory or via message passing. The key requirement for nodes to execute any distributed task successfully is coordination. In a pure distributed system, there are no existences any central controlling node that arbitrates decisions and thus, every node has to communicate with the remaining of the nodes in the network to make an actual decision. Many times during the decision process, not all nodes are able to make the same decision, thus the communication between nodes time-consuming and decision-making process. Coordination among nodes becomes tough task when consistency is required among all nodes. Centralized controlling nodes can be successfully chosen from the group of available nodes to reduce the complexity of decision making (Kim). But in all above three cases the leader election method is accomplished without evaluating node trust. But in Gopal (2012), leader election method is accomplished by considering the node trust, according to this method, five modes are implemented. They are sensing mode, voting mode, gossip mode, selection mode and regulation mode. According to sensing mode, trust values of each node are stored in a specific place, called as trust table. Trust is defined as the ratio between two entities. First entity is called as 'No. of messages transmitted' and the second entity is called as 'No. of messages received'. Finally, the trust table consists as trust value of current node as well as neighbor node and also the distance between the current node and its corresponding neighbor nodes. According to voting mode, the current node selects the top three neighbor nodes with respect of their trust values along with id. The trust values are selected as increasing order. According to gossip mode, the neighbor nodes compare their own trust values with the trust values of current node. The higher trust values are enjoying the advantage. According to selection mode, the node with highest trust value is broadcasting its set that consists of trust value. If any nodes from other networks have trust value which is equal or higher than current trust value, they can challenge the current node for selection of leader. If there are no nodes from other networks for challenging current node, the current node is selected as leader. Now a set is formed which consists of a leader node and various sub leader nodes. According to regulation mode, if a leader node is failed due to any specific reason such as vulnerable presence of any malicious nodes, at that one of the sub node from the set is activated for claiming itself as leader. Obviously this node must enjoy the next highest trust value to the trust value of the failed leader node. According to Secure Extrema Finding Algorithm or SEFA protocol (Shantanu 2011; Vasudevan, 2003), a single, Common Evaluation function is shared by all candidate nodes. It returns the same value at any candidate node when applied to any node. This function selects leader at first at one hop and then at two hop. In this way this function proceeds and selects leader at hop by hop. Finally, it selects the global leader. Certain factor plays a crucial role regarding the selection of global leader. These factors should be candidate node's id or identifier, computational power or certified level of trust within the system, battery life etc. According to Secure Preference-Based Leader Election Algorithm or SPLEA protocol (Shantanu, 2011; Vasudevan, 2003), different preferences of candidate nodes' are handled for electing a leader. This preference may be battery life or topological distance between the different nodes. So each candidate node should have a different value for electing a leader. According to Asynchronous Extrema Finding Algorithm or AEFA protocol (Shantanu, 2011), changing of topology is allowed during the process of leader election, though this protocol does not provide any security. In this protocol, each node has a specific value called as node weight. This node weight plays a important factor for accomplishing leader election process. In this way, the best node is selected as leader with the help of Asynchronous Extrema Finding Algorithm or AEFA protocol. According to Lee protocol (Shantanu, 2011; Lee, 2007), a list of leaders at each node is imposed for reducing the leader election phases. This protocol is totally based on Asynchronous Extrema Finding Algorithm or AEFA protocol. But this protocol has limited fault tolerance capability because this protocol is not capable to accomplish any major modification of Asynchronous Extrema Finding Algorithm. But one exception is there. It is the introduction of five leaders at each node. This process is accomplished with the help of decreasing order of node weight value. Thus the node with highest node weight value is elected as active leader. If this node is crashed in any reason, the node with second highest node value is elected as active leader and this process is continued. According to Boukerche protocol (Shantanu, 2011; Abrougui, 2006), a leader election procedure is presented which is performed in excellent manner under frequent network changes and node mobility. This protocol is successful for electing a leader in a connected cluster within a short period of time with the help of few messages un-like Asynchronous Extrema Finding Algorithm protocol. Also this protocol suffers from message complexity. According to Zhang protocol (Shantanu, 2011; Zhang, 2009), the fault tolerance version of leader election protocol is provided by imposing a hierarchy on the nodes with the help of Secure Extrema Finding Algorithm or SEFA protocol. To implement this process, a concept known as assistant leader is selected. According to this concept, once the leader is crashed, the assistant will take entire responsibility of leader as early as possible. According to this protocol, two level hierarchies of nodes are imposed. These two level hierarchies are known as high level of nodes and low level of nodes. These two levels are required to implement Secure Extrema Finding Algorithm or SEFA protocol. Like Lee protocol, this protocol also suffers from large message complexity. MANETs face challenge from this protocol when high level nodes use clock synchronization. Due to clock synchronization, high level nodes have less mobility. Only low level nodes have movement during leader election process. This protocol has another drawback. At the time of implementing Secure Extrema Finding Algorithm or SEFA protocol, this protocol does not provide any solution when frequent failure is happened at the time of leader election process. According to Leader Election Algorithm in Wireless Environments using Fibonacci Heap Structure (Sinha, 2014; Jain, 2012), it is assumed that each node of the distributed system consists of only one process. These remaining M-1 nodes are treated as candidate nodes for electing the leader. After certain amount of time, a node from remaining M-1 nodes is elected as new leader. In this way, it has been concluded that only one leader should be present at last. Here Fibonacci heap (Fredman, 1987) concept is implemented for electing the leader. Here communication model is nothing but a point to point communication network. This network is represented as undirected graph where the processes are represented by nodes or vertices and the direct communication link between two vertices is represented by an edge. Processes communicate with the help of message passing technique through these edges. Environment including presence of fault is suitable for implementing this algorithm. This algorithm finds minimum key of heap for electing the leader. According to Leader Election Algorithm based on Spanning Tree for Mobile Ad Hoc Networks (Sinha, 2014; Ramasubramarian, 2002), when absence of leader is detected by any node, an ELECTION message is sent by the detector node. This message is spread along the entire neighbor of the detector node like a spanning tree. After the arrival of message, the other nodes forward it towards their children and at the same time, the node, from which the message is sent to the other nodes, is declared as leader. This declaration should be performed by other nodes. Now all the other nodes send the ACKNOWLEDGEMENT message to the sender. After receiving ACKNOWLEDGEMENT message, sender conveys the information, which confirms that the sender is the new leader, through the entire network. But if network size is too large, the time, to convey the information, should be high. According to Asynchronous Leader Election Algorithm on Ad hoc Hierarchy Networks (Sinha, 2014; Zhang, 2009), a hierarchy is established by network within the election group. When a leader is lost and if this phenomenon is detected by a node or several nodes, they have to wait for a specified time interval, after this specified time interval, an ELECTION message is sent by the node. After receiving the message, the other node forwards this message towards it unvisited neighbors. These unvisited neighbors should be equipped with highest priority. The nodes are marked which receive the ELECTION message. The node resends the ELECTION message when the node has no neighbor. The next duty of this algorithm is to declare the new leader. Regarding this matter, the last unvisited node transfers the leader message with the identity of the leader to all the other nodes. According to Leader Election Algorithm based on Priority Candidates on Ad Hoc Networks (Sinha, 2014; Lee, 2007), network is partitioned and merged during the leader election process. By using the candidate list, such new concept to the original algorithms (Molina, 1982; Lamport, 1978.) is added. Candidate has the Unique Identifiers of the current leader and as well as four other candidates. When absence of leader is confirmed by the nodes, a number of ELECTION messages are initiated by the nodes. For knowing the highest Unique Identifier, these messages are spread throughout the spanning tree. Now one of the messages is able to reach at leaf nodes of the spanning tree, the leaf nodes send acknowledgement messages containing candidate lists to their parent nodes. During this time, the updating of the candidate list has occurred and this updated candidate list is sent back to the initiator. Updating is done for obtaining highest known Unique Identifier of the nodes. At last, that initiator is elected as new leader which is equipped with candidate lists and highest Unique Identifier. According to Cooperative Leader Election Algorithm based on Master/Slave Mobile Ad Hoc Network (R.Ali, 2009), the responsibility of the master is to assign and coordinate tasks and roles which include scheduling mutual exclusive access. The master's order is strictly followed by the slave. This algorithm is proposed on (Lann., 1977.). The algorithm has one specific assumption. It is that one unique leader is selected by MANET by utilizing the algorithm iteratively. The system is in synchronous mode and the channels are reliable. All nodes have Unique Identifiers. According to this election algorithm, each node maintains a record with two values. One is the identifier of the current leader and another is the current leader's master value. For wishing to be new leader, nodes replace their record with one of its slaves. If the master node finds a new slave node which has higher value than its master, the master node replaces its own value with value of new slave node and this information is broadcasted by the master node along the entire network with the value of the slave node. In other ways, it can be concluded that when a new node is joined at the network, its value is compared with the value of the current leader. If the value is lower than the value of the current leader, new node accepts the current leader. But if the value of the new node is higher than the value of the current leader, the new node replaces current leader and declares itself as the new leader.

PROPOSED SYSTEM WITH PSEUDO CODE

Proposed System

According to our proposed system, the following steps are applied:

1. Input the no. of nodes in a network.
2. Input positive no. of messages sent and as well as positive no. of acknowledgements received for each node. If no. of acknowledgements received is greater than no. of messages sent, we should rectify the error.

3. Calculate Node Trust Probability for each node by dividing the no. of acknowledgements received by the no. of messages sent. If Node Trust Probability is equal to or more than 0.50 or 50%, the particular node is trusted, otherwise, the node is untrustworthy. Now we should implement necessary steps so that the status of node is converted form 'Untrustworthy' to 'Trusted'.
4. Determine the node weight for each node within range between 1 and 20.
5. Calculate node priority for each node by multiplying node weight and Node Trust Probability. In this case it should be remembered that higher the node priority value, higher the priority. In case of tie of priority, last node is considered.
6. Now the activeness of each node is calculated. '1' indicates that node is active and '0' indicates that node is inactive.
7. Now select any node as leader. This leader sends the message to other nodes for electing new leader.
8. If no signal is received within a specific time (say t), this current node is remained as leader.
9. Otherwise, the active node with highest priority among the other nodes is elected as new leader.
10. Now the systems are asked to continue the above operation or not.
11. If yes, perform above operations to elect new leader. Otherwise, the systems are terminated.

Pseudo Code

```
1.        Start
2.         Read no., priority, active, next, proc under structure 'process'
3.         Main () function
        Read i, no_process, no_acknowledgement_received, no_message_sent,
node_priority, node_trust_probability, node_weight.
        Input no_process
        For i=0 to i<no_process do
        Under jay and jay3, input input no_message_sent for process(i+1)
        Input no_acknowledgement_received for process(i+1)
        If no_message_sent>=no_acknowledgement_received and no_message_sent>0
and no_acknowledgement_received>0    then
        node_trust_probability= no_acknowledgement_received / no_message_sent
        Write node_trust_probability for process(i+1)
        If node_trust_probability<0.50 then
        Write "Node is untrustworthy. Immediately rectify the error".
        Goto jay3
        endif
        Under jay4, input node_weight for process(i+1)
        If node_weight<1 or node_weight>20 then
        Write "Wrong input of Node Weight. Please try again."
        Goto jay4
        endif
         node_priority=node_weight * node_trust_probability
        Write node_priority for process(i+1)
        else
        Write "Not possible"
```

```
           Goto jay
           endif
           endfor
           Call bully (no_process, node_priority)
           End main () function
4.           bully (no_process, node_priority)
           Read head, p1, p2, i, a, pid, max, ch
           Head = p1 = p2 = NULL
           For i=0 to i<no_process do
           Under jay1, input activeness for process(i+1) as a
           If a<0 or a>1 then
           Goto jay1
           endif
           If head = NULL
           Head = (proc*) malloc(sizeof(proc))
           If head = NULL, then
           Write "Memory Cannot be allocated"
           Exit
           endif
           head ->no= i+1
           head ->priority= node_priority
           head ->active= a
           head ->next= head
           p1= head
           else
           p2 = (proc*)malloc(sizeof(proc))
           If p2= NULL, then
           Write "Memory Cannot be allocated"
           Exit
           endif
           p2 ->no= i+1
           p2 ->priority= node_priority
           p2 ->active= a
           p2 ->next= head
           p1= p2
           endif
           endfor
           Input process id or pid that invokes election algorithm
           Write "Election message is sent to process"
           while p2->next! =head do
           If p2->no>pid then
           Write process id as p2->no
           endif
           p2= p2->next
```

```
endwhile
Write process id as p2->no
p2= head
max= 0
while true do
if p2->priority>max and p2->active=1 then
max=p2->no
p2= p2->next
if p2= head then
break
endif
endif
endwhile
Write max
While true do
Input ch
If ch= 'n' or ch= 'N' then
break
else
p2= head
endif
while true do
Under jay2, input the activeness for process p2 as p2->active
If p2->active<0 or p2->active>1 then
goto jay2
endif
p2= p2->next
if p2=head then
break
endif
endwhile
Input process id or pid that invokes election algorithm
Write "Election message is sent to process"
while p2->next! =head do
If p2->no>pid then
Write process id as p2->no
endif
p2= p2->next
endwhile
Write process id as p2->no
p2= head
max= 0
while true do
if p2->no>max and p2->active=1 then
```

```
        max=p2->no
        p2= p2->next
        if p2= head then
        break
        endif
        endif
        endwhile
        Write max
        Endwhile
5       End bully (no_process, node_priority)
6       End
```

STRENGTH OF OUR ALGORITHM

- In the first time, leader is elected after evaluating the trust of the node.
- In case of untrustworthy node, it is converted into trusted node by denying the values for which the node becomes untrustworthy.

CONCLUSION

In this proposed system, the leader election is implemented after trust evaluation in the shadow of bully algorithm. In future, it will be targeted that the leader election is implemented after trust evaluation in the shadow of another advanced algorithm for minimizing overhead.

REFERENCES

Shantanu. (2011). *Highly Available Coordinators for Mobile Ad hoc Networks* (M.Tech. Dissertation). Dept. of CSE, NIT Kurukshetra.

Davis & McGuffin. (1995). *Wireless Local Area Networks*. McGraw-Hill.

Forouzan & Fegan. (2007). *Data Communications and Networking* (4th ed.). McGraw-Hill.

Goodchild, M., Johnston, D., Maguire, D., & Noronha, V. (2003). Distributed and Mobile Computing. In A Research Agenda for Geographic Information Science. Boca Raton, FL: CRC Press.

Shrivastava, Shanmogavel, Mistry, Chander, Patlolla, & Yadlapalli. (n.d.). *Overview of Routing Protocols in MANET's and Enhancements in Reactive Protocols*. Department of Computer Science, Lamar University.

Gawali, D. P. (2012). Leader Election Problem in Distributed Algorithm. *International Journal of Computer Science and Technology, 3*(1), 714–718.

Loutfi, Valerie, & Bruno. (2003). *Securing mobile adhoc networks*. MP71 Project.

Awerbuch, Curtmola, Holmer, Nita-Rotaru, & Rubens. (2000). Mitigating Byzantine Attacks in Ad Hoc Wireless Networks. *ACM MobiCom.*

Marti, , Giuli, Lai, & Baker. (2000). Mitigating Routing Misbehavior in Mobile Ad Hoc Networks. *Proceedings of the 6th annual international conference on Mobile computing and networking.*

Cho & Chen. (2011, Oct.). A Survey on Trust Management for Mobile Ad-Hoc Networks. *IEEE Communications Surveys & Tutorials, 13*(4).

Joa-Ng. (1999). A Peer-to-Peer Zone-Based Two-Level Link State Routing for Mobile Ad Hoc Networks. *IEEE Journal on Selected Areas in Communications, 17*(8).

Misra, P. (1999). *Routing Protocols for ad hoc mobile wireless Networks.* Retrieved from http://www.cse.ohio-state.edu /~jain/cis788-99/ftp/adhoc_routing/#TDRP

Altman & Jimenez. (2002). *NS for Beginners.* Retrieved from http://www-sop.inria.fr/maestro/personnel/Eitan.Altman/ COURS-NS/n3.pdf

Silberschatz, A., Galvin, P. B., & Gagne, G. (2009). Operating System Concepts. Wiley India.

Gopal, V. D., Subramaniam, S. M., & Jawahar, D. S. (2012). Gossip Originated Trusted Leader Selection with Reinforcement in Wireless Mesh Network. *2012 International Conference on Information and Network Technology* (ICINT 2012).

Dalal, Khari, & Singh. (2012). Different Ways to Achieve Trust in MANET. *International Journal on AdHoc Networking Systems, 2*(2).

Capra, L. (2004). Toward a Human Trust Model for Mobile Ad-hoc Network. *Proc. 2nd UK-UbiNet Workshop.* Cambridge University.

Josang and S. LoPresti. (2004). *Analyzing the Relationship between Risk and Trust. In Proc.2nd Int'1 Conf. Trust Management (I Trust' 04),* (pp. 135–145). Springer-Verlag.

Theodorakopoulos, G., & Baras, J. S. (2006, February). On Trust Models and Trust Evaluation Metrics for Ad-hoc Networks. *IEEE Journal on Selected Areas in Communications, 24*(2), 318–328. doi:10.1109/JSAC.2005.861390

Boukerche & Ren. (2008). A Security Management Scheme using a novel Computational Reputation Model for Wireless and Mobile Ad hoc Networks. In *Proc.Int'l Workshop on Modeling Analysis and Simulation of wireless and Mobile System.*

Yu, Shen, Miao, Leung, & Niyato. (2010). A Survey of Trust and Reputation Management System in Wireless Communications. *Proc. of the IEEE.*

Marti, S., Giuli, T. J., Lai, K., & Baker, M. (2000). Mitigating Routing Misbehavior in Mobile Ad-hoc Networks. In *ACM MobiCom Conference.*

Buchegger, S., & Le Boudec, J.-Y. (2002). Performance analysis of the confident protocol. In *MobiHoc '02, IEEE/ACM Symposium on Mobile Ad-hoc Networking and Computing.*

Michirardi, P., & Molva, R. (2002). Core: A collaborative reputation mechanism to encode node cooperation in mobile ad-hoc networks. In *CMS'02 Communication and Multimedia Security Conference.*

Bansal, S., & Baker, M. (2003). *Observation-based Cooperation Enforcement in Ad-hoc Networks.* arxiv:cs/0307012v2

He, Q., Wu, D., & Khosla, P. (2004). SORI: A Secure and Objective Reputation- based Incentive Schemes for Ad-hoc Networks. In *WCNC'04 IEEE Wireless Communications and Networking Conference.*

Liu, Z., Joy, A. W., & Thompson, R. A. (2004, May). A Dynamic Trust Model for Mobile Ad Hoc Networks. *Proceeding of 10th IEEE International Workshop on Future Trends of Distributed Computing Systems.*

Cho & Chen. (2011, Oct.). A Survey on Trust Management for Mobile Ad-Hoc Networks. *IEEE Communications Surveys & Tutorials, 13*(4).

Jacquet, S., & Varghese, M. (2014). Role Based and Energy Efficient Trust System for Clustered Wsn. *IOSR Journal of Computer Engineering, 16*(2), 44–48.

Das, A., Basu, S. S., & Chaudhuri, A. (2011). A Novel Security Scheme for Wireless Adhoc Network. *Wireless Communication, Vehicular Technology, Information Theory and Aerospace & Electronics Systems Technology (Wireless VITAE),20112nd International Conference on.*

Das, A., Rahman, A., Basu, S. S., & Chaudhuri, A. (2011). Energy Aware Topology Security Scheme for Mobile Ad Hoc Network. *Proceedings of the2011International Conference on Communication, Computing & Security.* doi:10.1145/1947940.1947965

Kaur, J. (2013). SBPGP Security based Model in Large Scale Manets. *International Journal of Wireless Networks and Communications, 5*(1), 1–10.

Mittal, N. (2013, June). Performance Evaluation of AODV and DSDV under Seniority based Pretty Good Privacy Model. *International Journal of Scientific and Engineering Research, 4*(6), 943–949.

Velloso, Laufer, Kunha, Duarte, & Pujjole. (2010). Trust Management in Mobile Ad Hoc Networks Using a Scalable Maturity-Based Model. *IEEE Transactions on Network and Service Management, 7*(3), 172-185.

Bhoir, S., & Vidhate, A. (2013, February). A Modified Leader Election Algorithm for Manet. *International Journal on Computer Science and Engineering, 5*(2), 78–86.

Kordafshari, M., Gholipour, M., Jahanshahi, M., & Haghighat, A. (2005, January). Two Novel Algorithms for Electing Coordinator in Distributed Systems based on Bully Algorithm. *WSEAS Transactions on Systems, 4*(1), 10–15.

Parvar, Bemana, & Dehghan. (2007). Determining a Central Controlling Processor with Fault Tolerant Method in Distributed System. In *Proceeding of IEEE-International Conference on Information Technology* (ITNG).

Singh, S., & Kurose, J. (1994). Electing Good Leaders. *Journal of Parallel and Distributed Computing, 21*(2), 184–201. doi:10.1006/jpdc.1994.1051

Raz, Shavitt, & Zhang. (2004). Distributed Council Election. *IEEE/ACM Transaction on Networking, 12*(3), 483-492.

Boukerche, A., & Abrougui, K. (2007). An Efficient Leader Election Protocol for Wireless Quasi-Static Mesh Networks: Proof of Correctness. In *Proceeding IEEE International Conference on Communication (ICC)*. doi:10.1109/ICC.2007.577

Raychoudhury, V., Cao, J., & Wu, W. (2008). Top K-leader Election in Wireless Ad Hoc Networks. In *Proceeding IEEE 17th International Conference on Computer Communications and Networks (ICCCN)*. doi:10.1109/ICCCN.2008.ECP.35

Sinha, S., & Yadav, N. (2014, January-February). Comparative Analysis and Enhancement of Leader Election Algorithms through Shared Memory in Mobile Ad-hoc Networks. *International Journal of Emerging Trends & Technology in Computer Science, 3*(1), 84–89.

Mohammad, R. E. P., Yazdani, N., Parvar, M. E., Dadlani, A., & Khonsari, A. (2010). Improved Algorithms for Leader Election in Distributed System. *Computer Engineering and Technology (ICCET),20102nd International Conference on*.

Kim. (n.d.). *A Leader Election Algorithm in a Distributed Computing System*. Department of Computer Science, Korea University-1.

Vasudevan, S., DeCleene, B., Immerman, N., Kurose, J., & Towsley, D. "Leader Election Algorithms for Wireless Ad Hoc Networks," In *Proceeding IEEE DARPA Information Survivability Conference and Exposition (DISCEX)*, pp. 261-272, 2003. doi:10.1109/DISCEX.2003.1194890

Lee, S., Muhammad, R., & Kim, C. (2007). A Leader Election Algorithm within Candidates on AdHoc Mobile Networks. In *Proceeding of the 3rd International Conference on Embedded Software and Systems* (ICESS), (LNCS) (vol. 4523, pp. 728-738). Berlin: Springer.

Boukerche, A., & Abrougui, K. (2006). An Efficient Leader Election Protocol for Mobile Networks. In *Proceeding ACM International Wireless Communications and Mobile Computing Conference (IWCMC)*. doi:10.1145/1143549.1143775

Zhang, G., Kuang, X., Chen, J., & Zhang, Y. (2009). Design and Implementation of a Leader Election Algorithm in Hierarchy Mobile Ad hoc Network. In *Proceeding IEEE 4th International Conference on Computer Science & Education* (ICCSE). doi:10.1109/ICCSE.2009.5228448

Sinha & Yadav. (2014). Comparative Analysis and Enhancement of Leader Election Algorithms through Shared Memory in Mobile Ad-hoc Networks. *International Journal of Emerging Trends & Technology in Computer Science, 3*(1), 84-89.

Jain & Sharma. (2012). Leader Election Algorithm in Wireless Environments Using Fibonacci Heap Structure. *Int. J. Computer Technology and Applications, 3*(3), 871-873.

Michael, L. (1987, July). Heaps and their uses in improved network optimization algorithms. *Journal of the Association for Computing Machinery, 34*(3), 596–615. doi:10.1145/28869.28874

Ramasubramarian, V. (2002). Providing a Birectional Abstraction for Unidirectional Ad Hoc Networks. *Proceedings - IEEE INFOCOM*.

Zhang, Chen, Zhang, & Liu. (2009). Research of Asynchronous Leader Election Algorithm on Hierarchy Ad Hoc Network. *WiCom '09.*

Lee, S., Rahman, M., & Kim, C. (2007). A Leader Election Algorithm Within Candidates on Ad Hoc Mobile Networks. In Embedded Software and Systems (LNCS), (Vol. 4523, pp. 728-738). Springer Berlin/Heidelberg. doi:10.1007/978-3-540-72685-2_67

Molina, G. H. (1982). Elections in a Distributed Computing System. *IEEE Transactions on Computers, 31*(1), 48–59. doi:10.1109/TC.1982.1675885

Lamport, L. (1978, July). Time, Clocks, and the Ordering of Events in a Distributed System. *Communications of the ACM, 21*(7), 558–565. doi:10.1145/359545.359563

Ali, Lor, Benouaer, & Rio. (2009). *Cooperative Leader Election Algorithm for Master/Slave Mobile Ad Hoc Network.* 2nd IFIP Wireless Days (WD), Paris, France.

Le Lann, G. (1977). Distributed systems: Towards a formal approach. *Information Processing 77, Proc. of the IFIP Congress.*

Chapter 12

Fuzzy-Topsis-Based Cluster Head Selection in Mobile Wireless Sensor Networks:
Cluster Head Selection in Mobile WSN

Bilal Muhammad Khan
National University of Sciences and Technology Islamabad, Pakistan

Rabia Bilal
Usman Institute of Technology, Pakistan

ABSTRACT

One of the critical and vital parameter of Wireless Sensor Networks (WSNs) is its lifetime. There are various methods to increase WSN lifetime, clustering technique is one of them. In clustering, selection of desired percentage of Cluster Head (CHs) is performed among the sensor nodes (SNs). Selected CHs are responsible to collect data from its member nodes, aggregates the data and finally send to the sink. In this chapter, Fuzzy-TOPSIS techniques based on multi criteria decision making to choose CH efficiently and effectively to maximize the WSN lifetime are presented. These five criteria includes; residual energy, node energy consumption rate, number of neighbor nodes, average distance between neighboring nodes and distance from sink. Threshold based intra-cluster and inter-cluster multi-hop communication mechanism is used to decrease energy consumption. Moreover impact of node density and different type mobility strategies are presented in order to investigate impact over WSN lifetime.

INTRODUCTION

Wireless Sensor Networks (WSNs) consists of large number of sensor nodes (SNs) randomly deployed to sense and monitor the physical and environmental. WSNs become a reality because of development and advancement in micro-electro-mechanical systems (MEMS), communication system and digital electronic circuitry; resulting in number of small chip fits SNs mechanic parts as well as wireless communication

DOI: 10.4018/978-1-5225-1785-6.ch012

components (Akyildiz, Weilian, Sankarasubramaniam, & Cayirci, 2002). The capabilities and function-alities of these tiny SNs have enable sensing, processing, data gathering and communication feasible.

WSNs have numerous applications, such as environmental monitoring, structural health monitoring, military and natural disasters (Li, Wang, & Guo, 2010). Cost-effectiveness in data sensing, gathering and communication is primary concern. Due to compactness of wireless SNs limited power and energy is available; therefore, the efficient and effective utilization of energy in WSNs is required (Lhadi, Rifai, & Alj, 2014).

Motivation

In recent years, WSNs is an emerging field in the broader area of wireless networking; with application ranges from surveillance to health care. Most of research is done on static cluster based protocols but they are less energy efficient compare fuzzy-TOPSIS based CH selection in mobile WSNs due to some of the following reasons.

1. Small lifetime and stability of WSNs is CH selection is based on few criteria i.e. one or two parameters.
2. Number of CHs varies from round to round.
3. High network energy consumption per round

Problem with power-efficient gathering in sensor information system (PEGASIS) protocol (Raghav-endra & Lindsey, 2002) is that distance between each node is not same therefore some nodes have to send their data from longer distance as than others, hence those nodes consume more energy.

In single hop communication, nodes away from BS die earlier compare to nodes closer to BS because former consume more energy to cover larger distance communication. Similarly, in simple multi hop communication nodes close to BS die earlier compare to nodes away from BS because former consume more energy to transport packets on the behalf of away nodes from BS. Which results in drastically reduces lifetime of WSNs.

To overcome above mentioned problems in this chapter several different techniques for CH selection is compared with MCDM approach. In order to select a potential node to act as a cluster head, MCDM approach uses five criteria; i.e. remaining energy of the node (residual energy), node energy consumption rate, number of neighbor nodes (node density), average distance between neighboring nodes and distance from the sink.. To overcome the problem of PEGASIS, the multi-hop communication model is considered mostly for both inter and intra-cluster communication based on threshold; it depends upon the distance from the CH or sink is greater than some threshold. In this way energy consumption of the sensor nodes can be minimized, which will result in improve network lifetime.

WIRELESS SENSOR NETWORKS

In recent years, a lot of research and development has been carried on Wireless Sensor Networks (WSNs) due to its enormous applications. As, there is no single set of requirement which clearly classifies all WSNs; therefore, many areas are need to be explored to support a lot of very different real world applications.

Figure 1. Architecture of WSNs
Source: Akyildiz, Weilian, Sankarasubramaniam, & Cayirci, 2002.

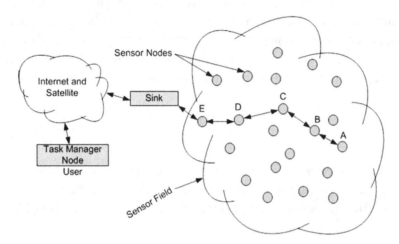

Architecture of WSNs

There are four main components in WSNs as shown in Figure 1. WSNs architecture includes SNs to perform sensing and processing tasks in order to accumulate data from the desired geographical area; an interconnection network basically a radio transceiver through which SNs transmit data to sink/gateway; a centrally data gathering mechanism known as sink or base station (BS); a set of computing resource at the user end for further storage, processing and analysis (Akyildiz, Weilian, Sankarasubramaniam, & Cayirci, 2002).

Protocol Stack of WSNs

WSNs protocol stack consists of five layers and six planes as shown in Figure 2. WSNs protocol stack manages power and routing awareness, integrates data with network protocols, communicates efficiently and effectively through the wireless medium, and promotes cooperative efforts of SNs. The brief detail of layers and planes of WSNs protocol stack is mentioned below.

Application Layer

The application layer supports different types of applications software depending upon sensing tasks. It also supports different management functionalities such as query processing and topology management.

Transport Layer

The transport layer provides congestion control, reliable data transport, multiplexing and de-multiplexing if WSNs application requires it.

Figure 2. WSNs protocol stack

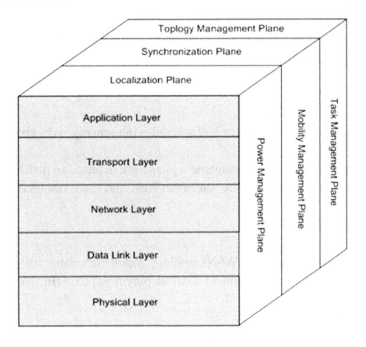

Network Layer

The network layer helps in routing the data supplied by the transport layer. It also provides internetworking with external networks.

Data Link Layer

The data link layer ensures reliable communication mechanism by point to point and point to multipoint connection, with help of error control techniques and manages collision mechanism during channel access.

Physical Layer

The physical layer helps frequency selection and generation, robust modulation, data encryption, transmission and receiving techniques.

Power Management Plane

The power management plane monitors power and manages how a SN uses its power by turn on-off receiver; avoid getting duplicated messages and not participating in routing by reserving remaining power for sensing.

Mobility Management Plane

The mobility management plane helps in the movements of SNs. Movement is control by keeping in view of speed, direction and data flow of SNs.

Task Management Plane

The task management plane helps to balance and schedules the sensing tasks given to a specific region of interest.

Therefore, power, mobility and task management planes are required so that, SNs can work together in power efficient way, route day in a mobile sensor network, and share resources between SNs.

Topology Management Plane

The topology management plane maintains WSNs topology. Maintenance and changes in topology divided in three phases, i.e. deployment, post deployment and re-deployment phase (Basha, Ravela, & Rus, 2008).

Synchronization Plane

The synchronization plane ensures synchronization of SNs. Each SN is WSNs is operates independently and relies on its own clock. Therefore, synchronization plane ensures that sensing time can be compared in a meaningful way.

Localization Plane

The localization plane determines the physical coordinates or spatial coordinates of SNs. Accurate location information of SNs is required for various tasks such as routing and object tracking etc.

Architecture of Sensor Node in WSNS

SNs are basic component for all WSNs. SN should meet the requirements that come from the specific application requirement; such as small, economical, power efficient, equipped with the right sensors, sufficient computation capability, adequate communicating facilities and memory resources. A typical SN consists of five basic parts: Sensing, controller, memory, communication and power supply. The Figure 3 shows the basic architecture of SNs in WSNs.

Sensors

The sensors are used to observe or monitor physical parameters of the environment. They are the hardware devices and play crucial role in WSNs architecture because they establish interface between the computation environment and the real-time world. The energy is transformed from one form to another by using transducers in SNs.

Figure 3. Architecture of SN in WSNs

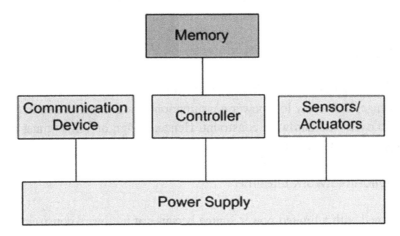

Controllers

The controller is main component of SN and responsible to process all the relevant data such as collects data from sensors, process it and decides where and when to send it. It is capable of executing code of operating system.

Communication

The communication subsystem is used to transmit and receive the sensed and gathered data over a wireless channel. Most of power consumed during the radio transmission and reception of data compare to sensing and computation. Therefore, design of communication protocol must be power-efficient.

Memory

The memory unit is used store programs and intermediate data. Different types of memory are used; such as the Random Access Memory (RAM) used to store intermediate sensor data and packets from other SNs while Read-Only Memory (ROM) stores program codes such as operating and application softwares.

Power Supply

The power supply is very crucial component and is responsible to provide energy in the voltage and current form to all subsystem as mentioned above. There are strict power constraints due to compactness of SNs; hence, efficiently and effectively power utilization is required. Life time of WSNs depends upon remaining power of SNs. Conventionally batteries are used to store power.

Factors Influencing WSNS Design

The major factors which significantly influence the WSNs design are hardware constraint, power consumption, scalability, fault tolerance, latency, throughput, data aggregation, transmission channel, node deployment and security. Similarly, good knowledge is required to design of WSNs in different field such as digital signal processing, wireless communication, embedded systems and software engineering.

Hardware Constraint

As, SNs are tiny is size, therefore, main challenges are limited energy capacity, low computation capabilities and low storage. Extremely low power consumption, low computation and optimized software code are required to overcome hardware constraint. Hence, design of WSNs must address mentioned issues to have longer network lifetime.

Power Consumption/Network Lifetime

A SN usually equipped with a limited power source because of hardware constraints. Therefore, management of SN's power consumption is one of the critical and challenging tasks because of most of SNs are operated by limited battery power. Mostly power is consumed in communication process. So power management and power conservation should be used in effective manner in order to improve the network lifetime.

Scalability

The scalability factor is important in WSNs and defined as any change in network density and size has negligible effect on the performance of WSNs. Therefore, routing protocol should be scalable in order to avoid any topological changes.

Fault Tolerance

The level of failures in network which allows network to function properly without complete network failure is known as fault tolerance. Due to hardware constraints, which may leads to SNs to fail because of lack of power, link failure, environmental interferences, software problems or by physical damage; which results SNs disconnected from the network

Latency

The main primary task in WSNs is to acquire exact information without any delay and distortions. Therefore, routing protocols should be designed with minimum possible delay and distortion to improve overall network performance.

Throughput

Throughput is also important factor which influence the WSNs design and defined as the rate of amount of information transmitted correctly starting from the source to the destination SN. Throughput could be affected with different factors including packet collision or loss, obstruction between SNs and the schemes of used topology.

Data Aggregation

Data aggregation is also main factor conserve energy in WSNs and is defined as combining of data arriving from different SNs by applying suppression technique in order to reduce the number data transmissions.

Transmission Channel

Wireless transmission channel used in WSNs which is prone to interference and errors. Therefore, successful operation of WSNs depends on reliable communication between SNs.

Node Deployment

Usually, SNs are randomly deployed to sense and monitor the physical environmental. This deployment considered as simple and low-cost strategy for large number of SNs. Another way of deployment is uniform distribution of SNs which is more efficient for small number of SNs.

Security

Protection of data accessed from unauthorized person is required in certain application such as for military use.

Application of WSNS

WSNs have wide range of applications; this is possible because of different sensors like temperature, pressure humidity, movement, speed, direction, thermal, magnetic, seismic visual, acoustic, infrared availability. Due to ever increasing applications of WSNs are categorized by five categories such as environmental monitoring, military, health, industry and home applications.

Environmental Monitoring

To monitor the environment is one of widely used and basic application of WSNs. Some environmental applications of WSNs are temperature and humidity monitoring, tracking of vehicles, animals, birds and insects, traffic control, wild life monitoring, flood detection, fire detection, disaster management, weather monitoring, pollution monitoring (Basha, Ravela, & Rus, 2008).

Military

The rapid deployment, self- organization and fault tolerance factors of WSNs enable them a very promising for military command, control, communication, computing, intelligence, surveillance, reconnaissance and targeting (C4ISRT) use. Some of other applications of military are battlefield surveillance, battle damage assessment, monitoring of friendly forces, attack detection, ammunition and nuclear, biological, and chemical (NBC) attack detection and reconnaissance (Ledeczi et al., 2005).

Figure 4. An example of environmental application in WSNs
Source: Mao et al., 2012.

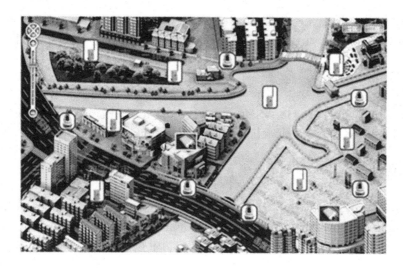

Figure 5. An example of military (battlefield) application in WSNs
Source: Yu & Lu, 2011.

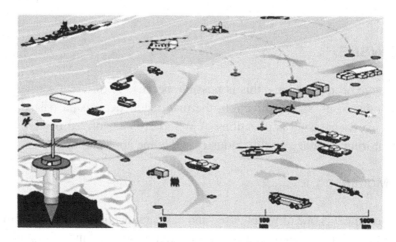

Health

The design and developments of biomedical devices with smart integrated sensors enable WSNs for health applications possible. Health applications in WSNs are used to monitoring of patient's physical and psychological condition, monitoring and tracking of patients and doctors within hospital premises. Health application of WSNs is also called as Wireless body area networks (WBANs) (Wod et al., 2006).

Figure 6. An example of health (BAN) application in WSNs
Source: Acampora, Cook, Rashidi, & Vasilakos, 2013.

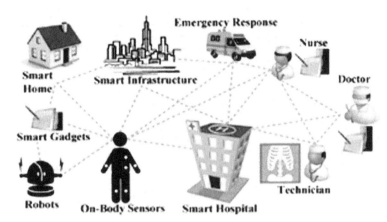

Industry

WSNs are also promising solution for industrial applications because of rapidly and easily deployment, high accuracy and high granularity. Some of industry applications are factory process and automation, monitoring product quality, machine diagnosis and semiconductor processing chambers monitoring (Fodor, Glaropoulos, & Pescosolido, 2009).

Home

With the help of home applications in WSNs, end users can easily manage their home devices remotely and locally. Some of home applications are to monitor and control the room temperature and humidity, remotely monitoring and control of vacuum cleaners, refrigerators, microwave oven and many other home appliances.

Figure 7. An example of industrial application in WSNs

Figure 8. An example of home monitoring application in WSNs

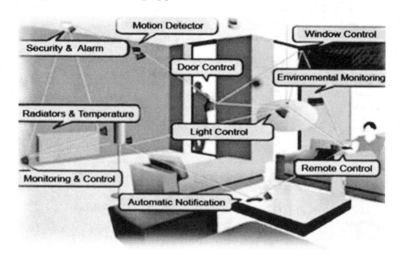

ROUTING PROTOCOLS LITERATURE REVIEW

In this section, a comprehensive study on sate of art routing protocols for WSNs is carried out In WSNs proximity data is sensed, processed and collected by SNs and then finally transfer toward a BS. In small-scale WSNs, direct communication also known as single-hop communication is feasible between SNs and BS because SNs and BS are close to each other. However, single-hop communication is not feasible for large-scale WSNs; this is because father nodes have to cover larger distance to send its data to BS hence consumes its energy quickly and die earlier than the nodes closer to BS. As most of WSNs are in large scale, therefore, multi-hop communication approach is use (Peng et al., 2015). In multi-hop communication, SNs sends their own data but also forward other nodes data. In this simple multi-hop communication, closer SNs to BS have to cover more data compare to father nodes and hence in this case closer SNs to BS die earlier. Single-hop and multi-hop communication concepts are shown in Figure 9.In order to overcome these problems, there is one technique, which enhances the lifetime of network and provides functioning procedure in effective manner is called clustering technique. In clustering WSNs is divided into different groups and in each group head by CH is responsible to collect data from its group SNs and then aggregate and forward to BS (Zheng, Liu, & Qi, 2012). Network lifetime in WSNs is widely improved if proper clustering algorithm is used for CH selection. A lot of work has been devoted to CH selection process; so for many clustering algorithms have been suggested. In this chapter, the literature review of routing and CH techniques is discussed.

Major Challenges and Issue in WSNs

To design a protocol for WSNs compare to Mobile Ad-hoc Networks (MANETs) is more difficult and challengeable task due to its characteristics and requirements. Energy consumption, scalability, mobility, robustness, topology, data aggregation, coverage and quality of service (QoS) etc are the major challenges and issues in design of WSNs algorithms (Wang & Liu, 2011).

Figure 9. Single-hop and multi-hop communication model
Source: Peng et al., 2015.

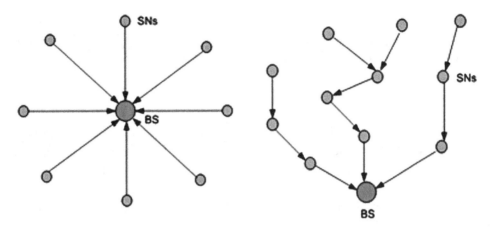

Routing Protocols in WSNs

The main responsibility of the routing protocols is to find best possible path from source to destination. Due to its importance, therefore, a lot of research has been carried out in this domain in recent years. The WSNs routing protocols are categorized in three ways, such as network organization or network structure, protocol operation and route discovery (Pantazis, Nikolidakis, & Vergados, 2013). The detail of three categories of routing protocols is shown in Figure 10.

Figure 10. Routing Protocols in WSNs
Source: Akyildiz & Mehmet, 2010.

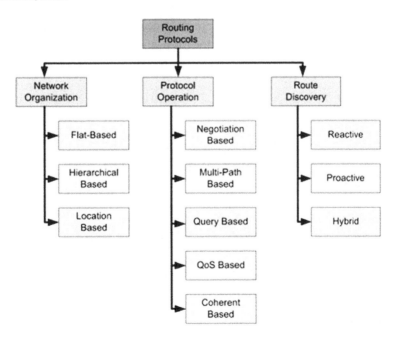

WSNs Protocols Based on Network Organization or Network Structure

WSNs protocols based on network organization or network structure are mainly divided into three ways, such as flat-based, hierarchical based and location based (Panda & Sethy, 2014). This section provides review of routing protocols based on network organization or network structure.

Flat Based

In flat-based WSNs networks, all nodes are equal and typically play the same role in the network. In flat-based networks it is not feasible to assign a global identifier to each node due to large number of SNs (Panda & Sethy, 2014). Therefore, the concept of data-centric routing has evolved, in which BS waits for data from SNs located in the selected regions after sending queries to certain region SNs. In data-centric routing protocols attribute-based naming is given to SNs instead of specific IDs to the each SN. Flooding, gossiping, SPIN and direct diffusion are some popular flat-based routing protocols.

Flooding

The flooding is simplest and oldest type of routing protocol designed for multi-hop networks (Subbu & Li, 2010). In this protocol data is propagate into network like flood, in order to information reach destination node at an unknown location. According to this protocol, whenever a SN receives a packet, it relay this packet to all of its neighboring nodes. This process continues until all the SNs in the network receive the packet as shown in Figure 11.

The advantages of flooding are in its simplicity and straightforward protocol implementation due to not require neighborhood information and complex route discovery. But, flooding has following disadvantages:

- **Implosion:** In this duplicate data packets are received by the nodes, this leads to resource wastage because of unnecessary transmit and receive process. Figure 12 (a) illustrates that node A sent packet to node B and C. Then B and C forward same packet to node D. The energy has been wasted even if node D discards the duplicate data packet.

Figure 11. Flooding routing protocol

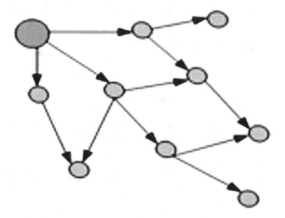

Figure 12. Implosion problem in left and Overlap problem in right
Source: Subbu & Li, 2010.

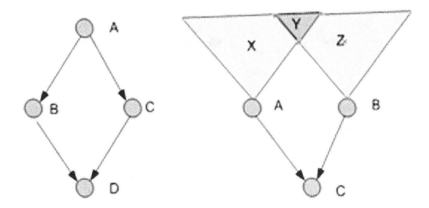

- **Overlap:** The two neighboring nodes may sense the data from overlap region. As a result, BS receives duplicate data packets. In Figure 12 (b), SN A and B have overlap region Y and hence this duplicate data packet from region Y is received by node C from node A and B. This problem is even difficult to figure out compare to implosion.
- **Resource Blindness:** Flooding protocols do not care of its resource specially energy. Therefore an energy resource-aware protocol must be used, in order to conserve energy in WSNs.

Gossiping

Gossiping routing protocol is used to overcome implosion problem in flooding protocol (AlShawi, Yan, Pan, & Luo, 2012). In gossiping, SNs employs probabilistic approach to forward data packets to its neighboring SN with probability p or discard data with probability 1-p, instead of broadcast data packets to its neighbors. The drawbacks of gossiping protocol are energy inefficient, overlapping and resource blindness.

SPIN

Sensor Protocol for Information via Negotiation (SPIN) routing protocol is designed to overcome all three problems in flooding routing protocol. In SPIN to overcome issue of implosion and overlap, SNs negotiate with their neighboring SNs before any data transmission; hence avoid unnecessary communication overheads (Jing, Liu, & Li, 2011). On the other hand to overcome the issue of resource blindness each SN monitors and control resource consumption such as energy. There are number of family members in SPIN protocol.

One of the first members of SPIN protocol is point-to-point (SPIN-PP). The basic operation of SPIN-PP is carried out with help of three types of messages, such as advertisement (ADV), request (REQ) and DATA. In this before sending DATA packet, a SN broadcast advertise (ADV) packet to its neighboring SNs, if a neighbor or number of neighboring SNs are interested in ADV packet, it replies back with a REQ message. After intention DATA packet is sent back to SNs which request it as shown in Figure 13. At each hop all these three types of messages are used to transfer data packets from source to destination.

Figure 13. The operation of SPIN protocol
Source: Jing, Liu, & Li, 2011.

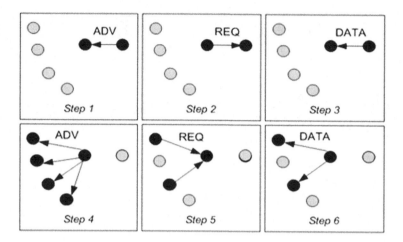

As, SPIN-PP does not address the issue of resource blindness of conventional flooding and gossiping protocols, therefore, energy conservation (SPIN-EC) protocol is used to overcome above problem. In SPIN-EC, whenever the remaining energy of a SN is lower than some defined threshold, the SN does not participant in the basic protocol operation like SPIN-PP.

Another variation of SPIN protocol is SPIN-BC. Both previous SPIN-PP and SPIN-EC protocols are to assumed point-to-point communication protocols, however, SPIN-EC used concept of broadcast transmission. In SPIN-BC, every data is sent to all SNs within sending SN's transmission range. Steps 4 to 6 mentioned in Figure 3. 5 are related to SPIN-BC protocol.

The final version of SPIN protocol is SPIN-RL. SPIN-RL is a reliable version of SPIN-broadcast protocol. In SPIN-RL, if SN receives and ADV packet but does not receive a DATA packet due to wireless radio errors, it request the DATA packet from its neighboring SNs, that may have received DATA packet from source node.

Directed Diffusion

Directed diffusion is also a data-centric protocol. As already discussed, the initiation or flow of data in SPIN protocol is from SNs to sink, however, this type of transmission may not require in some WSNs specific applications. In this algorithm, sink initiated the specific data from SNs or region of interest. This protocol is consists of four steps to establish route between the sink and the SN of interest (Intanagonwiwat, Govindan, Estrin, Heidemann, & Silva, 2003). The four steps are interest propagation, gradient setup, reinforcement and data delivery as shown in Figure 14.

The sink initiate interest message if any information require from SN of interest. In interest propagation step, interest message is flooded within network until reached to destination SN. SN after receiving interest message, it reply back to sink with gradient setup. Then sink reinforce to SN a particular path for data transmission by looking certain parameters like link quality, minimum delay etc. Finally desired data is delivered to sink as shown in Figure 14. The disadvantage of directed diffusion protocol is congestion and scalability (Liu, 2015).

Figure 14. Operation of directed diffusion protocol
Source: Intanagonwiwat, Govindan, Estrin, Heidemann, & Silva, 2003.

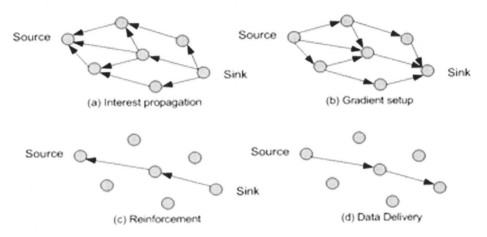

Hierarchical Based

The network is divided into groups called as clusters in order to improve WSNs efficiency and scalability is known as hierarchical based routing protocol. In flat based routing protocols SNs near to sink die earlier compare to SNs away from sink due to overwhelming traffic support and create holes in the network results disconnection of sink from WSNs. The idea behind hierarchical based routing protocol is that the SNs also called member nodes directly communicated with their leader known as Cluster Head (CH). Then CH aggregates data received from its member nodes and finally forward compressed data to sink directly or with help of other neighboring CHs (Liu, 2015). In hierarchical based routing protocol additional responsibilities of CH causes extra energy consumption, however, to overcome this problem the CHs are selected in rotation manner in order to energy consumption should be equally distributed among the SNs. Low-energy adaptive clustering hierarchy (LEACH), power-efficient gathering in sensor information system (PEGASIS), threshold-sensitive energy-efficient sensor network (TEEN) and adaptive threshold-sensitive energy-efficient sensor network (APTEEN) are some popular hierarchical-based routing protocols.

LEACH

One of the first hierarchical based algorithms (CH based) was proposed in Low Energy Adaptive Cluster Hierarchy (LEACH). LEACH algorithm is based on rounds and each round divided into two phases; set up phase and steady state phase. In set up phase, numbers of cluster heads are selected among the sensor nodes (SNs) if the random generated value of SN is greater than threshold mentioned in Equation 1. A SN cannot be elected as CH, if it already completed role as CH for last 1/p rounds. The selected CHs broadcast advertisement to other nodes within specific transmission range; the remaining nodes collect multiple broadcast advertisements from different CHs and becomes member of particular CH with high radio signal strength indicator (RSSI) value by sending associated request. Then CH creates TDMA scheduling, which depend upon the number of member nodes. Once the cluster formation is achieved in set up phase, the LEACH protocol is changed to steady phase. In steady state phase SNs send sensed information to their corresponding CHs, which compress and aggregate the received data and finally send to the sink. After some specific time re-clustering is performed. LEACH performs better as compared to other routing protocols in terms of load balancing and energy efficiency. The disadvantage in LEACH protocol is extra energy consumption due to periodical CH selection and formation. Compare to flat-based routing protocols, the energy consumption in LEACH protocol is reduced about 4 to 8 times (Heinzelman, Chandrakasan, & Balakrishnan, 2000).

$$T(n) = \begin{cases} \dfrac{p}{1 - p\left[r * \mathrm{mod}\left(\dfrac{1}{p}\right)\right]} & \text{if } n \in G \\ 0 & \text{otherwise} \end{cases} \tag{1}$$

where, P is the desired percentage to become a CH (probability), r is the current round and G is the group of SNs that not have been selected as CH in last 1/p rounds.

Another variation of LEACH protocol is Centralized LEACH (C-LEACH). It is designed to further improve the performance in LEACH protocol. In C-LEACH the selection and formation of CHs is performed by sink, instead of SNs themselves (Heinzelman, Chandrakasan, & Balakrishnan, 2002). C-LEACH algorithm has better results than the LEACH algorithm because of reduction of energy required due to formation of CHs. Sink uses central control algorithm to select CHs with some parameters like IDs, remaining energy and location of SNs during the setup phase.

PEGASIS

Power-efficient gathering in sensor information system (PEGASIS) protocol designed to improve issues in LEACH protocol. In PEGASIS protocol SNs are organized into a chain for relaying data packets to the sink instead of formation of clusters as in LEACH protocol. The construction of chain is performed with the help of greedy algorithm, in which the chain is constructed, when SN select their nearest neighbors as next hops. In this each SN only store track information of next and previous neighbor in the chain. The transmission of data packets to sink is controlled by the chain leader, which controls the communication sequence by passing a token among the SNs. The concept of chain communication is shown in Figure 15.

In Figure 15, the chain leader (SN-2) passes the token to SN-0 for communication initiation. Then SN-0 relays its data to SN-1, which compress this and its own data to produce a data packet of same length and forward it to SN-2. Similar way SN-2 passes token to SN-6 and gets information from SN-6, 5, 4 and 3. The aggregated received information in the chain, the SN-2 transmits the data to the sink by using single-hop communication. Compare to LEACH protocol, the energy consumption in PEGASIS protocol is reduced about 100 to 300%. The drawback of PEGASIS protocol is delay in data transmission due to the concept of chain.

TEEN

Threshold-sensitive energy-efficient sensor network (TEEN) protocol is event based, in which data is delivered to sink when any event occurs within the network. TEEN is one of the first protocols for reac-

Figure 15. Chain structure of PEGASIS
Source: Aliouat & Aliouat, 2012.

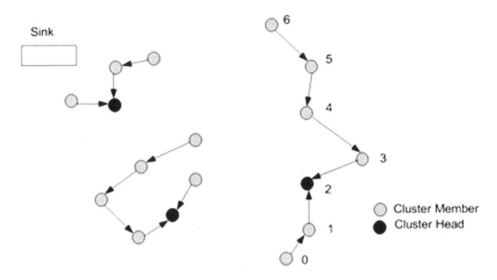

tive networks. It is different from LEACH and PEGASIS protocols, which support applications related to periodically data transmission to sink. TEEN is based on hard (H_T) and soft (S_T) thresholds. SNs continuously monitor the environment, when monitored attribute attains to its hard threshold value; the SN transmits sensed data by switch on transmitter and this sensed value *(SV)* is stored in internal variable. The SN will next transmit data in current CH, only when, current monitored attribute is greater than H_T and differs from SV by an amount equal or greater than the S_T. This will employ that H_T will reduce number of unnecessary transmissions and S_T ensures further eliminating unnecessary transmissions if there is little or no change in the sensed attribute in *SV* (Manjeshwar & Agrawal, 2001).

As, TEEN protocol is based on event based transmission and LEACH or PEGASIS based on periodical based transmission. APTEEN protocol (Manjeshwar & Agrawal, 2002) is designed so for to enjoy the flavor of both event based and periodical monitoring based transmission. These both TEEN and APTEEN protocols improves the overall energy consumption due to concept of H_T and S_T thresholds.

Location Based

Location based or geographical based routing protocols are used in WSNs to find out location information of the SNs for calculation of distance between SNs or to help forwarding data packet to the next hop. Location based routing protocols give various approaches to route that data for improvement in energy efficiency or latency. Minimum energy communication network (MECN), geographic adaptive fidelity (GAF), greedy perimeter stateless routing (GPSR), geographic and energy aware routing (GEAR)and trajectory based forwarding (TBF) are some popular examples related to location based routing protocols (Bokhari, Tamandani, & Makki, 2015).

WSNs Protocols Based on Protocol Operation

Depending upon protocol operation, routing WSNs are classified according to negotiation based, multipath based, query based, QoS based and coherent based (Sudevalayam & Kulkarni, 2011). The brief information related to these routing protocol operations is given below:

Negotiation Based

In negotiation based routing protocol operation data packets are sent after negotiation among the SNs in order to reduce redundant transmission. Normally, the negotiations are done between SN (source) and next hop SN or sink before start of data packet transmission. SPIN routing protocol is a good example of negotiation based routing protocols.

Multipath Based

The multipath based routing protocol utilized concept of multipath between the SN (source) and the destination instead of single path for enhancement of network performance. The direct diffusion routing protocol is a good example of multipath based routing algorithm.

Query Based

Query based routing protocol is depending upon the queries initiated from sink or SN (destination). The SN (source) receive query generated by destination SN and respond to the query accordingly. Rumor and directed diffusion routing protocols are good examples of query based routing protocols.

QoS Based

QoS a based routing protocol ensures the quality of service requirement for WSNs. This type of routing protocols must have to satisfy certain network parameters to achieve network QoS, like delay, jitter, data rate etc. It has to balance between energy consumption and provision of QoS as well. Stateless protocol for real time communication in sensor networks (SPEED) is a good example of QoS based routing protocol.

Coherent and Non-Coherent Based

Coherent and non-coherent are two types of data processing computation reduction techniques, used for reduction of energy consumption of the SN. In non-coherent based routing protocol, the SNs perform data processing methods locally and then send processed data to other SN or CH for aggregation and further forward to sink node. In coherent based routing protocol, the processing is not performed by SNs locally, in this CH or aggregator SN is responsible for processing and aggregation of data. Multiple Winner Algorithm (MWE) routing protocol is a good example of coherent based routing protocols and Single Winner Algorithm (SWE) routing protocol is a good example of non-coherent based routing protocols.

WSNs Protocols Based on Route Discovery

Route discovery based routing protocols are used to discover or identify routes from source SN to receiver SN. These protocols are classified according to reactive, proactive and hybrid based routing protocols (Al-Karaki & Kamal, 2004). The brief information related to route discovery based routing protocol is given below:

Reactive

Reactive based routing protocols find route on-demand. In this protocol route is not defined, therefore, whenever source SN desires to forward data packet to receiver SN; first route is require to establish before transmission of actual data. This is better protocol compare to proactive based routing protocol if route is broken, in terms of delay.

Proactive

In proactive based routing protocols route is already defined, therefore, whenever source SN desires to forward data packet to receiver SN; if transmit data packet. In this routing protocol delay is minimal compare to reactive based routing protocol.

Hybrid

Hybrid based routing protocol is used to take advantages of both reactive and proactive based routing protocols.

Table 1 shows brief summary of different routing protocols based on category.

FUZZY TOPSIS SCHEME

In this section, CH selection based on Fuzzy-TOPSIS; a Multi Criteria Decision Making (MCDM) technique is proposed. Fuzzy-TOPSIS based CH selection plays key role for energy utilization efficiently and effectively. Research on Fuzzy Technique for Preference by similarity to Ideal Solution (Fuzzy-TOPSIS) was performed by Yoon and Hwang and Yoon (1981). TOPSIS used in business as well as in engineering applications. Fuzzy TOPSIS choose the best alternatives based on concepts of compromise solution. It chooses the solution with the farthest Euclidean distance from the negative ideal solution and the shortest Euclidean distance from the positive ideal solution, it consists of matrix with m number of alternatives and n number of attributes for each alternative (Kavitha & Vijayalakshmi, 2010).

Proposed Scheme

In the proposed scheme, for CH selection, SNs take decision themselves, based on ranking index value by using five criteria parameters. The selected CH broadcast advertisement to its neighboring node transmission range, the remaining SNs receives multiple advertisement from different CH in their transmission rang, and decides to associate with the CH which has minimum distance or maximum RSSI value. The

Table 1. Summary of routing protocols

Routing Protocols	Category
Flooding	Flat based
Gossiping	Flat based
SPIN	Flat based
Directed Diffusion	Flat based
Rumor	Flat based
LEACH	Hierarchical based
PEGASIS	Hierarchical based
TEEN	Hierarchical based
APTEEN	Hierarchical based
MECN	Location based
GAF	Location based
GPSR	Location based
GEAR	Location based
TBF	Location based
SPEED	QoS based
SWE	Coherent based
MWE	Non-coherent based

proposed scheme, make sure that the CHs are not changed in every round in order to minimize overheads in set-up phase. Change of CHs is depending upon some threshold. If selected CHs threshold value is smaller than the other neighboring nodes, the re-clustering is performed.

The cluster selection process is divided it into six phases, i.e. random deployment of SNs, neighbor nodes discovery, CH selection, CH formation, intra-cluster and inter-cluster multi-hop communication mechanism and finally sink mobility with predictable octagonal and random trajectory. The detail procedure of proposed scheme is explained below.

Phase-1

Initially all SNs are deployed randomly in WSNs field because it is considered as effortless and low-cost strategy of deployment as shown in Figure 16 (a). After deployment sink node broadcast a Hello control packet in the network, which contains information about its location.

Phase-2

Neighbor discovery is performed in phase 2; all SNs broadcast a Hello control packet in their transmission range T_R, by using carrier sense multiple access (CSMA) technique. Hello control packet contains important information such as; residual energy (criteria-1, C1), nodes energy consumption rate C2, node density C3, average distance between this node and its neighbor nodes C4, distance from the sink node C5, node location and ID information. Initially, node has no information about its neighbors, so C2,

Figure 16. Neighbor discovery flowchart

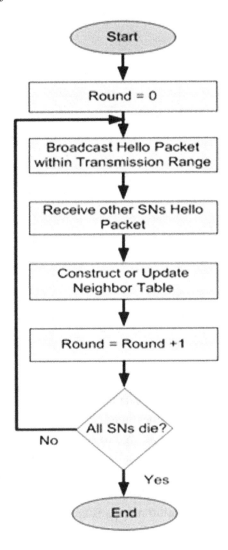

C3 and C4 fields are kept empty in Hello control packet. All SNs update their neighborhood table after receiving Hello control packet from neighboring nodes as shown in Equation 2.

$$T_k = \begin{array}{c|cccc} & C_1 & C_2 & C_3 & C_4 \\ \hline a_1 & x_{1,1} & x_{1,2} & x_{1,3} & x_{1,4} \\ a_2 & x_{2,1} & x_{2,2} & x_{2,3} & x_{2,4} \\ a_3 & \vdots & \vdots & \vdots & \vdots \\ \vdots & & & & \\ a_{n+1} & x_{n+1,1} & x_{n+1,2} & x_{n+1,3} & x_{n+1,4} \end{array} \qquad (2)$$

where, T_k is neighborhood table for node k, n is number of nodes.

Figure 17. Random deployment of SNs in WSN field

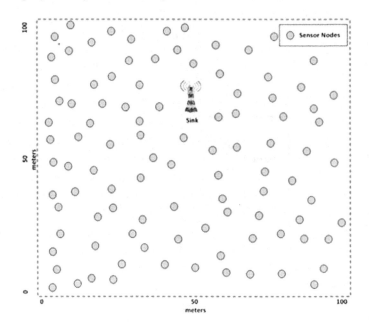

Phase-3

CH selection is performed in phase 3, using fuzzy-TOPSIS method. Since, all values in the neighborhood table are not in the same range, so, these values must be normalized to similar range in order to fairly select a CH. In C1 and C3 larger values are desired to select CH, so these values are normalized with Equation 3, on the other hand C2, C4 and C5 smaller values are desired to select CH, so these values are normalized with Equation 4. Then weighted decision matrix is formed by assigning criteria weights to each value of normalized matrix Xk. After that, maximum and minimum values are calculated from Equation 5 and 6 respectively. The separation measures are calculated with the help of n-dimensional Euclidean distances of each alternative from fuzzy negative ideal solution (FNIS) and fuzzy positive ideal solution (FPIS) are shown in Equation 8 and 9 respectively. Finally, Rank Index (R.I) calculated. The node with the highest R.I in its transmission range will be selected as CH.

$$X_{i,j} = \frac{x_{i,j} - \min_{\forall i}(x_{i,j})}{\left[\max_{\forall i}(x_{i,j}) - \min_{\forall i}(x_{i,j})\right]} \qquad (3)$$

$$X_{i,j} = \frac{\max_{\forall i}(x_{i,j}) - x_{i,j}}{\left[\max_{\forall i}(x_{i,j}) - \min_{\forall i}(x_{i,j})\right]} \qquad (4)$$

$$X_k = \begin{pmatrix} X_{1,1} & X_{1,2} & X_{1,3} & X_{1,4} \\ X_{2,1} & X_{2,2} & X_{2,3} & X_{2,4} \\ \vdots & \vdots & \vdots & \vdots \\ X_{n+1,1} & X_{n+1,2} & X_{n+1,3} & X_{n+1,4} \end{pmatrix} \tag{5}$$

where, X_k is normalized matrix for node k.

After normalization of decision matrix, each value is replaced with according to its rank value, and then transformed to fuzzy membership functions as shown in Table 2. It is not easy to assign exact values of the SNs for each fuzzy membership function.

$$X = \begin{pmatrix} X_{11} & X_{12} & X_{13} & X_{14} \\ X_{21} & X_{22} & X_{23} & X_{24} \\ \vdots & \vdots & \vdots & \vdots \\ X_{(n+1)1} & X_{(n+1)2} & X_{(n+1)3} & X_{(n+1)4} \end{pmatrix} \tag{6}$$

where, X is weighted decision matrix.

$$FPIS = \left(X_1^+, X_2^+, .., X_n^+ \right) = \left[\left(\max_i X_{ij} \mid i = 1, \cdots, m \right), j = 1.., \left(n+1 \right) \right] \tag{7}$$

$$FNIS = \left(X_1^-, X_2^-, .., X_n^- \right) = \left[\left(\min_i X_{ij} \mid i = 1, \cdots, m \right), j = 1.., \left(n+1 \right) \right] \tag{8}$$

$$D^+ = \sum_{i=1}^{5} \sqrt{\sum_{j=1}^{n+1} \left(X_{ij} - X_j^+ \right)^2} \tag{9}$$

$$D^- = \sum_{i=1}^{5} \sqrt{\sum_{j=1}^{n+1} \left(X_{ij} - X_j^- \right)^2} \tag{10}$$

Table 2. Transformed fuzzy membership functions

Rank		Membership Function
Very Low	VL	(0.00, 0.05, 0.15, 0.20, 0.25)
Low	L	(0.20, 0.25, 0.35, 0.40, 0.45)
Medium	M	(0.40, 0.48, 0.54, 0.60, 0.65)
High	H	(0.60, 0.68, 0.74, 0.80, 0.85)
Very High	VH	(0.80, 0.88, 0.93, 0.97, 1.00)

$$RankIndex = R.I = \frac{D^-}{D^+ + D^-} \tag{11}$$

Phase-4

In phase 4, clustering is formed. The CH announces itself as CH within its transmission range; the other nodes in that region will be associated with the CH by sending joining request as shown in Figure 18. Then CH creates TDMA scheduling depending upon number of node members associated with it. CHs are not changed in every round in order to minimize overheads due to set-up phase. Change of CHs is depending upon threshold with value of 0.11, when selected CHs threshold value is smaller than the other neighboring nodes, the re-clustering is performed.

Phase-5

Communication mechanism is used after the successfully CH selection and formation. Threshold based intra-cluster and inter-cluster multi-hop communication mechanism is used, because of more realistic and practical model considered as shown in Figure 19.If the nodes' distance from the CH is greater than 5m

Figure 18. Re-clustering process (CH change)

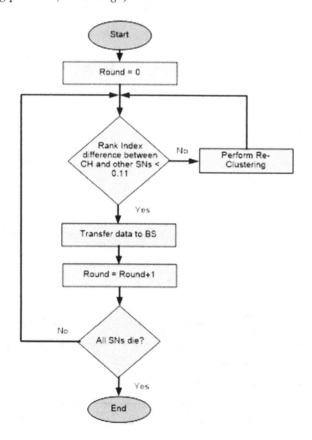

then most suitable neighboring node is selected to forward the data to CH with minimum energy usage as possible, similarly if the distance of CH from the sink is greater than 15m then the other suitable CH is selected to forward the data to sink with minimum energy usage as possible.

Phase-6

Finally, after every round completion sink moves its position by using sink predictable mobility with octagonal trajectory or random mobility. In the same way SNs and CHs move their position in random manner after every round. The sink random and predictable mobility is shown in Figure 21.

Figure 19. Clustering formation in WSN field

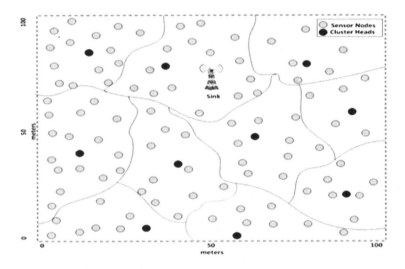

Figure 20. Proposed distance threshold based intra-cluster and inter-cluster multi-hop communication model

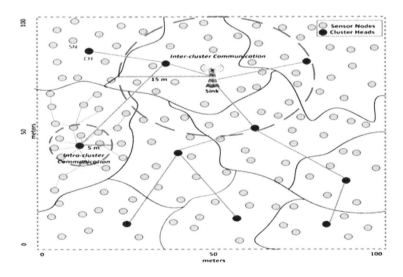

Figure 21. Random and predictable sink mobility patterns

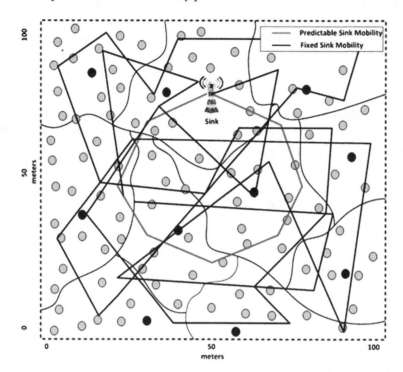

CONCLUSION

In this research paper, we recommend a routing algorithm for Cluster Head selection based on Fuzzy-TOPSIS with predictable sink mobility octagonal trajectory. We have considered five criteria; including residual energy, node energy consumption rate, number of neighbor nodes, average distance between neighboring node and distance from sink. Threshold based intra-cluster and inter-cluster multi-hop communication is also considered. Simulation results indicate, without AWGN channel model, the network lifetime of our proposed scheme increased as compared to LEACH and previous fuzzy based scheme around 140% and 72% respectively, and with AWGN channel model, the network lifetime of our proposed scheme increased as compare to LEACH and previous fuzzy based scheme around 60% and 15% respectively, on the other end, impact of node density on WSN lifetime is very negligible hence it is a robust network as well.

Figure 22. Proposed scheme flowchart

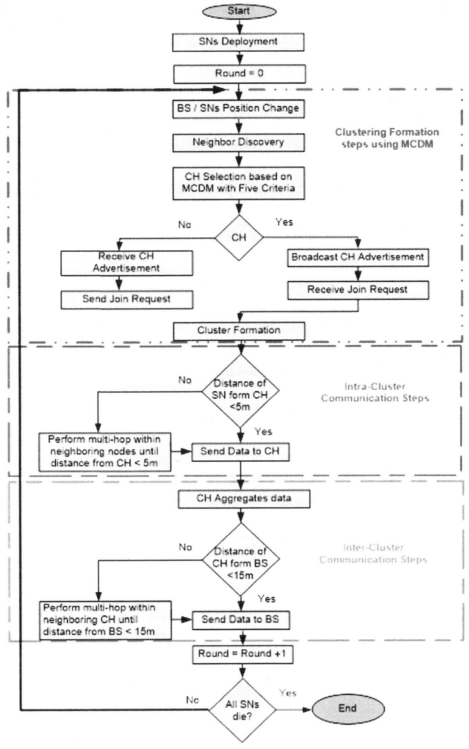

Table 3. Comparison with previous criteria based scheme

Protocol	No. of Parameters	Parameters Type	First Node Dead (Number of Iterations)	Last Node Dead (Number of Iterations)
Fault Tolerant Election Protocol (FTEP) (Heinzelman, Chandrakasan, & Balakrishnan, 2000).	1	Remaining Energy	565	1123
Improved-LEACH (P. Azada *et.al*,2013)	2	Remaining Energy and coverage	556	1179
Cluster-Head Election Algorithm Using a Takagi-Sugeno (CHEATS) (Mao et al., 2012)	2	Remaining energy and distance from Sink	616	1125
Fuzzy based Energy Efficient Clustering (Yu & Lu, 2011)	2	residual energy and Node centrality	634	1148
Hybrid, Energy Efficient Distributed clustering (HEED) (Ledeczi et al., 2005)	2	node residual energy and node degree	685	1276
Improved Fuzzy Unequal Clustering (IFUC) (Acampora, Cook, Rashidi, & Vasilakos, 2013)	3	Residual Energy, distance to sink and local density	803	1319
Analytical Hierarchy Process (AHP) (S. Shah *et.al*,2013)	3	Mobility, and the energy of nodes to the involved cluster centroid	775	1398
Previous Fuzzy (Fodor, Glaropoulos, & Pescosolido, 2009)	3	Residual energy, Distance from base station, number of neighbor,	589	1435
Decision Tree (DT) (Hennebert, C *et.al*,2014)	4	Remaining battery power, Distance of a node from the cluster centroid, vulnerability index and degree of mobility.	802	1619
Proposed Scheme	5	Residual energy, node energy consumption rate, number of neighbor nodes, average distance between neighboring nodes and distance from sink	1806	2473

REFERENCES

Acampora, G., Cook, J., Rashidi, P., & Vasilakos, V. (2013). A Survey on Ambient Intelligence in Health Care. *Proceedings of the IEEE, 101*(12), 2470–2494. doi:10.1109/JPROC.2013.2262913 PMID:24431472

Aijaz, A., & Aghvami, A. H. (2015). Cognitive machine-to-machine communications for Internet-of-Things: A protocol stack perspective. *IEEE Internet Things Journal, 2*(2), 103–112. doi:10.1109/JIOT.2015.2390775

Akyildiz, F., & Mehmet, V. (2010). *Wireless Sensor Networks*. New York, NY: John Wiley & Sons, Inc. doi:10.1002/9780470515181

Akyildiz, F., Weilian, Y., Sankarasubramaniam, & Cayirci, E. (2002). A survey on sensor networks. IEEE Communications Magazine, 40(8), 102-114.

Al-Karaki, J., & Kamal, A. (2004). Routing techniques in wireless sensor networks: A survey. *IEEE Wireless Communications, 11*(6), 6–28. doi:10.1109/MWC.2004.1368893

Aliouat, Z., & Aliouat, M. (2012). M Efficient Management of Energy Budget for PEGASIS Routing Protocol. In *Proceedings of 6th IEEE Conference on Sciences of Electronics, Technologies of Information and Telecommunications.* doi:10.1109/SETIT.2012.6481966

AlShawi, S., Yan, L., Pan, W., & Luo, B. (2012). A Fuzzy-Gossip routing protocol for an energy efficient wireless sensor networks. In *Proceedings of IEEE conference on Sensors.* doi:10.1109/IC-SENS.2012.6411162

Amine, R., Khalid, B., Elhoussaine, Z., & Mohammed, O. (2014). Energy consumption balancing in wireless sensors networks. In *Proceedings of the 4th IEEE International Conference on Multimedia Computing and Systems.* doi:10.1109/ICMCS.2014.6911348

Azada, P., & Sharma, V. (2013). Cluster Head Selection in Wireless Sensor Networks under Fuzzy Environment. ISRN Sensor Networks, 2013(2013), 1-9. doi:10.1155/2013/909086

Basha, A., Ravela, S., & Rus, D. (2008). Mode-based monitoring for early warning flood detection. In Proceedings of ACM Sensors and Systems.

Bokhari, U., Tamandani, K., & Makki, Q. (2015). A comprehensive study of position based routing protocols in WSNs. In *Proceedings of 4th International conference on Reliability, Infocom Technologies and Optimization (ICRITO).* doi:10.1109/ICRITO.2015.7359240

Borges, L., Velez, F., & Lebres, A. (2014). Survey on the characterization and classification of wireless sensor networks applications. *IEEE Communication. Surveys and Tutorials,* (99), 1860-1890.

Chanak, P., Banerjee, I., & Sherratt, S. (2015). Simultaneous mobile sink allocation in home environments with applications in mobile consumer robotics. *IEEE Transactions on Consumer Electronics, 61*(2), 181–188. doi:10.1109/TCE.2015.7150572

Ding, X., Zhang, P., Yin, S., & Ding, L. (2013). An integrated design framework of fault-tolerant wireless networked control systems for industrial automatic control applications. *IEEE Transaction on Ind. Informat, 9*(1), 462–471.

Fodor, V., Glaropoulos, I., & Pescosolido, L. (2009). Detecting low-power primary signals via distributed sensing to support opportunities spectrum access. In Proceedings of IEEE ICC'09.

Heinzelman, B., Chandrakasan, P., & Balakrishnan, H. (2002). An application-specific protocol architecture for wireless microsensor networks. *IEEE Transactions on Wireless Communications, 1*(4), 660–670. doi:10.1109/TWC.2002.804190

Heinzelman, R., Chandrakasan, A., & Balakrishnan, H. (2000). Energy efficient communication protocol for wireless micro-sensor networks. In *Proceedings of the 33rd Hawaii International Conference on System Sciences.* doi:10.1109/HICSS.2000.926982

Hennebert, C., & Dos Santos, J. (2014). Security Protocols and Privacy Issues into 6LoWPAN Stack: A Synthesis. *IEEE Internet of Things Journal, 1*(5), 384–398. doi:10.1109/JIOT.2014.2359538

Hwang, L., & Yoon, K. (1981). Multiple Attribute Decision Making.Lecture Notes in Economics and Mathematical Systems, 186. doi:10.1007/978-3-642-48318-9

Intanagonwiwat, C., Govindan, R., Estrin, D., Heidemann, J., & Silva, F. C. (2003). Directed Diffusion for Wireless Sensor Networking. *IEEE/ACM Transaction on Networking, 11*(1), 2-16.

Ji, S., Li, Y., & Jia, X. (2011). Capacity of dual-radio multi-channel wireless sensor networks for continuous data collection. In *Proceedings of IEEE INFOCOM*. doi:10.1109/INFCOM.2011.5934880

Jing, L., Liu, F., & Li, Y. (2011). Energy saving routing algorithm based on SPIN protocol in WSN. In *Proceedings of International conference on Image Analysis and Signal Processing (IASP)*.

Kavitha, C., & Vijayalakshmi, C. (2010). Implementation of fuzzy multi criteria decision technique to identify the best location for call centre. In *Proceedings of IEEE Trends in Information Sciences and Computing (TISC)*. doi:10.1109/TISC.2010.5714600

Ledeczi, A., Nadas, A., Volgyesi, P., Balogh, G., Kusy, B., Sallai, J., Pap, G., Dora, S., Molnar, K., Maroti, M., & Simon, G. (2005). Countersniper system for urban warfare. *ACM Transactions on Sensor Networks, 1*(2), 153-177.

Lhadi, I., Rifai, M., & Alj, S. (2014). An Energy-efficient WSN-based Traffic Safety System. In *Proceedings of 5th International Conference on Information and Communication Systems (ICICS)*.

Li, C., Wang, Y., & Guo, X. (2010). The Application Research of wireless sensor network based on ZigBee. In *Proceedings of International Conference on Multimedia and Information Technology*. doi:10.1109/MMIT.2010.143

Liu, X. (2015). Atypical hierarchical routing protocols for wireless sensor networks: A review. *IEEE Sensors Journal, 15*(10), 5372–5383. doi:10.1109/JSEN.2015.2445796

Liu, X., Li, F., Kuang, H., & Wu, X. (2006). The Study of Directed Diffusion Routing Protocol Based on Clustering for Wireless Sensor Networks. In *Proceedings of sixth world congress on intelligent control and automation (WCICA)*.

Manjeshwar, A., & Agrawal, D. P. (2001). TEEN: A Protocol for Enhanced Efficiency in Wireless Sensor Networks. In *Proceedings of the 1st International Workshop on Parallel and Distributed Computing Issues in Wireless Networks and Mobile Computing*. doi:10.1109/IPDPS.2001.925197

Manjeshwar, A., & Agrawal, D. P. (2002). APTEEN: A Hybrid Protocol for Efficient Routing and Comprehensive Information Retrieval in Wireless Sensor Networks. In *Proceedings of the 2nd International Workshop on Parallel and Distributed Computing Issues in Wireless Networks and Mobile Computing*. doi:10.1109/IPDPS.2002.1016600

Mao, X., Miao, X., He, Y., Zhu, T., Wang, J., Dong, W., & Liu, Y. et al. (2012). Citysee: Urban CO_2 monitoring with sensors. In *Proceedings of IEEE INFOCOM*.

Panda, M., & Sethy, K. (2014). Network structure based protocols for Wireless Sensor Networks. In *Proceedings of IEEE ICAETR*. doi:10.1109/ICAETR.2014.7012948

Pantazis, A., Nikolidakis, A., & Vergados, D. (2013). Energy-Efficient Routing Protocols in Wireless Sensor Networks: A Survey. *IEEE Communications Surveys and Tutorials*, *15*(2), 551–591. doi:10.1109/SURV.2012.062612.00084

Peng, H., Si, S., Awad, K., Cheng, N., Zhou, H., Shen, X., & Zhao, H. (2015). Energy-Efficient and Fault-Tolerant Evolution Models for Large-Scale Wireless Sensor Networks: A Complex Networks-Based Approach. In *Proceedings of IEEE Global Communication conference* (GLOBECOM). doi:10.1109/GLOCOM.2015.7417534

Raghavendra, S., & Lindsey, S. (2002). PEGASIS: Power-Efficient Gathering in Sensor Information Systems Stephanie Lindsey. In *Proceedings of Aerospace Conference*.

Sai, V., & Mickle, H. (2014). Exploring energy efficient architectures in passive wireless nodes for IoT applications. *IEEE Circuits Systems Magazines*, *14*(2), 48–54. doi:10.1109/MCAS.2014.2314265

Sha, M., Hackmann, G., & Lu, C. (2013). Real-world empirical studies on multi-channel reliability and spectrum usage for home-area sensor networks. *IEEE eTransactions on Network and Service Management*, *10*(1), 56–69. doi:10.1109/TNSM.2012.091312.120237

Shah, S., & Lozano, B. (2013). Joint sensor selection and multihop routing for distributed estimation in ad-hoc wireless sensor networks. *IEEE Transactions on Signal Processing*, *61*(24), 6355–6370. doi:10.1109/TSP.2013.2284486

Subbu, K., & Li, X. (2010). SFRP: A selective flooding-based routing protocol for clustered wireless sensor networks. In *Proceedings of IEEE Radio and Wireless Symposium*. doi:10.1109/RWS.2010.5434131

Sudevalayam, S., & Kulkarni, P. (2011). Energy Harvesting Sensor Nodes: Survey and Implications. *IEEE Communications Surveys and Tutorials*, *13*(3), 443–461. doi:10.1109/SURV.2011.060710.00094

Walravens, C., & Dehaene, W. (2014). Low-power digital signal processor architecture for wireless sensor nodes. *IEEE Transactions on Very Large Scale Integration (VLSI) Systems*, *22*(2), 313–321. doi:10.1109/TVLSI.2013.2238645

Wang, F., & Liu, J. (2011). Networked wireless sensor data collection: Issues, challenges, approaches. *IEEE Communications Surveys and Tutorials*, *13*(4), 673–687. doi:10.1109/SURV.2011.060710.00066

Wod, A., Virone, G., Doan, T., Cao, Q., Selav, L., Wu, Y., . . . Stankovic, J. (2006). *ALARMNET: Wireless sensor networks for assisted-living and residential monitoring*. Technical report CS-2006-11, Department of Computer Science, University of Virginia.

Yu, Y., & Lu, L. (2011). Intelligent Sensor Network Simulation for Battlefield Resources Management. In *Proceedings of IEEE Ninth International Conference on Dependable, Autonomic and Secure Computing* (DASC).

Zheng, Z., Liu, Y., & Qi, G. (2012). Clustering routing algorithm of wireless sensor networks based on the Bayesian game. *Journal of Systems Engineering and Electronics*, *23*(1), 154–159. doi:10.1109/JSEE.2012.00019

Chapter 13
Vehicular Cloud Computing Challenges and Security

Sunilkumar S. Manvi
REVA University, India

Nayana Hegde
Sri Krishna Institute of Technology, India

ABSTRACT

Vehicular Cloud Communication (VCC) is the latest technology in intelligent transport system. Vehicular cloud (VC) facilitates the customers to share resources ranging from storage to computing power to renting it to other users over the Internet. Security of VANET cloud covers various aspects of security, social impact, cost effective communication. Chapter highlights a cost effective, hassle free and secure communication between the cloud and moving vehicles. Communication is established via Network as a Service (Naas). The goal of this chapter is to give a broad overview of Vehicular cloud computing, vehicular cloud applications, mobile computing, and recent literature covering security of vehicular cloud.

INTRODUCTION

Vehicular cloud computing is a new technological model which combines the advantages of cloud computing with vehicular ad hoc network to serve the drivers at low cost and with pay as you go model. Minimize travel time, reduce traffic congestion, provide good computational power at low cost to drivers, reduce environmental pollution, reduce road accidents and make travel more enjoyable are the few objectives of VCC.

According to Whaiduzzaman (2014), the underutilized computing power, memory, sensing and internet connectivity, of large number of autonomous vehicles on roads, parking lots and streets can be coordinated and allocated to other authorized users. Internet access, computing power and storage capabilities can be rented to drivers and other customers exactly as similar to usual cloud computing service. Vehicular Clouds are technologically feasible and economically viable and will be the next paradigm shift. They will provide many benefits, including societal and technological impacts. Vehicular cloud scenario is shown in Figure 1.

DOI: 10.4018/978-1-5225-1785-6.ch013

Figure 1. Vehicular cloud

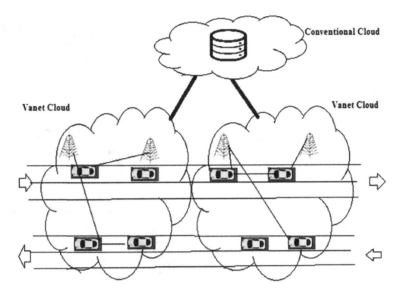

In the figure a group of vehicles are forming the cloud. This vehicular cloud can connect to the internet cloud.

Vehicular cloud is union of vehicular network, cloud computing and mobile computing. Figure 2(a) and Figure 2(b) shows cloud computing and mobile cloud computing. These are explained as follows:

Vehicular Network

In recent past, smarter vehicles have provided the travel experience with safer and delightful driving. Now a day's almost all vehicles are provided with cameras, GPS system, on board computers, small-scale collision radars, various sensors and radio transceivers. Different sensors are used to measure vehicle and road safety conditions, to alert drivers. It also takes care of mechanical malfunctions of vehicles. These vehicles when travel on road make ad hoc network by communicating with each other by wireless communication technology.

Cloud Computing

Cloud computing provides users with the computing, storing capability on demand. Advantage here is users need not invest for computation or storage but he/she can take it on rent from internet. The ever increasing demand for computing and storage has given rise to cloud computing. Customers rent processing, storage, networking and other fundamental computing resources for all purposes to authorized users.

Mobile Cloud Computing

Mobile cloud computing is combination of mobile communication and cloud computing. The drivers use their mobile devices (smart phones) and connect to the cloud via internet. Using mobile communication they can send safety related messages to other drivers and share data. But disadvantage of mobile

Figure 2. (a) Cloud computing, (b) mobile cloud computing

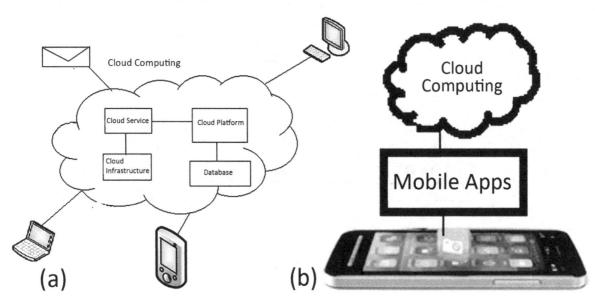

computation is it suffers from battery constraint, resource limitations. Vehicular cloud overcomes this disadvantage as power is generated when vehicle moves. So we consider VCC more advantageous in adhoc networks.

Need of Vehicular Cloud Computing

Vehicles represent an increasingly important source of computing and sensing resources for drivers as well as for urban communities. The concept of vehicular cloud computing borrows its architecture from mobile cloud computing. Modern day vehicular network needs to evolve as internet of vehicles. It uses intenet to keep the nodes connected while they travel. The advantage of VCC over mobile cloud computing is it has no power constraints. The strength of vehicular cloud is not only due to the computing resources they carry, but also due to the sensors available. Ideally vehicles are major sources of observation and can collect and store enourmous amount of local information. The ability to colect sensor information which is of local relevance is biggest advantage of vehicular cloud. This information is shared between the connected vehicles. It saves lot of time for upload and download of informaion from the internet. It saves cost of connecting to internet cloud.

Vehicular Cloud Computing Types

Vehicular Cloud can be formed by V2V communication and V2I to promote sharing information between vehicles. There are two different types of VCC, Roadside cloud and Central cloud. They are explained as follows.

Roadside Cloud

A network between base station or Road Side Units (RSUs) is known as Roadside cloud. Roadside cloud is mainly used for intermediator work. It does take care of communication between vehicular cloud and central cloud infrastructure. It takes care of inter-vehicle communication broadcasting. RSUs process data collected from moving vehicle to provide convenience to vehicles and it takes care of issueing session keys for secured cmmunication.

Central Cloud

The cloud that is formed by the service provider is known as Central Cloud. The authentication related data of the driver is stored in this cloud. When driver requests, service is provided by roadside cloud to the right driver. A role of intermediator is played by central cloud for trusting relationship for RSU and vehicle. (Altayeb, 2013), (Jungho, 2015) .

Comparision between VCC and CC

In this section we give a comparision of cloud computing and vehicular cloud computing. (Whaiduzzaman, 2015) summarized that both in CC and VCC services, applications and resources are accessed on demand. Several requestes can be run by one m/c and pretend to be as separate m/c. Payment is done only for the services used.VCC services are temporary but CC services are always available. Network as a Service is available in both model. Storage as a Service is avalable in both model. Cooporation as a Service is possible in CC and it is one of the main aim of VCC. Commercials, infotainment, information for drivers, planed and unplaned disaster management using roads and vehicles is an important application of VCC where as these applications are technically feasible for CC. VCC model can be described as moving network pool. Automatic cloud formation is possible in VCC and it is not possible in CC. One more advantage of VCC is cloud formation takes place autonomously for a vehicle and a running or standing vehicle. Also in VCC vehicle can provide service while it is moving. The VCC is based on CC and mobile computing architecture and it is a better network among the ad hoc networks. The Figure 3 shows the comparison of Vehicular Cloud and Cloud Computing in terms of resources and technologies.

Communication Model in Vehicular Cloud

There are two types of commnication in VANET, Vehicle to Vehicle (V2V) and Vehicle to Infrastructure (V2I) communication. Data is exchanged between vehicle and infrastructure. Base station or RSU and location based service providers are connected to cloud storage. Figure 4. shows the communication model of vehicular cloud.

In V2V communication data is collected by sensors and processed by OBU and shared between other vehicles.In V2I communication CA authenticates the vehicles and LSP collects the location details of the vehicle. RSU connects vehicle to the cloud.

There are three layers of communications in VANET clouds. At three different levels it incorporates different entities

Figure 3. Comparison between CC and VCC

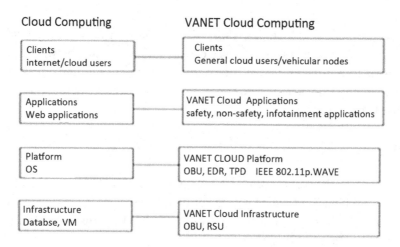

- First layer *is sensor layer* or inside car layer. -This layer deals with sensors, GPS, actuators, RADAR and wireless sensor network.
- Second layer is *vehicle to vehicle layer* or we call it as OBU – OBU or OBU-RSU layer. It uses IEEE 802.11p communication protocol.
- Third layer is *cloud layer*, where communication takes place between gateway to gateway.

Figure 5 gives details of the communication architecture of vehicular cloud. Communication in the first layer uses Wi-Fi or CAN. Inter-car level is second level of communication. In this level vehicles communicate with each other so called as OBU-OBU level. This communication can be either V2V or V2I by using IEEE 802.11p (WAVE) standard. Third level communication enables vehicles to commu-

Figure 4. Block diagram of vehicular cloud communication

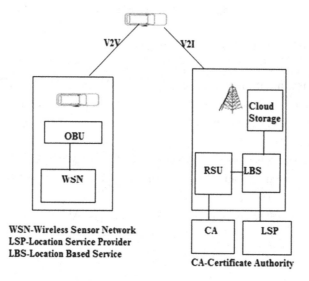

Figure 5. Communication architecture of vehicular cloud layers

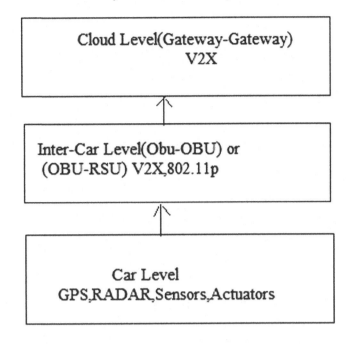

nicate at cloud level. This level uses vehicles or RSUs to serve as gateways. The nomination of vehicle or RSU as gateway will depend upon the underlying framework of VANET cloud.

Architecture of Vehicular Cloud Computing

Xi Chen (2015) and Khaleel Mershad (2013) explains VANET cloud service architecture which is popular as Network as a Service (NaaS), Storage as a Service (STaaS), and Cooperation as a Service (CaaS). These three services are explained next. Platform as a Service (PaaS) is not very popular in Vehicular clouds. Figure 6 shows the different layers of service architecture of VC.

1. **Network as a Service or NaaS (Internet Access):** Some smart vehicles will have a permanent Internet access through a cellular network. This helps other vehicles which don't have that facility to share the net by paying fee to it by such vehicles.
2. **Storage as a Service or SaaS (Virtual Network Hard-Disk):** Some smart vehicles will have high on-board storage capacity, which is not completely utilized. But others vehicles which have less storage facility may need it. This case can occur if several users are using a vehicle's hardware at the same time. Some users prefer to have backup of their data on an external harddisk for safety. The user pay nominal rate for the amount of data storage he uses for required amount of time to owner of the renting vehicle and make use of this service. (Arif, 2012).
3. **Data as a Service or DaaS (Virtual Data Provider):** Instead of requesting Internet access to view a website or work on a web application, a user in a smart vehicle may require specific data: for example, a video file, a city map, latest news, road conditions, etc. So vehicular cloud acts as data provider for travel related things like, nearest fuel stations, hotels, etc for requesting drivers.

Figure 6. Service architecture in VANET clouds

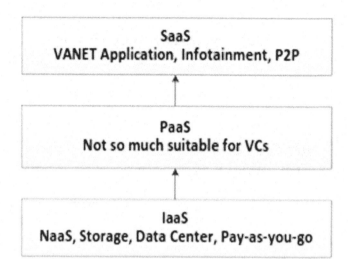

Applications of Vehicular Cloud Computing

Applications of vehicular cloud are: Airport as a Data Centre, Shopping mall as a data cloud, Traffic light management, and Traffic safety message. Some of the applications of vehicular cloud are discussed in detail.

Mallissery (2015) proposed that the concept of VANET cloud is used for helping the regulatory authorities in identifying the vehicles violating the traffic rules through sensors included as part of On Board Unit (OBU). When the vehicle is on fly the sensor values are periodically transferred to the cloud, controlled by the traffic police. So it is used for Transport and Traffic Rule Violation Monitoring Service in ITS. It is a Secured VANET Cloud Application.

Vignesh (2014) explains about stationary cloud to utilize the idle vehicle resources in cities. Vehicles parked at city railway station reach account of nearly 1200 during weekends. These vehicles have very good processing capability and resource poverty can be eliminated by utilizing these vehicular resources.

In a shopping mall if any incident occurred has to be traced with the help of Closed circuit television (CCTV) then lot of processing is required. For that computational ability of the vehicles in parking lot can be utilized.

Saini (2015) proposed a cloud based middleware framework for infotainment application in vehicular network. In this application a service based architecture deligates data fusion and data filtering functionalities to cloud environment. Since most of the processing is done on the cloud it reduces the resources for internet and platform inside the vehicles.

Mallissery (2014) proposed concept of vehicles using cloud(VuC). Here the cloud provides two services: Application as a Service (AaaS) and Storage as a Service (STaaS). It is assumed that all the vehicles are registered with the public cloud through the Certification Authority (CA). The use of public cloud will provide better storage facility; secure accessibility and easy availability of messages, public keys and certificates involved in VANET communication. The proposed system also addresses security attacks in VANET and reduces the overhead involved in communication.

Alazawi (2012) proposed a disaster management system which includes intelligent transport system, mobile cloud computing and VANET. Transportation and telecommunications play a critical role in disaster response and management in order to minimize loss of human life, economic cost and disruptions.

Jelassi (2015) explained an innovative solution in order to provide a satisfactory video streaming quality over a cloud-based VANET architecture. The improvement of video streaming delivery conditions over VANET is realized using cloudlets installed across roads and highways deployed by roadside infrastructure providers.

The main objective of this chapter is to highlight on the security of VCC. The recent works done in the area of security of VCC are listed in the section of literature survey. Next section explains the threat model of VCC which is followed by issues of VCC and challenges of VCC. Security scheme for VCC is explained in detail. The proposed model of secure data storage is explained.

Literature Survey of Vehicular Cloud Computing Security

Suqing Lin (2015) constructed a symmetric-key encryption scheme and a commitment scheme. According to their solution, hybrid encryption and a commitment can be used to add verification to the outsourced decryption more efficiently and a proper verification algorithm should be defined as a constraint during the final decryption for the data receiver.

Yu-Hsun Lin (2013) proposed a Private Circular Query Protocol with cross like search mechanism is proposed to simultaneously accomplish the location-based-NN query and the location privacy preservation, in a novel way.

Ning Cao(2011) proposed privacy-preserving multi-keyword ranked search over encrypted data in cloud computing (MRSE). They chose the efficient similarity measure of "coordinate matching," i.e., as many matches as possible, to capture the relevance of data documents to the search query.

M.Raya (2010) explains the importance of data aggregation and group communication. Here data aggregation is used to secure the communication VANET security. They used symmetric, asymmetric and hybrid cryptography in their work. Symmetric key encryption is used for inter vehicle communication. Efficiency of performance and security both are proved better.

R. Hussain (2014) Presents a less expensive and efficient method for secure and privacy procedure for route tracing and revocation mechanism which is based on the multiple pseudonym.

D. Huang (2011), proposed pseudonymous authentication-based conditional privacy (PACP) scheme. Pseudonyms are generated by roadside unit before communication. The pseudonyms are known only to the vehicles and no other participants in the network. In addition to this the proposed scheme gives a useful procedure for revocation of users.

Jian Shen (2016) proposed a novel lightweight authentication-based access control scheme, which is designed by exclusive-or operations, string concatenation and hash functions. Therefore, this scheme has lower computation cost. Moreover, the main computing work is transferred to the authorized agency, hence, the computation of the user side and the server side is lower than the related authentication scheme for cloud.

Security of Vehicular Cloud

Security Requirement of Vehicular Cloud

Security and privacy are two major challenges faced by all wired or wireless networks who share their resources as explained by (Md Waiduzzam, 2014). Wireless sensor network layer, Wireless communication architecture layer and cloud computing layer are the 3 layers of vehicular cloud architecture. Collecting information and events from the environment is the task of first layer. Second layer takes care of transferring transferring the data from etwr to the cloud through an access point. Storage and service is provided by the cloud layer. Security of vehicular cloud netwrok is depending the imlementation of security of these 3 layers.

Threats for Vehicular Cloud

Zeadally (2012) discussed on security of VANET cloud, as the usage of vehicular cloud service increases, the security requirements increases. Major thearts for vehicular cloud services are:

- Denial of services,
- Identity spoofing,
- Modification repudiation,
- Repudiation,
- Sybil attack, and
- Information disclosure.

To provide secure environment for vehicular cloud services following requirements should be considered:

- Confidentiality,
- Integrity,
- Availability,
- Authentication,
- Privacy,
- Real time constraints.

As per Mahmoud (2010) just like any other wireless networks, different types of attacks can happen on VANET. A vehicle is said to be adversary if it tries to harm or attempts to introduce any kind of misbehaviour in the network by causing problem to any other node, and thereby causing malfunctioning of the network. There are several types of attackers and each has different level of impact on the network. Some attackers are discussed in detail:

- **Drivers Looking Only for Their Interest:** A vehicle driver can send false message to all other vehicles as a road being blocked in order to clear vehicles in his destination road.
- **Users Who Misuse VCC:** A person can use VANET cloud to find out a place where there are no cars (means no people) in order to rob/theft a house in that area.

Table 1. Summary of attacks on VC

Type of Attack	Description	Impact
Access	Unauthorized person attempts to obtain information	Network confidentiality affected
Modification	Unauthorized person trying to alter the information	Network integrity affected
Denial of Service	Access or service not available for the legitimate/ authorized user.	Network availability affected
Repudiation	Incorrect information was given or deny the occurrence of event	Accountability affected.

- **People from within the Industry:** Manufacturers of vehicles know about the security of the vehicles and can steal information.
- **Malicious Attackers:** This is considered to be very dangerous category because it can cause severe damage to the network.

The Table 1 give the summary of attacks and their impacts on VC.
Most common attacks of vehicular cloud network:

- **Denial of Service:** Overload the communication channel by sending continuous messages from a node, in order to make network not available for other nodes to do communication.
- **Interception:** Some nodes act as man in middle so that all important information are passed through the nodes and they can get information that are intended for other destination.
- **Fabrication:** Some nodes send false information about traffic condition in order to get some information in the network.
- **Impersonation:** Adversary gives false identity to gather specific information in the network.
- **Alteration and Suppression of Data:** A malicious node receives data, alters it and resends it. A malicious node can send some false data between two nodes and destroy the communication and cause confusion.
- **The Sybil Attack:** A malicious node gives multiple identity of itself and it tries to get control over the network by destroying the communication.
- **Tampering:** A malicious node alters or modifies the data in the network.
- **Identity Spoofing:** Unauthorized user pretends as legitimate user and access the information from the network.
- **Information Disclosure:** A malicious node hides the identity of the node by an adversary in order to get some information forging from the network.

Vehicular Cloud Computing Issues

Architectural Issues

To accommodate the changing demands of the applications the resource availability is a problem and it caused due to high mobility of the nodes. The layered communication network like TCP/IP has been proved not efficient for the emerging technologies and applications.

Functional Challenges

Vehicular cloud is formed by cyber and physical resources. It is important to develop the trustworthy, efficient communication protocol and data processing methods in dynamic environment.

Policy Related Challenges

Standardization of setup, control access, establishment rules are still challenging and needs more attention from Researchers.

Security and Privacy Issues

In VCC communication takes place within vehicles, vehicle to vehicle and vehicle to infrastructure. These communications are either wired or wireless in nature. So there is requirement of security and privacy in all the 3 layers of communication of vehicular cloud system.

Single User Interface

Single-user access interface is another challenge to VCs. When the number of service accesses in a cloud increases, the number of VMs that provide the service will increase to guarantee quality of service. More VMs will be created and assigned. With the increase in VMs, security concerns grow as well.

Heterogeneous Network Nodes

Conventional cloud computing and fixed networks often have homogeneous end users. As it turns out, vehicles have a large array of (sometimes) vastly different onboard devices. Some high-end vehicles have several advanced devices, including a Global Positioning System (GPS) receiver, one or more wireless transceivers, and onboard radar devices. In contrast, some economy models have only a wireless transceiver. Some other vehicles have different combinations of GPS receivers, wireless transceivers, and radar. Different vehicle models have different device capabilities such as speed of processor, volume of memory, and storage. These heterogeneous vehicles as network nodes create difficulties to adapting security strategies as explained by (Gongjun,2012).

Scalability

Security schemes for VCs must be scalable to handle a dynamically changing number of vehicles. Security schemes must handle not only regular traffic but special traffic as well, e.g., the large volume of traffic caused by special events.

Vehicular cloud thus has many challenges and issues as listed above. In this chapter we concentrate on the security of VCC. So we elaborate on one of the issue that is security and privacy of vehicular cloud computing. Important security and privacy issues faced by the VCC are listed and discussed.

Security and Privacy Challenges of VCC

Authentication of High Mobility Nodes

The authentication in VC contains verifying the authentication of users and the integrity of messages. The VC environment is more challenging than vehicular network and cloud computing, due to the high mobility of nodes.

Secure Location and Localization

Location information plays a vital role in VC to transmit data and create connections because most applications in vehicular systems rely on location information such as traffic status reports, collision avoidance, emergency alerts, and cooperative driving. Therefore, the security of location information and localization should be provided among vehicles

Key Management

VCC is decentralized model of cloud computing. Key management is extremely important for mobile nodes. Most of VCC security solution depends on the Vehicular Public Key Infrastructure (VKPI).

Securing Vehicular Communication

Providing secure communication plays very important role in VCC. There is no centralized system in VCC. Communication is V2V or V2I and it is wireless mode. The attack is mostly possible in these layers of VCC. Mainly encryption is used for securing communication.

Data Security

VCC supports Storage as a Service (SaaS) and Cooperation as a Service (CaaS). Both services based on huge amount of Information exchange. This needs data security and integrity. All the sensitive data are encrypted at OBU using vehicle's public key so that data is not accessed by unauthorized users.

When static cloud is formed at a parking lot for temporarily data can be stored in vehicle's memory. Before vehicle moves out of the parking lot data should be backed up. VM should provide the isolation between the applications run on cloud, and users using it. When back up is taken the optimized usage of physical resources should be done. Data backup and recovery process should be simple and it should be secured.

Since we have discussed about the issues and challenges of VCC, now we present some of the solutions to the above discussed problem under the section scheme to protect vehicular communication. It discusses many security related solutions that are used to protect the attacks and threats of security as discussed above.

Schemes to Protect Vehicular Communication

Symmetric Key Approaches

Symmetric key systems were the first type of encryption system used to provide security to user's data. In this system node will have to first have an agreement for sharing of keys and then it should communicate on messages. There are few hybrid communication systems where both symmetric and public key crypto systems both are used for securing the system. As suggested by Brumister and Christolopous (2008) symmetric key algorithm should not be used for authentication as, it may prevent the non-repudiation. Also it is used to suggest the use of 1024 length of key for (AES) for encryption.

Vehicular Public Key Infrastructure

Public key schemes were used prior to the identity based encryption. The use of public key cryptography with manageable and robust PKI since symmetric key cryptography does not support accountability. Authentication is performed by digital signatures of communicated messages: The use of elliptical curve cryptography is done as it reduces processing time. Many vehicles are registered under different states registrations. Each registration authority has its own unique id. Based on their unique id we can identify, which vehicle is registered under which certificate authority. These vehicles will be travelling in different regions beyond their registered regions. So it becomes very important to manage these vehicles. Vehicle public key infrastructure manages the job of managing the vehicles in this way. It mainly consists of three steps.

1. **Key Assignment by Certificate Authority:** In this phase public key and private key are issued by certificate authority. Key assignment for each vehicle is based on the unique id of the vehicle and expiration date is decided by the certification authority.
2. **Key Verification:**
   a. Public Key verification can be done by the certificate authority. It can be explained by steps as follows:
   b. Vehicle 'X' requests for public key from Certificate authority 'Y' (CAy).
   c. Public key for vehicle 'X' (PUx) will be is issued by CAy.
   d. Certificate for this vehicle (Cert(X)) is calculated using PUx and Unique id of the CAy

(Cert(X))=PUx| SignPry(PUx|IDCAy).

3. **Certification Revocation:** Certificate revocation is one of the most significant ways to protect information from the attackers. Generally, when the attacker certification is detected or the certification of one node is exposed by attackers, the certificate should be revoked. As explained (Housley R 2002) The Certificate Revocation List (CLR) that is the most important revocation methods in a vehicular network. The CRL contains a list of the most recently revoked certificates which is broadcast among vehicles immediately. However, CLRs has several drawbacks: the length of list can be very long and the lifetime of certificates can be very short.

Pseudonym Based Approaches for Privacy

In a novel approach as explained by (Raya et al., 2006) for privacy preservation proposed by using a set of anonymous keys which have short life time. They have previously amount of time. Once a key is used it cannot be used again. All keys distribution and management is provided by the CA of the network. The stress is given on the point that these keys have to be traceable to the driver only in the case of emergencies and authority requirements.

Pseudonymous Authentication

(Park, 2015) explains some of the privacy preserving vehicle authentications. These schemes are designed on the basis of pseudonym-based techniques. It combines group signature based schemes and pseudonym-based algorithms. Conditional privacy preservation can be built using group signatures. In this method the signature size and computation costs are relatively long and high. In pseudonym-based technique widely used in vehicular networks, each vehicle possesses a lot of unlink able pseudonym certificates and frequently changes its pseudonyms to avoid tracking from global eavesdropper. One drawback of this system is revocation list is very large. Thus, the size of revocation list becomes getting longer depending on not the number of vehicles but the number of pseudonyms in the system.

Identity Based Cryptography

Recently the identity (Mahmoud Al-Q) based signature has become very important for security of VANET applications. This security framework is considered to be good choice due to unique characteristics of VANET. Earlier used symmetric key cryptography and public key cryptography methods are not suitable for VANET security applications. Since VANET is infrastructure less, public key cryptography needs infrastructure for key management and key distribution. Use of keys and its size in public key cryptography pose a constraint on the bandwidth usage of the dynamic wireless networks. Due to real time applications and delay constraints in the communications symmetric key cryptography is also not considered to be good solution. Therefore, Identity based cryptography is considered to be a viable solution for security of VANET.

Identity Based Signatures

As explained by (Shamir, 1984) identity based signature does not use any public key infrastructure like public/private key pairs. Instead it uses a cryptosystem which is built upon public key systems. Here public key is not generated but a general string that uniquely identifies the user is used to encrypt the data. Third Trusted Party will issue the private key to the user. It needs a random seed for generating public and private key pairs.

Signing and Verifying is done in 4 steps:

1. **Setup:** Third Trusted Party creates its own pair of private and public keys using the parameters given by the user. It distributes the public keys to users.
2. **Extraction:** The signer authenticates him/her to the TTP and then requests for his private key from TTP.
3. **Signing:** User after receiving the private key signs the message using the private key and then sends the message to the destination.
4. **Verifying:** Upon receiving the signed text the verifier uses public key of his and public key of TTP to verify the signature.

Identity Based Encryption

Identity based encryption was developed in 2001 and it was based on Elliptical Curve Cryptography. The encryption process is performed in 4 steps:

1. **Setup:** The TTP generates its own pair of public and private key pairs and distributes it within the network.
2. **Extraction:** The sender authenticates himself with the TTP and requests for private key from TTP. TTP generates the private key and gives it to sender.
3. **Encryption:** The sender uses the public key and uses public key of the TTP to encrypt the messages and send it to the receiver.
4. **Decryption:** Upon receiving the encrypted message receiver uses its private key to decrypt the message.

Strength of the identity based encryption:

1. It states the strength of the public key cryptosystem.
2. All level of secrecy is maintained in TTP.
3. Authentication is provided before the private key issued to the sender.
4. The method of calculation of private key is kept secret.

Attribute Based Encryption

Attribute based encryption is a public key encryption. In this algorithm secret key of user and cipher text is based on some attributes. Examples like University name, department name, designation of user etc. In this algorithm decryption of the cipher text is done only after matching the attributes of secret key with attributes of cipher text. An important property of ABE with respect to its security aspect is collusion-resistance. If an adversary has multiple keys, then user should be able to guess crucial security aspect of Attribute-Based Encryption is collusion-resistance: An adversary that holds multiple keys should only be able to access data if user grants permission. The concept of attribute-based encryption was first proposed by Amit Sahai and Brent Waters and later by Vipul Goyal, Omkant Pandey, Amit Sahai and Brent Waters. Recently, several researchers have further proposed Attribute-based encryption with multiple authorities who jointly generate users' private keys.

(Li, 2016) proposed a cipher text policy attribute based encryption (CP-ABE). In this scheme an efficient t user revocation policy is for cloud storage system. A user group is introduced and in this concept and user revocation is efficiently solved with this scheme. After a user leaves the group manager of the group updates all private keys. Additionally, CP-ABE scheme has heavy computation cost, as it grows linearly with the complexity for the access structure. To reduce the computation cost, they proposed outsource of high computation load to cloud service providers without leaking file content and secret keys. Notably, this scheme can withstand collusion attack performed by revoked users cooperating with existing users. They proved the security of scheme under the divisible computation Diffie-Hellman (DCDH) assumption.

Elliptical Curve Cryptosystem for Vehicular Cloud Security

As per (Sharma, 2015) Elliptic Curve Cryptography used for secure communication in the network that also ensures the security requirements such as confidentiality, integrity, privacy etc. The proposed scheme ensures the mutual authentication of both sender and receiver that wants to communicate. The scheme uses additional operation such as one-way hash function and concatenation to secure the network against various attacks i.e. spoofing attack, man-in-the-middle attack, replay attack etc. The effectiveness of the proposed scheme is evaluated using the different metrics such as packet delivery ratio, throughput and end-to-end delay and it is found better where it is not applied. Elliptical curve cryptography is used for authorization of users in vehicular cloud or cloud services (Singh, 2015; Divya, 2014).

Elliptical Curve Arithmetic

As explained by (Darrer, 2013) Elliptical curve cryptography is based on the points on curves. Cryptography is branch of mathematics that converts plaintext into cipher text. There are many algorithms to encrypt data and generate digital signatures. Elliptic Curve Cryptography (ECC) is very important among them. In 1985 a new cryptosystem was developed by Miller and Kolbitz which is dependent on the finite theory of and discrete logarithm problem. Elliptic curve cryptographic schemes can provide the same functionality as RSA schemes which are public-key mechanisms. Due to the reason of discrete logarithm property the key length of the elliptical curve cryptography system is smaller than the RSA. Advantage of ECC is, it gives same level of security to that of RSA and at the same time it has smaller key size compared to RSA. Other important features which make ECC popular for implementation is: it consumes low power, it is faster in computations. Since key size length is small, it takes smaller power and uses less bandwidth.

Wireless devices and smart cards present a good example for the constrained devices with limited resources. Arithmetic in elliptic curves requires a number of modules to calculate ECC operations:

- Modular multiplication,
- Modular division, and
- Modular addition/subtraction operations

The most critical operation, which is computationally expensive, is modular division. There are many applications using ECC as an authentication for encryption, transactions or signature for secure messaging.

Mathematics of Elliptical Curve Cryptography

Definition: An elliptic curve E over a field K is defined by an equation.

Mathematical details of Elliptical Curve Cryptography are given in Figure 7 with an example.

Elliptic Curve Digital Signature Algorithm

Authentication of a message or application in electronics and communication can be done using Digital Signature Algorithm (DSA). DSA has its own unique properties. Private Key in this signature is produced by one single individual. The produced key is verified by any recipient. If 'X' wants to send a message to Y, X should sign the message using her private key. By signing the message X will authenticate the message. Verification of the signature can be done using public key of X. Thus if Y is aware of X's public key, Y can verify the signature and confirm that it has come from authenticated user. Another version of DSA which works on elliptical curve theory is Elliptic Curve Digital Signature Algorithm (ECDSA).

Figure 7. Elliptical curves

$$E : y^2 + a_1xy + a_3y = x^3 + a_2x^2 + a_4x + a_6$$

where $a_1, a_2, a_3, a_4, a_6 \in K$ and $\Delta \neq 0$, where Δ is the *discriminant* of E and is defined as follows:

$$\Delta = -d_2^2 d_8 - 8d_4^3 - 27d_6^2 + 9d_2 d_4 d_6$$
$$d_2 = a_1^2 + 4a_2$$
$$d_4 = 2a_4 + a_1 a_3$$
$$d_6 = a_3^2 + 4a_6$$
$$d_8 = a_1^2 a_6 + 4a_2 a_6 - a_1 a_3 a_4 + a_2 a_3^2 - a_4^2.$$

If L is any extension field of K, then the set of L-*rational points* on E is

$$E(L) = \{(x, y) \in L \times L : y^2 + a_1xy + a_3y - x^3 - a_2x^2 - a_4x - a_6 = 0\} \cup \{\infty\}$$

where ∞ is the *point at infinity.*

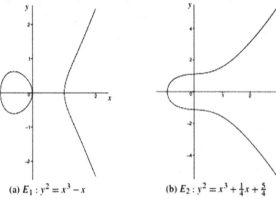

(a) $E_1 : y^2 = x^3 - x$ (b) $E_2 : y^2 = x^3 + \frac{1}{4}x + \frac{5}{4}$

Pairing Based Cryptosystem

The main concept of PBC is constructing a mapping between two suitable cryptographic groups. Then reduce the complexity of one of the group to match with another group. This method produces sufficient cryptographic schemes. DDHP and DLP can be solved with pairing methods. Examples of such pairings are Weil pairings and Tate pairings (Kristin,2004).

Chaos Theory Based Security for Vehicular Cloud

Chaos theory includes the properties of theory of nonlinear dynamics. In this theory simple deterministic equations help to predict the random events. Chaos means lack of orderliness and somewhat unpredictable behavior. They don't obey any rules or behaviors. Chaos theory is a very important theory for securing data on vehicular cloud. (Bahrami, 2016) proposed a scheme for security of cloud service which scrambles data on each multiple fields of a database. The proposed system uses predefined chaos based system to store data on the database. Main advantage of this scheme is data is scrambled and stored in database, so database users, authorized or unauthorized users or cloud administrators cannot get the original data.

Proposed Idea

In this section we present some of the ideas which will be implemented in VCC and beneficial for the society. These proposals are mainly for focused on the travelers and drivers.

Secure Storage Service for Vehicular Cloud Environment

Some of the vehicles have plenty of storage facility in their OBU and other vehicles which don't have storage facility may require it. It is predicted that vehicles will have multiple tera bytes of memory and they can be rented for other vehicles. The difference between the conventional cloud and VCC based SaaS is that, in VCC the service may be available for less time.

IoV (Internet of Vehicles)

By combining the emerging technology of Internet of Things (IoT) and VANET an autonomous framework can be formed which will be used for maintaining the network between the moving vehicles, hospitals and ambulances. These will help drivers and passengers in the emergency and accident places. It will save time of arrival of ambulances and saves lives.

Environment Sensing on Wheel

The sensors mounted on the vehicles can sense the pollution of the environment. So instead of deploying permanent infrastructure for environment pollution monitoring at large geographical area, the vehicles moving in that area can be used. The collected data can be uploaded to cloud or pollution control board for further processing.

Intelligent Transportation and Connected Vehicles

Intelligent Transportation helps users with the application like safety system, toll collection, trip planning, travel assistance, passenger information and intermodal communication. Communication is possible through IEEE 802.11u, 3G/4G, Wi-Fi, Hotspot, femtocells.

Open Research Issues

1. **Architectural Formation of Vehicular Cloud:** Due to the mobility of host and heterogeneity of nodes it is very difficult to manage computing, communication and storage facilities.
2. **Security and Privacy Issues:** VC is predicted to face same security issues like CC. This is because vehicles which are nodes of network share computational capability power, storage area, and internet facility from CC.
3. **Policy and Operational Management Issues:** There are no proper rules and regulations for setting up of VC and control structure of operation of VC. There is need for establishment of managing system for decision support at local and global level. Rules for incentive payment for vehicles participating in VC should be made.

CONCLUSION

Vehicular cloud has emerged due to high vehicle's computation and storage resources, sensing capabilities and traditional cloud computing. The VCC is considered as a complementary of traditional cloud computing but with more services and applications. In this chapter we presented introduction to vehicular cloud, architecture of vehicular cloud, applications of VC. The chapter gives details of vehicular cloud computing challenges and security. It focuses on security requirement, security threats and challenges. We also presented schemes for secure communications in VC. Secure data storage scheme is proposed. This chapter discusses many beneficial information about vehicular cloud computing and hope it motivates readers about VCC and its implementation about real time.

REFERENCES

Al-Quteyri. (2010). *Security and Privacy of Intelligent VANET*. Computational Intelligence and Modern Heuristics.

Alazawi, Z., Abdljabar, M. B., & Altowaijri, S. (2012). ICDMS: An Intelligent Cloud Based Disaster Management System for Vehicular Networks. *LNCS, 7266*, 40–56.

Altayeb, M., & Mahgoub, I. (2013). A survey of vehicular ad hoc networks routing protocols. *International Journal of Innovation and Applied Studies, 3*(3), 829–846.

Arif, S., Olariu, S., Wang, J., Yan, G., Yang, W., & Khalil, I. (2012). Datacenter at the airport: Reasoning about time-dependent parking lot occupancy. *IEEE Transactions on Parallel and Distributed Systems, 23*(11), 2067–2080. doi:10.1109/TPDS.2012.47

Auter. (2004). The Advantages of Elliptic Curve Cryptography For Wireless Security. *IEEE Wireless Communications*.

Bahrami, M., & Singhal, M. (2016). A light-weight Data Privacy schema for cloud based Databases. *International Conference on Computing, Networking and Communications*. doi:10.1109/ICCNC.2016.7440634

Cao, N., Wang, C., Li, M., Ren, K., & Lou, W. (2014, January). Privacy-Preserving Multi-Keyword Ranked Search over Encrypted Cloud Data. *IEEE Transactions on Parallel and Distributed Systems, 25*(1), 222–224. doi:10.1109/TPDS.2013.45

Chen, X., Rao, L., Yao, Y., Liu, X., & Bai, F. (2015). The Answer is Rolling On Wheels: Modelling and Performance Evaluation of in-cabin Wi-Fi Communications. *Vehicular Communications, 2*(1), 13–26. doi:10.1016/j.vehcom.2014.10.001

Divya, S. V. (2014). Security in Data Forwarding Through Elliptic Curve Cryptography in Cloud. *International Conference on Control, Instrumentation, Communication and Computational Technologies*.

Eltoweissy, M., Olariu, S., & Younis, M. (2010). Towards Autonomous Vehicular Clouds. *LNICST, 49*, 1–16.

Gerla, M. (2012). Vehicular Cloud Computing. *IEEE Vehicular Communications and Applications Workshop*.

Hankerson, Menezes, & Vanstone. (n.d.). *Guide to Elliptic Curve Cryptography.* Academic Press.

Housley, R., Polk, W., Ford, W., & Solo, D. (2002). *Internet X. 509 public key infrastructure certificate and certificate revocation list (CRL) profile.* RFC 3280.

Huang, D., Misra, S., Verma, M., & Xue, G. (2011, September). Pacp: An efcient pseudonymous authentication-based conditional privacy protocol for vanets. *IEEE Transactions on Intelligent Transportation Systems, 12*(3), 736–747. doi:10.1109/TITS.2011.2156790

Hussain, R., & Oh, H. (2014, October). A Secure and Privacy-Aware Route Tracing and Revocation Mechanism in VANET-based Clouds. *Journal of The Korea Institute of Information Security and Cryptology, 24*(5), 795–807. doi:10.13089/JKIISC.2014.24.5.795

Jelassi, S. (2015). QoE-Driven Video Streaming System over Cloud-Based VANET. *LNCS, 9066,* 84–93.

Kang & Park. (2015). *Design of Secure Protocol for Session Key Exchange in Vehicular Cloud Computing.* Advances in Computer Science and Ubiquitous Computing.

Lee & Chen. (2013). Cloud Server Aided Computation for ElGamal Elliptic Curve Cryptosystem. *IEEE 37th Annual Computer Software and Applications Conference Workshops.*

Li, J. (2016). *Flexible and Fine-Grained Attribute-Based Data Storage in Cloud Computing. IEEE Transactions on Services Computing.*

Lien & Lin. (2013). A Novel Privacy Preserving Location-Based Service Protocol With Secret Circular Shift for k-NN Search. *IEEE Transactions on Information Forensics and Security, 8*(6).

Lin, Zhang, Ma, & Wang. (2015). Revisiting Attribute-Based Encryption With Verifiable Outsourced Decryption. *IEEE Transactions on Information Forensics and Security, 10*(10).

Mallissery, S., Manohara, P. M. M., Ajam, N., Pai, R. M., & Mouzna, J. (2015). Transport and Traffic Rule Violation Monitoring Service in ITS: A Secured VANET Cloud Application. *Annual IEEE Consumer Communications and Networking Conference.* doi:10.1109/CCNC.2015.7157979

Mallissery, S., Manohara, P. M. M., & Pai, R. M. (2014). Cloud Enabled Secure Communication in Vehicular Ad-hoc Networks. *International Conference on Connected Vehicles and Expo2014.*

Mershad & Artail. (2013). *Finding a STAR in a Vehicular Cloud. IEEE Intelligent Transport on System Magazine.*

Park, Y. (2015). *Pseudonymous authentication for secure V2I services in cloudbased vehicular networks. J Ambient Intell Human Comput.*

Raya, M., Aziz, A., & Hubaux, J.-P. (2010). Efficient secure aggregation in Vanets. *Proceedings of the 3rd international workshop on Vehicular ad hoc networks.*

Saini, Alam, & Guo. (2015, December). InCloud: a cloud-based middleware for vehicular infotainment systems. *Multimed Tools Appl.*

Sharma, M. K., Bali, R. S., & Kaur, A. (2015). Dynamic key based authentication scheme for Vehicular Cloud Computing. *International Conference on Green Computing and Internet of Things (ICGCIoT)*. doi:10.1109/ICGCIoT.2015.7380620

Shen, J. (2016). *An Authorized Identity Authentication-based Data Access Control Scheme in Cloud*. ICACT.

Sherali Zeadally, S. C. A. I. A. H. (2012). Vehicular ad hoc networks (VANETs): Status, Results and Challenges. *Telecommunication Systems, 50*(10), 217–241. doi:10.1007/s11235-010-9400-5

Singh, S., & Kumar, V. (2015). Secured User's Authentication and Private Data Storage- Access Scheme in Cloud Computing Using Elliptic Curve Cryptography. *International Conference on Computing for Sustainable Global Development*.

Vignesh, N., Shankar, R., & Sathyamoorthy, S. (2014). Value Added Services on Stationary Vehicular Cloud. *LNCS, 8337*, 92–97.

Whaiduzzaman, M., Sookhak, M., Gani, A., & Buyya, R. (2014). A Survey On Vehicular Cloud Computing. *Journal of Network and Computer Applications, 40*, 325–344. doi:10.1016/j.jnca.2013.08.004

Yan, G., Wen, D., Olariu, S., & Weigle, M. C. (2012). Security Challenges in Vehicular Cloud Computing. *IEEE Transactions on Intelligent Transportation Systems*.

APPENDIX

Table 2. List of Acronyms

AVS	Autonomous Vehicular Cloud
CA	Certificate Authority
CaaS	Cooperation as a Service
CC	Cloud Computing
CRL	Certificate Revocation List
CRM	Customer Relationship Management
DoS	Denial of Services
DRP	Distributed Revocation Protocol
EBS	Elastic Book Store
EDR	Event Data Recorder
GPS	Global Positioning System
IaaS	Infrastructure as a Service
ITS	Intelligent Transportation Systems
SaaS	Software as a Service
STaaS	Storage as a Service
V2I	Vehicle to Interface
V2V	Vehicle to Vehicle
VANET	Vehicular Adhoc Network
VC	Vehicular Cloud
VCC	Vehicular Cloud Computing
V-Cloud	Vehicular Cloud
VM	Virtual Machine
VPKI	Vehicular Public Key Infrastructure
WSN	Wireless Sensor Network

Chapter 14

A Comprehensive Survey on Techniques Based on TPM for Ensuring the Confidentiality in Cloud Data Centers

Arun Fera M
Thiagarajar College of Engineering, India

M. Saravanapriya
Thiagarajar College of Engineering, India

J. John Shiny
Thiagarajar College of Engineering, India

ABSTRACT

Cloud computing is one of the most vital technology which becomes part and parcel of corporate life. It is considered to be one of the most emerging technology which serves for various applications. Generally these Cloud computing systems provide a various data storage services which highly reduces the complexity of users. we mainly focus on addressing in providing confidentiality to users' data. We are proposing one mechanism for addressing this issue. Since software level security has vulnerabilities in addressing the solution to our problem we are dealing with providing hardware level of security. We are focusing on Trusted Platform Module (TPM) which is a chip in computer that is used for secure storage that is mainly used to deal with authentication problem. TPM which when used provides a trustworthy environment to the users. A detailed survey on various existing TPM related security and its implementations is carried out in our research work.

INTRODUCTION

Trusted platform module is considered to be the core part of trusted computing group which provides various capabilities of cryptographic possibilities which protects PC from various threats to user's

DOI: 10.4018/978-1-5225-1785-6.ch014

Figure 1. Overview of TPM

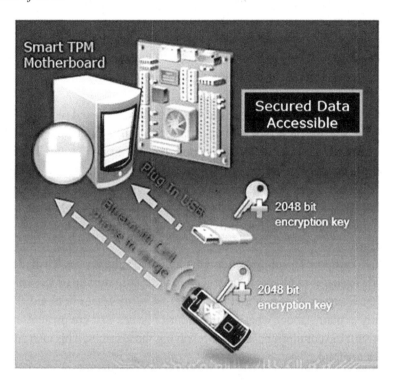

sensitive information. This paper explains about the trusted platform module features which help from preventing various threats.

Trusted platform module (TPM) is a microcontroller which stores the passwords, key and digital certificates. It is attached to motherboard which can be used in any devices for security purposes. We can save that TPM provides a secure place for storing all types of sensitive information which provides a secure space for key operations and protect from other security attacks. TPM is attached to motherboard of our PC and that can be used in any computing devices. TPM's overview is given in Figure 1.

SURVEY ON TRUSTED PLATFORM MODULE

A trusted platform module is used for generating secure asymmetric key. Goh W, Yeo CK (2013) describes the use of a secure key generating authority in Shamir identity-based signature scheme implementation. They proposed an idea of identity-based asymmetric cryptosystems (IBC) together with an identity-based asymmetric signature. The proposed IBS scheme in this paper has itself proven secure against forgery under chosen message attacks. This paper also proposed a new concept that assigns TPM as key generating authority and list out the various merits of implementing it.

Abbadi M, Muntaha (2012) lists out the challenges for establishing the trust in the cloud and then proposes a secure framework which helps in addressing the listed challenges. This paper is actually an extension of their previous work. In their previous work, they proposed a unique framework for establishing trust in the cloud environment. By extending their previous work, the current paper addresses those issue; it clearly covers applications data and their integration with infrastructure management data. The proposed framework by Abbadi M, Muntaha (2012) has four types of software agents, each run on trusted devices. The paper also explains about the controlled content sharing between devices.

In Huang et al (2013), security is ensured using C-code-like formal modeling at the application level. As a result of this approach, security of the protocol is ensured not only at the abstract level of protocol l, but also at the concrete level.

In Ramon et al. (2006), the authors propose the virtualization of trusted platform module, so that not only single machine can use the TPM but also any number of virtual machines can also use the TPM; doing so will support higher level services like remote attestation and so on. They also propose that the full TPM has been implemented in the form of software and integrate into hypervisor to make the TPM available to virtual machines also. In this environment, virtual TPM helps to establish trust using remote attestation and sealing capabilities. Establishing trust in computer platform is purely dependent upon validation. Validation allows external entity to keep up their trust on their platform based upon the specification of platform.

Schmidt et al. (2013) proposes a unique validation method to validate tree-formed data platform. This paper also uses Merkle hash tree to protect the integrity of the secure start up process of a trusted platform.

In Ali et al. (2015), a survey is done about the various security issues in cloud. This paper Ali et al. (2015) initially clearly explains about what are the security issues that are present in the various levels of cloud and suggest suitable countermeasures for resolving those issues. This also addresses some open issues and researches in cloud.

TPM usually contains a unique identity to provide security functions. This paper by Goh et al. (2011) proposes a new method of using TPM-enabled computer as client and server to detect anti-forensics. This paper presents and analyzes an anti-forensic system constructed by utilizing TPM-enabled security on a client-server system. It extends the basic system specification presented and pro- vides detailed analysis of its anti-forensic capabilities. The system design considers various vectors in which forensic examination can be conducted. Security analysis of the system showed how each component contributes to the overall objective of the system being anti-forensics capable. An important note is that the system is designed to hinder forensics, not prevent it. Therefore, as a hinderer, it works as it should. However, the system does not completely prevent forensics since human factor comes into play.

In Krautheim et al. (2010), a new mechanism is proposed for rooting trust in cloud environment called trusted virtual environment module. This paper introduces the high-level system architecture and design concepts of a necessarily somewhat TVEM system. In this paper [8], the TVEM protects information and conveys ownership in the cloud through the TEK generation process, which creates a dual rooted trust for the virtual environment and finally, when compared with other cloud computing security technologies such as private virtual infrastructure and locator bots, TVEMs enable a powerful solution to protecting information in cloud computing.

Trusted cloud computing platform provides a confidential execution of virtual machines by Santos et al (2009). Before launching their virtual machines, they allow the users to ensure whether the service is secure by VMware (2010).

The trusted computing group (TCG) claims the technology with TPMs has now reached about more than 600 million PCs by Ashford W (2012). TPM is tamper-resistant security chip that can be used for machine authentication, machine attestation, and data protection.

Table 1. A review on usage of TPM

Paper Details	Gist of the Paper
A framework for establishing trust in the cloud	This paper identifies the related challenges for establishing trust in the cloud and then proposes a foundation framework for identifying those challenges. Mainly focuses on IaaS. The framework presented in this paper is not enough by itself and it requires further extension as establishing trust in the cloud. Cloud provenance is not covered in this paper. It will be addressed in their future work
Design and implementation of a trusted monitoring framework for cloud platforms	In this paper, they have designed a trusted monitoring framework, which provides a chain of trust and have implemented this framework on Xen and integrate it with open nebula to improve the performance. But, this monitoring VM could crash under some circumstance. Therefore, recovering the monitoring functionality is something which is needed to be taken into consideration.
A hijacker's guide to communication interfaces of the trusted platform module	They proposed the some attacks in hijacking the trusted platform module. They have proposed active attack and implemented it. Though active attacks perform various activities, it does not allow direct retrieval of TPM protected data, like private parts of non-migratable keys. To extract this kind of information it is still necessary to resort to invasive high-effort method which directly targets the TPM chip by Winter et al (2013)
Security in cloud computing: Opportunities and challenges	This survey paper presented the security issues that arise due to the shared, virtualized, and public nature of the cloud computing paradigm. Subsequently, the counter measures presented in the literature are presented
Fine-grained refinement on TPM-based protocol applications	In this paper they formalize parts of the interfaces of TPM. Thus in their future work they try to expand our refinement framework to more general applications by formalizing all the interfaces of TPM

Though there exist a number of applications that makes use of TPM, there are number of problems that needs to be solved before we can fulfill the grand vision of trusted computing ISO/IEC-11889 (2009). In Sadeghi A-R, detailed explanation of TPM is given. It explains about the root of trust for storage (RTS), which is used for secure data storage implemented as hierarchy of keys.

TCG software stack (TSS) is the supporting software on the platform supporting the platform's TPM. TCG mainly explains with protected storage and protected capabilities. Since TPM is very expensive, the resources within the TPM should be kept in a restrictive manner BitLocker Drive Encryption Technical Overview (2012). The integration of various computing technologies into virtualized computing environments enables the protection of hardware Chen and Zhao (2012). Here, they addressed the problem of enabling secure migration in private clouds Danev et al (2011). The cloud networking (CloNe) infrastructure provides various services to virtualized network resources by Dhungana et al (2013). The framework supports AAI (authentication, authorization, and identity management) of entities in its infrastructure by Data Remanence solutions. A review on TPM usage is given in Table 1.

TPM FEATURES

Cryptographic Mechanisms and Algorithms

The following are the important features in cryptography that should be implemented in TPMs. These are explained and various cryptographic features are described in the following sections.

- Signing (RSA),
- Hashing (SHA-1),
- Keyed-Hash Message Authentication Code (HMAC),
- Random number generation (RNG),
- Asymmetric key (RSA) and nonce generation,
- Asymmetric encryption/decryption (RSA).

The specification that allows TPMs to implement various additional features or algorithms, such as elliptic curve asymmetric algorithms or DSA and there is no guarantee that these keys can migrate to other TPM devices or that other TPM devices will accept signatures from these additional algorithms. A minimum key length has been specified for some uses of TPM. Storage keys, for example, must be equivalent in strength to a 2048-bit or greater RSA key.

Random Number Generator

Nonce value can be generated by the TPM's random number generator which is used in key generation, and as randomness in signatures. The specification allows the RNG to be a Pseudo Random Number Generator implementation or a generator based on some source of hardware entropy. The RNG must be capable of providing at least 32 bytes of randomness at a time.

Key Generation

The Key Generation component of the TPM is capable of creating RSA key pairs as well as symmetric keys and nonce values. RSA key generation must follow the IEEE P1363 Standard Specifications for Public-Key Cryptography. The private key is held in a shielded location and usually does not leave the TPM unencrypted. Nonce values use the next n bits from the random number generator where n is the length of the nonce.

RSA Engine and Keys

TPMs use the RSA asymmetric algorithm encryption/decryption and digital signatures. While TPMs may support other algorithms for these purposes, they must support RSA, including key sizes of 512, 768, 1024, and 2048 bits. Other key sizes are also permissible, and the specification recommends a minimum key size is 2048 bits. The specification also states that the RSA public exponent must be $2^{16}+1$. The formats defined in the PKCS #1 standard are followed, but the TPM specification does specify how RSA algorithm should be implemented. This allows TPM implementations to use the Chinese Remainder Theorem or any other method of implementing RSA.

TPMs can sign both internal items and external data. TPMs do not perform signature verification, though, because verification does not use or expose private information and is better suited for software. Key pairs must be identified as either for signing or for encryption/decryption. TPMs do not allow a signature key to encrypt or an encryption key to sign because this can lead to attacks.

Secrets can also be assigned to keys so that use of the key requires knowledge of the secret. Keys can also be tied to specific system states or configurations (specified by PCR values). All keys have a parent key, which is used to encrypt the private part of the key if it needs to be stored off the TPM for future loading.

SHA-1 Engine

SHA-1 is the only hash algorithm that TPMs are required to support as of version 1.2 of the specification. This could become a concern since there are collision attacks against SHA-1. The SHA-1 functionality is used by the TPM and via exposed interfaces. These interfaces can be used for measurement taking during boot and to provide a hash function in platforms that have limited capabilities. The functionality is not intended to provide an accelerated hash capability, and there are no specific performance requirements for TPM hash services. Therefore, this engine should only be used to compute hash values of small chunks of data. Larger chucks of data should be hashed outside the TPM if possible.

HMAC Engine

TPMs support the calculation of HMACs according to RFC 2104 with a key size of 20 bytes and a block size of 64 bytes. The contents and order of the data depend on the TPM command that uses the HMAC engine

Symmetric Encryption Engine

TPMs use symmetric encryption to encrypt data during various operations (authentication and transport sessions). In these cases, a one-time pad is XORed with the data. In some cases, the nonce is large enough to perform a direct XOR, but in others, the entropy must be expanded using the MGF1 function from PKCS #1. (The specification allows for use of AES or Triple DES in use models where it would be beneficial.) Symmetric encryption is also used to encrypt protected data that is stored outside the TPM. For this purpose, the TPM specification allows the designer to use any symmetric algorithm that is deemed to have the proper level of protection.

While TPMs use symmetric encryption internally, they do not expose this functionality or the algorithm for general data encryption. As such, the TPM can only generate, store, and protect symmetric keys. The TCG FAQ does, however, leave the door open for use of AES or other symmetric encryption algorithms in future versions of the TPM specification.

Time Stamping

TPMs provide a type of time stamping service for various pieces of data. The time stamp that TPMs provide is the number of timer ticks the TPM has counted and not a universal time clock (UTC) value. The caller must associate the tick count with the actual UTC time, and the TPM specification provides a complex protocol that can be used to accomplish this. Time stamping is further complicated by the affect of various power states on the tick count and the differences in these states on various platforms.

Platform Configuration Registers

A Platform Configuration Register (PCR) is a 160-bit register for storing integrity measurements. TPMs must have at least 16 PCRs, all of which are protected and inside the TPM. While the number of PCRs is limited, they can each represent an unlimited number of measurements. This is accomplished by cryptographically hashing all updates to a PCR such that the new PCR value is dependent on the previous value and the value to add. The ordering and one-way properties of cryptographic hashes are particularly important for this use case.

The TPM_Seal operation can be used to encrypt data such that it can only be decrypted on a specific platform. Callers of this operation may specify PCR values required to unseal the data. Future TPM_Unseal operations will reveal the sealed data only if attempted on the same platform and the PCR value(s) match. In this way, the sealed data is protected from changes in the configuration. TPM_Seal and TPM_Unseal both require "AuthData" (similar to a password). This means that data can be sealed such that only a specific user can access it on a given client under a specific configuration.

Identities

Some TCG use cases require that the platform be identifiable or prove that it has a genuine TPM. There are two types of identifying keys, the Endorsement Key (EK) and Attestation Identity Keys (AIK).

Figure 2. Keys in TPM

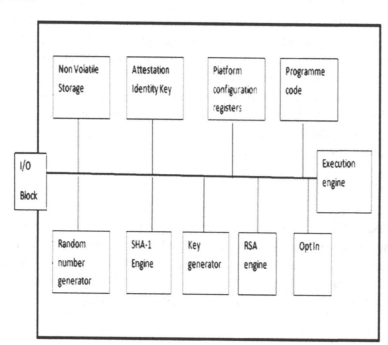

Endorsement Key

The Endorsement Key is a 2048-bit RSA key pair that is unique to the TPM and therefore the platform containing the TPM. The key pair is generated at manufacture time, and once it is set, it can never be changed. The private key is never exposed outside the TPM. The public key is used for attestation and for encryption of sensitive data sent to the TPM. Because of security reasons and privacy concerns, the EK cannot perform signatures. The EK (along with other infrastructure) is also used to recognize a genuine TPM.

Attestation Identity Keys

An Attestation Identity Key is an alias to the Endorsement Key. Like the EK, the AIK is a 2048-bit RSA key pair. Unlike the EK, there can be many (virtually unlimited) AIKs, and they can be generated at any time by the TPM Owner. Also unlike the EK, an AIK is a signature key and can perform signatures on information generated by the TPM, including PCR values, other keys, and TPM status information. AIKs cannot sign other data because this would make it possible for an attacker to create a fake PCR value.

Because many AIKs can be created, they cannot all be stored in the TPM. Therefore, AIKs may be stored on some general-purpose storage device. When stored outside the TPM, the AIK must be encrypted and its integrity must be protected.

An AIK can be used for platform authentication, platform attestation and certification of keys. A protocol known as Direct Anonymous Attestation uses zero-knowledge-proof technology to allow the EK to anonymously establish that an AIK was generated in a TPM. This allows the quality of an AIK to be confirmed without identifying which TPM generated it.

Use Models

Protecting Information

Clients contain a lot of information that should be protected from view, copying, and use by others. This includes keys, passwords, and other types of data. The first two are particularly important because some of them are used to authenticate to networks.

Protection of User Keys

Users can generate an RSA key pair in the TPM and specify that the private key never leave the chip unprotected. Even though the private key can is only known as plaintext inside the TPM, it can still be used for general signing and encryption purposes. If the private key is protected and an attacker gains control of the system, he or she may be able to execute encryption, decryption, and digital signing operations on any data he or she chooses while in control of the system, but this capability will cease once they lose control (i.e. the system is patched or powered off) because the private key cannot be copied to another system.

Additional security is possible that will prevent an attacker from even using the keys while in control of the system. Keys can be bound to specific PCR values such that use of the keys is not permitted if the PCR value is incorrect as would occur if the system has been improperly booted or the integrity of measured files has been compromised. In this way, the keys can be protected if a key logger, worm, etc. are installed.

Protection of User Passwords

Passwords can be encrypted by an RSA public key whose matching private key is protected by the TPM. If the private key requires specific a PCR value to be used, the password cannot be decrypted if a compromise has been detected. In this way, passwords cannot be obtained no matter what the attacker does. Protected storage could also be used to augment password storage programs, such as Password Safe these programs also encourage the use of strong (long, random) passwords.

Protection of User Data

The TPM can also be used to protect files and file system keys in the same way that user keys can be protected. Thus, if system compromise is detected, the TPM can prevent access to or use of the file or file system key. As a result, the encrypted files will be protected from theft or modification. Note that the user may still be able to destroy a file system depending on the file system and operating system implementation and configuration.

There are a couple options to protect large amounts of data. The easiest and quickest is to encrypt the large block of data using a one-time symmetric key then use the TPM to protect the symmetric key.

Trusted Boot

The TPM supports a trusted boot mechanism that can help detect root kits and other types of security compromises. During a trusted boot, hashes of configuration information throughout the boot sequence are stored in the PCRs. This configuration information may include the BIOS, option ROMs, Master Boot Record (MBR), OS loader, kernel, and other operating system information. Once the client has booted in a known clean state, keys and other information can be sealed – encrypted and tied to the PCR value(s). During subsequent boots, the sealed data will only be unsealed if the PCR values match. Consequently, if the configuration is changed or a virus, back door, or root kit has been installed, the PCR value(s) will be incorrect and the protected information will not be unsealed. The boot process itself is not stopped or changed by the TPM. This protects the sensitive information and any data it may protect. As a result, the user would also be informed of the compromise and could take action to address it.

The recorded measurements can also be used by multiple challengers to determine what boot process occurred and in turn whether they trust it. The TPM signs the stored measurement before sending it to challengers to prove that the measurement came from the TPM. The TPM provides the benefit that of measurement, storage, and reporting of integrity metrics in a secure manner.

Platform Authentication

Each TPM also has a unique identity (EK) that can be used to generate other identities (AIKs). Since the TPM is attached to the client and cannot be (easily) removed or replaced, the TPM can use these identities to prove that it is a specific client. This is different from user or even smart card authentication, which only proves that a specific user is using the system (or someone else is using their credentials).

If a challenger, say a network, has prior knowledge about permitted clients, it is possible for the TPM to authenticate itself to the challenger. That is, it can prove that it is one of the known and permitted clients. This allows a network or server to identify the clients that are accessing or requesting to access it and only permit access to clients that it knows and trusts.

Attestation

Attestation is one of the central features of Trusted Computing. It is the process of a client declaring the current state of the platform in a way that is trusted by the challenger. The challenger can then take actions based on the state. The basis for TPM attestation is the measuring of the platform – both the hardware and software – using the PCRs and/or digital signatures. TPMs allow a platform to attest that the platform configuration is as expected and has not been changed. The "configuration" can include as much information as is required. The TPM can also attest to a trusted boot and the information collected during that process. Attestation could also be used to prove that antivirus definitions are up to date. In this case, the client could measure the antivirus definitions file and create a digital signature of the measurement. The client could then send the signed message to the challenger. Attestation allows an administrative system to check the health (security, configuration, software, etc.) of a client to confirm that it meets a security policy and has not been compromised.

Threat Model

Sensitive Information

The TPM and other elements of the TCG specifications are designed to protect against or mitigate the potential damage caused by a variety of threats and attacks. This paper focuses on those that affect PC clients (desktops and notebooks).

PC clients have a large number of vulnerabilities, known and unknown, and this is unlikely to change given the nature and practices of the software industry. In addition, keeping patches up to date for all software installed on a system is time consuming and a large percentage of systems do not have all applicable patches. While networks and servers offer the most value for attackers, they are also better protected than PC clients.

In addition, PC clients often contain information, such as keys and passwords that can be used to access and compromise networks and servers or can be used for distributed attacks, such as Distributed Denial of Service (DDoS), against them. Keys could also be used to decrypt sensitive information, steal a digital identity, or forge signatures. PC clients also contain information, such as credit card and social security numbers, that is itself valuable. As a result of these and other factors, attackers are increasingly focused on PC clients. TPMs should support preventing attackers from being able to find information on a compromised client that can be used to compromise another system for which the client or its user has access. The TPM should also enable a network administrator to prevent a compromised client from being able to compromise or disrupt the rest of the network.

The information on clients could include encryption or signing keys, passwords, and personal or proprietary information. The TPM is designed to protect sensitive information on PC clients as well as the servers and networks they may connect to. In addition, some private RSA keys never leave the TPM, so it is impossible to obtain them directly by software means. The TPM does *not* attempt to reduce the number of vulnerabilities in software or prevent an attacker from exploiting those vulnerabilities. Instead, the TPM seeks to detect when the client is compromised and limit the damage and protect sensitive information when it occurs. If the TPM and related software are configured correctly, the attacker cannot access the sensitive information regardless of what he or she does. Attacks on sensitive information should be no better than a brute force attack.

One primary attack that the TPM seeks to thwart is attack on keys when cryptographic operations are performed in software. It has been definitively proven[1] that even very good encryption is vulnerable to attack performed in the usual locations, such as memory. TPM cryptography operations are performed in a closed hardware environment, protecting the keys at their most vulnerable point.

The TPM should prevent theft (copying to another system for use there) of RSA keys as well as improper use of keys when the system has been compromised. The latter is very dependent on the system firmware (i.e. BIOS), TPM Software Stack (TSS) and how they work detect that a system has been compromised, but the TPM provides all necessary framework.

The TPM also allows multiple users to protect sensitive information on a shared client. Even if a user has permission to use the client, they still may not have access to other user's secrets.

If any encryption key-pair is compromised, the data it protects and any data protected by keys that it protects may also be compromised. Once an encryption key-pair is compromised, all data ever encrypted with it is compromised and this cannot be recovered from, except by deleting all copies of the data encrypted with that key (including ones that may have been stolen). Likewise, once a digital signature key is compromised, the attacker can sign anything they wish. If certificates are used, the certificate could be revoked. The TPM cannot detect compromises of its own keys. Instead it protects them by not letting some private keys leave the TPM, encrypting its keys when they leave the TPM, and detecting compromise of the client software.

Keys and other sensitive information may be stored outside the TPM. For data stored outside the TPM, the protection of the sensitive information is only as strong as the encryption algorithm by which it is protected. The TPM cannot increase the strength of an algorithm with respect to algorithmic (i.e. brute force and differential cryptanalysis) attacks. For example, if a large file is encrypted with DES and the DES key is encrypted with a 2048-bit RSA key and stored in the TPM, the encrypted file is still subject to attacks on the DES encryption, which should be much easier than attacking the 2048-bit RSA key.

The TPM is intended to protect sensitive information even when hardware is physically stolen. This is important because the data on stolen clients, such as notebooks, is often more valuable than the hardware. Still, the TPM spec does not require protection against physical tampering. Thus, if the client is physically stolen, it may be possible for the attacker to steal sensitive information by means such as RF analysis, but it would be difficult. These attacks are not covered in this paper.

There is debate as to whether the TPM is designed to protect against attacks on digital rights management (DRM) mechanisms, and some of it is related to the physical protections of the TPM. DRM uses and attacks on those are also not covered in this paper.

Platform Authentication and Attestation

When a compromised client is connected to a network, it can be a threat to the entire network even if the sensitive information on the client is protected. Therefore, it is important to be able to identify unauthorized or compromised clients and prevent them from connecting to the network. Software-only methods of authenticating clients can be circumvented because the authentication information, such as the computer name or MAC address, can be forged. Network administrators should be able to prevent access to the network to specific authorized client hardware. They should also be able to prevent access to properly configured and uncompromised clients before they gain access. Furthermore, an attacker or rogue client should not be able to forge its authentication as an authorized client or its configuration and current state.

If one system is compromised, it should not enable the compromise of other systems or the network. If the prevention mechanism is defeated, the entire network infrastructure, clients, and servers could be compromised or prevented from serving their purpose.

CONCLUSION

Thus TPM has a lot to do with embedding trust in any kind of application by making the chip to be placed in all the machines and also network trust can be of future research direction where the data that travel across globe are to be protected and provided trust.

REFERENCES

Abbadi, I. M., & Muntaha, A. (2012). A framework for establishing trust in cloud. *Computers & Electrical Engineering*, *38*(5), 1073–1087. doi:10.1016/j.compeleceng.2012.06.006

Ali, M., Khan, S. U., & Vasilakos, A. V. (2015). Security in cloud computing: Opportunities and challenges. *Inf Sci*, *305*, 357–383. doi:10.1016/j.ins.2015.01.025

Ashford, W. (2012). *Will this be the year TPM comes of age?*. Retrieved from: http://www.computerweekly.com/news/2240157874/Analysis-2012-Will-this-be-the-year-TPM-finallycomes-of-age

BitLocker Drive Encryption Technical Overview. (n.d.). *Microsoft TechNet*. Retrieved from: http://technet.microsoft.com/en-us/library/cc732774(v=ws.10).aspx

Chen, D., & Zhao, H. (2012). The data security and privacy protection issues in cloud computing. In International Conference on Computer Science and Electron ICS Engineering (ICCSEE, IEEE). doi:10.1109/ICCSEE.2012.193

Cloud Computing. (n.d.a). Retrieved from: https://zapthink.com/2011/05/19 /data-remanence-cloud-computing-shellgame

Cloud Computing. (n.d.b). Retrieved from: http://www.cornwallcloud services.co.uk/index.php/easyblog/categories/listings/theinternetofthings

Cloud Computing Security. (n.d.a). Retrieved from: http://searchcompliance.techtarget.com/definition/cloudcomputing-security

Cloud Computing Security. (n.d.b). Retrieved from: http://www.forbes.com/sites/netapp/2012/12/12/cloud-security-1/

Cloud Storage. (n.d.). Retrieved from: http://securosis.com/blog/securing-cloud-data-withvirtual-private-storage/

Danev, B., Masti, R. J., Karame, G. O., & Capkun, S. (2011). Enabling secure VM migration in private clouds. In *Proceedings of the ACM 27th annual computer security applications conference*. doi:10.1145/2076732.2076759

Data Remanence. (n.d.). Retrieved from http://elastic-security.com/2010/01/07/data-remanence-in-the-cloud/

Data Remanence. (n.d.a). Retrieved from: http://www.itrenew.com/what-is-data-remanence

Data Remanence. (n.d.b). Retrieved from: http://en.wikipedia. org/wiki/Data_remanence

Data Remanence Solutions. (n.d.). Retrieved from http://fas.org/irp/nsa/rainbow tg025-2.htm

Deqing, Z., Wenrong, Z., Weizhong, Q., & Guofu, X. (2013). Design and implementation of a trusted monitoring framework for cloud platforms. *Future Generation Computer Systems*, *29*(8), 2092–2102. doi:10.1016/j.future.2012.12.020

Dhungana, R. D., Mohammad, A., Sharma, A., & Schoen, I. (2013). Identity management framework for cloud networking infrastructure. In *IEEE International conference on innovations in information technology (IIT)*. doi:10.1109/Innovations.2013.6544386

Fan, K., Mao, D., Lu, Z., & Wu, J. (2013). OPS: offline patching scheme for the images management in a secure cloud environment. In *IEEE International conference on services computing (SCC)*. doi:10.1109/SCC.2013.57

Goh, W., Leong, P. C., & Yeo, C. K. (2011). The plausibly-deniable, practical trusted platform module based anti-forensics client-server system. *IEEE Journal on Selected Areas in Communications*.

Goh, W., & Yeo, C.K. (2013). *Teaching an old trusted platform module: repurposing a tpm for an identity-based signature scheme*. Academic Press.

Huang, W., Xiong, Y., Miao, F., Wang, X., Wu, C., Lu, Q., & Xudong, G. (2013). Fine-grained refinement on tpm-based protocol applications. *IEEE Trans Info Forensics Sec, 8*(6).

ISO/IEC-11889:2009. (2009). *Information technology – Trusted Platform Module*. ISO.

Johannes, W., & Kurt, D. (2013). A hijacker guide to communication interfaces of the trusted platform module. *Computers & Mathematics with Applications (Oxford, England), 65*(5), 748–761. doi:10.1016/j.camwa.2012.06.018

John Krautheim, F., Phatak, D.S., & Sherman, A.T. (2010). *Introducing trusted virtual environment module: a new mechanism for rooting trust in cloud computing*. Academic Press.

Ramon, S., Caceres, R., Kenneth, A., Goldman, R., Sailer, P., & Leendert, R. (2006). vTPM: Virtualizing the Trusted Platform Module. *USENIX Association, Security'06:15th USENIX Security*.

Sadeghi, A-R. (n.d.). *Trusted platform module, lecture slides for secure, trusted and trustworthy computing.* Technische Universität Darmstadt. Retrieved from: http://www.trust.informatik.darmstadt.de/fileadmin/ user_upload/Group_TRUST/LectureSlides/STCWS2011/Chap3__Trusted_Platform_Module.pdf.pdf

Santos, N., Gummadi, K. P., & Rodrigues, R. (2009). Towards trusted cloud computing. In *Proceedings of the conference on cloud computing.* Berkeley, CA: USENIX Association.

Schmidt Andreas, U., Leicher, A., Brett, A., Shah, Y., & Cha, I. (2013). Tree-formed verification data for trusted platforms. *Computers & Security, 32,* 19–35. doi:10.1016/j.cose.2012.09.004

The TCG Software Stack (TSS) Specification-version 1.20 Errata A Golden Candidate 2. (n.d.). Trusted Computing Group.

VMware. (2010). *VMware vCenter Server.* Retrieved from http://www.vmware.com/products/vcenter-server/

Chapter 15

RFID and Dead–Reckoning–Based Indoor Navigation for Visually Impaired Pedestrians

Kai Li Lim
The University of Western Australia, Australia

Lee Seng Yeong
Sunway University, Malaysia

Kah Phooi Seng
Charles Sturt University, Australia

Li-Minn Ang
Charles Sturt University, Australia

ABSTRACT

This chapter presents an indoor navigation solution for visually impaired pedestrians, which employs a combination of a radio frequency identification (RFID) tag array and dead-reckoning to achieve positioning and localisation. This form of positioning aims to reduce the deployment cost and complexity of pure RFID array implementations. This is a smartphone-based navigation system that leverages the new advancements of smartphone hardware to achieve large data handling and fast pathfinding. Users interact with the system through speech recognition and synthesis. This approach allows the system to be accessible to the masses due to the ubiquity of smartphones today. Uninformed pathfinding algorithms are implemented onto this system based on our previous study on the implementation suitability of uninformed searches. Testing results showed that this navigation system is suitable for use for the visually impaired pedestrians; and the pathfinding algorithms performed consistently according to our algorithm proposals.

INTRODUCTION

Pedestrians who are visually impaired face numerous challenges whenever they are required to step out of their dwellings to move to another location. Assistive technologies exist to alleviate the mobility challenges faced by visually impaired pedestrians by utilising modern electronic innovations to guide the visually impaired user. With the advent of ubiquitous mobile and wireless technologies, there is a growing demand for assistive technologies from the visually impaired community. This is especially true whereby automotive navigation systems, along with many mainstream and modern pedestrian naviga-

DOI: 10.4018/978-1-5225-1785-6.ch015

tion systems implemented (e.g. on wearable technologies and smartphones) are evidently designed and developed for the sighted pedestrian, with little or no regard for the visually impaired. This, along with and other challenges faced in the mobility of the visually impaired is highlighted in (Williams, Hurst, & Kane, 2013), with extensive reviews and case studies. These reviews include those of assistive mobility aids for the visually impaired, where case studies are conducted by interviewing a selected group of visually impaired pedestrians across the United States. The authors queried the participants regarding their usage of smartphone-based assistive technologies and gathered that only 13% of the users do not use assistive navigation technologies. There is, therefore, a clear demand for assistive technologies.

According to (Dakopoulos & Bourbakis, 2010), navigation assistive technologies provides a form of visual substitution for the visually impaired. It can be categorised into three types of devices/aids:

1. Electronic travel aids (ETAs) for mobility and displacement,
2. Electronic orientation aids (EOAs) for orientation and bearings, and
3. Position locator devices (PLDs) for positioning and localisation.

The ETA is usually the main component in a navigation system for these pedestrians, and it is typically connected to an EOA and a PLD (aka ETA system). The ETA handles more vital processes for the system, which includes pathfinding computation and user guidance, among others. This chapter emphasises on pathfinding algorithms and their roles in ETA systems for blind pedestrians. An ETA system, like other pedestrian navigation systems, follows the process in Figure 1 to function.

ETAs remain an area of popular research interest, the growing smartphone adaptation rate, along with the ubiquity of navigation systems, catalysed the need of ETA systems for the visually impaired. These days, the processing capabilities of smartphones are improving immensely, with octa-core processors finding a commonplace within new smartphone launches. Hence, many current works on ETA systems proposed are smartphone-based (Au et al., 2013; Guy & Truong, 2012; Kamiński & Bruniecki, 2012; Uddin & Suny, 2015), where they are versatilely used to provide route calculation, speech input via speech-to-text, and speech output via text-to-speech, which is used in guidance (Ceipidor, Medaglia, & Sciarretta, 2010; Uddin & Suny, 2015). Alternative methods to guidance may involve external devices, such as a haptic device (Ando, Tsukahara, Seki, & Fujie, 2012; Todd, Mallya, Majeed, Rojas, & Naylor, 2014). ETA Route calculation (pathfinding) requires that the smartphone communicates with PLDs and EOAs such as a GPS receiver and a compass to localise and position the user before it can commence, as

Figure 1. Process of navigation in an ETA, texts on arrows depict the procedure for navigation

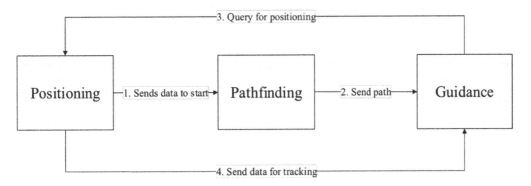

illustrated in Figure 1. Besides GPS receivers, PLDs can exist as different systems; in the case of indoor positioning, where GPS signals are unable to penetrate buildings, alternative positioning approaches are in active research. Examples include received signal strength indicator (RSSI) trilateration, where positioning is achieved by the measurement of signal strength from at least three wireless access points (AP) (Au et al., 2013; Ran, Helal, & Moore, 2004); radio frequency identification (RFID) arrays, where the pedestrian equipped with a RFID transponder traverses an environment fitted with RFID tags fixed on the floor (Di Giampaolo, 2010; Fernandes, Filipe, Costa, & Barroso, 2014; Liao et al., 2013); image positioning; where cameras are mounted on the pedestrian, which captures points of interests or barcodes that are matched within the database to achieve positioning (Beeharee & Steed, 2006; Filipe et al., 2012); dead-reckoning, which uses sensors to track the strides of the pedestrian (Hua, Marshall, & Wai, 2007; Kang & Han, 2015; Kourogi & Kurata, 2014); and visible light communication, where location data can also be relayed to the system (Hyun-Seung, Deok-Rae, Se-Hoon, Yong-Hwan, & Sang-Kook, 2013; Nakajima & Haruyama, 2012). A detailed review of the positioning methods for indoor navigation systems and their methods of pedestrian guidance is covered in (Fallah, Apostolopoulos, Bekris, & Folmer, 2013). Whichever the PLD system used, the positioning data obtained can then be sent to the ETA to start pathfinding.

Pathfinding is the computing process of finding the best route between two locational points on a map. The best route can be determined by a combination of the fastest route, the shortest route, and the simplest route (with the fewest number of turns). Pathfinding can either be informed or uninformed. Informed pathfinding is performed using informed search algorithms, where environmental information known as heuristics is fed into the algorithm to improve its search process. Examples of informed search algorithms include the A* search (Hart, Nilsson, & Raphael, 1968) and the iterative-deepening A* (IDA*) search (Korf, 1985).Conversely, uninformed pathfinding is performed using uninformed search algorithms, where pathfinding is performed sans the heuristics of informed algorithms, leading to an exhaustive search across the map. Examples of uninformed search algorithms include the Dijkstra's algorithm (Dijkstra, 1959) and the iterative-deepening depth-first search (IDDFS) (Korf, 1985). Out of the motivation to introduce a fast and memory efficient uninformed search algorithm, the boundary iterative-deepening depth-first search was proposed in (Lim, Seng, Yeong, Ang, & Ch'ng, 2015). Further improving on the speed of the BIDDFS, the findings in (Lim, Seng, Yeong, Ang, & Ch'ng, 2015) revealed that uninformed pathfinding is well-suited for use in indoor environments, especially when spaces are confined to corridors and walkways, and that indoor environments like these actually makes the heuristic calculation in informed algorithms redundant. Noting that most ETAs that implement pathfinding implements an informed search algorithm, this proposal of an ETA that uses uninformed search algorithm is a better alternative for indoor, path constricted environments.

On the prototyping front, an ETA that is built using modern wireless mobile technologies should incorporate recent devices such as a smartphone that is capable of performing route calculations and provides guidance for the user. The use of a smartphone should facilitate a wireless interface between the different modules and devices used within the ETA. For example, positioning devices can connect to the smartphone through ad-hoc Wi-Fi, whereby the smartphone will act as a hub for the positioning devices to connect to, which will then receive positioning data from these devices. A RFID positioning system is suitable for implementation for a wireless ETA, whereby ZigBee can be used to facilitate a many-to-many connection between the RFID tags. However, the accuracy of a RFID tag is limited to its effective tagging radius; increasing the signal output of the transponders using more powerful transponders, or by using signal amplifier is a method for improving the likelihood of successful tags.

In this chapter, the authors introduce an intelligent wireless ETA for visually impaired pedestrians with an emphasis on indoor environments, where positioning and localisation are achieved using a RFID/ dead-reckoning hybrid model. This is a portable and mobile navigation system and user communication is incorporated using speech recognition and synthesis. The main function of this system is to guide a visually impaired from one point to another in an indoor environment, and its performance benchmark is measured in this chapter as its pathfinding efficiency. A visually impaired pedestrian will initiate the navigation process by saying his/her intended destination after a voice prompt, then the system will perform pathfinding, and subsequently guides the user to his/her destination. The motivation for proposing this ETA is to address the current issues pertaining existing RFID-based ETAs whilst acknowledging the demand of accessible ETAs from the visually impaired community; as well as to offer a test bed for the authors' pathfinding algorithms to run on real-world hardware and scenarios. This ETA aims to be easily deployed by premise owners and adopted by the visually impaired community while providing simple and accurate navigational guidance.

The remainder of this chapter is organised as follows:

- Section 2 presents an in-depth look at the ETA and its components.
- Section 3 discusses the software requirement of this ETA, including the smartphone application and pathfinding programming.
- Section 4 documents the testing methodology and results conducted on the ETA.
- Finally, future directions the concluding remark is given in Section 5.

SYSTEM ARCHITECTURE AND COMPONENTS

This ETA system is conceptualised based on the reviews on currently available ETAs for the visually impaired, and it is able to harness the high processing performance of new smartphones. A smartphone is hence the core of this ETA device, where it will be paired with two PLDs and an EOA. This is an Android-based smartphone, meaning that the pathfinding algorithm will be programmed as part of an Android app, which interfaces with the PLDs and EOA. This system concept for the visually impaired is as illustrated in Figure 2, where the user attached module is worn by the pedestrian and communicates with the floor deployed RFID system in a one-to-many configuration. The smartphone communicates with the RFID system wirelessly through ZigBee (using the XBee Pro (Digi International, 2008)), which facilitates one-to-many connection. Within the main module, communications with the user can be performed via the Bluetooth headset using speech recognition and synthesis from an Android smartphone (the Samsung Galaxy Note II (Samsung Electronics Co. Ltd., 2014)). Positioning and tracking hardware can be connected to the computing device via RS232 through a microprocessor board (e.g. an Arduino), communicating with the Android application. The RFID module provides positioning relative to the map through strategically placed RFID transponders such as the Texas Instruments TRF7960A (Texas Instruments, 2014) module. The DRM provides positioning and tracking relative to the user's location, and the user's orientation is supplied by a digital compass, the Honeywell HMC6352 (Honeywell, 2006). These components constitute the ETA and they are as photographed in Figure 3, with Figure 3(a) illustrating the physical connections between the hardware modules.

Figure 2. System hardware block diagram

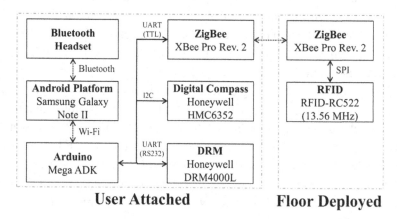

Figure 3. (a) The hardware components of the ETA (left), and (b) the Samsung Galaxy Note II smartphone

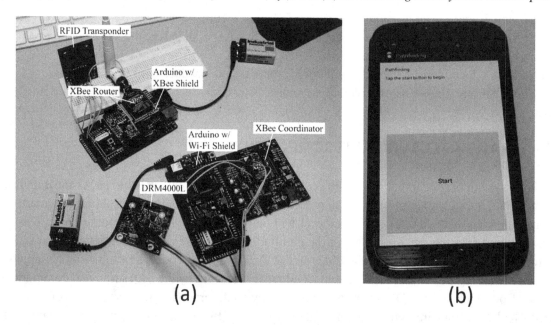

RFID Positioning with Dead-Reckoning Localization

This system employs two PLDs for positioning as an effort to reduce implementation cost and complexity when compared against conventional environment-wide fixtures such as using a dense RFID fixture layout. The PLDs consist of a dead-reckoning module (DRM) and a RFID positioning system. The Mifare RFID-RC522 (NXP Semiconductors, 2014) and the Honeywell DRM4000L (Honeywell, 2011) were used as the RFID transponder and the DRM in this system respectively. To alleviate the need of installing many RFID transponders for better positioning accuracy, the DRM is introduced in this system to complement the RFID transponders in tracking the pedestrian's movements. The DRM is able to ensure that the pedestrian is moving within his/her intended route (e.g. in a straight line) without having to resort to redundant RFID transmitters placed throughout the path of the pedestrian. The RFID positioning system then consists of a RFID tag (placed in the pedestrian's shoe sole), and RFID transponders; each successful tag positions the user on the map. Instead of installing the transponders with fixed distances from each other throughout the environment, they are installed on the floor at several critical locations within the navigation environment, such as at junctions, stairs, or dead-ends. This reduces the installation and maintenance cost on the navigation environment. The orientation of the user is provided by a digital compass, which is the dedicated EOA in this system. This is supplemented by the DRM, which is also able to provide orientation data.

The Android Platform

The Android platform is selected for implementation because of the wide availability of Android devices capable of fast mobile computing, and the ease of developing Android application using the Java programming language, royalty free. The recent advent of many multi-cored Android smartphone is an advantage for parallel processes such as pathfinding algorithms. The Samsung Galaxy Note II (Model: GT-7100) is used as the Android device for the development and implementation of this system. It functions as the main processing device in this navigation system. It is responsible for retrieving positioning data from the PLDs and EOA, and then processing it for pathfinding, and subsequently guiding the user over the Android application. Tethering is turned on and the smartphone functions as a Wi-Fi access point (AP), allowing the Arduino to connect to it, where the positioning data will be received. This allows the Arduino to find the Android AP and subsequently allowing User Datagram Protocol (UDP) communications over Wi-Fi. The user may then hold the home button to start the S-Voice to open the navigation application via the voice command "Open Pathfinding". Pathfinding will commence once the smartphone receives data from the Arduino. Once pathfinding is completed, guidance can be delivered by the device via Google's speech synthesis API, which is forwarded to the user via a paired Bluetooth headset (a wired headset works just as fine).

The Arduino Platform

This system prototype implements the Arduino Mega ADK for Android microcontroller board, with the ATmega2560 as the microcontroller. Two Arduino Mega ADK boards are used – one in the main module (attached with Wi-Fi shield, worn by the user), and another on the RFID module (attached with XBee shield, as a serial peripheral interface (SPI) to transistor-transistor logic (TTL) converter). This board is chosen for implementation due to its ability to support up to four serial communications simultaneously, along with SPI support. The Mega ADK features a Type-A USB port capable of connecting to an Android device via accessory mode. However, Wi-Fi was chosen over accessory mode to allow a wireless implementation, and that the Samsung Galaxy Note II does not support accessory mode.

Component Interfacing

Communications between the RFID flood-installed RFID transponders and the RFID module's Arduino handled via the ZigBee (IEEE 802.15.4) standard. For the purpose of this prototype, the XBee Pro Series 2 modules are used. ZigBee is chosen for this purpose due to its ability to support wireless data transfers in a mesh network with an advertised indoor range of 40m (Digi International, 2008). This is because multiple RFID readers will be interfacing with the navigation system simultaneously.

The XBees are programmed in two ways, and each connects to an Arduino board – the XBee connected to the smartphone-connected Arduino is programmed as the coordinator, where it receives incoming signals from the routers; the second set of XBees connects to the RFID transponders (via an Arduino Mega ADK), and are programmed as the routers. The coordinator XBees connects to the DRM and the DRM outputs in RS232. These XBees are not able to support the RS232 and hence an MAX3232CSE RS232 to TTL converter is used in tandem with the devices, which are connected as shown in Figure 4. To interface the DRM4000L to the Arduino, an initialisation parameter is required to be sent. The parameter "INIP" is sent to the DRM4000L from the Arduino to receive latitude and longitudinal data, and beginning position error for a connection without GPS. The DRM4000L ensures that the user follows the path from pathfinding; any deviation from the path would be detected by the system. On the router XBees' side, each device is connected directly to an Arduino that is programmed to convert the SPI signals from the RC522 into a UART signal that can be processed on the smartphone. As soon as a RFID tag is read by the RC522, the unique identification number (UID) of the tag is obtained, thus identifying the user treading on the transponder. A complete navigation system will use multiple RFID transponders placed at POIs around the navigation environment, each connected to an XBee through an SPI to UART converter. To provide absolute localisation to the system, each transponder is assigned a unique identification number, which is passed to the Arduino in a string datatype via the ZigBee mesh network to the ZigBee coordinator, which is connected to the Arduino in the main module. The effective range of the RFID transponder was measured with a ruler with the RFID tag moving increasingly closer to the transponder until the tag is read. Ten measurements were taken for the card tag and coin tag and the result was averaged to be 2.4cm. To increase the accuracy of absolute positioning, the density of implementation of the RFID transponders is to be increased, requiring more Transponder-ZigBee combinations to be implemented in an environment.

The UDP (User Datagram Protocol) is used for communications between the Android and Arduino platforms. The Arduino streams data from the positioning devices to the Android to be processed for user guidance on the route from pathfinding. Hence, the Arduino is made the transmitter and the Android device is made the receiver. UDP communications on the Arduino starts by defining the SSID name of the AP to connect and the DHCP server upon connection provides the IP address. The Arduino defines a listening port during initialisation. The listening port is used to wait for incoming connections before the data is streamed to the Android, henceforth known as the data request. Each set of data received from the positioning devices by the Arduino is cast and parsed as a single string, delimited by underscores ('_') (e.g. "3.0_128.5_31.5_A"). The Android device then splits the received string into their individual

Figure 4. The block diagram showing connections between the DRM4000L, MAX3232CSE, and the Arduino Mega ADK

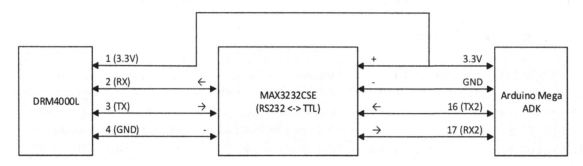

data set (using the String.split function) to be stored as variables to be processed by the Android device. Each string passed by the Arduino represents a set of data for an instance. The listening of data is set as a dedicated thread pool on the Android device and it is constantly listening to the UDP broadcast from the Arduino, it is able to receive UDP messages up to an interval of 10ms.

Based on the hardware block diagram in Figure 2, on the user attached side, the Arduino Mega ADK connects serially to the XBee and the DRM module through the TTL UART standard. It connects to the DRM through an RS232 to TTL converter, as the DRM outputs in the RS232 standard. The digital compass interfaces via the I2C standard and is connected to the analogue inputs on the Arduino. The Wi-Fi Shield attached to the Arduino in the main module allows the Arduino to connect to the Android AP. Once a Wi-Fi connection has been established, the Android is assigned an IP address via DHCP by the Android AP. On the floor-deployed side, these RFID transponders use the Arduino Mega ADK alongside the RFID reader to convert its SPI output of to UART usable by the XBee. In other words, the RFID reader connects to the SPI ports on the Arduino, which are then converted and serially outputted in UART to the XBee.

SOFTWARE REQUIREMENTS

Programming the Arduino

The Arduino devices are programmed using Arduino 1.5.4 for Mac. Every Arduino source code is separated into two functions – the initialisation (start()) and an infinite loop (loop()). This section describes the programming of the Arduino worn by the user. (The Arduino connected to the RFID transponder simply reads the RFID tags in SPI and outputs the signal in TTL) Before the loop begins, the Arduino is programmed to initialise the three serial connections with their baud rate, using the Serial0, Serial1, and Serial2 headers for the USB (connected to the Mac), XBee, and DRM respectively. During this initialisation, the Arduino is required to send the initialisation parameters "INIP" to the DRM and "A" to the digital compass (if attached), which are sent in strings. Finally, the Arduino connects to the Wi-Fi access point on the Android device through the defined service set identification (SSID) name. When a Wi-Fi connection is established, a confirmation is printed to Serial0, which can be viewed using Arduino's serial monitor. The loop then begins.

In the Arduino loop function, the Arduino is programmed to first wait for a packet from the Android device to enable the Arduino to identify the source IP address of the device before a reply can be sent. Once the data is received, the packet string is read, saved, and displayed in the serial monitor, together with the Android's IP address. The Android device now listens for replies on positioning data from the Arduino. To receive positioning data, the data streams from each of the positioning device is read at every 10ms interval and saved in variables. At every other 10ms, the positioning data from the positioning devices is parsed as a single string and sent to the Android device. A sample pseudocode used for reading the packet data is shown in Figure 5.

Pathfinding

Here, the pathfinding algorithm is implemented onto the Android platform. The uninformed pathfinding algorithms are programmed in Java and then packaged as an application, incorporating the features

Figure 5. A loop function for the retrieval of UDP data.

```
void loop() {

  receivePacket();

  if(packetReceived())

  {

    print("Received packet of size " + packetSize + "from " +
Udp.remoteIPAddress() + "from " + Udp.remotePortNumber());


    Udp.readPacketContent();

    print("Contents:" + contentBuffer);



    while (connection.isOpen()) {

      sendData();

    }

  }

  delay(10);

}
```

required to communicate with the other hardware devices. During this stage, the pathfinding algorithms are programmed as independent classes with their own methods, which can be called from the main class of the application. This enables the programming of multiple pathfinding algorithms onto the application, working independently from other processes such as hardware communications. Classes that interface with other hardware modules in this system are then programmed independently, alongside the pathfinding classes. A single goal algorithm and a multi-goal algorithm are selected for implementation. The single goal algorithm selected is the parallel bidirectional BIDDFS and the multi-goal algorithm is the multi-goal BIDDFS that the authors proposed in (Lim, Seng, Yeong, Ang, & Ch'ng, 2015), and are ported to Java in the same way that they did for (Lim, Seng, Yeong, Ang, & Ch'ng, 2015). The algorithms are programmed individually, and they will be used according to the pedestrian's need. For example, if a pedestrian requests to navigate directly to a destination, the single goal algorithm will be used; likewise, if the pedestrian decides to survey the distance from each destination, then the multi-goal algorithm will be used instead (the user will be prompted) These pathfinding algorithms are programmed onto the Android application using Android Studio 0.2 (Google), and the application is then installed on the Android device.

Smartphone Application

An Android application is designed in this system to interface with other hardware components, along with performing pathfinding and pedestrian navigation. The user interface (UI) is designed with the visually impaired in mind, offering a single, simplistic button on the main screen, and a text area to show navigational data for debugging purpose for the prototype (see Figure 6). All other interaction with the user is controlled through speech recognition and synthesis. The Android application performs speech recognition (speech-to-text) and synthesis (text-to-speech) by utilising Google's speech recognition and speech synthesis application programming interfaces (APIs). The Android application is programmed with the headers android.speech.RecognizerIntent and android.speech.tts respectively to enable speech recognition and speech synthesis. To use the Google speech recognition API, the Android device is connected to the internet as the speech database stored on Google's servers; the speech synthesis API is able to function without an Internet connection, as the text-to-speech algorithm is already built into the device.

Speech recognition and synthesis are used after pathfinding, during guidance. During navigation, the application will listen for speech input from the user. If a speech is recognised, it will be returned as text, which is then stored as a string in the Android application. The recognised string can then be manipulated by the Android application into input commands – if a test is matched with valid commands (e.g. "start"), the input is recognised. Speech synthesis is used as an alternative to visual feedback in a navigation device. The programming of the speech synthesis module in the Android application reads strings from the program and outputs the speech as an audio feedback. Examples of synthesised speech in this prototype include directional commands ("turn left", "go straight", etc.). If the Android device is

Figure 6. Android application user interface showing the time elapsed for multiple runs on the (a) parallel bidirectional BIDDFS runs (left), and (b) multi-goal BIDDFS runs using three goals (right).

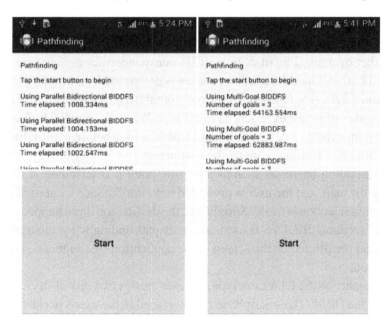

paired with a Bluetooth headset, the user will then receive the audio output via the Bluetooth headset. Otherwise, it will be outputted through the speaker. Speech synthesis is used to output responses from the Android application, such as directional guidance and application statuses.

Once pathfinding is completed, the Android device is required to interface with the Arduino to receive the user's current positioning data for guidance. A socket-programming module is programmed into the Android application as a standalone thread pool that is started after pathfinding. This enables UDP communications over the IEEE 802.11g Wi-Fi standard. The Android device acts as an AP using Android's tethering feature and the Arduino with an attached Wi-Fi shield connects to the Android device. The media access control address (MAC address) of the connected Arduino is used to look up its IP address from the address resolution protocol (ARP) table. Once the IP address of the Arduino has been identified, the application uses that IP address to send the first packet to the Arduino. An initialisation string (e.g. "start") is sent to the Arduino to commence the inflow of positioning data. Subsequently, the Arduino recognises the IP of the Android device from the packet sent and returns the positioning data in replies back to the Android device. The reply packets from the Arduino are received by the Android and are stored as variables to be processed for guidance.

TESTING AND RESULTS

The ETA is assembled according to Figure 2 and 3(a) as a prototype, where it is then subjected to testing. Testing is focused on the pathfinding algorithms with reference to the functionalities of the prototype. The implemented pathfinding algorithms are tested in two parts – the parallel bidirectional BIDDFS and the multi-goal BIDDFS. Prior to testing, a user is equipped with the ETA according to Figure 7. His objective is to navigate from his current location to a room as shown in Figure 8. This room is set to be the goal for single goal testing on the floor plan map. For multi-goal testing, this goal is used along with other predetermined goals scattered around the map as described in section pathfinding test results, where pathfinding on the smartphone will be benchmarked for its time efficiency to compare with the same instance as performed on a PC. Before pathfinding starts, the navigation system determines the user's starting position, either by manual input or by a RFID transponder; for the purpose of this testing, the manual input method is used. Once the starting position is determined, pathfinding tests begin first with the parallel bidirectional BIDDFS, followed by the multi-goal BIDDFS algorithm. Multi-goal and single goal pathfinding provide difference experiences to the user. When the parallel bidirectional BIDDFS is implemented, the system expects a destination input from the user before pathfinding begins, and then calculate the route from that starting point to the destination (goal). Conversely, when the multi-goal BIDDFS is used, pathfinding begins as soon as a starting point is determined; a single search is used to locate all goals on the map, and the user is presented with the distance from each goal relative to the user before a destination selection is made. Simply put, the destination input happens before pathfinding when the parallel bidirectional BIDDFS is used, and after pathfinding when the multi-goal BIDDFS is used. Pathfinding times are printed on the screen of the application (see Figure 6), and these results are tabulated and discussed.

To test the functionality of the ETA prototype, the user carries two sets of devices – the smartphone and the Arduino with the DRM. The smartphone can be placed in the user's pocket during navigation as communication can be performed through a connected Bluetooth headset. The other device set consists of the Arduino, the DRM, and the ZigBee coordinator, which are for now placed in a pouch bag worn by

Figure 7. (a) User carrying the ETA components, wearing the Bluetooth headset and holding the smartphone (left photo); and (b) user navigating in an environment with the navigation system prototype (right photo)

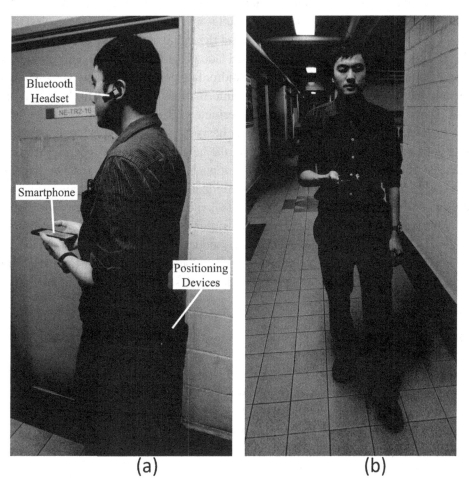

(a)   (b)

Figure 8. A simple illustration showing the devices worn by the user, and the path (in dashed line) obtained from pathfinding

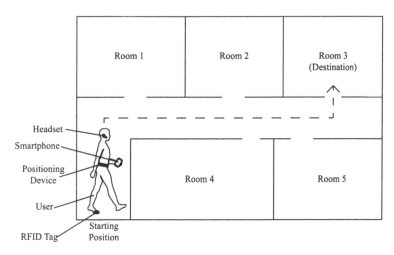

the user, the enclosure is awaiting fabrication. Figure 7(a) illustrates a user wearing the ETA prototype. To open the Android application, the user double taps the home button, launching SVoice, and say "Open Pathfinding". Once the application is opened and the starting position is determined, tapping on the start button initiates the pathfinding process. The result is a path(s) connecting the goal(s) to the starting point (this path is stored in the phone's memory), and then guidance for the user begins. The user can alternatively start pathfinding using the implemented Google speech-to-text module, which is also used to specify the destination. During navigation, the Android device provides only voice guidance. While the user is in motion, the device supplies directional information to the user. This begins by ensuring the orientation of the user after the starting point is determined by an audio feedback (e.g. "turn around", "turn right", "turn left", "go straight"). Once the user hears "go straight", he/she will proceed to walk in a straight line until the next feedback is delivered at the next turning point. The user travels according to the synthesised voice directions. This process continues until the goal is reached, where the RFID transponder is tagged. Turning points on the map are identified to set the locations to give directional cues to the user. The location of these turning points can be accurately identified by placing a RFID transponder at the location, allowing the absolute position to be delivered to the navigation system for directional cues. For testing purposes, the RFID transponder is placed on the goal and the DRM tracks the user's location, which is relative to the users starting location. The RFID tag placed in the user's shoe is detected by the transponder when it is within range. A successful tagging of the transponder will prompt an audio feedback to the user.

Pathfinding Test Results

The testing results of pathfinding algorithms running on the navigation system hardware are documented in this section. The algorithms are tested for the purpose to ensure their pathfinding times on hardware is consistent with the results obtained from (Lim, Seng, Yeong, Ang, & Ch'ng, 2015), where the single goal and multi-goal algorithms are run with maps of single and multiple goals, at varying sizes. The parallel bidirectional BIDDFS and the multi-goal BIDDFS are programmed onto the Samsung Galaxy Note II (N7100) Android device of the navigation system for testing. It is powered by a Quad-core 1.6 GHz Cortex-A9 processor with 2GB RAM, running on Android 4.3 Jellybean. Background applications are closed before running the pathfinding application, as they may interfere with the pathfinding speed.

The performance of pathfinding algorithms when the "Start" button is tapped on maps of different resolution is tabulated in Table 1 with different goal numbers using the two BIDDFS algorithms. Floor plans can be sub-divided into nodes for pathfinding, a division to more nodes constitutes to a higher resolution map. A map of higher resolution supports larger maps with a higher path and obstacle detail, but with longer pathfinding time, meaning that the user would have to wait longer before guidance begins. The maps used for testing introduces a virtual environment, where floor plans are superimposed on real environments for testing. A 50 by 50 node resolution map can be represented with 1 metre per node in a real environment; likewise, a 250 by 250 node map can be represented by 10 centimetres per node in a real environment. The pathfinding times are measured as an average of ten repeated runs on the Android device. The parallel bidirectional BIDDFS is faster than the multi-goal BIDDFS. On a 50×50 map, it is 10 times faster than the multi-goal BIDDFS and 4.4 times faster on the 250×250 map. This proves that the results obtained in this hardware testing between the algorithms and the map resolution are consistent with the results obtained in the simulations in (Lim, Seng, Yeong, Ang, & Ch'ng, 2015). It should be

Table 1. Pathfinding times for different map sizes used in testing with the parallel bidirectional and multi-goal BIDDFS

Map Resolution	BIDDFS	Goals	Time (s)
50×50	Parallel Bidirectional	1	0.02696
50×50	Multi-goal	1	0.26807
50×50	Multi-goal	3	0.27872
250×250	Parallel Bidirectional	1	14.736
250×250	Multi-goal	1	64.855
250×250	Multi-goal	3	65.925

taken into consideration that when the map size increases, pathfinding is slower on the Android smartphone since the computer has faster hardware. Therefore, it is deduced that a lowered map resolution on the Android smartphone allows it to perform pathfinding at speeds comparable with the computer.

CONCLUSION

This chapter presented a review of current ETAs and subsequently proposed an ETA system concept for visually impaired pedestrians. This ETA was developed and tested for indoor navigation with visually impaired pedestrians in mind. A detailed overview of the ETA is presented. The RFID-DRM indoor positioning solution reduces the need of installing many redundant RFID transponders while still being able to track the user's movements. With a focus on pathfinding algorithms, uninformed pathfinding algorithms were implemented onto this ETA. Testing results showed that the ETA is able to guide a visually impaired pedestrian for navigation, and pathfinding results are consistent with the tests performed during the authors' algorithm proposals. Further works relating to this ETA include more experiments to measure its hardware functionalities in the areas of positioning and guidance. For example, the PLDs will benefit from more experiments to measure their accuracy in positioning and tracking; whilst the guidance system can be subjected to a user experience survey.

ACKNOWLEDGMENT

This project has been supported by the Malaysian Ministry of Science, Technology and Innovation (MOSTI) eScienceFund number 01-02-16-SF0024.

REFERENCES

Ando, T., Tsukahara, R., Seki, M., & Fujie, M. G. (2012). A Haptic Interface "Force Blinker 2" for Navigation of the Visually Impaired. *Industrial Electronics. IEEE Transactions on*, *59*(11), 4112–4119. doi:10.1109/TIE.2011.2173894

Au, A. W. S., Chen, F., Valaee, S., Reyes, S., Sorour, S., Markowitz, S. N., & Eizenman, M. et al. (2013). Indoor Tracking and Navigation Using Received Signal Strength and Compressive Sensing on a Mobile Device. *Mobile Computing. IEEE Transactions on, 12*(10), 2050–2062. doi:10.1109/TMC.2012.175

Beeharee, A. K., & Steed, A. (2006). *A natural wayfinding exploiting photos in pedestrian navigation systems*. Paper presented at the 8th conference on Human-computer interaction with mobile devices and services, Helsinki, Finland. doi:10.1145/1152215.1152233

Ceipidor, U., Medaglia, C., & Sciarretta, E. (2010). SeSaMoNet 2.0: Improving a Navigation System for Visually Impaired People. In B. Ruyter, R. Wichert, D. Keyson, P. Markopoulos, N. Streitz, M. Divitini, & A. Mana Gomez et al. (Eds.), *Ambient Intelligence* (Vol. 6439, pp. 248–253). Springer Berlin Heidelberg. doi:10.1007/978-3-642-16917-5_25

Dakopoulos, D., & Bourbakis, N. G. (2010). Wearable Obstacle Avoidance Electronic Travel Aids for Blind: A Survey. *Systems, Man, and Cybernetics, Part C: Applications and Reviews. IEEE Transactions on, 40*(1), 25–35. doi:10.1109/TSMCC.2009.2021255

Di Giampaolo, E. (2010). *A passive-RFID based indoor navigation system for visually impaired people*. Paper presented at the Applied Sciences in Biomedical and Communication Technologies (ISABEL), 2010 3rd International Symposium on.

Digi International. (2008). *XBee™ ZNet 2.5/XBee-PRO™ ZNet 2.5 OEM RF Modules Datasheet*. Author.

Dijkstra, E. W. (1959). A Note on Two Problems in Connexion with Graphs. *NUMERISCHE MATHEMATIK, 1*(1), 269–271. doi:10.1007/BF01386390

Fallah, N., Apostolopoulos, I., Bekris, K., & Folmer, E. (2013). Indoor Human Navigation Systems: A Survey. *Interacting with Computers*. doi:10.1093/iwc/iws010

Fernandes, H., Filipe, V., Costa, P., & Barroso, J. (2014). Location based Services for the Blind Supported by RFID Technology. *Procedia Computer Science, 27*(0), 2–8. doi:10.1016/j.procs.2014.02.002

Filipe, V., Fernandes, F., Fernandes, H., Sousa, A., Paredes, H., & Barroso, J. (2012). Blind Navigation Support System based on Microsoft Kinect. *Procedia Computer Science, 14*, 94–101. doi:10.1016/j.procs.2012.10.011

Google. (n.d.). *Getting Started with Android Studio*. Retrieved from http://developer.android.com/sdk/installing/studio.html

Guy, R., & Truong, K. (2012). *CrossingGuard: exploring information content in navigation aids for visually impaired pedestrians*. Paper presented at the SIGCHI Conference on Human Factors in Computing Systems, Austin, TX. doi:10.1145/2207676.2207733

Hart, P. E., Nilsson, N. J., & Raphael, B. (1968). A Formal Basis for the Heuristic Determination of Minimum Cost Paths. *Systems Science and Cybernetics. IEEE Transactions on, 4*(2), 100–107. doi:10.1109/TSSC.1968.300136

Honeywell. (2006). *Digital Compass Solution - HMC6352 datasheet*. Author.

Honeywell. (2011). *DRM™4000L Dead Reckoning Module Datasheet*. Author.

Hua, W., Marshall, A., & Wai, Y. (2007). *Path Planning and Following Algorithms in an Indoor Navigation Model for Visually Impaired.* Paper presented at the Internet Monitoring and Protection, 2007. ICIMP 2007. Second International Conference on.

Hyun-Seung, K., Deok-Rae, K., Se-Hoon, Y., Yong-Hwan, S., & Sang-Kook, H. (2013). An Indoor Visible Light Communication Positioning System Using a RF Carrier Allocation Technique. *Lightwave Technology. Journalism, 31*(1), 134–144. doi:10.1109/JLT.2012.2225826

Kamiński, Ł., & Bruniecki, K. (2012). Mobile navigation system for visually impaired users in the urban environment. *Metrology and Measurement Systems, 19*(2), 245–256. doi:10.2478/v10178-012-0021-z

Kang, W., & Han, Y. (2015). SmartPDR: Smartphone-Based Pedestrian Dead Reckoning for Indoor Localization. *Sensors Journal, IEEE, 15*(5), 2906–2916. doi:10.1109/JSEN.2014.2382568

Korf, R. E. (1985). Depth-first iterative-deepening: An optimal admissible tree search. *Artificial Intelligence, 27*(1), 97–109. doi:10.1016/0004-3702(85)90084-0

Kourogi, M., & Kurata, T. (2014). *A method of pedestrian dead reckoning for smartphones using frequency domain analysis on patterns of acceleration and angular velocity.* Paper presented at the Position, Location and Navigation Symposium - PLANS 2014, 2014 IEEE/ION.

Liao, C., Choe, P., Wu, T., Tong, Y., Dai, C., & Liu, Y. (2013). RFID-Based Road Guiding Cane System for the Visually Impaired. In P. L. P. Rau (Ed.), *Cross-Cultural Design. Methods, Practice, and Case Studies* (Vol. 8023, pp. 86–93). Springer Berlin Heidelberg. doi:10.1007/978-3-642-39143-9_10

Lim, K. L., Seng, K. P., Yeong, L. S., Ang, L.-M., & Ch'ng, S. I. (2015). *Pathfinding for the Navigation of Visually Impaired People. International Journal of Computational Complexity and Intelligent Algorithms.*

Lim, K. L., Seng, K. P., Yeong, L. S., Ang, L.-M., & Chng, S. I. (2015). Uninformed pathfinding: A new approach. *Expert Systems with Applications, 42*(5), 2722–2730. doi:10.1016/j.eswa.2014.10.046

Nakajima, M., & Haruyama, S. (2012). *Indoor navigation system for visually impaired people using visible light communication and compensated geomagnetic sensing.* Paper presented at the Communications in China (ICCC), 2012 1st IEEE International Conference on.

Ran, L., Helal, S., & Moore, S. (2004). *Drishti: an integrated indoor/outdoor blind navigation system and service.* Paper presented at the Pervasive Computing and Communications, 2004. PerCom 2004.

Samsung Electronics Co. Ltd. (2014). *Samsung GALAXY Note2 - Samsung Mobile.* Retrieved from http://www.samsung.com/global/microsite/galaxynote/note2/spec.html

NXP Semiconductors. (2014). *MFRC522 - Standard 3V MIFARE reader solution Product data sheet.* Author.

Texas Instruments. (2014). *TRF7960A.* Retrieved from http://www.ti.com/product/trf7960a

Todd, C., Mallya, S., Majeed, S., Rojas, J., & Naylor, K. (2014). *VirtuNav: A Virtual Reality indoor navigation simulator with haptic and audio feedback for the visually impaired.* Paper presented at the Computational Intelligence in Robotic Rehabilitation and Assistive Technologies (CIR2AT), 2014 IEEE Symposium on.

Uddin, M. A., & Suny, A. H. (2015). *Shortest path finding and obstacle detection for visually impaired people using smart phone.* Paper presented at the Electrical Engineering and Information Communication Technology (ICEEICT), 2015 International Conference on.

Williams, M. A., Hurst, A., & Kane, S. K. (2013). *Pray before you step out: describing personal and situational blind navigation behaviors.* Paper presented at the 15th International ACM SIGACCESS Conference on Computers and Accessibility, Bellevue, WA. doi:10.1145/2513383.2513449

Chapter 16
Modified Differential Evolution Algorithm Based Neural Network for Nonlinear Discrete Time System

Uday Pratap Singh
Madhav Institute of Technology and Science, India

Rajeev Kumar Singh
Madhav Institute of Technology and Science, India

Sanjeev Jain
Shri Mata Vaishno Devi University, India

Mahesh Parmar
Madhav Institute of Technology and Science, India

ABSTRACT

Two main important features of neural networks are weights and bias connection, which is still a challenging problem for researchers. In this paper we select weights and bias connection of neural network (KN) using modified differential evolution algorithm (MDEA) i.e. MDEA-NN for uncertain nonlinear systems with unknown disturbances and compare it with KN using differential evolution algorithm (DEA) i.e. DEA-KN. In this work, MDEA is based on exploitation and exploration of capability, we have implemented differential evolution algorithm and modified differential evolution algorithm, which are based on the consideration of the three main operator's mutation, crossover and selection. MDEA-KN is applied on two different uncertain nonlinear systems, and one benchmark problem known as brushless dc (BDC) motor. Proposed method is validated through statistical testing's methods which demonstrate that the difference between target and output of proposed method are acceptable.

INTRODUCTION

A neural network is a processing device, whose design and functioning was inspired by the human brain. In computing world neural networks has a lot of gain, also known as artificial neural network. Before discussing neural network let us focus on functioning of human brain. Human brain consisting of spe-

DOI: 10.4018/978-1-5225-1785-6.ch016

cific type of cell known as neuron, which does not regenerated, because provide us with our abilities to remember, think and apply previous experiences. Human brain consisting of about 100 billion neurons, each neuron was connected with 200000 (approximately) other neurons. The power of human brain is depends upon number of neurons and their interconnections. Neurons convey information via a host of electrochemical pathways (Pratihar, 2013). These neurons and their connections form a process which is not binary, not stable and not synchronous. In short artificial neural network are more powerful than electronic computers.

An artificial neural network may be defined as information processing model that are inspired by the biological nervous systems. This model tries to replicate the most basic functions of brains. Neural network represent a meaningfully different approach such as pattern recognition or data classification through a learning process. A neural network is used to learn patterns and relationships in data. The data may be the results of academic investigations that use mathematical formulations to model. Regardless of the specifics involvement, applying a neural network is significantly different from traditional approaches.

Artificial neural network, like people, learn by examples. In biological system, learning involves adjustment of synaptic connections that exist between the neurons. Various neural networks are now designed that are quite accurate to the target. Neural network methods is looking to the future via analysing past experiences has generated its own set of problems. For the explanation that how network will learn and why it recommends a particular decision has been difficult, based on inner working of neural network i.e. black boxes. To justify these decision making process, several neural network tools are available that explain the whole process, from these information, expert in the application may be able to infer which data plays a major role in decision making and its importance (Pratihar, 2013; Hu & Hwang, 2001).

Neural network have self adaptability and self learning capability to derive meaning from complicated or imprecise data. A trained neural network is known as an expert in particular categories of information it has been given to analyze. Some advantages of artificial neural network are given below:

- **Self-Organization:** An ANN can create its own representation of the information it receives during learning time.
- **Adaptive Learning:** AN ANN is endowed with the ability to learn how to do task based on the given data for training.
- **Real-Time Operation:** ANN computation may be carried out in parallel. Hardware devices are being designed and manufactured to take advantages of capabilities of ANN.
- **Fault Tolerance:** Partial destruction of neural network leads to the corresponding degradation of performances.

Biological Neural Networks

It is well known that human brain contains a huge number of neurons and their interconnections. A biological neuron or a nerve cell (Pratihar, 2013) consists of Soma or cell body, Synapses, Dendrites and the Axon the elements are as follows:

- **Soma or Cell Body:** Where the cell nucleus is located.
- **Synapses:** A synapse is a biochemical device, which converts a pre-synaptic electrical signal into a chemical signal and then back into a post-synaptic electrical signal.

Figure 1. Biological neural network

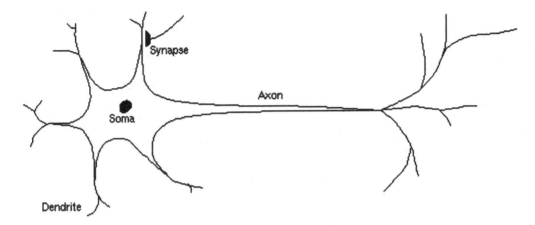

- **Dendrites:** Dendrites are tree like networks made for nerve fibre connected to the cell body.
- **Axon:** It is a single long connection extending from the cell body and carrying signals from the neurons. When a particular amount of input is received, then the cell fires. It transmits signal through axon to other cells.

Basically, a biological neuron receives inputs from other sources, combines them in some way, performs a generally nonlinear operation on the result, and then outputs the final result.

Artificial Neural Networks

An Artificial Neural Network (ANN) is information processing paradigm that is inspired by the way biological nervous system such as the brain, process information. The key element of this paradigm is the novel structure of the information processing system. In this information-processing system, the elements called as neurons, process the information. The signals are transmitted by means of connection links. The links possess an associated weight, which is multiplied along with the incoming signal for any typical neural net. The output signal is obtained by applying activation to the net input (Pratihar, 2013; Hu & Hwang, 2001; Chen & Pham, 2000).

An artificial neuron is characterized by:

- Architecture (connection between neuron),
- Training or Learning (determining weights on the connections),
- Activation function.

If a simple artificial neural network with two input neuron (x_1, x_2) and one output neuron y. The inter-connected weights are considered as w_1 and w_2. An artificial neuron is a p-input and single-output signal-processing element, which can be through of a simple model of non-branching biological neuron. Various input to the network are represented by the mathematical symbol, x_n. Each of these inputs, are multiplied by connection of weights. These weights are represented by w_n. In the simplest case, these products are simply summed, fed through a transfer function to generate a result, and then delivered as output. This process lends itself to physical implementation on a large scale in a small package. This electronic implementation is still possible with other network structure, which utilize different summing functions as well as different transfer functions.

Brains vs. Computers

A comparison between biological and artificial neurons could be made on the following criteria:

- **Speed:** The cycle time of the execution in the ANN is of few nanoseconds whereas in case of BNN are few milliseconds.
- **Processing:** The BNN can perform parallel operations simultaneously, ANN can also. In general ANN processing is faster than BNN.
- **Size and Complexity:** The number of neurons in BNN is very large in comparison to ANN; therefore structure of BNN is more complex than ANN.
- **Memory Capacity:** The biological neuron stores the information in its interconnections or in synapse strength but in an ANN it is stored in contiguous memory allocations.
- **Tolerance:** The biological neuron posses fault tolerance capability and artificial neuron posses no fault tolerance capability.
- **Control Mechanism:** In ANN model using computer there is a control unit presents in the central processing unit, which can transfer and control precise scalar values from unit to unit, but there are no such control units for monitoring the brain.

Evaluation of Neural Network

The evolution of neural network can be traced as follows (Pratihar, 2013):

1943 - McCulloch and Pitts: Start of the modern era of neural networks: This forms a logical calculus of neural networks. A network consists of sufficient number of neurons and properly set synaptic connection can compute any computable function.

1949 - Hebb's Book "The Organization of Behaviour": An explicit statement of a physiological learning rule for synaptic modification was presented for the first time. Hebb proposed that the connectivity of the brain is continually changing as an organism learns differing functional tasks, and the neural assemblies are created by such change.

1958 - Rosenblatt Introduces Perceptron, Minsky and Papert: In Perceptron network the weight on the connection paths can be adjusted. A method of iterative weight adjustment can be used in the perceptron net. The Perceptron net is found to converge if the weight obtained allow the net to reproduce exactly all the training input and target output vector pairs.

1985 - Parker, 1986-Lecum: During this period the backpropagation net paved its way into the Neural Ntworks. This method propagates the error information at the output units back to the hidden unit using a generalized dalta rules.

1987, 1988 - Carpenter and Grossberg: Carpenter and Grossberg invented Adaptive Resonance Theory (ART). ART was designed for both binary inputs and the continuous valued inputs. The design for the binary inputs formed ART1, and ART2 came into being when the design became applicable to the continuous valued input.

1990 - Vapnic: developed the support vector machine.

Application of Neural Network

Artificial neural network are very much useful in various field of applications, given below:

- **Science and Medicine:** Modelling, prediction, diagnosis, pattern recognition.
- **Manufacturing:** Process modelling and analysis.
- **Marketing and Sales:** Analysis, classification, customer targeting.
- **Finance:** Portfolio trading, investment support.
- **Banking and Insurance:** Credit and policy approval.
- **Security:** Bomb, iceberg, Fraud detection.
- **Engineering:** Dynamic load shedding, pattern recognition.

Evolutionary Computation

Evolutionary computation methods have become increasingly popular in recent years and these computations evolved over billions of years, providing a rich source of inspirations. Evolutionary computations can be used for optimization purpose in field of engineering, industries and business etc. Since time and money are always limited in real world applications, since various real world problems are highly nonlinear so they cannot be handle via mathematical modelling and mathematical tools (Chakraborty, 2008). Computer simulations become an indispensible tool for solving such optimization problems, for these simulations there are always an algorithms at work. Differential evolution is one of the most popular evolutionary computation techniques for solving such optimization problems discussed below.

Differential Evolution

Differential evolution (DE) was developed by R. Storn and K. Price in 1997 (Storn & Price, 1997), which has some similar pattern search like genetic algorithm due to use of similar selection, crossover and mutation operations. Indeed that DE can be viewed as further development of genetic algorithm with explicit updating equations. DE is a metaheuristic vector based computational methods that have good convergence properties. De is a stochastic search algorithm with self organizing tendency and free from gradients information. It is population based search algorithm, derivative free use real number as solution string and no encoding and decoding is needed (Chakraborty, 2008; Storn & Price, 1997).

As in genetic algorithm, design parameter in a n-dimensional search space are represented as vectors, and various genetic operators are operated over their bits of strings. However, unlike genetic algorithm differential evolution carries out operations over each dimension of the solution. In genetic algorithm mutation is carried out at one or multiple site of chromosome, whereas in differential evolution difference of two randomly chosen vectors is considered, such approach is more efficient for implementation point of view. Crossover operation is also vector based component-wise exchange of chromosomes.

Nonlinear Systems

A system in which the effect of external factors is not purely additive, and may even be disruptive. Nonlinear systems cannot be decomposed into parts and reassembled into the same thing, and do not change in proportion to a change in an input. Most economic and social processes are nonlinear where mathematical analysis is unable to provide general solutions. Typically, the behaviour of a nonlinear system is described in mathematics by a nonlinear system of equations, a nonlinear system of equations is a set of equations where one or more terms have a variable of degree two or higher and/or there is a product of variables in one of the equations. Most real-life physical systems are non-linear systems (Vidyasagar, 1993; Sakhre, Singh, & Jain, 2016). Solving nonlinear systems of equations is much complex than the solving linear equations. When the solutions are real, they will represent the coordinates of the points where the graphs of the two functions intersect but in case of complex solutions graphical representation are more difficult.

Why Nonlinear Systems?

1. Real-world systems are nonlinear time varying.
2. Linearization only valid for a small operational range.
3. Some models cannot be linearized (discontinuous nonlinearities).
4. Robust designs can sometimes be obtained by introducing nonlinearity.
5. Nonlinear feedback can sometimes give simpler controllers.

Classification of Nonlinearities

There are two types of nonlinearities

1. Naturally occurring versus artificially introduced.
2. Continuous versus discontinuous.

Table 1. Natural vs. artificial

Natural	Artificial
Natural: All physical systems for example	Artificial Introduced by control system designer
Mechanical: Coulomb friction, stiction, square law friction.	Relay in home heating system.
Electromagnetic: hysteresis in magnetization curves, relays, saturation.	Thrusters in aerospace applications.
Electronics: amplifier saturation.	Bang-bang control.
	Variable structure (switching) control.

Table 2. Continuous vs. discontinuous

Continuous	Discontinuous
Continuous (soft)	Discontinuous (hard)
Linearization possible	Linearization is not

Some Example of Nonlinear System

- **Aircraft (Sakhre, Singh, & Jain, 2016):** Physical systems where the control inputs appear non-linearly are rather uncommon. They are, however, indispensable in the high-fidelity modelling of aircraft dynamics, where the control surfaces such as the elevator, aileron, and rudder affect the aerodynamic forces and moments of the aircraft in a nonlinear manner.
- **Nonlinear Materials and Members (Sakhre, Singh, & Jain, 2016):** When strain of materials and deformation of members grow up due to increasing deformation of structures, the corresponding stress and restoring force are no longer proportional to the strain or deformation. Relation between stress and strain or force and deformation show softening type nonlinearity, which is favourable foe seismic design of structures.

LITERATURE REVIEW

Nonlinear discrete-time systems generally exhibit unpredictable behaviour. Many systems in nature including biological process (Xie, Guo, Gu, Li, & Stoica, 2006), chemical process (Watanbe, Matsuura, Abe, Kebota, & Himelblau, 1989) and control system (Chen & Billings, 1989) are uncertain. The dynamics nonlinear discrete-time systems, generally exhibit unpredictable behaviour and expressed via difference equation. Also, there exist many uncertain nonlinear dynamical systems such as robot manipulators and actuators, electric servomotors, piezoelectric translators, hydraulic servo valves etc. (Soderstrom & Stoica, 1989; Billings, 2013). Most of the physical processes are continuous in nature but they are generally modelled using discrete time with the use of derivative and integral as they are easily realizable. An enormous research has been focused on discrete time system and many techniques based on linear and nonlinear discrete-time systems have been developed. Linear system identification is less computational complexity whereas nonlinear systems have much computational complexity.

Self-adaptability and self-learning capability of Kohonen Network (KN) is used for approximation of nonlinear system and computing ability is more resilient (Ticknor, 2013). KN uses a group of artificial neurons based on a computational or mathematical model for transforming the information from one layer to another. On the basis of input, output, neurons and weight connections ANN's can be classified into two main categories feedforward neural network (FNN) and feedback neural network or backpropagation neural network (BPNN) (Zhang, 2002; Zhang & Zhang, 2011). Most of the systems are designed using feed forward network with gradient descent learning but the gradient descent encounters the problem of slow convergence. The problem of convergence can be overcome by use of some Cauchy-Newton (Bortoletti, Flore, Fanelli, & Zellini, 2003) Quasi-Newtonian method and polynomial identification methods (Dinga & Chenb, 2005), Winner-Hammerstein method (Lee & Jeng, 1998) used for the reasonable degree of accuracy for nonlinear systems but it suffers from computational complexities. Lyapunov-krasovskii function was used to study the convergence criterion (Alfaro-Ponce, Arguelles, & Chairez, 2014). Time delays are a common problem in nonlinear processes and it is overcome by use of Continuous Neural Network (CNN) which provide model over uncertain non-parametric systems. Identification of nonlinear dynamical system can be effectively approximated by the multi-layer neural network as fuzzy counter propagation network and with backpropagation network (Sakhre, Singh, & Jain, 2016; Narendra & Parthaasarathy, 1990). Adaptive dynamic programming was used to develop a control law which makes the iterative performance index function to reach the optimum. Studies on uncertain dynamical systems have been reported using adaptive neural network control and fuzzy-neuro control to approximate error by bounding the stability of the closed-loop system (Shigen, Hairon, Ning, & Chen, 2015; Zhouhua, Dan, Zhang, & Yejin, 2015; Zhang & Xiaonan, 2015; Jun & Shuping, 2015; Guozeng & Zhen, 2015; Yang, 2010). A nonlinear function can be estimated to a desired degree of accuracy by using some adaptive systems like neural networks (Ge & Wag, 2002; Li, Qiung, Zhuang, & Kaynak, 2004; Zhang, Yang, Liu, & Zhang, 2013; Zhang, Wang, & Liu, 2008; Zhang & Yang, 2008). An adaptive fuzzy control of dynamical or stochastic nonlinear systems with unknown disturbances and adaptive neural network feedback control of uncertain multiple input multiple output (MIMO) systems has been proposed (Wang, Zhang, & Wang, 2006; Yang & Chan, 2014; Wang & Huang, 2005; Tong, Li, Feng, & Li, 2011). Adaptive dynamic surface controls with uncertainty are approximated by type-2 fuzzy neural network (Yang & Chan, 2014). Robust hybrid intelligent controls for uncertain nonlinear systems with unknown disturbance are discussed in (Sakhre, Singh, & Jain, 2016; Singh, Jain, Singh, Parmar, Makwana, & Kumare, 2016). Many control techniques has been proposed for nonlinear dynamical systems such as neural network approach (Li, Qiung, Zhuang, & Kaynak, 2004; Zhang, Yang, Liu, & Zhang, 2013; Zhang, Wang, & Liu, 2008) fuzzy logic control (FLC) (Hsu, 2007; Laboid & Guerra, 2007; Tong, Li, & Wang, 2004; Johansson & Rantzer, 1998) hybrid algorithmic approach etc. (Sanchez, Shibata, & Zadeh, 1997). Accurate approximations of complex nonlinear dynamical surface control problems are almost impossible via the represented by linear models. FLC is a powerful method of approximation (Li, Wang, Feng, & Tong, 2010; Song & Hedrick, 2004; Wu, Wu, Luo, & Guan, 2012) and have many applications in industry e.g. ultra sonic motor-actuated servo drives.

In recent years, different metaheuristic algorithms which are computationally efficient have been developed for global optimization. Random walk is the main characteristic of any metaheuristic algorithms, which we can either do by the treasure hunting alone or whole path on trajectory basis search. Recently Storn and Price (1997) developed an evolutionary algorithm known as differential evolution (DE) used for solve real world and engineering optimization problems (Ge & Wang, 2002; Li, Qiung, Zhuang, & Kaynak, 2004; Zhang, Yang, Liu, & Zhang, 2013). DE has been preferred to many other evolutionary algorithms such as genetic algorithms, particle swarm optimization, firefly algorithm, harmony search, and Bat algorithms (Zhang, Wang, & Liu, 2008; Zhang & Yang, 2008; Wang, Zhang, & Wang, 2006; Yang & Chan, 2014; Wang & Huang, 2005; Tong, Li, Feng, & Li, 2011) due to the simple concept and fast convergence. Whereas all population based optimization techniques including DE, suffers from computational complexities because of their stochastic nature. The concept of chaos has been more attention in many fields including nonlinear dynamics (Yang & Chan, 2014). Chaotic sequence has been used to tune the parameters of different metaheuristic algorithms like genetic algorithm (Wang & Huang, 2005; Tong, Li, Feng, & Li, 2011), particle swarm optimization (Zhang & Yang, 2008), firefly algorithm (Wang, Zhang, & Wang, 2006), harmony search (Yang & Chan, 2014) and bat algorithm (Chen & Pham, 2000). Empirical studies indicate that chaos can have a high level of mobility and diversity when a fixed parameter is replaced by a chaos map (Singh, Jain, Singh, Parmar, Makwana, & Kumare, 2016).

The objectives of this chapter are to presents modified differential evolution algorithm for uncertain nonlinear systems. After optimization problem is formulated correctly, the main task is to find optimal solutions by using MDEA. We have designed artificial neural network model in which initial weight connection are chosen via MDEA. The MDEA-KN model is trained by unsupervised learning from input to hidden layer and supervised learning from hidden to the output layer. The unsupervised and supervised learning is used for adjusting weights and used for optimization of tracking error. The main contributions of this research are as follows:

1. This paper contributes the approximation for a class of uncertain nonlinear dynamical systems using MDEA-KN approach.
2. This approach is used to the tracking of an uncertain nonlinear system subject to the addition of dead zone control input.
3. This method is employed to optimize the Mean Absolute Error, Mean Square Error, Mean Absolute Percentage Error etc.

The paper is organized as follows.

*   In Section 2 problem formulation and preliminaries for a class of uncertain non-linear dynamical systems are discussed.
*   Section 3 contains description of the Kohonen network (KN), MDEA-KN algorithm for dynamical system.
*   Section 4 implementation and statistical analysis for uncertain nonlinear dynamical systems with MDEA.
*   Section 5 gives conclusion and future study.

PROBLEM FORMULATION

In this work we solve following different tasks: nonlinear discrete time system (Hsu, 2007), BDC motor problem (Wang & Huang, 2005). Numerous algorithms have been extensively used to solve these types of problems which give significant results in the area of prediction and forecasting. Nonlinear discrete time systems have many applications in control theory. The goal in this paper is to test neural network prediction for nonlinear discrete time system, forecasting and exchange rate prediction and their statistical analysis. We consider two different models of discrete time nonlinear discrete time systems for multiple input and single output (MISO), they are described by difference Equation 1 to Equation 4. Let $f: R^n \rightarrow R$ and $g: R^m \rightarrow R$ is the nonlinear function of the type model I-model IV are assumed to be continuous differentiable functions and approximated by MDEA-KN to the desired degree of accuracy. Once the system has been parameterized as given below like any of model I-model IV, the performance evaluation has been carried out by MDEA-KN:

Model I:

$$y(k+1) = \sum_{i=0}^{n-1} \alpha_i y(k-i) + g\big[u(k),...,u(k-m+1)\big]$$ (1)

Model II:

$$y(k+1) = f\big[y(k),...,y(k-n+1)\big] + \sum_{i=0}^{m-1} \beta_i u(k-i)$$ (2)

Model III:

$$y(k+1) = f\left[y(k),...,y(k-n+1)\right] + g\left[u(k),...,u(k-m+1)\right] \tag{3}$$

Model IV:

$$y(k+1) = f\left[y(k),...,y(k-n+1); u(k),...,u(k-m+1)\right] \tag{4}$$

where $[\,u(k),y(k)\,]$ represent the input-output pair of the system at time k and (n, m) are input and output order. A feedforward neural network is used to learn the system (1)-(4) and MDEA is employed to training. Performance of the MDEA-KN can be measured by cost functions given (5):

$$E(k) = \left(\frac{1}{2}\right)\left[y\left(k\right) - \overline{y}(k)\right]^2 \tag{5}$$

where $y(k)$ is target and $\overline{y}(k)$ neural network output.

KOHONEN NETWORK

When learning is based on only input data and independent of the output data no error is calculated to train the network. This type of learning is called unsupervised learning and input data are called unlabeled data. In such cases the network may respond to several output categories on training but only one of the several neurons has to respond. Hence additional structure can be included in the network so that network is forced to make decision as to which one unit will respond. Such mechanism in which only one unit is chosen to respond is called competition (Laboid & Guerra, 2007; Tong, Li, & Wang, 2004).

Kohonen Network is based on theory of competition, as a result the competitive processing elements are referred as Kohonen self organizing unit and this structure is known as Kohonen self organizing map (SOM). These SOM also termed as topology preserving map. In topology preserving map, units located physically next to each other will respond to classes of input vectors that are likewise located to next to each other. In SOM, the entire unit in the neighbourhood that receive positive feedback from the winning unit participate in the learning process.

Differential Evolution (DE)

DE is a vector based metaheuristic algorithm that possess the properties of god convergence. DE is stochastic search algorithm with self organizing tendency and it is gradient free optimization i.e. it is population based, derivative free optimization technique. DE uses solution string of real numbers and no encoding and decoding is needed. DE can be considered as further development of genetic algorithm (GA), which also uses crossover and mutation operator. Apart from these operators DE has explicit updating equations (Johansson & Rantzer, 1998). Mathematically DE is explained in brief as follows:

Let us assume that, we have to optimize the given objective function:

$$\min_{x} f(x) \tag{6}$$

where x is a vector containing n tuples in a continuous decision space $\Omega = \prod_{i=1}^{n} \left[L_i, U_i \right]$ and $f : \Omega \subseteq R^n \to R$ is called objective function. The procedure of DE for solving such optimization problems is given in algorithm 1. Initialize DE with a random selection of population in the search space

$$P_G = \left\{ x_{i,G} \mid i = 1, 2, \ldots, P \right\}.$$

Then, DE iteratively uses the trial vector generation strategy (i.e., mutation and crossover operators) and the selection operator to evolve the population until a stopping criterion is met. DE algorithmic procedure is given below:

DE Algorithm 1

```
1. Initialize a population
```
$$P_G = \left\{ x_{i,G} \mid i = 1, 2, \ldots, P = popsize \right\},$$
```
P_G is randomly generated also set weight F ∈ [0,2] and crossover probability
```
$$C_r \in [0,1].$$
```
2. while (stopping criterion)
3. for each  x_{i,G}  in  P_G do
4.  v_{i,G} =Mutate ( P_G )
5.  u_{i,G} = Crossover ( x_{i,G} , v_{i,G} )
6.  P_{G+1} = P_{G+1} ∪ Select ( x_{i,G} ,  u_{i,G} )
7. end for
8. Set G = G + 1
9. end while
```

MDE Algorithm 2

```
        Input: The objective function  f(x) :
     maximal number of generations, MaxGen;
     candidate strategies:"DE/rand/1/bin", "DE/rand/2/bin", and
     "DE/current-to-rand/1";

1.            Set popsize (P), MaxGen, G = 0, eval = 0, DB = Φ
2.            Initialize a population  P_G = { x_{i,G} | i = 1,2,....,P }
```

```
3.                   for all (x_{i,G}, f(x_{i,G})) into DB
4.                  eval = eval + P
5.               while eval < MaxEval do
6.                    if G < MaxGen then
7.                        Generate P_{G+1} based on P_G
8.                    else
9.                        for each x_{i,G} in P_G do
10.                          Generate five trials vectors using the five
combinations
a.          of strategies of mutation
11.                          Build a ranking model S based on DB
12.                          if The prediction accuracy of S is larger than 0.5
a.        then
13.                              Select the best trial vector according to S
(denoted as u_{i,G})
14.                          else
15.                              Randomly select one trial vector as u_{i,G}
16.                          end if
17.                          Evaluate u_{i,G} with f
18.                          P_{G+1} = P_{G+1} ∪ Select (x_{i,G}, u_{i,G})
19.                          eval = eval+1
20.                      end for
21.                  end if
22.                  all exact evaluations into DB e.g. step 3
23.                  G = G+1
end while
```

Output: the best individual in the current population.

Variants of Mutation Vector

Main focus in differential evolution algorithm is choice of *F*, C_r and *n* as well as modifications of mutation operation. To generate mutation vectors, we can use many different ways of formulation. Mutation naming convention is given by: DE/*x*/*y*/*z*, where *x* is mutation scheme e.g. best or rand, *y* is the number of difference vectors and *z* is crossover scheme e.g. exponential or binomial. For the mutation operator, there are five frequently use mutation schemes for generating a mutant vector:

"DE/rand/1/*Bin*":

$$v_{i,G} = x_{r_1,G} + F(x_{r_2,G} - x_{r_3,G}) \tag{7}$$

"DE/best/1/*Bin*":

$$v_{i,G} = x_{best,G} + F(x_{r_1,G} - x_{r_2,G}) \qquad (8)$$

"DE/target-to-best/1/*Bin*":

$$v_{i,G} = x_{i,G} + F(x_{best,G} - x_{i,G}) + F(x_{r_1,G} - x_{r_2,G}) \qquad (9)$$

"DE/best/2/*Bin*":

$$v_{i,G} = x_{best,G} + F(x_{r_1,G} - x_{r_2,G}) + F(x_{r_3,G} - x_{r_4,G}) \qquad (10)$$

"DE/rand/2/*Bin*":

$$v_{i,G} = x_{r_1,G} + F(x_{r_2,G} - x_{r_3,G}) + F(x_{r_4,G} - x_{r_5,G}) \qquad (11)$$

where the indices r_1, r_2, r_3, r_4 and r_5 are distinct integers randomly chosen from the range $[1, P]$ and also differ from i, and $x_{best,G}$ is the best individual at the Gth generation . The parameter F is called the scale factor and typically ranges on the interval [0.4, 1.0] according to (Chakraborty, 2008). For the crossover operator, there exist two crossover schemes for creating a trial vector with the mutant vector $v_{i,G}$ and the target vector $x_{i,G}$ i.e., exponential and binomial crossover schemes, and the latter is the more frequently used one, which can be described by the following formula:

$$\begin{cases} u_{j,i,G} = v_{j,i,G} & if\ rand_j(0,1) \le C_R\ or\ j = j_{rand} \\ x_{j,i,G} & Otherwise \end{cases} \qquad (12)$$

where $j = 1, 2, \cdots, n, j_{rand}$ is a randomly selected integer such that $j_{rand} \in [0,1]$, $rand_j(0,1)$ represents a number drawn uniformly between 0 and $x_{j,i,G}$, $u_{j,i,G}$ and $v_{j,i,G}$ denote the j-th element of $x_{i,G}, u_{i,G}, v_{i,G}$ respectively, $C_r \in [0,1]$ is called the crossover rate. In conjunction with the binomial crossover scheme, the above mentioned mutation schemes yield a total of five trial vector generation strategies. They are "DE/rand/1/bin", "DE/best/1/bin", "DE/target-to-best/1/bin", "DE/best/2/bin", "DE/rand/2/bin".

MDEA-KN

A good balance between global search and local search using MDEA used with adaptive chaos map, and has the perceptible merits of global convergence ability (Johansson & Rantzer, 1998). Good solution and fast convergence of neural network it is necessary to have optimum initial weight and threshold. The initial weights and bias connections of KN are selected by optimization of fitness function mean square error

(MSE) given by Equation 5 using MDEA-KN. The MDEA is used for preliminaries search for global optimal weights and bias connection. After initialization of weights using MDEA, KN is trained using unsupervised learning between inputs to hidden and supervised learning between hidden to output. So the KN with weight initialization by MDEA can obtain acceptable performance by especially avoiding the local minima and slow rate of convergence. So, KN optimized by MDEA may be a better option for uncertain nonlinear discrete-time systems, forecasting and prediction.

A group of weights and bias is obtained from every time step of MDEA are assigned to KN and an output value $\overline{y}(t)$ $(t = 1, 2, \cdots, k)$, k is the number of predictions is generated based on the connection of weights and bias. Objective function given in Equation 6 is formed on the basis of difference between the MDEA-KN output $\overline{y}(t)$ and the target $y(t)$. Generally, the mean square error (MSE), given by equation (5), is chosen as the objective function. Initial weights and bias connection of KN, optimum individual from MDEA is used. Network is trained with the training sample, and applies to testing data and thus, the best-fitting network is created. Proposed method is applied on nonlinear discrete time system, BDC motor (Yang & Chan, 2014). The flow chart of the proposed MDEA-KN is shown in Figure 2. Algorithm of MDEA-KN method is as follows:

MDEA-KN Algorithm

There are following steps for training of KN is as follows:

Step 0: Initialize weights of KN using MDEA.
Step 1: while (stopping criteria), perform step 2–5 //stopping criteria (maximum number of generation).

Figure 2. The flowchart of MDEA-KN algorithm

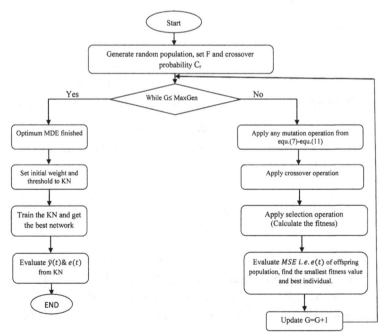

Step 2: Compute the winning node (J) using Euclidean distances $\left(\left\|x_i - v_{i,j}\right\|_2\right)$ between input and weight vectors.

$$D_j = \sum_{i=1}^{n} \left(x_i - v_{ij}\right)^2 : \text{where } j=1,2,\ldots,p. \tag{13}$$

and

$$z_{inJ} = \sum_{i=1}^{n} x_i v_{iJ} \tag{14}$$

Step 3: Set learning rate $\alpha \in [0,1]$

Step 4: update weight for unit Z_j.

$$v_{iJ}(\text{new}) = v_{iJ}(\text{old}) + \alpha\, h(\text{J}:i,j)(x_i - v_{iJ}) \tag{15}$$

where $i=1,2,3,\ldots,n$ and $h(.\,;\,.)$ is neighborhood function around winning node.

$$h(\text{J}:i,j) = \exp\left(\frac{-\left\|v_{i,j} - v_{iJ}\right\|}{2\bar{\sigma}^2(t)}\right) \text{Where } h(\text{J}:i,j) \in [0,1] \tag{16}$$

and

$$\bar{\sigma}(t) = \sigma_0 \exp\left(\frac{-t}{T}\right), \text{ where } t \text{ is current iteration and } T \text{ is maximum number of iterations.} \tag{17}$$

Step 5: Test the stopping criteria.

Step 6: Updating the weights from node Z_j to the output unit as:

$$w_{iJ}(\text{new}) = w_{iJ}(\text{old}) + \beta\, h(\text{J}:i,j)(y_i - w_{Jk}) \text{ for} 1 \leq k \leq m \tag{18}$$

where β is *learning rate*.

Step 7: Test the stopping condition (i.e. fixed number of epoch or its learning rate has reduced to negligible value)

Testing Phase

Step 0: Set the initial weights i.e. the weights obtain during training.

Step 1: Apply MDEA-KN to the input vector X.
Step 2: Find unit J that is closet to vector X.
Step 3: Set activations of output units.
Step 4: Apply activation function at y_k, where $y_k = \sum_j z_j w_{jk}$.

SIMULATION RESULTS

In this section we will discuss some benchmark problem and numerical simulation to demonstrate the effectiveness of proposed TS-model. The main objective of proposed model is to design a control law such that output of the system can approximately track a given reference signal with significant error. For simulation of uncertain nonlinear system with MATLAB platform with ODE45 function.

Example 1: Let uncertain nonlinear dynamical system (Hsu, 2007) is:

$$
\begin{aligned}
x_1(k+1) &= x_2(k) \\
x_2(k+1) &= f(x(k)) + u(k)
\end{aligned}
\tag{19}
$$

where

$$
f(x(k)) = -\frac{5}{8}\left[\frac{x_1(k)}{1 + x_2^2(k)}\right] + 0.65\, x_2(k)
\tag{20}
$$

is nonlinear.

The objective is to track reference signal $x_d(k)$ is given by:

$$
x_d(k) = 0.1\sin(wkT + \xi)
\tag{21}
$$

where $w = 0.1$, $\xi = \pi / 2$ and T is sampling interval taken as 250 and the desired signal is sine wave.

Figure 3 and Figure 4 shows the error $e(k) = y(k) - \bar{y}(k)$ and outputs of the uncertain dynamical system using MDEA-KN. If bounded unknown disturbance $d(k)$ and sampling interval T=250. Figure 4 shows that accuracy of MDEA-KN. Chi-square and t-test for the null hypothesis H_0 that the error vector $e(k) = y(k) - \bar{y}(k)$ for example 1 which is random in nature is acceptable from a normal distribution with mean and variance estimated from $e(k)$ against the H_1 that the data are not normally distributed with the estimated mean and variance. Chi-square and t-test show that H_0 is accepted at 5% level of significance.

Example 2: One-Link Manipulator with a BDC Motor.

Figure 3. Error of system using MDEA-KN of example 1

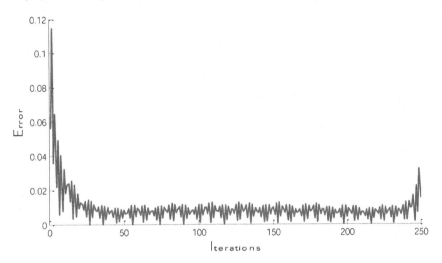

Figure 4. Performance of MDEA-KN for example 1

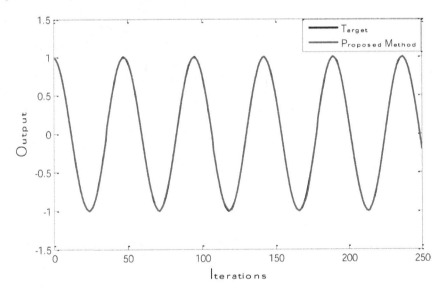

For validation of proposed TS-model is tested on a popular benchmark problem, known as one-link manipulator actuated by brush dc (BDC) motor (Wang & Huang, 2005). Differential equation of BDC motor is given in equation (22)

$$\begin{cases} D\ddot{\alpha} + B\dot{\alpha} + N\sin\alpha = I + \Delta_I \\ M\dot{I} = -HI - K_m\dot{\alpha} + V \end{cases} \tag{22}$$

where α, $\dot{\alpha}$ and $\ddot{\alpha}$ be the angular position, velocity and acceleration respectively. Whereas, I denotes the current, Δ_I denotes the unknown disturbances and V is the input voltage, values of parameter are

Figure 5. $\left(t, x_1, x_2\right)$ *space representation*

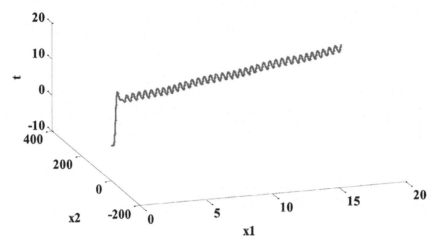

Figure 6. Tracking performance of TS model output and reference signal

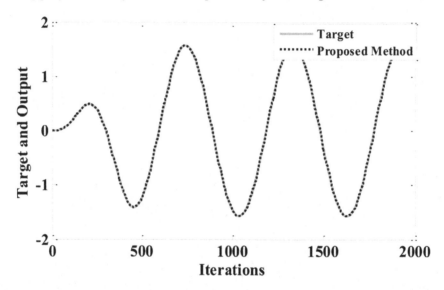

given by: *D=1, B=1, M=0.05, H=0.5, N=10, K_m =10*, and current disturbance Δ_I = *4sin(t)*. In Equation 22 first part represent one-link robot and second part represents BDC electrical system. Introducing some new cartesian variable, Equation 22 is converted into following form of uncertain nonlinear system.

Let $v_1 = \alpha$, $v_2 = \dot{\alpha}$, $v_3 = I$ and *u=V*, then Equation 22 can be expressed as

$$
\begin{cases}
\dot{v}_1 = v_2 \\
\dot{v}_2 = -10\sin v_1 - v_2 + v_3 + 4\sin k \\
\dot{v}_3 = -200v_2 - 10v_3 + 20u \\
y = v_1
\end{cases}
\tag{23}
$$

Figure 7. Trajectory of tracking error using proposed method

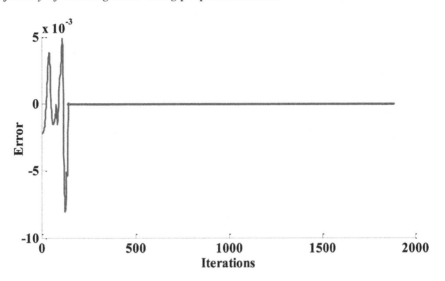

The reference signal is

$$y_r = (\pi / 2)\sin(k)\left(1 - e^{-0.2k^2}\right)$$

and $v_1 \in [-1,1]$, $v_2 \in [-3,3]$ and $v_3 \in [-5,5]$. Figure 5 and Figure 6, shows the $\left(t, x_1, x_2\right)$ space and tracking performance of TS model, where as Figure 7 shows the tracking error.

Example 3: Benchmark problem.

In this example we will consider another important benchmark problem i.e. following second order uncertain nonlinear system in the general form

$$\dot{x}_1 = 0.5x_1 + \left(1 + 0.1x_1^2\right)x_2 + 0.1\left(1 - \cos^2(x_1 x_2)\right)$$

$$\dot{x}_2 = x_1 x_2 + (2 + \cos x_1)u + 0.2\sin(x_1 x_2)$$

$$y = x_1 \tag{24}$$

The reference signal $y_r = \sin(t)$ for ODE45 the centers for $x_1 \in [-1,1]$ and $x_2 \in [-3,3]$ are evenly spaced.

Figure 8. $\left(t, x_1, x_2\right)$ *space representation*

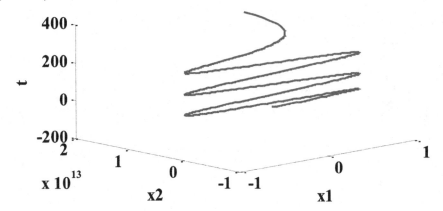

Figure 9. Tracking performance of TS model output (dotted line) and reference signal (solid line)

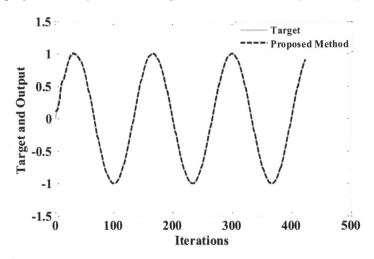

Figure 10. Trajectory of tracking error using proposed method

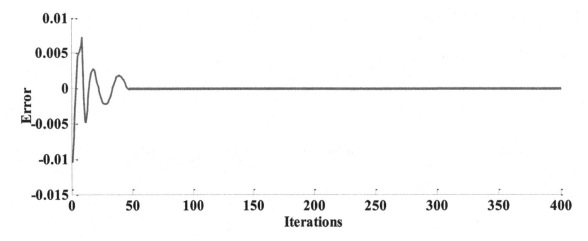

4.1 COMPUTATIONAL COMPLEXITY

Algorithmic complexities of all metaheuristic are easy to calculate and implement. MDEA contains one while loop based on maximum iteration and two inner for loop depends on size of population. So the time complexity of MDEA in worst case is $O\left(nt\right)$, if n is much smaller in comparison to t then complexity of MDEA is linear i.e. $O(t)$. The main computational cost is evaluation of objective functions, for all optimization problems. If n is relatively large it is possible to use for loop by sorting of positions using some sorting algorithm, then time complexity of MDEA will be $O(tn\log(n))$. Time complexity of training neural network for input data size N is $O(N)$ and complexity of choosing offspring for all vectors to obtain best solution is $O(tn\log(n))$. Hence, the overall time complexity of MDEA-KN is compounded as $O(tn\log(n)) + O(N)$.

CONCLUSION

Uncertain nonlinear discrete time systems and forecasting problems are a dynamic research area having fundamental importance for industries. The work presented in this paper for improving the accuracy of forecasting and milk production using MDEA-KN. The combination of MDEA with some modification based Kohonen neural network is developed with the scope of creating an improved balance between premature convergence and stagnation. Firstly, optimize the MSE function using MDEA, select output as initial weights from input to hidden layer of KN for good results. Experimental study demonstrates that the proposed MDEA-KN model achieves good performance. Numerical results show that MDEA-KN has more admirable performance in terms of solution quality, speed convergence and approximation capability. It is shown that the MDEA-KN models can generally be considered adequate in representing the approximation of nonlinear discrete-time systems, forecasting and exchange rate prediction. In future the other variety of metaheuristic algorithm and neural network can be used as well for recognizing such type problems also we can consider stochastic nonlinear problems.

REFERENCES

Alfaro-Ponce, M., Arguelles, A., & Chairez, I. (2014). Continuous neural identifier for certain nonlinear systems with time in the input signal. *Neural Networks*, *60*, 53–66. doi:10.1016/j.neunet.2014.07.002 PMID:25150629

Billings, S. A. (2013). *Nonlinear System Identification: NARMAX methods in the time, Frequency, andSaptio-Temporal Domains*. Chichester, UK: Wiley. doi:10.1002/9781118535561

Bortoletti, A., Flore, C., & Di, . (2003). A new class of Quasi-Newtonian methods for optimal learning in MLP-networks. *IEEE Transactions on Neural Networks*, *14*(2), 263–273. doi:10.1109/TNN.2003.809425 PMID:18238010

Chakraborty, U. K. (2008). *Advances in Differential Evolution: Studies in Computational Intelligence*. Heidelberg, Germany: Springer. doi:10.1007/978-3-540-68830-3

Chen, G., & Pham, T. T. (2000). *Introduction to fuzzy set, fuzzy logic and fuzzy control system*. New York: CRC Press. doi:10.1201/9781420039818

Chen, S., & Billings, S. A. (1989). Representation of nonlinear systems: The NARMAX model. *International Journal of Control, 49*(3), 1013–1032. doi:10.1080/00207178908559683

Dinga, F., & Chenb, T. (2005). Identification of Hammerstein nonlinear ARMAX systems. *Automatica, 41*(9), 1479–1489. doi:10.1016/j.automatica.2005.03.026

Ge, S., & Wang, C. (2002). Direct adaptive NN control of a class of nonlinear systems. *IEEE Transactions on Neural Networks, 13*(1), 214–221. doi:10.1109/72.977306 PMID:18244420

Guozeng, C., & Zhen, W. (2015). Adaptive Centralized NN control of large scale stochastic nonlinear time delay systems with unknown dead zone inputs. *Neurocomputing, 158*, 194–203. doi:10.1016/j.neucom.2015.01.048

Hernandez, E., & Arkun, Y. (1993). Control of nonlinear system using polynomial ARMA models. *AIChE Journal. American Institute of Chemical Engineers, 39*(3), 446–460. doi:10.1002/aic.690390308

Hsu, C. F. (2007). Self-organizing adaptive fuzzy neural network for a class of nonlinear system. *IEEE Transactions on Neural Networks, 18*(4), 1232–1241. doi:10.1109/TNN.2007.899178 PMID:17668674

Hu, Y. H., & Hwang, J. N. (2001). Handbook of Neural Network Signal Processing. CRC Press.

Johansson, M., & Rantzer, A. (1998). Computation of piecewise quadratic Lyapunov functions for hybrid systems. *IEEE Transactions on Automatic Control, 43*(4), 555–559. doi:10.1109/9.664157

Jun, S., & Shuping, H. (2015). Finite time robust passive control for a class of uncertain Lipschitz nonlinear systems with time delays. *Neurocomputing, 159*, 275–281. doi:10.1016/j.neucom.2015.01.038

Laboid, S., & Guerra, T. (2007). Adaptive fuzzy control of a class of SISO nonaffine nonlinear systems. *Fuzzy Sets and Systems, 158*(10), 1126–1137. doi:10.1016/j.fss.2006.11.013

Lee, T.T., & Jeng, J.T. (1998). The Chebyshev polynomial based unified model neural network for functional approximation. *IEEE Trans. Syst. Man Cybern B, 28*, 925-935.

Li, T., Wang, D., Feng, G., & Tong, S. (2010). A DSC approach to robust adaptive NN tracking control for strict-feedback nonlinear systems. *IEEE Transactions on Systems, Man, and Cybernetics. Part B, Cybernetics, 40*(3), 915–927. doi:10.1109/TSMCB.2009.2033563 PMID:19887321

Li, Y., Qiung, S., Zhuang, X., & Kaynak, O. (2004). Robust and adaptive backstepping control for nonlinear system using RBF neural networks. *IEEE Transactions on Neural Networks, 15*(3), 693–701. doi:10.1109/TNN.2004.826215 PMID:15384556

Narendra, K. S., & Parthaasarathy, K. (1990). Identification and control of dynamical systems using neural networks. *IEEE Transactions on Neural Networks, 1*(1), 4–27. doi:10.1109/72.80202 PMID:18282820

Pratihar, D. K. (2013). *Soft Computing: Fundamentals and Applications* (1st ed.). Alpha Science International Ltd.

Sakhre, V., Singh, U. P., & Jain, S. (2016). FCPN Approach for Uncertain Nonlinear Dynamical System with Unknown Disturbance. *International Journal of Fuzzy Systems*. doi:10.1007/s40815-016-0145-5

Sanchez, E., Shibata, T. & Zadeh, L.A. (1997). *Genetic algorithm and fuzzy logic system, Soft Computing Perspective*. World Scientific Singapore.

Shigen, G., Hairong, D., Ning, B., & Chen, L. (2015). Neural adaptive control for uncertain nonlinear system with input: State transformation based output feedback. *Neurocomputing*, *159*, 117–125. doi:10.1016/j.neucom.2015.02.012

Singh, U. P., Jain, S., Singh, R. K., Parmar, M., Makwana, R. R. S., & Kumare, J. S. (2016). Dynamic Surface Control Based TS-Fuzzy Model for a Class of Uncertain Nonlinear Systems. *International Journal of Control Theory and Applications*, *9*(2), 1333–1345.

Soderstrom, T., & Stoica, P. (1989). *System Identification*. New York: Prentice Hall.

Song, B., & Hedrick, J. K. (2004). Observer-based dynamic surface control for a class of nonlinear systems: An LMI approach. *IEEE Transactions on Automatic Control*, *49*(11), 1995–2001. doi:10.1109/TAC.2004.837562

Storn, R., & Price, K. (1997). Differential Evolution: A Simple and Efficient Heuristic for Global Optimization Over Continuous Space. *Journal of Global Optimization*, *11*(4), 341–359. doi:10.1023/A:1008202821328

Ticknor, J. L. (2013). A Bayesian regularized artificial network for stock market forecasting. *Expert Systems with Applications*, *40*(14), 5501–5506. doi:10.1016/j.eswa.2013.04.013

Tong, S., Li, Y., Feng, G., & Li, T. (2011). Observer based adaptive fuzzy backstepping dynamic surface control for a class of MIMO nonlinear systems. *IEEE Transactions on Systems, Man, and Cybernetics*, *41*(4), 1124–1134. doi:10.1109/TSMCB.2011.2108283 PMID:21317084

Tong, S. C., Li, H. X., & Wang, W. (2004). Observer based adaptive fuzzy control for SISO nonlinear systems. *Fuzzy Sets and Systems*, *148*(3), 355–376. doi:10.1016/j.fss.2003.11.017

Vidyasagar, M. (1993). *Nonlinear System Analysis* (2nd ed.). Prentice Hall.

Wang, D., & Huang, J. (2005). Neural network based adaptive dynamic surface control for a class of uncertain nonlinear system in strict feedback form. *IEEE Transactions on Neural Networks*, *16*(1), 195–202. doi:10.1109/TNN.2004.839354 PMID:15732399

Wang, Y., Zhang, H., & Wang, Y. (2006). Fuzzy adaptive control of stochastic nonlinear systems with unknown virtual gain function. *ActaAutom. Sin*, *32*, 170–178.

Watanbe, K., Matsuura, I., Abe, M., Kebota, M., & Himelblau, D. M. (1989). Incipient fault diagnosis of chemical processes via artificial neural networks. *AIChE Journal. American Institute of Chemical Engineers*, *35*(11), 1803–1812. doi:10.1002/aic.690351106

Wu, X., Wu, X., Luo, X., & Guan, X. (2012). Dynamic surface control for a class of state constrained nonlinear systems with uncertain time delays. *IET Control Theory Appl*, *6*(12), 1948–1957. doi:10.1049/iet-cta.2011.0543

Xie, Y., Guo, B., Gu, L., Li, J., & Stoica, P. (2006). Multistatic adaptive microwave imaging for early breast cancer detection. *IEEE Transactions on Bio-Medical Engineering, 53*(8), 1647–1657. doi:10.1109/TBME.2006.878058 PMID:16916099

Yang, Y., & Chan, W. (2014). Adaptive dynamic surface control for uncertain nonlinear systems with interval type-2 fuzzy neural networks. *IEEE Trans. Cybern, 44*(2), 293–304. doi:10.1109/TCYB.2013.2253548 PMID:23757550

Yang, Y., & Chan, W. (2014). Adaptive dynamic surface control for uncertain nonlinear systems with interval type-2 fuzzy neural networks. *IEEE Trans. Cybern, 44*(2), 293–304. doi:10.1109/TCYB.2013.2253548 PMID:23757550

Yang, X.S. (2010). A new metaheuristic bat inspired algorithm, in Nature Inspired Cooperative Strategies for Optimization (NISO 2010). *Studies in Computational Intelligence, 284,* 65-74.

Zhang, H., Wang, Z., & Liu, D. (2008). Global asymptotic stability of recurrent neural network with multiple time-varying delays. *IEEE Transactions on Neural Networks, 19*(5), 855–873. doi:10.1109/TNN.2007.912319 PMID:18467214

Zhang, H., Yang, F., Liu, S., & Zhang, Q. (2013). Stability analysis for neural network with time-varying delay based on quadratic convex combination. *IEEE Trans. Neural Netw. Learn Syst, 24*(4), 513–521. doi:10.1109/TNNLS.2012.2236571 PMID:24808373

Zhang, H., & Yang, W. (2008). Stability analysis of Markovian jumping stochastic cohen-Grossberg neural network with mixed time delays. *IEEE Transactions on Neural Networks, 19*(2), 366–370. doi:10.1109/TNN.2007.910738 PMID:18269968

Zhang, T., & Xiaonan, X. (2015). Decentralized adaptive fuzzy output feedback control of stochastic nonlinear large scale systems with dynamic un certainties. *Information Sciences, 315,* 17–18. doi:10.1016/j.ins.2015.04.002

Zhang, Y. (2002). *Analysis and design of recurrent neural networks and their applications to control and robotic systems* (Ph.D. dissertation). The Chinese University of Hong Kong, Hong Kong.

Zhang, Y., & Zhang, C. Yi. (2011). Neural Network and Neural dynamic method. NOVA Science Publishers.

Zhouhua, P., Dan, W., Zhang, H., & Yejin, L. (2015). Coopeative output feedback adaptive control of uncertain nonlinear multi-agent systems with a dynamic leader. *Neurocomputing, 149,* 132–141. doi:10.1016/j.neucom.2013.12.064

Chapter 17
A Brief Insight into Nanorobotics

Sanchita Paul
Birla Institute of Technology, India

ABSTRACT

The construction of a practical nanorobot is a definite futuristic reality. However development of a Nanorobot is associated with a multitude of challenges and limitations related mainly to its control and behavior aspects in different dynamic work environments. In this chapter a novel Nanorobot movement control algorithms in dynamic environment has being introduced. To avoid obstacles during movement trajectory, swarm intelligence based approach and for sensing, path planning, obstacle avoidance and target detection of nano-robot Quorum and RFID based approach has been utilized. Major proportion of work has been done on Microsoft Robotics Developer Studio 2008 (MSRD, 2008) along with two kinds of programming environment VPL and SPL. The chapter also includes a description of how nanorobotics technology has been applied in medical field. In this context, a non invasive method to treat a brain blood clot using nanorobots has being explained. Various other aspects of application of nanorobots has also been briefly mentioned.

INTRODUCTION

Richard P. Feynman once said "A friend of mine (Albert R. Hibbs) suggested a very interesting possibility for relatively small machines. He says that, although it is a very wild idea, it would be interesting in surgery if you could swallow the surgeon. You put the mechanical surgeon inside the blood vessel and it goes into the heart and looks around (of course the information has to be fed out.) It finds out which valve is the faulty one and takes a little knife and slices it out. Other small machines might be permanently incorporated in the body to assist some inadequately functioning organ.".However conventional techniques of robotics were found incapable to assist in the diagnosis and cure of cell or molecular scale diseases like cancer or cardiac diseases. This called for the development of nanoscale robots which can perform medical operations inside human body with nanoscale precision.

DOI: 10.4018/978-1-5225-1785-6.ch017

Nanotechnology based robots namely nanorobots have enabled science to associate with engineering activities at the cellular level. Nano-sized nanorobots can investigate any biological environment (cell culture or human body) at the microscopic level. For example treatment of medical conditions such as cancer and thrombi can be done by following a temporal pattern and employing definite artificial intelligence based methods to find the affected region in the body. Future medical nanotechnologies have been imagined to employ nanorobots injected into the human body to perform treatment on a cellular level. Every nanorobot placed inside the human body will encounter immune system as an obstacle while circulating within a human body. Thus nanorobot must formulate a strategy to avoid and bypass such immune system. To avoid obstacles during movement trajectory, swarm intelligent based approach and Quorum and RFID based approach for sensing, path planning, obstacle avoidance and target identification of nano-robot has been also proposed in this chapter. Today, nanorobots have found a wide application in a spectrum of medical treatment technologies. Moreover since Nanorobot have to work in a human body based environment, numerous additional requirements in size, reliability, efficiency, security and bio-computability are essentially required. This will enable it to access capillary vessels and cells; deliver drugs quantitatively at desired positions, repair cells and gene. While these nanorobots have not being fabricated yet, a study of the theoretical and simulation aspects for defining design strategies, capabilities, applications and limitations alongwith an innovative algorithm for movement control have been discussed comprehensively in this chapter.

The most recent applications of nanorobots in medical treatment include treatment of brain blood clot (clot in brain blood vessel) and has been discussed briefly in this chapter (first nanorobot movement control algorithm was described by Cavalcanti, A., et.al (2004)) .

In the present chapter:

- Section 2 describes how Nanotechnology and Bionanotechnology support a broad range of scientific disciplines and engineering.
- Section 3 presents nanorobot design, in which all the components have been described with their individual working in a nano environment.
- Section 4 describes nanorobot movement control algorithms in dynamic environment.
- Section 5 describes MRDS 2008 which is a 3D simulation tools for simulating Nanorobot control and movement.
- Section 6 presents a non invasive method to treat brain blood clot through nanorobot.
- Section 7 describes the summary of the work, state its major contributions, and hints on future directions.

NANOSCIENCE AND NANOTECHNOLOGY

Nanoscience is the study of phenomena and manipulation of materials at atomic, molecular and macro-molecular scales, where properties differ significantly from those at a larger scale.

Nanotechnologies are the design, characterisation, production and application of structures, devices and systems by controlling shape and size at nanometre scale.The prefix of nanotechnology derives from 'nanos' – the Greek word for dwarf. A nanometer is a billionth of a meter, or to put it comparatively, about 1/80,000 of the diameter of a human hair. The size-related challenge is the ability to measure, manipulate, and assemble matter with features on the scale of 1-100nm. Nanotechnology, in its tradi-

Figure 1. Size comparison of particles in nanometers

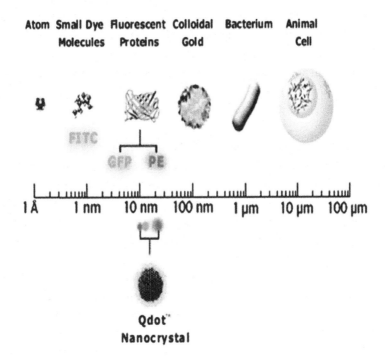

tional sense, means building things from the bottom up, with atomic precision .When K. Eric Drexler popularized the word 'nanotechnology' in the 1980's, he was talking about building machines on the scale of molecules, a few nanometers wide motors, robot arms, and even whole computers, far smaller than a cell. The U.S. National Nanotechnology Initiative was created to fund this kind of nanotech: their definition includes anything smaller than 100 nanometers with novel properties (Figure 1). In order to achieve a cost-effective mean of nanotechnology, automation of molecular manufacturing is necessary.

Nanotechnology has the ability to see and control individual atoms and molecules. However observing something as small as an atom with the naked eye or even with typical scientific microscopes is impossible. The microscopes needed to see things at the nanoscale were invented relatively recently—about 30 years ago. Once scientists had the right tools, such as the scanning tunneling microscope (STM) and the atomic force microscope (AFM), the age of nanotechnology was born.

Nanobiotechnology or Bionanotechnology

Nanobiotechnology, bionanotechnology, and nanobiology are terms that refer to the intersection of nanotechnology and biology. Given that the subject is one that has only emerged very recently, Bionanotechnology and Nanobiotechnology serve as blanket terms for various related technologies. Nanotechnology is the key technology of the 21st century. This discipline helps to indicate the merger of biological research with various fields of nanotechnology. Concepts that are enhanced through nanobiology include: nanodevices, nanoparticles, and nanoscale phenomena that occurs within the discipline of nanotechnology. This technical approach to biology allows scientists to imagine and create systems that can be used for biological research. Biologically inspired nanotechnology uses biological systems as the inspirations for technologies not yet created. However, as with nanotechnology and biotechnology, bionanotechnology does have many potential ethical issues associated with it.

The most important objectives that are frequently found in nanobiology involve applying nanotools to relevant medical/biological problems and refining these applications. Developing new tools, such as peptoid nanosheets, for medical and biological purposes is another primary objective in nanotechnology.

DNA Nanotechnology

The field of structural DNA nanotechnology utilizes DNA's powerful base-pairing molecular recognition criteria to help solve a number of problems facing researchers in material science and nanotechnology. In this, DNA is stripped away from its preconceived biological role, and is treated as a synthetic polymer. A key principle in the study of DNA nanostructures is the use of self-assembly processes to actuate the molecular assembly. Since self-assembly operates naturally at the molecular scale, it does not suffer from the limitation in scale reduction that so restricts lithography or other more conventional top-down manufacturing techniques.

DNA nanotechnology uses reciprocal exchange between DNA double helices or hairpins to produce branched DNA motifs, like Holliday junctions, or related structures, such as double crossover (DX), triple crossover (TX), paranemic crossover (PX) and DNA parallelogram motifs. We combine DNA motifs to produce specific structures by using sticky-ended cohesion (below, left). The strength of sticky-ended cohesion is that it produces predictable adhesion combined with known structure. From simple branched junctions, DNA stick polyhedra, such as a cube (below, right) and a truncated octahedron, several deliberately designed knots, and Borromean rings can be constructed (Figure 2).

DNA as Nano Material

DNA can be also recognized as a promising functional nanomaterial (See Table 1).

NANOROBOTICS

Nanorobotics is the emerging technology field creating machines or robots whose components are at or close to the scale of a nanometre (10^{-9} meters). More specifically, nanorobotics refers to the nanotechnology engineering discipline of designing and building nanorobots, with devices ranging in size from 0.1–10 micrometers and constructed of nanoscale or molecular components. The names nanobots, nanoids, nanites, nanomachine, or nanomites have also been used to describe these devices currently under research and development.

Nanorobot

A nanorobot is essentially a controllable machine at the nano meter or molecular scale that is composed of nano-scale components and algorithmically to input force and information. Nanorobots would constitute any active structure (nano-scale) capable of actuation, sensing, signaling, information processing, intelligence, and swarm behavior at nano-scale. Some of the characteristic abilities that are desirable for a nanorobot to function may include:

Figure 2. DNA Nano structures

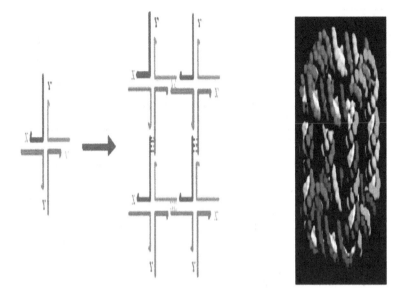

1. **Swarm Intelligence:** Decentralization and distributive intelligence.
2. **Self-Assembly and Replication:** Assemblage at nano-scale and "nano-maintenance".
3. **Nano-Information Processing and Programmability:** For programming and controlling nano-robots (autonomous nanorobots).
4. **Nano- to Macro-World Interface Architecture:** An architecture enabling instant access to the nanorobots and its control and maintenance.

Requirements for Nanorobot Design

- Due to its functions in human bloodstream and tissues it must be mobile and have powerful navigation system.
- It may have a wide range of sensors to navigate through human body and fast molecular and cell identification.
- It may have powerful transport subsystem to molecular deliver system (it must deliver molecules and atoms to the working nanomanipulators from storage systems).
- Wide range of computer-guided nanomanipulators also required.
- It may have broadcasting system which can connect to other nanorobots and to macro computers.
- Finally, it may have long telescopic manipulators to holding cells or surfaces.

Different Types of Nanorobot used for Medicine

- **Microbivore Nanorobots:** These nanorobots would function similarly to the white blood cells in our bodies, but they are designed to be much faster at destroying bacteria.
- **Respirocyte Nanorobots:** These nanorobots would function in a similar way to the red blood cells in our bodies; however, they are designed to carry much more oxygen than natural red blood cells.

Table 1. Role of DNA as a Nanomaterial

S No.	Roles of DNA as a Nanomaterial	Description of Roles
1	DNA as a conductive nanowire	• Preparation of a conducting nanowire derived from DNA has been reported by Braun, et.al. (1998) and Willner (2002). • Braun, et.al (1998) attached DNA of different sequences onto two microelectrodes respectively. A connection between the two electrodes was then made, with the DNA fragment complementary to both electrode-linked DNA sequences, using DNA-DNA hybridization. • Later on Keren, et.al (2002) proposed molecular lithography using single stranded DNA binding protein and Kawasaki (2003) proposed a photoelectric transfer material.
2	DNA as a molecular recognition element	• Molecular recognition, as for antibodies, the methodology is called 'in vitro selection' or systematic evolution of ligands by exponential enrichment (SELEX), which is one of the combinatorial bioengineering techniques was proposed by Ellington, Szostak (1990), Tuerk (1990) and Gold (1995). • The oligonucleotide obtained by SELEX is called an aptamer (retrieved from the aptamer databaes http://aptamer.icmb.utexas.edu/index.html), was first proposed by Ito, et.al. (2000) and then again by Ito (2004) who reported advence nature of Aptamer. An example of a medical drug is the recent development, by Rusconi et al (2002)., of an aptamer that acts as an anti-thrombogenic agent by targeting the blood coagulation factor IXa.
3	DNA as a catalyst	• There are two methods for the preparation of catalytic DNA. • One is the 'indirect method', similar to the preparation method for catalytic antibodies, in which specific DNA molecules that bind to a transition state analog as a target molecule are selected. For example, the method affords the methylporphyrin-binding of RNA or DNA (Ito, 2004). • The second method for acquiring a DNAzyme is the 'direct method'. This method can result in catalytic DNA that catalyzes an amide formation, an ester formation, or a Diels–Alder reaction was proposed by Seeling, et.al. (2000).
4	DNA as nanoarchitecture	• Seeman succeeded in preparing several architectures using an overlap width for adhesion and with branched structures (Seeman, 2003). • There are different examples that have considered the use of DNA as a nanoarchitecture and the interaction of DNA with a carbon nanotube.A DNA-modified nanotube has been widely illustrated by Baker, et.al. (2002), Gao, et.al. (2003) and Nguyen, (2003). • A gold nanoparticle–DNA complex was investigated by Mirkin(2000)and Harnack, et.al. (2002) for DNA sequencing and protein detection was proposed by Stojanovic, et. al (2002).
5	DNA as nanodevice	• Many types of nanodevices have been designed using the functions of DNA. An example of nanodevice is aptamer beacons. • Recently, a nanodevice based on the visible light analytical system has been designed (Stojanovic, 2002). • Moreover, integrated nanodevice systems including 'molecular recognition' and 'catalytic function' have been frequently reported.
6	DNA as nanomachine	Yurke et al. (2000) has developed a DNA machine that worked with DNA fuel.

- **Clottocyte Nanorobots:** These robots function similarly to the platelets in our blood. Platelets stick together in a wound to form a clot, stopping blood flow.
- **Cellular Repair Nanorobots:** These little nanorobots could be built to perform surgical procedures more precisely. By working at the cellular level, such nanorobots could prevent much of the damage caused by the comparatively clumsy scalpel.

Bio-Nanorobotics

In nano electronics, DNA could be used as molecular switches for molecular memories or electronic circuitry to assemble future nano-electronics transistors which was proposed by Diez, et.al.(2003), and Hoummady, Fujita (1999). In nanorobotics (Figure 3), structural elements could be carbon nanotubes while the passive/active joints are formed by appropriately designed DNA elements which was reported by Dwyer, et.al. (2004). In such nanodevices, nature assembles nano-scene components using molecular recognition and was described by Montegano, et.al.(1999). In the case of DNA, hydrogen bonding provides the specificity behind the matching of complementary pairs of single-stranded (ss) DNA to hybridize into a double strand (ds) of helical DNA. To achieve these, prototyping tools based on molecular dynamic (MD) simulators should be developed in order to understand the molecular mechanics of proteins and develop dynamic and kinematic models to study their performances and control aspects. The ability to visualize the atom-to-atom interaction in real-time and see the results in a fully immersive 3-D environment is an additional feature of such simulations can be done using Virtual Reality (VR) technology, which not only provides immersive visualization but also gives an added functionality of CAD-based design, simulation, navigation and interactive manipulation of molecular graphical objects which was desibribed by Hamdi, et.al., (2005). Using simulated biological nano-environments in virtual environments, the operator can design and characterize through physical simulation the behavior of molecular robots. Adding haptic interaction, the operator can explore and prevent the problems of bionanorobots in their native environment.

Medical Nanorobot Architecture

The architecture for a nanorobot must include the necessary devices for monitoring the most important aspects of its operational workspace: the human body. The main components used for the medical nanorobot architecture are described next in Table 2

Estimated Integrated Hardware Architecture of Nanorobot

The nanorobot model includes Generic differential drive (GDD), sicklaser rangefinder, multiplexer, demultiplexer for avoiding the obstacle and locating the target region. Integrated sicklaser range finder (SLRF) and generic differential drive (GDD) incorporated in the nanorobot model provides the movement control of the nanorobot and also helps it to avoid the obstacles. It also provides laser signals for

Figure 3. Basic DNA-based molecular components; (a) and (b) represent passive joint (c) active joint

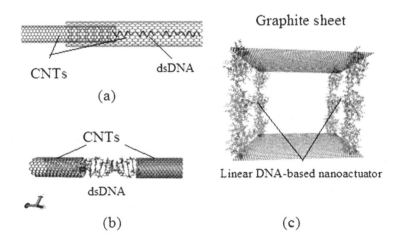

Table 2. Components of a Nanorobot

Parameters	Description
Manufacturing Technology	CMOS and VLSI design using extreme ultraviolet lithography provides high precision and a commercial way for manufacturing early nanodevices and nanoelectronics systems.
Sensors	**(I) Chemical Sensor** • Silicon based chemical sensor architecture on two level system has been used from past so many years. Some other sensors based on CMOS have resulted in satisfied efficiency but there costs are found to be quite expensive. • The nanosensors are based on fact of low energy and high sensitivity. These sensors have sometimes faces some problems in quantum mechanical tunneling where they are found to be inefficient in providing information. • The sensors are typically sensitive in the range of 8-12 micrometers where electrons can be detected and amplified into signal. Thus, the change in the thermal and chemical concentration inside the vessel will be used as a guiding principle by the nanorobots to detect the targeted area. **(II) Thermal Sensor** • Human has skin temperature of about 93F infrared energy with wavelength between 9 to 10 micrometers. For controlling the cell signaling process, Ca++ (calcium ion) serves as an intracellular mediator in a wide variety of cell response including neurotransmission, cellular metabolism and signal cascade that are regulated by calcium calmodulin – dependent protein fibrinogen . • These sensors has a characteristics resonance frequency which shifts the response signal with the change in fluid velocity which can be calculated by the following equation: • Where the densities of the sensor material and fluid, η are is the fluid viscosity, d is the sensor thickness and is the resonance frequency of the sensor. • These sensors are quite useful in target detection based on temperature, change and measurement in body temperature which provides high thermal conductivity and fast frequency response. **(III) Bio- Sensor** • The nanorobot uses sensors allowing it to detect nearby objects in the environment or its target region like Cancer cell. • Rhodopsin is a light sensor. • Nanosensors include long distance sensor and short distance sensor, the former navigate the nanorobot to the target tissue, other nanorobots or obstacle. • Biochemical sensors can perceive chemical grads, pH, temperature, and radiation of the environment as described by Huai-wei, et.al.(2005). • There are many groups utilize the mechanical, light, chemical, electrical, biological characteristics to construct nanosensors. **(IV) Temperature Sensor** • CMOS as a thermoelectric sensor has advantage of linear self-generated response with system integration without requiring bias or temperature stabilization. • Thus the infrared array could be integrated on a single chip within amplifiers and signal processing capabilities. Such approach allows a fast pace towards miniaturization with no loss of efficiency due electromagnetic noise. • CMOS could be operated at very low voltage levels, which is also a positive aspect, presenting good functionality and requiring little energy. Cantilever and bridge types are also valid techniques for possible different ways to implement CMOS thermoelectric sensors.

continued on following page

the target detection and attracting other nanorobots to reach the targeted area. The distance measured (Dist) is based on the position of Right, Left and Centre (Rt, Lt, C) of the nanorobot and the object. These are decided by the data transmission generated by the multiplexer and demultiplexer in the form of bits. The two modes of operation i.e. manual and automatic mode of operations are used.

If it is being operated manually, the three buttons Trigger, Thumbstick and Button change are used to operate the nanorobots, otherwise the nanorobots move automatically. Since the size of nanorobots is few nanometers, it can freely move inside our body. The computation is being performed by a nanosensor and the other parameters. The nanorobot exterior material consists of carbon nanotubes (CNT) that minimizes fibrinogen protein and other blood proteins adsorption providing biocompatibility to avoid immune system attack. The nanorobot has sensory ability to detect nearby obstacles as well as the chemical signals for its task such as Calcium ion protein concentrations (CC).

Table 2. Continued

Parameters	Description
Actuators	**CNT-ATP (nano-bio-actuator)** • For a bio- nanorobot the ATP has been used as an actuator based on biological patterns and CNTs as an architecture along with fibrinogen protein which serves for ionic flux used for integrating the devices of molecular machine. • The ion channels from the electrochemical signals of calcium are made necessary for actuator operation, enabling the nanorobots for active interaction with the bloodstream patterns. **CNT-SOI-CMOS (nano-electronic-actuator)** • The use of CNTs as conductive structures permits electrostatically driven motions providing the forces necessary for nanomanipulation. • CNTs can be used as a material for commercial applications on building devices and nanoelectronics such as nanotweezers and memory systems. • Siliconon- insulator (SOI) technology has been used for transistors with high performance, low heating and energy consumption for very-large-scale integration (VLSI) devices. • CNT selfassembly and SOI properties can be combined in a CMOS design to enable high-performance nanoelectronics and nanoactuators to be manufactured. **MOTORS** **(I) ATP (Nano-bio-motor)** • ATP synthesis is the process within the mitochondria of a cell by which a rotary engine uses the potential difference across the lipid bilayer to power a chemical transformation of Adenosine Di-Phosphate (ADP) into ATP. • Therefore it can be used as a motor in DNA nanorobotics. The positive ions try to move to a lower potential, and the negative ions try to move to a higher one, thus creating a force which is used to spin the rotor and was first described by Huai-wai, et.al (2005) and further explained by Ummat, et.al. (2005). **(II) VPL Motor (Nano-bio-motor)** • Computational studies are performed to predict and verify the performance of a new nanoscale bimolecular motor: The Viral Protein Linear (VPL) Motor was proposed by Montegano, Bachand (1999). • The motor is based on a conformational change observed in a family of viral envelope proteins when subjected to a changing pH environment. • The conformational change produces a motion of about 10 nm, making the VPL a basic linear actuator which can be further interfaced with other organic/inorganic nanoscale components such as DNA actuators and carbon nanotubes.
Data transmission	**(I) RFID** • The application of devices and sensors implanted inside the human body to transmit data about the health of patients can provide great advantages in continuous medical monitoring. Most recently, the use of RFID for in vivo data collecting and transmission was successfully tested for Electroencephalograms. • For communication in liquid workspaces, depending on the application, acoustic, light, RF, and chemical signals may be considered as possible choices for communication and data transmission. **(II) CMOS** • CMOS sensors embedded in the nanorobot, which enable sending and receiving data through electromagnetic fields. • The nanorobots monitoring data convert the wave propagation generated by the emitting devices through a well defined protocol.
Joints and storage information	**DNA (For Bio nano- bot)** • There has been a great interest and many reports in use of DNA specifically to actuate and assemble micro and nano sized system. • In nano electronics, DNA could be used as molecular switches for molecular memories or electronic circuitry to assemble future nano-electronics transistors. • In this model, structural elements could be carbon nanotubes while the passive/active joints are formed by appropriately designed DNA elements.
CNT-Structural material	• Carbon Nano Tubes (CNT) are cylindrical sheets of carbon. CNT have diameters of ~1nm and lengths up to a few centimeters was first introduced by Merced (2008). • In DNA nanorobotics, CNT could be used as structural element while the passive/active joints are formed by appropriate designed DNA elements. • CNT and DNA are combined to create new genetically programmed self assembly materials for facilitating the selection placement on CNTs on a substrate by functionalizing CNTs with DNA. • CNT is able to improve performance with low power consumption for nanosensor.

Figure 4. Block diagram of different components of nanorobot and estimated nanocircuit architecture

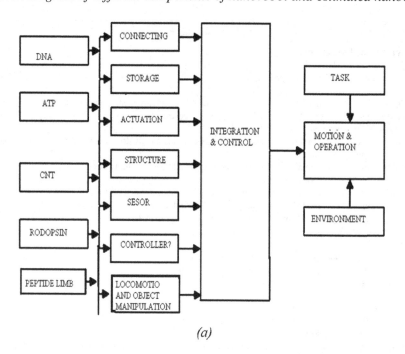

(a)

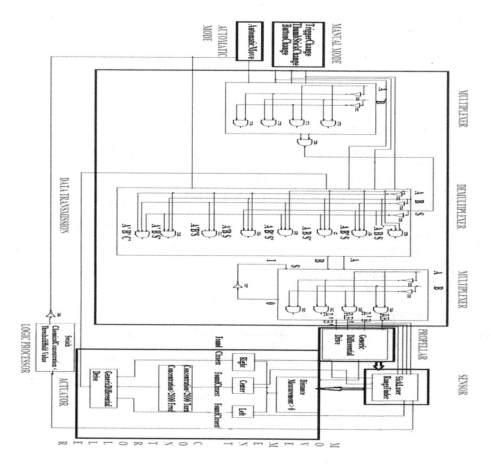

The chemical detection in a complex environment is an important factor for nanorobots for interacting within the human body as was described by Cavalcanti, et al. (2004), Hamdi, et al. (2005), Cavalcanti, et al. (2007) and further by Cavalcanti, et.al (2008) described nanorobot architecture for medical target identification. In the proposed architecture of nanorobot, the integrated system comprises for movement control, obstacle avoidance and target detection.

The overall block diagram of nanorobot and Hardware Architecture of Nanorobot are given in Figure 4.

Advantages and Disadvantages of Nanorobotics

Advantages

- The process is very fast.
- Since the scale of operation is very small, the results are very accurate.
- The process is less painful unlike angioplasty, where the patient takes months to recover from the physical trauma of the operation.
- The process is technologically very advanced and reliable.
- The patients when placed below continuous X-rays during diagnosis, is not subjected to harmful rays like in angioplasty
- The chances of any effects or recurrences are completely eliminated.

Disadvantages

- Nanotechnology is a very costly technology.
- The technology may take several years to be implemented practically.
- The technology may lead to further technological problems like the introduction of artificial reconstruction and artificial intelligence which will result in the robots going out of control of humans.

MOVEMENT CONTROL, OBSTACLES AVOIDANCE, AND TARGET DETECTION THROUGH NANO-BOTS

How Do We Introduce the Device into the Body?

A way needs to be found out to introduce the nano-bot into the body, and allow it to access the operations site without causing too much ancillary damage.

- The first is that the size of the nano-bot determines the minimum size of the blood vessel that it can traverse.
- Not only do we want to avoid damaging the walls of whatever blood vessel the device is in, we also do not want to block it too much, which would either cause a clot to form, or just slow or stop the blood flow, precipitating the problem we want to cure in the first place.
- What this means, of course, is that the smaller the nano-robot the better. However, this must be balanced against the fact that the larger the nano-bot the more versatile and effective it can be.

- This is especially important in light of the fact that external control problems become much more difficult if we are trying to use multiple machines, even if they don't get in each other's way.
- The second consideration is an even simpler one; we have to get it into the body without being too destructive in the first place.
- This requires that we gain access to a large diameter artery that can be traversed easily to gain access to most areas of the body in minimal time.
- The obvious candidate is the femoral artery in the leg. This is in fact the normal access point to the circulatory system for operations that require access to the bloodstream for catheters, dye injections, etc., so it will suit our purposes nicely.

How Do We Move the Device Around the Body?

One of the first problems to solve is how to get our device to the problem area in the first place. We start with a basic assumption: we will use the circulatory system to allow our device to move about. We must then consider two possibilities: should it be carried to the site of operations, or should it be propelled? We will start by dismissing the idea of using a probe, catheter or umbilicus to move the device around since this would be very difficult to make versatile enough.

- The first possibility is to allow the device to be carried to the site of operations by means of normal blood flow. There are a number of requirements for this method to be practical. We must be able to navigate the bloodstream; to be able to guide the device so as to make use of the blood flow. This also requires that there be an uninterrupted blood flow to the site of operations.
- In the case of blood clots, of course, the flow of blood is dammed and thus our device would not be carried to the site without the capability for active movement. Another problem with this method is that it would be difficult to remain at the site without some means of maintaining position, either by means of an anchoring technique, or by actively moving against the current. While the above objections do not eliminate any possibility of using this technique, they do point out the need for at least a supplementary means of locomotion.

There are a number of means available *for active propulsion* of our device.

1. **Propeller/ Motor/Actuator:** See section Bio- Nanorobotics
2. **Cilia/Flagella:** In this scenario, we are using some sort of vibrating cilia (similar to those of a paramecium) to propel the device.
3. **Electromagnetic Pump:** This is a device with no moving parts that takes conductive fluid in at the front end and propels it out the back, in a manner similar to a ramjet, although with no minimum speed. It uses magnetic fields to do this. It would require high field strengths, which would be practical with high capacity conductors.
4. **Membrane Propulsion:** A rapidly vibrating membrane can be used to provide thrust, as follows: Imagine a concave membrane sealing off a vacuum chamber, immersed in a fluid under pressure, which is suddenly tightened. This would have the effect of pushing some of the fluid away from the membrane, producing thrust in the direction toward the membrane. The membrane would then be relaxed, causing the pressure of the fluid to push it concave again.

5. **Crawl Along Surface:** Rather than have the device float in the blood, or in various fluids, the device could move along the walls of the circulatory system by means of appendages with specially designed tips, allowing for a firm grip without excessive damage to the tissue. It must be able to do this despite surges in the flow of blood caused by the beating of the heart, and do it without tearing through a blood vessel or constantly being torn free and swept away.

How Do We Know Where the Device Should Go?

The next problem to consider is exactly how to detect the problem tissue that must be treated. We need two types of sensors. Long-range sensors will be used to allow us to navigate to the site of the unwanted tissue. We must be able to locate a tumor, blood clot, patches in the heart of new born baby closely enough so that the use of short-range sensors is practical. These would be used during actual operations, to allow the device to distinguish between healthy and unwanted tissue. There are many different types of sensors, each suited for different purposes. Without any way of determining location from internal references, we need to be able to track the device by external means.

1. **Ultrasonic:** This technique can be used in either the active or the passive mode. In the active mode, an ultrasonic signal is beamed into the body, and either reflected back, received on the other side of the body, or a combination of both. The received signal is processed to obtain information about the material through which it has passed.
2. **NMR/MRI:** This technique involves the application of a powerful magnetic field to the body, and subsequent analysis of the way in which atoms within the body react to the field. It usually requires a prolonged period to obtain useful results, often several hours, and thus is not suited to real-time applications.
3. **Radioactive Dye:** This technique is basically one of illumination. A radioactive fluid is introduced into the circulatory system and its progress throughout the body is tracked by means of a fluoroscope or some other radiation-sensitive imaging system.

Several Parameters for Environment, Nanorobots and Signal Used in Medical Diagnosis Field

In order to analyze the effectiveness of movement control algorithms, several simulation parameters shown in Table 3 is used.

Algorithm for Movement Control, Obstacle Avoidance, and Target Detection

Quorum and RFID Based Approach for Sensing, Path Planning, Obstacle Avoidance, and Target Identification of Nano-Robot

Communication can improve through group coordination like ants use pheromone trails as they forage for food. This type of coordination may be achieved through chemical signals, visual cues, etc. communicated between agents. At micro- or nano-levels, communication through chemical signals is preferred. Quorum sensing is the ability of bacteria to coordinate behavior via signaling molecules. Quorum sensing is a highly evolved and effective tool for many activities. For example, communication in a bacterial

Table 3. Parameters for environment, nanorobots, and signal used for medical diagnosis

Parameters	Values
Vessel and Target	
• Vessel Radius • Workspace Length.	• R=5μm • L= 50μm
Fluid	
• Fluid Density • Fluid Viscosity • Skin Temperature	• $2*10^7$W/m^3 • 100μm/sec • 93F
Nanorobots	
• Radius • Density of Robot • Robot Diffusion Coefficient • No. of Nanorobots	• R=1μm • $r_{obot=}$ 2 x 10^{-4} robots/(μm)^3 • 108.18 μm^2/sec • 5
Chemical Signal	
• Production Flux • Diffusion Coefficient • Fitness Threshold • Concentration near Source • Background Concentration	• 70.12 molecules/s/μm^3 • 100μm^2/s • $0.1<\varepsilon<0.9$ • 1.8 molecules/(μm)^3 • $6x10^{-3}$ molecules/μm^3
Acoustic Signal	
Speed of Sound	1.5 x 10^9 μm/s

colony infecting a host is accomplished using chemical signals. Inspired by the quorum sensing chemical dispersion and sensing abilities of bacteria, these capabilities can be used for collaborative goal seeking. The new group coordination behavior of the nano-robots emerges based on a communication process using chemical signaling.

Problem in Nano -Robotics Movement and Group Communication

The foremost problem encountered in nano robotics is capability to avoid of obstruction faced by immune system. Many research papers have proposed obstruction avoidance by means of swarm based approach where even if one nano robots succeed in reaching near to target, it alerts or send signal to other nano robots so that they can tackle or neutralize target (affected) cells in collective manner.

In the context of the nano sensor network, autonomous arrangement of nodes is the main problem. This problem is studied as a problem of pattern formation in the field of swarm robots.

In research of a pattern formation, there are various techniques, such as method based on molecule combination, assuming a potential field virtually and the method expressing the relation of robots by the spring model. These techniques are suitable for overall severances and the military application of unknown environment. But these methods are unsuitable the purpose building the net- work infrastructure by multi-hop for gathering sensing data on distance place.

Here a comprehensive approach to reduce the communication link and delay has been presented. The research purpose is to develop a self-deployment algorithm for nano based sensor network comprising nano-bots which is adapted for very sensitive and fragile environment. The network relocation problem is equivalent to considering decision-making problem of each nano robots. In the various constraints, such as physical obstacle, communication range of each robot, the robots have to decide what to do next for the global purpose. A self-alignment priority criterion for a nano sensor network has been proposed. This algorithm was combined with the obstacle avoidance algorithm.

RFID Module

RFID is an automatic identification method that relies on storing and remotely retrieving data using data-carrying devices called RFID tags or transponders. The power required to operate the data-carrying device is transferred using a contactless technology from a data-capturing device called an RFID reader. The basic communication between the reader and the transponder of an RFID system is based on radio frequency (RF) technology.

A Simplified RFID system's architecture is depicted in Figure 5. A communication antenna is usually built within the tag, whereas the reader is typically equipped with one or two antennas. The RF transceiver on the reader illuminates a short pulse of electromagnetic waves. The transponder receives the RF transmission, rectifies the received signal to obtain the dc power supply for the IC memory, reads the ID stored in the memory, and backscatters it in response to the interrogation. The signal generated by the transponder is then received by the reader to extract the tag's ID number.

Behavioral Control Algorithm: Quorum Based Group Communication Using RFID

Assumptions

It is assumed that nano-robots are operating in small blood vessels. The fluid in the vessels contains numerous cells, several microns in diameter. Viscosity dominates the nano-robots motion through the fluid in the environment, with physical behaviors quite different from what is experienced with larger organisms and robots. The ratio of inertial to viscous forces for an object of size R moving with velocity v through a fluid with viscosity η and density ρ is given by the Reynolds number as follows:

Figure 5. Simplified RFID system's architecture

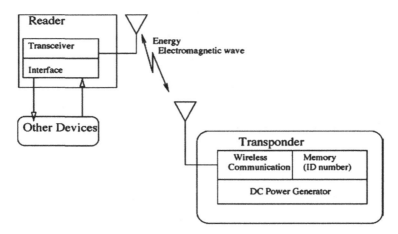

$$\text{Re} \equiv \frac{R\rho v}{\eta} \tag{1}$$

Typical values for density and viscosity in blood plasma are represented by Equations 2 and 3 respectively.

$$\rho = 1g / cm^3 \tag{2}$$

$$\eta = 10^{-2} g / cm.s \tag{3}$$

Flow speeds in small blood vessels are about 1mm/s. This is also a reasonable speed for nano-robot motion with respect to the fluid, providing **Re≈10⁻³** for a 1-micron nanorobot, and thus viscous forces dominate. Consequently, nano-robots applying a locomotive force quickly reach a desired velocity in the fluid. Hence, applied force is proportional to velocity rather than the direct correlation applied in the acceleration of Newton's law F=ma. Diffusion arising from thermal motion of molecules (Brownian motion) is also important. Depending on the object's size, the diffusion coefficient D characterizes the resulting random motion. In a time t, the root-mean-square displacement due to diffusion may be defined as:

$$k = \sqrt{6Dt} \tag{4}$$

Parameters for chemical signal and corresponding nominal values is as shown in Table 4

Consider a fluid moving uniformly with velocity v in the positive x-direction past a plane. It contains a point source of chemical produced at a rate · Q, which is the chemical signal as molecules per second. The diffusion coefficient is represented by D, and the diffusion equation is:

$$D\nabla^2 C = v\partial C / \partial x \tag{5}$$

Table 4. The nominal values for the parameters for chemical signal

Chemical Signal	
Production rate molecules	Q=10⁴ molecule/s
Diffusion coefficient	D=100μm^2/s
Background concentration	6×10^{-3} molecule/$(\mu m)^3$
Parameter	**Nominal Value**
Average fluid velocity	v =1000 μm/s
Vessel diameter	d= 20 μm
Workspace length	L= 50 μm
Density of cells	2.5×10^{-3} cell/$(\mu m)^3$
Density of nano-robots	2×10^{-4} robot/$(\mu m)^3$

Origin and no net flux across the boundary plane at y = 0, determines the steady-state concentration C, which is molecules per $(\mu m)^3$ or chemical concentration at point (x, y, z):

$$C(x, y, z) = \frac{Q}{2\pi Dr} e^{v(r-x)/(2D)} \tag{6}$$

'r' is the distance to the chemical signal source

$$r = \sqrt{x^2 + y^2 + z^2}$$

Initialization

- Initialize, minimum number of nano-robots 'm' as per requirement (Suppose if 10 nano-robots are required to neutralize /break a cancer tissue. Minimum number of members= 10 chosen).
- Assign NODE_ID and GR_ID (if a node is members of 1st group its GR_ID= 1 and so on).
- **Communication Setup:** Communication is performed in bi-direction mode; each node is capable of communicating with other node using Radio frequency signals via serial communication channel.
- **Chemical Gradient Level (C.G.L):** Each node is capable of sensing chemical-gradient present at any location at any given time (t). Chemical gradient at point C(X, Y, Z) is calculated as per formula (6).
- **STATUS (Behavior):** Four levels of status can be defined
  - **OBS-Free (0):** If status/flag is '0' a node is assumed to be obstacle free (by nano-robot, immune system, target).
  - **SENS (1):** In this node nano-robot is busy in sensing the micro environment through its movement. This bit is generally kept at active state all the phase.
  - **OBST (2):** It signifies that obstacle has been detected and it is within the range of nano-robot. We treat all type of entity present in body as obstacle except the target size where gradient level is the most.
  - **TARG (3):** It signifies that a node has arrived at target site and signals should be send to perform neutralization operation.
- **Current Position/ Centroids:** Current position is the position attained at a given time t.

Look-Up table initial configuration of RFID TAGs for two group_id's is as shown in Table 5 and Table 6

Inter Group Communication and Movement

- A group is formed so that the desired number of nano-robots to reach at target site same time, can be achieved.
- Movement/alignment towards group leader is performed during collision free time. (STATUS BIT= OBS-free).
- If any obstacle is found/sensed at any time by any node within the group. First it will try to avoid the obstacle and then it will try to move towards Group leader.

Table 5. Look-up table initial configuration of RFID TAGs present at each node of a group (GR_ID=1) having 5 members

Node_ID	GR_ID	Target Set	CGL (Chemical Gradient)	Gr_Leader	Status	Cur. Position/ Centroids
1	1	{2,3,4,5}	0.33	0	OBS_free	(X_1, Y_1)
2	1	{1,3,4,5}	0.34	0	OBS_free	(X_2, Y_2)
3	1	{1,2,4,5}	0.86	1	SENS	(X_3, Y_3)
4	1	{1,2,3,5}	0.84	0	OBST	(X_4, Y_4)
5	1	{1,2,3,4}	0.26	0	OBS_free	(X_5, Y_5)

Update Group Information:

Table 6. Look-up intermediate configuration of RFID TAGs present at each node of a group (GR_ID=5) having 5 members

Node_ID	GR_ID	Target Set	CGL (Chemical Gradient)	Gr_Leader	Status	Cur. Position
3	5	{5,7,8,9}	0.86	0	SENS	(X_1, Y_1)
5	5	{3,7,8,9}	0.95	1	SENS	(X_2, Y_2)
7	5	{3,5,8,9}	0.74	0	OBS_free	(X_3, Y_3)
8	5	{3,7,5,9}	0.34	0	OBS_free	(X_4, Y_4)
9	5	{3,5,7,8}	0.28	0	OBS_free	(X_5, Y_5)

Figure 6. Resultant net movement vector of obstacle avoidance position and centroid vector

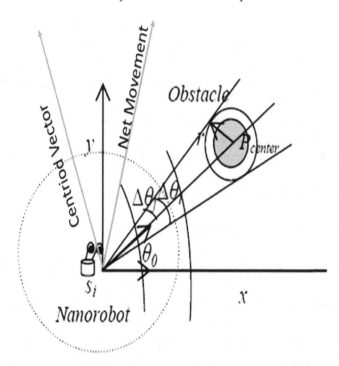

- To achieve this task specific inter group alignment algorithm is executed.
- The node which is having highest-level of chemical gradient becomes a group leader by raising the alarm "Gr_Leader" to 1 at any time. Then it emits its centroid towards group members and writes CGL at HASH_MAP.
- All nodes within a group are able to sense the micro-environment quorum as well as compare its CGL by RFID communication with other nodes.
- If a node becomes a Group-Leader subsequent node will set their GR-Leader Bit to '0' zero.
- Gr_Leader emits its centroid C (X, Y, Z) to all member nodes within a group.
- All sub-nodes try to reach at this centroid by calculating Euclidian distance. If a node is moving towards centroid, detects an obstacle then Pso-based obstacle avoidance algorithm is run and best possible position is calculated (Pbest). Net movement/direction is towards the resultant vector of GR-Leader direction and Pbest (Figure 6 and Figure 7).

Figure 7. Algorithm for net movement towards resultant vector of Pbest and centroid vector

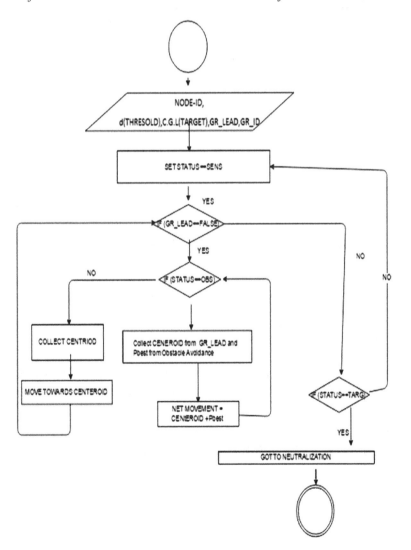

Figure 8. New group creation

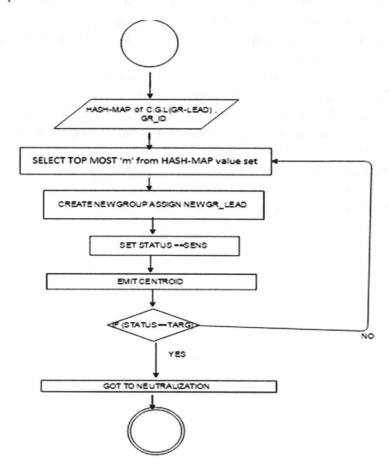

Intra-Group Communication and New Group Creation

- All Group-Leaders are able to communicate with other group leaders.
- They compare their CGL (chemical gradient levels) using RFID communication (Figure 8).

Status of Group Leaders at any time is shown in Table 7

- Select top (m) Group-Leaders and form a HASH_MAP where m is minimum no group members this dynamic structure is achieved by bubble sorting the top most element of HASH_MAP.

Table 7. Status Of group leader's –C.G.L HASH_MAP at any time t (there are more elements present in the MAP and size of MAP is not fixed)

Gr_Leader	1	2	3	4	5	6	...
CGL	0.95	0.86	0.15	0.99	0.68	0.54	...

- Update all the information and assign a new group ID to group/generation (see Figure 8).
- If a redundant node having higher CGL. It is eligible to become a Group-Leader.

Target Identification

In this scenario Group is nearing towards target as chemical gradient level attains approx. value to chemical gradient level of target site. After reaching near to target nano-robots present in specific group performs the neutralization operation. Overall scenario is depicted in Figure 9, Figure 10 and Figure 11.

Future Direction/Implications

- It is assumed that both sender and receiver RFID modules are present at nano-robots; to achieve this task current technology should be improvised accordingly.
- Degree of freedom can be applied based on predictive analysis so that nano-robots can take optimal decision (how much degree a nano-robot should adhere towards centroid or towards Pbest).
- Multithreaded and synchronization should be introduced to make the system more robust and effective.
- HASH-MAPPING procedure should be enhanced further so that it can provide best result at any given time.
- Computing power of each nano-robot should be such that it can compute and reconfigure its memory dynamically and should be able to cope with multiple READ-WRITE operation.

Figure 9. Group of nanorobots moving towards Target Site

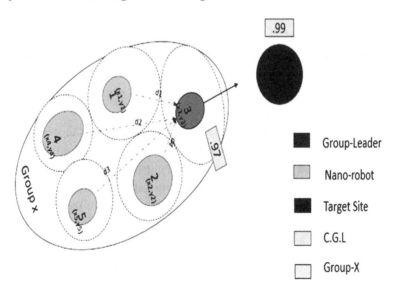

Figure 10. Overall movement of nanorobots by behavior control mechanism

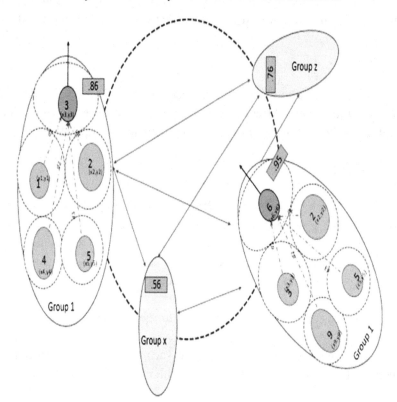

Bacterial Foraging Optimization Algorithm (BFO)

Bacterial Foraging Optimization Algorithm (BFO) [BFO was first introduced by Das, et.al (2009)] belongs to the family of nature-inspired optimization algorithms. This optimization technique imitates the foraging behaviour of the E. coli bacterium and involves four major steps.

They are:

- **Chemotaxis:** This process involves moving of the bacterium in the positive nutrient gradient. An E.coli bacterium can move in two different ways, it can swim for a period of time in the same direction or it may tumble. It alternates between these two modes of operation for the entire life-time. Assuming that $\Theta^i(j, k, l)$ represents i-th bacterium at j-th chemotactic, k-th reproductive and l-th elimination-dispersal step. C (i) is the size of the step taken in the random direction specified by the tumble (run length unit). Then mathematically, the movement of the bacterium may be represented by

$$\theta^i(j+1,k,l) = \theta^i(j,k,l) + C(i)\Delta(i) / \sqrt{(\Delta^t(i)\Delta(i))} \qquad (1)$$

where Δ indicates a vector in the random direction whose elements lie in [-1, 1].

Figure 11. Flow chart of overall behavioral control algorithm

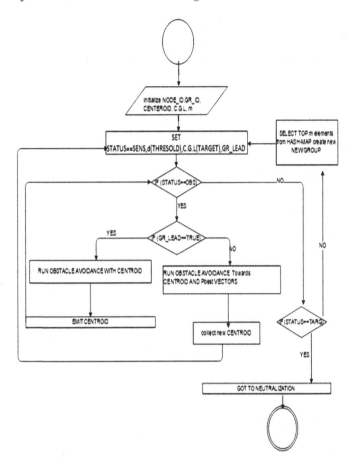

- **Swarming:** The cells when moving up a nutrient gradient release an attractant aspirate, which helps them to aggregate into groups and thus move in concentric patterns of swarms with high bacterial density. The cell-to-cell signalling is represented by the following function:

$$Jcc(\theta, P(j,k,l)) = \sum_{i=1}^{s} Jcc(\theta, \theta^i(j,k,l))$$

$$= \sum_{i=1}^{s} \left[-d_{attractant} \exp(-w_{attractant} \sum_{m=1}^{s} (\theta_m - \theta_m^{\ i})^2) \right] \\ + \sum_{i=1}^{s} \left[-h_{repellant} \exp(-w_{repellant} \sum_{m=1}^{p} (\theta_m - \theta_m^{\ i})^2) \right] \qquad (2)$$

Here $J_{cc}(\Theta, P(j, k, l))$ is the objective function value to be added to the actual objective function (to be minimized) to present a time varying objective function, S is the total number of bacteria, p is the number of variables to be optimized. $d_{attractant}$, $W_{atractant}$, $h_{repellant}$, $W_{repellant}$ are different coefficients that should be chosen properly.

- **Reproduction:** The least healthy bacteria eventually die while the healthier ones asexually split into two bacteria, which are then placed in the same location.
- **Elimination and Dispersal:** Due to gradual or sudden changes in the local environment certain bacteria may get killed. Events can take place in such a fashion that all the bacteria in a region are killed or a group is dispersed into a new location.

Optimized Energy Based Bacteria Forage Algorithm to Locate Affected Tissues

Step 1: Experimental Setup

Optimized Energy based Bacteria Forage Algorithm to locate affected tissue:

1. **Initial Nano-Robot Swarm Setup:**
   a. All Nano-robots must have the same goal finding characteristics.
   b. All Nano-robots are injected at the same place into the body of human being.
   c. The working of Nano-robots assumes to be successful when some percentage of the Nano-robots will reach the affected part of the body.
2. **Nano-Robot Setup:**
   a. It is considered that each Nano-robot has some definite and pre-defined lifetime.
   b. Each Nano-robot has some kind of chemicals and also has sensors, which is capable of sensing the signals present in the environment.
   c. Each Nano-robot stops its movement when it senses the chemicals that are releasing from the affected portion of body and starts sending its own chemical signals to other Nano-robots about the finding of the affected part of the body.
3. It is assumed that the blood particles are moving with velocity 'v', so that the Nano–robots know that any obstacle that they find during their movement that are moving with the velocity other than 'v' is definitely another Nano-robot.

Step 2: Movement and Finding of Target Based on B.F.O

1. Population: All Nano-robots
2. **For (j=0 to Nc)** // Chemotaxis loop

Chemotaxis _And _Swim (Population, Ns) //Searching for the target area
    End- For

3. **If** (the concentration levels of chemical signals released by Nano- robots are present in sufficient percentage around the tissue or affected part of the body)

then
Other Nano-robots continue to move along the blood stream in random directions and will get dissolved after their life- span.
   else
Move towards the direction of chemical signals that are coming from the other Nano-robots.
Chemotaxis _And _Swim (Population, Ns) //Definition here.

Begin:

For (each cell in population) {

- Nanorobot moves via the blood stream in the body for finding one new position based on its own velocity and velocity of blood. We assume that velocity of Nano-robot is 'u' and velocity of blood stream is 'v'. The conditional statement checks, if it has enough coverage based on its neighbors.
- For becoming a neighbor in the vicinity of each Nano –robot checks for the information about its distance, whether the distance between them is satisfied by the experimental criteria/setup or not.
- For each Nano-robot S_i, calculate the coverage value based on the neighbor Nano-robot and blood -particles position. We assume that (x_i,y_i) is the position of one Nano-robot and (x_j,y_j) is the position of other Nano-robot / blood particles.

$$\Delta d = \sqrt{\begin{array}{l}((x_j + (u + \Delta v)x_j * \Delta t - x_i + (u + \Delta v)x_i * \Delta t)^2 + \\ (y_j + (u + \Delta v)y_j * \Delta t - y_i + (u + \Delta v)y_i * \Delta t)^2)\end{array}} \tag{1}$$

(Applicable for distance between two Nano-robots only).

$$\Delta d = \sqrt{\left(\begin{array}{l}\left(x_j + (v)x_j * \Delta t - x_i + (u + \Delta v)x_i * \Delta t\right)^2 + \\ \left(y_j + (v)y_j * \Delta t - y_i + (u + \Delta v)y_i * \Delta t\right)^2\end{array}\right)} \tag{2}$$

(Applicable for distance between Nano-robot and blood particle only).

=> If coverage value < threshold value (Maximum allowed distance between two Nano-robots / blood- particles), it will find out the new position using the given equation below.

$$\theta^i(j+1) = \theta^i(j) + C(i)\Delta(i) / \sqrt{(\Delta^T(i)\Delta(i))} \tag{3}$$

Here Δ is the random number between [0, 1].

- The new position is selected randomly, then the new neighbors will be found out based on new position and coverage over the new position is carried out.
- The fitness function is evaluated at the new position, based on the coverage of the current position and coverage over global best position. Here we define fitness function in form of the "Euclidean distance" which is the distance between nanorobot and each of the obstacles. Our main aim is to maximize the Euclidean distance.
- If the Nano-robot finds out the best position, update the velocity and move to the next location.
- Whenever a Nano-robot detects an obstacle, the obstacle –avoidance algorithm is initiated.
- Time to collision ΔTc, will find out to predict the next possible position of the Nano-robot.
- Based on the previously calculated value of ΔTc, Nano-robot will head towards collision free position $\Delta\theta i$ and move to the new location.

If the Nano-robot is moving with the velocity "u + Δv", Then the energy required by the Nano-robot to go to new position is:

$$\Delta E = 1/2 \times (u + \Delta v)^2 m - 1/2m \times u^2 \qquad (4)$$

where

(Δ*v* ranges from 0 to v)
m = mass of the Nano-robot and we consider the Nano-robot of unit mass.
u = velocity at which the nano-robot is travelling in blood stream.

- ○ The position of the Nano-robot is now changed and if there is any loss in energy it has experienced, below some optimum energy level that was defined at the initial stage of robot. Loss in energy is regained to the optimum level at this state.
- ○ The fitness of the current position is evaluated again; if the fitness is less than threshold value then new position will be found out by Nano-robot.
- ○ After reaching at the new position it senses the environment around it, and if there is any sign of chemicals that is releasing from the cancer/affected tissue it stops moving further.
- ○ After finding the affected part inside the body, Nano-robot starts sending chemical signals to the other Nano-robots.

End – For loop here.}

Here, the parameters N_c represent the number of Chemotaxis steps. It would be interesting to analyse the result with different values of N_c. A 'coverage value' represents the conditional statement checks if it has enough coverage based on its neighbors and 'Current optimum' is the best solution after each Chemotaxis step. The 'fitness function' is evaluated over the new position based on the coverage over current position and coverage over global best position. 'N_s' represents the total number of swim steps.

Illustration

Assumptions:

- Velocity of any particle should be considered according to Brownian's motion.
- (X_i, Y_i) is the co-ordinate of the center of the nano-robot (Figure 12).
- (X_j, Y_j) is the co-ordinate of the center of the other nano-robot or blood particle (Figure 12).
- Radius of the nano-robot as well as the blood particle is r=2mm
- It is assumed that the mass of the nano-robot and the blood particle is of Unit mass.
- Now consider the velocity of the nano-robot is U=5mm/s.
- And the velocity of the blood particle is V=3mm/s.
- Consider the time unit Δ*t*=1*s*.
- Consider that work is being performed in 2D plane (for simulation purpose consider micro-environment is 2D).

Let the initial position of one nano-robot is (1, 1) (Figure 13)

Figure 12. Representation of nano-robot /blood particle

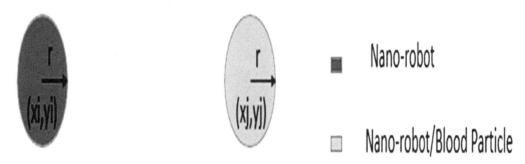

Figure 13. Initial representation of one nano-robot at its possible position at given time

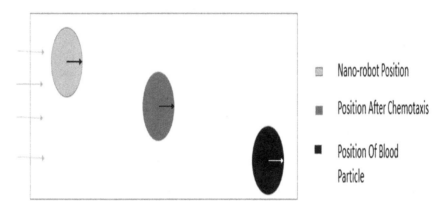

After applying the equation of chemotaxis

$$\theta^i(j+1) = \theta^i(j) + C(i)\Delta(i) / \sqrt{(\Delta^T(i)\Delta(i))}$$

where

Δ is a number in the range [-1, 1], C (i) is the step-length of the nano-robot
$\Theta^i(j)$ is the current position of the ith nano-robot in i[th] chemotaxis loop
$\Theta^i(j+1)$ is the new position in (j+1)[th] chemotaxis loop.

Let the new position in the (j+1)[th] Chemotaxis loop of our nano-robot is (2, 1) (Figure 14)
Now the Euclidean distance is calculated considering it as the fitness function;
Let the position of the other Blood Particle is (5, 1), consider the obstacle to be a Blood Particle.
So with respect to the Equation 2, the Euclidean distance is calculated as:

$$\Delta d = \sqrt{\left[(2 + 6*2*1) - (5 + 3*5*1)\right]^2 + \left[(1 + 3*1*1)\right]^2}$$

Figure 14. Movement of nano-robot to the new position after satisfying the fitness function

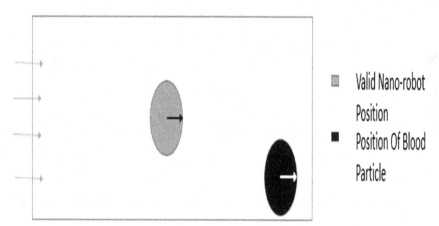

$$\Delta d = \sqrt{\left[14 - 20\right]^2 + \left[7 - 4\right]^2}$$

$$\Delta d = \sqrt{45} = 3\sqrt{5} \text{ mm}$$

Here (Xi, Yi) is the new position of nano-robot after Chemotaxis (2, 1)

(Xj, Yj) is the position of the blood particle (5, 1)

Let at the point of time $\Delta v = 1mm/s$, is the velocity of blood stream by which the nano-robot is travelling in addition with its own velocity.

Now consider two scenarios:

- Let threshold value be 7mm. Now as the Δd is less than the threshold value then nano robot moves to the new position as the new position is free from the obstacle and start sensing its neighboring environment for chemicals that are being releasing from the affected tissue.
- Let threshold value be 5mm. Now the value of $\Delta\theta$ is calculated; the angle at which the nano-robot moves from its current location and direction

$$\Delta\theta = \arctan * r / (d(s_i - P_{centre}))$$

d (S_i. P_{centre}) in the present case is $3\sqrt{5}$, and then above equation looks like

$$\Delta\theta = \arctan * 2 / 3\sqrt{5}$$

Consider the value of $\Delta\theta$ obtained as 110 degree (Figure 15)

Now the Energy is calculated that is needed by nano-robot to change its direction due to obstacle.

Figure 15. Movement of nano-robot to the valid position that satisfies the fitness function after a deviation with angle $\Delta\theta$

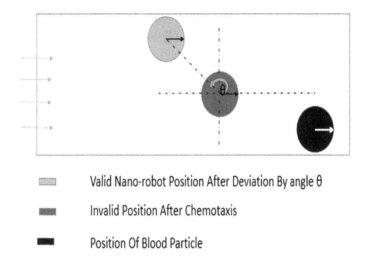

▦	Valid Nano-robot Position After Deviation By angle θ
▬	Invalid Position After Chemotaxis
▬	Position Of Blood Particle

$$\Delta E = 0.5 * m \left[(u + \Delta v)^2 - (u)^2 \right]$$

$$\Delta E = 0.5 * 1 * \left[36 - 25 \right]$$

ΔE=5.5

ΔE is the amount of energy that is needed by nano-robot for changing its current position by utilizing it.

If, the energy level of nano-robot becomes lower than the optimum level that is defined during the designing of the nano-robot due to change in location the robot reset its energy level to the optimum level.

MICROSOFT ROBOTICS DEVELOPER STUDIO

Microsoft Robotics Developer Studio 2008 (MSRD, 2008) is a window based environment for robot control and simulation. MRDS is based on CCR: A .Net based concurrent library implementation for managing asynchronous parallel tasks. This technique involves using message-passing and a lightweight services-oriented runtime, DSS (Decentralized Software Services), which allows the orchestration of multiple services to achieve complex behaviors.

The Microsoft Robotics Developer Studio SDK consists of a number of components. The Concurrency and Coordination Runtime (CCR) and Decentralized Software Services (DSS) comprise the run - time environment. They are both managed libraries, so the robotics services that operate within their environments are also implemented using managed code. The Visual Simulation Environment is a 3D simulator with full physics simulation that can be used to prototype new algorithms for robots. The Visual Programming Language (VPL) is a graphical programming environment that can be used to simulate robotics functionalities. In addition to all of these components, the MRDS team has implemented numerous samples and complete applications to provide programming examples and building blocks for user applications. Another programming language which has been used in MRDS is SPL which is mainly a scripted programming language for robot simulation. Here VPL acts as a modeling tool whereas SPL acts as a programming language and both have been applied for robot simulation.

Tools

The tools that allow to develop an MRDS application contain a graphical environment (Microsoft Visual Programming Language: VPL) command line tools allow to deal with Visual Studio projects in C#, and 3D simulation tools and SPL uses Microsoft Robotics Developer Studio as a simulation environment and provides scripted programming interfaces for this simulation.

Operating System

- Tested on Windows 8 consumer preview but not supported until final release of windows 8.
- Windows XP SP 2, Vista, Windows 7, Server 2003 up to 2008 R3.
- Windows 7, Windows Embedded 7, Server 2003 R2.
- CE 5.0, CE 6.0 up to 2008 R2.

Creating Environment using Virtual Programming Language

Virtual Programming Language (Vpl): Vpl Design

The VPL design is being divided into two modes of operation.

- Manual Mode,
- Automatic Mode.

The manual mode is being controlled by a dashboard where machine is connected with a port number: 50001 with service directory. The differential drives are being connected and are controlled by the dash controller through x, y and z axis. Figure 16 shows the manual control of a single nanorobot in an environment.

The automatic modes are being generated automatically. The nanorobots are made self decisive for the movement control and target detection. The two xinput controller are merged together with Thumbstick button change and trigger button to set a vibration and provides a state of variables (right, left and centre) to get the values (float).The left shoulder button and rights shoulder button propels the generic differential drive in the direction based on the state of the variables. The SicklaserRange Finder acts as a sensor which runs in a continuous monitoring mode at 0.5 degree of intervals which is decided by the distance covered by the nanorobots. The Workers (activity) helps to find the target and also avoid the obstacle based on the best fitness function. Figure 17 illustrates the worker (activity) connection for the movement control and obstacle avoidance.

These movement controls is based on the angle between the nanorobot (object) and the obstacle. The SickLaserRangeFinder (sensors) if detects an object less than 2000nm of range, it will turn back the nanorobots from the current position and if the range crosses above 3000nm between an object and

Figure 16. Manual control of a nanorobot in an simulated environment

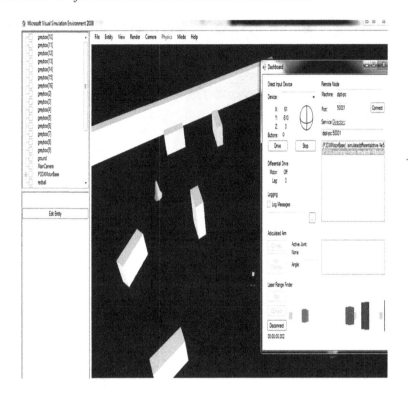

an obstacle, the generic differential drive will move the nanorobot in a forward state of direction. The overall design based on visual programming language is shown in Figure 18.

Simulation Experiment

A virtual programming language (VPL) can be implemented to design the virtual environment for the obstacle avoidance, control movement and target detection of the nanorobots. After the simulation of the designed block diagram Figure 18, the nanorobot will move in designed workspace region Figure 20 and follow the path by avoiding obstacles and reaches the goal by detecting the correct path through SickLaserRangeFinder (sensor). The design scenario will be change with adding an environment with viscous medium along with numbers of robots searching for the goal applying global search method using swam intelligence.

In order to examine the performance of the proposed obstacle avoidance algorithm, we use random obstacles in dynamic environment. Figure 21 depicts the illustration representation of obstacle avoidance a nanorobots, which is based on the global path planning and local path planning. While any robot identify the target, it send signal to rest of the target represented by Figure 22.

Figure 17. Worker activity connections in VPL screen

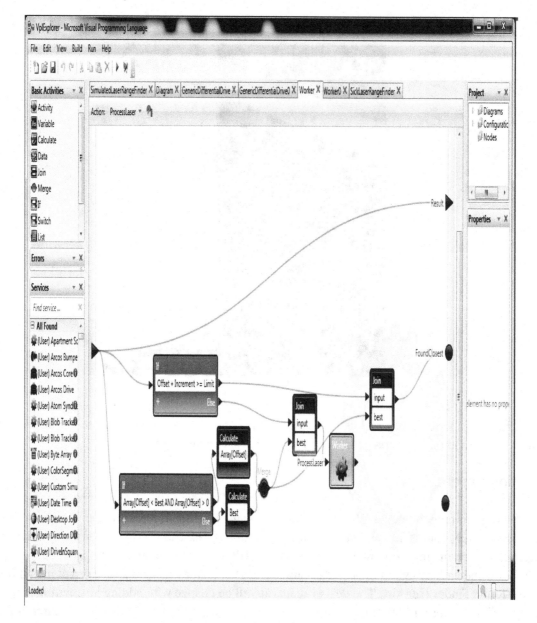

SPL: Simple Programming language

SPL Introduction

SPL (Simple Programming Language) is the result of open source project which aims at helping novices or beginners to start programming with easy and fun by simplifying complicated coding pattern into the simple script. This makes SPL particularly suited for creating applications as compositions of commands and expressions regardless of whether these scripts are running PC, mobile phone, or embedded

Figure 18. (a) and (b) Nanorobot trajectory for avoiding obstacle and target detection

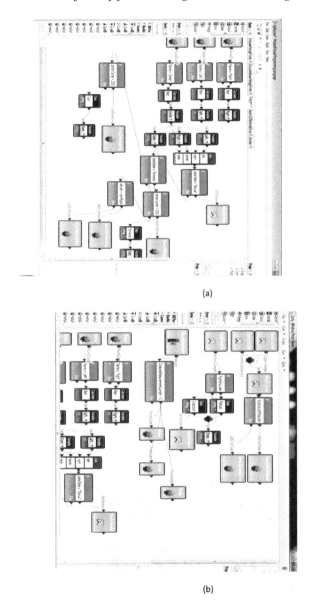

(a)

(b)

board. The result is a flexible yet simple for writing a broad set of applications. The final goal of the SPL project is to launch a community for the user-created-contents which supports all platforms with a unified simple script.

There are so many apps communities currently such as for Apple, Google, or MS's platform, and all these apps are required totally different dev environment. Also these dev environments are not easy for most general users or student to engage in.

Figure 19. Decentralized software services runtime on debugging

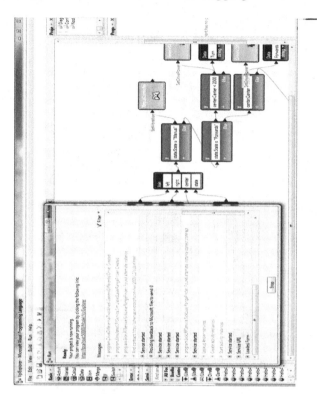

Figure 20. Apparent environment for the simulation experiment

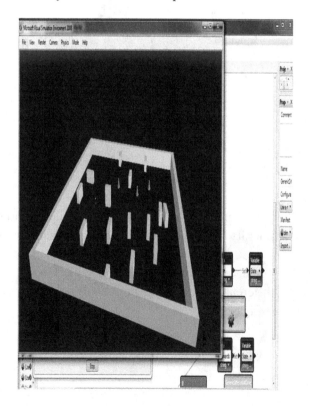

Figure 21. Obstacle avoidance by Nanorobot in a simulated environment

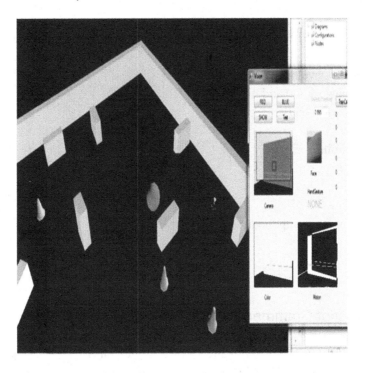

Figure 22. Target detection by Nanorobot in a simulated environment

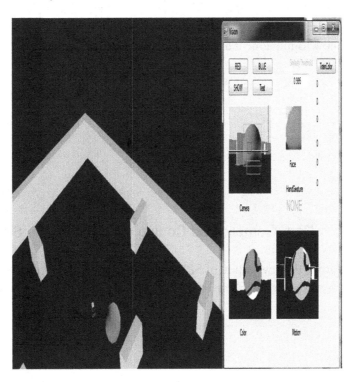

Status of the SPL Project

SPL script is executed on the SPL script engine and current SPL script engines are implemented on the;

- Microsoft Robotics Developer Studio 2008 R3,
- .NET Micro Framework 4.0 and 4.1,
- General C# application on the PC,
- Windows 7,
- WPF 3D Programming.

SPL Overview

SPL scripting has two major components:

- Expression,
- Command & Option.

Expression Part (Script Grammar)

Expression part of SPL is almost same with any Script coding pattern except the defining of procedure. SPL expression part took a merit of BASIC and Python languages that it doesn't need to consider data or variable type when you deal with variable or data within the script.

Although SPL is based on the general C style grammar, it provides a number of useful utilities and math functions so that you can use these resources as in the general Java or C# programming.

Below script shows how to implement a simple function with SPL script.

```
a = 10
b = 20
c = Sum (a, b)
Print "Sum is"+ c
Procedure Sum (a1, b1)
Return a1 + b1
End
```

Command and Option Part (Complicated Coding Pattern into the Simple Script)

Simplifying coding pattern is the key feature of SPL among the number of valuable features. In the SPL script, you can define a broad set of complicated object or entities just by using command & option pattern.

SPL Command

```
/option1:value1
/option2:value2
```

This command & option pattern can simplify quite complicated coding pattern into the just same pattern for all cases.

For example, if you want to implement a simple simulation environment with MSRDS without SPL, you should use C# in order to implement it.

C# Code to Show How to Implement a Simple Simulation Environment

```
Private void Populate World ()
        {
        AddSky ();
        AddGround ();
        AddBox (new Vector3 (1, 1, 1));
        AddTexturedSphere (new Vector3 (3, 1, 0));
        }
        Void AddSky ()
        {
        // add a sky using a static texture.
        // to do per pixel lighting on each simulation visual entity
SkyDomeEntity sky = new SkyDomeEntity ("skydome.dds","sky_diff.dds");
SimulationEngine.GlobalInstancePort.Insert (sky);
        // add a directional light to simulate the sun.
            LightSourceEntity sun = new LightSourceEntity ();
        sun.State.Name = "Sun";
        sun.Type = LightSourceEntityType.Directional;
        sun.Color = new Vector4 (0.8f, 0.8f, 0.8f, 1);
        sun.Direction = new Vector3 (0.5f, -.75f, 0.5f);
        SimulationEngine.GlobalInstancePort.Insert (sun);
                }
```

One should invest quite a time to study C# before start MSRDS programming and after then, also you should be familiar with DSS/CCR technologies as well as simulation entity programming.

Due to these several steps in starting simulation programming, most of beginners give up further progress in simulation programming.

SPL Script

Below samples shows how to implement simple simulation environment.

```
StartSimulationEngine
AddSkyEntity     sky1
AddLightSourceEntity     sun1
AddHeightFieldEntity     ground1
```

It is seen in above script, there are only simple commands needed in order to implement same functions as in the C#.

Customization of Commands

```
StartSimulationEngine
AddSkyEntity      sky1
        /VisualCubeTextureFile:"sky.dds"
        /LightingCubeTextureFile:"sky_diff.dds"
AddLightSourceEntity      sun1
        /LightType: Omni
        /Color: 0.8 0.8 0.8 1
        /Direction:-1.0 -1.0 0.5
AddHeightFieldEntity       ground1
```

In the above samples, SPL script enables novices to start programming without preparation of complicated coding pattern (Figure 23).

Code in SPL Editor for Obstacles Avoidance and Target Detection by Multiple Bots

```
StartSimulationEngine  "SimState/basicmaze.xml"
AddNewEntity ent1 /Position: 0 0 0
AddSphereShape
```

Figure 23. Screenshot of SPL script

```
        /Radius: 0.4          /Mass: 0.5
        /Diffuse Color: 1 0 0 1
AddBoxShape
        /Dimensions: 0.4 0.4 0.4          /Mass: 0.1
        /Position: 4 0 0.5
        /Diffuse Color: 0 1 0 1
AddCapsuleShape
        /Radius: 0.2          /Height: 0.2          /Mass: 0.1
        /Position: 3 0 0.5
        /Diffuse Color: 0 0 1 1
//------------------------------Bot 1------------------------------start
AddDifferentialDriveEntity    base1
        /Position: -1 0 0
        /Orientation: 0 90 0
AddLaserRangeFinderEntity    lrf1
        /Position: 0 0.4 0
        /ParentEntity: base1
AddBumperEntity    bumper1
        /ParentEntity: base1
AddWebCamEntity    cam1
        /Position: 0 0.5 0
        /ParentEntity: base1
//AddFollowingChaseCamera    cam1
//        /Position: 0 0.5 2.0
//        /ChaseTarget: base1
AddColorSensorEntity    color1
        /Position: 0 0.4 -0.3
        /ParentEntity: base1
        /Procedure_SensorNotify:proc1
//------------------------------Bot 1------------------------------end
AddPioneer3DX    p3dx1
        /Position: 4 1 1
//------------------------------Bot 2------------------------------start
AddDifferentialDriveEntity    base2
        /Position:-0 0 1
//------------------------------Bot 2------------------------------end
//------------------------------Bot 3------------------------------start
AddDifferentialDriveEntity    base3
        /Position: 1 -0 1.5
//------------------------------Bot3------------------------------end
//AddWebCamEntity    cam2
//        /Position: 0 0.5 0
//        /ParentEntity:base2
//AddWebCamEntity    cam3
```

```
//          /Position:0  0.5  0
//          /ParentEntity:base3
//SimpleVision     simplevision1
//          /CameraName:cam1
//          /CapturingInterval:300
//          /Procedure_ResultNotify:proc1
//AddBumperEntity     bumper2
//          /ParentEntity:base1
// /Procedure_SensorNotify:
//type the name of proceedure which will be triggered
// /DiffuseColor:1  0  0  1 //Red Green Blue Alpha
//add this option from "Entities->AddColorSensorEntity"
FlushScript
base1.Go(-0.2, 0.2)
base2.Go(-0.1,0.1)
base3.SetDrivePower(-0.03, 0.03)
//base1.Go()
Procedure  proc1
        r = value.NormalizedAverageRed
        g = value.NormalizedAverageGreen
        b = value.NormalizedAverageBlue
        print "[Color] " + r.ToString() + " / " + g.ToString() + " / " +
b.ToString()
                if (r > 0.9 && g < 0.3 && b < 0.3)
        {
                base1.Go(0)
                base2.Go(0)
                base3.Go(0)
        }
        End
SimpleDashboard
//FlushScript
//Procedure  proc1
//        r = value.Results[0]
//        print  r.XMea
```

Using SPL when simulating multiple robots, their movements can be controlled automatically through the simulation engines or through manual dashboard (Figure 24 and Figure 25). The manual dashboard gives user the freedom to move robots freely according to the obstacles present in the simulation environment.

Figure 24. Screenshot of a simulation scenario with multiple robots (using SPL language)

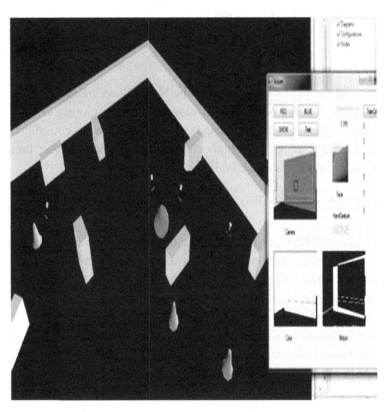

Figure 25. Screenshot of the dashboard used to manually control the robots

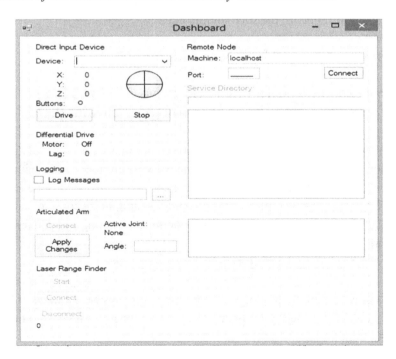

A NON-INVASIVE METHOD TO TREAT BRAIN BLOOD CLOT THROUGH NANOROBOT

Description of Blood Clot

Blood clots are semi-solid masses of blood. Normally, blood flows freely through veins and arteries. Some blood clotting, or coagulation, is necessary and normal. Blood clotting helps stop bleeding if you are injured. However, when too much clotting occurs, it can cause serious complications. When a blood clot forms, it can be stationary (called a thrombosis) and block blood flow or break loose (called an embolism) and travel to various parts of the body.

Causes of Blood Clot in Brain

Head injuries or trauma to the brain, head and neck can cause these clots to form in the brain. Blood clots in the brain are caused when bleeding occurs between the skull and the brain. The body will form a clot to stop the bleeding, which will put pressure on the surrounding brain tissue. Trauma to the head can also cause blood clots formed outside of the brain to break loose and become lodged in the brain, which can cause an ischemic stroke.

Travelling clots from other parts of the body will travel to a blood vessel that leads to the brain, causing a blockage that can lead to an embolic stroke or cerebral embolism. These travelling clots are more likely to cause damage to other parts of the body before they reach the brain.

Inflammation of a superficial vein can also cause an increased risk of blood clots. If a vein is damaged due to a high trauma injury it can become inflamed. A bacterial infection in the vein can also cause this type of inflammation which will reduce blood flow to the surrounding area. These damaged areas will be at a higher risk for leaking, which will result in a blood clot. If the area is inflamed then this blood clot could cut off the blood supply to the surrounding cells.

Blood Clots Identification and Removal Technique

Blood Clots Identification Using Thrombin-Sensitive Synthetic Biomarkers and Removal Process by Using Tissue Plasminogen Activator (tPA)

Thrombin is a serine protease and regulator of hemostasis that plays a critical role in the formation of obstructive blood clots, or thrombosis. To detect thrombi in living animals, trials to implement conjugate thrombin-sensitive peptide substrates to the surface of nanorobots has been done earlier. These "synthetic biomarkers" survey the host vasculature for coagulation and, in response to substrate cleavage by thrombin, transmit signal to others nanorobots through chemical signaling and deliver the "clot-blusters" (Figure 26 and Figure 27).

Overall Process can be classified as follows:

1. All nanorobots move randomly in blood vessel/ vasculature system along with blood stream.
2. If any nanorobot identifies the thrombin activity then it transmits signal to others nanorobots and release "clot-blusters".
3. Repeat step 2, until thrombin activity is being identified.

Figure 26. Nano robots architecture composing Thrombin Substrate and Payload

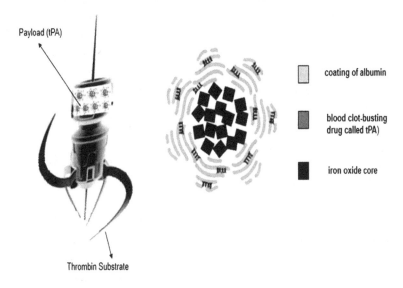

Figure 27. Process of overall clot detection and removal

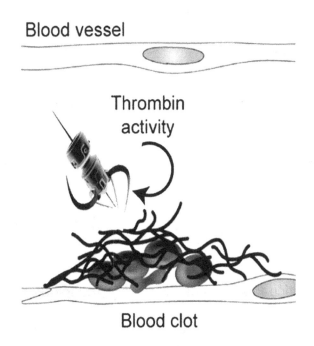

Engineering Thrombin-Sensitive Synthetic Biomarkers was first described by Lin, K.Y., et. al (2013) Mitchell, et al. (1978) and Rijkers, et al. (1995) explained the construction of synthetic biomarkers for thrombosis involves modifying the surface of iron oxide nanorobots. To first develop a suitable substrate, extension of the thrombin cleavable sequence fPR–x–S (x= site of cleavage, $k_{cat}/K_m \sim 9.33 \times 10^6$) to include glycine spacers and a C-terminal cysteine to allow coupling to nanorobots *via* sulfhydryl chemistry has been done (Park & Von Maltzahn, (2009)). To test substrate specificity, it has been conjugated with fluorophore-labeled derivatives onto nanorobots (sequence = (K-Flsc) GGfPRSGGGC at a valency ~40 peptides per nanorobot by absorbance spectroscopy, sufficient to reduce fluorescence by over 90% *via* homo quenching and followed by incubation of the nanorobots (200 nM by peptide, 5 nM by nanorobot) with purified thrombin (2 μM) or a panel of blood clotting proteases (FXa (160 nM), APC (60 nM), FIXa (90 nM), FVIIa (10 nM), FXIa (31 nM)), each present at its maximal physiological concentration. Freely emitting peptide fragments that were released by thrombin activity rapidly increased sample fluorescence. By contrast, negligible proteolysis was observed from the panel of no cognate proteases, as well as by thrombin in the presence of bivalirudin (Bival), a clinically approved direct thrombin inhibitor. To further investigate the ability to sense thrombin activity from blood, nanorobots have been spiked into human plasma samples inactivated with sodium citrate (an anticoagulant that chelates the cofactor calcium) and monitored plasma fluorescence after the addition of excess calcium chloride ($CaCl_2$) to trigger coagulation, or phosphate buffered saline (PBS) as a control. Aligned with previous observations with purified enzymes, plasma fluorescence markedly increased upon activation of the clotting cascade but not in control samples or in the presence of bivalirudin. To test stability, fluorogenic nanorobots were incubated in 10% serum at 37 °C overnight and any significant differences in size that would indicate precipitation or increases in sample fluorescence that would indicate nonspecific substrate cleavage was not detected. Collectively, these results established the ability of the specified nanorobots to specifically sense the proteolytic activity of thrombin within the complex milieu of plasma, consistent with previously described thrombin-specific fluorogenic probes as described by Tung et al. (2002).

Peptide Nanorobots Synthesis

Aminated iron oxide nanorobots were synthesized according to previously published protocols presented by Mitchell et al. (1978), Rijker et al. (1995) and Park et al. (2009). Peptides (biotin-eGvndneeGffsar (K-Flsc) GGfPRSGGGC, lower case= d-isomer) were synthesized by the Tufts University Core Facility peptide synthesis service. To conjugate peptides to nanorobots, nanorobots were first reacted with succinimidyl iodoacetate (Pierce) to introduce sulfhydryl-reactive handles. Cysteine terminated peptides and 20 kDa polyethylene glycol–SH (Laysan Bio.) were then mixed with nanorobots (95:20:1 molar ratio) for one hour at room temperature (RT) and purified by fast protein liquid chromatography. Stock solutions were stored in PBS at 4 °C. The number of fluorescein-labeled peptides per nanorobots was determined by absorbance spectroscopy using the absorbance of fluorescein (490 nm) and its extinction coefficient (78000 cm^{-1} M^{-1}).

Thrombolysis Using Anticoagulents (Clot Bursting) Technique

Thrombotic strokes can affect large or small arteries in the brain. Strokes that affect large arteries block flow to greater portions of the brain. When a thrombotic stroke (Figure 28) occurs in a small artery, the artery is usually one that is deep within the brain.

The most effective treatment for thrombotic stroke is a clot-busting drug, such as tissue plasminogen activator (tPA). Nanorobots are used to deliver the Clot-Busters directly to the spot needed. tPA one of the most important treatments over the last few years for the immediate treatment of a stroke is a medicine called tPA (which stands for tissue plasminogen activator). tPA is a very powerful "clot – buster" that is infused through the veins. If given within the first three hours after the onset of the symptoms. tPA

Figure 28. Thrombotic stroke

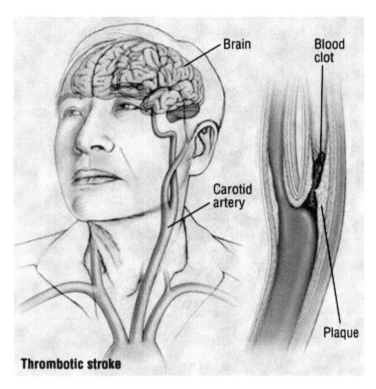

can significantly improve the patients' outcome from the stroke over the long term. The sooner the tPA is started the better outcome, so time is of the essence.

Magnetic nanoparticles quickly bust blood clots to promise improved stroke prevention (The research was published in the journal a advance functional materils. Source: House Methodist Research Institute, 2010) (See Figure 29)

Problem

Tissue plasminogen activator (tPA) is a drug commonly used by surgeons to bust open blood clots in a patient's bloodstream, but it does have its limitations. Once injected, there's no guarantee it will reach the site of the blood clot, and even then, having it arrive in the correct dosage can be tricky, with the risk of hemorrhage a very real possibility. Researchers have now found that using a new type of magnetic nanoparticle to deliver the drug offers a much more efficient journey to the site, promising to destroy blood clots 100 to 1,000 times faster and aid significantly in the prevention of heart attacks and strokes.

When using clot-busting tPA (an enzyme that also occurs naturally in the blood) in treatment, surgeons will generally inject a small quantity upstream of where the clot is thought to be. While there is the chance that the tPA will travel directly to the clot, there is also a chance that it will bypass the clot and never serve its intended purpose. Furthermore, the drug is broken down quickly in the blood, necessitating higher volumes in order to achieve an effective dose, something that heightens the risk of hemorrhage, which can prove fatal.

Figure 29. The new nanoparticles that help break up blood clots feature an iron oxide core (red), a coating of albumin (gray) and carry a blood clot-busting drug called tPA (green) (Image: Paolo Decuzzi laboratory/Houston Methodist Research Institute)

In looking to improve on these current methods, scientists from Houston Methodist Research Institute loaded magnetic nanoparticles with tPA, the idea being that the drug wouldn't be broken down so quickly once injected. To offer further shielding, the team then coated the nanoparticles in a protein found in the blood called albumin. This acts as a camouflage, tricking the body's immune system so the nanoparticles aren't identified as invaders and destroyed before they reach the site of the clot. This design has the potential to solve two problems inherent in current treatment techniques.

The nanoparticle protects the drug from the body's defenses, giving the tPA time to work, But it also allows the use of less tPA, which could make hemorrhage less likely. There is chance that the method could yet prove even more efficient. The team used iron oxide for the core of the nanoparticles, which not only enables the team to use them for magnetic resonance imaging, but opens up possibilities in remote guidance and localized magnetic heating to hasten the breaking up of the clots.

It is possible to use a static magnetic field first to help guide the nanoparticles to the clot, and then alternate the orientation of the field to increase the nanoparticles' efficiency in dissolving clots. tPA is normally injected at room temperatures; it performs better at higher temperatures (around 40° C (104° F)). Iron oxide particles is exposed to external magnetic fields with the aim of creating friction and heat, and indeed found that the warmed tPA acted faster, raising the speed of clot-busting by another factor of 10 (1,000 in total).

Drugs and Blood Clots: A Complicated Relationship

The different categories of patients suffering from blood clots and their suggested drug treatment is as shown in Table 8

Table 8. Drugs and blood clots

Category	Description	Treatment
Person at high risk of forming blood clots	Some people are at high risk of forming blood clots and are intentionally given drugs to decrease the risk. Drugs may be given that reduce the stickiness of platelets, so that they will not clump together to block a blood vessel.	Aspirin, ticlopidine, clopidogrel,abciximab, tirofiban are examples of drugs that interfere with the activity of platelets
People at moderate risk of forming blood clots	People at risk of forming blood clots may be given an anticoagulant, a drug that inhibits the action of blood proteins called clotting factors. Although often called "blood thinners," anticoagulants do not really thin the blood.	Commonly used anticoagulants are warfarin (given by mouth), and heparin (given by injection). People who take these drugs must be under close medical supervision. Lepirudin, bivalirudin, and argatrobanare newer types of anticoagulants that directly act on thrombin, a potent protein that induces clotting.
Person already suffering from blood clot	If a person already has a blood clot, a thrombolytic (fibrinolytic) drug can be given to help dissolve the clot	Thrombolytic drugs, which include streptokinase and tissue plasminogen activators (tPA), are sometimes used to treat heart attacks and strokes caused by blood clots

FUTURE APPLICATIONS OF NANOROBOTIC SYSTEM

- **Parasite Removal:** Nanorobots could wage micro-war on bacteria and small parasitic organisms inside a patient. It might take several nanorobots working together to destroy all the parasites.
- **Gout**: Gout is a condition where the kidneys lose the ability to remove waste from the breakdown from the bloodstream. A nanorobot could break up the crystalline structures at the joints, providing relief from the symptoms, though it wouldn't be able to reverse the condition permanently.
- **Breaking Up Kidney Stones:** Kidney stones can be intensely painful — the larger the stone the more difficult it is to pass. A nanorobot could break up kidney stones using a small laser.
- **Cleaning Wounds:** Nanorobots could help remove debris from wounds, decreasing the likelihood of infection.

Other Applications of Nanobots

1. Transmigration of the white blood cells (WBC) and other inflammatory cells to the inflamed tissues by attaching to them for accelerating the healing process.
2. Drug delivery nanorobots, known as 'pharmacytes', will be applied in future therapeutics against HIV.
3. Nanorobots can help in the control and monitoring of glucose levels in diabetic patients.

CONCLUSION

The chapter has presented the background, approach, implementation and result of research work involved in the development of nanorobots in extensive details. In the aforementioned research work, attempt has been made to solve medical problem through non invasive techniques by making a control movement of nanorobot through obstacle avoidance and making it to reach the targeted region. Realizing application of nanorobot to health issue raises new control challenges. The intelligent control system for nanorobot may have great impact on the development of future medical nanorobotic systems. The simulations results have proved that the proposed scheme effectively constructs an obstacle free self organized trajectory.

REFERENCES

Baker, S. E., Cai, W., Lasseter, T. L., Weidkamp, K. P., & Hamers, R. J. (2002). Covalently bonded adducts of DNA oligonucleotide with single wall carbon nanotube: Synthesis and hybridization. *Nano Letters*, *2*, 1413–1417. doi:10.1021/nl025729f

Braun, E., Eichen, Y., Sivan, U., & Ben-Yoseph, G. (1998). DNA-templated assembly and electrode attachment of a conducting silver wire. *Nature*, *391*(6669), 775–778. doi:10.1038/35826 PMID:9486645

Cavalcanti, A. (2007). Hardware architecture for nanorobots application in cerebral aneurysm. *IEEE-Nano Conf.*

Cavalcanti, A., & Freitas, R. A. Jr. (2002). Collective Robotics Coherent Behaviour for Nanosystems with Sensor-Based Neural Motion. *IEEE International Conference on Artificial Intelligence Systems (ICAIS'02)*, Divnomorskoe, Russia. doi:10.1109/ICAIS.2002.1048090

Cavalcanti, A., & Rosen, L. (2004). Nanorobotic challenges in Biomedical applications. *Design and Control, IEEE ICECS Int'l conf. on Electronics, Circuits and systems.*

Cavalcanti, A., & Shirinzadeh, B., Jr. (2008). Nanorobot architecture for medical target identification. IOP Science.

Das, S., Biswas, A., Dasgupta, S., & Abraham, A. (2009). Bacterial Foraging Optimization Algorithm: Theoretical Foundations, Analysis, and Applications, in Foundations of Computational Intelligence Volume 3. *Studies in Computational Intelligence*, *203*, 23–55.

Diez, S., Reuther, C., Dinu, C., Seidel, R., Mertig, M., Pompe, W., & Howard, J. (2003). Stretching and Transporting DNA Molecules using Motor Proteins. *Nano Letters*, *3*(9), 1251–1254. doi:10.1021/nl034504h

Dwyer, C., Johri, V., Cheung, M., Patwardhan, J., Lebeck, A., & Sori, D. (2004). Design tools for a DNA-guided self-assembling carbon nanotube technology. *Nanotechnology*, *15*(9), 1240–1245. doi:10.1088/0957-4484/15/9/022

Ellington, A. D., & Szostak, J. W. (1990). In vitro selection of RNA molecules that bind specific ligands. *Nature*, *346*(6287), 818–822. doi:10.1038/346818a0 PMID:1697402

Freitas Jr. (2005). Progress in Nanomedicine and Medical Nanorobotics. In Handbook of Theoretical and Computational Nanotechnology. American Scientific Publishers.

Freitas Jr. (n.d.). Current Status of Nanomedicine and Medical Nanorobotics (Invited Survey). *J. Comput. Theor. Nanosci., 2*, 1-25.

Gao, H., Kong, Y., Cui, D., & Ozkan, C. S. (2003). Spontaneous Insertion of DNA Oligonucleotides into Carbon Nanotubes. *Nano Letters*, *3*(4), 471–473. doi:10.1021/nl025967a

Gold, J. L. (1995). Oligonucleotides as research, diagnostic, and therapeutic agents. *Biological Chemistry*, *270*(23), 13581–13584. doi:10.1074/jbc.270.23.13581 PMID:7775406

Hamdi, M., Sharma, G., Ferreira, A., & Mavroidis, D. (2005). Molecular Mechanics Study on Bionanorobotic Components using Force Feedback. *IEEE International Conference on Robotics and Biomimetics, Hong Kong.*

Harnack, O., Ford, W. E., Yasuda, A., & Wessels, J. M. (2002). Tris (hydroxymethyle) phosphine capped gold particles templated by DNA as nano wire precursors. *Nano Letters*, *2*(9), 919–923. doi:10.1021/nl020259a

Hla, Choi, & Park. (2008). Obstacle Avoidance Algorithm for Collective Movement in Nanorobots. *International Journal of Computer Science and Network Security, 8*(11), 302-309.

Hogg, T., & Freitas, R. A., Jr. (2012). *Acoustic communication for medical nanorobots.* arXiv:1202.0568 vi [cs.RD]

Hoummady, M., & Fujita, Y. (1999). Micromachines for nanoscale science and technology. *Nanotechnology*, *10*(1), 29–33. doi:10.1088/0957-4484/10/1/007

Huai-wei, J., Shi-gang, W., & Wei, X. U. (2005). Construction of Medical Nanorobot. *IEEE International Conference on Robotics and Biomimetics (ROBIO).*

Ito, Y. (2004). Design and synthesis of functional polymers by *in vitro* selection. *Polymers for Advanced Technologies*, *15*(12), 3–14. doi:10.1002/pat.455

Ito, Y., Kawazoe, N., & Imanishi, Y. (2000). In vitro selected oligonucleotides as receptors in binding assays. *Methods (San Diego, Calif.)*, *22*(1), 107–114. doi:10.1006/meth.2000.1041 PMID:11020323

Kawasaki, T. (2003). DNA use as a photoelectric transfer material. High Polym., 52, 143.

Keren, K., Krueger, M., Gilad, R., Ben-Yoseph, G., Sivan, U., & Braun, E. (2002). Sequence specific molecular lithography on single DNA. *Science*, *297*(5578), 72–75. doi:10.1126/science.1071247 PMID:12098693

Lin, K. Y., Kwong, G. A., Warren, A. D., Wood, D. K., & Bhatia, S. N. (2013). Nanoparticles That Sense Thrombin Activity As Synthetic Urinary Biomarkers of Thrombosis. Department of Chemical Engineering, Massachusetts Institute of Technology.

Magnetic nanoparticles quickly bust blood clots to promise improved stroke prevention. (2010). House Methodist Research Institute.

Merced. (2008). Study of Stable Conformations CNT-DNA Hybrids by Means of Principle Component Analysis. In *Proceedings of The National Conference on Undergraduate Research* (NCUR). Salisbury University.

Mirkin, C. A. (2000). A DNA-Based Methodology for Preparing Nanocluster Circuits, Arrays, and Diagnostic Materials. *MRS Bulletin*, *25*, 43–54.

Mitchell, G. A., Gargiulo, R. J., Huseby, R. M., Lawson, D. E., Pochron, S. P., & Sehuanes, J. A. (1978). Assay for Plasma Heparin Using a Synthetic Peptide Substrate for Thrombin: Introduction of the Fluorophore Aminoisophthalic Acid, Dimethyl Ester. *Thrombosis Research*, *3*(1), 47–52. doi:10.1016/0049-3848(78)90108-1 PMID:694832

Montegano, C. D., & Bachand, G. D. (1999). Constructing nanomechanical devices powered by biomolecular motors. *Nanotechnology*, *10*(3), 225–331. doi:10.1088/0957-4484/10/3/301

Nguyen, C. V., Delzeit, L., Cassell, A. M., Li, J., Han, J., & Meyyappan, M. (2003). Preparation of Nucleic Acid Functionalized Carbon Nanotube Arrays. *Nano Letters*, *2*(10), 1079–1081. doi:10.1021/nl025689f

Requicha, A. A. G. (2003). Nanorobots, NEMS, and Nanoassembly. *Proceedings of the IEEE*, *91*(11).

Rijkers, D. S., Wielders, S. J. H., Tesser, G. I., & Hemker, H. C. (1995). Design and Synthesis of Thrombin Substrates with Modified Kinetic Parameters Thromb. *Res.*, *79*, 491–499. PMID:7502275

Rusconi, C. P., Scardino, E., Layzer, J., Pitoc, G. A., Ortel, T. L., Monroe, D., & Sullenger, B. A. (2002). RNA aptamers as reversible antagonists of coagulation factor IXa. *Nature*, *419*(6902), 90–94. doi:10.1038/nature00963 PMID:12214238

Seeling, B., Keiper, S., Stuhlmann, F., & Jaeschke, A. (2000). Enantioselective ribozyme catalysis of a bimolecular cycloaddition reaction. *Angewandte Chemie International Edition*, *39*(24), 4576–4579. doi:10.1002/1521-3773(20001215)39:24<4576::AID-ANIE4576>3.0.CO;2-J PMID:11169675

Seeman. N. C. (2003). DNA in a material world. *Nature, 421*, 427-431.

Sitti, M. (2009). Miniature Devices: Voyage of the microrobots. *Nature, 458*(30).

Stojanovic, M. N., Landry, D. W., & Am, J. (2002). Aptamer-based colorimetric probe for cocaine. *Chem. Soc.*, *124*(33), 9678–9679. doi:10.1021/ja0259483 PMID:12175205

Tuerk, C., & Gold, L. (1990). Systematic evolution of ligands by exponential enrichment: RNA ligands to bacteriophage T4 DNA polymerase. *Science*, *249*(4968), 505–510. doi:10.1126/science.2200121 PMID:2200121

Tung, C. H., Gerszten, R. E., Jaffer, F. A., & Weissleder, R. A. (2002). *Novel Near-Infrared Fluorescence Sensor for Detection of Thrombin Activation in Blood. ChemBioChem*, *3*, 207–211. PMID:11921399

Ummat, A., Dubey, A., & Mavroidis, C. (2005). *Bionanorobotics: A Field Inspired by Nature*. In *Biomimetics - Biologically Inspired Technologies* (pp. 201–227). CRC Press.

Willner, I. (2002, December20). Biomaterials for Sensors, Fuel Cells, and Circuitry. *Science*, *298*(5602), 2407–2408. doi:10.1126/science.298.5602.2407 PMID:12493919

Yurke, B., Turberfield, A. J., Mills, A. P. Jr, Simmel, F. C., & Neumann, J. L. (2000). A DNA-fuelled molecular machine made of DNA. *Nature*, *406*(6796), 605–608. doi:10.1038/35020524 PMID:10949296

Chapter 18

A Linear Time Series Analysis of Fetal Heart Rate to Detect the Variability:
Measures Using Cardiotocography

Sahana Das
Narula Institute of Technology, India

Kaushik Roy
West Bengal State University, India

Chanchal Kumar Saha
Biraj Mohini Matrisadan and Hospital, India

ABSTRACT

Real time analysis and interpretation of fetal heart rate (FHR) is the challenge posed to every clinician. Different algorithms had been developed, tried and subsequently incorporated into Cardiotocograph (CTG) machines for automated diagnosis. Feature extraction and accurate detection of baseline and its variability has been the focus of this chapter. Algorithms by Dawes and Redman and Ayres-de-Campos have been discussed in this chapter. The authors are pleased to propose an algorithm for extracting the variability of fetal heart. The algorithm's accuracy and degree of agreement with clinician's diagnosis had been established by various statistical methods. This algorithm has been compared with an algorithm proposed by Nidhal and the new algorithm is found to be better at detecting variability in both ante-partum and intra-partum period.

INTRODUCTION

It is important to monitor the fetus during late pregnancy (ante partum) and labor (intrapartum). Since the fetus is not directly accessible the fetal status can be best determined by monitoring its heart rate and rhythm. Under normal circumstances the fetal heart rate is between 110 – 160 beats per minute (bpm).

DOI: 10.4018/978-1-5225-1785-6.ch018

It may vary by 5 – 25 bpm. The heart rate may be affected by various factors ranging from external stimuli to maternal health to any sort of fetal distress. Primary aim of fetal monitoring is to maximize the likelihood of detecting a fetus at risk and make a timely intervention to avoid fetal compromise.

It has been found by National Center for Health Statistics, USA, that perinatal mortality rate (PMR) was 10.14/1000 live births. In USA stillbirth contribute to 55% of perinatal mortality (Macdorman & Gregory, 2015). The Indian scenario is even more staggering. According to a WHO report of 2009 the PMR in rural India is 47/1000 live births and 30/1000 in urban area and 44/1000 in combined rural and urban areas (United Nations Children's Fund [UNCF], 2009).

Main causes of perinatal mortality are intrauterine and birth related hypoxia and asphyxia. These are reflected in the fetal heart rate (FHR) pattern. Imperfection in the fetal heart rate pattern reflects developing acidosis which precedes major neurological damage to the fetus.

Risk factors in the perinatal stage of a fetus may produce adverse effects which range from cardiovascular problems, cognitive learning and behavioral disorder such as cerebral- palsy to even fetal demise. This makes it necessary to monitor the fetus during ante-partum and intrapartum period.

Fetal monitoring primarily aims to prevent metabolic acidosis by evaluating whether or not the fetus is suffering from lack of oxygen during labor. During intrapartum period hypoxia can set in due to umbilical cord compression or decreased placental perfusion during the uterine contraction of the mother. This is exhibited by the late deceleration of FHR. There are other factors that affect the FHR changes but are not directly related to hypoxia. These are maternal fever, infection, medications etc. (Heelen, 2015).

(FHR) produces an automatic rate controlled by the autonomic nervous system (ANS) and its activities are reflected in the heart rate patterns which can provide information regarding the status of the fetus. ANS has two branches: parasympathetic and sympathetic. They have complementary effect on the FHR. Sympathetic branch tends to increase the heart rate while parasympathetic branch tend to reduce it (Fanelli, Giovanni, Companile, & Signorini, 2013). These two opposing effects tend to produce moment-to-moment change in the FHR, known as fetal heart rate variability (FHRV). Its presence thus implies that both branches of ANS are adequately oxygenated and are working well. This makes FHRV one of the most important characteristics of FHR.

Since fetus is not directly accessible, monitoring heart rate signals can be done only noninvasive way to evaluate the condition of the fetus. Cardiotocograph is the predominantly established method for fetal monitoring.

This chapter explores various algorithms including a novel method proposed by the authors for estimating FHRV by analyzing and interpreting fetal heart rate patterns from CTG signals. This method has been compared with another method proposed by Shahad Nidhal, another researcher currently working in this field.

PHYSIOLOGY OF FETUS

Placenta exchanges oxygen and carbon dioxide between the mother and the fetus. There are two types of metabolism: anaerobic and aerobic. Waste products of aerobic metabolism are carbon dioxide and water. The energy produced controls the fetal growth and activity. Aerobic metabolism is dependent on the oxygen.

In anaerobic metabolism oxygen is not available. The waste product is lactic acid and the energy produced controls the basal/ vital activity. Since anaerobic metabolism only provides energy for vital

Figure 1. Relationship between blood gas and fetal heart rate
Source: Spilka, 2013.

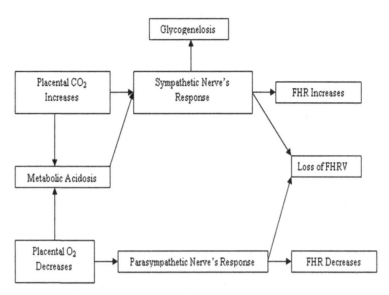

activity, the fetal growth is inhibited. Anaerobic metabolism thus should not last long. If the supply of oxygen is not restored on time oxygen saturation in the fetal blood gets reduced and gradually hypoxemia, hypoxia and finally the most dangerous stage, the asphyxia sets in. This relationship is depicted in Figure 1.

Autonomic nervous system reacts to the oxygen deficiency. Parasympathetic nervous system responds by reducing the heart rate (bradycardia) and sympathetic nervous system tries to counter by increasing the heart rate (tachycardia). This tends to reduce the moment-to-moment changes in FHR, i.e. it results in reduced FHRV. A hypoxic fetus is identified if the FHR is above 180 bpm for fifteen minutes or more, decreased FHRV, little or no acceleration, late deceleration (Murray, 2006).

Hypoxemia

This is the primary stage of oxygen insufficiency. Though oxygen is depleted at the fringe, there is still enough oxygen for aerobic metabolism. Fetus responds by reducing movements; growth is also restricted too to save oxygen. Hypoxemia can be sustained for days and weeks. But during intrapartum period hypoxemia reduces the fetal ability to handle the stress of the labor.

Hypoxia

It is the second stage of oxygen insufficiency. Anaerobic metabolism develops at the peripheral tissues. Sympathetic nerve is activated. Hypoxia can last for hours without damaging the fetus.

Asphyxia

This is the most serious stage. Oxygen reaches a dangerously low level. Main organs resort to anaerobic metabolism. Brain at this point has very low glucose level. Fetus responds by activating sympathetic nervous system.

METHODS OF MONITORING THE FETUS

There are two ways to monitor the fetus:

1. The external method, and
2. The internal method.

External Monitoring

A toco-transducer is placed over the fundus to measure the uterine contraction pressure (UCP) of the mother and ultrasound transducer is placed over the abdomen to measure the fetal heart rate.

External method is non-invasive, easy to perform, cost-effective and continuously records the FHR pattern. Disadvantage is that any movement of the patient may produce an inaccurate trace. It also cannot measure the basal tone of the uterus. FHR may also be lost if the fetus is active or changes position.

Internal Monitoring

It involves inserting a transducer through the cervix of the mother and attaching to the scalp of the fetus. A problem with this monitoring it involves the risk of infection or injury to the fetus. It may also cause perforation of the uterus or separation of the low-lying placenta. Also partial dilation of the cervix is necessary to access the fetus. As a result, this method is not suitable for ante-partum fetal surveillance.

Though this method is able to accurately measure the UCP and basal tone of the uterus and is not subject to artifacts, external monitoring method is mostly preferred.

CARDIOTOCOGRAPH

Until the 1960s fetal condition was assessed by the growth of the fetus, movement of the fetus perceived by the mother and by listening to fetal hear beat using stethoscope. Absence of fetal movement posed a serious diagnostic predicament. X-ray images would show overlapping fetal skull bones and softened and broken down fetal tissues; all indicative of fetal demise.

These recurrent dilemmas about the viability of the fetus provided the major impetus for the Cardiotocograph (CTG). Electrocardiography and phonocardiography were initially pursued but were later abandoned due to technical problems. Later when it was found that Doppler-shift or direct electrocardiography could be used to successfully detect the fetal heart rate and reassure the condition of the fetus, that CTG became an established method of monitoring the fetus (van Gejin, 2011).

Figure 2. Huntleigh Sonicaid FetalCare used by the authors to collect CTG trace

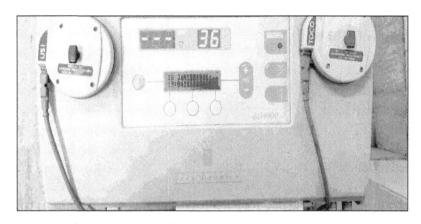

These days Cardiotocograph is the most widely used non-invasive electronic fetal monitoring (EFM) technique to continuously measures the FHR and uterine contractions (UC). Hunteleigh Sonicaid Fetal-Care shown in Figure 2 is used by authors to collect data for their research work.

Doppler ultrasound transducer picks up the heart rate of the fetus while pressure transducer detects the UCP. These are electronically recorded on a strip of thermal paper or stored in computer for farther reference. A sample CTG trace is shown in Figure 3. The signal at the top is the FHR signal measured in beats per minute (bpm) and the bottom signal is the uterine contraction pressure (UCP) of the mother and is measured in mmHg.

Figure 3. A CTG trace with FHR at the top and uterine contraction pressure is shown at the bottom

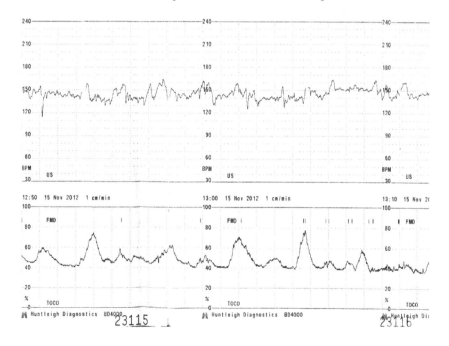

Features of CTG

The four major features of FHR are:

- Acceleration,
- Deceleration,
- Baseline of fetal heart and
- Baseline variability.

They are defined as follows:

- Baseline is the mean fetal heart rate rounded to increments of 5 bpm in a ten minutes period, measured in the absence of acceleration and deceleration. Normal baseline is between 110 – 160 bpm. Fall of FHR below 110 bpm is called bradycardia and rise of FHR above 160 bpm is called tachycardia.
- Fetal heart rate variability is the fluctuations in baseline over a ten minutes period. It is measured as the difference in amplitude from the peak to trough in a ten minutes interval. Variability is said to be absent if the amplitude range is undetectable. If amplitude range is less than 5 bpm variability is minimal. Amplitude range 6 – 25 bpm means variability is moderate and more than 25 bpm is classified as marked variability.
- Acceleration is defined as an abrupt increase in FHR at least 15 bpm above the baseline and lasting for 15 seconds or longer but less than 2 minutes. Onset to peak should be in less than 30 seconds. Acceleration is classified as prolonged if the duration is more than 2 minutes but less than 10 minutes. Any acceleration that lasts for more than 10 minutes is considered a baseline change.
- Deceleration is defined as an abrupt decrease in FHR at least 15 bpm below the baseline and lasting for 15 seconds or longer but less than 2 minutes. Onset to nadir should be in less than 30 seconds. Deceleration is classified as 'early' if the nadir of the deceleration coincides with the peak of the uterine contraction; it is classified as 'late' if the nadir of the deceleration occurs after the peak of the contraction; 'variable' deceleration is an abrupt decrease in FHR below the baseline and may or may not coincide with uterine contractions.

In Figure 4 baseline, deceleration and uterine contractions are marked on CTG trace from CTU-UHB database by the authors.

Classification of CTG

A CTG trace can be classified into one of three categories depending on the acid-base status of the fetus and the corresponding FHR pattern. The classifications are shown in Table 1.

GUIDELINES OF CTG INTERPRETATION

CTG was first introduced in the 1960s. But there was not any consensus regarding the definition, terminology and clinical interpretation of FHR patterns. In order to standardize the interpretation and

Figure 4. A CTG trace with the baseline, deceleration nadir and uterine contraction peaks are marked

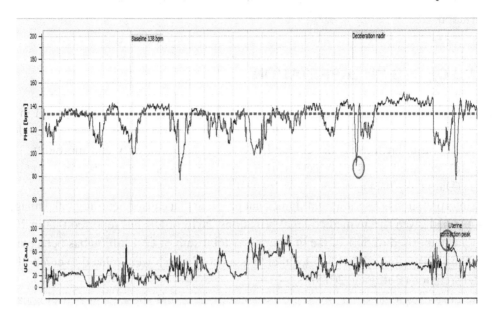

Table 1. Classification of CTG trace

	Interpretations	Features
Category I: .Normal	Tracings suggest normal acid base status.	• Baseline: 110 – 160 bpm • Variability: Moderate • Deceleration: Late or variable decelerations absent. • Early decelerations present or absent.
Category II: Suspicious	Tracings do not predict abnormal acid-base status.	Traces that do not fall into either into Category I or Category III are classified as Category II
Category III: Abnormal	Tracings are predictive of abnormal acid-base status.	• Absent variability. • Bradycardia. • Recurrent late deceleration or recurrent variable deceleration. • Sinusoidal heart rate pattern.

classification of CTG, Federation International de Gynecologie et d'Obstetrique (FIGO) first proposed an interpretation of CTG signals in 1986. These were later modified and adopted by other obstetrics organizations such as Royal College of Obstetricians and Gynecologists (RCOG) in 2001 and National Institute of Health and Care Excellence (NICE) in 2007 (Das, Roy, & Saha, 2011).

National Institute of Child Health and Development (NICHD) took up this issue in 1997 and provided its own set of guidelines. The guidelines were further reviewed in 2008 by NICHD and ACOG and a set of standardized guidelines was established. Though the definitions were mainly for visual analysis, it was also possible to adapt these definitions for computerized interpretation (NICHD, 2008). Though the definitions were mainly for visual analysis, it was also possible to adapt these definitions for computerized interpretation (NICHD, 2008). A 3-tier classification system is followed by all the guidelines. Authors in their work have chosen to follow the NICHD guidelines as it is more thorough and takes into consideration different factors to determine the features of FHR (Das et al., 2011).

In spite of several guidelines, the interpretation of CTG is still biased with high inter and intra-observer variation.

PROBLEMS OF CTG INTERPRETATION

CTG was first introduced it was expected that it would be a good decision making tool in the hands of the physicians and its use would prevent adverse outcomes during labor. Though there had been a significant reduction in birth asphyxia, cerebral palsy, perinatal mortality and morbidity, debate and controversy still remained on its usefulness as there had been cases of inaccurate interpretation of the FHR patterns (Das et al., 2011).

CTG misinterpretation is a serious and significant problem that caused neurological damage or death of the fetus and had given rise to medico-legal litigations. NHS of UK has reported that in 2011, 'birth asphyxia' alone comprised of 50% of the litigations. A total sum of £3.1 billion has been paid by NHS between 2000 and 2010 towards medico-legal claims most of which were related to cerebral palsy and CTG misinterpretation (Buttigieg, 2015).

Of all the obstetrics legal cases involving intrapartum care and subsequent neurological damage, 70% are due to abnormalities or interpretation of CTG traces (RCOG, 2001). Majority of medico-legal problems have their roots in the inability to accurately interpret the CTG trace and thus failing to take appropriate actions on time (Sinai & Arulkumaran, 2013).

One of the main problems in classifying the CTG trace arises when interpreting the FHR patterns that lie in the gray zone between what is clearly normal and what is grossly abnormal. It is known that accumulation of lactic acid in the fetal blood over a period of time leads to metabolic acidosis. During this period the fetus tries to compensate for this stress. This is evident from early deceleration as the fetus is trying to recover from the stress of a brief period of reduced oxygen supply. But if the fetus is too distressed and is unable to deal with it, it would be apparent from the FHR pattern. Identification of this gray zone from fetal stress to distress making timely intervention is of utmost importance. The heart rate pattern involved are varied and complex and are not always discernible by visual inspection alone (Das, Roy, & Saha, 2015a).

Lack of objective definition of some of the features led to the limitation of these guidelines. Non-existent universally accepted guideline for CTG interpretation and objective definition of the parameters limited the efficacy of CTG monitoring (Das, Roy, & Saha, 2015b). There are also discrepancies in the classifications given in these guidelines. For example, there is an inconsistency in the FIGO classification of deceleration. It is stated that absence of deceleration except for mild irregular deceleration of very short duration is consistent with 'normal' FHR patterns. But again, the guideline says irregular deceleration of any type unless severe are part of the definition of 'suspicious' FHR pattern. Thus in cases where deceleration are difficult to identify, it is not obvious whether a CTG should be classified as 'normal' or 'suspicious' (Buttigieg, 2016).

Another major problem is vast degree of inter-observer and intra-observer variation in patterns recognition. The standard way of assessment till date is visual interpretation. Since there is a lack of standardization in the guidelines, a feature that may be recognized by a physician may be completely missed by another. Studies have shown that not only clinicians differ with one another; a clinician may also disagree with himself when assessing the same trace at different times (Das et al., 2015a).

Visual estimations are thus educated guesses which depend upon the experience and expertise of the clinicians. But it is not possible even for the most expert clinician to remember all the possible range of patterns and their significance. These at times can be a big hindrance to accurate assessment. Measurement of the FHR parameters should be reliable and precise as the mortality and morbidity of the fetus depend on it.

The interpretation of FHR requires experience and knowledge. Often there are subtle changes in the CTG trace that are indicative of early signs of asphyxia. But these signs may be completely missed if analyzed visually. It is therefore crucial for obstetricians to have an automated decision making tool to help in the analysis and interpretation of CTG trace.

Prof. Phil Steer (2008) (Emeritus professor of Obstetrics, Imperial College London) famously stated that the major weakness of CTG lies in poor standard of interpretation and the human factor demonstrated by high inter and intra observer variations.

AUTOMATION OF CTG ANALYSIS AND ONGOING SCENARIO

The above problems provided the incentives to automate the interpretation of CTG. Automation of the CTG signal analysis need to deal with two main problems: *parameter extraction* and *classifications*, i.e. FHR patterns recognition and subsequent *interpretation* of patterns to make a diagnosis (Guijarro-Berdinas, Alonso-Betanzos, & Fontella-Romero, 2002).

The first problem is mainly due to the imprecision and incompleteness in the definition of the features of CTG by various obstetric and gynecological bodies and guidelines for their extraction and classification. It has been concluded by de Campos and Bernardes that the guidelines are consistent for normal patterns but they disagree widely for suspicious and pathological patterns (Guijarro-Berdinas et al., 2002).

Interpretation on the other hand needs to take into account the circumstantial analysis of all the pathological, physiological and clinical aspects of fetal monitoring. Even though many automated systems are available in the market, the fallacy in the feature extraction and analysis failed to cease.

Automation of CTG Analysis: Early Works

Keeping in mind the problems encountered in visual estimation and analysis, several attempts over the years have been made to automate FHR evaluation. The very first attempt at the automation of CTG analysis and classification was by Dawes and Redman in 1981 (Dawes & Redman, 1981). Following the guidelines provided by FIGO, they proposed an algorithm for the estimation of baseline and for the extraction of acceleration and deceleration of FHR. Based on their algorithm System 8000 was created for antenatal fetal monitoring. It was later upgraded to SonicAid FetalCare which uses an additional parameter called short term variability (STV).

In 1990 Mantel et al developed an iterating procedure to extract the features of CTG using FIGO guidelines (Mantel et al., 1990a, 1990b). Features extraction method was further improved by J. Bernardes et al (Bernardes, Moura, de Sa, & Leite, 1991) when SisPorto project was stated in 1987 in University of Porto, Portugal. The outcome of this project was Porto System for computerized analysis of CTG signals. In 1997 this system was farther upgraded to SisPorto 2.0 by Ayres-de-Campos and Bernardes. The latest version Sisporto 3.5 was developed in 2008 and is now commercially available (de-Campos, Sousa, Costa, & Bernardes, 2008).

2CTG2, an ante-partum fetal monitoring system was developed by Magenes and Signorini in 2003 (Magenes et al., 2003). NST-EXPERT was developed in 1995 by Alonso-Betanzos for non-invasive fetal assessment. It is an expert system capable of making diagnosis and proposing a treatment (Alonso-Betanzos, 1995). CAFE (Computer Aided Fetal Evaluation) which is a successor of NST-EXPERT, was developed in 2002 by Guijarro-Berdinas and Alonso-Betanzos. It uses neuro-fuzzy approach to automate all the tasks associated with CTG evaluation (Guijarro-Berdinas & Alonso-Betanzos, 2002).

Green and Smith developed K2 Medical System in University of Plymouth, UK. It is a distributed system with a central unit and multiple local units by the bedsides of the bedsides of the patients. An alarm is sounded if abnormalities are noticed in the FHR pattern (Green, & Keith, 2002). This system was later renamed INFANT. It can be viewed as an intelligent system as it is capable of providing logical reasoning for its assessment (INFANT study, 2009).

PeriCALM was developed in 2010 by LMS Medical System, Canada and PeriGen, USA. The system is based on the NICHD guideline (PeriCALM, 2010). Though there had been lot of efforts to improve the reliability of CTG evaluation and interpretation, none of them showed the dependability that the clinicians expect. None of the systems described above has any wide applications. Obstetricians till now mostly depend on visual evaluation of CTG trace (Spilka, 2013). The authors have discussed some of the algorithms in detail in terms of how they estimated the variability of fetal heart rate.

FHR VARIABILITY INTERPRETATION

It has already been mentioned previously how the interplay of sympathetic and parasympathetic nervous system play a role in producing the variation in the baseline of FHR. Thus accurate estimation and classification of FHRV is vital to the recognition of fetal status.

Fetal heart rate variability is the fluctuation of FHR in the absence of uterine contraction, acceleration and deceleration. Variability can be long term or short term. Long term variability (LTV) is the fluctuation range of the heart beat interval epochs in analyzable one minute sections. It is influenced by sympathetic nervous system. Presence of LTV indicates that the fetus is adequately oxygenated. The fluctuation range is calculated as a difference between maximal deviation above and below the baseline. The fluctuation ranges of all analyzed one minute sections are averaged.

Short term variability (STV) is independent of baseline. It is the beat-to-beat variation in FHR i.e. how fast the heart rate varies. STV is vital for detecting fetal well-being. Low STV implies that the fetus is growth restricted and persistently stressed. It is influenced by parasympathetic nervous system. STV proves to be a useful measure of fetal condition if measured after at least 60 minutes of recording.

STV cannot be visually estimated (Wretlar et al., 2016). STV is computed as mean difference between successive heart beat interval epochs in all analyzable one minute sections. The results of all one minute sections are averaged.

In both cases samples containing more than 50% signal loss are discarded during signal analysis. Presence of FHRV (LTV & STV) indicates normal cardiac response. The physiological components of STV and LTV are interrelated and hence can be interpreted as a single entity as done by NICHD, i.e. no distinction is made between STV and LTV. There are certain factors to consider while analyzing variability:

1. Presence of FHRV along with decelerative patterns indicates the fetus is not in metabolic acidosis.
2. Usually LTV and STV change simultaneously resulting in uniform change in overall variability of the baseline.
3. Absent FHRV may indicate fetal hypoxia, central nervous system anomaly, cardiovascular anomaly or fetal brain injury.
4. Absent variability along with persistent late or variable deceleration may imply hypoxemia and resultant metabolic acidosis.

Variability is classified as 'absent' if FHRV is absent, 'minimal' if 0 bpm ≤ FHRV ≤ 5 bpm, 'moderate' if 6 bpm ≤ FHRV ≤ 25 bpm and 'marked' if FHRV ≥ 25 bpm.

Guidelines for Estimation of FHR Variability

According to Federation International de Gynecologie et d'Obstetrique (FIGO) guideline variability of fetal heart rate is the oscillation of FHR signal, estimated as the average bandwidth amplitude of the signal in one minute duration (de-Campos & Arulkumaran, 2015).

Royal College of Obstetricians and Gynecologists (RCOG) defines variability as minor fluctuations in baseline FHR occurring at 3-5 cycles/minute. It is measured by estimating the difference in bpm between the highest peak and the lowest trough of fluctuation in one minute segment of the trace (RCOG, 2001).

National Institute of Child Health and Development (NICHD) excludes sinusoidal patterns. Variability is defined as the fluctuations in the FHR baseline of 2 cycles/ minute or more, with irregular amplitude and inconsistent frequency. Fluctuations are visually quantitated as the amplitude of the peak to trough in bpm (Macones et al., 2008).

SOME EXISTING ALGORITHMS FOR VARIABILITY ESTIMATION

Algorithm of Dawes and Redman

A lot of research work was devoted to improve the reliability of interpretation of CTG trace. Automatic interpretation of CTG began evolving around the early 1980s with the pioneering work of Dawes and Redman, resulting in the first commercial system called Sonicaid FetalCare (Dawes et al., 2001).

Dawes-Redman system is software that provides numeric analysis of the CTG trace based on a set of criteria called Dawes-Redman criteria. There are two possible outcomes: 'criteria met' and 'criteria not met' (Dawes et al., 2001).

Dawes and Redman incorporated FIGO risk scores along with STV and LTV of fetal heart rate in their algorithm (Redman & Moulden, 2014). The first value is displayed after 10 minutes. Thus, new values are added and the STV is updated continuously for 60 minutes.

Dawes and Redman's Algorithm for the Estimation of Long Term FHR Variability

1. If Samples Have > 50% Signal Loss: Discard
2. Else
   a. Divide The Sample Into N Samples Of 1 Min. Duration
   b. For Each 1 minute duration
      i. Detect The Maximum And Minimum deviation from the Base Value.
      ii. Minute Range (MR) = Maxdev – Mindev
3. If 5 of 6 MR Are < 30 Msec: Record for 2 more minutes
4. If 5 of 6 MR Are > 32 Msec: Period of High Variation
5. If Mean LTV of all High Variation < 10th percentile Of gestational age
   a. If Time < 60 Minutes: Record for 2 More Minutes
   b. Else: Stop
6. Else: Consider other factors related To FHR

Dawes and Redman's Algorithm for the Estimation of Short Term FHR Variability

1. If samples has > 50% signal loss: Discard
2. Else
   a. Divide the sample into N samples of 1 min. duration
   b. For each 1 min duration
      i. STV_i = mean difference between consecutive heart beat interval epochs.
      ii. $STV = \sum_i STV_i$
3. If STV < 3.0 msec
   a. If time < 60 mins: Record for 2 more mins
   b. Else: Stop
4. Else
   a. If STV > 4.5 msec and mean LTV of all high variation > 3rd percentile of the gestational age consider other factors related to FHR
   b. Else
      i. If time < 60 mins: Record for 2 more mins
      ii. Else: Stop
5. If STV > 5.0 msec: Consider other factors related to FHR
6. Else:
   a. If time < 60 mins: Record for 2 more mins
   b. Else: Stop

Sonicaid uses this technique for antenatal monitoring. Effectiveness of STV analysis has not yet been properly evaluated for intrapartum monitoring. Though STV is an important measure of fetal condition it can only be applicable if measured after at least 60 minutes of recording (Wretlar et al., 2016).

A new CTG monitor launched by EDAN instruments in China is able to estimate STV both externally and internally using a scalp electrode (Wretlar et al., 2016). The algorithm by Dawes and Redman is only applicable during the contraction free period i.e. the ante partum period.

Algorithm of Diego Ayres-de-Campos

The algorithm developed Prof. Diego Ayres-de-Campos and his team in University of Porto, Portugal developed a fetal monitoring system which is known as Omiview SisPorto system. The Porto project was undertaken in 1987 with the aim of creating a system for the computer analysis of FHR signals. FIGO guidelines for FHR interpretation had been followed for its development (de-Campos & Bernardes, 2004, 2010).

The latest version of Omniview fetal monitor is Omniview SisPorto3.5 which is designed for centralized monitoring and computerized CTG analysis along with online alert system to warn the health care professionals about an impending hypoxic situation

Like Huntleigh's Soniaid FetalCare SisPorto too distinguishes between LTV and STV. If the difference between signals is less than 1 bpm then the STV is said to be abnormal. After estimation of STV each value of FHR is substituted by an average of 5 values centered on it (de-Campos et al., 2004, 2010). Algorithm for STV calculation is as follows:

Ayres-de-Campos's Algorithm for the Estimation of Short Term FHR Variability

1 Start estimation after 10 mins. of signal acquisition.
2. Compute $STV_i = FHR_{i+1} - FHR_i$ the difference between two adjacent FHR signals.
3. If $STV_i < 1$bpm

The point has abnormal STV

With N values of FHR signal

$$STV = \sum_i STV_i / N$$

LTV is calculated in those segments without acceleration and deceleration. Difference between the maximum and minimum values of FHR in a sliding 1 minute window is estimated. If this value is less than 5 bpm then the LTV is said to be abnormal (de-Campos et al, 2004, 2010).

Ayres-de-Campos's Algorithm for the Estimation of Long Term FHR Variability

1. Divide the trace into N segments of 60 sec duration each.
2. Segments without acceleration or deceleration are considered for computation of LTV.
3. Compute $LTV_i = FHR_{i+1} - FHR_i$.
4. If $LTV_i < 5$ bpm: The point has abnormal LTV.
5. $LTV = \sum_i LTV_i / N$.

A NOVEL METHOD OF ESTIMATION OF FHR VARIABILITY

Even though many algorithms had been proposed over the years, none of them guaranteed the correct estimated value of baseline variability. Thus there is no consensus on the best method for automated estimation of FHRV. Though most of these algorithms show a satisfactory result for regular and stable FHR trace, they fail for complex or irregular traces.

An analysis of fetal heart rate pattern had been performed by the authors to estimate the FHRV and statistical methods had been applied to compare the result obtained with the visual estimate given by physicians. The algorithm is based on the guideline given by the NICHD. The authors opted to follow this guideline as it is thorough and more suitable for implementing in an automated system.

Linear time series analysis of FHR was performed on the FHR data obtained from CTU-UHB (CTU-UHB, 2010) database of Czech Technical University. Fifty samples were used to test the algorithm. For each sample first 30 minutes of CTG trace had been used. Each 30 min sample was divided into 10 min windows and each window was separately analyzed.

A given FHR signal was decomposed to its single frequencies where each frequency is represented by its amplitude expressed in bpm. At time t measured in seconds, amplitude of the FHR signal is *fhr(t)*, i = 1, 2, ..., N where, N is the length of FHR. FHRV is calculated in discreet time windows of length n < N by standard deviation.

$$SDN = \left(\frac{1}{n-1} \sum_{i=1}^{n} \left[\left(fhr(i) - B \right)^2 \right]^{1/2} \right)$$

B is the mean heart rate or the baseline value for the segment of length n. The proposed novel algorithm is outlined below (Das et al, 2015b):

Author's Proposed Algorithm for the Estimation of FHR Variability

1. For each 10 mins. window, calculate the baseline B in this segment
2. Divide each 10 min segment to 1 min subintervals
3. Count the no. of cycles C in each 1 min
4. If $C \geq 1$ consider this interval for calculation of FHRV
    a. Find the variability $FHRV_i$ by standard deviation
    b. Increment the count by 1 min.
5. Else: Ignore the current interval and go to the next interval
6. Repeat steps 1 – 5 till the segment is covered
7. $FHRV = \sum FHRV_i$
8. If $FHRV \leq 0$: Amplitude = 'absent'
9. Else if $FHRV \leq 5$ && $FHRV \geq 0$: Amplitude = 'minimal'
10. Else if $FHRV \leq 25$ && $FHRV \geq 6$: Amplitude = 'moderate'
11. Else: Amplitude = 'marked'

Table 2. Average of the FHRV values for each window given by three clinicians and the estimated value obtained using the algorithm

	Window 1		Window 2		Window 3	
	Algorithm	Physician_avg	Algorithm	Physician_avg	Algorithm	Physician_avg
1	6.1631	6.0	5.6667	5.0	8.0424	5.0
2	2.3274	4.6667	3.2572	4.0	2.6642	4.0
3	2.2887	6.5	4.1251	6.5	5.1564	6.5
4	4.625	4.6667	5.9103	5.6667	4.9568	6.6667
5	3.5184	7.0	9.4065	6.0	12.7187	9.0
6	9.4950	6.0	4.6667	4.173	4.038	3.0
7	6.7282	7.6667	9.6322	10.6667	9.2591	12.3333
8	9.6657	8.0	6.9336	9	4.4715	6.5
9	6.1846	10.0	7.8799	8.3333	4.8277	5.3333
10	3.1414	5.0	11.836	5.5	4.4830	8.0

The result was compared with the average of the readings provided by three obstetricians using various statistical methods like confidence interval, paired sample t-test, and Bland-Altman approach etc. Levels of agreement on classification were measured using Cohen's Kappa.

Agreement between the Physician's Estimate and Algorithmic Estimate of FHRV

Authors needed to ensure that the FHRV values calculated using the algorithm tallies with the visual estimate given by the physicians. The estimates of FHRV using the algorithm and the average of the estimates given by three physicians are shown in Table 2.

Since there exists no direct way to measure the accuracy of the results, paired sample *t*-test had been used to assess the agreement between two sets of estimates (Petrie, & Sabin, 2009).

Using paired sample *t*-test the Null Hypothesis and the Alternate Hypothesis respectively are

H_0 = *the mean difference between two sets of readings is zero* i.e. μ_d =0.

H_d = *the mean difference between two sets of readings is non-zero* i.e. $\mu_d \neq 0$

Significance level was chosen to be $\alpha=0.05$. Authors opted for two-tailed tests as deviation of the FHRV values is possible in either direction. The calculated *p*-values are given in Table 3.

Table 3. p-value for each window

	Window1	Window2	Window3
p-value	0.077	0.106	0.068
95% CI Lower	-1.044	-0.253	-0.062
95% CI Upper	1.902	2.844	1.671

But since for all windows p-value was greater than 0.05 the Null Hypothesis couldn't be rejected. But that does not automatically mean that the assumption can be accepted either (Altman & Bland, 2008). Hence, the average discrepancy between observer's estimate and algorithmic estimates were assessed using Bland-Altman Plot. Bland-Altman plots are shown in Figure 5, Figure 6 and Figure 7. The lines at the top and bottom are the lower and upper limits of agreement (LoA), while the line in the middle indicates mean.

A-priori precision measurements were defined by the clinicians as ±14. Bland-Altman plot shows that all the windows fall within the defined limit. Table 4 shows the mean, standard deviation, lower and upper limit of Bland-Altman plot.

Figure 5. Bland-Altman plot for the first 10 minutes window

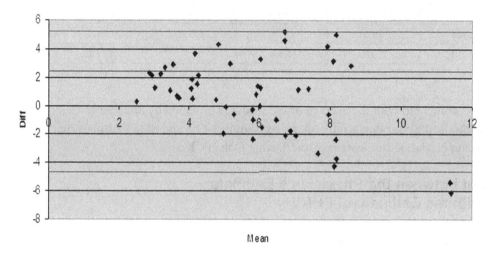

Figure 6. Bland-Altman plot for the second 10 minutes window

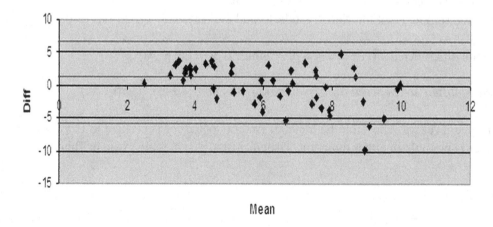

Figure 7. Bland-Altman plot for the third 10 minutes window

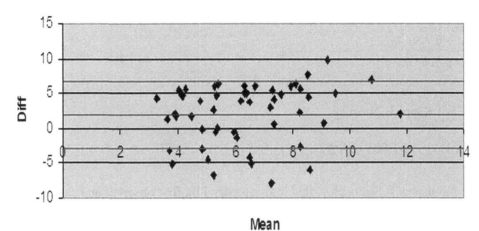

Table 4. Mean, std. deviation and LoA of Bland- Altman plot

	Window1	Window2	Window3
Mean	0.2685	0.0820	0.9611
Std. deviation	2.5740	2.9617	2.2237
95% CI Lower	5.2836	5.8553	5.3168
95% CI Upper	-4.7367	-5.6933	-3.3751

Assessment of Agreement on the Classification of FHRV

Physicians classified the FHRV according to NICHD guidelines into 'absent', 'minimal', 'moderate' and 'marked'. The same classifications had been done by the novel algorithm proposed by the authors. As it is an automated decision making tool, it is necessary to evaluate the ability of the method to assist the clinicians.

Medical literature is abounding with emphasis on sensitivity and specificity. While these estimations address the validity of the method, those who interpret the outcome may not always agree. Researchers need to show that the interpretation is not a 'guesstimate' i.e. the *precision* should be measured. It is thus important to check the degree of agreement on the classification between the clinicians and the algorithm. This is done by the Cohen's Kappa statistics (Vierra & Garret, 2005).

The calculation of Kappa is thus based on the difference between *observed agreement* and the *expected agreement*. Kappa lies between -1 and +1, with -1, 0 and +1 representing potential disagreement, agreement by chance and perfect agreement respectively. Estimated Kappa value may also be by chance. Thus it may be necessary to compute the confidence interval or CI of the Kappa. CI is sample size dependent. If sample size is large, any Kappa value greater than 0 is considered significant. The Kappa value is calculated as

$$\kappa = \frac{p_0 - p_e}{1 - p_e}$$

The standard error of Kappa is calculated as

$$SE(\kappa) = \frac{\sqrt{x+y-z}}{\left[(1-p_e)N^{1/2}\right]}$$

The 95% CI of Kappa is given by

$$\kappa - 1.96 * SE(\kappa) \text{ to } \kappa + 1.96 * SE(\kappa)$$

$\{p_{ii}\}$ is the number of subjects classified into category I by first observer and category j by second observer. $\{p_{iX}\}$ and $\{p_{Xj}\}$ are the proportion of subjects classified into each category by each of the observers separately.

$$p_{iX} = \sum_{j=1}^{k} p_{ij}, \ p_{Xj} = \sum_{i=1}^{k} p_{ij} \text{ and } p_0 = \sum_{i=1}^{k} p_{ii}$$

$$p_e = \sum_{i=1}^{k} p_{iX} p_{Xj}$$

$$x = \sum_{i=1}^{k} p_{ii} \left[1 - (p_i + p_{Xi})(1-\kappa)\right]^2$$

$$y = (1-\kappa)^2 \sum \sum_{i \neq j}^{k} p_{ij} \left(p_{iX} + p_{Xj}\right)^2$$

$$z = \left[\kappa - p_e(1-\kappa)\right]^2$$

The results obtained by the authors are shown in Table 5.

The range of values of Kappa show *substantial agreement* in classification between the clinicians and the algorithm. Strength of agreement between clinicians and the algorithm is good.

Table 5. Cohen's Kappa values for the three windows showing the agreement between clinician's and algorithmic classification

	Window 1	Window 2	Window 3
κ	0.715	0.610	0.727
SE(κ)	0.099	0.102	0.103
95% CI	0.522 to 0.909	0.419 to 0.809	0.525 to .930

COMPARISON OF THE PROPOSED ALGORITHM WITH OTHER WORK

The proposed algorithm had been compared with the works of Shahad Nidhal et al of University Kebangsan, Malaysia. Their algorithms for the estimation of baseline and variability are given below (Nidhal, Mohammed, & Mohammed, 2010).

Algorithm of Shahad Nidhal et. al

Shahad Nidhal et al, a researcher in this field, has calculated the baseline variability by following the guidelines provided by RCOG.

Algorithm for the Estimation of FHR Baseline

1. Calculate the virtual imaginary baseline R by taking the, mean of FHR.
2. The maximum and minimum limit of FHR signal estimated as H=R+10 and L=R-10.
3. The mean of the FHR signal within this boundary is the true baseline RL.

Algorithm for the Estimation of FHRV

1. Detect the first occurrence of acceleration.
2. Detect maximum and minimum values of FHR signal for a period of two minutes.
3. Compute the difference between maximum and minimum values to obtain baseline variability

$$V = Y_{max} - Y_{min}$$

Though the algorithm is simple, the accuracy of the result obtained had not been verified by the proposers using any statistical means. No proper comparison had been made with the estimates given by various physicians.

In Nidhal's work FHRV is calculated by taking the difference between the maximum and minimum values of FHR signals in a two minutes period after the occurrence of first acceleration. There is no mention of what should be done:

1. If there is no detectable signal in that two minutes period.
2. If there is no acceleration.

This is illustrated in Figure 8. Since there is no acceleration Nidhal's algorithm failed to calculate the FHRV value. The proposed algorithm of the author was able to estimate the FHRV in three different windows of 10 minutes each. The values are marked in the figure.

These problems were overcome in the author's algorithm as baseline and variability both were estimated in the 10 minutes window and FHRV was estimated in one minute sub-interval with at least one cycle. In absence of any cycle the next sub-interval was considered.

This algorithm is simple and easy to implement. It is found that Nidhal's method is in agreement with the physicians for regular traces and the CTG traces of ante-partum period, but the method fails to give

Figure 8. A CTG trace with no acceleration

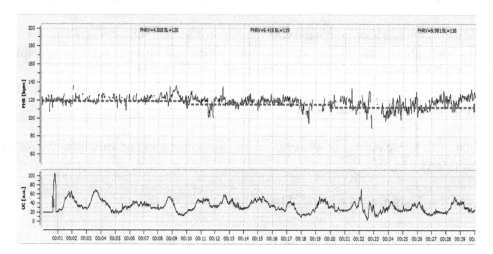

accurate result for traces in intra-partum period when there are irregularities in the CTG due to uterine contractions. FHRV values calculated using Nidhal's algorithm and the estimate given by the clinicians are given in Table 6. Trace numbers 1, 11 and12 are traces taken during ante-partum period and both the author's result and that of Nidhal's are in good agreement. Rests of the traces are taken during the labor.

A Bland-Altman plot for the Nidhal et al algorithm is given in Figure 9. The upper LoA and lower LoA are 19.827 and -10.842 respectively. Bias line is at 4.493 and the standard deviation is 7.824. Thus, the difference between the two limits is much higher than the a-priori precision measurement provided by the clinicians.

Table 6. Estimated values of FHRV by the Nidhal's algorithm, algorithm of the author and the visual estimation given by the clinicians

	Observer1	Observer2	Observer3	Nidhal's Result	Author's Resullt
1	8	10	6	9.9898	7.7807667
2	6	4	5	14.9957	4.2557667
3	3	4	5	14.9722	2.9324
4	8	9	8	4.7297	8.6110333
5	8	4	9	1.3048	6.1218333
6	10	6	4	0.2882	6.9843333
7	5	4	2	8.5058	5.0395667
8	6	6	7	13.6662	6.1591
9	3	4	5	14.3143	5.7847333
10	10	10	8	23.3703	8.768446
11	5	10	5	6.5125	5.5681333
12	10	7	6	7.009	7.5264333

Figure 9. Bland-Altman plot for the Nidhal's algorithm

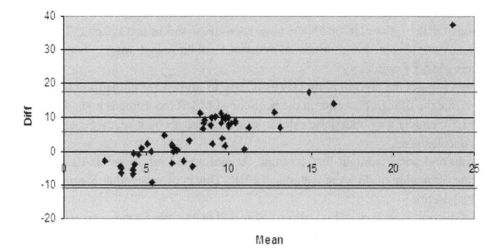

FUTURE RESEARCH SCOPE

One of the problems in the classification of variability is when the FHRV values lie in the gray zone between 'absent' and 'minimal' or between 'minimal' and 'moderate' or between 'moderate' and 'marke'. Diagnostic accuracy has been found to be lower in this gray region. This lack of precision may prove fatal for the fetus. Traditional crisp method is thus not good enough for the FHRV values at the boundary.

Also, clinicians put across their opinion in fuzzy language, rather than in crisp terms, i.e. they use imprecise terms to convey the conclusion, e.g. if FHRV = 2 bpm, the clinician may opine that the *fetus is not quite normal and variability seems to tend towards absent*. This kind of dilemma is quite common in bio-medical signal analysis and pattern recognition.

Crisp boundaries which can handle hard boundaries only are thus not suitable for medical diagnostics and pattern recognition. Fuzzy based classification technique which is capable of handling soft and continuous boundaries is best suited for medical decision support system.

Artificial Neural Network (ANN) is capable of handling quantitative data, while fuzzy system can handle qualitative data. Thus instead of using crisp logic for the classification, authors are planning to use neuro-fuzzy technique to create a robust decision making system.

The interpretation of FHR requires expensive equipments that need to be operated by trained personnel. Thus for women living in remote places without proper of infrastructure, there is no option for regularly monitoring the status of the fetus. One of the ways to get around this problem is to run the software application on mobile phones. An inexpensive fetal monitor when placed on the mother's abdomen can pick up the FHR signal which will be fed to the mobile phone. The installed software will extract the features of FHR, analyze it and relay the data to a central system in a health care centre or to a doctor who is in a far away location.

CONCLUSION

Four algorithms for the estimation of FHRV have been discussed in this chapter. Two of these algorithms are already implemented in commercial systems. Both these systems, i.e. Sonicaid and SisPorto distinguish between STV and LTV.

SisPorto that follows the algorithm by Dawes is easy to implement but suffers from certain flaws. One of them is that the fitting of baseline at the beginning of FHR recording is poor. This may affect the estimation of LTV and STV as both these calculations take into account segments of CTG that doesn't contain large decelerations.

SisPorto uses traditional 'straight-line' baseline. According to Prof. Ayres-de-Campos this provides a more accurate estimation of different features of FHR. This is because other features of FHR are dependent on the baseline.

No signal reduction is performed by SisPorto. Sonicaid on the other hand averages signal every 3.75 sec. Also, SisPorto combines the guideline of FIGO and NICHD, making it more robust. But one big problem with SisPorto is that the details of the algorithm for variability calculation are not properly documented (de-Campos et al., 2004, 2010).

The algorithms by Nidhal and the authors aim to counter the shortcomings of the existing methods, though they are yet to be implemented in any commercial system.

Accuracy of Nidhal's algorithm has not yet been verified statistical means by the authors and the algorithm is found to be in good agreement with the physicians estimate in case of stable FHR. But for irregular pattern there is a lack of agreement with the clinician's estimate. Also, they have used a method for the calculation of variability that is not followed in the guideline of any standard body.

Author's follow the guidelines provided by NICHD which probably has the widest possible criteria for visual analysis. Though the proposed algorithm is yet to be incorporated into any commercial system, it has the potential to be a good decision making tool for the physicians, as the results are in strong agreement with the physicians. The proposed algorithm is able to estimate the fetal heart rate variability values for both the intra-partum and ante-partum period and in both cases the estimations are in good agreement with the clinician's estimates. This had been established by various statistical analyses.

REFERENCES

Alonso-Betanzos, A., Guijarro-Berdiñas, B., Moret-Bonillo, V., & López-Gonzalez, S. (1995). The NST-EXPERT project: The need to evolve. *Artificial Intelligence in Medicine*, *7*(4), 297–313. doi:10.1016/0933-3657(95)00007-S PMID:7581626

Altman, D. G., & Bland, J. M. (2008). Design, Analysis, and Interpretation of Method Comparison-Studies. *AACN Advanced Critical Care*, *19*(2), 223–234. PMID:18560291

Bernardes, J., Moura, C., de Sa, J. P., & Leite, L. P. (1991). The Porto system for automated cardiotocographic signal analysis. *Journal of Perinatal Medicine*, *19*(1-2), 61–65. doi:10.1515/jpme.1991.19.1-2.61 PMID:1870058

Buttigieg, G. G. (2015). When electronic fetal monitoring becomes court business. *Malawi Medical Journal*, *27*(1), 40–46. PMID:26405509

Buttigieg, G. G. (2016). Cerebral palsy: Medico-legal issues. *Phys Med Rehabil. Int*, *3*(2), 1–7.

Czech Technical university (CTU) in Prague and University Hospital in Brno (UHB) database. (2010). Retrieved August 8th, 2014 from http://physionet.nlm.nih.gov/pn3/ctu-uhb-ctgdb/

Das, S., Roy, K., & Saha, C. K. (2011). A novel approach for extraction and analysis of variability of baseline. In *Proceedings of International Conference on Recent Trends in Information Systems* (pp.336 – 339). Kolkata: IEEE Press. doi:10.1109/ReTIS.2011.6146892

Das, S., Roy, K., & Saha, C. K. (2015a). Determination of Window Size for Baseline Estimation of Fetal Heart Rate Using CTG. In *Proceedings of 2015 Third International Conference on Computer, Communication, Control and Information Technology (C3IT)* (pp. 1 – 5). Hooghly: IEEE Press. doi:10.1109/C3IT.2015.7060179

Das, S., Roy, K., & Saha, C. K. (2015b). A novel step towards machine diagnosis of fetal status in-utero: Calculation of baseline variability. In *Proceedings of 2015 IEEE International Conference on Research in Computational Intelligence and Communication Networks (ICRCICN)* (pp. 230-234). Kolkata: IEEE Press. doi:10.1109/ICRCICN.2015.7434241

Dawes, G. S., & Redman, C. W. G. (1981). Numerical analysis of the human fetal heart rate: The quality of ultrasound records. *American Journal of Obstetrics and Gynecology*, *141*(1), 43–52. doi:10.1016/0002-9378(81)90673-6 PMID:7270621

de-Campos, D. A., & Arulkumaran, S. (2015). FIGO consensus guidelines on intrapartum fetal monitoring: Introduction. *International Journal of Gynaecology and Obstetrics: the Official Organ of the International Federation of Gynaecology and Obstetrics*, *131*(1), 3–4. doi:10.1016/j.ijgo.2015.06.017 PMID:26433398

de Campos, D. A., & Bernardes, J. (2004). Comparison of fetal heart rate baseline estimation by SisPorto 2.01 and a consensus of clinicians. *Euopeanr Journal of Obstet Gynecol Reprod Biol*, *117*(2), 174–178. doi:10.1016/j.ejogrb.2004.03.013 PMID:15541853

de Campos, D. A., & Bernardes, J. Twenty-five years after the FIGO guidelines for the use of fetal monitoring: Time for a simplified approach? *International Journal of Gynecology & Obstetrics, 110*(1), 1 – 6.

de Campos, D. A., Sousa, P., Costa, A., & Bernardes, J. (2008). Omniview-SisPorto® 3.5 - A central fetal monitoring station with online alerts based on computerized cardiotocogram+ST event analysis. *Journal of Perinatal Medicine*, *36*(3), 260–264. PMID:18576938

Fanelli, A., Giovanni, M., Companile, M., & Signorini, M. (2013). Quantitative assessment of fetal well-being through CTG recordings: A new parameter based on phase-rectified signal average. *IEEE Journal Biomedical and Health Informatics*, *17*(5), 959–966. doi:10.1109/JBHI.2013.2268423 PMID:25055375

Greene, K., & Keith, R. (2002). *K2 Medical System*. Retrieved August 12, 2015, from http://www.k2ms.com/

Guijarro-Berdiñas, B., & Alonso-Betanzos, A. (2002). Empirical Evaluation of a Hybrid Intelligent Monitoring System using Different Measures of Effectiveness. *Journal of Artificial Intelligence Medicine*, *24*(1), 1–6. doi:10.1016/S0933-3657(01)00091-4 PMID:11779686

Guijarro-Berdinas, B., Alonso-Betanzos, A., & Fontella-Romero, O. (2002). Intelligent analysis and pattern recognition in cardiotocographic signals using a tightly coupled hybrid system. *Elsevier. Artificial Intelligence*, *136*(1), 1–27. doi:10.1016/S0004-3702(01)00163-1

Heelen, L. (2013). Fetal monitoring: Creating a culture of safety with informed choice. *Journal of Perinatal Education*, *22*(3), 156–165. doi:10.1891/1058-1243.22.3.156 PMID:24868127

INFANT Study. (2009). Retrieved August 12, 2015, from http://www.k2ms.com/products/infant.aspx

Macdormen, M. F., & Gregory, E. C. W. (2015). Fetal and perinatal mortality: United States, 2013. *National Vital Statistics Reports*, *64*(8), 1–23. PMID:26222771

Macones, G. A., Hankins, G. D., Spong, C. Y., Hauth, J., & Moore, T. (2008). The 2008 National Institute of Child Health and Human Development workshop report on electronic fetal monitoring: Update on definitions, interpretation, and research guidelines. *Journal of Obstetric, Gynecologic, and Neonatal Nursing*, *37*(5), 510–515. doi:10.1111/j.1552-6909.2008.00284.x PMID:18761565

Magenes, G., Signorini, M. G., Ferrario, M., Pedrinazzi, L., & Arduini, D. (2003). Improving the fetal cardiotocographic monitoring by advanced signal processing. In *Proceedings of 25th Annual International Conference of the IEEE Engineering in Medicine and Biology Society*. IEEE Press.

Mantel, R., van Geijn, H. P., Caron, F. J., Swartjes, J. M., van Woerden, E. E., & Jongsma, H. W. (1990a). Computer analysis of antepartum fetal heart rate: 1. Baseline determination. *International Journal of Bio-Medical Computing*, *25*(4), 261–272. doi:10.1016/0020-7101(90)90030-X PMID:2194979

Mantel, R., van Geijn, H. P., Caron, F. J., Swartjes, J. M., van Woerden, E. E., & Jongsma, H. W. (1990b). Computer analysis of antepartum fetal heart rate: 2. Detection of accelerations and decelerations. *International Journal of Bio-Medical Computing*, *25*(4), 273–286. doi:10.1016/0020-7101(90)90031-O PMID:2194980

Murray, M. (2006). *Antepartum and intrapartum fetal monitoring* (3rd ed.). Springer Publishing Company.

National Institute of Child Health and Development. (2008). Workshop report on electronic fetal monitoring. Update on definitions, interpretation, and research guidelines. *Obstet. Gynaecol.*, *112*, 661 – 666.

Nidhal, S. A., Mohammed, A., & Mohammed, A. (2010). Cardiotocograph parameter estimation using MATLAB programming. In *Proceedings of International Conference on Intelligent and Advanced Systems*. IEEE Press.

PeriCALM. (2010). Retrieved August 12, 2015, from http://perigen.com/products/pericalm-tracings/

Petrie, A., & Sabin, C. (2009). *Medical Statistics at a Glance*. Oxford, UK: Wiley-Blackwell.

Redman, C. W. G., & Moulden, M. (2014). Avoiding CTG misinterpretation: A review of the latest Dawes Redman CTG analysis. *British Journal of Midwifery*, *22*(1), 2–5.

Royal College of Obstetricians and Gynecologists. (2001). *The use of electronic fetal monitoring: The use and interpretation of cardiotocography in intrapartum fetal surveillance*. London: RCOG Press.

Spilka, J. (2013). *Complex approach to fetal heart rate analysis: A hierarchical classification model* (Unpublished doctoral dissertation). Czech Technical University, Prague, Czech Republic.

Steer, P. J. (2008). Has Electronic Fetal Heart Rate Monitoring Made a Difference. (2008). *PubMed. Seminars in Fetal & Neonatal Medicine*, *13*(1), 2–7. doi:10.1016/j.siny.2007.09.005 PMID:18271079

Talaulikar, T. V., & Arulkumaran, S. (2013). Medico-legal issues with CTG interpretation. *Current Women's Health Reports*, *9*(3), 143–157.

United Nations Children's Fund. (2009). *Coverage Evaluation Survey*. New Delhi: Author.

Van Gejin, H. P. (2011). Cardiotocography. In A. Kurjak (Ed.), *Textbook of Perinatal Medicine* (pp. 1424–1428). London: Pantheon Publishing.

Vierra, A. J., & Garrett, J. M. (2005). Understanding inter-observer agreement: The kappa statistic. *Family Medicine*, *37*(5), 360–363. PMID:15883903

Wretlar, S., Holzmann, M., Graner, S., Lindqvist, P., Falck, S., & Nordström, L. (2016). Fetal Heart Rate Monitoring of Short Term Variation (STV): A Methodological Observational Study. *BMC Pregnancy and Childbirth*, *16*(1), 1–6. PMID:26728010

KEY TERMS AND DEFINITIONS

Baseline of Fetal Heart Rate: Baseline of fetal heart is the mean fetal heart rate rounded to 5 beats per minute in the absence of acceleration and deceleration. It is measured over a period of 10 minutes.

Bland-Altman Plot: In medical statistics is a method of data plotting used to analyze the agreement between two different methods.

Cardiotocography: Cardiotocography is the electronic recording of fetal heart beat and mother's uterine contraction pressure simultaneously.

Fetal Heart Rate Variability: It is defined as the fluctuations in fetal heart rate of more than 2 cycles/minute in the absence of acceleration and deceleration.

Kappa Statistics (κ): It is a measure of agreement between categorical variables X and Y. Kappa can be used to compare the ability of different raters to classify subjects into one of different groups.

Long Term Variability (LTV): It is the fluctuation range of the heart beat interval period in analyzable one minute sections. The fluctuation range is calculated as a sum between maximal deviation above and below the baseline.

p-**value:** It is used in the context of null hypothesis testing in order to quantify the idea of statistical significance of evidence.

Short Term Variability (STV): It is the beat-to-beat variation in fetal heart rate. STV is computed as mean difference between successive heart beat interval epochs in all analyzable one minute sections.

Chapter 19
A Comparative Study on DNA–Based Cryptosystem

Thangavel M
Thiagarajar College of Engineering, India

Varalakshmi P
Madras Institute of Technology, India

Sindhuja R
Thiagarajar College of Engineering, India

ABSTRACT

Information security plays a vital role in almost every application that we handle in our day-to-day life since the communication needs to be protected in terms of the messages that we send and receive. Thus, cryptography the science of encoding the secret information provides security from being known by the unintended receivers. It ensured confidentiality, integrity, and authentication of messages. To simplify the methodology of traditional cryptography with the usage of genetic concepts lead to the field of DNA cryptography. This chapter gives an insight on various methods so far proposed related to DNA cryptography that involves the characteristics of DNA incorporating the traditional cryptographic techniques and a detailed comparison of these techniques thereby proposing the requirements for an efficient DNA-based cryptographic system. These techniques also include the area of steganography that conceals the message within a cover or a career media to eschew the attacks from the intruders.

INTRODUCTION

In this era, every piece of information that is communicated needs a security measure. It is quite challenging to provide security to the big data that dynamically evolves at a faster pace. To overcome these challenges, the traditional cryptographic techniques provided security by encoding the messages transferred from the sender to the receiver and the receiver used to decode the encoded message to view the original message. Those techniques were commonly classified as public key encryption or asymmetric encryption and private key encryption or symmetric encryption. These approaches increased the time

DOI: 10.4018/978-1-5225-1785-6.ch019

and space complexity. In certain cases the intruders were able to compromise the system to view the original message. It resulted with the concept that, increase in complexity increased the security.

To provide an alternative approach towards less complexity in order to gain high level of security became the goal of DNA cryptography. The major part of DNA cryptography was based on the prominent nature of the DNA molecules. Leonard Adleman used the DNA molecules to solve the NP-Complete problem in 1994, which lead to the remarkable innovations in DNA computing, the backbone of DNA cryptography that inherits the properties of DNA to design the cryptographic techniques.

DNA is a deoxyribonucleic acid made up of two strands comprising the four nucleotide bases namely Adenine (A), Thymine (T), Cytosine (C), and Guanine (G) (Doublehelix 2016). DNA acts as a carrier of the genetic information in the living organisms. So, these DNA molecules were incorporated to carry the encrypted information in it for secure data transfer.

By the concept of Watson and Crick, these nucleotides form the complementary pairs such as Adenine pairs with Thymine (A-T) and Cytosine pairs with Guanine (C-G). This concept is almost included in every technique that includes both biological and arithmetic operations. The biological operation involves like Polymerase Chain Reaction (PCR), hybridization, and transcription (Flashcards, 2016) whereas the arithmetic operation involves XOR, insertion, substitution, complement and generation of random functions. The various works in DNA cryptography dealt with laboratory processes such as DNA synthesis, generation of probes, using of fluorophores, PCR amplification and DNA chips.

These processes provide utmost security but at the same time it relies on biological equipments and so the DNA cryptographic approach has to be computable with minimum biological resources that must be easily available for anyone to encrypt and decrypt their information. At the same time it should serve security needs by maintaining computational complexity and time complexity. Thus, the reliability and security of the information is to be enhanced efficiently with reduced complexity in the system.

The DNA cryptography has a wider scope to provide data confidentiality in real time applications that handle large amount of data for its operations. The several algorithms that have been proposed in different ways to achieve better security and data confidentiality have also been proved by various experimental results. These experimental results are of both theoretical and practical implementations that support the novel ideas of the proposed work. All these dimensions of the different works are analyzed and are studied in this following chapter.

BACKGROUND

Until today, there are so many DNA cryptosystems proposed either as an algorithmic approach or implemented as a part of an application to provide data confidentiality to the application data. Among algorithmic approach there are very few authors who incorporate both the biological and arithmetic operations to satisfy the optimality of the system (Hussain, 2015). Other than that, DNA cryptosystems are used for providing layered security in applications that also includes other cryptographic algorithms like traditional cryptosystems (Raju, 2015).

THE STUDY ON DNA CRYPTOGRAPHY

Traditional, Quantum vs. DNA Cryptography

Implementation

Traditional cryptography comprising of encryption and decryption is based on mathematical problems. But the methodologies that involve DNA passwords are not based on mathematical problems. It is implemented using cryptographic algorithms. Quantum cryptography is based on quantum physics especially the concept of single photon and the quantum properties (Kilor, 2014). According to Heisenberg's Uncertainty principle the quantum password is strong against any attacks. It is implemented using the concepts of Uncertainty principle, Bell principle and Non-orthogonal quantum states. Using these techniques the information is encrypted and transferred to the satellite and the satellite transmits the information to the receiving station making it available to the receiver who decodes the information. The information is passed through the channel of optical fibers. DNA cryptography involves nucleotides, their complementary pairs, encoding of the message and mapping it into the DNA sequences. Initially the keys to encrypt and decrypt are formed through DNA sequences using primer sequences, Watson-Crick complementary pairs, etc (Jiang, 2013). The plaintext is converted to any coding scheme and here it is encoded using the nucleotide bases such as A, C, T, G. The message sequence number is found with respect to the reference sequence. The reference DNA sequence of a single string is taken and it acts as a carrier of the encoded message. The message sequence is then appended with primers that are shared among the receiver and the sender; finally it is stored as micro points and is transmitted to the receiver. The receiver amplifies the message through the concept of Polymerase Chain Reaction (PCR amplification is done to amplify single or few copies of DNA) to get the DNA sequence that is further decrypted with the pre-shared encodings and primers to restore the original plaintext. The algorithmic steps are,

Step 1: Convert the plaintext to DNA coding system where letters are mapped to the DNA sequences. For example, GGC represents the character A, CAG represents the character B, etc.,
Step 2: The message sequence number is found in order to add the primers of 20 nucleotides to the DNA message sequence.
Step 3: The reference sequence is chosen and converted into single chain then the message sequence is shuffled for sending it to the receiver through a micro point.
Step 4: Receiver extracts the DNA sequence from the micro point using the primers that were pre-shared.
Step 5: Amplifies the sequence using PCR amplification.
Step 6: On sequencing the DNA sequence, the plaintext is found based on the agreed encoding method.

Challenges

Quantum cryptography needs consistent and better computing power, reliable transmission of the data between the sender and the receiver. The metrics to measure the security implementation is minimal. The DNA techniques require a well-equipped biological laboratory for its execution. So far there has been no theoretical support for the generation of DNA passwords.

Advantages

Quantum cryptography which is based on quantum physics guarantees unconditional security (Mehrdad, 2011). The quantum laws ensure that even if the attacker intercepts, the password could not be deciphered. DNA encryption and decryption is quicker to perform, it increases accuracy of the original message on decryption and it can resist quantum attack and also reduces time complexity providing efficient authentication and data storage (Murugan, 2014). It is advantageous because of its smaller size, conveniently parallel for execution, its storage as micro points could not be intercepted by any adversary or the adversary would not be able to mix the sequence as the message sequence number is unknown.

Disadvantages

Quantum cryptography needs lower temperature for encryption and the quanta getting scattered makes it hard to be received by the satellite. Thus, the chance for the receiver to receive the encrypted message on time is lower. The speed of encryption also varies based on the strength of the photons. Hence quantum cryptography does not provide complete security for data transfer in all scenarios. DNA cryptography requires human intervention and the support of traditional cryptography, to withstand computational power. It needs a larger DNA sequence for a larger text to be encoded. The availability of a larger DNA sequence is limited and not surplus. The methodology of biological process requires a well equipped laboratory with biological resources and the increased cost of laboratory resources makes it less feasible and as a whole it acts as a disadvantage.

But still it can act as a one-time password for traditional approaches, functionality in public key encryption, and an authentication code for any real time applications. The various parameters that differentiate the three cryptographic approaches are stated in Table 1.

Classification Among DNA Cryptography

DNA Cryptography is classified into three subfields namely (Jain, 2014b),

- Symmetric Key DNA Cryptography,
- Asymmetric Key DNA Cryptography,
- Pseudo DNA Cryptography.

Table 1. Cryptographic techniques

Parameters	Traditional Cryptography	Quantum Cryptography	DNA Cryptography
Theoretical basis	Mathematical approach	Quantum physics	Biological approach
Transmission	Serial transmission	Quantum channel	DNA carrier
Security	Based on mathematical principles	Based on Uncertainty principle	Based on biological techniques

Symmetric Key DNA Cryptography

Here, the sender and the receiver share the same key for encryption and decryption. It is susceptible to linear cryptanalysis and plaintext attacks. It is also said as shared key cryptography. Based on the algorithmic implementation the security can be increased in the proposed system.

Asymmetric Key DNA Cryptography

This method uses two keys, one key to encrypt and the other key to decrypt the data. These keys are known to be public key and private key. It is also said as public key cryptography. The public key is known to everyone and it is distributed whereas the private key or the secret key is known only to a particular person who uses that key.

Pseudo DNA Cryptography

It relies on the functions of DNA and not on the DNA strands. It simulates the transcription and translation process of the DNA without performing any biological processes with the equipments. It adds as an advantage of enhancing the security needs with reduced complexity.

Types of Operations

The biological operations that are mostly used in DNA cryptography are,

- Polymerase Chain Reaction,
- DNA Hybridization,
- DNA Fragment assembly,
- Transcription,
- Translation,
- DNA Fabrication,
- Splicing.

The polymerase chain reaction is used to amplify the DNA sequences, DNA hybridization is to combine two double-stranded DNA molecule or RNA molecule that are complement to each other to form a single strand of molecule through base pairing, DNA fragment assembly to reconstruct many fragments of DNA into an original long chain of DNA sequence, transcription is to convert a DNA sequence into a mRNA sequence and translation is to relate a DNA sequence to the amino acids in the proteins (Anam, 2010), DNA fabrication is to form a DNA sequence through combining the artificial DNA sequence and the natural DNA sequence, Splicing in DNA means to split the DNA nucleotides of one sequence and combine it in another sequence. Among these operations few can be simulated without the need for biological equipments.

The usual arithmetic operations in DNA cryptography are:

- Substitution,
- XOR operation,
- Insertion,
- Random number generation,
- Binary addition,
- Binary subtraction.

The substitution operation replaces the plaintext based on a coding scheme to form a cipher text, XOR operation is a logic gate function that outputs true only when one of its input is true, insertion is to add a DNA sequence to the existing sequence to form a larger DNA sequence, random number generation to generate random numbers for robustness in the proposed system, binary addition and subtraction which are similar to the decimal system (Cui, 2008).

The biological process has the disadvantage of feasibility and increased cost where as the disadvantage of arithmetic operations includes key dependency, key transmission, and complexity of the operation which can cause great threats to the proposed system if it is less sufficient to serve the security purposes. An effective cryptosystem should have both biological and arithmetic operations that overcome the above discussed drawbacks.

Block Based DNA Encoding

The properties of DNA sequences are adopted in the proposed algorithm (Majumdar, 2014b) that works on a block of 256 bit. The operations like swapping of DNA nucleotides are performed in this algorithm. The existing two phases are key selection phase and message encryption phase.

Key Selection

In key selection phase, a key of 256 bit is chosen randomly and it is transformed into an 8X8 matrix each having a 4 bit value in row wise. The key bits are read in column wise considering two columns at a time. Thus it generates four blocks of sub-keys from the 64 values which are labeled as A, C, T, and G (Mandge, 2013). Select a DNA sequence of 4 characters having no repetition in the bases randomly. In general, there are 24 such combinations and they are ATCG, ATGC, ACGT, ACTG, AGTC, AGCT, CTAG, CTGA, CGTA, CGAT, CAGT, CATG, GATC, GACT, GTAC, GTCA, GCAT, GCTA, TAGC, TACG, TCGA, TCAG, TGAC and TGCA. Among these a unique sequence is selected in a random fashion for the round key selection. Each nucleotide in the sequence is mapped to the four sub-keys that have been generated.

The steps for key generation are:

Step 1: A 256 bit key of binary digits is chosen.
Step 2: Transform the binary key into an 8X8 matrix having its entries as 4 bits that are written in row wise.
Step 3: Read two columns at a time to produce four sub-keys from the matrix.

Step 4: Map the four sub-keys with the DNA nucleotides A, C, T and G such that A represents first sub-key, C represents second sub-key, T represents third sub-key and G represents fourth sub-key.

Step 5: Select a random DNA sequence of four nucleotides that has all the four nucleotides generated in any order.

For example, a key of 256 bit is taken as "1011 1010 0011 0011 1100 1100 1010 0011 0000 0000 0000 0000 1110 1110 1110 1110 1110 1110 1001 0011 0000 1010 1110 0100 1011 1100 0101 1001 0011 1011 0001 1010 0011 1001 0011 0100 1010 1100 1001 1010 0000 0001 1000 1010 1110 0001 1010 0101 0000 0001 1010 1100 1000 1110 1000 1110 0001 1110 0011 0010 1100 0001 1110 1000". It is then placed in a matrix and read column wise. The sub-keys are mapped to the four nucleotides such as,

A is mapped to the sequence - 1011 0000 1110 1011 0011 0000 0000 0001 1010 0000 1110 1100 1001 0001 0001 1110.

C is mapped to the sequence - 0011 0000 1001 0101 0011 1000 1010 0011 0011 0000 0011 1001 0100 1010 1100 0010.

G is mapped to the sequence - 1100 1110 0000 0011 1010 1110 1000 1100 1100 1110 1010 1011 1100 0001 1110 000.1

T is mapped to the sequence - 1010 1110 1110 0001 1001 1010 1000 1111 0011 1110 0100 1010 1010 0101 1110 1000.

Let the random sequence be selected as "AGTC" then A will be the round key 1, G will be the round key 2, T will be the round key 3 and C will be the round key 4.

Message Encryption

The byte values from the message or the input file is extracted and it is transformed into 8 bit binary data which is further divided into 256 bit blocks. Each 256 bit block is divided into four 64 bit blocks. There are four rounds incorporating cipher block chaining method. Consider the randomly selected DNA sequence is AGTC, then in the first round the round key 1 will be the block labeled as A. XOR operation is performed between the fourth 64 bit block of plaintext and the 64 bit block of Key 1 (A). The result is then performed XOR with the third block of plaintext and its result is again performed XOR with the second block of plaintext. Finally, the result is performed XOR operation with the first block. Then the resulting four 64 bit blocks goes through a straight D-Box having four input and four output terminals to permute based on the label with DNA bases. The output of D-box is sent as the input for the second round. In the second round, XOR operation is performed between the first 64 bit block of plaintext and the round key 2 (G) continuing in a similar fashion as the before round for the next three complete rounds (Roy, 2011b). It is shown in Figure 1.

For example, the four inputs to straight D-Box are named as V1, V2, V3, and V4 where each block is mapped to one of the four nucleotides. If the input V1 is mapped to A, V2 is mapped to T, V3 is mapped to C and V4 is mapped to G then they are swapped to the four blocks of output based on the random sequence. If the random sequence is "AGTC" then V1 will be permuted to the first output block, V4 will be permuted to the second output block, V2 will be permuted to the third output block and V3 will be permuted to the fourth output block. Similarly, it is done in the remaining three rounds.

Figure 1. Message encoding scheme

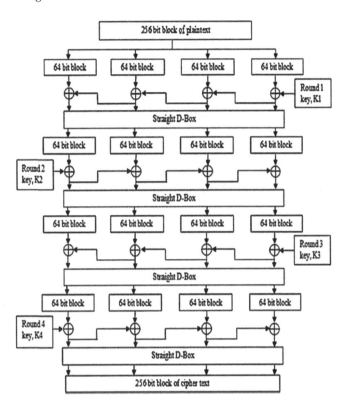

The final cipher by the end of four rounds is padded along with a starting primer (SP), file type code (FTC), CRC code (CRC) and ending primer (EP) in the pattern like 'SP, CTB_1, FTC, CTB_2, CRC, CTB_3, EP'. After that it is mapped to a modified DNA sequence using the randomly selected 16 characters that are transformed into 4X4 matrix representing alphabets as its values in random. It takes 4 bit at a time, first 2 bit for selecting the column and the next 2 bit to select a row. This algorithm suits every file type such as .txt, .mp3, .avi, etc. The sender sends the clue to the receiver that contains the positions to place the primers, the secret key and the selected DNA sequences. The receiver decrypts the cipher text with the clue which is the reverse process of encryption. The algorithmic steps for message encryption are:

Step 1: Convert the plaintext into 8 bit binary code.
Step 2: Divide the binary plaintext into blocks where each block is consisting of 256 bits.
Step 3: Divide each 256 bit block into blocks of 64 bits which eventually produces four 64 bit blocks.
Step 4: Perform four rounds of XOR operation with all the four 64 bit blocks of each 256 bit block by using the round keys or sub-keys in the following manner.
    Step 4.1: For round 1, XOR the fourth block of 64 bits with the first sub-key selected from the random sequence. The result is then performed XOR with the third block of 64 bits. This result is again XORed with the second block of 64 bits and finally this result is performed XOR with the first block of 64 bits.
    Step 4.2: For round 2, XOR the first block of 64 bits with the second sub-key selected from the random sequence. The result is then performed XOR with the second block of 64 bits. This

result is again XORed with the third block of 64 bits and finally this result is performed XOR with the fourth block of 64 bits.

Step 4.3: For round 3, XOR the fourth block of 64 bits with the third sub-key selected from the random sequence. The result is then performed XOR with the third block of 64 bits. This result is again XORed with the second block of 64 bits and finally this result is performed XOR with the first block of 64 bits.

Step 4.4: For round 4, XOR the first block of 64 bits with the fourth sub-key selected from the random sequence. The result is then performed XOR with the second block of 64 bits. This result is again XORed with the third block of 64 bits and finally this result is performed XOR with the fourth block of 64 bits.

Step 5: Every 64 bit blocks generated on every XOR operation among the 256 bit sized blocks are sent as input to the straight D-Box having four inputs and four outputs.

Step 6: A random sequence is chosen for every straight D-Box and the input blocks of 64 bits are permuted based on the four nucleotide characters of the sequence that are assigned to the four output terminals.

Step 7: Repeat the steps from step 4 to step 6 for all the 64 bit blocks of each 256 bit block for four rounds.

Step 8: After completing four rounds, combine all the blocks of the output together forming a single binary sequence.

Step 9: Append extra bits at both the ends of the sequence as well as at two specific positions within the sequence. These extra bits are to denote the starting primer, ending primer, file type and Cyclic Redundancy Code (CRC).

Step 10: The obtained sequence is then mapped to a modified DNA sequence.

Step 11: Construct a 4X4 matrix taking a two bit binary values for the four columns and two bit binary values for four rows.

Step 12: Choose 16 alphabets in random, and place them randomly as the matrix entries.

Step 13: The cipher text binary values are grouped into four bits together.

Step 14: Read the first two bits for the column and the next two bits for the row and map the matrix alphabet value for the taken four bits.

Step 15: Repeat the step 14 for all the four bits taken consecutively from the cipher text.

Step 16: Form the final cipher text sequence and send the clue having the secret key, random DNA sequences and the positions of the primers attached to the receiver through a secure channel.

The algorithmic steps for decryption are the complete reverse of these encryption steps. This algorithm is checked for efficiency by calculating the performance with respect to the metrics like encryption time, decryption time, plaintext file size and the cipher text file size. For a file of document type (.doc) of size 11264 KB, the cipher file size is 22534 KB and the time to encrypt is 9531 milliseconds and time taken to decrypt is 10672 milliseconds. When an input file of .jpeg file format of size 2304 KB is encrypted the cipher file size becomes 4609.5 KB and the time taken for encryption was 18966 milliseconds and the decryption time was 21345 milliseconds. For an .mp3 file of 5990.4 KB the ciphered file size was 11981.6 KB and it took 46936 milliseconds to encrypt and 53406 milliseconds to decrypt. The .avi file of 14950 KB led to the ciphered text file of size 299002 KB. The time taken for encryption is 119281 milliseconds and the decryption time was 133500 milliseconds. The file size is measured in kilobytes and the time taken is measured in milliseconds. In all the above cases, the file size gets increased after encoding and also the time taken for decryption is more than the encryption time. Similarly, the time taken for both encryption and decryption is linearly increased with the increase in the file size.

Block Based DNA Cryptography and Steganography

(Majumdar, 2014a) proposed a scheme that holds two methods, one method is DNA based encryption and the other method is embedding the resultant DNA sequence into an image. The encryption method is further divided into two phases namely key selection and message encryption.

Key Selection

In key selection phase, a key of 256 bit is chosen randomly (Roy, 2011a) and it is divided into four 64 bit blocks as sub-keys. The sub-keys are labeled as A, C, T and G. Select a DNA sequence of 4 bit without repetition from the 24 such combinations as a key from TAGC, TACG, TCGA, TCAG, TGAC, TGCA, GATC, GACT, GTAC, GTCA, GCAT, GCTA, ATCG, ATGC, ACGT, ACTG, AGTC, AGCT, CTAG, CTGA, CGTA, CGAT, CAGT and CATG. The steps for key generation are as follows:

Step 1: Choose a key of 256 bits in random.
Step 2: Divide the bits of the key into blocks having 64 bits that results in four 64 bit blocks.
Step 3: Name these four blocks with respective to the four nucleotide bases of the DNA. These four blocks are the four sub-keys to be used.
Step 4: Select a random DNA sequence of four characters that has the four unique nucleotides taken in any order.

For example, the key of 256 bit chosen randomly be

"1001 1010 1001 1001 0010 0001 0000 1101 1010 1110 1000 1111 1000 1111 1000 1010 0011 0001 1100 0100 1011 0001 0111 0000 0010 0100 1111 1100 0100 1011 1111 0000 1011 1100 1101 1011 1011 1011 1111 0011 1110 1110 0011 1010 0001 1110 0001 1000 0011 0110 1010 1111 1000 1110 0001 0000 0100 1111 1100 1110 0011 1010 1110".

From this key, the four sub keys are generated and labeled as,

T – 1001 1010 1001 1001 0010 0001 0000 1101 1010 1110 1000 1111 1000 1111 1000 1010.
A – 0011 0001 1100 0100 1011 0001 0111 0000 0010 0100 1111 1100 0100 1011 1111 0000.
C – 1100 1101 1011 1011 1011 1111 0011 1110 1110 0011 1010 0001 1110 0001 1000 0011.
G – 1010 1111 1000 1110 0001 0000 0100 1111 1100 1110 0011 1010 1110 0011 1010 0001.

The random sequence is chosen as "CTAG" which acts as the key.

Message Encryption

The plaintext is converted into ASCII. The ASCII values are transformed into its equivalent 8 bit binary form which is further divided into 256 bit blocks. Each 256 bit blocks are divided into four 64 bit blocks namely PT1, PT2, PT3 and PT4. For round 1, perform XOR operation between the four 64 bit blocks of plaintext and 64 bit blocks of sub-keys for the randomly selected key "CTAG". In round 2, the key is right shifted by 1 block of 64 bits then the key would be "GCTA". It is then performed XOR with the result of first round and it continues for the next two rounds where the key for round 3 is "AGCT" and the key for round 4 is "TAGC".

For example, in round 1 the plaintext block PT1 is XOR with sub-key C, PT2 is XOR with sub-key T, PT3 is XOR with sub-key A, PT4 is XOR with sub-key G. Let PT1 be "1111 1100 1110 0011 1010 1110 0011 1010 0001 0011 0001 1100 0100 1011 0001 0111" and sub-key C be "1100 1101 1011 1011 1011 1111 0011 1110 1110 0011 1010 0001 1110 0001 1000 0011" then the result on XOR of both after round 1 becomes as "0011 0001 0101 1000 0001 0001 0000 0100 1111 0000 1011 1101 1010 1010 1001 0100". Similarly, it is done for all the other blocks in all the rounds whereas the values of the plaintext blocks and the sub-keys change in every round.

Then generate a random table of ASCII values ranging from 0-255 corresponding to each 8 bit binary combination. The 8 bit binary value need not be equal to the ASCII value generated in the random table. For example, an 8 bit binary value is "0000 0100" and it is assigned to an ASCII value 75, instead of 4, the actual value of the binary string. These ASCII values are again transformed to their actual binary values of 8 bits and each two bit are converted to DNA bases in a randomly chosen manner (Roy 2012). A primer of length [2 x (1/100 x length of the cipher text (resulted DNA sequence))] is taken from EBI or NCBI databases (Genbank 2016). It is then split into two equal parts and appended as starting and ending primer of the DNA sequence which forms the cipher text. The decryption is the reverse process of encryption which is done by the receiver with the help of the keys sent by the sender. The algorithmic steps for encryption is as follows:

Step 1: Take the plaintext message and convert it into ASCII format.

Step 2: Convert the ASCII values into 8 bit binary form.

Step 3: Divide the binary sequence into 256 bit blocks.

Step 4: Divide each 256 bit block of the plaintext into 64 bit blocks of plaintext that forms four plaintext blocks for every 256 bit block.

Step 5: Perform four rounds of XOR operation on the plaintext blocks as follows,

    Step 5.1: For first round, do XOR operation on the four 64 bit blocks of plaintext with the four 64 bit blocks of sub-keys in the order of the random DNA sequence.

    Step 5.2: For second round, do XOR operation on the four 64 bit blocks of plaintext generated in the previous round with the four 64 bit blocks of sub-keys after performing a right shift of one block of sub-key in the order of the random sequence.

    Step 5.3: For third round, do XOR operation on the four 64 bit blocks of plaintext generated in the previous round with the four 64 bit blocks of sub-keys after performing a right shift of one block of sub-key in the order of the previous random sequence.

    Step 5.4: For fourth round, do XOR operation on the four 64 bit blocks of plaintext generated in the previous round with the four 64 bit blocks of sub-keys after performing a right shift of one block of sub-key in the order of the previous random sequence.

Step 6: Perform Step 5 for all the four rounds of every 256 bit block of the plaintext.

Step 7: The final output of the fourth round is combined together to form a 256 bit blocks of cipher text.

Step 8: Divide each 256 bit block into 8 bit values.

Step 9: Perform random mapping with the 8 bit binary values to any ASCII value.

Step 10: Convert the ASCII value to its original binary sequence of 8 bits for all the blocks of the cipher text.

Step 11: Map every 2 bits of the obtained binary sequence with the four DNA bases based on the mapping scheme defined.

Step 12: Select a random DNA sequence from the publically available repository such as EBI database.

Step 13: Divide the selected DNA sequence into two parts.

Step 14: Attach the two parts as the starting primer and the ending primer of the cipher text DNA sequence at both of its ends.

The secret key and the random sequences are sent to the receiver for decryption. The algorithmic steps for decryption are the reverse process of the encryption steps.

Embedding

The algorithmic steps for embedding are as follows:

Step 1: Take a cover image in order to carry the encrypted message in a hidden manner.

Step 2: Choose 'n' number of pixels from the cover image, where n refers to the bit length of the DNA sequence that was encrypted.

Step 3: Collect all the Most Significant Bits (MSB) of these collected pixels.

Step 4: Do XOR operation on the MSB with the DNA sequence in its binary representation for its complete length.

Step 5: Choose another set of pixels of 'n' values where n is the length of the binary representation of the DNA sequence.

Step 6: Retrieve the Least Significant Bits (LSB) of these n pixels.

Step 7: These LSB are replaced with the XOR resulted binary represented output of the corresponding DNA sequence.

Step 8: The receiver is provided with the clue of having these pixels to retrieve the original message from the cover image.

Once the message is encrypted, the embedding phase begins. Initially, take 'n' number of pixels from the cover image randomly where 'n' refers to the bit length of the overall encrypted DNA sequence. The most significant bits (MSB) of these pixels are performed XOR with the bits of the encrypted DNA sequence. Again take 'n' number of pixels from the image randomly and replace with the resulted value after XOR operation, in the chosen pixels' least significant bits (LSB).

Thus, this method is more secure and reliable and it exhibits the approach of both cryptography and steganography. The most significant bits of the pixels act as the key which are carried by the image itself. It makes a tedious process for the attacker to understand the information.

DNA Cryptosystem with OTP Key

In this approach (Aich, 2015) a symmetric key based cryptosystem is proposed. The generated key acts as an OTP key that is used for both encryption and decryption. The key and the cipher text are hidden in the DNA sequence before sending it to the receiver in a secure channel for communication. It involves three phases such as key generation, encryption and decryption. They are as follows,

Key Generation

The original key gets encrypted in two stages before it is sent to the receiver. In the first stage, the original key generated randomly is made to the equal length of the binary plain text and it is divided into two equal parts producing the dummy key with the first part filled with '0' and the second part filled with '1' and it is concatenated to produce a full dummy key which was initialized with '1' and it is done XOR with the original key to obtain an encrypted key (OTP key). In the second stage, the OTP key is converted to alphabet form and then converted to the DNA sequence to obtain a final encrypted key. The algorithmic steps are as follows:

Step 1: Generate a random key as a DNA sequence and convert it into binary format.
Step 2: The random binary key is adjusted to the length of the binary representation of original message. It forms as the adjusted random binary key.
Step 3: To produce a dummy key,
    Step 3.1: Initialize it with the single bit '1'.
    Step 3.2: Divide the adjusted random binary key into two parts equally.
    Step 3.3: Replace the first part with all zeros.
    Step 3.4: Replace the second part with all ones.
Step 4: Produce the OTP key on first stage of encryption by performing XOR operation between the adjusted random binary key and the dummy key.
Step 5: For the second stage, convert the OTP key into alphabetical form.
Step 6: Convert the alphabets into DNA sequence using the pre-defined table that provides mapping of DNA sequence with the capital letters, numbers and punctuation marks.

For example, let the adjusted random binary key be,

"1010 1001 0001 1110 0001 1101 0100 1000 0011 0000 1110 0000 1100 0001 1010 1001 0000 1110 0000 1101 0100 1010 1001 0001 1110 0000 1100 0011 1010 1001 0000 1110 1010 0101 0100 1000 0011 0000 1110 0000 1100 0001 1010 1001 0000 1110 1010 0100" .

It is then divided into two equal parts. Initialize the dummy key with a bit '1' then replace the first part with zeros and the second part with ones. Thus the dummy key is,

"1000 0000 0000 0000 0000 0000 0000 0000 0000 0000 0000 0000 0000 0000 0000 0000 0000 0000 0000 0000 0000 0000 1111 1111 1111 1111 1111 1111 1111 1111 1111 1111 1111 1111 1111 1111 1111 1111 1111 1111 1111 1111 1111 1111 1111 1111".

The encrypted key on first stage is known as OTP key, XOR the dummy key and the adjusted random binary key to obtain the OTP key as,

"0010 1001 0001 1110 0001 1101 0100 1000 0011 0000 1110 0000 1100 0001 1010 1001 0000 1110 0000 1101 0100 1010 1001 0001 0001 1111 0011 1100 0101 0110 1111 0001 0101 1010 1011 0111 1100 1111 0001 1111 0011 1110 0101 0110 1111 0001 0101 1011".

Encryption

The algorithmic steps for encryption are:

Step 1: Convert the plaintext into ASCII format.
Step 2: Convert the ASCII values into binary format.
Step 3: Check the length of the binary values of the plaintext, if it is of odd length append the bit '1' or else being even length leave it as it is.
Step 4: Compute the first stage of encrypted key or otherwise called as OTP key.
Step 5: Perform XOR between the binary plaintext and the OTP key which is represented as binary values. This forms the first stage of cipher text.
Step 6: For the second stage, convert the cipher text into alphabet form.
Step 7: Convert the alphabet form into DNA sequences of three nucleotides based on the pre-defined encoding table which forms the final cipher text.
Step 8: Send the cipher text and the encrypted key to the receiver through two separate secure channels.

The plaintext is transformed into corresponding ASCII values and then to a binary format. If the length of the binary sequence is odd, append '1' and then generate the DNA sequence based on the coding scheme such as, A – 00, C – 01, G – 10, T – 11.

Generate a random key which is a DNA sequence and convert it to binary format. Make the length of the key (OTP Key) equal to the length of the binary sequence of the plaintext. XOR both, the resulting sequence is converted into alphabet format. The second stage of encryption is transforming the obtained alphabet format into DNA sequence of 3 bit length where the alphabets, digits, and punctuation marks can be converted into DNA sequences (Yi 2013). This encrypted cipher and the encrypted key is sent to the receiver through a secure channel.

Consider the plaintext binary values as,

"0101 0100 0110 1000 0110 0101 0111 1001 0010 0000 0110 0001 0111 0010 0110 0101 0010 0000 0110 0111 0110 1111 0110 1001 0110 1110 0110 0111 0010 0000 0111 0100 0110 1111 0010 0000 0100 1101 0111 0101 0110 1101 0110 0010 0110 0001 0110 1001".

On performing XOR operation with the OTP key, the first stage of cipher text results as,

"1111 1101 0111 0110 0111 1000 0011 0001 0001 0000 1000 0001 1011 0011 1100 1100 0010 1110 0110 1010 0010 0101 1111 1000 1000 1110 1010 0100 1000 1001 0111 1010 1100 1010 0110 1000 0111 1101 1001 0101 1010 1100 1100 1011 0110 1111 1100 1101".

The above values are further converted into alphabet form and then to DNA sequence as the second stage of encryption.

Decryption

The algorithmic steps for decryption are:

Step 1: Convert the encrypted key from DNA sequences into alphabet form.
Step 2: Convert the alphabet values into binary values.
Step 3: Transform the encrypted cipher text from DNA sequences into alphabet form using the generated encoding table.
Step 4: The alphabet values are further converted into binary sequences.
Step 5: Perform XOR operation with the binary key values and the binary values of the cipher text.
Step 6: Retrieve the original plaintext which is in binary format.
Step 7: Convert the binary values into ASCII values.
Step 8: Convert the ASCII values into original plaintext message.

The above steps goes by converting the cipher text into alphabet format which is converted to the corresponding binary format. The key is again decrypted to the original OTP key. XOR operation is performed between the original cipher text and the original key to get back the original message. Thus, the plaintext is recovered.

Thus, this system causes biological difficulties for an attacker to gain the plaintext. Similarly the attacker cannot predict the random key generation. Thus, it proves that it is more secure than the traditional symmetric key cryptosystem (Cui 2007). But it produces high computational complexity especially when the plaintext message is large in size. The algorithm has supported security analysis that emphasis on the usage of encoding table and the randomly generated one time pad key.

Password Authentication Using Dual Server

This authentication system (Raju, 2015) holds two servers such as Server1, Server2 (Yang, 2010). When a client enters his password and submits it during registration, the password is sent to the Server1, which in turn divides it into two parts namely, Pwd1 and Pwd2, as shown in Figure 2.

The Pwd1 is then encrypted using Elgamal encryption and then encoded using DNA sequences and stored in the database1. The Pwd2 is sent from the Server1 to the Server2. The Pwd2 is then encrypted using Elgamal encryption and then encoded using DNA sequences and stored in the database2.

Figure 2. Encryption mechanism to authenticate the password

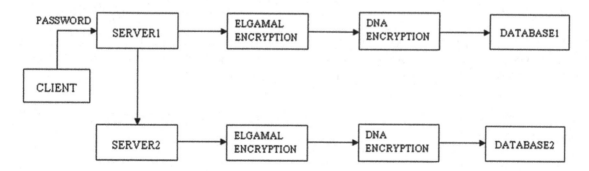

Figure 3. Decryption mechanism to authenticate the password

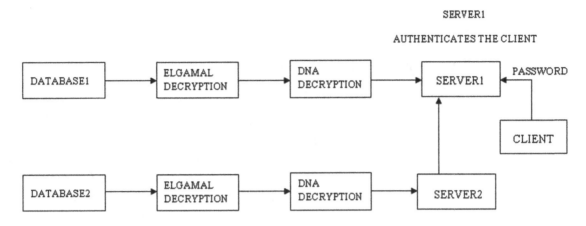

As the client logs in, the encrypted password stored in the database1 and database2 will be decrypted and compared with the client entered password. If it matches, the client is authenticated or else he is not authenticated (Madhulika, 2014). The decryption is the complete reverse process of encryption where the encrypted password is decrypted with DNA sequences and then by Elgamal decryption and combined at Server1 which authenticates the client as shown in Figure 3.

The Elgamal encryption involves the selection of a largest prime number N, and a generator number G. The receiver selects the secret number as S which should be lesser than the length of N-2. Based on this, the value D is computed as G^S mod N where S is the private key and (N, G, D) is a public key. An integer K is selected in a way that it lies between 1 and N-2. The plaintext is represented as an integer M which lies between 0 and N-1. Now the two parameters Y and Z are computed as $Y = G^K$ mod N and $Z = (D^K \times M)$ mod N. The cipher text is the pair of (Y, Z). On receiving the cipher text the receiver calculates the value of R as $R = Y^{N-1-S}$ mod N and recovers the plaintext as $M = (R \times Z)$ mod N.

For DNA encryption, the random DNA sequences are generated using the DNA bases A, G, C, and T for all possible characters. The sequence is then stored in the database. The cipher text after Elgamal encryption is replaced with the stored sequence for the corresponding characters. The received sequence is then performed XNOR operation with a randomly generated DNA sequence known as public key. The result is the twice encrypted part of the password. The XNOR operation is performed by the selection of a single base value for the two base input from the DNA 4 x 4 matrix. The complement of the public key is the private key. In order to decrypt, the XOR operation is performed between the DNA encrypted password and the private key where the XOR table is again a 4 x 4 matrix having a two base input and the output is a single base output.

The general algorithmic steps for DNA encryption described above is as follows:

Step 1: Generate random DNA sequences for all characters and store it in a database.
Step 2: Get the cipher text obtained from the Elgamal encryption.
Step 3: Convert the characters in the Elgamal cipher text into DNA sequences by mapping the characters with the DNA sequence stored in the database.
Step 4: A random DNA sequence is generated and it is considered as a public key.

Step 5: Do XNOR operation between the random DNA sequence and the DNA sequence of the ciphered text based on the values in the XNOR table.

    Step 5.1: Generate the XNOR table with four nucleotides of DNA considering each as the column value and the row value.

    Step 5.2: Generate the matrix entries with random values of each having one DNA nucleotide.

Step 6: The result obtained forms the final ciphered password.

The DNA decryption algorithm is performed in the reverse order of the above encryption algorithm. This approach is recent and the novel application of DNA cryptosystem towards securing the password in transit from the client to the server's database emphasize on security of sensitive data and also it ensures secure authentication of the client with the system. This method has the password in the form of numbers from 0 – 9, letters such as A-Z and a – z, and special characters of 29 characters. Thus, it needs (number of the possible characters) $^{\text{length of the password}}$ to attain the password by brute force attack (BFA 2016). But the minimum password length is 10 and so it definitely takes 91^{10} computations which are approximately more than 6100 years. It ensures the efficiency of this technique in terms of security.

Spiral Approach Using DNA Sequence

This method (Jain, 2014a) encrypts any form of data such as text, image, audio or a video file. It begins with the conversion of data into binary values and further divided into blocks of 64 bit each. These bits are arranged in 8 x 8 matrix form. If the data is an image, then it is converted into ASCII and then to binary using the ASCGEN software.

It is then followed by the method of spiral transposition that changes the position of bits in the matrix either row wise or column wise as shown in Figure 4.

It is scrambled in a spiral motion from the starting element of the matrix as in Figure 5.

Now, these bits are converted into their equivalent decimal value by taking 8 bits of the row or the column (Borda, 2010). These 8 bits can yield decimal values ranging from 0 to 256. A dictionary table consisting of 256 decimal numbers mapped with a DNA sequence of length 4. As this method is randomized it is used as a key between the sender and the receiver and it also offers security easily when compared with the other approaches.

Figure 4. The matrix before and after the spiral transposition

2	1	32	31	34	33	64	63
3	4	29	30	35	36	61	62
6	5	28	27	38	37	60	59
7	8	25	26	39	40	57	58
10	9	24	23	42	41	56	55
11	12	21	22	43	44	53	54
14	13	20	19	46	45	52	51
15	16	17	18	47	48	49	50

1	2	3	4	5	6	7	8
9	10	11	12	13	14	15	16
17	18	19	20	21	22	23	24
25	26	27	28	29	30	31	32
33	34	35	36	37	38	39	40
41	42	43	44	45	46	47	48
49	50	51	52	53	54	55	56
57	58	59	60	61	62	63	64

Figure 5. Spiral transformation

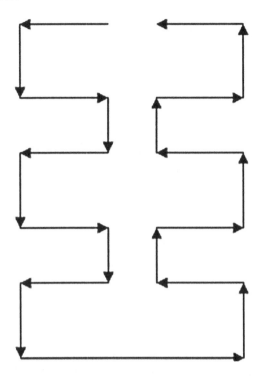

This method has been implemented using MATLAB software and it proves experimentally that the time taken for encryption is minimally low for the given size of the data. Thus, the two level of security is provided with the first level of security through binary data encryption and the second level of security is achieved through the encryption using DNA sequences (Gao, 2011). It has been achieved with less computational effort and in less time.

DNA Technologies Based Cryptosystem

A DNA technology generally means the usage of codons, primers and so on. Here, the concept of primers is widely used (Cui, 2014). The message begins its transformation through ASCII code to form 8 bit binary code for every character. It is then converted into DNA sequence by using the DNA digital coding rule which operates like encoding of binary data into DNA base as A=00, C=11, G=01 and T=10 (Shiu, 2010).

It is further converted using the rules as: (A-G), (G-T), (T-C), (C-A) where the first base is the complement of the second base in every pair. These rules are known to be complementary rules. To increase the potential of this method incorporating security altogether, the DNA sequences are cut into three fragments.

In prior, the sender and receiver agree to the same number of primers to be used for encryption and decryption. Both of them designed the primers on their own and numbered it. The primer sequence with same number is paired up to be used as a primer pair. The primers are exchanged in a secure channel. Consider that the primers count agreed upon is three. These three pairs of primers are appended to the both ends of the three DNA fragments. Thus, the message gets encrypted in a secure manner as in Figure 6.

Figure 6. Encryption technique

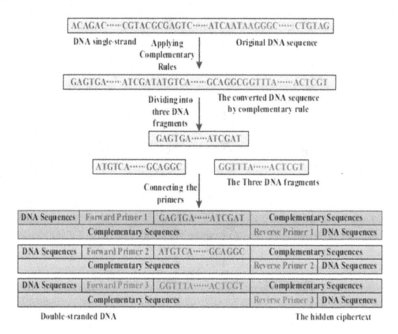

The encrypted message is decrypted at the receiver's side by PCR amplification and DNA sequencing. This method has been tested for a sample message encryption and decryption by performing PCR and analyzed using gel electrophoresis.

When considered in terms of security, the attacker cannot obtain the primers easily as it takes huge computation depending upon the count of primers, primer length (Lai, 2010). This method has a hard security barrier as the techniques and methodology is not easy to interpret by an intruder.

Encryption Using DNA Microdots

The sender and the receiver share the secret key in advance and through a secure channel. The secret key includes a primer sequence set K and a software for pre-processing of the original messages (Cui-Han, 2014).

The sender and the receiver designs same number of DNA sequences. The DNA sequences designed by the sender is KS1, KS2, ..., KS6 becomes the front primer set and the DNA sequences designed by the receiver is KR1, KR2, ..., KR6 becomes the rear primers set (Goff, 2013). These primers used for encryption and decryption are transmitted to each other in a secure way before the message encryption takes place.

The encryption phase initiates by converting the plaintext into binary format based on ASCII code. This binary code is again encrypted using DES algorithm to obtain the binary cipher text (Yanfeng, 2014). From this, the odd number bits are extracted to form an odd-bit sequence and the remaining sequences are framed to be even-bit sequence.

The sender then divides the odd-bit sequence into three parts at any position and links the primer in sequence as the front end and the back end of the DNA sequence fragments. Once linking the primers, it forms the artificially synthesized chain groups as odd-bit chain group and even-bit chain group.

Security is preserved by mixing the redundant chains of odd-bit chain group and even-bit chain group to get a mixed solution of DNA sequences such as mixed solution odd-bit and mixed solution even-bit. It is sprayed on a filter paper to get an odd-bit sequence paper (OP) and an even-bit sequence paper (EP). The OP is sent first and then if it gets received securely the EP is sent or else the OP is again encrypted to get transmitted to the receiver.

It analyzes and provides security in many ways such as the properties of DNA microdot which is more advantageous because of its colorlessness and it is hard to find the binary encoding schemes and the primers involved throughout the process.

Pseudo DNA Cryptography

This methodology (Misbahuddin, 2014) inherits the concept of transcription, splicing, and translation processes. Splicing is to remove the introns or the non-coding areas based on random tags and the remaining extrons or the coding areas are combined and transcribed into a single stranded sequence of mRNA. This mRNA usually moves from the nucleus into the cytoplasm are known to be transcription. Translation happens by translating the mRNA sequence into an amino acid sequence that takes three bases at a time based on the codon table.

The encryption process initiates by converting the message into 8 bit binary code through ASCII. A key p is selected and now split the binary coded message into a block of size p. Now a DNA strand from the publically available DNA database is chosen in random (DDBJ 2016). Convert this DNA sequence into binary using the base pair rules as, A=00, T=11, G=10, C=01. Again a key s is selected and the DNA sequence in binary form is split into blocks of size s. The index value is marked in this sequence. Append the encoded message blocks from the starting index of the primer and the last message block is appended to the ending index of the primer. Meantime, all the other index positions can be filled with random values of block size p. Convert the obtained result into DNA sequence through the base pair rules. The complementary rules are applied to receive the completely encrypted cipher text. The tuple of key with the values of p, s, starting primer, ending primer and complementary rule is sent along with the cipher text to the receiver securely through a channel.

In order to decrypt, the cipher text is first applied with complementary rule, and then converted into binary form through the base pair rules to convert from DNA notation into binary value. The values of the key p and s are added and the result is used to split the obtained binary sequence. The index values are marked and then the primers are checked and then spliced (Yunpeng, 2011). Separate the sequences with the values of p and s and append the resulting 8 bit binary values with all the resulting output sequences. It is then converted into ASCII values to get the original message. Thus, the original message has been obtained by decrypting it completely (Menaka, 2014).

This approach is less prone to any intrusion as the process involved is time consuming and computations are need to be handled in biological aspects. As randomization is involved, security could be least compromised in this system.

DNA Computing Based Cryptosystem

This proposed algorithm (Hussain, 2015) has its own uniqueness in its techniques implemented. It consists of two parts such as,

- The DNA Computing based on an encoding algorithm.
- The DNA Computing based on an encryption and decryption algorithm.

The encoding algorithm is a well-designed process based on the generation of the encoding table. The encoding table is generated as an 8 x 4 matrix (Hussain, 2012). Initially, two DNA sequences of 4 unique nucleotides are taken and formed a matrix by considering them as row and column of the matrix. The entries of the matrix are the elements of the row and column. It is then extended to a three character sequence by combining either the row or the column element with all the entries. Finally, a four character DNA sequence is obtained as the entries of the matrix by adding the intron sequence which is the random values involving date and time converted to binary and to DNA nucleotides. Thus, the matrix is further extended from 64 elements to 96 elements by adding two rows from the existing matrix and replacing the intron character with the complementary nucleotide. They are produced in a systematic approach because it follows the sequential procedure of transformation and generation of values in a random order altogether.

This encoding table is generated for every pre-defined session intervals (Sabry, 2012). This encoding table is used to encode the alphabets of upper case and lower case, numbers and special characters. In total there are 96 plaintext characters that can be encoded with this encoding table. One such table is designed by the sender and other table is designed by the receiver and they exchange the clues to each other in order to generate the other encoding table.

The encryption phase begins after generating the two encoding tables by the sender. The plaintext is divided into two halves equally. If it is not even then it is padded with a random element (Sadeg, 2010). The first half is encoded using the Encoding Table 1 generated by the sender with his own sequence and the other part is encoded with Encoding Table 2 generated by the sender with the receiver's sequence obtained from the clue.

For example, consider the plaintext as 'BANK' it is divided into two halves as BA and NK. BA is encoded with the values of encoding Table 1 and NK is encoded with the values of Encoding Table 2. Assume the sequences for the characters as of here as, B – AAGG, A – ACAT, N – GCTT, K – GAAG. Thus it becomes, BA – AAGGACAT and NK – GCTTGAAG.

The next procedure is a multi round function and each functions perform various operations in sequence. Out of which, the first step is transformation by doing XNOR between the DNA encoded plaintext with the intron sequences used during the generation of encoding tables. XNOR operation is performed by the logic gate that outputs true (1) if and only if both the inputs are true (1) or both the inputs are false (0). It outputs false (0) if one of the inputs is true (1) and the other input is false (0). It is done based on the base rule pair such as A-00, T-01, C-10, and G-11 where it is carried out on the binary sequence and again represented as a DNA sequence. Thus in the example it becomes, CACACCAG and CTGTTAAT.

It is then performed an operation of transcription by replacing Thymine (T) with Uracil (U) on both the parts. It then again converted into tRNA sequence by replacing each DNA sequence character with its complement using the complementary rules as A-U, U-A, G-C, C-G. This process is known to be translation process. The tRNA sequence undergoes the conversion by replacing Uracil (U) with Thymine (T). It is the simulated process of reverse transcription. It is right shifted once for both the parts (Sabry 2015). These multi step functions are performed for some number of rounds agreed by both the sender and the receiver. Thus in the example, it is first converted into the sequences as CACACCAG and CUGUUAAC, then on tRNA conversion it becomes GUGUGGUC and GACAAUUA. On reverse

Table 2. Comparison of DNA cryptosystems

Author	Operators used	Functionalities	Advantage	Disadvantage	Experimental Results
Jun Jiang (Jiang 2013)	Both Arithmetic and Biological process	Quantum cryptography, DNA cryptography and traditional cryptography are compared.	The efficiency of DNA cryptography is identified with respect to quantum and traditional cryptography.	DNA cryptosystem depends on biological laboratory for implementation. DNA passwords cannot be reused.	Practical implementation of DNA cryptosystem and its challenges are identified completely.
Shipra Jain (Jain 2014b)	Both Arithmetic and Biological process	Gives an overview of the various security algorithms.	Gives insights on different parameters of the security algorithms.	Parameters compared are focused mainly on the operators involved.	Generic ideology of security based on the type of operators is obtained.
Abhishek Majumdar (Majumdar 2014a)	Arithmetic process	Cipher block chaining method and DNA primers are used.	Easy computation to make and it is highly secure.	The size of ciphered file is greater than the size of input file size.	The time and size of file after encryption and decryption reveals that the decryption process takes more time and storage space for the file to be decrypted.
Abhishek Majumdar (Majumdar 2014b)	Arithmetic process	Implements by 64-bit EXOR operation for encryption along with embedding the result within the image.	Easy implementation in less time.	Have comparatively many computations and processing.	Algorithmic implementation is executed.
Asish Aich (Aich 2015)	Arithmetic process	In this approach, XOR operation plays a vital role.	Since OTP key is used, it is not possible for the attacker to gain access to the key and the message.	The computational complexity is increasingly high with respect to the size of message.	Security analysis ensures the scalability and reliability of this proposed technique.
P.V.S.S. Raju (Raju 2015)	Arithmetic process	Elgamal cryptosystem and DNA cryptosystem is used.	Provides best authentication methodology and overcomes brute force attack.	It is time consuming for authenticating the client.	Algorithmic implementation is done.
Noorul Hussain Ubaidur Rahman (Hussain 2015)	Both Arithmetic and Biological process	DNA computing based encoding algorithm and encryption, decryption algorithm is proposed.	This method is highly randomized involving both arithmetic and biological operations.	It involves large number of computations.	Here, the decryption time is lesser than the encryption time. Similarly, the decoding time is lesser than the encoding time. Pearson's correlation coefficient method is used to analyze the association between two cipher texts.

continued on following page

Table 2. Continued

Author	Operators used	Functionalities	Advantage	Disadvantage	Experimental Results
S.Jain (Jain 2014a)	Arithmetic process	Spiral Transposition and DNA sequence dictionary is implemented.	Easy to implement and accepts various data input formats.	Biological functions are not highly depended for encryption.	It compares the time taken for encryption of different file formats of varying size.
Guangzhao Cui (Cui 2014)	Biological process	Usage of primers and additional complementary sequences.	Less computation to achieve secure communication.	Requires receiver to do PCR amplification and sequencing to obtain the original plaintext.	It states its security in terms of biological security and computing security, making impossible for the attackers to breach the system.
Yan Wang (Cui-Han 2014)	Biological process	Primers and Microdots technique is implemented.	Provides four layers of security namely, physical concealing, stepwise transmission, mathematical security, and biological security.	Requires filter papers for implementing encryption in real time.	The probability of synthesizing right primers is highly impossible and so it maintains confidentiality and integrity.
M.Hashim N.P (Misbahuddin 2014)	Both Arithmetic and Biological process	Splicing, Indexing techniques are used along with the usage of complementary rules of DNA sequences.	This method involves easy implementation of the algorithm dynamically.	Iterative approach is quite time consuming.	It ensures biological security using the DNA primers.
O. Tornea (Torena 2009)	Biological process	Implements RSA algorithm in one approach and the concept of DNA tiles in another approach.	Both approaches ensure security rather the computational complexity is high.	Laboratory implementations using tiles is expensive and time consuming.	The proposed methodology has been implemented and the output is obtained.
Lu Ming Xin (MingXin 2007)	Biological process	Uses DNA probes for encryption and decryption keys. It also implements DNA hybridization technique involving DNA chip.	Forms a complete symmetric cryptosystem.	It is completely a biological process that requires biological resources that makes it less flexible to the real time application.	The significance of biological security and computational difficulty ensures the strength of this secure system.
Jing Yang (Yang 2014)	Biological process	Strand displacement process and fluorescent signal detection is incorporated.	Obtains the right cipher text for the given plain text though it involves self-assembly structure of DNA.	It depends mainly on laboratory equipments for both encryption and decryption.	The results show that the system is prone less to interdependency of DNA strands causing errors due to the leakage of fluorescent signals.

transcription it is converted into GTGTGGTC and GACAATTA. By shifting the sequence it ends as, CGTGTGGT and AGACAATT.

The resulting tRNA sequence is replaced by an amino acid sequence correspondingly. The amino acid sequence generation has a procedure for implementation. Initiate by generating two DNA sequences randomly consisting of all 4 DNA base alphabets occurring once. Convert these two sequences into mRNA sequences. It is then assigned randomly row wise and column wise in 4 x 4 matrix. The matrix elements are product of the row and column headers. It is then extended into 16 x 16 matrix by assigning the matrix elements as row and column headers randomly. The element of this matrix is the product of row and column headers which is of length 4 DNA alphabets. The usual amino acid table comprises of 20 amino acids and so it is made up of 256 amino acids. It is divided into four groups namely A, U, C, and G. These amino acids are assigned to the 16 x 16 matrix elements using one of the 24 possible collating sequence such as (A, U, C, G), (A, C, U, G), (C, G, A, U) and so on. These collating sequences are mapped with the amino acid group to get assigned for the matrix elements either row wise or column wise. The resulting protein sequence is the cipher text when it is mapped with the tRNA sequences. In our example, based on the values of amino acid table entries the cipher text will be like Q5L2D1T7.

Decryption is exactly the reverse of the encryption procedure. Initially the cipher text is divided into two halves equally. It is then converted into tRNA sequence using amino acid table generated. It is transformed into mRNA sequence by replacing every DNA alphabet with its complement DNA alphabet, which further replaces Uracil with Thymine on both the parts. Then the multi round function is applied on both the sides where the DNA sequence is XNORed with the intron sequence and right shifted to both the parts. Reverse transcription of converting Uracil with Thymine is performed. It is then converted into tRNA sequence by replacing every DNA alphabet with its complement DNA alphabet. The tRNA sequence is converted into DNA sequence by replacing Uracil with Thymine in both the parts. In the last round, both the parts of DNA sequences are transformed into intron sequence 1 and intron sequence 2. These sequences are converted into plaintext using DNA encoding tables and both the half parts are merged altogether.

This method is analyzed for efficiency by comparing the time taken for encryption and decryption algorithm and for encoding and decoding technique. The time taken for encryption and decryption is greater than the time taken for encoding and decoding procedure. In general the decoding and decryption process takes more time than encoding and encryption process. The frequency analysis is done by Pearson's correlation coefficient method and reports that the two cipher text for the two plaintexts generated, differs completely. It reduces the possibility of cryptanalysis and breaking of cipher.

Thus, this method provides a complete character set fulfillment, dynamic generation of encoding table, unique character encoding procedure, includes biological process of simulation and dynamicity of encryption of the original message. But it is highly randomized and involves greater computational complexity which marks the strength of this proposed work.

DNA Cryptography Using DNA Structures

This method (Tornea, 2009) involves two DNA cryptographic algorithms. The first one deals about public key encryption of binary data followed by its transformation into DNA sequence. And the other one is based on XOR one-time-pad cryptographic algorithm where the binary data is transformed into DNA structures of tiles.

Data Stored as DNA

The binary data, text or image is transformed into ASCII values which are encrypted using RSA algorithm. Here, the two large prime numbers P and Q are considered to be of 100 decimal digits at least. The product of these two numbers is N, where N = P x Q and Euler's totient is computed as $\varphi(N) = (P-1) \times (Q-1)$. The public key used for encryption is (N, E) where E is the co prime of $\varphi(N)$. The private key (N, D) is used for decryption where $(D \times E) \bmod \varphi(N) = 1$. The cipher text on encryption is $C = P^E \bmod N$ and the plaintext on decryption is $P = C^D \bmod N$. The encrypted message is a set of numerical values.

The plaintext is converted into ASCII values and these numeric values are arranged in a string by taking several digits together of same length as the public key length. It is then encrypted using the public key. The resulted numbers are transformed into binary form and then converted into DNA sequence using the base pair rules. All the sequences are appended together in a single strand and the cipher text is transformed on a DNA chip. The decryption is the reverse process where it uses private key for decryption.

Consider the original message as "my secret!". It is converted into ASCII values as

109 121 32 115 101 99 114 101 11633.

It is then grouped in a string with the length equal to the public key length. Let us assume it to be seven digits. Then the string becomes,

1091213 2115101 9911410 111633.

It is further encrypted with the public key and the result is also a set of numbers as:

417310496328959 129126952185213 373906236380070 367568882589235

The entire string is transformed into a binary sequence. Take the first part of the string

417310496328959,

it is transformed as

0101111011100010101010101111100101000001100111111111.

It is then converted into a DNA sequence with the nucleotides corresponding to the binary values as

A – 00, C – 01, G – 10, T -11

and so the above string becomes

CCTGTGAGGGGGTTGCCAATATTTT.

Finally it is combined with all the parts of the string resulting in the cipher text having the value as,

CCTGTGAGGGGGTTGCCAATATTTTCTCCCTAAGTCGACTCGGTCCTTCCTCCCTAAGTC-
GACTCGGTCCTTCCCCCAACAATCCACGCGACATGGCGCCCCAACAATCCACGCGACATG-
GCGCCATGCATCCATAGGTCCCTGATAT.

The decryption process is the reverse of the above process instead the private key values are used.

Data Stored as DNA Structures

The tile structure and its principle were invented in 1961 by Hao Wang. It is an equal sized square with colored edge that can be arranged side by side that neighboring edges of adjacent tiles have the same color. DNA tiles are multi-strand complexes containing two or more double helical domains (Zeng, 2011). Here, triple-helix-tiles (Hirabayashi, 2011) are assembled by the complementary hybridization of four DNA strands.

During hybridization, a link of two strands having sticky ends to create a phosphodiester bond between two tiles is made. Binary data is encoded using a single tile for each bit. The XOR operation is performed between the plaintext binary message and the one-time pad where it assembles along with the results in a linear structure. The result is the cipher text as in Figure 7.

It is accomplished by binding of the message tiles in as string by choosing a start bit tile and the first bit of the message. Thus, two types of tiles are prepared for the start bit and two stacks are used to store tiles for the bits from the message. Here, a microcontroller is used to take the next tile for the next bit from the corresponding stack. The message assembling is stopped by the last tile. For an example, consider that the message begins with the binary values as "100", then the first tile for assembling is "1" and it is taken from stack 1 and the second bit is "0" now the microcontroller will take the tile "0" from stack 2.

XOR operation is performed between message and the one-time pad which is a large non-repeating set of truly random letters. The tiles from pad which hybridize with the message become the encryption key. Their labels are copied in a string and transmitted along with the cipher text. Thus, the result or the encrypted message is self assembled and finally the cleavage process is done to keep the cipher text alone with the help of the string of labels. Decryption is done by using XOR operations where the tiles are assembled in reverse order to obtain the plain text.

Figure 7. DNA tiles formation

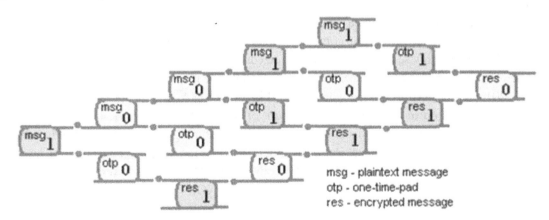

This method is implemented in MATLAB using bio informatics toolbox. Though it can be done by laboratory implementation it is expensive and time consuming. This method is effective but still it is highly complex for implementation. It involves the biological process of DNA hybridization, complementary pairing, and tile binding which are tedious for a larger sized plaintext to be encrypted and decrypted.

Cryptosystem Using DNA Molecules and DNA Probes

(MingXin, 2007) proposes that the encryption process is a fabrication of a specially designed DNA chip and the decryption process is done by DNA hybridization. Here, both the encryption and decryption keys are formed by DNA probes while the cipher text is transferred by DNA chip.

Initially, a DNA hybridization experiment is done to generate the probes. It is purely biological process involving biological laboratory resources. Here an experiment is performed with the microarray data that represents the shifting of gene transcription spectrum of yeast that transforms from the anaerobic process to aerobic process. It involves the usage of fluorophores, a microscope and DNA chip. The probes obtained after the experiment are taken.

The probes printed on the chip are grouped into subsets and it is considered as the encryption key and the hybridization conditions with the target probes are considered as the decryption key. The decryption key is a set of corresponding complementary probes of the encryption key. The sender selects the probes and sends the decryption key to the receiver. The plaintext is translated into a binary matrix of 21 x 24 through ASCII code (Xue Jia, 2010). It is then written into a binary virtual chip. The probes are then randomized in the subsets to form a spot that denotes the positions of '1' and '0' where the accurate number of probes selection is impossible since the probes are selected among thousands of test tubes. The receiver uses the decryption key to hybridize the cipher text and receives the hybridization signals which are processed and translated into binary matrix using signal processing. The coloured spots denote the binary value 1 and the black spots denote the binary value 0. These binary values are then converted into ASCII values further obtaining the original plaintext (Pramanik, 2012).

For example, in key generation process, the sender 'X' selects probes as an encryption key and the decryption key which are the complementary probes are found by X and it is sent to the receiver 'Y' through a secure channel for communication between them. Then X translates the plain text into a binary matrix. By using randomization process it behaves like a one-time-pad encryption thereby making it a dynamic form of encryption. Y uses the decryption key and hybridizes the DNA chip containing the cipher text and receives hybridization signals. These signals when processed in a computer, plaintext is obtained.

Thus, this method ensures biological security and computational complexity. This method cannot be implemented using a modern electronic computer but it could be possible for the future DNA computer. This methodology is highly secure as the adversary needs the correct probes and laboratory facilities to obtain the plaintext without which the exact signals could not be retrieved.

(Yang, 2014) proposes a technique where several kinds of DNA strands are synthesized and used (Zhang, 2011). Based on the self-assembly structure of the DNA, a symmetric key cryptosystem is designed. The DNA self assembly structure is formed by combining various DNA strands using hybridization technique in a biological environment under particular temperature, concentration level with specific to time constraint. Initially, the plaintext is converted to ASCII then converted into binary form and then encryption is carried out by strand displacement by XOR operation using fluorescent signal detection where if the fluorescent signal is produced it indicates '1' and if the signals are not produced it is indicated as '0'. The hybridization of the DNA strands and DNA self structures are used to perform XOR operation. The DNA self assembly structure and the key sequence is sent through the secure channel. Decryption is the reverse of the encryption process where the receiver decrypts the cipher text with the key generated from the DNA structure. The electrophoresis method and fluorescent signal are used to compute the results. This process is tough to implement for real time applications or scenario as it highly requires biological resources that reduces the adaptability on implementation (Heiss, 2009).

COMPARATIVE ANALYSIS OF THE STUDY

From the study on various approaches there are so many parameters that differ among every methodology. They are compared in the following Table 2.

PROPOSED IDEAS

From the study of various novel ideas proposed and implemented so far, an insight on the parameters and the requirements for a mechanism to design an efficient model that is compatible with the real time network communications and that must also be capable of working efficiently on the replacement of existing traditional strategies without being compromised at any time is proposed.

The features that are needed are as follows,

- **Complete Character Set Encoding:** It should be capable of encoding every DNA sequence to the complete character set of ASCII such that the printable elements of the entire ASCII character set should be mapped with the DNA sequences which must eventually hold the property of uniqueness on every time when the encoding table is generated. It is done to avoid having two characters mapped with a same DNA sequence.
- **Dynamic Encryption:** It must be able to encrypt and encode in a faster pace independent of the input size. It should also be able to encrypt dynamically that goes by the fact that each plaintext should produce different cipher text on every encryption process and it should be capable of producing different cipher text for the same plaintext on using with the same encoding table. This denotes the dynamicity of encryption process.
- **Reduced Biological Complexity:** The computations involving biological resources reduces the feasibility of this technique for implementation in real time. Thus, the DNA concepts must also be handled by the arithmetic operations. It must be able to verify the system at real time based on the need. It has to equally balanced that the computations should involve both arithmetic and biological properties of DNA that are to exhibited and possible for implementing in a real time computer paving a way towards real time application of the cryptographic algorithm. It should be feasible for any sender and any intended receiver to transfer their data at anytime and anywhere without restricting the scope for encryption through the usage of biological resources like DNA chips, probes and test tubes which are hard to find for every encryption process. For example, the properties of DNA like transcription, translation, complementary pairing, amino sequences, reverse transcription and reverse translation could be exploited.

- **Randomization:** The approach can have randomization steps but it must be able to decrypt the encrypted original message. The steps to achieve randomization also need to be in minimal in order to have better time and computational complexity tradeoff. The main goal of randomization is to make the system completely robust from cryptanalysis and the malicious attacks by an unintended user. On using unique encoding table values for every generation of the encoding table in every session of the communication would certainly make the system prudent. The time taken to break the system should always be higher than the time taken to complete the particular process which could be either encryption or decryption.

Finally, the tradeoff between security and computation involved must be well maintained. The approach must be capable of reducing the computations in terms of computational time where as the goal of preserving security is achieved in higher ratio. An efficient system is said to be the one that have average number of computations but executing it in lesser time. It would also be able to compute in minimum time involving minimum memory space for maximum performance and maximum security that suits the plaintext with alphabets of both uppercase and lowercase, numbers, special characters of any larger size it could be. Thus, if a method being proposed incorporates all the above features will gain implementation in real time making a remarkable innovation in DNA cryptography.

FUTURE RESEARCH DIRECTIONS

DNA cryptography is the recent research area where enhanced data confidentiality is sought for. Though there are many DNA cryptosystems exist, a DNA cryptosystem that satisfies the necessary requirements is hard to find. Other challenging feature is to establish a set of metrics to measure the complexity of the cryptosystem.

CONCLUSION

The importance for the need of security techniques is the common goal among various researchers in the field of DNA cryptography. It is revealed through various proposed ideas and results obtained. The concepts of DNA cryptography like DNA bases, primers are used with base rules and complementary rules involving arithmetic operations such as XOR operation, binary addition and so on. Few approaches ensure security with reduced computational complexity whereas the computational time increases. This establishes a tradeoff of increased computations resulting in increased security. Every novel approach has its own way of preserving security for the existing communication process. In future, an approach holding the tradeoff between computational complexity and security implementation must be well designed and managed to model a robust and a reliable system with maximum efficiency achieved incorporating the significant properties of the DNA molecules.

REFERENCES

Aich, Sen, Dash, & Dehuri. (2015). A Symmetric Key Cryptosystem Using DNA Sequence with OTP Key. *Advances in Intelligent Systems and Computing*, 207 – 215.

Anam, Sakib, Hossain, & = Dahal. (2010). Review on the Advancements of DNA Cryptography. *IJARCS, 3*.

Rahman, Balamurugan & Mariappan. (2015). A Novel DNA Computing based Encryption and Decryption Algorithm. *ICICT*, 463 – 475.

Borda, M., & Tornea, O. (2010). DNA Secret Writing Techniques.*International Conference on Communications, IEEE*.

Cui, Qin, Wang, & Zhang. (2008). An Encryption Scheme Using DNA Technology. *Bio-Inspired Computing: Theories and Applications*, 37-42.

Cui, G., Han, D., & Wang, Y. (2014). An Improved Method of DNA Information Encryption. BIC-TA, CCIS. Springer.

Cui, G., Han, D., & Wang, Y. (2014). An Encryption Scheme Based on DNA Microdots Technology. BIC-TA, CCIS. Springer.

Cui, G., Qin, L., Wang, Y., & Zhang, X. (2007). Information security technology based on DNA computing.*IEEE International Workshop on Anti-counterfeiting, Security and Identification*, (pp. 288-291). doi:10.1109/IWASID.2007.373746

DDBJ. (2016). *DNA Data Bank of Japan*. Retrieved from http://www.ddbj.nig.ac.jp/

Fancher. (2016). *Double Helix*. Retrieved from http://www.cod.edu/people/faculty/fancher/DoubleHelix.htm

Gao, Q. (2011). A Few DNA Based Security Techniques. *Systems, Applications and Technology Conference, IEEE*.

Heiss, G., Lapiene, V., & Kukolka, F. (2009). Single-molecule investigations of a photo switchable nanodevice. *Small, 5*(10), 1169–1175. PMID:19263427

Hirabayashi, M., Nishikawa, A., Tanaka, F., Hagiya, M., Kojima, H., & Oiwa, K. (2011). Analysis on secure and effective applications of a DNA-based cryptosystem. Bio-Inspired Computing: Theories and Applications, IEEE.

Jain & Bhatnagar. (2014a). A Novel DNA Sequence Dictionary method for Securing Data in DNA using Spiral Approach and Framework of DNA Cryptography. *IEEE, ICAETR*.

Jain & Bhatnagar. (2014b). Analogy of Various DNA Based Security Algorithms Using Cryptography and Steganography. *IEEE, ICICT*.

Jiang & Yin. (2013). The Advantages and Disadvantages of DNA Password in the Contrast to the Traditional Cryptography and Quantum Cryptography. *Bio-Inspired Computing: Theories and Applications*, 307-316.

Kilor, P. P., & Soni, P. D. (2014). Quantum Cryptography: Realizing next generation information security. *IJAIEM*, *3*(2), 286–289.

Lai, X. J., Lu, M. X., Qin, L., Han, J. S., & Fang, X. W. (2010). Asymmetric encryption and signature method with DNA technology. *Science China Information Sciences*, *53*(3), 506–514. doi:10.1007/s11432-010-0063-3

Le Goff, G. C., Blum, L. J., & Marquette, C. A. (2013). Shrinking hydrogel-DNA spots generates 3D microdots arrays. *Macromol Biosci Journal*, *13*(2), 227–233. doi:10.1002/mabi.201200370 PMID:23335561

Lu, Lai, Xiao, & Qin. (2007). Symmetric-key cryptosystem with DNA technology. *Information Sciences. Science in China*, 324–333.

Madhulika, G., & Rao, C. S. (2014). Generating digital signature using DNA coding. FICTA, AISC. Springer.

Majumdar, Podder, Majumder, Kar, & Sharma. (2014). Secure Data Communication and Cryptography Based on DNA Based Message Encoding. *IEEE, ICACCCT*.

Majumdar, Podder, Majumder, Kar, & Sharma. (2014). DNA-Based Cryptographic Approach Toward Information Security. *Advances in Intelligent Systems and Computing*, 209-219.

Mandge, T., & Choudhary, V. (2013). A DNA encryption technique based on matrix manipulation and secure key generation scheme. ICICES, IEEE.

Menaka, K. (2014). Message Encryption Using DNA Sequences. Computing and Communication Technologies (WCCCT), IEEE.

Misbahuddin, M., & Mohammed, H. N. (2014). DNA for Information Security: A Survey on DNA Computing and a Pseudo DNA Method Based On Central Dogma of Molecular Biology. ICCCT, IEEE.

Murugan & Jacob. (2014). On the secure storage and transmission of health care records based on DNA sequences. *Intelligent Computing Applications (ICICA), IEEE*.

NCBI. (2016). *Genbank*. Retrieved from www.ncbi.nlm.nih.gov/genbank

Noorul Hussain, U., & Chithralekha, T. (2012). *A Novel DNA Encoding Technique for DNA Cryptography*. India Patent 5107.

OWASP. (2016). *Brute Force Attack*. Retrieved from https://www.owasp.org/index.php/Brute_force_attack

Pramanik, S., & Setua, S. K. (2012). DNA cryptography. Electrical & Computer Engineering (ICECE), IEEE.

Quizlet. (2016). *Flash Cards*. Retrieved from https://quizlet.com/90321024/flashcards

Raju & Parwekar. (2015). DNA Encryption Based Dual Server Password Authentication. *Advances in Intelligent Systems and Computing*, 29-37.

Roy, Rakshit, Singha, Majumder, & Datta. (2011). A DNA based Symmetric key Cryptography. *ICSSA*, 68-72.

Roy, B., & Majumder, A. (2012). An improved concept of cryptography based on DNA sequencing. *International Journal of Electronics and Communication Computer Engineering*, *3*(6), 1475–1478.

Roy, B., Rakshit, G., Singha, P., Majumder, A., & Datta, D. (2011). An Improved symmetric key cryptography with DNA based strong cipher.*International Conference on Devices and Communications*, (pp. 1-5). doi:10.1109/ICDECOM.2011.5738553

Sabry, M., Hashem, M., & Nazmy, T. (2012). Three reversible Data Encoding Algorithms based on DNA and Amino Acids Structure. *IJCA*, *54*(8), 24–30.1. doi:10.5120/8588-2339

Sabry, M., Hashem, M., Nazmy, T., & Khalifa, M. E. (2015). Design of DNA based advanced encryption standard (AES).*International Conference on Intelligent Computing and Information Systems (ICICIS), IEEE*. doi:10.1109/IntelCIS.2015.7397250

Sadeg, S., Gougache, M., Mansouri, N., & Drias, H. (2010). An encryption algorithm inspired from DNA.*International Conference on Machine and Web Intelligence, IEEE*.

Sharbaf, M. S. (2011). Quantum Cryptography: An emerging technology in network security. Technologies for Homeland Security, IEEE.

Shiu, H. J., Ng, K. L., Fang, J. F., Lee, R. C. T., & Huang, C. H. (2010). Data hiding methods based upon DNA sequences. *Information Sciences*, *180*(11), 2196–2208. doi:10.1016/j.ins.2010.01.030

Tornea, O., & Borda, M. E. (2009). DNA Cryptographic Algorithms. *IFMBE Proceedings*, *26*, 223–226. doi:10.1007/978-3-642-04292-8_49

Yanfeng, W., Qinqin, H., & Dong, H. (2014). Information security technology based on nucleic acids. *Chinese Academy of Sciences*, *29*(1), 83–93.

Yang, D., & Yang, B. (2010). A Novel Two-Server Password Authentication Scheme with Provable Security. Computer and Information Technology, IEEE.

Yang, J., Ma, J., Liu, S., & Zhang, C. (2014). A molecular cryptography model based on structures of DNA self-assembly. *Chinese Science Bulletin*, *59*(11), 1192–1198. doi:10.1007/s11434-014-0170-4

Yi, X., Ling, S., & Wang, H. (2013). Efficient Two-Server Password-Only Authenticated Key Exchange. *IEEE Transactions on Parallel and Distributed Systems*, *24*(9), 1773–1782. doi:10.1109/TPDS.2012.282

Yunpeng, Yu, Zhong, & Sinnott. (2011). Index-based symmetric DNA encryption algorithm. *Image and Signal Processing (CISP)*, 2290-2294.

Zeng, J., & Zhang, M. (2011). Virtual genome-based cryptography. Multimedia Information Networking and Security, IEEE.

Zhang, C., Yang, J., & Xu, J. (2011). Molecular logic computing model based on self-assembly of DNA nanoparticles. *Chinese Science Bulletin*, *56*(33), 3566–3571. doi:10.1007/s11434-011-4725-3

KEY TERMS AND DEFINITIONS

Authentication: To ensure that the users are they who are claimed to be. It identifies and assures the origin of information.

Confidentiality: The key feature of security to ensure the data or the information is accessed only by the authorized users.

Cryptosystem: It is a complete system that possesses the algorithms for key generation, encryption and decryption techniques to achieve confidentiality of data.

DNA Cryptography: DNA Cryptography is the cryptographic technique to encrypt and decrypt the original data using DNA sequences based on its biological processes.

DNA Hybridization: It is process to anneal two double stranded DNA or RNA molecule that are complement to each other forming a single strand of DNA molecule.

Encoding: Encoding is the process of converting data into a defined data format for enabling secure transmission and storage of original data.

Integrity: Integrity is to assure that the data is reliable, accurate and it remains in its original form from being modified by unintended users.

Network Attacks: Network attacks are the methods like session hijacking, IP spoofing, denial of service, accessing the unintended data, etc., that exploit the vulnerabilities causing adverse effects in the network.

Security: The concept of achieving confidentiality, integrity and availability of data protected from its issues.

Steganography: The art of concealing the original data within another data that acts as the carrier.

Chapter 20
Micro–Electromechanical Systems for Underwater Environments

Gurkan Tuna
Trakya University, Turkey

Vehbi Cagri Gungor
Abdullah Gul University, Turkey

ABSTRACT

Underwater networking technologies have brought us unforeseen ways to explore the unexplored aquatic environment and this way provided us with a large number of different kinds of applications for environmental, scientific, commercial, and military purposes. Although precise and continuous aquatic environment monitoring capability is highly important for various underwater applications, due to the unique characteristics of underwater networks such as low communication bandwidth, high error rate, node mobility, large propagation delay, and harsh underwater environmental conditions, existing solutions cannot be applied directly to underwater networks. Therefore, new solutions considering the unique features of underwater environment are highly demanded. In this chapter, the authors mainly focus on the use of wireless micro-electromechanical systems for underwater networks and present its advantages. In addition, the authors investigate the challenges and open research issues of wireless MEMS to provide an insight into future research opportunities.

INTRODUCTION

Thanks to Underwater Networks (UNs), the desire and significant interest in monitoring aquatic environments are satisfied. UNs are used for various applications requiring precise and continuous data transfers including oceanographic data collection, pollution monitoring, scientific exploration, commercial exploitation, and coastline protection (Akyildiz, Pompili, & Melodia, 2005; Erol-Kantarci, Mouftah, & Oktug, 2010; Erol-Kantarci, Mouftah, & Oktug, 2011; Ren & Cheng, 2010; Han, Zhang, Shu, & Rodrigues, 2015). Although UNs and ground communication networks have common properties, they

DOI: 10.4018/978-1-5225-1785-6.ch020

have two distinct differences. First and foremost, radio communications do not work well under the water and hence they are replaced by acoustic communications (Heidemann, Stojanovic, & Zorzi, 2011; Akkaya & Newell, 2009). Second, although most ground nodes are static, underwater nodes are mostly mobile since they may move with water currents, waves, and other underwater activities (Heidemann, Stojanovic, & Zorzi, 2011).

Micro-Electromechanical Systems (MEMS) is a rapidly growing, innovative technology which combines micro computers with various tiny mechanical devices such as sensors, actuators, valves, gears, mirrors, and other parts in semiconductor chips. Basically, MEMS devices contain micro-circuitry on tiny silicon chips into which mechanical devices have been manufactured. MEMS is a foundational technology at the present and will continue to be so into the next decade; this technology has already successfully replaced many other devices in several applications since MEMS devices are built in large quantities at low cost and thereby are cost-effective for many uses.

Recently, the use of wireless MEMS in UNs has emerged as a powerful, reliable and low cost technique for many UN applications addressing monitoring, measurement, control, and surveillance needs (Yu, Ou, Zhang, Zhang, & Li, 2009; Chaimanonart & Young, 2006; Sarisaray-Boluk, Gungor, Baydere, & Harmanci, 2011). Due to the significant differences and unique features of UNs, this has received unprecedented interest, although the idea of applying wireless MEMS into monitoring and/or control applications is not new.

MEMS are miniature devices, which integrate processors, sensors, and actuators and their functional subsystems could be electronic, mechanical, optical, fluidic, or thermal. MEMS technology has numerous attributes, which can mitigate challenges to meet future military and non-military application requirements. For instance, MEMS allows miniaturization, reduced cost of fabrication through the use of micro-electronics processing technologies, real-time control, and control of macro physical processes through micro action. Specifically, MEMS can enable enhanced functionality for the following applications:

- Inter-linked communication channels (radio frequency (RF) or optical);
- Optical devices and systems, and displays;
- Micro-satellite and unmanned surveillance systems;
- Multi-sensing capabilities; distributed, agent-based, or sensor array systems;
- Inertial Navigation Systems (INSs);
- Autonomous, unmanned ground sensors, detection and treatment systems
- Intelligent/unmanned operations;
- Power generators and management;
- Integrated fluidic systems including fluid sensing, control & transport;
- Nuclear and bio/chemical sensing;
- Micro thrusters;
- Fuze/safety & arming;
- Health monitoring and utilization monitoring systems;
- Logistic tagging systems;
- Self assembly/healing and reusable modules/subsystems.

The abovementioned generic, functional elements can be integrated across the various platforms for land, sea, air, space and missile applications. Also, as well as underwater vehicles, MEMS can enable the realization of advanced platforms for avionics and aircraft systems, miniaturised spacecraft, smart unmanned land vehicles, robots and sentinels, stabilized platforms and launch-pads, smart missiles and bombs.

In this chapter, a survey on the use of wireless MEMS in UNs, with a special focus on potential underwater applications, is given. Moreover, the challenges in meeting the requirements posed by both emerging and existing wireless MEMS-based applications are presented. The remainder of the chapter is constructed as follows.

- Section 2 reviews wireless MEMS technologies.
- A review of UNs along with potential application scenarios and communication standards are presented in Section 3.
- Section 4 presents the use of Wireless MEMS in UN scenarios and reviews existing and emerging power sources for this.
- Challenges of wireless MEMS and Open research issues are given in Section 5 and Section 6, respectively.
- Finally, the chapter is concluded in Section 7.

Wireless Micro-Electromechanical Systems (Wireless MEMS)

Basically, MEMS are miniature devices in dimensions from a few hundred microns to millimeters which consist of integrated mechanical components such as springs, vibrating structures, levers, and deformable membranes, and electrical components such as capacitors, resistors, and inductors. Since MEMS technology makes the integration of microelectronic circuits with mechanical structures on the same chip possible, it considerably reduces the system size and cost. Although silicon is the most commonly used material for the fabrication of MEMS devices, micromachining methods for the fabrication of the MEMS devices is not restricted to silicon and non-silicon materials such as polymers, ceramics, plastics, and metals can also be used in the fabrication processes (Elwenspoek & Wiegerink, 2001).

Due to the increasing low-cost availability of low-power and small-size sensors and actuators, MEMS technology has numerous application areas including automotive, biomedical, telecommunication, household appliances, consumer applications, and defence applications. The components in MEMS are designed to work in concert for various goals such as sensing the physical properties of the immediate or local environment, performing physical interaction or actuation with the immediate or local environment. Although the traces of MEMS technology can be found in many different types of devices and uses, a few examples where MEMS technology is used in everyday life are motion and orientation detection in smart phones and tablets, roll-over detection systems, read/write heads in disk drives, ink-jet heads in printers, deployment sensors for airbag systems, microsurgery tools, hearing/visual aid devices, pacemakers, body fluid analysis systems, smart drug delivery systems, frost sensors for refrigerators, pressure sensors for water level detection, micro fluidic pumps, smart antennas, micromirrors for fiber optic switching, low cost night vision systems, homeland security systems, weapon systems, smart munitions, and micro telemetry devices (Elwenspoek & Wiegerink, 2001; Chowdhury, Ahmadi, & Miller, 2002; Arshad, 2009; Madou, 2002; Madou, 2011; Nguyen, 2006).

With the advancements in communication technology, the demand for increased mobility and more bandwidth can now be fulfilled and hence different wireless applications are spreading to new markets. To handle the various needs of growing wireless device market, with their unique features wireless MEMS are one of the best candidates. While different communication technologies can be used, the most commonly used enabling technology for MEMS based wireless applications is radio frequency (RF) as the above integrated circuit (IC) technique enables the placement of RF MEMS devices directly on top of the IC by using a thick copper technology compatible with Complementary Metal Oxide Semiconductor (CMOS), Bipolar CMOS (BiCMOS), and gallium arsenide processes (Enz & Kaiser, 2013; Nabki, Dusatko, & El-Gamal, 2008; Wen, Guo, Haspeslagh, Severi, Witvrouw, & Puers, 2011). Typically, wireless MEMS technology is based on passive components, phase shifters and antennas, and it is used for various purposes and devices including the monitoring of telecommunications reliability, automatic drug delivery, implantable health devices, intraocular pressure sensors, and automotive radars.

UNDERWATER NETWORKS

Because of the unique nature of underwater applications and the harsh, complex properties of aquatic environment, the devices and protocols developed for terrestrial communication networks are not directly applicable to UNs. Acoustic communications exhibit different travel time and characteristics than radio communications used in terrestrial wireless networks (Heidemann, Stojanovic, & Zorzi, 2011; Akkaya & Newell, 2009). In particular, they feature low bandwidth capacity, high error rates, and large propagation latency. Different from the very early implementations of underwater monitoring systems which were generally small-scale and based on point-to-point communication links, nowadays underwater applications are highly sophisticated and demand scalable networked solutions.

Underwater communication channels often display high attenuation characteristics, frequency dispersion, limited bandwidth, and time-varying multi-path fading. In addition, for UN applications, there exists a unique set of other challenges due to the large signal propagation delays and variable speed of sound. However, in the last decade, overcoming these challenges and exploring the numerous advantages of UNs were possible as a result of the advancements in communication technologies and progress in the development of sophisticated coding and decoding techniques. Therefore, many underwater multi-point communication systems and multi-hop ad hoc networks have been deployed.

Application Scenarios

UNs consist of a large number of underwater nodes with onboard modems and a limited number of surface stations and/or autonomous underwater vehicles, and enable the accurate and energy efficient monitoring of aquatic environment as shown in Figure 1. As a result of the significant and increasing interest in aquatic environments, UNs are used for various environmental, scientific, commercial, safety and security reasons, and many different applications such as oceanographic data collection, pollution monitoring, offshore exploration, tactical surveillance, disaster prevention through earthquake and tsunami warnings, mine reconnaissance, and assisted navigation (Akyildiz, Pompili, & Melodia, 2005; Erol-Kantarci, Mouftah, & Oktug, 2010; Erol-Kantarci, Mouftah, & Oktug, 2011; Ren & Cheng, 2010; Han, Zhang, Shu, & Rodrigues, 2015).

Communication Standards

Underwater networks are designed to enable applications for oceanographic data collection, disaster prevention, pollution monitoring, assisted navigation, offshore exploration, and tactical surveillance.

Figure 1. Typical UN monitoring scenario

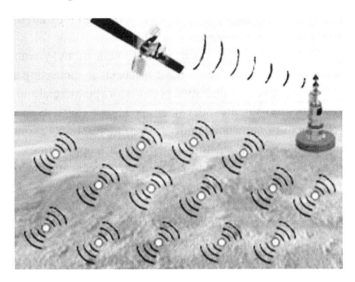

Therefore, there is a need for underwater communications among underwater nodes which are used to explore undersea resources and gather scientific data. Underwater nodes and vehicles such as Autonomous Underwater Vehicles (AUVs) should be capable of coordinate their operations, exchanging their location and movement information, and relaying gathered data to an onshore base station.

Communication is a very important process in underwater applications since it enables data transfers between two or more onshore/underwater entities. Those data transfers are used for various purposes including monitoring, identification, localization, and navigation. Although communication in underwater applications can be established by wired or wireless connections, wireless communication is the preferred way since wired connections are generally not practical or impossible (Johnstone et al., 2008). On the other hand, different from terrestrial applications, underwater wireless communication is not a straightforward process and a number of design issues and major problems such as instrumentation, underwater channel model, modulation strategy, transmission distance, power consumption, symbol interference, attenuation, signal to noise (SNR) ratio, bit error, and interference should always be considered (Akyildiz, Pompili, & Melodia, 2005; Lanbo, Shengli, & Jun-Hong, 2008; Stojanovic, 2003; Heidemann, Li, Syed, Wills, & Ye, 2006).

Although the history of underwater communications goes back to the Second World War, underwater networking still remains as a relatively unexplored area. For wireless communication in underwater applications, there are three types of carrier wave. Acoustic communication is the typical physical layer technology in UNs due to the following reasons. Through conductive sea water, because of high absorption and attenuation which has significant effect on the transmitted signal, radio waves propagate at long distances only at extra low frequencies between 30 and 300 Hz and hence require large antennas with high transmission power (Kilfoyle & Baggeroer, 2000. Therefore, this type of communication severely affects the cost and design complexity. Optical waves do not suffer from the high attenuation experienced in underwater communication and offer high data transmission rates; however, they are affected by scattering and the signals are rapidly absorbed in water (Akyildiz, Pompili, & Melodia, 2005; Lanbo, Shengli, & Jun-Hong, 2008; Stojanovic, 2003; Heidemann, Li, Syed, Wills, & Ye, 2006).

Furthermore, high precision in pointing the narrow laser beams is required to transmit optical signals. Although tethered communication is also possible, it only works well for stationary underwater objects and Peer-to-Peer (P2P) systems.

Until the last couple of decades, underwater acoustics communications systems were exclusively used in military applications. However, in recent years, there has been an increasing interest in research and development of underwater acoustics communication systems for commercial and consumer applications due to the need for such systems existing in underwater applications such as speech and data transmission between divers, autonomous or unmanned underwater vehicles, remote control in oil industry, and environmental monitoring systems. In the existing systems of such applications, transmitted signals can be typically grouped in four main categories: control, telemetry, speech, and video, respectively. Sending commands to submerged instrumentations and underwater robots is realized using control signals with small data rate requirements. However, reliability of such signals is critical. Telemetry signals collected by hydrophones and sonar systems require high data rates but they always do not need high reliability. Speech signals with usually data rates of few Kbps are transmitted between divers or between surface stations and divers. Although utilizing image compression techniques, video signals require huge data rates per sec.

Although the data rates of underwater communication technologies are much less than those used in terrestrial networks (Kilfoyle & Baggeroer, 2000; Heidemann, Stojanovic, & Zorzi, 2011) and there are several challenges in the acoustics domain such as limited bandwidth (Akyildiz, Pompili, & Melodia, 2005; Erol-Kantarci, Mouftah, & Oktug, 2010), compared to RF and optical, acoustics is more reliable medium for underwater communications. Because acoustic signals attenuate less than those in RF and optical and hence are able to travel further distances in UNs. Signal propagation speed in underwater acoustic channels is around 1500 m/s and most acoustic systems used in UN applications operate under 30 KHz and (Kilfoyle & Baggeroer, 2000; Heidemann, Stojanovic, & Zorzi, 2011). However, there are commercially available acoustic systems which operate at higher frequencies.

Considering the difficulties and constraints for underwater sensor node deployments, a heterogeneous multi-hop network solution which relies on a combination of ultrasonic, optical and RF networks as supplements to wires can be useful for some application scenarios (Dalbro et al., 2008). In this approach, redundancy for robust and uninterrupted communication for critical applications can be provided so that real-time information exchange and integration can be ensured. In addition, equipment position, movements and orientation can be monitored via sensor nodes placed on.

Compared to terrestrial networks, in meeting the requirements of UN applications, there are challenges and constraints such as large propagation delays, node mobility and high error probability of acoustic underwater channels (Katiyar, Chand, and Chauhan, 2010). Besides, for localization and navigation goals, there is another challenge. The Global Positioning System (GPS) does not work under water since the GPS signal get highly attenuated if it passes through just few centi meters inside water. To address this challenge, GPS-free routing protocols such as Distributed Underwater Clustering Scheme (DUCS) can be used (Domingo & Prior, 2007). DUCS is a GPS free routing protocol which minimizes the proactive routing message exchange, does not use flooding techniques, and uses data aggregation to eliminate redundant information.

WIRELESS MEMS FOR UNDERWATER NETWORKS

Unlike terrestrial applications, the challenges for underwater wave propagation in UNs are quite different because water itself is the main source for signal interference. As well as water and its composition and dissolved impurities, depth pressure and temperature affect the underwater wave propagation. Similar to terrestrial applications, reflection, scattering, and refraction also occur in underwater communication. In this respect, the design phase of communication systems plays a critical role. Therefore, in the design process, transducer parameters such as transduction mechanism, impedance, directivity, resolution, power consumption, sensitivity and noise immunity must be taken into consideration (Akyildiz, Pompili, & Melodia, 2005; Lanbo, Shengli, & Jun-Hong, 2008; Stojanovic, 2003; Heidemann, Li, Syed, Wills, & Ye, 2006). Nowadays, thanks to the advancements in electronic technology, MEMS technology can be used in the transducer design and this way, several existing issues can be overcome because of the advantages of MEMS technology over conventional design approaches.

MEMS technology allows sensors, actuators, and electronics to be integrated on the same silicon chip. MEMS devices are micro-machined and their components with typical dimensions about 50-100 μm are physically functional. Common examples of MEMS devices are micromotors, microscopic gears, fluid pumps, hinges, and levers. Different from ICs which only provide strictly electronic functions, electronic, mechanical, fluidic, and optical functions can be provided by MEMS devices on the same chip (Elwenspoek & Wiegerink, 2001; Rai-Choudhury, 2000; Kovacs, 1998; Griffiths, 2003).

For UN applications, packaging is one of the most difficult issues which MEMS designers must address. Because harsh underwater environments impose some constraints related to physical properties and chemical compatibility (Griffiths, 2003). In addition, MEMS devices may have the energy density problem. MEMS require interfaces for physical connections and certainly the most significant physical connection for underwater MEMS sensors is water (Griffiths, 2003). Therefore, considering the adverse effects of potentially corrosive elements, appropriate materials and assembly techniques must be chosen. Similar to terrestrial MEMS devices, design optimization plays a key role in making an underwater MEMS device ready for harsh environments.

Reduction in size enabled by MEMS technology offers many distict advantages in terms of portability, power consumption, production, and cost. As well as the advantages brought by the reduction in size, MEMS technology has theoretically countless other advantages even though the use of MEMS technology in underwater environments is still new and many researchers mainly concentrate on other aspects of UNs such as signal processing, communication protocols, deployment and routing (Nasri, Andrieux, Kachouri, & Samet, 2008). One of those distinct advantages is the ability to overcome the problems caused by the size and power consumption (Pandya, Engel, Chen, Fan, & Liu, 2006). For instance, in an AUV, the utilisation of a MEMS device with a small battery instead of a conventional device can significantly reduce the overall weight of the AUV and thus can reduce the power needed to drive the vehicle. Besides AUVs, MEMS devices can be attached to a variety of objects including anchors on the bottom of the ocean, sea or river, floating devices such as buoys, fixed objects such as rigs, and ships. For real-time monitoring in the oceans and seas, AUVs can be equipped with Lab on a Chip (LOC) which is a set of sensors developed on a single chip by the use of MEMS technology. A LOC device can simultaneously sense many chemical pollutants.

MEMS technology can greatly help to realize new UN systems with enhanced levels of perception, monitoring, control, and performance. However, the requirements of proposed underwater applications strictly affect processing, assembly, packaging, testing, and manufacturing techniques to employed

(Griffiths, 2003). Therefore, to successfully handle the requirements of underwater applications, a multi-disciplinary approach must be followed.

Potential Applications of MEMS Technology in Underwater Networks

Environmental sensing has always been important. However, after cataclysmic events in recent years, the prospect of human-caused climate changes, and the need for more energy sources, targeted sensing has become a necessity for individuals and governments. In this respect, MEMS sensors can help protect and preserve underwater life by doing the following:

- Monitor environmental conditions;
- Monitor energy, fluid, machinery, and other systems in underwater facilities, buildings and structures;
- Sense underwater vehicles and related transportation infrastructure;
- Sense potential security and safety problems.

Parameters which can be measured, monitored and sensed in the marine environment using MEMS sensor technology are:

- Temperature;
- pH;
- Pressure;
- Light;
- Tidal and current velocity;
- Plant pigmentation;
- Dissolved gases;
- Metal concentration;
- Pesticide concentration;
- Seabed characteristics such as seismic signals.

Although basic parameters measured in UN applications are physical parameters such as salinity, density, pressure, temperature, and velocity of sound, MEMS technology is used in the manufacturing of many kinds of versatile underwater devices. Different from the initial efforts, with the advancements in fabrication processes and as a result of mass production, nowadays many types of useful and low-cost underwater MEMS devices including the well-known ones such as micropumps, acoustic systems, accelerometers, and spectrometers are available. In this section, a brief summary of typical underwater MEMS devices used in fixed UN nodes and mobile UN nodes, sometimes called AUVs, are given.

Micropumps are one of the most used MEMS types in UN applications. They enable UN nodes to be capable of sampling fluids. While the sampling of fluids can be realized using alternative techniques, micropumps are preferred due to their advantages. MEMS pumps utilizing different methodologies such as piezoelectrics (van Lintel, van De Pol, & Bouwstra, 1988), magnetohydrodynamics (Lemoff, Lee, Miles, & McConaghy, 1999), and thermoneumatics (Grosjean & Tai, 1999) are available. However, integrating micropumps into MEMS sensor systems is a highly precise process. Since most micro AUVs do not require large pump pressure and their battery resources are limited, a micropump actuated by continuous electrowetting is proposed in (Yun, Cho, Bu, Kim, & Yoon, 2002; Yun et al., 2001). With low voltage operation and highly low power consumption, the proposed micropump achieves comparable performance, pumping up to 63 ml/min at the applied voltage of 2.3 Vpp, compared to other micropumps operated by various actuation mechanisms. It was fabricated using a continuous electrowetting actuator, silicone rubber pumping membranes and copper flap check valves, and uses the surface-tension-induced motion of a mercury drop in the microchannel filled with an electrolyte as actuation energy (Yun, Cho, Bu, Kim, & Yoon, 2002; Yun et al., 2001).

MEMS sensors, detectors, and transducers are commonly used in UN applications. While in the past the use of MEMS sensors for detecting molecules was quite challenging due to the size constraints defining the MEMS device, in the last decade the efficacy of MEMS sensors has been shown many times and commercially available MEMS sensors such as flow sensors, pressure sensors, shear stress sensors, humidity sensors, conductivity sensors, chemical detectors, biological sensors, gas analysers, temperature detectors, accelerometers, acoustic sensors, and optical sensors can easily be obtained. MEMS transducers overcome the shortcomings of conventional transducers in terms of size, power consumption, sensitivity and accuracy (Chowdhury, Ahmadi, & Miller, 2002; Shevtsov et al., 2012; Barlian et al., 2006; Vinoy, Ananthasuresh, Pratap, & Krupanidhi, 2014; Asadnia et al., 2015; Kottapalli, Asadnia, Miao, Barbastathis, & Triantafyllou, 2012; Kottapalli et al., 2012; Pandya, Yang, Jones, Engel, & Liu, 2006), and are required in many UN applications for various goals including current measurement, seismic measurement, biological noise measurement, object classification, target detection, platform localization, ocean topography and profiling, acoustic holography, bathy-velocimeter, sub-bottom geological mapping, and control and position marking (Sathishkumar, Vimalajuliet, Prasath, Selvakumar, & Veer Reddy, 2011; Bernstein et al., 1997; Arshad, 2009). MEMS transducers are especially important for AUVs since mini AUVs are typically battery-powered.

Increasing interest in homeland security, harbour and water-side infrastructure protection have resulted in the increasing interest of the research community in vector sensors (de Bree, Gur, & Akal, 2009; Tijs, Bree, & Akal, 2013). Vector sensors are another sensor type MEMS technology can be utilized. Instead of measuring sound pressure, a vector sensor measures the particle velocity in air and hence has a great potential in many applications including underwater acoustic communication systems, AUVs, harbour and water-side infrastructure protection, and seismic towed arrays for underwater oil and mineral prospecting (de Bree, Gur, & Akal, 2009; Tijs, Bree, & Akal, 2013). A commercially-available transducer called "Microflown" which consists of two closely spaced heated wires and operates in flow ranges of 10 nm/s up to about 1 m/s is presented in (de Bree, Gur, & Akal, 2009).

It has been already proven that MEMS technology will make AUVs smarter and prolong their operational time (Griffiths, 2003). Underwater vehicles generally rely on a combination of INSs, dead reckoning (DR), acoustic navigation and geophysical navigation techniques since the Global Positioning System (GPS) does not work in deep underwater environments. Although tactical inertial sensors used in underwater vehicles provide very detail measurements, they are not suitable for small size and low cost AUVs. In this respect, low cost MEMS Inertial Measurement Units (IMUs) and MEMS 3 axis gyroscopes combined with accelerometers and magnetometers are good navigation tools for the low cost AUVs (Hwang, Yoon, Kim, Lee, Hong, & Parmentier, 2011). Because, by providing accurate pitch, angle and acceleration measurements, MEMS IMUs and gyroscopes can perform with precision in AUV operations.

In an effort to improve and enhance the environmental awareness of AUVs, MEMS pressure sensor arrays which are based on flexible polydimethylsiloxane (PDMS), liquid crystal polymer (LCP) and

LCP/PDMS substrates were developed (Asadnia et al., 2015). The design of an array of 2×10 silicon piezoresistive pressure sensors with a resolution ≈ 10 Pa fabricated on flexible LCP substrates and encapsulated in PDMS is explained in (Asadnia et al., 2015). By mimicking the biological neuromasts on the body of many fish, these sensor arrays can guide AUVs to navigate in dark, unsteady and cluttered environments where vision and sonar-based systems may fail (Asadnia et al., 2013). They have power dissipation ≈ 2 μW per sensor and offer low power passive sensing while their low footprint and flexible backing make them mounted on the streamlined bodies of AUVs conveniently (Asadnia et al., 2015). Under various pressure signals, the accuracy of these MEMS sensors was compared with a set of commercial sensors in a pool test (Asadnia et al., 2015). It was shown that the MEMS sensors generated the same output signals as the commercial sensors. A sample image of piezoresistive sensor array readily mountable on stream line bodies is shown in Figure 2.

Many complex behaviors of fish may be attributed to this sensory organ (Yaul, 2011). For instance, Astyanax fasciatus uses its lateral line to navigate in cluttered environments in the absence of light (Montgomery, Coombs, & Baker, 2001; von Campenhausen, Riess, & Weissert, 1981). Other behaviors of fish including tracking prey by their wake (Pohlmann, Atema, & Breithaupt, 2004), and discriminating the size, shape, and velocity of nearby objects (Vogel & Bleckmann, 2000) may also be attributed to the lateral line. Since certain types of fish have an excellent ability to navigate blindly in a complex underwater environment by relying on their lateral line which consists of arrays of biological sensors called neuromast that interact with surrounding flow, aquatic flow sensors inspired by the function of neuromast organ of the lateral line system of fish can be very useful for hydrodynamic imaging of noisy and complex underwater environments to provide information for obstacle detection, navigation and surveillance (Izadi, 2012; Fernandez, Hou, Hover, Lang, & Triantafyllou, 2007). Providing such functionality to underwater vehicles is a topic of research (Yang et al., 2006; Yang et al. 2007), and is highly useful for mobile underwater sensor nodes such as AUVs. Compared to active sonar systems, these sensors provide AUVs a passive object detection system which operates silently and this way enable AUVs to manoeuvre in murky or dark water environments. The design of a bio-inspired MEMS flow sensor is presented in (Asadnia et al., 2011). The bio-inspired MEMS flow sensor shown in Figure 3 consists of a LCP diaphragm and an SU-8 standing pillar to imitate the cupula of the fish sensor (Asadnia

Figure 2. Piezoresistive sensor array
Source: "Piezoelectric and Piezoresistive Array Pressure Sensors", 2014.

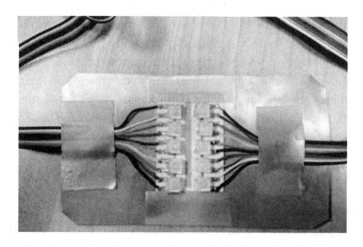

Figure 3. Bio-inspired MEMS flow sensor
Source: Asadnia et al., 2011.

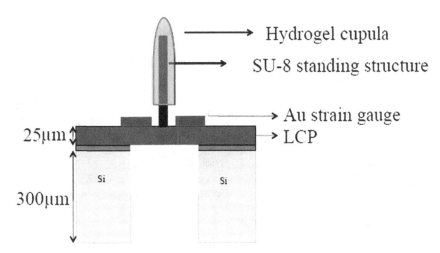

et al., 2011). SU-8 is a negative tone, epoxy-based, near Ultra-Violet photoresist and is used to realize chemically, thermally and mechanically stable structures at various aspect ratios (Maluf & Williams, 2004; Krijnen, Lammerink, Wiegerink, & Casas, 2007; Skordos, Chan, Vincent, & Jeronimidis, 2002).

The MEMS flow sensor mounted on an autonomous surface vehicle (see Figure 4) demonstrated a detection limit as low as 0.46 Pa. Due to LCP's low chemical attack and very low moisture absorption coefficient, it offers sensitivity and high reliability. In addition, the MEMS flow sensor is low-cost and low-powered and more importantly is capable of withstanding harsh seawater environments. A flexible underwater pressure sensor array for artificial lateral line applications mounted on a curved hull is shown in Figure 5.

As shown in the literature, miniaturized, in addition to being used in navigation and maneuvering of underwater robots, low-powered and low-cost sensors are useful in microfluidic devices. For instance, nanofibril scaffold assisted MEMS artificial hydrogel neuromasts can meet the stringent demands on high sensitivity and low threshold detection limits of enhanced sensitivity flow sensing (Kottapalli et

Figure 4. MEMS pressure sensor arrays mounted on an autonomous surface vehicle
Source: "Bio-inspired MEMS sensors for underwater sensing applications", 2014.

Figure 5. MEMS sensor array mounted on a curved hull with a 0.5m curvature
Source: Yaul, 2011.

Perspective view   *Front view*

al., 2016). By replicating the functionality of a lateral line of fish, array of such sensors aid in artificial vision, energy-efficient maneuvering, improved control and maneuverability of underwater vehicles. Importantly, such sensors can detect flow separation on the hulls of underwater vehicles and sense minute flow velocities within the vortices.

In recent years, Surface Acoustic Wave (SAW) devices have gained popularity, and much research has been done in the area of SAW sensors (Benes, Gröschl, & Seifert, 1998). SAW devices have become very important in the implementation of chemical and biological warfare agent detectors, sensors, resonators and wireless applications as a filter (Khalil, Zaki, Saleh, & Ali, 2006). SAW devices can be implemented with MEMS to be compatible with CMOS technology. Basically, SAW is an acoustic wave travelling along the surface of a material exhibiting elasticity, with amplitude which typically decays exponentially with depth into the substrate (Rayleigh, 1885). SAWs have a longitudinal and a vertical shear component which can couple with any media in contact with the surface and hence SAW sensors can directly sense mechanical and mass properties. Sensor applications of SAWs include almost all areas of sensing such as optical, thermal, pressure, chemical, acceleration, torque, and biological. Different from the past, in the last decade, SAW sensors have seen high commercial success and have been commonly used in touchscreen displays. Based on the transduction of acoustic waves from electric energy to mechanical energy which is accomplished by the use of one or more interdigital transducers (IDTs) and piezoelectric materials, SAWs are used in a number of electronic components such as filters, correlators, oscillators, transformers, and DC-to-DC converters (Weigel et al., 2002). Since they provide significant advantages in size, performance, and cost over other filter technologies such as waveguide filters, LC filters and quartz crystals, SAWS filters are now commonly used in mobile telephones. As well as mobile phones, SAW filters are used in wireless communication system applications (Khalil, Zaki, Saleh, & Ali, 2006).

MEMS sensors could be the answer to an effective warning system. MEMS hydrophones are being used in seafloor seismic recording systems as well as seismic sensors for the oil and gas industry. Just as microphones collect sounds in air, hydrophones are small devices which detect sounds in water. Such sounds could be generated by ships, submarines, ocean waves or marine animals. A hydrophone can be anchored to the ocean bottom or dragged behind a ship. Hydrophones also hear tertiary waves created by earthquakes or any movements within the earth's crust. As well as earthquake warning systems, MEMS sensors can also be used in tsunami warning systems. Seismic, current, pressure and velocity asensors are the types of sensors which can be used in tsunami warning systems (Milburn et al., 1996). At present, a tsunami warning system, Deep-ocean Assessment and Reporting of Tsunamis (DART) system of the National Oceanic and Atmospheric Administration (NOAA) shown in Figure 6 is in place. The DART I system was established in the Pacific Ocean in 2003 with sensors positioned at strategic locations throughout the ocean and plays a critical role in tsunami forecasting (Gonzalez et al., 1998). Different from the DART I system which transmitted four estimated sea-level height observations at 15-minute intervals, the DART II became operational in 2005 (Green, 2006). The DART II relies on a two-way communications infrastructure provided by the Iridium commercial satellite communications system (Meinig et al., 2005) and thus allows retrieving high resolution data, transmitted at 15-second intervals, for detailed analysis.

Recently, exciting new sensor array concepts such as MEMS have revolutionized how we approach surface mounted acoustic sensor systems for underwater vehicles (Houston, Bucaro, & Romano, 2001). In this regard, Houston et al. (2001) proposed two schemes: *virtual sonar concept* and *wireless concept*, respectively. In the virtual sonar concept formulated around Helmholtz integral processing, an interesting framework is provided through which structure-borne vibration and variations in structure-backing impedance can be combatted. In the wireless concept, the necessity of a complex wiring or fiberoptic

Figure 6. DART II sytem
Source: "Deep-ocean Assessment and Reporting of Tsunamis (DART®)", 2008.
Copyright info: http://www.photolib.noaa.gov/about.html.

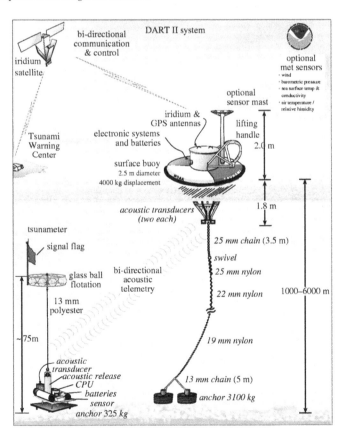

external network is eliminated by transferring sensor information through radiated RF signals while minimizing vehicle penetrations.

To sum up, MEMS technology is a capable platform to realize small, sensitive, reliable and low-cost sensory systems. Since potential applications of MEMS technology in underwater environments are countless and compared to conventional precision engineering approaches MEMS technology brings numerous advantages such as reliability, high spatial resolution, robustness, batch fabrication, and high accuracy at a lower cost, MEMS will have a strong impact on the future of marine research with its opportunities to existing and emerging UN applications. Table 1 lists a summary of common, existing UN applications of MEMS technology.

Existing and Emerging MEMS Power Sources

Very low power consumption is one of the most distinct advantages of MEMS devices. However, due to size limitations, there is a need for an energy source on a size scale commensurate with the MEMS device (Griffiths, 2003). Although, wireless transmission of energy is possible and practically applicable in terrestrial wireless networks, due to harsh underwater environments, except for acoustic medium, continuous delivery of energy using wireless transmission is questionable. Therefore, in wireless MEMS devices, energy is provided autonomously from different types of energy harvesting techniques or batteries. Regardless of the way how the energy is provided, the complexity and dimensions of the device is significantly influenced by the level of power consumption (Pavlin, Belavic, & Novak, 2011). Hence, the power consumption of wireless MEMS devices should be minimized as much as possible. Reduc-

Table 1. Existing UN applications of MEMS technology

MEMS Device	Used for
Acoustic wave sensors	Measure sound levels
Electro-optical sensors	Convert light or a change in light into an electronic signal
Transducers	Converting power from one form to another for purposes of measurement or control
Hydrophones	Detecting sounds in water
Accelerometers	Measuring the acceleration of a moving body
SAW sensors	Directly sensing mechanical and mass properties
Flow sensors	Navigation and maneuvering of underwater robots
Pressure sensors	Detecting pressure
Vector sensors	Measuring particle velocity in air
Micropumps	Enabling UN nodes to be capable of sampling fluids
Temperature detectors	Detecting temperature
Chemical detectors	Analysing chemical properties
Conductivity sensors	Measuring conductivity
Biological sensors	Measuring a set of biological parameters
Gas analysers	Analysing gases

ing the power consumption of the components accordingly reduces the generated heat and improves the stability (Zarnik, Belavic, & Macek, 2010).

The common way to power a wireless MEMS device is to integrate an energy supply into the device such as a battery based on conventional electrochemical cells. Since the commercially available cells cannot be feasibly integrated into a MEMS device due to their form factors, due to occupying minimal volume, tape-cells are preferred. Although the primary way to power wireless MEMS devices is conventional battery technologies, other micro-scale and emerging power generation technologies such as thermal and vibration-based energy harvesters, micro fuel cells and microscale combustors can also be used as renewable energy sources such as solar, wind, and geothermal cannot be easily adopted in MEMS due to the difficulties in storage and intermittency in their availability. Therefore, one of the best sources to harvest energy for MEMS devices is by creating electricity from the chemical energy available in hydrocarbon fuels.

Essentially, fuel cells can produce much more electrical energy per unit weight than conventional battery technologies can. For instance, even when the low conversion efficiency of around 10% taken into account, the use of hydrocarbon fuels in power generation provides advantages in terms of energy storage per unit mass and power generation per unit volume (Chia & Feng, 2007) since hydrocarbon fuels can provide the high energy density of 40 to 50 MJ/kg while most modern lithium ion batteries can provide energy density of 0.4 to 0.7 MJ/kg (Madou, 2002; Madou, 2011). Since fuel cells are not heat engines, they are not subject to the thermodynamic limitations on efficiency suffered by heat engines.

MEMS Communication

Although wired communication is also possible, it is not practically implemented since the MEMS device is likely be damaged or destroyed while the connector is being attached to set a physical data connection. Hence, wireless communication technologies such as acoustics, optics, and RF are suited to MEMS devices. Considering the possibility of intermittent availability of wireless communication, most MEMS devices are equipped with onboard data storage. A fully integrated underwater MEMS device includes microelectronic components for control and data storage/communication.

RF is the most popular communication option for MEMS devices. Through air, frequencies in the 10s of GHz and long distance data transmissions (around a few kilometers) can be achieved. Optical communication is another choice for MEMS communication and ranges from very simple communication systems using asynchronous opto-electronic communication to highly complex active systems (Griffiths, 2003). The asynchronous opto-electronic communication uses an LED detector pair to transmit and receive frequency shift keyed (FSK) amplitude modulated light. Although, it can transfer data as high as a few Mpbs through air over very short distances, active optical communication systems can achieve long-range high-speed data transfers. However, different from their prevalence in terrestrial applications, neither RF nor optical communication is common in underwater applications. On the other hand, although they can provide lower data transfer rates than RF; certainly acoustic systems are well suited for underwater data communications. Acoustic MEMS are constructed using piezoelectric and other materials. Similar to conventional acoustic systems, two-way communications can be achieved.

RESEARCH CHALLENGES

In recent years, underwater communication technologies have progressed with the advances in modulation, demodulation, coding and decoding techniques and moved to multi-hop ad hoc networks. At the same time, here have been advances at higher communication stack layers to establish reliable underwater communications. However, in spite of all these advances and changes, it is clear that there is no single-solution for UN applications since underwater communication channel bandwidth is generally limited and underwater communication systems need to reconfigure themselves to the changing network topology and environment. In addition, there is an important interoperability problem as different from the terrestrial networks, standardization efforts for UNs have not been completed yet and each device manufacturer generally develops proprietary schemes and modems which are mostly unable to communicate with systems from a different manufacturer.

UNs enable the realization of numerous underwater applications, namely a few of them are tactical surveillance, commercial exploitation, aquatic data collection, coral reef monitoring, and earthquake and tsunami warning. However, the requirements of each underwater application are different from the others. Therefore, to select feasible standards, ranking the performance of existing and emerging candidates for realistic topologies, applications and environments plays a key role. Since carrying out extensive trials of underwater applications over a wide range of parameters is costly and logistically complex, physics-based simulation platforms, emulation and hardware-in-the-loop technologies, and experimental testbeds are needed for implementing, testing and comparing the proposed solutions for underwater applications.

In accordance with the prevalence of wireless communication technologies in many application domains and due to the demands of the market for new functions, wireless system manufacturers add more functionality to the devices they produce. However, adding more functionality necessities the use of more components. As well as this, the market expects reduced power consumption, smaller form factors, and lower cost per unit. Furthermore, there are other common expectations such as higher performance and reliability. All these needs can be addressed by cost-effective and tighter integration techniques such as the emerging trend: a single-chip RF circuit. By the single-chip RF circuit approach, MEMS devices can be directly integrated on the RF chip itself, and this way several discrete components such as RF switches, varactor diodes, high Q-factor resonators and filters can be replaced (Nguyen, 2006). As a consequence of the high-yield IC-compatible manufacturing processes, this approach offers benefits such as lower costs, smaller form factors, and higher performance and reliability. Moreover, this approach enables tighter integration and faster communication with the IC. While the integration of RF MEMS devices can replace all passive RF chips with on-chip devices to achieve the long-awaited single-chip RF solution, the limitations in technology and manufacturing processes hinder placement of all passive components with on-chip MEMS components.

Wireless MEMS devices face several energy related research challenges. Due to the limitations of power generation systems and parasitic electrical power requirements, almost all small-scale power generation systems even without moving parts require some form of pump. However, micromotors and micropumps are not efficient at converting electrical power into pumping power (Bhat, Bloomquist, Ahn, Kim, & Kim, 2009). Hence, for wireless MEMS with high power consumption, a large fraction of the weight and total system size must be devoted to batteries (Bhat, Bloomquist, Ahn, Kim, & Kim, 2009). In recent years, many researchers have considered Proton Exchange Membrane (PEM) cells. PEM fuel cells require hydrogen which has both pros and cons (Peighambardoust, Rowshanzamir, & Amjadi, 2010). Hydrogen's energy content per unit weight is nearly three times that of hydrocarbons, but it does not exist in nature in significant quantities. In addition, although hydrogen is very clean-burning, it is easy to burn even in low temperature flames. Moreover, its storage is really problematic due to the production and safety related issues. Due to the all these reasons, hydrocarbon is more practical than hydrogen. An alternative to PEM cells is Direct Methanol (DM) fuel cells. While DM fuel cells can be used for power generation and have some advantages as methanol can be stored easier than hydrogen, methanol has around 6 times lower energy density than hydrogen and cannot be used in pure form without fuel dilution with water (Liu et al., 2006). Moreover, the efficiency of DM fuel cells is low due to the high permeation of methanol through the membrane (Zhang & Liu, 2009). One of the emerging fuel cell types which use hydrocarbon fuels is Solid Oxide (SO) fuel cells. SO fuel cells do not suffer from the limitations DM fuel cells encounter and hence have received considerable attention (Stambouli & Traversa, 2002). However, they work at very high temperatures and are difficult to maintain at small scale because of significant heat losses. Therefore, SO fuel cells have limited applicability in small scale.

Usually, underwater acoustics are band limited and suffer from the following features:

- Different from a point sound of sound in air, in water, the intensity of sound near a point source is highly variable because of reflection from the oscillating surface boundary. Rapid and large fluctuation in intensity or amplitude is produced by reflection at the water surface (Mahmoud & Ososanya, 2006).

- As well as affecting the amplitude, the vertical motion of the surface wave superimposes itself upon the frequency of the sound incident upon it in the manner of frequency modulation. Hence, it produces lower and upper sidebands in the spectrum of the reflected sound producing the frequency smearing effect on a constant frequency signal. Therefore, frequencies different from the input frequencies appear at the output. Moreover, the generation of harmonics of the fundamental frequency occurs at the expense of the fundamental and portion of the power of the fundamental is converted into harmonics.

- Underwater reverberation creates a shift in the center frequency of sinusoidal pulses causing the Doppler shift. Also, it causes a spreading out of the frequency band, i.e., the spread of frequency spectrum and a change in the mean frequency (Mahmoud & Ososanya, 2006).

- Sound waves travelling in water encounter changes in pressure and temperature in different layers. For instance, in shallow waters, water temperature changes with seasons and with depth. Therefore, sound speed and signal refraction is affected.

- Water is more resistant substance than air; hence, underwater transducers use hard piezoelectric ceramics with a reasonable displacement which force their energy into the water. Therefore, designs working in air may not work underwater and depending on the design technique and construction materials, some designs may work better than others. Also, the quality of the water affects underwater transmission systems. In other words, systems working well in fresh water may not work in heavily contaminated water or seawater, and systems working in testbed aquariums may not work well in realistic scenarios.

In many, if not in the majority of future applications, underwater systems will rely entirely on devices developed for the commercial and consumer market. Mass-market products available for potential underwater applications include wireless communication components, embedded sensors, lab-on-chip devices, chemical sensors, flow sensors, fluidic valves, accelerometers, gyroscopes, micro-thrusters, pressure sensors, temperature sensors, and other devices. On the other hand, the performance of such devices must satisfy the stringent specifications and environmental conditions required by the market. For the selected high pay-off applications, Commercial off-the-shelf (COTS) and new developments should be considered and discussed thoroughly in insertion strategies because currently MEMS technology for most of those applications such as micro flow control and IMUs is immature with new areas of research continuously being identified. The expectations in the insertion strategies mainly depend on technology pull and sufficient funding both from commercial and military users. Hence, it is highly critical to find the right application opportunity where MEMS technology can identify road maps for technology implementation, provide new functionalities, demonstrate and quantify benefits, and build confidence. For this goal, international collaborations may be required to maintain a critical mass and develop realistic MEMS devices. For the insertion strategies, reliability is one of the most important concerns since the sensitivity, stability and performance required for underwater applications is high. The high cost and complexity of military and commercial underwater systems has traditionally made it essential that they are repairable under severe conditions. Therefore, major suppliers have set up worldwide support facilities to complement those run by the services themselves. However, in general, MEMS devices are not considered to be repairable or salvageable, and, failure in service will inevitably require replacement of the entire system. Besides reliability, process availability and product obsolescence is another major concern. As expected, since military product life cycle exceeds the others, the total product life cycle for MEMS technology in military applications is much higher than commercial and consumer products. Therefore, the expected life of state-of-the-art commercial fabrication facilities and processes for military applications may require periodic update or renewal and raise the question of process availability and product obsolescence. Also, the stringent operational and environmental standards, dictated by military applications may also include electromagnetic compatibility, resilience to radiation, high temperatures, and vibration and shock. There are a number of possible routes for military requirements to exploit the cost and volume advantages of commercial and consumer MEMS production. Dual use of technology developed entirely in the commercial sector is clearly the most desirable option, but this assumes that the performance and environmental capability will be adequate for the intended military application. For critical security applications, it would be essential not just to make the device unusable in a military system by a third party, but also to physically destroy or remove the design details of how the improved performance or functionality was achieved in the first place.

Finally, to sum up, there are common major design related challenges for UN applications. First of all, since UN nodes have limited battery power and their batteries cannot easily be recharged or practically be replaced, energy harvesting techniques must be employed during long-term monitoring applications. Second, UN nodes are prone to failures due to harsh environmental conditions and if such failures occur, it may not be possible to detect them before the nodes are recovered or replaced. This may lead to the failure of the mission. Third, the amount of data which can be recorded during a mission by UN nodes is limited by not only the capacity of the onboard storage devices but also the unique characteristics and limitations of underwater channels. Finally, in most UN applications, there is no interaction between onshore control systems and UN nodes. Therefore, adaptive tuning and reconfiguration of the UN nodes may not be possible.

FUTURE RESEARCH DIRECTIONS

Use of sophisticated manufacturing technologies, such as MEMS and nanotechnology, has considerably reduced the size of instruments. Increase of platform functionality while reducing operational costs substantially has been achieved by integration of multiple sensors on a single platform (Peach & Yarali, 2013). It is expected that MEMS technology will play a key role in meeting future requirements considering current demands for more compact, more intelligent and more efficient systems, which would improve efficiency and performance, and extend functionalities, including increasing autonomy, reliability, maneuverability, range, affordability, and enhanced service life (Schadow, 2004). In other words, MEMS will enable the development of new capabilities which will allow the introduction of low-cost and high-end functionality to existing systems, thus, will extend their lifetimes and performance. Examples of such enhanced capabilities for UN applications include the development of the following devices and systems:

- Miniaturized RF or optical transmit/receive units for networked communication and tagging;
- Miniaturized optical elements for display and mass storage techniques;
- Multi-parameter smart autonomous sensors and monitoring chips;
- Distributed and networked sensing and smart structures for surveillance and control;
- Intelligent guidance and control through inertial navigation units integrated onto electronic chips;
- Integrated multifunctional components for sensing and monitoring;
- Miniaturized mechanical actuators for fuzing, safeing, and arming;
- Miniaturized and integrated fluid control actuators for fluid/gas manipulation;
- Miniaturized, unmanned, autonomous vehicles;
- Enhanced capabilities for more compact and light-weight engine designs for AUVs.

Although considerable research effort has been directed to UNs and their applications, there are still several open research issues waiting to be addressed. As one of the most important requirements of all wireless devices is energy, the demand for energy and the interest in alternative energy sources to power wireless MEMS devices have increased enormously in recent years and it is expected that they will continue to do so. However, although battery technologies have significantly advanced in recent years, but their power density is still far inferior to combustion devices. Therefore, combustion devices remain as a versatile and cost-effective approach in a wide variety of wireless sensor network applications (Warneke & Pister, 2002) and MEMS-based UN applications. However, such micro conventional power generation devices with moving parts face more friction and heat losses than the ordinary conventional power generation devices due to higher surface to volume ratios (Bhat, Bloomquist, Ahn, Kim, & Kim, 2009). In addition, at such small scales, due to the difficulty of reducing the size, sealing, fabrication, and assembly are much harder. In this regard, one of the most important researches issues for the use of wireless MEMS technology in UN applications is the development of practical and low-cost combustion devices.

The unique characteristics of underwater acoustic communication channels call for very reliable and efficient novel data communication protocols (Heidemann, Li, Syed, Wills, & Ye, 2006). It is expected that such protocols can effectively handle the following issues.

- High bit error rates are experienced by underwater communication channels.

- Available bandwidth of underwater communication channels in most cases is severely limited (Han, Zhang, Shu, & Rodrigues, 2015).
- Typical channel characteristics of underwater communication such as variable and long propagation delays, fading and multi-path problems affect the quality of underwater communication (Heidemann, Li, Syed, Wills, & Ye, 2006; Cui, Kong, Gerla, & Zhou, 2006).

CONCLUSION

Although there is an increasing demand for various applications based on underwater networks and considerable research effort has been directed to UNs, due to the harsh underwater environment conditions, most of the UN applications are imperfect. One of the main issues with UN applications is high implementation and operational costs. In this respect, as a result of the advancements in wireless MEMS technologies, wireless MEMS can play a key role in minimizing the implementation and operational costs and thus in the long-term success of the UN applications. However, due to the unique requirements and challenges of UNs, new research efforts at every layer of protocol stacks are needed.

MEMS technology is very versatile and has countless application areas including marine research. The challenges associated with the enhanced capabilities for marine research are high temperature, need for novel materials, distributed control, active control, reduced lifecycle costs, management of volumes of data, increased intelligence and versatility, and signal and power connectivity. MEMS technology has the potential to mitigate or eliminate these challenges. However, both the industry and academia are challenged to define their own specific applications, which would utilize the benefits of MEMS technologies to enable more compact, more efficient, and more intelligent systems to improve performance and efficiency and to extend capabilities at reduced cost and volume/weight.

When fitted with the appropriate MEMS devices, UNs can provide researchers with an expanding set of capabilities and tools. As well as stationary nodes, mobile autonomous UN nodes coupled with vehicle technology, sensor technologies, intelligent navigation and remote intelligence capabilities can be effectively used to study underwater environments. Because continuing advancement of sensors through MEMS and nano-technologies and advances in software and hardware technologies along with sophisticated data analysis capabilities enable mobile UN nodes to more accurately monitor and measure the underwater environments and thus provide scientists and researchers with accurate and reliable low-cost tools to gather data in order to help them better understand the underwater world.

To conclude, in this chapter, a detailed review of potential UN applications has been given and the use of wireless MEMS for these applications has been discussed. Accordingly, communication standards employed in UNs and existing and emerging power sources for wireless MEMS have been investigated. In addition, open research issues have been outlined and research challenges have been presented.

ACKNOWLEDGMENT

This work was supported by the Turkish Scientific and Technical Research Council (TUBITAK) under Grant no. 114E248.

REFERENCES

Akkaya, K., & Newell, A. (2009). Self-deployment of sensors for maximized coverage in underwater acoustic sensor networks. *Computer Communications*, *32*(7-10), 1233–1244. doi:10.1016/j.comcom.2009.04.002

Akyildiz, I., Pompili, D., & Melodia, T. (2005). Underwater acoustic sensor networks: Research challenges. *Ad Hoc Networks*, *3*(3), 257–279. doi:10.1016/j.adhoc.2005.01.004

Arshad, M. R. (2009). Recent advancement in sensor technology for underwater applications. *Indian Journal of Marine Sciences*, *38*(3), 267–273.

Asadnia, M., Kottapalli, A., Haghighi, R., Cloitre, A., Alvarado, P., Miao, J., & Triantafyllou, M. (2015). MEMS sensors for assessing flow-related control of an underwater biomimetic robotic stingray. *Bioinspiration & Biomimetics*, *10*(3), 036008. doi:10.1088/1748-3190/10/3/036008 PMID:25984934

Asadnia, M., Kottapalli, A., Tan, C., Woo, M., Lang, J., Miao, J., & Triantafyllou, M. (2011). *Bioinspired MEMS Pressure and Flow Sensors for Underwater Navigation and Object Imaging*. Retrieved 25 December 2015, from http://web.mit.edu/towtank/www/posters/MEMS_bldg5display.pdf

Asadnia, M., Kottapalli, A. G. P., Shen, Z., Miao, J. M., & Triantafyllou, M. S. (2013). Flexible and surface mountable piezoelectric sensor arrays for underwater sensing in marine vehicles. *IEEE Sensors Journal*, *13*(10), 3918–3925. doi:10.1109/JSEN.2013.2259227

Barlian, A. A., Narain, R., Li, J. T., Quance, C. E., Ho, A. C., Mukundan, V., & Pruitt, B. L. (2006). Piezoresistive MEMS Underwater Shear Stress Sensors. In *Proceedings of 19th IEEE International Conference on Micro Electro Mechanical Systems (MEMS 2006)* (pp. 626-629). doi:10.1109/MEMSYS.2006.1627877

Benes, E., Gröschl, M., Seifert, F., & Pohl, A. (1998). Comparison Between BAW and SAW Sensor Principles. *IEEE Transactions on Ultrasonics, Ferroelectrics, and Frequency Control*, *45*(5), 1314–1330. doi:10.1109/58.726458 PMID:18244294

Bernstein, J., Finberg, S., Houston, K., Niles, L., Chen, H., Cross, L., & Udayakumar, K. et al. (1997). Micromachined high frequency ferroelectric sonar transducers. *IEEE Transactions on Ultrasonics, Ferroelectrics, and Frequency Control*, *44*(5), 960–969. doi:10.1109/58.655620

Bhat, A., Bloomquist, C., Ahn, J., Kim, Y., & Kim, D. (2009). Thermal Transpiration Based Micro-Scale Pumping and Power Generation Devices. In *Proceedings of 7th International Energy Conversion Engineering Conference*. doi:10.2514/6.2009-4561

Bio-inspired MEMS sensors for underwater sensing applications. (2014). *Center for Environmental Sensing and Modeling*. Retrieved 25 December 2015, from http://censam.mit.edu/research/Pages/Bioinspired%20MEMS%20sensors%20for%20underwater%20sensing%20applications.aspx

Chaimanonart, N., & Young, D. (2006). Remote RF powering system for wireless MEMS strain sensors. *IEEE Sensors Journal*, *6*(2), 484–489. doi:10.1109/JSEN.2006.870158

Chia, L., & Feng, B. (2007). The development of a micropower (micro-thermophotovoltaic) device. *Journal of Power Sources*, *165*(1), 455–480. doi:10.1016/j.jpowsour.2006.12.006

Chowdhury, S., Ahmadi, M., & Miller, W. (2002). Design of a MEMS acoustical beamforming sensor microarray. *IEEE Sensors Journal*, *2*(6), 617–627. doi:10.1109/JSEN.2002.807773

Cui, J.-H., Kong, J., Gerla, M., & Zhou, S. (2006). The challenges of building scalable mobile underwater wireless sensor networks for aquatic applications. *IEEE Network*, *20*(3), 12–18. doi:10.1109/MNET.2006.1637927

Dalbro, M., Eikeland, E., Veld, A. J., Gjessing, S., Lande, T. S., & Riis, H. K. (2008), Wireless sensor networks for off-shore oil and gas installations. In *Proceedings of the 2nd International Conference on Sensor Technologies and Applications* (pp. 258-263). doi:10.1109/SENSORCOMM.2008.111

de Bree, H.-E., Gur, B. M., & Akal, T. (2009). The hydroflown: Mems-based underwater acoustical particle velocity sensor the sensor, its calibration and some possible localization techniques. In *Proceedings of 3rd International Conference & Exhibition on "Underwater Acoustic Measurements: Technologies & Results"* (pp. 35-42).

Deep-ocean Assessment and Reporting of Tsunamis (DART®). (2008). *The National Oceanic and Atmospheric Administration (NOAA)*. Retrieved 21 February 2015, from http://www.ndbc.noaa.gov/dart/dart.shtml

Domingo, M. C., & Prior, R. (2007). A Distributed Clustering Scheme for Underwater Wireless Sensor Networks. In *Proceedings of 2007 IEEE 18th International Symposium on Personal, Indoor and Mobile Radio Communications* (pp. 1-5). doi:10.1109/PIMRC.2007.4394038

Elwenspoek, M., & Wiegerink, R. (2001). *Mechanical microsensors*. Berlin: Springer. doi:10.1007/978-3-662-04321-9

Enz, C., & Kaiser, A. (2013). *MEMS-based circuits and systems for wireless communication*. New York: Springer. doi:10.1007/978-1-4419-8798-3

Erol-Kantarci, M., Mouftah, H., & Oktug, S. (2010). Localization techniques for underwater acoustic sensor networks. *IEEE Communications Magazine*, *48*(12), 152–158. doi:10.1109/MCOM.2010.5673086

Erol-Kantarci, M., Mouftah, H., & Oktug, S. (2011). A Survey of Architectures and Localization Techniques for Underwater Acoustic Sensor Networks. *IEEE Communications Surveys and Tutorials*, *13*(3), 487–502. doi:10.1109/SURV.2011.020211.00035

Fernandez, V. I., Hou, S. M., Hover, F. S., Lang, J. H., & Triantafyllou, M. S. (2007). Lateral line inspired MEMS-array pressure sensing for passive underwater navigation. In *Proceedings of the International Symposium on Unmanned Untethered Submersible Technology*.

Gonzalez, F. I., Milburn, H. M., Bernard, E. N., & Newman, J. C. (1998). Deep-ocean Assessment and Reporting of Tsunamis (DART®): Brief Overview and Status Report. In *Proceedings of the International Workshop on Tsunami Disaster Mitigation*.

Green, D. (2006). Transitioning NOAA Moored Buoy Systems From Research to Operations. In *Proceedings of OCEANS'06 MTS/IEEE Conference*. doi:10.1109/OCEANS.2006.307068

Griffiths, G. (2003). *Technology and Applications of Autonomous Underwater Vehicles*. London: Taylor & Francis.

Grosjean, C., & Tai, Y. C. (1999). A thermoneumatic peristaltic micropump. In Proceedings of Transducers'99.

Han, G., Zhang, C., Shu, L., & Rodrigues, J. (2015). Impacts of Deployment Strategies on Localization Performance in Underwater Acoustic Sensor Networks. *IEEE Transactions on Industrial Electronics*, *62*(3), 1725–1733. doi:10.1109/TIE.2014.2362731

Heidemann, J., Li, Y., Syed, A., Wills, J., & Ye, W. (2006). Research Challenges and Applications for Underwater Sensor Networking. In *Proceedings of the IEEE Wireless Communications and Networking Conference* (pp. 228-235). doi:10.1109/WCNC.2006.1683469

Heidemann, J., Stojanovic, M., & Zorzi, M. (2011). Underwater sensor networks: applications, advances and challenges. *Philosophical Transactions of the Royal Society A: Mathematical, Physical and Engineering Sciences, 370*(1958), 158-175.10.1098/rsta.2011.0214

Houston, B. H., Bucaro, J., & Romano, A. J. (2001). New virtual sonar and wireless sensor system concepts. *The Journal of the Acoustical Society of America*, *115*(5), 2614–2615. doi:10.1121/1.4784795

Hwang, A., Yoon, S., Kim, M. H., Lee, S., Hong, J. S., & Parmentier, G. (2011). Performance Evaluation of AHRS Based MEMS For Unmanned Underwater Vehicle. In *Proceedings of the Twenty-first International Offshore and Polar Engineering Conference*.

Izadi, N. (2012). *Bio-inspired mems aquatic flow sensor arrays* (Ph.D.). University of Twente. Retrieved from http://eprints.eemcs.utwente.nl/19216/01/Final-HighQ.pdf

Johnstone, R., Caputo, D., Cella, U., Gandelli, A., Alippi, C., Grimaccia, F., & Zich, R. E. et al. (2008). Smart Environmental Measurement & Analysis Technologies (SEMAT): Wireless sensor networks in the marine environment. In *Proceedings of the Wireless Sensor and Actuator Network Research on Opposite Sides of the Globe (SENSEI)*.

Katiyar, V., Chand, N., & Chauhan, N. (2010). Recent advances and future trends in Wireless Sensor Networks. *International Journal of Applied Engineering Research*, *1*(3), 330–342.

Khalil, N., Zaki, A., Saleh, M. B., & Ali, H. (2006). Optimum design of MEMS-SAW filter for wireless system applications. In *Proceedings of the 5th WSEAS International Conference on Circuits, Systems, Electronics, Control & Signal Processing (CSECS'06)* (pp. 14-19). World Scientific and Engineering Academy and Society (WSEAS).

Kilfoyle, D., & Baggeroer, A. (2000). The state of the art in underwater acoustic telemetry. *IEEE Journal of Oceanic Engineering*, *25*(1), 4–27. doi:10.1109/48.820733

Kottapalli, A., Asadnia, M., Barbastathis, G., Triantafyllou, M., Miao, J., & Tan, C. (2012). Polymer MEMS pressure sensor arrays for fish-like underwater sensing applications. *Micro & Nano Letters*, *7*(12), 1189–1192. doi:10.1049/mnl.2012.0604

Kottapalli, A., Asadnia, M., Miao, J., Barbastathis, G., & Triantafyllou, M. (2012). A flexible liquid crystal polymer MEMS pressure sensor array for fish-like underwater sensing. *Smart Materials and Structures*, *21*(11), 115030. doi:10.1088/0964-1726/21/11/115030

Kottapalli, A. G. P., Bora, M., Asadnia, M., Miao, J., Venkatraman, S., & Triantafyllou, M. (2016). Nanofibril scaffold assisted MEMS artificial hydrogel neuromasts for enhanced sensitivity flow sensing. *Scientific Reports*, *6*, 19336. doi:10.1038/srep19336 PMID:26763299

Kovacs, G. (1998). *Micromachined Transducers Sourcebook*. Boston, MA: Mcgraw-Hill.

Krijnen, G., Lammerink, T., Wiegerink, R., & Casas, J. (2007). Cricket Inspired Flow-Sensor Arrays. In *Proceedings of the IEEE Sensors* (pp. 539-546). doi:10.1109/ICSENS.2007.4388455

Lanbo, L., Shengli, Z., & Jun-Hong, C. (2008). Prospects and problems of wireless communication for underwater sensor networks. *Wireless Communications & Mobile Computing*, *8*(8), 977–994. doi:10.1002/wcm.654

Lemoff, A. V., Lee, A. P., Miles, R. R., & McConaghy, C. F. (1999). An AC magnetohydrodynamic micropump: Towards a true integrated microfluidic system. In Proceedings of Transducer'99.

Liu, H., Song, C., Zhang, L., Zhang, J., Wang, H., & Wilkinson, D. (2006). A review of anode catalysis in the direct methanol fuel cell. *Journal of Power Sources*, *155*(2), 95–110. doi:10.1016/j.jpowsour.2006.01.030

Madou, M. (2002). *Fundamentals of Microfabrication*. Boca Raton, FL: CRC Press.

Madou, M. (2011). *Fundamentals of Microfabrication and Nanotechnology*. Boca Raton, FL: CRC.

Mahmoud, W., & Ososanya, E. T. (2006). *The Development of a MEMS-based Integrated Wireless Remote Biosensors: Annual Progress Report for FY 2005*. University of the District of Columbia. Retrieved from http://www.udc.edu/docs/dc_water_resources/technical_reports/report_201_development_of_a_MEMS-based_integrated_wireless_r.pdf

Maluf, N., & Williams, K. (2004). *Introduction to microelectromechanical systems engineering*. Boston: Artech House.

Meinig, C., Stalin, S. E., Nakamura, A. I., & Milburn, H. B. (2005). *Real-Time Deep-Ocean Tsunami Measuring, Monitoring, and Reporting System: The NOAA DART II Description and Disclosure*. Academic Press.

Milburn, H. B., Nakamura, A. I., & Gonzalez, F. I. (1996). Real-time tsunami reporting from the deep ocean. In *Proceedings of the Oceans 96 MTS/IEEE Conference* (pp. 390-394). doi:10.1109/OCEANS.1996.572778

Montgomery, J. C., Coombs, S., & Baker, C. F. (2001). The mechanosensory lateral line system of the hypogean form of Astyanax fasciatus. *Environmental Biology of Fishes*, *62*(1-3), 87–96. doi:10.1023/A:1011873111454

Nabki, F., Dusatko, T. A., & El-Gamal, M. N. (2008). Frequency tunable silicon carbide resonators for MEMS above IC. In *Proceedings of IEEE Custom Integrated Circuits Conference* (pp. 185-188). doi:10.1109/CICC.2008.4672054

Nasri, N., Andrieux, L., Kachouri, A., & Samet, M. (2008). Design Considerations for Wireless Underwater Communication Transceiver. In *Proceedings of IEEE International Conference on Signals, Circuits and Systems* (pp. 1-5). doi:10.1109/ICSCS.2008.4746954

Nguyen, C. (2006). MEMS Technologies and Devices for Single-Chip RF Front-Ends. *Journal of Microelectronics and Electronic Packaging*, *3*(4), 160–168. doi:10.4071/1551-4897-3.4.160

Pandya, S., Engel, J., Chen, J., Fan, Z., & Liu, C. (2005). CORAL: miniature acoustic communication subsystem architecture for underwater wireless sensor networks. In *Proceedings of IEEE Sensors*. doi:10.1109/ICSENS.2005.1597661

Pandya, S., Yang, Y., Jones, D., Engel, J., & Liu, C. (2006). Multisensor Processing Algorithms for Underwater Dipole Localization and Tracking Using MEMS Artificial Lateral-Line Sensors. *EURASIP Journal on Advances in Signal Processing*, *2006*, 1–9. doi:10.1155/ASP/2006/76593

Pavlin, M., Belavic, D., & Novak, F. (2011). Ceramic MEMS Designed for Wireless Pressure Monitoring in the Industrial Environment. *Sensors (Basel, Switzerland)*, *12*(12), 320–333. doi:10.3390/s120100320 PMID:22368471

Peach, C., & Yarali, A. (2013). An Overview of Underwater Sensor Networks. In *Proceedings of the Ninth International Conference on Wireless and Mobile Communications (ICWMC 2013)* (pp. 31-36).

Peighambardoust, S., Rowshanzamir, S., & Amjadi, M. (2010). Review of the proton exchange membranes for fuel cell applications. *International Journal of Hydrogen Energy*, *35*(17), 9349–9384. doi:10.1016/j.ijhydene.2010.05.017

Piezoelectric and Piezoresistive Array Pressure Sensors. (2014). MIT Towing Tank Lab. Retrieved 25 December 2015, from http://web.mit.edu/towtank/www/pcbarray.html

Pohlmann, K., Atema, J., & Breithaupt, T. (2004). The importance of the lateral line in nocturnal predation of piscivorous catfish. *The Journal of Experimental Biology*, *207*(17), 2971–2978. doi:10.1242/jeb.01129 PMID:15277552

Rai-Choudhury, P. (2000). *MEMS and MOEMS technology and applications*. Bellingham, WA: SPIE Optical Engineering Press.

Rayleigh, L. (1885). On Waves Propagated along the Plane Surface of an Elastic Solid. *Proc. London Math. Soc.*, *17*(1), 4-11. 10.1112/plms/s1-17.1.4

Ren, Q., & Cheng, X. (2010). Latency-Optimized and Energy-Efficient MAC Protocol for Underwater Acoustic Sensor Networks: A Cross-Layer Approach. *EURASIP Journal on Wireless Communications and Networking*, *2010*, 1–8. doi:10.1155/2010/323151

Sarisaray-Boluk, P., Gungor, V., Baydere, S., & Harmanci, A. (2011). Quality aware image transmission over underwater multimedia sensor networks. *Ad Hoc Networks*, *9*(7), 1287–1301. doi:10.1016/j.adhoc.2011.02.007

Sathishkumar, R., Vimalajuliet, A., Prasath, J. S., Selvakumar, K., & Veer Reddy, V. H. S. (2011). Micro size ultrasonic transducer for marine applications. *Indian Journal of Science and Technology*, *4*(1), 8–11.

Schadow, K. (2004). MEMS Military Applications-RTO Task Group Summary. In *Proceedings of CANEUS 2004 Conference on Micro-Nano-Technologies*. doi:10.2514/6.2004-6749

Shevtsov, S., Parinov, I., Zhilyaev, I., Chang, S.-H., Lee, J. C.-Y., & Wu, P.-C. (2012). Modeling and Optimization of MEMS-Based Acoustic Sensor for Underwater Applications. In Proceedings of Recent Researches in Applied Mechanics (pp. 88-93).

Skordos, A., Chan, P., Vincent, J., & Jeronimidis, G. (2002). A novel strain sensor based on the campaniform sensillum of insects. *Philosophical Transactions of The Royal Society A: Mathematical, Physical and Engineering Sciences, 360*(1791), 239-253.10.1098/rsta.2001.0929

Stambouli, A., & Traversa, E. (2002). Solid oxide fuel cells (SOFCs): A review of an environmentally clean and efficient source of energy. *Renewable & Sustainable Energy Reviews, 6*(5), 433–455. doi:10.1016/S1364-0321(02)00014-X

Stojanovic, M. (2003). Acoustic (Underwater) Communications. In Encyclopedia of Telecommunications. John Wiley & Sons.

Tijs, E., de Bree, H.-E., & Akal, T. (2013). Sea-Bottom Mounted Trials with Hydroflown Sensors. In *Proceedings of 1st International Conference and Exhibition on Underwater Acoustics* (pp. 673-678).

van Lintel, H., van De Pol, F., & Bouwstra, S. (1988). A piezoelectric micropump based on micromachining of silicon. *Sensors and Actuators, 15*(2), 153–167. doi:10.1016/0250-6874(88)87005-7

Vinoy, K. J., Ananthasuresh, G. K., Pratap, R., & Krupanidhi, S. B. (2014). *Micro and smart devices and systems*. Academic Press.

Vogel, D., & Bleckmann, H. (2000). Behavorial discrimination of water motions caused by moving objects. *Journal of Comparative Physiology. A, Neuroethology, Sensory, Neural, and Behavioral Physiology, 186*(12), 1107–1117. doi:10.1007/s003590000158 PMID:11288823

von Campenhausen, C., Riess, I., & Weissert, R. (1981). Detection of stationary objects by the blind cave fish Anoptichthys jordani (characidae). *Journal of Comparative Physiology. A, Neuroethology, Sensory, Neural, and Behavioral Physiology, 143*(3), 369–374. doi:10.1007/BF00611175

Warneke, B. A., & Pister, K. S. J. (2002). MEMS for distributed wireless sensor networks. In *Proceedings of 9th International Conference on Electronics, Circuits and Systems* (vol. 1, pp. 291-294). doi:10.1109/ICECS.2002.1045391

Weigel, R., Morgan, D. P., Owens, J. M., Ballato, A., Lakin, K. M., Hashimoto, K., & Ruppel, C. C. W. (2002). Microwave acoustic materials, devices, and applications. *IEEE Transactions on Microwave Theory and Techniques, 50*(3), 738–749. doi:10.1109/22.989958

Wen, L., Guo, B., Haspeslagh, L., Severi, S., Witvrouw, A., & Puers, R. (2011). Thin film encapsulated SiGe accelerometer for MEMS above IC integration. In *Proceedings of 16th International on Solid-State Sensors, Actuators and Microsystems Conference (TRANSDUCERS)* (pp. 2046-2049). doi:10.1109/TRANSDUCERS.2011.5969217

Yang, Y., Chen, J., Engel, J., Pandya, S., Chen, N., Tucker, C., & Liu, C. et al. (2006). Distant touch hydrodynamic imaging with an artificial lateral line. *Proceedings of the National Academy of Sciences of the United States of America, 103*(50), 18891–18895. doi:10.1073/pnas.0609274103 PMID:17132735

Yang, Y., Chen, J., Tucker, C., Pandya, S., Jones, D., & Liu, C. (2007). Biomimetic flow sensing using artificial lateral lines. *Proceedings of ASME Conf. Proc, 43025*, 1331-1338. doi:10.1115/IMECE2007-43870

Yaul, F. M. (2011). *A Flexible Underwater Pressure Sensor Array for Artificial Lateral Line Applications* (MSc Thesis). Massachusetts Institute of Technology.

Yu, Y., Ou, J., Zhang, J., Zhang, C., & Li, L. (2009). Development of Wireless MEMS Inclination Sensor System for Swing Monitoring of Large-Scale Hook Structures. *IEEE Transactions on Industrial Electronics, 56*(4), 1072–1078. doi:10.1109/TIE.2009.2012469

Yun, K.-S., Cho, I.-J., Bu, J.-U., Kim, C.-J., & Yoon, E. (2002). A surface-tension driven micropump for low-voltage and low-power operations. *Journal of Microelectromechanical Systems, 11*(5), 454–461. doi:10.1109/JMEMS.2002.803286

Yun, K.-S., Cho, I.-J., Bu, J.-U., Kim, G.-H., Jeon, Y.-S., Kim, C.-J., & Yoon, E. (2001). A Micropump Driven by Continuous Electrowetting Actuation for Low Voltage and Low Power Operations. In *Proceedings of IEEE International MEMS 2001 Conference* (pp. 487-490). doi:10.1109/MEMSYS.2001.906585

Zarnik, M., Belavic, D., & Macek, S. (2010). The warm-up and offset stability of a low-pressure piezoresistive ceramic pressure sensor. *Sensors and Actuators. A, Physical, 158*(2), 198–206. doi:10.1016/j.sna.2009.12.035

Zhang, J., & Liu, H. (2009). *Electrocatalysis of direct methanol fuel cells*. Weinheim: Wiley-VCH.

KEY TERMS AND DEFINITIONS

Acoustic Modem: An acoustic modem offers the possibility of wireless communication under water. However, underwater acoustic communication is relatively slow compared to radio communication. This has to do mainly with the speed of sound in water which is roughly 1500 meters per second. The result is a relatively low baud rate.

Autonomous Underwater Vehicle: An Autonomous Underwater Vehicle is a programmable, robotic vehicle that, depending on its design, can drift, drive, or glide through the ocean without real-time control by a human operator.

Fuel Cell: A fuel cell is a device which generates electricity by a chemical reaction. Every fuel cell has two electrodes, the anode and cathode. Electricity is produced by the reactions taking place at the electrodes.

MEMS above IC: MEMS above IC technology has developed in order to allow the elaboration of post-processed micro-machined passive components on top of other circuits. It presents many advantages, as it uses conventional equipments of microelectronics and is in adequation with high frequency applications.

MEMS: MEMS are miniature devices in dimensions from a few hundred microns to millimeters which consist of integrated mechanical components such as springs, vibrating structures, levers, and deformable membranes, and electrical components such as capacitors, resistors, and inductors.

Sensor Array: A sensor array is a group of sensors, usually deployed in a certain geometry pattern. Using a sensor array adds new dimensions to the observation, helping to estimate more parameters and improve the estimation performance.

Single-Chip RF Circuit: By the single-chip RF circuit approach, MEMS devices can be directly integrated on the RF chip itself, and this way several discrete components such as RF switches, varactor diodes, high Q-factor resonators and filters can be replaced.

Underwater Network: A network which consists of a number of underwater nodes with onboard modems and a limited number of surface stations and/or autonomous underwater vehicles, and enables the accurate and energy efficient monitoring of aquatic environment.

Chapter 21

Some Aspects of QoS for High Performance of Service–Oriented Computing in Load Balancing Cluster–Based Web Server

Abhijit Bora
Gauhati University, India

Tulshi Bezboruah
Gauhati University, India

ABSTRACT

Quality estimation for viability of data processing and delivering through the paradigm of service oriented computing and load balancing cluster based web server for high performance of services against extensive load of consumers is an important concern in the domain of grid and distributed computing, big data analysis and internet of things. As such, this chapter proposes a quality estimation framework considering a prototype architecture for multi service multi-functional web services deploying in load balancing cluster based Apache Tomcat web server and developing a clinical database for processing disease related queries through the architecture. The high quality of service is monitored by generating extensive load of users over the system through Mercury LoadRunner load testing tool. In this chapter, the authors will discuss the methodology to study the quality of service, recorded quality metrics against different load of users and the statistical analysis along with results to establish the feasibility, applicability and adaptability of proposed quality estimation framework.

INTRODUCTION

Service Oriented Architecture (SOA) introduces the flexibility of services over internet. It enhances the applicability of distributed and grid computing, interoperability of Internet of Things (IoT) through Service Oriented Computing (SOC) over network based protocol. SOC based system primarily includes

DOI: 10.4018/978-1-5225-1785-6.ch021

binding, publishing and consuming activity of service over network. Among different techniques of SOC based system, Web Services (WSs) are popularly used for its flexibility in power of binding, publishing and discovering over network. WSs support interoperable node to node interaction and use the infrastructure of SOA for delivering the service over network (Booth, 2004). Due to the exponential growth of WSs over internet, the framework of SOA provides the excellent platform for service developing and delivering in the era of Web 2.0 (O'Reilly, 2007). The SOC based system consists of multiple numbers of homogeneous or heterogeneous WSs that work together for the functional objective. How to assess the overall quality of such SOC based system against load of users becomes a crucial problem in research community, software practitioners and among research organizations.

With the increase in consumers of WSs over internet, the load in the server side increases gradually. As such, quality estimation of service has become critical. At peak time of usage, it is highly essential to handle and respond each incoming request properly, so that the consumers do not face the invalid response of such a system. In such cases, cluster based load balancing web server deployment can enhance the ability to process incoming request properly against massive load of consumers.

From the articles of research community presented elsewhere, evidences are acquired that inclusion of cluster based web server for deployment of growing business oriented process in today's era can retain large extend of users, and can handle the challenges of bulks of request processing in server side (Cardellini et al., 2001; Zhu et al., 2001; Andreolini et al., 2002; Andreolini et al., 2004; Hong et al., 2006; Urgaonkar et al., 2007; Vercauteren et al., 2007).

In general WSs are viewed as black box, where the knowledge of internal architecture is omitted. So quality evaluation primarily depends upon the views of users (Zheng et al., 2014). The quality metrics usually vary over exposure period of service time against different stresses of users. As such we emphasize here on quality estimation of multi service multi-functional Simple Object Access Protocol (SOAP) based WSs using load balancing cluster based web server through the analysis of performance and reliability records against high load of users at a peak time of usage.

The Background

SOA is an evolutionary framework for distributed computing over internet that exposes software agents, functional process, and modular business oriented process as service over network based protocol. It is most popular standard model for SOC based system that utilizes WSs, tightly or loosely coupled software agents for service delivery. It provides programmable interface to consumers for consuming self describing modular oriented application in their system (Matthew et al., 2005). It provides a conceptual method to deploy the distributed architecture of WSs. In SOA, the client is not aware of internal programming data structure and the platform that it is running on. The client simply uses the service for their computational logic over network.

The system, running service in the server side is usually termed as SOC based system. The SOC based system contains WSs for the operational purpose. It may contain atomic or composite WSs for implementation of business logic (BL).

WSs contain three foundation layers for service delivery, namely:

1. SOAP,
2. Web Service Description Language (WSDL), and
3. Universal Description Discovery and Integration (UDDI).

Figure 1. Block diagram of WS communication

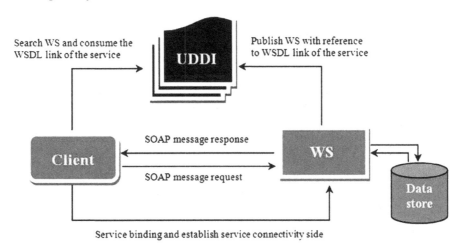

The SOAP supports exchanging of information among software agents. It generates SOAP message using Extensible Markup Language (XML) nodes (SOAP, 2016). The WSDL is an interface for the service that consumers generally consume to establish the connectivity and generate server side class files (WSDL, 2016). The UDDI describes and publishes the functionality of the service, key methods and their types of parameters for the execution of computational logic in the server side (Peiris et al., 2007).

A basic block diagram of WS along with the functionality of the layers is given Figure 1.

The WS is created and stored in server side. The particular WSDL link of the service is registered and published in UDDI. The consumer searches for the particular service of specific operation over UDDI and obtains the WSDL link of the server side WS. The consumer consumes the WSDL link through programme and creates SOAP message. They invoke the WSs by sending the SOAP message to the service. The service in the server side captures the SOAP message and processes it for execution of BL methods. The response is generated in SOAP messaging format and sent back to the client. Thus the client receives the response and utilizes it for its own business purpose. The block diagram focuses the concept of platform independent utilization power of WS over network. The WS can be viewed as Broker (B), Parent (P) and Child (C) WS to the consumers. In Figure 2, the different ways of WS implementation architecture are given.

The implementation of the architecture can serve over internet only if we deploy them using web servers. The web server is solely responsible for managing the incoming request response to the WSs. As per some investigation carried out by different researchers (Saddik, 2006; Kalita et al., 2011; Bora et al., 2013; Bora et al., 2014), it is observed that web servers are limited to specific stress level of incoming request and beyond that it fails or gives invalid response in general. The lack of inability to handle massive request can be reduced by load balancing and clustering the web server (Bryhni et al., 2000). The Figure 3 demonstrates the block diagram for the theoretical concept of load balancing cluster based web server. The web server load can be distributed by clustering a single machine, running a web server, or multiple machines can also be utilized. As support of load balancer, usually a third party web server can be utilized to manage the load routine among the clustered nodes of the web server. It executes parallel servers for the same application as worker nodes for the service. The load is distributed in such a way that if a particular cluster node or worker of server fails in serving request then the request is redirected

Figure 2. Some of the different possibilities of WS implementation and their inter communications

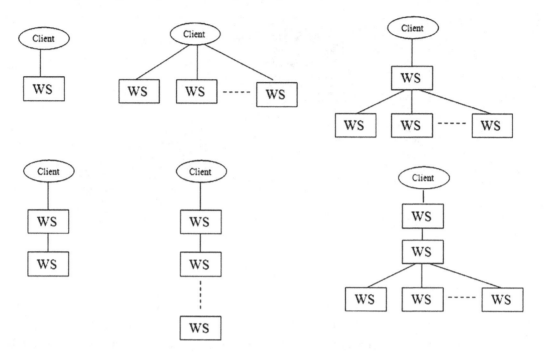

to the other active cluster node of server. Thus request is handled and processed properly, and response is sent back to the client. This technique usually enhances the performance of the system over network. The performance can even be increased by adding more nodes in the cluster. The clustering load balancing web server primarily supports high availability, load balancing for better response, scalability and fault tolerance against massive requests. Figure 3 shows the basic block diagram for different possibility of load balancing cluster based web server.

Figure 3. Basic block diagram for different possibility of load balancing cluster based web server

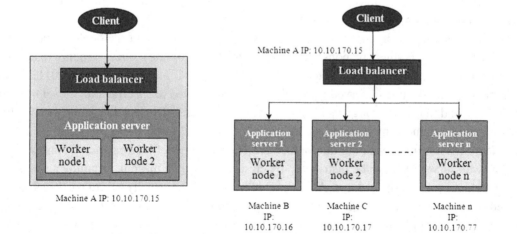

Overview of Evaluation Metrics

Response Time

It is the time taken from the submission of the request to the WS, processing of the parameter, parsing of SOAP messages, executing the BL methods in server side to get the reply from the WS. In short it is the time perceived by the consumer to get response of a request from the WS. It is generally measured in time units (Menasce et al., 2002).

Throughput

It is the number of requests processed in the server side, usually measured in bytes per second unit. It reflects the amount of work executed by server after submission of the request to the WS (Menasce et al., 2002).

Hits/s

It is the number of HTTP call made by the requester to the web server, usually measured in second. A request may have many calls to web server during the exposure period of the WS.

CPU Utilization

It reflects the processing resource utilization in the server side that helps to identify system performance during execution of heavy work load. It is usually measured in percentage of overall cycle of system execution (Singh et al., 2015).

Disk Time Utilization

It is the busyness of the disk during the input output operation against each request made by the client to the WS. It refers to amount of space utilization during reading and writing of data in the server side (Singh et al., 2015).

Reliability

Reliability of SOC based system is the quality of being capable of delivering service over network. WS reliability is the probability that the WS will process and respond request without failure during its execution period of time under a specific operational environment. It reveals the time measurement between failure and the number of occurrences of fault during the operational period of time. Different reliability models that can be employed for analysis of reliability are discussed elsewhere (Goel, 1985).

Related Work

Many researchers are working in the domain of quantifying WS performance, system metrics, development of algorithms for clustering and managing load distribution, fault tolerances of internet based service through clustering web server techniques (Shirazi et al., 1995; Chen et al., 2002; Kalita et al., 2011; Singh et al., 2015). However, there is a lack of study carried out for QoS aspects of multi service based SOC in load balancing cluster based web server against massive load of users.

In the year 2005, Pacifici et al. had proposed an architecture for performance management of web service oriented cluster based system. They demonstrated a prototype implementation that dynamically increases request response time and optimized the resource utilization for enhancing the overall performance, resource allocation, protection of server overload and load balancing aspects of server side.

In the year 2006, Guo et al. had proposed load balancing algorithms for clustering multimedia web server and discussed some scheduling algorithms; key point of media units to increase the overall streaming performance of a multimedia based application.

In the year 2007, Zhang et al. studied the performance of load balancing web server through a queuing model. They measured the response time, rejection rate of the model and compared three routing policies for the load balancing. They observed an experimental investigation for an optimal routing policy that have a minimal response time.

In the year 2011, Sharifian et al. had proposed a novel load balancing and dispatching technique to improve the overall response time and throughput factors of web servers. They classified the incoming request into classes and utilized them to enhance the overall performance of the system. They established the acceptability of the algorithm through some bench mark results comparing with the results of two existing algorithms.

In the year 2012, Tekli et al. had surveyed on the research effort made in enhancing SOAP performance through parsing, serialization, deserialization, security aspects and compression technique of SOAP messages in SOA and grid computing system. They focused some key metrics that must be processed properly to reduce overhead in a system.

In the year 2013, Agustin et al. had proposed a model driven architecture for the development of web based application. They stated that cost and complexity of the program can be reduced through the model along with high availability and reusability of the system that can be obtained through cache management of the application. They established the applicability of the proposed model in a holiday web portal with some experimental investigations.

In the year 2014, Medhi et al. had illustrated a WS based prototype for Automatic Teller Machine (ATM) and had discussed some system metrics for the feasibility of such implementation. The prototype was implemented in .NET framework and monitored against different stress level. However, there is a lack of study for the observed connection refusals that were occurred during the exposure period of the system. In the same year, Çekyay et al. had analyzed a system for the reliability and fault tolerance through a mathematical model and presented some mathematical expression for the performance characterization of such a system.

In the year 2015, Ismail et al. had approached a novel methodology for design, development and implementation of a prototype telemedicine WS based application. A detail discussion was given through internal and external assessment of the service. In the internal evaluation the performance key points of the telemedicine based WS were shown, and in the external assessment, the experimental results were compared to other's existing service over internet. They had established the applicability of their approach through some experimental analysis.

Similar work had been done among other research communities who had utilized the mathematical and statistical model for web server performance analysis against arrival of different incoming request. The different incoming requests may invoke operational logic for retrieval of plain text, graphical image, audio or visual data considering the different data sizes. Those studies primarily highlight some key aspects of such system before implementation in the real world.

In the year 2006, Saddik had proposed and implemented a testing methodology for WS based implementation technique considering a real world scenario of e-learning system. He had used a distributed environment for the experiment and carried out some investigation considering the performance and scalability measurement of such WS based system. From the development point of view, the author had introduced a novel WS based learning system that he named as UbiLearn. The features included:

1. Learning of contents,
2. Management, and
3. Collaboration of service entities.

He had used Java Server Pages (JSP) and Java Beans along with Java Database Connection (JDBC) for capturing and processing user requests against data store. A test bed with hardware specification of Intel Pentium 4 processor with 2.20 GHz, 512 MB of RAM and a hard disk of 80 GB was used. The software specifications included:

1. MySQL Server as database server,
2. Sun One version 7 as application server, and
3. Windows XP as operating system (OS).

A test suite had been generated through a testing tool TestMaker version 3.3 (Cohen, 2001). The testing tool can create multiple SOAP connection and send SOAP request to the application server. He had tested the overall system against different load of test agents at 10, 100, 500 and 1000 respectively. He had monitored the number of successful and error responses, total sessions and error percentage during each load execution over the WS based e-learning system. All test agents had executed same test suite at the same time so that the load can be generated over the WS hosted application server. During the end of load exposure period, the testing tool had recorded the response time in an array format. Additionally, he had tested the system using different networking configuration and observed the performance and scalability metrics against different work load of test agents. He had suggested that to avail better performance and scalability measurement for the load of more than 1000 test agents or requesters, a proxy based system with different available scheduling criteria can be implemented.

In the year 2009, Orallo et al. had introduced a pre implementation system analysis framework through a histogram calculus models. Their primary concern in this work was to bring out the system performance considering the real world web traffic that was calculated through some other system parameters. Their proposed model can estimate the probability of incoming request rejection rate along with the delay time in response. The experimental results had highlighted some comparative work in between predicted and calculated results considering a real scenario of single site hosted web server. The overall performance of the server was monitored through varied workload of users over the server machine. They had discussed the influence of client and network over the performance of web server against different workload intensity level. They had emphasized the static and dynamic request processing and receiving workload in the web server. The workload model had varied over web traffic distribution model. The study had demanded that the proposed model can highlight better estimation than other simulation and classic queuing model. At the end, they had proposed to implement and extend their model for estimation of workload intensity level in the load balancing web server by deploying a complete package of web site with different web methods.

In the year 2011, Sharifian et al. had predicted that there was an exponential growth of users in the database driven dynamic content generation over web for which optimizing and improving the response time and throughput of web hosted web server had become an important concern. The exponential trade-off for high performance of service delivery led to clustering of web server. As such the authors had proposed an algorithm for the load balancing of web servers that primarily categorises incoming request into different classes. The algorithm selects a request from the classes and assigns it to a particular web server node. Some experimental benchmark was developed to establish and confirm that the proposed algorithm can be implemented for better utilization of clustered web server. The experimental setup had utilized 33 machines that consisted of 1 web switch, 16 web server and 16 dedicated database server. Additionally, variable number of client machines was used to access the overall web based system. The hardware configuration, such as 512 MB of RAM for each of web server and database server along with 2 GB of RAM for web switch was used during the investigation. The processors of the machines were AMD Athlon at 2 GHz speed. The software specification consisted of Linux as OS for all machines. The Apache was utilized as web server and MySQL as database server for real world data processing and implementation of web methods. The concurrent load of client was generated through the features of emulator called as RUBiS and Httperf that periodically generates load over the cluster web server (Mosberger et al., 1997). Each concurrent load had interacted with web server and thrown HTTP request for necessary query execution. Each load generating clients were assigned a waiting time, usually a think time was assigned before next request generation. The experimental outcome of the algorithm had predicted that the response time, throughput and scalability of the clustered web server could be improved in contrast to Content Aware Policy (CAP) and Weighted Round Robin (WRR) algorithm.

In the year 2011, Palviainen et al. had emphasized on the evaluation techniques of reliability estimation and its importance over software quality predictions before implementation in the organization. They had stated that software system produces sensitive information to the business process. As such, design consideration, considering architecture and different tightly coupled software component needs to be evaluated thoroughly. The authors had proposed a novel methodology for reliability evaluation of such component based system that can be carried out in design and implementation stage of software development life cycle (SDLC). They had predicted that the reliability estimation of the system through a mathematical model and compared the results against a heuristic approach. The approach had provided a framework for smooth functioning of reliability estimation and future prediction process. The methodology had included was an experimental set up that was configured for the overall investigation. A test script was developed which can access the different internal and inter related components of the system. The test script was designed particularly to evaluate the reliability goal of an organization. The failure behaviour evaluation of the tightly coupled components was carried out. Additionally, the authors had developed a tool that utilized the information from different investigation of the approach and helped in predicting the reliability of the overall system. As part of future investigation, the authors are keen interested in moving their investigation that focuses particularly on the distributed system.

In the year 2012, Kalita et al. had developed a novel framework for comparing the performance of web applications that were developed in different techniques and hosted in different application servers. They had predicted that investigation prior to real time hosting over web is necessary from the perspective of better service delivery over network based protocol. As such, a prototype web based model was created and developed the same in Microsoft .NET and Java framework. A detailed comparative study was carried out considering the system metrics that primarily highlighted the scalability and reliability of service, efficiency and stability of service along with performance against different stress level of end users. An algorithm was developed for fetching records from data store. The experimental set up was developed and implemented with the following hardware specification: Intel Pentium processor at 2.20 GHz speed, 1 GB of RAM and 150 GB of disk drive storage. The different software specification that were utilized for developing one of the two prototype model included:

- Internet Information Service (IIS) version 5.1 as web server,
- Microsoft SQL Server version 2005,
- Visual Studio version 2005, and
- Internet Explorer version 6.1.

The other one was developed with software specification such as Apache Tomcat version 6 as web server, MySQL version 5.0 as database server, and Integrated Development Environment (IDE) NetBeans of version 6.5. The OS for both the systems was Windows XP. The authors had developed a test case for data insert operation. They had generated the stress over each system and monitored the connection refusal rate and performance parameters up to 125 stress agents. The stress was generated and recorded the system metrics over a bandwidth of 128 KBPS. Some statistical results were discussed. The study reveals that percentage of connection refusal is higher in .NET technique as compared to Java technique that is used for web development. As such, scalability was observed to be better in Java technique as compared to .NET technique. Some additional system metrics were monitored which were increasing with increase in load level in both cases. They had also observed some correlation in between system metrics that primarily reflects the performance parameters of both the systems.

In the year 2012, Misra et al. had introduced a novel framework for evaluating and estimating the software quality and complexity metrics. They had utilized the different available evaluation and validation criteria for practical measurement of software quality metrics. The study strongly suggests that success of web based software depends upon validation criteria, behaviours of end users and the relationship in between system metrics and measuring attributes. According to the proposed framework, the practical utility of the system metrics were evaluated first. Then they estimated a scale of measurement for the system metrics which is admissible for feasible consideration. Then they had characterised the practical feasibility response of the system metrics. After practical and theoretical estimation, the desirable sets of properties are introduced that predominantly reflects the robustness of the measurement and usefulness of the system metrics. The study also had given a comparative report, considering a set of existing framework and methodology for web based software quality estimation and measurement. Though the report had some limitation in discussion, but it had covered most of the specific parameters and measurements of software testability. Overall an in-depth guideline was given which can be considered for complexity measurement of web based software in the real world scenario.

In the year 2014, Rahmani et al. had proposed a novel methodology for evaluating the reliability and performance metrics of WS based system considering different middle ware layer of implementation techniques. They had developed a prototype experimental set up to establish the fact that the middle ware configurations have impact on overall performance and reliability measurement issues of real life scenario. They had deployed their prototype WSs in JBoss web server. The loads were generated considering different middle ware configuration over the system. The overall stress was executed for a specific period of time and then the system metrics were recorded for further investigation. The simulation models and remarks were generated considering a Petri net methods. The simulation model had specified the internal architecture and operational view of the WS that were utilized for service delivery. Some key parameters such as HTTP request and rejection rate, error rate of WS, JBoss web server errors against simultaneous users. The database connection and rejection rate were investigated in detail. The system was tested under different system work load and configuration set up. The study had highlighted the importance of middleware entity in the overall reliability of the system. The authors also had developed one analytical model which can calculate the failure and success rate of the service delivery along with the consecutive response time of the system. The proposed model had highlighted some key aspects of overall reliability and performance measurement of the WS based system considering together the application server, database server, WSs and internal configuration of WS settings.

Medhi et al. (2014) had performed an investigation to study the interoperability and flexibility of WS along with their performance against different loads of user. A prototype model was prepared and designed considering the features of ATM in WS paradigm. The detail study had explored the scalability of such a system for implementation in real world. They had categorised the overall WS based ATM system into three atomic parts of services. The first one was the WS for client request handling operation usually a client application. The second one was the WS for handling authenticity of request among end users. The third one was the WS for handling server side computational logic that basically included database operation. The overall communications among WSs were established in hierarchical fashion. The software specifications that were utilized in the development of overall system includes the following:

- Microsoft IIS as web server,
- C# as scripting language,
- Microsoft SQL Express version 2005 as database software, and
- Microsoft Visual Studio version 2010 as framework.

The WS based ATM was implemented in a remote server machine with OS as Windows 2008 server. The authors had created a test suite that periodically access the system for certain amount of time interval. Each access creates an activity of SOAP parsing in server side. As such, it executes a request over web server and fetches records from the data store. The response was generated in SOAP format and sent back to requester node. During the exposure period of service against different stress level of users, the authors had recorded the response time. The system metrics such as hits/s and number of bytes which were processed in the server side was also recorded. They had captured those system parameters against stress level in the range of 10 to 1500 consumers. The study had revealed that some parameters have combine influence over the generation of other system metrics. A statistical evaluation methodology was also demonstrated which can be followed for predicting the system behaviour in real world scenario of implementation. The authors had also demonstrated a comparative study of their work against other authors work to establish the applicability, feasibility and scalability of hierarchical WS against different stress level of users.

In the year 2015, Singh et al. had proposed a novel framework for evaluating the performance of sensor based system over network based protocol through a web application. The study emphasized on the performance key metrics of such web based system for monitoring sensor data and the quality aspects considering the server side resource utilization against concurrent load of users. The authors also had highlighted the importance of disk and processor utilization in server side during concurrent execution of incoming requests. Standard system testing software was used for monitoring the overall responses and server side data bytes that are being processed by execution of load in the system. The experimental set up was developed that particularly captures temperatures through a remote machine over network. A web based application was also developed in ASP.NET technique that particularly captured the temperature data of the sensor. The web based system actually had worked as the presentation logic of the sensor based system for the end users. The additional features such as log in, view record, controlling the sensor over network were provided for the users so that the incoming requests do not collide and serialization of the incoming request can be maintained properly. The web based system had communicated the hardware for accessing the temperature sensor data. The performance and quality of the system was evaluated through two test cases that execute 60 VU to access the system. Additionally, some system constraints were set for the investigation. The influence of VU over the sensor based system and the web application was monitored. A total of 2 VU were allowed to visit the web based system at a time and likewise the load was increased gradually. As soon as all VU initialized to a load of 60, the system was executed for 5 minutes. After the exposure period, all VU had stopped simultaneously. A varied number of data sizes such as 1 KB, 30 KB, 70 KB and 100 KB were used to monitor the influence of varied data size over the performance parameter considering the response time and server side data byte processing. Some statistical interpretation of the system response time was carried out against the test cases. The results had revealed that the performance parameters such as response time, utilization ratio of disk and processor, and the throughput of the server side processing had raised gradually with the increase in varied data sizes and VU. They had given some runtime estimation of the system for quality measurement. The study had concluded that hardware configuration can also influence the overall performance metrics in accessing the sensor data over network.

In the year 2016, Medhi et al. had performed some investigation considering the security policies of SOC. A prototype experimental set up was developed considering Windows Communication Foundation (WCF) services. The WS paradigm was followed for the implementation. The system was evaluated for monitoring the scalability and execution quality of the WS against different security policies. The security policies were implemented in the hierarchical communication of WS. The architecture of the prototype work had included three services for the execution of the service towards end users. The development of the WCF based WS was carried out through the utilization of C# programming language, Microsoft IIS as web server along with Microsoft SQL Server 2005 for database processing and BL implementation. A database of 10,000 records were prepared that was implemented in the server for the database processing. A testing tool was deployed for testing the system. A test bed set up was configured considering a 128 Kbps of network bandwidth. The load was generated over the system through the specified bandwidth of the network. The authors had collected a data sample considering SQL insert operation. The load testing for 5, 10 and 15 end user was carried out. A repetitive execution of each stress of user was run for 30 times. That means, 30 data sample of repetitive execution by considering stress of 5, 10 and 15 end users were taken for each. Each execution in turn had executed SOAP request over SOC. The different stress level of the end user was executed continuously for 5 minutes over the SOC based security system. A framework for statistical investigation was also implemented for estimating the overall response time, server side hits over clock time and the execution of server side throughput metrics. The outcome of the statistical analysis had shown the mean response time of SOC against WS security policies. The normal distribution of performance metrics through scatter plots was observed. The study had predicted that the security policies have its own influence factor over the execution parameters of the system. As such, the performance metrics were observed to be proportionally related to different WS security policies.

The proposed work is novel from previous work, because, we focused on the study of the QoS aspects of multi service based SOC system for high performance against massive users through load balancing cluster based web server. The emphasis is given on performance and reliability quality metrics of SOAP based WS for the service delivery, as the end user client visualizes theses metrics comparatively of higher priority than other quality metrics.

Need of Service Oriented System and Future Scope of Implementation

The research communities and the software practitioners have highlighted many area of implementation and future scope of high performance service delivery system considering the architecture of SOC and cluster based web server. They emphasize the importance of service delivery techniques through SOC for it's highly interoperability nature among heterogeneous and homogenous platform independent components. Some of the selected highlight is discussed below:

Tewoldeberhan et al. (2008) had shown a new direction of implementing WS considering the business process of supply chain system. The development of simulation framework to study the efficiency and reliability of such system was observed to be important from the perspective of the author's experimental work. They had discussed that execution of simulation based framework to estimate the quality metrics of supply chain business considering WS can improve the supply chain process in an organization before implementation in the business world.

A need of the work and the service implementation scope considering SOC and cluster based web server were discussed in the study of Piro et al. (2014). They highlighted the importance of Information and Communication Technique (ICT) services in the urban development of smart cities. Through the interoperability of service delivery considering the framework of e-government, citizen security, social and health care, and water resources and other citizen services, the innovative system can be developed and implemented for the citizen of smart city for better quality of life. The study had also discussed the importance of such methodology in the sectors of road safety to avoid accidents, waste material management among geographically separated locations, people centric health care system and remote management of traffic control. The discussion and issues raised by the authors had successfully demonstrated that service delivery through ICT can resolve many issues that usually occur in urban development of cities.

Jiang et al. (2014) had emphasized the need of SOC in e-government web portal for better service to the users. The different e-government SOC based system can be developed that can be either the visa application, property tax for official process, passport application or other governmental citizen service. The development of the e-government service is carried out considering the mind set and basic day to day requirement of citizen from governmental departments. They had highlighted the user perspective satisfaction level as well as service quality aspects of e-government portal considering the service adaptation and information acquisition over web. The authors had implemented an experimental framework over a sample of service consumer. The outcome had varied over different groups of user. The authors had stated that the internal functionality, availability, reliability, security aspects and performance quality can impact a lot over the adaptation of e-government services. As such service quality estimation framework can be developed and implemented for user perspective service quality estimation over web.

Another need of service oriented system was discussed in the study of Hussain et al. (2015). They had said that the remote service delivery considering the health care diagnostic system in smart cities needs a service oriented system for effective response to the patient and other concern person. A typical standard needs to be developed through service oriented system that focuses on the health monitoring system of disabled and elderly people. It relies over the internal execution of server side sensing, data processing, data storing and other system parameters. They had also discussed a human centric framework for emergency health care service that comprises existing medical services to provide collaborative service towards disabled and elderly people of smart city.

The utilization of collaborative service towards emergency situation in location specific zones through ICT helps the management in decision making. As such Palmieri et al. (2016) had demonstrated an architecture that can be implemented through remote services for better utilization of online storage constraint and computing resources during emergency situation in a city. They had highlighted the real time response context and integration of different ICT based service during emergency scenario in a place. For the context of urban area, with growing needs of industries and population, the importance of remote service availability and efficient server side processing capability is getting a focal point from the perspective of emergency management system. According to the authors, monitoring the traffic control and processing the environmental data through highly reliable, available and efficient system during emergency situation and helping management in decision making can also be an important concern. During emergency situation, the execution of users over remote services increases, as such, network congestion situation and system failure issues may generate. In that case hybrid cloud based system and remote service can work collaboratively as the fast responders to emergency management unit in an organization or in cities.

OBJECTIVE AND METHODOLOGY OF INVESTIGATION

The objective of the proposed work is to study the overall performance and reliability quality of multi service based SOC in load balancing cluster based web server against massive load of user accesses. An architecture of multi WS communication is designed for the study which contains broker (B-WS), parent (P-WS), and child WS (C-WS) and executes together to fetch record from database. The web server load is distributed in round robin scheduling fashion. The web server clustering is carried out through configuration of Apache Tomcat Application Server (Tomcat, 2016), mod_jk tomcat connector (Mod jk connector, 2015) and Apache HTTP Web Server (Apache Web Server, 2014). A detail discussion on clustering Apache Tomcat web server is given elsewhere (Cluster Configuration, 2016). The WS is developed and implemented using JAVA with Spring framework Model View Controller (MVC) version 2.5 and MySQL database server. A database mapping of 15000 records for disease medicine clinical remarks is taken for the investigation. The load in SOC based system is given through a load testing tool Mercury LoadRunner version 8.1 (Mercury LoadRunner, 2016). The tool generates virtual user (VU) that can access the system. A test case is designed that contains instructions about how to access the system. All VU follow the test case. The experimental arrangement for the work is given in Figure 4. Here the Tomcat Application Server is clustered into two nodes, running the same multi WS. The load distribution of incoming request is handled by configuring Apache HTTP Web Server along with mod_jk tomcat connector.

Motivation of the Proposed Work

In today's era of SOA, service delivery against high load of consumers is gaining importance among organizations, software practitioners and research communities. The system should always be active in

Figure 4. Experimental arrangement for SOC in load balancing cluster based web server

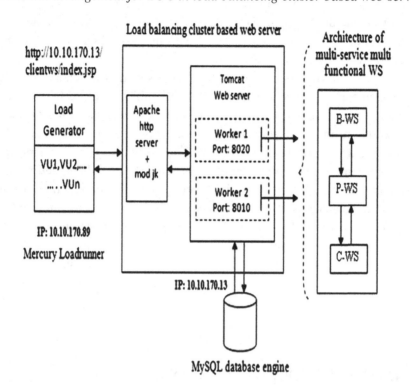

delivering the functional requirements of the end users. However, the software industries and practitioners are always concerned about their online products towards their consumers. With day to day activity and online market demand, the business organizations have given more importance in delivering their support and service to consumers over web based system. In that context, the platform independent online SOC comprise of WSs is getting an important limelight among industries. However, the role of web server clustering along with WS together can have greater impact in service delivery. The overall system can perform better up to a particular maximum stress level and then degrade gradually with increase in incoming server request. The observation of failure transaction in server side against different incoming request and at different stress level is also an important concern that can't be neglected from the perspective of consumers, industries and software testers. Additionally, the server side resource utilization in processing incoming request and generating necessary response against each incoming load of request is also a concern from the perspective of quality in service delivery. These quality metrics evaluations of WSs can have significant impact on the overall success of SOC. Some quality metrics are correlated and that too can impact the overall performance and reliability of service delivery through SOC. If the quality metrics degrades gradually and the rate of degradation is increasing exponentially, then a special consideration or a limitation of service delivery marking is necessary to be recorded and evaluated. As such, assessing such SOC based system and that too in clustered web server needs an efficient evaluation framework that can be implemented to estimate the overall performance and reliability against different execution of user load level. However, it is seen that the concerned developer involved at design and development stage of SDLC, have lack of idea about the performance and reliability estimation about their practical implementation. As such, the assessor or software tester should generate a quality estimation report for the SOC based system. The generated report can be considered as real time evaluation report that the SOC along with clustered web server will perform in real word scenario during the exposure period of service against different stress level at a time together. Additionally, that evaluated report should be compared against some existing system, to prioritize the quality of their service and market demanding product.

The motivation of the work is to study the performance and reliability of the SOC in load balancing cluster based web server for service delivery and to estimate some quality metrics of such system. Such motivation leads to an assessment of real SOC based system along with the evaluation of system parameters and the correlation of different server side system attributes. The study will also highlight a framework that can be implemented statistically to assess the overall performance and reliability metrics of such system in near future. However, many authors have implemented different architecture for information retrieval over web. Those can be implemented in the practical scenario of service delivery (Saddik, 2006; Kalita et al.; 2011, Medhi et al.; 2014). Though through their methodology, some milestones of service delivery can be observed and evaluated against different stress level of users, it is necessary to compare their work at different stress level. As such the motivation of the study also leads to a comparative evaluation of such implementation technique considering SOC and clustered web server against some other implementation methodology, so that, the evaluation can highlight the betterment of proposed service delivery methodology. If the assessment results can highlight the system metrics at different stress of request, then it can be assumed that, the SOC based system along with the clustered web server will be able to deliver service without degradation of performance and reliability up to a specific stress of incoming requests from end users. In that case, the developers will be able to predict the quality metrics of the SOC based system or how the clustered web server will react against different load of end users in the real world scenario, when bulks of request will arrive at the same time.

Software and Hardware Configuration

The software and hardware specifications for the present study which are followed in the work are given in Table 1.

TESTING AND EVALUATION

The quality of SOC based system along with load balancing cluster based web server is studied by testing against 100, 300, 500, 1000, 1200, 1400, 1600, 1800, 2000 VU level. The Mercury LoadRunner is used to create the VU. It creates test case for accessing the SOC based system. The VU follows the test case. The execution of a test case causes a SOAP transaction to occur in between WS for the necessary BL method invocation. The load is gradually increased by a ramp up setting of 2 VU entering each after a time of 15 second. After initiating all VU, the whole group of VU executes together for 5 minutes. During this ramp up period we monitor the average CPU utilization, disk time utilization, response time, throughput, hits/sec, total transaction passed and failed metrics of the system. After the ramp up period, the load ramps down and all VU stop simultaneously. We have tested the system continuously till the transaction failures occur. The SOC based system throws failure transaction at 1800 VU and the failure increases with increase in stress level of VU. That is, the failure records observed against 1800 and 2000 VU load level. The recorded performance metrics against different stress level of VU are given in Table 2.

Table 1. Software and hardware specification for the experiment

Specification	SOC Based System	Load Generator System
Operating system	64-bit Windows Server 2008 R2 Standard	Windows XP
Processor	Intel® Xeon® CPU E5620 @ 2.40 GHz	Intel® Pentium® Dual CPUE2200 @ 2.20 GHz
RAM	8 GB	1 GB
Application server	Apache Tomcat version 7	Not applicable (NA)
Web server	Apache HTTP server 2.2.4	NA
Database software	MySQL version 5.0	NA
Hard disk	600 GB	150 GB
Software support tool	• Mod JK Tomcat connector, • Java Development Kit of Version 7, • Java Runtime Environment of Version 7, • Spring MVC 2.5 framework, • Metro WS stack, • NetBeans Integrated Development Environment of Version 7.0, • Google Chrome web browser.	Mercury load runner Load testing tool (version 8.1)

Table 2. Recorded average values of observed metric for QoS against VU

VU Stress Level	CPU UT	DT UT	RT	THP	HTS	TP	TF	TT	FR = TF/TT
100	22.48	0.24	1.4	10752.37	5.48	892	0	892	0
300	24.09	0.25	1.9	12203.21	8.5	3286	0	3286	0
500	29.57	0.28	2.1	22880.97	21.46	12829	0	12829	0
1000	31.37	0.27	2.2	26128.34	24.94	28489	0	28489	0
1200	33.31	0.27	2.35	30099.004	29.68	40186	0	40186	0
1400	34.89	0.29	3.33	34174.78	34.13	53895	0	53895	0
1600	35.45	0.29	3.44	47272.44	36.69	68228	0	68228	0
1800	38.69	0.29	25.85	102666.33	58.58	80495	42127	122622	0.34
2000	38.81	0.28	51.74	100756.29	59.18	81410	57476	138886	0.41

CPU UT: % of CPU utilization, DT UT: % of disk time utilization, RT: Response time (sec), THP: Throughput (bytes/s), HTS: Hits/sec, TP: Transaction passed, TF: Transaction fail, TT: Total transaction, FR: Failure rate

Statistical Analysis for Performance and Reliability Quality Estimation

Since the recorded metrics of 1800 VU stress level shows the first transaction failure records, we have taken 30 data sample of repeated test for further analysis of performance and reliability at this stress level. The statistical analysis is carried out using Microsoft Excel 2007 over that data sample. At 95% confidence level, the analysis shows the responses of the data sample as given in Table 3.

The distribution nature of the recorded data sample is observed through the interpretation of histogram. The histogram reveals that the distribution of CPU utilization is normal with slightly left skewed. The distribution of disk time utilization, response time (s), throughput (bytes/s) and hits/s is normal in

Table 3. Recorded metrics mean and frequency range of data sample

Recorded Quality Metrics	Mean	Lies Between
% of CPU utilization	39.13	37.26 – 40.94
% of Disk utilization	0.28	0.26 – 0.3
Response time (s)	25.28	14.3 – 36.97
Throughput (bytes/s)	105729.1	98290.53 – 112591.5
Hits/s	60.27	58.08 – 62.98
Total transaction	126223.5	122622 – 130191
Transaction passed	82387.4	74527 – 88931
Transaction failed	43836.1	37306 – 53424

nature. The frequency tables with bin ranges and the histograms are shown in Tables 4-5 and Figures 5-9 respectively. However, based on different used bin sizes, the interpretation of histogram may be different. As such evaluating normal probability plot is a better technique. If the data samples are following a straight line then it can be concluded that data samples are normal in distribution. The normal probability plots of the recorded data sample are shown in Figures. 10 – 14. From the normal probability plot, it reveals that the recorded metrics are linear and follows the mean value.

Table 4. Frequency and bin ranges for CPU utilization and disk time utilization

CPU Utilization		Disk Time Utilization	
Bin	Frequency	Bin	Frequency
0 - 37.26	1	0 - 0.257	1
37.26 - 37.996	2	0.257 - 0.2662	3
37.996 - 38.732	8	0.2662 - 0.2754	6
38.732 - 39.468	7	0.2754 - 0.2846	10
39.468 - 40.204	6	0.2846 - 0.2938	7
>40.204	6	>0.2938	3

Table 5. Frequency and bin ranges for response time, throughput and hits/s

Response Time(s)		Throughput (Bytes/s)		Hits/s	
Bin	Frequency	Bin	Frequency	Bin	Frequency
0 - 14.3	1	0 - 98290.529	1	0 - 58.08	1
14.3 - 18.834	3	98290.529 - 101150.717	3	58.08 - 59.06	4
18.834 - 23.368	8	101150.717 - 104010.905	6	59.06 - 60.04	9
23.368 - 27.902	8	104010.905 - 106871.093	9	60.04 - 61.02	7
27.902 - 32.436	7	106871.093 - 109731.281	6	61.02 - 62	7
>32.436	3	>109731.28	5	>62	2

Figure 5. Histogram of CPU utilization

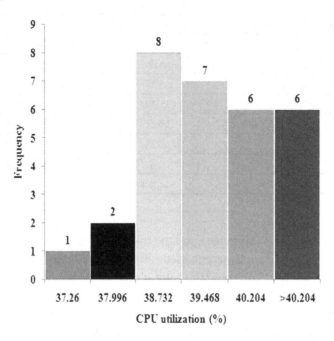

Figure 6. Histogram of disk time utilization

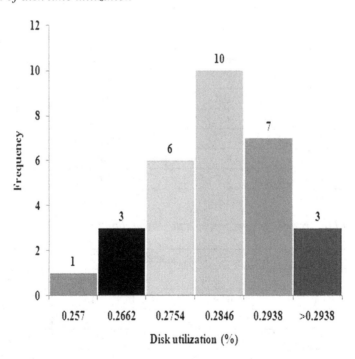

Figure 7. Histogram of response time

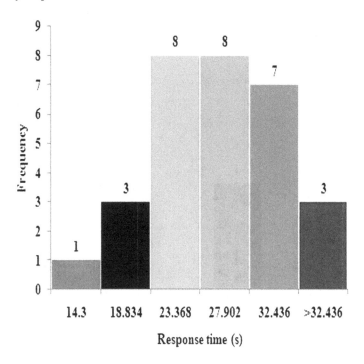

Figure 8. Histogram of throughput

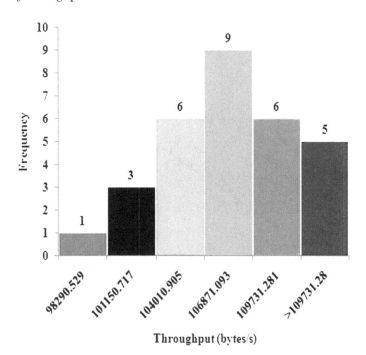

Figure 9. Histogram of hits/s

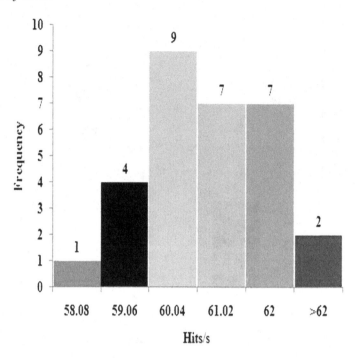

Figure 10. Normal probability plot of CPU utilization

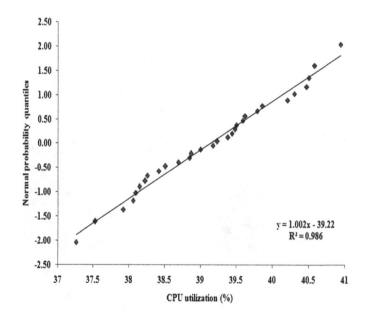

Figure 11. Normal probability plot of disk time utilization

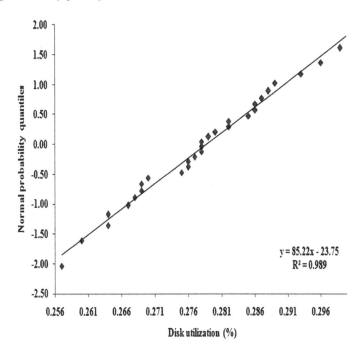

Figure 12. Normal probability plot of response time

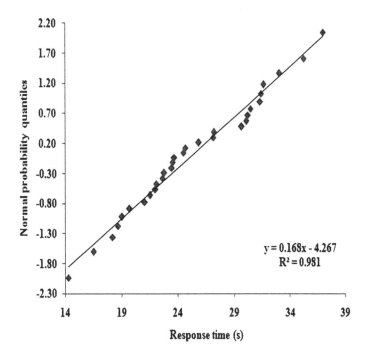

Figure 13. Normal probability plot of throughput

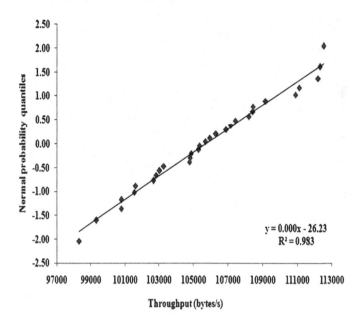

Figure 14. Normal probability plot of hits/s

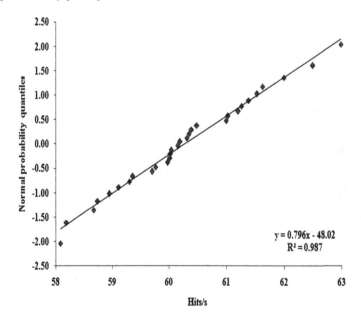

Kolmogornov Smirnov (KS) Test for Normality and Goodness of Fit (GoF) Evaluation

We have carried out the KS test of normality to verify the hypothesis that the observed recorded data sample is from a specified continuous distribution. The test evaluates the observed and expected cumulative distribution function (CDF) and finds the differences between them. It has two key metrics to be calculated as given below.

$$KS + = \sqrt{n} \max (\frac{i}{n} - y_i) \tag{1}$$

$$KS - = \sqrt{n} \max (y_i - \frac{i-1}{n}) \tag{2}$$

The KS+ and KS- describe the maximum deviation when the observed CDF is above and below the expected CDF. If the calculated KS+ and KS- values are smaller than KS (1± confidence level; n), then we can conclude that n observations are coming from a specified distribution at ± level of significance. (Jain, 2012)

We have used NORMDIST function of Microsoft Excel to calculate the normal cumulative distribution of the recorded metrics for the specified mean and standard deviation. Evaluated CPU utilization CDF metrics and different KS test results are shown in Table 6.

KS+ and KS- are observed to be 0.46 and 0.38 respectively. At 99% confidence level and for n=30, the KS(0.99, n) is 1.4801. Since both KS+ and KS- are less than KS table value, the data sample of CPU utilization metrics signifies the KS test of normality and passes the GoF. Hence, the hypothesis is accepted with an interpretation that CPU utilization CDF values follow the normal distribution at mean value =39.13, standard deviation=0.963. That means, the population of the data sample for CPU utilization is normally distributed.

Similar situation is observed for the data sample of disk time utilization, response time, throughput and hits/s. That is, the disk time utilization passes the KS test of GoF with KS+ and KS- values equal to 0.65 and 0.15 respectively and follows the normal distribution at mean value = 39.13, standard deviation=0.963. The response time utilization passes the KS test of GoF with KS+ and KS- values equal to 0.61 and 0.6 respectively and follows the normal distribution at mean value=25.28, standard deviation=5.71. The throughput utilization passes the KS test of GoF with KS+ and KS- values equal to 0.38 and 0.4 respectively and follows the normal distribution at mean value=105729.1, standard deviation=3893.74. The hits/s utilization passes the KS test of GoF with KS+ and KS- values equal to 0.54 and 0.38 respectively and follows the normal distribution at mean value=60.27, standard deviation=1.21.

Fault Count and Confidence Interval of Observation

The recorded data sample for the transaction failure of the SOC based system is divided in to six classes. The frequency table and histogram of fault count is given in Table 7 and Figure 15 respectively. The

Table 6. KS GoF test for adequacy of distribution for CPU utilization

i	CDF y	i/n	i-1/n	i/n-y	y-(i-1)/n
1	0.026	0.033333	0	0.007256	0.026078
2	0.048	0.066667	0.033333	0.018358	0.014976
3	0.104	0.1	0.066667	-0.00447	0.037802
4	0.133	0.133333	0.1	7.31E-05	0.03326
5	0.142	0.166667	0.133333	0.024261	0.009072
6	0.154	0.2	0.166667	0.045579	-0.01225
7	0.175	0.233333	0.2	0.058331	-0.025
8	0.183	0.266667	0.233333	0.083517	-0.05018
9	0.230	0.3	0.266667	0.069524	-0.03619
10	0.260	0.333333	0.3	0.073488	-0.04015
11	0.324	0.366667	0.333333	0.042797	-0.00946
12	0.386	0.4	0.366667	0.014382	0.018952
13	0.394	0.433333	0.4	0.039749	-0.00642
14	0.446	0.466667	0.433333	0.020359	0.012975
15	0.517	0.5	0.466667	-0.01657	0.049899
16	0.541	0.533333	0.5	-0.00802	0.041353
17	0.602	0.566667	0.533333	-0.03575	0.069083
18	0.626	0.6	0.566667	-0.02624	0.059573
19	0.642	0.633333	0.6	-0.00853	0.041865
20	0.650	0.666667	0.633333	0.017076	0.016257
21	0.684	0.7	0.666667	0.016441	0.016892
22	0.695	0.733333	0.7	0.03877	-0.00544
23	0.753	0.766667	0.733333	0.013226	0.020108
24	0.776	0.8	0.766667	0.024211	0.009122
25	0.869	0.833333	0.8	-0.03563	0.068961
26	0.888	0.866667	0.833333	-0.02114	0.054475
27	0.918	0.9	0.866667	-0.01796	0.051294
28	0.923	0.933333	0.9	0.010754	0.022579
29	0.934	0.966667	0.933333	0.032737	0.000596
30	0.970	1	0.966667	0.030085	0.003248
-	-	-	Max	0.083517	0.069083

y: Observed CDF; i: Rows; n: number of dataset i.e. 30

histogram shows that the highest fault count observation is in the range of 40529.6 to 43753.2. The VU access the system through test case execution which in turn creates HTTP transactions. Each invocation of HTTP transaction causes a processing of SOAP request and response in server side. In this case, for 1800 VU, an average of 126223.5 transactions occurred in one day and out of that an average of 43836.1 transactions had failed due to high stress in server side.

Table 7. Bin and frequency ranges for the fault count

Bin	Frequency
0 – 37306	1
37306 - 40529.6	5
40529.6 - 43753.2	12
43753.2 - 46976.8	7
46976.8 - 50200.4	2
>50200.4	3

Figure 15. Histogram of fault count

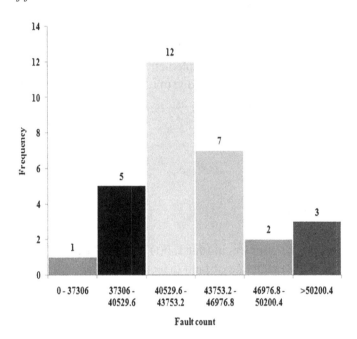

At 95% confidence level, the population mean μ of fault count observation is evaluated for 1800 VU per day. The μ is evaluated by using the Equation 3 as follows (Spiegel, 2000; Pal, 1998; Kalita et al., 2011).

$$\mu = \overline{x} \pm \frac{t_c SDV}{\sqrt{N}} \tag{3}$$

where $\overline{x}$, $t_{c(0.05,29)}$, SDV, N and ($t_c SDV/\sqrt{N}$) are mean, critical value, standard deviation, sample size 30 and margin of errors respectively. The fault count observed against 1800 VU per day is taken for the evaluation of the μ. Table 8 shows the estimated values for the μ.

From Table 8, the following can be concluded at 95% confidence level: that for a load of 1800 VU in one day the mean fault count lies between 43836.1 ± 1549.94 that is in between 45386.04 to 42286.16.

Table 8. Estimated values for fault count and μ

N	$t_{c(0.05,29)}$	Parameter	$\bar{x}$	SDV	$\dfrac{t_c SDV}{\sqrt{N}}$
30	2.045	Fault count	43836.1	4151.29	1549.94

Reliability Evaluation

Reliability of SOC reflects the probability of failure free during the run time period of the WS against heavy load of usage. A reliability model is deployed considering the recorded fault count against 1800 VU. The reliability model plays a vital role for this analysis. Among the research community, many reliability models are introduced that have different methodology of implementation for the evaluation of reliability metrics. In the present work we implement "Non Homogeneous Poison Process (NHPP) model of Goel and Okumoto" (Goel et al., 1979) due to its flexibility and applicability nature over many system testing. This model evaluates two metrics as:

mean value function $\alpha(t) = m(1- e^{-kt})$ (4)

and

failure intensity function $\beta(t) = mke^{-kt}$ (5)

where $\alpha(t)$ is the expected failure numbers in time t, $\beta(t)$ is the failure rate, 'm' is the observed average failure numbers and 'k' is the average rate of fault detection per day. In this case, the values are evaluated to be m= $\bar{x}$ i.e. m=43836.1 and k=FR i.e. k=0.35. So,

$\alpha(t) = 43836.1 (1- e^{-0.35t})$

$\beta(t) = 43836.1 . 0.35. e^{-0.35t}$

The evaluation of reliability is done over execution of calendar time so that the SOC based system can accurately reflect its usage. In this work time 't' is 30 days. So, $\alpha(t)$ and $\beta(t)$ is evaluated to be 43834.89 and 0.42 respectively.

The estimation of overall reliability metric for a SOC based system is defined as (Shooman, 2002; Rahmani et al., 2014):

$R = e^{-\lambda t}$ (6)

The Equation 6 represents the reliability of a system during the execution period of WS against a failure rate λ. It states that during the exposure period of the server, the SOC based system will show valid information and respond properly against the usage of massive load of users. In other case, the SOC based system will fail for which the HTTP rejection rate will arise. With the failure of HTTP request no SOAP processing will occur in between the WS, for which the user will not get the searchable information from SOC based system. The reliability metric is usually measured in the range of 0 to 1. A value near to 1 reflects strong reliability of service and a value near to 0 will reflect unreliable or moderate reliability of service against load of users. In this work, using Equation 6, the reliability against 1800 VU per day is evaluated to be R=0.66. That means, the SOC based system will respond 66% of its exposure period against a stress level of 1800 VU in one day. It will very if the number of VU is varied above 1800VU.

OVERALL ASSESSMENT OF QOS

The overall quality of the SOC based system in load balancing cluster based web server is shown in Table 9. The performance metrics of SOC based system increases proportionally with increase in stress level in the server side. With increased stress level, the massive numbers of requests are initiated by VU, which in turn causes SOAP processing in between WS, functional invocation, parameter processing through SQL query execution in the server side. For which the CPU and disk utilization, response time, throughput and hits/s increase gradually. The recorded test case responses against different level of VU are observed. The load balancing cluster based web server is not showing any transactional refusal for VU up to 1600. The mean CPU utilization for this stress level is recorded to be 35.45% with 0.29% of disk time utilization. For 1600 VU, the mean response time, throughput and hits/s of SOC along with load balancing web server is observed to be 3.44 s, 47272.44 bytes/s and 36.69 respectively. Here, the TF and FR are observed to be 0 up to 1600 VU. Above this stress level, an increasing FR of transaction is observed. These metrics increase gradually as there is an increase in VU level. The frequency table and histogram of fault count shows that highest density of failure is in the range of 40529.6 to 43753.2. At 95% confidence level, the population mean of failure count lies between 45386.04 and 42286.16. A highly reliable SOC based system along with load balancing cluster based web server is observed up to 1600 VU. It degrades gradually with 1800 and 2000 VU level, that means the reliability of SOC based system may be expected up to a specific stress level and then the reliability degrades gradually as there is an increase in stress level. For 1800 VU level in one day, the reliability metric is observed to be R=0.66. It states that the SOC based system expected to serve approximately about 66% of its service time against a massive level of 1800 VU in one day. In other cases, HTTP transactional failure will occur and user dissatisfactory results will arise. The occurrence of failure during the massive stress level of VU may be due the memory management heap error, SOAP parsing error in between WS, database connection pool error, and collision of requests in the server side. A massive failure of transaction is observed for 1800 and 2000 VU, for which the reliability of the system degrades. The decline of reliability with increased VU level may be due to memory release error, and data base engine error that are necessary for processing of HTTP request in the server side

Comparative Assessment

A comparative study, by considering the experimental results of the present work and the experimental results of the works of the other group of researcher's is given in Table 10. The Table highlights the observed results against different stresses of VU request over the web server. In the proposed study, for 100 VU stress level, the observed response time is 1.4 s, throughput is 10752.37 bytes/s and hits/s is

Table 9. Overall assessment for QoS

Experimental Observations	Results
Stability of SOC and load balancing cluster based web server	Observed up to 1600 VU
Performance metrics	Increases with increase in VU stress
Mean of performance metrics against 1800VU per day	39.13% of CPU utilization, 0.28% of disk time utilization, 25.28 s response time, 105729.1 bytes/s throughput, 60.27 hits/s, 126223.5 total transaction, 82387.4 transaction passed, 43836.1transaction failed
Minimum of performance metrics against 1800VU per day	37.26% of CPU utilization, 0.26% of disk time utilization, 14.3 s response time, 98290.53 bytes/s throughput, 58.08 hits/s, 122622 total transaction, 74527 transaction passed, 37306 transaction failed
Maximum of performance metrics against 1800VU per day	40.94% of CPU utilization, 0.3% of disk time utilization, 36.97 s response time, 112591.5 bytes/s throughput, 62.98 hits/s, 130191 total transaction, 88931transaction passed, 53424 transaction failed
Histogram and normal probability plot of performance metrics	Normal distribution
KS test of GoF for normality	Passes at 99% confidence level
TF and FR against 100, 300, 500, 1000, 1200, 1400, 1600 VU	NIL
TF and FR against 1800, 2000 VU	Observed and increases gradually
Histogram of fault count data sample	Highest density of failure is in the range of 40529.6 to 43753.2
$\bar{x}$ of fault count	43836.1
μ of fault count	43836.1 ± 1549.94 that is population mean of fault count lies between 45386.04 and 42286.16.
Goel Okumoto α (t); t=30th day	43834.89
Goel Okumoto β (t); t=30th day	0.42
Reliability of SOC up to 1600 VU per day	Strong reliability with R=1; Consumer will get valid searchable information without failure
Reliability of SOC against 1800 VU per day	Moderate reliability with R=0.66; There is a probability of user observable dissatisfactory information
Reliability of SOC against >1800 VU per day	Reliability degrades gradually as FR increases; There is a probability of frequently occurring user observable dissatisfactory information

5.48. There are no transaction failures of incoming request during this stress level. However, in the study of Kalita et al. (2011) that utilizes .NET framework, the 100 VU stress level highlights the response time as 49.859 s, throughput as 308799 bytes/s and hits/s as 8.963. In this case, the failure of transaction considering the incoming request is observed. In the study of Kalita et al. (2011) that utilizes Java Server Faces (JSF), the experimental outcome of 100 VU stress level highlights the response time as 112.34 s, throughput as 122645 bytes/s and hits/s as 2.524. In their methodology, the failure of transaction against incoming request was also observed. In the study of Medhi et al. (2014) that utilizes .NET framework, the 100 VU stress level over the system highlights the response time as 15.228 s, throughput as 16717.475 bytes/s and hits/s as 45.033. However, the failure of transaction against incoming request over the web server was not recorded in this case. Now, for the incoming stress of 100 VU at a time, if we observe and compare the response time of the proposed methodology, it is recorded to be 1.4 s against its counterpart 49.859 s (Kalita et al., 2011), 112.34 s (Kalita et al., 2011) and 15.228 s (Medhi et al., 2014). As such the response time of the proposed work is much better than the response time recorded in other author's work. Similar situation can be observed considering the system metrics of throughput and hits/s. In the proposed methodology, the throughput is recorded to be 10752.37 bytes/s against its counterpart 308799 bytes/s (Kalita et al., 2011), 122645 bytes/s (Kalita et al., 2011) and 16717.475 bytes/s (Medhi et al., 2014). As such the throughput of the proposed work is much better than the throughput recorded in the other author's work. The recorded hits/s of the proposed work is also compared with other authors work. In the proposed methodology, the hits/s for 100 VU stress level is recorded to be 5.48 against its counterpart 8.963 (Kalita et al., 2011), 45.033 (Medhi et al., 2014). But, in case of Kalita et al. (2011) that utilizes the JSF technique, the hits/s was evaluated to be 2.524 which is lower than recorded hits/s of the proposed work. This is observed because in their work the failure of transaction against incoming request was generated. As such number of hits to the web server decreases. However, comparatively the throughput and hits/s of the proposed work is much better than other author's work.

Though Kalita et al. (2011) had not performed the investigation against high load of different VU, we compare the results of the proposed work against the work of Medhi et al. (2014). At 1000 VU, the proposed study highlights that, the observed response time is 2.2 s, throughput is 26128.34 bytes/s and hits/s is 24.94. There is not any transaction failure of incoming request during this stress level. However, in the study of Medhi et al. (2014) that utilizes .NET framework, the 1000 VU stress level highlights the response time as 107.412 s, throughput as 16992.061 bytes/s and hits/s as 6.556. In this case, the failure of transaction considering the incoming request was observed. Now, for the incoming stress level of 1000 VU at a time, if we observe and compare the response time of the proposed methodology, it is recorded to be 2.2 s against its counterpart 107.412 s (Medhi et al., 2014). However, the throughput and hits/s of the proposed methodology is recorded to be 26128.34 bytes/s and 24.94 hits against 1000 VU which is comparatively higher than its counterpart 16992.061 bytes/s and 6.556 hits (Medhi et al., 2014). This is due to fact that during this stress level a failure of transaction against incoming request towards web server was observed, as such the throughput and hits/s in the work of Medhi et al. (2014) decreases.

Though we have not recorded the performance metrics against 1500 VU stress level to compare its counterpart Medhi et al. (2014), we can compare the performance metrics of 1600 VU stress level against 1500 VU of Medhi et al. (2014). In the proposed study, for the stress level of 1600 VU at a time over the system, the response time is recorded to be 3.44 s, throughput is 47272.44 bytes/s and hits/s is 36.69. There is no recorded transaction failure against the incoming request. However, in the study of Medhi et al. (2014), the 1500 VU stress level highlights the response time as 95.756 s, throughput as 17558.763 bytes/s and hits/s as 13.635. In this case, the failure of transaction considering the incoming request was observed. Now, if we observe and compare the performance metrics of 1600 VU stress level of the proposed work and 1500 VU stress level of the study carried out by Medhi et al. (2014), it is observed that the response time for 1600 VU is 3.44 s against its counterpart 95.756 s for 1500 VU (Medhi et al., 2014). However, the throughput and hits/s in the proposed methodology is recorded to be 47272.44 bytes/s and 36.69 hits against 1600 VU which is comparatively higher than its counterpart 17558.763 bytes/s and 13.635 hits at 1500 VU level (Medhi et al., 2014). This is due to the fact that during the 1500 stress level, a failure of transaction against incoming request towards web server was observed, as such the throughput and hits/s in the work of Medhi et al. (2014) decreases.

Though at the stress level of 1800 and 2000 VU, the proposed work highlights the transaction failure against incoming request towards web server, the response time during this stress level is observed to be

Table 10. A comparison of experimental result with other group of authors against different load of VU level

VU Stress Level	Parameter	Present Work	Kalita et al, 2011	Kalita et al, 2011	Medhi et al, 2014
		J2EE	.NET	JSF	.NET
50	RT	Not monitored	51.5	52.4	37.011
	THP		228690	112628	11389.726
	HTS		8	3.261	10.349
	TFO		No	Yes	No
100	RT	1.4	49.859	112.34	15.228
	THP	10752.37	308799	122645	16717.475
	HTS	5.48	8.963	2.524	45.033
	TFO	No	Yes	Yes	No
300	RT	1.9	Not monitored	Not monitored	Not monitored
	THP	12203.21			
	HTS	8.5			
	TFO	No			
500	RT	2.1	Not monitored	Not monitored	Not monitored
	THP	22880.97			
	HTS	21.46			
	TFO	No			
1000	RT	2.2	Not monitored	Not monitored	107.412
	THP	26128.34			16992.061
	HTS	24.94			6.556
	TFO	No			Yes
1200	RT	2.35	Not monitored	Not monitored	Not monitored
	THP	30099.004			
	HTS	29.68			
	TFO	No			
1400	RT	3.33	Not monitored	Not monitored	Not monitored
	THP	34174.78			
	HTS	34.13			
	TFO	No			
1500	RT	Not monitored	Not monitored	Not monitored	95.756
	THP				17558.763
	HTS				13.635
	TFO				Yes
1600	RT	3.44	Not monitored	Not monitored	Not monitored
	THP	47272.44			
	HTS	36.69			
	TFO	No			
1800	RT	25.85	Not monitored	Not monitored	Not monitored
	THP	102666.33			
	HTS	58.58			
	TFO	Yes			
2000	RT	51.74	Not monitored	Not monitored	Not monitored
	THP	100756.29			
	HTS	59.18			
	TFO	Yes			

RT: Response time per second, THP: Throughput in bytes per seconds, HTS: Hits per second, TFO: Transaction failure observed

much better than the last highest stress level observation carried out by Medhi et al. (2014). That means, in the proposed work the response time at 1800 and 2000 VU level is recorded to be 25.85 s and 51.74 s. But, in case of Medhi et al. (2014), the last response time metrics at 1500 VU level was recorded to be 95.756 s. This reveals that even at high stress of VU level and that too with generation of transaction failure, the response time of the SOC based system in load balancing cluster based web server can be assumed to be better than other methodology of system implementation.

From the overall assessment, it can be concluded that the performance metrics of the proposed methodology is better than the performance metrics of other authors work.

Additionally, a comparative study considering the percentage of HTTP failure in the server side for the reliability and stability estimation of the proposed work against other group of researchers is also performed and is given in Table 11. At 100 VU stress level, the proposed methodology does not highlight the percentage of HTTP failure. That means 0% occurrence of HTTP failure rate against incoming request toward the system. However, in case of Saddik (2006) that utilizes J2EE technique, the percentage of HTTP failure rate is recorded to be 60.28%. In case of Kalita et al. (2011) that utilizes .NET technique, the percentage of HTTP failure rate is recorded to be 50%. In case of Kalita et al. (2011) that utilizes J2EE technique, the percentage of HTTP failure rate is recorded to be 35%. However, in case of Medhi et al. (2014), the percentage of HTTP failure rate is recorded to be 0%. That means, for the stress level of 100 VU at a time, the stability and reliability of the proposed work comparatively same against its counterpart Medhi et al. (2014), but better than its counterpart Saddik (2005) and Kalita et al. (2011).

During the load test of 500 VU, though Kalita et al. (2011) had not recorded percentage of HTTP failure rate, we compare our proposed work against Saddik (2005) and Medhi et al. (2014). In case of Saddik (2006) that utilizes J2EE technique, the percentage of HTTP failure rate for 500 VU stress level is recorded to be 87.9%. However, in case of Medhi et al. (2014), the percentage of HTTP failure rate is recorded to be 0%. That means for the stress level of 500 VU at a time, the stability and reliability of

Table 11. A comparative study of the proposed work with other group of authors considering the HTTP transaction failure rate against different load of VU level.

VU Level	Recorded % of HTTP Failure Rate				
	Proposed Study	**Saddik, 2006**	**Kalita et al., 2011**	**Kalita et al., 2011**	**Medhi et al., 2014**
	J2EE	**J2EE**	**.NET**	**JSF**	**.NET**
50	Not monitored	Not monitored	0%	5%	0%
100	0%	60.28%	50%	35%	0%
300	0%	Not monitored	Not monitored	Not monitored	Not monitored
500	0%	87.9%	Not monitored	Not monitored	0%
1000	0%	92.06%	Not monitored	Not monitored	37%
1200	0%	Not monitored	Not monitored	Not monitored	Not monitored
1400	0%	Not monitored	Not monitored	Not monitored	Not monitored
1500	0%	Not monitored	Not monitored	Not monitored	75%
1600	0%	Not monitored	Not monitored	Not monitored	Not monitored
1800	34%	Not monitored	Not monitored	Not monitored	Not monitored
2000	41%	Not monitored	Not monitored	Not monitored	Not monitored

the proposed work is comparatively same against its counterpart Medhi et al. (2014), but better than its counterpart Saddik (2005).

During the load test of 1000 VU, though Kalita et al. (2011), had not recorded the percentage of HTTP failure, we compare the proposed work against Saddik (2005) and Medhi et al. (2014). In case of Saddik (2006) that utilizes J2EE technique, the percentage of HTTP failure rate for 1000 VU stress level is recorded to be 60.28%. In case of Medhi et al. (2014) that utilizes .NET technique, the percentage of HTTP failure rate for 1000 VU stress level is recorded to be 37%. In the proposed study, the system is not showing any percentage of HTTP failure rate for 1000 VU stress level. As such, the proposed methodology is better than other author's methodology during this stress level.

In the proposed study, a 0% of HTTP failure rate is observed up to 1600 VU stress level. That means the reliability and stability of the proposed work can be estimated up to 1600 VU and then HTTP failure rate generates. However, the first percentage of HTTP failure rate is observed to be 34% at 1800 VU stress level and then it increases proportionally. Although the other authors had not recorded the percentage of HTTP failure rate at 1800 stress level of VU, but evaluating their last observation of HTTP failure rate percentage that is 92.06% for 1000 VU (Saddik, 2006), 50% for 50 VU (Kalita et al., 2011) and 75% for 1500 VU stress level (Medhi et al., 2014), it can be easily concluded that the proposed SOC based system in cluster based web server is comparatively better in reliability and stability than the methodology of system implementation proposed by other authors.

CONCLUSION

In this work, we introduce a novel framework for evaluating the QoS considering a SOC based system for high performance through load balancing cluster based web server. We can conclude that the performance metrics increase proportionally with the increased stress level in the server side. The system is tested against different load level of users. The HTTP transaction failure is observed after a specific load point. The stability and reliability of the SOC based system along with load balancing cluster based Tomcat application server and MySQL database engine is observed up to 1600 VU. Beyond that, HTTP transaction failure occurs and increases gradually with increase in load in the server side. Degradation of reliability is observed for 1800 and 2000 VU. With increase in VU, numbers of request to the server increases for which number of SOAP request response transaction processing increases in between the WS. This in turn increases proportionally the server side CPU and disk time utilization along with response time, throughput and hits/s metrics. The distribution of the recorded data sample is normal. KS test of GoF for normality is observed. This reveals that population from where the data sample is extracted follows normal distribution.

From the study of the experimental results of the proposed works we can conclude that the quality evaluation framework considering SOC based system in load balancing cluster based web server is viable, acceptable and applicable. The experimental results and evaluation of the work will help the researchers and software developers to acquire an idea about the quality of service oriented system in load balancing cluster based web server. However, an in depth study is necessary to monitor the degradation of quality metrics against massive load of user considering different system key metrics along with the correlation in between them. The study of different test cases along with different data set sizes and combination of hardware and software specification that primarily imputes the overall quality of SOC based system for high performance of service over network based protocol is also necessary.

ACKNOWLEDGMENT

We are thankful to the All India Council of Technical Education (AICTE), Govt. of India, New Delhi for financial support towards the work (Grant No. 8023/BOR/RID/RPS (NER)-84/2010-2011, 31st March 2011).

REFERENCES

Agustin, J. L. H., & Barco, P. C. D. (2013). A model-driven approach to develop high performance web applications. *Journal of Systems and Software*, *86*(12), 3013–3023. doi:10.1016/j.jss.2013.07.028

Andreolini, M., Casalicchio, E., Colajanni, M., & Mambelli, M. (2004). A cluster-based web system providing differentiated and guaranteed services. *Cluster Computing*, *7*(1), 7–19. doi:10.1023/B:CLUS.0000003940.34740.be

Andreolini, M., Colajanni, M., Morselli, R. (2002). Performance study of dispatching algorithms in multi-tier web architectures. *ACM Performance Evaluation Review, 30*(2).

Apache Web Server. (2016). Retrieved on 21.1.2016, 2016 from, http://httpd.apache.org/docs/

Booth, D. (2004). *W3C working group note 11: Web services architecture*. World Wide Web Consortium (W3C). Retrieved from http://www.w3.org/TR/ws-arch/#whatis

Booth, D. (2004). *W3C working group note 11: Web services architecture*. World Wide Web Consortium (W3C). Retrieved from http://www.w3.org/TR/ws-arch/#stakeholder

Bora, A., & Bezboruah, T. (2014). Testing and Evaluation of a Hierarchical SOAP based Medical Web Service. *International Journal of Database Theory Application*, *7*(5), 145–160. doi:10.14257/ijdta.2014.7.5.11

Bora, A., Bhuyan, M. K., & Bezboruah, T. (2013). Investigations on Hierarchical Web service based on Java Technique. In *Proceedings of the World Congress on Engineering (WCE)*.

Bryhni, H., Klovning, E., & Kure, O. (2000). A Comparison of Load Balancing Techniques for Scalable Web Servers. *IEEE Network*, *14*(4), 58–64. doi:10.1109/65.855480

Cardellini, V., Casalicchio, E., Colajanni, M., & Tucci, S. (2001). Mechanisms for quality of service in web clusters. *Computer Networks*, *37*(6), 761–771. doi:10.1016/S1389-1286(01)00252-3

Çekyay, B., & Ozekici, S. (2014). *Reliability, MTTF and steady-state availability analysis of systems with exponential lifetimes. Appl. Math. Modell*. Elsevier; doi:10.1016/j.apm.2014.05.029

Chen, X., & Mohapatra, P. (2002). Performance Evaluation of Service Differentiating Internet Servers. *IEEE Transactions on Computers*, *51*(11), 1368–1375. doi:10.1109/TC.2002.1047760

Cluster Configuration. (2016). Retrieved on January 21, 2016 from, http://tomcat.apache.org/tomcat-5.5-doc/cluster-howto.html

Cohen, F. (2001). Performance Testing SOAP-Based Applications: Is your Web Service Production Ready? *IBM Developer Works*.

El Saddik, A. (2006). Performance measurement of Web Service based application. *IEEE Transactions on Instrumentation and Measurement*, 55(5), 1599–1605. doi:10.1109/TIM.2006.880288

Goel, A.L. (1985). Software Reliability Models: Assumptions, Limitations, and Applicability. *IEEE Transaction of Software Computing*, SE-11(12), 1411-1423. DOI: 10.1109/TSE.1985.232177

Goel, A. L., & Okumoto, K. (1979). A time dependent error detection rate model for software reliability and other performance measures. *IEEE Transactions on Reliability*, R-28(3), 206–211. doi:10.1109/TR.1979.5220566

Guo, J., & Bhuyan, L. N. (2006). Load Balancing in a Cluster-Based Web Server for Multimedia Applications. *IEEE Transactions on Parallel and Distributed Systems*, 17(11).

Hong, Y. S., No, J. H., & Kim, S. Y. (2006). DNS-based load-balancing in distributed web server systems. In *Proceedings of Fourth IEEE Workshop on Software Technologies for Future Embedded and Ubiquitous Systems*.

Hussain, A., Wenbi, R., Silva, A. L. D., Nadher, M., & Mudhisha, M. (2015). Health and emergency-care platform for the elderly and disabled people in the Smart City. *Journal of Systems and Software*, 110, 253–263. doi:10.1016/j.jss.2015.08.041

Ismail, H., Issa, K., Abdallah, K. (2015). Designing High Performance Web-Based Computing Services to Promote Telemedicine Database Management System. *IEEE Transaction on Services Computing*, 8(1).

Jain, R. (2012). The art of computer systems performance analysis: Technique for experimental Design, Measurement, Simulation and Modeling. *Wiley Professional Computing*, 462-465

Jiang, X., & Ji, S. (2014). E-Government Web Portal Adoption: A Service Level and Service Quality Perspective. In *Proceedings of 47th Hawaii International Conference on System Science*, (pp. 2179-2188). DOI doi:10.1109/HICSS.2014.275

Kalita, M., & Bezboruah, T. (2011). Investigation on performance testing and evaluation of PReWebD: A. NET technique for implementing web application. *IET Software*, 5(4), 357–365. doi:10.1049/iet-sen.2010.0139

Kalita, M., & Bezboruah, T. (2012). Investigations on implementation of web applications with different techniques. *IET Software*, 6(6), 474–478. doi:10.1049/iet-sen.2011.0136

Kalita, M., Khanikar, S., & Bezboruah, T. (2011). Investigation on performance testing and evaluation of PReWebN: A JAVA technique for implementing web application. *IET Software*, 5(5), 434–444. doi:10.1049/iet-sen.2011.0030

Matthew, M. C., Laskey, K., McCabe, F., Brown, P., & Metz, R. (2005). *Reference Model for Service Oriented Architectures. Published on theinternet*. OASIS Working Draft.

Medhi, S., & Bezboruah, T. (2014). Investigations on implementation of e-ATM Web Services based on. NET technique. *International Journal of Information Retrieval Research*, 4(2), 42–51.

Medhi, S., Bora, A., & Bezboruah, T. (2016). Security Impact on e-ATM Windows Communication Foundation Services using Certificate based Authentication and Protection: An implementation of Message Level Security based on. NET Technique. *International Journal of Information Retrieval Research*, *6*(3), 37–51. doi:10.4018/IJIRR.2016070103

Menasce, D. A., & Almeida, V. A. F. (2002). *Capacity Planning for Web Services - Metrics, Models and Methods*. Prentice Hall.

Mercury Load runner tutorial - Mercury Roadrunner Quick Start. (n.d.). Available online: https://qageek.files.wordpress.com/2007/05/loadrunner_tutorial.pdf

Misra, S., Akman, I., & Colomo-Palacios, R. (2012). Framework for evaluation and validation of software complexity measures. *IET Software*, *6*(4), 323–334. doi:10.1049/iet-sen.2011.0206

Mod jk connector. (2016). Retrieved on 24.1.2016 from, https://tomcat.apache.org/tomcat-3.3-doc/mod_jk-howto.html

Mosberger, D., & Jin, T. (1997). Httperf a tool to measure web server performance.*InProceedings of USENIX Symposium on Internet Technologies and Systems*, (pp. 59 – 76).

O'Reilly, T. (2007). What is Web 2.0: Design patterns and business models for the next generation of software. *Communications in Statistics*, *65*(1), 17.

Orallo, E. H., & Carbo, J. V. (2009). Web server performance analysis using histogram workload models. *Computer Networks*, *53*(15), 2727–2739. doi:10.1016/j.comnet.2009.06.005

Pacifici, G., Spreitzer, M., Tantawi, A. N., & Youssef, A. (2005). Performance Management for Cluster-Based Web Services. *IEEE Journal on Selected Areas in Communications*, *23*(12), 2333–2343. doi:10.1109/JSAC.2005.857208

Pal, S. K. (1998). *Statistics for Geo scientists, techniques and applications*. Concept Publishing Company.

Palmieri, F., Ficco, M., Pardi, S., & Castiglione, A. (2016). A cloud-based architecture for emergency management and First responders localization in smart city environments. *Computers & Electrical Engineering*, 1–21. doi:10.1016/j.compeleceng.2016.02.012

Palviainen, M., Evesti, A., & Ovaska, E. (2011). The reliability estimation, prediction and measuring of component-based software. *Journal of Systems and Software*, *84*(6), 1054–1070. doi:10.1016/j.jss.2011.01.048

Peiris, C., Mulder, D., Cicoria, S., Bahree, A., & Pathak, N. (2007). *Pro WCF: Practical Microsoft SOA Implementation*. Apress Press.

Piro, G., Cianci, I., Grieco, L. A., Boggia, G., & Camarda, P. (2014). Information centric services in Smart Cities. *Journal of Systems and Software*, *88*, 169–188. doi:10.1016/j.jss.2013.10.029

Rahmani, M., Azadmanesh, A., & Siy, H. (2014). Architectural reliability analysis of framework-intensive applications: A web service case study. *Journal of Systems and Software*, *94*, 186–201. doi:10.1016/j.jss.2014.03.070

Sharifian, S., Motamedi, S. A., & Akbari, M. K. (2011). A predictive and probabilistic load-balancing algorithm for cluster-based web Servers. *Applied Soft Computing, 11*(1), 970–981. doi:10.1016/j.asoc.2010.01.017

Shirazi, B. A., Hurson, A. R., & Kavi, K. M. (1995). *Scheduling and Load Balancing in Parallel and Distributed Systems.* CS Press.

Shooman, M. L. (2002). *Reliability of Computer Systems and Networks: Fault Tolerance, Analysis, and Design.* New York: John Wiley & Sons. doi:10.1002/047122460X

Singh, H. K., & Bezboruah, T. (2015). Performance Metrics of a Customized Web Application Developed for Monitoring Sensor Data. In *Proceedings of the IEEE 2nd International Conference on Recent Trends in Information Systems (ReTIS).* doi:10.1109/ReTIS.2015.7232870

SOAP. (n.d.). Retrieved online on 31.1.2016, Available at http://www.w3.org/TR/soap12-part1/

Spiegel, M.R. (2000). *Theory and problems of probability and statistics.* McGraw-Hill Book Company.

Tekli, J.M., Damiani, E., Chbeir, R., & Gianini, G. (2012). SOAP Processing Performance and Enhancement. *IEEE Transaction on Services Computing, 5*(3).

Tewoldeberhan, T., & Janssen, M. (2008). Simulation-based experimentation for designing reliable and efficient Web service orchestrations in supply chains. *Electronic Commerce Research and Applications, 7*(1), 82–92. doi:10.1016/j.elerap.2006.11.007

Tomcat. (2016). Retrieved on 20.1.2016, from http://tomcat.apache.org/

Urgaonkar, B., Shenoy, P., & Roscoe, T. (2007). Resource overbooking and application profiling in shared internet hosting platforms. *ACM Transactions on Internet Technology.*

Vercauteren, T., Aggarwal, P., Wang, X., & Li, T. H. (2007). Hierarchical Forecasting of web server workload using sequential Monte Carlo training. *IEEE Transactions on Signal Processing, 55*(4), 1286–1297. doi:10.1109/TSP.2006.889401

WSDL. (n.d.). Retrieved online on 31.1.2016, Available at http://www.w3.org/TR/wsdl20-primer/

Zhang, Z., Fan, W. (2008). Stochastics and Statistics Web server load balancing: A queueing analysis. *European Journal of Operational Research, 186,* 681–693. DOI:10.1016/j.ejor.2007.02.011

Zheng, Y., & Lyu, M. R. (2014). Investigating QoS of real-world web services. *IEEE Transaction Service Computing, 7*(1), 32–39. doi:10.1109/TSC.2012.34

Zhu, H., Tang, H., & Yang, T. (2001). Demand-driven service differentiation for cluster based network servers. *Proceedings - IEEE INFOCOM.*

Compilation of References

Abbadi, I. M., & Muntaha, A. (2012). A framework for establishing trust in cloud. *Computers & Electrical Engineering*, *38*(5), 1073–1087. doi:10.1016/j.compeleceng.2012.06.006

Abdelhaq, M., Hassan, R., & Ismail, M. (2014). Performance evaluation of mobile ad hoc networks under flooding-based attacks. *International Journal of Communication Systems*, *27*(12), 4328–4345. doi:10.1002/dac.2615

Abu-Shanab, E., & Yamin, E. (2014). RFID utilization in public university libraries in Jordan. *International Journal of Digital Library Systems*, *4*(2), 29–43. doi:10.4018/IJDLS.2014070103

Acampora, G., Cook, J., Rashidi, P., & Vasilakos, V. (2013). A Survey on Ambient Intelligence in Health Care. *Proceedings of the IEEE*, *101*(12), 2470–2494. doi:10.1109/JPROC.2013.2262913 PMID:24431472

Adam, H., Yanmaz, E., & Bettstetter, C. (2014). Medium Access with Adaptive Relay Selection in Cooperative Wireless Networks. *IEEE Transactions o Mobile Computing*, *13*(9), 2042-2057.

Adarbah, H. Y., Ahmad, S., & Duffy, A. (2015). Impact of noise and interference on probabilistic broadcast schemes in mobile ad-hoc networks. *Computer Networks*, *88*, 178–186. doi:10.1016/j.comnet.2015.06.013

Afyf, A., Bellarbi, L., Riouch, F., Achour, A., Errachid, A., & Sennouni, M. A. (2015). Antenna for Wireless Body Area Network (WBAN) Applications Flexible Miniaturized UWB CPW II- shaped Slot. In *IEEE Third International Workshop on RFID And Adaptive Wireless Sensor Networks* (pp. 52–56).

Afyf, A., Bellarbi, L., Riouch, F., Achour, A., Errachid, A., & Sennouni, M. A. (2015). Flexible Miniaturized UWB CPW II- shaped Slot. In *IEEE Third International Workshop on RFID And Adaptive Wireless Sensor Networks* (pp. 52–56).

Agarwal, S. K., & Rishiwal, A. (2013). Fallout of different routing structures for mobility patterns in large ad-hoc network. In *Proceedings of IEEE Confluence 2013, The Next Generation Information Technology Summit, 4th International Conference*.

Agustin, J. L. H., & Barco, P. C. D. (2013). A model-driven approach to develop high performance web applications. *Journal of Systems and Software*, *86*(12), 3013–3023. doi:10.1016/j.jss.2013.07.028

Ahamad, S. S., Sastry, V., & Udgata, S. K. (2014). A secure and optimized proximity mobile payment framework with formal verification. *International Journal of E-Services and Mobile Applications*, *6*(1), 66–92. doi:10.4018/ijesma.2014010104

Ahmed, N. (2012). Widespread adoption of RFID technology. In M. Khan & A. Ansari (Eds.), *Handbook of research on industrial informatics and manufacturing intelligence: Innovations and solutions* (pp. 297–314). Hershey, PA: IGI Global. doi:10.4018/978-1-4666-0294-6.ch013

Aich, Sen, Dash, & Dehuri. (2015). A Symmetric Key Cryptosystem Using DNA Sequence with OTP Key. *Advances in Intelligent Systems and Computing*, 207 – 215.

Aijaz, A., & Aghvami, A. H. (2015). Cognitive machine-to-machine communications for Internet-of-Things: A protocol stack perspective. *IEEE Internet Things Journal*, 2(2), 103–112. doi:10.1109/JIOT.2015.2390775

Ajana, M. E., Harroud, H., Boulmalf, M., & Elkoutbi, M. (2011). FlexRFID middleware in the supply chain: Strategic values and challenges. *International Journal of Mobile Computing and Multimedia Communications*, 3(2), 19–32. doi:10.4018/jmcmc.2011040102

Akkaya, K., & Newell, A. (2009). Self-deployment of sensors for maximized coverage in underwater acoustic sensor networks. *Computer Communications*, 32(7-10), 1233–1244. doi:10.1016/j.comcom.2009.04.002

Akyildiz, F., Weilian, Y., Sankarasubramaniam, & Cayirci, E. (2002). A survey on sensor networks. IEEE Communications Magazine, 40(8), 102-114.

Akyildiz, F., & Mehmet, V. (2010). *Wireless Sensor Networks*. New York, NY: John Wiley & Sons, Inc. doi:10.1002/9780470515181

Akyildiz, I. F., Lee, W. Y., Vuran, M. C., & Mohanty, S. (2006). NeXt generation/dynamic spectrum access/cognitive radio wireless networks: A survey. *Computer Networks, Elsevier*, 50(13), 2127–2159. doi:10.1016/j.comnet.2006.05.001

Akyildiz, I., Pompili, D., & Melodia, T. (2005). Underwater acoustic sensor networks: Research challenges. *Ad Hoc Networks*, 3(3), 257–279. doi:10.1016/j.adhoc.2005.01.004

Alagheband, M. R., & Aref, M. R. (2013). Unified privacy analysis of new-found RFID authentication protocols. *Security and Communication Networks*, 6(8), 999–1009. doi:10.1002/sec.650

Alampalayam, S. K., & Natsheh, E. F. (2008). Multivariate fuzzy analysis for mobile ad hoc network threat detection. *International Journal of Business Data Communications and Networking*, 4(3), 1–30. doi:10.4018/jbdcn.2008070101

Alazawi, Z., Abdljabar, M. B., & Altowaijri, S. (2012). ICDMS: An Intelligent Cloud Based Disaster Management System for Vehicular Networks. *LNCS, 7266*, 40–56.

Alden, A., & Ohno, T. (1992). Single foreplane high power rectenna. *Electronics Letters*, 21(11), 1072–1073. doi:10.1049/el:19920679

Alfaro-Ponce, M., Arguelles, A., & Chairez, I. (2014). Continuous neural identifier for certain nonlinear systems with time in the input signal. *Neural Networks*, 60, 53–66. doi:10.1016/j.neunet.2014.07.002 PMID:25150629

Ali, Lor, Benouaer, & Rio. (2009). *Cooperative Leader Election Algorithm for Master/Slave Mobile Ad Hoc Network*. 2nd IFIP Wireless Days (WD), Paris, France.

Ali, M., & Jawandhiya, P. (2012). Security aware routing protocols for mobile ad hoc networks. In K. Lakhtaria (Ed.), *Technological advancements and applications in mobile ad-hoc networks: Research trends* (pp. 264–289). Hershey, PA: IGI Global. doi:10.4018/978-1-4666-0321-9.ch016

Ali, M., Khan, S. U., & Vasilakos, A. V. (2015). Security in cloud computing: Opportunities and challenges. *Inf Sci, 305*, 357–383. doi:10.1016/j.ins.2015.01.025

Aliouat, Z., & Aliouat, M. (2012). M Efficient Management of Energy Budget for PEGASIS Routing Protocol. In *Proceedings of 6th IEEE Conference on Sciences of Electronics, Technologies of Information and Telecommunications.* doi:10.1109/SETIT.2012.6481966

Alipour, S., Parvaresh, F., Ghajari, H., & Kimball, D. F. (2010). Propagation Characteristics for a 60 GHz Wireless Body Area Network (WBAN). In *The 2010 Military Communications Conference - Unclassified Program - Waveforms and Signal Processing Track* (pp. 719–723).

Al-Karaki, J., & Kamal, A. (2004). Routing techniques in wireless sensor networks: A survey. *IEEE Wireless Communications*, *11*(6), 6–28. doi:10.1109/MWC.2004.1368893

Alomainy, A., Hao, Y., & Pasveer, F. (2007). Numerical and experimental evaluation of a compact sensor antenna for healthcare devices. *IEEE Transactions on Biomedical Circuits and Systems*, *1*(4), 242–249. doi:10.1109/TB-CAS.2007.913127 PMID:23852005

Alomainy, A., Sani, A., Rahman, A., Santas, J. G., & Hao, Y. (2009). Transient characteristics of wearable antennas and radio propagation channels for ultrawideband body-centric wireless communications. *IEEE Transactions on Antennas and Propagation*, *57*(4), 875–884. doi:10.1109/TAP.2009.2014588

Alonso-Betanzos, A., Guijarro-Berdiñas, B., Moret-Bonillo, V., & López-Gonzalez, S. (1995). The NST-EXPERT project: The need to evolve. *Artificial Intelligence in Medicine*, *7*(4), 297–313. doi:10.1016/0933-3657(95)00007-S PMID:7581626

Al-Quteyri. (2010). *Security and Privacy of Intelligent VANET*. Computational Intelligence and Modern Heuristics.

Alshabtat, A., & Dong, L. (2011). Low Latency Routing Algorithm for Unmanned Aerial Vehicles Ad-Hoc Networks. *Iranian Journal of Electrical and Computer Engineering*, *6*(1), 48–54.

AlShawi, S., Yan, L., Pan, W., & Luo, B. (2012). A Fuzzy-Gossip routing protocol for an energy efficient wireless sensor networks. In *Proceedings of IEEE conference on Sensors*. doi:10.1109/ICSENS.2012.6411162

Altayeb, M., & Mahgoub, I. (2013). A survey of vehicular ad hoc networks routing protocols. *International Journal of Innovation and Applied Studies*, *3*(3), 829–846.

Altman & Jimenez. (2002). *NS for Beginners*. Retrieved from http://www-sop.inria.fr/maestro/personnel/Eitan.Altman/COURS-NS/n3.pdf

Altman, D. G., & Bland, J. M. (2008). Design, Analysis, and Interpretation of Method Comparison-Studies. *AACN Advanced Critical Care*, *19*(2), 223–234. PMID:18560291

Alwidian, S. A., Ababneh, I. M., & Yassein, M. O. (2013). Neighborhood-based route discovery protocols for mobile ad hoc networks. *International Journal of Mobile Computing and Multimedia Communications*, *5*(3), 68–87. doi:10.4018/jmcmc.2013070105

Al-Yamin, A. M., Harb, K., & Abduljauwad, S. (2013). Industrial Wireless Sensor Networks in the perspective of Diversity and Spectral Efficiency. In *Proceeding of 11ᵗʰ IEEE international Conference on Communications*.

Amal, A., Larbi, B., & Anouar, A. (2016). Miniaturized Wideband Flexible CPW Antenna with Hexagonal Ring Slots for Early Breast Cancer Detection. In S. S. M. Singapore (Ed.), *Ubiquitous Networking* (pp. 211–222). Springer. doi:10.1007/978-981-287-990-5_17

Amine, R., Khalid, B., Elhoussaine, Z., & Mohammed, O. (2014). Energy consumption balancing in wireless sensors networks. In *Proceedings of the 4th IEEE International Conference on Multimedia Computing and Systems*. doi:10.1109/ICMCS.2014.6911348

Amini, M., Otondo, R. F., Janz, B. D., & Pitts, M. G. (2007). Simulation modeling and analysis: A collateral application and exposition of RFID technology. *Production and Operations Management*, *16*(5), 586–598. doi:10.1111/j.1937-5956.2007.tb00282.x

An experience of health technology assessment in new models of care for subjects with Parkinson's disease by means of a new wearable device. (2008). *Telemed J E Health*, 467–472.

Anam, Sakib, Hossain, & = Dahal. (2010). Review on the Advancements of DNA Cryptography. *IJARCS*, *3*.

Ando, T., Tsukahara, R., Seki, M., & Fujie, M. G. (2012). A Haptic Interface "Force Blinker 2" for Navigation of the Visually Impaired. *Industrial Electronics. IEEE Transactions on, 59*(11), 4112–4119. doi:10.1109/TIE.2011.2173894

Andreolini, M., Colajanni, M., Morselli, R. (2002). Performance study of dispatching algorithms in multi-tier web architectures. *ACM Performance Evaluation Review, 30*(2).

Andreolini, M., Casalicchio, E., Colajanni, M., & Mambelli, M. (2004). A cluster-based web system providing differentiated and guaranteed services. *Cluster Computing, 7*(1), 7–19. doi:10.1023/B:CLUS.0000003940.34740.be

Andriole, S. J. (2009). Enterprise investing in radio frequency identification (RFID): The Oracle case. In S. Andriole (Ed.), *Technology due diligence: Best practices for chief information officers, venture capitalists, and technology vendors* (pp. 191–209). Hershey, PA: IGI Global. doi:10.4018/978-1-60566-018-9.ch007

Apache Web Server. (2016). Retrieved on 21.1.2016, 2016 from, http://httpd.apache.org/docs/

Arif, S., Olariu, S., Wang, J., Yan, G., Yang, W., & Khalil, I. (2012). Datacenter at the airport: Reasoning about time-dependent parking lot occupancy. *IEEE Transactions on Parallel and Distributed Systems, 23*(11), 2067–2080. doi:10.1109/TPDS.2012.47

Arjmandi, H., & Lahouti, F. (2011). Resource Optimized Distributed Source Coding for Complexity Constrained Data Gathering Wireless Sensor Networks. *IEEE Sensors Journal, 11*(9), 2094–2101. doi:10.1109/JSEN.2011.2109947

Arrawatia, M., Baghini, M. S., & Kumar, G. (2011), RF energy harvesting system from cell towers in 900MHz band. *Proceedings of National Conference on Communications* (pp. 1 – 5). doi:10.1109/NCC.2011.5734733

Arrawatia, M., Baghini, M. S., & Kumar, G. (2016). Broadband bent triangular omnidirectional antenna for RF energy harvesting. *IEEE Antennas and Wireless Propagation Letters, 15*, 36–39.

Arshad, M. R. (2009). Recent advancement in sensor technology for underwater applications. *Indian Journal of Marine Sciences, 38*(3), 267–273.

Asadnia, M., Kottapalli, A., Tan, C., Woo, M., Lang, J., Miao, J., & Triantafyllou, M. (2011). *Bio-inspired MEMS Pressure and Flow Sensors for Underwater Navigation and Object Imaging*. Retrieved 25 December 2015, from http://web.mit.edu/towtank/www/posters/MEMS_bldg5display.pdf

Asadnia, M., Kottapalli, A. G. P., Shen, Z., Miao, J. M., & Triantafyllou, M. S. (2013). Flexible and surface mountable piezoelectric sensor arrays for underwater sensing in marine vehicles. *IEEE Sensors Journal, 13*(10), 3918–3925. doi:10.1109/JSEN.2013.2259227

Asadnia, M., Kottapalli, A., Haghighi, R., Cloitre, A., Alvarado, P., Miao, J., & Triantafyllou, M. (2015). MEMS sensors for assessing flow-related control of an underwater biomimetic robotic stingray. *Bioinspiration & Biomimetics, 10*(3), 036008. doi:10.1088/1748-3190/10/3/036008 PMID:25984934

Aschenbruck, N., Ernst, R., Gerhards-Padilla, E., & Schwamborn, M. (2010). BonnMotion - a Mobility Scenario Generation and Analysis Tool. In *3rd International ICST Conference on Simulation Tools and Techniques (SIMUTools)*, Brussels, Belgium. doi:10.4108/ICST.SIMUTOOLS2010.8684

Ashford, W. (2012). *Will this be the year TPM comes of age?*. Retrieved from: http://www.computerweekly.com/news/2240157874/Analysis-2012-Will-this-be-the-year-TPM-finallycomes-of-age

Au, A. W. S., Chen, F., Valaee, S., Reyes, S., Sorour, S., Markowitz, S. N., & Eizenman, M. et al. (2013). Indoor Tracking and Navigation Using Received Signal Strength and Compressive Sensing on a Mobile Device. *Mobile Computing. IEEE Transactions on, 12*(10), 2050–2062. doi:10.1109/TMC.2012.175

Auter. (2004). The Advantages of Elliptic Curve Cryptography For Wireless Security. *IEEE Wireless Communications*.

Automatic recognition of postures and activities in stroke patients. (2009). In IEEE Eng Med Biol Soc (pp. 2200–2203).

Awerbuch, Curtmola, Holmer, Nita-Rotaru, & Rubens. (2000). Mitigating Byzantine Attacks in Ad Hoc Wireless Networks. *ACM MobiCom*.

Ayu, M. A., Ahmad, B. I., & Mantoro, T. (2016). Managing students' attendance using NFC-enabled mobile phones. In N. Mohamed, T. Mantoro, M. Ayu, & M. Mahmud (Eds.), *Critical socio-technical issues surrounding mobile computing* (pp. 184–203). Hershey, PA: IGI Global. doi:10.4018/978-1-4666-9438-5.ch009

Azada, P., & Sharma, V. (2013). Cluster Head Selection in Wireless Sensor Networks under Fuzzy Environment. ISRN Sensor Networks, 2013(2013), 1-9. doi:10.1155/2013/909086

Azad, A. K., Kamruzzaman, J., & Karmakar, N. C. (2012). Wireless sensor network protocols applicable to RFID system. In N. Chandra Karmakar (Ed.), *Chipless and conventional radio frequency identification: Systems for ubiquitous tagging* (pp. 251–284). Hershey, PA: IGI Global. doi:10.4018/978-1-4666-1616-5.ch013

Aziz, B., & Nafkha, A. (2014). Implementation of blind cyclostationary feature detector for cognitive radios using USRP. In *Proceedings of 21st International Conference on Telecommunications (ICT)*. doi:10.1109/ICT.2014.6845077

Azmi, N., & Kamarudin, L. M. (2014). Interfernce issues and mitigitaion method in WSN 2.4GHz ISM band: A survey. In *Proceeding of IEEE 2nd International conference on Electronic design* (ICED).

Badawy, A., & Khattab, T. (2014). A novel peak search & save cyclostationary feature detection algorithm. In *Proceedings of Wireless Communications and Networking Conference (WCNC)*. doi:10.1109/WCNC.2014.6951976

Bagchi S & Rakshit M. (2014). Cognitive Radio: A Non-parametric Approach by Approximating Signal Plus Noise Distribution by Kaplansky Distributions in the Context of Spectrum Hole Search. *Smart Innovation, Systems and Technologies, 28*, 553-559.

Bagchi, S. (2014). Cognitive Radio: Spectrum Sensing Under Unknown Signal and Noise Distributions. *2014 Sixth International Conference on Computational Intelligence and Communication Networks*. IEEE Computer Society. doi:10.1109/CICN.2014.101

Bahrami, M., & Singhal, M. (2016). A light -weight Data Privacy schema for cloud based Databases. *International Conference on Computing, Networking and Communications*. doi:10.1109/ICCNC.2016.7440634

Bahr, W., & Price, B. (2016). Radio frequency identification and its application in e-commerce. In I. Lee (Ed.), *Encyclopedia of e-commerce development, implementation, and management* (pp. 1841–1857). Hershey, PA: IGI Global. doi:10.4018/978-1-4666-9787-4.ch130

Baker, S. E., Cai, W., Lasseter, T. L., Weidkamp, K. P., & Hamers, R. J. (2002). Covalently bonded adducts of DNA oligonucleotide with single wall carbon nanotube: Synthesis and hybridization. *Nano Letters, 2*, 1413–1417. doi:10.1021/nl025729f

Bal, M. (2014). Industrial Applications of collaborative Wireless Sensor Networks: A Survey. *IEEE 23rd International Symposium on Industrial Electronics*. doi:10.1109/ISIE.2014.6864830

Balanis, C. A. (2005). *Antenna Theory* (3rd ed.). New York: John Wiley & Sons.

Balanis, C. A. (2005). *Antenna Theory Analysis and Design* (3rd ed.). John Wiley Sons, Inc.

Baldini, G., Guiliani, R., Capriglione, D., & Sithamparanathan, K. (2012). A Practical Demonstration of Spectrum Sensing for WiMAX Based on Cyclostationary Features. In *Foundation of Cognitive Radio Systems*. Available from: http://www.intechopen.com/books/foundation-of-cognitive-radio-systems/a-practical-demonstration-of-spectrum-sensing-for-wimax-based-on-cyclostationary-features

Banerjee, A., Chakrabarti, C., & Chakraborty, A. (2014). A New Approach to Trace the Behaviour Pattern of Nodes in Delay Tolerant Network. In Proceedings of the ICCACCS 2014, 229-237. Kolkata, India: Springer.

Banerjee, A., Chakrabarti, C., Chakraborty, A., & Chakrabarti, S. (2014). A Comparative Survey on Detection and Prevention of Different Routing Attacks on MANET. In Proceedings of the IEMCON-2014. Kolkata, India: Elsevier Publications.

Banerjee, A., Chakraborty, A. & Chakrabarti, C. (2014). Survey on Analysis of Damage and Need Assessment in Post-Disaster Environment. *International Journal of Innovative Research in Science, Engineering and Technology, 3*(12), 18274-18279.

Bansal, S., & Baker, M. (2003). *Observation-based Cooperation Enforcement in Ad-hoc Networks*. arxiv:cs/0307012v2

Baqar, M. A., Aldabbas, H., Alwadan, T., Alfawair, M., & Janicke, H. (2014). Review of security in VANETs and MANETs. In A. Amine, O. Mohamed, & B. Benatallah (Eds.), *Network security technologies: Design and applications* (pp. 1–27). Hershey, PA: IGI Global. doi:10.4018/978-1-4666-4789-3.ch001

Barlian, A. A., Narain, R., Li, J. T., Quance, C. E., Ho, A. C., Mukundan, V., & Pruitt, B. L. (2006). Piezoresistive MEMS Underwater Shear Stress Sensors. In *Proceedings of 19th IEEE International Conference on Micro Electro Mechanical Systems (MEMS 2006)* (pp. 626-629). doi:10.1109/MEMSYS.2006.1627877

Barrado, C., Messeguer, R., Lopez, J., Pastor, E., Santamaria, E., & Royo, P. (2010). Wildfire monitoring using a mixed air-ground mobile network. *IEEE Pervasive Computing / IEEE Computer Society [and] IEEE Communications Society, 9*(4), 24–32. doi:10.1109/MPRV.2010.54

Barratt, M., & Choi, T. (2007). Mandated RFID and institutional responses: Cases of decentralized business units. *Production and Operations Management, 16*(5), 569–585. doi:10.1111/j.1937-5956.2007.tb00281.x

Basha, A., Ravela, S., & Rus, D. (2008). Mode-based monitoring for early warning flood detection. In Proceedings of ACM Sensors and Systems.

Batchelor, J. C. (2008). A dual band belt antenna. In *International Workshop on Antenna Technology: Small Antennas and Novel Metamaterial* (pp. 374–377).

Beeharee, A. K., & Steed, A. (2006). *A natural wayfinding exploiting photos in pedestrian navigation systems*. Paper presented at the 8th conference on Human-computer interaction with mobile devices and services, Helsinki, Finland. doi:10.1145/1152215.1152233

Bekmezci, İ., Sahingoz, O., & Temel, Ş. (2013). Flying Ad-Hoc Networks (FANETs): A survey. *Ad Hoc Networks, 11*(3), 1254–1270. doi:10.1016/j.adhoc.2012.12.004

Bellotti, F., Berta, R., Margarone, M., & de Gloria, A. (2008). oDect: An RFID-based object detection API to support applications development on mobile devices. *Software: Practice and Experience, 38*(12), 1241–1259. doi:10.1002/spe.864

Belza, B., Steele, B., Hunziker, J., Lakshminaryan, S., Holt, L., & Buchner, D. (2001). Correlates of physical activity in chronic obstructive pulmonary disease. In Nurs Res (pp. 195–202). doi:10.1097/00006199-200107000-00003

Bendoly, E., Citurs, A., & Konsynski, B. (2007). Internal infrastructural impacts on RFID perceptions and commitment: Knowledge, operational procedures, and information-processing standards. *Decision Sciences*, *38*(3), 423–449. doi:10.1111/j.1540-5915.2007.00165.x

Benes, E., Gröschl, M., Seifert, F., & Pohl, A. (1998). Comparison Between BAW and SAW Sensor Principles. *IEEE Transactions on Ultrasonics, Ferroelectrics, and Frequency Control*, *45*(5), 1314–1330. doi:10.1109/58.726458 PMID:18244294

Benssalah, M., Djeddou, M., & Drouiche, K. (2014). Security enhancement of the authenticated RFID security mechanism based on chaotic maps. *Security and Communication Networks*, *7*(12), 2356–2372. doi:10.1002/sec.946

Bernardes, J., Moura, C., de Sa, J. P., & Leite, L. P. (1991). The Porto system for automated cardiotocographic signal analysis. *Journal of Perinatal Medicine*, *19*(1-2), 61–65. doi:10.1515/jpme.1991.19.1-2.61 PMID:1870058

Bernstein, J., Finberg, S., Houston, K., Niles, L., Chen, H., Cross, L., & Udayakumar, K. et al. (1997). Micromachined high frequency ferroelectric sonar transducers. *IEEE Transactions on Ultrasonics, Ferroelectrics, and Frequency Control*, *44*(5), 960–969. doi:10.1109/58.655620

Bhat, A., Bloomquist, C., Ahn, J., Kim, Y., & Kim, D. (2009). Thermal Transpiration Based Micro-Scale Pumping and Power Generation Devices. In *Proceedings of 7th International Energy Conversion Engineering Conference*. doi:10.2514/6.2009-4561

Bhattacharya, M., & Wamba, S. F. (2015). A conceptual framework of RFID adoption in retail using TOE framework. *International Journal of Technology Diffusion*, *6*(1), 1–32. doi:10.4018/IJTD.2015010101

Bhoir, S., & Vidhate, A. (2013, February). A Modified Leader Election Algorithm for Manet. *International Journal on Computer Science and Engineering*, *5*(2), 78–86.

Bigwood, G., & Henderson, T. (2011). Ironman: Using social networks to add incentives and reputation to opportunistic networks. In *Proceedings of the IEEE International Conference on Privacy, Security, Risk, and Trust, and IEEE International Conference on Social Computing*, (pp. 65-72). Boston, MA: IEEE. doi:10.1109/PASSAT/SocialCom.2011.60

Billings, S. A. (2013). *Nonlinear System Identification: NARMAX methods in the time, Frequency, andSaptio-Temporal Domains*. Chichester, UK: Wiley. doi:10.1002/9781118535561

Bio-inspired MEMS sensors for underwater sensing applications. (2014). *Center for Environmental Sensing and Modeling*. Retrieved 25 December 2015, from http://censam.mit.edu/research/Pages/Bio-inspired%20MEMS%20sensors%20 for%20underwater%20sensing%20applications.aspx

Bisoy, S. K., & Pattnaik, P. K. (2016). Transmission control protocol for mobile ad hoc network. In P. Mallick (Ed.), *Research advances in the integration of big data and smart computing* (pp. 22–49). Hershey, PA: IGI Global. doi:10.4018/978-1-4666-8737-0.ch002

BitLocker Drive Encryption Technical Overview. (n.d.). *Microsoft TechNet*. Retrieved from: http://technet.microsoft.com/en-us/library/cc732774(v=ws.10).aspx

Bodanese, J., de Araujo, G., Steup, C., Raffo, G., & Becker, L. (2014). Wireless Communication Infrastructure for a Short-Range Unmanned Aerial. In *28th International Conference on Advanced Information Networking and Applications Workshops (WAINA)*, Victoria, BC. doi:10.1109/WAINA.2014.154

Bokhari, S. A., Zürcher, J. F., Mosig, J. R., & Gardiol, F. E. (1996). A small microstrip patch antenna with a convenient tuning option. *IEEE Transactions on Antennas and Propagation*, *44*(11), 1521–1528. doi:10.1109/8.542077

Bokhari, U., Tamandani, K., & Makki, Q. (2015). A comprehensive study of position based routing protocols in WSNs. In *Proceedings of 4th International conference on Reliability, Infocom Technologies and Optimization (ICRITO)*. doi:10.1109/ICRITO.2015.7359240

Booth, D. (2004). *W3C working group note 11: Web services architecture*. World Wide Web Consortium (W3C). Retrieved from http://www.w3.org/TR/ws-arch/#stakeholder

Booth, D. (2004). *W3C working group note 11: Web services architecture*. World Wide Web Consortium (W3C). Retrieved from http://www.w3.org/TR/ws-arch/#whatis

Bora, A., & Bezboruah, T. (2014). Testing and Evaluation of a Hierarchical SOAP based Medical Web Service. *International Journal of Database Theory Application, 7*(5), 145–160. doi:10.14257/ijdta.2014.7.5.11

Bora, A., Bhuyan, M. K., & Bezboruah, T. (2013). Investigations on Hierarchical Web service based on Java Technique. In *Proceedings of the World Congress on Engineering (WCE)*.

Borda, M., & Tornea, O. (2010). DNA Secret Writing Techniques. *International Conference on Communications, IEEE.*

Borges, L., Velez, F., & Lebres, A. (2014). Survey on the characterization and classification of wireless sensor networks applications. *IEEE Communication. Surveys and Tutorials*, (99), 1860-1890.

Bortoletti, A., Flore, C., & Di, . (2003). A new class of Quasi-Newtonian methods for optimal learning in MLP-networks. *IEEE Transactions on Neural Networks, 14*(2), 263–273. doi:10.1109/TNN.2003.809425 PMID:18238010

Bose, I., & Lam, C. W. (2009). Facing the challenges of RFID data management. In J. Symonds, J. Ayoade, & D. Parry (Eds.), *Auto-identification and ubiquitous computing applications* (pp. 230–246). Hershey, PA: IGI Global. doi:10.4018/978-1-60566-298-5.ch014

Bouachir, O., Abrassart, A., Garcia, F., & Larrieu, N. (2014). A Mobility Model for UAV Ad-hoc Network. In *International Conference on Unmanned Aircraft Systems*, Orlando, FL. doi:10.1109/ICUAS.2014.6842277

Boukerche & Ren. (2008). A Security Management Scheme using a novel Computational Reputation Model for Wireless and Mobile Ad hoc Networks. In *Proc.Int'l Workshop on Modeling Analysis and Simulation of wireless and Mobile System.*

Boukerche, A., & Abrougui, K. (2006). An Efficient Leader Election Protocol for Mobile Networks. In *Proceeding ACM International Wireless Communications and Mobile Computing Conference (IWCMC)*. doi:10.1145/1143549.1143775

Boukerche, A., & Abrougui, K. (2007). An Efficient Leader Election Protocol for Wireless Quasi-Static Mesh Networks: Proof of Correctness. In *Proceeding IEEE International Conference on Communication (ICC)*. doi:10.1109/ICC.2007.577

Braun, E., Eichen, Y., Sivan, U., & Ben-Yoseph, G. (1998). DNA-templated assembly and electrode attachment of a conducting silver wire. *Nature, 391*(6669), 775–778. doi:10.1038/35826 PMID:9486645

Brown, W. C., Mims, J. R., & Heenan, N. I. (1965), An experimental microwave-powered helicopter. *IEEE International Convention Record* (vol. 13, part 5, pp. 225 – 235).

Brown, M. (2011). Ubiquitous use of RFID in the health industry. In S. Brown & M. Brown (Eds.), *Ethical issues and security monitoring trends in global healthcare: Technological advancements* (pp. 166–178). Hershey, PA: IGI Global. doi:10.4018/978-1-60960-174-4.ch012

Brown, S., & Sreenan, C. J. (2007). Study on Data Aggregation and Reliability in managing Wireless Sensor Networks. In *Proceedings of IEEE International Conference on Mobile Adhoc and Sensor Systems*. doi:10.1109/MOBHOC.2007.4428743

Brown, W. A., & Loomis, H. (1993). Digital Implementations of Spectral Correlation Analyzers. *IEEE Transactions on Signal Processing, 41*(2), 703–720. doi:10.1109/78.193211

Brown, W. C. (1984). The history of power transmission by radio waves. *IEEE Transactions on Microwave Theory and Techniques*, *32*(9), 1230–1242. doi:10.1109/TMTT.1984.1132833

Brown, W. C., & Triner, J. F. (1982), Experimental thin-film, etched-circuit rectenna.*IEEE MTT-S International Microwave Symposium Digest* (pp. 185–187). doi:10.1109/MWSYM.1982.1130655

Broyles, D., Jabbar, A., & Sterbenz, J. (2010). *Design and analysis of a 3-D Gauss-Markov mobility model for highly-dynamic airborne networks*. In International Telemetering Conference (ITC), San Diego, CA.

Bryhni, H., Klovning, E., & Kure, O. (2000). A Comparison of Load Balancing Techniques for Scalable Web Servers. *IEEE Network*, *14*(4), 58–64. doi:10.1109/65.855480

Buchegger, S., & Le Boudec, J.-Y. (2002). Performance analysis of the confident protocol. In *MobiHoc'02, IEEE/ACM Symposium on Mobile Ad-hoc Networking and Computing*.

Burmester, M., & Munilla, J. (2013). RFID grouping-proofs. In P. Lopez, J. Hernandez-Castro, & T. Li (Eds.), *Security and trends in wireless identification and sensing platform tags: Advancements in RFID* (pp. 89–119). Hershey, PA: IGI Global. doi:10.4018/978-1-4666-1990-6.ch004

Burns. (2002). *Software Defined Radio for 3G*. Artech House.

Buttigieg, G. G. (2015). When electronic fetal monitoring becomes court business. *Malawi Medical Journal*, *27*(1), 40–46. PMID:26405509

Buttigieg, G. G. (2016). Cerebral palsy: Medico-legal issues. *Phys Med Rehabil. Int*, *3*(2), 1–7.

Buttyan, L., Dora, L., Felegyhazi, M., & Vajda, I. (2007). Barter-based cooperation in delay-tolerant personal wireless networks. In *Proceedings of the IEEE International Symposium on a World of Wireless, Mobile and Multimedia Networks. (WoWMoM 2007)*.Espoo, Finland: IEEE. doi:10.1109/WOWMOM.2007.4351689

Buttyan, L., Dora, L., Felegyhazi, M., & Vajda, I. (2010). Barter trade improves message delivery in opportunistic networks. *Ad Hoc Networks*, *8*(1), 1–14. doi:10.1016/j.adhoc.2009.02.005

Cabric, D., Tkachenko, A., & Brodersen, R. W. (2006). Spectrum Sensing Measurements of Pilot, Energy and Collaborative Detection. *IEEE Military Communications Conference (MILCOM)*. doi:10.1109/MILCOM.2006.301994

Cai, Y., Yu, F., Li, J., Zhou, Y., & Lamont, L. (2012). MAC performance improvement in UAV ad-hoc networks with full-duplex radios and multi-packet reception capability. In *IEEE International Conference on Communications (ICC)*, Ottawa, Canada. doi:10.1109/ICC.2012.6364116

Calderbank, P. R. (1984). *Technology as Driver of Change in Telecommunications ne Bell System – It Worked The Changing Face of Telecommunications Research*. Academic Press.

Camdereli, A. Z., & Swaminathan, J. M. (2010). Misplaced inventory and radio-frequency identification (RFID) technology: Information and coordination. *Production and Operations Management*, *19*(1), 1–18. doi:10.1111/j.1937-5956.2009.01057.x

Camp, T., Boleng, J., & Davies, V. (2002). A survey of mobility models for ad hoc network research. *Wireless Communication and Mobile Computing*, *2*(5), 483–502. doi:10.1002/wcm.72

Cao, N., Wang, C., Li, M., Ren, K., & Lou, W. (2014, January). Privacy-Preserving Multi-Keyword Ranked Search over Encrypted Cloud Data. *IEEE Transactions on Parallel and Distributed Systems*, *25*(1), 222–224. doi:10.1109/TPDS.2013.45

Capra, L. (2004). Toward a Human Trust Model for Mobile Ad-hoc Network. *Proc. 2nd UK-UbiNet Workshop*. Cambridge University.

Cardellini, V., Casalicchio, E., Colajanni, M., & Tucci, S. (2001). Mechanisms for quality of service in web clusters. *Computer Networks*, *37*(6), 761–771. doi:10.1016/S1389-1286(01)00252-3

Carmo, J. P., Dias, N., Mendes, P. M., Couto, C., & Correia, J. H. (2006). Low-power 2.4-GHz RF transceiver for wireless EEG module plug-and-play. In *13th IEEE International Conference on Electronics, Circuits and Systems* (pp. 1144–1147). doi:10.1109/ICECS.2006.379642

Carreton, A. L., Pinte, K., & Meuter, W. D. (2013). Software abstractions for mobile RFID-enabled applications. *Software: Practice and Experience*, *43*(10), 1219–1239. doi:10.1002/spe.1114

Carter, J., Saberin, J., Shah, T., Sai Ananthanarayanan, P. R., & Furse, C. (2010). Inexpensive fabric antenna for off-body wireless sensor communication. In *IEEE International Symposium on Antennas and Propagation* (pp. 9–12). http://doi.org/ doi:10.1109/APS.2010.5561753

Casula, G., Montisci, G., & Mazzarella, G. (2013). A wideband PET inkjet-printed antenna for UHF RFID. *Antennas and Wireless Propagation Letters*, *12*, 1400–1403. doi:10.1109/LAWP.2013.2287307

Catarinucci, L., Cappelli, M., Colella, R., & Tarricone, L. (2008). A novel low-cost multisensor-tag for RFID applications in healthcare. *Microwave and Optical Technology Letters*, *50*(11), 2877–2880. doi:10.1002/mop.23837

Catarinucci, L., Colella, R., & Tarricone, L. (2012). Design, development, and performance evaluation of a compact and long-range passive UHF RFID tag. *Microwave and Optical Technology Letters*, *54*(5), 1335–1339. doi:10.1002/mop.26777

Cavalcanti, A. (2007). Hardware architecture for nanorobots application in cerebral aneurysm. *IEEE-Nano Conf.*

Cavalcanti, A., & Rosen, L. (2004). Nanorobotic challenges in Biomedical applications. *Design and Control, IEEE ICECS Int'l conf. on Electronics, Circuits and systems.*

Cavalcanti, A., & Shirinzadeh, B., Jr. (2008). Nanorobot architecture for medical target identification. IOP Science.

Cavalcanti, A., & Freitas, R. A. Jr. (2002). Collective Robotics Coherent Behaviour for Nanosystems with Sensor-Based Neural Motion. *IEEE International Conference on Artificial Intelligence Systems (ICAIS'02)*, Divnomorskoe, Russia. doi:10.1109/ICAIS.2002.1048090

Ceipidor, U., Medaglia, C., & Sciarretta, E. (2010). SeSaMoNet 2.0: Improving a Navigation System for Visually Impaired People. In B. Ruyter, R. Wichert, D. Keyson, P. Markopoulos, N. Streitz, M. Divitini, & A. Mana Gomez et al. (Eds.), *Ambient Intelligence* (Vol. 6439, pp. 248–253). Springer Berlin Heidelberg. doi:10.1007/978-3-642-16917-5_25

Çekyay, B., & Ozekici, S. (2014). *Reliability, MTTF and steady-state availability analysis of systems with exponential lifetimes. Appl. Math. Modell.* Elsevier; doi:10.1016/j.apm.2014.05.029

Cetin, O., & Zagli, I. (2011). Continuous Airborne Communication Relay Approach Using Unmanned Aerial Vehicles. *Journal of Intelligent & Robotic Systems*, *65*(1-4), 549–562. doi:10.1007/s10846-011-9556-6

Chaimanonart, N., & Young, D. (2006). Remote RF powering system for wireless MEMS strain sensors. *IEEE Sensors Journal*, *6*(2), 484–489. doi:10.1109/JSEN.2006.870158

Chakrabarti, C. (2014). A Secured Message Exchange Scheme in Post–Disaster Environment Using Delay Tolerant Network. *Global Journal for Research Analysis, 3*(10), 64-66.

Chakrabarti, C., & Roy, S. (2015). Adapting Mobility of Observers for Quick Reputation Assignment in a Sparse Post-Disaster Communication Network. In Proceedings of the Applications and Innovation in Mobile Coputing (AIMOC 2015), (pp. 29-35). Kolkata, India: IEEE. doi:10.1109/AIMOC.2015.7083826

Chakrabarti, C., Banerjee, A., & Chakrabarti, S. (2014). A Secured Group-based Communication Scheme in Disaster Response Environment using Delay Tolerant Network. In *Proceedings of the ICCACCS 2014*, (pp. 217- 227). Kolkata, India: Springer.

Chakrabarti, C., Banerjee, A., & Roy, S. (2014). An Observer based Distributed Scheme for Selfish node Detection in a Post-disaster Communication Environment using Delay Tolerant Network. In *Proceedings of the Applications and Innovation in Mobile Coputing (AIMOC 2014)*, (pp. 151 – 156). Kolkata, India: IEEE. doi:10.1109/AIMOC.2014.6785534

Chakrabarti, C., Banerjee, A., Chakrabarti, S., & Chakraborty, A. (2014a). A Novel Approach for Non-Cooperative Node Detection and Avoidance using Reputation based Scheme in Mobile Ad-hoc Network. In *Proceedings of the ICCACCS 2014*, (pp. 279-289). Kolkata, India: Springer.

Chakrabarti, C., Chakrabarti, S., & Chakrabarti, S. K. (2014). Towards Cluster Based Mobility Aware Secured Ad-hoc Network. In *Proceedings of the IEMCON-2014*, (pp. 123-128). Kolkata, India: Elsevier Publications.

Chakrabarti, C., Banerjee, A., Chakrabarti, S., & Chakraborty, A. (2014b). A Dynamic Reputation Estimation Technique For Selfish Node Detection And Avoidance Of Non-Cooperative Nodes. In *Mobile Ad-hoc Network. Proceedings of the IEMCON-2014*. Kolkata, India: Elsevier Publications.

Chakrabarti, C., & Chaki, R. (2011). Improved Cluster based Route Discovery Algorithm for Ad-hoc Networks. In *Proceedings of the IEEE International Conference on Communication and Industrial Application (ICCIA 2011)*, (pp. 1-4). Kolkata, India: IEEE. doi:10.1109/ICCIndA.2011.6146657

Chakrabarti, C., Chakrabarti, S., & Banerjee, A. (2015). A dynamic two hops reputation assignment scheme for selfish node detection and avoidance in delay tolerant network. In *Proceedings of the 2015 IEEE International Conference on Research in Computational Intelligence and Communication Networks (ICRCICN)*, (pp. 345-350). Kolkata, India: IEEE. doi:10.1109/ICRCICN.2015.7434262

Chakraborty, U. K. (2008). *Advances in Differential Evolution: Studies in Computational Intelligence*. Heidelberg, Germany: Springer. doi:10.1007/978-3-540-68830-3

Chanak, P., Banerjee, I., & Sherratt, S. (2015). Simultaneous mobile sink allocation in home environments with applications in mobile consumer robotics. *IEEE Transactions on Consumer Electronics*, *61*(2), 181–188. doi:10.1109/TCE.2015.7150572

Chand, N. (2007). Data caching in mobile ad-hoc networks. In D. Taniar (Ed.), *Encyclopedia of mobile computing and commerce* (pp. 172–177). Hershey, PA: IGI Global. doi:10.4018/978-1-59904-002-8.ch030

Chandran, A. R., Conway, G. A., & Scanlon, W. G. (2008). Compact Low Profile Patch Antenna For Medical Body Area Netowrks at 868 MHz. In *IEEE Antennas and Propagation Society International Symposium* (pp. 8–11).

Chang, K. (1996). *Microwave Circuits and Antennas*. New York: Wiley.

Chatterjee, S., Maity, S. P., & Acharya, T. (2014). Energy Efficient Cognitive Radio System for Joint Spectrum Sensing and Data Transmission. *IEEE J. on Emerging and Selected Topics in Circuits and Systems*, *4*(3), 292–300. doi:10.1109/JETCAS.2014.2337191

Chen, B. B., & Chan, M. C. (2010). Mobicent: a Credit-Based Incentive System for Disruption Tolerant Network. In *Proceedings of the INFOCOM, 2010*, (pp. 1–9). San Diego, CA: IEEE. doi:10.1109/INFCOM.2010.5462136

Chen, D., & Zhao, H. (2012). The data security and privacy protection issues in cloud computing. In *International Conference on Computer Science and Electron ICS Engineering (ICCSEE, IEEE)*. doi:10.1109/ICCSEE.2012.193

Chen, E. T. (2015). RFID technology and privacy. In I. Lee (Ed.), RFID technology integration for business performance improvement (pp. 140–155). Hershey, PA: IGI Global. doi:10.4018/978-1-4666-6308-4.ch007

Chen, X. L., Kuster, N., Tan, Y. C., & Chavannes, N. (2012). Body effects on the GPS antenna of a wearable tracking device. In *6th European Conference on Antennas and Propagation, EuCAP* (pp. 3313–3316). http://doi.org/ doi:10.1109/ EuCAP.2012.6205889

Chen, B., Jiao, Y.-C., Ren, F.-C., & Zhang, L. (2012). Broadband monopole antenna with wideband circular polarization. *Progress In Electromagnetics Research Letters, 32*, 19–28. doi:10.2528/PIERL12032807

Chen, C. L., & Wu, C. Y. (2014). An RFID system yoking-proof protocol conforming to EPCglobal C1G2 standards. *Security and Communication Networks, 7*(12), 2527–2541. doi:10.1002/sec.383

Cheney, M. (1981). *Tesla, Man Out of Time*. Englewood Cliffs, NJ: Prentice-Hal.

Chen, G., & Pham, T. T. (2000). *Introduction to fuzzy set, fuzzy logic and fuzzy control system*. New York: CRC Press. doi:10.1201/9781420039818

Cheng, H. (2012). Dynamic genetic algorithms with hyper-mutation schemes for dynamic shortest path routing problem in mobile ad hoc networks. *International Journal of Adaptive, Resilient and Autonomic Systems, 3*(1), 87–98. doi:10.4018/ jaras.2012010105

Cheng, H., Cao, J., Wang, X., Das, S. K., & Yang, S. (2009). Stability-aware multi-metric clustering in mobile ad hoc networks with group mobility. *Wireless Communications and Mobile Computing, 9*(6), 759–771. doi:10.1002/wcm.627

Cheng, Z. Y., Liu, Y., Chang, C. C., & Chang, S. C. (2013). Authenticated RFID security mechanism based on chaotic maps. *Security and Communication Networks, 6*(2), 247–256. doi:10.1002/sec.709

Chen, K. C., & Prasad, R. (2009). *Cognitive Radio Networks*. John Wiley & Sons. Ltd. doi:10.1002/9780470742020

Chen, N. K., Chen, J. L., & Lee, C. C. (2009). Array-based reader anti-collision scheme for highly efficient RFID network applications. *Wireless Communications and Mobile Computing, 9*(7), 976–987. doi:10.1002/wcm.646

Chen, S., & Billings, S. A. (1989). Representation of nonlinear systems: The NARMAX model. *International Journal of Control, 49*(3), 1013–1032. doi:10.1080/00207178908559683

Chen, W. S., Huang, C.-C., & Wong, K.-L. (2001). Microstrip-line-fed printed shorted ring-slot antennas for circular polarization. *Microwave and Optical Technology Letters, 31*(2), 137–140. doi:10.1002/mop.1380

Chen, X., & Mohapatra, P. (2002). Performance Evaluation of Service Differentiating Internet Servers. *IEEE Transactions on Computers, 51*(11), 1368–1375. doi:10.1109/TC.2002.1047760

Chen, X., Rao, L., Yao, Y., Liu, X., & Bai, F. (2015). The Answer is Rolling On Wheels: Modelling and Performance Evaluation of in-cabin Wi-Fi Communications. *Vehicular Communications, 2*(1), 13–26. doi:10.1016/j.vehcom.2014.10.001

Chen, Z. N. (2007). *Antennas for Portable Devices* (1st ed.). Wiley-VCH. doi:10.1002/9780470319642

Chia, L., & Feng, B. (2007). The development of a micropower (micro-thermophotovoltaic) device. *Journal of Power Sources, 165*(1), 455–480. doi:10.1016/j.jpowsour.2006.12.006

Chiam, T. M., Ong, L. C., Karim, M. F., & Guo, Y. X. (2009), 5.8 GHz circularly polarized rectennas using schottky diode and LTC5535 rectifier for RF energy harvesting.*Proceedings of Asia-Pacific Microwave Conference* (pp. 32 – 35).

Childers, D. G., Skinner, D. P., & Kemerait, R. C. (1977). The cepstrum: A guide to processing. *Proceedings of the IEEE, 65*(10), 1428–1443. doi:10.1109/PROC.1977.10747

Chin, C. H. K., Xue, Q., & Chan, C. H. (2005). Design of a 5.8-GHz rectenna incorporating a new patch antenna. *IEEE Antennas and Wireless Propagation Letters, 4*(1), 175–178. doi:10.1109/LAWP.2005.846434

Cho & Chen. (2011, Oct.). A Survey on Trust Management for Mobile Ad-Hoc Networks. *IEEE Communications Surveys & Tutorials, 13*(4).

Choi, S. H., Cheung, H. H., Yang, B., & Yang, Y. X. (2015). Item-level RFID for retail Business improvement. In I. Lee (Ed.), RFID technology integration for business performance improvement (pp. 1–26). Hershey, PA: IGI Global. doi:10.4018/978-1-4666-6308-4.ch001

Choi, K. W., Jeon, W. S., & Jeong, D. G. (2009). Sequential Detection of Cyclostaionary Signal for Cognitive Radio Systems. *IEEE Transactions on Wireless Communications, 8*(9), 4480–4485. doi:10.1109/TWC.2009.090288

Cho, K., Pack, S., Kwon, T., & Choi, Y. (2010). An extensible and ubiquitous RFID management framework over next-generation network. *International Journal of Communication Systems, 23*(9/10), 1093–1110. doi:10.1002/dac.1073

Chowdhury, M. U., & Ray, B. R. (2014). Security risks/vulnerability in a RFID system and possible defenses. In *Crisis management: Concepts, methodologies, tools, and applications* (pp. 1667–1681). Hershey, PA: IGI Global. doi:10.4018/978-1-4666-4707-7.ch084

Chowdhury, S., Ahmadi, M., & Miller, W. (2002). Design of a MEMS acoustical beamforming sensor microarray. *IEEE Sensors Journal, 2*(6), 617–627. doi:10.1109/JSEN.2002.807773

Christin, D., Mogre, P. S., & Hollick, M. (2010). Survey on Wireless Sensor Network Technologies for Industrial Automation the Security and Quality of Service Perspectives. *Future Internet, 2*(2), 96–125. doi:10.3390/fi2020096

Chu, L. J. (1948). Small antennas. *Journal of Applied Physics, 19*(12), 1163–1175. doi:10.1063/1.1715038

Cibin, C., Leuchtmann, P., Gimersky, M., Vahldieck, R., & Moscibroda, S. (2004). A flexible wearable antenna. In IEEE Antennas and Propagation Society (pp. 3589–3592). doi:10.1109/APS.2004.1330122

Cibin, C., Leuchtmann, P., Gimersky, M., & Vahldieck, R. (2004). Modified E-Shaped Pifa Antenna for Wearable Systems. In *URSI International Symposium on Electromagnetic Theory (URSI EMTS)* (pp. 873–875).

Cloud Computing Security. (n.d.a). Retrieved from: http://searchcompliance.techtarget.com/definition/cloudcomputing-security

Cloud Computing Security. (n.d.b). Retrieved from: http://www.forbes.com/sites/netapp/2012/12/12/ cloud-security-1/

Cloud Computing. (n.d.a). Retrieved from: https://zapthink.com/2011/05/19/data-remanence-cloud-computing-shellgame

Cloud Computing. (n.d.b). Retrieved from: http://www.cornwallcloud services.co.uk/index.php/easyblog/categories/listings/theinternetofthings

Cloud Storage. (n.d.). Retrieved from: http://securosis.com/blog/securing-cloud-data-withvirtual-private-storage/

Cluster Configuration. (2016). Retrieved on January 21, 2016 from, http://tomcat.apache.org/tomcat-5.5-doc/cluster-howto.html

Cohen, F. (2001). Performance Testing SOAP-Based Applications: Is your Web Service Production Ready? *IBM Developer Works.*

Coifman, B., McCord, M., Mishalani, R., Iswalt, M., & Ji, Y. (2006). Roadway traffic monitoring from an unmanned aerial vehicle. *IEEE Proceedings on Intelligent Transport Systems.*

Constantinou, C., Nechayev, Y., Wu, X., & Hall, P. (2012). Body-area Propagation at 60 GHz. In Loughborough Antennas & Propagation Conference (pp. 1–4).

Cook, B., & Shamim, A. (2013). Utilizing wideband AMC structures for high-gain inkjet-printed antennas on lossy paper substrate. *IEEE Antennas and Wireless Propagation Letters*, *12*, 76–79. doi:10.1109/LAWP.2013.2240251

Corner, A. A. (2013). Body-Worn Antennas Making a Splash: Lifejacket-Integrated Antennas for Global Search and Rescue Satellite System. *IEEE Antennas and Propagation Magazine, 55*(2).

Cornetta, G., Touhafi, A., Santos, D. J., & Vázquez, J. M. (2011). Power issues and energy scavenging in mobile wireless ad-hoc and sensor networks. In M. Cruz-Cunha & F. Moreira (Eds.), *Handbook of research on mobility and computing: Evolving technologies and ubiquitous impacts* (pp. 994–1020). Hershey, PA: IGI Global. doi:10.4018/978-1-60960-042-6.ch061

Cui, G., Han, D., & Wang, Y. (2014). An Encryption Scheme Based on DNA Microdots Technology. BIC-TA, CCIS. Springer.

Cui, G., Han, D., & Wang, Y. (2014). An Improved Method of DNA Information Encryption. BIC-TA, CCIS. Springer.

Cui, Qin, Wang, & Zhang. (2008). An Encryption Scheme Using DNA Technology. *Bio-Inspired Computing: Theories and Applications*, 37-42.

Cui, B., Wang, Z., Zhao, B., & Chen, X. (2016). Design and analysis of secure mechanisms based on tripartite credibility for RFID systems. *Computer Standards & Interfaces*, *44*, 110–116. doi:10.1016/j.csi.2015.06.003

Cui, G., Qin, L., Wang, Y., & Zhang, X. (2007). Information security technology based on DNA computing.*IEEE International Workshop on Anti-counterfeiting, Security and Identification*, (pp. 288-291). doi:10.1109/IWASID.2007.373746

Cui, J.-H., Kong, J., Gerla, M., & Zhou, S. (2006). The challenges of building scalable mobile underwater wireless sensor networks for aquatic applications. *IEEE Network*, *20*(3), 12–18. doi:10.1109/MNET.2006.1637927

Curone, D., Dudnik, G., Loriga, G., Luprano, J., Magenes, G., Paradiso, R., … Bonfiglio, A. (2007). Smart Garments for Safety Improvement of Emergency/Disaster Operators. In *29th Annual International Conference of the IEEE Engineering in Medicine and Biology Society (EMBS)* (pp. 3962–3965). doi:10.1109/IEMBS.2007.4353201

Curran, K., & Norrby, S. (2011). RFID-enabled location determination within indoor environments. In K. Curran (Ed.), *Ubiquitous developments in ambient computing and intelligence: Human-centered applications* (pp. 301–324). Hershey, PA: IGI Global. doi:10.4018/978-1-60960-549-0.ch026

Curto, S., McEvoy, P., Bao, X., & Ammann, M. J. (2009). Compact patch antenna for electromagnetic interaction with human tissue at 434 MHz. *IEEE Transactions on Antennas and Propagation*, *57*(9), 2564–2571. doi:10.1109/TAP.2009.2027040

Czech Technical university (CTU) in Prague and University Hospital in Brno (UHB) database. (2010). Retrieved August 8th, 2014 from http://physionet.nlm.nih.gov/pn3/ctu-uhb-ctgdb/

D'Andrea, A., Ferri, F., & Grifoni, P. (2013). RFID technologies in the health sector. In A. Moumtzoglou & A. Kastania (Eds.), *E-health technologies and improving patient safety: Exploring organizational factors* (pp. 140–147). Hershey, PA: IGI Global. doi:10.4018/978-1-4666-2657-7.ch009

Dahshan, H., & Irvine, J. (2010). A robust self-organized public key management for mobile ad hoc networks. *Security and Communication Networks*, *3*(1), 16–30. doi:10.1002/sec.131

Dakopoulos, D., & Bourbakis, N. G. (2010). Wearable Obstacle Avoidance Electronic Travel Aids for Blind: A Survey. *Systems, Man, and Cybernetics, Part C: Applications and Reviews. IEEE Transactions on, 40*(1), 25–35. doi:10.1109/TSMCC.2009.2021255

Dalal, Khari, & Singh. (2012). Different Ways to Achieve Trust in MANET. *International Journal on AdHoc Networking Systems, 2*(2).

Dalbro, M., Eikeland, E., Veld, A. J., Gjessing, S., Lande, T. S., & Riis, H. K. (2008), Wireless sensor networks for off-shore oil and gas installations. In *Proceedings of the 2nd International Conference on Sensor Technologies and Applications* (pp. 258-263). doi:10.1109/SENSORCOMM.2008.111

Danev, B., Masti, R. J., Karame, G. O., & Capkun, S. (2011). Enabling secure VM migration in private clouds. In *Proceedings of the ACM 27th annual computer security applications conference.* doi:10.1145/2076732.2076759

Dang, K., Shen, J. Z., Dong, L. D., & Xia, Y.-X. (2013). A Graph route –Based Superframe Scheduling Scheme in WirlelessHART Mesh Networks for High Robustness. *Wireless Personal Communications, 71*(4), 2431–2444. doi:10.1007/s11277-012-0946-2

Danyang, Q., Lin, M., Xuejun, S., & Yubin, X. (2011). Realization of route reconstructing scheme for mobile ad hoc network. In I. Khalil & E. Weippl (Eds.), *Innovations in mobile multimedia communications and applications: New technologies* (pp. 62–79). Hershey, PA: IGI Global. doi:10.4018/978-1-60960-563-6.ch005

Das, A., Basu, S. S., & Chaudhuri, A. (2011). A Novel Security Scheme for Wireless Adhoc Network. *Wireless Communication, Vehicular Technology, Information Theory and Aerospace & Electronics Systems Technology (Wireless VITAE), 2011 2nd International Conference on.*

Das, A., Rahman, A., Basu, S. S., & Chaudhuri, A. (2011). Energy Aware Topology Security Scheme for Mobile Ad Hoc Network. *Proceedings of the 2011 International Conference on Communication, Computing & Security.* doi:10.1145/1947940.1947965

Das, S., Roy, K., & Saha, C. K. (2015a). Determination of Window Size for Baseline Estimation of Fetal Heart Rate Using CTG. In *Proceedings of 2015 Third International Conference on Computer, Communication, Control and Information Technology (C3IT)* (pp. 1 – 5). Hooghly: IEEE Press. doi:10.1109/C3IT.2015.7060179

Da, S., Xiaoying, G., Hsiao-Hwa, C., Liang, Q., & Miao, X. (2009). Significant Cycle Frequency based Feature Detection for Cognitive Radio Systems. In *Proceedings of the 4th International Conference on CROWNCOM.* doi:10.1109/CROWNCOM.2009.5189106

Das, A., & Chaudhuri, A. (2017). Derivation and simulation of an efficient QoS scheme in MANET through optimised messaging based on ABCO using QualNet. In *Nature-inspired computing: Concepts, methodologies, tools, and applications* (pp. 396–425). Hershey, PA: IGI Global. doi:10.4018/978-1-5225-0788-8.ch016

Das, S., Biswas, A., Dasgupta, S., & Abraham, A. (2009). Bacterial Foraging Optimization Algorithm: Theoretical Foundations, Analysis, and Applications, in Foundations of Computational Intelligence Volume 3. *Studies in Computational Intelligence, 203*, 23–55.

Das, S., Roy, K., & Saha, C. K. (2011). A novel approach for extraction and analysis of variability of baseline. In *Proceedings of International Conference on Recent Trends in Information Systems* (pp. 336 – 339). Kolkata: IEEE Press. doi:10.1109/ReTIS.2011.6146892

Das, S., Roy, K., & Saha, C. K. (2015b). A novel step towards machine diagnosis of fetal status in-utero: Calculation of baseline variability. In *Proceedings of 2015 IEEE International Conference on Research in Computational Intelligence and Communication Networks (ICRCICN)* (pp. 230-234). Kolkata: IEEE Press. doi:10.1109/ICRCICN.2015.7434241

Data Remanence Solutions. (n.d.). Retrieved from http://fas.org/irp/nsa/rainbow tg025-2.htm

Data Remanence. (n.d.). Retrieved from http://elastic-security.com/2010/01/07/data-remanence-in-the-cloud/

Data Remanence. (n.d.a). Retrieved from: http://www.itrenew.com/what-is-data-remanence

Data Remanence. (n.d.b). Retrieved from: http://en.wikipedia. org/wiki/Data_remanence

Davis & McGuffin. (1995). *Wireless Local Area Networks*. McGraw-Hill.

Dawes, G. S., & Redman, C. W. G. (1981). Numerical analysis of the human fetal heart rate: The quality of ultrasound records. *American Journal of Obstetrics and Gynecology*, *141*(1), 43–52. doi:10.1016/0002-9378(81)90673-6 PMID:7270621

DDBJ. (2016). *DNA Data Bank of Japan*. Retrieved from http://www.ddbj.nig.ac.jp/

de Bree, H.-E., Gur, B. M., & Akal, T. (2009). The hydroflown: Mems-based underwater acoustical particle velocity sensor the sensor, its calibration and some possible localization techniques. In *Proceedings of 3rd International Conference & Exhibition on "Underwater Acoustic Measurements: Technologies & Results"* (pp. 35-42).

de Campos, D. A., & Bernardes, J. Twenty-five years after the FIGO guidelines for the use of fetal monitoring: Time for a simplified approach? *International Journal of Gynecology & Obstetrics, 110*(1), 1 – 6.

de Campos, D. A., & Bernardes, J. (2004). Comparison of fetal heart rate baseline estimation by SisPorto 2.01 and a consensus of clinicians. *Euopeanr Journal of Obstet Gynecol Reprod Biol*, *117*(2), 174–178. doi:10.1016/j.ejogrb.2004.03.013 PMID:15541853

de Campos, D. A., Sousa, P., Costa, A., & Bernardes, J. (2008). Omniview-SisPorto® 3.5 - A central fetal monitoring station with online alerts based on computerized cardiotocogram+ST event analysis. *Journal of Perinatal Medicine*, *36*(3), 260–264. PMID:18576938

de-Campos, D. A., & Arulkumaran, S. (2015). FIGO consensus guidelines on intrapartum fetal monitoring: Introduction. *International Journal of Gynaecology and Obstetrics: the Official Organ of the International Federation of Gynaecology and Obstetrics*, *131*(1), 3–4. doi:10.1016/j.ijgo.2015.06.017 PMID:26433398

Declercq, F., Couckuyt, I., Rogier, H., & Dhaene, T. (2010). Complex permittivity characterization of textile materials by means of surrogate modeling. In *IEEE Antennas and Propagation Society International Symposium* (pp. 1–4).

Deep-ocean Assessment and Reporting of Tsunamis (DART®). (2008). *The National Oceanic and Atmospheric Administration (NOAA)*. Retrieved 21 February 2015, from http://www.ndbc.noaa.gov/dart/dart.shtml

Degenford, J., Sirkis, W., & Steier, W. (1964). The reflecting beam waveguide. *IEEE Transactions on Microwave Theory and Techniques*, *12*(4), 445–453. doi:10.1109/TMTT.1964.1125845

DeJean, G., Bairavasubramanian, R., Thompson, D., Ponchak, G. M. T., & Papapolymerou, J. (2005). Liquid crystal polymer (LCP): A new organic material for the development of multilayer dual-frequency dual-polarization flexible antenna arrays. *IEEE Antennas and Wireless Propagation Letters*, *4*(1), 22–26. doi:10.1109/LAWP.2004.841626

Deqing, Z., Wenrong, Z., Weizhong, Q., & Guofu, X. (2013). Design and implementation of a trusted monitoring framework for cloud platforms. *Future Generation Computer Systems*, *29*(8), 2092–2102. doi:10.1016/j.future.2012.12.020

Dhar, S. (2007). Applications and future trends in mobile ad hoc networks. In J. Gutierrez (Ed.), *Business data communications and networking: A research perspective* (pp. 272–300). Hershey, PA: Idea Group Publishing. doi:10.4018/978-1-59904-274-9.ch011

Dhar, S. (2009). Mobile ad hoc network. In D. Taniar (Ed.), *Mobile computing: Concepts, methodologies, tools, and applications* (pp. 952–960). Hershey, PA: IGI Global. doi:10.4018/978-1-60566-054-7.ch077

Dhungana, R. D., Mohammad, A., Sharma, A., & Schoen, I. (2013). Identity management framework for cloud networking infrastructure. In *IEEE International conference on innovations in information technology (IIT)*. doi:10.1109/Innovations.2013.6544386

Di Giampaolo, E. (2010). *A passive-RFID based indoor navigation system for visually impaired people*. Paper presented at the Applied Sciences in Biomedical and Communication Technologies (ISABEL), 2010 3rd International Symposium on.

Diez, S., Reuther, C., Dinu, C., Seidel, R., Mertig, M., Pompe, W., & Howard, J. (2003). Stretching and Transporting DNA Molecules using Motor Proteins. *Nano Letters*, *3*(9), 1251–1254. doi:10.1021/nl034504h

Digham, F., Alouini, M. S., & Simon, M. K. (2007). On the energy detection of unknown signals over fading channels. *IEEE Transactions on Communications*, *55*(1), 21–24. doi:10.1109/TCOMM.2006.887483

Digi International. (2008). *XBee™ ZNet 2.5/XBee-PRO™ ZNet 2.5 OEM RF Modules Datasheet*. Author.

Dijkstra, E. W. (1959). A Note on Two Problems in Connexion with Graphs. *NUMERISCHE MATHEMATIK*, *1*(1), 269–271. doi:10.1007/BF01386390

Dimic, F., Baldini, G., & Kandeepan, S. (2014). Experimental detection of mobile satellite transmissions with cyclostationary features. *International Journal of Satellite Communications and Networking*, *33*(2), 163–183. doi:10.1002/sat.1081

Dimitriou, T. (2016). Key evolving RFID systems: Forward/backward privacy and ownership transfer of RFID tags. *Ad Hoc Networks*, *37*, 195–208. doi:10.1016/j.adhoc.2015.08.019

Dinga, F., & Chenb, T. (2005). Identification of Hammerstein nonlinear ARMAX systems. *Automatica*, *41*(9), 1479–1489. doi:10.1016/j.automatica.2005.03.026

Ding, X., Tian, Y., & Yan, Yu. (2016). A Real-Time Big Data Gathering Algorithm Based on Indoor Wireless Sensor Networks for Risk Analysis of Industrial Operations. *IEEE Transaction on Industrial Informatics*, *12*(3), 1232–1242. doi:10.1109/TII.2015.2436337

Ding, X., Zhang, P., Yin, S., & Ding, L. (2013). An integrated design framework of fault-tolerant wireless networked control systems for industrial automatic control applications. *IEEE Transaction on Ind. Informat*, *9*(1), 462–471.

Dini, G., & Duca, A. L. (2010). A reputation-based approach to tolerate misbehaving carriers in delay tolerant networks. In *Proceedings of the IEEE Symposium on Computers and Communications (ISCC 2010)*, (pp. 772–777). Riccione, Italy: IEEE. doi:10.1109/ISCC.2010.5546701

Divya, S. V. (2014). Security in Data Forwarding Through Elliptic Curve Cryptography in Cloud. *International Conference on Control, Instrumentation, Communication and Computational Technologies*.

Djenouri, D., & Badache, N. (2008). Struggling against selfishness and black hole attacks in MANETs. *Wireless Communications and Mobile Computing*, *8*(6), 689–704. doi:10.1002/wcm.493

Domingo, M. C., & Prior, R. (2007). A Distributed Clustering Scheme for Underwater Wireless Sensor Networks. In *Proceedings of 2007 IEEE 18th International Symposium on Personal, Indoor and Mobile Radio Communications* (pp. 1-5). doi:10.1109/PIMRC.2007.4394038

Dominikus, S., & Kraxberger, S. (2014). Secure communication with RFID tags in the Internet of Things. *Security and Communication Networks*, *7*(12), 2639–2653. doi:10.1002/sec.398

Dong, Q., Ding, W., & Wei, L. (2015). Improvement and optimized implementation of cryptoGPS protocol for low-cost radio-frequency identification authentication. *Security and Communication Networks*, *8*(8), 1474–1484. doi:10.1002/sec.1096

Dutta, A., Lee, H. L., & Whang, S. (2007). RFID and operations management: Technology, value, and incentives. *Production and Operations Management*, *16*(5), 646–655. doi:10.1111/j.1937-5956.2007.tb00286.x

Dwyer, C., Johri, V., Cheung, M., Patwardhan, J., Lebeck, A., & Sori, D. (2004). Design tools for a DNA-guided self-assembling carbon nanotube technology. *Nanotechnology*, *15*(9), 1240–1245. doi:10.1088/0957-4484/15/9/022

El Khaddar, M. A., Harroud, H., Boulmalf, M., & El Koutbi, M. (2013). FlexRFID middleware in the supply chain: Strategic values and challenges. In I. Khalil & E. Weippl (Eds.), *Contemporary challenges and solutions for mobile and multimedia technologies* (pp. 163–177). Hershey, PA: IGI Global. doi:10.4018/978-1-4666-2163-3.ch010

El Saddik, A. (2006). Performance measurement of Web Service based application. *IEEE Transactions on Instrumentation and Measurement*, *55*(5), 1599–1605. doi:10.1109/TIM.2006.880288

Ellington, A. D., & Szostak, J. W. (1990). In vitro selection of RNA molecules that bind specific ligands. *Nature*, *346*(6287), 818–822. doi:10.1038/346818a0 PMID:1697402

Eltoweissy, M., Olariu, S., & Younis, M. (2010). Towards Autonomous Vehicular Clouds. *LNICST*, *49*, 1–16.

Elwenspoek, M., & Wiegerink, R. (2001). *Mechanical microsensors*. Berlin: Springer. doi:10.1007/978-3-662-04321-9

Engel, T., Goswami, S., Englschalk, A., & Krcmar, H. (2015). CostRFID: Design and evaluation of a cost estimation method and tool for RFID integration projects. In I. Lee (Ed.), *RFID technology integration for business performance improvement* (pp. 27–51). Hershey, PA: IGI Global. doi:10.4018/978-1-4666-6308-4.ch002

Enserink, S., & Cochran, D. (1994). A Cyclostationary Feature Detector. *Signals, Systems and Computers*, *1994*, 806–810.

Enz, C., & Kaiser, A. (2013). *MEMS-based circuits and systems for wireless communication*. New York: Springer. doi:10.1007/978-1-4419-8798-3

Ernst, R., & Martini, P. (2012). Adaptive HELLO for the Neighborhood Discovery Protocol. In *Proceedings of 37th Annual IEEE Conference on Local Computer Networks LCN*. doi:10.1109/LCN.2012.6423663

Erol-Kantarci, M., Mouftah, H., & Oktug, S. (2010). Localization techniques for underwater acoustic sensor networks. *IEEE Communications Magazine*, *48*(12), 152–158. doi:10.1109/MCOM.2010.5673086

Erol-Kantarci, M., Mouftah, H., & Oktug, S. (2011). A Survey of Architectures and Localization Techniques for Underwater Acoustic Sensor Networks. *IEEE Communications Surveys and Tutorials*, *13*(3), 487–502. doi:10.1109/SURV.2011.020211.00035

Fallah, N., Apostolopoulos, I., Bekris, K., & Folmer, E. (2013). Indoor Human Navigation Systems: A Survey. *Interacting with Computers*. doi:10.1093/iwc/iws010

Fancher. (2016). *Double Helix*. Retrieved from http://www.cod.edu/people/faculty/fancher/DoubleHelix.htm

Fanelli, A., Giovanni, M., Companile, M., & Signorini, M. (2013). Quantitative assessment of fetal well-being through CTG recordings: A new parameter based on phase-rectified signal average. *IEEE Journal Biomedical and Health Informatics*, *17*(5), 959–966. doi:10.1109/JBHI.2013.2268423 PMID:25055375

Fan, K., Mao, D., Lu, Z., & Wu, J. (2013). OPS: offline patching scheme for the images management in a secure cloud environment. In *IEEE International conference on services computing (SCC)*. doi:10.1109/SCC.2013.57

Farhang-Boroujeny, B. (2008). Filter Bank Spectrum Sensing for Cognitive Radios. *IEEE Transactions on Signal Processing, 56*(5), 1801–1811. doi:10.1109/TSP.2007.911490

FCC. (2003). *In the Matter of Facilitating Opportunities for Flexible, Efficient and Reliable Spectrum Use Employing Cognitive Radio Technologies*. ET Docket No.03-108.

Federal Communications Commission (FCC). (2014). Retrieved from HTTP: //transition.fcc.gov/Bureaus/Engineering_Technology/Orders/2002/fcc02048.pdf

Fernandes, H., Filipe, V., Costa, P., & Barroso, J. (2014). Location based Services for the Blind Supported by RFID Technology. *Procedia Computer Science, 27*(0), 2–8. doi:10.1016/j.procs.2014.02.002

Fernandez, V. I., Hou, S. M., Hover, F. S., Lang, J. H., & Triantafyllou, M. S. (2007). Lateral line inspired MEMS-array pressure sensing for passive underwater navigation. In *Proceedings of the International Symposium on Unmanned Untethered Submersible Technology*.

Ferrag, M. A., Nafa, M., & Ghanemi, S. (2014). Security and privacy in mobile ad hoc social networks. In D. Rawat, B. Bista, & G. Yan (Eds.), *Security, privacy, trust, and resource management in mobile and wireless communications* (pp. 222–243). Hershey, PA: IGI Global. doi:10.4018/978-1-4666-4691-9.ch010

Filipe, V., Fernandes, F., Fernandes, H., Sousa, A., Paredes, H., & Barroso, J. (2012). Blind Navigation Support System based on Microsoft Kinect. *Procedia Computer Science, 14*, 94–101. doi:10.1016/j.procs.2012.10.011

Firoozy, N., & Shirazi, M. (2011). Planar Inverted-F Antenna (PIFA) Design Dissection for Cellular Communication Application. *Journal of Electromagnetic Analysis and Applications, 03*(10), 406–411. doi:10.4236/jemaa.2011.310064

Fleury, M., Qadri, N. N., Altaf, M., & Ghanbari, M. (2011). Robust video streaming over MANET and VANET. In C. Zhu, Y. Li, & X. Niu (Eds.), *Streaming media architectures, techniques, and applications: Recent advances* (pp. 170–200). Hershey, PA: IGI Global. doi:10.4018/978-1-61692-831-5.ch008

Fodor, V., Glaropoulos, I., & Pescosolido, L. (2009). Detecting low-power primary signals via distributed sensing to support opportunities spectrum access. In Proceedings of IEEE ICC'09.

Forouzan & Fegan. (2007). *Data Communications and Networking* (4th ed.). McGraw-Hill.

Forsmann, J., Hiromoto, R., & Svoboda, J. (2007). A time-slotted on-demand routing protocol for mobile ad hoc unmanned vehicle systems. In *SPIE Defense and Security Symposium, Unmanned Systems Technology*, Orlando, FL. doi:10.1117/12.719355

Freitas Jr. (2005). Progress in Nanomedicine and Medical Nanorobotics. In Handbook of Theoretical and Computational Nanotechnology. American Scientific Publishers.

Freitas Jr. (n.d.). Current Status of Nanomedicine and Medical Nanorobotics (Invited Survey). *J. Comput. Theor. Nanosci., 2*, 1-25.

Frew, E., & Brown, T. (2008). Networking Issues for Small Unmanned Aircraft Systems. *Journal of Intelligent & Robotic Systems, 54*(1-3), 21–37. doi:10.1007/s10846-008-9253-2

Fuentes, G., Barbe, L., Moer, K. V., & Björsell, N. (2013). Discriminant Analysis for Automatic Signal Detection in Measured Power Spectra. *IEEE Transactions on Instrumentation and Measurement, 62*(12), 3351–3360. doi:10.1109/TIM.2013.2265607

Fujimoto, K. (2008). Mobile Antenna Systems Handbook. Artech House.

Fujino, Y., & Ogimura, K. (2004). A rectangular parabola rectenna with elliptical beam for SPS test satellite experiment. *Proc. of the Institute of Electronics, Information and Communication Engineers* (SBC-1-10, pp.S29-S20).

Fujino, Y., Fujita, M., Kaya, N., Kunimi, S., Ishii, M., Ogihata, N., & Ida, S. et al. (1996), A dual polarization microwave power transmission system for microwave propelled airship experiment.*Proceedings of International Symposium on Antennas and Propagation* (vol. 2, pp.393-396).

Fung, L. C., Chan, K. H., Lam, W. K., Leung, S. W., Wong, Y. F., Wu, P. W. K., & Tang, C. K. (2007). Electromagnetic assessment on human safety of RFID system at Hong Kong International Airport. *Microwave and Optical Technology Letters*, *49*(4), 924–928. doi:10.1002/mop.22311

Gaetano, D., McEvoy, P., Ammann, M. J., Browne, J. E., Keating, L., & Horgan, F. (2013). Footwear antennas for body area telemetry. *IEEE Transactions on Antennas and Propagation*, *61*(10), 4908–4916. doi:10.1109/TAP.2013.2272451

Gallo, C., Perilli, M., & de Bonis, M. (2011). Mobile ad hoc networks: Protocol design and implementation. In M. Cruz-Cunha & F. Moreira (Eds.), *Handbook of research on mobility and computing: Evolving technologies and ubiquitous impacts* (pp. 31–47). Hershey, PA: IGI Global. doi:10.4018/978-1-60960-042-6.ch003

Gandino, F., Sanchez, E. R., Montrucchio, B., & Rebaudengo, M. (2009). RFID technology for agri-food tracability management. In J. Symonds, J. Ayoade, & D. Parry (Eds.), *Auto-identification and ubiquitous computing applications* (pp. 54–72). Hershey, PA: IGI Global. doi:10.4018/978-1-60566-298-5.ch004

Gao, Q. (2011). A Few DNA Based Security Techniques. *Systems, Applications and Technology Conference, IEEE*.

Gao, H., Kong, Y., Cui, D., & Ozkan, C. S. (2003). Spontaneous Insertion of DNA Oligonucleotides into Carbon Nanotubes. *Nano Letters*, *3*(4), 471–473. doi:10.1021/nl025967a

Gardner, W. A. (1988). Signal Interception: A Unifying Theoretical Framework for Feature Detection. *IEEE Transactions on Communications*, *36*(8), 897–906. doi:10.1109/26.3769

Gardner, W. A. (1994). *Cyclostationarity in Communications and Signal Processing* (W. A. Gardner, Ed.). New York: IEEE Press.

Gavalas, D., Konstantopoulos, C., Mamalis, B., & Pantziou, G. (2011). Mobility prediction in mobile ad-hoc networks. In S. Pierre (Ed.), *Next generation mobile networks and ubiquitous computing* (pp. 226–240). Hershey, PA: IGI Global. doi:10.4018/978-1-60566-250-3.ch021

Gawali, D. P. (2012). Leader Election Problem in Distributed Algorithm. *International Journal of Computer Science and Technology*, *3*(1), 714–718.

Ge, F., & Bostian, C. W. (2008). A Parallel Computing Based Spectrum Sensing Approach for Signal Detection under Conditions of Low SNR and Rayleigh Multipath Fading. In *Proceedings of 3rd IEEE Symposium on New Frontiers in Dynamic Spectrum Access Networks*. doi:10.1109/DYSPAN.2008.12

Geirhofer, S., Tong, L., & Sadler, B. M. (2007). Dynamic Spectrum Access in the Time Domain: Modeling and Exploiting White Space. *IEEE Communications Magazine*, *45*(5), 66–72. doi:10.1109/MCOM.2007.358851

Geng, L., Zhang, Y., Wang, J., Fuh, J., & Teo, S. (2013). Mission planning of autonomous UAVs for urban surveillance with evolutionary algorithms. In *10th IEEE International Conference on Control and Automation (ICCA)*, Hangzhou, China. doi:10.1109/ICCA.2013.6564992

George, J., & Sousa, J. (2010). Search Strategies for Multiple UAV Search and Destroy Missions. *Journal of Intelligent & Robotic Systems*, *61*(1-4), 355–367. doi:10.1007/s10846-010-9486-8

Gerla, M. (2012). Vehicular Cloud Computing. *IEEE Vehicular Communications and Applications Workshop.*

Ge, S., & Wang, C. (2002). Direct adaptive NN control of a class of nonlinear systems. *IEEE Transactions on Neural Networks, 13*(1), 214–221. doi:10.1109/72.977306 PMID:18244420

Ghada, K., Li, J., & Ji, Y. (2012). Cross-layer design for topology control and routing in MANETs. *Wireless Communications and Mobile Computing, 12*(3), 257–267. doi:10.1002/wcm.957

Ghaderi, M., Towsley, D., & Kurose, J. (2008). Reliability gain of network coding in lossy wireless networks. In *Proceedings of 28th IEEE Conference in Computer Communications.* doi:10.1109/INFOCOM.2008.284

Ghasemi, A., & Sousa, E. S. (2005). Collaborative spectrum sensing for opportunistic access in fading environment. In *Proc. IEEE DySPAN,* (pp. 131-136). doi:10.1109/DYSPAN.2005.1542627

Ghasemi, A., & Sousa, E. S. (2008). Spectrum Sensing in Cognitive Radio Networks: Requirements, Challenges and Design Trade-offs. *IEEE Communications Magazine, 46*(4), 32–39. doi:10.1109/MCOM.2008.4481338

Ghauri, A., Qureshi, I., Shah, I., & Khan, N. (2014). Modulation Classification using Cyclostationary Features on Fading Channels. Research Journal of Applied Sciences. *Engineering and Technology, 7*(24), 5331–5339.

Ghosh, S. (2015), Design and testing of RF energy harvesting module in GSM 900 band using circularly polarized antenna. *Proceedings of IEEE International Conference on Research in Computational Intelligence and Communication Networks* (pp. 386 – 389). doi:10.1109/ICRCICN.2015.7434269

Ghosh, S., & Chakrabarty, A. (2016). Dual band circularly polarized monopole antenna design for RF energy harvesting. *Journal of the Institution of Electronics and Telecommunication Engineers, 62*(1), 9–16.

Ghosh, S., Ghosh, S. K., & Chakrabarty, A. (2014), Design of RF energy harvesting system for wireless sensor node using circularly polarized monopole antenna. In *Proceedings of IEEE 9th International Conference on Industrial and Information Systems* (pp. 1-6).

Girard, A., Howell, A., & Hedrick, J. (2014). Border patrol and surveillance missions using multiple unmanned air vehicles. In *43rd IEEE Conference on Decision and Control* (CDC), Nassau.

Goel, A.L. (1985). Software Reliability Models: Assumptions, Limitations, and Applicability. *IEEE Transaction of Software Computing, SE-11*(12), 1411-1423. DOI: 10.1109/TSE.1985.232177

Goel, A. L., & Okumoto, K. (1979). A time dependent error detection rate model for software reliability and other performance measures. *IEEE Transactions on Reliability, R-28*(3), 206–211. doi:10.1109/TR.1979.5220566

Goh, W., & Yeo, C.K. (2013). *Teaching an old trusted platform module: repurposing a tpm for an identity-based signature scheme.* Academic Press.

Goh, W., Leong, P. C., & Yeo, C. K. (2011). The plausibly-deniable, practical trusted platform module based anti-forensics client-server system. *IEEE Journal on Selected Areas in Communications.*

Gold, J. L. (1995). Oligonucleotides as research, diagnostic, and therapeutic agents. *Biological Chemistry, 270*(23), 13581–13584. doi:10.1074/jbc.270.23.13581 PMID:7775406

Gómez, C., García, J. A., Mediavilla, A., & Tazón, A. (2004), A high efficiency rectenna element using E-pHEMT technology.*Proceedings of 12th GAAS Symposium* (pp.315-318).

Gonzalez, F. I., Milburn, H. M., Bernard, E. N., & Newman, J. C. (1998). Deep-ocean Assessment and Reporting of Tsunamis (DART®): Brief Overview and Status Report. In *Proceedings of the International Workshop on Tsunami Disaster Mitigation.*

Goodchild, M., Johnston, D., Maguire, D., & Noronha, V. (2003). Distributed and Mobile Computing. In A Research Agenda for Geographic Information Science. Boca Raton, FL: CRC Press.

Google. (n.d.). *Getting Started with Android Studio.* Retrieved from http://developer.android.com/sdk/installing/studio.html

Gopal, V. D., Subramaniam, S. M., & Jawahar, D. Š. (2012). Gossip Originated Trusted Leader Selection with Reinforcement in Wireless Mesh Network. *2012 International Conference on Information and Network Technology* (ICINT 2012).

Green, D. (2006). Transitioning NOAA Moored Buoy Systems From Research to Operations. In *Proceedings of OCEANS'06 MTS/IEEE Conference.* doi:10.1109/OCEANS.2006.307068

Greene, K., & Keith, R. (2002). *K2 Medical System.* Retrieved August 12, 2015, from http://www.k2ms.com/

Griffiths, G. (2003). *Technology and Applications of Autonomous Underwater Vehicles.* London: Taylor & Francis.

Grosjean, C., & Tai, Y. C. (1999). A thermoneumatic peristaltic micropump. In Proceedings of Transducers'99.

Gudmundson, E., Sandgren, N., & Stoica, P. (2008). Automatic Smoothing of Periodogram. In *Proceedings of the 2006 IEEE International Conference on Acoustics, Speech and Signal Processing (ICASSP).*

Guenther, E. (2009). *Multi-User Signal Classification via Cyclic Spectral Analysis* (Master's Dissertation). Wright State University.

Guijarro-Berdiñas, B., & Alonso-Betanzos, A. (2002). Empirical Evaluation of a Hybrid Intelligent Monitoring System using Different Measures of Effectiveness. *Journal of Artificial Intelligence Medicine, 24*(1), 1–6. doi:10.1016/S0933-3657(01)00091-4 PMID:11779686

Guijarro-Berdinas, B., Alonso-Betanzos, A., & Fontella-Romero, O. (2002). Intelligent analysis and pattern recognition in cardiotocographic signals using a tightly coupled hybrid system. *Elsevier. Artificial Intelligence, 136*(1), 1–27. doi:10.1016/S0004-3702(01)00163-1

Guo, J., & Bhuyan, L. N. (2006). Load Balancing in a Cluster-Based Web Server for Multimedia Applications. *IEEE Transactions on Parallel and Distributed Systems, 17*(11).

Guozeng, C., & Zhen, W. (2015). Adaptive Centralized NN control of large scale stochastic nonlinear time delay systems with unknown dead zone inputs. *Neurocomputing, 158,* 194–203. doi:10.1016/j.neucom.2015.01.048

Gupta, S., Garg, M., Xu, H., & Goh, M. (2009). RFID and supply chain visibility. In B. Unhelkar (Ed.), Handbook of research in mobile business, second edition: Technical, methodological and social perspectives (pp. 368–374). Hershey, PA: IGI Global. doi:10.4018/978-1-60566-156-8.ch034

Gupta, M. (2014). Enhanced Flooding Scheme for AODV Routing Protocol in Mobile Ad Hoc Networks. In *Proceedings of Electronic Systems Signal Processing and Computing Technologies.* ICESC. doi:10.1109/ICESC.2014.60

Gustafsson, M., Sohl, C., & Kristensson, G. (2007). Physical limitations on antennas of arbitrary shape. In Royal Society a-Mathematical Physical and Engineering Sciences (Vol. 463, pp. 2589–2607). http://doi.org/ doi:10.1098/rspa.2007.1893

Gutmann, R. J., & Gworek, R. B. (1979). Yagi-uda receiving elements in microwave power transmission system rectennas. *The Journal of Microwave Power, 14*(4), 313–320. doi:10.1080/16070658.1979.11689166

Guy, R., & Truong, K. (2012). *CrossingGuard: exploring information content in navigation aids for visually impaired pedestrians.* Paper presented at the SIGCHI Conference on Human Factors in Computing Systems, Austin, TX. doi:10.1145/2207676.2207733

Hagerty, J. A., Helmbrecht, F. B., McCalpin, W. H., Zane, R., & Popovic, Z. V. (2004). Recycling ambient microwave energy with broad-band rectenna arrays. *IEEE Transactions on Microwave Theory and Techniques*, *52*(3), 1014–1024. doi:10.1109/TMTT.2004.823585

Hamdi, M., Sharma, G., Ferreira, A., & Mavroidis, D. (2005). Molecular Mechanics Study on Bionanorobotic Components using Force Feedback. *IEEE International Conference on Robotics and Biomimetics, Hong Kong.*

Hanada, E. (2013). Effective use of RFID in medicine and general healthcare. In T. Issa, P. Isaías, & P. Kommers (Eds.), *Information systems and technology for organizations in a networked society* (pp. 335–352). Hershey, PA: IGI Global. doi:10.4018/978-1-4666-4062-7.ch018

Hancke, G. P. (2012). Industrial Wireless Sensor Networks: A selection of challenging applications. In *Proceedings of 6th European conference on Antennas and Propagation (EUCAP).* doi:10.1109/EuCAP.2012.6206686

Händel, P., & Zetterberg, P. (2010). Receiver I/Q imbalance: Tone test, sensitivity analysis, and the universal software radio peripheral. *IEEE Transactions on Instrumentation and Measurement*, *59*(3), 704–714. doi:10.1109/TIM.2009.2025989

Han, G., Zhang, C., Shu, L., & Rodrigues, J. (2015). Impacts of Deployment Strategies on Localization Performance in Underwater Acoustic Sensor Networks. *IEEE Transactions on Industrial Electronics*, *62*(3), 1725–1733. doi:10.1109/TIE.2014.2362731

Hankerson, Menezes, & Vanstone. (n.d.). *Guide to Elliptic Curve Cryptography.* Academic Press.

Hanzo, L. II, & Tafazolli, R. (2011). The effects of shadow-fading on QoS-aware routing and admission control protocols designed for multi-hop MANETs. *Wireless Communications and Mobile Computing*, *11*(1), 1–22. doi:10.1002/wcm.912

Hanzo, L., & Tafazolli, R. (2006). Quality of Service Routing and Admission Control for Mobile Ad-hoc Networks with a Contention-based MAC Layer. In *Proceedings of IEEE International Conference Mobile Adhoc and Sensor Systems (MASS).* doi:10.1109/MOBHOC.2006.278594

Hao, Y., Alomainy, A., Hall, P. S., Nechayev, Y. I., Parini, C. G., & Constantinou, C. C. (2012). *Antennas and Propagation for Body Centric Wireless Communications* (2nd ed.; pp. 38–41). Norwood, MA: Artech House, Inc.

Hardgrave, B. C., Aloysius, J. A., & Goyal, S. (2013). RFID-enabled visibility and retail inventory record inaccuracy: Experiments in the field. *Production and Operations Management*, *22*(4), 843–856. doi:10.1111/poms.12010

Harnack, O., Ford, W. E., Yasuda, A., & Wessels, J. M. (2002). Tris (hydroxymethyle) phosphine capped gold particles templated by DNA as nano wire precursors. *Nano Letters*, *2*(9), 919–923. doi:10.1021/nl020259a

Harous, S., Aldubai, M., & Nasir, Q. (2008). An energy aware multi-path routing algorithm for mobile ad hoc networks. *International Journal of Business Data Communications and Networking*, *4*(2), 58–75. doi:10.4018/jbdcn.2008040104

Harrington, R. F. (1960). Effect of antenna size on gain, bandwidth, and efficiency. *Journal of Research of the National Bureau of Standards, Section D. Radio Propagation*, *64D*(1), 1–12. doi:10.6028/jres.064D.003

Hart, P. E., Nilsson, N. J., & Raphael, B. (1968). A Formal Basis for the Heuristic Determination of Minimum Cost Paths. *Systems Science and Cybernetics. IEEE Transactions on*, *4*(2), 100–107. doi:10.1109/TSSC.1968.300136

Haskou, A., Ramadan, A., Al-Husseini, M., Kasem, F., Kabalan, K. Y., & ElHajj, A. (2012). A simple estimation and verification technique for electrical characterization of textiles. In *Middle East Conference on Antennas and Propagation* (pp. 1–4). doi:10.1109/MECAP.2012.6618190

Hawrylak, P. J., & Hart, C. (2014). Using radio frequency identification technology to store patients' medical information. In V. Michell, D. Rosenorn-Lanng, S. Gulliver, & W. Currie (Eds.), *Handbook of research on patient safety and quality care through health informatics* (pp. 159–178). Hershey, PA: IGI Global. doi:10.4018/978-1-4666-4546-2.ch009

Hawrylak, P. J., Schimke, N., Hale, J., & Papa, M. (2012). RFID in e-health: Technology, implementation, and security issues. In J. Rodrigues, I. de la Torre Díez, & B. Sainz de Abajo (Eds.), *Telemedicine and e-health services, policies, and applications: Advancements and developments* (pp. 347–368). Hershey, PA: IGI Global. doi:10.4018/978-1-4666-0888-7.ch013

Haykin, S. (2005). Cognitive Radio: Brain-empowered wireless communications. *IEEE Journal on Selected Areas in Communications*, *23*(2), 201–220. doi:10.1109/JSAC.2004.839380

He, Q., Wu, D., & Khosla, P. (2004). SORI: A Secure and Objective Reputation- based Incentive Schemes for Ad-hoc Networks. In *WCNC'04 IEEE Wireless Communications and Networking Conference*.

Hecht, A., Ma, S., Porszasz, J., & Casaburi, R. (2009). *Methodology for using long-term accelerometry monitoring to describe daily activity patterns in COPD*. COPD.

Heelen, L. (2013). Fetal monitoring: Creating a culture of safety with informed choice. *Journal of Perinatal Education*, *22*(3), 156–165. doi:10.1891/1058-1243.22.3.156 PMID:24868127

Heese, H. S. (2007). Inventory record inaccuracy, double marginalization, and RFID adoption. *Production and Operations Management*, *16*(5), 542–553. doi:10.1111/j.1937-5956.2007.tb00279.x

Heidemann, J., Stojanovic, M., & Zorzi, M. (2011). Underwater sensor networks: applications, advances and challenges. *Philosophical Transactions of the Royal Society A: Mathematical, Physical and Engineering Sciences, 370*(1958), 158-175.10.1098/rsta.2011.0214

Heidemann, J., Li, Y., Syed, A., Wills, J., & Ye, W. (2006). Research Challenges and Applications for Underwater Sensor Networking. In *Proceedings of the IEEE Wireless Communications and Networking Conference* (pp. 228-235). doi:10.1109/WCNC.2006.1683469

Heimfarth, T., & De Araujo, J. (2014). *Using Unmanned Aerial Vehicle to Connect Disjoint Segments of Wireless Sensor Network*. In IEEE 28th International Conference on Advanced Information Networking and Applications (AINA), Victoria, BC.

Heim, G. R., Wentworth, W. R. Jr, & Peng, X. (2009). The value to the customer of RFID in service applications. *Decision Sciences*, *40*(3), 477–512. doi:10.1111/j.1540-5915.2009.00237.x

Heinzelman, B., Chandrakasan, P., & Balakrishnan, H. (2002). An application-specific protocol architecture for wireless microsensor networks. *IEEE Transactions on Wireless Communications*, *1*(4), 660–670. doi:10.1109/TWC.2002.804190

Heinzelman, R., Chandrakasan, A., & Balakrishnan, H. (2000). Energy efficient communication protocol for wireless micro-sensor networks. In *Proceedings of the 33rd Hawaii International Conference on System Sciences*. doi:10.1109/HICSS.2000.926982

Heiss, G., Lapiene, V., & Kukolka, F. (2009). Single-molecule investigations of a photo switchable nanodevice. *Small*, *5*(10), 1169–1175. PMID:19263427

Hennebert, C., & Dos Santos, J. (2014). Security Protocols and Privacy Issues into 6LoWPAN Stack: A Synthesis. *IEEE Internet of Things Journal*, *1*(5), 384–398. doi:10.1109/JIOT.2014.2359538

Hernandez, E., & Arkun, Y. (1993). Control of nonlinear system using polynomial ARMA models. *AIChE Journal. American Institute of Chemical Engineers*, *39*(3), 446–460. doi:10.1002/aic.690390308

Hertel, T. W., & Smith, G. S. (2003). On the dispersive properties of the conical spiral antenna and its use for pulsed radiation. *IEEE Transactions on Antennas and Propagation, 51*(7), 1426–1433. doi:10.1109/TAP.2003.813602

Hertleer, C., Rogier, H., Member, S., Vallozzi, L., & Van Langenhove, L. (2009). A Textile Antenna for Off-Body Communication Integrated Into Protective Clothing for Firefighters. *IEEE Transactions on Antennas and Propagation, 57*(4), 919–925. doi:10.1109/TAP.2009.2014574

Hirabayashi, M., Nishikawa, A., Tanaka, F., Hagiya, M., Kojima, H., & Oiwa, K. (2011). Analysis on secure and effective applications of a DNA-based cryptosystem. Bio-Inspired Computing: Theories and Applications, IEEE.

Hla, Choi, & Park. (2008). Obstacle Avoidance Algorithm for Collective Movement in Nanorobots. *International Journal of Computer Science and Network Security, 8*(11), 302-309.

Hogg, T., & Freitas, R. A., Jr. (2012). *Acoustic communication for medical nanorobots.* arXiv:1202.0568 vi [cs.RD]

Honeywell. (2006). *Digital Compass Solution - HMC6352 datasheet.* Author.

Honeywell. (2011). *DRM™4000L Dead Reckoning Module Datasheet.* Author.

Hong, Y. S., No, J. H., & Kim, S. Y. (2006). DNS-based load-balancing in distributed web server systems. In *Proceedings of Fourth IEEE Workshop on Software Technologies for Future Embedded and Ubiquitous Systems.*

Hossain, M. A., & Quaddus, M. (2014). Mandatory and voluntary adoption of RFID. In J. Wang (Ed.), *Encyclopedia of business analytics and optimization* (pp. 1457–1475). Hershey, PA: IGI Global. doi:10.4018/978-1-4666-5202-6.ch132

Hommady, M., & Fujita, Y. (1999). Micromachines for nanoscale science and technology. *Nanotechnology, 10*(1), 29–33. doi:10.1088/0957-4484/10/1/007

Housley, R., Polk, W., Ford, W., & Solo, D. (2002). *Internet X. 509 public key infrastructure certificate and certificate revocation list (CRL) profile.* RFC 3280.

Houston, B. H., Bucaro, J., & Romano, A. J. (2001). New virtual sonar and wireless sensor system concepts. *The Journal of the Acoustical Society of America, 115*(5), 2614–2615. doi:10.1121/1.4784795

Hozak, K., & Collier, D. A. (2008). RFID as an enabler of improved manufacturing performance. *Decision Sciences, 39*(4), 859–881. doi:10.1111/j.1540-5915.2008.00214.x

Hsin, W., & Harn, L. (2013). Offline/online security in mobile ad hoc networks. In A. Elçi, J. Pieprzyk, A. Chefranov, M. Orgun, H. Wang, & R. Shankaran (Eds.), *Theory and practice of cryptography solutions for secure information systems* (pp. 199–222). Hershey, PA: IGI Global. doi:10.4018/978-1-4666-4030-6.ch009

Hsu, C. F. (2007). Self-organizing adaptive fuzzy neural network for a class of nonlinear system. *IEEE Transactions on Neural Networks, 18*(4), 1232–1241. doi:10.1109/TNN.2007.899178 PMID:17668674

Hu, Y. H., & Hwang, J. N. (2001). Handbook of Neural Network Signal Processing. CRC Press.

Hua, W., Marshall, A., & Wai, Y. (2007). *Path Planning and Following Algorithms in an Indoor Navigation Model for Visually Impaired.* Paper presented at the Internet Monitoring and Protection, 2007. ICIMP 2007. Second International Conference on.

Huai-wei, J., Shi-gang, W., & Wei, X. U. (2005). Construction of Medical Nanorobot. *IEEE International Conference on Robotics and Biomimetics (ROBIO).*

Hua, M., & Dong, L. (2011). A Closed-loop Adjusting strategy for wireless HART Time Synchronization. In *Proceedings of 11th International Symposium on Communication and Information Technology (ISCIT 2011)*. doi:10.1109/ISCIT.2011.6089716

Huang, W., Xiong, Y., Miao, F., Wang, X., Wu, C., Lu, Q., & Xudong, G. (2013). Fine-grained refinement on tpm-based protocol applications. *IEEE Trans Info Forensics Sec, 8*(6).

Huang, D., Misra, S., Verma, M., & Xue, G. (2011, September). Pacp: An efcient pseudonymous authentication-based conditional privacy protocol for vanets. *IEEE Transactions on Intelligent Transportation Systems, 12*(3), 736–747. doi:10.1109/TITS.2011.2156790

Huang, J., & Liang, S. (2011). Reliability Gain of Network Coding in complicated network topology. In *Proceedings of 7th International Conference on Wireless Communication, Networking and Mobile Computing*. doi:10.1109/wicom.2011.6040178

Huang, Y., Thomson, S., Hoffmann, W., Lan, Y., & Fritz, B. (2013). Development and prospect of unmanned aerial vehicle technologies for agricultural production management. *International Journal of Agricultural and Biological Engineering, 6*(3), 1–10.

Huba, W., & Shenoy, N. (2012). Airborne surveillance networks with directional antennas. In *8th International Conference on Networking and Services (ICNS)*.

Hussain, A., Wenbi, R., Silva, A. L. D., Nadher, M., & Mudhisha, M. (2015). Health and emergency-care platform for the elderly and disabled people in the Smart City. *Journal of Systems and Software, 110*, 253–263. doi:10.1016/j.jss.2015.08.041

Hussain, R., & Oh, H. (2014, October). A Secure and Privacy-Aware Route Tracing and Revocation Mechanism in VANET-based Clouds. *Journal of The Korea Institute of Information Security and Cryptology, 24*(5), 795–807. doi:10.13089/JKIISC.2014.24.5.795

Hwang, L., & Yoon, K. (1981). Multiple Attribute Decision Making.Lecture Notes in Economics and Mathematical Systems, 186. doi:10.1007/978-3-642-48318-9

Hwang, A., Yoon, S., Kim, M. H., Lee, S., Hong, J. S., & Parmentier, G. (2011). Performance Evaluation of AHRS Based MEMS For Unmanned Underwater Vehicle. In *Proceedings of the Twenty-first International Offshore and Polar Engineering Conference*.

Hyun-Seung, K., Deok-Rae, K., Se-Hoon, Y., Yong-Hwan, S., & Sang-Kook, H. (2013). An Indoor Visible Light Communication Positioning System Using a RF Carrier Allocation Technique. *Lightwave Technology. Journalism, 31*(1), 134–144. doi:10.1109/JLT.2012.2225826

INFANT Study. (2009). Retrieved August 12, 2015, from http://www.k2ms.com/products/infant.aspx

Intanagonwiwat, C., Govindan, R., Estrin, D., Heidemann, J., & Silva, F. C. (2003). Directed Diffusion for Wireless Sensor Networking. *IEEE/ACM Transaction on Networking, 11*(1), 2-16.

Ismail & Ja'afar. (2007). Mobile Ad Hoc Network Overview. In *IEEE Asia Pacific Conference on Applied Electromagnetics Proceedings*.

Ismail, H., Issa, K., Abdallah, K. (2015). Designing High Performance Web-Based Computing Services to Promote Telemedicine Database Management System. *IEEE Transaction on Services Computing, 8*(1).

ISO/IEC-11889:2009. (2009). *Information technology – Trusted Platform Module*. ISO.

Isomursu, M., & Ervasti, M. (2009). Touch-based access to mobile Internet: User experience findings. *International Journal of Mobile Human Computer Interaction, 1*(4), 58–79. doi:10.4018/jmhci.2009062605

Ito, T., Fujino, Y., & Fujita, M. (1993). Fundamental experiment of a rectenna array for microwave power receptions. *IEICE Transactions on Communications* (Vol. E *(Norwalk, Conn.), 76-B*(12), 1508–1513.

Ito, Y. (2004). Design and synthesis of functional polymers by *in vitro* selection. *Polymers for Advanced Technologies, 15*(12), 3–14. doi:10.1002/pat.455

Ito, Y., Kawazoe, N., & Imanishi, Y. (2000). In vitro selected oligonucleotides as receptors in binding assays. *Methods (San Diego, Calif.), 22*(1), 107–114. doi:10.1006/meth.2000.1041 PMID:11020323

Izadi, N. (2012). *Bio-inspired mems aquatic flow sensor arrays* (Ph.D.). University of Twente. Retrieved from http://eprints.eemcs.utwente.nl/19216/01/Final-HighQ.pdf

J., R.-T., Roa, L. M., & Prado, M. (2006). Design of antennas for a wearable sensor for homecare movement monitoring. *IEEE Engineering in Medicine and Biology Society*, (pp. 5972–5976).

Jabbar, H., Song, Y. S., & Jeong, T. T. (2010). RF energy harvesting system and circuits for charging of mobile devices. *IEEE Transactions on Consumer Electronics, 56*(1), 247–253. doi:10.1109/TCE.2010.5439152

Jacquet, S., & Varghese, M. (2014). Role Based and Energy Efficient Trust System for Clustered Wsn. *IOSR Journal of Computer Engineering, 16*(2), 44–48.

Jain & Bhatnagar. (2014a). A Novel DNA Sequence Dictionary method for Securing Data in DNA using Spiral Approach and Framework of DNA Cryptography. *IEEE, ICAETR*.

Jain & Bhatnagar. (2014b). Analogy of Various DNA Based Security Algorithms Using Cryptography and Steganography. *IEEE, ICICT*.

Jain & Sharma. (2012). Leader Election Algorithm in Wireless Environments Using Fibonacci Heap Structure. *Int. J. Computer Technology and Applications, 3*(3), 871-873.

Jain, R. (2012). The art of computer systems performance analysis: Technique for experimental Design, Measurement, Simulation and Modeling. *Wiley Professional Computing*, 462-465

Jamali, N. N., & El Ouadghiri, D. (2013). An enhanced on ad hoc wireless network routing based on AODV. In Proceedings of Wireless Days (WD).

Jang, W. M. (2014). Blind Cyclostationary Spectrum Sensing in Cognitive Radios. *IEEE Communications Letters, 18*(3), 393–396. doi:10.1109/LCOMM.2014.012714.132507

Jawhar, I., Mohamed, N., Al-Jaroodi, J., & Sheng Zhang, J. (2013). Data communication in linear wireless sensor networks using unmanned aerial vehicles. In *International Conference on Unmanned Aircraft Systems (ICUAS)*, Atlanta, GA. doi:10.1109/ICUAS.2013.6564725

Jelassi, S. (2015). QoE-Driven Video Streaming System over Cloud-Based VANET. *LNCS, 9066*, 84–93.

Jeong, B., Cheng, C., & Prabhu, V. (2011). Performance modeling and analysis of surgery patient identification using RFID. In J. Wang (Ed.), *Information systems and new applications in the service sector: Models and methods* (pp. 279–292). Hershey, PA: IGI Global. doi:10.4018/978-1-60960-138-6.ch016

Jiang & Yin. (2013). The Advantages and Disadvantages of DNA Password in the Contrast to the Traditional Cryptography and Quantum Cryptography. *Bio-Inspired Computing: Theories and Applications*, 307-316.

Jiang, X., & Ji, S. (2014). E-Government Web Portal Adoption: A Service Level and Service Quality Perspective. In *Proceedings of 47th Hawaii International Conference on System Science*, (pp. 2179-2188). DOI doi:10.1109/HICSS.2014.275

Jia, X., & Feng, Q. Y. (2015). An improved anti-collision protocol for radio frequency identification tag. *International Journal of Communication Systems*, 28(3), 401–413. doi:10.1002/dac.2629

Jing, L., Liu, F., & Li, Y. (2011). Energy saving routing algorithm based on SPIN protocol in WSN. In *Proceedings of International conference on Image Analysis and Signal Processing (IASP)*.

Ji, S., Li, Y., & Jia, X. (2011). Capacity of dual-radio multi-channel wireless sensor networks for continuous data collection. In *Proceedings of IEEE INFOCOM*. doi:10.1109/INFCOM.2011.5934880

Joa-Ng. (1999). A Peer-to-Peer Zone-Based Two-Level Link State Routing for Mobile Ad Hoc Networks. *IEEE Journal on Selected Areas in Communications*, 17(8).

Johannes, W., & Kurt, D. (2013). A hijacker guide to communication interfaces of the trusted platform module. *Computers & Mathematics with Applications (Oxford, England)*, 65(5), 748–761. doi:10.1016/j.camwa.2012.06.018

Johansson, M., & Rantzer, A. (1998). Computation of piecewise quadratic Lyapunov functions for hybrid systems. *IEEE Transactions on Automatic Control*, 43(4), 555–559. doi:10.1109/9.664157

John Krautheim, F., Phatak, D.S., & Sherman, A.T. (2010). *Introducing trusted virtual environment module: a new mechanism for rooting trust in cloud computing*. Academic Press.

Johnstone, R., Caputo, D., Cella, U., Gandelli, A., Alippi, C., Grimaccia, F., & Zich, R. E. et al. (2008). Smart Environmental Measurement & Analysis Technologies (SEMAT): Wireless sensor networks in the marine environment. In *Proceedings of the Wireless Sensor and Actuator Network Research on Opposite Sides of the Globe (SENSEI)*.

Josang and S. LoPresti. (2004). *Analyzing the Relationship between Risk and Trust. In Proc.2nd Int'1 Conf. Trust Management (I Trust' 04)*, (pp. 135–145). Springer-Verlag.

Jr, H., & Williams, C. S. (1965). Transients in wide-angle conical antennas. *IEEE Transactions on Antennas and Propagation*, 13(2), 236–246. doi:10.1109/TAP.1965.1138399

Jun, S., & Shuping, H. (2015). Finite time robust passive control for a class of uncertain Lipschitz nonlinear systems with time delays. *Neurocomputing*, 159, 275–281. doi:10.1016/j.neucom.2015.01.038

Juntunen, A., Tuunainen, V. K., & Luukkainen, S. (2012). Critical business model issues in deploying NFC technology for mobile services: Case mobile ticketing. *International Journal of E-Services and Mobile Applications*, 4(3), 23–41. doi:10.4018/jesma.2012070102

Kadri, B., Feham, M., & M'hamed, A. (2009). Securing reactive routing protocols in MANETs using PKI (PKI-DSR). *Security and Communication Networks*, 2(4), 341–350. doi:10.1002/sec.63

Kaija, T., Lilja, J., & Salonen, P. (2010). Exposing textile antennas for harsh environment. In *Military Communications Conference (MILCOM)* (pp. 737–742).

Kaivanto, E., Berg, M., Salonen, E., & Maagt, P. (2011). Wearable circularly polarized antenna for personal satellite communication and navigation. *IEEE Transactions on Antennas and Propagation*, 59(12), 4490–4496. doi:10.1109/TAP.2011.2165513

Kalita, M., & Bezboruah, T. (2011). Investigation on performance testing and evaluation of PReWebD: A. NET technique for implementing web application. *IET Software*, 5(4), 357–365. doi:10.1049/iet-sen.2010.0139

Kalita, M., & Bezboruah, T. (2012). Investigations on implementation of web applications with different techniques. *IET Software*, *6*(6), 474–478. doi:10.1049/iet-sen.2011.0136

Kalita, M., Khanikar, S., & Bezboruah, T. (2011). Investigation on performance testing and evaluation of PReWebN: A JAVA technique for implementing web application. *IET Software*, *5*(5), 434–444. doi:10.1049/iet-sen.2011.0030

Kamiński, Ł., & Bruniecki, K. (2012). Mobile navigation system for visually impaired users in the urban environment. *Metrology and Measurement Systems*, *19*(2), 245–256. doi:10.2478/v10178-012-0021-z

Kamoun, F. (2013). Mobile NFC services: Adoption factors and a typology of business models. In I. Lee (Ed.), *Mobile services industries, technologies, and applications in the global economy* (pp. 254–272). Hershey, PA: IGI Global. doi:10.4018/978-1-4666-1981-4.ch016

Kamoun, F., & Miniaoui, S. (2015). Towards a better understanding of organizational adoption and diffusion of RFID technology: A case study approach. *International Journal of Technology Diffusion*, *6*(3), 1–20. doi:10.4018/IJTD.2015070101

Kamruzzaman, J., Azad, A. K., Karmakar, N. C., Karmakar, G., & Srinivasan, B. (2013). Security and privacy in RFID systems. In N. Karmakar (Ed.), *Advanced RFID systems, security, and applications* (pp. 16–40). Hershey, PA: IGI Global. doi:10.4018/978-1-4666-2080-3.ch002

Kang & Park. (2015). *Design of Secure Protocol for Session Key Exchange in Vehicular Cloud Computing*. Advances in Computer Science and Ubiquitous Computing.

Kang, W., & Han, Y. (2015). SmartPDR: Smartphone-Based Pedestrian Dead Reckoning for Indoor Localization. *Sensors Journal, IEEE*, *15*(5), 2906–2916. doi:10.1109/JSEN.2014.2382568

Karmakar, N. C. (2009). Smart antennas for automatic radio frequency identification readers. In C. Sun, J. Cheng, & T. Ohira (Eds.), *Handbook on advancements in smart antenna technologies for wireless networks* (pp. 449–473). Hershey, PA: IGI Global. doi:10.4018/978-1-59904-988-5.ch021

Karmakar, N. C. (2012). Introduction to chipless and conventional radio frequency identification system. In N. Karmakar (Ed.), *Chipless and conventional radio frequency identification: Systems for ubiquitous tagging* (pp. 1–8). Hershey, PA: IGI Global. doi:10.4018/978-1-4666-1616-5.ch001

Karnouskos, S. (2007). NFC-capable mobile devices for mobile payment services. In D. Taniar (Ed.), *Encyclopedia of mobile computing and commerce* (pp. 706–710). Hershey, PA: IGI Global. doi:10.4018/978-1-59904-002-8.ch118

Kasemsap, K. (2015a). The role of radio frequency identification in modern libraries. In S. Thanuskodi (Ed.), *Handbook of research on inventive digital tools for collection management and development in modern libraries* (pp. 361–385). Hershey, PA: IGI Global. doi:10.4018/978-1-4666-8178-1.ch021

Kasemsap, K. (2015b). The role of customer relationship management in the global business environments. In T. Tsiakis (Ed.), *Trends and innovations in marketing information systems* (pp. 130–156). Hershey, PA: IGI Global. doi:10.4018/978-1-4666-8459-1.ch007

Kasemsap, K. (2015c). The role of cloud computing adoption in global business. In V. Chang, R. Walters, & G. Wills (Eds.), *Delivery and adoption of cloud computing services in contemporary organizations* (pp. 26–55). Hershey, PA: IGI Global. doi:10.4018/978-1-4666-8210-8.ch002

Kasemsap, K. (2016a). Encouraging supply chain networks and customer loyalty in global supply chain. In N. Kamath & S. Saurav (Eds.), *Handbook of research on strategic supply chain management in the retail industry* (pp. 87–112). Hershey, PA: IGI Global. doi:10.4018/978-1-4666-9894-9.ch006

Kasemsap, K. (2016b). Investigating the roles of mobile commerce and mobile payment in global business. In S. Madan & J. Arora (Eds.), *Securing transactions and payment systems for m-commerce* (pp. 1–23). Hershey, PA: IGI Global. doi:10.4018/978-1-5225-0236-4.ch001

Kasemsap, K. (2016c). The fundamentals of business intelligence. *International Journal of Organizational and Collective Intelligence*, *6*(2), 12–25. doi:10.4018/IJOCI.2016040102

Kasemsap, K. (2017a). Professional and business applications of social media platforms. In V. Benson, R. Tuninga, & G. Saridakis (Eds.), *Analyzing the strategic role of social networking in firm growth and productivity* (pp. 427–450). Hershey, PA: IGI Global. doi:10.4018/978-1-5225-0559-4.ch021

Kasemsap, K. (2017b). Mastering web mining and information retrieval in the digital age. In A. Kumar (Ed.), *Web usage mining techniques and applications across industries* (pp. 1–28). Hershey, PA: IGI Global. doi:10.4018/978-1-5225-0613-3.ch001

Kaspar, C. (2009). RFID technologies and applications. In M. Pagani (Ed.), *Encyclopedia of multimedia technology and networking* (2nd ed., pp. 1232–1239). Hershey, PA: IGI Global. doi:10.4018/978-1-60566-014-1.ch167

Kathirvel, A., & Srinivasan, R. (2011). ETUS: An enhanced triple umpiring system for security and performance improvement of mobile ad hoc networks. *International Journal of Network Management*, *21*(5), 341–359. doi:10.1002/nem.761

Katiyar, V., Chand, N., & Chauhan, N. (2010). Recent advances and future trends in Wireless Sensor Networks. *International Journal of Applied Engineering Research*, *1*(3), 330–342.

Kaur, J. (2013). SBPGP Security based Model in Large Scale Manets. *International Journal of Wireless Networks and Communications*, *5*(1), 1–10.

Kaur, R., Gaur, M., Suresh, L., & Laxmi, V. (2011). DoS attacks in MANETs: Detection and countermeasures. In R. Santanam, M. Sethumadhavan, & M. Virendra (Eds.), *Cyber security, cyber crime and cyber forensics: Applications and perspectives* (pp. 124–145). Hershey, PA: IGI Global. doi:10.4018/978-1-60960-123-2.ch010

Kavitha, C., & Vijayalakshmi, C. (2010). Implementation of fuzzy multi criteria decision technique to identify the best location for call centre. In *Proceedings of IEEE Trends in Information Sciences and Computing (TISC)*. doi:10.1109/TISC.2010.5714600

Kawasaki, T. (2003). DNA use as a photoelectric transfer material. High Polym., 52, 143.

Keren, K., Krueger, M., Gilad, R., Ben-Yoseph, G., Sivan, U., & Braun, E. (2002). Sequence specific molecular lithography on single DNA. *Science*, *297*(5578), 72–75. doi:10.1126/science.1071247 PMID:12098693

Khader, O. H. (2007). FSR evaluation using the suboptimal operational values. *International Journal of Information Technology and Web Engineering*, *2*(1), 47–56. doi:10.4018/jitwe.2007010104

Khaleel, H., Al-Rizzo, H. M., Rucker, D. G., & Mohan, S. (2012). A compact polyimide based UWB antenna for flexible electronics. *Antennas and Wireless Propagation Letters*, *11*, 564–567. doi:10.1109/LAWP.2012.2199956

Khalil, N., Zaki, A., Saleh, M. B., & Ali, H. (2006). Optimum design of MEMS-SAW filter for wireless system applications. In *Proceedings of the 5th WSEAS International Conference on Circuits, Systems, Electronics, Control & Signal Processing (CSECS'06)* (pp. 14-19). World Scientific and Engineering Academy and Society (WSEAS).

Khan, M. S. S., Kumar, A., Xie, B., & Sahoo, P. K. (2015). Network tomography application in mobile ad-hoc network using stitching algorithm. *Journal of Network and Computer Applications*, *56*, 77–87. doi:10.1016/j.jnca.2015.07.003

Kilfoyle, D., & Baggeroer, A. (2000). The state of the art in underwater acoustic telemetry. *IEEE Journal of Oceanic Engineering*, 25(1), 4–27. doi:10.1109/48.820733

Kilor, P. P., & Soni, P. D. (2014). Quantum Cryptography: Realizing next generation information security. *IJAIEM*, 3(2), 286–289.

Kim, Hekland, Petersen, & Doyle. (2008). When HART Goes Wireless: Understanding and Implementing the WirelessHART Standard. In *Proceedings of IEEE International Conference of Emerging Technologies and Factory Automation*.

Kim. (n.d.). *A Leader Election Algorithm in a Distributed Computing System*. Department of Computer Science, Korea University-1.

Kim, J., & Rahmat-Samii, Y. (2004). Implanted antennas inside a human body: Simulations, designs, and characterizations. *IEEE Transactions on Microwave Theory and Techniques*, 52(8), 1934–1943. doi:10.1109/TMTT.2004.832018

Kim, S. C., Cho, J. S., & Kim, S. K. (2013). Performance improvement of hybrid tag anti-collision protocol for radio frequency identification systems. *International Journal of Communication Systems*, 26(6), 705–719. doi:10.1002/dac.2389

Kim, Y., Kim, H., & Yoo, H. (2010). Electrical characterization of screen-printed circuits on the fabric. *IEEE Transactions on Advanced Packaging*, 33(1), 196–205. doi:10.1109/TADVP.2009.2034536

Kiourti, A., Member, S., Costa, J. R., Member, S., Fernandes, C. A., Member, S., & Member, S. et al. (2012). Miniature Implantable Antennas for Biomedical Telemetry: From Simulation to Realization. *IEEE Transactions on Bio-Medical Engineering*, 59(11), 3140–3147. doi:10.1109/TBME.2012.2202659 PMID:22692865

König, A., Hollick, M., Krop, T., & Steinmetz, R. (2009). GeoSec: Quarantine zones for mobile ad hoc networks. *Security and Communication Networks*, 2(3), 271–288. doi:10.1002/sec.68

Konstantopoulos, C., Mpitziopoulos, A., Gavalas, D., & Pantziou, G. (2010). Effecting Determination of Mobile Agent Itineraries for Data aggregation on Sensor Network. *IEEE Transactions on Knowledge and Data Engineering*, 22(12), 1679–1693. doi:10.1109/TKDE.2009.203

Koohestani, M., Zurcher, J.-F., Moreira, A. A., & Skrivervik, A. K. (2014). A Novel, Low-Profile, Vertically-Polarized UWB Antenna for WBAN. *IEEE Transactions on Antennas and Propagation*, 62(4), 1888–1894. doi:10.1109/TAP.2014.2298886

Koo, T., Kim, D., Ryu, J., Seo, H., Yook, J., & Kim, J. (2011). Design of a label typed UHF RFID tag antenna for metallic objects. *Antennas and Wireless Propagation Letters*, 10, 1010–1014. doi:10.1109/LAWP.2011.2166370

Kordafshari, M., Gholipour, M., Jahanshahi, M., & Haghighat, A. (2005, January). Two Novel Algorithms for Electing Coordinator in Distributed Systems based on Bully Algorithm. *WSEAS Transactions on Systems*, 4(1), 10–15.

Korf, R. E. (1985). Depth-first iterative-deepening: An optimal admissible tree search. *Artificial Intelligence*, 27(1), 97–109. doi:10.1016/0004-3702(85)90084-0

Kothari, M., Postlethwaite, I., & Gu, D. (2013). UAV Path Following in Windy Urban Environments. *Journal of Intelligent & Robotic Systems*, 74(3-4), 1013–1028. doi:10.1007/s10846-013-9873-z

Kottapalli, A. G. P., Bora, M., Asadnia, M., Miao, J., Venkatraman, S., & Triantafyllou, M. (2016). Nanofibril scaffold assisted MEMS artificial hydrogel neuromasts for enhanced sensitivity flow sensing. *Scientific Reports*, 6, 19336. doi:10.1038/srep19336 PMID:26763299

Kottapalli, A., Asadnia, M., Barbastathis, G., Triantafyllou, M., Miao, J., & Tan, C. (2012). Polymer MEMS pressure sensor arrays for fish-like underwater sensing applications. *Micro & Nano Letters*, 7(12), 1189–1192. doi:10.1049/mnl.2012.0604

Kottapalli, A., Asadnia, M., Miao, J., Barbastathis, G., & Triantafyllou, M. (2012). A flexible liquid crystal polymer MEMS pressure sensor array for fish-like underwater sensing. *Smart Materials and Structures*, *21*(11), 115030. doi:10.1088/0964-1726/21/11/115030

Kourogi, M., & Kurata, T. (2014). *A method of pedestrian dead reckoning for smartphones using frequency domain analysis on patterns of acceleration and angular velocity.* Paper presented at the Position, Location and Navigation Symposium - PLANS 2014, 2014 IEEE/ION.

Kovacs, G. (1998). *Micromachined Transducers Sourcebook*. Boston, MA: Mcgraw-Hill.

Krijnen, G., Lammerink, T., Wiegerink, R., & Casas, J. (2007). Cricket Inspired Flow-Sensor Arrays. In *Proceedings of the IEEE Sensors* (pp. 539-546). doi:10.1109/ICSENS.2007.4388455

Kuiper, E. (2008). *Mobility and Routing in a Delay-tolerant Network of Unmanned Aerial Vehicles* (PhD Dissertation). Linköping University.

Kuiper, E., & Nadjm-Tehrani, S. (2006). Mobility Models for UAV Group Reconnaissance Applications. In *International Conference on Wireless and Mobile Communications (ICWMC)*, Bucharest, Romania. doi:10.1109/ICWMC.2006.63

Kumar, L. (2012). Scalability Performance of AODV, TORA and OLSR with Reference to Variable Network Size. *International Journal of Engineering Research and Applications*, *2*(6), 82–92.

Kumar, P., Reinitz, H. W., Simunovic, J., Sandeep, K. P., & Franzon, P. D. (2009). Overview of RFID technology and its applications in the food industry. *Journal of Food Science*, *74*(8), R101–R106. doi:10.1111/j.1750-3841.2009.01323.x PMID:19799677

Kumar, S., & Dutta, K. (2016). Security issues in mobile ad hoc networks: A survey. In *Mobile computing and wireless networks: Concepts, methodologies, tools, and applications* (pp. 1940–1985). Hershey, PA: IGI Global. doi:10.4018/978-1-4666-8751-6.ch086

Kuphaldt, T. R. (2009). *Lessons in Electric Circuits*. Retrieved from www.ibiblio.org/obp/electricCircuits

Laboid, S., & Guerra, T. (2007). Adaptive fuzzy control of a class of SISO nonaffine nonlinear systems. *Fuzzy Sets and Systems*, *158*(10), 1126–1137. doi:10.1016/j.fss.2006.11.013

Lai, X. J., Lu, M. X., Qin, L., Han, J. S., & Fang, X. W. (2010). Asymmetric encryption and signature method with DNA technology. *Science China Information Sciences*, *53*(3), 506–514. doi:10.1007/s11432-010-0063-3

Lamport, L. (1978, July). Time, Clocks, and the Ordering of Events in a Distributed System. *Communications of the ACM*, *21*(7), 558–565. doi:10.1145/359545.359563

Lanbo, L., Shengli, Z., & Jun-Hong, C. (2008). Prospects and problems of wireless communication for underwater sensor networks. *Wireless Communications & Mobile Computing*, *8*(8), 977–994. doi:10.1002/wcm.654

Lapinski, M., Feldmeier, M., & Paradiso, J. A. (2011). Wearable wireless sensing for sports and ubiquitous interactivity. *IEEE Sensors*, *1425–1428*. doi:10.1109/ICSENS.2011.6126902

Le Goff, G. C., Blum, L. J., & Marquette, C. A. (2013). Shrinking hydrogel-DNA spots generates 3D microdots arrays. *Macromol Biosci Journal*, *13*(2), 227–233. doi:10.1002/mabi.201200370 PMID:23335561

Le Lann, G. (1977). Distributed systems: Towards a formal approach. *Information Processing 77, Proc. of the IFIP Congress*.

Ledeczi, A., Nadas, A., Volgyesi, P., Balogh, G., Kusy, B., Sallai, J., Pap, G., Dora, S., Molnar, K., Maroti, M., & Simon, G. (2005). Countersniper system for urban warfare. *ACM Transactions on Sensor Networks, 1*(2), 153-177.

Lee & Chen. (2013). Cloud Server Aided Computation for ElGamal Elliptic Curve Cryptosystem. *IEEE 37th Annual Computer Software and Applications Conference Workshops.*

Lee, S., Muhammad, R., & Kim, C. (2007). A Leader Election Algorithm within Candidates on AdHoc Mobile Networks. In *Proceeding of the 3rd International Conference on Embedded Software and Systems* (ICESS), (LNCS) (vol. 4523, pp. 728-738). Berlin: Springer.

Lee, S., Rahman, M., & Kim, C. (2007). A Leader Election Algorithm Within Candidates on Ad Hoc Mobile Networks. In Embedded Software and Systems (LNCS), (Vol. 4523, pp. 728-738). Springer Berlin/Heidelberg. doi:10.1007/978-3-540-72685-2_67

Lee, T.T., & Jeng, J.T. (1998). The Chebyshev polynomial based unified model neural network for functional approximation. *IEEE Trans. Syst. Man Cybern B, 28,* 925-935.

Lee, C., & Shim, J. P. (2009). Ubiquitous healthcare: Radio frequency identification (RFID) in hospitals. In A. Lazakidou & K. Siassiakos (Eds.), *Handbook of research on distributed medical informatics and e-health* (pp. 273–281). Hershey, PA: IGI Global. doi:10.4018/978-1-60566-002-8.ch019

Lee, G. Y., Psychoudakis, D., Chen, C. C., & Volakis, J. L. (2011). Omnidirectional vest-mounted body-worn antenna system for UHF operation. *IEEE Antennas and Wireless Propagation Letters, 10,* 581–583. doi:10.1109/LAWP.2011.2158381

Lee, I. (2013). Justifying RFID investment to enable mobile service applications in manufacturing and supply chain. In I. Lee (Ed.), *Strategy, adoption, and competitive advantage of mobile services in the global economy* (pp. 325–348). Hershey, PA: IGI Global. doi:10.4018/978-1-4666-1939-5.ch018

Lee, I. (2015). *RFID technology integration for business performance improvement* (pp. 1–317). Hershey, PA: IGI Global. doi:10.4018/978-1-4666-6308-4

Lee, J. (2008). Blind Spectrum Sensing Techniques for Cognitive Radio System. *International Journal of Multimedia and Ubiquitous Engineering, 3*(2), 117–128.

Leema, A. A., & Hemalatha, M. (2015). Data management issues in RFID applications. In I. Lee (Ed.), RFID technology integration for business performance improvement (pp. 179–198). Hershey, PA: IGI Global. doi:10.4018/978-1-4666-6308-4.ch009

Lemoff, A. V., Lee, A. P., Miles, R. R., & McConaghy, C. F. (1999). An AC magnetohydrodynamic micropump: Towards a true integrated microfluidic system. In Proceedings of Transducer'99.

Lhadi, I., Rifai, M., & Alj, S. (2014). An Energy-efficient WSN-based Traffic Safety System. In *Proceedings of 5th International Conference on Information and Communication Systems (ICICS).*

Liang, J., Chiau, C. C., Chen, X., & Parini, C. G. (2004). Printed circular disc monopole antenna for ultra-wideband applications. *Electronics Letters, 40*(20), 1246. doi:10.1049/el:20045966

Liangkaia, L., Jian, C., Yongtao, L., & Tao, L. (2011). Estimation of BPSK Carrier Frequency Based on the High-Order Cyclic Cumulants. In *Proceedings of International Conference on Computer Science and Information Technology (ICCSIT 2011).*

Liang, Y. C., Chen, K. C., Li, G. Y., & Mahonen, P. (2011). Cognitive Radio Networking and Communications: An Overview. *IEEE Transactions on Vehicular Technology, 60*(7), 3386–3407. doi:10.1109/TVT.2011.2158673

Liao, C., Choe, P., Wu, T., Tong, Y., Dai, C., & Liu, Y. (2013). RFID-Based Road Guiding Cane System for the Visually Impaired. In P. L. P. Rau (Ed.), *Cross-Cultural Design. Methods, Practice, and Case Studies* (Vol. 8023, pp. 86–93). Springer Berlin Heidelberg. doi:10.1007/978-3-642-39143-9_10

Li, C., Wang, G., & Zheng, J. (2014). An aggregated signature-based fast RFID batch detection protocol. *Security and Communication Networks*, 7(9), 1364–1371. doi:10.1002/sec.838

Li, C., Wang, Y., & Guo, X. (2010). The Application Research of wireless sensor network based on ZigBee. In *Proceedings of International Conference on Multimedia and Information Technology*. doi:10.1109/MMIT.2010.143

Lien & Lin. (2013). A Novel Privacy Preserving Location-Based Service Protocol With Secret Circular Shift for k-NN Search. *IEEE Transactions on Information Forensics and Security, 8*(6).

Li, J. (2016). *Flexible and Fine-Grained Attribute-Based Data Storage in Cloud Computing. IEEE Transactions on Services Computing.*

Li, J. S., & Liu, K. H. (2011). A hidden mutual authentication protocol for low-cost RFID tags. *International Journal of Communication Systems*, 24(9), 1196–1211. doi:10.1002/dac.1222

Like, E., Chakravarthy, V., Ratazzi, P., & Wu, Z. (2009). Signal Classification in Fading Channels Using Cyclic Spectral Analysis. *EURASIP Journal on Wireless Communications and Networking*, 20(1), 879–812.

Li, L., Cai, Y., & Xu, X. (2009). Domain-based autoconfiguration framework for large-scale MANETs. *Wireless Communications and Mobile Computing*, 9(7), 938–947. doi:10.1002/wcm.642

Lilja, J., & Salonen, P. (2009). Textile material characterization for software antennas. In *IEEE Military Communications Conference* (pp. 1–7).

Lim, C., Park, S., Ryoo, C., Choi, K., & Cho, J. (2010). *A path planning algorithm for Surveillance UAVs with timing mission constrains*. In International Conference on Control Automation and Systems (ICCAS), Gyeonggi.

Lim, K. L., Seng, K. P., Yeong, L. S., Ang, L.-M., & Ch'ng, S. I. (2015). *Pathfinding for the Navigation of Visually Impaired People. International Journal of Computational Complexity and Intelligent Algorithms.*

Lim, K. L., Seng, K. P., Yeong, L. S., Ang, L.-M., & Chng, S. I. (2015). Uninformed pathfinding: A new approach. *Expert Systems with Applications*, 42(5), 2722–2730. doi:10.1016/j.eswa.2014.10.046

Lim, M. K. (2013). Exploring value-added applications of chipless RFID systems to enhance wider adoption. In N. Karmakar (Ed.), *Advanced RFID systems, security, and applications* (pp. 221–240). Hershey, PA: IGI Global. doi:10.4018/978-1-4666-2080-3.ch010

Lin, C. H., Li, Z., Ito, K., Takahashi, M., & Saito, K. (2012). A small tunable and wearable planar inverted-F antenna (PIFA). In *6th European Conference on Antennas and Propagation, EuCAP* (pp. 742–745). http://doi.org/ doi:10.1109/EuCAP.2012.6206554

Lin, K. Y., Kwong, G. A., Warren, A. D., Wood, D. K., & Bhatia, S. N. (2013). Nanoparticles That Sense Thrombin Activity As Synthetic Urinary Biomarkers of Thrombosis. Department of Chemical Engineering, Massachusetts Institute of Technology.

Lin, Zhang, Ma, & Wang. (2015). Revisiting Attribute-Based Encryption With Verifiable Outsourced Decryption. *IEEE Transactions on Information Forensics and Security, 10*(10).

Li, N., & Das, S. K. (2010). Radon: reputation-assisted data forwarding in opportunistic networks. In *Proceedings of the Second International Workshop on Mobile Opportunistic Networking, ser. (MobiOpp '10)*, (pp. 8–14). New York: ACM. doi:10.1145/1755743.1755746

Li, N., Mu, Y., Susilo, W., Guo, F., & Varadharajan, V. (2015). Vulnerabilities of an ECC-based RFID authentication scheme. *Security and Communication Networks*, 8(17), 3262–3270. doi:10.1002/sec.1250

Lin, L., Sung, Q., Li, J., & Yang, F. (2012). A novel geographic position mobility oriented routing strategy for UAVs. *Journal of Computer Information Systems*, *8*(2), 709–716.

Lin, Y., He, C., Jiang, L., & He, D. (2009). A Spectrum Sensing Method in Cognitive Radio Based on the Third Order Cyclic Cumulant. In *Proceedings of International Conference on Wireless Communications & Signal Processing (WCSP)*. doi:10.1109/WCSP.2009.5371428

Li, T., Deng, R. H., & Wang, G. (2008). The security and improvement of an ultra-lightweight RFID authentication protocol. *Security and Communication Networks*, *1*(2), 135–146. doi:10.1002/sec.8

Li, T., Wang, D., Feng, G., & Tong, S. (2010). A DSC approach to robust adaptive NN tracking control for strict-feedback nonlinear systems. *IEEE Transactions on Systems, Man, and Cybernetics. Part B, Cybernetics*, *40*(3), 915–927. doi:10.1109/TSMCB.2009.2033563 PMID:19887321

Littman, M. K. (2008). Implementing RFID technology in hospital environments. In N. Wickramasinghe & E. Geisler (Eds.), *Encyclopedia of healthcare information systems* (pp. 705–710). Hershey, PA: IGI Global. doi:10.4018/978-1-59904-889-5.ch089

Liu, X., Zhang, Q., Yan, X., Feng, Z., Liu, J., Zhu, Y., & Zhang, J. (2013). A Feature Detector Based on Compressed Sensing and Wavelet Transform for Wideband Cognitive Radio. In *Proceedings of 24th IEEE International Symposium on Personal, Indoor and Mobile Radio Communications: Mobile and Wireless Networks*.

Liu, A. X., Bailey, L. A., & Krishnamurthy, A. H. (2010). RFIDGuard: A lightweight privacy and authentication protocol for passive RFID tags. *Security and Communication Networks*, *3*(5), 384–393. doi:10.1002/sec.138

Liu, H., Song, C., Zhang, L., Zhang, J., Wang, H., & Wilkinson, D. (2006). A review of anode catalysis in the direct methanol fuel cell. *Journal of Power Sources*, *155*(2), 95–110. doi:10.1016/j.jpowsour.2006.01.030

Liu, X. (2015). Atypical hierarchical routing protocols for wireless sensor networks: A review. *IEEE Sensors Journal*, *15*(10), 5372–5383. doi:10.1109/JSEN.2015.2445796

Liu, X., Han, Q., Liu, Z., & Wu, Z. (2013). Novel Modulation Detection Scheme for Underwater Acoustic Communication Signal Through Short-Time Detailed Cyclostationary Features.*IEEE Wireless Communications and Networking Conference (WCNC)*.

Liu, X., Li, F., Kuang, H., & Wu, X. (2006). The Study of Directed Diffusion Routing Protocol Based on Clustering for Wireless Sensor Networks. In *Proceedings of sixth world congress on intelligent control and automation (WCICA)*.

Liu, Y., Lin, T., Ram, S., & Su, X. (2010). A non-invasive software architecture style for RFID data provisioning. *International Journal of Applied Logistics*, *1*(1), 1–15. doi:10.4018/jal.2010090201

Liu, Z., Joy, A. W., & Thompson, R. A. (2004, May). A Dynamic Trust Model for Mobile Ad Hoc Networks. *Proceeding of 10th IEEE International Workshop on Future Trends of Distributed Computing Systems*.

Li, Y., Qiung, S., Zhuang, X., & Kaynak, O. (2004). Robust and adaptive backstepping control for nonlinear system using RBF neural networks. *IEEE Transactions on Neural Networks*, *15*(3), 693–701. doi:10.1109/TNN.2004.826215 PMID:15384556

Li, Z., Yu, F., & Huang, M. (2009). A cooperative spectrum sensing consensus scheme in cognitive radios. *Proceedings - IEEE INFOCOM*, *2009*, 2546–2550.

Lockman, M. T., & Selamat, A. (2011). Multi-agent based formal verification of data in RFID middleware. In T. Matsuo & T. Fujimoto (Eds.), *E-activity and intelligent web construction: Effects of social design* (pp. 63–74). Hershey, PA: IGI Global. doi:10.4018/978-1-61520-871-5.ch006

Loebecke, C. (2008). RFID in the retail supply chain. In A. Becker (Ed.), *Electronic commerce: Concepts, methodologies, tools, and applications* (pp. 659–666). Hershey, PA: IGI Global. doi:10.4018/978-1-59904-943-4.ch054

Loutfi, Valerie, & Bruno. (2003). *Securing mobile adhoc networks.* MP71 Project.

Low, A. (2013). *Evolution of Wireless Sensor Networks for Industrial Control. Technology Innovation Management Review.*

Lu, Lai, Xiao, & Qin. (2007). Symmetric-key cryptosystem with DNA technology. *Information Sciences. Science in China*, 324–333.

Lunden, J., & Koivunen, V. (2007). Spectrum sensing in cognitive radios based on multiple cyclic frequencies. In *Proceedings of 2nd International Conference on Cognitive Radio Oriented Wireless Network Communication* (CrownCom). doi:10.1109/CROWNCOM.2007.4549769

Lu, R., Lin, X., Zhu, H., Shen, X., & Preiss, B. (2010). Pi: A practical incentive protocol for delay tolerant networks. *IEEE Transactions on Wireless Communications, 9*(4), 1483–1493. doi:10.1109/TWC.2010.04.090557

Ma, L., Edwards, R., & Bashir, S. (2008). A wearable monopole antenna for ultra wideband with notching function. In *IET Seminar on Wideband and Ultrawideband Systems and Technologies: Evaluating current Research and Development* (pp. 1–5). doi:10.1049/ic.2008.0695

Macdormen, M. F., & Gregory, E. C. W. (2015). Fetal and perinatal mortality: United States, 2013. *National Vital Statistics Reports, 64*(8), 1–23. PMID:26222771

Macones, G. A., Hankins, G. D., Spong, C. Y., Hauth, J., & Moore, T. (2008). The 2008 National Institute of Child Health and Human Development workshop report on electronic fetal monitoring: Update on definitions, interpretation, and research guidelines. *Journal of Obstetric, Gynecologic, and Neonatal Nursing, 37*(5), 510–515. doi:10.1111/j.1552-6909.2008.00284.x PMID:18761565

Ma, D., & Saxena, N. (2013). Towards sensing-enabled RFID security and privacy. In P. Lopez, J. Hernandez-Castro, & T. Li (Eds.), *Security and trends in wireless identification and sensing platform tags: Advancements in RFID* (pp. 65–88). Hershey, PA: IGI Global. doi:10.4018/978-1-4666-1990-6.ch003

Ma, D., & Saxena, N. (2014). A context-aware approach to defend against unauthorized reading and relay attacks in RFID systems. *Security and Communication Networks, 7*(12), 2684–2695. doi:10.1002/sec.404

Madhulika, G., & Rao, C. S. (2014). Generating digital signature using DNA coding. FICTA, AISC. Springer.

Madou, M. (2002). *Fundamentals of Microfabrication.* Boca Raton, FL: CRC Press.

Madou, M. (2011). *Fundamentals of Microfabrication and Nanotechnology.* Boca Raton, FL: CRC.

Magenes, G., Signorini, M. G., Ferrario, M., Pedrinazzi, L., & Arduini, D. (2003). Improving the fetal cardiotocographic monitoring by advanced signal processing. In *Proceedings of 25th Annual International Conference of the IEEE Engineering in Medicine and Biology Society.* IEEE Press.

Magnetic nanoparticles quickly bust blood clots to promise improved stroke prevention. (2010). House Methodist Research Institute.

Mahmoud, W., & Ososanya, E. T. (2006). *The Development of a MEMS-based Integrated Wireless Remote Biosensors: Annual Progress Report for FY 2005.* University of the District of Columbia. Retrieved from http://www.udc.edu/docs/dc_water_resources/technical_reports/report_201_development_of_a_MEMS-based_integrated_wireless_r.pdf

Majumdar, Podder, Majumder, Kar, & Sharma. (2014). DNA-Based Cryptographic Approach Toward Information Security. *Advances in Intelligent Systems and Computing*, 209-219.

Majumdar, Podder, Majumder, Kar, & Sharma. (2014). Secure Data Communication and Cryptography Based on DNA Based Message Encoding. *IEEE, ICACCCT.*

Majumder, K., De, D., Kar, S., & Singh, R. (2016). Genetic-algorithm-based optimization of clustering in mobile ad hoc network. In J. Mandal, S. Mukhopadhyay, & T. Pal (Eds.), *Handbook of research on natural computing for optimization problems* (pp. 128–158). Hershey, PA: IGI Global. doi:10.4018/978-1-5225-0058-2.ch006

Malek, B., & Miri, A. (2014). Identification and authentication for RFID systems. In *Crisis management: Concepts, methodologies, tools, and applications* (pp. 1682–1704). Hershey, PA: IGI Global. doi:10.4018/978-1-4666-4707-7.ch085

Mallissery, S., Manohara, P. M. M., Ajam, N., Pai, R. M., & Mouzna, J. (2015). Transport and Traffic Rule Violation Monitoring Service in ITS: A Secured VANET Cloud Application. *Annual IEEE Consumer Communications and Networking Conference.* doi:10.1109/CCNC.2015.7157979

Mallissery, S., Manohara, P. M. M., & Pai, R. M. (2014). Cloud Enabled Secure Communication in Vehicular Ad-hoc Networks. *International Conference on Connected Vehicles and Expo2014.*

Maluf, N., & Williams, K. (2004). *Introduction to microelectromechanical systems engineering*. Boston: Artech House.

Mandal, S., Turicchia, L., & Sarpeshkar, R. (2010). A low-power, battery-free tag for body sensor networks. *IEEE Pervasive Computing / IEEE Computer Society [and] IEEE Communications Society, 9*(1), 71–77. doi:10.1109/MPRV.2010.1

Mandge, T., & Choudhary, V. (2013). A DNA encryption technique based on matrix manipulation and secure key generation scheme. ICICES, IEEE.

Manjeshwar, A., & Agrawal, D. P. (2001). TEEN: A Protocol for Enhanced Efficiency in Wireless Sensor Networks. In *Proceedings of the 1st International Workshop on Parallel and Distributed Computing Issues in Wireless Networks and Mobile Computing*. doi:10.1109/IPDPS.2001.925197

Manjeshwar, A., & Agrawal, D. P. (2002). APTEEN: A Hybrid Protocol for Efficient Routing and Comprehensive Information Retrieval in Wireless Sensor Networks. In *Proceedings of the 2nd International Workshop on Parallel and Distributed Computing Issues in Wireless Networks and Mobile Computing*. doi:10.1109/IPDPS.2002.1016600

Mantash, M., Tarot, A., Collardey, S., & Mahdjoubi, K. (2011). Wearable monopole zip antenna. *Electronics Letters, 47*(23), 1266–1267. doi:10.1049/el.2011.2784

Mantel, R., van Geijn, H. P., Caron, F. J., Swartjes, J. M., van Woerden, E. E., & Jongsma, H. W. (1990a). Computer analysis of antepartum fetal heart rate: 1. Baseline determination. *International Journal of Bio-Medical Computing, 25*(4), 261–272. doi:10.1016/0020-7101(90)90030-X PMID:2194979

Mantel, R., van Geijn, H. P., Caron, F. J., Swartjes, J. M., van Woerden, E. E., & Jongsma, H. W. (1990b). Computer analysis of antepartum fetal heart rate: 2. Detection of accelerations and decelerations. *International Journal of Bio-Medical Computing, 25*(4), 273–286. doi:10.1016/0020-7101(90)90031-O PMID:2194980

Manzoor, A. (2016). RFID applications in healthcare-state-of-the-art and future trends. In T. Iyamu & A. Tatnall (Eds.), *Maximizing healthcare delivery and management through technology integration* (pp. 184–206). Hershey, PA: IGI Global. doi:10.4018/978-1-4666-9446-0.ch012

Mao, X., Miao, X., He, Y., Zhu, T., Wang, J., Dong, W., & Liu, Y. et al. (2012). Citysee: Urban CO2 monitoring with sensors. In *Proceedings of IEEE INFOCOM.*

Marriwala, N., Sahu, O. P., & Vohra, A. (2013). 8-QAM Software Defined Radio Based Approach for Channel Encoding and Decoding Using Forward Error Correction. *Wireless Personal Communications, 72*(4), 2957–2969. doi:10.1007/s11277-013-1191-z

Marriwala, N., Sahu, O. P., & Vohra, A. (2015). Novel Design of a Low Cost Flexible Transceiver Based on Multistate Digitally Modulated Signals Using Wi-Fi Protocol for Software Defined Radio. *Wireless Personal Communications.* doi:10.1007/s11277-015-3052-4

Marti, , Giuli, Lai, & Baker. (2000). Mitigating Routing Misbehavior in Mobile Ad Hoc Networks. *Proceedings of the 6th annual international conference on Mobile computing and networking.*

Marti, S., Giuli, T. J., Lai, K., & Baker, M. (2000). Mitigating Routing Misbehavior in Mobile Ad-hoc Networks. In *ACM MobiCom Conference.*

Martian, A., Sandu, B. T., Fratu, O., Marghescu, I., & Craciunescu, R. (2014). Spectrum sensing based on spectral correlation for cognitive radio systems. In *Proceedings of 4th International conference on Wireless Communications Vehicular Technology Information Theory Aerospace & Electronics Systems (VITAE).* doi:10.1109/VITAE.2014.6934448

Martinez-de Dios, J., Lferd, K., de San Bernabé, A., Núñez, G., Torres-González, A., & Ollero, A. (2012). Cooperation Between UAS and Wireless Sensor Networks for Efficient Data Collection in Large Environments. *Journal of Intelligent & Robotic Systems.* doi:10.1007/s10846-012-9733-2

Maskell, D. L., & Vinod, A. P. (2008). *Efficient Multiplierless Channel Filters for Multi-Standard SDR.* Academic Press.

Matthew, M. C., Laskey, K., McCabe, F., Brown, P., & Metz, R. (2005). *Reference Model for Service Oriented Architectures. Published on theinternet.* OASIS Working Draft.

Matthews, J., & Pettitt, G. (2009). Development of flexible, wearable antennas. In *3rd European Conference on Antennas and Propagation (EuCAP)* (pp. 273–277).

Ma, Y., & Jamalipour, A. (2009). Optimized message delivery framework using fuzzy logic for intermittently connected mobile ad hoc networks. *Wireless Communications and Mobile Computing, 9*(4), 501–512. doi:10.1002/wcm.693

McLean, J. S. (1996). A re-examination of the fundamental limits on the radiation Q of\nelectrically small antennas. *IEEE Transactions on Antennas and Propagation, 44*(5), 672–676. doi:10.1109/8.496253

Medhi, S., & Bezboruah, T. (2014). Investigations on implementation of e-ATM Web Services based on. NET technique. *International Journal of Information Retrieval Research, 4*(2), 42–51.

Medhi, S., Bora, A., & Bezboruah, T. (2016). Security Impact on e-ATM Windows Communication Foundation Services using Certificate based Authentication and Protection: An implementation of Message Level Security based on. NET Technique. *International Journal of Information Retrieval Research, 6*(3), 37–51. doi:10.4018/IJIRR.2016070103

Medical Device Radiocommunications Service (MedRadio). (2009). Retrieved from www.fcc.gov

Meghanathan, N. (2012). Node stability index: A stability metric and an algorithm to determine long-living connected dominating sets for mobile ad hoc networks. *International Journal of Interdisciplinary Telecommunications and Networking, 4*(1), 31–46. doi:10.4018/jitn.2012010102

Meghanathan, N., & Sugumar, M. (2010). A beaconless minimum interference based routing protocol to minimize end-to-end delay per packet for mobile ad hoc networks. *International Journal of Interdisciplinary Telecommunications and Networking, 2*(1), 12–26. doi:10.4018/jitn.2010010102

Meinig, C., Stalin, S. E., Nakamura, A. I., & Milburn, H. B. (2005). *Real-Time Deep-Ocean Tsunami Measuring, Monitoring, and Reporting System: The NOAA DART II Description and Disclosure.* Academic Press.

Menaka, K. (2014). Message Encryption Using DNA Sequences. Computing and Communication Technologies (WCCCT), IEEE.

Menasce, D. A., & Almeida, V. A. F. (2002). *Capacity Planning for Web Services - Metrics, Models and Methods.* Prentice Hall.

Mendel, J. M. (1991). Tutorial on Higher-Order Statistics (Spectra) in Signal Processing and System Theory: Theoretical Results and Some Applications. *Proceedings of the IEEE, 79*(3), 278–305. doi:10.1109/5.75086

Merced. (2008). Study of Stable Conformations CNT-DNA Hybrids by Means of Principle Component Analysis. In *Proceedings of The National Conference on Undergraduate Research* (NCUR). Salisbury University.

Mercury Load runner tutorial - Mercury Roadrunner Quick Start. (n.d.). Available online: https://qageek.files.wordpress.com/2007/05/loadrunner_tutorial.pdf

Merli, F. (2008). Implantable antennas for biomedical applications. In *Antennas and propagation society international Symposium* (Vol. 5110, pp. 1642–1649). http://doi.org/ doi:<ALIGNMENT.qj></ALIGNMENT>10.5075/epfl-thesis-5110

Mershad & Artail. (2013). *Finding a STAR in a Vehicular Cloud. IEEE Intelligent Transport on System Magazine.*

Miao, J., Hasan, O., Mokhtar, S B., Brunie, L., & Yim, K. (2012). An Analysis of Strategies for Preventing Selfish Behavior in Mobile Delay Tolerant Networks. In *Proceedings of the Sixth International Conference on Innovative Mobile and Internet Services in Ubiquitous Computing (IMIS-2012),* (pp. 208-215). Palermo, Italy: IEEE.

Michael, K., & Michael, M. (2009). RFID tags and transponders: The new kid on the block. In K. Michael & M. Michael (Eds.), *Innovative automatic identification and location-based services: From bar codes to chip implants* (pp. 234–272). Hershey, PA: IGI Global. doi:10.4018/978-1-59904-795-9.ch009

Michaelides, Z., & Forster, R. (2014). The use of RFID technologies for e-enabling logistics supply chains. In *Crisis management: Concepts, methodologies, tools, and applications* (pp. 1145–1164). Hershey, PA: IGI Global. doi:10.4018/978-1-4666-4707-7.ch057

Michael, L. (1987, July). Heaps and their uses in improved network optimization algorithms. *Journal of the Association for Computing Machinery, 34*(3), 596–615. doi:10.1145/28869.28874

Michirardi, P., & Molva, R. (2002). Core: A collaborative reputation mechanism to encode node cooperation in mobile ad-hoc networks. In *CMS'02 Communication and Multimedia Security Conference.*

Micoach. (2014). Retrieved from http://micoach.adidas.com/

Milburn, H. B., Nakamura, A. I., & Gonzalez, F. I. (1996). Real-time tsunami reporting from the deep ocean. In *Proceedings of the Oceans 96 MTS/IEEE Conference* (pp. 390-394). doi:10.1109/OCEANS.1996.572778

Miorandi, D., Sicari, S., de Pellegrini, F., & Chlamtac, I. (2012). Internet of Things: Vision, applications and research challenges. *Ad Hoc Networks, 10*(7), 1497–1516. doi:10.1016/j.adhoc.2012.02.016

Mirkin, C. A. (2000). A DNA-Based Methodology for Preparing Nanocluster Circuits, Arrays, and Diagnostic Materials. *MRS Bulletin, 25,* 43–54.

Misbahuddin, M., & Mohammed, H. N. (2014). DNA for Information Security: A Survey on DNA Computing and a Pseudo DNA Method Based On Central Dogma of Molecular Biology. ICCCT, IEEE.

Mishra, S. M., Sahai, A., & Brodersen, R. W. (2006). Cooperative sensing among cognitive radios. In *Proc. IEEE Conference on Communications.*

Misra, P. (1999). *Routing Protocols for ad hoc mobile wireless Networks.* Retrieved from http://www.cse.ohio-state.edu/~jain/cis788-99/ftp/adhoc_routing/#TDRP

Misra, S., Akman, I., & Colomo-Palacios, R. (2012). Framework for evaluation and validation of software complexity measures. *IET Software, 6*(4), 323–334. doi:10.1049/iet-sen.2011.0206

Mitchell, G. A., Gargiulo, R. J., Huseby, R. M., Lawson, D. E., Pochron, S. P., & Sehuanes, J. A. (1978). Assay for Plasma Heparin Using a Synthetic Peptide Substrate for Thrombin: Introduction of the Fluorophore Aminoisophthalic Acid, Dimethyl Ester. *Thrombosis Research, 3*(1), 47–52. doi:10.1016/0049-3848(78)90108-1 PMID:694832

Mitola, J., & Maguire, G., Jr. (1999). Cognitive Radio: Making Software Radios More Personal. *IEEE Personal Communication, 6*(4), 13-18.

Mitola, I. J. III. (2001). Cognitive Radio for Flexible Mobile Multimedia Communications. *Mobile Networks and Applications, 6*(5), 435–441. doi:10.1023/A:1011426600077

Mitola, J. (1995). The software radio architecture. *IEEE Communications Magazine, 33*(5), 26–38. doi:10.1109/35.393001

Mittal, N. (2013, June). Performance Evaluation of AODV and DSDV under Seniority based Pretty Good Privacy Model. *International Journal of Scientific and Engineering Research, 4*(6), 943–949.

Moamen, A. A., Hamza, H. S., & Saroit, I. A. (2014). Secure multicast routing protocols in mobile ad-hoc networks. *International Journal of Communication Systems, 27*(11), 2808–2831. doi:10.1002/dac.2508

Mod jk connector. (2016). Retrieved on 24.1.2016 from, https://tomcat.apache.org/tomcat-3.3-doc/mod_jk-howto.html

Mohajer, M., Mohammadi, A., Abdipour, A., & Lo, C. Z. (n.d.). *A Software Defined Radio Direct Conversion Receiver.* Academic Press.

Mohammad, R. E. P., Yazdani, N., Parvar, M. E., Dadlani, A., & Khonsari, A. (2010). Improved Algorithms for Leader Election in Distributed System. *Computer Engineering and Technology (ICCET), 2010 2nd International Conference on.*

Molina, G. H. (1982). Elections in a Distributed Computing System. *IEEE Transactions on Computers, 31*(1), 48–59. doi:10.1109/TC.1982.1675885

Moloney, M. (2014). State of the art for near field communication: Security and privacy within the field. In D. Rawat, B. Bista, & G. Yan (Eds.), *Security, privacy, trust, and resource management in mobile and wireless communications* (pp. 408–431). Hershey, PA: IGI Global. doi:10.4018/978-1-4666-4691-9.ch017

Montegano, C. D., & Bachand, G. D. (1999). Constructing nanomechanical devices powered by biomolecular motors. *Nanotechnology, 10*(3), 225–331. doi:10.1088/0957-4484/10/3/301

Montgomery, J. C., Coombs, S., & Baker, C. F. (2001). The mechanosensory lateral line system of the hypogean form of Astyanax fasciatus. *Environmental Biology of Fishes, 62*(1-3), 87–96. doi:10.1023/A:1011873111454

Monti, G., & Congedo, F. (2012). UHF rectenna using a bowtie antenna. *Progress In Electromagnetics Research C, 26,* 181–192. doi:10.2528/PIERC11102706

Monti, G., Corchia, L., & Tarricone, L. (2013). UHF wearable rectenna on textile materials. *IEEE Transactions on Antennas and Propagation, 61*(7), 3869–3873. doi:10.1109/TAP.2013.2254693

Morishita, H., Hirasawa, K., & Fujimoto, K. (1991). Analysis of a cavity backed annular slot antenna with one point shorted. *IEEE Transactions on Antennas and Propagation, 39*(10), 1472–1478. doi:10.1109/8.97378

Mosberger, D., & Jin, T. (1997). Httperf a tool to measure web server performance. *InProceedings of USENIX Symposium on Internet Technologies and Systems,* (pp. 59 – 76).

Moy, M., Mentzer, S., & Reilly, J. (2003). Ambulatory monitoring of cumulative freeliving activity. *IEEE Engineering in Medicine and Biology Magazine, 22*(3), 89–95. doi:10.1109/MEMB.2003.1213631 PMID:12845824

Mukherjee, A., Dey, N., Kausar, N., Ashour, A. S., Taiar, R., & Hassanien, A. E. (2016). A disaster management specific mobility model for flying ad-hoc network. *International Journal of Rough Sets and Data Analysis, 3*(3), 72–103. doi:10.4018/IJRSDA.2016070106

Murray, M. (2006). *Antepartum and intrapartum fetal monitoring* (3rd ed.). Springer Publishing Company.

Murugan & Jacob. (2014). On the secure storage and transmission of health care records based on DNA sequences. *Intelligent Computing Applications (ICICA), IEEE.*

Nabki, F., Dusatko, T. A., & El-Gamal, M. N. (2008). Frequency tunable silicon carbide resonators for MEMS above IC. In *Proceedings of IEEE Custom Integrated Circuits Conference* (pp. 185-188). doi:10.1109/CICC.2008.4672054

Nafkha, A., Naoues, M., Cichon, K., & Kliks, A. (2014). Experimental Spectrum Sensing Measurements using USRP Software Radio Platform and GNU-Radio. In *Proceedings of 9th International Conference on Cognitive Radio Oriented Wireless Networks CROWNCOM.* doi:10.4108/icst.crowncom.2014.255415

Nakajima, M., & Haruyama, S. (2012). *Indoor navigation system for visually impaired people using visible light communication and compensated geomagnetic sensing.* Paper presented at the Communications in China (ICCC), 2012 1st IEEE International Conference on.

Napolitano, A. (2014). Cyclostationary Signal Processing and its Generalizations. In *Proceedings of IEEE Statistical Signal Processing Workshop.*

Narendar, M., Krishna, A., Vinod, A. P., & Madhukumar, A. S. (2012). Robust Two-Stage Spectrum Sensing and Policy Management for Cognitive Radios Using Fourth Order Cumulants. *International Journal of Information Engineering IJIE., 3*(2), 45–55.

Narendra, K. S., & Parthaasarathy, K. (1990). Identification and control of dynamical systems using neural networks. *IEEE Transactions on Neural Networks, 1*(1), 4–27. doi:10.1109/72.80202 PMID:18282820

Nasimuddin, X., Qing, X., & Chen, Z. N. (2011). Compact asymmetric-slit microstrip antennas for circular polarization. *IEEE Transactions on Antennas and Propagation, 59*(1), 285–288. doi:10.1109/TAP.2010.2090468

Nasri, N., Andrieux, L., Kachouri, A., & Samet, M. (2008). Design Considerations for Wireless Underwater Communication Transceiver. In *Proceedings of IEEE International Conference on Signals, Circuits and Systems* (pp. 1-5). doi:10.1109/ICSCS.2008.4746954

National Institute of Child Health and Development. (2008). Workshop report on electronic fetal monitoring. Update on definitions, interpretation, and research guidelines. *Obstet. Gynaecol., 112,* 661 – 666.

National Instruments Coorporation. (n.d.). *LabVIEW User Manual.* Ni.com.

National Swiss Plan. (2014). Swiss National Frequency Allocation Plan and Specific Assignments.

Natsheh, E. (2009). Fuzzy linguistic knowledge for active queue management in wireless ad-hoc networks. In I. Bose (Ed.), *Breakthrough perspectives in network and data communications security, design and applications* (pp. 243–257). Hershey, PA: IGI Global. doi:10.4018/978-1-60566-148-3.ch016

Natsheh, E., Jantan, A., Khatun, S., & Subramaniam, S. (2007). Adaptive Optimizing of Hello Messages in Wireless Ad-Hoc Networks. In: The International Arab. *Journal of Information Technology, 4*(3), 191–200.

NCBI. (2016). *Genbank.* Retrieved from www.ncbi.nlm.nih.gov/genbank

Nejad, K. K., Jiang, X., & Kameyama, M. (2013). RFID-based localization with non-blocking tag scanning. *Ad Hoc Networks*, *11*(8), 2264–2272. doi:10.1016/j.adhoc.2013.05.007

Netlab Online. (n.d.). *The Opportunistic Network Environment simulator (The ONE), in netlab online. Retrieved from* http://www.netlab.tkk.fi/tutkimus/dtn/theone/Ver.1.4.0

Newaz, A., Pratama, F., & Chong, N. (2013). Exploration Priority Based Heuristic Approach to UAV path planning. In RO-MAN IEEE, Gyeongju.

Ngai, E. W. T., Cheng, T. C. E., Lai, K. H., Chai, P. Y. F., Choi, Y. S., & Sin, R. K. Y. (2007). Development of an RFID-based traceability system: Experiences and lessons learned from an aircraft engineering company. *Production and Operations Management*, *16*(5), 554–568. doi:10.1111/j.1937-5956.2007.tb00280.x

Nguyen, C. (2006). MEMS Technologies and Devices for Single-Chip RF Front-Ends. *Journal of Microelectronics and Electronic Packaging*, *3*(4), 160–168. doi:10.4071/1551-4897-3.4.160

Nguyen, C. V., Delzeit, L., Cassell, A. M., Li, J., Han, J., & Meyyappan, M. (2003). Preparation of Nucleic Acid Functionalized Carbon Nanotube Arrays. *Nano Letters*, *2*(10), 1079–1081. doi:10.1021/nl025689f

Nidhal, S. A., Mohammed, A., & Mohammed, A. (2010). Cardiotocograph parameter estimation using MATLAB programming. In *Proceedings of International Conference on Intelligent and Advanced Systems*. IEEE Press.

Nikolaou, S., Ponchak, G., Papapolymerou, J., & Tentzeris, M. (2006). Conformal double exponentially tapered slot antenna (DETSA) on LCP for UWB applications. *IEEE Transactions on Antennas and Propagation*, *54*(6), 1663–1669. doi:10.1109/TAP.2006.875915

Ning, Z. (2014). Computer system attacks. In *Crisis management: Concepts, methodologies, tools, and applications* (pp. 1–24). Hershey, PA: IGI Global. doi:10.4018/978-1-4666-4707-7.ch001

Noël, G. P. J. C., & Connolly, C. C. (2016). Monitoring the use of anatomical teaching material using a low-cost radio frequency identification system: A comprehensive assessment. *Anatomical Sciences Education*, *9*(2), 197–202. doi:10.1002/ase.1575 PMID:26441139

Noorul Hussain, U., & Chithralekha, T. (2012). *A Novel DNA Encoding Technique for DNA Cryptography*. India Patent 5107.

Norris, J., Taylor, B., & Tyler, W. (2013). Methods of Detection of Bandlimited Signals on UHF MILSATCOM Downlinks. In *Proceedings of IEEE Military Communications Conference*. doi:10.1109/MILCOM.2013.307

Numakura, D. (2007). Flexible Circuit Applications and Materials. In Printed Circuit Handbook (6th ed.). McGraw-Hill.

NXP Semiconductors. (2014). *MFRC522 - Standard 3V MIFARE reader solution Product data sheet*. Author.

O'Reilly, T. (2007). What is Web 2.0: Design patterns and business models for the next generation of software. *Communications in Statistics*, *65*(1), 17.

Onat, I., & Miri, A. (2013). RFID wireless link threats. In A. Miri (Ed.), *Advanced security and privacy for RFID technologies* (pp. 24–32). Hershey, PA: IGI Global. doi:10.4018/978-1-4666-3685-9.ch003

Orallo, E. H., & Carbo, J. V. (2009). Web server performance analysis using histogram workload models. *Computer Networks*, *53*(15), 2727–2739. doi:10.1016/j.comnet.2009.06.005

Osmany, S. A., Herzel, F., & Scheytt, J. C. (2010). *Software-Defined Radio Applications*. Academic Press.

Ouyang, Y., Hou, Y., Pang, L., Wang, D., & Xiong, Z. (2008). *An intelligent RFID reader and its application in airport baggage handling system*. Paper presented at the 2008 4th IEEE International Conference on Wireless Communications, Networking and Mobile Computing (WiCOM 2008), Dalian, China. doi:10.1109/WiCom.2008.710

Ouyang, Y., & Chappell, W. (2008). High-frequency properties of electro-textiles for wearable antenna applications. *IEEE Transactions on Antennas and Propagation, 56*(2), 381–389. doi:10.1109/TAP.2007.915435

OWASP. (2016). *Brute Force Attack*. Retrieved from https://www.owasp.org/index.php/Brute_force_attack

Pacifici, G., Spreitzer, M., Tantawi, A. N., & Youssef, A. (2005). Performance Management for Cluster-Based Web Services. *IEEE Journal on Selected Areas in Communications, 23*(12), 2333–2343. doi:10.1109/JSAC.2005.857208

Paisana, F., Prasad, N., Rodrigues, A., & Prasad, R. (2012). An alternative implementation of a cyclostationary detector. In *Proceedings of Wireless Personal Multimedia Communications*. Taipei: WPMC.

Palanisamy, R., & Mukerji, B. (2013). The RFID technology adoption in e-government: Issues and challenges. In V. Weerakkody (Ed.), *E-government services design, adoption, and evaluation* (pp. 93–106). Hershey, PA: IGI Global. doi:10.4018/978-1-4666-2458-0.ch006

Palmieri, F., Ficco, M., Pardi, S., & Castiglione, A. (2016). A cloud-based architecture for emergency management and First responders localization in smart city environments. *Computers & Electrical Engineering*, 1–21. doi:10.1016/j.compeleceng.2016.02.012

Pal, S. K. (1998). *Statistics for Geo scientists, techniques and applications*. Concept Publishing Company.

Palviainen, M., Evesti, A., & Ovaska, E. (2011). The reliability estimation, prediction and measuring of component-based software. *Journal of Systems and Software, 84*(6), 1054–1070. doi:10.1016/j.jss.2011.01.048

Panda, M., & Sethy, K. (2014). Network structure based protocols for Wireless Sensor Networks. In *Proceedings of IEEE ICAETR*. doi:10.1109/ICAETR.2014.7012948

Pandya, S., Engel, J., Chen, J., Fan, Z., & Liu, C. (2005). CORAL: miniature acoustic communication subsystem architecture for underwater wireless sensor networks. In *Proceedings of IEEE Sensors*. doi:10.1109/ICSENS.2005.1597661

Pandya, S., Yang, Y., Jones, D., Engel, J., & Liu, C. (2006). Multisensor Processing Algorithms for Underwater Dipole Localization and Tracking Using MEMS Artificial Lateral-Line Sensors. *EURASIP Journal on Advances in Signal Processing, 2006*, 1–9. doi:10.1155/ASP/2006/76593

Pang, L., Morgan-Morris, V., & Howell, A. (2010). RFID in urban planning. In C. Silva (Ed.), *Handbook of research on e-planning: ICTs for urban development and monitoring* (pp. 388–403). Hershey, PA: IGI Global. doi:10.4018/978-1-61520-929-3.ch020

Pantazis, A., Nikolidakis, A., & Vergados, D. (2013). Energy-Efficient Routing Protocols in Wireless Sensor Networks: A Survey. *IEEE Communications Surveys and Tutorials, 15*(2), 551–591. doi:10.1109/SURV.2012.062612.00084

Park, Y. (2015). *Pseudonymous authentication for secure V2I services in cloudbased vehicular networks. J Ambient Intell Human Comput*.

Parry, D., & Symonds, J. (2009). RFID and assisted living for the elderly. In J. Symonds, J. Ayoade, & D. Parry (Eds.), *Auto-identification and ubiquitous computing applications* (pp. 119–136). Hershey, PA: IGI Global. doi:10.4018/978-1-60566-298-5.ch007

Parvar, Bemana, & Dehghan. (2007). Determining a Central Controlling Processor with Fault Tolerant Method in Distributed System. In *Proceeding of IEEE-International Conference on Information Technology* (ITNG).

Patel, B. N., & Prajapati, S. (2012). Performance comparison of AODV and DSDV routing protocols of MANET. In K. Lakhtaria (Ed.), *Technological advancements and applications in mobile ad-hoc networks: Research trends* (pp. 144–151). Hershey, PA: IGI Global. doi:10.4018/978-1-4666-0321-9.ch008

Patel, K., Vasavada, T., & Vegas, M. (2011). Effect of Hello Message on Performance on Ad-hoc On-demand Routing Protocol. In *Proceedings of National Conference on Recent Trends in Engineering & Technology*.

Paul, C. R. (2006). *Introduction to Electromagnetic Compatibility* (2nd ed.). Wiley-Interscience.

Pavlin, M., Belavic, D., & Novak, F. (2011). Ceramic MEMS Designed for Wireless Pressure Monitoring in the Industrial Environment. *Sensors (Basel, Switzerland)*, *12*(12), 320–333. doi:10.3390/s120100320 PMID:22368471

Peach, C., & Yarali, A. (2013). An Overview of Underwater Sensor Networks. In *Proceedings of the Ninth International Conference on Wireless and Mobile Communications (ICWMC 2013)* (pp. 31-36).

Pei, G., & Ravindran, B. (2010). Event-based system architecture in mobile ad hoc networks (MANETs). In A. Hinze & A. Buchmann (Eds.), *Principles and applications of distributed event-based systems* (pp. 346–368). Hershey, PA: IGI Global. doi:10.4018/978-1-60566-697-6.ch015

Peighambardoust, S., Rowshanzamir, S., & Amjadi, M. (2010). Review of the proton exchange membranes for fuel cell applications. *International Journal of Hydrogen Energy*, *35*(17), 9349–9384. doi:10.1016/j.ijhydene.2010.05.017

Pei-hua, L., Hong-xin, Z., Xu-ying, W., Nan, X., & Yuan-yuan, X. (2012). Modulation recognition of communication signals based on high order cumulants and support vector machine. *Journal of China Universities of Posts and Telecommunications*, *19*(1), 61–65.

Peiris, C., Mulder, D., Cicoria, S., Bahree, A., & Pathak, N. (2007). *Pro WCF: Practical Microsoft SOA Implementation*. Apress Press.

Pellegrini, A., Brizzi, A., Zhang, L., Ali, K., Hao, Y., Wu, X., & Sauleau, R. et al. (2013). Antennas and propagation for body-centric wireless communications at millimeter-wave frequencies: A review. *IEEE Antennas and Propagation Magazine*, *55*(4), 262–287. doi:10.1109/MAP.2013.6645205

Peng, H., Si, S., Awad, K., Cheng, N., Zhou, H., Shen, X., & Zhao, H. (2015). Energy-Efficient and Fault-Tolerant Evolution Models for Large-Scale Wireless Sensor Networks: A Complex Networks-Based Approach. In *Proceedings of IEEE Global Communication conference* (GLOBECOM). doi:10.1109/GLOCOM.2015.7417534

Percival, D. B., & Walden, A. T. (1993). *Spectral Analysis for Physical applications*. Cambridge, UK: Cambridge University Press. doi:10.1017/CBO9780511622762

PeriCALM. (2010). Retrieved August 12, 2015, from http://perigen.com/products/pericalm-tracings/

Permala, A., Rantasila, K., Pilli-Sihvola, E., & Hinkka, V. (2014). RFID: From closed manufacturers' systems to supply chain-wide tracking. In J. Wang (Ed.), *Management science, logistics, and operations research* (pp. 53–64). Hershey, PA: IGI Global. doi:10.4018/978-1-4666-4506-6.ch004

Petersen & Carlsen. (2011). Wireless HART versus ISA100.11a: The Format War Hits the Factory Floor. *IEEE Industrial Electronics Magazine, 5*(4), 23-34.

Petrie, A., & Sabin, C. (2009). *Medical Statistics at a Glance*. Oxford, UK: Wiley-Blackwell.

Picazo-Sanchez, P., Ortiz-Martin, L., Peris-Lopez, P., & Bagheri, N. (2015). Weaknesses of fingerprint-based mutual authentication protocol. *Security and Communication Networks*, *8*(12), 2124–2134. doi:10.1002/sec.1161

Picazo-Sanchez, P., Ortiz-Martin, L., Peris-Lopez, P., & Hernandez-Castro, J. C. (2013). Security of EPC Class-1. In P. Lopez, J. Hernandez-Castro, & T. Li (Eds.), *Security and trends in wireless identification and sensing platform tags: Advancements in RFID* (pp. 34–63). Hershey, PA: IGI Global. doi:10.4018/978-1-4666-1990-6.ch002

Piezoelectric and Piezoresistive Array Pressure Sensors. (2014). MIT Towing Tank Lab. Retrieved 25 December 2015, from http://web.mit.edu/towtank/www/pcbarray.html

Piro, G., Cianci, I., Grieco, L. A., Boggia, G., & Camarda, P. (2014). Information centric services in Smart Cities. *Journal of Systems and Software, 88*, 169–188. doi:10.1016/j.jss.2013.10.029

Pohlmann, K., Atema, J., & Breithaupt, T. (2004). The importance of the lateral line in nocturnal predation of piscivorous catfish. *The Journal of Experimental Biology, 207*(17), 2971–2978. doi:10.1242/jeb.01129 PMID:15277552

Pojda, J., Wolff, A., Sbeiti, M., & Wietfeld, C. (2011). Performance analysis of mesh routing protocols for UAV swarming applications. In *8th International Symposium on Wireless Communication Systems (ISWCS)*, Aachen. doi:10.1109/ISWCS.2011.6125375

Popovic, Z., Momenroodaki, P., & Scheeler, R. (2014). Toward wearable wireless thermometers for internal body temperature measurements. *IEEE Communications Magazine, 52*(10), 118–125. doi:10.1109/MCOM.2014.6917412

Potyrailo, R. A., Morris, W. G., Sivavec, T., Tomlinson, H. W., Klensmeden, S., & Lindh, K. (2009). RFID sensors based on ubiquitous passive 13.56-MHz RFID tags and complex impedance detection. *Wireless Communications and Mobile Computing, 9*(10), 1318–1330. doi:10.1002/wcm.711

Pramanik, S., & Setua, S. K. (2012). DNA cryptography. Electrical & Computer Engineering (ICECE), IEEE.

Pratihar, D. K. (2013). *Soft Computing: Fundamentals and Applications* (1st ed.). Alpha Science International Ltd.

Preetha, K. G., Unnikrishnan, A., & Poulose Jacob, K. (2010). A probabilistic approach to reduce the route establishment overhead in aodv algorithm for MANET. *International Journal of Distributed and Parallel Systems, 3*(2), 207–214. doi:10.5121/ijdps.2012.3218

Premalatha, J., & Balasubramanie, P. (2010). Enhancing Quality of service in MANETS by Effecting routing. In *Proceedings of International Conference on Wireless Communication and Sensor Computing*.

Priyadsrini, , & Navamani, , & Mahadevan. (2012). An Efficient Route Discovery in Manets with Improved Route Lifetime. *International Journal of Information and Electronics Engineering, 2*(4), 493–496.

Psychoudakis, D., Lee, G., Chen, C., & Volakis, J. (2010). Military UHF body-worn antennas for armored vests. In *6th European Conference on Antennas and Propagation (EuCAP) IEEE* (pp. 1–4).

Psychoudakis, D., & Volakis, J. L. (2009). Conformal Asymmetric Meandered Flare (AMF) Antenna for Body-Worn Applications. *IEEE Antennas and Wireless Propagation Letters, 8*, 931–934. doi:10.1109/LAWP.2009.2028662

Pursley, M. B., & Royster, T. C. (2008). Low-Complexity Adaptive Transmission for Cognitive Radios in Dynamic Spectrum Access Networks. *IEEE Journal on Selected Areas in Communications, 26*(1), 83–94. doi:10.1109/JSAC.2008.080108

Qadri, N. N., & Fleury, M. (2012). Overview of mobile ad hoc networks and their modeling. In M. Fleury & N. Qadri (Eds.), *Streaming media with peer-to-peer networks: Wireless perspectives* (pp. 96–117). Hershey, PA: IGI Global. doi:10.4018/978-1-4666-1613-4.ch006

Qadri, N. N., & Liotta, A. (2011). Peer-to-peer over mobile ad-hoc networks. In S. Pierre (Ed.), *Next generation mobile networks and ubiquitous computing* (pp. 105–121). Hershey, PA: IGI Global. doi:10.4018/978-1-60566-250-3.ch011

Qian, C., Ngan, H., Liu, Y., & Ni, L. M. (2011). Cardinality estimation for large-scale RFID systems. *IEEE Transactions on Parallel and Distributed Systems*, *22*(9), 1441–1454. doi:10.1109/TPDS.2011.36

Qian, Z., Tian, X., Chen, X., Huang, W., & Wang, X. (2014). Multicast capacity in MANET with infrastructure support. *IEEE Transactions on Parallel and Distributed Systems*, *25*(7), 1808–1818. doi:10.1109/TPDS.2013.79

Quan, Z., Cui, S., Sayed, A. H., & Poor, H. V. (2009). Optimal Multiband Joint Detection for Spectrum Sensing in Cognitive Radio Networks. *IEEE Transactions on Signal Processing*, *57*(3), 1128–1140. doi:10.1109/TSP.2008.2008540

Quaritsch, M., Kruggl, K., Wischounig-Strucl, D., Bhattacharya, S., Shah, M., & Rinner, B. (2010). Networked UAVs as aerial sensor network for disaster management applications. *Elektrotechnik und Informationstechnik*, *127*(3), 56-63.

Quizlet. (2016). *Flash Cards*. Retrieved from https://quizlet.com/90321024/flashcards

Qu, Y., Li, X., Zhou, R., Chakravarthy, V., & Wu, Z. (2013). Software-Defined Radio Based Automatic Blind Hierarchical Modulation Detector via Second-Order Cyclostationary Analysis and Fourth-Order Cumulant.*IEEE Military Communications Conference*. doi:10.1109/MILCOM.2013.82

Raghavendra, S., & Lindsey, S. (2002). PEGASIS: Power-Efficient Gathering in Sensor Information Systems Stephanie Lindsey. In *Proceedings of Aerospace Conference*.

Rahman, Balamurugan & Mariappan. (2015). A Novel DNA Computing based Encryption and Decryption Algorithm. *ICICT*, 463 – 475.

Rahmani, M., Azadmanesh, A., & Siy, H. (2014). Architectural reliability analysis of framework-intensive applications: A web service case study. *Journal of Systems and Software*, *94*, 186–201. doi:10.1016/j.jss.2014.03.070

Rahmat-Samii, Y. (2007). Wearable and implantable antennas in body-centric communications. In *2nd European Conference on Antennas and Propagation (EuCAP)* (pp. 1–5).

Rai-Choudhury, P. (2000). *MEMS and MOEMS technology and applications*. Bellingham, WA: SPIE Optical Engineering Press.

Rais, N., Soh, P., Malek, F., Ahmad, S., Hashim, N., & Hall, P. (2009). A review of wearable antenna. In *Loughborough Antennas and Propagation Conference(LAPC)* (pp. 225–228).

Raju & Parwekar. (2015). DNA Encryption Based Dual Server Password Authentication. *Advances in Intelligent Systems and Computing*, 29-37.

Ramacher, U., & Ag, I. T. (2007). Software-Defined Radio Prospects for Multistandard Mobile Phones. *IEEE Computer Society Press Los Alamitos, CA, USA*, *40*(10), 62–69. doi:10.1109/MC.2007.362

Ramanathan, R., Ko, L. W., Chen, H., & Ramanathan, U. (2015). Green characteristics of RFID technologies: An exploration in the UK logistics sector from innovation diffusion perspective. In I. Lee (Ed.), *RFID technology integration for business performance improvement* (pp. 156–178). Hershey, PA: IGI Global. doi:10.4018/978-1-4666-6308-4.ch008

Ramanathan, R., Ramanathan, U., & Ko, L. W. (2015). An analysis of the diffusion of RFID in the UK logistics sector using a technology-acceptance perspective. In I. Lee (Ed.), *RFID technology integration for business performance improvement* (pp. 247–259). Hershey, PA: IGI Global. doi:10.4018/978-1-4666-6308-4.ch012

Ramanathan, R., Ramanathan, U., & Ko, L. W. (2016). Some lessons for promoting RFID by applying TAM theory. In I. Lee (Ed.), *Encyclopedia of e-commerce development, implementation, and management* (pp. 1900–1912). Hershey, PA: IGI Global. doi:10.4018/978-1-4666-9787-4.ch134

Ramasubramarian, V. (2002). Providing a Birectional Abstraction for Unidirectional Ad Hoc Networks. *Proceedings - IEEE INFOCOM.*

Ramon, S., Caceres, R., Kenneth, A., Goldman, R., Sailer, P., & Leendert, R. (2006). vTPM: Virtualizing the Trusted Platform Module. *USENIX Association, Security'06:15th USENIX Security.*

Ran, L., Helal, S., & Moore, S. (2004). *Drishti: an integrated indoor/outdoor blind navigation system and service.* Paper presented at the Pervasive Computing and Communications, 2004. PerCom 2004.

Ranck, J. (n.d.). *The wearable computing market: A global analysis.* Retrieved from http://go.gigaom.com/rs/gigaom/ images/ wearable-computing-the-next-big-thing-in-tech.pdf

Randriatsiferana, R., Lorion, R., Alicalapa, F., & Harivelo, F. (2013). Energy-efficient clustering algorithm based on energy variance for wireless sensor networks. In *IEEE International Conference on Smart Communications in network technologies* (SaCoNeT).

Rao, J. S., & Das, B. N. (1978). Impedance characteristics of transverse slots in the ground plane of a stripline. *Proceedings of the Institution of Electrical Engineers, 125*(1), 29–32. doi:10.1049/piee.1978.0007

Raya, M., Aziz, A., & Hubaux, J.-P. (2010). Efficient secure aggregation in Vanets. *Proceedings of the 3rd international workshop on Vehicular ad hoc networks.*

Raychoudhury, V., Cao, J., & Wu, W. (2008). Top K-leader Election in Wireless Ad Hoc Networks. In *Proceeding IEEE 17th International Conference on Computer Communications and Networks (ICCCN).* doi:10.1109/ICCCN.2008.ECP.35

Rayleigh, L. (1885). On Waves Propagated along the Plane Surface of an Elastic Solid. *Proc. London Math. Soc., 17*(1), 4-11. 10.1112/plms/s1-17.1.4

Raz, Shavitt, & Zhang. (2004). Distributed Council Election. *IEEE/ACM Transaction on Networking, 12*(3), 483-492.

Razafindralambo, T., & Mitton, N. (2007). Analysis of the Impact of Hello Protocol Parameters over a Wireless Network Self Organization. In *Proceedings of the 4th ACM workshop on Performance evaluation of wireless ad hoc, sensor and ubiquitous networks.* doi:10.1145/1298197.1298206

Rebeiz, E., & Cabric, D. (2011). Blind modulation classification based on spectral correlation and its robustness to timing mismatch. In *Proceedings of Military Communications Conference.* doi:10.1109/MILCOM.2011.6127676

Redman, C. W. G., & Moulden, M. (2014). Avoiding CTG misinterpretation: A review of the latest Dawes Redman CTG analysis. *British Journal of Midwifery, 22*(1), 2–5.

REED., F. (2007). 60 GHz WPAN Standardization within IEEE. In *International Symposium on Signals, Systems and Electronics, (ISSSE '07)* (pp. 103–105).

Regattieri, A., Santarelli, G., Gamberi, M., & Gamberini, R. (2014). The use of radio frequency identification technology in packaging systems: Experimental research on traceability. *Packaging Technology and Science, 27*(8), 591–608. doi:10.1002/pts.2052

Rekleitis, E., Rizomiliotis, P., & Gritzalis, S. (2014). How to protect security and privacy in the IoT: A policy-based RFID tag management protocol. *Security and Communication Networks, 7*(12), 2669–2683. doi:10.1002/sec.400

Renard, J., Lampe, L., & Horlin, F. (2013). Nonparametric Cyclic Polyspectrum-Based Spectrum Sensing. *IEEE Wireless Communications Letters, 2*(1), 98–101. doi:10.1109/WCL.2012.120312.120749

Ren, Q., & Cheng, X. (2010). Latency-Optimized and Energy-Efficient MAC Protocol for Underwater Acoustic Sensor Networks: A Cross-Layer Approach. *EURASIP Journal on Wireless Communications and Networking, 2010*, 1–8. doi:10.1155/2010/323151

Requicha, A. A. G. (2003). Nanorobots, NEMS, and Nanoassembly. *Proceedings of the IEEE, 91*(11).

Richard, K., & Martin, W., & Zhiqiang, W. (2011). Using Spectral Correlation For Non-cooperative RSS-based Positioning. In *Proceedings of IEEE Statistical Signal Processing Workshop* (SSP).

Rijkers, D. S., Wielders, S. J. H., Tesser, G. I., & Hemker, H. C. (1995). Design and Synthesis of Thrombin Substrates with Modified Kinetic Parameters Thromb. *Res., 79*, 491–499. PMID:7502275

Rishani, N. R., Al-Husseini, A. E.-H., & Kabalan, K. Y. (2012). Design and relative permittivity determination of an EBG-based wearable antenna. In Progress in Electromagnetics and Radio Frequency (pp. 96–99). Moscow, Russia: PIERS.

Rivet, F., Deval, Y., Begueret, J., Dallet, D., & Belot, D. (2007). *A Universal Radio Frequency Receiver Architecture Based on Sampled Analog Signal Processing*. Academic Press.

Roberts, R., Brown, W., & Loomis, H. (1991). Computationally Efficient Algorithms for Cyclic Spectral Analysis. *IEEE Signal Processing Magazine, 8*(2), 38–49. doi:10.1109/79.81008

Rohankar, R., Bhatia, R., & Shrivastava, V. (2012). Performance Analysis of Various Routing Protocols (Proactive and Reactive) for Random Mobility Models of Adhoc Networks. In *Proceedings of 1st International conference on Recent Advances in Information Technology (RAIT)*. doi:10.1109/RAIT.2012.6194441

Roy, Rakshit, Singha, Majumder, & Datta. (2011). A DNA based Symmetric key Cryptography. *ICSSA*, 68-72.

Royal College of Obstetricians and Gynecologists. (2001). *The use of electronic fetal monitoring: The use and interpretation of cardiotocography in intrapartum fetal surveillance*. London: RCOG Press.

Roy, B., & Majumder, A. (2012). An improved concept of cryptography based on DNA sequencing. *International Journal of Electronics and Communication Computer Engineering, 3*(6), 1475–1478.

Roy, B., Rakshit, G., Singha, P., Majumder, A., & Datta, D. (2011). An Improved symmetric key cryptography with DNA based strong cipher.*International Conference on Devices and Communications*, (pp. 1-5). doi:10.1109/ICDE-COM.2011.5738553

Running, G. P. S. Watches. (2014). Retrieved from http://sports.tomtom.com/en_us/

Rusconi, C. P., Scardino, E., Layzer, J., Pitoc, G. A., Ortel, T. L., Monroe, D., & Sullenger, B. A. (2002). RNA aptamers as reversible antagonists of coagulation factor IXa. *Nature, 419*(6902), 90–94. doi:10.1038/nature00963 PMID:12214238

Sabry, M., Hashem, M., & Nazmy, T. (2012). Three reversible Data Encoding Algorithms based on DNA and Amino Acids Structure. *IJCA, 54*(8), 24–30.1. doi:10.5120/8588-2339

Sabry, M., Hashem, M., Nazmy, T., & Khalifa, M. E. (2015). Design of DNA based advanced encryption standard (AES).*International Conference on Intelligent Computing and Information Systems (ICICIS), IEEE*. doi:10.1109/Intel-CIS.2015.7397250

Sadeghi, A-R. (n.d.). *Trusted platform module, lecture slides for secure, trusted and trustworthy computing*. Technische Universität Darmstadt. Retrieved from: http://www.trust.informatik.darmstadt.de/fileadmin/user_upload/Group_TRUST/LectureSlides/STCWS2011/Chap3__Trusted_Platform_Module.pdf.pdf

Sadeg, S., Gougache, M., Mansouri, N., & Drias, H. (2010). An encryption algorithm inspired from DNA.*International Conference on Machine and Web Intelligence, IEEE*.

Saini, Alam, & Guo. (2015, December). InCloud: a cloud-based middleware for vehicular infotainment systems. *Multimed Tools Appl.*

Sai, V., & Mickle, H. (2014). Exploring energy efficient architectures in passive wireless nodes for IoT applications. *IEEE Circuits Systems Magazines, 14*(2), 48–54. doi:10.1109/MCAS.2014.2314265

Saka, T., Fujino, Y., Fujita, M., & Kaya, N. (1997). An experiment of a C Band rectenna.*Proceedings of SPS* (pp.251-253).

Sakhre, V., Singh, U. P., & Jain, S. (2016). FCPN Approach for Uncertain Nonlinear Dynamical System with Unknown Disturbance. *International Journal of Fuzzy Systems.* doi:10.1007/s40815-016-0145-5

Sakpere, W. E., & Adeyeye, M. O. (2015). Can near field communication solve the limitations in mobile indoor navigation? In I. Lee (Ed.), *RFID technology integration for business performance improvement* (pp. 52–79). Hershey, PA: IGI Global. doi:10.4018/978-1-4666-6308-4.ch003

Salman, L. K. H., & Talbi, L. (2010). G-shaped wearable cuff button antenna for 2.45 GHZ ISM band applications. In *2010 14th International Symposium on Antenna Technology and Applied Electromagnetics and the American Electromagnetics Conference, ANTEM/AMEREM 2010* (pp. 14–17). http://doi.org/ doi:<ALIGNMENT.qj></ALIGNMENT>10.1109/ANTEM.2010.5552573

Salonen, P., Sydanheimo, L., Keskilammi, M., & Kivikoski, M. (1999). A Small Planar Inverted-F Antenna for Wearable Applications. In *IEEE Conference Publications* (pp. 95–100). http://doi.org/ doi:10.1109/ISWC.1999.806679

Salonen, P., Rahmat-Samii, Y., Hurme, H., & Kivikoski, M. (2004). Effect of conductive material on wearable antenna performance: A case study of WLAN antennas. *Antennas and Propagation Society, 1,* 455–458. doi:10.1109/APS.2004.1329672

Samsung Electronics Co. Ltd. (2014). *Samsung GALAXY Note2 - Samsung Mobile.* Retrieved from http://www.samsung.com/global/microsite/galaxynote/note2/spec.html

Sanchez, E., Shibata, T. & Zadeh, L.A. (1997). *Genetic algorithm and fuzzy logic system, Soft Computing Perspective.* World Scientific Singapore.

Sánchez, M. M., Nieto, J. A., Gallinas, R. B., & Vidales, M. Á. (2014). CommunicaME: A new proposal for facilitating communication using NFC. In M. Cruz-Cunha, F. Moreira, & J. Varajão (Eds.), *Handbook of research on enterprise 2.0: Technological, social, and organizational dimensions* (pp. 89–106). Hershey, PA: IGI Global. doi:10.4018/978-1-4666-4373-4.ch005

Sankaralingam, S., & Gupta, B. (2009). A circular disk microstrip WLAN antenna for wearable applications. In *IEEE India Council Conference* (pp. 3–6). http://doi.org/ doi:10.1109/INDCON.2009.5409355

Santas, J., Alomainy, A., & Hao, Y. (2007). Textile Antennas for On-Body Communications: Techniques and Properties. In *2nd European Conference on Antennas and Propagation (EuCAP)* (pp. 1–4.). doi:10.1049/ic.2007.1064

Santos, N., Gummadi, K. P., & Rodrigues, R. (2009). Towards trusted cloud computing. In *Proceedings of the conference on cloud computing.* Berkeley, CA: USENIX Association.

Sanz-Izquierdo, B., Huang, F., & Batchelor, J. C. (2006). Small size wearable button antenna. In *First European Conference on Antennas and Propagation* (pp. 1–4).

Sanz-Izquierdo, B., Miller, J. A., Batchelor, J. C., & Sobhy, M. I. (2010). Dual-Band Wearable Metallic Button Antennas and Transmission in Body Area Networks. *IET Microw. Antennas Propag., 4*(2), 182–190. doi:10.1049/iet-map.2009.0010

Sari, A. (2015). Security issues in mobile wireless ad hoc networks: A comparative survey of methods and techniques to provide security in wireless ad hoc networks. In M. Dawson & M. Omar (Eds.), *New threats and countermeasures in digital crime and cyber terrorism* (pp. 66–94). Hershey, PA: IGI Global. doi:10.4018/978-1-4666-8345-7.ch005

Sarisaray-Boluk, P., Gungor, V., Baydere, S., & Harmanci, A. (2011). Quality aware image transmission over underwater multimedia sensor networks. *Ad Hoc Networks*, *9*(7), 1287–1301. doi:10.1016/j.adhoc.2011.02.007

Sarwar, K., & Shah, M. A. (2015). Cost effective design of an RFID based healthcare service system. *International Journal of Privacy and Health Information Management*, *3*(2), 51–65. doi:10.4018/IJPHIM.2015070103

Sathishkumar, R., Vimalajuliet, A., Prasath, J. S., Selvakumar, K., & Veer Reddy, V. H. S. (2011). Micro size ultrasonic transducer for marine applications. *Indian Journal of Science and Technology*, *4*(1), 8–11.

Schadow, K. (2004). MEMS Military Applications-RTO Task Group Summary. In *Proceedings of CANEUS 2004 Conference on Micro-Nano-Technologies*. doi:10.2514/6.2004-6749

Schmidt Andreas, U., Leicher, A., Brett, A., Shah, Y., & Cha, I. (2013). Tree-formed verification data for trusted platforms. *Computers & Security*, *32*, 19–35. doi:10.1016/j.cose.2012.09.004

Schmidt-knorreck, C., Knorreck, D., Knopp, R., & Antipolis, S. (2012). *IEEE 802. Receiver Design for Software Defined Radio Platforms*. doi:10.1109/DSD.2012.76

Seeling, B., Keiper, S., Stuhlmann, F., & Jaeschke, A. (2000). Enantioselective ribozyme catalysis of a bimolecular cycloaddition reaction. *Angewandte Chemie International Edition*, *39*(24), 4576–4579. doi:10.1002/1521-3773(20001215)39:24<4576::AID-ANIE4576>3.0.CO;2-J PMID:11169675

Seeman. N. C. (2003). DNA in a material world. *Nature, 421*, 427-431.

Selva, A. F. B., Reis, A. L. G., Lenzi, K. G., Meloni, L. G. P., & Barbin, S. E. (2012). *Introduction to the Software-defined Radio Approach*. Academic Press.

Semsch, E., Jakob, M., & Pavlicek, D. (2009). *Autonomous UAV Surveillance in Complex Urban Environments*. In IEEE/WIC/ACM International Joint Conferences on Web Intelligence and Intelligent Agent Technologies (WI-IAT), Milan, Italy.

Serra, A. A., Nepa, P., & Manara, G. (2011). Cospas Sarsat rescue applications.*IEEE International Symposium on Antennas and Propagation (APSURSI)*, *3*, 1319–1322. doi:10.1109/APS.2011.5996532

Shah, S. C. (2015). Energy efficient and robust allocation of interdependent tasks on mobile ad hoc computational grid. *Concurrency and Computation*, *27*(5), 1226–1254. doi:10.1002/cpe.3297

Shah, S., & Lozano, B. (2013). Joint sensor selection and multihop routing for distributed estimation in ad-hoc wireless sensor networks. *IEEE Transactions on Signal Processing*, *61*(24), 6355–6370. doi:10.1109/TSP.2013.2284486

Sha, M., Hackmann, G., & Lu, C. (2013). Real-world empirical studies on multi-channel reliability and spectrum usage for home-area sensor networks. *IEEE eTransactions on Network and Service Management*, *10*(1), 56–69. doi:10.1109/TNSM.2012.091312.120237

Shantanu. (2011). *Highly Available Coordinators for Mobile Ad hoc Networks* (M.Tech. Dissertation). Dept. of CSE, NIT Kurukshetra.

Sharbaf, M. S. (2011). Quantum Cryptography: An emerging technology in network security. Technologies for Homeland Security, IEEE.

Sharifian, S., Motamedi, S. A., & Akbari, M. K. (2011). A predictive and probabilistic load-balancing algorithm for cluster-based web Servers. *Applied Soft Computing*, *11*(1), 970–981. doi:10.1016/j.asoc.2010.01.017

Sharma, M. K., Bali, R. S., & Kaur, A. (2015). Dynamic key based authentication scheme for Vehicular Cloud Computing. *International Conference on Green Computing and Internet of Things (ICGCIoT)*. doi:10.1109/ICGCIoT.2015.7380620

Shellhammer, S. J., Sadek, A. K., & Zhang, W. (2009). Technical Challenges for Cognitive Radio in the TV White Space Spectrum. *Information Theory and Applications Workshop*. doi:10.1109/ITA.2009.5044964

Shen, J. (2016). *An Authorized Identity Authentication-based Data Access Control Scheme in Cloud*. ICACT.

Sherali Zeadally, S. C. A. I. A. H. (2012). Vehicular ad hoc networks (VANETs): Status, Results and Challenges. *Telecommunication Systems*, *50*(10), 217–241. doi:10.1007/s11235-010-9400-5

Sherrill, D. M., Moy, M. L., Reilly, J. J., & Bonato, P. (2005). Using hierarchical clustering methods to classify motor activities of COPD patients from wearable sensor data. *Neuroeng Rehabil*, *2*(1), 16. doi:10.1186/1743-0003-2-16 PMID:15987518

Shetty, V., Sudit, M., & Nagi, R. (2008). Priority-based assignment and routing of a fleet of unmanned combat aerial vehicles. *Computers & Operations Research*, *35*(6), 1813–1828. doi:10.1016/j.cor.2006.09.013

Shevtsov, S., Parinov, I., Zhilyaev, I., Chang, S.-H., Lee, J. C.-Y., & Wu, P.-C. (2012). Modeling and Optimization of MEMS-Based Acoustic Sensor for Underwater Applications. In Proceedings of Recent Researches in Applied Mechanics (pp. 88-93).

Shigen, G., Hairong, D., Ning, B., & Chen, L. (2015). Neural adaptive control for uncertain nonlinear system with input: State transformation based output feedback. *Neurocomputing*, *159*, 117–125. doi:10.1016/j.neucom.2015.02.012

Shih, D., Chiu, Y., Chang, S., & Yen, D. C. (2010). An empirical study of factors affecting RFID's adoption in Taiwan. In J. Symonds (Ed.), *Ubiquitous and pervasive computing: Concepts, methodologies, tools, and applications* (pp. 1122–1143). Hershey, PA: IGI Global. doi:10.4018/978-1-60566-960-1.ch070

Shin, K. G., Kim, H., Min, A. W., & Kumar, A. (2010). Cognitive Radios for Dynamic Spectrum Access: From Concept to Reality. *IEEE Wireless Communications*, *17*(6), 64–74. doi:10.1109/MWC.2010.5675780

Shirazi, B. A., Hurson, A. R., & Kavi, K. M. (1995). *Scheduling and Load Balancing in Parallel and Distributed Systems*. CS Press.

Shiu, H. J., Ng, K. L., Fang, J. F., Lee, R. C. T., & Huang, C. H. (2010). Data hiding methods based upon DNA sequences. *Information Sciences*, *180*(11), 2196–2208. doi:10.1016/j.ins.2010.01.030

Shooman, M. L. (2002). *Reliability of Computer Systems and Networks: Fault Tolerance, Analysis, and Design*. New York: John Wiley & Sons. doi:10.1002/047122460X

Shrivastava, Shanmogavel, Mistry, Chander, Patlolla, & Yadlapalli. (n.d.). *Overview of Routing Protocols in MANET's and Enhancements in Reactive Protocols*. Department of Computer Science, Lamar University.

Silberschatz, A., Galvin, P. B., & Gagne, G. (2009). Operating System Concepts. Wiley India.

Sim, M. L., Chin, C. M., & Tan, C. M. (2007). Mobile ad-hoc networks. In D. Taniar (Ed.), *Encyclopedia of mobile computing and commerce* (pp. 424–428). Hershey, PA: IGI Global. doi:10.4018/978-1-59904-002-8.ch070

Simon, M. K., & Alouini, M. S. (2005). Digital Communications over Fading Channels. John Wiley & Sons.

Singh, S., & Kumar, V. (2015). Secured User's Authentication and Private Data Storage- Access Scheme in Cloud Computing Using Elliptic Curve Cryptography. *International Conference on Computing for Sustainable Global Development*.

Singh, H. K., & Bezboruah, T. (2015). Performance Metrics of a Customized Web Application Developed for Monitoring Sensor Data. In *Proceedings of the IEEE 2nd International Conference on Recent Trends in Information Systems (ReTIS)*. doi:10.1109/ReTIS.2015.7232870

Singh, J., Bhardwaj, M., & Sharma, A. (2015). Experimental analysis of distributed routing algorithms in ad hoc mobile networks. *Procedia Computer Science, 57*, 1411–1416. doi:10.1016/j.procs.2015.07.459

Singh, R. K. (2016). Issues related to network security attacks in mobile ad hoc networks (MANET). In N. Mohamed, T. Mantoro, M. Ayu, & M. Mahmud (Eds.), *Critical socio-technical issues surrounding mobile computing* (pp. 234–256). Hershey, PA: IGI Global. doi:10.4018/978-1-4666-9438-5.ch012

Singh, S. (2012). Security threats and issues with MANET. In K. Lakhtaria (Ed.), *Technological advancements and applications in mobile ad-hoc networks: Research trends* (pp. 247–263). Hershey, PA: IGI Global. doi:10.4018/978-1-4666-0321-9.ch015

Singh, S. P., McCartney, M., Singh, J., & Clarke, R. (2008). RFID research and testing for packages of apparel, consumer goods and fresh produce in the retail distribution environment. *Packaging Technology and Science, 21*(2), 91–102. doi:10.1002/pts.782

Singh, S., & Kurose, J. (1994). Electing Good Leaders. *Journal of Parallel and Distributed Computing, 21*(2), 184–201. doi:10.1006/jpdc.1994.1051

Singh, S., Singh, D. K., & Mondal, M. S. (2012). Potential area of research in MANET. In K. Lakhtaria (Ed.), *Technological advancements and applications in mobile ad-hoc networks: Research trends* (pp. 391–407). Hershey, PA: IGI Global. doi:10.4018/978-1-4666-0321-9.ch021

Singh, U. P., Jain, S., Singh, R. K., Parmar, M., Makwana, R. R. S., & Kumare, J. S. (2016). Dynamic Surface Control Based TS-Fuzzy Model for a Class of Uncertain Nonlinear Systems. *International Journal of Control Theory and Applications, 9*(2), 1333–1345.

Sinha & Yadav. (2014). Comparative Analysis and Enhancement of Leader Election Algorithms through Shared Memory in Mobile Ad-hoc Networks. *International Journal of Emerging Trends & Technology in Computer Science, 3*(1), 84-89.

Sinha, S., & Yadav, N. (2014, January-February). Comparative Analysis and Enhancement of Leader Election Algorithms through Shared Memory in Mobile Ad-hoc Networks. *International Journal of Emerging Trends & Technology in Computer Science, 3*(1), 84–89.

Sinodinou, T. (2009). RFID technology and its impact on privacy: Is society one step before the disappearance of personal data protection? In D. Politis, P. Kozyris, & I. Iglezakis (Eds.), *Socioeconomic and legal implications of electronic intrusion* (pp. 89–107). Hershey, PA: IGI Global. doi:10.4018/978-1-60566-204-6.ch005

Sithamparanathan, K., & Giorgetti, A. (2012). Cognitive Radio Techniques: Spectrum Sensing, Interference Mitigation, and Localization. Artech House. Available http://www.artechhouse.com/static/sample/Sith-203_CH03.pdf

Sitti, M. (2009). Miniature Devices: Voyage of the microrobots. *Nature, 458*(30).

Skordos, A., Chan, P., Vincent, J., & Jeronimidis, G. (2002). A novel strain sensor based on the campaniform sensillum of insects. *Philosophical Transactions of The Royal Society A: Mathematical, Physical and Engineering Sciences, 360*(1791), 239-253.10.1098/rsta.2001.0929

Skrivervik, A. K., & Merli, F. (2011). Design strategies for implantable antennas. In *Loughborough Antennas and Propagation Conference* (pp. 1–5). http://doi.org/ doi:10.1109/LAPC.2011.6114011

Skrivervik, A. K., & Zürcher, J. F. (2007). Miniature antenna design at LEMA. In *19th International Conference on Applied Electromagnetics and Communications* (pp. 4–7). http://doi.org/ doi:<ALIGNMENT.qj></ALIGNMENT>10.1109/ICECOM.2007.4544410

Smith, A. D. (2014). Case studies of RFID practices for competitive inventory management systems. In J. Wang (Ed.), *Management science, logistics, and operations research* (pp. 1–25). Hershey, PA: IGI Global. doi:10.4018/978-1-4666-4506-6.ch001

Snow flaik tracks skiers. (2011). Retrieved from http://news.discovery.com/tech/ snow-flaik-tracks-skiers.htm

So, J., Kim, & Gupta. (2005). Cushion: Autonomically Adaptive Data Fusion in Wireless Sensor Network. In *Proceedings of IEEE International Conference on Mobile Adhoc and Sensor Systems Conference.*

SOAP. (n.d.). Retrieved online on 31.1.2016, Available at http://www.w3.org/TR/soap12-part1/

Soderstrom, T., & Stoica, P. (1989). *System Identification.* New York: Prentice Hall.

Soh, P. J., Vandenbosch, G. A. E., Volski, V., & Nurul, H. M. R. (2010). Characterization of a Simple Broadband Textile Planar Inverted-F Antenna (PIFA) for on Body Communications. In *22nd International Conference on Applied Electromagnetics and Communications (ICECom)* (pp. 1–4).

Soh, P., Boyes, S., Vandenbosch, G., Huang, Y., & Ma, Z. (2012). Dual-band Sierpinski textile PIFA efficiency measurements. In *6th European Conference on Antennas and Propagation (EuCAP)*, (pp. pp. 3322–3326).

Somappa, K., Ovsthus, K., & Kristensen, L. (2014). An industrial perspective on wireless sensor networks-A survey of requirement, protocols and challenges. *IEEE Communications Surveys and Tutorials*, *16*(3), 1391–1412. doi:10.1109/SURV.2014.012114.00058

Song, B., & Hedrick, J. K. (2004). Observer-based dynamic surface control for a class of nonlinear systems: An LMI approach. *IEEE Transactions on Automatic Control*, *49*(11), 1995–2001. doi:10.1109/TAC.2004.837562

Song, H., Xiuming, Z., & Mok, A. K. (2011). Reliable and Real-time communication in Industrial Messh Networks. In *Proceedings of 17th IEEE Real-Time and Embedded Technology and Applications Symposium.*

Song, J., Han, S., Mok, A. K., Chen, D., Lucas, M., Nixon, M., & Pratt, W. (2008). WirelessHART: Applying Wireless Technology in Real-Time Industrial Process Control. In *Proceedings of IEEE Real-Time and Embedded Technology and Applications Symposium*, (pp. 22-24). doi:10.1109/RTAS.2008.15

Soon, C. B. (2010). Radio frequency identification history and development. In J. Symonds (Ed.), *Ubiquitous and pervasive computing: Concepts, methodologies, tools, and applications* (pp. 65–81). Hershey, PA: IGI Global. doi:10.4018/978-1-60566-960-1.ch007

Soon, C. B., & Gutiérrez, J. A. (2011). Adoption of RFID in supply chains: A motivation and ability perspective. In J. Wang (Ed.), *Supply chain optimization, management and integration: Emerging applications* (pp. 54–63). Hershey, PA: IGI Global. doi:10.4018/978-1-60960-135-5.ch004

Sornil, O. (2010). QoS signaling security in mobile ad hoc networks. In P. Bhattarakosol (Ed.), *Intelligent quality of service technologies and network management: Models for enhancing communication* (pp. 322–332). Hershey, PA: IGI Global. doi:10.4018/978-1-61520-791-6.ch017

Spiegel, M.R. (2000). *Theory and problems of probability and statistics.* McGraw-Hill Book Company.

Spilka, J. (2013). *Complex approach to fetal heart rate analysis: A hierarchical classification model* (Unpublished doctoral dissertation). Czech Technical University, Prague, Czech Republic.

Srinivasan, S., & Alampalayam, S. P. (2011). Intrusion detection algorithm for MANET. *International Journal of Information Security and Privacy*, *5*(3), 36–49. doi:10.4018/jisp.2011070103

Stambouli, A., & Traversa, E. (2002). Solid oxide fuel cells (SOFCs): A review of an environmentally clean and efficient source of energy. *Renewable & Sustainable Energy Reviews*, *6*(5), 433–455. doi:10.1016/S1364-0321(02)00014-X

Staub, O., Zurcher, J.-F., Skrivervik, A. K., & Mosig, J. R. (1999). PCS antenna design: the challenge of miniaturisation. *IEEE Antennas and Propagation Society International Symposium*, *1*. http://doi.org/ doi:10.1109/APS.1999.789198

Staub, O., Zürcher, J.-F., & Skrivervik, A. (1998). Some considerations on the correct measurement of the gain and bandwidth of electrically small antennas. *Microwave and Optical Technology Letters*, *17*(3), 156–160. doi:10.1002/(SICI)1098-2760(19980220)17:3<156::AID-MOP2>3.0.CO;2-I

Steele, B. L. H., Belza, B., Ferris, S., Lakshminaryan, S., & Buchner, D. (2000). *Quantitating physical activity in COPD using a triaxial accelerometer*. Chest.

Steer, P. J. (2008). Has Electronic Fetal Heart Rate Monitoring Made a Difference. (2008). *PubMed. Seminars in Fetal & Neonatal Medicine*, *13*(1), 2–7. doi:10.1016/j.siny.2007.09.005 PMID:18271079

Stoica, P., & Sandgren, N. (2006). Cepstrum Thresholding Scheme for Nonparametric Estimation of Smooth Spectra. *IMTC 2006 - Instrumentation and Measurement Technology Conference Sorrento*, (pp. 874-878).

Stoica, P., & Moses, R. (2005). *Spectral Analysis of Signals*. Upper Saddle River, NJ: Prentice Hall.

Stoica, P., & Sandgren, N. (2006). Smoothed nonparametric spectral estimation via cepstrum Thresholding. *IEEE Signal Processing Magazine*, 34–45. doi:10.1109/SP-M.2006.248710

Stojanovic, M. (2003). Acoustic (Underwater) Communications. In Encyclopedia of Telecommunications. John Wiley & Sons.

Stojanovic, M. N., Landry, D. W., & Am, J. (2002). Aptamer-based colorimetric probe for cocaine. *Chem. Soc.*, *124*(33), 9678–9679. doi:10.1021/ja0259483 PMID:12175205

Storn, R., & Price, K. (1997). Differential Evolution: A Simple and EfficientHeuristic for Global Optimization Over Continuous Space. *Journal of Global Optimization*, *11*(4), 341–359. doi:10.1023/A:1008202821328

Stutzman, W., & Thiele, G. (1997). *Antenna Theory and Design* (2nd ed.). Wiley.

Subbu, K., & Li, X. (2010). SFRP: A selective flooding-based routing protocol for clustered wireless sensor networks. In *Proceedings of IEEE Radio and Wireless Symposium*. doi:10.1109/RWS.2010.5434131

Sudevalayam, S., & Kulkarni, P. (2011). Energy Harvesting Sensor Nodes: Survey and Implications. *IEEE Communications Surveys and Tutorials*, *13*(3), 443–461. doi:10.1109/SURV.2011.060710.00094

Suh, Y. H., & Chang, K. (2000). A circularly polarized truncated-corner square patch microstrip rectenna for wireless power transmission. *Electronics Letters*, *36*(7), 600–602. doi:10.1049/el:20000527

Sungsoon, C. (2009). *Adaptive Management schemes for mobile Ad-hoc Networks* (Dissertation for PHD). The University of Michigan.

Sun, Q., Zhang, H., & Mo, L. (2011). Dual-reader wireless protocols for dense active RFID identification. *International Journal of Communication Systems*, *24*(11), 1431–1444. doi:10.1002/dac.1225

Sutton, P. D., Nolan, K. E., & Doyle, L. E. (2008). Cyclostationary signatures in practical cognitive radio applications. *IEEE Journal on Selected Areas in Communications*, *26*(1), 13–24. doi:10.1109/JSAC.2008.080103

Swami, A., & Sadler, M. (2000). Hierarchical Digital Modulation Classification Using Cumulants. *IEEE Transactions on Communications, 48*(3), 416–429. doi:10.1109/26.837045

Tajima, M. (2012). Small manufacturers vs. large retailers on RFID adoption in the apparel supply chain. In T. Choi (Ed.), *Fashion supply chain management: Industry and business analysis* (pp. 74–99). Hershey, PA: IGI Global. doi:10.4018/978-1-60960-756-2.ch004

Talaulikar, T. V., & Arulkumaran, S. (2013). Medico-legal issues with CTG interpretation. *Current Women's Health Reports, 9*(3), 143–157.

Tandra, R., Mishra, M., & Sahai, A. (2009). What is a spectrum hole and what does it take to recognize one? *Proceedings of the IEEE, 97*(5), 824–848. doi:10.1109/JPROC.2009.2015710

Tandra, R., & Sahai, A. (2005). Fundamental Limits on Detection in Low SNR Under Noise Uncertainty. *International Conference on Wireless Networks, Communication and Mobile Computing.* doi:10.1109/WIRLES.2005.1549453

Tandra, R., & Sahai, A. (2008). SNR Walls for Signal Detection. *IEEE Journal of Selected Topics in Signal Processing, 2*(1), 4–17. doi:10.1109/JSTSP.2007.914879

Tang, Z. J., Wu, X. F., Zhan, J., & Hu, S. G. (2014). Broadband UHF RFID tag antenna design matched with different RFID chips. *Microwave and Optical Technology Letters, 56*(1), 55–57. doi:10.1002/mop.28046

Tarchi, D., Guidotti, A., Icolari, V., Varelli-Coralli, A., Sharma, S. K., Chatzinotas, S., . . . Grotz, J. (2014). Technical Challenges for Cognitive Radio Application in Satellite Communications. In *Proceedings of 9th International Conference on Cognitive Radio Oriented Wireless Networks* (CROWNCOM). doi:10.4108/icst.crowncom.2014.255727

Tekli, J.M., Damiani, E., Chbeir, R., & Gianini, G. (2012). SOAP Processing Performance and Enhancement. *IEEE Transaction on Services Computing, 5*(3).

Temel, S., & Bekmezci, I. (2013). *On the performance of Flying Ad-hoc Networks (FANETs) utilizing near space high altitude platforms* (HAPs). In *6th International Conference on Recent Advances in Space Technologies (RAST)*, Istanbul, Turkey. doi:10.1109/RAST.2013.6581252

Tesla, N. (1892). Experiments with alternate currents of high potential and high frequency. *Journal of the Institution of Electrical Engineers, 21*(97), 51–162. doi:10.1049/jiee-1.1892.0002

Tetrapol. (2015). *Tetrapol Factsheet Trunked radio system for emergency services.* Author.

Tewoldeberhan, T., & Janssen, M. (2008). Simulation-based experimentation for designing reliable and efficient Web service orchestrations in supply chains. *Electronic Commerce Research and Applications, 7*(1), 82–92. doi:10.1016/j.elerap.2006.11.007

Texas Instruments. (2014). *TRF7960A.* Retrieved from http://www.ti.com/product/trf7960a

Thayananthan, V., Alzahrani, A., & Qureshi, M. S. (2015). Efficient techniques of key management and quantum cryptography in RFID networks. *Security and Communication Networks, 8*(4), 589–597. doi:10.1002/sec.1005

The TCG Software Stack (TSS) Specification-version 1.20 Errata A Golden Candidate 2. (n.d.). Trusted Computing Group.

Thenral, B., & Sikamani. (2013). Proficient routing method that exploits the lifetime of wireless sensor network. In *Proceedings of IEEE International Conference of Current trends in engineering and technology* (ICCTET). doi:10.1109/ICCTET.2013.6675954

Theodorakopoulos, G., & Baras, J. S. (2006, February). On Trust Models and Trust Evaluation Metrics for Ad-hoc Networks. *IEEE Journal on Selected Areas in Communications, 24*(2), 318–328. doi:10.1109/JSAC.2005.861390

Ticknor, J. L. (2013). A Bayesian regularized artificial network for stock market forecasting. *Expert Systems with Applications*, *40*(14), 5501–5506. doi:10.1016/j.eswa.2013.04.013

Tijs, E., de Bree, H.-E., & Akal, T. (2013). Sea-Bottom Mounted Trials with Hydroflown Sensors. In *Proceedings of 1st International Conference and Exhibition on Underwater Acoustics* (pp. 673-678).

Todd, C., Mallya, S., Majeed, S., Rojas, J., & Naylor, K. (2014). *VirtuNav: A Virtual Reality indoor navigation simulator with haptic and audio feedback for the visually impaired.* Paper presented at the Computational Intelligence in Robotic Rehabilitation and Assistive Technologies (CIR2AT), 2014 IEEE Symposium on.

Toh, B. Y., Cahill, R., & Fusco, V. F. (2003). Understanding and measuring circular polarization. *IEEE Transactions on Education*, *46*(3), 313–318. doi:10.1109/TE.2003.813519

Tomcat. (2016). Retrieved on 20.1.2016, from http://tomcat.apache.org/

Tong, S. C., Li, H. X., & Wang, W. (2004). Observer based adaptive fuzzy control for SISO nonlinear systems. *Fuzzy Sets and Systems*, *148*(3), 355–376. doi:10.1016/j.fss.2003.11.017

Tong, S., Li, Y., Feng, G., & Li, T. (2011). Observer based adaptive fuzzy backstepping dynamic surface control for a class of MIMO nonlinear systems. *IEEE Transactions on Systems, Man, and Cybernetics*, *41*(4), 1124–1134. doi:10.1109/TSMCB.2011.2108283 PMID:21317084

Tornea, O., & Borda, M. E. (2009). DNA Cryptographic Algorithms. *IFMBE Proceedings*, *26*, 223–226. doi:10.1007/978-3-642-04292-8_49

Trajkovikj, J., Fuchs, B., & Skrivervik, A. (2011). *LEMA internal report.* LEMA.

Trivedi, A. K., Arora, R., Kapoor, R., & Sanyal, S. (2009). Mobile ad hoc network security vulnerabilities. In M. Khosrow-Pour (Ed.), *Encyclopedia of information science and technology* (2nd ed., pp. 2557–2561). Hershey, PA: IGI Global. doi:10.4018/978-1-60566-026-4.ch407

Tseng, L. Y., & Han, T. Y. (2008). Microstrip-fed circular slot antenna for circular polarization. *Microwave and Optical Technology Letters*, *50*(4), 1056–1058. doi:10.1002/mop.23290

Tuerk, C., & Gold, L. (1990). Systematic evolution of ligands by exponential enrichment: RNA ligands to bacteriophage T4 DNA polymerase. *Science*, *249*(4968), 505–510. doi:10.1126/science.2200121 PMID:2200121

Tung, C. H., Gerszten, R. E., Jaffer, F. A., & Weissleder, R. A. (2002). *Novel Near-Infrared Fluorescence Sensor for Detection of Thrombin Activation in Blood. ChemBioChem*, *3*, 207–211. PMID:11921399

Uddin, M. A., & Suny, A. H. (2015). *Shortest path finding and obstacle detection for visually impaired people using smart phone.* Paper presented at the Electrical Engineering and Information Communication Technology (ICEEICT), 2015 International Conference on.

Ullah, S., & Kwak, K. S. (2011). *Body Area Network for Ubiquitous Healthcare Applications: Theory and Implementation.* http://doi.org/<ALIGNMENT.qj></ALIGNMENT>10.1007/s10916-011-9787-x

Ummat, A., Dubey, A., & Mavroidis, C. (2005). *Bionanorobotics: A Field Inspired by Nature.* In *Biomimetics - Biologically Inspired Technologies* (pp. 201–227). CRC Press.

United Nations Children's Fund. (2009). *Coverage Evaluation Survey.* New Delhi: Author.

Unnithan, C., & Fraunholz, B. (2015). Radio frequency identification technology as an analytical lens and solution in hospitals: A novel approach in BPR/BPM. In M. Tavana, A. Ghapanchi, & A. Talaei-Khoei (Eds.), *Healthcare informatics and analytics: Emerging issues and trends* (pp. 194–211). Hershey, PA: IGI Global. doi:10.4018/978-1-4666-6316-9.ch010

Urgaonkar, B., Shenoy, P., & Roscoe, T. (2007). Resource overbooking and application profiling in shared internet hosting platforms. *ACM Transactions on Internet Technology*.

Vales-Alonso, J., Parrado-García, F. J., & Alcaraz, J. J. (2016). OSL: An optimization-based scheduler for RFID dense-reader environments. *Ad Hoc Networks*, *37*, 512–525. doi:10.1016/j.adhoc.2015.10.004

Vallozzi, L., Van Torre, P., Hertleer, C., Rogier, H., Moeneclaey, M., & Verhaevert, J. (2010). Wireless communication for firefighters using dual-polarized textile antennas integrated in their garment. *IEEE Transactions on Antennas and Propagation*, *58*(4), 1357–1368. doi:10.1109/TAP.2010.2041168

Vallozzi, L., Vandendriessche, W., Rogier, H., Hertleer, C., & Scarpello, M. L. (2010). Wearable textile GPS antenna for integration in protective garments. In *4th European Conference on Antennas and Propagation (EuCAP)* (pp. 1–4).

Van Gejin, H. P. (2011). Cardiotocography. In A. Kurjak (Ed.), *Textbook of Perinatal Medicine* (pp. 1424–1428). London: Pantheon Publishing.

van Lintel, H., van De Pol, F., & Bouwstra, S. (1988). A piezoelectric micropump based on micromachining of silicon. *Sensors and Actuators*, *15*(2), 153–167. doi:10.1016/0250-6874(88)87005-7

Vasudevan, S., DeCleene, B., Immerman, N., Kurose, J., & Towsley, D. "Leader Election Algorithms for Wireless Ad Hoc Networks," In *Proceeding IEEE DARPA Information Survivability Conference and Exposition (DISCEX)*, pp. 261-272, 2003. doi:10.1109/DISCEX.2003.1194890

Velloso, Laufer, Kunha, Duarte, & Pujjole. (2010). Trust Management in Mobile Ad Hoc Networks Using a Scalable Maturity-Based Model. *IEEE Transactions on Network and Service Management, 7*(3), 172-185.

Verb for shoe - very intelligent shoes. (2004). Retrieved from http://www.gizmag. com/go/3565/picture/7504/

Vercauteren, T., Aggarwal, P., Wang, X., & Li, T. H. (2007). Hierarchical Forecasting of web server workload using sequential Monte Carlo training. *IEEE Transactions on Signal Processing*, *55*(4), 1286–1297. doi:10.1109/TSP.2006.889401

Vidyasagar, M. (1993). *Nonlinear System Analysis* (2nd ed.). Prentice Hall.

Vierra, A. J., & Garrett, J. M. (2005). Understanding inter-observer agreement: The kappa statistic. *Family Medicine*, *37*(5), 360–363. PMID:15883903

Vignesh, N., Shankar, R., & Sathyamoorthy, S. (2014). Value Added Services on Stationary Vehicular Cloud. *LNCS*, *8337*, 92–97.

Vijaya, M., & Dash, R. (2011). Influence of Routing Protocols in Performance of Wireless Mobile Adhoc Network. *Emerging Applications of Information Technology (EAIT),Second International Conference*. doi:10.1109/EAIT.2011.65

Vinoy, K. J., Ananthasuresh, G. K., Pratap, R., & Krupanidhi, S. B. (2014). *Micro and smart devices and systems*. Academic Press.

Vinoy, K. J., & Prabhakar, T. V. (2014). *A universal energy harvesting scheme for operating low-power wireless sensor nodes using multiple energy resources. In Micro and Smart Devices and Systems* (pp. 453–466). Springer.

Virtanen, J., Björninen, T., Ukkonen, L., & Sydänheimo, L. (2010). Passive UHF inkjet-printed narrow-line RFID tags. *Antennas and Wireless Propagation Letters*, *9*, 440–443. doi:10.1109/LAWP.2010.2050050

Visotsky, E., Kuffner, S., & Peterson, R. (2005). On collaborative detection of TV transmissions in support of dynamic spectrum sharing. In *Proc. of IEEE DySPAN 2005*, (pp. 338–345). doi:10.1109/DYSPAN.2005.1542650

VMware. (2010). *VMware vCenter Server*. Retrieved from http://www.vmware.com/products/vcenter-server/

Vogel, D., & Bleckmann, H. (2000). Behavorial discrimination of water motions caused by moving objects. *Journal of Comparative Physiology. A, Neuroethology, Sensory, Neural, and Behavioral Physiology, 186*(12), 1107–1117. doi:10.1007/s003590000158 PMID:11288823

von Campenhausen, C., Riess, I., & Weissert, R. (1981). Detection of stationary objects by the blind cave fish Anoptichthys jordani (characidae). *Journal of Comparative Physiology. A, Neuroethology, Sensory, Neural, and Behavioral Physiology, 143*(3), 369–374. doi:10.1007/BF00611175

Voss, M., Heinemann, A., & Muhlhauser, M. (2005). A privacy preserving reputation system for mobile information dissemination networks. In *Proceedings of the First International Conference on Security and Privacy for Emerging Areas in Communications Networks (SecureComm 2005)*, (pp. 171– 181). Athens, Greece: IEEE. doi:10.1109/SECURECOMM.2005.7

Vowels, S. A. (2009). Understanding RFID (radio frequency identification). In A. Cartelli & M. Palma (Eds.), *Encyclopedia of information communication technology* (pp. 782–790). Hershey, PA: IGI Global. doi:10.4018/978-1-59904-845-1.ch103

Walravens, C., & Dehaene, W. (2014). Low-power digital signal processor architecture for wireless sensor nodes. *IEEE Transactions on Very Large Scale Integration (VLSI) Systems, 22*(2), 313–321. doi:10.1109/TVLSI.2013.2238645

Wang, D., & Huang, J. (2005). Neural network based adaptive dynamic surface control for a class of uncertain nonlinear system in strict feedback form. *IEEE Transactions on Neural Networks, 16*(1), 195–202. doi:10.1109/TNN.2004.839354 PMID:15732399

Wang, F., & Liu, J. (2011). Networked wireless sensor data collection: Issues, challenges, approaches. *IEEE Communications Surveys and Tutorials, 13*(4), 673–687. doi:10.1109/SURV.2011.060710.00066

Wang, J., Ghosh, M., & Challapali, K. (2011). Emerging Cognitive Radio Applications: A Survey. *IEEE Communications Magazine, 49*(3), 74–81. doi:10.1109/MCOM.2011.5723803

Wang, J., & Lu, K. (2014). On the mobile relay placement in hybrid MANETs with secure network coding. *Security and Communication Networks, 7*(4), 738–749. doi:10.1002/sec.775

Wang, S. S., Li, C. C., Lin, H. W., & Shih, K. P. (2015). A passive self-configuration MAC protocol for supporting network management in IEEE 802.11-based multi-hop mobile ad hoc networks. *Journal of Network and Computer Applications, 56*, 149–157. doi:10.1016/j.jnca.2015.05.019

Wang, S., Zhang, Z., & Naït-Abdesselam, F. (2015). Towards cross-layer approaches to coping with misbehavior in mobile ad hoc networks: An anatomy of reputation systems. *Security and Communication Networks, 8*(2), 232–244. doi:10.1002/sec.976

Wang, W., Guan, X., Wang, B., & Wang, Y. (2010). A novel mobility model based on semi-random circular movement in mobile ad hoc networks. *Information Sciences, 180*(3), 399–413. doi:10.1016/j.ins.2009.10.001

Wang, Y., Li, L., Wang, B., & Wang, L. (2009). A body sensor network platform for in-home health monitoring application. In *4th International Conference on Ubiquitous Information Technologies Applications* (pp. 1–5). doi:10.1109/ICUT.2009.5405731

Wang, Y., Zhang, H., & Wang, Y. (2006). Fuzzy adaptive control of stochastic nonlinear systems with unknown virtual gain function. *ActaAutom. Sin, 32*, 170–178.

Wan, Y., Namuduri, K., Zhou, Y., & Fu, S. (2013). A Smooth-Turn Mobility Model for Airborne Networks. *IEEE Transactions on Vehicular Technology, 62*(7), 3359–3370. doi:10.1109/TVT.2013.2251686

Warneke, B. A., & Pister, K. S. J. (2002). MEMS for distributed wireless sensor networks. In *Proceedings of 9th International Conference on Electronics, Circuits and Systems* (vol. 1, pp. 291-294). doi:10.1109/ICECS.2002.1045391

Watanbe, K., Matsuura, I., Abe, M., Kebota, M., & Himelblau, D. M. (1989). Incipient fault diagnosis of chemical processes via artificial neural networks. *AIChE Journal. American Institute of Chemical Engineers*, 35(11), 1803–1812. doi:10.1002/aic.690351106

Watfa, M. K., Kaur, M., & Daruwala, R. F. (2013). RFID applications in e-healthcare. In *User-driven healthcare: Concepts, methodologies, tools, and applications* (pp. 259–287). Hershey, PA: IGI Global. doi:10.4018/978-1-4666-2770-3.ch014

Wei, L., Cao, Z., & Zhu, H. (2011). MobiGame: A User-Centric Reputation based Incentive Protocol for Delay/Disruption Tolerant Networks. In Proceedings of the IEEE Globecom 2011, (pp. 1-5). Houston, TX: IEEE.

Wei, L., Zhu, H., Cao, Z., & Shen, X. (2011). Mobiid: A user-centric and socialaware reputation based incentive scheme for delay/disruption tolerant networks. In Ad-hoc, Mobile, and Wireless Networks, ser. Lecture Notes in Computer Science. Springer.

Weigel, R., Morgan, D. P., Owens, J. M., Ballato, A., Lakin, K. M., Hashimoto, K., & Ruppel, C. C. W. (2002). Microwave acoustic materials, devices, and applications. *IEEE Transactions on Microwave Theory and Techniques*, 50(3), 738–749. doi:10.1109/22.989958

Weiner, M. M. (2003). *Monopole Antennas* (1st ed.). Taylor and Francis. doi:10.1201/9780203912676

Wen, L., Guo, B., Haspeslagh, L., Severi, S., Witvrouw, A., & Puers, R. (2011). Thin film encapsulated SiGe accelerometer for MEMS above IC integration. In *Proceedings of 16th International on Solid-State Sensors, Actuators and Microsystems Conference (TRANSDUCERS)* (pp. 2046-2049). doi:10.1109/TRANSDUCERS.2011.5969217

Whaiduzzaman, M., Sookhak, M., Gani, A., & Buyya, R. (2014). A Survey On Vehicular Cloud Computing. *Journal of Network and Computer Applications*, 40, 325–344. doi:10.1016/j.jnca.2013.08.004

Wheeler, H. A. (1975). Small antennas. *IEEE Transactions on Antennas and Propagation*, 23(4), 462–469. doi:10.1109/TAP.1975.1141115

Whitaker, J., Mithas, S., & Krishnan, M. S. (2007). A field study of RFID deployment and return expectations. *Production and Operations Management*, 16(5), 599–612. doi:10.1111/j.1937-5956.2007.tb00283.x

Wiedmann, K., Reeh, M., & Schumacher, H. (2012). Employment and acceptance of near field communication in mobile marketing. In *Wireless technologies: Concepts, methodologies, tools and applications* (pp. 1868–1890). Hershey, PA: IGI Global. doi:10.4018/978-1-61350-101-6.ch709

Williams, M. A., Hurst, A., & Kane, S. K. (2013). *Pray before you step out: describing personal and situational blind navigation behaviors*. Paper presented at the 15th International ACM SIGACCESS Conference on Computers and Accessibility, Bellevue, WA. doi:10.1145/2513383.2513449

Willner, I. (2002, December20). Biomaterials for Sensors, Fuel Cells, and Circuitry. *Science*, 298(5602), 2407–2408. doi:10.1126/science.298.5602.2407 PMID:12493919

Wod, A., Virone, G., Doan, T., Cao, Q., Selav, L., Wu, Y., . . . Stankovic, J. (2006). *ALARMNET: Wireless sensor networks for assisted-living and residential monitoring*. Technical report CS-2006-11, Department of Computer Science, University of Virginia.

Wong, K. (2002). *Compact and Broadband Microstrip Antennas* (1st ed.). Wiley-VCH. doi:10.1002/0471221112

Wretlar, S., Holzmann, M., Graner, S., Lindqvist, P., Falck, S., & Nordström, L. (2016). Fetal Heart Rate Monitoring of Short Term Variation (STV): A Methodological Observational Study. *BMC Pregnancy and Childbirth, 16*(1), 1–6. PMID:26728010

WSDL. (n.d.). Retrieved online on 31.1.2016, Available at http://www.w3.org/TR/wsdl20-primer/

Wu, B., Wu, J., & Cardei, M. (2008). A survey of key management in mobile ad hoc networks. In Y. Zhang, J. Zheng, & M. Ma (Eds.), *Handbook of research on wireless security* (pp. 479–499). Hershey, PA: IGI Global. doi:10.4018/978-1-59904-899-4.ch030

Wu, F., Chen, T., Zhong, S., Qiao, C., & Chen, G. (2013). A Game-Theoretic Approach to Stimulate Cooperation for Probabilistic Routing in Opportunistic Networks. *IEEE Transactions on Wireless Communications, 12*(4), 1573–1583. doi:10.1109/TWC.2013.022113.120282

Wu, H. C., & Iyengar, S. S. (2011). A Novel Robust Detection Algorithm for Spectrum Sensing. *IEEE Journal on Selected Areas in Communications, 29*(2), 305–315. doi:10.1109/JSAC.2011.110204

Wu, X. Y., Akhoondzadeh-Asl, L., Wang, Z. P., & Hall, P. S. (2010). Novel Yagi-Uda antennas for on-body communication at 60GHz. In *Loughborough Antennas* (pp. 153–156). Propagation Conference. doi:10.1109/LAPC.2010.5666188

Wu, X., Wu, X., Luo, X., & Guan, X. (2012). Dynamic surface control for a class of state constrained nonlinear systems with uncertain time delays. *IET Control Theory Appl, 6*(12), 1948–1957. doi:10.1049/iet-cta.2011.0543

Wu, Y., Sheng, Q. Z., Shen, H., & Zeadally, S. (2013). Modeling object flows from distributed and federated RFID data streams for efficient tracking and tracing. *IEEE Transactions on Parallel and Distributed Systems, 24*(10), 2036–2045. doi:10.1109/TPDS.2013.99

Wu, Z., Yang, T. C., Liu, Z., & Chakarvarthy, V. (2012). Modulation Detection of Underwater Acoustic Communication Signals Through Cyclostationary Analysis. In *Proceedings of IEEE Military Communications Conference (MILCOM)*. doi:10.1109/MILCOM.2012.6415832

Wyld, D. C. (2008). Radio frequency identification (RFID) technology. In G. Garson & M. Khosrow-Pour (Eds.), *Handbook of research on public information technology* (pp. 425–440). Hershey, PA: IGI Global. doi:10.4018/978-1-59904-857-4.ch041

Xia, W., Saito, K., Takahashi, M., & Ito, K. (2009). Performances of an implanted cavity slot antenna embedded in the human arm. In IEEE Transactions on Antennas and Propagation (Vol. 57, pp. 894–899). http://doi.org/ doi:10.1109/TAP.2009.2014579

Xiao, Y., Yu, S., Wu, K., Ni, Q., Janecek, C., & Nordstad, J. (2007). Radio frequency identification: Technologies, applications, and research issues. *Wireless Communications and Mobile Computing, 7*(4), 457–472. doi:10.1002/wcm.365

Xie, X., Chen, H., & Wu, H. (2009). Bargain-based stimulation mechanism for selfish mobile nodes in participatory sensing network. In *Proceedings of the Sixth Annual IEEE Communications Society Conference on Sensor, Mesh and Ad Hoc Communications and Networks*. Rome: IEEE. doi:10.1109/SAHCN.2009.5168911

Xie, Y., Guo, B., Gu, L., Li, J., & Stoica, P. (2006). Multistatic adaptive microwave imaging for early breast cancer detection. *IEEE Transactions on Bio-Medical Engineering, 53*(8), 1647–1657. doi:10.1109/TBME.2006.878058 PMID:16916099

Xu, T., Chen, H., & Hu, H. (2014). A Low-Complexity Detection Method for Statistical Signals in OFDM Systems. *IEEE Communications Letters, 18*(4), 632–635. doi:10.1109/LCOMM.2014.030614.140193

Yanfeng, W., Qinqin, H., & Dong, H. (2014). Information security technology based on nucleic acids. *Chinese Academy of Sciences, 29*(1), 83–93.

Yang, D., & Yang, B. (2010). A Novel Two-Server Password Authentication Scheme with Provable Security. Computer and Information Technology, IEEE.

Yang, X.S. (2010). A new metaheuristic bat inspired algorithm, in Nature Inspired Cooperative Strategies for Optimization (NISO 2010). *Studies in Computational Intelligence, 284,* 65-74.

Yan, G., Wen, D., Olariu, S., & Weigle, M. C. (2012). Security Challenges in Vehicular Cloud Computing. *IEEE Transactions on Intelligent Transportation Systems.*

Yang, C., He, J., & Kun, Y. (2013). RFID tag anti-collision protocols. In N. Karmakar (Ed.), *Advanced RFID systems, security, and applications* (pp. 133–154). Hershey, PA: IGI Global. doi:10.4018/978-1-4666-2080-3.ch007

Yang, J., Ma, J., Liu, S., & Zhang, C. (2014). A molecular cryptography model based on structures of DNA self-assembly. *Chinese Science Bulletin, 59*(11), 1192–1198. doi:10.1007/s11434-014-0170-4

Yang, S. J. (2010). Design issues and performance analysis for DSR routing with reclaim-based caching in MANETs. *International Journal of Network Management, 20*(1), 21–34.

Yang, Y., & Chan, W. (2014). Adaptive dynamic surface control for uncertain nonlinear systems with interval type-2 fuzzy neural networks. *IEEE Trans. Cybern, 44*(2), 293–304. doi:10.1109/TCYB.2013.2253548 PMID:23757550

Yang, Y., Chen, J., Engel, J., Pandya, S., Chen, N., Tucker, C., & Liu, C. et al. (2006). Distant touch hydrodynamic imaging with an artificial lateral line. *Proceedings of the National Academy of Sciences of the United States of America, 103*(50), 18891–18895. doi:10.1073/pnas.0609274103 PMID:17132735

Yang, Y., Chen, J., Tucker, C., Pandya, S., Jones, D., & Liu, C. (2007). Biomimetic flow sensing using artificial lateral lines.*Proceedings of ASME Conf. Proc, 43025,* 1331-1338. doi:10.1115/IMECE2007-43870

Yan, Q., Li, Y., & Deng, R. H. (2013). Malware protection on RFID-enabled supply chain management systems in the EPCglobal Network. In A. Miri (Ed.), *Advanced security and privacy for RFID technologies* (pp. 153–175). Hershey, PA: IGI Global. doi:10.4018/978-1-4666-3685-9.ch010

Yao, F., & Lee, T. C. M. (2007). Spectral density estimation using sharpened periodograms. *IEEE Transactions on Signal Processing, 55*(9), 4711–4716. doi:10.1109/TSP.2007.896297

Yaul, F. M. (2011). *A Flexible Underwater Pressure Sensor Array for Artificial Lateral Line Applications* (MSc Thesis). Massachusetts Institute of Technology.

Yeh, T. C., Wang, Y. J., Kuo, T. C., & Wang, S. S. (2010). Securing RFID systems conforming to EPC Class 1 Generation 2 standard. *Expert Systems with Applications, 37*(12), 7678–7683. doi:10.1016/j.eswa.2010.04.074

Yi, X., Ling, S., & Wang, H. (2013). Efficient Two-Server Password-Only Authenticated Key Exchange. *IEEE Transactions on Parallel and Distributed Systems, 24*(9), 1773–1782. doi:10.1109/TPDS.2012.282

Yoon, W., & Vaidya, N. H. (2012). RFID reader collision problem: Performance analysis and medium access. *Wireless Communications and Mobile Computing, 12*(5), 420–430. doi:10.1002/wcm.972

Yu, Shen, Miao, Leung, & Niyato. (2010). A Survey of Trust and Reputation Management System in Wireless Communications. *Proc. of the IEEE.*

Yu, Y., & Lu, L. (2011). Intelligent Sensor Network Simulation for Battlefield Resources Management. In *Proceedings of IEEE Ninth International Conference on Dependable, Autonomic and Secure Computing* (DASC).

Yucek, T., & Arslan, H. (2009). A survey of spectrum sensing algorithms for cognitive radio applications. *IEEE Communications Surveys and Tutorials, 11*(1), 116–130. doi:10.1109/SURV.2009.090109

Yuce, M. R., Tekin, A., & Liu, W. (2008). Design and performance of a wideband sub-sampling front-end for multi-standard radios. *AEÜ. International Journal of Electronics and Communications*, *62*(1), 41–48. doi:10.1016/j.aeue.2007.02.005

Yun, K.-S., Cho, I.-J., Bu, J.-U., Kim, C.-J., & Yoon, E. (2002). A surface-tension driven micropump for low-voltage and low-power operations. *Journal of Microelectromechanical Systems*, *11*(5), 454–461. doi:10.1109/JMEMS.2002.803286

Yun, K.-S., Cho, I.-J., Bu, J.-U., Kim, G.-H., Jeon, Y.-S., Kim, C.-J., & Yoon, E. (2001). A Micropump Driven by Continuous Electrowetting Actuation for Low Voltage and Low Power Operations. In *Proceedings of IEEE International MEMS 2001 Conference* (pp. 487-490). doi:10.1109/MEMSYS.2001.906585

Yunpeng, Yu, Zhong, & Sinnott. (2011). Index-based symmetric DNA encryption algorithm. *Image and Signal Processing (CISP)*, 2290-2294.

Yurke, B., Turberfield, A. J., Mills, A. P. Jr, Simmel, F. C., & Neumann, J. L. (2000). A DNA-fuelled molecular machine made of DNA. *Nature*, *406*(6796), 605–608. doi:10.1038/35020524 PMID:10949296

Yu, Y., Ou, J., Zhang, J., Zhang, C., & Li, L. (2009). Development of Wireless MEMS Inclination Sensor System for Swing Monitoring of Large-Scale Hook Structures. *IEEE Transactions on Industrial Electronics*, *56*(4), 1072–1078. doi:10.1109/TIE.2009.2012469

Zadin, A., & Fevens, T. (2015). Minimizing communication interference for stable position-based routing in mobile ad hoc networks. *Procedia Computer Science*, *52*, 460–467. doi:10.1016/j.procs.2015.05.015

Zarnik, M., Belavic, D., & Macek, S. (2010). The warm-up and offset stability of a low-pressure piezoresistive ceramic pressure sensor. *Sensors and Actuators. A, Physical*, *158*(2), 198–206. doi:10.1016/j.sna.2009.12.035

Zayou, R., Besbe, M. A., & Hamam, H. (2014). Agricultural and environmental applications of RFID technology. *International Journal of Agricultural and Environmental Information Systems*, *5*(2), 50–65. doi:10.4018/IJAEIS.2014040104

Zegna Sport Bluetooth iJacket incorporates smart fabric. (2007). Retrieved from http://www.gizmag.com/go/7856/

Zeng, J., & Zhang, M. (2011). Virtual genome-based cryptography. Multimedia Information Networking and Security, IEEE.

Zhai, Z., Zhang, Y., & Chen, G. (2010). A Reliable and Adaptive AODV Protocol based on Cognitive Routing for Ad Hoc Networks. In *Proceedings of 12th International Conference on Advanced Communication Technology* (ICACT).

Zhang, Chen, Zhang, & Liu. (2009). Research of Asynchronous Leader Election Algorithm on Hierarchy Ad Hoc Network. *WiCom '09*.

Zhang, F., Meng, F–Y., Lee, J.-C., & Wu, Q. (2013). Study of a novel compact rectenna for wireless energy harvesting. *Proceedings of IEEE International Wireless Symposium* (pp. 1 – 4). doi:10.1109/IEEE-IWS.2013.6616837

Zhang, G., Kuang, X., Chen, J., & Zhang, Y. (2009). Design and Implementation of a Leader Election Algorithm in Hierarchy Mobile Ad hoc Network. In *Proceeding IEEE 4th International Conference on Computer Science & Education* (ICCSE). doi:10.1109/ICCSE.2009.5228448

Zhang, Y. (2002). *Analysis and design of recurrent neural networks and their applications to control and robotic systems* (Ph.D. dissertation). The Chinese University of Hong Kong, Hong Kong.

Zhang, Y., & Zhang, C. Yi. (2011). Neural Network and Neural dynamic method. NOVA Science Publishers.

Zhang, Z., Fan, W. (2008). Stochastics and Statistics Web server load balancing: A queueing analysis. *European Journal of Operational Research*, *186*, 681–693. DOI:10.1016/j.ejor.2007.02.011

Zhang, C., Yang, J., & Xu, J. (2011). Molecular logic computing model based on self-assembly of DNA nanoparticles. *Chinese Science Bulletin*, *56*(33), 3566–3571. doi:10.1007/s11434-011-4725-3

Zhang, H., Wang, Z., & Liu, D. (2008). Global asymptotic stability of recurrent neural network with multiple time-varying delays. *IEEE Transactions on Neural Networks*, *19*(5), 855–873. doi:10.1109/TNN.2007.912319 PMID:18467214

Zhang, H., Yang, F., Liu, S., & Zhang, Q. (2013). Stability analysis for neural network with time-varying delay based on quadratic convex combination. *IEEE Trans. Neural Netw. Learn Syst*, *24*(4), 513–521. doi:10.1109/TNNLS.2012.2236571 PMID:24808373

Zhang, H., & Yang, W. (2008). Stability analysis of Markovian jumping stochastic cohen-Grossberg neural network with mixed time delays. *IEEE Transactions on Neural Networks*, *19*(2), 366–370. doi:10.1109/TNN.2007.910738 PMID:18269968

Zhang, J., & Liu, H. (2009). *Electrocatalysis of direct methanol fuel cells*. Weinheim: Wiley-VCH.

Zhang, T., & Xiaonan, X. (2015). Decentralized adaptive fuzzy output feedback control of stochastic nonlinear large scale systems with dynamic un certainties. *Information Sciences*, *315*, 17–18. doi:10.1016/j.ins.2015.04.002

Zhang, X., Wang, X., Liu, A., Zhang, Q., & Tang, C. (2011). Reputation-based Scheme for Delay Tolerant Networks. In *Proceedings of the IEEE International Conference on Computer Science and Network Technology*, (pp. 974-978). Harbin: IEEE.

Zhang, Z., Lu, Z., Chen, Q., Yan, X., & Zheng, L. R. (2012). Code division multiple access/pulse position modulation ultra-wideband radio frequency identification for Internet of Things: Concept and analysis. *International Journal of Systems*, *25*(9), 1103–1121. doi:10.1002/dac.2312

Zheng, Y., & Lyu, M. R. (2014). Investigating QoS of real-world web services. *IEEE Transaction Service Computing*, *7*(1), 32–39. doi:10.1109/TSC.2012.34

Zheng, Z., Liu, Y., & Qi, G. (2012). Clustering routing algorithm of wireless sensor networks based on the Bayesian game. *Journal of Systems Engineering and Electronics*, *23*(1), 154–159. doi:10.1109/JSEE.2012.00019

Zhou, H., Mutka, M. W., & Ni, L. M. (2010). Secure prophet address allocation for MANETs. *Security and Communication Networks*, *3*(1), 31–43. doi:10.1002/sec.126

Zhouhua, P., Dan, W., Zhang, H., & Yejin, L. (2015). Coopeative output feedback adaptive control of uncertain nonlinear multi-agent systems with a dynamic leader. *Neurocomputing*, *149*, 132–141. doi:10.1016/j.neucom.2013.12.064

Zhou, R., Li, X., Yang, T., Liu, Z., & Wu, Z. (2012). Real-time Cyclostationary Analysis for Cognitive Radio via Software Defined Radio. In *Proceedings of IEEE Globe-com*. doi:10.1109/GLOCOM.2012.6503325

Zhu, H., Tang, H., & Yang, T. (2001). Demand-driven service differentiation for cluster based network servers. *Proceedings - IEEE INFOCOM*.

Zurcher, J.-F., Skrivewik, A. K., & Staub, O. (2000). SMILA: a miniaturized antenna for PCS applications. *IEEE Antennas and Propagation Society International Symposium*, *3*, 1646–1649. http://doi.org/ doi:10.1109/APS.2000.874556

Zürcher, J. F., Staub, O., & Skrivervik, A. K. (2000). SMILA: A compact and efficient antenna for mobile communications. *Microwave and Optical Technology Letters*, *27*(3), 155–157. doi:10.1002/1098-2760(20001105)27:3<155::AID-MOP1>3.0.CO;2-P

About the Contributors

Siddhartha Bhattacharyya did his Bachelors in Physics, Bachelors in Optics and Optoelectronics and Masters in Optics and Optoelectronics from University of Calcutta, India in 1995, 1998 and 2000 respectively. He completed PhD in Computer Science and Engineering from Jadavpur University, India in 2008. He is the recipient of the University Gold Medal from the University of Calcutta for his Masters in 2012. He is also the recipient of the coveted ADARSH VIDYA SARASWATI RASHTRIYA PURASKAR for excellence in education and research in 2016. He is currently the Professor and Head of Information Technology of RCC Institute of Information Technology, Kolkata, India. In addition, he is serving as the Dean of Research and Development of the institute from November 2013. Prior to this, he was an Associate Professor of Information Technology of RCC Institute of Information Technology, Kolkata, India from 2011-2014. Before that, he served as an Assistant Professor in Computer Science and Information Technology of University Institute of Technology, The University of Burdwan, India from 2005-2011. He was a Lecturer in Information Technology of Kalyani Government Engineering College, India during 2001-2005. He is a co-author of 4 books and the co-editor of 8 books and has more than 150 research publications in international journals and conference proceedings to his credit. He has got a patent on intelligent colorimeter technology. He was the convener of the AICTE-IEEE National Conference on Computing and Communication Systems (CoCoSys-09) in 2009. He was the member of the Young Researchers' Committee of the WSC 2008 Online World Conference on Soft Computing in Industrial Applications. He has been the member of the organizing and technical program committees of several national and international conferences. He served as the Editor-In-Chief of International Journal of Ambient Computing and Intelligence (IJACI) published by IGI Global, Hershey, PA, USA from 17th July 2014 to 06th November 2014. He was the General Chair of the IEEE International Conference on Computational Intelligence and Communication Networks (ICCICN 2014) organized by the Department of Information Technology, RCC Institute of Information Technology, Kolkata in association with Machine Intelligence Research Labs, Gwalior and IEEE Young Professionals, Kolkata Section and held at Kolkata, India in 2014. He is the Associate Editor of International Journal of Pattern Recognition Research. He is the member of the editorial board of International Journal of Engineering, Science and Technology and ACCENTS Transactions on Information Security (ATIS). He is also the member of the editorial advisory board of HETC Journal of Computer Engineering and Applications. He is the Associate Editor of the International Journal of BioInfo Soft Computing since 2013. He is the Lead Guest Editor of the Special Issue on Hybrid Intelligent Techniques for Image Analysis and Understanding of Applied Soft Computing, Elsevier, B. V. He was the General Chair of the 2015 IEEE International Conference on Research in Computational Intelligence and Communication Networks (ICRCICN 2015) organized by the Department of Information Technology, RCC Institute of Information Technology, Kolkata in association with IEEE Young Professionals, Kolkata Section and held at Kolkata, India in 2015. He is the Lead Guest Editor of the Special Issue on Computational Intelligence and Communications in International Journal of Computers and Applications (IJCA); Publisher: Taylor & Francis, UK in 2016. He is the Issue Editor of International Journal of Pattern Recognition Research since January 2016. He was the General Chair of the 2016 International Conference on Wireless Communications, Network Security and Signal Processing (WCNSSP2016) held during June 26-27, 2016 at Chiang Mai, Thailand. He is the member of the editorial board of Applied Soft Computing, Elsevier, B. V. Dr. Bhattacharyya has visited Kyushu Institute of Technology, Izuka, Japan; Fukuoka Institute of Technology, Fukuoka, Japan and University of Hyogo, Himeji, Japan as an invited lecturer. His research interests include soft computing, pattern recognition, multimedia data processing, hybrid intelligence and quantum computing. Dr. Bhattacharyya is a Fellow of Institute of Electronics and Telecommunication Engineers (IETE), India. He is a senior member of Institute of Electrical and Electronics Engineers (IEEE), USA, Association for Computing Machinery (ACM), USA and International Engineering and Technology Institute (IETI), Hong Kong. He is a member of International Rough Set Society, International Association for Engineers (IAENG), Hong Kong, Computer Science Teachers Association (CSTA), USA and International Association of Academicians, Scholars, Scientists and Engineers (IAASSE), USA. He is a life member of Computer Society of India, Optical Society of India, Indian Society for Technical Education and Center for Education Growth and Research, India.

Nibaran Das received his B.Tech degree in Computer Science and Technology from Kalyani Govt. Engineering College under Kalyani University, in 2003. He received his M.C.S.E degree from Jadavpur University, in 2005. He received his Ph. D.(Engg.) degree thereafter from Jadavpur University, in 2012. He joined Jadavpur University, Kolkata, India as an Assistant Professor in 2006. His areas of current research interest are OCR of handwritten text, optimization techniques, machine learning and image processing. He has been an editor of Bengali monthly magazine "Computer Jagat" since 2005. He has published around 85 research papers in international journals and conference proceedings. He was the one of the organizing chairs of International Conference of RETIS-15 and convener of National Conference RETIS-06. He was the one of the co-editors of the conference proceedings of ReTIS-15, ReTIS-08 and ReTIS-06. Dr. Das is a member of Institute of Electrical and Electronics Engineers (IEEE), USA and Executive committee member of IEEE young professional affinity group and computer Chapter, Kolkata Section. He is a life member of Computer Society of India, Institution of Electronics and Telecommunication Engineers (IETE).

Debotosh Bhattacharjee received the Master of Computer Science and Engineering and the Ph. D(Engineering) degrees from Jadavpur University, India, in 1997 and 2004 respectively. He was associated with different institutes in various capacities until March 2007. After that, he joined his Alma Mater, Jadavpur University. Currently, he is working as a full professor in the Department of Computer Science and Engineering there. His research interests pertain to the applications of computational intelligence techniques like Fuzzy Logic, Artificial Neural Network, Genetic Algorithm, Rough Set Theory in Face Recognition, Gait Analysis, Hand Geometry Recognition, Histopathological Image Analysis and Biomedical imaging. He has authored or coauthored more than 200 journals, conference publications, including several book chapters in the areas of Biometrics and Medical Image Processing. For postdoctoral research, Dr. Bhattacharjee has visited different universities abroad like the University of Twente, The Netherlands; Instituto Superior Técnico, Lisbon, Portugal; University of Bologna, Italy; ITMO National

Research University, St. Petersburg, Russia; University of Ljubljana, Slovenia and Heidelberg University, Germany. He is a life member of Indian Society for Technical Education (ISTE, New Delhi), Indian Unit for Pattern Recognition and Artificial Intelligence (IUPRAI), and a senior member of IEEE (USA).

Anirban Mukherjee did his Bachelors in Civil Engineering in 1994 from Jadavpur University, Kolkata. While in service he achieved a professional Diploma in Operations Management (PGDOM) in 1998 and completed his PhD on 'Automatic Diagram Drawing based on Natural Language Text Understanding' from Indian Institute of Engineering, Science and Technology (IIEST), Shibpur in 2014. Serving RCC Institute of Information Technology (RCCIIT), Kolkata since inception (in 1999), he is currently an Associate Professor and Head of the Department of Engineering Science & Management at RCCIIT. Before joining RCCIIT he served as an Engineer in the Scientific & Technical Application Group in erstwhile RCC, Calcutta for 6 years. His research interest includes Computer Graphics, Computational Intelligence, Optimization and Assistive Technology. He has co-authored two UG engineering textbooks: one on 'Computer Graphics and Multimedia' and another on 'Engineering Mechanics'. He has also co-authored more than 18 books on Computer Graphics/Multimedia for distance learning courses BBA/MBA/BCA/MCA/B.Sc (Comp. Sc.)/M.Sc (IT) of different Universities of India. He has few international journal, book chapters and conference papers to his credit. He is in the editorial board of International Journal of Ambient Computing and Intelligence (IJACI).

***

Amal Afyf was born in Kingdome of Morocco . She received her B.E. degree in Electrical and computer engineering from Abdelmalek Essaidi University Faculty of Sciences-Tétouan in 2009. She received her M.S. degree in Telecommunication Systems Engineering in 2011. She is currently pursuing her PhD degree at Higher National School of Technical Education (ENSET) and Higher National School of Computer Science and Systems Analysis (ENSIAS), University Mohammed V Rabat. Her research area is involving on research, Modeling and Designing RF circuits and sensors for biomedical applications.

Li-Minn Ang received his BEng (first class) and PhD from Edith Cowan University, Australia, in 1996 and 2001, respectively. He is currently attached with the School of Computing and Mathematics, Charles Sturt University. His research interests include the fields of video compression, visual processing, wireless visual sensor networks and reconfigurable computing.

Srijibendu Bagchi did his Bachelors of Technology in Electronics and Communication Engineering from JIS College of Engineering under the University of Kalyani in 2004 and Master of Technology in Radio Physics and Electronics from the University of Calcutta in 2006. He is currently pursuing his PhD from the Department of Radio Physics and Electronics, University of Calcutta. His research interest includes wireless communication and statistical signal processing. Mr. Bagchi is currently working as an Assistant Professor in Electronics and Communication Engineering Department, RCC Institute of Information Technology, Kolkata, India. Before that he worked as an Assistant Professor in Electronics and Communication Engineering Department, GNIT, India. He has more than ten publications to his credit. Also he acts as a reviewer for some reputed international journals. He acted as a convener in two one-week Faculty Development Programs and a one-day National Level Seminar. In addition he acted as a coordinator in a one-week Faculty Development Program. He is also a program committee member in two conferences. He is a member of IEEE GRSS Chapter, IEEE Kolkata Section and Indian Association for Productivity, Quality and Reliability.

Larbi Bellarbi was born in Rabat, Morocco. He received the Ph.D. degree in electronics and Tele-communication systems from Mohamadia School of Engineers of University of Mohammed V Agdal, Rabat, Morocco, in 1994. He is currently a Professor of electronics and nanotechnologies in the Higher National School of Technical Education (ENSET) of Rabat in Morocco and he is the head of nano-biotechnologies and sensors team of LRGE laboratory. He is involved in the design and implementaion of nano-biosensors, also the design of hybrid, monolithic active and passive microwave electronic for biomedical application.

Tulshi Bezboruah was graduated in Physics from North Lakhimpur College under Dibrugarh University (Now Autonomous), Assam, India, in 1990. He received his M. Sc and Ph. D degree in Radio Physics and Electronics from Gauhati University, Guwahati, Assam, India, in 1999. He had joined as a Lecturer in the department of Electronics and Communication Technology (Formerly Electronics Science), University of Gauhati in 2000. He is currently a Professor and the Head of the Department of Electronics and Communication Technology, University of Gauhati. His current research interests include instrumentation and control, Communication Systems, and Web Services. Prof. Bezboruah was a Junior Associate Member of the Abdus Salam International Centre for Theoretical Physics (ICTP), Trieste, Italy (2003-2010). He is also a Senior Member of IEEE and a member of the IEEE Geoscience and Remote Sensing Society.

Rabia Bilal holds an Assistant professor position in the Department of Electrical Engineering at Usman Institute, Karachi, Pakistan. She has an MPhil in Engineering from the University of Sussex, UK, and a BS degree in Electronic Engineering and MS degree in Electronic with specialization in Telecommunication from Sir Syed University of Engineering and Technology, Karachi, Pakistan. She has decade of experience in engineering universities and industry where she was involved in teaching engineering undergraduates, research and publications. Her publications include refereed journal, conference papers, book chapters and books. She is a lifetime member of Pakistan Engineering Council (PEC).

Abhijit Bora did his Bachelor of Computer Applications (BCA) from Institute of Management & Information Technology, Guwahati, India (Under MCRPV University) in the year 2004. He did his Master of Computer Applications (MCA) from Jorhat Engineering College, Jorhat, India (Under Dibrugarh University) in the year 2008. He is currently the Research Scholar of Department of Electronics and Communication Technology, Gauhati University, India and pursuing Ph.D. in the domain of Web Services. He is also the active resource person in the Indian Sign Language Education & Recognition System (a Ministry of Human Resource Development, Govt. Of India sponsored project under National Mission Education for dumb & deaf, hearing impaired students) at IIT Guwahati. He has played many active roles as the member of the organizing and technical program committees of several national and international conferences and workshops. He had developed and implemented successfully the e-governance projects for Directorate of Agriculture and Horticulture, Govt. of Meghalaya, India under the supervision of National Informatics Centre (NIC), Shillong, India. He has published 8 International Journals and 4 International Proceedings. Many of his research publications got citations by other authors in the research community. He has presented several research papers in International and National

Conferences. He has delivered lectures in several seminars and national workshops. His research interest includes web service, web security, software engineering and software reliability.

Chandrima Chakrabarti, M.TECH (Computer Science and Engineering), B.TECH (Information Technology), is presently working as an Assistant Professor, Department of Computer Science and Engineering, Narula Institute of Technology, Kolkata, India. She has overall 10 years of teaching and 3 years of research experience. She received M.TECH (Computer Science and Engineering) degree in 2007 from Netaji Subhash Engineering College under West Bengal University of Technology. Before that in 2005 Miss. Chakrabarti received B.TECH (Information Technology) degree from Narula Institute of Technology under West Bengal University of Technology, Kolkata, India. Miss. Chakrabarti is pursuing PhD (Engineering) from Maulana Abul Kalam Azad University of Technology (formerly known as West Bengal University of Technology). Her research interest includes, Delay Tolerant Network, Opportunistic Network, Applications of Mobile Computing in Disaster Management, Mobile Ad-hoc Network, Network Security, Database Management System, Internet Technology, Web Technology, Mobile Computing, Computer Graphics and Multimedia and so on. She has 3 International Journal publications and 11 International Conference publications (including IEEE, Springer, Elsevier proceedings) till date. She has the hobbies of Reciting, Singing, Painting etc.

Abhijit Das has completed his B.Tech. in IT in the year 2003 from University of Kalyani, M.Tech. in IT in the year 2005 from University of Calcutta and submitted his PhD thesis (Engg.) in the year 2016 at Jadavpur University, Kolkata, India. Being an Assistant Professor of RCC Institute of Information Technology, he has over 12 years of experience in academia. His working areas are Ad hoc and Sensor Network, Music Categorization, Bio-informatics etc, and he has over twenty numbers of publications on his credit. Abhijit is a professional singer and his favorite pastimes are watching movies, travelling and spending time with his family.

Jayanta Das has done his Diploma in Mechanical Engineering Course in 1994 with First Class under State Council of Engineering and Technical Education, Govt. of West Bengal, Masters in Computer Application in 2004 with First Class under Indira Gandhi National Open University and passed Masters in Technology (Information Technology) in 2009 with First Class under Bengal Engineering and Science University, Shibpur (Currently Indian Institute of Engineering Science and Technology, Shibpur). He was engaged as Maintenance Supervisor under Hindustan Motors Ltd. from November, 1995 to August, 2001 and as Computer Programmer under Hindustan Motors Ltd. from August, 2001 to May, 2006. He then joined academia and after serving different institutes, he is now engaged as Principal of Krishnanagar-I Govt. ITI from July, 2016. Jayanta is presently working in the area of Wireless and Sensor Network and he has five publications in different peer reviewed journals.

Sahana Das did her Bachelors with Mathematics and Physics double major from University of Swaziland, Southern Africa in 1995. She obtained first class in her graduation and was the university topper. She was the recipient of Dean's Award for the Best Student of the Faculty of Science and Vice-Chancellor's Award for the Best Student of the University. In 2004 she completed Masters in Computer Application from Indira Gandhi National Open University with first class. Her areas of interest are in the applications of Pattern Recognition, Image processing, Soft Computing techniques in the field of Medical diagnosis. Currently she is pursuing PhD in Computer Science from West Bengal State University, Barasat. Her research work involves development of a diagnostic tool to predict the status of the fetus from its heart rate using soft computing based technique. She published several papers in many international conferences. Her paper 'A Novel Approach for Baseline Estimation of FHR Signal' was awarded the best paper in International Conference on Intelligent Healthcare in 2011. In 2004 Ms. Das joined Narula Institute of Technology as a Lecturer in the Department of Computer Application where she is presently an Assistant Professor.

M. Arun Fera is currently working as an Assistant Professor in the Dept of Information Technology, Thiagarajar College of Engineering, Madurai. He completed his B.Tech (InformationTechnology) in Mepco Schlenk Engineering College, affiliated to Anna University-Chennai in 2008. While doing his Final Year project, he was awarded FIRST prize for the paper "Fault tolerant approach for mobile IP in wireless systems" presented in National Level Technical symposium in Dhanalaskhmi Srinivasan Engineering College, Tamil Nadu. Also in his Final year of B.Tech degree, he presented a paper in Sothern regional conference organized by CSI' Students Branch at National Engineering College, Kovilpatti. During his UG college days, he played a role as Office Bearer for Computer Society of India. Then he had good industry exposure particularly in the software industry "Cognizant" for nearly two years (Nov 2008 – Sep 2010). There he was involved in both developmental and maintenance projects some of which notably are Corporate Billing Systems (system used by MetLife for billing Group Insurance Products) and Metpay (Systems for Auto and Home Insurance in US). He then joined SSN college of Engineering, Chennai to pursue his Masters in Engineering in Computer science and completed in 2012. He got the Chairman Medal for achieving state level rank in Anna University Examinations. Thereafter he joined Thiagarajar College of Engineering as an Assistant Professor and currently he is in that designation. He has three years of teaching experience especially in cloud security and databases for both UG and PG degrees. He is a certified programmer from Sun microsystems as a "Sun Certified Programmer" for Java 2 Platform, Standard Edition 5.0. His was involved in developing community certificate automation project in collaboration with the Madurai District Collectorate. He is also a department coordinator in Oracle's "Software in Silicon Technology" project done in the college. He has organized one credit courses in the college in association with Cognizant and Dell, Bangalore. He is also the department coordinator for "European Business and Technology Centre" in TCE campus. He has given lectures like "Databases and Android Application", "Grid and cloud computing" etc in various colleges. He acts as a reviewer for Elsevier's Computers in Biology and Medicine, KSII Transactions, IGI Global. He was a Technical Committee member for CoCoNet 2015, IITM Kerala and technical Committee Member in ICCCA 2015, Galgotias University, Uttar Pradesh, India. Also he is member of ACM.

Saswati Ghosh did her Bachelors in Physics, Masters in Radio Physics and Electronics and MTech in Microwaves from University of Burdwan, India in 1992, 1995 and 1997 respectively. She completed PhD in RF and Microwave Engineering from Indian Institute of Technology, Kharagpur, India in 2004. Currently she is working as a scientist (under the Women Scientist scheme, DST, India) in the Kalpana Chawla Space Technology Cell, Indian Institute of Technology, Kharagpur. She had received the Young Scientist Fellowship of Fast Track Scheme by Department of Science and Technology, New Delhi, India, in 2006 and 2010 and worked at Indian Institute of Technology, Kharagpur. She had served as a Professor in Durgapur Institute of Advanced Technology and Management, Durgapur, West Bengal, India during 2009 – 2010. She is actively involved in research projects on different areas of RF and Microwave Engineering for the last seventeen years at Indian Institute of Technology, Kharagpur. During this period, she has participated as instructor (theory and practical classes) in various short term courses on Electromagnetic Interference (EMI), Electromagnetic Compatibility (EMC), Electromagnetic Pulse (EMP) and Microwave & EMI Measurement organized at IIT Kharagpur. She has twenty publications in reputed journals/book chapters and around sixty papers in proceedings of different international and national conferences. She had received the grant from Indo-Sri Lanka Foundation for presenting paper in the Fourth IEEE International conference on Industrial and Information Systems (ICIIS 2009) at University of Peradeniya, Sri Lanka in 2009. She received the best paper award in the Seventh International Conference and Workshop on Electromagnetic Interference and Compatibility (INCEMIC) held at Bangalore, India in 2001. She has served as the reviewer of different reputed journals e.g. IEEE Transactions on Antennas and Propagation, IEEE Transactions on Electromagnetic Compatibility, IEEE Antennas and Wireless Propagation Letters, Journal of Electrostatics, Elsevier publication, Journal of Electromagnetic Waves and Applications and Progress in Electromagnetics Research. Her research interests include the Radio frequency energy harvesting, ultra wideband antennas, electromagnetic interference (EMI) and electromagnetic compatibility (EMC) measurements, EMI sensors, estimation of EMC of high frequency electronic systems, EMI/EMC/ESD on spacecraft bodies etc. She is a Member of IEEE, Life member of SEMCEI and Senior Member IACSIT.

Vehbi Cagri Gungor received his B.S. and M.S. degrees in Electrical and Electronics Engineering from Middle East Technical University, Ankara, Turkey, in 2001 and 2003, respectively. He received his Ph.D. degree in electrical and computer engineering from the Broadband and Wireless Networking Laboratory, Georgia Institute of Technology, Atlanta, GA, USA, in 2007 under the supervision of Prof. Ian F. Akyildiz. He was an Associate Professor and the Graduate Programs (Ph.D. and M.S.) Coordinator at the Department of Computer Engineering, Bahcesehir University, Istanbul, Turkey. He is currently an Associate Professor at Abdullah Gul University (Turkey). His current research interests are in smart grid communications, machine-to-machine communications, next-generation wireless networks, wireless ad hoc and sensor networks, cognitive radio networks, and IP networks. Dr. Gungor has authored several papers in refereed journals and international conference proceedings, and has been serving as an Editor, and program committee member to numerous journals and conferences in these areas. He is also the recipient of the IEEE Transactions on Industrial Informatics 2012 Best Paper Award, the IEEE ISCN 2006 Best Paper Award, the European Union FP7 Marie Curie IRG Award in 2009, Turk Telekom Research Grant Awards in 2010 and 2012, and the San-Tez Project Awards supported by Alcatel-Lucent, and the Turkish Ministry of Science, Industry and Technology in 2010.

Nayana Hegde did her Bachelors in Electronics and Communication from Karnataka University, India in year 2001 and Masters in Digital Communication and Networking from VTU, India in 2014. She is pursuing her PhD in Electronics and Communication and Engineering from Reva University Bangalore, India. She is currently Assistant Professor in Sri Krishna Institute of Technology Bangalore, India. Before that she worked as Lecturer in Impact College of Engineering Bangalore from 2011-2012. Before that she worked for Infosys Technologies Bangalore from 2003to 2009. She was Graduate Engineer Trainee at NTTF from 2002-2003.

Aruna Jain is currently working as Associate Professor in Computer Science and Engineering department of Birla Institute of Technology Mesra Ranchi Jharkhand. She has an experience of more than 24 years in Teaching and research and working in Birla Institute of Technology from 1989 holding different positions. She completed her M.Sc. (in Physics with specialization in Electronics) from Nagpur University in 1983, and the M.Tech. degree in Computer Science and Engineering from BIT Mesra Ranchi Jharkhand in 1999.In 2008 she received Ph.D. degree in Engineering from BIT Mesra Ranchi. She is currently guiding three research scholars. Her area of interest is computer network and security, Data mining and Speech processing. She is a member of board of studies for MCA and B.E. programs of BIT Ranchi and Ranchi University, Ranchi. Dr. Jain is a life member of the Indian Society for Technical Education, The Computer Society of India, and the co-editor of GSTF International Journal on Computing (ISSN 2010-2283).

Sanjeev Jain was born on September 11, 1967 in Vidisha, M.P., India. He is Vice Chancellor of Shri Mata Vaishno Devi University, Katra, Jammu, India. He completed his B.E. at the Samrat Ashok Technological Institute, Vidisha, M.P., his M.Tech. at the Indian Institute of Technology, Delhi, India, and received his Ph.D. in Computer Science & Engineering from Barkatullah University, Bhopal. He has published/presented 88 research papers in International/National Journals and Conferences on image processing and soft computing techniques. His areas of research include Computer Network, Image Processing, Neural Networks, etc. He is a life member of various technical societies.

Kijpokin Kasemsap received his BEng degree in Mechanical Engineering from King Mongkut's University of Technology, Thonburi, his MBA degree from Ramkhamhaeng University, and his DBA degree in Human Resource Management from Suan Sunandha Rajabhat University. Dr. Kasemsap is a Special Lecturer in the Faculty of Management Sciences, Suan Sunandha Rajabhat University, based in Bangkok, Thailand. Dr. Kasemsap is a Member of the International Economics Development and Research Center (IEDRC), the International Foundation for Research and Development (IFRD), and the International Innovative Scientific and Research Organization (IISRO). Dr. Kasemsap also serves on the International Advisory Committee (IAC) for the International Association of Academicians and Researchers (INAAR). Dr. Kasemsap is the sole author of over 250 peer-reviewed international publications and book chapters on business, education, and information technology. Dr. Kasemsap is included in the TOP 100 Professionals–2016 and in the 10th edition of 2000 Outstanding Intellectuals of the 21st Century by the International Biographical Centre, Cambridge, England.

Bilal Muhammad Khan holds PhD and Post Doc in wireless communication networks from the University of Sussex UK. He was affiliated with Sussex University UK as Teaching Fellow and Visiting Research Fellow. Currently he is working as Assistant Professor at National University of Sciences and Technology. He is involved in various projects on design of wireless sensor networks, programmable logic controllers, Microcontrollers, Systems administration and Software training. He has published number of journal papers and written many book chapters and also serving in the editorial boards of journals. His research interests are in the area of wireless sensor networks, wireless local area networks.

Kai Li Lim received his BEng degree (with first-class honours) in Electronic and Computer Engineering from the University of Nottingham in 2012, and the MSc degree (with distinction) in Computer Science from Lancaster University and Sunway University in 2014. He is currently a PhD candidate at the University of Western Australia with the School of Electrical, Electronic and Computer Engineering. His research interests cover the fields of navigational algorithms, autonomous mobile robots, and ubiquitous computing.

Sunilkumar Manvi received M.E., and Ph.D., from the University of Visweshwariah College of Engineering (UVCE),and Indian Institute of Science (IISc.), Bengaluru, India, respectively. He is currently working as a Professor and Director of School of Computing and IT, REVA University, Bengaluru, India. He has experience of around 29 years in teaching and research. He is involved in research of agent based applications, multimedia communications, grid/cloud computing, mobile ad-hoc networks, sensor networks, e-commerce, vehicle networks and mobile computing. He has published 5 books, 10 book chapters, 108 refereed journal papers, and about 150 refereed conference papers. He has presented many invited lectures and has conducted several workshops/seminars/conferences. He is reviewer for many journals/conferences including IEEE and Elsevier Publications. He is a senior member of IEEE, Member CSI (India), Fellow of IETE (India) and Fellow of IE (India).

Nikhil Marriwala is working as Assistant Professor in Electronics and Communication Engineering Department at University Institute of Engineering and Technology, Kurukshetra University, Kurukshetra. He did his post graduation in Electronics and Communication Engineering from IASE University, Sardarshahar, Rajasthan and did his B-Tech Electronics and Instrumentation from MMEC, Mullana affiliated to Kurukshetra University, Kurukshetra. He was also the M-Tech Coordinator of ECE in U.I.E.T, KUK for more than 3 years and is currently having the additional charge of Training and Placement cell of U.I.E.T, KUK. He has more than 13 years of experience of teaching graduate and post graduate students. More than 24 students have completed their dissertation under his guidance. His areas of interests are Software Defined Radios, Wireless Communication, Fuzzy system design, and Advanced Microprocessors.

S. Nithya did her Bachelors of Technology in Information Technology from KSR Institute For Engineering and Technology in 2015. She is currently pursuing Master of Engineering in Computer Science and Information Security at Thiagarajar College of Engineering. Her research interests include Cloud Computing and Security in Cloud. Her research works contributing towards Resource allocation and Capacity planning in cloud.

K. PandiSelvi did her Bachelors of Engineering in Computer Science and Engineering from K.L.N College of Information Technology in 2015. She is currently pursuing Master of Engineering in Computer Science and Information Security at Thiagarajar College of Engineering. Her research interests include Cryptography, Cloud Computing and Security in Cloud.

Mahesh Parmar was born on May 30, 1980. He is currently working as an Assistant Professor in the Department of CSE & IT, Madhav Institute of Technology & Science, Gwalior, India. He completed his B.E. at the Samrat Ashok Technological Institute, Vidisha, M.P., his M.Tech. at the SGSITS Indore, India. He has published/presented 09 research papers in International/National Journals and Conferences. His area of expertise is Soft Computing and Computer Network.

Sanchita Paul did her Bachelors in Engineering in Computer Science and Engineering from Burdwan University, followed by Master of Engineering in Software Engineering and Ph.D from Birla Institute of Technology, Mesra in 2004, 2006 and 2012 respectively. She is currently the Assistant Professor in Department of Computer Science and Engineering, Birla Institute of Technology, Mesra, Jharkhand, India. She is a co-author of 1 book and has more than 45 research publications in international journals and conference proceedings to her credit. She has been the member of the organizing and technical program committees of several International conferences and Workshop. She has also acted as Principal Investigator in an AICTE funded project. Her research interests include soft computing, cloud computing, Big Data, IoT and NLP and Bioinformatics.

Saravana Priya is a Masters Student in Computer Science and Information Security Program in the Dept of Information Technology, Thiagarajar College of Engineering, Madurai during the year 2014-2016. Her areas of interest include security, trust in cloud computing and TPM concepts.

Kaushik Roy obtained his Bachelor's degree from NIT Silchar, Masters and Ph.D. from Jadavpur University in computer science and engineering in 1998, 2002 and 2008, respectively. He is currently working as an Professor and Head in the Department of Computer Science at West Bengal State University, Barasat, He has worked as lecturer in West Bengal University of Technology and as Scientific Officer in Centre for Development of Advanced Computing (CDAC) Kolkata. He has also worked as Asst. Professor in Narula Institute of Technology, Kolkata and as Project Linked Personnel in Computer Vision and Pattern Recognition Unit of Indian Statistical Institute Kolkata on the development of a complete system for postal automation. He has acted as Principal Investigator in one of AICTE funded projects. His areas of interests are in image processing, pattern recognition, handwriting recognition, and document processing, etc. He has published more than 19 International Journals and 81 papers/book chapters in reputed National International conferences. He was a champion in the National Competition for Young IT Professional Awards 2004 (YITPA-04), conferred by the Computer Society of India. He is a life member of the Indian Unit for Pattern Recognition and Artificial Intelligence (affiliated to the International Association of Pattern Recognition) and Computer Society of India.

Chanchal K Saha graduated from Institute of Medical Sciences, Banaras Hindu University in 1993. On completion of rotatory internship training he received his MBBS degree in 1994. He joined the Post-graduate Institute of Medical Education and Research (PGIMER), Chandigarh in 1995 as House staff in the Department of Pharmacology for a brief stint. As a research team member he worked on Cognitive and behavioural modification of Gingko biloba in primates and lower mammals. He joined the Department of Obstetrics and Gynaecology as a Junior Resident in 1996. He was the recipient of Institute Research Scholarship for his MD research during his stay at PGIMER. His work on Preterm Labor (PTL) and premature rupture of membranes (PROM) earned him accolades from the various quarters. He worked on acute phase reactants as serum marker for these complications of pregnancy. His work on serum ferritin as a marker of PTL and PROM was published in the International Journal of Obstetrics and Gynecology (IJOG) in Nov, 2000. He successfully completed his MD in 1999 and joined Biraj Mohini Matri Sadan Hospital, Barrackpore as a Consultant in 2000. Dr Saha works closely with local communities and his endeavour to reduce maternal and child mortality has been recognised locally. As a surgeon he performs most obstetric, gynaecologic and laparoscopic surgeries. He imparts training to his junior colleagues, residents and trainee midwives for conducting safe obstetric and operative procedures. He is a member of Bengal Obstetric and Gynaecologic Society and Federation of Obstetric and Gynaecologic Societies of India. Presently he is working as a guide for development of a research module using Cardiotocograph traces as diagnostic tool.

O. P. Sahu received his B.E. degree in 1989 and M.Tech degree in 1991 both in Electronics and Communication Engineering from Rani Durgavati Vishvavidyalaya Jabalpur and Kurukshetra University Kurukshetra respectively. He received his Ph.D. degree in 2005 from Kurukshetra University Kurukshetra in the area of Multirate Filter Banks. He joined NIT (then REC) Kurukshetra as a Lecturer in 1991 in the department of Electronics and Communication Engineering and was promoted as an Assistant Professor in 1999 and as professor in 2009 and is still working there. He has about 100 research papers in his credit in National and International Conferences and Journals. His Research interests include Signals and Systems, Digital Signal Processing, Digital Communication and Fuzzy Systems.

Kah Phooi Seng received her BEng (first class) and PhD from University of Tasmania, Australia, in 1997 and 2001, respectively. She is currently with the School of Computing and Mathematics, Charles Sturt University. She was a Professor at Sunway University before returning to Australia. Prior to joining Sunway University, she was an Associate Professor at School of Electrical and Electronic Engineering, Nottingham University. Her research interests include the fields of visual processing, multi-biometrics, artificial intelligence and wireless visual sensor networks.

Mohamed Adel Sennouni was born in Wazzane, Morocco. He received his B.Sc. degree in physic 'Electronic option' in 2009 from faculty of sciences, Ibn Tofail University in Morocco and a M.Sc. degree in Telecommunication systems engineering from faculty of sciences of Abd Elmalek Essaadi University in Tétouan Morocco in 2011. Since January 2012 he is following researches at LITEN laboratory at the faculty of sciences and technologies of SETTAT, Hassan the first University in Morocco. His research interests include analysis and design of microstrip antennas and filters, design and modeling of microwave devices and their applications in RF energy harvesting and wireless power transmission.

J. John Shiny is currently working as an Assistant Professor in the Dept of Information Technology, Thiagarajar College of Engineering, Madurai. She completed her B.Tech (InformationTechnology) in Hindustan College of Engineering, affiliated to Anna University-Chennai in 2011. She then joined SSN college of Engineering, Chennai to pursue her Masters in Engineering in Computer science and completed in 2013. Thereafter she joined Thiagarajar College of Engineering as an Assistant Professor and currently she is in that designation. She has two years of teaching experience especially in Network security and Distributed Systems for both UG and PG degrees. She has organized one credit courses in the college in association with Cognizant and Dell, Bangalore.

Vaibhav Shukla has received B. Sc. and M.Sc. in Mathematics from CSJM University Kanpur (UP), India in 2005, and the MCA degree from Kamla Nehru Institute of Technology Sultanpur (UP), India in 2009. He is currently pursuing Ph.D. in Computer Science and Engineering from Birla Institute of Technology Mesra Ranchi (Jharkhand), India. He has published number of International and national papers in international journals indexed in SCI, Scopus etc. Mr. Shukla is a life member of IACSIT, ISOC, ACM and SDIWC. His research area includes optical packet switching design and analysis and computer networks.

R. Sindhuja did her Bachelors of Engineering in Computer Science and Engineering from Kamaraj College of Engineering and Technology in 2015. She is currently pursuing Master of Engineering in Computer Science and Information Security at Thiagarajar College of Engineering. Her research interests include Cryptography, Cloud Computing and Security in Cloud. She has done research works contributing towards novelty in DNA based Cryptosystem.

Rajeev Kumar Singh is currently working as an Assistant Professor in the Department of CSE & IT, Madhav Institute of Technology & Science, Gwalior, India. He completed his M.Tech. at the Lakshmi Narain College of Technology, Bhopal, India. He has published/presented 14 research papers in International/National Journals and Conferences. His area of expertise is Evolutionary Computation and Computer Network.

Uday Pratap Singh was born on February 6, 1979 in Sultanpur, U.P., India. He is currently working as an Assistant Professor in the Department of Applied Mathematics, Madhav Institute of Technology & Science, Gwalior, India. He completed B.Sc. at the K.N.I.P.S.S., Sultanpur, U.P., M.Sc. at the Indian Institute of Technology, Guwahati, India, and received Ph.D. in Computer Science from Barkatullah University, Bhopal. He has published/presented about 30 research papers in International/National Journals and at Conferences on Soft Computing, Image Processing, etc. His areas of research include Computational Intelligence, Soft Computing, Image Processing etc. He has also qualified from CSIR (NET). He is a life member of the Computer Society of India.

M. Thangavel is an Assistant Professor at the Department of Information Technology at Thiagarajar College of Engineering, Madurai, Tamilnadu, India. He is also presently pursuing his PhD under the guidance of Dr. P. Varalakshmi, Supervisor in Faculty of Information and Communication, Anna University, Chennai, Tamilnadu, India. He completed his post graduate in Computer Science and Engineering at the J.J. College of Engineering, Trichy, Tamilnadu, India. His research interests include cryptography and network security, compiler design and data structures.

Gurkan Tuna received his B. S. degree in computer engineering from Yildiz Technical University, Istanbul, Turkey, in 1999, and his M.S. degree in computer engineering from Trakya University, Edirne, Turkey, in 2008. He received his Ph.D. degree in electrical engineering from Yildiz Technical University, Istanbul, Turkey, in 2012. He is currently an Associate Professor at Edirne Vocational School of Technical Sciences, Trakya University, Turkey. He has authored several papers in international conference proceedings and refereed journals, and edited three book chapters. He has been serving as an associate editor for IEEE Access and Australian Journal of Electrical and Electronics Engineering. He has been a reviewer of many prestigious international journals and conferences. His current research interests include underwater acoustic communication, underwater sensor networks, ad hoc and sensor networks, robotic sensor networks, smart grid, and smart cities.

P. Varalakshmi is an Associate Professor at the Department of Computer Technology, Madras Institute of Technology, Anna University, Chennai, Tamilnadu, India. She received her PhD under Information and Communication Engineering-Trust Management in Grid Computing at the Anna University, Chennai, Tamilnadu, India. Her research interests include compiler design, network security in grid and cloud computing.

Anil Vohra Received M.Sc. Degree in 1985 and Ph.D. in 1991 from Panjab University Chandigarh. He joined Kurukshetra University as Reader in 1991 and as Professor since 1999 in Electronic Science

Department, Kurukshetra University, Kurukshetra. He is the Chairman of the department and is the member of several academic bodies and administrative committees of Kurukshetra University and other neighboring Institutes and Universities. He is involved in research and teaching of M.Sc. (Electronic Science) and M.Tech (Microelectronics and VLSI Design) and M.Tech (Nano Science & Technology) courses. He has also coordinating a number of UG/PG courses from Directorate of Distance Education of the University. He has visited several academic and research institutes in India and abroad. He was awarded a Commonwealth Commission fellowship in 1998. During this period he worked on development of new technology for solar cell applications at Engineering Department, Cambridge University, UK. His present areas of research include materials and devices for microwave applications, nano-devices and nano-materials, Semiconductor Devices, Electronic/VLSI Design, Software reuse, Industrial Control Applications. He has published more than 70 research papers in various national/international journals and conferences. He has chaired several sessions in conferences. Presently, four students are working for Ph.D. under his guidance.

Lee Seng Yeong graduated from the University of Nottingham in 2015 with a PhD in Engineering. He is currently a Lecturer at Sunway University. His topics of research include wireless sensor networks, image processing and embedded systems.

Index

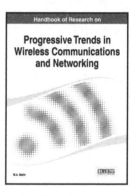

Support Your Colleagues and Stay Current on the Latest Research Developments

Become a Reviewer

In this competitive age of scholarly publishing, constructive and timely feedback significantly decreases the turn-around time of manuscripts from submission to acceptance, allowing the publication and discovery of progressive research at a much more expeditious rate.

The overall success of a refereed journal is dependent on quality and timely reviews.

Several IGI Global journals are currently seeking highly qualified experts in the field to fill vacancies on their respective editorial review boards. Reviewing manuscripts allows you to stay current on the latest developments in your field of research, while at the same time providing constructive feedback to your peers.

Reviewers are expected to write reviews in a timely, collegial, and constructive manner. All reviewers will begin their role on an ad-hoc basis for a period of one year, and upon successful completion of this term can be considered for full editorial review board status, with the potential for a subsequent promotion to Associate Editor.

Join this elite group by visiting the IGI Global journal webpage, and clicking on **"Become a Reviewer"**.

Applications may also be submitted online at:
www.igi-global.com/journals/become-a-reviewer/.

Applicants must have a doctorate (or an equivalent degree) as well as publishing and reviewing experience.

If you have a colleague that may be interested in this opportunity, we encourage you to share this information with them.

Any questions regarding this opportunity can be sent to:
journaleditor@igi-global.com.

Printed in the United States
By Bookmasters